Reading Comprehension

Grade 6

Recently, many students have been taught to read using such "no-fail" techniques as sight reading, picture reading, and whole language.

While it is probable that some students responded well to some of these new techniques, it is also likely that many others were unable to learn to read using these alternative methods. It is for these students that the *Basics First* books were created.

The back-to-basics method is tried and true. It provides students with an approach they can use to learn all of the skills needed for a particular subject. Many of these fundamental techniques may even have helped you learn to read when you were a child!

To help students learn to comprehend what they read, this *Basics First* features an interesting fact- or fiction-based story on every other page. Each narrative has been written so that a student at a sixth-grade level can read it successfully. After each story, there are activities that will help students practice the following skills: locating the main idea, reading for details, putting events in order, following directions, determining the cause and the effect of an action, recognizing similarities and differences, analyzing characters, predicting outcomes, drawing inferences, and much more. The carefully thought-out questions help students learn to think, respond, create, imagine, and even do research to learn more about a subject.

You will be thrilled when students using this book want to read more as they begin to better understand what they are reading. They will also learn to question and will develop higher-level thinking skills that are necessary in so many important aspects in life. Most of all, this book will help students recognize reading as an enjoyable way to spend their time.

Dog-gone It!

Name _____

"Don't look now, but there's a dog following us," whispered Daniel as the sixth-graders of Room 22, Snodgrass School, played at recess. He was right. A small gray dog with shaggy hair was trying to play soccer with them. The bell rang, and everyone got in line. The dog got in line, too.

"I haven't seen that dog around the neighborhood, have you?" kids started asking. Everyone wondered about the dog, who then followed them into the classroom.

"Hide the dog from Mrs. Fine," said David.

"No way!" exclaimed Linnette. "She loves animals." The teacher noticed the dog.

"What is that smell?" she asked. The dog came up to her and licked her ankle.

"Phew!" said the teacher, holding her nose. "This poor animal hasn't had a bath in months, I bet. Whose dog is it?" The kids told her the dog just followed them.

"I've seen that dog around the neighborhood," said Lance. "Her name is Jackie. She wanders all over and nobody takes care of her, but she has a home."

"Well," said Mrs. Fine, "take her into the classroom, and we'll see what we can do."

Mrs. Fine saw that Jackie was wearing a license. It was expired. She called the phone number on the license from the classroom phone. It was the wrong number. Bo said, "I've seen her come out of a house. She squeezes through a fence. She's going to get hit by a car."

Everyone was worried about Jackie. After school, the kids showed Mrs. Fine where Jackie lived, and she deposited her over the gate and crossed her fingers. Nobody was home. Jackie watched Mrs. Fine as she left. The next day, Jackie was back.

"Let's give her a bath. Then she'll smell good. Maybe we can keep her since her own family doesn't take care of her," suggested Emily. Mrs. Fine explained that a classroom wasn't the best place for a dog. Jackie stayed for the day.

The next day, someone brought soap, someone else a tub, and they washed Jackie. Then they rinsed her off. She was dried and brushed. She looked beautiful. Mrs. Fine took Jackie home again. The kids hoped that maybe Jackie's family would like her better since she was nice and clean.

The next day, Daniel came with a note for Mrs. Fine. "I was passing by Jackie's house, and a woman came out and asked if I would take this note to you. She knew you were a teacher at Snodgrass. I told her you were my teacher." The note said, *Thank you for taking care of Jackie. I have been sick so I couldn't take care of her. I'm better now. Maybe Jackie and I can visit your classroom and thank you in person.*

The students felt sad and glad at the same time. The next day, Daniel said he saw a man walking Jackie on a leash. She looked happy. The class missed Jackie. Everyone was very quiet, just thinking about the small dog they had grown to love in such a short time. Emily noticed that Mrs. Fine had something under her desk. It was a cage. In it was a small, caramel-colored hamster.

"Do you know you have a hamster under your desk?" teased Brett.

"This is Stinky," said Mrs. Fine. "I realize she's no Jackie, but I'm sure we'll love her, too." And they did.

Dog-gone It!

Name _____

Understanding and Enjoying What You Read

Answer the questions below about the story. Reread the story if necessary.

1. Write a different ending to the story. _____

   _____

2. What did you think would happen in the story? _____

   _____

3. Why did the kids feel both sad and glad at the same time? _____

   _____

4. Why wouldn't it be a good idea to keep a dog in the classroom? _____

   _____

5. Why did Mrs. Fine bring a pet for the class? _____

6. Write words from the story that mean the following: light-brownish color _____

   long, messy hair _____   smells bad _____   saw, observed _____

   goes from place to place _____   a long chain or ropelike lead for a dog _____

7. Why did the kids care so much about a strange dog? _____

   _____

8. Put a check next to the main idea of the story.

   ___ Jackie was a dirty dog.   ___ The class took time out to care for a neglected dog.

   ___ A kind teacher let kids bathe a dog.   ___ A stray dog plays with kids.

9. What do you think your teacher would do if a dog was following your class?

   _____

10. Are there any dangers in picking up a stray dog? What are they? _____

    _____

11. Find out what the laws are in your town about dog licenses and keeping dogs on a leash. Write

    the laws here. _____

    _____

12. Write, in order, how the class took care of Jackie. First, they _____

    Then, they _____

    After that, they _____

    Finally, they _____

13. Why is a hamster better than a dog for a classroom pet? _____

    _____

Try This!   Write a story about an unusual animal that was lost and then found.

Name _____

Drawing conclusions, inference, predicting outcomes, details, grammar, vocabulary, illustrating, recalling facts

The class really did love their new hamster, Stinky. Everyone wanted to hold her, feed her, put her in the plastic hamster ball and watch her roll around the classroom. They didn't even mind cleaning her cage. The class was warned that hamsters are very good escape artists. Mrs. Fine assigned one person each week to take care of the new pet.

One morning, Mrs. Fine entered the classroom. It was nice and quiet. She put her things down on her desk. Then, as was her habit, she walked over to Stinky's cage.

"Hi, Stinky," the teacher said cheerfully. "How did you sleep?" Mrs. Fine really didn't expect an answer, but when she looked inside Stinky's house, she saw that Stinky was gone! Mrs. Fine looked all over the small cage. Then she noticed that the top of the cage was open. Pretty smart for a baby hamster, she thought. There was no time to waste. Mrs. Fine looked on the playground and saw Linnette and Daniel playing tetherball. She called them, "Kids! Pssst! Come here." The two students ran over. Mrs. Fine tried to keep calm.

"Don't panic," she warned, "but Stinky isn't in her cage. Come in and find her before all the kids come in." Daniel and Linnette opened closets, looked under and inside desks, and even opened the drawers to Mrs. Fine's desk. No sign of Stinky!

"Let's leave some food on the floor," suggested Linnette. "When she finds it, she'll come out to grab it, then we'll grab her!" Mrs. Fine cautioned them. "Hamsters have very poor eyesight. She won't see the food. She'll have to smell it."

They decided to try. Just as they were laying the trail of food, Daniel whispered, "There she is, sitting in the corner of the closet." Stinky was chewing on lined writing paper. She held it in her paws and ate it as though it were something really delicious. Daniel sneaked up on her. Stinky tried to bite him. She went into reverse and tried to run away.

"Hey! That hamster's gone crazy!" he declared.

"Hamsters want to be free," said Mrs. Fine. "They are rodents originally from Asia and Europe. They've been bred as pets for many years, but how would you like to spend your life in a cage?" Daniel had an idea.

"Then why don't we just not catch her? She can be free and happy." Mrs. Fine shook her head. "That's a good idea, but this is the city, and there are many dangers for a little animal like Stinky. Cats, dogs, people, other rodents—she wouldn't last long out there by herself. Stinky was born in captivity. She shouldn't roam by herself."

The teacher bent down and picked up Stinky. She brushed her off and put her back in the cage. Daniel and Linnette thought about the Stinky situation.

The next day, Lance and Brett brought tiny locks with keys to lock up the doors of the cage. Emily brought a little fake tree stump for the hamster. David brought a little plastic shoe for her to play in. Bo brought a tiny hamster toy. They put the new things in the cage. Stinky started playing with them right away.

"We thought about what you said," said Linnette. "We decided that it's for Stinky's own good to be in a cage, but we want her to be as happy as a hamster can be."

The Adventures of Stinky the Hamster

Name _____

Understanding and Enjoying What You Read

Answer the questions below about the story. Reread the story if necessary.

1. Where do hamsters come from? _____

2. Write how you think everyone would have felt if Stinky had not been found. _____
_____

3. What else could they have done to find her? _____

4. Put the events below in the order in which they occurred.

   ___ Stinky tries to bite Daniel. ___ Stinky is missing. ___ Stinky starts playing with her toys.

   ___Stinky gets toys. ___ Stinky eats paper. ___ Mrs. Fine tells about hamsters.

5. Write five true facts about hamsters. _____
_____
_____

6. On the back of this paper, design and draw a good toy for a hamster. Explain how it works and
   why a hamster would enjoy using it.

7. What is the difference between prey and predator? _____
_____

8. Write the names of five animals you know that are prey. Write the names of five that are
   predators.

   Prey _____

   Predators_____

9. A noun is a person, place, or thing. Circle all the nouns in the story that have to do with animals.

10. Hamsters were originally desert animals. What kind of weather do you think they might not like,
    or that might make them sick? _____

11. Why didn't Mrs. Fine want the whole class to know that Stinky was missing?

    _____

12. Hamsters have long whiskers. What sense do they provide and how do long whiskers help
    hamsters? _____

    _____

13. Hamsters are rodents. Name as many rodents as you know. _____
_____

Try This! Write a story in which Stinky the hamster escapes from the school.

FS-30025 Reading Comprehension

The Case of the Missing Lunch

Name _____

Emily watched the clock from her desk. She was supposed to be doing math.

Linnette said, "Mrs. Fine is watching you. You're going to get in trouble if you don't finish your math. What's the matter?"

"I'm so hungry," said Emily. "I can hear my stomach growling. I'm going to die!"

"It isn't even recess time," said Linnette grimly. "We have more than two hours."

"Emily, is your math assignment finished?" asked Mrs. Fine.

"Almost," Emily said, as she got back to the book.

Finally, lunchtime came. Emily reached into her backpack for her lunch. The apple was there. The juice was there. But the sandwich, her very favorite kind, was gone.

"Someone took my sandwich," she cried. "An apple and some juice isn't enough. Who would steal my sandwich? Everybody knew I was hungry! And I brought my special sandwich! A criminal did it!" Her face got red, and her stomach rumbled again.

"I would share with you, but I ate mine already," said Brett sympathetically.

"I wouldn't have liked it anyway," said Emily grimly. "I want my sandwich!"

"Beggars can't be choosers," Brett grinned as he walked away, leaving Emily in her misery.

"Don't worry, we'll investigate," said David and Daniel. "We'll be back fast! And with your sandwich, too."

Daniel looked at David. "Why did you say we'd be right back with her sandwich? Who knows who took it?"

"Oh, I have a feeling we'll find it pretty fast," David said mysteriously. They asked a lot of people a lot of questions, but no one seemed to know anything. Or, as Daniel said, "They're not talking." He wanted to be a detective when he grew up.

Suddenly, David and Daniel heard loud meowing.

"It's those cats from across the street," said David. "There's a man in that white house near the school who has about a kazillion cats, and they roam around the streets all day. That's got to be them! My theory is correct!"

"What theory?" asked Daniel. "If we're working together, isn't it time to share your idea with me?" He was clearly annoyed.

"Follow that meowing!" commanded David. Before Daniel knew what was happening, he was running behind David. They stopped short at an amazing sight. It was so astonishing that kids were already gathered to watch. Lance was surrounded by about a kazillion cats, and he didn't like it at all.

"Hey, you guys! I'm glad you came along. Everybody else is just standing there staring. What's wrong with these crazy cats?"

"I think I know," said David as he reached into Lance's pocket and fished out the remains of a sandwich. "You took Emily's sandwich. Here's the evidence. Why did you do it?"

"It was a joke," said Lance. "She was whining about being hungry all day. I was tired of listening to her. How did you know it was me?" He talked to David as he shooed the meowing, hungry cats away.

"The cat was in the bag," said David. "I've known Emily since kindergarten, and I know her favorite sandwich—sardines! It's the cat's meow, as my great-granddad says!"

The Case of the Missing Lunch

Name _____

Understanding and Enjoying What You Read

Answer the questions below about the story. Reread the story if necessary.

1. What other kinds of sandwiches might give someone away? _____
   _____

2. Do you think "a kazillion cats" is an exaggeration? An exaggeration means saying something is more than it really is, on purpose. What else in the story is an exaggeration? _____
   _____

3. What do you think of Lance for taking Emily's sandwich? _____
   _____

4. On the back of this page, write directions for making the best sandwich ever.

5. Do you think Emily made too big a fuss about her sandwich? Explain.
   _____

6. How would you speak *sympathetically* to someone? Pretend that a friend just told you that he or she didn't get a good grade on a science test. What would you say?
   _____

7. Put the events below in the order in which they occurred.

   ___ Lance is surrounded by cats.   ___ Emily discovers that her sandwich is missing.

   ___ Emily complains that she's hungry.   ___ Emily watches the clock.

   ___ David and Daniel get on the case.

8. Find and write a synonym (a word that means the same) for *amazing* in the story. _____

9. What do you think the following saying means: "Beggars can't be choosers"?_____
   _____

10. Put a check next to the main idea of the story.

    ___ Cats love sardines.   ___ Daniel and David help Emily find the sandwich thief.

    ___ Emily can't wait for lunch.   ___ Lance takes Emily's sandwich.

11. A theory is an idea that has not been proven. *There are people on other planets* is a theory.
    Write another theory that you know. _____

12. What did Emily find when she reached into her backpack? _____

13. Why do you think Lance wasn't happy about being surrounded by cats? _____
    _____

14. Why didn't the kids who were watching help get the cats away from Lance? _____
    _____

Try This! Make up sentences using these exaggerated phrases: He would burst; she would blow up like a balloon; he was bouncing off the walls; he ate like he hadn't eaten in a year.

7

Let's Communicate!

Name _____

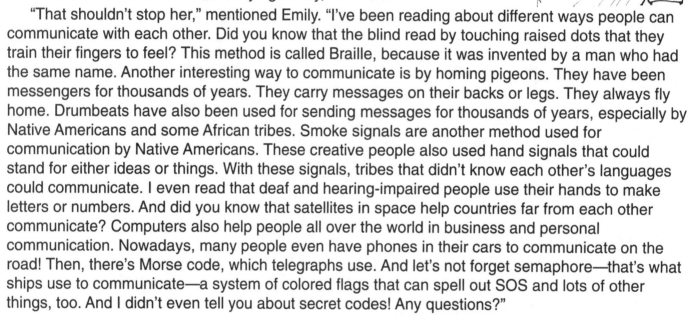

"Linnette has been very quiet today," commented Brett. "She's just sitting around looking glum. She's no fun, and there's no school, either. What's going on?"

"What a way to spend the weekend," agreed Bo.

"Linnette has laryngitis," said Emily. "Don't tease her."

"What's laryngitis?" asked Brett.

"She went to her parents' college football game," Emily commented. "She yelled and screamed for hours. Now she can't talk, not even a whisper."

Linnette started making hand signals to her friends.

"I can't understand what she's trying to say," said Lance.

"That shouldn't stop her," mentioned Emily. "I've been reading about different ways people can communicate with each other. Did you know that the blind read by touching raised dots that they train their fingers to feel? This method is called Braille, because it was invented by a man who had the same name. Another interesting way to communicate is by homing pigeons. They have been messengers for thousands of years. They carry messages on their backs or legs. They always fly home. Drumbeats have also been used for sending messages for thousands of years, especially by Native Americans and some African tribes. Smoke signals are another method used for communication by Native Americans. These creative people also used hand signals that could stand for either ideas or things. With these signals, tribes that didn't know each other's languages could communicate. I even read that deaf and hearing-impaired people use their hands to make letters or numbers. And did you know that satellites in space help countries far from each other communicate? Computers also help people all over the world in business and personal communication. Nowadays, many people even have phones in their cars to communicate on the road! Then, there's Morse code, which telegraphs use. And let's not forget semaphore—that's what ships use to communicate—a system of colored flags that can spell out SOS and lots of other things, too. And I didn't even tell you about secret codes! Any questions?"

"No, but Linnette is trying to say something," said David.

Linnette was flapping her arms around frantically. Nobody could understand what she was trying to say.

"That's interesting," said Emily. "Linnette is doing just what our cave ancestors used to do, communicate with gestures. People still use a lot of gestures today. When we shake our heads up and down, it means 'yes.' When we shake our heads from side to side, it means 'no.' When we lift our shoulders, it means 'I don't know.' Folding our arms in front of us means we're angry. Clapping our hands together shows approval for something we saw or heard. Thumbs up means we like something, thumbs down means we don't. How about our faces? We frown when we're unhappy and smile when we are happy. We stick out our tongues when we want to send a message to someone that we don't like him or her. Placing your index finger in front of your mouth means you want someone to be quiet. See, just like Linnette is doing now. That's good, Linnette. You'll be better in no time at all."

Her friends were pointing to Emily. "Right," she continued. "That's another one. Pointing your finger. What? Are you trying to tell me something? Oh, Linnette means me? Well, I was just trying to help."

FS-30025 Reading Comprehension

Let's Communicate!

Name _____

Understanding and Enjoying What You Read

Answer the questions below about the story. Reread the story if necessary.

1. Why do you think Linnette screamed so much at the game? _____

_____

2. What is *semaphore*? _____

3. Laryngitis is just one of many diseases. List five others. _____

_____

4. If you were Linnette, how would you communicate with your friends? _____

_____

5. Name some ways the animals below communicate with each other.

cat _____ horse _____ chimpanzee _____

rabbit _____ dog _____ whale _____

6. Why do you think Emily told her friends about communication? _____

_____

7. How would you signal that you were in trouble if you couldn't speak? _____

_____

8. Write three kinds of communication mentioned in the story. _____

_____

_____

9. What do you think makes pigeons fly home? _____

10. Why was Linnette flapping her arms? What was she trying to tell Emily? _____

_____

_____

11. Why do you think Linnette appeared to be annoyed with Emily? _____

_____

12. What did you learn about Emily's character in this story? _____

_____

13. How do blind people read? _____

14. How do deaf people communicate? _____

15. How could drumbeats be used for communication? _____

Make up some drumbeatlike signals to use with your friends. Write them on the back of this paper. Try them out.

Try This! Make up some hand signals you could use if you got laryngitis. Share them with your friends.

© Frank Schaffer Publications, Inc.   FS-30025 Reading Comprehension

The Field Trip

Name _____

The kids in Room 22 had been working very hard to earn a field trip. They had sold candy, cookies, popcorn, and other assorted goodies at recess. It was time to decide where they would go on their trip.

"Let's vote on where we want to go on our field trip," suggested Mrs. Fine. The class began to shout out, "Disneyland!" "Universal Studios!" "Water Slide!"

"We have to take an educational trip," Mrs. Fine gently reminded them. "Perhaps a museum." Everyone groaned.

"We always go to museums," said Bo. "We like them, but let's do something not so educational." The students murmured their approval.

"Well, if you're going to argue, I'll decide," said the teacher. "We'll go to the opera." Now everybody really groaned.

"People screaming! Ladies with horns on their heads! Boring!" The reaction was unanimous. That is, except for Emily. "My father and mother have taken me to lots of operas," she sniffed, nose high in the air. "They are very cool, and I can't wait to go!"

"You're kidding!" said Daniel. "Nobody likes operas except rich, snooty people."

"That's not true," said Mrs. Fine. "Opera is enjoyed by regular people throughout the world. You don't have to be rich to enjoy opera."

"Not if you're Emily," said Bo as he patted his friend on the shoulder.

Mrs. Fine told them about the opera called "The Barber of Seville." It was about a young man who disguised himself to win the love of a young lady. Another man was in love with her, but in the end, she and the young man marry.

"Opera flourished in several countries of Europe," she said. "Some of the greatest composers wrote operas. Italians such as Verdi, Puccini, and the composer of 'The Barber of Seville', Rossini. The French had Bizet, the Germans had Wagner and Beethoven (who wrote one opera), and the Austrians had Mozart. Russia had operatic composers too, and their works are still performed. Some opera stars are real celebrities and are appreciated by people who don't even like opera. Stars like Luciano Pavarotti sing to sold-out performances at concerts and operas."

So, the kids in Room 22 went to the opera. A woman called a docent, someone who conducts tours through museums or art galleries, showed them through the opera house. The kids saw pictures of opera stars of long ago and of the present. They were shown to their seats. The kids were surprised to see that the whole theater was full of students of all ages.

"I guess lots of teachers decided to drag their helpless students to the opera today, huh Mrs. Fine?" said Daniel.

"Today is student day at the opera," said the teacher. The kids were led high up to the very topmost balcony of the theater.

"I think I'm getting dizzy," said Linnette. "I have acrophobia, you know, fear of high places. I feel sick." Mrs. Fine had to find a lower seat for Linnette.

"I have to go to the bathroom," said David. Mrs. Fine pointed the way.

The words appeared on big screens in English, although the singers sang in Italian. The kids already knew the story, so they could follow along.

"This isn't too bad," admitted Daniel. "You were right, Emily. Emily?" He looked over at his friend who was sound asleep and snoring very softly.

10

The Field Trip

Understanding and Enjoying What You Read

Answer the questions below about the story. Reread the story if necessary.

1. Put a check next to the main idea of the story.

    ___ Emily likes opera. ___ The class goes on a field trip to the opera.

    ___ Emily falls asleep. ___ The kids don't want to go to the opera.

2. What is your favorite kind of music? Why? _____

    _____

3. Would you like to go to an opera? Why or why not? _____

    _____

4. Where would you like to go on a field trip? Write directions for getting there. _____

    _____

    _____

5. Do you think Mrs. Fine was fair not to let the kids vote? Explain. _____

    _____

6. What is the name of the opera the students went to? _____

7. What does a composer do? _____

8. What is a disguise? _____

    _____

    _____

9. Name five composers. _____

    _____

    _____

10. How did the kids in Room 22 earn a field trip? _____

11. Name three countries that produced operas. _____

12. What did the docent show the students? _____

13. Where did the kids get their idea of opera before they attended one? _____

    _____

14. Circle all the adjectives in the story. Remember that adjectives describe nouns. For example, *old house*: *House* is a noun and *old* describes it.

15. What do you think Emily's friends thought of her when she said she wanted to go to the opera?

    _____

16. What would have happened if Linnette hadn't sat in a seat on a lower floor?_____

    _____

Try This! Write about the best field trip you ever took.

Stuck in the Mall

Sequencing, drawing
conclusions, recalling facts,
details, predicting outcomes,
character analysis

Name _____

Emily's mother gave the girls a lecture before she left them at the mall.

"Now, don't forget, meet me at entrance fourteen in exactly two hours. Not two hours and two minutes—two hours exactly. Don't talk to strangers, don't buy anything you don't need, and don't eat junk food. Oh, and Emily, don't even waste your time asking me for my credit card, because the answer is no." With that, Mrs. Johansson left the girls alone. "Boy," said Linnette, "your mother doesn't want us to have much fun, does she?"

"Sure she does," said Emily, smiling, "she just wants us to be safe. Maybe she goes a little overboard sometimes. Anyway, time flies, so let's cruise the mall!"

"Let's take the elevator to the third floor," said Emily. "My mom isn't going to pick us up for two hours. Just think! Two glorious hours in the mall! Just one problem: She said we shouldn't eat junk food."

"What's junk food, anyway?" asked Linnette. "We'll have some French fries, that's a vegetable, with ketchup, which is made out of tomatoes, which is really a fruit, and a milk shake, which is a dairy product. That's not junk food!"

"You sure have a way of making things sound right!" Emily was convinced too! The girls walked toward the elevator. It was very crowded.

"Let's just take the escalator," said Linnette. But Emily didn't want to. "The escalator's on the other side of the mall. I don't feel like walking all the way over there."

The girls waited for a few minutes. People with baby carriages left no room in the elevator. Finally, an empty elevator came down.

"Okay, here comes the elevator again," said Emily. "This time, it's empty." The girls got on. Several people began coming toward them but Linnette pressed the "Close Door" button fast so she and Emily wouldn't have to share the ride.

"Now we have it all to ourselves. I love these glass elevators. You can see everybody on every floor. Press the third floor button." Linnette pressed the button. The elevator went up. When it reached the third floor, the girls waited for it to stop. It didn't.

"Hey!" said Linnette. "What's going on?" The elevator went up and down, past the second floor, down to the first, and up again. Soon, a crowd gathered to watch the two girls go up and down, up and down. Emily began counting how many times they were going up and down. "Thirty-one, or was that thirty?" Linnette saw a phone in the elevator.

She picked it up. "May I help you?" asked a pleasant voice.

"We're going up and down," said Linnette.

"That's what an elevator is for," said the voice.

"But we've gone up and down 33 times," said Linnette.

"Then get off the elevator, little girl. Other people need to use it."

"But we can't get off!" yelled Linnette. "It won't stop. It passes right by every floor."

"Oh," said the voice. "I'll get help for you. Don't get excited."

Soon, a huge crowd had gathered. A security guard kept them calm. Maintenance men came and suddenly the elevator stopped. The girls got out. Everybody applauded.

continued on next page

Emily and Linnette quickly ran to the exit to meet Emily's mother. Just then, Mom came along. "Well, girls, did you enjoy the mall?" she asked.

"It has its ups and downs," said Emily, giggling.

Understanding and Enjoying What You Read

Answer the questions below about the story. Reread the story if necessary.

1. What could the girls have done if there had been no phone in the elevator? _____
_____

2. How many times did they go up and down before they spoke to the phone voice?
_____ Why did a security guard come? _____

3. On the back of this paper, draw a map of your favorite mall or shopping center.

4. Suppose the elevator couldn't be stopped. What would have happened? _____
_____
_____
_____

5. Put the events below in the order in which they occurred. ___ A security guard came.
___ Emily's mother left her and Linnette at the mall. ___ The elevator wouldn't stop.
___ Mom came to pick up the girls. ___ The girls wanted to go up to the third floor.

6. Why is the last line a joke? _____
_____

7. What kind of person is Emily's mother? _____

8. Why was there no room in the first elevator for the girls? _____

9. Why didn't the girls want to share the elevator? _____
_____

10. Why was a security guard needed? _____

11. Why do you think the girls were so excited to be by themselves at the mall?_____
_____

12. What would Emily's mother have said if she knew about the girls' adventure? _____
_____

13. How would you spend two hours in a mall? _____
_____

14. Why did everybody applaud when the girls were rescued? _____
_____

15. On the back of this paper, write a story about an experience you have had in a mall.

Try This! Write a different ending for the story.

The Big Sleepover

Name _____

The girls were giggling at recess. They were giggling again at lunch.

"What's going on?" asked David with great curiosity.

"It's for girls only!" said Celia, a new girl in class.

"Is that so?" exclaimed Daniel. "It's probably so boring that we would start snoring if we heard it anyway!" He snorted, imitating heavy snoring.

"Well, if you must know," said Emily, "since you're so nosy, we might tell you."

"I'm so excited!" exclaimed Linnette. "I can't wait for Emily's sleepover."

"Sleepover! I knew it would be dumb! What could be more boring than a bunch of girls talking, giggling, fixing each other's hair, gossiping, and playing stupid songs on the radio. And they sing-along, too!"

"David, how do you know so much about sleepovers?" asked Linnette.

"I have a sister. She kicks me out when she has a sleepover," he answered.

"That's because you eavesdrop and make fun of her and her friends. I also heard that you ate half the cake she baked for the sleepover. I'd kick you out, too," Linnette assured him.

"I liked being kicked out," asserted David. "If I hadn't, I would have kicked myself out."

David and Daniel left the girls and walked on together. Daniel was muttering.

"Boys should have sleepovers too," he finally said. "Only better than the girls have."

"Let's do it!" said David. "We'll have it at my house. Then I'll get to kick out my sister." He and Daniel made a list. They invited all their friends. Guy friends, that is!

He made sure his sister Betsy left. "Good riddance," he said. Betsy just smirked. When the guys arrived, David told them they'd make their own dinner.

Bo said, "But I came hungry. I thought your mom or dad would make stuff."

They looked in the refrigerator. There wasn't a big choice. So they put everything they could find in a bowl. Peanut butter, mayonnaise, hard-boiled eggs, pickles, tuna, jelly, spaghetti, and some stuff in cans that nobody recognized. They mixed it all together and made sandwiches.

"We'll call them garbage sandwiches," suggested Lance.

"That's a good idea," said David. "My dad was probably going to throw a lot of this stuff in the garbage. It's past its prime, as he would say." They made the sandwiches. Lance was the first one who dared try one.

"Hey! This is good. No, it's great! I bet the girls don't have anything like this to eat."

Soon, all the guys were chomping on garbage sandwiches. They were a big success.

"What should we do now?" asked Brett. "Nothing the girls do!"

So they watched TV, talked about kids at school, saw a scary movie, told jokes and laughed. They turned on the radio and sang along with some songs. They had burping contests, too. The boys fell asleep at about three o'clock in the morning.

On the next school day, Emily and Linnette asked about the sleepover.

"It was great," said Daniel proudly. "Nothing like a girls' sleepover."

"That's not what I heard," giggled Linnette. "Your sister recorded the whole thing. She's going to let us play it at our next sleepover." The girls kept giggling and left.

Emily told Linnette, "I can't wait to see that tape."

"There is no tape," confessed Linnette. "I just made it up. We'll let them squirm for awhile!"

14

The Big Sleepover

Name _____

Understanding and Enjoying What You Read

Answer the questions below about the story. Reread the story if necessary.

1. Why did the girls want the boys to squirm for awhile? _____
   _____

2. What would you plan if you were having a sleepover? _____
   _____

3. Put the events below in the order in which they occurred.
   ___ The boys told jokes.   ___ The boys turned on the radio.
   ___ The boys decided to have a sleepover.   ___ The boys invented "garbage sandwiches."
   ___ The boys laughed at the girls' sleepovers.

4. Make up an original "garbage sandwich." Write the ingredients. _____
   _____

5. Circle all the past tense verbs in the story.

6. What does "eavesdrop" mean? _____

7. Why did Emily call Daniel nosy? _____

8. Compare the girls' sleepover with the boys'. What was alike? What was different? _____
   _____
   _____

9. Match the following words with the meanings below by writing the correct numbers:
   1. asserted   2. sleepover   3. chomping   4. prime   5. snort
   ___ to force air violently through the nose   ___ declared forcefully
   ___ a slumber or pajama party   ___ chewing or biting something
   ___ the most active, best stage of the life of something or someone

10. What does Lance trying the garbage sandwich first tell you about him? _____
    _____

11. Why do you think the boys were in competition with the girls? _____
    _____

12. Write another name for "garbage sandwiches." _____

13. On the back of this page, write about a sleepover you may have had or one you'd like to have.

14. What do you think the boys would do if there really had been a tape? _____
    _____

15. Why did the girls want the boys to think they had a tape of their sleepover? Did the boys have
    anything to be embarrassed about? _____
    _____

Try This!   Write a scary story that you would tell at a sleepover.

The "Weirdest Fish" Contest

Name _____

"My goldfish is so cool," said Brett. "I've had him all my life. He's eight inches long, and when I got him, he was only an inch long! When I come into the room, he swims toward me. He's a really weird fish."

"You think that's weird!" said Emily. "My grandpa went fishing off the coast of Mexico. He caught an enormous fish called a marlin. Actually, the fish caught him. It wouldn't let go, and it dragged grandpa's boat way out to sea. Then when the fish was tired of the game, he dropped the line, stuck his tongue out at grandpa, and swam away."

"I didn't know fish had tongues!" said Daniel. "And it stuck it out at him? That sounds like a fish story to me."

Everyone agreed that fish could be very strange indeed. "Did you see that piranha in the zoo?" asked Brett. "It had teeth that could tear anybody to pieces in a few minutes. It's small but deadly. If an animal falls in piranha-infested waters, these frenzied fish eat the whole thing in a couple of minutes. Even a dog wouldn't have a chance. It's the world's weirdest fish."

"I don't think so," said Bo. "The world's weirdest fish is the stonefish. It's the most poisonous fish in the world. Its spines are as sharp as a hypodermic needle. It injects poison into its victim, too. It's hard to spot because it has all these bumps and warty things all over it. It looks like a stone. That's why it's called a stonefish, I guess. A human victim can die in two hours from its sting! In Japan, people eat a poisonous fish called fugu. It's considered a rare delicacy. Special chefs prepare the fish so no poison will remain, but sometimes they make a mistake, and people in the restaurant eat the poison and die. I guess that's what they mean when they say something is so good it's to die for."

"I nominate the anglerfish," said Daniel. "It lives thousands of feet under the sea. It has a lure that sticks out of its head like a headlight to attract fish for food. The lure glows like a light. And, guess what! This lure looks like an eye on a stick. Gross!"

"My candidate is the mudskipper," Emily joined in. "It actually comes onto land and skips like a frog out of water. It's cute, with bulging eyes. It's a fish that breathes air."

"Cute!" scoffed Linnette. "How about the moray eel! It's anything but cute! It has a body that looks kind of like a snake, razor-sharp teeth, and nasty habits. It hides in holes and can jump out and scare you when you're diving. Divers have died from its bite!"

"Have you all forgotten about the great white shark? It's the king of predators! This shark is the most feared of all sharks. Supposedly a sports fisherman caught one and found an entire horse in its stomach! If it smells blood anywhere in the water, watch out! The great white has killed lots of people, not just in the movies!" Linnette was out of breath.

"Wow!" said Daniel. "I had no idea there were such weird fish in the world. But which is the weirdest?"

"We haven't said it yet," remarked Bob. "It's the sea horse. It's not big, has no sharp teeth, and doesn't hurt anybody. But the male carries the eggs around and gives birth to the babies. That's weird!" Everyone agreed.

The "Weirdest Fish" Contest

Name _____

Understanding and Enjoying What You Read

Answer the questions below about the story. Reread the story if necessary.

1. Look at the pictures below. From the descriptions in the story, decide which is which. Write the name of each fish under the correct picture.

2. Write two facts about each fish pictured above. _____

   _____

   _____

   _____

3. Which fish do you think is the weirdest? Why? _____

   _____

   _____

4. Write **T** or **F** for each statement to show if it is True or False.

   ___ Sea horses have sharp teeth.   ___ Sharks don't kill people.   ___ The stonefish is hard to see.   ___ The piranha is poisonous.   ___ Mudskippers can "skip" on land.

5. Circle all the adjectives in the story. Remember, adjectives describe nouns.
   (Examples: <u>scary</u> fish, <u>long</u> teeth, <u>scaly</u> body—all the underlined words are adjectives.)

6. Do you believe Emily's grandpa's story? Explain. _____

   _____

7. What's a "fish story?" _____

8. Find a word in the story that means "full of piranha" _____, "a special kind of food," _____, "to propose as a candidate," _____.

9. Why would people eat a fish that they know is poisonous? Would you try to eat fugu? Why or why not? _____

10. Which do you nominate as the world's weirdest fish? Why? If your nominee isn't one of those named in the story, tell about it. _____

11. On the back of this paper, create a fish that's stranger than any mentioned in the story. Label what's weird about it and tell about your fish.

12. On another sheet of paper, write a short story entitled "The One That Got Away."

13. What would you do if you were confronted by a moray eel? _____

    _____

Try This!   Write a story entitled "The Weirdest Fish on Earth."

17

The Mystery of Stonehenge

Name _____

"Have you seen those weird rocks on the hillside?" asked David. "Everybody is talking about them. They're the greatest find in our part of the country."

"What are you talking about?" asked Daniel with great interest.

"Some rock climbers were rappelling down the cliffs and discovered a cave. Inside it were these incredible rock formations. They say Indians probably made them a few thousand years ago. Nobody knew about that cave. Scientists from all over the world want to examine the cave. And it's right here in our town!"

"It's just like Stonehenge!" exclaimed Emily. "This is so exciting! I bet the Druids sailed here from Britain and made megaliths in our cave just like they did at Stonehenge. Then they got back in their boats and went home. Maybe they got stuck here and died out after awhile. The possibilities are endless!"

"I think your imagination is running away here," said Linnette.

"I wish we lived near Stonehenge," sighed Emily. "It would be so exciting."

"What's exciting about a bunch of rocks standing up?" asked Daniel.

"They're not just rocks," answered Emily. "They're history. They're mysterious. They're in Great Britain."

"You're just saying that because Mrs. Fine told us about her trip to Stonehenge," said Bo. "You like being the teacher's pet."

"I do not!" yelled Emily. "But I'm doing an extra credit report. Want to know what I found out so far?"

"Do I have a choice?" groaned Daniel. "I'm just sitting here eating lunch. Okay. Go."

"Well," began Emily in her best teacher's voice, "Stonehenge was built about 4,000 years ago. We don't know who did it or why. It may have been used to track the movement of the stars and planets. Some think ancient people named Druids put them up, but that's not certain."

"Okay," said Daniel. "Thanks a lot. Now I know."

"I'm not finished yet," said Emily. "There's more. The vertical stones are called *sarsens*. They each weigh up to 50 tons. The stones that go across the top are called *lintels*. It took 1,100 men about seven weeks to drag each stone 25 miles from the quarry where they found the stones. They used leather ropes and rollers to move the stones. Some of the stones are gone. People carried them away to make bridges or dams. But the ones that remain are excellent tourist attractions."

"Speaking of tourist attractions, we have our own Stonehenge, remember?" said David.

"I almost forgot! Hey! Let's ask Mrs. Fine." They approached the teacher.

"Have you heard about the discovery on the cliffs?" asked Emily.

"Yes, it's a shame it's not real," the teacher said.

"What do you mean?" asked Daniel.

"Oh, some surfers confessed they did it as a prank. All the scientists have left. The town's not going to be famous after all," said Mrs. Fine.

"Emily," asked David, "what were you saying about Stonehenge?"

The Mystery of Stonehenge

Name _____

Understanding and Enjoying What You Read
Answer the questions below about the story. Reread the story if necessary.

1. Why do you think Stonehenge was built? _____
   _____

2. On another sheet of paper, write a short story entitled "A Tourist Attraction in My Town."

3. Answer the questions:
   1. How old is Stonehenge? _____
   2. Who built Stonehenge? _____
   3. Why was Stonehenge built? _____
   4. How far away was the quarry? _____
   5. What is a quarry? _____
   6. Where is Stonehenge? _____

4. Why do you think Stonehenge is such a popular spot for tourists? _____
   _____

5. How do you think Stonehenge could be used to track the movements of the stars and planets?
   _____
   _____

6. Why would surfers fake the rock formations? _____

7. Write the numbers of the correct definitions next to the words.
   ___ rappel   ___ incredible   ___ megalith   ___ prank   ___ quarry
   1. a huge stone used in an ancient monument   2. to descend on a rope passed under the thigh, across the body and over the shoulder   3. a trick   4. an open pit from which stone is obtained   5. unbelievable

8. Why did Linnette think Emily's imagination was running away? _____
   _____

9. Circle all the proper nouns in the story. Remember: Proper nouns are specific persons, places, or things. They are capitalized.

10. What are the vertical stones at Stonehenge called? _____
    What are the stones that lie across the top called? _____

11. What is taken from a quarry? _____

12. How much did the sarsens weigh? _____

13. How long did it take to drag each stone to the site? _____

14. What do you think of Emily and her teacher voice? What does it tell you about her?
    _____

Try This! What would be a modern way of moving the huge stones at Stonehenge?

© Frank Schaffer Publications, Inc.   FS-30025 Reading Comprehension

Cracking the Code

Name _____

Bo was writing the alphabet. A,B,C,D...

"I thought you already knew the alphabet," teased Linnette.

"Of course I do," he said, "but I'm inventing a new one, for a code. Then I can send secret messages to my friends."

"How are they going to be able to figure out the messages?" asked Linnette. "I'll teach them the code. I'll teach it to you, too," said Bo.

"Thanks," grinned Linnette. "That'll be fun. People have been writing and making up codes for thousands of years," she mentioned.

"I know," said Bo. "The ancient Sumerians, in the Middle East, were pretty smart. They invented pictographs–pictures that stood for words or ideas. A lot of them looked like the real things. A sword might mean a sword, or it might stand for power. The Egyptians had pictographs called hieroglyphics."

"That makes sense," agreed Linnette. "Then, in the same area, people invented cuneiform, which was the same idea, but simpler. Cuneiform was wedge-shaped strokes that stood for sounds in their language. It was a mystery for years, but then archaeologists and other scientists figured it out by comparing it to two other languages that they found side by side in a message," noted Bo.

"The Phoenicians, who were great traders, shortened writing even more. They invented 22 symbols that stood for sounds of words. That's our alphabet, plus four more letters. I wonder what ever happened to the Phoenicians," said Linnette.

"Lots of ancient people have disappeared," said Bo, "but I read that many of the people native to the country of Lebanon in the Middle East consider themselves the descendants of the Phoenicians. It's nice to know that these smart people aren't really gone."

"That's true," agreed Linnette, "but I found out some fascinating facts about codes. Putting messages into code is called *cryptography*. The message is called a *cryptogram*. *Cryptanalysis* is what you do when you break the code. All these words have *crypto* in them. That's an ancient Greek word meaning *hidden*. Cryptography means *hidden writing*. Cryptography and cryptanalysis make up the science of *cryptology*."

"Wow!" said Bo, impressed, "you've really researched this stuff. You sound like Emily."

"What do you mean?" asked Linnette indignantly. "She's not the only smart person around here, although she is the biggest know-it-all!"

"Well, I know something about codes, too," said Bo. "One great code is called *transposition*. You can take words and rearrange the letters. For example, suppose I said, 'Og ot het vomesi hwit em.' Can you figure out what I said?"

"I've been wanting to see that new horror movie," answered Linnette. "Let's ask Emily and David and Brett and Daniel to see the movie, too."

"That's a good idea," agreed Bo. "Back to codes, you could also put words together that don't normally belong together. You can even make up words for a whole new language. That way, people won't know what you're talking about at all. But that would take a long time. You'd have to find people to teach it to. I think I'll stick to Pig Latin. Ee-say ou-yay ater-lay."

Linnette thought for a minute. "Oh, I'll see you later, too!" she responded.

Name _____

Understanding and Enjoying What You Read

Answer the questions below about the story. Reread the story if necessary.

1. Number in order the types of writing as they appear in the story from 1 to 4.

    ___ alphabet

    ___ hieroglyphics

    ___ cuneiform

    ___ pictographs

2. Put a check next to the main idea of the story. ___ Emily is a know-it-all. ___ Writing and codes have been around for thousands of years. ___ Bo knows quite a bit about codes. ___ Anyone can learn a code. ___ It's fun to send secret messages.

3. Fill in the missing words. The Phoenicians were famous _____. The Sumerians invented a system of writing called _____. Bo spoke to Linnette in a made-up language called _____. Bo was inventing a new _____. The descendants of the Phoenicians are from the modern-day country of _____. The word cryptography comes from the _____ language. Linnette wanted to see a _____ movie.

4. Why do you think Bo and Linnette were so interested in language and codes? _____

    _____

5. How many more letters are in the English alphabet than in the Phoenician? ____

6. What does *indignantly* mean? Put a check next to what you think is the best meaning:

    ___ happily ___ angrily ___ sadly ___ glumly

7. Write the names of all the ancient peoples mentioned in the story.

    _____

8. What is a know-it-all? Why do you think Bo and Linnette think Emily is one? _____

    _____

9. Why would it be a good idea to know a secret code? _____

    _____

10. What is a disadvantage of pictographs? Why wouldn't they work today? _____

    _____

11. Try this code on your friends: Write the alphabet from A to Z. Then write the numbers 1-26 under the letters. Write a secret message and have your friends translate it. Read this message, too, and write it. 12 5 1 18 14   20 8 5   3 15 4 5

    Try this code backwards, too, using Z as number 1.

12. On the back of this paper, draw ten pictographs that stand for something common around school. See if a friend can understand them.

Try This!   Using an atlas, write the names of the countries in the Middle East.

Name _____

"Earth really does look like a big blue marble from space," said Emily. "All you can see is swirls of blue water and white clouds. I really liked those pictures that Mrs. Fine showed us."

"I don't think it looks like a big blue marble," said Brett. "It looks just like my mother's bowling ball."

"Anyway," said Emily, "I hope I can go into space someday. Maybe I'll be an astronaut."

"That's about the zillionth thing you've wanted to be since I've known you," said David. "Let's see, first it was a model, then a singer, then a writer, then. . ."

"Okay, okay, you've made your point," said Emily, annoyed at her friend.

"Anyway, you're wrong about the big blue marble. I know something on Earth that you can see from space," said David. "Do you know what it is?"

"Is this a riddle or a joke?" asked Emily.

"Nope. Give up? Good! It's the Great Wall of China. It's so long that you can see it from space. The wall is over 1,500 miles long. It was built by an emperor who wanted to keep out invaders. So he figured that guards would be posted all along the wall. But the invaders found the wall pretty easy to conquer. They went around it or over it. It didn't keep people out for long. China was invaded anyway. The wall is a great tourist attraction for people all over the world. Nowadays, people ride bikes on it or hike it." said David.

"The wall didn't work for the purpose for which it was made, even though it's 30 feet high and wide enough for five horses to run side by side on top of it. The emperor Ch'in was the first emperor of China. They named the country after him. But he wanted this wall so much that thousands of lives were lost building it." Emily shook her head just thinking about it.

"Three hundred thousand men were used to build the wall," David said. "Thousands died just making the journey to the site. Thousands more died building the wall. They were buried where they died. Guards were stationed on top of the wall when it was finished, but they couldn't ever have enough guards to keep out invaders."

"There's a story about the emperor's son, Fu Su," replied David. "Supposedly he was tricked into going to the site of the wall when he received a message from his father to go there. Since no one disobeyed the emperor, not even his son, he went. But once there, he died, and his father didn't know the truth, that the message had come from his uncle, who feared that the young man might prevent him from having power. It's a sad story."

"I feel sorry for the men who never returned to their families," Emily said sadly.

"Me too," said David. "I'm glad nobody builds giant walls anymore."

"How about the Berlin wall in Germany?" asked Bo. "It was there for almost 30 years to keep Germans apart. It's gone now, crumbled to rubble. When it was coming down, people took chunks of it as souvenirs. My father has a piece of it. He bought it at a store. At least, he was told it's part of the Berlin wall. The destruction of the wall represents freedom."

"But there are lots of places in the world where people still don't have freedom," Emily said. "Maybe that's like building the Great Wall."

The Great Wall of China

Name _____

Understanding and Enjoying What You Read

Answer the questions below about the story. Reread the story if necessary.

1. What does Emily mean by the last sentence? _____

_____

2. Answer these questions about the Great Wall of China.

   a. Who was the first Emperor of China? _____ b. How long is the wall? _____

   c. What is one reason the wall was built? _____

   d. Why didn't the wall keep out invaders? _____

   e. What happened to thousands of workers? _____ f. How high is the wall? _____

3. Why do you think the men who died weren't sent home for burial? _____

_____

4. What are methods used today to keep enemies out of a country? _____

_____

5. A man once rode his bicycle down the length of the wall. What would be some problems in

   doing that? _____

_____

6. Why do you think Emily keeps changing her mind about what she wants to be when she grows

   up? _____

7. Write three facts about the first emperor of China. _____

_____

8. Suppose Fu Su had refused to obey his father. What do you think would have happened to

   him? _____

9. Fences and walls have been used for thousands of years to keep people in or out of an area.

   What do you think the old saying, "Good fences make good neighbors" means? _____

_____

10. What happened to the Berlin wall? _____

11. Why do you think the Great Wall was made to be so long? _____

12. Put the events below in the order in which they occurred.

    ___ The emperor wanted to build a wall. ___ Men were sent to build the wall.

    ___ The emperor's son died. ___ Fu Su thought his father had sent for him.

    ___ Many men died while building the wall. ___ The wall can be seen from space.

13. Why do you think the friends are so interested in the Great Wall? _____

_____

14. Why do walls represent a lack of freedom? _____

Try This!   Look in an atlas and find out where the Great Wall of China is. Trace it.

FS-30025 Reading Comprehension

Native Americans

Name _____

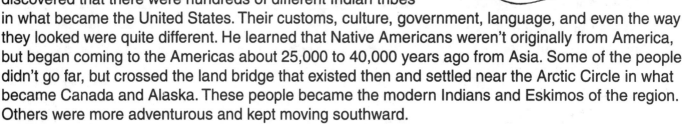

Brett's report on Native Americans of the Woodlands was a lot more interesting to do than he thought it would be. He handed it in before the due date. Mrs. Fine was really surprised. So was Brett. He had thought that all Indians were the same. He thought they all wore war paint and ran around yelling war whoops all the time. This, however, is a stereotype.

People often make stereotypes when they think they know everything about people when they really don't. Brett discovered that there were hundreds of different Indian tribes in what became the United States. Their customs, culture, government, language, and even the way they looked were quite different. He learned that Native Americans weren't originally from America, but began coming to the Americas about 25,000 to 40,000 years ago from Asia. Some of the people didn't go far, but crossed the land bridge that existed then and settled near the Arctic Circle in what became Canada and Alaska. These people became the modern Indians and Eskimos of the region. Others were more adventurous and kept moving southward.

The southward-moving people settled throughout the Americas in what is now Canada, the United States, Mexico, and Central and South America. They were bound to clash with Europeans when these people explored the Americas. The Europeans had many stereotypes about Indians. They decided that the natives were brutal, savage, stupid, and uncivilized. It was their duty to change them, they believed. This was tragic for the Indians, whose descendants are still bitter about what happened.

Brett decided to find out more about the Indians of the Eastern Woodlands as a focus. He discovered many interesting facts. For example, the Eastern Woodland Indians included the Cherokee, Chippewa, Creek, Huron, and Mohawks. They were called Woodland Indians by the white settlers who met them. Depending on their culture and environment, they lived in wigwams or long houses. Some lived in small villages, others in what would be considered Indian towns or cities. Some Indian nations, like those belonging to the Iroquois League, had such well-organized tribes that the new country of the United States borrowed some of their ideas for its government.

These Native Americans had been cultivating corn for at least 5000 years. Brett found that they taught the new settlers all about this crop that was not grown in Europe. Europeans discovered that corn could also be dried and made into meal and that they could fry, cook, and bake with it. Corn was so important to the Indians that many even had a legend that told how corn was first given to the people.

In one story Brett read about, it seems that a young man spied an unusual girl. She had golden hair and was very beautiful. He fell in love with her instantly, but when he approached her, she moved away. He asked what he could do so she wouldn't leave. He would do anything she wished. She asked if he really meant that, and he assured her that he did. She said he was to get two dry sticks. She rubbed the sticks together and made a fire. She set the grass afire, and it burned. Then she told him to drag her by the hair across the burned ground. When he refused, she reminded him that he said he'd do anything she asked. He did it, and she said, "Remember, when you see a kind of grass that has what looks like my hair in it, take its seeds and plant it. There will be food for the people." That was the beginning of corn.

Brett liked this story. He just hoped Mrs. Fine was as impressed with his report as he was with the Native Americans.

 FS-30025 Reading Comprehension

Name _____

Understanding and Enjoying What You Read

Answer the questions below about the story. Reread the story if necessary.

1. Unscramble the letters below to find the names of six Woodland tribes.

   aciphpwe   oruhn   khowma   kerce   recheoek   siqoriou

   _____   _____   _____   _____   _____   _____

2. Why would a golden-haired woman be unusual among the Indians? _____
   _____

3. Two houses mentioned in the story are wigwams and long houses. Write the names of other
   types of houses that you can think of. _____
   _____

4. Which tribe gave the government of the United States some ideas? _____

5. What do you think would have happened to the Indians if no Europeans would ever have come
   to their lands? _____

6. Put a check next to the main idea of this story.

   ___ Indians of the Woodlands are small in number today. ___ Woodland Indians have an
   interesting culture. ___ Indians have known about corn for a long time. ___ Indians have an
   interesting and long history.

7. Why do you think the woman in the corn story would let the young man drag her around like
   that? Who might she have been? _____
   _____

8. What is a stereotype? _____
   "All girls like to play with dolls, but they don't like to play sports." Why is this a stereotype? ____
   _____
   _____

9. From where did the Indians originate? _____ How long ago did they come? _____
   Where did they settle? _____
   What is one type of person who settled near the Arctic Circle? _____

10. Why do you think the Indians left their native homelands in Asia? _____
    _____

11. If you were an Indian, how do you think you would feel about the Europeans invading your
    land? _____

12. What do you think happened to all the Indians who used to live in the United States? _____
    _____

Try This! Make up a legend about how something that is important to you began.
Illustrate your story.

The Community Garden

Name _____

"It's time to plant our garden," said Mrs. Fine. "The ground is nice and warm, and I've arranged a spot in the garden."

"Can we vote on it?" asked Daniel.

Mrs. Fine was surprised. "I thought everyone would want to plant a garden," she said. "We can plant vegetables and make a salad in a couple of months. We can plant flowers. What's the problem?"

"It's Mr. Grinch," said David.

Mrs. Fine laughed. "You mean Mr. Lynch, I believe. Well, I know he's a bit grumpy, but it is his garden, too. It is a community garden. Although it's on school grounds, Mr. Lynch and a few other people have permission to plant there."

"Last year, he chased us out every time we went with Ms. Dawes. He ran after Bo with a shovel. He kept yelling, 'Stay on the path, keep away from my squash' and stuff like that. I can't stand him. He's not grumpy, he's a creep!" Linnette finished her speech.

"I had no idea you all felt this way," said Mrs. Fine. "There's only one thing to do, we'll take the bull by the horns." Mrs. Fine was always saying things like that, and sometimes it took a while to figure them out.

"I think she's going to make us go into the garden," said Bo. "What she said means we should meet the problem head on." Mrs. Fine smiled. Bo was right.

The next morning, the class dragged themselves to the garden. Mrs. Fine unlocked the chainlink gate. Their spot was overgrown with weeds from the year before.

"This looks like hard work," said Emily. "I'm going to get dirty. I hate to get dirty."

The kids entered the garden, looking around for any sign of Mr. Lynch. He was nowhere to be found. Mrs. Fine unlocked the shed and passed out the tools. Soon, kids were pulling weeds, softening the dirt, and watering it to make it easier to dig in.

"Hey!" yelled Lance. "Brett got me all wet." He grabbed the hose from Brett and turned it on him. Pandemonium resulted. Kids started throwing dirt clods at each other. Emily was yelling, "I'm getting dirty!" Enraged, she tried to stuff a big weed in Bo's mouth. Mrs. Fine was angry. "We're going back right now," she shouted. "You children don't know how to act in a garden. No wonder Mr. Lynch threw you out last year."

She stopped. Mr. Lynch, glowering at her and the kids, appeared before them. "I know this bunch," he snorted. "Hooligans. Hoodlums. Criminals. Get out of my garden!"

David stood his ground. "I'm sorry, Mr. Lynch," he said, "but we're not any of that stuff you said. But we sure were right about you!"

Mrs. Fine interrupted. "I think everyone is wrong here. Mr. Lynch, we want a garden. You'll have to live with that. You can either help us or ignore us. The kids won't act like this again—will you?" She looked sternly at her class, most of whom were pretty ashamed of their behavior. Mr. Lynch seemed to soften.

"Well, I'll give this bunch a chance. Now, don't step on my babies—those are the little seedlings, you know. I'll give you a tour. I'll even show you Mr. Choi's Chinese garden and Mr. Cifuentes' cactus and pepper garden. I'll tell you about good bugs and bad ones, how to water properly, and make your plants love you. I might even show you where the black and white rabbits live." He led the way.

FS-30025 Reading Comprehension

The Community Garden

Name _____

Understanding and Enjoying What You Read

Answer the questions below about the story. Reread the story if necessary.

1. Put a check next to the main idea of the story.   ___ Mr. Lynch was a mean man.
   ___ Mrs. Fine wanted a garden.   ___ Rabbits were in the garden.
   ___ The class made peace with Mr. Lynch. ___ The kids went crazy in the garden.

2. Put the events below in the order in which they occurred.
   ___ Mr. Lynch confronted the class. ___ The class went into the garden.
   ___ Mr. Lynch helped the gardeners.
   ___ There was pandemonium. ___ Mr. Lynch called the kids names.

3. Write **T** or **F** to indicate whether the facts below are true or false.
   ___ The kids were eager to go into the garden.   ___ The class garden was full of weeds.
   ___ Mrs. Fine unlocked the garden gate and the shed. ___ There were rabbits in the garden.
   ___ Mr. Lynch was a very nice man who welcomed the kids. ___ Mrs. Fine yelled at Mr. Lynch.

4. What did you think Mr. Lynch would do when David apologized? _____
   _____

5. Put a check next to what you believe is the meaning of *pandemonium.*
   ___ tears and crying ___ a wild uproar ___ laughing ___ fighting

6. What would you plant in a class garden? Write your selections below, then draw your garden on
   the back of this paper. Don't forget any animals you might want. _____
   _____

7. Why might it not be a great idea to have rabbits in a garden? _____
   _____

8. What did Emily do to Bo? _____
   What did Brett do to Lance? _____

9. Why do you think the kids acted the way they did in the garden? _____
   _____

10. How do you think the kids and Mr. Lynch will treat each other in the future? _____
    _____

11. Why did Mrs. Fine become angry? _____

12. On the back of this page, write a letter to your teacher telling him or her why you would or would
    not like to have a garden for your class.

13. What do you think a dirt clod is? Look it up if necessary. _____

14. Why is gardening hard work? Is it worth it? Explain. _____
    _____

Try This! Find out if there's a community garden in your neighborhood. Make a report on it or a
pretend one.

Drawing conclusions, predicting outcomes, sequencing, character analysis, recalling facts

Name _____

"My mother says that when she was a kid, nobody used computers," said David. "They barely knew what they were."

"My grandmother says that when she was working as an engineer, they didn't even have calculators," said Daniel. "They used something called a slide rule. You had to move this wooden ruler around or something. That's really primitive!"

"Imagine what our kids and grandkids will say about us," grinned Emily. "They'll probably think we rode around on the backs of dinosaurs!"

"I wonder what the future will really be like," Linnette wondered out loud.

"I bet I know," answered Emily.

"Oh, you think you know everything!" said Bo.

"Okay, then, what do you think the world will be like?" Emily challenged him.

"I don't have a crystal ball," said Bo, "but here it goes. We won't have to drive our own cars. We'll just get in, program it to where we want to go, and it'll get us there–avoiding traffic, accidents, and all that stuff. We can watch cartoons on TV in the car."

"You won't want to watch cartoons when you're an adult," laughed Emily.

"Wrong!" said Linnette. "Bo will always watch cartoons. But I wouldn't like a car like that. I can't wait to learn to drive!"

"We'll be driving little airplanes on highways in the sky," said Daniel. "The streets will be reserved for people to walk around."

"Schools will have no teachers," declared Brett. "Kids will have school on TV piped into their living rooms. A teacher or maybe a robot will instruct us."

"When would we play with our friends?" asked Linnette.

"Well, there are bugs in everything at first," said Brett.

"There will be a law that says parents can't punish their kids," said Bo.

"Wait!" said Emily. "We'll be the parents by then. Is that a good idea?"

"Sure," Bo said. "We'll remember when we were kids, and we'll be great parents. Our kids will think we're really cool."

"I wonder what kind of clothes we'll wear?" said Lance, who had been pretty quiet.

Everyone thought. "That's a hard one," said David. "Something comfortable, I guess, because we'll be speeding all over the place in our little airplanes, or aircars, or whatever we'll call them."

"Computers will be as tiny as a wristwatch," said Linnette.

"I think they have that already," mentioned Daniel. "I read about it."

"People will have time to have fun," said Lance. "Maybe nobody will have to work."

continued on next page

It's All in the Future

Name _____

"How will people live if they don't work?" asked Linnette.

"I don't know," said Lance, "that's why it's for the future."

"That doesn't make sense," said Brett. "But it would be nice to have more time for vacations and fun. Maybe we could fly to France in an hour."

"I don't like to fly much," said Bo. "Maybe they can build long highways across the oceans. Maybe I'll be the one to design them!" The kids laughed.

"Hey!" said Bo. "This is the present, and we'll get in trouble if we don't do that social studies homework!"

Understanding and Enjoying What You Read

Answer the questions below about the story. Reread the story if necessary.

1. Do you think the kids are correct in any of their predictions? Explain. _____
   _____

2. How do you think you will live when you become an adult? How will the world have changed?
   _____

3. What do you think of Bo's ideas? _____

4. What kind of person does Bo show himself to be? _____

5. What does "There are bugs in everything at first" mean? _____
   _____

6. Put the events below in the order in which they occurred. ___ Cars will drive themselves.
   ___ The kids wonder about the future.   ___ There will be highways in the sky.
   ___ Computers will be tiny.   ___ School will be at home on TV.

7. What is a *crystal ball* used for? _____

8. What kind of school would you like right now? _____
   _____

9. Do you think Bo likes Emily? Explain. _____

10. Why does Bo think they'll be great parents? _____
    _____

11. Will you want to watch cartoons when you're an adult? Why or why not? _____
    _____

12. On the back of this paper, draw yourself in the future, wearing the clothes of the time.

13. Who do the kids think might teach them in the future? _____

14. Would you prefer to drive or have a car that drives itself? Explain. _____
    _____

Try This!   Write a report on what your vision for the future is.

29

Neither a Borrower nor a Lender Be

Name _____

"Aw, I forgot that we can get ice cream for only a quarter after lunch today," said Bob. "I love ice cream. I didn't bring any money, though. Hey, David, my best friend, how about giving me a quarter so I can get ice cream?"

"Neither a borrower nor a lender be," said David, quite seriously.

"What does that mean?" asked Bob as he got ready to buy his ice cream.

"Neither a borrower nor a lender be means that you shouldn't borrow or lend money," explained David. "My dad taught me that. So I don't borrow, and I don't lend."

"Come on, just give me the quarter. I know you have it. Don't be like that."

"No, Bob, friends become enemies when money is involved," insisted David.

"You're just stingy and cheap," replied Bob, "and so is your father."

"You take that back or I'll. . . I won't be your friend," answered David.

"Okay, but just this once, please. It's only a quarter. Come on, give it to me."

David reluctantly gave Bob the quarter. Bob bought ice cream.

Understanding and Enjoying What You Read

Answer the questions below about the story. Reread the story if necessary.

1. How do you feel about someone who doesn't pay his or her debts? (Debts are what is owed.)

   _____

2. Why was Bob annoyed with David? _____

3. Have you ever loaned money to anyone? If so, what happened? _____

   _____

4. What can you buy with a quarter? _____

5. How do you think David felt when Bob called his father stingy and cheap? _____

   _____

6. Write the opposite (antonym) of each word below. Use a dictionary if necessary.

   reluctantly _____   lend _____   stingy _____

7. Do you agree with what David's father says? Explain. _____

   _____

8. Why might friends become enemies when money is involved? What does this mean and do you agree? _____

   _____

9. Make up a new saying similar to "Neither a borrower nor a lender be."

   _____

Try This!   Write what you should do if someone doesn't pay off a loan.

Page 3

1. Answers will vary.
2. Answers will vary.
3. Answers may vary.—They wanted Jackie, but they were happy to have a pet.
4. Answers will vary.
5. Answers may vary.—to help the kids feel better after Jackie was gone
6. caramel, shaggy, stinky, noticed, wanders, leash
7. Answers will vary.
8. The class took time out to care for a neglected dog.
9. Answers will vary.
10. Answers may vary.—You could get bitten.
11. Answers will vary.
12. First, they took her into the classroom. Then, they took her home. After that, they gave her a bath. Finally, they took her home clean.
13. Answers will vary.

Page 5

1. Asia and Europe
2. Answers will vary.
3. Answers will vary.
4. 3, 1, 6, 5, 2, 4
5. Answers will vary.
6. Answers will vary.
7. Prey is an animal hunted or caught by a predator for food.
8. Answers will vary.
9. Check students' stories.
10. Answers will vary.—perhaps cold, damp weather
11. Answers will vary.
12. Answers may vary.—They can't see well, and their whiskers may help them feel their way.
13. Answers may vary.—mice, rats, beavers, squirrels, chipmunks Note: Do not accept rabbits, they are not rodents.

Page 7

1. Answers may vary.—onion, garlic, cheese
2. Emily says she's going to die, and she says whoever stole her sandwich is a criminal.
3.-6. Answers will vary.
7. going across: 5, 3, 2, 1, 4
8. astonishing
9. Answers may vary. - If you don't have anything, you can't be picky.
10. Daniel and David help Emily find the sandwich thief.
11. Answers will vary.
12. an apple and juice
13. Answers may vary.—Perhaps he was afraid of them, or knew they'd give him away.
14. Answers will vary.

Page 9

1. Answers will vary.
2. A system of colored flags that are waved to send messages
3.-7. Answers will vary.
8. Answers may vary.—drumbeats, Morse code, smoke signals, Braille, body gestures, semaphore
9. Answers may vary.—instinct
10. Answers may vary.—She was telling her to be quiet.
11.-12. Answers will vary.
13. Braille
14. sign language
15. Answers will vary.

Page 11

1. The class goes on a field trip to the opera
2.-5. Answers will vary.
6. "The Barber of Seville"
7. A composer writes music.
8. A disguise is clothing and/or make-up used to make someone look different.
9. Verdi, Puccini, Bizet, Wagner, Beethoven, Mozart

10. They sold candy, popcorn, cookies, and other goodies.
11. Italy, Germany, France, Russia, Austria
12. Pictures of opera stars
13. Answers may vary.—cartoons, TV, movies
15. Answers will vary.
16. Answers may vary.—She may have fainted.

Page 13

1. Answers will vary.
2. 31 or 30; to calm down the crowd
3.-4. Answers will vary.
5. 4, 1, 3, 5, 2
6. Answers may vary.—because elevators go up and down
7. Answers will vary.
8. There were people with baby carriages.
9. Answers may vary.—so they could enjoy the ride alone
10. Answers may vary.—A crowd gathered.
11.-13. Answers will vary.
14. Answers may vary.—They were happy to see them free.

Page 15

1. Answers may vary.—because they had laughed at the girls
2. Answers will vary.
3. going across: 4, 5, 2, 3, 1
4. Answers will vary.
5. Check students' stories.
6. to listen in on a private conversation secretly
7. Answers will vary.
8. Answers may vary.—Both listened to the radio, laughed, talked, ate, sang. The girls fixed each other's hair, the boys made garbage sandwiches, had burping contest.
9. 5, 1, 2, 3, 4
10. Answers may vary.—He's daring.

Answers

11.-15. Answers will vary.

Page 17

1. stonefish, anglerfish, sea horse, piranha
2.-3. Answers will vary.
4. F, F, T, F, T
5. See students' stories.
6. Answers will vary.
7. Answers may vary.—a story that's exaggerated or made up
8. piranha-infested, delicacy, nominate
9.-13. Answers will vary.

Page 19

1.-2. Answers will vary.
3. 1. about 4,000 years old
   2. Maybe Druids, ancient people, we're not sure
   3. Perhaps to track the movement of the stars and planets
   4. 25 miles
   5. a place with many rocks
   6. in Great Britain
4.-6. Answers will vary.
7. 2, 5, 1, 3, 4
8. Answers will vary.
9. See students' stories.
10. sarsens, lintels
11. stones or rocks
12. up to 50 tons
13. 7 weeks
14. Answers will vary.

Page 21

1. 1, 3, 4, 2
2. Writing and codes have been around for thousands of years.
3. traders, cuneiform, Pig Latin, alphabet, Lebanon, Greek, horror
4. Answers will vary.
5. 4
6. angrily
7. Sumerians, Egyptians, Phoenicians, Greeks

8. Answers may vary.—someone who thinks he or she knows everything
9.-10. Answers will vary.
11. Learn the code.

Page 23

1. Answers may vary.—possible: Walls keep people apart; they're not free.
2. a. Ch'in
   b. 1,500 miles long
   c. to keep out invaders
   d. It was easy to get over or around, and it couldn't be guarded.
   e. They died on the job.
   f. 30 feet
3. Answers may vary.—They weren't considered to be important; it was too far from their homes; the wall was more important.
4.-6. Answers will vary.
7. Answers may vary.—He wanted to build a wall. He was the first emperor. China was named for him.
8.-9. Answers will vary.
10. It was destroyed, torn down.
11. Answers may vary.—Because China is a huge country
12. 2, 3, 6, 5, 4, 1
13.-14. Answers will vary.

Page 25

1. Chippewa, Huron, Mohawk, Creek, Cherokee, Iroquois
2. Answers may vary.—Most Indians are dark.
3. Answers will vary.—hut, apartment, igloo, trailer, mobile home, yurt, tent, tree house
4. Iroquois
5. Answers will vary.
6. Indians have an interesting and long history.
7. Answers will vary.
8. a false idea about individuals or

a group based on limited experience or accepted ideas
9. Asia, 25,000-40,000 years ago, the Americas, Eskimo
10. Answers will vary.
11. Answers will vary.
12. Answers will vary.

Page 27

1. The class made peace with Mr. Lynch.
2. 3, 1, 5, 2, 4
3. F, T, F, T, F, F
4. Answers will vary.
5. a wild uproar
6. Answers will vary.
7. Answers may vary.—They'd eat the vegetables and flowers.
8. Emily tried to stuff a weed in his mouth. He got him wet.
9.-12. Answers will vary.
13. a clump of dirt
14. Answers will vary.

Page 29

1.-4. Answers will vary.
5. Answers may vary.—There are mistakes, flaws in everything.
6. 2, 1, 3, 5, 4
7. to see into the future
8.-9. Answers will vary.
10. because they won't punish their kids
11. Answers will vary.
13. TV's
14. Answers will vary.

Page 30

1. Answers will vary.
2. Because David wouldn't lend him money at first.
3.-5. Answers will vary.
6. gladly, willingly; generous; borrow
7.-9. Answers will vary.

Dietary Reference Intakes (DRIs): Recommended Intakes for Individuals, Elements
Food and Nutrition Board, Institute of Medicine, National Academies

Life Stage Group	Calcium (mg/d)	Chromium (μg/d)	Copper (μg/d)	Fluoride (mg/d)	Iodine (μg/d)	Iron (mg/d)	Magnesium (mg/d)	Manganese (mg/d)	Molybdenum (μg/d)	Phosphorus (mg/d)	Selenium (μg/d)	Zinc (mg/d)
Infants												
0–6 mo	210*	0.2*	200*	0.01*	110*	0.27*	30*	0.003*	2*	100*	15*	2*
7–12 mo	270*	5.5*	220*	0.5*	130*	11	75*	0.6*	3*	275*	20*	3
Children												
1–3 y	500*	11*	340	0.7*	90	7	80	1.2*	17	460	20	3
4–8 y	800*	15*	440	1*	90	10	130	1.5*	22	500	30	5
Males												
9–13 y	1,300*	25*	700	2*	120	8	240	1.9*	34	1,250	40	8
14–18 y	1,300*	35*	890	3*	150	11	410	2.2*	43	1,250	55	11
19–30 y	1,000*	35*	900	4*	150	8	400	2.3*	45	700	55	11
31–50 y	1,000*	35*	900	4*	150	8	420	2.3*	45	700	55	11
51–70 y	1,200*	30*	900	4*	150	8	420	2.3*	45	700	55	11
>70 y	1,200*	30*	900	4*	150	8	420	2.3*	45	700	55	11
Females												
9–13 y	1,300*	21*	700	2*	120	8	240	1.6*	34	1,250	40	8
14–18 y	1,300*	24*	890	3*	150	15	360	1.6*	43	1,250	55	9
19–30 y	1,000*	25*	900	3*	150	18	310	1.8*	45	700	55	8
31–50 y	1,000*	25*	900	3*	150	18	320	1.8*	45	700	55	8
51–70 y	1,200*	20*	900	3*	150	8	320	1.8*	45	700	55	8
>70 y	1,200*	20*	900	3*	150	8	320	1.8*	45	700	55	8
Pregnancy												
≤18 y	1,300*	29*	1,000	3*	220	27	400	2.0*	50	1,250	60	12
19–30 y	1,000*	30*	1,000	3*	220	27	350	2.0*	50	700	60	11
31–50 y	1,000*	30*	1,000	3*	220	27	360	2.0*	50	700	60	11
Lactation												
≤18 y	1,300*	44*	1,300	3*	290	10	360	2.6*	50	1,250	70	13
19–30 y	1,000*	45*	1,300	3*	290	9	310	2.6*	50	700	70	12
31–50 y	1,000*	45*	1,300	3*	290	9	320	2.6*	50	700	70	12

NOTE: This table presents Recommended Dietary Allowances (RDAs) in **bold type** and Adequate Intakes (AIs) in ordinary type followed by an asterisk (*). RDAs and AIs may both be used as goals for individual intake. RDAs are set to meet the needs of almost all (97 to 98 percent) individuals in a group. For healthy breastfed infants, the AI is the mean intake. The AI for other life stage and gender groups is believed to cover needs of all individuals in the group, but lack of data or uncertainty in the data prevent being able to specify with confidence the percentage of individuals covered by this intake.

SOURCES: Dietary Reference Intakes for Calcium, Phosphorus, Magnesium, Vitamin D, and Fluoride (1997); Dietary Reference Intakes for Thiamin, Riboflavin, Niacin, Vitamin B-6, Folate, Vitamin B-12, Pantothenic Acid, Biotin, and Choline (1998); Dietary Reference Intakes for Vitamin C, Vitamin E, Selenium, and Carotenoids (2000); and Dietary Reference Intakes for Vitamin A, Vitamin K, Arsenic, Boron, Chromium, Copper, Iodine, Iron, Manganese, Molybdenum, Nickel, Silicon, Vanadium, and Zinc (2001). These reports may be accessed via www.nap.edu.

Dietary Reference Intakes (DRIs): Recommended Intakes for Individuals, Macronutrients

Food and Nutrition Board, Institute of Medicine, National Academies

Life Stage Group	Carbohydrate (g/d)	Total Fiber (g/d)	Fat (g/d)	Linoleic Acid (g/d)	α-Linolenic Acid (g/d)	Protein[a] (g/d)
Infants						
0–6 mo	60*	ND	31*	4.4*	0.5*	9.1*
7–12 mo	95*	ND	30*	4.6*	0.5*	**13.5**
Children						
1–3 y	**130**	19*	ND[b]	7*	0.7*	**13**
4–8 y	**130**	25*	ND	10*	0.9*	**19**
Males						
9–13 y	**130**	31*	ND	12*	1.2*	**34**
14–18 y	**130**	38*	ND	16*	1.6*	**52**
19–30 y	**130**	38*	ND	17*	1.6*	**56**
31–50 y	**130**	38*	ND	17*	1.6*	**56**
51–70 y	**130**	30*	ND	14*	1.6*	**56**
>70 y	**130**	30*	ND	14*	1.6*	**56**
Females						
9–13 y	**130**	26*	ND	10*	1.0*	**34**
14–18 y	**130**	26*	ND	11*	1.1*	**46**
19–30 y	**130**	25*	ND	12*	1.1*	**46**
31–50 y	**130**	25*	ND	12*	1.1*	**46**
51–70 y	**130**	21*	ND	11*	1.1*	**46**
>70 y	**130**	21*	ND	11*	1.1*	**46**
Pregnancy						
14–18 y	**175**	28*	ND	13*	1.4*	**71**
19–30 y	**175**	28*	ND	13*	1.4*	**71**
31–50 y	**175**	28*	ND	13*	1.4*	**71**
Lactation						
14–18 y	**210**	29*	ND	13*	1.3*	**71**
19–30 y	**210**	29*	ND	13*	1.3*	**71**
31–50 y	**210**	29*	ND	13*	1.3*	**71**

NOTE: This table presents Recommended Dietary Allowances (RDAs) in **bold type** and Adequate Intakes (AIs) in ordinary type followed by an asterisk (*). RDAs and AIs may both be used as goals for individual intake. RDAs are set to meet the needs of almost all (97 to 98 percent) individuals in a group. For healthy breastfed infants, the AI is the mean intake. The AI for other life stage and gender groups is believed to cover needs of all individuals in the group, but lack of data or uncertainty in the data prevent being able to specify with confidence the percentage of individuals covered by this intake.

[a]Based on 0.8g protein/kg body weight for reference body weight.

[b]ND = not determinable at this time

SOURCES: Dietary Reference Intakes for Energy, Carbohydrate, Fiber, Fat, Fatty Acids, Cholesterol, Protein, and Amino Acids (2002). This report may be accessed via www.nap.edu.

Eighth Edition

NUTRITION

FOR HEALTH, FITNESS, & SPORT

Melvin H. Williams

Old Dominion University

Boston   Burr Ridge, IL   Dubuque, IA   New York   San Francisco   St. Louis   Bangkok
Bogotá   Caracas   Kuala Lumpur   Lisbon   London   Madrid   Mexico City   Milan
Montreal   New Delhi   Santiago   Seoul   Singapore   Sydney   Taipei   Toronto

Higher Education

NUTRITION FOR HEALTH, FITNESS, & SPORT, EIGHTH EDITION

Published by McGraw-Hill, a business unit of The McGraw-Hill Companies, Inc., 1221 Avenue of the Americas, New York, NY 10020.

 This book is printed on recycled, acid-free paper containing 10% postconsumer waste.

1 2 3 4 5 6 7 8 9 0 DOW/DOW 0 9 8 7 6

ISBN-13 978-0-07-294371-9
ISBN-10 0-07-294371-8

Publisher: *Michelle Watnick*
Publisher: *Colin H. Wheatley*
Senior Developmental Editor: *Lynne M. Meyers*
Marketing Manager: *Tami Petsche*
Project Manager: *April R. Southwood*
Senior Production Supervisor: *Kara Kudronowicz*
Senior Media Producer: *Jeffry Schmitt*
Designer: *Rick D. Noel*
Cover Designer: *John Rokusek*
Lead Photo Research Coordinator: *Carrie K. Burger*
Compositor: *Carlisle Publishing Services*
Typeface: *10/12 Times Roman*
Printer: *R. R. Donnelley Willard, OH*

(USE) Cover Images: Fruit: © Jonelle Weaver/Getty Images; Swimmer: © Art Explosion; Rowing team: © Lawrence M. Sawyer/Getty Images; Runners: © Art Explosion; Soccer game: © Geoff Manasse/Getty Images.

The credits section for this book begins on page 562 and is considered an extension of the copyright page.

Library of Congress Cataloging-in-Publication Data

Williams, Melvin H.
  Nutrition for health, fitness, & sport / Melvin H. Williams.—8th ed.
    p. cm.
  title: Nutrition for health, fitness, and sport.
  Includes index.
  ISBN 978-0-07-294371-9 - ISBN 0-07-294371-8 (hard copy : alk. paper)
  1. Nutrition. 2. Physical fitness. 3. Sports—Physiological aspects. I. Title: Nutrition for health, fitness, & sport. II. Title.

QP141.W514   2007
612.3—dc22   2006006202
                                              CIP

www.mhhe.com

To Jeanne,
Sara and Nik May
Serena, Jeff, and Daniel Newsom

and

To My Teachers,
Colleagues, and Students

Brief Contents

Contents

CHAPTER EIGHT

Minerals: The Inorganic Regulators 279

CHAPTER NINE

Water, Electrolytes, and Temperature Regulation 319

CHAPTER TEN

Body Weight and Composition for Health and Sport 363

CHAPTER ELEVEN

Weight Maintenance and Loss through Proper Nutrition and Exercise 399

CHAPTER TWELVE

Weight Gaining through Proper Nutrition and Exercise 451

CHAPTER THIRTEEN

Food Drugs and Related Supplements 477

Preface

In this new millennium, our love affair with fitness and sports continues to grow. Worldwide, although physical inactivity is still very prevalent in developed nations, more of us are joining fitness facilities or initiating fitness programs, such as bicycling, running, swimming, walking, and weight training. Improvement in health and fitness is one of the major reasons that more and more people initiate an exercise program. Research has shown that adults who become physically active also may become more interested in other aspects of their lifestyles—particularly nutrition—that may affect their health in a positive way.

Nutrition is the study of foods and their effects upon health, development, and performance. Although a relatively young science, nutrition research has made a significant contribution to our knowledge of essential nutrient needs. During the first part of the twentieth century, most nutrition research focused on identification of essential nutrients and amounts needed to prevent nutrient-deficiency diseases, such as scurvy from inadequate vitamin C. More recently, medical researchers have focused on the effects of foods and their specific constituents as a means to help prevent major chronic diseases, such as heart disease and cancer, that are epidemic in developed countries. *Nutriceutical* is a relatively new term used to characterize the drug, or medical, effects of a particular nutrient. Recent research findings continue to indicate that our diet is one of the most important determinants of our health status, and although individual nutrients are still being evaluated for possible health benefits, research is also focusing on dietary patterns, or the totality of the diet, and resultant health benefits.

Other than the health benefits of exercise and fitness, many physically active individuals also are finding the joy of athletic competition, participating in local sport events such as golf tournaments, tennis matches, triathlons, and road races. Individuals who compete athletically are always looking for a means to improve performance, be it a new piece of equipment or an improved training method. In this regard, proper nutrition may be a very important factor in improving exercise and sport performance. The United States Anti-Doping Agency (USADA), in its *Optimal Dietary Intake* guidelines for competitive athletes, notes that now more than ever, athletes need accurate sports nutrition information, indicating that optimal nutrition is an integral part of peak performance, while an inadequate diet and lack of fuel can limit an athlete's potential for maximum performance. Although the effect of diet on sport and exercise performance had been studied only sporadically prior to 1970, subsequently numerous sport scientists and sport nutritionists have studied the performance-enhancing effects of nutrition, such as diet composition and dietary supplements. Results of these studies have provided nutritional guidance to enhance performance in specific athletic endeavors.

With the completion of the Human Genome Project, gene therapies are currently being developed for the medical treatment of various health problems. Moreover, some contend that genetic manipulations may be used to enhance sports performance. For example, gene doping to increase insulin-like growth factor, which can stimulate muscle growth, may be applied to sport.

Our personal genetic code plays an important role in determining our health status and our sports abilities, and futurists speculate that one day each of us will carry our own genetic chip that will enable us to tailor food selection and exercise programs to optimize our health and sport performance. Such may be the case, but for the time being we must depend on available scientific evidence to provide us with prudent guidelines.

Each year literally thousands of published studies and reviews analyze the effects of nutrition on health or exercise and sports performance. The major purpose of this text is to evaluate these scientific data and present prudent recommendations for individuals who want to modify their diet for optimal health or exercise/sport performance.

Textbook Overview

This book uses a question-answer approach, which is convenient when you may have occasional short periods to study, such as riding a bus or during a lunch break. In addition, the questions are arranged in a logical sequence, the answer to one question often leading into the question that follows. Where appropriate, cross-referencing within the text is used to expand the discussion. No deep scientific background is needed for the chemical aspects of nutrition and energy expenditure, as these have been simplified. Instructors who use this book as a course text may add details of biochemistry as they feel necessary.

Chapter 1 introduces you to the general effects of exercise and nutrition on health-related and sports-related fitness, including the importance of well-controlled scientific research. Chapter 2 provides a broad overview of sound guidelines relative to nutrition for optimal health and physical performance. Chapter 3 focuses upon energy and energy pathways in the body, the key to all exercise and sport activities.

Chapters 4 through 9 deal with the six basic nutrients—carbohydrate, fat, protein, vitamins, minerals, and water—with emphasis on the health and performance implications for the physically active individual. Chapters 10 through 12 review concepts of body composition and weight control, with suggestions on how to gain or lose body weight through diet and exercise, as well as the implications of such changes for health and athletic performance. Chapter 13 is a new chapter for this edition, covering several drug foods, such as alcohol and caffeine, and other related dietary supplements that previously had been integrated in other chapters. Instructors who prefer to adhere to the chapter content of previous editions may have students read the relevant sections of chapter 13. Several appendixes complement the text, providing data on caloric expenditure during exercise, methods to determine body composition, nutritional value of fast foods, and other information pertinent to physically active individuals.

New to the Eight Edition

The content throughout each chapter of the book has been updated, where merited, based on contemporary research findings regarding the effects of nutritional practices on health, fitness, and sport performance. Over 450 new references, including clinical studies, reviews, and meta-analyses, have been added to the text. Some key changes regarding specific chapters follow.

Chapter 1—Introduction to Nutrition for Health, Fitness, and Sports Performance
- New reviews on the role of exercise may play as a means to enhance health.

Chapter 2—Healthful Nutrition for Fitness and Sport
- Detailed coverage for the new *MyPyramid* food guide, the United States Department of Agriculture's sixth edition detailing healthy eating guidelines for Americans.
- New information on food colors and potential health benefits.

Chapter 3—Human Energy
- New information on factors contributing to fatigue during exercise, including overreaching and overtraining.

Chapter 4—Carbohydrate: The Main Energy Food
- New viewpoints on how impaired carbohydrate stores in the body may contribute to fatigue during exercise.
- Optimizing the type of carbohydrate to ingest during exercise as a means to enhance performance.
- Expanded discussion of the role of *healthy* carbohydrates in the diet.

Chapter 5—Fat: An Important Energy Source during Exercise
- Enhanced discussion of the role that modification of dietary fat intake, such as *trans* ft and omega-3 fatty acids, may play in determining health status.
- New National Cholesterol Education Program guidelines involving when it may be appropriate to recommend use of drugs to reduce serum cholesterol.

Chapter 6—Protein: The Tissue Builder
- Updated information on protein and carbohydrate intake to promote protein synthesis following exercise.
- New research findings with branched-chain amino acid supplementation and glucosamine-chondroitin supplementation.

- Updated research findings regarding creatine supplementation and its effect on exercise performance and health status.

Chapter 7—Vitamins: The Organic Regulators
- New viewpoints on the possible role of vitamin D in health.
- New research findings regarding the limitations to health improvement or performance enhancement from antioxidant vitamin supplementation.

Chapter 8—Minerals: The Inorganic Regulators
- An evaluation of the role that dietary calcium may play in weight control.
- Discussion of the new American College of Sports Medicine position stand on physical activity and bone health.

Chapter 9—Water, Electrolytes, and Temperature Regulation
- An expanded discussion of exercise-associated hyponatremia (EAH), including its etiology and potential dangers.
- Discussion of the new American College of Sports Medicine position stand on exercise and hypertension.

Chapter 10—Body Weight and Composition for Health and Sport
- Updated discussion of the relationship of body mass index (BMI) and waist circumference to health status and mortality.
- Updated information on the role of dietary supplements in weight loss.

Chapter 11—Weight Maintenance and Loss through Proper Nutrition and Exercise
- Recent research comparing the effectiveness of various diets, such as low-fat and low-carbohydrate, for weight loss.
- Twenty ways to decrease caloric intake.

Chapter 12—Weight Gaining through Proper Nutrition and Exercise
- Incorporated some general guidelines for percent macronutrient (carbohydrate, fat, protein) intake for competitive bodybuilders.

Chapter 13—Food Drugs and Related Supplements
- A new chapter incorporating recent information on alcohol, caffeine, ephedrine, sodium bicarbonate, selected herbals, and anabolic dietary supplements and their effects on health and sport performance.

Enhanced Pedagogy

Each chapter contains several features to help enhance the learning process. **Chapter Learning Objectives** are presented at the beginning of each chapter, highlighting the key points and serving as a studying guide. **Key Terms** also are listed at the beginning of each chapter, along with the page number on which they are first highlighted and defined. Although some terms may appear in the text before they are defined, a thorough glossary includes the key terms as well as other terms warranting definition. **Key Concept Check** provides a summary of essential information presented in each main section. Students are encouraged to participate in several practical activities to help reinforce learning. **Check for Yourself** includes individual activities, such as checking food labels at the supermarket or measuring your body fat percentage, while the **Application Exercise** at the end of each chapter may involve more extensive involvement, such as a case study in weight control involving yourself or a survey of an athletic team. Students may wish to peruse all application exercises at the beginning of the course, as some may take several weeks or months to complete.

The bibliographic references are of three types. *Books* listed provide broad coverage of the major topics in the chapter. *Reviews* are detailed analyses of selected topics, usually involving a synthesis and analysis of specific research studies. The *specific studies* listed are primary research studies. The reference lists have been completely updated for this eighth edition, with the inclusion of nearly 450 new references, and provide the scientific basis for the new concepts or additional support for those concepts previously developed. These references provide greater in-depth reading materials for the interested student. Although the content of this book is based on appropriate scientific studies, a reference-citation style is not used, that is, each statement is not referenced by a bibliographic source. However, names of authors may be used to highlight a reference source where deemed appropriate.

This book is designed primarily to serve as a college text in professional preparation programs in health and physical education, exercise science, athletic training, sports medicine, and sports nutrition. It is also directed to the physically active individual interested in the nutritional aspects of physical and athletic performance.

Those who may desire to initiate a physical training program may also find the nutritional information useful, as well as the guidelines for initiating a training program. This book may serve as a handy reference for coaches, trainers, and athletes. With the tremendous expansion of youth sports programs, parents may find the information valuable relative to the nutritional requirements of their active children.

In summary, the major purpose of this book is to help provide a sound knowledge base relative to the role that nutrition, complemented by exercise, may play in the enhancement of both health and sport performance. Hopefully, the information provided in this text will help the reader develop a more healthful and performance-enhancing diet. Bon appetit!

Acknowledgements

This book would not be possible without the many medical/health scientists and exercise/sport scientists throughout the world who, through their numerous studies and research, have provided the scientific data that underlie its development. I am fortunate to have developed a friendship with many of you, and I extend my sincere appreciation to all of you.

The reviewers of the seven previous editions have played an integral role in the changes that are made, and this edition is no exception. I wish to extend a special note of appreciation to those who reviewed the seventh edition text and provided many valuable suggestions for improving the eighth edition manuscript.

Eight Edition

Gale Carey	Tom Kelly
Alana Cline	George Langford
Sandra Graham	Kathy Munoz
Jie Kang	Roy Wohl

Seventh Edition

John L. Bergen *University of West Florida*	Kathy Hosig *Virginia Tech*
Rebecca Cole *Utah State University*	Thomas Kelly *Western Oregon University*
Susan Fullmer *Brigham Young University*	Diana Kirk *San Jose State University*
Candance Gabel *University of Missouri–Columbia*	Nweze Nnakwe *Illinois State University*
Shelley R. Hancock *The University of Alabama*	Christine Rosenbloom *Georgia State University*

Sixth Edition

Jack Benson *Eastern Washington University*	Donna R. Potacco *William Paterson University*
Barbara Bushman *Southwest Missouri State University*	Susan J. Rudge *Miami University*
Dorothy Chen-Maynard *California Sate University—San Bernardino*	J. Andres Vasconcellos *Chapman University* *Universidad de las Americas*
Marie Dunford *California State University—Fresno*	Michael J. Webster *University of Southern Mississippi*
David Gee *Central Washington University*	Suzy Weems *Stephen F. Austin State University*
Sharlene Holladay *George Mason University*	Roy Wohl *Washburn University*
Cherie Moore *Cuesta College*	

I would like to acknowledge deep gratitude to Lynne Meyers, Senior Developmental Editor, for her friendly and cooperative support during the developmental process of this book, to April Southwood, Project Manager, for her assistance during the production process, and to Colin Wheatley, Publisher, for his continued support. Many thanks also to Jane Stembridge for her meticulous review as a copyeditor. Finally, to the memory of Pat McSwegin for her friendship and input during the first five editions of this book.

Melvin H. Williams
Norfolk, Virginia

Introduction to Nutrition for Health, Fitness, and Sports Performance

CHAPTER ONE

LEARNING OBJECTIVES

After studying this chapter, you should be able to:

1. Explain the role of both genetics and environment, particularly nutrition and exercise, in the determination of optimal health and successful sport performance.

2. List each of the components of health-related fitness, and then identify the potential health benefits of a physical fitness program designed to enhance both aerobic and musculoskeletal fitness.

3. List the twelve guidelines underlying the Prudent Healthy Diet and discuss, in general, the importance of proper nutrition, including the role of dietary supplements, to optimal health.

4. Understand the importance of proper nutrition, including the role of dietary supplements as ergogenic aids, to sports performance.

5. Define nutritional quackery and understand the various strategies you can use to determine whether the claims of a dietary supplement are valid.

6. Explain what types of research have been used to evaluate the relationship between nutrition and health or sport performance, and evaluate the pros and cons of each type.

Introduction

There are two major focal points of this book. One is the role that nutrition, complemented by physical activity and exercise, may play in determining one's health status. The other is the role that nutrition may play in the enhancement of fitness and sports performance. People of all ages today are physically active, and athletic competition spans all ages. Healthful nutrition is important throughout the life span of the physically active individual because suboptimal health status may impair training and competitive performance. In general, the diet that is optimal for health is also optimal for exercise and sports performance.

Nutrition, fitness, and health. At a national level, the health care of Americans and Canadians has improved tremendously over the past century. Primarily because of the dedicated work of medical researchers, we no longer fear the scourge of acute infectious diseases such as polio, smallpox, or tuberculosis. However, we have become increasingly concerned with the treatment and prevention of chronic diseases. Six of the ten leading causes of death in the United States are chronic diseases. Given with rank in parentheses, they include: (1) diseases of the heart, (2) cancer, (3) stroke, (4) chronic lung diseases, (7) diabetes, and (10) chronic liver disease and cirrhosis. These diseases cause over 80 percent of all deaths, and this figure is destined to rise as the U.S. population becomes increasingly older, particularly during the first quarter of this century when the baby boomers of the 1940s and 1950s reach their senior years.

The two primary factors that influence one's health status are genetics and lifestyle. Most chronic diseases have a genetic basis. The Human Genome Project, which deciphered the DNA code of our 80,000 to 100,000 genes, has identified various genes associated with many chronic diseases, such as breast and prostate cancer. Genetically, females whose mothers had breast cancer are at increased risk for breast cancer, while males whose fathers had prostate cancer are at increased risk for prostate cancer.

Completion of the Human Genome Project is believed to be one of the most significant medical advances of all time and, according to Futterman and Lemberg, will change the field of medicine forever. Scientists now have the ability to analyze the genetic basis and molecular mechanisms underlying various diseases, and genetic health risk profiles may be developed to evaluate individual susceptibility. Although multiple genes are involved in the etiology of most chronic diseases and research regarding the application of the findings of the Human Genome Project to improve health is in its initial stages, the future looks bright. For individuals with genetic profiles predisposing them to a specific chronic disease, such as cancer, genetic therapy may provide an effective treatment or cure.

Although genetic influences may play an important role in the development of chronic diseases, so too does lifestyle. According to Mokdad and others, poor diet and physical inactivity may soon overtake tobacco as the leading cause of death in the United States. In a recent review Ward indicated that lifestyle, particularly one incorporating a healthful diet and exercise, may provide the best hope for living a healthier, longer life. Indeed, LaRosa indicated that even with the current use of powerful medicines to treat chronic health problems, diet and exercise are important nonpharmacological interventions not only because they

may augment the effect of therapeutic drugs but, probably more importantly, may prevent chronic disease in the first place.

The role of a healthful diet and exercise are intertwined with your genetic profile, and various organizations, such as the Center for Genetics, Nutrition and Health, have as one of their goals the evaluation of scientific knowledge regarding genetic variation in nutrition and fitness as these relate to health. What you eat and how you exercise may influence your genes. Cousins suggests that research involving nutritional regulation of gene expression may help identify specific nutrients in the diet that may either promote or repress gene expression. For example, nutrients may be identified that repress expression of a specific cancer gene. Additionally, Shephard and Shek indicate that exercise may induce various chemical changes, such as hormone secretion, in the body that may repress gene expression for certain cancers. If your personal genetic code indicates that your genetic profile predisposes you to certain forms of cancer, and if your genetic profile indicates that you will respond favorably to specific nutritional or exercise interventions, then a preventive diet and an exercise plan may be individualized for you. The terms *nutrigenomics* and *exercisenomics* have been coined to identify the study of the genetic aspects of nutrition and exercise, respectively, as related to health benefits.

Treatment of chronic diseases is very expensive. Foreseeing a financial health care crisis associated with an increasing prevalence of such diseases during the first half of this century, most private and public health professionals have advocated health promotion and disease prevention as the best approach to address this potential major health problem. For example, James Rippe, a renowned physician, has coined the term "lifestyle medicine" to characterize this focus on health promotion behaviors to help prevent disease. The United States Public Health Service, beginning in the 1980s, has published a series of reports designed to increase the nation's health, the latest version entitled *Healthy People 2010: National Health Promotion/ Disease Prevention Objectives. Physical activity/fitness and overweight/obesity* are two major focus areas in *Healthy People 2010.* In these reports, lifestyle behaviors that promote health and reduce the risk of chronic diseases are basically under the control of the individual. For the full *Healthy People 2010* report, consult www.health.gov/healthypeople.

Over the years, scientists in the field of epidemiology have identified a number of lifestyle factors considered to be health risks; these lifestyle factors are known as risk factors. A **risk factor** is a health behavior that has been associated with a particular disease, such as cigarette smoking being linked to lung cancer. As we shall see, proper exercise and proper nutrition, both individually and combined, may reduce many of the risk factors associated with the development of chronic diseases. These healthful benefits will be addressed at appropriate points throughout the book.

Nutrition, fitness, and sport. Sport is now most commonly defined as a competitive athletic activity requiring skill or physical prowess, for example, baseball, basketball, soccer, football, track, wrestling, tennis, and golf. As with health status, athletic ability and subsequent success in sport are based primarily upon two factors: natural genetic endowment and state of training.

To be successful at high levels of competition, athletes must possess the appropriate biomechanical, physiological, and psychological genetic characteristics associated with success in a given sport. International-class athletes have such genetic traits. Enhancement of athletic performance of elite athletes via genetic therapy, or genetic engineering, is a current concern among international sport organizations such as the International Olympic Committee (IOC) and the World Anti-Doping Agency (WADA). Research by Claude Bouchard, James Skinner, and James Hagberg and their associates have identified specific genetic markers for various sport performance attributes, which Wolfarth and others have assembled as a human gene map for performance and health-related fitness.

Several recent genetic engineering studies with rodents have produced "endurance" and "He-Man" mice. Although some sports scientists such as Skinner do not believe that genetic engineering can be used to reliably produce champion athletes, sports scientists and administrators interviewed by Fitzpatrick indicate it is only a matter of time and may even be in use now. Adam suggests gene therapy for athletes may be in effect for the 2008 Olympic games.

To be successful at high levels of competition, athletes must also develop their genetic characteristics maximally through proper biomechanical, physiological, and psychological coaching and training. Whatever the future holds for genetic enhancement of athletic performance, specialized exercise training will still be the key to maximizing genetic potential. Training programs at the elite level have become more intense and individualized, resulting in significant performance gains, and world records continue to improve.

Proper nutrition also is an important component in the total training program of the athlete. Certain nutrient deficiencies can seriously impair performance, while supplementation of other nutrients may help delay fatigue and improve performance. Over the past four decades, research has provided us with many answers about the role of nutrition in athletic performance, but unfortunately some findings have been misinterpreted or exaggerated so that a number of misconceptions still exist.

The purpose of this chapter is to provide a broad overview of the role that exercise and nutrition may play relative to health, fitness, and sport, and how prudent recommendations may be determined. More detailed information regarding specific relationships of nutritional practices to health and sports performance is provided in subsequent chapters.

Key Concept Recap

▶ The two primary determinants of health status are genetics and lifestyle.

▶ Six of the ten chronic diseases in the United States and Canada (heart diseases, cancer, stroke, lung diseases, diabetes, and liver diseases) may be prevented by appropriate lifestyle behaviors.

▶ Two of the key health promotion objectives set by the U.S. Department of Health and Human Services in *Healthy People 2010* are increased levels of physical activity and fitness and reduced levels of overweight and obesity.

Check for Yourself

Discuss with your parents any health problems they or your grandparents may have, such as high blood pressure or diabetes, to determine whether you may be predisposed to such health problems in the future. Having such knowledge may help you develop a preventive exercise and nutrition plan early in life.

Nutrition, Exercise, and Health-Related Fitness

Physical fitness may be defined, in general terms, as a set of abilities individuals possess to perform specific types of physical activity. The development of physical fitness is an important concern of many professional health organizations, including the American Alliance for Health, Physical Education, Recreation, and Dance (AAHPERD), which has categorized fitness components into two different categories. In general, these two categories may be referred to as health-related fitness and sports-related fitness. Both types of fitness may be influenced by nutrition and exercise.

Exercise and Health-Related Fitness

What is health-related fitness?

As mentioned above, one's health status or wellness is influenced strongly by hereditarian predisposition and lifestyle behaviors, particularly appropriate physical activity and a high-quality diet. As we shall see in various sections of this book, one of the key factors in preventing the development of chronic disease is maintaining a healthful body weight.

Proper physical activity may certainly improve one's health status by helping to prevent excessive weight gain, but it may also enhance other facets of health-related fitness as well. **Health-related fitness** includes not only a healthy body weight and composition, but also cardiovascular-respiratory fitness, adequate muscular strength and endurance, and sufficient flexibility (figure 1.1). Other measures used as markers of health-related fitness include blood pressure, bone strength, postural control, and various indicators of lipid and carbohydrate metabolism. Several health professional organizations, such as the American College of Sports Medicine (ACSM), have indicated that various forms of physical activity may be used to enhance health.

In general, **physical activity** involves any bodily movement caused by muscular contraction that results in the expenditure of energy. For purposes of studying its effects on health, epidemiologists classify physical activity as either unstructured or structured.

Unstructured physical activity includes many of the usual activities of daily life, such as leisurely walking and cycling, climbing stairs, dancing, gardening and yard work, various domestic and occupational activities, and games and other childhood pursuits. These unstructured activities are not planned to be exercise.

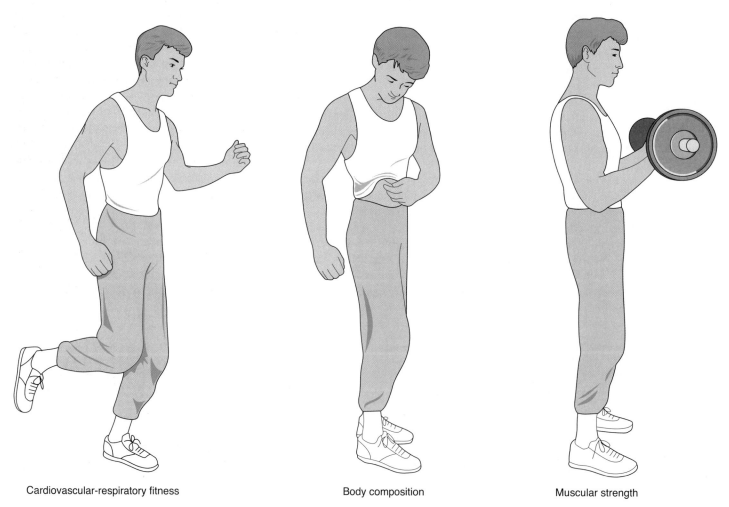

Cardiovascular-respiratory fitness   Body composition   Muscular strength

FIGURE 1.1   Health-related fitness components. The most important physical fitness components related to personal health include cardiovascular-respiratory fitness, body composition, muscular strength, muscular endurance, and flexibility.

Structured physical activity, as the name implies, is a planned program of physical activities usually designed to improve physical fitness, including health-related fitness. For the purpose of this book, we shall refer to structured physical activity as **exercise,** particularly some form of planned vigorous exercise, such as brisk, not leisurely, walking.

What is the role of exercise in health promotion?

The beneficial effect of exercise on health has been known for centuries. For example, Plato noted that "Lack of activity destroys the good condition of every human being while movement and methodical physical exercise save and preserve it." Plato's observation is even more relevant in contemporary society. Frank Booth, a prominent exercise scientist at the University of Missouri, has coined the term **Sedentary Death Syndrome,** or **SeDS,** and recently highlighted over thirty health problems that are caused or worsened by a sedentary lifestyle.

The Consumers Union, reporting on the use of alternative treatments to treat various health problems, noted that exercise was one of the most effective for numerous conditions. In support of this viewpoint, the National Center for Chronic Disease Prevention and Health Promotion indicated that regular physical activity reduces people's risk for heart attacks, certain cancers, diabetes, and high blood pressure, and may reduce their risk for stroke. It also helps to control weight; contributes to healthy bones, muscles, and joints; reduces falls among older adults; helps to relieve the pain of arthritis; reduces symptoms of anxiety and depression; and is associated with fewer hopitalizations, physician visits, and medications. Indeed, some physicians indicate that exercise is the best medicine of all because it offers such an array of health benefits.

Clinical, epidemiological, and basic research evidence clearly supports the inclusion of regular physical activity as a tool for the prevention of chronic disease and the enhancement of overall health. In his excellent book, *The Exercise-Health Connection,* David C. Nieman quantified the health benefits of exercise from such reports, and his findings are presented in table 1.1. These benefits may accrue to males and females of all races across all age spans. You are never too young or too old to reap the health benefits of exercise. For example, recent research indicates that physically active older people may have a lower risk for Alzheimer's disease than the sedentary.

In essence, physically active individuals enjoy a higher quality of life, a *joie de vivre,* because they are less likely to suffer the disabling symptoms often associated with chronic diseases, such as loss of ambulation experienced by some stroke victims. Physical activity may also increase the quantity of life. Lee, Paffenbarger, and associates estimated that a physically active lifestyle may add approximately two years of life by averting premature mortality.

How does exercise enhance health?

The mechanisms whereby exercise may help to prevent the development of various chronic diseases are not completely understood, but there may be multiple processes. Exercise stimulates metabolism, increasing the release of various hormones, and the skeletal muscles also produce and release numerous hormones and metabolites into the blood. These hormones and metabolites may enter various body tissues, influencing gene expression that may induce adaptations favorable to health. For example, exercise may influence genes within the muscle, inducing the formation of cell membrane receptors that transport glucose from the blood into the cell, an effect that may help regulate blood glucose and prevent type 2 diabetes. Some of these adaptations may occur with a single bout of exercise. Thompson and others have noted that a single exercise session can acutely improve the blood lipid profile, reduce blood pressure, and improve insulin sensitivity, all beneficial responses. However, such adaptations will regress unless exercise becomes habitual. The role that exercise may play in the prevention of some chronic diseases, such as heart disease, and associated risk factors, such as obesity, are discussed throughout this book where relevant.

Do most of us exercise enough?

In general, no. Surveys reveal that most adult Americans and Canadians have little or no physical activity in their daily lives. The Consumers Union notes that our addiction to physical inactivity

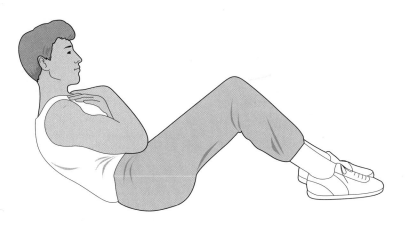

Muscular endurance

Flexibility

FIGURE 1.1 (continued)

TABLE 1.1   The health benefits of physical activity

The table is based on a total physical fitness program that includes physical activity designed to improve both aerobic and musculoskeletal fitness.

Physical Activity Benefit	Surety Rating
Fitness of Body	
Improves heart and lung fitness	****
Improves muscular strength/size	****
Cardiovascular Disease	
Coronary heart disease prevention	****
Regression of atherosclerosis	**
Treatment of heart disease	***
Prevention of stroke	**
Cancer	
Prevention of colon cancer	****
Prevention of breast cancer	**
Prevention of uterine cancer	**
Prevention of prostate cancer	**
Prevention of other cancers	*
Treatment of cancer	*
Osteoporosis	
Helps build up bone density	****
Prevention of osteoporosis	***
Treatment of osteoporosis	**
Blood Cholesterol/Lipoproteins	
Lowers blood total cholesterol	*
Lowers LDL-cholesterol	*
Lowers triglycerides	***
Raises HDL-cholesterol	***
Low Back Pain	
Prevention of low back pain	**
Treatment of low back pain	**
Nutrition and Diet Quality	
Improvement in diet quality	**
Increase in total energy intake	***
Weight Management	
Prevention of weight gain	****
Treatment of obesity	**
Helps maintain weight loss	***
Children and Youth	
Prevention of obesity	***
Controls disease risk factors	***
Reduction of unhealthy habits	**
Improves odds of adult activity	**

Physical Activity Benefit	Surety Rating
Elderly and the Aging Process	
Improvement in physical fitness	****
Counters loss in heart/lung fitness	**
Counters loss of muscle	***
Counters gain in fat	***
Improvement in life expectancy	****
Improvement in life quality	****
Cigarette Smoking	
Improves success in quitting	**
Diabetes	
Prevention of type 2	****
Treatment of type 2	***
Treatment of type 1	*
Improvement in diabetic life quality	***
Infection and Immunity	
Prevention of the common cold	**
Improves overall immunity	**
Slows progression of HIV to AIDS	*
Improves life quality of HIV-infected	****
Arthritis	
Prevention of arthritis	*
Treatment/cure of arthritis	*
Improvement life quality/fitness	****
High Blood Pressure	
Prevention of high blood pressure	****
Treatment of high blood pressure	****
Asthma	
Prevention/treatment of asthma	*
Improvement in life quality	***
Sleep	
Improvement in sleep quality	***
Psychological Well-Being	
Elevation in mood	****
Buffers effects of mental stress	***
Alleviates/prevents depression	****
Anxiety reduction	****
Improves self-esteem	****
Special Issues for Women	
Improves total body fitness	****
Improves fitness while pregnant	****
Improves birthing experience	**
Improves health of fetus	**
Improves health during menopause	***

****Strong consensus, with little or no conflicting data
***Most data are supportive, but more research is needed for clarification
**Some data are supportive, but much more research is needed
*Little or no data support

From David C. Nieman. *The Exercise-Health Connection.* Champaign, IL: Human Kinetics Publishers, 1998. Used with permission from Human Kinetics.

remains as strong as ever. In a recent review of the goals of *Healthy People 2010,* Spain and Franks noted that most adult Americans were not getting enough physical activity. The physical activity objectives of *Healthy People 2010* are to reduce the percentage of people who engage in no leisure-time physical activity, which is currently 40 percent; to increase the percentage who engage regularly, preferably daily in moderate physical activity for 30 minutes per day, which is currently only 15 percent; and, to increase the proportion of adults who engage in vigorous physical activity that promotes the development of cardiovascular fitness 3 or more days per week for 20 or more minutes per occasion. Similar objectives have been set for muscular strength/endurance and flexibility.

Although the percentage of children and adolescents participating in physical activity was somewhat higher compared to adults, participation was still considered to be low and thus similar physical activity objectives were established.

How much physical activity is enough for health benefits?

This is a difficult and complex question, and an appropriate answer may depend on the type of exercise and the specific health benefit. In essence, this question was the topic of a recent Consensus Symposium, sponsored by Health Canada and the United States Centers for Disease Control and Prevention, and focusing on the dose-response issue of physical activity and health. The symposium has been summarized by Rankinen and Bouchard.

In his introduction to the symposium, Bouchard indicated that physical activity may have a direct effect on health, such as improving heart function, or it may have an indirect effect by influencing a risk factor for health, such as excess body weight. Bouchard also noted that there may be three specific dose-response patterns between physical activity and health outcomes, with the dose of physical activity being represented by weekly energy expenditure (see figure 1.2). The first pattern is nonlinear with significant health benefits occurring at low to moderate levels (doses) of physical activity and diminishing returns with higher levels of exercise. A second pattern is also nonlinear, but opposite the first pattern, with few health benefits occurring at low levels of physical activity and increased benefits with higher levels. The third pattern is linear in nature, indicating some health benefits at low levels of physical activity and increased benefits with increasing levels of physical activity. Thus, dependent on the desired health outcome, the dose (intensity, duration, frequency) of physical activity may vary accordingly, as will the type of physical activity (aerobic exercise for cardiovascular fitness; resistance exercise for musculoskeletal fitness). Heck and others also note that genetic and environmental factors may contribute to considerable interindividual differences in responses to exercise training, with some individuals benefitting more so than others from similar amounts of training.

Most physical activity recommendations for health incorporate increased levels of both unstructured and structured physical activity. For example, one of the key points of the *Surgeon General's Report on Physical Activity and Health* is that physical

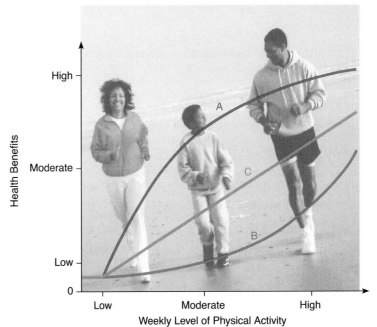

FIGURE 1.2 Dose-response patterns between levels of physical activity and possible health benefits. Pattern A is nonlinear with significant health benefits occurring at low to moderate levels of physical activity and diminishing returns with higher levels. Pattern B is also nonlinear, with few health benefits at low levels of physical activity and increased benefits with higher levels. Pattern C is linear, indicating increasing health benefits with increasing levels of physical activity. See text for discussion. Adapted from Bouchard, C. 2001. Physical activity and health: Introduction to the dose-response symposium. *Medicine and Science in Sports and Exercise.* 33:S347–50.

activity need not be strenuous to achieve health benefits. Children, adolescents, and men and women of all ages may benefit from a moderate amount of daily unstructured physical activity, such as washing the car or raking leaves. Moderate structured exercise, such as brisk walking for 30 minutes or three 10-minute walks daily, may also confer significant health benefits. Some examples of moderate amounts of physical activity are presented in table 1.2.

Although Blair and others concluded that 30 minutes of moderate-intensity physical activity daily provides substantial benefits across a broad range of health outcomes for sedentary adults, it may be insufficient to prevent unhealthful weight gain for some persons who may need additional exercise or caloric restriction to minimize the likelihood of further weight gain. Furthermore, they note that persons who get 30 minutes of moderate-intensity exercise per day are likely to achieve additional health benefits if they exercise more. The caloric equivalent of various forms of exercise will be presented in chapter 3, and a discussion of the role of exercise in weight control will be detailed in chapter 11.

The American College of Sports Medicine (ACSM) has developed recommendations for the quantity and quality of exercise for developing and maintaining health-related fitness, including exercise programs for the development of cardiovascular fitness, muscular strength and endurance, and flexibility (see www.mhhe.com/williams).

TABLE 1.2 Some examples of moderate amounts of physical activity*

Washing and waxing a car for 45–60 minutes

Washing windows or floors for 45–60 minutes

Playing various team sports for 45 minutes

Gardening for 30–45 minutes

Wheeling self in wheelchair for 30–40 minutes

Walking 2 miles in 40 minutes (20 minutes/mile)

Bicycling 5 miles in 30 minutes (10 miles/hour)

Dancing (social) fast for 30 minutes

Walking briskly 2 miles in 30 minutes (15 minutes/mile)

Water aerobics for 30 minutes

Swimming laps for 20 minutes

Bicycling 4 miles in 15 minutes (3.75 minutes/mile)

Jumping rope for 15 minutes

Running 1.5 miles in 15 minutes (10 minutes/mile)

Stairwalking for 15 minutes

*A moderate amount of physical activity is roughly equivalent to physical activity that uses 150 Calories per day, or 1,000 Calories per week. Note that exercising at lower intensity levels requires more time (walking 2 miles in 40 minutes) than exercising at higher intensity levels (running 1.5 miles in 15 minutes). Adapted from U.S. Department of Health and Human Services. *The Surgeon General's Report on Physical Activity and Health.*

What are some general guidelines for exercising properly for someone who wants to be more physically active?

Chuck Corbin and Robert Pangrazi, exercise scientists at Arizona State University, used the ACSM guidelines to develop the Physical Activity Pyramid, comparable to the MyPyramid food guide discussed in chapter 2. A modification of their Physical Activity Pyramid is presented in figure 1.3. Key guidelines are established for five levels of the pyramid as follows:

Level 1—Every day for at least 30 minutes: Do low-intensity activities such as playing golf, walking, gardening, climbing stairs, and active household chores.

Level 2—At least three, preferably six, days a week for at least 20 minutes: Do aerobic exercise that increases your heart rate up to 50 to 85 percent of your maximal through exercise tasks such as running, bicycling, tennis, soccer, or other active sports.

Level 3—At least three, preferably seven, days a week: Do stretching exercises to increase the flexibility of the major muscles in your body, particularly in your lower back and your legs.

Level 4—At least two, preferably three, days per week: Do resistance (strength) type exercises, such as weight lifting or calisthenics, to improve muscular strength and endurance.

Level 5—Rarely: Physical inactivity, such as television viewing and computer games.

The Physical Activity Pyramid is in accord with the guidelines to obtain adequate amounts of moderate aerobic physical activity, complemented with several days of vigorous aerobic activity and muscular strength, endurance, and flexibility training.

The ACSM guidelines, the Physical Activity Pyramid, and guidelines provided by the President's Council on Physical Fitness and Sports underlie the basis of designing an aerobics program for cardiovascular-respiratory fitness and proper weight control presented in chapter 11 and the principles of resistance training for muscular strength and endurance presented in chapter 12. If you are interested in starting an exercise program, you may preview those chapters or access excellent programs at www.smallstep.gov, www.Americaonthemove.org, or www.acsm.org; for the latter click on "Health and Fitness Information." Considerable information on physical fitness may also be accessed at www.fitness.gov.

Can too much exercise be harmful to my health?

In general, the health benefits outweigh the risks of exercise. Although individuals training for sport may need to undergo prolonged, intense exercise training, such is not the case for those seeking health benefits of exercise. Given our current state of knowledge, adhering to the guidelines of the Physical Activity Pyramid, preferably at the upper time limits, should be safe and provide optimal health benefits associated with physical activity. In this regard, the Surgeon General's report indicates that care should be taken to avoid excessive amounts of high-intensity exercise because of increased risk of injury or other health problems, such as menstrual abnormalities. Excessive exercise may also lead to impaired immune function and predisposition to various infections.

It is important to note that although a properly planned exercise program may be safe and confer multiple health benefits to most individuals, exercise may be hazardous to some. In an article entitled "Exercise can kill you—or save your life," the Consumers Union notes that exercise may aggravate heart problems in susceptible individuals, leading to a heart attack, possibly a fatal one. Individuals who have any concerns about their overall health, particularly those over age 35, should have a medical screening to detect risk factors for heart disease, such as high blood pressure, before increasing their level of physical activity. Such a medical screening might include an exercise stress test during which your heart rate and blood pressure are monitored for abnormal responses. The Consumers Union notes that although exercise may be a temporary risk, it conveys lasting protection. The best protection for the heart is to exercise frequently, mainly because regular exercise helps prevent heart disease in the first place. See chapter 5, and activities in chapters 3, 11, and 12.

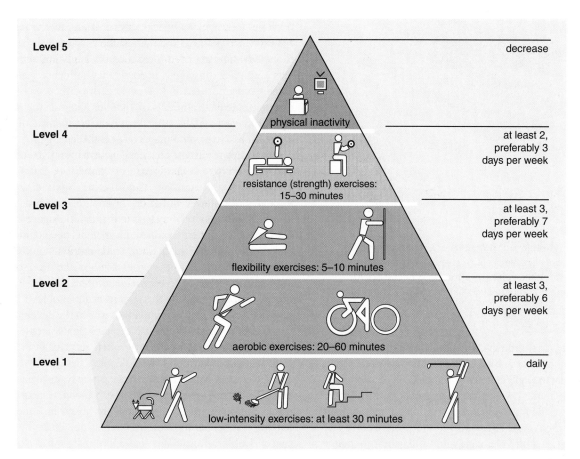

Level 5 — decrease

physical inactivity

Level 4 — at least 2, preferably 3 days per week

resistance (strength) exercises: 15–30 minutes

Level 3 — at least 3, preferably 7 days per week

flexibility exercises: 5–10 minutes

Level 2 — at least 3, preferably 6 days per week

aerobic exercises: 20–60 minutes

Level 1 — daily

low-intensity exercises: at least 30 minutes

FIGURE 1.3 One version of a Physical Activity Pyramid, modeled after the My Pyramid Food Guide. See text for discussion about the importance of physical activity for health and fitness.

Key Concept Recap

▶ Health-related fitness includes a healthy body weight, cardiovascular-respiratory fitness, adequate muscular strength and endurance, and sufficient flexibility.

▶ Physical inactivity may be dangerous to your health. As documented in the *Surgeon General's Report on Physical Activity and Health,* exercise, as a form of physical activity, is becoming increasingly important as a means to help prevent, and even treat, many chronic diseases.

▶ One of the key points of the Surgeon General's report is that physical activity need not be strenuous to achieve health benefits, but additional benefits may be gained through greater amounts of physical activity.

Check for Yourself

As a prelude to activities presented in later chapters, make a detailed record of all your physical activities for a full day, from the moment you arise in the morning until you go to bed at night.

Nutrition and Health-Related Fitness

What is nutrition?

Nutrition usually is defined as the sum total of the processes involved in the intake and utilization of food substances by living organisms, including ingestion, digestion, absorption, transport, and metabolism of nutrients found in food. This definition stresses the biochemical or physiological functions of the food we eat, but the American Dietetic Association notes that nutrition may be interpreted in a broader sense and be affected by a variety of psychological, sociological, and economic factors.

Although our food selection may be influenced by these latter factors, particularly economic ones in the case of many college students, the biochemical and physiological roles of many different types of food are similar. From a standpoint of health and sport performance, it is the biochemical and physiological role or function of food that is important.

The primary purpose of the food we eat is to provide us with a variety of nutrients. A **nutrient** is a specific substance found in food that performs one or more physiological or biochemical functions in the body. There are six major classes of essential nutrients found in

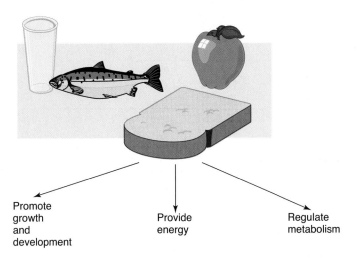

Promote
growth
and
development

Provide
energy

Regulate
metabolism

FIGURE 1.4 Three major functions of nutrients in food. Many nutrients have only one key role (e.g., glucose provides energy), whereas others have multiple roles (e.g., protein is necessary for growth and development and regulation of metabolism, and it may also be used as a source of energy).

foods: carbohydrates, fats, proteins, vitamins, minerals, and water. However, as noted in chapter 2, food contains substances other than essential nutrients that may affect body functions.

As illustrated in figure 1.4, the major nutrients perform three basic functions. First, they provide energy for human metabolism (see chapter 3). Carbohydrates and fats are the prime sources of energy. Protein may also provide energy, but this is not its major function. Vitamins, minerals, and water are not energy sources. Second, all nutrients are used to promote growth and development by building and repairing body tissue. Protein is the major building material for muscles, other soft tissues, and enzymes, while certain minerals such as calcium and phosphorus make up the skeletal framework. Third, all nutrients are used to help regulate metabolism, or body processes. Vitamins, minerals, and proteins work closely together to maintain the diverse physiological processes of human metabolism. For example, hemoglobin in the red blood cell (RBC) is essential for the transport of oxygen to muscle tissue via the blood. Hemoglobin is a complex combination of protein and iron, but other minerals and vitamins are needed for its synthesis and for full development of the RBC.

In order for our bodies to function effectively, we need more than forty specific essential nutrients, and we need these nutrients in various amounts as recommended by nutrition scientists. Dietary Reference Intakes (DRI) represent the current recommendations in the United States, and include the Recommended Dietary Allowances (RDA). These recommendations are detailed in chapter 2. Nutrient deficiencies or excesses may cause various health problems, some very serious.

What is the role of nutrition in health promotion?

As noted previously, your health is dependent upon the interaction of your genes and your environment, and the food you eat is part of your personal environment. *Let food be your medicine and medicine be your food.* This statement has been attributed to Hippocrates for over two thousand years, and it is becoming increasingly meaningful as the preventative and therapeutic health values of food relative to the development of chronic diseases are being unraveled. Nutrients and other substances in foods may influence gene expression, some having positive and others negative effects on our health. For example, adequate amounts of vitamins and minerals may help prevent damage to DNA, the functional component of your genes, while excessive alcohol may lead to DNA damage.

Most chronic diseases have a genetic basis; if one of your parents has had coronary heart disease or cancer, you have an increased probability of contracting that disease. Such diseases may go through three stages: initiation, promotion, and progression. Your genetic predisposition may lead to the initiation stage of the disease, but factors in your environment promote its development and eventual progression. In this regard, some nutrients are believed to be **promoters** that lead to the progression of the disease, while other nutrients are believed to be **antipromoters** that deter the initiation process from progressing to a serious health problem.

What you eat plays an important role in the development or progression of a variety of chronic diseases. For example, the National Center for Chronic Disease Prevention and Health Promotion indicates that good nutrition lowers people's risk for many chronic diseases, including heart disease, stroke, some types of cancer, diabetes, and osteoporsis (see figure 1.5). The National Cancer Institute estimates that one-third of all cancers are linked in some way to diet, ranking just behind tobacco smoking as one of the major causes of cancer. DeMarini estimates that appropriate dietary changes could reduce by 50 percent the deaths due to prostate, colorectal, pancreatic, and breast cancer. The future of healthful nutrition will unquestionably involve nutritional genomics and personalization of dietary recommendations.

Do we eat right?

Surveys indicate that most people are aware of the role of nutrition in health and want to eat better for healthful purposes, but they do not translate their desires into appropriate action. Poor eating habits span all age groups. For example, in a recent survey of female college students by Anding and others, not one student adhered to all of the seven healthy guidelines recommended for Americans. The diets of children are also poor. Brady and others found that less than 10 percent of the children studied met dietary recommendations, and 50 percent of the diet was composed of foods least recommended, those with high amounts of sugar and fat. As a nation, young and older Americans still eat too many Calories, too much fat and saturated fat, too much sugar and other sweeteners, too much salt, too much meat and cheese, too few fruits and vegetables, and too few complex-carbohydrate and fiber-containing foods. Many are overweight and chronically dieting. Many women and children do not consume enough foods rich in calcium and iron. Analyzing recent changes in the American diet for intake of nine different food categories associated with health status, Liebman noted that we are becoming worse in several areas, remaining stable in others, and making only marginal progress toward recommended goals in other areas.

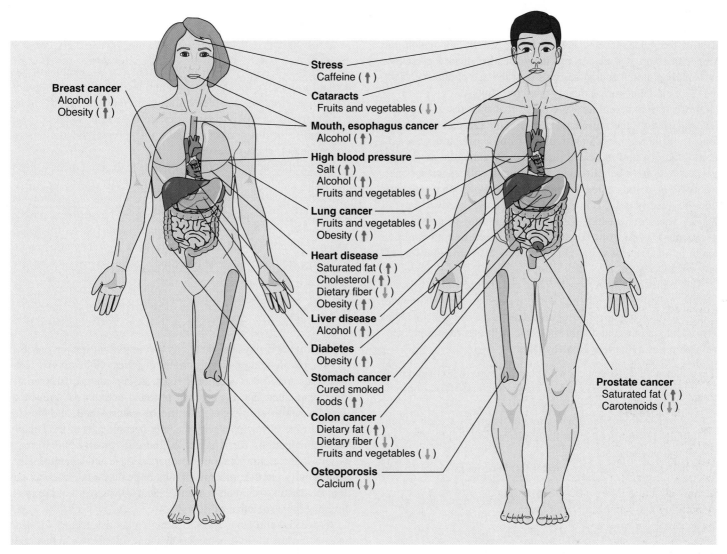

Stress
Caffeine (↑)

Cataracts
Fruits and vegetables (↓)

Mouth, esophagus cancer
Alcohol (↑)

High blood pressure
Salt (↑)
Alcohol (↑)
Fruits and vegetables (↓)

Lung cancer
Fruits and vegetables (↓)
Obesity (↑)

Heart disease
Saturated fat (↑)
Cholesterol (↑)
Dietary fiber (↓)
Obesity (↑)

Liver disease
Alcohol (↑)

Diabetes
Obesity (↑)

Stomach cancer
Cured smoked foods (↑)

Colon cancer
Dietary fat (↑)
Dietary fiber (↓)
Fruits and vegetables (↓)

Osteoporosis
Calcium (↓)

Breast cancer
Alcohol (↑)
Obesity (↑)

Prostate cancer
Saturated fat (↑)
Carotenoids (↓)

FIGURE 1.5 Some possible health problems associated with poor dietary habits. An upward arrow (↑) indicates excessive intake while a downward arrow (↓) indicates low intake or deficiency.

To relate these nutrition findings to health in simplistic terms, most Americans eat more food (Calories) than they need, due in part to the increase in food portion sizes in recent years, and eat less of the food that they need more. As a rule, according to Hill, children and most adults eat what they like and leave the rest, and what they like are foods high in sugar and fat. In essence, the major nutrition goal of *Healthy People 2010* is to get more Americans to change their faulty dietary habits.

What are some general guidelines for healthy eating?

Because the prevention of chronic diseases is of critical importance, thousands of studies have been and are being conducted to discover the intricacies of how various nutrients may affect our health. Particular interest is focused on nutrient function within cells at the molecular level, the interactions between various nutrients, and the identification of other protective factors in certain foods. All of the answers are not in, but sufficient evidence is available to provide us with some useful, prudent guidelines for healthful eating practices.

Over the past two decades, in response to the need for healthier diets, a variety of public and private health organizations analyzed the research relating diet to health and developed some basic guidelines for the general public. The details underlying these recommendations may be found in several voluminous governmental reports, most recently the totally revamped sixth edition of *Nutrition and Your Health: Dietary Guidelines for Americans,* released by the U.S. Departments of Agriculture and Health and Human Services in 2005. Additionally, governmental health agencies in other countries, such as Britain, Canada, Germany, Japan, and Mexico, have developed dietary guidelines for health promotion in their countries. Recently, the American Heart Association released a set of dietary guidelines to help prevent heart disease, the American Cancer Society released a similar set to help prevent cancer, and the American Diabetes Association did likewise for prevention of diabetes. Other organizations, such as the American Dietetic Association, have also proposed dietary guidelines to promote general health. Although most of the guidelines are directed to the general population, the American Heart Association has recommended dietary guidelines for healthy children and adolescents over the age of about 2 years, and these guidelines are similar to those for adults.

McCarron and Reusser have noted that past research efforts have focused on the individual roles of specific dietary components to influence health, particularly cardiovascular disease and its risk factors, and indicated that although manipulation of single nutrients may benefit some individuals with specific health problems, it is improving the total dietary profile that will provide the most benefit. Bowen and Beresford also recently noted that 25 years of research has provided us with some valuable information as to how the diet may be modified to improve health in a variety of ways. However, they also note that we still have much to learn.

Although we do have considerable research to support dietary recommendations to promote health, the research is incomplete. Thus, the following dozen recommendations may be considered to be prudent, and throughout this book we will refer to these recommendations as a **Prudent Healthy Diet.**

1. Balance the food you eat with physical activity to maintain or improve your weight. Consume only moderate food portions. Be physically active every day.
2. Eat a nutritionally adequate diet consisting of a wide variety of nutrient-rich foods. Let the MyPyramid Food Guide guide your food choices.
3. Choose a diet moderate in total fat, but low in saturated and *trans* fat and cholesterol.
4. Choose a diet with plenty of fruits and vegetables, whole grain products, and legumes, which are rich in complex carbohydrates, phytochemicals, and fiber.
5. Choose beverages and foods that moderate your intake of sugars.
6. Choose and prepare foods with less salt and sodium.
7. If you drink alcoholic beverages, do so in moderation. Pregnant women should not drink any alcohol.
8. Maintain protein intake at a moderate, yet adequate level, obtaining much of your daily protein from plant sources, complemented with smaller amounts of fish, skinless poultry, and lean meat.
9. Choose a diet adequate in calcium and iron. Individuals susceptible to tooth decay should obtain adequate fluoride.
10. Practice food safety, including proper food storage, preservation, and preparation.
11. Avoid excess intake of questionable food additives and dietary supplements.
12. Enjoy your food. Eat what you like, but balance it within your overall healthful diet.

An expanded discussion of these guidelines along with practical recommendations to help you implement them is presented in chapter 2. Additional details on how each specific recommendation may affect your health status is presented in appropriate chapters throughout this book. For example, inadequate dietary intake of calcium and iron may cause, respectively, osteoporosis and anemia. These topics are covered in chapter 8, Minerals: The Inorganic Regulators.

Am I eating right?

As part of this course, you may be required to document your actual food intake for several days and then conduct a computerized dietary analysis to determine your nutrient intake. Many computerized dietary analysis programs assess the quality of your diet from a health perspective, and make recommendations for improvement where necessary.

For the time being, you may wish to take the brief dietary inventory in the Application Exercise at the end of this chapter to provide you with a general analysis of your current eating habits. Another useful in depth, dietary (and physical activity) assessment may be found online at www.mypyramid.gov. Click on MyTracker for details, which will be discussed further in chapter 2. You may also want to access the Nutrition Analysis Tools and System at www.nat.uinc.edu.

Are there additional health benefits when both exercise and diet habits are improved?

A poor diet and physical inactivity are individual major risk factors for the development of chronic diseases. Collectively, however, they may pose additional risks. In this regard, Brooks and others indicated that dietary and physical activity recommendations for healthful living are inextricably intertwined, and thus for the first time physical activity recently became part of the Dietary Recommendations for Americans. Indeed, Roberts and Barnard believe that the combination of proper exercise and a healthful diet is the solution to the epidemic of metabolic diseases—such as cardiovascular disease, diabetes, and cancer—diseases that are inundating today's societies worldwide.

As indicated in table 1.3, which highlights risk factors for heart disease, the key lifestyle behaviors that may be effective in favorably modifying heart disease risk factors are proper nutrition and exercise. Moreover, several of the risk factors for heart disease are diseases themselves, such as diabetes, obesity, and high blood pressure, all of which may benefit from the combination of proper nutrition and exercise. The National Institute of Aging recently cited research revealing that lack of exercise and poor dietary habits, taken together, were the second-largest underlying cause (smoking was the largest) of all deaths in the United States, not counting genetic causes.

Vuori indicates that in the genesis of most chronic diseases, a lack of physical activity and inadequate nutrition act synergistically and in part, additively, so both must be given high priority in plans to improve the health of the public. And many organizations have already done so. Recommendations to improve general health by the United States Department of Health and Human Services, as well as recommendations to help prevent specific chronic diseases, such as heart disease and cancer, by the American Heart Association and the American Cancer Society, include considerations of both diet and physical activity. A healthy lifestyle incorporating proper diet and exercise would help to maximize related health benefits. The possible complementary effect of exercise and nutrition on chronic diseases will be presented in later chapters as appropriate.

However, although appropriate lifestyle behaviors, such as exercise, a healthful diet, and maintaining a healthy body weight may help prevent the development of chronic diseases, individuals with a strong genetic predisposition to various risk factors, such as high serum cholesterol levels and high blood pressure, may need medication to reduce these to a level compatible with protective effects.

Key Concept Recap

▶ The primary purpose of the food we eat is to provide us with nutrients essential for the numerous physiological and biochemical functions that support life.

▶ Poor eating habits span all ages. The *Healthy People 2010* report notes that poor nutrition is a major health problem in the United States.

▶ Basic guidelines for a Prudent Healthy Diet include maintenance of proper body weight and consumption of a wide variety of natural foods high in complex carbohydrates and low in fat.

▶ Although both proper exercise and sound nutrition habits may confer health benefits separately, health benefits may be maximized when both healthy exercise and nutrition lifestyles are adopted.

TABLE 1.3 Risk factors associated with coronary heart disease

Risk Factors	Classification	Positive Health Lifestyle Modification
High blood pressure	Major	Proper nutrition, aerobic exercise
High blood lipids	Major	Proper nutrition, aerobic exercise
Smoking	Major	Stop smoking
Sedentary lifestyle	Major	Aerobic exercise
ECG abnormalities	Major	Proper nutrition, aerobic exercise
Obesity	Major	Low-Calorie diet, aerobic exercise
Diabetes	Major	Proper nutrition, weight loss, aerobic exercise
Stressful lifestyle	Contributory	Stress management
Dietary intake	Contributory	Proper nutrition
Oral contraceptives	Contributory	Alternative methods of birth control
Family history	Major	Not modifiable
Gender	Contributory	Not modifiable
Race	Contributory	Not modifiable
Age	Contributory	Not modifiable

Check for Yourself

As a prelude to activities presented in later chapters, make a detailed record of everything you eat for a full day, from breakfast until your late snack at night.

Nutrition, Exercise, and Sports-Related Fitness

As with health, genetic endowment plays an important underlying role in the development of success in sport, but so too do lifestyle behaviors, such as appropriate sports training and sports nutrition.

What is sports-related fitness?

One of the key factors determining success in sport is the ability to maximize your genetic potential with appropriate physical and mental training to prepare both mind and body for intense competition. In this regard, athletes develop **sports-related fitness,** that is, fitness components such as strength, power, speed, endurance, and neuromuscular motor skills specific to their sport.

Training of elite athletes at the United States Olympic Training Center (USOTC) focuses on three attributes: physical power, mental strength, and mechanical edge. Coaches and scientists work with athletes to maximize physical power production for their specific sport, to optimize mental strength in accordance with the psychological demands of the sport, and to provide the best mechanical edge by improving specific fitness and sport skills, sportswear, and sports equipment. Jay Kearney, former senior sports scientist at the USOTC, has noted that sports science and technology provide elite competitors with the tiny margins needed to win in world-class competition (figure 1.6).

Athletes at all levels of competition, whether an elite international competitor, a college wrestler, a high school baseball player, a seniors age-group distance runner, or a youth league soccer player, can best improve their performance by intense training appropriate for their age, physical and mental development, and sport. For example, in a recent review as to how we should spend our time and money to improve cycling performance, Jeukendrup and Martin indicated that, of the many ways possible, training is the first and most effective means. As the saying goes, "Do the best with what you got." However, sports and exercise scientists have investigated a number of means to improve athletic performance beyond that attributable to training, and one of the most extensively investigated areas has been the effect of nutrition.

What is sports nutrition?

As noted above, state-of-the-art physical and mental training is one of the most important factors underlying success in sports. At high levels of athletic competition, athletes generally receive

FIGURE 1.6 Elite athletes are exposed to state-of-the-art physiological, psychological, and biomechanical training that may mean the difference between the gold and silver medal in world-class competition.

excellent coaching to enhance their biomechanical skills (mechanical edge), sharpen their psychological focus (mental strength), and maximize physiological functions (physical power) essential for optimal performance. Clyde Williams, a renowned sport scientist from England, notes that, in addition to specialized training, from earliest times certain foods were regarded as essential preparation for physical activity, whether this was for confrontation on the battlefields of history or competition in the stadiums of ancient Greece, the aim being to achieve greater strength, power, and stamina than one's opponent.

As we shall see, there are various dietary factors that may influence biomechanical, psychological, and physiological considerations in sport. For example, losing excess body fat will enhance biomechanical efficiency; consuming carbohydrates during exercise may maintain normal blood sugar levels and prevent psychological fatigue; and providing adequate dietary iron may ensure optimal oxygen delivery to the muscles. All these sports nutrition factors may impact favorably upon athletic performance.

Sports nutrition is a relatively new area of study involving the application of nutritional principles to enhance sports performance. Louise Burke, a prominent sports nutritionist from Australia, defines sports nutrition as the application of eating strategies to promote good health and adaptation to training, to recover quickly after each exercise training session, and to perform optimally during competition. Although investigators have studied the interactions between nutrition and various forms of sport or exercise for more than a hundred years, it is only within the past few decades that extensive research has been undertaken regarding specific recommendations to athletes.

Several factors suggest that sports nutrition is becoming increasingly important for optimal athletic performance, and is a viable career opportunity.

Research Productivity Numerous exercise-science research laboratories at major universities are dedicated to sports nutrition research. Almost every scientific journal in sport/exercise science, and even in general nutrition, appears to contain at least one study or review in each issue that is related to sports nutrition.

International Meetings Numerous international meetings have focused on sports nutrition, some meetings highlighting nutritional principles for a specific sport, such as soccer or track and field.

Professional Associations Several professional associations, such as the Sports and Cardiovascular Nutritionists (SCAN) subsection of the American Dietetic Association, and the International Society of Sports Nutrition, are involved in the application of nutrition to sport, health, and wellness.

Sports Magazines and Books Numerous magazines have been developed for individuals with active lifestyles, while others are targeted to specific groups of athletes pursuing almost every kind of sport, such as runners, swimmers, triathletes, bodybuilders, and weight lifters. Invariably, each issue contains a nutrition-related article. Dozens of books have focused on sports nutrition in general, but also for specific sports.

College Courses Many colleges and universities throughout the world have developed courses in sports nutrition to help prepare future coaches, athletic trainers, and other sports medicine personnel to better advise athletes on sound nutritional practices. Some universities that have departments of nutrition and sport/exercise science have developed complete curricular programs of study in sports nutrition.

Career Opportunities Sports nutritionists are employed by professional sport teams and athletic departments of major universities to design optimal nutritional programs for their athletes. Some dieticians market themselves as full-time or part-time sports nutritionists within their communities.

Sports nutrition as we know it today has a relatively short history, but it appears to be an important aspect in the total preparation of the athlete, as documented by the developments cited above and the recent position stand entitled "Nutrition and Athletic Performance" issued jointly by the American Dietetic Association, Dietitians of Canada, and The American College of Sports Medicine. You may access this position statement at www.acsm.org. Click on Publications and then Position Stands.

Are athletes today receiving adequate nutrition?

Survey data evaluating the dietary habits of athletes may vary tremendously, particularly when different sports are compared. An excellent review is presented by Sarah Short of Syracuse University who provides a critique of the validity and usefulness of various survey techniques used to assess average nutrient intake. The usual method in these studies is to obtain a three- to seven-day record of the food intake of the athletes and then use computer analyses to compare their intake with the RDA for a variety of nutrients. One of the problems with dietary survey research is improper responses to the survey by the athletes. For example, in a study evaluating the diet of female gymnasts, Jonnalagadda and others noted that some athletes may under-report energy intake, which may distort the nutritional analysis and indicate a dietary deficiency when there is none. Nevertheless, numerous dietary surveys of various athletic groups provides a broad view of dietary adequacy.

Recent surveys regarding dietary intake of athletes present mixed results. Some studies find that athletes may be eating as well as or better than nonathletes and meeting or exceeding the RDA for many nutrients, while other studies reveal diets inadequate in energy intake or specific nutrients. However, as Mullins and others note, even though the dietary status of the group of athletes as a whole may appear appropriate, wide individual variability indicates that individual athletes may be undernourished.

Inadequate nutrient intakes have been reported for athletes of both genders and all age levels, ranging in athletic ability from the high school level to Olympic caliber. Athletes involved in weight-control sports, such as dancers, gymnasts, bodybuilders, distance runners, and wrestlers, are most susceptible to poor nutrient intake. Female athletes were much more likely than males to incur inadequate nutrient intake. The most significant dietary deficiency in most studies was iron, although zinc, calcium, protein, and several of the B vitamins also were found to be inadequate by several investigators.

In many of these studies, including a nationwide survey of elite athletes, inadequate nutrient intake was due to a very low caloric intake. In addition, several studies have revealed a high incidence of eating disorders in these groups of athletes as they adopted bizarre techniques in attempts to control body weight. Although this problem is more prevalent in females, a small percentage of male athletes also exhibit disordered eating behaviors. This topic is addressed in chapter 10.

This brief review indicates that some athletic groups are not receiving the recommended allowances for a variety of essential nutrients or may not be meeting certain recommended standards. It should be noted, however, that these surveys have analyzed the diets of the athletes only in reference to a standard, such as the RDA, and many studies have not analyzed the actual nutrient or biochemical status (such as by a blood test) of the athlete or the effects that the dietary deficiency exerted on exercise performance capacity or sport performance. The RDA for vitamins and minerals incorporates a safety factor, so an individual with a dietary intake of essential nutrients below the RDA may not necessarily suffer a true nutrient deficiency. On the other hand, if the athlete does develop a nutrient deficiency, then athletic performance may deteriorate and health may be impaired. For example, Daly and others note that adolescent athletes may be at risk of restricted growth and delayed maturation when intense training is combined with insufficient energy intake, which may impair optimal growth if done long-term. This viewpoint is supported by the American Academy of Pediatrics which indicated decreased bone density could be a related health problem in these athletes.

For a number of reasons, dietary surveys indicate that many athletes do not appear to be getting adequate nutrition. For example, one recent study found that only 15 and 26 percent of athletes had adequate intakes of carbohydrate and protein, respectively, based on recommendations for athletes. Part of the problem may be that athletes do not possess sufficient knowledge to make appropriate food choices. Christine Rosenbloom, a distinguished sports nutritionist at Georgia State University, and her colleagues indicate that athletes continue to have misconceptions about the roles of specific nutrients in sport performance, and if they chose foods based on these misconceptions then sports performance may suffer.

Many athletes may not be getting sound sport nutrition information. In a survey of nutrition practices and knowledge of college varsity athletes, Jacobson and others reported that although some athletes received nutrition information from reliable sources, such as dietitians and athletic trainers (who are required to have a nutrition course for certification), considerable nutrition information was obtained from less reliable sources such as magazines. Many athletes receive nutrition information from their coaches, who may not have the background to provide proper advice. Surveys of coaches indicated that 60 to 80 percent had not had a formal course in nutrition or were in need of a better nutrition background. Other constraints, such as finances and time, may limit food selection and preparation.

Given the numerous dietary surveys indicating that some athletes may not be eating appropriately for their sport, Ziegler and others suggest the need to develop dietary intervention and education programs targeted at promoting optimal nutrient intakes by these athletes, not only to maintain performance, but also to improve long-term health status.

How important is nutrition to athletic performance?

As mentioned previously, the ability to perform well in an athletic event is dependent primarily upon two factors: genetic endowment and state of training. First and foremost is genetic endowment. The individual athlete must possess the characteristics that are necessary for success in his or her chosen sport. For example, a world-class male marathoner must have a high aerobic capacity and a low body fat percentage in order to run over 26 sub-five-minute miles. However, unless he has undergone a strenuous training program and maximized his genetic potential, his performance will be suboptimal. The state of training is the most important factor differentiating athletes of comparable genetic endowment. The better-trained athlete has the advantage. No matter at what level the athlete is competing, be it a world championship or a high school swimming meet, genetic endowment and state of training are the two most critical factors determining success. Nevertheless, the nutritional status of the athlete may also exert a significant impact upon athletic performance. Ron Maughan, a world authority on sports nutrition, recently noted that when talented, motivated, and highly trained athletes meet for competition, the margin between victory and defeat is usually small. When everything else is equal, nutrition can make the difference between winning and losing.

Malnutrition represents unbalanced nutrition and may exist as either undernutrition or overnutrition, that is, an individual does not receive an adequate intake (undernutrition) or consumes excessive amounts of single or multiple nutrients (overnutrition). Either condition can hamper athletic performance. As noted previously, the three major functions of foods are to supply energy, regulate metabolism, and build and repair body tissues. Thus, an inadequate intake of certain nutrients may impair athletic performance due to an insufficient energy supply, an inability to regulate exercise metabolism at an optimal level, or a decreased synthesis of key body tissues or enzymes. On the other hand, excessive intake of some nutrients may also impair athletic performance, and even the health of the athlete, by disrupting normal physiological processes or leading to undesirable changes in body composition.

Sports nutrition for the physically active person may be viewed from two aspects: nutrition for competition and nutrition for training. Of the three basic purposes of food—to provide energy, to regulate metabolic processes, and to support growth and development—the first two are of prime importance during athletic competition, while all three need to be considered during the training period in preparation for competition.

Nutrition for Competition In competition an athlete will utilize specific body energy sources and systems, depending upon the intensity and duration of the exercise. The three human energy systems will be discussed in detail in chapter 3. Briefly, however, high energy compounds stored in the muscle are utilized during very short, high-intensity exercise; carbohydrate stored in the muscle as glycogen may be used without oxygen for intense exercise lasting about 1 to 3 minutes; and the oxidation of glycogen and fats becomes increasingly important in endurance activities lasting longer than 5 minutes. The release of energy in each of these three systems may require certain vitamins and minerals for optimal efficiency.

If an individual is well nourished, athletic competition normally will not impose any special demands for any of the six major classes of nutrients. Body energy stores of carbohydrate and fat are adequate to satisfy the energy demands of most activities lasting less than 1 hour. Protein is not generally considered a significant energy source during exercise. The vitamin and mineral content of the body will be sufficient to help regulate the increased levels of metabolic activity, and body-water supply will be adequate under normal environmental conditions.

However, certain dietary modifications may enhance performance when used prior to or during competition. For example, on the basis of the available research evidence, carbohydrate intake prior to and during exercise bouts of long duration at moderate to high intensity and adequate fluid intake prior to and during similar endurance events conducted in warm or hot environmental conditions are two dietary practices that have consistently been shown to increase performance capacity. Specific dietary recommendations will be presented in chapters 4 and 9.

Although not all research findings are in agreement, a number of well-designed studies with several other nutrients or related compounds have documented beneficial effects upon laboratory and field exercise tasks. Some of these tasks are comparable to competitive athletic events. With some of these compounds, such as creatine, the scientific evidence supportive of a beneficial effect is somewhat strong whereas with others, such as sodium phosphate, the data are less conclusive. The potential for all nutrients to enhance competitive performance will be discussed where relevant in the remaining chapters, as will the efficacy of various commercial nutritional supplements targeted for athletes.

Nutrition for Training Proper nutrition during training is one of the keys to success in competition. Chris Carmichael, coach and nutritionist for seven-time Tour de France champion Lance Armstrong, indicates that athletes need to match their nutritional intake to the demands of their training in order to achieve peak performance. Because energy expenditure increases during a training period, the caloric intake needed to maintain body weight may increase considerably—an additional 500–1,000 Calories or more per day in certain activities. By selecting these additional Calories wisely from a wide variety of foods, you should obtain an adequate amount of all nutrients essential for the formation of new body tissues and proper functioning of the energy systems that work harder during exercise. A balanced intake of carbohydrate, fat, protein, vitamins, minerals, and water is all that is necessary. For endurance athletes, dietary carbohydrates should receive even greater emphasis.

However, there may be some circumstances during sport training that particular attention to the diet is important. For example, during the early phases of training, the body will begin to make adjustments in the energy systems so that they become more efficient. This is the so-called **chronic-training effect,** and many of the body's adjustments incorporate specific nutrients. For example, one of the chronic effects of long distance running is an increased hemoglobin content in the blood and increased myoglobin and cytochromes in the muscle cells; all three compounds need iron in order to be formed. Hence, the daily diet would need to contain adequate amounts of iron not only to meet normal needs but also to make effective body adjustments due to the chronic effects of training.

Timing of nutrient intake during training may also be very important. As we shall see in chapters 4 and 6, proper timing of both carbohydrate and protein intake following exercise may be associated with optimal recovery.

Based on the available scientific data, nutrient supplementation does not appear to be necessary for the well-nourished athlete during training. However, nutrient supplementation may be warranted in some cases. For example, in activities where excess body weight may serve to handicap performance, a loss of some body fat may be helpful. Although the use of a very low-Calorie diet to achieve a desirable competitive weight is not advised, vitamin-mineral supplements may be recommended to prevent a nutrient deficiency in athletes who use such a procedure. Recommended procedures for weight loss will be presented in chapter 11.

What should I eat to help optimize my athletic performance?

Melinda Manore, an expert in sport nutrition, noted that there is no doubt that the type, amount, composition, and timing of food intake can dramatically affect exercise performance, recovery from exercise, body weight and composition, and health. The importance of nutrition to your athletic performance may depend on a variety of factors, including your gender, your age, your body weight status, your eating and lifestyle patterns, the environment, the type of training you do, and the type of sport or event in which you participate. As an example of the latter point, the nutrient needs of a golfer or baseball player may vary little from those of the nonathlete, whereas those of a marathon runner or ultraendurance triathlete may be altered significantly during training and competition.

The opinions offered by researchers in the area of exercise and nutrition relative to optimal nutrition for the athlete run the gamut. At one end, certain investigators note that the daily food requirement of athletes is quite similar to the nutritionally balanced diet for everyone else, and therefore no special recommendations are needed. On the other extreme, some state that it is almost impossible to obtain all the nutrients the athlete requires from the normal daily intake of food, and for that reason nutrient supplementation is absolutely necessary. Other reviewers advocate a compromise between these two extremes, recognizing the importance of a nutritionally balanced diet but also stressing the importance of increased consumption of specific nutrients or dietary supplements for athletes under certain situations.

The review of the scientific literature presented in this book supports the latter point of view. In general, athletes who consume enough Calories to meet their energy needs and who meet the requirements for essential nutrients should be obtaining adequate nutrition. The dietary guidelines for better health, as discussed previously and expanded upon in chapter 2, are the same for optimal physical performance. The key to sound nutrition for the athletic individual is to eat a wide variety of healthful foods.

The need for sound nutrition is especially important for all females and for young males who engage in strenuous physical training. Females need to pay special attention to the iron and calcium content of their diet, as well as energy intake, because of possible health problems, which will be noted in chapters 8 and 10. During the growth and development years of childhood and adolescence, the need for protein, calcium, and iron, as well as many other nutrients, is relatively high because the muscle, bone, and

other body tissues are growing rapidly. Strenuous exercise may increase these needs slightly, but obtaining adequate caloric intake from healthful foods should easily provide the nutrients needed.

A nutritionally balanced diet is still the keystone of sports nutrition, but some athletes may benefit from dietary modifications. The implications of specific nutrients or dietary supplements for optimization of physical performance are discussed briefly below, but will be addressed in more detail in the following chapters where applicable.

Key Concept Recap

▶ Success in sports is primarily dependent on genetic endowment and proper training, but nutrition also can be an important contributing factor.

▶ Sports nutrition involves dietary strategies to optimize physiological responses for adaptation to training and for sports competition.

▶ Studies reveal that although athletes desire to eat a diet that may enhance sport performance, their knowledge of nutrition is inadequate, and many are not meeting the dietary recommendations of sports nutritionists.

Dietary Supplements and Health

Nutrition scientists indicate that foods, particularly fruits and vegetables, contain numerous nutrients or other food substances that may have pharmaceutical properties when taken in appropriate dosages. The potential health benefits of various food substances will be discussed in chapter 2, whereas the benefits of specific nutrients will be covered in appropriate chapters. The purpose of this section is to provide a broad overview of possible health effects of dietary supplements.

What are dietary supplements?

The dietary supplement industry is a multi-billion dollar business. Over 40 percent of Americans use dietary supplements. In the United States, the Dietary Supplement Health and Education Act (DSHEA) defines a **dietary supplement** as a food product, added to the total diet, that contains at least one of the following ingredients: a vitamin, mineral, herb or botanical, amino acid, metabolite, constituent, extract, or combination of any of these ingredients (figure 1.7). It is important to note that the DSHEA stipulates that a dietary supplement cannot be represented as a conventional food or as the sole item of a meal or diet.

As noted by this definition, dietary supplements may contain essential nutrients such as essential vitamins, minerals, and amino acids, but also other nonessential substances such as ginseng, ginkgo, yohimbe, ma huang, and other herbal products. The technical definition of a supplement is something added, particularly to correct a deficiency. Theoretically then, dietary supplements should be used to correct a deficiency of a specific nutrient, such as vitamin C. However, numerous dietary supplements contain

FIGURE 1.7 Dietary supplements are marketed as a means of enhancing both health and physical performance.

substances other than essential nutrients and are marketed not to correct a deficiency, but rather to increase the total dietary intake of some food or plant substance that allegedly may enhance one's health status.

Will dietary supplements improve my health?

Dietary supplements are usually advertised to the general public as a means to improve some facet of their health, and are usually under governmental regulation. In the United States, dietary supplements are regulated under food law by the Food and Drug Administration (FDA), and thus are eligible for FDA-authorized health claims, which will be discussed in chapter 2. Dietary supplement health claims in Canada are governed by Health Canada's Natural Health Products Directorate. In some countries, such as Germany, a medical prescription is needed to obtain some dietary supplements containing strong herbal products. Blendon and others noted that a substantial percentage of Americans regularly take dietary supplements as a part of their routine health regimen. Can dietary supplements improve your health? Possibly, but there are several caveats.

In its position statement on dietary supplements, the American Dietetic Association (ADA) indicated that the best nutritional strategy for promoting health and reducing the risk of chronic disease is to wisely choose a wide variety of foods. Essential nutrients and phytochemicals found in most dietary supplements are readily available for us in fruits, vegetables, legumes, fish and other healthy foods. However, the ADA also notes that additional vitamins and minerals from supplements can help some people

meet their nutritional needs as specified by the Dietary Reference Intakes. Two recent *Journal of the American Medical Association (JAMA)* reports regarding the scientific evidence and clinical applications of vitamin supplementation to prevent chronic disease provide support for this position statement. Fletcher and Fairfield noted that some individuals, such as the elderly, vegans, women of childbearing age, and those at risk for cardiovascular disease, may not be obtaining adequate amounts of various vitamins. Moreover, they note that most people do not consume an optimal amount of vitamins by diet alone. Pending strong evidence of effectiveness from randomized trials, they indicate that it appears *prudent* for all adults to take vitamin supplements. Nevertheless, along with Troppman and others, they noted that consumers should be aware of exceeding recommended upper limits of fat-soluble vitamins that may be harmful. The American Dietetic Association reinforces this viewpoint in their position statement. Prudent recommendations for vitamin supplementation will be presented in chapter 7.

The other two essential nutrients marketed as dietary supplements, amino acids and minerals, have also been studied for potential health benefits. In general, as shall be noted in chapter 6, individual amino acid supplements may not enhance health if adequate protein is consumed in the diet. However, research is ongoing with several amino acids. As with vitamins, supplementation with several minerals may confer health benefits to certain individuals, and prudent recommendations will be presented in chapters 7 and 8.

Of the other classes of nonvitamin, nonmineral dietary supplements (herb or botanical, metabolite, constituent, extract, or combinations), numerous products are marketed for their purported health benefits. In a recent survey of college students by Newberry and others, nearly 50 percent had used such supplements within the past year. Although we have no specific requirement for these substances as they are not essential for normal physiological function, some may affect physiological functions in the body associated with health benefits. Using a broad interpretation of the FDA health claim regulations for dietary supplements, some supplement companies advertise their supplements as "miracle products" that can produce "magical results" in a short period of time.

The Consumers Union notes that, under current federal law, any dietary supplement can be marketed without advance testing. The only restriction is that the label cannot claim that the product will treat, prevent, or cure a disease. However, the label may make vague claims, referred to as structure/function claims, like "enhances energy" or "supports testosterone production." Unfortunately, as Nesheim notes, for most of these dietary supplements there are few research data to support their claims. Most advertisements are based on theory alone, testimonials or anecdotal information, or on the exaggeration or misinterpretation of research findings relative to the health effects of specific nutrients or other food constituents. Moreover, although advertisers may not make unsubstantiated health claims, the 1994 DSHEA stipulates that the burden of proving the claims false rests with the government. Currently, under the DSHEA, the FDA must show in court that an unreasonable risk is posed by consumption of a dietary supplement. Thus, numerous unsupported health claims are being made in advertisements and even on dietary supplement labels.

Help is on the way. The Center for Food Safety and Applied Nutrition of the FDA recently launched a ten-year plan to develop a science-based regulatory program that will provide consumers with a high level of confidence in the safety, composition, and labeling of dietary supplement products by the year 2010. In the meantime, the Federal Trade Commission recently indicated that marketers of dietary supplements must have above-board scientific evidence to support any health claims. Additionally, U.S. Pharmacopeia, a respected nonprofit medical agency, recently launched a certification program for dietary supplements. If the dietary supplement contains what the label indicates, then it may carry the USP seal of approval. However, the USP seal does not mean the product is effective or even that it is safe to use, just simply that it contains what the label promises.

It should be noted that some of these types of dietary supplements, such as herbals and food extracts, have been the subject of recent research to evaluate their health effects. Such effects will be discussed in later chapters as appropriate.

Again, to reiterate the point, dietary supplements may exert some beneficial healthful effects in certain cases, but as Thomas points out, for most of us the substances found in most dietary supplements are readily available in familiar and attractive packages called fruits, vegetables, legumes, fish, and other healthy foods. Although the Prudent Healthy Diet is the optimal means to obtain the nutrients we need, dietary supplements may be recommended under certain circumstances. When deemed to be prudent behavior, such recommendations will be provided at specific points in this text.

Can dietary supplements harm my health?

In his review of dietary supplements, Thomas noted that although they may be beneficial to some individuals their use may be harmful in some ways. Some of his key points, and others, are:

1. Nutrition is only one factor that influences health, well-being, and resistance to disease. Individuals who rely on dietary supplements to guarantee their health may disregard other very important lifestyle behaviors, such as appropriate exercise and a healthy diet.
2. Dietary supplements may provide a false sense of security to some individuals who may use them as substitutes for a healthful diet, believing they are eating healthfully and not attempting to eat right.
3. Taking supplements of single nutrients in large doses may have detrimental effects on nutritional status and health. Although large doses of some vitamins may be taken to prevent some conditions, excesses may lead to other health problems.
4. Individuals who use dietary supplements as an alternative form of medicine may avoid seeking effective medical treatment.
5. Dietary supplements vary tremendously in quality. Numerous independent analyses of specific dietary supplements, such as those by ConsumerLab.com, reveal that some may contain less than that listed, sometimes even none of the main ingredient. Some products often contain substances not listed on the label. This may pose a health risk.
6. Numerous case studies have shown that the use of various dietary supplements may impair health, and may even be fatal. Use of ephedrine-containing dietary supplements for weight loss have resulted in deaths.

Nonetheless, some research suggests that use of several herbal products may have some healthful effects. In some countries, such as Germany, herbs are approved for medical use by agencies comparable to the U.S. FDA.

On the other hand, in a recent Consumers Union report various herbal preparations were associated with stomach disorders, non-viral hepatitis (rapid liver damage), obstructed blood flow to the liver and possible cirrhosis, and even death.

Where appropriate, the effectiveness and safety of various dietary supplements will be discussed in later sections of this book, but some general safeguards recommended by the Consumers Union to protect your health will be presented at this point:

- Before trying a dietary supplement to treat a health problem, try changing your diet or lifestyle first.
- Check with your doctor before taking any dietary supplement, particularly herbal preparations. This is especially important for pregnant and nursing women, children, and individuals taking prescribed drugs whose effects may be impaired by herbal interactions.
- Buy standardized products. Most dietary supplements in the United States should be standardized according to federal regulations. "Supplement Facts" labels should provide information comparable to the "Nutrition Facts" food label. Consumer Lab (www.ConsumerLab.com) provides an analysis of many popular dietary supplements.
- Use only single-ingredient dietary supplements. Use of combination supplements may make it difficult to determine the cause of any side effects.
- Be alert to both the positive and negative effects of the supplement. Try to keep an objective record of the effects.
- Stop taking the supplement immediately if you experience any health-related problems. Contact your physician and local health authorities to report the problem. This may help establish a data base for the safety of dietary supplements.

Key Concept Recap

▶ As defined by the Dietary Supplement Health and Education Act (DSHEA) a dietary supplement is a food product, added to the total diet, that may contain vitamins, minerals, herbs or botanicals, amino acids, metabolites, constituents, extracts, or any combination of the above.

▶ Although some people may need dietary supplements for various reasons, particularly vitamins and minerals, the use of supplements should not be routine practice for most individuals. Obtain nutrients through natural foods.

Dietary Supplements and Sports Performance

Although many athletes may take dietary supplements for health reasons, numerous dietary supplements are marketed to athletes specifically to enhance sports performance. In sport and exercise science terminology, such supplements are referred to as **ergogenic aids.**

What is an ergogenic aid?

As mentioned previously, the two key factors important to athletic success are genetic endowment and state of training. At certain levels of competition, the contestants generally have similar genetic athletic abilities and have been exposed to similar training methods, and thus they are fairly evenly matched. Given the emphasis placed on winning, many athletes training for competition are always searching for the ultimate method or ingredient to provide that extra winning edge. Indeed, one report suggests that two of the key factors leading to better athletic records in recent years are improved diet and ergogenic aids.

The word *ergogenic* is derived from the Greek words *ergo* (meaning work) and *gen* (meaning production of), and is usually defined as *to increase potential for work output.* In sports, various ergogenic aids, or ergogenics, have been used for their theoretical ability to improve sports performance by enhancing physical power, mental strength, or mechanical edge. There are several different classifications of ergogenic aids, grouped according to the general nature of their application to sport. The first two classifications are often referred to as *performance-enhancing techniques,* whereas the last three classifications involve taking some substance into the body and are known as *performance-enhancing substances.* We have listed several major categories with an example of one theoretical ergogenic aid for each.

Mechanical Aids Mechanical, or biomechanical, aids are designed to increase energy efficiency, to provide a mechanical edge. Lightweight racing shoes may be used by a runner in place of heavier ones so that less energy is needed to move the legs and the economy of running increases.

Psychological Aids Psychological aids are designed to enhance psychological processes during sport performance, to increase mental strength. Hypnosis, through posthypnotic suggestion, may help remove psychological barriers that may limit physiological performance capacity.

Physiological Aids Physiological aids are designed to augment natural physiological processes to increase physical power. Blood doping, or the infusion of blood into an athlete, may increase oxygen transport capacity and thus increase aerobic endurance.

Pharmacological Aids Pharmacological aids are drugs designed to influence physiological or psychological processes to increase physical power, mental strength, or mechanical edge. Ana-bolic steroids, drugs that mimic the actions of the male sex hormone, testosterone, may increase muscle size and strength. The potential dangers of anabolic steroids, as well as several other drugs used to enhance sports performance, are discussed in later chapters.

Nutritional Aids Nutritional aids are nutrients designed to influence physiological or psychological processes to increase physical power, mental strength, or mechanical edge. Protein supplements may be used by strength-trained athletes in attempts to increase muscle mass because protein is the major dietary constituent of muscle.

Why are nutritional ergogenics so popular?

Probably the most used ergogenic aids are dietary supplements. Dietary supplements marketed as nutritional aids are commonly known as sports nutrition supplements, or simply **sports supplements.** Companies market their products as "Supplements for the Competitive Athlete," and the overall sports supplement business is brisk. According to Dancho and Manore, sports supplements constitute approximately 10 percent of total dietary supplement sales.

Sport supplements are popular worldwide. Fomous and others recently summarized the proceedings of a conference on performance-enhancing supplements organized by the Office of Dietary Supplements, noting that sports supplements are used by all types of athletes: male and female, young and old, professional and amateur. As reported at this conference, about 99 percent of American athletes in the 2000 Olympic games used dietary supplements. Other surveys document significant use among high school and collegiate athletes, military personnel in elite groups such as SEALS, and fitness club members.

Sports supplements are popular for several reasons. Athletes have believed that certain foods may possess magical qualities, so it is no wonder that a wide array of nutrients or special preparations have been used since time immemorial in attempts to run faster, jump higher, or throw farther. Shrewd advertising and marketing strategies promote this belief, enticing many athletes and physically active individuals to try sports supplements. Many of these products may be endorsed by professional athletes, giving the product an aura of respectability. Specific supplements also may be recommended by coaches and fellow athletes. Additionally, as drug testing in sports gets increasingly sophisticated, leading to greater detection of pharmacological ergogenics, many athletes may resort to sports supplements, believing them to be natural, safe, and legal. However, as noted below, this may not be the case.

Are nutritional ergogenics effective?

There are a number of theoretical nutritional ergogenic aids in each of the six major classifications of nutrients, and athletes have been known to take supplements of almost every nutrient in attempts to improve performance. Here are a few examples:

Carbohydrate. Special compounds have been developed to facilitate absorption, storage, and utilization of carbohydrate during exercise.

Fats. Special fatty acids have been used in attempts to provide an alternative fuel to carbohydrate.

Protein. Special amino acids derived from protein have been developed and advertised to be more potent than anabolic steroids in stimulating muscle growth and strength development.

Vitamins. Special vitamin mixtures and even "nonvitamin vitamins," such as vitamin B_{15}, have been ascribed ergogenic qualities ranging from increases in strength to improved vision for sport.

Minerals. Special mineral supplements, such as chromium, vanadium and boron, have been advertised to be anabolic in nature.

Water. Special oxygenated waters have been developed specifically for aerobic endurance athletes, theoretically designed to increase oxygen delivery.

In addition to essential nutrients derived from foods, there are literally hundreds of nonessential substances or compounds that are classified as food supplements and targeted to athletes as potent ergogenics, such as creatine, L-carnitine, coenzyme Q_{10}, inosine, octacosanol, and ginseng. Moreover, many products contain multiple ingredients, each purported to enhance sports performance. For example, one of the "Energy" drinks on the market includes carbohydrates, amino acids, vitamins, minerals, metabolites, herbs, and caffeine.

Nutrient supplementation above and beyond the RDA is not necessary for the vast majority of athletes. In general, consumption of specific nutrients above the RDA has not been shown to exert any ergogenic effect on human physical or athletic performance. However, there are some exceptions. As noted in chapters 4 through 10, there may be some justification for nutrient supplementation or dietary modification in certain athletes under specific conditions, particularly in cases where nutrient deficiencies may occur. Some specific dietary supplements and food drugs may also possess ergogenic potential under certain circumstances.

The effectiveness of almost all of the popular nutritional ergogenics, including the essential nutrients, the nonessential nutrients, the food drugs caffeine and alcohol, the steroid precursor androstenedione, and other agents, will be covered in this book.

Are nutritional ergogenics safe?

The majority of over-the-counter dietary supplements, particularly those containing essential nutrients, appear to be safe for the general population when taken in recommended dosages. However, some dietary supplements, including sports supplements, may contain ingredients that pose health risks in several ways. First, using the "if one is good, then ten is better" mentality, athletes may overdose. The FDA has noted that some sports supplements contain chemicals that have been linked to numerous serious illnesses and even death. Second, the product label may not contain all the ingredients or may contain ingredients not listed. Several products analyzed independently have been shown to contain powerful stimulants which could have adverse effects.

Hermann Engels, a noted exercise scientist at Wayne State University, says that medical authorities are concerned about possible adverse reactions [...] ments, and that th[...] recent *Consumer* [...] likely to use spo[...] may have a sense [...] use appropriate d[...] athletes, the Cou[...] association promo[...] plement industry, [...] *letes: Responsibl[...]* guidelines encom[...] "Stop Light" appr[...] vide normal nutri[...] vitamins; a yello[...] qualified because [...] the red light represents products that should not be used because of possible health problems, such as steroid hormone precursors. This system would appear to be very useful for use by youth sports administrators.

Supplements that are mislabeled and contain unlisted substances pose a serious health threat. Some companies are unscrupulous and may not list a chemical, such as ephedrine, that could provide a stimulant effect which, unknowingly, you may attribute to the *listed* ingredients and thus think the product is effective. Fortunately, the government is working to have all ingredients listed on dietary supplement labels, and hopefully appropriate warnings of any potential health risks will be provided as new laws take effect. Currently, some companies are voluntarily adding warnings in their advertisements and product labels.

Throughout this text, possible health risks associated with nutritional ergogenics will be discussed when such information is available.

Are nutritional ergogenics legal?

The use of pharmaceutical agents to enhance performance in sport has been prohibited by the governing bodies of most organized sports. The use of drugs in sports is known as **doping,** and the Medical Commission of the International Olympic Committee has provided an extensive list of drugs and doping techniques that have been prohibited.

At the present time, all essential nutrients are not classified as drugs and are considered to be legal for use in conjunction with athletic competition. Most other food substances and constituents sold as dietary supplements are also legal. However, some dietary supplements are prohibited, such as DHEA (dehydroepiandrosterone) and androstenedione, because they are classified as anabolic steroids, which are prohibited. Other dietary supplements may contain substances that are prohibited; for example, Chinese Ephedra and some forms of ginseng may contain ephedrine, a prohibited stimulant drug. The National Football League (NFL) has developed strict requirements for the manufacturing of dietary supplements approved for use by its players. The National Collegiate Athletic Association (NCAA) prohibits member institutions from providing ergogenic nutritional supplements to student athletes at

ogenic nutritional supplements
AA-banned substances.

national expert in sports nutrition,
of sports supplements that may cause an
test is widespread. The scientific literature
reports of athletes testing positive for doping
they have not taken drugs, only dietary supple-
gh the risk of an inadvertant positive doping test
e use of sports supplements is small, Baylis and others
is a real problem facing athletes who may be tested for
use. Supporting this viewpoint, independent analyses of
ports supplements, such as those reported by the research groups
of Green and Kamber, revealed prohibited substances not listed
on the product label.

It is hoped that, with pending legislation, all ingredients will be
listed in correct amounts on dietary supplement labels. In the
meantime, athletes should consult with appropriate authorities
before using any sports nutrition supplements marketed as performance enhancers. Nevertheless, the United States Anti-Doping
Agency notes that the use of nutritional or dietary supplements is
completely at the athlete's own risk, even if the supplements are
"approved" or "verified." Websites such as www.supplement-
watch.com and others noted previously concerning dietary supplements may provide helpful information.

Key Concept Recap

▶ Probably the most prevalent ergogenic aids used to increase
sport performance are those classified as nutritional, for
theoretical nutritional aids may be found in all six classes of
nutrients.

▶ Although most dietary supplements are safe and legal, most are
not effective ergogenic aids, and some are unsafe or illegal.
Before using a sports supplement, athletes should try to determine if it is effective, if it is safe, and if it is legal.

Check for Yourself

Go to a health food store, peruse the multiple dietary
supplements available, and ask the clerk for advice on a supplement to treat a minor health condition, such as symptoms of a
cold or headaches, or help you enhance your sport
performance, such as increasing your muscle mass or losing
body fat. Write down the advice and check out advertisements
on the Internet. Then, go to www.supplementwatch.com, check
their comments on the supplement, and compare the findings.

Nutritional Quackery in Health and Sports

Increasing numbers of dietary supplements are being marketed to
the general population as health enhancers and to athletes as performance enhancers. Unfortunately, many of the products that

advertise extravagant claims of enhanced health or performance
are promoted by unscrupulous entrepreneurs, have no legitimate
basis, and may be regarded as quackery.

What is nutritional quackery?

According to the Food and Drug Administration (FDA), **quackery,** as the term is used today, refers not only to the fake practi-
tioner but also to the worthless product and the deceitful
promotion of that product. Untrue or misleading claims that are
deliberately or fraudulently made for any product, including food
products, constitute quackery. The American Dietetic Association,
in its position statement on food and nutrition misinformation,
notes that such misinformation can have harmful effects on the
health and economic status of consumers.

Knowledge relative to all facets of life, the science of nutrition
included, has increased phenomenally in recent years. Thousands
of studies have been conducted, revealing facts to help unravel
some of the mysteries of human nutrition. The ADA indicates that
consumers are taking greater responsibility for self-care and are
eager to receive food and nutrition information. However, that creates opportunities for nutrition *mis*information, health fraud, and
quackery to flourish. The ADA further notes that the media are
consumers' leading source of nutrition information, but that news
reports of nutrition research often provide inadequate depth for
consumers to make wise decisions. Certain individuals may capitalize on these research findings for personal financial gain. For
example, isolated nutritional facts may be distorted or the results
of a single study will be used to market a specific nutritional product. Health hustlers will use this information to capitalize on people's fears and hopes, be it the fear that the nutritional quality of
our food is being lessened by modern processing methods or the
hope of improved athletic performance capacity.

Quackery is big business. It has been estimated that over
twenty-five billion dollars a year are spent on questionable health
practices in the United States. A substantial percentage of this
amount has been spent on unnecessary nutritional products.
Authorities in this area have noted that the amount of misinformation about nutrition is overwhelming, and it is circulated
widely, particularly by those who may profit from it. Although we
may still think of quacks as sleazy individuals selling patent medicine from a covered wagon, the truth is quite different. Nutritional quacks today are super salespeople, using questionable
scientific information to give their products a sense of authenticity and credibility and using sophisticated advertising and marketing techniques.

As noted previously, there are some bona fide health benefits
associated with the foods we eat, but as shall be noted in chapter 2,
federal legislation provides strict guidelines regarding the place-
ment of health claims on food labels for most of the packaged
foods that we buy. Such may not be the case, however, with
dietary supplements.

Before the passage of the 1994 Dietary Supplements Health
and Education Act (DSHEA), many extravagant health claims
were made by some unscrupulous companies in the food supplement industry. As an example, the label of one secret formula

noted that it would help you lose excess body fat while sleeping, which is untrue. Although the DSHEA was designed to eradicate such fraudulent health claims, dietary supplements appear to have more leeway than packaged foods to infer health benefits. Technically, labels on dietary supplements are not permitted to display scientifically unsupported claims. However, companies are allowed to make general claims like "boosts the immune system" if, for example, the product contains a nutrient, such as zinc, that has been deemed important in some way to immune functions in the body. Although companies may not claim that the product prevents diseases associated with impaired immune functions, such as the common cold, cancer, or AIDS, the consumer may erroneously make such an assumption.

Many companies now use a disclaimer on their labels, indicating that the effectiveness of their products has not been evaluated by the FDA. They may also provide information in the form of a reprint of an article, a brochure with highlighted research, or other printed materials that are distributed in connection with the sale of the product. Many dietary supplement companies have developed infomercials for television or home pages on the Internet to provide comparable biased advertising information to potential consumers.

Although these advertising strategies may contain fraudulent information, the federal agencies that monitor such practices are understaffed and cannot litigate every case of misleading or dishonest advertising. Thus, unsuspecting consumers may be lured into buying an expensive health-food supplement that has no scientific support of its effectiveness. As mentioned previously, however, the FDA has plans in motion to remedy this problem by the year 2010.

Nutritional quackery is widespread as documented in the recent position stand on food and nutrition misinformation by the American Dietetic Association. Years ago J.V. Durnin, an international authority on nutrition and exercise, stated that there is still no sphere of nutrition in which faddism, misconceptions, ignorance, and quackery are more obvious than in athletics, a situation which continues today.

Why is nutritional quackery so prevalent in athletics?

As with nutritional quackery in general, hope and fear are the motivating factors underlying the use of nutritional supplements by athletes. They hope that a special nutrient concoction will provide them with a slight competitive edge, and they fear losing if they do not do everything possible to win. In this regard, there are four factors within the athletic environment that help nurture these hopes and fears.

First, eating behavior may be patterned after some star athlete who is successful in a given sport, such as an Olympic champion or professional athlete who attributed part of their success to a sport supplement. For example, sales of androstenedione skyrocketed when Mark McGwire, baseball's home-run record holder at the time, revealed that he had used it as a dietary supplement.

Second, many coaches may suggest to their athletes that certain foods or food supplements are essential to success. Surveys reveal

that many athletes still receive nutritional information from their coaches, but as noted previously, these surveys also reveal that many coaches have poor backgrounds in nutrition. Thus, misconceptions adopted by coaches in the past may be perpetuated in their athletes.

Third, misinformation also may be found in leading sports magazines and books, which often present articles on nutrition for the athlete based upon very questionable research. As noted previously, Jacobson and others reported that athletes receive considerable nutrition information from magazines. Unfortunately, many people believe that if it is in print, then it is true. Some of these magazines and books are published by companies that sell nutritional ergogenics, so the information in the article may be biased.

Fourth, and probably the most significant factor contributing to nutritional quackery in sports, is direct advertising of nutritional products marketed specifically for the athlete, as suggested by the fabricated example presented in figure 1.8. Literally hundreds of nutritional supplements are advertised for athletic consumption. For example, in a survey of only five magazines targeted to body-building athletes, Grunewald and Bailey reported that over 800 performance claims were made for 624 commercially available supplements ranging from amino acids to yohimbine. The authors noted that most claims were not supported by research.

Direct advertising is often combined with several of the methods above for perpetuating nutritional information. Often star athletes

FIGURE 1.8 Simulated nutritional supplement advertisement for athletes.

are hired to endorse a particular product. One advertisement pictured one of America's leading marathoners with the name of a nutritional supplement emblazoned across his running shirt and the statement that this product was an important part of his training program. Also, many sports magazines will run articles on the ergogenic benefits of a particular nutrient, and in close proximity to the article place an advertisement for a product that contains that nutrient. Freedom of speech guaranteed by the First Amendment permits the author of the article to make sensational and deceptive claims about the nutrient. However, freedom of speech does not extend to advertising, so that fraudulent or deceptive claims may be grounds for prosecution by the FDA or the Federal Trade Commission (FTC). Thus, by cleverly positioning the article and the advertisement, the promoter can make the desired claims about the value of the product and yet avoid any illegality. Classic examples of this technique may be found with protein and amino acid supplement advertising in magazines for bodybuilders.

Most of these advertised products are economic frauds. The prices are exorbitant in comparison to the same amount of nutrients that may be obtained in ordinary foods. Besides being an economic fraud, these products are an intellectual fraud, for there is very little scientific evidence to support their claims. Simple basic facts about the physiological functions of the nutrients in these products are distorted, magnified, and advertised in such a way as to make one believe they will increase athletic performance. Unfortunately, in the area of nutrition and sport, it is very easy to distort the truth and appeal to the psychological emotions of the athlete. Dr. Robert Voy, former chief medical officer of the United States Olympic Training Center, has noted that we have abandoned athletes to the hucksters and charlatans. Athletes are wasting their money on worthless, and sometimes harmful, substances.

How do I recognize nutritional quackery in health and sports?

It is often difficult to differentiate between quackery and reputable nutritional information, but the following may be used as guidelines in evaluating the claims made for a nutritional supplement or nutritional practice advertised or recommended to athletes and others. If the answer to any of these questions is yes, then one should be skeptical of such supplements and investigate their value before investing any money.

1. Does the product promise quick improvement in health or physical performance?
2. Does it contain some secret or magical ingredient or formula?
3. Is it advertised mainly by use of anecdotes, case histories, or testimonials?
4. Are currently popular personalities or star athletes featured in its advertisements?
5. Does it take a simple truth about a nutrient and exaggerate that truth in terms of health or physical performance?
6. Does it question the integrity of the scientific or medical establishment?
7. Is it advertised in a health or sports magazine whose publishers also sell nutritional aids?

8. Does the person who recommends it also sell the product?
9. Does it use the results of a single study or dated and poorly controlled research to support its claims?
10. Is it expensive, especially when compared to the cost of equivalent nutrients that may be obtained from ordinary foods?
11. Is it a recent discovery not available from any other source?
12. Is its claim too good to be true? Does it promise the impossible?

Where can I get sound nutritional information to combat quackery in health and sports?

The best means to evaluate claims of enhanced health or sport performance made by dietary supplements or other nutritional practices is to possess a good background in nutrition and a familiarity with related high-quality research. Unfortunately, most individuals, including most athletes, coaches, athletic trainers, and physicians, have not been exposed to such an educational program, so they must either take formal course work in nutrition or sport nutrition, develop a reading program in nutrition for health and sport, or consult with an expert in the field.

This book has been designed to serve as a text for a college course in nutrition for health-related and sports-related fitness, but it may also be read independently. It is an attempt to analyze and interpret the available scientific literature as to how nutrition may impact upon health and sports performance, and to provide some simple guidelines for physically active individuals to help improve their health or athletic performance. It should provide the essential science-based (evidence-based) information you need to plan an effective nutritional program, either for yourself, other physically active individuals, or athletes, and to evaluate the usefulness of many nutritional supplements or practices designed to improve health or sport performance. Here are some key resources.

Books Numerous reputable books that detail the relationship of nutrition to health and sports performance are available, and many are cited in the reference list at the end of this chapter.

Government, Health Professional, Consumer, and Commercial Organizations Accurate information relating nutrition to health is published by governmental agencies such as the FDA and USDA; health professional groups such as the American Dietetic Association, Dietitians of Canada, American College of Sports Medicine, and the American Medical Association; consumer groups such as Consumers Union and Center for Science in the Public Interest; and commercial groups such as the National Dairy Council and the PepsiCo's Gatorade Sports Science Institute. Excellent materials relative to nutrition may be obtained free or at small cost from some of these organizations. A list of reputable Website addresses is provided for you at www.mhhe.com/williams.

Scientific Journals Many scientific journals publish reputable findings about nutrition, exercise, and health. These technical journals may not be readily available in public libraries but may be found in university and medical libraries. Examples of such publications include *Medicine & Science in Sports & Exercise, The Journal of the American Dietetic Association, American Journal of Clinical Nutrition, Sports Medicine,* and the *International Journal of Sport Nutrition and Exercise Metabolism.* Abstracts of original research studies and excellent reviews may be obtained at the National Library of Medicine Website, www.pubmed.gov.

Popular Magazines Articles in popular health and sports magazines may or may not be accurate. The credentials of the author, if listed, should be a good guide to an article's authenticity. A Ph.D. listed after the author's name may not guarantee accuracy of the content of the article. Be wary of publications emanating from organizations or publishers that also sell nutritional supplements.

Consultants Nutritional consultants are another source of information. Such consultants should have a solid background in nutrition, particularly sports nutrition if they are to advise athletes. The consultant should be a registered dietician (R.D.) or clinical nutritionist (C.N.). He or she should be a member of a reputable organization of nutritionists, such as the American Dietetic Association (ADA). You may contact the ADA at the Website address www.eatright.org and they will provide you with the name of a local dietician. Other recognized nutritional organizations include the American Society for Nutrition Sciences and the American Society for Clinical Nutrition. Qualified nutritionists are able to provide you with nutritional advice to help you meet your health goals.

A subunit of SCAN, Sports Dietetics-USA, is currently in the process of developing a certification as a Specialist in Sports Dietetics, with the slogan *Winning with Sports Nutrition.* A qualified sports nutritionist will be able to assess your nutritional status, including such variables as body composition, dietary analysis, and eating and lifestyle patterns, and relate these nutritional factors to the physiological and related nutritional demands of your sport or exercise program, providing you with a plan to help you reach your performance goals. The International Olympic Committee (IOC) is also in the process of developing a program of study leading to the IOC Diploma in Sports Nutrition.

Be wary of individuals who do not possess professional degrees or appropriate certification, such as "experts" in nutrition or fitness. Many states do not have regulations restricting the use of various terms, such as "nutritionist" or "fitness professional." Although these individuals may have some practical experience to help people change their diets and initiate exercise programs, they normally do not have the depth of knowledge required in many cases. For example, Healey and others recently reported that employees of natural/health food stores did not provide appropriate health information to investigators posing with symptoms of severe asthma. For proper nutritional advice, be certain to ask for proof of certification from recognized nutrition professional groups as cited above. For fitness professionals, check for certification by such groups as the American College of Sports Medicine (ACSM), the American Council on Exercise (ACE), or the National Strength and Conditioning Association (NSCA).

Websites Several Websites mentioned previously provide reputable information. Other Websites are available, but not all are reputable as they may be sponsored by unethical supplement companies. Dancho and Manore provide guidelines for evaluating dietary supplement Websites and provide a list of reputable sites, most of which are also listed at www.mhhe.com/williams.

Key Concept Recap

▶ There appears to be no sphere of nutrition in which faddism, misconceptions, ignorance, and quackery are more obvious than with dietary supplements marketed to athletes.

▶ There are a number of guidelines to help identify quackery and false claims of dietary supplements, but one of the critical points to consider is if the claim simply appears to be too good to be true.

▶ The best means to counteract nutritional quackery is to possess a good background in nutrition. Reputable sources of information are available to help provide contemporary viewpoints on the efficacy, safety, and legality of various dietary supplements for health or sport.

Research and Prudent Recommendations

By now you should realize that nutrition and exercise may influence our health and sport performance. But how do we know what effect a nutrient, food, or dietary supplement we consume or exercise program we undertake will have on our health or performance? To find answers to specific questions, we should rely on the findings derived from scientific research which is the heart of evidence-based medicine. As sophisticated sciences, nutrition and exercise science have a relatively short history. Not too long ago, nutrition scientists were concerned primarily with identifying the major constituents of the foods we eat and their general functions in the human body, while those investigating exercise concentrated more on its application to enhance sports performance. More recently, however, numerous scientists have turned their attention to the possible health benefits of certain foods and various forms of exercise, and, in the case of sport scientists, the possible applications to athletic performance. These scientists are not only attempting to determine the general effects of diet and exercise on health and performance, but are also investigating the effects of specific nutrients at the molecular and genetic level to determine possible mechanisms of action to improve health or performance in sport.

Because this book makes a number of nutritional (and some exercise) *evidence-based* recommendations relative to sports and health, it is important to review briefly the nature and limitations of nutritional and exercise research with humans. For the purpose of this discussion, our emphasis will be on nutritional research, although the same research considerations apply to exercise as well.

What types of research provide valid information?

Several research techniques have been used to explore the effect of nutrition on health or athletic performance. The two major general categories have been epidemiological research and experimental research, and Temple provides an excellent overview of the challenges of research design in the study of nutrition and disease.

Epidemiological research involves studying large populations to find relationships between two or more variables. There are various forms of epidemiological research. One general form uses retrospective techniques. In this case, individuals who have a certain disease are identified and compared with a group of their peers, called a cohort, who do not have the disease. Researchers then trace the history of both groups through interviewing techniques to identify dietary practices that may have increased the risk for developing the disease. Another general form of epidemiological research uses prospective techniques. In this case, individuals who are free of a specific disease are identified and then followed for years, during which time their diets are scrutinized. As some individuals develop the disease and others do not, the investigators then attempt to determine what dietary behaviors may increase the risk for the disease.

Epidemiological research helps scientists identify important relationships between nutritional practices and health. For example, years ago several epidemiological studies reported that individuals who consumed a diet high in fat were more likely to develop heart disease. One should note that such research does not prove a cause and effect relationship. Although these studies did note a deleterious association between a diet high in fat and heart disease, they did not actually prove that fat consumption (possible cause) leads to heart disease (possible effect), but only that some form of relationship between the two existed. However, in some cases the relationship between a lifestyle behavior and a disease is so strong that causality is inferred. In this regard, epidemiologists often calculate and report relative risks (RR) or odds ratios (OR), which are probability estimates of getting some disease by practicing some unhealthful behavior. A RR of 1.0 is normal probability, so if a study reports a RR of 2.5 for developing heart disease in individuals who consumed a diet rich in saturated fatty acids, such diets may increase one's risk 2.5 times normal. Conversely, if a study reports a RR of 0.5 for developing heart disease by consuming a pure vegetarian diet, such diets may cut heart disease risk in half.

Epidemiological research is useful in identifying relationships between variables, but **experimental research** is essential to establishing a cause and effect relationship (figure 1.9). In human nutrition research, experimental studies are often referred to as clinical trials or clinical intervention studies, usually involving a treatment group and a control, or placebo, group. Clinical studies may involve studying a smaller group of subjects under tightly controlled conditions for a short time frame, or larger population groups living freely over a long time frame. In such studies, often called intervention studies, an independent variable (cause) is manipulated so that changes in a dependent variable (effect) can be studied. If we continue with the example of fat and heart disease, a large (and expensive) clinical intervention study could be designed to see whether a low-fat diet could help prevent heart disease. Two groups of subjects would be matched on several risk factors associated with the development of heart disease, and over a certain time, say 10 years, one group would receive a low-fat diet (treatment, or cause) while the other would continue to consume their normal high-fat diet (control or placebo). At the end of the experiment, the differences in the incidence of heart disease (effect) between the two groups would be evaluated to determine whether or not the low-fat diet was an effective preventive strategy. Bouchard presents an excellent detailed overview of the quality of different research-based sources of evidence, noting that randomized controlled clinical trials with large populations represent the richest source of data. If the results of such a study showed that consumption of a low-fat diet had no effect upon the incidence rate of heart disease, should you continue to consume a high-fat diet? The answer to this question, as we shall see later, is "not necessarily."

Most of the research designed to explore the effect of nutrition on sport performance is experimental in nature, and of a much shorter time frame compared to those studies investigating the relationship of nutrition and health. Additionally, most sports nutrition studies are conducted in a laboratory with tight control of extraneous variables. Very few studies have actually investigated the effect of nutritional strategies on actual competitive sport performance. Nevertheless, although most of our information about the beneficial effects of various nutritional strategies on sport performance is derived from laboratory-based research, many of these studies use laboratory protocols designed to mimic the physiologic demands of the sport. In later chapters, as we discuss the effects of various nutritional strategies or dietary supplements on sports performance, we will often refer to studies that have problems with their experimental methodology, but we will also note studies that are well controlled. Following are some major questions you should ask when evaluating the experimental methodology of a study to see if it has been well designed. We shall use research with creatine supplementation as an example.

1. Is there a legitimate reason for creatine supplementation? Theoretically, creatine may add to the stores of creatine phosphate in the muscle, an important energy source.
2. Were appropriate subjects used? As creatine phosphate may theoretically benefit power performance, trained strength athletes would be ideal subjects.
3. Are the performance tests valid? Validated tests should be used to collect data on the dependent variable, in this case valid power tests.
4. Was a placebo control used? A placebo similar in appearance and taste to creatine should be used in the control trial.
5. Were the subjects randomly assigned to treatments? Subjects should be randomly assigned to separate groups, either the treatment (creatine) or the control (placebo) group. In a repeated-measures design, in which all subjects take both the creatine and the placebo in different trials, the order of administration of the creatine and placebo are counterbalanced, which is known as a crossover design. In general, a repeated-measures design is preferable because each subject serves as his or her own control.

6. Was the study double-blind? Neither the investigators nor the subjects should know which groups received the treatment or the placebo until the conclusion of the study.

7. Were extraneous factors controlled? Investigators should try to control other factors that may influence power, such as physical training, diet, and activity prior to testing.

8. Were the data analyzed properly? Appropriate statistical techniques should be used to reduce the risk of statistical error. Using a reasonable number of subjects also helps to minimize statistical error.

Most experienced contemporary investigators generally use similar sophisticated research designs to generate meaningful data. However, some researchers do not apply such strict protocols, and thus may produce erroneous conclusions.

FIGURE 1.9 Well-controlled experimental research serves as the basis underlying recommendations for the use of nutritional strategies to enhance health status or sport performance.

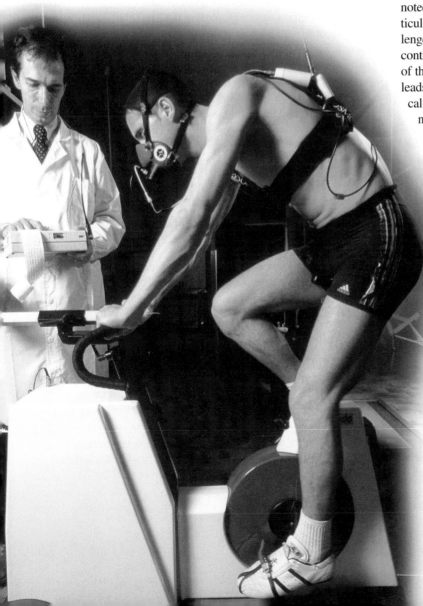

Why do we often hear contradictory advice about the effects of nutrition on health or physical performance?

It is very difficult to conduct nutritional research about health and athletic performance with human subjects. For example, many diseases such as cancer and heart disease are caused by the interaction of multiple risk factors and may take many years to develop. It is not an easy task to control all of these risk factors in freely living human beings so that one independent variable, such as dietary fat, could be isolated to study its effect on the development of heart disease over 10 or 20 years. In a similar manner, numerous physiological, psychological, and biomechanical factors also influence athletic performance on any given day. Why can't athletes match their personal records day after day, such as the 19.32 second 200-meter dash performance by Michael Johnson? Because their physiology and psychology vary from day to day, and even within the day.

Although well-designed studies in peer-reviewed (reviewed by several other experts) scientific journals serve as the basis for making an informed decision as to whether or not to use a particular nutritional strategy or dietary supplement to enhance health or sport performance, it is important to realize that the results from one study with humans do not prove anything. For example, Ioannidis recently noted that even the most highly cited randomized clinical trials, particularly small ones with a limited number of subjects, may be challenged and refuted over time. Although most investigators attempt to control extraneous factors that may interfere with the interpretation of the results of their study, there may be some unknown factor that leads to an erroneous conclusion. For example, early epidemiological studies investigating the role of dietary fat in heart disease may not have adjusted their findings for the type of fat or intake of dietary fiber, which may help retard the development of heart disease. Thus, the results of such a study may lead to the conclusion that diets high in fat do not contribute to the development of heart disease. Consequently, for this and other reasons, the results of single studies, whether epidemiological or experimental, should be taken with a grain of salt, figuratively speaking of course.

Wellman and others indicated that, unfortunately, all too often the media make bold headlines based on the findings of an individual study, and often these headlines may inadvertently exaggerate the findings of the study and their importance to health or physical performance. For example, a newspaper headline might blare that "Coffee drinking causes heart disease" after a study is published that indicated coffee drinking could increase blood cholesterol levels slightly. The study did not show coffee drinking caused heart disease, but only that it may have adversely affected one of its risk factors. A year or so later one may read headlines that report "Coffee drinking does not cause heart disease" because a more recent individual study did not find an association between coffee use and serum cholesterol levels. Is it no wonder consumers are often confused about nutrition and its effects on health or sport performance? Wellman and others note that nutrition scientists should be more involved in helping the media accurately convey diet and health messages.

Scientists consider each single study as only one piece of the puzzle in attempting to find the truth. To evaluate the effects of nutritional strategies or dietary supplements on health or sport performance, individual studies need to be repeated by other scientists and, if possible, a consensus developed. Reviews and meta-analyses provide a stronger foundation than the results of an individual study.

In reviews, an investigator analyzes most or all of the research on a particular topic, and usually offers a summarization and conclusion. However, the conclusion may be influenced by the studies reviewed or by the reviewer's orientation. There have been instances in which different reviewers evaluated the same studies and came up with diametrically opposed conclusions.

Meta-analysis, a review process that involves a statistical analysis of previously published studies, may actually provide a quantification and the strongest evidence available relative to the effect of nutritional strategies or dietary supplements on health or sport performance.

The value of reviews and meta-analyses is based on the quantity and quality of studies reviewed. If the number of studies is limited and they are not well controlled, or if improper procedures are used in analyzing and comparing the findings of each study, the conclusions may be inaccurate. Nevertheless, well-designed reviews and, in particular, meta-analyses provide us with valuable data to make prudent decisions.

For the purpose of improving public understanding, the National Cancer Institute provided for journalists and others in the communications business some guidelines for reporting health-related nutrition research. Key points included the quality and credibility of the study; peer-reviewed study or presentation at a meeting; comparison of findings to other studies; funding sources; and putting findings in context, such as risk/benefit trade-offs. As an example of the latter point, some behavior may increase a health risk from one in a million to three in a million; if reported as a three-fold increase in risk, it may appear to be more unhealthful than it really is. Although these guidelines were presented in 1998, their use by the media does not appear to have increased appreciably.

What is the basis for the dietary recommendations presented in this book?

Within the lifetime of many students a tremendous amount of both epidemiological and experimental research has been concerned with the effect nutrition may have upon health and athletic performance. Based on evolving research findings, dietary recommendations change over time. For example, in a twenty-fifth anniversary issue, *Environmental Nutrition* compared 10 different dietary recommendations based on current research and that available 25 years ago. Here is one of the ten: Then, fat was at the root of most illnesses, including heart disease and cancer, and there was no distinction between different types of fat. Now, fat is in good favor if amounts are moderate, and unsaturated fats, especially monounsaturated, may even help reduce the risk of some chronic diseases.

Although in many cases we still do not have absolute proof that a particular nutritional practice will produce the desired effect, we do have sufficient information to make a recommendation that is prudent, meaning that it is likely to do some good and cause no harm. Thus, the recommendations offered in this text should be considered prudent; they are based upon a careful analysis and evaluation of the available scientific literature, primarily comprehensive reviews and meta-analyses of the pertinent research by various scientists or public and private health or sports organizations. In cases where the research data are limited, recommendations may be based on several individual studies if they have been well designed.

Nevertheless, remember that we all possess biological individuality and thus might react differently to a particular nutritional intervention. For example, relative to health, most of us have little or no reaction to an increase in dietary salt, but some individuals are very sensitive to salt intake and will experience a significant rise in blood pressure with increased dietary salt. Relative to athletic performance, some, but not all, individuals experience gastrointestinal distress when they ingest certain forms of carbohydrate before performing. Such individual reactions have been noted in some research studies, and are discussed where relevant in the following chapters. With advances in genetic technology, diets may one day be individualized to conform to our genetically determined favorable responses to particular dietary strategies.

Thus, recommendations offered in this text should not be regarded as medical advice. Individuals should consult a physician or an other appropriate health professional for advice on taking any dietary supplement for health purposes. Additionally, although information presented in this book may help athletes make informed decisions regarding the use of nutritional strategies as a means to improve sport performance, athletes should confer with an appropriate health professional before using dietary supplements or nutritional ergogenics.

Key Concept Recap

▶ Prudent nutritional recommendations for enhancement of health or athletic performance are based on reputable research.

▶ Epidemiological research helps to identify relationships between nutritional practices and health or sport performance, but experimental studies are needed to establish a cause-effect relationship. Such experimental studies should adhere to appropriate research design protocols.

Check for Yourself

Obtain a scientific article from your library that involves the use of a dietary supplement to improve some facet of sport performance. To get a list of studies, you may go to www.pubmed.gov, and type in the name of the supplement and the term "exercise" in the search column, or simply scan some sports medicine journals in your library. Compare the methodology to the recommended criteria presented on pages 26–27.

Rate and score your diet by completing the quiz on the next several pages. Also, determine your Healthy Eating Index at www.usda.gov/cnpp and then compare the two ratings. Keep these results until the end of the course and retake the quizzes to see if your dietary practices have changed.

Instructions

These 39 questions will give you a rough sketch of your typical eating habits. The (+) or (–) number for each answer instantly pats you on the back for good eating habits or alerts you to problems you didn't even know you had. The quiz focuses on fat, saturated fat, cholesterol, sodium, sugar, fiber, and fruits and vegetables. It doesn't attempt to cover everything in your diet. Also, it doesn't try to measure precisely how much of the key nutrients you eat.

Next to each answer is a number with a + or – sign in front of it. **Circle the number that corresponds to the answer you choose.** That's your score for the question. If two or more answers apply, circle each one. Then average them to get your score for the question.

How to average. In answering question 19, for example, if your sandwich-eating is equally divided among tuna salad (–2), roast beef (+1), and turkey breast (+3), add the three scores (which gives you +2) and then divide by three. That gives you a score of +2/3 for the question. Round it to +1.

Pay attention to serving sizes, which we give when needed. For example, a serving of vegetables is 1/2 cup. If you usually eat one cup of vegetables at a time, count it as two servings.

The Quiz
Fruits, vegetables, grains, and beans

1. How many servings of fruit or 100% fruit juice do you eat per day? *(OMIT fruit snacks like Fruit Roll-Ups and fruit-on-the-bottom yogurt. One serving = one piece or 1/2 cup of fruit or 6 oz. of fruit juice.)*
   - (a) 0   –3   (d) 2   +1
   - (b) less than 1 –2   (e) 3   +2
   - (c) 1   0   (f) 4 or more +3

2. How many servings of non-fried vegetables do you eat per day? *(One serving = 1/2 cup. INCLUDE potatoes.)*
   - (a) 0   –3   (d) 2   +1
   - (b) less than 1 –2   (e) 3   +2
   - (c) 1   0   (f) 4 or more +3

3. How many servings of vitamin-rich vegetables do you eat per week? *(One serving = 1/2 cup. Count ONLY broccoli, Brussels sprouts, carrots, collards, kale, red pepper, spinach, sweet potatoes, or winter squash.)*
   - (a) 0   –3   (c) 4 to 6   +2
   - (b) 1 to 3   +1   (d) 7 or more +3

4. How many servings of leafy green vegetables do you eat per week? *(One serving = 1/2 cup cooked or 1 cup raw. Count ONLY collards, kale, mustard greens, romaine lettuce, spinach, or Swiss chard.)*
   - (a) 0   –3   (d) 3 to 4   +2
   - (b) less than 1 –2   (e) 5 or more +3
   - (c) 1 to 2   +1

5. How many times per week does your lunch or dinner contain grains, vegetables, or beans, but little or no meat, poultry, fish, eggs, or cheese?
   - (a) 0   –1   (c) 3 to 4   +2
   - (b) 1 to 2   +1   (d) 5 or more +3

6. How many times per week do you eat beans, split peas, or lentils? *(OMIT green beans.)*
   - (a) 0   –3   (d) 2   +1
   - (b) less than 1 –1   (e) 3   +2
   - (c) 1   0   (f) 4 or more +3

7. How many servings of grains do you eat per day? *(One serving = 1 slice of bread, 1 oz. of crackers, 1 large pancake, 1 cup pasta or cold cereal, or 1/2 cup granola, cooked cereal, rice, or bulgur. OMIT heavily sweetened cold cereals.)*
   - (a) 0   –3   (d) 5 to 7   +2
   - (b) 1 to 2   0   (e) 8 or more +3
   - (c) 3 to 4   +1

8. What type of bread, rolls, etc., do you eat?
   - (a) 100% whole wheat as the only flour   +3
   - (b) whole wheat flour as the 1st or 2nd flour   +2
   - (c) rye, pumpernickel, or oatmeal   +1
   - (d) white, French, or Italian   0

9. What kind of breakfast cereal do you eat?
   - (a) whole-grain (like oatmeal or Wheaties)   +3
   - (b) low-fiber (like Cream of Wheat or Corn Flakes)   0
   - (c) sugary low-fiber (like Frosted Flakes) or low-fat granola   –1
   - (d) regular granola   –2

Meat, poultry, and seafood

10. How many times per week do you eat high-fat red meats *(hamburgers, pork chops, ribs, hot dogs, pot roast, sausage, bologna, steaks other than round steak, etc.)?*
    - (a) 0   +3   (d) 2   –2
    - (b) less than 1 +2   (e) 3   –3
    - (c) 1   –1   (f) 4 or more –4

11. How many times per week do you eat lean red meats *(hot dogs, or luncheon meats with no more than 2 grams of fat per serving, round steak, or pork tenderloin)?*
    - (a) 0   +3   (d) 2–3   –1
    - (b) less than 1 +1   (e) 4–5   –2
    - (c) 1   0   (f) 6 or more –3

12. After cooking, how large is the serving of red meat you eat? *(To convert from raw to cooked, reduce by 25%. For example, 4 oz. of raw meat shrinks to 3 oz. after cooking. There are 16 oz. in a pound.)*
    - (a) 6 oz. or more   –3
    - (b) 4 to 5 oz.   –2
    - (c) 3 oz. or less   0
    - (d) don't eat red meat   +3

13. If you eat red meat, do you trim the visible fat when you cook or eat it?
    - (a) yes   +1   (b) no   –3

14. What kind of ground meat or poultry do you eat?
    - (a) regular ground beef   –4
    - (b) ground beef that's 11% to 25% fat   –3
    - (c) ground chicken or 10% fat ground beef   –2
    - (d) ground turkey   –1
    - (e) ground turkey breast   +3
    - (f) don't eat ground meat or poultry   +3

15. What chicken parts do you eat?
    (a) breast   +3   (d) wing   −2
    (b) drumstick   +1   (e) don't eat
    (c) thigh   −1   poultry   +3
16. If you eat poultry, do you remove the skin before eating?
    (a) yes   +2   (b) no   −3
17. If you eat seafood, how many times per week? *(OMIT deep-fried foods, tuna packed in oil, and mayonnaise-laden tuna salad—low-fat mayo is okay.)*
    (a) less than 1   0   (c) 2   +2
    (b) 1   +1   (d) 3 or more +3

Mixed foods

18. What is your most typical breakfast? *(SUBTRACT an extra 3 points if you also eat sausage.)*
    (a) biscuit sandwich or croissant sandwich   −4
    (b) croissant, Danish, or doughnut   −3
    (c) eggs   −3
    (d) pancakes, French toast, or waffles   −1
    (e) cereal, toast, or bagel (no cream cheese)   +3
    (f) low-fat yogurt or low-fat cottage cheese   +3
    (g) don't eat breakfast   0
19. What sandwich fillings do you eat?
    (a) regular luncheon meat, cheese, or egg salad   −3
    (b) tuna or chicken salad or ham   −2
    (c) peanut butter   0
    (d) roast beef   +1
    (e) low-fat luncheon meat   +1
    (f) tuna or chicken salad made with fat-free mayo   +3
    (g) turkey breast or hummus   +3
20. What do you order on your pizza? *(Subtract 1 point if you order extra cheese, cheese-filled crust, or more than one meat topping.)*
    (a) no cheese with at least one vegetable topping   +3
    (b) cheese with at least one vegetable topping   −1
    (c) cheese   −2
    (d) cheese with one meat topping   −3
    (e) don't eat pizza   +3
21. What do you put on your pasta? *(ADD one point if you also add sautéed vegetables.)*
    (a) tomato sauce or red clam sauce   +3
    (b) meat sauce or meat balls   −1
    (c) pesto or another oily sauce   −3
    (d) Alfredo or another creamy sauce −4

22. How many times per week do you eat deep-fried foods *(fish, chicken, french fries, potato chips, etc.)?*
    (a) 0   +3   (d) 3   −2
    (b) 1   0   (e) 4 or more −3
    (c) 2   −1
23. At a salad bar, what do you choose?
    (a) nothing, lemon, or vinegar   +3
    (b) fat-free dressing   +2
    (c) low- or reduced-Calorie dressing +1
    (d) oil and vinegar   −1
    (e) regular dressing   −2
    (f) cole slaw, pasta salad, or potato salad   −2
    (g) cheese or eggs   −3
24. How many times per week do you eat canned or dried soups or frozen dinners? *(OMIT lower-sodium, low-fat ones.)*
    (a) 0   +3   (d) 3 to 4   −2
    (b) 1   0   (e) 5 or more −3
    (c) 2   −1
25. How many servings of low-fat calcium-rich food do you eat per day? *(One serving = 2/3 cup low-fat or nonfat milk or yogurt, 1 oz. low-fat cheese, 1 1/2 oz. sardines, 3 1/2 oz. canned salmon with bones, 1 oz. tofu made with calcium sulfate, 1 cup collards or kale, or 200 mg. of a calcium supplement.)*
    (a) 0   −3   (d) 2   +2
    (b) less than 1 −1   (e) 3 or more +3
    (c) 1   +1
26. How many times per week do you eat cheese? *(INCLUDE pizza, cheeseburgers, lasagna, tacos or nachos with cheese, etc. OMIT foods made with low-fat cheese.)*
    (a) 0   +3   (d) 3   −2
    (b) 1   +1   (e) 4 or more −3
    (c) 2   −1
27. How many egg yolks do you eat per week? *(ADD 1 yolk for every slice of quiche you eat.)*
    (a) 0   +3   (d) 3   −1
    (b) 1   +1   (e) 4   −2
    (c) 2   0   (f) 5 or more −3

Fats and oils

28. What do you put on your bread, toast, bagel, or English muffin?
    (a) stick butter or cream cheese   −4
    (b) stick margarine or whipped butter   −3
    (c) regular tub margarine   −2
    (d) light tub margarine or whipped light butter   −1

    (e) jam, fat-free margarine, or fat-free cream cheese   0
    (f) nothing   +3
29. What do you spread on your sandwiches?
    (a) mayonnaise   −2
    (b) light mayonnaise   −1
    (c) catsup, mustard, or fat-free mayonnaise   +1
    (d) nothing   +2
30. With what do you make tuna salad, pasta salad, chicken salad, etc?
    (a) mayonnaise   −2
    (b) light mayonnaise   −1
    (c) fat-free mayonnaise   0
    (d) low-fat yogurt   +2
31. What do you use to sauté vegetables or other foods? *(Vegetable oil includes safflower, corn, sunflower, and soybean.)*
    (a) butter or lard   −3
    (b) margarine   −2
    (c) vegetable oil or light margarine −1
    (d) olive or canola oil   +1
    (e) broth   +2
    (f) cooking spray   +3

Beverages

32. What do you drink on a typical day?
    (a) water or club soda   +3
    (b) caffeine-free coffee or tea   0
    (c) diet soda   −1
    (d) coffee or tea (up to 4 a day)   −1
    (e) regular soda (up to 2 a day)   −2
    (f) regular soda (3 or more a day)   −3
    (g) coffee or tea (5 or more a day) −3
33. What kind of "fruit" beverage do you drink?
    (a) orange, grapefruit, prune, or pineapple juice   +3
    (b) apple, grape, or pear juice   +1
    (c) cranberry juice blend or cocktail 0
    (d) fruit "drink," "ade," or "punch" −3
34. What kind of milk do you drink?
    (a) whole   −3   (c) 1% low-fat +2
    (b) 2% fat −1   (d) skim   +3

Desserts and snacks

35. What do you eat as a snack?
    (a) fruits or vegetables   +3
    (b) low-fat yogurt   +2
    (c) low-fat crackers   +1
    (d) cookies or fried chips   −2
    (e) nuts or granola bar   −2
    (f) candy bar or pastry   −3

36. Which of the following "salty" snacks do you eat?
    - (a) potato chips, corn chips, or popcorn   −3
    - (b) tortilla chips   −2
    - (c) salted pretzels or light microwave popcorn   −1
    - (d) unsalted pretzels   +2
    - (e) baked tortilla or potato chips or homemade air-popped popcorn   +3
    - (f) don't eat salty snacks   +3

37. What kind of cookies do you eat?
    - (a) fat-free cookies   +2
    - (b) graham crackers or reduced-fat cookies   +1
    - (c) oatmeal cookies   −1
    - (d) sandwich cookies (like Oreos)   −2
    - (e) chocolate coated, chocolate chip, or peanut butter   −3
    - (f) don't eat cookies   +3

38. What kind of cake or pastry do you eat?
    - (a) cheesecake   −4
    - (b) pie or doughnuts   −3
    - (c) cake with frosting   −2
    - (d) cake without frosting   −1
    - (e) muffins   0
    - (f) angelfood, fat-free cake, or fat-free pastry   +1
    - (g) don't eat cakes or pastries   +3

39. What kind of frozen dessert do you eat? *(SUBTRACT 1 point for each of the following toppings: hot fudge, nuts, or chocolate candy bars or pieces.)*
    - (a) gourmet ice cream   −4
    - (b) regular ice cream   −3
    - (c) frozen yogurt or light ice cream   −1
    - (d) sorbet, sherbet, or ices   −1
    - (e) non-fat frozen yogurt or fat-free ice cream   +1
    - (f) don't eat frozen desserts   +3

Scoring your diet

Add your score for each question.

Score

Score		
0 or below	**Oops!**	We don't staple *Nutrition Action* shut, you know.
1 to 29	**Hmmm.**	Don't be discouraged. This eating business is tough.
30 to 59	**Yesss!**	Congratulations. You can invite us over to eat any day.
60 or above	**C-o-o-o-l.**	Our photographer should be at your door any second.

Review Questions: Multiple Choice

1. Which of the following would not be regarded as unstructured physical activity, sometimes referred to as activities of daily living?
   - (a) gardening
   - (b) housework
   - (c) jogging
   - (d) leisurely walking
   - (e) driving the car

2. In general, what appears to be a recommended minimum weekly caloric expenditure believed to be needed to provide health benefits?
   - (a) 50–100 Calories
   - (b) 150–200 Calories
   - (c) 250–400 Calories
   - (d) 450–500 Calories
   - (e) 1,000 Calories

3. Increased levels of both aerobic and musculoskeletal fitness through physical activity may produce numerous health benefits. Which of the following is least likely to occur from a combined aerobic and resistance exercise training program?
   - (a) prevention of heart disease
   - (b) building of bone density
   - (c) prevention of weight gain
   - (d) prevention of type 1 diabetes
   - (e) improvement of life expectancy

4. Which of the following is not a recommended dietary guideline associated with the Prudent Healthy Diet?
   - (a) Maintain a healthy body weight.
   - (b) Eat a variety of wholesome, natural foods.
   - (c) Choose a diet with plenty of simple, refined carbohydrates.
   - (d) Abstain from alcohol if you are pregnant.
   - (e) Choose a diet low in saturated fat.

5. Poor nutrition may contribute to the development of numerous chronic diseases. For example, obesity, high blood pressure, diabetes, and heart disease are most associated with which of the following nutritional problems?
   - (a) diets rich in vitamins and minerals
   - (b) diets rich in dietary fiber
   - (c) diets rich in fat and Calories
   - (d) diets rich in complex carbohydrates
   - (e) diets rich in plant proteins

6. Which group of athletes are most likely to suffer from nutritional inadequacies?
   - (a) male baseball players
   - (b) female gymnasts
   - (c) male tennis players
   - (d) female basketball players
   - (e) male football players

7. Recent research suggests that because most individuals do not consume enough of these in their daily diet, taking them may be prudent for all adults.
   - (a) vitamins
   - (b) amino acids
   - (c) herbals
   - (d) metabolites
   - (e) extracts

8. Which of the following statements regarding ergogenic aids is false?
   - (a) They are designed to enhance sports performance.
   - (b) Use of any aid that enhances sport performance is illegal and is grounds for disqualification.
   - (c) Although most nutritional ergogenics are safe, some dietary supplements pose significant health risks.
   - (d) Endorsement of a nutritional ergogenic by a professional athlete does not necessarily mean that it is effective as advertised.
   - (e) Some nutritional supplements marketed as ergogenics may contain prohibited drugs.

9. In an experimental study to evaluate the effect of creatine supplementation on

muscular power for sport, which of the following would not be considered acceptable for the research methodology to be followed in the conduct of the study?

(a) Use well-trained power sport athletes.

(b) Use a double-blind protocol.

(c) Use a placebo control group.

(d) Use a sport-related performance task.

(e) Use males in one group and females in the other.

10. A meta-analysis is

(a) an ergogenic aid for mathematicians.

(b) a technique to evaluate the presence of drug metabolites in athletes.

(c) a statistical evaluation of a collection of studies in order to derive a conclusion.

(d) an evaluation of the daily metabolic rate.

(e) an analytical technique to evaluate biomechanics in athletes.

Answers to multiple choice questions:

1. c; 2. e; 3. d; 4. c; 5. c; 6. b; 7. a; 8. b; 9. e; 10. c.

Review Questions: Essay

1. Describe the Physical Activity Pyramid, highlighting the types and importance of the activities on the five levels of the pyramid.

2. Define the term *sports nutrition* and explain how appropriate eating strategies may enhance sports performance.

3. Explain the ways in which use of dietary supplements may possibly impair one's health status.

4. List at least five guideline questions one may use to evaluate advertised claims for dietary supplements.

5. Differentiate between epidemiological research and experimental research, discussing the protocols used in each and the pros and cons of each.

References

Books

American Dietetic Association. 2002. *The Health Professional's Guide to Popular Dietary Supplements*. Chicago: American Dietetic Association.

Antonio, J., and Stout, J. 2001. *Sports Supplements*. Philadelphia: Lippincott, Williams & Wilkins.

Bahrke, M., and Yesalis, C. 2002. *Performance-Enhancing Substances in Sport and Exercise*. Champaign, IL: Human Kinetics.

Benardot, D. 2000. *Nutrition for the Serious Athlete*. Champaign, IL: Human Kinetics.

Carmichael, C. 2004. *Food for Fitness: Eat Right to Train Right*. New York: G.P. Putnam's Sons.

Center for Food Safety and Applied Nutrition. January 2000. *Diet supplement strategy (Ten-year plan)*. Washington, DC: United States Food and Drug Administration.

Clark, N. 1997. *Nancy Clark's Sports Nutrition Guidebook: Eating to Fuel Your Active Lifestyle*. Champaign, IL: Human Kinetics.

Driskell, J., and Wolinsky, I. 2002. *Nutritional Assessment of Athletes*. Boca Raton, FL: CRC Press.

Driskell, J. A. 2000. *Sports Nutrition*. Boca Raton, FL: CRC Press.

Dunford, M. 2006. *Sports Nutrition: A Practice Manual for Professionals*. Chicago: SCAN and the American Dietetic Association.

Duyff, R. 2002. *The American Dietetic Association's Complete Food and Nutrition Guide*. New York: Wiley.

Institute of Medicine, Food and Nutrition Board. 2002. *Dietary Reference Intakes for Energy, Carbohydrates, Fiber, Fat, Protein and Amino Acids (Macronutrients)*. Washington, DC: National Academy Press.

Ivy, J., and Portman, R. 2004. *Nutrient Timing: The Future of Sports Nutrition*. North Bergen, NJ: Basic Health Publications.

Jeukendrup, A., and Gleeson, M. 2004. *Sport Nutrition*. Champaign, IL: Human Kinetics.

Manore, M., and Thompson, J. 2000. *Sport Nutrition for Health and Performance*. Champaign, IL: Human Kinetics.

Maughan, R. J. 2000. *Nutrition in Sport*. Oxford: Blackwell Science.

McArdle, W. D., et al. 2005. *Sports and Exercise Nutrition*. Baltimore: Lippincott, Williams & Wilkins.

National Academy of Sciences. 1999. *Dietary Reference Intakes*. Washington, DC: National Academy Press.

National Institutes of Health. 2002. *The Interaction of Physical Activity and Nutrition: Biological Remodeling and Plasticity*. Bethesda, MD: NIH.

Rippe, J. M. 1999. *Lifestyle Medicine*. Boston: Blackwell Science.

Shils, M., et al. 2006. *Modern Nutrition in Health and Disease*. Philadelphia: Lippincott Williams & Wilkins.

United States Anti-Doping Agency. 2005. *Optimal Dietary Intake*. Colorado Springs, CO: USADA.

U.S. Department of Agriculture and U.S. Department of Health and Human Services. 2005. *Nutrition and Your Health: Dietary Guidelines for Americans*. Washington, DC: U.S. Government Printing Office.

U.S. Department of Health and Human Services. Public Health Service. 1996. *The Surgeon General's Report on Physical Activity and Health.* Washington, DC: U.S. Government Printing Office.

U.S. Department of Health and Human Services. 2000. *Healthy People 2010.* Washington, DC: U.S. Government Printing Office.

Voy, R. 1991. *Drugs, Sports, and Politics.* Champaign, IL: Leisure Press.

Wardlaw, G. 2003. *Contemporary Nutrition: Issues and Insights.* Boston: McGraw-Hill.

Wolinsky, I. and Driskell, J. 2004. *Nutritional Ergogenic Aids.* Boca Raton, FL: CRC Press.

Reviews

Adam, D. 2001. Gene therapy may be up to speed for cheats at 2008 Olympics. *Nature* 414:569–70.

American Academy of Pediatrics. 2000. Medical concerns in the female athlete. *Pediatrics* 106:610–3.

American Cancer Society. 2001. Nutrition and Physical Activity Guidelines Advisory Committee. 2002. American Cancer Society guidelines on nutrition and physical activity for cancer prevention: Reducing the risk of cancer with healthy food choices and physical activity. *CA: A Cancer Journal for Clinicians* 52:92–119.

American College of Sports Medicine. 1998. American College of Sports Medicine Position Stand. The recommended quantity and quality of exercise for developing and maintaining cardiorespiratory and muscular fitness, and flexibility in healthy adults. *Medicine & Science in Sports & Exercise* 30:975–91.

American Diabetes Association. 2003. Evidence-based nutrition principles and recommendations for the treatment and prevention of diabetes and related complications. *Diabetes Care* 26:S51–61.

American Dietetic Association. 2000. *10 Tips to Healthy Eating.* Chicago: The American Dietetic Association.

American Dietetic Association. 2001. Position of the American Dietetic Association: Food fortification and dietary supplements. *Journal of the American Dietetic Association* 101:115–25.

American Dietetic Association. 2002. Position of the American Dietetic Association: Food and nutrition misinformation. *Journal of the American Dietetic Association* 102:260–66.

American Dietetic Association, Dietitians of Canada, and American College of Sports Medicine. 2000. Nutrition and athletic performance. *Journal of the American Dietetic Association* 100:1543–56.

American Heart Association. 2000. *AHA Dietary Guidelines: Revision 2000.* Circulation 102:2284–99.

Ames, B. 2001. DNA damage from micronutrient deficiencies is likely to be a major cause of cancer. *Mutation Research* 475:7–20.

Anding, J., et al. 2001. Dietary intake, body mass index, exercise, and alcohol; Are college women following the dietary guidelines for Americans? *Journal of the American College of Health* 49:167–71.

Balon, T. 2004. Exercisenomics: A wave of the future? *Medicine & Science in Sports and Exercise* 36:745.

Baracos, V. 2001. Nutrition and athletic performance. *Canadian Journal of Applied Physiology* 26:S1–3.

Bauman, A. 2004. Updating the evidence that physical activity is good for health: An epidemiological review 2000–2003. *Journal of Science and Medicine in Sport* 7:6–19.

Baylis, A., et al. 2001. Inadvertent doping through supplement use by athletes: Assessment and management of the risk in Australia: *International Journal of Sport Nutrition and Exercise Metabolism* 11:365–83.

Bieler, K. 2004. Eat like a champion. *Runner's World* 39 (7):43–44.

Blair, S., et al. 2004. The evolution of physical activity recommendations: How much is enough? *American Journal of Clinical Nutrition* 79:919SS–920S.

Blendon, R., et al. 2001. American's views on the use and regulation of dietary supplements. *Archives of Internal Medicine* 161:805–10.

Booth, F., and Chakravarthy, M. 2002. Cost and consequences of sedentary living: New battleground for an old enemy. *President's Council on Physical Fitness and Sports Research Digest* 3 (13):1–8.

Bouchard, C. 2001. Physical activity and health: Introduction to the dose-response symposium. *Medicine & Science in Sports & Exercise* 33:S347–50.

Bouchoux, A. 2001. The human genome: A master code for better health. *Food Insight.* (July/August): 1–5.

Bowen, D., and Beresford, S. 2002. Dietary interventions to prevent disease. *Annual Review of Public Health* 23:255–86.

Brooks, G., et al. 2004. Chronicle of the Institute of Medicine physical activity recommendation: How a physical activity recommendation came to be among

dietary recommendations. *American Journal of Clinical Nutrition* 79:921S–930S.

Burke, L. 2001. Nutritional practices of male and female endurance cyclists. *Sports Medicine* 31:521–32.

Burke, L. 1999. Nutrition for sport: Getting the most out of training. *Australian Family Physician* 28:561–7.

Byers, T., et al. 2002. American Cancer Society guidelines on nutrition and physical activity for cancer prevention: Reducing the risk of cancer with healthy food choices and physical activity. *CA:A Cancer Journal for Clinicians* 52:92–119.

Consumers Union. 2005. The new do's and don'ts for protecting your heart. *Consumers Reports on Health* 17(7):1–46.

Consumers Union. 2005. Which alternative treatments work? *Consumers Reports* 70(8):39–43.

Consumers Union. 2004. Dangerous supplements: Still at large. *Consumers Reports* 69(5):12–17.

Consumers Union. 2001. Sports-supplement dangers. *Consumer Reports* 66 (6):40–42.

Consumers Union. 1999. Checkup for the new millennium. *Consumer Reports on Health* 11 (2):1–6.

Consumers Union. 1998. Exercise can kill you—or save your life. *Consumer Reports on Health* 10 (7):1–4.

Corbin, C. B., et al. 2000. Definitions: Health, fitness and physical activity. *President's Council on Physical Fitness and Sports* 3 (9):1–8.

Cordain, L., et al. 2005. Origins and evolution of the Western diet: Healthy implications for the 21st century. *American Journal of Clinical Nutrition* 81:341–54.

Cotman, C., and Engesser-Cesar, C. 2002. Exercise enhances and protects brain function. *Exercise & Sport Sciences Reviews* 30:75–79.

Council for Responsible Nutrition. 2002. *Guidelines for Young Athletes: Responsible Use of Sports Nutrition Supplements.* Washington, DC: CRN.

Cousins, R. J. 1999. Nutritional regulation of gene expression. In *Modern Nutrition in Health and Disease,* eds. M. Shils et al. Baltimore: Williams & Wilkins.

Daly, R., et al. 2002. Does training affect growth? *The Physician and Sportsmedicine* 30 (10):21–29.

Dancho, C., and Manore, M. 2001. Dietary supplement information on the World Wide Web. *ACSM's Health & Fitness Journal* 5 (6):7–12.

DeBusk, R., et al. 2005. Nutritional genomics in practice: Where do we begin? *Journal* of the *American Dietetic Association* 105:589–98.

DeMarini, D. M. 1998. Dietary interventions and human carcinogenesis. *Mutation Research* 400:457–65.

Draeger, J., et al. 2005. The obligatory exerciser. *Physician and Sportsmedicine* 33(6):13–23.

Durnin, J.V. 1967. The influence of nutrition. *Canadian Medical Association Journal* 96:715–20.

Engels, H. J. 1999. Publication of adverse events in exercise studies involving nutritional agents. *International Journal of Sport Nutrition* 9:89–91.

Environmental Nutrition Editors. 2002. Celebrating 25 years of *Environmental Nutrition*: What we believed then, what we think we know now. *Environmental Nutrition* 25 (1):8.

Fairfield, K., and Fletcher, R. 2002. Vitamins for chronic disease prevention in adults: Scientific review. *JAMA* 287:3116–26.

Febbraio, M., and Pedersen, B. 2005. Contraction-induced myokine production and release: Is skeletal muscle an endocrine organ? *Exercise and Sport Sciences Reviews* 33:114–19.

Fitzpatrick, F. 2002. The ageless athlete may not be too far off. *Philadelphia Inquirer,* 4 August, D1, D11.

Fletcher, R., and Fairfield, K. 2002. Vitamins for chronic disease prevention in adults: Clinical applications. *JAMA* 287:3127–29.

Fomous, C., et al. 2002. Symposium: Conference on the science and policy of performance-enhancing products. *Medicine & Science in Sports & Exercise* 34:1685–90.

Friedenreich, C., and Orenstein, M. 2002. Physical activity and cancer prevention: etiologic evidence and biological mechanisms. *Journal of Nutrition* 132:3456S–64S.

Futterman, L., and Lemberg, L. 2001. The mysteries of the human genome uncovered: Medicine is changed forever. *American Journal of Critical Care* 10:125–32.

Grunewald, K., and Bailey, R. 1993. Commercially marketed supplements for bodybuilding athletes. *Sports Medicine* 15:90–103.

Hagberg, J., et al. 2001. Specific genetic markers of endurance performance and VO$_2$max. *Exercise & Sport Sciences Reviews* 29:15–19.

Heck, A., et al. 2004. Genenutrition interaction in human performance and exercise response. *Nutrition* 20:598–602.

Hill, A. 2002. Developmental issues in attitudes to food and diet. *Proceedings of the Nutrition Society* 61:259–66.

Hoffman-Goetz, L., et al. 1998. Possible mechanisms mediating an association between physical activity and breast cancer. *Cancer* 83 (3 Suppl):621–8.

Jeukendrup, A., and Martin, J. 2001. Improving cycling performance: How should we spend our time and money. *Sports Medicine* 31:559–69.

Kearney, J. 1996. Training the Olympic athlete. *Scientific American* 274 (June):52–63.

Kell, R., et al. 2001. Musculoskeletal fitness, health outcomes and quality of life. *Sports Medicine* 31:863–73.

Krauss, R., et al. 2000. AHA Dietary Guidelines: Revision 2000. *Circulation* 102:2284–99.

LaRosa, J. C. 1998. The role of diet and exercise in the statin era. *Progress in Cardiovascular Diseases* 41:137–50.

Lawrence, M., and Kirby, D. 2002. Nutrition and sports supplements: Fact or fiction. *Journal of Clinical Gastroenterology* 35:299–306.

Lee, C., and Blair, S. 2002. Cardiorespiratory fitness and smoking-related and total cancer mortality in men. *Medicine & Science in Sports & Exercise* 34:735–39.

Lee, I. M., et al. 1997. Physical activity, physical fitness and longevity. *Aging (Milano)* 9:2–11.

Lee, I-Min., and Paffenbarger, R. 1996. Do physical activity and physical fitness avert premature mortality? *Exercise & Sport Sciences Reviews* 24:135–172.

LeLorier, J., et al. 1997. Discrepancies between meta-analyses and subsequent large, randomized, controlled trials. *New England Journal of Medicine* 337:559–61.

Liebman, B. 2005. While you wait: The cost of inactivity. *Nutrition Action Health Letter* 32 (10):1–6.

Manore, M. 2004. Nutrition and physical activity: Fueling the active individual. *President's Council on Physical Fitness and Sports Research Digest* 5(1):1–8.

Maughan, R., et al. 2004. Dietary supplements. *Journal of Sports Sciences* 22:95–113.

Maughan, R. 2002. The athlete's diet: Nutritional goals and dietary strategies. *Proceedings of the Nutrition Society* 61:87–96.

McCarron, D., and Reusser, M. 2000. The power of food to improve multiple cardiovascular risk factors. *Current Atherosclerosis Reports* 2:482–86.

Meadows, M. 2005. Genomics and personalized medicine. *FDA Consumer* 39(6):12–17.

Melzer, K., et al. 2004. Physical activity: The health benefits outweigh the risks. *Current Opinion in Clinical Nutrition and Metabolic Care* 7:641–47.

National Cancer Institute. 1998. Commentary: Improving Public Understanding: Guidelines for communicating emerging science on nutrition, food safety, and health. *Journal of National Cancer Institute* 90 (3): 194–99.

Nesheim, M. C. 1999. What is the research base for the use of dietary supplements? *Public Health Nutrition* 2:35–38.

Nieman, D. 2000. Is infection risk linked to exercise workload? *Medicine & Science in Sports & Exercise* 32:S406–11.

Oguma, Y., and Shinoda-Tagawa, T. 2004. Physical activity decreases cardiovascular disease risk in women: Review and meta-analysis. *American Journal of Preventive Medicine* 26:407–18.

Ornish, D. 1999. Healing broken hearts. *Nutrition Action Health Letter* 26 (5):1–7.

Pollock, M. L., and Evans, W. J. 1999. Resistance training for health and disease; Introduction. *Medicine & Science in Sports & Exercise* 31:10–11.

Prentice, R., et al. 2004. Nutrition and physical activity and chronic disease prevention: Research strategies and recommendations. *Journal of the National Cancer Institute* 96:1276–87.

Rankinen, T., and Bouchard, C. 2002. Dose-response issues concerning the relations between regular physical activity and health. *President's Council on Physical Fitness and Sports Research Digest* 3 (18):1–8.

Roberts, C., and Barnard, R. 2005. Effects of exercise and diet on chronic disease. *Journal of Applied Physiology* 98:3–30.

Shephard, R. J., and Shek, P. N. 1998. Immunological hazards from nutritional imbalance in athletes. *Exercise and Immunology Review* 4:22–48.

Shephard, R. J., and Shek, P. N. 1998. Associations between physical activity and susceptibility to cancer: Possible mechanisms. *Sports Medicine* 26:293–315.

Short, S. 1994. Surveys of dietary intake and nutrition knowledge of athletes and their coaches. In *Nutrition in Exercise and Sport,* eds. I. Wolinsky and J. Hickson. Boca Raton, FL: CRC Press.

Skinner, J. 2001. Do genes determine champions? *Sports Science Exchange* 14 (4):1–4.

Spain, C., and Franks, B. D. 2001. Healthy People 2010: Physical activity and fitness.

President's Council on Physical Fitness and Sports Research Digest 3(13):1–16.

Stover, P., and Garza, C. 2002. Bringing individuality to public health recommendations. *Journal of Nutrition* 132:2476S–2480S.

Temple, N. 2002. Nutrition and disease: Challenges of research design. *Nutrition* 18:343–47.

Thomas, P. 1996. Food for thought about dietary supplements. *Nutrition Today* 31 (March/April):46–54.

Thompson, P., et al. 2001. The acute versus the chronic response to exercise. *Medicine & Science in Sports & Exercise* 33:S438–45.

Vuori, I. 2001. Health benefits of physical activity with special reference to interaction with diet. *Public Health Nutrition* 4:517–28.

Ward, E. 2002. Lifestyle, not genes, offers best hope of living healthier, longer. *Environmental Nutrition* 25 (4):1–4.

Wellman, N., et al. 1999. Do we facilitate the scientific process and the development of dietary guidance when findings from single studies are publicized? An American Society for Nutritional Sciences controversy session report. *American Journal of Clinical Nutrition* 70:802–5.

Williams, C. 1998. Diet and sports performance. In *Oxford Textbook of Sports Medicine,* eds. M. Harries et al. Oxford: Oxford University Press.

Williams, M. H. 2006. Sports Nutrition. In *Modern Nutrition in Health and Disease,* eds. M. Shils et al. Philadelphia: Lippincott Williams & Wilkins.

Williams, M. H., and Branch, J. D. 2000. Ergogenic aids for improved performance. In *Exercise and Sport Science,* eds. W. E. Garrett and D. T. Kirkendall. Philadelphia: Lippencott Williams & Wilkins.

Wolfarth, B., et al. 2005. The human gene map for performance and health-related fitness phenotypes: The 2004 update. *Medicine & Science in Sports & Exercise* 27:881–903.

Specific Studies

Bouchard, C., et al. 2000. Genomic scan for maximal oxygen uptake and its response to training in the HERITAGE family study. *Journal of Applied Physiology* 88:551–59.

Brady, L., et al. 2000. Comparison of children's dietary intake patterns with US dietary guidelines. *British Journal of Nutrition* 84:361–7.

Green, G., et al. 2001. Analysis of over-the-counter dietary supplements. *Clinical Journal of Sports Medicine* 11:254–59.

Healey, B., et al. 2002. Do natural health food stores require regulation? *New Zealand Medical Journal* 115:U165.

Hinton, P., et al. 2004. Nutrient intakes and dietary behaviors of male and female collegiate athletes. *International Journal of Sport Nutrition and Exercise Metabolism* 14:389–405.

Ioannidis, J. 2005. Contradicted and initially stronger effects in highly cited clinical research. *JAMA* 294:218–28.

Jacobson, B., et al. 2001. Nutrition practices and knowledge of college varsity athletes: A follow-up. *Journal of Strength and Conditioning Research* 15:63–68.

Johnson, M. F., et al. 1998. Interrelationships between physical activity and other health behaviors among university women and men. *Preventive Medicine* 27:536–44.

Jonnalagadda, S., et al. 2000. Assessment of underreporting of energy intake of elite female gymnasts. *International Journal of Sport Nutrition and Exercise Metabolism* 10:315–25.

Kamber, M., et al. 2001. Nutritional supplements as a source for positive doping cases? *International Journal of Sport Nutrition and Exercise Metabolism* 11:258–63.

Kristiansen, M., et al. 2005. Dietary supplement use by varsity sthletes at a Canadian University. *International Journal of Sport Nutrition and Exercise Metabolism* 15:195–210.

Mokdad, A., et al. 2004. Actual causes of death in the United States, 2000. *JAMA* 291:1238–45.

Morrison, L., et al. 2004. Prevalent use of dietary supplements among people who exercise at a commercial gym. *International Journal of Sport Nutrition and Exercise Metabolism* 14:481–92.

Mullins, V., et al. 2001. Nutritional status of U.S. elite female heptathletes during training. *International Journal of Sport Nutrition and Exercise Metabolism* 11:299–314.

Newberry, H., et al. 2001. Use of nonvitamin, nonmineral dietary supplements among college students. *Journal of the American College of Health* 50:123–29.

Ornish, D., et al. 1998. Intensive lifestyle changes for reversal of coronary heart disease. *Journal of the American Medical Association* 280:2001–7.

Rosenbloom, C. 2002. Nutrition knowledge of collegiate athletes in a Division I National Collegiate Athletic Association institution. *Journal of the American Dietetic Association* 102:418–20.

Rovio, S., et al. 2005. Leisure-time physical activity at midlife and the risk of dementia and Alzheimer's disease. *Lancet Neurology* 4:705–11.

Sossin, K., et al. 1997. Nutrition beliefs, attitudes, and resource use of high school wrestling coaches. *International Journal of Sport Nutrition* 7:219–28.

Troppmann, L., et al. 2002. Supplement use: Is there any nutritional benefit? *Journal of the American Dietetic Association* 102:818–25.

Williams, P. 1998. Relationships of heart disease risk factors to exercise quantity and intensity. *Archives of Internal Medicine* 158:237–45.

Ziegler, P., et al. 1999. Nutritional and physiological status of U. S. national figure skaters. *International Journal of Sport Nutrition* 9:345–60.

Healthful Nutrition for Fitness and Sport

CHAPTER TWO

LEARNING OBJECTIVES

After studying this chapter, you should be able to:

1. List the six major classes of nutrients that are essential for human nutrition and identify specific nutrients within each class.

2. Explain the development of the DRI and explain the meaning of its various components, including the RDA, AI, AMDR, UL, and EAR.

3. Discuss the concept of the balanced diet as applied to the MyPyramid food guide.

4. Explain the concept of nutrient density and provide an example.

5. Outline the twelve guidelines for healthy eating and provide several examples for each as to how food might be selected or prepared in order to adhere to these guidelines.

6. Describe the various classes of vegetarians, what foods they may consume in their diets and the potential health benefits.

7. List the nutrients that must be included on a food label and explain how reading food labels may help one consume a healthier diet.

8. Describe how commercial and home food processing may enhance or impair the quality of food we eat.

9. Understand how dietary practices as related to training and competition may help optimize sport performance.

What you eat can have a significant effect on your health. Hippocrates, the Greek physician known as the father of medicine, recognized the value of nutrition and the power of food to enhance health when he declared that you should let food be your medicine and medicine be your food. As noted in chapter 1, the foods we eat contain various nutrients to sustain life by providing energy, promoting growth and development, and regulating metabolic processes. Basically, healthful nutrition is designed to optimize these life-sustaining properties of nutrients and other substances found in food.

As the human race evolved over the aeons, a natural diet of plant and animal foods provided the nutrients necessary to sustain the lives of our hunter/gatherer ancestors. As human civilization developed, however, human food consumption patterns gradually changed as the emerging food industry developed newer and increasingly more technological methods to plant, grow, process, and prepare foods. Overall, modern developments in the food industry have improved food quality and safety, but there are still some practices that are cause for consumer concern. For example, provision of a wide variety of foods has helped to eradicate most nutrient-deficiency diseases in industrialized nations. Conversely, provision of a wide variety of high-fat, high-sugar, high-Calorie, low-fiber foods appears to have increased the possibility of the development of various chronic diseases.

The three keys to a healthful diet are balance, variety, and moderation. In general, a healthful diet is simply one that provides a balanced proportion of foods from different food groups, a variety of foods from within the different food groups, and moderation in the consumption of any food. Such a diet should provide us with the nutrients we need to sustain life. In this regard, several governmental and professional health organizations have developed dietary guidelines to help us obtain the nutrients we need.

Additionally, the current major focus of nutrition research, both epidemiological and experimental, is how our diets—and even specific foods or nutrients in our diets—affect our health, primarily as related to the development of chronic diseases. Again, specific dietary guidelines have been recommended as a means to enhance one's health status, and these recommendations underlie the Prudent Healthy Diet. In essence, the basic premise of the Prudent Healthy Diet is to consume foods in as natural a state as possible, primarily relying on plant foods and a movement toward a vegetarian or semivegetarian diet.

Although the basic guidelines underlying the Prudent Healthy Diet are rather simple, selecting the appropriate foods in modern society may be somewhat confusing. Fortunately, nutrition labels should provide the knowledgeable consumer with sufficient information to make intelligent choices and select high-quality foods. Food safety is also another consumer concern, and appropriate food selection and preparation practices may help minimize most of the health risks associated with certain foods.

The Prudent Healthy Diet also serves as the basic diet for those interested in optimal physical performance, although it may be modified somewhat for specific types of athletic endeavors as shall be noted as appropriate throughout the book.

Essential Nutrients and Recommended Nutrient Intakes

"You are what you eat" is a popular phrase that contains some truth, particularly in its implications for both health and athletic performance. The foods you eat contain a wide variety of nutrients, both essential and nonessential, as well as other substances that may affect your body functions. Careful selection of wholesome, natural foods will provide you with the proper amounts of nutrients to optimize energy sources, to build and repair tissues, and to regulate body processes. However, as we shall see in later chapters, poor food selection with an unbalanced intake of some nutrients may contribute to the development of significant health problems and impair sport performance.

What are essential nutrients?

As noted in chapter 1, six classes of nutrients are considered necessary in human nutrition: carbohydrates, fats, proteins, vitamins, minerals, and water. Within most of these general classes (notably protein, vitamins, and minerals) are a number of specific nutrients necessary for life. For example, more than a dozen vitamins are needed for optimal physiological functioning.

In relation to nutrition, the term **essential nutrients** describes nutrients that the body needs but cannot produce at all or cannot produce in adequate quantities. Thus, in general, essential nutrients must be obtained from the food we eat. Essential nutrients also are known as indispensable nutrients.

Table 2.1 lists the specific nutrients currently known to be essential or probably essential to humans. Some of the nutrients

TABLE 2.1 Nutrients essential or probably essential to humans

Carbohydrates

Fiber
Sugars and starches

Fats (essential fatty acids)

Linoleic fatty acid
Alpha linolenic fatty acid

Protein (essential amino acids)

Histidine	Phenylalanine and tyrosine
Isoleucine	Threonine
Leucine	Tryptophan
Lysine	Valine
Methionine and cysteine	

Vitamins

Water soluble	Fat soluble
B_1 (thiamin)	A (retinol)
B_2 (riboflavin)	D (calciferol)
Niacin	E (tocopherol)
B_6 (pyridoxine)	K
Pantothenic acid	
Folacin	
B_{12} (cyanocobalamin)	
Biotin	
Choline	
C (ascorbic acid)	

Minerals

Major	Trace/Ultratrace	
Calcium	Boron	Manganese
Chloride	Chromium	Molybdenum
Magnesium	Cobalt	Nickel
Phosphorus	Copper	Selenium
Potassium	Fluorine	Silicon
Sodium	Iodine	Vanadium
Sulfur	Iron	Zinc

Water

Some foods, such as whole wheat bread, may contain all six general classes of nutrients, whereas others, such as table sugar, contain only one nutrient class. However, whole wheat bread cannot be considered a complete food because it does not contain a proper balance of all essential nutrients.

The human body requires substantial amounts of some nutrients, particularly those that may provide energy and support growth and development of the body tissues, namely carbohydrate, fat, protein, water, and several minerals and electrolytes. These nutrients are referred to as **macronutrients** because the daily requirement is greater than a few grams. Most nutrients that help to regulate metabolic processes, particularly vitamins and minerals, are needed in much smaller amounts (usually measured in milligrams or micrograms) and are referred to as **micronutrients,** although as noted in chapter 8, minerals may be classified by other terminology according to the daily requirement.

Essential nutrients are necessary for human life. An inadequate intake may lead to disturbed body metabolism, certain disease states, or death. Conversely, an excess of certain nutrients may also disrupt normal metabolism and may even be lethal (see figure 2.1).

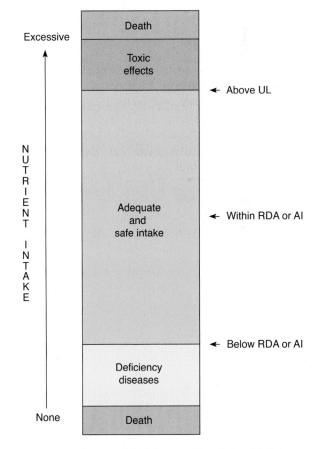

FIGURE 2.1 One model of the possible relationship between nutrient intake and health status. An inadequate intake may lead to nutrient-deficiency diseases, while excessive amounts may cause various toxic reactions. Both deficiencies and excesses may be fatal if carried to extremes. Nutrient intakes within the Recommended Dietary Allowance (RDA) or Adequate Intake (AI) levels are normally adequate and safe, while those below these levels may lead to deficiency diseases. Nutrient intakes above the Tolerable Upper Intake Level (UL) may lead to toxic reactions.

listed have been shown to be essential for various animals and are theorized to be essential for humans. Curing a nutrient-deficiency disease by a specific nutrient has been the key factor underlying the determination of nutrient essentiality. However, the concept of nutrient essentiality is evolving to include substances that may help prevent the development of chronic diseases. Most recently, the essentiality of choline was included with the B vitamin group, and the list is likely to expand in the future as research reveals health benefits of various plant substances.

What are nonessential nutrients?

Those nutrients found in food but that also may be formed in the body are known as **nonessential nutrients,** or dispensable nutrients. A good example of a nonessential nutrient is creatine. Although we may obtain creatine from food, the body can also manufacture creatine from several amino acids when necessary. As we shall see later, creatine combined with phosphate is a very important nutrient for energy production during very high intensity exercise.

Other than nonessential nutrients, foods contain other nonessential substances that may be involved in various metabolic processes in the body. These substances, sometimes referred to as nonnutrients, include those found naturally in foods and those added either intentionally or inadvertently during the various phases of food production and preparation. Classes of these substances include drugs, phytochemicals, extracts, herbals, food additives, and even antinutrients (substances that may adversely affect nutrient status). Many of these nonessential nutrients and other substances are marketed as a means to enhance health or sports performance. Table 2.2 provides some examples that will be covered later in this text.

How are recommended dietary intakes determined?

As noted in table 2.1, humans have an essential requirement for more than forty specific nutrients. A number of countries, as well as the Food and Agriculture and World Health Organizations (FAO/WHO), have estimated the amount of each nutrient that individuals should consume in their diets. In the United States, the recommended amounts of certain of these nutrients have been established by the Food and Nutrition Board, Institute of Medicine, of the National Academy of Sciences. The first set of recommendations, **Recommended Dietary Allowances (RDA),** was published in 1941 and revised periodically over the years. In general, scientists with considerable knowledge of a specific nutrient would meet to evaluate the totality of scientific data concerning the need for that nutrient in the diet. Based on their analysis, specific dietary intake recommendations were made.

In the past the Recommended Dietary Allowances (RDA) were developed to prevent deficiency diseases. For example, the RDA for Vitamin C was set to prevent scurvy. However, more recently scientists have discovered that higher amounts of some nutrients may confer some health benefits in specific population groups, such as prevention of birth defects by adequate folic acid intake in the early stages of pregnancy and the prevention of various chronic diseases by sufficient intake of nutrients found in fruits and vegetables. Conversely, scientists have also noted that overconsumption of some nutrients may increase health risks.

Expert scientists still meet to evaluate the available scientific data that serve as the basis for dietary recommendations, but the basis for such recommendations has been expanded beyond the objective of simply preventing deficiency diseases. The current philosophy relative to the development of recommendations for dietary intake focuses on a continuum of nutrient intake. Several points along this continuum for a specific nutrient may be (1) the amount that prevents a nutrient-deficiency disease, (2) the amount that may reduce the risk of a specific health problem or chronic diseases, and (3) the amount that may increase health risks.

Based on this concept, the Food and Nutrition Board, working with Health Canada, is involved in a multiyear project to develop new standards for nutrient intake, the **Dietary Reference Intakes (DRI),** for Americans and Canadians. The DRI replace and expand on the Recommended Dietary Allowances (RDA). The DRI is an umbrella term. Allison Yates, director of the Food and Nutrition Board, noted that the DRI consist of various reference intakes:

The Recommended Dietary Allowance (RDA) The RDA represents the average daily dietary intake that is sufficient to meet the nutrient requirement of nearly all (97 percent to 98 percent) healthy individuals in a group. The RDA is to be used as a goal for the individual. You may use the RDA to evaluate your intake of a specific nutrient. The *RDA* term will be used throughout this book as the means to express nutritional adequacy.

The Adequate Intake (AI) The AI is a recommended daily intake level based on observed or experimentally determined approximations of nutrient intake by a group of healthy people. When an RDA cannot be set because extensive scientific data are not available, an AI may be established because the limited data available may provide grounds for a reasonable judgment. You may also use the AI to evaluate your intake of a specific nutrient, but remember that it is not as well established as the RDA. The *AI* term will be used throughout this book as appropriate.

TABLE 2.2 Nonessential nutrients and other substances found in foods
Nonessential nutrients
Carnitine
Creatine
Glycerol
Drugs
Caffeine
Ephedrine
Phytochemicals
Phenols
Plant sterols
Terpenes
Extracts
Bee pollen
Ginseng
Yohimbe
Antinutrients
Phytates
Tannins

The Acceptable Macronutrient Distribution Range (AMDR) The AMDR is defined as a range of intakes for a particular energy source that is associated with reduced risk of chronic disease while providing adequate intakes of essential nutrients. The AMDR is expressed as a percentage of total energy intake and has both an upper an lower level. Individuals consuming below or above this range are at more risk for inappropriate intake of essential nutrients and development of chronic diseases. AMDRs have been set for carbohydrate, fat, and protein.

The Tolerable Upper Intake Level (UL) The UL is the highest level of daily nutrient intake that is likely to pose no risks of adverse health effects to most individuals in the general population. The UL is given to assist in advising individuals what levels of intake may result in adverse effects if habitually exceeded. The UL is not intended to be a recommended dietary intake; you should consider it as a maximum for your daily intake of a specific nutrient on a long-term basis. The UL will be cited throughout this book when data are available.

The Estimated Average Requirement (EAR) The EAR represents a nutrient intake value that is estimated to meet the requirement of half the healthy individuals in a group. Conversely, half of the individuals consuming the EAR will not meet their nutrient needs. The EAR is used to establish the RDA. Depending on the data available, the RDA is some multiple of the EAR, mathematically calculated to provide adequate amounts to 97 percent to 98 percent of the general population. When sufficient scientific data are not available to calculate an EAR, then an AI may be provided.

Figure 2.1 highlights several of these terms in relation to nutritional deficiency, adequacy, and excess. These terms, and others, are described in detail in the National Academy of Sciences series on Dietary Reference Intakes.

Currently, DRI have been established for all classes of essential nutrients, including carbohydrate, fat, protein and amino acids, vitamins, minerals, and water. The new DRI also, for the first time, provide recommendations for those 70 years and older. Tables containing the current DRI may be found on the inside of the front and back covers of this text. They may also be accessed in full at www.nap.edu. The current DRI will be updated, with inclusion of additional substances like phytochemicals, as future research data merits.

The DRI have been developed for several purposes, one of the most important being the assessment of dietary intake and planning diets for individuals and groups. In this context, the DRI for specific nutrients will be provided in the appropriate chapter. However, another term, Daily Value (DV), is used with food labels and may be useful in helping you plan your dietary intake. The DV is discussed later in this chapter.

These new standards are designed to ensure adequate nutrition for most individuals in the population. They may also be used to plan diets for individuals with special needs. If individuals in a population consume foods in amounts adequate to meet these standards, there will be very little likelihood of nutritional inadequacy or impairment of health. An individual does not necessarily have a deficient diet if the recommendation for a given nutrient is not received daily. The daily recommendation for any nutrient should average over a five- to eight-day period, so that one may be deficient in iron consumption one day but compensate for this one-day deficiency during the remainder of the week. Thus, comparison of our nutrient intake to these standards over a sufficient period may be useful in estimating our risk for deficiency. However, one should realize that only a clinical and biochemical evaluation can reveal an individual's nutritional status in regard to any specific nutrient.

Although the RDA are useful because they state approximately how much of all the essential nutrients we need, they are not designed to inform us as to which specific foods we may need to consume to obtain these nutrients. Other dietary guidelines have been developed to help us select foods that will provide us with the RDA for all essential nutrients.

Key Concept Recap

▶ Balance, variety, and moderation are the three keys to a healthful diet.
▶ The principal purposes of the nutrients in the food we eat are to provide energy, build and repair body tissues, and regulate metabolic processes in the body.
▶ More than forty specific nutrients are essential to life processes. They may be obtained in the diet through consumption of the six major nutrient classes: carbohydrates, fats, proteins, vitamins, minerals, and water.
▶ The Dietary Reference Intakes (DRIs) provide us with a set of standards for our nutritional needs and are being developed with the goal of promoting optimal health.

Check for Yourself

Using the tables on the inside of the front and back covers of the text, list the DRI for yourself, including the RDA, AI, and UL.

The Balanced Diet and Nutrient Density

One of the major concepts advanced by nutritionists over the years to teach proper nutrition is that of the balanced diet, stressing variety and moderation. In order to obtain the nutrients that we need, guides to food selection have been developed, establishing various food groups with key nutrients, and in more recent years focusing on the concept of nutrient density.

What is a balanced diet?

As noted previously, the human body needs more than forty different nutrients to function properly. The concept of the balanced diet is that by eating a wide variety of foods in moderation you will obtain all the nutrients you need to support growth and development of all tissues, regulate metabolic processes, and provide adequate energy for proper weight control (see figure 2.2). You should obtain the RDA or AI for all essential nutrients and adequate food energy to achieve a healthy body weight.

Although everyone's diet requires the essential nutrients and adequate energy, the proportions differ at different stages of the life cycle. The infant has needs differing from his grandfather, and the pregnant or lactating woman has needs differing from her adolescent daughter. There also are differences between the needs of males and females, particularly in regard to the iron content of the diet. Moreover, individual variations in lifestyle may impose different nutrient requirements. A long-distance runner in training for a marathon has some distinct nutritional needs compared to a sedentary colleague. The individual trying to lose weight needs to balance Calorie losses with nutrient adequacy. The diabetic individual needs strict nutritional counseling for a balanced diet. Thus, there are a number of different conditions that may influence nutrient needs and the concept of a balanced diet.

The food supply in the United States is extremely varied, and most individuals who consume a wide variety of foods do receive an adequate supply of nutrients. However, there appears to be some concern that many Americans are not receiving optimal nutrition because they consume excessive amounts of highly processed foods. This may be true, as improper food processing may lead to depletion of key nutrients and the addition of high-Calorie and low-nutrient ingredients, such as fat and sugar. Over half of the Calories that the average American eats are derived from fat and sugar.

An unbalanced diet is due not to the unavailability of proper foods but rather to our choice of foods. To improve our nutritional habits we need to learn to select our foods more wisely.

What foods should I eat to obtain the nutrients I need?

Although the RDA, AI, and AMDR provide us with information relative to the nutrients we need, they don't guide us in appropriate food selection. Thus, over the years a number of different educational approaches have been used to convey the concept of a balanced diet to help individuals select foods that will provide sufficient amounts of all essential nutrients. In essence, foods with similar nutrient content were grouped into categories.

In the past, foods were grouped into the Basic Seven or the Basic Four Food Groups, but today there is some consensus that six general categories of foods may be used to represent the grouping of various nutrients. Although different terminology may be used with various food guides, the six categories are: (1) milk, yogurt, and cheese; (2) meat, poultry, fish, eggs, dry beans, and nuts; (3) bread, cereal, rice, and pasta; (4) vegetables; (5) fruits; and (6) fats, oils, and sweets. Table 2.3 lists some of the major nutrients found in each of these six food categories.

One concept of balance focuses on the macronutrients, from which we derive our food energy. Although a RDA for protein had previously been established, the National Academy of Sciences recently released DRI for carbohydrate, fat, and protein as a guide to provide adequate energy but also to help minimize the risk of chronic disease. For adults, the AMDR should be composed of approximately 45–65 percent of carbohydrate, 20–35 percent of fat, and 10–35 percent of protein. Similar percentages are recommended for children, except younger children need a slightly higher percentage of fat. Carbohydrates are found primarily in the bread, cereal, rice, pasta category, the vegetable category, and the fruit category, but also in beans and sweets in other categories. Protein and fats are both found primarily in the milk, yogurt, cheese category, and the meat, poultry, fish, dry beans, eggs, nuts category, while solid fats and added sugars are major components of the fats, oils, sweets category.

Two contemporary food guides using a six-level classification system are the MyPyramid and the Food Exchange System.

What is the MyPyramid Food Guide?

The most recent food guide designed to provide sound nutritional advice for daily food selection is the **MyPyramid,** developed by the United States Department of Agriculture (USDA). MyPyramid represents the 2005 Dietary Guidelines for Americans, and the full document is available at www.healthierus.gov/dietaryguidelines. Health Canada has developed a similar Food Guide to Healthy Eating, as have many other countries.

MyPyramid, *Steps to a Healthier You*, designed to stress variety, proportionality, and moderation in your diet and the value of physical activity, is presented in figure 2.3. The figure also stresses personalization and gradual improvement in both diet and physical activity.

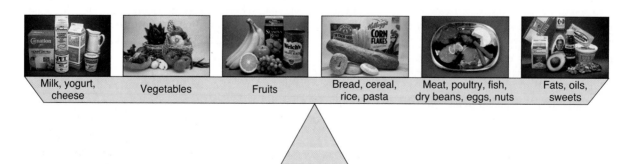

| Milk, yogurt, cheese | Vegetables | Fruits | Bread, cereal, rice, pasta | Meat, poultry, fish, dry beans, eggs, nuts | Fats, oils, sweets |

FIGURE 2.2 The key to sound nutrition is a balanced diet that is high in nutrients and low in Calories. For balance, select a wide variety of foods from among and within the food groups in the MyPyramid food guide or the Exchange Lists (appendix E).

TABLE 2.3 Major nutrients found in the six food categories of the MyPyramid food guide

Milk, Yogurt, Cheese	Meat, Poultry, Fish, Dry beans, Eggs, Nuts	Bread, Cereal, Rice, Pasta	Vegetables	Fruits	Fats, Oils, Sweets*
Calcium	Protein	B Vitamins	Vitamin A (carotene)	Vitamin A (carotene)	Vitamin A
Protein	B Vitamins	Iron	Vitamin C	Vitamin C	Vitamin D
Riboflavin	Iron	Fiber	Iron	Fiber	Vitamin E
Vitamins A, D	Zinc		Fiber		

*Mainly contains Calories. Fat-soluble vitamins found in some foods.

Variety is symbolized by the six color bands, representing the five food groups (orange, green, red, blue, purple) and oils (yellow), illustrating that foods from all groups are needed daily for good health. Although there are six food groups represented in MyPyramid, the USDA does not regard oils as an actual food group; thus, officially there are only five food groups in MyPyramid.

Proportionality, or balance, is shown by the different widths of the food group bands. The widths at the base serve as a general guide to how much food a person should choose from each group.

Moderation is represented by the narrowing of each food group from bottom to top. Each color band is wider at the base and narrows as it reaches the top of the pyramid. Although implied but not depicted in the pyramid, the wide base for each food group represents those foods which should be consumed more often, while the narrow segment represents those foods which should be eaten less often. For example, in the grain group, whole wheat, high fiber foods are represented at the base while highly refined grains, those with added sugar and fat, are represented at the top of the pyramid.

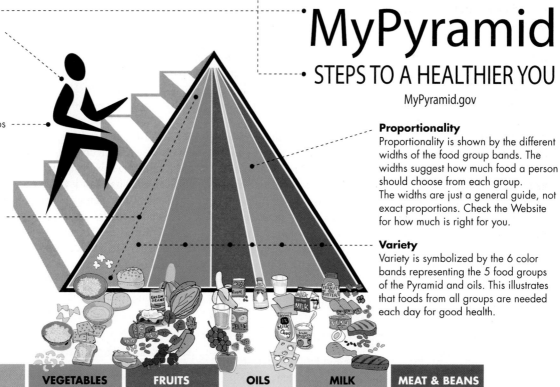

Gradual Improvement
Gradual improvement is encouraged by the slogan. It suggests that individuals can benefit from taking small steps to improve their diet and lifestyle each day.

Personalization
Personalization is shown by the person on the steps, the slogan, and the Website. Find the kinds and amounts of food to eat each day at MyPyramid.gov.

Activity
Activity is represented by the steps and the person climbing them, as a reminder of the importance of daily physical activity.

Moderation
Moderation is represented by the narrowing of each food group from bottom to top. The wider base stands for foods with little or no solid fats or added sugars. These should be selected more often. The narrower top area stands for foods containing more added sugars and solid fats. The more active you are, the more of these foods can fit into your diet.

MyPyramid
STEPS TO A HEALTHIER YOU
MyPyramid.gov

Proportionality
Proportionality is shown by the different widths of the food group bands. The widths suggest how much food a person should choose from each group. The widths are just a general guide, not exact proportions. Check the Website for how much is right for you.

Variety
Variety is symbolized by the 6 color bands representing the 5 food groups of the Pyramid and oils. This illustrates that foods from all groups are needed each day for good health.

GRAINS   VEGETABLES   FRUITS   OILS   MILK   MEAT & BEANS

FIGURE 2.3   The new food guide for *Dietary Guidelines for Americans* is MyPyramid. The guide contains five food groups, plus oils, and emphasizes the concepts of variety, proportionality, and moderation. Physical activity is incorporated in the design for the first time. Overall, personalization is the key to MyPyramid, and it may be assessed at www.MyPyramid.gov. See text for discussion.

Source: U.S. Department of Agriculture/U.S. Department of Health and Human Services.

Activity is represented by the steps and the person climbing them, as a reminder of the importance of daily physical activity.

Gradual improvement is encouraged by the slogan, *Steps to a Healthier You*. It suggests that individuals can benefit from taking small steps to improve their diet and lifestyle each day.

Personalization is shown by the person on the steps, the slogan, and the URL *MyPyramid*.

MyPyramid is designed to be simple, yet motivational, with the intent to help individuals make healthier lifestyle choices relative to diet and exercise. Serving sizes for each food group are presented in table 2.4, while key points for healthful eating and physical activity are presented in figure 2.4. One of the key points of MyPyramid is to make changes in your diet and physical activity levels gradually, or in small steps one at a time. A list of 120 small steps to improve your diet and physical activity is presented in appendix H.

The beauty of the new MyPyramid, as the name implies, is its design to individualize dietary recommendations. When you go to the Website, www.MyPyramid.gov, you are asked to input your age, gender, and activity level, which will provide you with one of 12 dietary patterns, ranging from 1,000 to 3,200 Calories, based on your individual nutrition needs. You can develop an individualized food plan of the types and amount of foods to suit your dietary preferences and daily caloric needs. You can print a personalized pyramid to use as a guide for one day or a week, and a worksheet to help you track your process and choose goals for tomorrow and the future. An example of a 7-day meal plan for 2,000 Calories is presented in appendix I.

For a more detailed assessment and analysis of your current eating and physical activity habits, use *MyPyramid Tracker*, whose database contains more than 8,000 foods and 600 physical activities. *MyPyramid Tracker* can be used to analyze your daily food intake and physical activity level, and provide you with comparison to the 2005 Dietary Guidelines recommendations, nutrient intake, and energy balance. An overall *Healthy Eating Index* is in development on the Website. A history function will permit you to track your progress for up to one year.

You may also use the MyPyramid Website to obtain detailed information about each food group and physical activity. For example, for each food group information is provided relative to the foods in that group, an appropriate serving size (accompanied by a food photo gallery to illustrate serving sizes), associated nutrients and health benefits. The Website also contains information on needs for specific populations, such as pregnant women, overweight children and adults, and the elderly. Of particular interest, MyPyramid for Kids presents the first food guide for children age 6-11. Computer games are designed to promote healthy eating and daily exercise as a means of preventing childhood obesity.

What is the Food Exchange System?

A food guide similar to MyPyramid is the **Food Exchange System,** a grouping of foods developed by the American Dietetic Association, American Diabetes Association, and other professional and governmental health organizations. Foods in each of the six exchanges contain similar amounts of Calories, carbohydrate, fat, and protein. As with the MyPyramid food guide, eating a wide vari-

TABLE 2.4 Serving sizes for the MyPyramid food guide

MyPyramid food group	Serving size
Milk	1 cup of milk or yogurt 1 1/2 ounces natural cheese 2 ounces of processed cheese
Meat	1 ounce of cooked lean meat, poultry, or fish 1/4 cup of cooked dry beans 1 egg 1 tablespoon peanut butter
Grains	1 slice of bread 1 ounce of ready-to-eat cereal 1/2 cup of cooked cereal, rice, or pasta
Vegetable	1 cup of raw, leafy vegetables 1/2 cup of other vegetables, cooked or chopped raw 1 cup vegetable juice
Fruit	1 medium apple, banana, or orange 1 cup of chopped, cooked, or canned fruit 1 cup of fruit juice 1/2 cup dried fruit
Oils (Not an official food group)	1 Teaspoon

ety of foods from the various food exchanges will help guarantee that you receive the RDA for essential nutrients. The basic content of the six primary food exchanges is presented in table 2.5. There are several differences between the food groups in MyPyramid and the Food Exchange Lists. First, the milk exchange list has three levels based on fat content. Second, cheese is found in the meat and meat substitutes exchange list. Third, the meat and meat substitutes exchange list has four levels based on fat content. Fourth, the starch exchange list includes starchy vegetables. And fifth, nuts and seeds are found in the fat exchange list. A detailed list of common foods in the various exchanges may be found in appendix E. The Food Exchange System was developed for diabetics and for weight control and because it may be an effective means to judge the caloric content of foods during a weight management program, it will be covered in greater detail in chapter 11.

What is the key-nutrient concept for obtaining a balanced diet?

As already noted, humans require many diverse nutrients, including twenty amino acids, thirteen vitamins, and more than fifteen minerals. To plan our daily diet to include all of these nutrients would be mind-boggling, so simplified approaches to diet planning have been developed.

GRAINS Make half your grains whole	VEGETABLES Vary your veggies	FRUITS Focus on fruits	MILK Get your calcium-rich foods	MEAT & BEANS Go lean with protein
Eat at least 3 oz. of whole-grain cereals, breads, crackers, rice, or pasta every day 1 oz. is about 1 slice of bread, about 1 cup of breakfast cereal, or ½ cup of cooked rice, cereal, or pasta	Eat more dark-green veggies like broccoli, spinach, and other dark leafy greens Eat more orange vegetables like carrots and sweet potatoes Eat more dry beans and peas like pinto beans, kidney beans, and lentils	Eat a variety of fruit Choose fresh, frozen, canned, or dried fruit Go easy on fruit juices	Go low-fat or fat-free when you choose milk, yogurt, and other milk products If you don't or can't consume milk, choose lactose-free products or other calcium sources such as fortified foods and beverages	Choose low-fat or lean meats and poultry Bake it, broil it, or grill it Vary your protein routine — choose more fish, beans, peas, nuts, and seeds

For a 2,000-Calorie diet, you need the amounts below from each food group. To find the amounts that are right for you, go to MyPyramid.gov.

Eat 6 oz. every day	Eat 2½ cups every day	Eat 2 cups every day	Get 3 cups every day; for kids aged 2 to 8, it's 2	Eat 5½ oz. every day

Find your balance between food and physical activity
- Be sure to stay within your daily Calorie needs.
- Be physically active for at least 30 minutes most days of the week.
- About 60 minutes a day of physical activity may be needed to prevent weight gain.
- For sustaining weight loss, at least 60 to 90 minutes a day of physical activity may be required.
- Children and teenagers should be physically active for 60 minutes every day, or most days.

Know the limits on fats, sugars, and salt (sodium)
- Make most of your fat sources from fish, nuts, and vegetable oils.
- Limit solid fats like butter, stick margarine, shortening, and lard, as well as foods that contain these.
- Check the Nutrition Facts label to keep saturated fats, *trans* fats, and sodium low.
- Choose food and beverages low in added sugars. Added sugars contribute Calories with few, if any, nutrients.

Source: United States Department of Agriculture; MyPyramid.gov

FIGURE 2.4 MyPyramid provides guidelines for healthful eating and physical activity.

TABLE 2.5 Carbohydrate, fat, protein, and Calories in the six food exchanges (typical serving sizes)

Food exchange	Carbohydrate	Fat	Protein	Calories
Milk (1 cup)				
Skim/very low fat	12	0–3	8	90
Low fat	12	5	8	120
Whole	12	8	8	150
Meat and meat substitutes (1 ounce)				
Very lean	0	0–1	7	35
Lean	0	3	7	55
Medium fat	0	5	7	75
High fat	0	8	7	100
Starch (1 ounce; 1/2 cup)	15	0–1	3	80
Fruit (1 medium; 1/2 cup)	15	0	0	60
Vegetable (1/2 cup)	5	0	2	25
Fat (1 teaspoon)	0	5	0	45

Carbohydrate, fat, and protein in grams (g)
  1 g carbohydrate = 4 Calories
    1 g fat = 9 Calories
  1 g protein = 4 Calories				

The nutritional composition of foods varies tremendously. If you wish, you may evaluate the nutrient content of your favorite foods on the MyPyramid Website, or for a more detailed evaluation go to the USDA Website, www.nal.usda.gov/fnic/foodcomp. This site analyzes for nearly 120 nutrients and food components. If you examine a food-composition table, you will quickly see that no two foods are exactly alike in nutrient composition. However, certain foods are similar enough in nutrient content to be grouped accordingly. This fact is the basis for approaching nutrition education by way of the MyPyramid food guide and the Food Exchange Lists. In essence, foods are grouped or listed according to approximate caloric content and nutrients in which they are rich.

Eight nutrients are central to human nutrition: protein, thiamin, riboflavin, niacin, vitamins A and C, iron, and calcium (figure 2.5). When found naturally in plant and animal sources, these nutrients are usually accompanied by other essential nutrients. The central theme of the **key-nutrient concept** is simply that if these eight key nutrients are adequate in your diet, you will probably receive an ample supply of *all* nutrients essential to humans. It is important to note that in order for the key-nutrient concept to work, you must obtain the nutrients from a wide variety of minimally processed whole foods. For example, highly processed foods to which some vitamins have been added will not contain all of the trace elements, such as chromium, that were removed during processing.

Table 2.6 presents the eight key nutrients and some significant plant and animal sources. You can see that the food groups and food exchanges can be a useful guide to securing these eight key nutrients. Keep in mind, however, that there is some variation in the proportion of the nutrients, not only between the food groups but also within each food group. For example, the grain food group does contain some protein, but it is not as good a source as the meat or milk group. Within the fruit group, oranges are an excellent source of vitamin C, but peaches are not, although peaches are high in vitamin A. If you select a wide range of foods within each group, the nutrient intake should be balanced over time. Table 2.7 presents a daily diet based upon the food exchanges. An example of a low-Calorie diet plan based upon the food exchanges is presented in chapter 11, together with methods for planning a diet based upon a specific number of Calories.

What is the concept of nutrient density?

As mentioned before, the nutrient content of foods varies considerably, and the differences between food groups are more distinct than the differences between foods in the same group. **Nutrient density** is an important concept relative to the proportions of essential nutrients such as protein, vitamins, and minerals that are found in specific foods. In essence, a food with high nutrient density possesses a significant amount of a specific nutrient or nutrients per serving compared to its caloric content. We refer to these as quality Calories.

Let's look at an extreme example between two different food groups. Consider the nutrient differences between six ounces of baked Yellowfin tuna (meat and meat substitute exchange) and six strips of fried bacon (fat exchange), each containing about 220 Calories. The tuna fish would provide a young adult female with 100 percent of her requirement for two key nutrients (protein and niacin) along with substantial amounts of several other vitamins, and minerals, but very little fat. The bacon would contain less than 25 percent of the protein requirement and about 10 percent of the niacin requirement, with greater amounts of total and saturated fat. Hence, the tuna fish has greater nutrient density and considerably greater nutritional value. Another example is presented in figure 2.6, which compares the nutrient density of milk and sweetened cola.

Let's also look at a comparison of two foods within the same group, the meat and meat substitute exchange. Consider the following nutritional data for three ounces of tuna fish and three ounces of clams:

	Calories	Protein	Iron
3 oz. tuna:	118	24 g	0.8 mg
3 oz. clams:	126	22 g	24 mg

The protein density is similar in the two foods. However, clams contain more than thirty times the amount of iron per serving. Both foods are excellent sources of protein for the amount of Calories consumed, and although tuna fish is also a good source of iron, clams are a much superior source. This illustrates the need to consume a wide variety of foods within each food group to satisfy your nutrient needs.

Will use of MyPyramid Food Guide or the Food Exchange System guarantee me optimal nutrition?

If you use the key-nutrient and nutrient density concepts, MyPyramid or the Food Exchange System may be an effective means to obtain optimal nutrition and help sustain a healthful body weight. However, although the MyPyramid food guide and the Food Exchange System represent a significant improvement over previous food guides to

Protein
Vitamin A
Thiamin
Riboflavin
Niacin
Vitamin C
Iron
Calcium

FIGURE 2.5 The key-nutrient concept. Obtaining the RDA or AI for these eight key nutrients from a balanced diet of wholesome, natural foods among the six food exchanges will most likely support your daily needs for all other essential nutrients.

TABLE 2.6 Eight key nutrients and significant food sources from plants and animals

Nutrient	RDA or AI		Plant source	Animal source	Food group/ food exchange
	M	F			
Protein	58 g	46 g	Dried beans and peas, nuts	Meat, poultry, fish, cheese, milk	Meat, milk
Vitamin A	0.9 mg	0.7 mg	Dark-green leafy vegetables, orange-yellow vegetables, margarine	Butter, fortified milk, liver	Vegetable, fat, meat
Vitamin C	90 mg	75 mg	Citrus fruits, broccoli, potatoes, strawberries, tomatoes, cabbage, dark-green leafy vegetables	Liver	Fruit, vegetable
Thiamin (vitamin B$_1$)	1.2 mg	1.1 mg	Breads, cereals, pasta, nuts	Pork, ham	Grain (starch), meat
Riboflavin (vitamin B$_2$)	1.3 mg	1.1 mg	Breads, cereals, pasta	Milk, cheese, liver	Grain (starch), milk
Niacin	16 mg	14 mg	Breads, cereals, pasta, nuts	Meat, fish, poultry	Grain (starch), meat
Iron	8 mg	18 mg	Dried peas and beans, spinach, asparagus, dried fruits	Meat, liver	Meat, grain (starch)
Calcium	1000 mg	1000 mg	Turnip greens, okra, broccoli, spinach, kale	Milk, cheese, sardines, salmon	Milk, meat (fish) vegetable

Recommended Dietary Allowance (RDA) or Adequate Intake (AI) for males (M) and females (F) age 19–50. See inside of text cover for other age groups.

TABLE 2.7 Example of a daily menu based on the food exchanges

Exchange	Food selections	Exchange	Food selections
Breakfast		*Dinner*	
Meat	Canadian bacon	Meat substitute	Baked beans
Starch	English muffin	Starch	Rice or pasta
Milk	Skim milk		Bagel
Fruit	Orange juice	Milk	Yogurt
Fat	Low-fat margarine	Fruit	Sliced peaches (in yogurt)
		Vegetable	Mixed salad
Lunch		Fat	Low-fat salad dressing
Meat	Tuna fish (water pack)	*Snacks*	
Starch	Whole wheat bread		
Milk	Skim milk	Fruit	Banana
Fruit	Apple		
Vegetable	Lettuce and tomato		
Fat	Low-fat mayonnaise		

Note: This table presents some common examples of foods within each of the six food exchanges. As discussed in the text, however, you should select food wisely among exchanges and within each exchange. For example, to avoid excessive amounts of Calories, cholesterol, and saturated fats, you should select skim milk, lean meats such as skinless turkey and chicken, water-packed tuna fish, low-fat yogurt, and low-fat, soft tub margarine.

FIGURE 2.6 Comparison of the nutrient density of a sugared soft drink with that of nonfat milk. Both contribute fluid to the diet. However, choosing a glass of nonfat milk makes a significantly greater contribution to nutrient intake in comparison with a sugared soft drink. An easy way to determine nutrient density is to see how many of the nutrient bars in the graph are longer than the Energy (Calories) bar. The soft drink has no longer nutrient bars. Nonfat milk has longer nutrient bars for protein, vitamin A, thiamin, riboflavin, and calcium. Including many nutrient-dense foods in your diet aids in meeting nutrient needs.

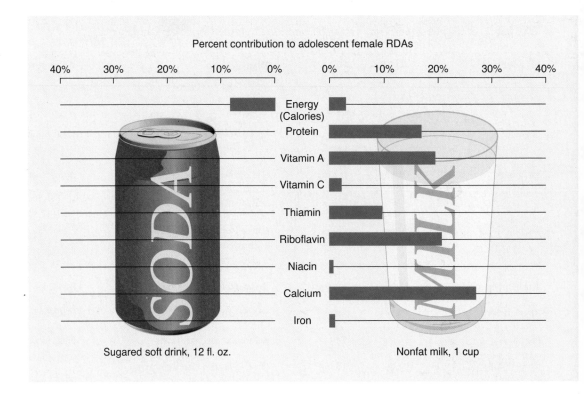

Percent contribution to adolescent female RDAs

Sugared soft drink, 12 fl. oz.

Nonfat milk, 1 cup

help ensure proper nutrition, both have some flaws if foods are not selected carefully. For example, the Food Exchange System does provide some classification for high-fat and low-fat foods in the milk and meat exchanges, but individuals who predominantly choose the high-fat and high-sugar foods from among the food lists may be more susceptible to the development of chronic health problems.

The new MyPyramid has been criticized by various health professionals for various reasons. One of the main criticisms is MyPyramid by itself lacks clarity because it does not indicate what specific foods may be more healthful and which foods may be less healthful. Another criticism indicates the basic diet plan does not use height and weight to help determine caloric requirement. Still another is that you need to be computer literate and have access to a computer with an Internet connection to access the Website. These, as well as others, may be legitimate criticisms, but are not insurmountable. Although the MyPryamid figure by itself does not indicate which foods are healthful or unhealthful, the accompanying guidelines do. For example, the seven key guidelines presented in figure 2.4 provide individuals with suggestions for selecting healthier foods and limiting less healthful foods. More detailed information concerning healthful food selection is presented on the Website. Although the basic diet plan does not use your height and weight to calculate caloric needs, the MyPyramid Tracker program does. Those without Internet access may find assistance available in local libraries.

Prior to the development of the MyPyramid food guidelines, the previous Food Guide Pyramid received

considerable criticism, so much so that other more healthful models were proposed, such as the Mediteranean Food Guide Pyramid, the California Cuisine Food Pyramid, the Harvard Pyramid, and the Vegetarian Food Guide Pyramid. Basically, all proposed healthy modifications to the former Food Guide Pyramid attempt to reduce the consumption of or modify the type of fat, to increase the consumption of whole-grain products, and to increase the consumption of plant products, particularly beans and other legumes, fruits, and vegetables.

The American Dietetic Association developed a position stand focusing on the message that healthful eating should emphasize the total diet, or overall pattern of food eaten, rather than any one food or meal, and that if consumed in moderation all foods can fit into a healthful diet. In concert with this ADA viewpoint, and reflecting healthful recommendations in MyPyramid, the major guidelines for healthier food choices are presented in the following section.

Key Concept Recap

▶ If most healthy individuals in a given population consume wholesome, natural foods in amounts adequate to meet their RDA, there will be very little likelihood of nutritional inadequacy or impairment of health.

▶ The MyPyramid food guide and the related Food Exchange System—meat, milk, starch, fruit, vegetable, and fat—should be viewed as an educational approach to help individuals obtain proper nutrition. Foods of similar nutrient value are found in each of the six exchanges.

Healthful Dietary Guidelines

In the past most morbidity and mortality in industrialized nations were caused by nutrient-deficiency diseases and infectious diseases, but advances in nutritional and medical science have almost eliminated most of the adverse health consequences associated with these diseases. Today, most morbidity and mortality are associated with various chronic diseases (e.g., coronary heart disease, stroke, cancer, diabetes, osteoporosis, obesity), and most dietary guidelines for healthful nutrition are targeted to prevent these chronic diseases.

Nutrition scientists are using both epidemiological and experimental research in attempts to determine what types of diet, specific foods, and specific nutrients or food constituents may either cause or prevent the development of chronic diseases. Such research, coupled with the application of nutrigenomics, may provide each of us with individualized diets for optimal health.

What is the basis underlying the development of healthful dietary guidelines?

In general, healthful dietary guidelines are based on appropriate research. Over the years, epidemiologists have attempted to determine the relationship between diet and the development of chronic diseases. In early research, the focus was simply on the overall diet and its relationship to disease, such as comparing the typical American diet to the Mediterranean (Greece, Italy, Spain) or Japanese diet. If a significant relationship was found between the diets of two nations, say more heart disease among Americans compared to those consuming the Mediterranean diet, scientists then attempted to determine what specific foods, particularly which macronutrients (carbohydrate, fat, and protein) in those foods, may have been related to either an increased or decreased risk for heart disease. In more recent years, scientists have been investigating the roles of specific nutrients or food constituents, especially certain vitamins and nonessential nutrients, and their potential to prevent or deter chronic diseases. Although most of the research relating diet to disease is epidemiological in nature, a number of experimental studies have been conducted and are underway to evaluate the effect of specific nutrient interventions, particularly studies involving the use of various vitamins and nonessential nutrients such as phytochemicals. In summary, Schneeman and Mendelson noted that the relationship between food, nutrition, and health should be evidence-based, involving data from all types of studies ranging from large randomized trials to *in vitro* laboratory research.

Based on the evaluation of current research findings, nutritional scientists believe that the development of most chronic diseases may be associated with either deficiencies or excesses of various nutrients or food constituents in the diet. As mentioned previously, most Americans eat more food than they need and eat less of the food they need more.

In general, many Americans eat too many Calories, consume too much fat, saturated fat, cholesterol, refined sugars, and salt and sodium, and drink too much alcohol. Such dietary practices may predispose one to several chronic diseases, including obesity, heart disease, hypertension, and cancer.

Conversely, possibly because they rely more on highly processed foods, many Americans do not consume a diet rich in whole grain products, legumes, fruits, and vegetables, foods that are rich in dietary fiber and other healthful nutrients such as antioxidant vitamins. Some may not obtain adequate amounts of calcium and iron. These dietary practices may lead to such chronic diseases as cancer, osteoporosis, and anemia.

To help prevent chronic diseases, numerous governmental and professional health organizations have developed general dietary guidelines for good health. Some of these guidelines, such as *Dietary Guidelines for Americans (MyPyramid)*, also include recommendations for physical activity and for maintenance of a healthy body weight since both may help prevent major chronic diseases.

Unfortunately, few studies have evaluated the relationship between adherence to *Dietary Guidelines for Americans*, and chronic disease. Specific guidelines have been criticized, possibly because they may not be based on the best science or they may not apply to everyone in the population. Nevertheless, even given these constraints, the scientists involved in the development of healthful dietary guidelines believe that they are prudent recommendations.

What are the recommended dietary guidelines for reducing the risk of chronic disease?

Although there is no absolute proof that dietary changes will enhance the health status of every member of the population, the guidelines presented below appear to be prudent recommendations for most individuals and are based upon the available scientific evidence. These recommendations represent a synthesis of various recent reports from both governmental and professional health organizations, such as the American Heart Association, the American Cancer Society, the American Dietetic Association, and the American Diabetes Association. These recommendations are also in accord with *Dietary Guidelines for Americans,* 2005. The guidelines are not considered to be static, and may be modified somewhat as we gain more knowledge through research. In particular, healthful dietary recommendations may be individualized in the future when the full impact of nutrigenomics is realized.

Taken together, these recommendations may be helpful in preventing most chronic diseases, including cardiovascular diseases and cancer. The rationale as to how these dozen healthful dietary recommendations may promote good health is presented in later chapters where appropriate. These guidelines do, however, come with several caveats.

Remember, diet is only one factor that may influence the development of chronic diseases. Exercise, as discussed in chapter 1, is also important, as are other positive lifestyle behaviors, such as avoiding tobacco use.

Most dietary guidelines have been developed for Americans over age 2, but some organizations, such as the American Heart Association, have developed separate dietary guidelines for children. Children and adolescents need energy to support growth and development, so it is important that adequate Calories be provided if dietary fat is restricted. Several of the guidelines presented below have special implications for children.

Although research may show that some foods, such as fruits and vegetables, may be protective against the development of chronic diseases, it is the total diet that is important. The benefits that may accrue from adhering to only a few healthful eating recommendations may be negated if most dietary guidelines are ignored. You can maximize your health benefits by adopting as many of these healthful dietary guidelines as possible.

1. *Balance the food you eat with physical activity to maintain or achieve a healthy body weight.* Consume only moderate food portions. Be physically active every day. Preventing obesity helps to reduce the risk of numerous chronic diseases, such as heart disease and cancer. To avoid becoming overweight, you should consume only as many Calories as you expend daily. Methods of regulating your body weight are presented in detail in chapter 11. An appropriate exercise program and adherence to the concept of nutrient density, which includes a number of the following recommendations, could serve as the basis for a sound weight-control program.

2. *Eat a nutritionally adequate diet consisting of a wide variety of nutrient-rich foods.* Build a healthy base. Eating a wide variety of natural foods from within (and among) the MyPyramid food groups or the Food Exchange Lists will assure you of obtaining a balanced and adequate intake of all essential nutrients. Stress foods that are nutrient dense, particularly those that are rich in the key nutrients.

   However, keep the concept of variety in perspective. Research has shown that the more food choices we have, the more likely we are to eat more. Our supermarket society, with over 50,000 food products in the typical store, provides us with so many choices that it is very easy to overeat and become overweight. Thus, although consuming a wide variety of foods is a good strategy to get the nutrients we need, we must keep in mind the first point, to maintain or achieve a healthy body weight.

3. *Choose a diet moderate in total fat, but low in saturated and trans fats and cholesterol.* There is no specific requirement for fat in the diet. However, a need exists for essential fatty acids (linoleic and alpha-linolenic fatty acids) and vitamins that are

components of fat. Since almost all foods contain some fat, sufficient amounts of the essential fatty acids and related vitamins are found in the average diet. Even on a vegetarian diet of fruits, vegetables, legumes, and grain products, about 5 to 10 percent of the Calories are derived from fat, thus supplying enough of these essential nutrients. Fat, however, currently comprises almost 35 percent of our Calories; the AMDR is 20–35 percent of Calories from fat. In addition, the amount of saturated fat in the diet should be 10 percent or less, and cholesterol intake should be limited to 300 milligrams or less per day. However, it should be noted that some healthful diet plans recommend lower values, such as 10–20 percent total fat, less than 7 percent saturated fat, and less than 200 milligrams of cholesterol.

The following practical suggestions will help you meet the recommended dietary goal.

a. Eat less meat with a high-fat content. Avoid hot dogs, luncheon meats, sausage, and bacon. Trim off excess fat before cooking. Eat only limited amounts of meat, mostly lean red meat and white meat, such as turkey and chicken, which have less fat. Remove the skin from poultry. Eat more fish. Many fish, such as sardines, salmon, tuna, and mackerel, are rich in omega-3 fatty acids. White fish, such as flounder, is very low in fat Calories. However, as noted in chapter 5, children and some women should avoid fish that may be polluted with mercury. Eat no more than 3–6 ounces of animal meat per day.

b. Eat only several eggs per week. One egg yolk contains about 220–250 milligrams of cholesterol, close to the limit of 300 milligrams per day. Egg whites have no cholesterol and are an excellent source of high-quality protein. You may use commercially prepared egg substitutes, particularly those that are low in fat.

c. Eat fewer dairy products that are high in fat. Switch from whole milk to low-fat or skim milk. Eat other dairy products made from skim or nonfat milk, such as yogurt and cottage cheese. Most cheeses, except low-fat cottage cheese, are high in fat and Calories, but some fat-free cheeses are now available.

d. Eat less butter, which is high in saturated fats, by substituting soft margarine made from liquid oils that are monounsaturated or polyunsaturated, such as corn oil. Avoid hard margarine made from hydrogenated or partially hydrogenated oils that produce *trans* fatty acids, which basically are metabolized like saturated fats. Eat butter and margarine sparingly. Some fat-free and other healthier margarines are also available.

e. Eat fewer commercially prepared baked goods made with eggs and saturated or hydrogenated fats. Many of these foods may also contain significant amounts of *trans* fatty acids.

f. Limit your consumption of fast foods. Although fast-food chains generally serve grade A foods, many of their products are high in fat. The average fast-food sandwich contains approximately 50 percent of its Calories in fat. Appendix F provides a breakdown of the fat Calories and milligrams of cholesterol in products served by popular fast-food restau-

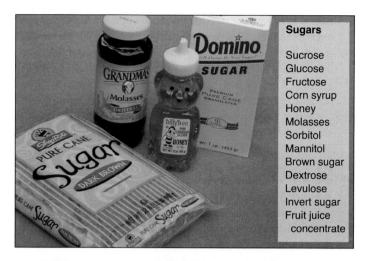

Sugars

Sucrose
Glucose
Fructose
Corn syrup
Honey
Molasses
Sorbitol
Mannitol
Brown sugar
Dextrose
Levulose
Invert sugar
Fruit juice
    concentrate

Fats

Oil
Lard
Palm oil
Coconut oil
Monoglycerides
Diglycerides
Triglycerides
Stearate
Palminate
Vegetable shortening
Hydrogenated oils

FIGURE 2.7 Nutritional labeling as a guide to sugar and fat in processed foods. Refined sugar and fats may appear in processed foods in a variety of forms. Check for these terms on nutrition labels.

rants. Some fast-food restaurants do serve nutrient-dense foods. Wise choices, such as baked fish, grilled skinless chicken, lean meat, baked potatoes, and salads can provide healthy nutrition. But, avoid high-fat sauces. For example, the mayonnaise serving on a Burger King Chicken Whopper adds 160 Calories, or 18 grams of fat, which accounts for 28 percent of the total Calories of the sandwich.

g. Use food labels to help you select foods low in total fat, saturated fat, *trans* fat, and fat Calories, all of which are listed on the food label for most products. In the ingredients list, look for the terms presented in figure 2.7, all of which contain fat.

h. Broil, bake, or microwave your foods. Limit frying. If you must use oil in your cooking or food preparation, try to use monounsaturated oils such as olive, canola, or peanut oil. For other health reasons, as noted later, avoid charring foods when grilling or broiling.

In general, most dietary fat should come from sources of polyunsaturated and monounsaturated fatty acids, such as fish, nuts, seeds, and vegetable oils.

4. *Choose a plant-rich diet with plenty of fruits and vegetables, whole-grain products, and legumes, foods which are rich in complex carbohydrates, phytochemicals, and fiber* (see figure 2.8). In general, about 45–65 percent or more of your daily Calories should come from carbohydrates, about

FIGURE 2.8 Include in your diet foods high in plant starch and fiber. Eat more fruits, vegetables, and whole-grain products.

35–55 percent from complex carbohydrates, and the other 10 percent from simple, naturally occurring carbohydrates. To accomplish this, you need to eat more whole-grain products (breads and cereals), legumes (beans and peas), and fruits and vegetables.

Numerous epidemiological studies have shown that diets rich in plant foods confer significant health benefits, which are attributable mainly to the complex mixture of phytochemicals and dietary fibers. The health benefits of phytochemicals and dietary fiber are discussed, respectively, in the next section on vegetarianism and in chapter 4.

Whole-grain products are rich in dietary fiber and phytochemicals as well as several key nutrients. Select whole wheat bread where you can see the grain, whole-grain cereals such as Cheerios, Wheaties, and Quaker Oatmeal, and whole-grain pasta. Consume three or more ounce equivalents of whole-grain products per day, and check food labels that provide for grams of fiber per serving.

In particular, eat a wide variety of fruits and vegetables, including legumes. The slogan *Eat Your Colors Every Day to Stay Healthy and Fit* refers to the health benefits associated with eating fruits and vegetables of different colors and the associated phytochemicals that appear to protect you against heart disease, strokes, and several forms of cancer. Eat at least five servings of fruits and vegetables daily, but this is a minimum. Grill vegetables and bake fruits to add flavor. Eat larger portions. For example, one-half cup of cooked vegetables is a standard serving size, so a full cup represents two servings.

5. *Choose beverages and foods to moderate your intake of added sugars.* Natural sugars are found in fruits and milk, while added sugars are defined as sugars eaten separately, such as table sugar to sweeten coffee, or used as ingredients in processed or prepared foods. The National Academy of Sciences recently recommended that the maximum amount of added sugars in the diet be 25 percent. However, this recommendation has been challenged by dietitians who indicate that taking in a quarter of your Calories from added sugars does

not appear to represent healthful dietary advice, and trying to reduce intake to 10 percent is a healthier alternative.

Excessive consumption of refined sugar has been associated with high blood triglyceride levels. Sticky sugars are a major contributing factor to dental cavities. Sugars also significantly increase the caloric content of foods without an increase in nutritional value, so they may contribute to body weight problems. Americans eat the equivalent of about 30 teaspoons of added sugar daily, which is the equivalent of about 500 Calories.

To meet this goal you should reduce your intake of common table sugar and products high in refined sugar, such as nondiet soft drinks, the largest source of added sugars in the American diet. Sugar is one of the major additives to processed foods, so check the labels. If sugar is listed first, it is the main ingredient. Also look for terms such as corn syrup, dextrose, fructose, malt sugar, and even fruit juice concentrate which are also primarily refined sugars (figure 2.7). Food labels list the total amount of sugar per serving.

Use naturally occurring sugars to satisfy your sweet tooth. Most fruits have a high sugar content, but also contain vitamins, minerals, and fiber as well.

6. *Choose and prepare foods with less salt and sodium.* Restrict sodium intake to less than 1,500 mg daily, which is the equivalent of 3,750 milligrams, or 3.75 grams, of table salt. This lower amount will provide sufficient sodium for normal physiological functioning.

Sodium is found naturally in a wide variety of foods, so it is not difficult to get an adequate supply. Several key suggestions may help you reduce the sodium content in your diet.

a. Get rid of your salt shaker. One teaspoon of salt is 2,000 mg of sodium; the average well-salted meal contains about 3,000 to 4,000 mg. Put less salt on your food both in your cooking pot and on your table.

b. Reduce the consumption of obviously high-salt foods such as most pretzels and potato chips, pickles, and other such snacks.

c. Check food labels for sodium content. Salt is a major additive in many processed foods, and food labels list the sodium content per serving.

d. Eat more fresh fruits and vegetables, which are very low in sodium. Fruits, both fresh and canned, have less than 8 mg of sodium per serving. Fresh and frozen vegetables may have 35 mg or less, but if canned may contain up to 460 mg.

e. Use fresh herbs, spices that do not contain sodium, or lite salt as seasoning alternatives.

The DASH (Dietary Approaches to Stop Hypertension) diet, discussed in chapter 9, is a low-sodium diet.

7. *If you drink alcoholic beverages, do so in moderation.* The current available scientific evidence does not suggest that light to moderate daily alcohol consumption will cause any health problems to the healthy, nonpregnant adult. A drink is defined as one 12-ounce bottle of beer, one 4-ounce glass of wine, or 1.5 ounces of 80-proof distilled spirits. Current guidelines for moderate alcohol intake recommend no more than two drinks per day for males and one for females. However, even small amounts may pose health problems to some individuals. Certainly, excessive alcohol consumption is one of the most serious health problems in our society today. An expanded discussion is presented in chapter 13.

8. *Maintain protein intake at a moderate, yet adequate level, obtaining much of your daily protein from plant sources complemented with smaller amounts of fish, skinless poultry, and lean meats.* The recommended dietary intake is 0.8 grams of protein per kilogram body weight, which averages out to about 50 to 60 grams per day for the average adult male and somewhat less for the average adult female or about 10 percent of daily Calories. The current recommendation of the National Academy of Sciences is to obtain 10–35 percent of daily Calories from protein. Since the average daily American intake of protein is about 100 grams, we appear to be staying within the guidelines. However, most of the protein Americans eat is of animal origin. Although animal products are an excellent source of complete protein, they tend to be higher in saturated fats and cholesterol compared with foods rich in plant protein. On the other hand, animal protein is usually a better source of dietary iron and other minerals like zinc and copper than plant protein is.

Three to six ounces of lean meat, fish, or poultry, together with two glasses of skim or soy milk, will provide the average individual with the daily RDA for protein, totaling about 40–60 grams of high-quality protein. Combining this animal protein intake with plant foods high in protein, such as whole-grain products, soy-protein meat substitutes, beans and peas, and vegetables, will substantially increase your protein intake and more than meet your needs.

Soy protein products, such as tofu, soy milk, tempeh, and miso, as well as commercial products such as soy sausages and burgers, are excellent meat substitutes. Soy offers a complete protein profile and may also provide some health benefits, as highlighted in chapter 6.

The general recommendation is to eat less meat, and that which is eaten preferably should be fish. White poultry meat, such as turkey breast, and lean red meats such as beef eye of round or pork tenderloin, may also be incorporated into the diet. One healthful recommendation is to use meat as a condiment, such as helping to add flavor to stir-fried vegetable dishes.

In a recent review, Mann noted scientific evidence is accumulating that meat itself is not a risk factor for chronic disease, but rather the risk stems from the excessive fat found in modern-day domesticated animals. Lean meat is a healthy and beneficial component of any well-balanced diet as long as it is fat trimmed and consumed as part of a varied diet. On average, the recommended total meat intake should range between 3 to 6 ounces daily; of that total, men and women should consume, respectively, less than 3 and 2 ounces of red or processed meat.

Why this recommendation? Epidemiological studies report that a diet rich in red and processed or well-done meat is associated with an increased risk of colon cancer, breast cancer, and lung cancer. Possible reasons may be that red and processed meat tends to contain lots of fat (particularly saturated fat), cooking meat at high temperatures can create potentially cancer-causing compounds, and meat of hormone-treated animals may have adverse effects on human health.

9. *Choose a diet adequate in calcium and iron. Individuals susceptible to tooth decay should obtain adequate fluoride.* Adequate calcium and iron are particularly important for women and children. Skim or low-fat milk and other low-fat dairy products are excellent sources of calcium. For example, one glass of skim milk provides nearly one-third the RDA for calcium. Certain vegetables, such as broccoli, are also good sources of calcium. Iron is found in good supply in the meat and starch exchanges. Small amounts of lean or very-lean meats should be selected so as to limit fat intake, and whole-grain or enriched products should be chosen over those made with bleached, unenriched white flour. Some foods rich in calcium and iron are listed in table 2.8.

Adequate flouride is particularly important during childhood when the primary and secondary teeth are developing, for fluoride helps prevent tooth decay by strengthening the tooth enamel. Your water supply may contain sufficient fluoride—naturally or artificially—to provide an adequate amount, but if not, fluoride supplements or use of fluoride toothpaste may be recommended.

10. *Practice food safety, including proper food preservation and preparation.* Food should be stored in ways that minimize contamination with bacteria. Use refrigeration to preserve perishable foods. Food preparation techniques should also minimize possible bacteria contamination. Using careful washing techniques is very helpful.

One specific recommendation, as related to the preceding point discussing meat consumption, is to avoid excess grilling or broiling of foods, particularly meat. Charring meats may lead to the formation of various carcinogens known as heterocyclic amines (HCA). Frying foods may also produce HCA, but steaming, boiling and microwaving meat is much safer because these techniques produce fewer HCA that may cause cancer. If you enjoy the flavor of grilled or broiled foods, marinating meats may dramatically reduce HCA formation. A healthful technique is to precook marinated meat in a microwave, and then grill or broil briefly for flavor, but not to the point of charring.

More detailed information on food safety is presented later in this chapter.

11. *Avoid excess intake of questionable food additives and dietary supplements.*

The general consensus is that most additives used in processed foods are safe, but several health agencies, such as the Center for Science in the Public Interest, recommend caution with additives such as nitrates, which have been linked to the development of cancer in laboratory animals, and other substances such as sulfites and certain food colors, which may cause allergic reactions in some individuals. Eating fresh, natural foods is one of the best approaches to avoiding additives. However, nutrients such as vitamins and minerals are often used as food additives to increase the nutritional quality of a food product.

As noted in chapters 7 through 9, dietary supplements of most vitamins and minerals are not necessary for individuals consuming a balanced diet. If you adhere to the recommendations listed here, you are not likely to need any supplementation at all, for the consumption of nutrient-dense foods should guarantee adequate vitamin and mineral nutrition. If you feel a supplement is needed, the ingredients should not exceed 100 percent of the daily RDA for any vitamin or mineral. Many one-a-day vitamin-mineral supplements do adhere to this standard.

Moreover, many health professionals are recommending dietary supplements for certain segments of the population. For example, in their position statement the American Dietetic Association notes that additional vitamins and minerals from fortified foods and/or supplements can help some people meet their nutritional needs as specified by such standards as the DRI. The Consumers Union, in recommending nutrition to help lessen the adverse health effects of aging, suggested the possibility of vitamin (B_{12}, D) and mineral (calcium) supplementation as one ages past 50. The American Academy of Pediatrics recommends fluoride supplementation for children if the water supply does not contain fluoride, or if the child drinks only bottled water. As shall be noted in chapter 7, some health professionals believe it may be prudent for most individuals to take a daily multivitamin.

Conversely, excess supplementation with some vitamins and minerals, as well as other dietary supplements, may elicit some serious adverse health effects.

The possible health benefits of dietary supplements, as well as possible adverse effects, will be discussed in later chapters where appropriate.

12. *Enjoy your food. Eat what you like, but balance it within your overall healthful diet.*

It is important to note that you can eat whatever you want with the Prudent Healthy Diet. There are no unhealthy foods, only unhealthy diets. The dietary advice to moderate intake of certain foods, such as high-fat meats and ice cream, does

TABLE 2.8	Foods rich in calcium and iron
Mineral	**Food source**
Calcium	All dairy products: milk, cheese, ice milk, yogurt; egg yolk; dried peas and beans; dark-green leafy vegetables such as beet greens, spinach, and broccoli; cauliflower
Iron	Organ meats such as liver; meat, fish, and poultry; shellfish, especially clams and oysters; dried beans and peas; whole-grain products such as breads and cereals; dark-green leafy vegetables such as spinach and broccoli; dried fruits such as figs, raisins, apricots, and dates

not mean that they have to be eliminated from the diet, but that their intake be limited and balanced with other nutrient-dense foods in the total diet. Portion control is an important concept to limit caloric intake. It is balance, variety, and moderation in the overall diet that is important, not any single food.

In this context, it is important to note that although healthful eating may confer numerous health benefits, some may take it to extremes whereby it may become counterproductive. In his book, *Health Food Junkies: Overcoming the Obsession with Healthful Eating*, Bratman indicates that taking the quest for a healthful diet to excess can become a disease in its own.

Enjoy eating; it is one of life's pleasures.

The Healthy Prudent Diet   Your health depends on a variety of factors such as heredity and certain aspects of your environment. Adherence to these twelve simple guidelines will not guarantee you good health; however, the available data indicate that these dietary changes have the potential to keep you healthy or even to improve upon your current health status.

The sooner in life one develops healthy eating habits, the better. Research has shown that preadolescent children can modify their lifestyle, eating healthier foods and engaging in exercise. The National Institute of Health has launched a national public education program entitled We Can! Ways to Enhance Children's Activity & Nutrition, which may be accessed at http://wecan. nhlbi.nih.gov.

A Dietary Guidelines Alliance, with representatives from several leading health, government, and food industry organizations has proposed five simple messages to motivate you into positively changing your eating and physical activity routines. They are:

- Be realistic. Make small changes over time in what you eat and the level of activity you do. Small steps work better than giant leaps.
- Be adventurous. Expand your tastes to enjoy a variety of foods.
- Be flexible. Balance what you eat and the physical activity you do over several days. No need to worry about just one meal or one day.
- Be sensible. Enjoy all foods, just don't overdo it.
- Be active. Start moving, even in small steps. Walk the dog, don't just watch the dog walk. (See appendix H.)

Although it may not appear obvious, the general nature of the Prudent Healthy Diet is a shift toward vegetarianism, so it may be important to address the nature of this dietary regimen.

Key Concept Recap

Here are twelve recommendations for healthier nutrition.

1. Maintain or improve a healthy weight.
2. Consume a wide variety of nutrient-rich foods.
3. Choose a diet moderate in total fat and low in saturated and *trans* fats and cholesterol.

4. Choose a diet with plenty of whole-grain products, legumes, fruits, and vegetables.
5. Choose a diet moderate in sugars.
6. Choose a diet with less salt and sodium.
7. Drink alcoholic beverage in moderation, if at all.
8. Eat protein at a moderate, yet adequate level.
9. Choose a diet adequate in calcium, iron, and fluoride.
10. Practice food safety.
11. Avoid questionable food additives and excess dietary supplements.
12. Enjoy your food!

Check for Yourself

Think about your dietary habits and then determine how many of the twelve healthful dietary guidelines you follow.

Vegetarianism

Many individuals have been changing their diets to improve their health. One of the major changes has been a shift toward a vegetarian-type diet.

What types of foods does a vegetarian eat?

There are a variety of ways to be a vegetarian. A strict vegetarian, known also as a **vegan,** eats no animal products at all. Most nutrients are obtained from fruits, vegetables, breads, cereals, legumes, nuts, and seeds. **Ovovegetarians** include eggs in their diet, while **lactovegetarians** include foods in the milk group such as cheese and other dairy products. An **ovolactovegetarian** eats both eggs and milk products. These latter classifications are not strict vegetarians, because eggs and milk products are derived from animals.

Others may call themselves **semivegetarians** because they do not eat red meat such as beef and pork products, although they may eat fish and white poultry meat. Those who eat fish, but not poultry, are known as **pescovegetarians.** In practice, then, vegetarians range on a continuum from those who eat nothing but plant foods to those who eat a typical American diet with the exception of red meat. The concern over obtaining a balanced intake of nutrients depends upon where the vegetarian is on that continuum. The more you restrict your food groups, the more difficult it is to get the nutrients you need.

As a general guide, table 2.9 presents the amounts of food that should help meet daily nutrient requirements for the vegan. The amounts may be increased to provide additional Calories. Foods rich in iron, calcium, zinc, and riboflavin should be included daily. Use of fortified foods or supplements can be helpful in meeting recommendations for individual nutrients. Other classes of vegetarians may obtain nutrients from cow milk, eggs, cheese, yogurt, and in the case of semivegetarians, from fish or poultry.

TABLE 2.9 Daily food guidelines for a vegetarian (vegan) diet

Grains and starchy vegetables

Servings: 4 or more daily

Note: Use whole wheat or other whole grains. Products made of oats, rice, rye, corn, and whole wheat are good sources of protein, B vitamins, and iron, more so if they are fortified products. Fortified cereals may provide adequate vitamin B_{12}.

Food examples:

Barley	Macaroni, enriched
Bran flakes	Oatmeal
Bread, whole wheat	Potatoes
Buckwheat pancakes	Rice, brown
Corn	Rye wafers
Corn muffins	Spaghetti, enriched
Farina, cooked	Sweet potatoes
Fortified cereals	Wheat, shredded

Legumes

Servings: 2 or more daily

Note: Good sources of protein, niacin, iron, and Calories.

Food examples:

Great northern beans	Soybeans
Navy beans	Tofu
Red kidney beans	Split peas
Pinto beans	Chickpeas
Lima beans	Lentils

Nuts and seeds

Servings: 2 or more daily

Note: Good sources of Calories, protein, niacin, and iron. May be excellent snack foods.

Food examples:

Almonds	Pecans
Brazil nuts	Walnuts
Cashew nuts	Sesame seeds
Peanuts	Sunflower seeds
Peanut butter	Pumpkin seeds

Fruits

Servings: 3 or more daily

Note: Fruits are generally good sources of vitamins and minerals. At least one fruit should come from the citrus group and one from the high-iron group. Select fruits of different colors.

Food examples:

Regular	Citrus	High iron
Apples	Oranges	Dried apricots
Bananas	Orange juice	Dried prunes
Grapes	Grapefruit	Dried dates
Peaches	Grapefruit juice	Dried figs
Pears	Lemon juice	Dried peaches
Pineapple		Raisins
		Prune juice

Vegetables

Servings: 2 or more daily

Note: Vegetables are good sources of vitamins and minerals. At least one serving should come from the dark-green or deep-yellow vegetables. Select other color vegetables as well.

Food examples:

Regular	Dark-green or deep-yellow
Artichokes	Beet greens
Asparagus	Broccoli
Beans, green	Carrots
Cabbage	Collard greens
Cauliflower	Lettuce
Cucumbers	Spinach
Eggplant	Squash
Radishes	
Tomatoes	

Milk products (calcium-rich foods)

Servings: 2 or more daily

Note: Good source of protein and calcium, if fortified.

Food examples:

Non-dairy soy milk
Non-dairy rice milk

Sweets and vegetable oils may be added to increase caloric intake.

What are some of the nutritional concerns with a vegetarian diet?

In their position statement, the American Dietetic Association and Dietitians of Canada noted that planned vegetarian diets are healthful, nutritionally adequate, and provide health benefits in the prevention and treatment of certain diseases. However, if foods are not selected carefully, the vegetarian may suffer nutritional deficiencies involving Calories, vitamins, minerals, and protein.

Vegetarian diets, particularly vegan diets, should be well-planned, especially for children. Messina and Mangels noted that vegetarian diets can be, but are not necessarily, adequate for children. The major threats to the diet of children are lack of variety of foods and too much reliance on vegetarian convenience foods, which may not possess the nutritional quality of unprocessed plant foods.

Calories   Caloric deficiency is one of the lesser concerns of a vegetarian diet. However, because plant products are generally low in caloric content, a vegetarian may be on a diet with insufficient Calories for proper body weight maintenance. This may be particularly true for children, who need energy for growth and development, and for the active individual who may be expending over 1,000 Calories per day through exercise. The solution is to eat greater quantities of the foods that constitute the diet, and to include some of the higher-Calorie foods like nuts, beans, corn, green peas, potatoes, sweet potatoes, avocados, orange juice, raisins, dates, figs, whole wheat bread, and pasta products. These foods may be used in main meals and as snacks.

On the other hand, the low caloric content of vegetarian diets may be a desirable attribute for some, as it may be useful in weight-reduction programs or helpful in maintenance of proper body weight. However, Martins and others have voiced concern that some individuals may adopt a vegetarian dietary style in an attempt to mask their dieting behavior from others. Adopting a vegetarian-type diet may be a very useful strategy for weight control, but may be detrimental if associated with an eating disorder.

Vitamins Strict vegetarians may incur a vitamin B_{12} deficiency because this vitamin is not found in plant foods. Vitamin B_{12} is found in many animal products such as meat, eggs, fish, and dairy products, so the addition of these foods to the diet will help prevent a deficiency state. An ovolactovegetarian should have no problem getting the required amounts. A vegan will need a source of B_{12}, such as fortified soy milk, fortified breakfast cereal, or a B_{12} supplement. If not exposed to sunlight, vegans will also need dietary supplements of vitamin D, which is not found in plant foods.

Minerals Mineral deficiencies of iron, calcium, and zinc may occur. During the digestion process, some plant foods form compounds known as phytates and oxalates that can bind these minerals so that they cannot be absorbed into the body. Avoidance of unleavened bread helps reduce this effect, as does thorough cooking of legumes such as beans. In general, research has revealed that a balanced intake of grains, legumes, and vegetables will not significantly impair mineral absorption. Foods rich in iron, calcium, and zinc should also be included in the vegetarian diet. Iron-rich plant foods include nuts, beans, split peas, dates, prune juice, raisins, green leafy vegetables, and many iron-enriched grain products. Special attention should be given to dietary practices that promote absorption of iron and zinc from plant foods. For example, consuming foods rich in vitamin C will increase the absorption of dietary iron from plant sources. Semivegetarians may obtain high-quality iron in fish and poultry. Calcium-rich plant foods include many green vegetables like broccoli, cabbage, mustard greens, and spinach.   Dairy

products added to the diet supply very significant amounts of calcium, as do calcium-fortified soy milk or orange juice. Zinc-rich plant foods include whole wheat bread, peas, corn, and carrots. Egg yolk and seafood also add substantial zinc to the diet.

Iodine deficiency may occur with strict vegetarian diets, particularly when plant foods grown in iodine-depleted soils are ingested. In such cases, use of iodized salt will prevent iodine deficiency.

Protein The major concern of the vegetarian is to obtain adequate amounts of the right type of protein, particularly in the case of young children. Generally speaking, consuming enough Calories to maintain an optimal body weight will provide adequate amounts of protein.

As will be noted in chapter 6, proteins are classified as either complete or incomplete. A protein is complete if it contains all of the essential amino acids that the human body cannot manufacture. Animal products generally contain complete proteins, whereas plant proteins are incomplete. However, certain vegetable products may also provide good sources of protein. Grain products such as wheat, rice, and corn, as well as beans (particularly soybeans), peas, and nuts, have a substantial protein content. However, most vegetable products lack one or more essential amino acids in sufficient quantity. They are incomplete proteins and, eaten individually, are not generally adequate for maintaining proper human nutrition. But, if certain plant foods are eaten together, they may supply all the essential amino acids necessary for human nutrition and may be as good as animal protein (see figure 2.9).

The strict vegetarian must receive nutrients from breads and cereals, nuts and seeds, legumes, fruits, and vegetables. To receive a balanced distribution of the essential amino acids, the vegan must eat plant foods that possess **complementary proteins.** In essence, a vegetable product that is low in a particular amino acid is eaten with a food that is high in that same amino acid. For example, grains and cereals, which are low in lysine, are complemented by legumes, which have adequate amounts of lysine. The low level of methionine in the legumes is offset by its high concentration in the grain products. These types of food combinations are practiced throughout the world. Traditionally, many Hispanic peoples have eaten beans and corn; many Asians, soybeans and rice. Through the proper selection of foods that contain complementary proteins, the vegan can get an adequate intake of the essential amino acids. Because all amino

FIGURE 2.9 It is important for the vegetarian to eat protein foods that complement each other (e.g., nuts and bread, rice and beans) so that all the essential amino acids are obtained in the diet.

TABLE 2.10 Combining foods for protein complementarity

Milk and grains

Pasta with milk or cheese
Rice and milk pudding
Cereal with milk
Macaroni and cheese
Cheese sandwich
Cheese on nachos*

Milk and legumes

Creamed bean soups*
Cheese on refried beans*

Grains and legumes

Rice and bean casserole
Wheat bread and baked beans
Corn tortillas and refried beans*
Pea soup and toast
Peanut-butter sandwich

*Low-fat, low-sodium versions should be selected to minimize excessive saturated fat and sodium intake.

acids need to be present for tissue formation, a deficiency of one or two essential amino acids will limit the proper development of protein structures in the body.

In their position statement regarding vegetarian diets, the American Dietetic Association stated that complementary proteins should be consumed over the course of the day. The ADA noted that since endogenous sources of amino acids are available, it is not necessary that complementation of amino acids occur at the same meal.

Table 2.10 provides some examples of food combinations that achieve protein complementarity. Milk is included because it is a common means of enhancing the quality of plant protein for lactovegetarians, but eggs could also be substituted by ovovegetarians where appropriate. The two most common plant foods that vegans combine to achieve protein complementarity are grains and legumes. Grains such as wheat, corn, rice, and oats are combined with legumes such as soybeans, peanuts, navy beans, kidney beans, lima beans, black-eyed peas, and chickpeas.

Is a vegetarian diet more healthful than a nonvegetarian diet?

Numerous epidemiological studies have suggested that a vegetarian diet, when compared to the typical nonvegetarian Western diet, is associated with reduced risk for numerous chronic diseases and health problems, including obesity, hypertension, blood sugar and lipid control, heart disease, stroke, and some types of cancer. For example, Bazzano and others recently reported that an increased intake of fruits and vegetables was associated with a decreased risk of strokes, cardiovascular disease, and all-cause mortality in nearly 10,000 Americans over a 19-year period. The nature of the vegetarian diet is based on certain nutritional concepts that may reduce health risks, including the following.

Low Fat and Cholesterol The total fat and saturated fat content in a vegetarian diet is usually low because the small amounts of fats found in plant foods are generally polyunsaturated. Plants also do not contain cholesterol; this compound is found only in animal products. These two factors account for the finding that vegetarians generally have lower blood triglycerides and cholesterol than meat eaters, and these lower levels may be important to the prevention of coronary heart disease.

High Fiber Plant foods possess a high content of fiber, which may help reduce levels of serum cholesterol and help in the prevention of heart disease. Diets rich in fiber may also prevent certain disorders in the gastrointestinal tract. Moreover, increased fiber intake may help maintain normal blood glucose levels and a healthy body weight, two factors involved in the prevention of diabetes. More details on the health benefits of fiber are presented in chapter 4.

Low Calorie If the proper foods are selected, the vegetarian diet supplies more than an adequate amount of nutrients and is rather low in caloric content. Plant foods can be high in nutrient density, providing bulk in the diet without the added Calories of fat. Hence, the vegetarian diet can be an effective dietary regimen for losing excess body weight. However, vegetarians who consume dairy products need to select low-fat versions instead of high-fat cheeses and whole milk.

High Vitamin and Phytochemical Content Plant foods are rich in various vitamins, including folic acid. As discussed in chapter 7, diets containing good sources of folic acid may be associated with lower risks of cardiovascular disease.

Plant foods are also rich in antioxidant vitamins, particularly vitamin C and beta-carotene, a precursor to vitamin A. Polyunsaturated plant oils provide substantial amounts of vitamin E. Selenium, an antioxidant mineral, is found in other plant foods.

Other than nutrients, plants also contain numerous **phytochemicals** (plant chemicals), compounds, such as phenols, plant sterols, and terpenes, which have no nutritional value but may still influence various metabolic processes in the body. Collectively, these antioxidant nutrients and phytochemicals are referred to as **nutraceuticals,** parts of food that may provide a medical or health benefit, as suggested in a recent position stand of the American Dietetic Association on phytochemicals. Table 2.11 provides a list of some antioxidant nutrients and phytochemicals and their common plant sources.

Although the exact mechanisms whereby antioxidant nutrients and phytochemicals may help prevent chronic diseases such as cancer or heart disease have not been identified, several hypotheses are being studied. Potential health benefits of antioxidants and

TABLE 2.11 Some antioxidant nutrients and phytochemicals with common food sources

Antioxidant nutrients	Common plant sources
Vitamin C	Citrus fruits
	Potatoes
	Strawberries
Vitamin E	Dark-green leafy vegetables
	Margarine
	Vegetable oils
	Wheat germ
	Whole grains

Phytochemicals	Common plant sources
Allium sulfides	Garlic
	Onions
Anthocyanins	Blueberries
Capsaicin	Hot peppers
Carotenoids	Carrots
Beta-carotene	Dark-green leafy vegetables
Lycopene	Sweet potatoes
Lutein	Tomatoes
Flavonoids	Citrus fruits
Quercetin	Broccoli
Indoles	Cruciferous vegetables
	Broccoli
	Brussels sprouts
	Cabbage
	Cauliflower
	Kale
Isoflavones	Soybeans
Phytoestrogens	Peanuts
Genistein	Soy milk
Isothiocyanates	Cruciferous vegetables
Sulforaphane	Broccoli
	Brussels sprouts
	Cabbage
	Cauliflower
	Kale
Phenolic acids	Carrots
	Citrus fruits
	Tomatoes
	Whole grains
Polyphenols	Grapes
Resveratrol	Green tea
	Wine
Saponins	Beans
	Legumes
Terpenes	Cherries
Limonene	Citrus fruits

phytochemicals may be related to one or more of their possible roles in human metabolism:

- affect enzyme activity
- detoxify carcinogenic compounds
- block cell receptors for natural hormones

- prevent formation of excess oxygen-free radicals
- alter cell membrane structure and integrity
- suppress DNA and protein synthesis

Some of these actions may favorably affect health, as in the following two examples. Antioxidants, such as carotenoids, may block the oxidation of certain forms of serum cholesterol, reducing their potential to cause atherosclerosis and possible heart disease. Also, phytochemicals known as phytoestrogens may compete with natural forms of estrogen in the body for estrogen receptors in various tissues, blocking estrogen's natural proliferative activity and possibly suppressing cancer development.

Considerable epidemiological research has suggested that foods rich in antioxidants and phytochemicals may possess therapeutic value. Conversely, a few studies have suggested that excess of some phytochemicals may be harmful. For example, Skibola and Smith note that excess flavonoid intake may be mutagenic or pro-oxidant, generating free radicals. Experimental research in this area is limited. Studies involving supplementation with soy protein, which contains numerous phytochemicals, have reported beneficial health effects. However, Mares-Perlman and others noted that although certain phytochemicals in foods, such as the carotenoids lutein and zeaxanthin, may protect against the development of several chronic diseases, research is needed to evaluate the effect of their consumption independent of other nutrients in fruits and vegetables. If you wish, you may obtain a list of all the vitamins and other phytochemicals found in your favorite food or plant, like strawberries, at the Website, www.ars-grin.gov/duke/plants.html.

Most nutrition scientists indicate that many of these nutrients and phytochemicals share the same food sources, so the protective health effect associated with a plant-rich diet may not be attributed to a single food constituent, but may be due to the collective effect of multiple nutraceuticals. Thus, health professionals currently recommend that consuming natural plant foods, rather than supplements, is the best way to obtain these purported nutraceuticals.

To help insure that you obtain a wide variety of healthful phytochemicals in your diet, eating foods of many different colors is one proposed strategy. In the recommendation to eat five or more per day (5 a Day-The Color Way), health professionals indicate that people should eat fruits and vegetables of varying colors. Details are provided in several books, including *The Color Code: A Revolutionary Eating Plan for Optimal Health* by Joseph and Nadeau. Fruits and vegetables may contain numerous vitamins and phytochemicals, each of which may have some beneficial health effect. Table 2.12 lists the key colors and some examples of foods found within each color group. In brief, the following highlights one of the main health effects for one food of each color.

Red—Tomatoes and tomato products contain lycopene, which may help prevent prostate cancer.
Blue/purple—Blueberries contain anthocyanins, which may help lower blood pressure and risk of heart disease.
Yellow/orange—Carrots contain carotenoids, which may reduce risk of heart disease.
Green—Broccoli contains sulforaphane, which may help prevent cancer.
White/brown—Onions contain allicin, which may help lower cholesterol and risk of heart disease.

TABLE 2.12 Food colors of various fruits and vegetables

Red	Yellow/Orange	Green	Blue/Purple	White/Brown
Cherries	Apricots	Artichokes	Blackberries	Bananas
Cranberries	Cantaloupe	Avocados	Blueberries	Cauliflower
Raspberries	Corn	Collards	Dried plums	Garlic
Red cabbage	Carrots	Cucumbers	Eggplant	Jicama
Red grapes	Lemons	Green grapes	Plums	Onions
Strawberries	Mangos	Kiwi fruit	Purple cabbage	Pears
Tomatoes	Oranges	Lettuce	Purple grapes	Potatoes
Watermelon	Pineapple	Spinach	Raisins	Turnips

In summary, although a vegetarian diet is more healthful than a typical high-fat diet, it should be emphasized that the nonvegetarian who carefully selects foods from the meat and milk group, including limited amounts of lean red meat, may attain the same health benefits as the vegetarian. The major nutritional difference between a vegetarian and a nonvegetarian diet appears to be the higher content of saturated fats and cholesterol and lower amounts of fruits and vegetables in the latter. Selection of animal products with a low-fat and low-cholesterol content helps avoid one of these problems and also assures consumption of very high-quality proteins. In two recent reviews, Mann and Truswell noted that lean meat may not be as detrimental to health as once assumed, although adverse health effects may be associated with high-fat meats and methods of preparation. The National Research Council, in *Diet and Health: Implications for Reducing Chronic Disease Risk,* did not recommend against eating meat, but advised eating leaner meat in smaller and fewer portions than is customary in the United States.

How can I become a vegetarian?

People become vegetarians for a number of reasons, including weight control, improved health, religion, love for all animals, and taste preferences. Choosing to adopt a vegetarian diet is up to the individual and represents a significant change in dietary habits. Anyone desiring to make an abrupt change to a vegetarian diet should do some serious reading on the matter beforehand. Once you have done some reading on vegetarianism, there may be several ways to gradually phase yourself into a vegetarian diet.

- You may become a part-time vegetarian simply by eating less red meat. For example, you may have several meatless meals each day by skipping the ham or sausage at breakfast and having a big salad for lunch. Eventually, you may move toward having several meatless days per week, possibly incorporating vegetarian "meats" such as meatless chicken, meatless smoked turkey, or tasty veggie burgers in your meals.
- You may become a semivegetarian, substituting white meat such as chicken and turkey breast, with its generally lower fat content, for red meat. You may become a pescovegetarian, eating fish as your main animal food.

- You may wish to become an ovolactovegetarian, eating eggs and dairy products. These excellent sources of complete protein can be blended with many vegetable products or eaten separately.
- You may use the above methods as forerunners to a strict vegan diet, gradually phasing out animal products altogether as you learn to select and prepare vegetable foods to obtain protein complementarity and adequate intake of essential nutrients.

The following simple suggestions may help you incorporate more fruits, vegetables, and whole grains in your diet.

- Keep 100-percent fruit juices available, but limit those which provide few nutrients, such as apple and white grape juice.
- Buy only bread products that list whole wheat as the first ingredient on the food label.
- Keep a variety of raw fruits handy for snacks, such as bananas, grapes, apples, and oranges.
- Keep a bowl of raw vegetables in the refrigerator, such as small carrots, cut-up celery, broccoli, cauliflower, and radishes, along with a tasty dip, for handy snacks.
- Use frozen vegetables for quick stir-fry meals.
- Add vegetables, such as onions, tomatoes, lettuce, spinach, and peppers to your sandwiches.
- Load up on fresh vegetables at the supermarket salad bar, putting meal-sized portions in small containers to take for lunch during the week.
- Add cut-up vegetables to canned beans, soups, or omelets to increase their nutrient value.
- Use your microwave to cook sweet potatoes and baked potatoes, and to steam vegetables with a little water.
- Bake fruits for dessert.

The scope of this book does not permit a discussion of food preparation. A number of excellent cookbooks for vegetarian meals are available at local bookstores, the titles of which may be obtained from a local dietician or local branch of the American Heart Association. These cookbooks provide the vegetarian with a variety of appetizing recipes that not only incorporate complementary proteins with a balance of vitamins and minerals but also make vegetarianism a gastronomical delight. An excellent example is the *Vegetarian Times Complete Cookbook.*

Will a vegetarian diet affect physical performance potential?

As noted previously, a diet that follows vegetarian principles is considered to be more healthful than the typical American diet today. But will such a diet have any significant impact upon physical performance? In a recent review of nutritional considerations for vegetarian athletes, Barr and Rideout noted that well-controlled long-term studies assessing the effects of vegetarian diets on athletes have not been conducted. Nevertheless, based on their review and the reviews of others, the following observations can be made.

- Well-planned, appropriately supplemented vegetarian diets appear to effectively support athletic performance.
- Plant and animal protein sources appear to provide equivalent support to athletic training and performance provided protein intakes are adequate to meet needs for total nitrogen and the essential amino acids.
- Vegetarian athletes (particularly women) are at increase risk for non-anemic iron deficiency, which may limit endurance performance.
- Vegetarian diets may be low in creatine, and thus vegetarian athletes may have lower muscle creatine concentrations than meat-eating athletes. Lower creatine levels may impair very-high intensity exercise. Details are presented in chapter 6.
- Vegetarian diets may be high in healthful carbohydrates and be effective for weight control, which could be to the advantage of some athletes, particularly endurance runners. However, if used improperly as a strategy for weight control, vegetarian diets could lead to eating disorders and impaired performance and health, a topic discussed in chapter 10.

Some world-class athletes have been vegetarians, and on occasion their diets have been cited as a reason for their success. On the other hand, there are a far greater number of world-class athletes who eat a balanced diet including animal products. Both types of diet may supply the nutrients necessary for the physically active individual if foods are selected properly.

However, as noted above, if you want to shift toward a vegetarian diet, you would need to do some careful reading beforehand and then could initiate the process gradually. During the process, you should listen to your body—a common phrase among many athletes today. If you are active, how do you feel during your workouts? Do you have more or less stamina? Are you gaining or losing weight? Is your physical performance getting better or worse? The answers to these questions, together with other body reactions, may offer you some feedback as to whether the dietary change is beneficial.

Remember, there is nothing magical about a vegetarian diet that will increase your physical performance capacity. It can be a healthful way to obtain the nutrients your physically active body needs, but so too is a well-balanced diet containing animal products.

Consumer Nutrition— Food Labels and Health Claims

Guidelines for a healthful diet will not be effective unless people change their behavior to buy and eat healthier foods. A model often used to explain the development of a set of behaviors involves a sequence of (1) acquisition of knowledge, (2) formation of an attitude or set of values, and (3) development of a particular behavior. In this sequence, knowledge is the first step that may enhance the development of proper health behaviors. Knowing how to interpret food labels may guide you in developing a nutritious, safe, and healthful diet.

What nutrition information do food labels provide?

Food manufacturers view labels as a device for persuading you to buy their product instead of a competitor's product. Just walk down the cereal aisle next time you visit the supermarket and notice the bewildering number of choices. As manufactured food products multiplied over the years, and as competition for your food dollar intensified, food companies began to manipulate their labels to enhance sales. Unfortunately, many of these practices were deceptive, and the consumer had a difficult time determining the nutritional quality of many processed foods. Thus, Congress passed a law designed to establish a set of standards to help Americans base their food choices on sound nutritional information.

This set of standards resulted in **nutritional labeling,** whereby major nutrients found in a food product must be listed on the label. It is not the total solution to the problem of poor food selection existing among many Americans, but combined with an educational program to increase nutritional awareness, it may effectively improve the nutritional health of our nation.

Initial food labeling legislation was passed in 1973, but it contained numerous flaws. Because of pressure from a variety of consumer interest groups, a major overhaul of the nutritional labeling program was signed into law as the Nutrition Labeling and Education Act in 1990, and it was in full effect in 1994. Under this law, nutrition labeling is mandatory for almost all foods regulated by the Food and Drug Administration (FDA). However, there are some exceptions. Food produced by very small businesses; food served in restaurants, hospital cafeterias, and airplanes; ready-to-eat food prepared primarily on site; and several other categories are exempt from these regulations. Other modifications may be used for children under the age of 2, and others for children under the age of 4. Additionally, providing nutrition information is currently voluntary for many raw foods such as fresh fruits, vegetables, meat, and fish, but may become mandatory in the future.

The food label illustrated in figure 2.10 is called *Nutrition Facts,* and it is designed to provide information on the nutrients that are of major concern for consumers. Food labels must contain the following information:

List of ingredients
  Ingredients will be listed in descending order by weight.
Serving size
  Serving size has been standardized.
Servings per container
Amount per serving of the following:
  Total Calories
    Calories from fat
  Total fat
    Saturated fat
    Trans fat
  Cholesterol
  Sodium
  Total carbohydrate
    Dietary fiber
    Sugars
  Protein
  Vitamin A
  Vitamin C
  Calcium
  Iron

The following are optional:

Calories from saturated fat	Phosphorus
Polyunsaturated fat	Magnesium
Monounsaturated fat	Zinc
Potassium	Selenium
Soluble fiber	Copper
Insoluble fiber	Manganese
Sugar alcohols	Molybdenum
Other carbohydrates	Iodine
Vitamins D, E, K	Potassium
All B vitamins	Chloride

How can I use this information to select a healthier diet?

The **Daily Value (DV),** which is based on dietary standards discussed earlier in this chapter, represents how much of a specific nutrient you should obtain in your daily diet. DVs have been established for macronutrients and micronutrients that may affect our health. In essence, a food label indicates how much of a given nutrient is present in that product, and for some nutrients, what percentage of the DV is provided by one serving.

The DVs cover the macronutrients that are sources of energy, consisting of carbohydrate (including fiber), fat, and protein, as well as cholesterol, sodium, and potassium, which contain no Calories. The DVs for the energy-producing nutrients are based on the number of Calories consumed daily. On the food label, the percent of the DV that a single serving of a food contains is based on a 2,000 Calorie diet, which has been selected because it is believed to have the greatest public health benefit for the nation. However, the DV may be higher or lower depending on your Calorie needs. Values for some of the macronutrients are also provided for a 2,500 Calorie diet on the food label.

The DVs are based on certain minimum and maximum allowances, including the following for a 2,000 Calorie diet:

Total fat: Maximum of 30 percent of Calories, or less than 65 grams.
Saturated fat: Maximum of 10 percent of Calories, or less than 20 grams.
Carbohydrate: Minimum of 60 percent of Calories, or more than 300 grams.
Protein: Based on 10 percent of Calories. Applicable only to adults and children over age 4; 50 grams for a 2,000 Calorie diet.
Fiber: Based on 12.5 grams of fiber per 1,000 Calories.
Cholesterol: Less than 300 milligrams.
Sodium: Less than 2,400 milligrams.

The DVs for vitamins and minerals, based on previously established RDA, are presented in table 2.13. The list includes those whose listing is mandatory and some selected others. Although the RDA for several nutrients has changed with recent DRI updates, the DV are still based on older interpretations of the RDA. However, the Food and Drug Administration, along with Health Canada, is collaborating with the Institute of Medicine in the process of revamping current food labels, changing the DV for various nutrients and focusing on caloric content. For example, one proposal is to reduce the DV for iron from 18 to 8 milligrams and another is to develop a DV for Calories and to list caloric content on the front of the label.

Some important points to consider in reading a food label are as follows:

1. The DV for a nutrient represents the percentage contribution one serving of the food makes to the daily diet for that nutrient based on current recommendations for healthful diets. A lower DV is desirable for total fat, saturated fat, cholesterol, and

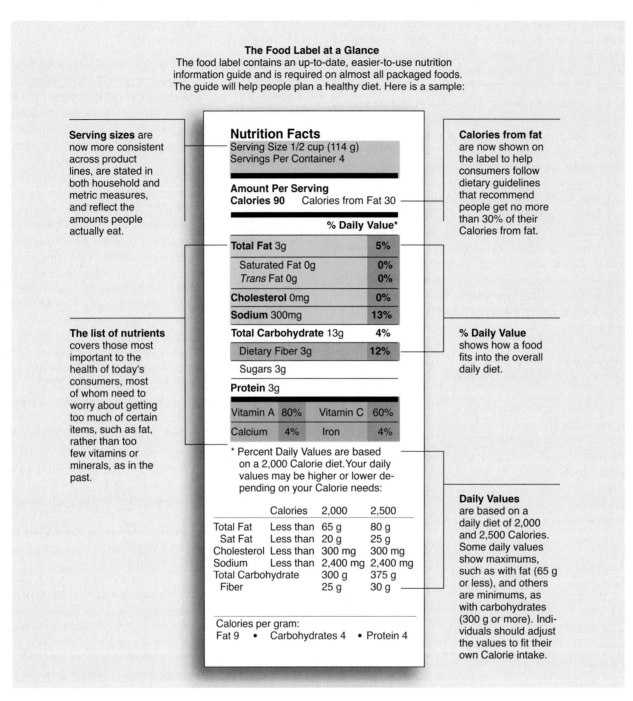

The Food Label at a Glance
The food label contains an up-to-date, easier-to-use nutrition information guide and is required on almost all packaged foods. The guide will help people plan a healthy diet. Here is a sample:

Serving sizes are now more consistent across product lines, are stated in both household and metric measures, and reflect the amounts people actually eat.

The list of nutrients covers those most important to the health of today's consumers, most of whom need to worry about getting too much of certain items, such as fat, rather than too few vitamins or minerals, as in the past.

Calories from fat are now shown on the label to help consumers follow dietary guidelines that recommend people get no more than 30% of their Calories from fat.

% Daily Value shows how a food fits into the overall daily diet.

Daily Values are based on a daily diet of 2,000 and 2,500 Calories. Some daily values show maximums, such as with fat (65 g or less), and others are minimums, as with carbohydrates (300 g or more). Individuals should adjust the values to fit their own Calorie intake.

Nutrition Facts
Serving Size 1/2 cup (114 g)
Servings Per Container 4

Amount Per Serving
Calories 90   Calories from Fat 30

% Daily Value*

Total Fat 3g	**5%**
Saturated Fat 0g	0%
Trans Fat 0g	0%
Cholesterol 0mg	**0%**
Sodium 300mg	**13%**
Total Carbohydrate 13g	**4%**
Dietary Fiber 3g	**12%**
Sugars 3g	
Protein 3g	

Vitamin A	80%	Vitamin C	60%
Calcium	4%	Iron	4%

* Percent Daily Values are based on a 2,000 Calorie diet. Your daily values may be higher or lower depending on your Calorie needs:

		Calories	2,000	2,500
Total Fat	Less than		65 g	80 g
Sat Fat	Less than		20 g	25 g
Cholesterol	Less than		300 mg	300 mg
Sodium	Less than		2,400 mg	2,400 mg
Total Carbohydrate			300 g	375 g
Fiber			25 g	30 g

Calories per gram:
Fat 9 • Carbohydrates 4 • Protein 4

FIGURE 2.10   An example of a Nutrition Fact food label with some explanatory material.

Source: Food and Drug Administration, 1992.

sodium; a DV of 5 percent or less is a good indicator. A higher DV is desirable for total carbohydrates, dietary fiber, iron, calcium, vitamins A and C, and other vitamins and minerals that may be listed, with 10 percent or more representing a good source.

2. To calculate the percentage of fat Calories in one serving, divide the value for Calories from fat by the total Calories and multiply by 100. For example, if one serving contains 70

Calories from fat and the total number of Calories is 120, the food consists of 58 percent fat Calories (70/120 × 100). It should be noted that this percentage is not the same as the DV percentage for fat, which is based on your total daily diet, not an individual serving of the food product.

3. Related to carbohydrates, sugars include both natural and added sugars. Dietary fiber is total dietary. Other carbohydrates represent total carbohydrates minus sugars and dietary fiber.

TABLE 2.13	DVs for protein, dietary fiber, and some vitamins and minerals on food labels

Mandatory listing

Protein	56 grams
Vitamin A	5,000 IU; 1 milligram
Vitamin C	60 milligrams
Calcium	1,000 milligrams
Iron	18 milligrams
Dietary Fiber	25 grams

Optional listing

Thiamin	1.5 milligrams
Riboflavin	1.7 milligrams
Niacin	20 milligrams
Vitamin D	400 IU
Vitamin E	30 IU
Vitamin B_6	2 milligrams
Folic acid	400 micrograms
Vitamin B_{12}	6 micrograms
Zinc	15 milligrams
Copper	2 milligrams
Magnesium	400 milligrams

4. Be aware of serving size tricks. A serving size for a cola drink may be 8 ounces (100 Calories), so a 20-ounce bottle of soda is 2.5 servings (250 Calories). However, most people drink it all at one time, thinking it is only one serving and may consume more than twice the Calories as expected. Recommended changes are to provide nutrition information for a single serving as well as for the entire package; so for a 20-ounce bottle of soda, you will get the nutrition breakdown for 8 ounces as well as for the entire 20 ounces.

Labels also must disclose certain ingredients, such as sulfites, certain food dyes, and milk proteins, so food-sensitive consumers may avoid foods that may cause allergic responses. Others may be added as deemed necessary.

In the past, many terms used on food labels, such as "lean" and "light," had no definite meaning. However, under the new regulations, most terms used have specific definitions. A summary of these terms is presented in table 2.14. Additionally, new milk labels are based on fat content, expressed as percent or grams of fat, as follows: fat-free, skim, or nonfat milk (0 grams); low-fat or light milk (1% or 2.5 grams); reduced fat milk (2% or 5 grams); and whole milk (8 grams).

Several studies have shown that reading food labels carefully helps individuals to limit their fat intake, one of the most significant changes we can make in our diet. Individuals with high blood pressure have also used food labels to reduce their consumption of sodium, a dietary risk factor for some. Take time to learn to read food labels; it's a smart thing to do.

What health claims are allowed on food products?

Food manufacturers want your business. Given the public's growing awareness of the relationship between nutrition and health, many food labels now list various health claims that may entice you to buy that product. However, health claims may be deceptive. For example, terms such as "High Energy" or "All Natural" may be used to convey the impression of a healthful food, but that food may not be healthful. One product marketed as *All Natural Banana Chips* did contain sliced bananas, but they were fried and sweetened, containing 150 Calories per serving with 8 grams of fat, including 7 grams of saturated fat. This is certainly no health food. A comparable serving of natural banana would contain only 60 Calories and no fat.

The FDA permits food manufacturers to make specific health claims on food labels only if the food meets certain minimum standards. These health claims are permitted because the FDA believes there may be significant scientific agreement supporting a relationship between consumption of a specific nutrient and possible prevention of a certain chronic disease. However, there are several requirements, such as not stating the degree of risk reduction, using only terms such as "may" or "might" in reference to reducing health risks, and indicating that other foods may provide similar benefits. Figure 2.11 provides an example. Currently, fourteen health claims are allowed on food labels. Although additional constraints may be required before a food can carry a health claim, the following are the conditions that must be met:

1. Calcium and osteoporosis: A food must contain 20 percent or more of the DV for calcium.
2. Fat and cancer: A food must meet the definition for low fat or fat free.
3. Saturated fat and cholesterol and coronary heart disease: A food must meet the definition for low saturated fat, low cholesterol, and low fat.
4. Fiber containing grain products, fruits and vegetables and cancer: A food must meet the definition for low fat and be, without fortification, a good source of fiber.

FIGURE 2.11 An example of a Nutrition Fact food label with an approved health claim.

Credit: Sabina Dowell

TABLE 2.14 Definitions of terms for food labels

The following terms refer to one serving. A reference food is a standard food containing set proportions of nutrients.

Free (None or trivial amount; if the product is inherently free of the ingredient, it must be noted so on the label.)

Fat free: Less than 0.5 gram per serving
Saturated fat free: Less than 0.5 gram per serving
Cholesterol free: Less than 2 milligrams per serving
Sugar free: Less than 0.5 gram per serving
Sodium free: Less than 5 milligrams per serving
Calorie free: Less than 5 Calories per serving

Low (very little, or low source of)

Fat: No more than 3 grams
Sodium: Fewer than 140 milligrams; very low, 35 milligrams
Calories: Fewer than 40
Saturated fat: No more than 1 gram
Cholesterol: Less than 20 milligrams

High or Good Source

Based on Daily Value (DV), high is 20% or more of the DV; good source is 10–19%. For example, to be high in fiber, a cereal must have 5 grams because the DV is 25 grams

Reduced, Less, or Fewer

At least 25% less of a nutrient per serving compared to the particular nutrient in the reference food

More or Added

Must be 10% or more of the DV for the particular nutrient in the reference food

Light or Lite

If a food normally derives 50% or more of its Calories from fat, it can be labeled light or lite if it is reduced in fat by 50%. If it derives less than 50% of its Calories from fat, the food must be reduced in fat by at least 50% or reduced in Calories by at least one-third.

Light foods must carry the percentage reduction. Light in sodium may be used if the sodium content is reduced by 50%

Lean (meat, fish, and game)

Contains fewer than 10 grams of fat, 4 grams of saturated fat, and 95 milligrams of cholesterol per 100 grams (3.5 ounces)

Extra lean

Contains fewer than 5 grams of fat, 2 grams of saturated fat, and 95 milligrams of cholesterol per 100 grams (3.5 ounces)

Fresh

If the food is unprocessed, it must be in its raw state, having not been frozen or subjected to other forms of processing. Fresh does not apply to processed foods such as fresh milk or fresh bread

Meals and Main Dishes (per 100 grams)

Low Calorie is defined as fewer than 120 Calories. To be called light, the meal must meet the definition for a low-Calorie or a low-fat meal, and it must signify which, e.g., a low-Calorie meal. A low-cholesterol meal must contain less than 20 milligrams of cholesterol and no more than 2 grams of saturated fat

Milk

Fat-free, skim, or nonfat contains 0 grams of fat; lowfat or light milk contains 1% or 2.5 grams of fat; reduced fat milk contains 2% or 5 grams of fat; and, whole milk contains 8 grams of fat.

Source: Data from The Food and Drug Administration, United States Department of Agriculture.

5. Fruits, vegetables, and grain products that contain fiber and risk of coronary heart disease: Fruits and vegetables must meet the definition for low saturated fat, low cholesterol, low fat, and contain, without fortification, at least 0.6 grams of soluble fiber.

6. Sodium and hypertension: A food must meet the description for low sodium.

7. Fruits and vegetables and cancer: Fruits and vegetables must meet the definition for low fat and, without fortification, be a good source of at least one of the following: dietary fiber, vitamin A, or vitamin C.

8. Fiber from psyllium or whole oats and heart disease: A food must be low fat and contain at least 0.75 gram of soluble fiber.

9. Folic acid, or folate, and neural tube defects: A food, including fortified foods, must be a good or high source of folic acid.

10. Sugarless gum and dental caries: The gum needs to meet the definition of sugar free.

11. Soy protein and risk of coronary heart disease: The food must contain at least 6.25 grams of soy protein per serving.

12. Plant sterol and stanol esters and reduced risk of heart disease: The product must be consumed in two servings at different times of the day with other foods.

13. Whole grain and heart disease: Whole-grain foods and other plants must be low in total fat, saturated fat, and cholesterol.

14 Potassium and high blood pressure or stroke: The food must be a good source of potassium, at least 350 milligrams, and be low in sodium.

Although these health claims have been approved by the FDA because there appears to be substantial supportive evidence, the

FDA has recently approved the first of new "qualified health claims" for foods which scientific evidence suggests, but does not prove, may reduce disease risk. For example, a qualified health claim was recently passed indicating that supportive, but not conclusive, research shows that consumption of omega-3 fatty acids may reduce the risk of coronary heart disease. Additionally, other food products are being marketed with similar purposes in mind, but in many cases without substantial scientific support.

What are functional foods?

In 1994, the Dietary Supplement Health and Education Act (DSHEA) permitted dietary supplement manufacturers to make structure and function claims on their products. Basically, a structure and function claim simply means that the food product may affect body physiology in some way, usually in some way beneficial to health or performance. These claims may not be as authoritative as the FDA-approved claims cited above (such as preventing heart disease or cancer), but these claims may use such terminology as "helps to maintain healthy cholesterol levels" or "supports your immune system" that the consumer may interpret as preventing heart disease or cancer. Technically, these health claims must be correct, but they do not need to have as much supportive scientific evidence nor do they have to have approval from the FDA.

Dietary supplements sales have skyrocketed following passage of the DSHEA, and the food industry jumped on the bandwagon. In recent years, numerous food manufacturers, including some giants such as Kellogg, Tropicana, and Procter & Gamble, have marketed products that have been referred to as functional foods.

Functional foods are food products designed to provide health benefits beyond basic nutrition, the benefits being attributed mostly to vitamins, minerals, phytochemicals, and herbals. In an excellent review, Bidlack and Wang note that many natural foods have been modified to make them more healthful. For example, meat animals have been bred for lower fat content and plant fatty acid content has been altered to achieve desired ratios of beneficial fatty acids in the extracted oil. In its position stand, the American Dietetic Association indicated that functional foods, including whole foods and fortified, enriched, or enhanced foods, have a potentially beneficial effect on health when consumed as part of a varied diet on a regular basis.

Fortification with nutrients or nutraceuticals is a current technique to make functional foods. In a sense, functional foods have been around for nearly a century, as salt was fortified with iodine, and milk was fortified with vitamins A and D, to help prevent nutrient deficiencies. More recently, calcium-fortified orange juice and multivitamin/mineral-fortified cereals are breakfast mainstays designed, in part, to help us obtain adequate amounts of specific nutrients. Some of these products may be worthwhile, for they may be in accord with the principles underlying FDA approval of food health claims. For example, calcium-fortified orange juice may be an excellent source of calcium for someone who does not drink milk. Cereals fortified with psyllium may be an excellent source of soluble dietary fiber. On the other hand, many food products may contain nutraceuticals with little scientific support.

Some examples of nutraceutical-fortified foods available include soups with Echinacea or St. John's wort, snack foods with kava kava, cereals with ginkgo biloba or gota cola, margarine with plant sterols, and sodas or energy drinks with ginseng and yohimbe. Almost any food may be fortified with these, and other, nutraceuticals.

In a review of functional foods in *Nutrition Action Health Letter,* Brophy and Schardt noted that each functional food needs to be evaluated independently, with four questions to ask.

Does it work? Quality research is needed to support any health claims, and in many cases, health claims are based on theory and not reputable research. In some cases research is available, but only with certain groups of individuals, not the general population.

How much does it contain? Some food products contain only a fraction of the amount that may be beneficial.

Is it safe? Unfortunately, many herbs or other ingredients used in functional foods need not undergo strict governmental testing for approval. Although most herbs that have been used for years are most likely safe, use of some may be associated with several health problems.

Is it healthy? Although there may be some healthful benefits of added nutrients to some foods, such as calcium-fortified orange juice, creating a calcium-fortified orange drink with sugar and water is much less healthful because the additional nutrients found in orange juice are missing.

These same four questions may be directed to evaluate the benefits of dietary supplements, which are the purportedly active ingredients in functional foods. Relative to any health or sport benefits, the role of specific vitamins and minerals will be discussed in the appropriate chapters. Popular nutraceuticals will also be discussed as relevant.

In the meantime, remember that fruits, vegetables, whole grains, and other plant foods are the optimal functional foods. Their health benefits have been well established.

Key Concept Recap

▶ Information provided through nutritional labeling on most food products may serve as a useful guide in finding foods that have a high nutrient density and are healthful choices.

▶ The Daily Value (DV) for a single serving on a food label represents the percentage of a nutrient, such as saturated fat or carbohydrate, that is recommended for an individual consuming 2,000 Calories daily.

▶ Terms used on food labels, such as fat free, must meet specific standards. In this case, use of fat free indicates that a serving of the food contains less than 0.5 grams of fat.

▶ Health claims may be placed on food labels only if they have been approved by the Food and Drug Administration (FDA) and are supported by adequate scientific data.

Check for Yourself

Go to a supermarket and compare food labels for various products. In particular, compare the caloric content of some fat-free products with their non–fat-free counterparts to see the Calorie reduction, if there is any.

Consumer Nutrition— Food Quality and Safety

We Americans and Canadians have the basic assumption that the food we eat is safe and of high quality. Several federal agencies, such as the FDA's Center for Food Safety and Applied Nutrition (www.fda.gov) effectively regulate food quality and safety, so in general this assumption is correct. However, foods are not necessarily risk free or high quality. Many factors may influence food quality and safety in the development of a food product. For example, from the time a plant seed is created until the final food product hits our kitchen table, the food may have been treated with plant chemicals, loaded with additives, contaminated with bacteria, or prepared improperly, all of which may affect food quality and safety. Food safety is an important consideration in healthful eating, and thus has been included in the *2005 Dietary Guidelines for Americans*. The purpose of this section is to discuss several of the major factors and concerns influencing food quality and safety in developed nations.

Is current food biotechnology effective and safe?

Food biotechnology has been around for thousands of years as farmers used plant breeding techniques to enhance desired traits, such as the ability of plants to produce higher yields or to resist pests and diseases. Today, genetic engineering, which involves the insertion of favorable genes into plants or animals, is a key feature of food biotechnology. Genetically engineered (GE) foods are also known as genetically modified (GM) foods. Ackerman noted that genetic engineering is designed to enhance human nutrition in both developing and developed countries. Genetic engineering may enable the production of greater quantities of foods or prevention of food spoilage to meet the needs of the world's growing population without damaging the environment. Genetic engineering may also enhance food quality by increasing the nutrient content. For example, rice could be designed to contain more beta-carotene, a precursor to vitamin A, and help prevent several million deaths per year that are caused by vitamin A deficiency. Fish, such as salmon, could be engineered to grow much faster and larger, producing a source of high-quality, healthful protein. Although GM plants and animals are designed to enhance food quality, the technique has raised some public concern over the safety of GM foods.

In a recent review, the International Food Information Council (IFIC) discussed some myths and facts about genetic engineering of plants. In the United States, since 1992 the FDA determined that crops produced by biotechnology must meet the same rigorous standards for safety as those created through traditional means. Although nutrition scientists indicate that there is no such thing as "zero risk" for any food, the scientific consensus is that the risks associated with food biotechnology products are basically the same as for other foods. Bioengineered foods are regulated by three federal agencies, the FDA, the USDA, and the Environmental Protection Agency (EPA). The IFIC notes that consumers can be confident that foods produced through genetic engineering meet the government's most stringent safety standards, and the FDA is not aware of any information that bioengineered foods differ from conventional foods in quality, safety, or any other characteristic.

Although most of us are probably unaware of the fact, we have eaten GM products. More than 60 percent of all processed foods in the United States, such as pizza and salad dressing, contain ingredients from GM foods. Are they safe for us to eat? In her review, Ackerman answers this question with the response, "Yes, as far as we know." In its review, the Center for Science in the Public Interest (CSPI) also indicated that GM foods currently on the market are safe.

However, Ackerman notes that although GM foods represent a field of promise, they are also a subject of debate. Critics fear that GM products have been marketed without adequate research. One of the key problems with GM foods may be the development of a protein that may cause an allergic response in some individuals. Another concern is the possible long-term effect on children. Thus, although GM foods are generally regarded as safe for the present, the CSPI also notes that governmental agencies should become increasingly involved to help assure safety in the future. One possible future action may be to mandate labeling of GM foods. Currently, genetically modified (GM) foods need not be identified on food labels in the United States unless the food is significantly different in nutrient content from its conventional counterpart, unless a known food allergen has been introduced, or unless the food is to be exported.

Is current food production safe?

Modern production techniques are designed to increase both the quantity and quality of plant and animal food and yet maintain appropriate safety standards. One potential problem is bacterial contamination, discussed later, and another is the potential health risks of pesticides.

As noted previously, plants contain substances called phytochemicals, which may contribute to various health benefits associated with a diet high in fruits, vegetables, and other wholesome plant foods. Many of these phytochemicals also help the plant survive, primarily by acting as herbicides or pesticides to prevent damage from naturally occurring weeds and insects. Nevertheless, over two thousand insects, weeds, or plant diseases damage nearly one-third of our nation's farm crop each year. To help minimize crop damage from these pests, agriculturalists have developed synthetic herbicides and pesticides to augment plants' natural defenses.

Although synthetic herbicides and pesticides may effectively control weeds and pests harmful to plants, they appear to function differently in the human body than do natural plant phytochemicals. Synthetic chemicals may cause health problems. A number of illnesses, including cancer and nervous system disorders, along with genetic mutations, birth defects, miscarriages, and deaths, have been attributed to prolonged exposure to these chemicals. On the one hand, we need to control those pests destructive to our food supply, but on the other hand, the health of the public should not be harmed by the chemicals being used. This is the dilemma concerning the use of pesticides and similar chemicals.

Most of the serious diseases from pesticide use have been among farm workers who may be exposed to high concentrations on a daily basis or in people who live near sprayed areas. However, direct exposure to even small amounts of household insect spray has been known to alter brain function, causing irritability, insomnia, and reduced concentration. The prudent individual should avoid direct contact with these substances as much as possible, for even thorough washing with soap and water has little effect upon the absorption through the skin of some insect sprays.

Ames and Gold note that 99.99 percent of the pesticides we eat are naturally present in plants, but synthetic pesticides may also be on the food we eat and in the water we drink. The FDA and state government agencies conduct spot surveys to analyze the pesticide content of produce for sale. In a recent report that analyzed data on more than 200 known carcinogens in foods, the National Research Council of the National Academy of Sciences concluded that both synthetic and naturally occurring pesticides are consumed at such low levels that they pose little threat to human health. Moreover, in a review of over 4,500 research studies from around the world, the American Institute for Cancer Research found no convincing evidence that eating foods containing trace amounts of chemicals, such as pesticides and herbicides, and drugs used on farm animals, changes our risk for cancer.

There is increasing concern that children may be exposed to higher levels of pesticides because children are smaller and normally consume greater amounts of fruits and vegetables per unit of body weight. However, available evidence is inconclusive. Weiss and others have noted that in the absence of direct conclusive evidence, some observations have led some investigators to infer that chronic low-dose exposure to certain pesticides may pose a potential hazard to the health and development of infants and children, but others have noted such inferences can be neither supported nor refuted at the present time.

Government agencies are attempting to reduce pesticide residues in the food we eat, and more farmers are turning to pesticide-free farming, producing more organic foods certified to be free of any pesticide residue. Genetically engineered plants may also reduce the need for pesticides. Unfortunately, at the present time there is little understanding of how varying levels of pesticide exposure will affect human health. Based on current knowledge, the following points appear to be sound advice to help reduce, but may not completely eliminate, the pesticide content in the foods we eat.

1. Avoid direct skin contact or breathing exposure to pesticides.
2. Food preparation may reduce pesticide residues. Wash produce thoroughly; some, but not all, pesticides on fruits and vegetables are water soluble. Washing may be particularly helpful to remove pesticide residues from apples, bananas, corn, grapes, lettuce, peaches, and tomatoes. Peeling some fruits and vegetables also helps. Peeling is effective for apples, carrots, cucumbers, grapes, oranges, peaches, and potatoes. Remove outer leaves of produce. Cooking may also help, particularly with broccoli, green beans, potatoes, and tomatoes.
3. Eat less animal fat and seafood from contaminated waters. Pesticides may concentrate in animal fat. In particular, farmed fish such as Atlantic salmon may contain high concentrations of several contaminants.
4. Buy fruits and vegetables locally and in season. Farmers are less likely to use pesticides if the food is to be sold locally.
5. Eat a wide variety of foods. A food that contains pesticides will then contribute only a small amount as part of your overall diet.
6. Buy certified **organic foods.** According to recently released USDA rules with regard to organically grown foods, the use of certain synthetic pesticides and fertilizers in plant production and the use of antibiotics and growth hormones in animal production are prohibited. Other prohibitions include irradiation and genetically modified organisms. Foods that are 95–100 percent organic can carry the USDA organic label (see figure 2.12), while foods marketed with the notation "Made With Organic Ingredients" must contain at least 70 percent organic ingredients, but cannot use the organic label. Such foods may reduce pesticide levels. Baker and others, analyzing data representing over 94,000 food samples, concluded that organically grown foods have fewer and generally lower pesticide residues than conventionally grown foods. However, organic foods were not pesticide free, possibly due to windborne contamination from neighboring farms. They concluded that consumers who wish to minimize their dietary pesticide exposure can do so with confidence by buying organic foods. Additionally, Worthington noted that there appear to be genuine differences in the nutrient content of organic and conventional foods, with higher amounts of vitamin C, iron, and magnesium in organic foods. However, Williams notes that whether or not organic foods are healthier than conventional foods is debatable, and indicates we need higher quality research than that currently available. Moreover, there are numerous organic products in the marketplace, such as peanut butter cookies, potato chips, cream cheese, ice cream, and even soda, which may contain significant amounts of added sugar and fat.

Organic foods are becoming increasingly available. However, most health professionals agree that if you cannot find organic produce, you should not cut back on fruits and vegetables, because the associated health benefits discussed previously far outweigh potential risks from pesticides. Relative to meat, because of possible contamination of beef, chicken and farm-raised fish, the Consumers Union recommends looking for beef and

FIGURE 2.12 The USDA organic label. Foods that are 95 to 100 percent organic can carry the USDA organic label. Foods containing at least 70 percent organic ingredients may use the notation "Made with Organic Ingredients" but cannot use the label.

chicken certified organic; standards for organic fish have not yet been developed, but wild (rather than farm-raised) fish may have lower levels of some contaminants.

Does commercial food processing affect food quality and safety?

Ideally, commercial food processing would make food more healthy, safe, delicious, attractive, and stable. In many cases it does, but certain commercial food-processing practices may be detrimental to our health in several ways. Potential health risks of several food-processing practices, such as the intentional inclusion of food additives and the unintentional inclusion of bacteria, are discussed later in this chapter. The major problem with some forms of commercial food-processing techniques is adding the wrong stuff and taking away the good stuff.

One potential health risk of commercial food processing is the conversion of a healthful food into potentially harmful one. The major feature of the Prudent Healthy Diet is the consumption of wholesome, natural, low-fat foods. But most of us do consume a wide variety of packaged foods, some of which may be highly processed and may be of questionable nutritional value. There has been increasing concern over the years that the nutritional quality of our food has been declining because many of our foods are overprocessed. They contain too much refined sugar, extracted oils, or white flour, all products of a refinement process. Refined sugar is pure carbohydrate with no nutritional value except Calories. The same can be said for extracted oils, which are pure fat. In the bleaching and processing of wheat to white flour, at least twenty-two known essential nutrients are removed, including the B vitamins, vitamin E, calcium, phosphorus, potassium, and magnesium. In addition, many fruits and vegetables are artificially ripened before they have reached maturity and contain smaller quantities of vitamins and minerals than naturally ripened ones do. We also consume many totally synthetic products such as artificial orange juice, nondairy creamers, and imitation ice cream, which do not possess the same nutrient value as their natural counterparts. Concern about the declining nutritional value of our food supply appears to be legitimate. Much of the blame is assigned to the processing of food, rightfully so but not necessarily so.

In the mind of the public, processed foods more and more are thought to be inferior foods as compared with natural sources—for example, frozen peas versus fresh peas. The major purpose of food processing is to prevent waste through deterioration or spoilage. There are a variety of ways to do this, including heat, irradiation, dehydration, refrigeration, freezing, and the use of chemicals. Commercial food processing results in the loss of some nutrients, but preservation techniques in common use today do not cause major nutrient losses in the foods we eat. Commercial food processing may actually cause less nutrient loss than home processing. For example, some frozen foods may have higher concentrations of nutrients than their fresh counterparts because they are usually "flash-frozen" soon after picking. Processed tomatoes may increase the bioavailability of phytochemicals, such as lycopene, by breaking cell walls. In addition, food companies may enrich or fortify certain products before marketing. Examples include the addition of some B vitamins and iron to grain products, vitamins A and D to milk, vitamin A to margarine, and iodine to table salt. In some cases not all of the nutrients that were removed in processing are returned, but in some products a greater amount is returned or added.

Nevertheless, a few nutrients may be susceptible to loss through processing. Finley and others indicated that heat is particularly destructive to nutrients, especially vitamins. However, processing at optimal temperature and time may minimize nutrient loss.

The key point is that commercial processing of food will not necessarily lead to a nutritionally inferior product. Even if commercial food processing does cause a slight decrease in nutritional quality, it helps provide a greater and more varied food supply with adequate amounts of dietary nutrients.

The major problem with food processing is the excessive use of highly refined products like sugar, oils, fats, unenriched white flour, and salt. Additionally, some foods are fortified with vitamins and minerals up to 100 percent of the RDA. Consumption of multiple servings of such products may exceed the UL for several nutrients. Wise food selection can help avoid these problems, though this may be somewhat tricky in today's food marketplace. It requires careful reading of food labels.

Another potential health problem with commercial food processing is the inadvertent inclusion of bacteria. Although bacteria may be added unintentionally during commercial processing, improper food preparation at home also may contribute to the development of health problems, as discussed below.

Does home food processing affect food quality and safety?

Somewhat like commercial food processing, you process food at home. You may wash, cut, blend, freeze, and cook a variety of foods at home in preparation for a meal, and home food processing, like commercial food processing, may lead to loss of some nutrients, particularly several water-soluble vitamins. You can minimize nutrient losses and preserve the healthful quality of foods by following these procedures at home:

- Keep most fruits and vegetables chilled in the refrigerator to prevent enzymatic destruction of nutrients. For similar reasons, keep frozen foods in the freezer until ready for preparation to eat.
- After cutting, wrap most fruits and vegetables tightly to prevent exposure to air, which may accelerate oxidation and spoiling, and store them in the refrigerator.
- Buy milk in cardboard or opaque plastic containers to prevent light from destroying riboflavin, a B vitamin. For similar reasons, keep most grain products stored in opaque containers or dark cupboards.
- Steam or microwave vegetables in very little water to prevent the loss of water-soluble vitamins and some minerals. Microwaving is very effective in preserving the nutrient value of food. Use microwave-safe dishes or glass cookware. Do not use plastic wrap, plastic containers, or Styrofoam because chemicals can leach into the food when heated.

- Avoid cooking with high temperatures and prolonged cooking of foods, particularly in hot water, which may increase nutrient losses such as water-soluble vitamins.
- Avoid excess cooking of foods, which may produce several carcinogens. Recent research indicates prolonged, high-temperature cooking, such as when French fries and other starchy foods are fried or baked at high temperatures (over 250° F), may produce acrylamide, a cancer-causing agent. In particular, avoid grilling or broiling foods, especially meats, over open flames on a daily basis as charring may lead to the formation of heterocyclic amines (HCA), a known carcinogen. Frying foods may also produce HCA, but steaming, boiling, stir frying, poaching, or microwaving meat are probably the healthiest cooking methods.

Using these techniques, nutrient losses incurred with home food processing are minimal, and an adequate nutrient intake will be obtained if you consume a wide variety of foods.

What is food poisoning?

The major health problem associated with home food processing is the presence of foodborne bacteria. Food bacteria are of two types. One type causes food spoilage, which probably won't make you sick, while the other type doesn't spoil food, but can make you sick.

Food poisoning is caused primarily by consuming foods contaminated with certain bacteria, particularly Salmonella, Escherichia, Staphylococcus, Clostridium, Campylobacter, and Listeria. Campylobacter jejuni and Salmonella are the most commonly reported bacterial causes of food poisoning in the United States. With increasing globalization of food distribution, foodborne illness is likely to become a major public health focus worldwide.

Bacteria that cause food poisoning are found mainly in animal foods, but may also be found in produce. The most common sources of food poisoning are

- Raw and undercooked meat and poultry
- Raw or undercooked eggs
- Raw or undercooked shellfish
- Contaminated produce
- Improperly canned foods

The most common symptoms of food poisoning include nausea, vomiting, or diarrhea, which normally clear up in a day or two. However, the Center for Science in the Public Interest indicates that individuals should seek medical help in cases involving headache, stiff neck, and fever occurring together; bloody diarrhea; diarrhea lasting longer than three days; fever that lasts more than 24 hours; or sensations of weakness, numbness, and tingling in the arms and legs. Some cases of food poisoning may lead to lifelong health problems and may be fatal if not treated properly.

Most cases of food poisoning occur at home, and may be associated with inappropriate commercial food processing. Although governmental health agencies attempt to control the spread of bacteria to food through appropriate regulations governing the food industry, the Consumers Union recently noted occasional outbreaks do occur because of food contamination during industrial processing, such as ground meat contamination with Escherichia coli (E. coli). E. coli can lead to kidney failure. Millions of Americans experience a significant foodborne illness each year, with several thousand fatalities.

Food poisoning may be prevented by improving both commercial and home food processing. The Consumers Union notes that government action within recent years has reduced bacterial contamination of the food supply. New processes to eradicate bacteria are being used, such as pulsed electrical fields and ultrasound. One procedure is **irradiation,** a process whereby food products are subjected to powerful gamma rays from ionizing radiation, such as radioactive cobalt-60. Parnes and Lichtenstein indicates that irradiating food can greatly reduce illness from foodborne pathogens and extend food shelf life by delaying ripening, inhibiting spoilage, and minimizing contamination, and may do so without affecting nutritional or taste qualities. Irradiation may also reduce the need for many food preservatives. The FDA has approved irradiation for poultry, beef, pork, and lamb, and irradiated food products must have a label containing a statement that they have been treated and the international symbol of irradiation known as a "radura" which is depicted in figure 2.13. The position of the American Dietetic Association, developed by Wood and Bruhn, is that food irradiation enhances the safety and quality of the food supply and helps protect consumers from foodborne illness.

If you prefer to not purchase irradiated meats, at the minimum the following guidelines should be helpful in preventing the spread of bacteria in food prepared at home. Even if you buy organic or irradiated foods, which may reduce the possibility of bacterial contamination, these guidelines are still recommended.

1. Wash hands thoroughly and often before and during food preparations.
2. Treat all raw meat, poultry, fish, seafood, and eggs as if they were contaminated. When shopping, place meat in separate bags, and store them that way in the refrigerator. Rinsing raw meat is more likely to contaminate the kitchen than decontaminate the food. Handle raw meat in just one part of the kitchen, on a cutting board used only for such food. Prevent juices from getting on other foods.

FIGURE 2.13 The radura, the international symbol of irradiation.

3. Eating raw fruits and vegetables is healthy. However, produce is often coated with wax, which can trap potentially dangerous pesticides. Wash all fruits and vegetables thoroughly with running water, even if you are going to peel them with a knife. The knife can transfer bacteria to the fruit as you recut it.

4. Thoroughly clean with hot soapy water all utensils used in food preparation. Microwaving your sponges and other food preparation utensils for about 30 to 60 seconds may help kill bacteria.

5. Use a clean preparation surface. After preparing poultry or other animal foods, clean the preparation surface thoroughly before using it to prepare other foods. When using the same surface, prepare animal foods last.

6. Do not use canned foods that are extensively dented or bulging.

7. Cook all meat, poultry, seafood, and eggs thoroughly according to directions. Use a meat thermometer inserted deep into the meat, especially with ground meat, because bacteria may get from the surface to the interior. Heat meat to the desired temperature, usually noted on the meat package. Guidelines include heating beef, pork, lamb, and veal to 160° and poultry to 170°–180°. However, do not overcook or char meats, as this process may produce carcinogens.

8. Do not eat raw shellfish.

9. Store heated foods promptly in the refrigerator or freezer. Reheat foods thoroughly.

10. Use leftovers within a few days. When in doubt, throw it out.

Are food additives safe?

Do you ever read the list of ingredients on the labels of highly processed food products? If not, check one out soon. My guess is you will not know what half the ingredients are or why they are there (unless the reason is listed). A recently purchased box of Long Grain & Wild Rice with Herb Seasoning, thought to be totally natural, had the main ingredients of enriched parboiled long grain rice, wild rice, and dehydrated vegetables (onion, parsley, spinach, garlic, celery) as the herb seasoning—along with hydrolyzed vegetable protein, salt, sugar, monosodium glutamate, autolyzed yeast, sodium silicoaluminate, disodium inosinate, disodium guanylate, and sodium sulfite. The rice was delicious, but were all the additives necessary?

The Food and Drug Administration (FDA) classifies a **food additive** as any substance added directly to food. There are more than forty different purposes for the additives in the foods we eat, but the four most common are to add flavor, to enhance color, to improve texture, and to preserve the food. For example, vanilla extract may be added to ice cream to impart a vanilla flavor, vitamin C (ascorbic acid) may be added to fruits and vegetables to prevent discoloration, emulsifiers may be added to help blend oil evenly throughout a product, and sodium propionate may be used to prolong shelf life. Nutrients may also be added to increase the quality of the product, a process called fortification.

To earn FDA approval, additives must be **generally recognized as safe (GRAS).** The FDA determines an acceptable daily intake (ADI) for all food additives. The ADI represents the amount of food additive that an individual may consume daily without any adverse effect, and includes a 100-fold safety factor. Additives may be added only to specific foods for specific purposes, and in general must improve the quality of the food without posing any hazards to humans. Only the minimum amount necessary to achieve the desired purpose may be added.

Although we realize that absolute safety does not exist in anything we do, including eating, we do have a right to expect that the food we purchase is generally safe for consumption. The government and food manufacturers must take utmost care to ensure that food additives do not create any appreciable health risks. On the other hand, we as consumers also have a responsibility to select foods necessary for good nutrition. Food product labeling has helped us in this regard, for we now can tell what ingredients we are eating, although we may not always know why they are there.

In the past, the major concern with most additives was the possibility that they could cause cancer. The Delaney Clause to the Food, Drug, and Cosmetic Act prohibits the addition of any additive to foods if it has been shown to cause cancer in animals or humans at any dose. Saccharin, which has been shown to cause cancer in laboratory animals when given in high doses, was exempted from the Delaney Clause by an act of Congress. More recently, in its position statement on food and water safety, the American Dietetic Association cited a National Research Council report indicating that people should worry less about the risk of cancer from food additives and be more concerned about the carcinogenic effects of excess macronutrients, evidenced by the linkage of obesity to various cancers.

In general, the additives in today's food are regarded safe. Nevertheless, in a recent review of over 70 food additives, the Center for Science in the Public Interest (CSPI) noted that although most were safe, others could pose some health problems. The CSPI recommended that individuals cut back on some additives because, although not toxic, large amounts may be unsafe or unhealthy. Included in this list are corn syrup, partially hydrogenated vegetable oil, and sugar, all products with high caloric content.

Some additives were recommended to be treated with caution, as they may pose a risk and need to be better tested, such as some artificial colorings and aspartame. The CSPI noted that certain people should avoid other additives, such as caffeine and sulfites. Finally, the CSPI recommended everyone should avoid several products because they are unsafe or very poorly tested and not worth the risk, such as the fat-substitute olestra. The health aspects of many of these food additives will be discussed in later chapters where appropriate.

Why do some people experience adverse reactions to some foods?

Although most food we eat is safe and causes no acute health problems, some individuals may experience mild to severe reactions, or possibly death, from eating certain foods. These reactions may be attributed to food intolerance or food allergy.

Food intolerance, the most common problem, is a general term for any adverse reaction to a food or food component that does not involve the immune system. The body cannot properly digest a portion of the food because it lacks the appropriate enzyme, resulting in gastrointestinal distress such as nausea and diarrhea. For example, many African Americans lack lactase, the enzyme needed to digest lactose (milk sugar), and thus suffer from lactose intolerance, a topic that is covered in chapter 4.

Food allergy, also known as food hypersensitivity, involves an adverse immune response to an otherwise harmless food substance. Many foods contain allergens, usually proteins, that may stimulate the immune system to manufacture antibodies (immunoglobulin E, or IgE) specific to that food. When individuals who have inherited a food allergy are first exposed to that food, their immune system produces millions of IgE antibodies. These antibodies reside in some white blood cells and mast cells in the body, particularly in the skin, respiratory tract, and gastrointestinal tract, the parts of the body that come into contact with air and the food we eat. These cells also contain substances, such as histamine, that are released when the antibodies are exposed again to the offending food allergen. Histamine and other chemicals cause the allergic reaction, which may involve the skin (swelling, hives, itchy skin and eyes), gastrointestinal tract (nausea, vomiting, abdominal cramps, diarrhea), or respiratory tract (runny nose, sneezing, coughing). In severe cases, an allergic response may involve anaphylactic shock and death. Food allergies affect approximately 2–3 percent of the population in the United States, or more than 6 million individuals.

Over 700 food allergens have been identified. Although allergens may be found in many foods, 90 percent of the offenders are proteins found in milk, eggs, fish and seafood, nuts, peanuts, soy protein, and wheat. Some additives also may cause allergic responses, particularly sulfites used as preservatives. Shellfish is the number one cause of food allergy in American adults. Peanuts are also one of the most common allergens, so much so that some commercial airlines have "peanut free" zones. For individuals who know which food substances may trigger an allergic response, food labels may be helpful in determining the allergen's presence. Increasingly, food manufacturers are placing notices on food labels for "Food Allergic Consumers" to see the ingredient list.

If you experience problems when you consume certain foods, you may be able to make a self-diagnosis by simply avoiding that food and noting whether or not you experience a recurrence. But, because there may be many causes of food-related illness, you should consult an allergist or other appropriate physician to determine whether you have either food intolerance or food allergy. Once the offending food is determined, you may need to eliminate that food from your diet or reduce the amount you consume. In some cases this is relatively simple. For example, if you develop a reaction to clams, a common problem, you should have no difficulty finding other sources of high-quality protein. However, if you react to milk, it may be more difficult to obtain an adequate dietary intake of calcium. A dietician will be able to assist you in planning a diet that compensates for the reduced intake of calcium. Some suggestions are presented in chapter 8.

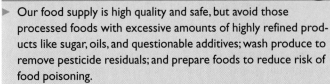

Healthful Nutrition Recommendations for Better Physical Performance

Articles about nutrition for athletes in popular sports magazines, and food supplements advertised therein, give the impression that athletes have special nutritional requirements above those of nonathletes. In general, however, the diet that is optimal for health is also optimal for physical or sport performance. The Prudent Healthy Diet will provide adequate food energy and nutrients to meet the need of almost all athletes in training and competition.

Nevertheless, modifications to the Prudent Healthy Diet may help enhance performance for certain athletic endeavors, and subsequent chapters will focus on specific recommendations relative to the use of various nutrients and dietary supplements to enhance physical performance. The purpose of this section is to provide some general recommendations regarding the use of the Prudent Healthy Diet by the athlete for training and competition.

What should I eat during training?

Ron Maughan, an expert in exercise metabolism and sports nutrition, recently noted that the main role of nutrition for the athlete may be to support consistent intensive training. As noted in chapter 1, optimal training is the most important factor contributing to improved sport performance.

Athletes involved in daily physical activity of a prolonged, intensive nature, such as long-distance running and swimming or prolonged tennis bouts, need to maintain adequate energy balance to sustain workout intensity. Heavy prolonged exercise also may adversely affect the immune system, predisposing the athlete to illness that may interrupt training. To help optimize training and prevent illness, athletes should consume a daily diet rich in nutrient-dense carbohydrates and high-quality protein in order to provide adequate energy for muscular activity and maintenance of an optimal body weight and composition. Such a diet will also provide adequate amounts of vitamins, minerals, and other nutrients to help maintain optimal immune system functions. Athletes should also maintain optimal fluid intake, particularly in high heat-stress environments.

Proper nutrition should enhance the physiological responses to training, and thus enhance competitive sports performance. The nutrient needs of athletes in training will be highlighted throughout the remainder of this text where relevant.

When and what should I eat just prior to competition?

It is a well-established fact that the ingestion of food just prior to competition will not benefit physical performance in most athletic events, yet the pregame meal, so to speak, is one of the major topics of discussion among athletes. A number of special meals have been utilized throughout the years because of their alleged benefits to physical performance, and special products have been marketed as pre-event nutritional supplements. Although research has not substantiated the value of any one particular precompetition meal, some general guidelines have been developed from practical experience over the years.

There are several major goals of the precompetition meal that may be achieved through proper timing and composition. In general, the precompetition meal should do the following:

1. Allow for the stomach to be relatively empty at the start of competition.
2. Help to prevent or minimize gastrointestinal distress.
3. Help avoid sensations of hunger, lightheadedness, or fatigue.
4. Provide adequate fuel supplies, primarily carbohydrate, in the blood and muscles.
5. Provide an adequate amount of body water.

In general, a solid meal should be eaten about 3 to 4 hours prior to competition. This should allow ample time for digestion to occur so that the stomach is relatively empty, and yet hunger sensations are minimized. However, pre-event emotional tension or anxiety may delay digestive time, as will a meal with a high-fat or high-protein content. Hence, the composition of the meal is critical. It should be high in carbohydrate, low in fat, and low to moderate in protein, providing for easy digestibility.

The composition of the precompetition meal should not contribute to any gastrointestinal distress, such as flatulence, increased acidity in the stomach, heartburn, or increased bulk that may stimulate the need for a bowel movement during competition. In general, foods to be avoided include gas formers like beans, spicy foods that may elicit heartburn, and bulk foods like bran products. High-sugar compounds may delay gastric emptying or create a reverse osmotic effect, possibly increasing the fluid content of the stomach, which may lead to a feeling of distress, cramps, or nausea. High-sugar loads, particularly fructose, may

also lead to other forms of gastrointestinal distress, such as diarrhea. Large amounts of concentrated sugar can cause a reactive drop in blood sugar in susceptible individuals. Individuals with known food intolerances, such as lactose intolerance, should use due caution. Through experience, you should learn what foods disagree with you during performance, and of course, you should avoid these prior to competition.

Adequate fluid intake should be assured prior to an event, particularly if the event will be of long duration or conducted under hot environmental conditions. Diuretics such as alcohol, which increase the excretion of body water, should be avoided. Large amounts of protein increase the water output of the kidneys and thus should be avoided. Fluids may be taken up to 15 to 30 minutes prior to competition to help ensure adequate hydration.

A wide variety of foods may be selected for the precompetition meal. The meal should consist of foods that are high in complex carbohydrates with moderate to low amounts of protein. Examples of such foods are presented in later chapters and also may be found in appendix E, particularly those in the starch list. The foods should be agreeable to you. You should eat what you like within the guidelines presented above.

Two examples of precompetition meals, each containing about 500–600 Calories with substantial amounts of carbohydrate, are presented in table 2.15. Bloch and Wheeler recently presented an excellent overview of practical approaches to feeding athletes. A similar approach, based on the Food Exchange System, is presented in chapter 11 as a means of designing comprehensive diet plans for physically active individuals. Such an approach has been used successfully with athletes, as noted recently by Frentsos and Baer.

One important last point. Meals other than the precompetition meal eaten on the same day should not be skipped. They should adhere to the basic principles set forth earlier in this chapter. Follow these general recommendations.

1. For events in the morning, eat a precompetition meal similar to breakfast; for example, meal A in table 2.15.
2. For events in early to mid-afternoon, eat breakfast and lunch. You might consume a more substantial breakfast, along with meal B in table 2.15 as a precompetition meal for lunch.
3. For events in the late afternoon, eat breakfast, lunch, and a snack. Again, eat a substantial breakfast and lunch and consume snacks that appeal to you, such as fruit, bagels with jelly, or other easily digestible foods.
4. For events in the evening, eat breakfast, lunch, and a precompetition meal for dinner.

TABLE 2.15 Two examples of precompetition meals containing 500–600 Calories

Meal A	Meal B
Glass of orange juice	One cup low-fat yogurt
One bowl of oatmeal	One banana
Two pieces of toast with jelly	One toasted bagel
Sliced peaches with skim milk	One ounce of turkey breast
	One-half cup of raisins

Pre-event nutritional strategies will vary somewhat for athletes involved in prolonged exercise tasks, such as running a marathon. As noted by prominent Australian exercise scientist Mark Hargreaves, body stores of both carbohydrate and fluids should be optimized. To achieve this goal, athletes may engage in practices such as carbohydrate loading and water hyperhydration, which will be detailed in chapters 4 and 9.

What should I eat during competition?

There is no need to consume anything during most types of athletic competition with the possible exception of carbohydrate and water. Carbohydrate may provide additional supplies of the preferred energy source during prolonged exercise, while water intake may be critical for regulation of body temperature when exercising in warm environments. In ultradistance competition, a hypotonic salt solution may be recommended. Appropriate details are presented in chapters 4 and 9. However, in some sport events such as prolonged daily cycling tours, Burke notes that current strategies appear to favor pre-stage intake and post-stage recovery meals to achieve nutritional goals.

What should I eat after competition?

In general, a balanced diet is all that is necessary to meet your nutrient needs and restore your nutritional status to normal following competition or daily, hard physical training. Carbohydrate and fat are the main nutrients used during exercise and can be replaced easily from foods among the food exchange lists. The increased caloric intake that is needed to replace your energy expenditure also will help provide you with the additional small amounts of protein, vitamins, minerals, and electrolytes that may be necessary for effective recovery. Thirst will normally help replace water losses on a day-to-day basis; you can check this by recording your body weight each morning to see if it is back to normal.

Simple sugars eaten immediately after a hard workout may help restore muscle glycogen fairly rapidly. Consuming a small amount of high-quality protein may also be prudent. Specific guidelines are presented in chapters 4 and 6.

For those who must compete several times daily and eat between competitions, such as in tennis tournaments or swim meets, the principles relative to pregame meals may be relevant, with a focus on carbohydrate-rich foods or fluids and moderate protein intake.

How important is breakfast for the physically active individual?

Breakfast may be especially important. A balanced breakfast provides a significant amount of Calories and other nutrients in the daily diet of the physically active person. A breakfast of skim milk, a poached egg, whole-grain toast, fortified high-fiber cereal, and orange juice will help provide a substantial part of the RDA for protein, calcium, iron, fiber, vitamin C, and other nutrients and is also relatively high in complex carbohydrates. A balanced breakfast high in fiber with an average amount of protein also will help prevent the onset of mid-morning hunger. The fiber and protein may help maintain a feeling of satiety throughout the morning, whereas a breakfast of refined carbohydrates, like doughnuts, may trigger an insulin response and produce hypoglycemia (low blood sugar) in the middle of the morning. The resultant hunger is typically satisfied by eating other refined carbohydrates, which will satisfy the hunger urge only until about lunch time. A balanced breakfast having a high nutrient density is therefore preferable to a breakfast based on refined carbohydrate products. Nontraditional breakfast foods, such as pizza, may also provide a balanced meal for breakfast.

Skipping breakfast would be comparable to a small fast, as the individual might not eat for 12 to 14 hours. This could conceivably produce hypoglycemia with resultant symptoms of weakness and possible impairment of training. Indeed, Schabort and others recently reported that when compared to no breakfast after an overnight fast, subjects who ate a breakfast containing 100 grams of carbohydrate improved their cycling endurance time by 36 percent. Moreover, for young athletes, Nicklas and others have noted that breakfast consumption is an important factor in their nutritional well-being, enhancing their academic performance, an important consideration for those aspiring to college scholarships. Although individual preferences should be taken into account, a balanced breakfast could provide a good source of some major nutrients to the individual who is involved in a physical conditioning program. For those on a tight time schedule, a bowl of ready-to-eat, fortified high-fiber cereal with skim milk and fruit may be an ideal choice. Nancy Clark, a nationally acclaimed sports nutritionist, notes that this breakfast is not only quick, easy, and convenient but also rich in carbohydrate, fiber, iron, calcium, and vitamins, and low in fat, cholesterol, and Calories.

How about the use of liquid meals, sports bars, and dietary supplements?

Liquid meals have some advantages over solid meals for precompetition nutrition. The available **liquid meals** are well balanced in nutrition value, have a high-carbohydrate content, have no bulk, are easily digested and assimilated, and may be more practical and economical than a solid meal.

A number of different liquid meal products are available commercially in various flavors, including Nutrament, Ensure, Ensure-Plus, and others associated with weight loss programs, such as Slim-Fast. The composition of each may vary somewhat, but checking the label will reveal the exact nutrient content. The energy content is usually about 250–400 Calories. Most liquid meals are high in carbohydrates, moderate in protein, and low in fat. Vitamins and minerals may be added in varying amounts.

Because a liquid meal may be assimilated more readily than a solid meal, it may be taken closer to competition, say 2 to 3 hours before. Research has shown that there is no difference between a liquid meal and a solid meal relative to subsequent hunger, nausea, diarrhea, or weight changes prior to competition. In addition, liquid meals will not affect physical performance any differently than a well-planned solid precompetition meal.

From a practical standpoint, liquid meals may save time and money. The time and expense of stopping for a solid meal prior to an event may be avoided by the proper use of liquid meals. Although they are rather economically priced in comparison to a solid meal, liquid meals may be prepared even more economically at home. Non-fat dry milk powder can be purchased in any supermarket, while various glucose polymer powders can be obtained at stores specializing in sports merchandise, particularly running and cycling shops. The following formula will provide one quart of a tasty liquid meal:

1/2 cup water
1/2 cup of nonfat dry milk powder
1/4 cup of a glucose polymer
3 cups of skim milk
1 teaspoon of flavoring for palatability (cherry, vanilla, or chocolate extract)

Sports bars have become increasingly popular in recent years, and several dozen products are targeted to physically active individuals. **Sports bars** vary in composition. Some are high carbohydrate, some high protein, and some have nearly equal mixtures of carbohydrate, protein, and fat. Many are vitamin and mineral fortified, and some are designed to serve as a meal replacement. Others contain drugs, such as caffeine. As with liquid meals, the food label on the sports bar will describe its contents. When compared to comparable energy sources from ordinary food, sports bars do not possess any magical qualities to enhance physical performance, but they possess some advantages similar to liquid meals, such as convenience. Because the major ingredient in many sports bars is carbohydrate, an expanded discussion is presented in chapter 4.

It is important to note that although liquid meals and sports bars may be convenient and appropriate for a pregame, post-training or post-competition meal, they do not contain all the healthful nutrients found in natural foods and thus should not be used on a long-term basis to replace the Prudent Healthy Diet.

Numerous dietary supplements are marketed to athletes as a means to enhance sport performance, but, with few exceptions, have not been shown to exert any potent ergogenic effects. Research evaluating the effectiveness of purported sport ergogenics is presented throughout the book. Pertinent discussion topics include the following:

Chapter 4: Carbohydrate ergogenics
Chapter 5: Ergogenics that affect fat metabolism
Chapter 6: Amino acids, creatine, and other protein-related ergogenics
Chapter 7: Vitamins and other vitamin-related ergogenics, such as ginseng
Chapter 8: Mineral ergogenics
Chapter 9: Glycerol
Chapter 13: Alcohol, caffeine and related ergogenics.

How do gender and age influence nutritional recommendations for enhanced physical performance?

The diet that is optimal for health is the optimal diet for physical performance. This is the key principle of sports nutrition and it applies to physically active males and females of all ages. However, as shall be noted at certain points in this text, specific nutrient needs may vary by gender and age, and various forms of exercise training may influence nutrient requirements as well.

Metabolic differences between males and females could influence nutritional requirements. For example, as shall be noted in chapter 5, female endurance athletes oxidize more fat and less carbohydrate during exercise as compared to males, which may influence various dietary strategies such as carbohydrate loading.

Adolescent and adult premenopausal females need more dietary iron than males. Female athletes, especially those participating in aerobic endurance sports such as distance running, must include iron-rich foods in their diet or risk incurring iron-deficiency anemia and impaired running ability. Being smaller in size, women need fewer Calories than men, yet many may not consume adequate energy and may develop disordered eating practices as they attempt to lose body mass for competition purposes. Disordered eating in female athletes may contribute to the development of premature osteoporosis, prompting the American College of Sports Medicine to develop a position stand on the Female Athlete Triad, an important issue discussed in chapter 8. Because of gender differences, some sports nutrition products have been designed for women only.

Petrie and others have noted that child and adolescent athletes typically consume more food to meet their energy expenditure and thus are more likely to obtain an adequate supply of nutrients. However, one of the leading authorities on sports nutrition for children, Oded Bar-Or from McMaster University in Canada noted that while nutritional considerations are similar for all athletes irrespective of age, children have several physiological characteristics that may require specific nutritional considerations. For example, their relative protein needs may be greater to support growth, and their relative calcium needs may be greater for optimal bone development. Moreover, young athletes may experience greater thermal stress during exercise and those that participate in weight-control sports involving excessive exercise and inadequate energy intake may be at risk for nutrient deficiencies and impaired growth and development.

On the other end of the age spectrum, older athletes may have special nutrient needs. In general, resting metabolism declines in older age, so caloric need may decrease. Older people also eat less, so they need to make wiser food choices, that is, foods with high nutrient density. Campbell and Geik recently noted that nutrition is a tool that the older athlete should use to enhance exercise performance and health. In particular, they noted that older athletes may need to focus on obtaining sufficient micronutrients, such as the B vitamins and vitamin D. Supplements may be recommended to obtain adequate vitamin B_{12} and calcium if not obtained from the diet, such as from fortified foods. Older individuals also need to ensure adequate fluid intake because of increased susceptibility to dehydration.

The special nutrient requirements of females, the young, and the elderly, as they relate to physical activity, will be incorporated in the text where relevant. However, most of the nutritional principles underlying exercise and sport performance that are presented in this text apply to most physically active individuals.

How can I eat more nutritiously while traveling for competition?

Athletes who must travel to compete are often faced with the problem of obtaining proper pre-event and postevent nutrition. After reading this chapter, you should be aware of how to select foods that are high in carbohydrate, low in fat, and moderate in protein. More guidelines are presented in chapters 4 through 6. One possible solution is to pack your own food and fluids in a traveling bag or cooler. Foods from each of the Food Exchange Lists can be easily packed or kept on ice, such as skim milk; precooked low-fat meats; bagels and cereal; fruits, juices, and vegetables; sports drinks; and high-carbohydrate snacks including whole wheat crackers and pretzels, and low-fat cookies such as Fig Newtons and vanilla wafers. Small containers of condiments can also be easily transported in the cooler, along with proper eating utensils. Taking your own food means you can eat your pre-event or postevent meal as planned, and you may save money as well. Such an approach may be very effective for short, one-day trips and may also be used to complement other meals on longer journeys. Some easily packed snack foods are presented in table 2.16.

While traveling, you have a variety of eating places from which to select your food, including full-service restaurants, restaurants with all-you-can-eat buffets, steakhouses and fishhouses, fast-food restaurants, pizza parlors, sub shops, supermarkets, convenience stores, and even vending machines. With a solid background on the nutritional principles presented in this chapter, you should be able to select healthful, high-carbohydrate and low-fat foods at any of these establishments, but of course the variety of food choices will vary depending on the place you choose. Keep in mind that you can always ask to see if they will create a meal for you. For example, order a salad and ask to have extra vegetables and fish or chicken breast added, with the dressing on the side.

Although all fast foods can be part of a healthy diet when consumed in moderation, many are relatively high in fat content, and their intake should be restricted. However, many restaurants do provide a few healthier choices with individual sandwiches containing less than 30 percent of their Calories from fat, including grilled or broiled chicken, lean roast beef, and veggie burgers. In some cases, particularly with grilled, skinless chicken sandwiches, much of the fat content is in the sauce added to the sandwich, so ordering the sauce on the side allows you to control the amount added. Other sandwich shops, such as Au Bon Pain and Subway may serve healthful sandwiches, but unwise selections in these stores may also contain substantial amounts of fat.

You can eat fast food and stay within the recommended nutrition guidelines for a healthy diet, but obtaining a healthful diet requires careful selection of foods. Fast-food restaurants provide materials detailing the nutrient content of each of their products.

In some cases the materials may be obtained in the restaurant, and all have Websites detailing nutrient analysis of their products. See appendix F for the fat percentages of specific fast-food products and appropriate Websites.

The following suggestions may be helpful if you are dining in a fast-food or budget-type restaurant, such as McDonald's, Wendy's, Arby's, Pizza Hut, Baja Fresh, Applebee's, or Ruby Tuesday. Many supermarkets also have takeout departments or salad bars from which to select lunch or dinner.

Breakfast selections
    English muffins, unbuttered, with jelly
    English muffins with Canadian bacon
    Whole wheat pancakes with syrup
    French toast
    Bran muffins, fat-free or low-fat
    Hot whole-grain cereal, oatmeal
    Ready-to-eat fortified, high-fiber cereal
    Skim or low-fat milk
    Orange juice
    Hot cocoa
Lunch or dinner selections
    Any low-fat sandwiches, no mayonnaise or high-fat sauces
    Grilled chicken breast sandwich, on whole-grain bun
    Baked or broiled fish sandwich
    Lean roast beef sandwich, on whole-grain bun
    Single, plain hamburger, on whole-grain bun
    Baked potato, with toppings on the side (add sparingly)
    Pasta dishes, spaghetti, and macaroni, with low-fat sauces
    Rice dishes
    Lo mein noodles, not chow mein (fried noodles)
    Soups, rice and noodle
    Salsas, made with tomatoes
    Chicken or seafood tostadas, made with cornmeal tortillas
    Bean and rice dishes
    All whole-grain and other breads
    Salads, low-fat dressing
    Salad bar, focus on vegetables and high-carbohydrate foods; avoid high-fat items
    Pizza, thick crust, vegetable type with minimum cheese topping
    Skim or low-fat milk
    Orange juice
    Frozen yogurt, fat-free or low-fat
    Sherbet

With any of these selections, it is always a good idea to order toppings, for example, mayonnaise, salad dressing, etc., on the side so that you can control portions. When selecting sandwiches, ask for those that are either baked, broiled, or grilled.

For the most part, research supports the general finding that the diet that is optimal for your health is also the optimal diet for your performance. Eating right, both for health and performance, does not mean you need to eat bland foods because all foods, some in moderation, can be tastefully prepared and blended into the Prudent Healthy Diet.

TABLE 2.16 Easily packed snacks for traveling or brown bag lunches

Grains	Meats	Vegetables
Bagels	Small can of baked beans	Sliced carrots
Pita bread	Cooked chicken or turkey, small 2-ounce commercial	Broccoli stalks
Muffins	packages, packed in airtight plastic bags	Cauliflower pieces
Fig Newtons	Small can of sardines	Tomatoes
Vanilla wafers	Peanut butter	Canned vegetable juices
Whole wheat crackers	Reduced-fat cheese slices	
Graham crackers	String cheese	
Dry cereals		
Wheat Chex		
Grapenuts		
Plain popcorn		

Fruits	Milk	Nuts
Small cans of fruit in own juice	Small containers of skim or low-fat milk, aseptic	Almonds
Small containers of fruit juice,	packaging if available	Walnuts
aseptic packages	Dried skim milk powder, to be reconstituted	
Oranges	Packaged yogurt	
Apples		
Other raw fruits		
Dried fruits		

Key Concept Recap

▶ The precompetition meal should be easily digestible, high in complex carbohydrates, moderate in protein, and low in fat, and it should be consumed about 3 or 4 hours prior to competition.
▶ In general, nutritional guidelines for the improvement of health are completely compatible with those for improvement of physical performance.

Check for Yourself

Interview a coach or some athletes at your school about their meal strategies prior to competition. How do their strategies compare with general recommendations?

APPLICATION EXERCISE

In chapter 1 we recommended that you consume your normal daily diet, record the foods you have eaten, and then rate your diet using the quiz on pp. 29–31. Do the same but switch to a vegetarian diet, as close to a vegan diet as possible, for the day and compare the two rating scores.

Review Questions—Multiple Choice

1. The guide to eating from the United States Department of Agriculture, MyPyramid, has six colors representing foods, but which of the following is not considered a food group by the USDA?
   (a) grains
   (b) meat
   (c) oils
   (d) fruits
   (e) milk
   (f) vegetables

2. Which of the following is not an acceptable definition for food labels with the listing "free"?
   (a) fat free—less than 0.5 grams of total fat per serving
   (b) cholesterol free—less than 2 milligrams per serving
   (c) sugar free—less than 0.5 grams per serving
   (d) Calorie free—less than 40 calories per serving
   (e) sodium free—less than 5 milligrams per serving

3. Approximately how many Calories are in a meal with two starch/bread exchanges, four lean meat exchanges, one fruit exchange, two vegetable exchanges, three fat exchanges, and one skim milk exchange?
   (a) 450
   (b) 540
   (c) 670
   (d) 715
   (e) 780

4. How many Calories are in a "Big Mac" sandwich, a large order of French fries, and a medium soft drink if this meal contains 31 grams of protein, 82 grams of carbohydrate, and 50 grams of fat?
   (a) 686
   (b) 811
   (c) 902

(d) 1066
(e) 1140

5. Which of the following is not a key (indicator) nutrient as defined by the key nutrient concept?
   (a) iron
   (b) calcium
   (c) vitamin A
   (d) protein
   (e) vitamin D
   (f) riboflavin
   (g) niacin
   (h) all are key nutrients

6. The recommended dietary goals for healthy Americans suggest that the intake of saturated fat, as a percentage of daily Calories, be less than what percent?
   (a) 10
   (b) 20
   (c) 30
   (d) 40
   (e) 50

7. Which key nutrient is not usually found in substantial amounts in the meat group?
   (a) vitamin C
   (b) iron
   (c) protein
   (d) niacin
   (e) thiamin

8. A food label lists the amount of complex carbohydrates as 5 grams, the amount of simple sugars as 10 grams, the amount

of protein as 5 grams, and the amount of fat as 10 grams. Which of the following is true?
   (a) Simple sugars make up the majority of the Calories.
   (b) Carbohydrate makes up the majority of the Calories.
   (c) The amount of Calories from protein and carbohydrate is equal.
   (d) The majority of the Calories is derived from fat.
   (e) None of the above statements is true.

9. A vegetarian-type diet may be more healthful than the current typical American diet for all of the following reasons *except* which?
   (a) higher in iron
   (b) higher in fiber
   (c) lower in saturated fats
   (d) a higher polyunsaturated to saturated fat ratio
   (e) lower in cholesterol

10. Which of the following nutrients is of *least* concern to a vegan relative to incurring a deficiency?
   (a) iron
   (b) vitamin C
   (c) zinc
   (d) calcium
   (e) vitamin B$_{12}$

Answers to multiple choice questions:
1. c; 2. d; 3. d; 4. c; 5. e; 6. a; 7. a; 8. d; 9. a; 10. b.

1. Name the eight key nutrients and identify a food source that is particularly rich in that nutrient. For example, lean meat is a rich source of iron.

2. Discuss the six categories of foods depicted in the MyPyramid design in respect to the concepts of variety, proportionality, and moderation.

3. Compare and contrast the MyPyramid food guide with the Food Exchange System. What similarities and differences do you note?

4. List and explain the potential health benefits of a vegan diet as compared to the typical American diet today.

5. Identify the nutrients that must be listed on food labels, how the DV is determined for each, and why you may want to have a high percent of the DV for some and a low percent for others.

Books
American Dietetic Association and American Diabetes Association. 1995. *Exchange Lists for Meal Planning.* Chicago: American Dietetic Association.

Bratman, S. 2000. *Health Food Junkies: Overcoming the Obsession with Healthful Eating.* New York: Bantam Doubleday.
Dorfman, L. 1999. *The Vegetarian Sports Nutrition Guide: Peak Performance for*

Everyone from Beginners to Gold Medalists. New York: John Wiley & Sons.
Hawley, J., and Burke, L. 1998. *Peak Performance: Training and Nutritional*

Strategies for Sport. St. Leonards, NSW: Allen & Unwin Australia.

Heber, D. 2001. *What Color Is Your Diet?* New York: Regan Books.

Joseph, J., and Nadeau, D. 2002. *The Color Code: A Revolutionary Eating Plan for Optimal Health.* New York: Hyperion.

National Academy of Sciences. Institute of Medicine, Food and Nutrition Board. 2004. *Dietary Reference Intakes for Water, Potassium, Sodium, Chloride, and Sulfate.* Washington, DC: National Academy Press.

National Academy of Sciences. Institute of Medicine. Food and Nutrition Board. 2003. *Dietary Reference Intakes: Guiding Principles for Nutrition Labeling and Fortification.* Washington, DC.: National Academy Press.

National Academy of Sciences. Institute of Medicine, Food and Nutrition Board. 2002. *Dietary Reference Intakes for Vitamin A, Vitamin K, Arsenic, Boron, Chromium, Copper, Iodine, Iron, Manganese, Molybdenum, Nickel, Silicon, Vanadium, and Zinc.* Washington, DC: National Academy Press.

National Academy of Sciences. Institute of Medicine, Food and Nutrition Board. 2002. *Dietary Reference Intakes for Energy, Carbohydrates, Fiber, Fat, Protein and Amino Acids (Macronutrients).* Washington, DC: National Academy Press.

National Academy of Sciences. Institute of Medicine, Food and Nutrition Board. 2000. *Dietary Reference Intakes for Thiamin, Riboflavin, Niacin, Vitamin B_6, Folate, Vitamin B_{12}, Pantothenic Acid, Biotin, and Choline.* Washington, DC: National Academy Press.

National Academy of Sciences. Institute of Medicine, Food and Nutrition Board. 2000. *Dietary Reference Intakes for Vitamin C, Vitamin E, Selenium, and Carotenoids.* Washington, DC: National Academy Press.

National Academy of Sciences. Institute of Medicine, Food and Nutrition Board. 1999. *Dietary Reference Intakes for Calcium, Phosphorus, Magnesium, Vitamin D, and Fluoride.* Washington, DC: National Academy Press.

National Research Council. 1989. *Diet and Health: Implications for Reducing Chronic Disease Risk.* Washington, DC: National Academy Press.

Shils, M., et al. (Eds.). 2006. *Modern Nutrition in Health and Disease.* Philadelphia: Lippincott Williams & Wilkins.

U.S. Department of Agriculture and U.S. Department of Health and Human Services. 2005. *Nutrition and Your Health: Dietary Guidelines for Americans.* Washington, DC: U.S. Government Printing Office.

U.S. Department of Health and Human Services. 1988. *The Surgeon General's Report on Nutrition and Health.* Washington, DC: U.S. Government Printing Office.

U.S. Department of Health and Human Services. 2000. *Healthy People 2010: National Health Promotion and Disease Prevention Objectives.* Washington, DC: U.S. Government Printing Office.

Review Articles

Ackerman, J. 2002. *Food: How safe; How altered?* National Geographic 201 (5):2–51.

American Cancer Society 2001 Nutrition and Physical Activity Guidelines Advisory Committee. 2002. American Cancer Society guidelines on nutrition and physical activity for cancer prevention: Reducing the risk of cancer with healthy food choices and physical activity. *CA: A Cancer Journal for Clinicians* 52:92–119.

American Diabetes Association. 2003. Evidence-based nutrition principles and recommendations for the treatment and prevention of diabetes and related complications. *Diabetes Care* 26:S51–61.

American Dietetic Association. 2004. Position of the American Dietetic Association: Functional Foods. *Journal of the American Dietetic Association* 104:814–26.

American Dietetic Association. 2003. Position of the American Dietetic Association and Dietitians of Canada: Vegetarian Diets. *Journal of the American Dietetic Association* 103:748–65.

American Dietetic Association. 2002. Position of the American Dietetic Association: Total diet approach to communicating food and nutrition information. *Journal of the American Dietetic Association* 102:100–108.

American Dietetic Association. 2001. Position of the American Dietetic Association: Food fortification and dietary supplements. *Journal of the American Dietetic Association* 101:115–25.

American Dietetic Association. 2000. *10 tips to healthy eating.* Chicago: The American Dietetic Association.

American Dietetic Association. 1997. Position of the American Dietetic Association: Food and water safety. *Journal of the American Dietetic Association* 97:184–89.

American Dietetic Association. 1995. Position of the American Dietetic Association: Phytochemicals and functional foods. *Journal of the American Dietetic Association* 95:493–95.

American Heart Association. 2002. *Dietary Guidelines for Healthy Children.* Dallas: AHA.

American Heart Association. 2000. AHA Dietary Guidelines: Revision 2000. *Circulation* 102:2284–99.

American Institute for Cancer Research. 1997. Pesticides and cancer risk. *American Institute for Cancer Research Newsletter* 55: 5.

Ames, B. N., and Gold, L. S. 1998. The causes and prevention of cancer: The role of environment. *Biotherapy* 11:205–20.

Bar-Or, O. 2001. Nutritional considerations for the child athlete. *Canadian Journal of Applied Physiology* 26:S186–91.

Barr, S., and Rideout, C. 2004. Nutritional considerations for vegetarian athletes. *Nutrition* 20:696–703.

Bidlack, W. R., and Wang, W. 1999. Designing functional foods. In *Modern Nutrition in Health and Disease,* eds. M. Shils et al. Baltimore: Williams & Wilkins.

Bloch, T. D, and Wheeler, K. B. 1999. Dietary examples: A practical approach to feeding athletes. *Clinics in Sports Medicine* 18:703–11.

Bren, L. 2003. Turning up the heat on acrylamide. *FDA Consumer* 37 (1):10–11.

Brophy, B., and Schardt, D. 1999. Functional foods. *Nutrition Action Health Letter* 26 (3):1–7.

Burke, L. 2001. Nutritional practices of male and female endurance cyclists. *Sports Medicine.* 31:521–32.

Burks, W. 2002. Current understanding of food allergy. *Annals of the New York Academy of Sciences* 964:1–12.

Byers, T., et al. 2002. American Cancer Society guidelines on nutrition and physical activity for cancer prevention: Reducing the risk of cancer with healthy food choices and physical activity. *CA: A Cancer Journal for Clinicians* 52:92–119.

Caine, D., et al. 2001. Does gymnastics training inhibit growth of females? *Clinician Journal of Sport Medicine* 11:260–70.

Campbell, W., and Geik, R. 2004. Nutritional considerations for the older athlete. *Nutrition* 20:603–8.

Center for Science in the Public Interest. 2002. Genetically engineered foods: Are they safe? *Nutrition Action Health Letter* 28 (9):1–8.

Center for Science in the Public Interest. 1999. Chemical cuisine. *Nutrition Action Health Letter* 26 (2):4–9.

Clark, N. 1987. Breakfast of champions. *Physician and Sportsmedicine* 15(January):209–12.

Consumers Union. 2005. 'Super' foods: Do you really need them. *Consumer Reports on Health* 17 (6):1, 4–6.

Consumers Union. 2005. The new do's and don'ts for protecting your heart. *Consumer Reports on Health* 17 (7):1, 4–6.

Consumers Union. 2005. You are what they eat. *Consumer Reports* 70 (1):26–31.

Consumers Union. 2003. The truth about irradiated meat. *Consumer Reports* 68 (8):34–37.

Consumers Union. 2002. How safe is that burger? *Consumer Reports* 67 (11):29–35.

Consumers Union. 2000. Debate over genetically engineered food heats up. *Consumer Reports* 65 (6):48.

Consumers Union. 1999. Live longer, feel younger. *Consumer Reports on Health* 11 (3):1–6.

Consumers Union. 1999. The new foods: Functional or dysfunctional? *Consumer Reports on Health* 11 (6):1–5.

Consumers Union. 1998. Fruits and vegetables: Nature's best protection. *Consumer Reports on Health* 10 (6):1–5.

Consumers Union. 1998. Greener greens: The truth about organic food. *Consumer Reports* 63:12–18.

Consumers Union. 1997. Food poisoning: How to protect yourself from pathogens. *Consumer Reports* 62:64–65.

Corliss, R. 2002. Should we all be vegetarians? Would we be healthier? Would the planet? The risks and benefits of a meat-free life. *Time* 160 (3):48–56.

de la Torre Boronat, M. C. 1999. Scientific basis for the health benefits of the Mediterranean diet. *Drugs under Experimental and Clinical Research* 25:155–61.

Felton, J., et al. 2002. Human exposure to heterocyclic amine food mutagens/carcinogens: Relevance to breast cancer. *Environmental Molecular Mutagenesis* 39:112–18.

Finley, J., et al. 2006. Food processing: Nutrition, safety, and quality. In *Modern Nutrition in Health and Disease,* eds. M. Shils et al. Philadelphia: Lippincott Williams & Wilkins.

Formanek, R. 2001. Proposed rules issued for bioengineered foods. *FDA Consumer* 35(2):9–11.

Giovanucci, E. 2002. A review of epidemiologic studies of tomatoes, lycopene, and prostate cancer. *Experimental Biology and Medicine* 227:852–59.

Gleeson, M., and Bishop, N. 2000. Elite athlete immunology: Importance of nutrition. *International Journal of Sports Medicine* 21:S44–50.

Guarderas, J. 2001. Is it food allergy? Differentiating the causes of adverse reactions to food. *Postgraduate Medicine* 109:125–134.

Hargreaves, M. 2001. Pre-exercise nutritional strategies: Effects on metabolism and performance. *Canadian Journal of Applied Physiology* 26:S64–70.

Hasler, C. 2000. The changing face of functional foods. *Journal of the American College of Nutrition* 19:499S–506S.

Heber, D. 2004. Vegetables, fruits and phytoestrogens in the prevention of diseases. *Journal of Postgraduate Medicine* 50:145–49.

Hefle, S., and Taylor, S. 2004. Food allergy and the food industry. *Current Allergy and Asthma Reports* 4:55–59.

Hunt, J. 2002. Moving toward a plant-based diet: Are iron and zinc at risk? *Nutrition Reviews* 60:127–34.

Hurley, J., and Liebman, B. 2005. Fast food in '05. *Nutrition Action Health Letter* 32(2):12–15.

International Food Information Council Foundation. 1999. Myths and facts about food biotechnology. *Food Insight* September/October:2–3.

Jacobs, D. R., et al. 1998. Whole-grain intake and cancer: An expanded review and meta-analysis. *Nutrition and Cancer* 30:85–96.

Johnston, P., and Sabate, J. 2006. Nutritional implications of vegetarian diets. In *Modern Nutrition in Health and Disease,* eds. M. Shils et al. Philadelphia: Lippincott Williams & Wilkins.

Kennedy, D. 2004. Dietary diversity, diet quality, and body weight regulation. *Nutrition Reviews* 62:S78–S81.

King, J. 2002. Biotechnology: A solution for improving nutrient bioavailability. *International Journal of Vitamin and Nutrition Research* 72:7–12.

Kratz, V. 2001. The hidden life of a bioengineered meal. *Sierra* 86 (1):24–25.

LaChance, P. A. 1998. Overview of key nutrients: Micronutrient aspects. *Nutrition Reviews* 56:S34–39.

Liu, R. 2004. Potential synergy of phytochemicals in cancer prevention: Mechanism of action. *Journal of Nutrition* 134:3479S–85S.

Mann, N. 2000. Dietary lean meat and human evolution. *European Journal of Nutrition* 39:71–79.

Mares-Perlman, J., et al. 2002. The body of evidence to support a protective role for lutein and zeaxanthinin delaying chronic disease: Overview. *Journal of Nutrition* 132:518S–24S.

Massey, B. 2002. Dietary supplements. *Medical Clinics of North America* 86:127–47.

Maughan, R. 2002. The athlete's diet: Nutritional goals and dietary strategies. *Proceedings of the Nutrition Society* 6:87–96.

Meadows, M. 2002. Plastics and the microwave. *FDA Consumer* 36 (6):30.

Medeiros, L., et al. 2001. Food safety education: What should we be teaching to consumers? *Journal of Nutrition Education* 33:108–13.

Messina, V., and Mangels, A. 2001. Considerations in planning vegan diets: Children. *Journal of the American Dietetic Association* 110:661–69.

Munoz de Chavez, M., and Chavez, A. 1998. Diets that prevent cancer: Recommendations from the American Institute for Cancer Research. *International Journal of Cancer Supplement* 11:85–89.

Murphy, S., et al. 2002. Using the new dietary reference intakes to assess diets: A map to the maze. *Nutrition Reviews* 60:267–75.

Neuhouser, M. 2004. Dietary flavonoids and cancer risk: Evidence from human population studies. *Nutrition and Cancer* 50:1–7.

Neville, K. 1999. Worried about pesticides on produce? EN offers advice on minimizing risk. *Environmental Nutrition* 22 (8):1, 6.

Nicklas, T. A., et al. 1998. Nutrient contribution of breakfast, secular trends, and the role of ready-to-eat cereals: A review of data from the Bogalusa Heart Study. *American Journal of Clinical Nutrition* 67:757S–763S.

Parnes, R., and Lichtenstein, A. 2004. Food irradiation: A safe and useful technology. *Nutrition in Clinical Care* 7:149–55.

Petrie, H., et al. 2004. Nutritional concerns for the child and adolescent competitor. *Nutrition* 20:620–31.

Pusztai, A. 2002. Can science give us the tools for recognizing possible health risks of GM food? *Nutrition and Health* 16:73–84.

Reinhardt, W., and Brevard, P. 2002. Integrating the Food Guide Pyramid and Physical Activity Pyramid for positive dietary and physical activity behaviors in adolescents. *Journal of the American Dietetic Association* 102:S96–99.

Sampson, H. A. 1999. Food allergy. Part 1: Immunopathogenesis and clinical disorders. *Journal of Allergy and Clinical Immunology* 103:717–28.

Sampson, H. A. 1999. Food allergy. Part 2: Diagnosis and management. *Journal of*

Allergy and Clinical Immunology 103:981–89.

Schardt, D. 2002. Food poisoning's long shadow. *Nutrition Action Health Letter* 29 (4):1–5.

Schneeman, B., and Mendelson, R. 2002. Dietary guidelines: Past experience and new approaches. *Journal of the American Dietetic Association* 102:1498–500.

Setchell, K. D., and Cassidy, A. 1999. Dietary isoflavones: Biological effects and relevance to human health. *Journal of Nutrition* 129:758S–767S.

Shi, J., and Le Maguer, M. 2000. Lycopene in tomatoes: Chemical and physical properties affected by food processing. *Critical Reviews in Food Science and Nutrition* 40:1–42.

Sicherer, S. 2002. Food allergy. *Lancet* 360:701–10.

Skibola, C., and Smith, M. 2000. Potential health impacts of excessive flavonoid intake. *Free Radicals in Biology and Medicine* 29:375–83.

Steinmetz, K. A., and Potter, J. D. 1996. Vegetables, fruit, and cancer prevention: A review. *Journal of the American Dietetic Association* 96:1027–39.

Tauxe, R. 2002. Emerging foodborne pathogens. *International Journal of Food Microbiology* 78:31–41.

Thompson, L. 2000. Are bioengineered foods safe? *FDA Consumer* 34 (1):18–23.

Trichopoulou, A. 2001. Mediterranean diet: The past and present. *Nutrition, Metabolism, and Cardiovascular Disease* 11:1–4.

Truswell, A. 2002. Meat consumption and cancer of the large bowel. *European Journal of Clinical Nutrition* 56:S19–24.

Tucker, K. 2001. Eat a variety of healthful foods: Old advice with new support. *Nutrition Reviews* 59:156–58.

Van Duyn, M. and Pivonka, E. 2000. Overview of the health benefits of fruit and vegetable consumption for the dietetics professional: Selected literature. *Journal of the American Dietetic Association* 100:1511–21.

Vogt, T. M., et al. 1999. Dietary Approaches to Stop Hypertension: Rationale, design, and methods. DASH Collaborative Research Group. *Journal of the American Dietetic Association* 99:S12–18.

Weiss, B., et al. 2004. Pesticides. *Pediatrics* 113:1030–36.

Williams, C. 2002. Nutritional quality of organic food: Shades of grey or shades of green? *Proceedings of the Nutrition Society* 61:19–24.

Wood, O., and Bruhn, C. 2000. Position of the American Dietetic Association: Food irradiation. *Journal of the American Dietetic Association* 100:246–53.

Worthington, V. 2001. Nutritional quality of organic versus conventional fruits, vegetables, and grains. *Journal of Alternative and Complementary Medicine* 7:161–73.

Yates, A. A., et al. 1998. Dietary Reference Intakes: The new basis for recommendations for calcium and related nutrients, B vitamins, and choline. *Journal of the American Dietetic Association* 98:699–706.

Specific Studies

Baker, B., et al. 2002. Pesticide residues in conventional, integrated pest management (IPM)-grown and organic foods: Insights from three US data sets. *Food Additives and Contaminants* 19:427–46.

Bazzano, L., et al. 2002. Fruit and vegetable intake and risk of cardiovascular disease in US adults: The first National Health and Nutrition Examination Survey Epidemiologic Follow-up Study. *American Journal of Clinical Nutrition* 76:93–99.

Chao, A., et al. 2005. Meat consumption and risk of colorectal cancer. *JAMA* 293:172–82.

Frentsos, J. A., and Baer, J. T. 1997. Increased energy and nutrient intake during training and competition improves elite triathletes' endurance performance. *International Journal of Sport Nutrition* 7:347–49.

Giovannucci, E., et al. 2002. A prospective study of tomato products, lycopene, and prostate cancer risk. *Journal of the National Cancer Institute* 94:391–98.

Harnack, L., et al. 2002. An evaluation of the Dietary Guidelines for Americans in relation to cancer occurrence. *American Journal of Clinical Nutrition* 76:889–96.

Hunt, J. R., et al. 1998. Zinc absorption, mineral balance, and blood lipids in women consuming controlled lactoovovegetarian and omnivorous diets

for 8 wk. *American Journal of Clinical Nutrition* 67:421–30.

Jensen, M., et al. 2004. Intakes of whole grains, bran, and germ and the risk of coronary heart disease in men. *American Journal of Clinical Nutrition* 80:1492–99.

Key, T., et al. 1996. Dietary habits and mortality in 11,000 vegetarians and health conscious people: Results of a 17-year follow up. *British Medical Journal* 313:775–79.

Kristal, A., et al. 2001. Predictors of self-initiated, healthful dietary change. *Journal of the American Dietetic Association* 101:762–66.

Larsson, C., and Johansson, G. 2002. Dietary intake and nutritional status of young vegans and omnivores in Sweden. *Journal of the American Dietetic Association* 102:100–106.

Maffucci, D. M., and McMurray, R. G. 2000. Towards optimizing the timing of the pre-exercise meal. *International Journal of Sport Nutrition and Exercise Metabolism* 10:103–13.

Martins, Y., et al. 1999. Restrained eating among vegetarians: Does a vegetarian eating style mask concerns about weight? *Appetite* 32:145–54.

Neuhouser, M. L. et al. 1999. Use of food nutrition labels is associated with lower fat intake. *Journal of the American Dietetic Association* 99:45–53.

Nicholson, A. S., et al. 1999. Toward improved management of NIDDM: A randomized, controlled, pilot intervention using a lowfat, vegetarian diet. *Preventive Medicine* 29:87–91.

Remer, T., et al. 1999. Increased risk of iodine deficiency with vegetarian nutrition. *British Journal of Nutrition* 81:45–49.

Schabort, E. J., et al. 1999. The effect of a preexercise meal on time to fatigue during prolonged cycling exercise. *Medicine & Science in Sports & Exercise* 31:464–71.

Toohey, M. L., et al. 1998. Cardiovascular disease risk factors are lower in African-American vegans compared to lacto-ovovegetarians. *Journal of the American College of Nutrition* 17:425–34.

Zheng, W., et al. 1998. Well done meat and the risk of breast cancer. *Journal of the National Cancer Institute* 90:1724–29.

Human Energy

CHAPTER THREE

LEARNING OBJECTIVES

After studying this chapter, you should be able to:

1. Understand the interrelationships among the various forms of chemical, thermal, and mechanical energy, and be able to perform mathematical conversions from one form of energy to another.

2. Identify the three major human energy systems, their major energy sources as stored in the body, and various nutrients needed to sustain them.

3. List the components of total daily energy expenditure (TDEE) and how each contributes to the total amount of caloric energy expended over a 24-hour period.

4. Describe the various factors that may influence resting energy expenditure (REE).

5. List and explain the various means whereby energy expenditure during exercise, or the thermic effect of exercise (TEE), may be measured, and be able to calculate conversions among the various methods.

6. Explain the relationship between exercise intensity, particularly walking and running, and energy expenditure, and relate walking and running intensity to other types of physical activities.

7. Understand the concept of the physical activity level (PAL) and how it relates to estimated energy expenditure (EER). Calculate your EER based on an estimate of your PAL and the physical activity coefficient (PA).

8. Describe the role of the three energy systems during exercise.

9. Explain the various causes of fatigue during exercise and discuss nutritional interventions that may help delay the onset of fatigue.

As noted in chapter 1, the body uses the food we eat to provide energy, to build and repair tissues, and to regulate metabolism. Of these three functions, the human body ranks energy production first and will use food for this purpose at the expense of the other two functions in time of need. Energy is the essence of life.

Through technological processes, humans have harnessed a variety of energy sources such as wind, waterfalls, the sun, wood, and oil to operate the machines invented to make life easier. However, humans cannot use any of these energy sources for their own metabolism but must rely on food sources found in nature. The food we eat must be converted into energy forms that the body can use. Thus, the human body is equipped with a number of metabolic systems to produce and regulate energy for its diverse needs, such as synthesis of tissues, movement of substances between tissues, and muscular contraction.

Sport energy! The underlying basis for the control of movement in all sports is human energy, and successful performance depends upon the ability of the athlete to produce the right amount of energy and to control its application to the specific demands of the sport. Sports differ in their energy demands. In some events, such as the 100-meter dash, success is dependent primarily upon the ability to produce energy very rapidly. In others, such as the 26.2-mile marathon, energy need not be produced so rapidly but must be sustained for a much longer period. In still other sports, such as golf, the athlete need not only produce energy at varying rates (compare the drive with the putt) but must carefully control the application of that energy. Thus, each sport imposes specific energy demands upon the athlete.

A discussion of the role of nutrition as a means to help provide and control human energy is important from several standpoints. First, inadequate supplies of necessary energy nutrients, such as muscle glycogen or blood glucose, may cause fatigue. Fatigue also may be caused by the inability of the energy systems to function optimally because of a deficiency of other nutrients, such as selected vitamins and minerals. In addition, the human body is capable of storing energy reserves in a variety of body forms, including body fat and muscle tissue. Excess body weight in the form of fat or decreased body weight due to losses of muscle tissue may adversely affect some types of athletic performance.

One purpose of this chapter is to review briefly the major human energy systems and how they are used in the body under conditions of exercise and rest. Following this, chapters 4 through 9 discuss the role of each of the major classes of nutrients as they relate to energy production in the human body, with the primary focus on prevention of fatigue caused by impaired energy production; chapter 13 details the effects of various food drugs and supplements on human energy systems. Another purpose of this chapter is to discuss the means by which humans store and expend energy. Chapters 10 through 12 focus on weight control methods and expand on some of the concepts presented in this chapter.

Measures of Energy

What is energy?

For our purposes, **energy** represents the capacity to do work. **Work** is one form of energy, often called mechanical energy. When we throw a ball or run a mile, we have done work; we have produced mechanical energy.

Energy exists in a variety of other forms in nature, such as the light energy of the sun, nuclear energy in uranium, electrical energy in lightning storms, heat energy in fires, and chemical energy in oil. The six forms of energy—mechanical, chemical, heat, electrical, light, and nuclear—are interchangeable according to various laws of thermodynamics. We take advantage of these laws every day. One such example is the use of the chemical energy in gasoline to produce mechanical energy—the movement of our cars.

In the human body, four of these types of energy are important. Our bodies possess stores of chemical energy that can be used to produce electrical energy for creation of electrical nerve impulses, to produce heat to help keep our body temperature at 37°C (98.6°F) even on cold days, and to produce mechanical work through muscle shortening so that we may move about.

The sun is the ultimate source of energy. Solar energy is harnessed by plants, through photosynthesis, to produce either plant carbohydrates, fats, or proteins, all forms of stored chemical energy. When humans consume plant and animal products, the carbohydrates, fats, and proteins undergo a series of metabolic changes and are utilized to develop body structure, to regulate body processes, or to provide a storage form of chemical energy (figure 3.1).

The optimal intake and output of energy is important to all individuals, but especially for the active person. To perform to capacity, body energy stores must be used in the most efficient manner possible.

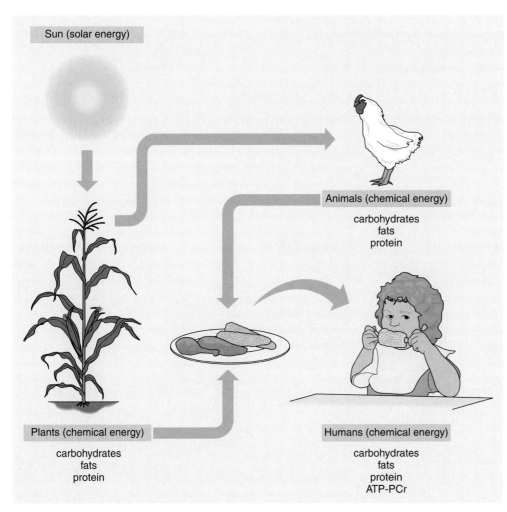

FIGURE 3.1 Through photosynthesis, plants utilize solar energy and convert it to chemical energy in the form of carbohydrates, fats, or proteins. Animals eat plants and convert the chemical energy into their own stores of chemical energy—primarily fat and protein. Humans ingest food from both plant and animal sources and convert the chemical energy for their own stores and use.

In the figure:

Sun (solar energy)

Animals (chemical energy)
carbohydrates
fats
protein

Plants (chemical energy)
carbohydrates
fats
protein

Humans (chemical energy)
carbohydrates
fats
protein
ATP-PCr

How do we measure work and energy?

Energy has been defined as the ability to do work. According to the physicist's definition, work is simply the product of force times vertical distance, or in formula format, Work = Force × Distance. When we speak of how fast work is done, the term **power** is used. Power is simply work divided by time, or Power = Work/Time.

Two major measurement systems have been used in the past to express energy in terms of either work or power. The metric system has been in use by most of the world, while England, its colonies, and the United States have used the English system. In an attempt to provide some uniformity in measurement systems around the world, the International Unit System (*Systeme International d'Unites,* or SI) has been developed. Most of the world has adopted the SI. Although legislation has been passed by Congress to convert the United States to the SI, and terms such as *gram, kilogram, milliliter, liter,* and *kilometer* are becoming more prevalent, it appears that it will take some time before this system becomes part of our everyday language.

The SI is used in most scientific journals today, but the other two systems appear in older journals. Terms that are used in each system are presented in table 3.1. For our purposes in this text, we shall use several English terms that are still in common usage in the United States, but if you read scientific literature, you should be able to convert values among the various systems if necessary. For example, work may be expressed as either foot-pounds, kilogram-meters (kgm), joules, or watts. If you weigh 150 pounds and climb a 20-foot flight of stairs in one minute, you have done 3,000 foot-pounds of work. One kgm is equal to 7.23 foot-pounds, so you would do about 415 kgm. One **joule** is equal to about 0.102 kgm, so you have done about 4,062 joules of work. One watt is equal to one joule per second, so you have generated about 68 watts of power. Some basic interrelationships among the measurement systems are noted in table 3.2. Other equivalents may be found in appendix A.

In general, exercise scientists and nutritionists are interested in measuring work output under two conditions. One condition involves specific exercise tasks. Various laboratory techniques have been developed to accurately record work output during exercise, such as measurement of kgm or watts on a cycle ergometer. The other condition involves measurement of work output during normal daily activities over prolonged periods of time, such as a 24-hour period.

TABLE 3.1 Terms in the English, metric, and international systems

Unit	English system	Metric system	International system
Mass	slug	kilogram (kg)	kilogram (kg)
Distance	foot (ft)	meter (m)	meter (m)
Time	second (s)	second (s)	second (s)
Force	pound (lb)	newton (N)	newton (N)
Work	foot-pound (ft-lb)	kilogram-meter (kgm)	joule (J)
Power	horsepower (hp)	watt (W)	watt (W)

TABLE 3.2   Some interrelationships between work measurement systems

Weight	Distance	Work	Power
1 kilogram = 2.2 pounds	1 meter = 3.28 feet	1 kgm = 7.23 foot-pounds	1 watt = 1 joule per second
1 kilogram = 1,000 grams	1 meter = 1.09 yards	1 kgm = 9.8 joules	1 watt = 6.12 kgm per minute 1 watt = 0.0013 horsepower
454 grams = 1 pound	1 foot = 0.30 meter	1 foot-pound = 0.138 kgm	1 horsepower = 550 foot-pounds per second
1 pound = 16 ounces	1,000 meters = 1 kilometer	1 foot-pound = 1.35 joules	1 horsepower = 33,000 foot-pounds per minute
1 ounce = 28.4 grams	1 kilometer = 0.6215 mile	1 newton = 0.102 kg	1 horsepower = 745.8 watts
3.5 ounces = 100 grams	1 mile = 1.61 kilometers 1 inch = 2.54 centimeters 1 centimeter = 0.39 inch	1 joule = 1 newton meter 1 kilojoule = 1,000 joules 1 megajoule = 1,000,000 joules 1 joule = 0.102 kgm 1 joule = 0.736 foot-pound 1 kilojoule = 102 kgm	

To measure work we need to know the weight of an object and the vertical distance through which it is moved. This is fine according to the formal definition of work, but are you doing work while holding a stationary weight out in front of your body? According to the formal definition, the answer is no, because the distance the weight moved is zero. How about when you come down stairs as compared to going up? It is much easier to descend the stairs, and yet according to the formula you have done the same amount of work. Also, how about when you run a mile? You know you have worked, but most of the distance you covered was horizontal, not vertical. Various devices, such as pedometers and accelerometers attached to the body, detect motion throughout the day and provide an approximation of daily work output. However, research comparing such devices to more accurate determinations of energy expenditure has shown that they may underestimate energy expenditure for some activities and overestimate it for others. Thus, measuring work output is not the same as measuring energy expenditure, and so we need to have means to express the energy expenditure of the human body other than simply the amount of work done.

Another means for measuring energy expenditure in the body involves chemical and heat energy. Without going into much detail, look briefly at several different methods for measuring energy production in humans. First, a device known as a **calorimeter** may be used to measure the energy content of a given substance. Figure 3.2 shows how a bomb calorimeter works. For example, a gram of fat contains a certain amount of chemical energy. When placed in the calorimeter and oxidized completely, the heat it gives off can be recorded. We then know the heat energy of one gram of fat and can equate it to chemical or work units of energy if needed. Large, expensive whole-room calorimeters (metabolic chambers) are available that can accommodate human

beings and measure their heat production under normal home activities and some conditions of exercise. This technique is known as *direct calorimetry.*

A second, more commonly used method of measuring energy is to determine the amount of oxygen an individual consumes, an *indirect calorimetry* technique. This procedure is normally done

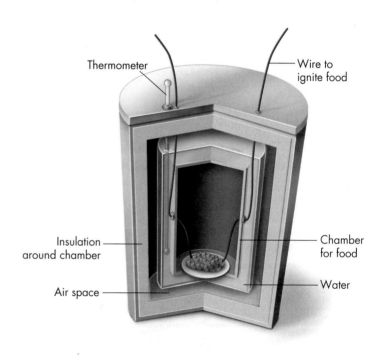

FIGURE 3.2   A bomb calorimeter. The food in the calorimeter is combusted via electrical ignition. The heat (Calories) given off by the food raises the temperature of the water, thereby providing data about the caloric content of specific foodstuffs.

under laboratory conditions (see figure 3.3), but lightweight portable oxygen analyzers are also available. The volume of oxygen one uses is usually expressed in liters (L) or milliliters (ml); one L is equal to 1,000 ml. One liter is slightly larger than a quart. In general, humans need oxygen, which helps metabolize the various nutrients in the body to produce energy. It is known that when oxygen combines with a gram of carbohydrate, fat, or protein, a certain amount of energy is released. If we can accurately measure the oxygen consumption (and carbon dioxide production) of an individual, we can get a pretty good measure of energy expenditure. The amount of oxygen used can be equated to other forms of energy, such as work done in foot-pounds or heat produced in Calories.

A third method is the doubly labeled water (DLW) technique in which stable isotopes of hydrogen and oxygen in water ($^2H_2^{18}O$) are ingested. This is a safe procedure as the isotopes are stable and emit no radiation. Analysis of urine and blood samples provide data on ^2H and ^{18}O excretion. The labeled oxygen is eliminated from the body as water and carbon dioxide, whereas the hydrogen is eliminated only as water. Subtracting the hydrogen losses from the oxygen losses provides a measure of carbon dioxide fluctuation, which may be converted to energy expenditure. Although expensive, the advantage of this technique is that it may be used with individuals while they perform their normal daily activities, and they need not be confined to a metabolic chamber or be attached to equipment to measure oxygen consumption.

Newer techniques have been developed to measure daily energy expenditure. Fully portable devices can be worn throughout the day and may monitor physiological functions such as muscle contraction, heart rate, oxygen consumption, and joint movements. Zhang and others indicated that the Intelligent Device for Energy Expenditure and Activity (IDEEA), a portable device that records body motion and postural changes second by second on a 24-hour basis,

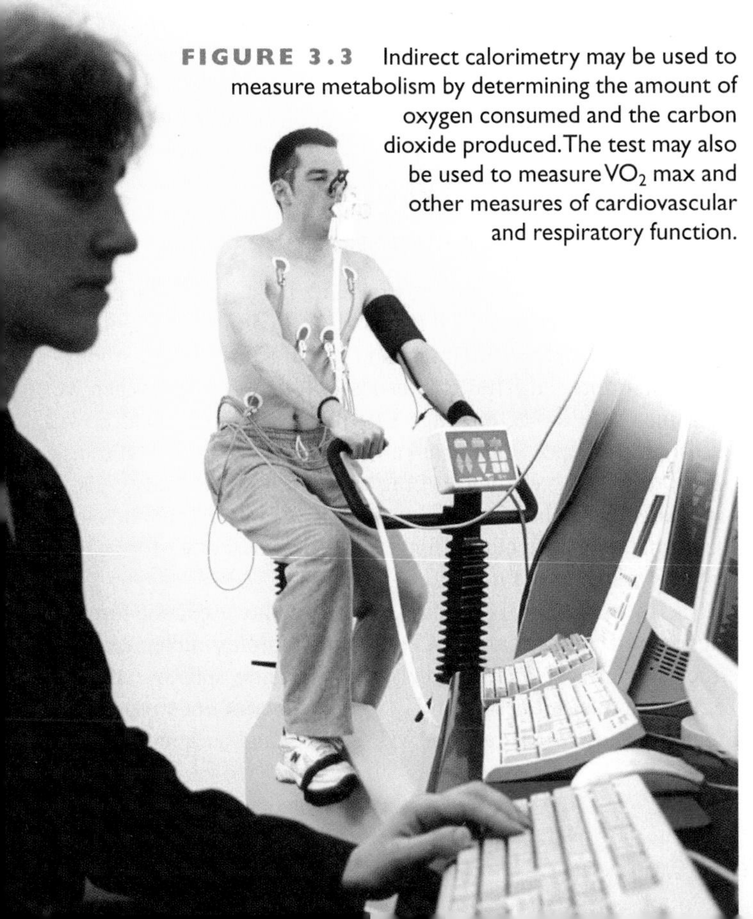

FIGURE 3.3 Indirect calorimetry may be used to measure metabolism by determining the amount of oxygen consumed and the carbon dioxide produced. The test may also be used to measure VO_2 max and other measures of cardiovascular and respiratory function.

has shown promise as a means to evaluate total daily body energy expenditure. Although all of these techniques to measure energy expenditure have limitations, they do provide useful data relative to the approximate energy cost of exercise and normal daily activities.

What is the most commonly used measure of energy?

Although there are a number of different ways to express energy, the most common term used in the past and still most prevalent and understood in the United States by most people is **Calorie.**

A calorie is a measure of heat. One gram calorie represents the amount of heat needed to raise the temperature of one gram of water one degree Celsius; it is sometimes called the gram calorie. A kilocalorie is equal to 1,000 small calories. It is the amount of heat needed to raise 1 kg of water (1 L) one degree Celsius. In human nutrition, because the gram calorie is so small, the kilocalorie is the main expression of energy. It is usually abbreviated as kcal, kc, or C, or capitalized as Calorie. Throughout this book, *Calorie* or *C* will refer to the kilocalorie.

According to the principles underlying the first law of thermodynamics, energy may be equated from one form to another. Thus, the Calorie, which represents thermal or heat energy, may be equated to other forms of energy. Relative to our discussion concerning physical work such as exercise and its interrelationships with nutrition, it is important to equate the Calorie with mechanical work and the chemical energy stored in the body. As will be explained later, most stored chemical energy must undergo some form of oxidation in order to release its energy content as work.

The following represents some equivalent energy values for the Calorie in terms of mechanical work and oxygen utilization. Some examples illustrating several of the interrelationships will be used in later chapters.

$$1\ C = 3,086\ \text{foot-pounds}$$
$$1\ C = 427\ \text{kgm}$$
$$1\ C = 4.2\ \text{kilojoules (kJ) or 4,200 joules}$$
$$1\ C = 200\ \text{ml oxygen (approximately)}$$

Although the Calorie is the most commonly used expression in the United States for energy, work, and heat, **kilojoule** is the proper term in the SI. It is important for you to be able to convert from Calories to kilojoules, and vice versa. To convert Calories to kilojoules, multiply the number of Calories by 4.2 (4.186 to be exact); to convert kilojoules to Calories, divide the number of kilojoules by 4.2. Simply multiplying or dividing by 4 for each respective conversion will provide a ballpark estimate. In some cases megajoules (MJ), a million joules, are used to express energy. One MJ equals about 240 Calories, or 4.2 MJ is the equivalent of about 1,000 Calories.

Through the use of a calorimeter, the energy contents of the basic nutrients have been determined. Energy may be derived from the three major foodstuffs—carbohydrate, fat, and protein—plus alcohol. The caloric value of each of these three nutrients may vary somewhat, depending on the particular structure of the different forms. For example, carbohydrate may exist in several forms—as glucose, sucrose, or starch—and the caloric value of each will differ slightly. In general, one gram of each of the three nutrients, measured in a calorimeter, yields the following Calories:

$$1 \text{ gram carbohydrate} = 4.30 \text{ C}$$

$$1 \text{ gram fat} = 9.45 \text{ C}$$

$$1 \text{ gram protein} = 5.65 \text{ C}$$

$$1 \text{ gram alcohol} = 7.00 \text{ C}$$

Unfortunately, or fortunately if one is trying to lose weight, humans do not extract all of this energy from the food they eat. The human body is not as efficient as the calorimeter. For one, the body cannot completely absorb all the food eaten. Only about 97 percent of ingested carbohydrate, 95 percent of fat, and 92 percent of protein are absorbed. In addition, a good percentage of the protein is not completely oxidized in the body, with some of the nitrogen waste products being excreted in the urine. In summary, then, the caloric value of food is reduced somewhat in relation to the values given above. Although the following values are not exactly precise, they are approximate enough to be used effectively in determining the caloric values of the foods we eat. Thus, the following caloric values are used throughout this text as a practical guide:

$$1 \text{ gram carbohydrate} = 4 \text{ C}$$

$$1 \text{ gram fat} = 9 \text{ C}$$

$$1 \text{ gram protein} = 4 \text{ C}$$

$$1 \text{ gram alcohol} = 7 \text{ C}$$

For our purposes, the Calories in food represent a form of potential energy to be used by our bodies to produce heat and work (figure 3.4). However, the fact that fat has about twice the amount of energy per gram as carbohydrate does not mean that it is a better

1 teaspoon sugar = 5 grams carbohydrate = 20 Calories

1 teaspoon salad oil = 5 grams fat = 45 Calories

FIGURE 3.5 The Calorie as a measure of energy.

energy source for the active individual (figure 3.5), as we shall see in later chapters when we talk of the efficient utilization of body fuels.

Key Concept Recap

► Energy represents the capacity to do work, and food is the source of energy for humans.
► The Calorie, or kilocalorie, is a measure of chemical energy stored in foods; this chemical energy can be transformed into heat and mechanical work energy in the body. A related measure is the kilojoule. One Calorie is equal to 4.2 kilojoules.

Check for Yourself

Measure the height of a step on a flight of stairs or bleachers and convert it to feet (9 inches = 0.75 foot). Stepping in place, count the total number of steps you do in one minute. Multiply your count by the step height to determine the number of feet you have climbed. Next, multiply this value by your body weight in pounds to determine the number of foot-pounds of work you have done. Then, convert this number of foot-pounds to the equivalent amount of kilogram-meters (kgm), kilojoules (kJ), and Calories.

FIGURE 3.4 Eight ounces of orange juice will provide enough chemical energy to enable an average man to produce enough mechanical energy to run about one mile.

Human Energy Systems

How is energy stored in the body?

The ultimate source of all energy on earth is the sun. Solar energy is harnessed by plants, which take carbon, hydrogen, oxygen, and nitrogen from their environment and manufacture either carbohydrate, fat, or protein. These foods possess stored energy. When we consume these foods, our digestive processes break them down into simple compounds that are absorbed into the body and transported to various cells. One of the basic purposes of body cells is to transform the chemical energy of these simple compounds into forms that may be available for immediate use or other forms that may be available for future use.

Energy in the body is available for immediate use in the form of **adenosine triphosphate (ATP).** It is a complex molecule constructed with high-energy bonds, which, when split by enzyme action, can release energy rapidly for a number of body processes, including muscle contraction. ATP is classified as a high-energy compound and is stored in the tissues in small amounts. It is important to note that ATP is the immediate source of energy for all body functions, and the other energy stores are used to replenish ATP at varying rates. Myburgh notes that muscle contraction is totally dependent on ATP, so the body has developed an intricate system to help replenish ATP as rapidly as needed.

Another related high-energy phosphate compound, **phosphocreatine (PCr),** is also found in the tissues in small amounts. Although it cannot be used as an immediate source of energy, it can rapidly replenish ATP.

ATP may be formed from either carbohydrate, fat, or protein after those nutrients have undergone some complex biochemical changes in the body. Figure 3.6 represents a basic schematic of how ATP is formed from each of these three nutrients. PCr is actually derived from excess ATP.

Because ATP and PCr are found in very small amounts in the body and can be used up in a matter of seconds, it is important to have adequate energy stores as a backup system. Your body stores of carbohydrate, fat, and protein can provide you with ample amounts of ATP, enough to last for many weeks even on a starvation diet. The digestion and metabolism of carbohydrate, fat, and protein are discussed in their respective chapters, so it is unnecessary to present that full discussion here. However, you may wish to preview figure 3.12 in order to visualize the metabolic interrelationships between the three nutrients in the body. For those who desire more detailed schematics of energy pathways, appendix G provides some of the major metabolic pathways for carbohydrate, fat, and protein.

It is important to note that parts of each energy nutrient may be converted to the other two nutrients in the body under certain circumstances. For example, protein may be converted into carbohydrate during prolonged exercise, whereas excess dietary carbohydrate may be converted to fat in the body during rest.

Table 3.3 summarizes how much energy is stored in the human body as ATP, PCr, and various forms of carbohydrate, fat, and

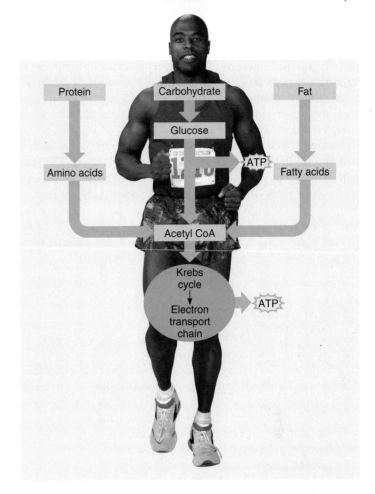

FIGURE 3.6 Simplified schematic of ATP formation from carbohydrate, fat, and protein. All three nutrients may be used to form ATP, but carbohydrate and fat are the major sources via the aerobic metabolism of the Krebs cycle. Carbohydrate may be used to produce small amounts of ATP under anaerobic conditions, thus providing humans with the ability to produce energy rapidly without oxygen for relatively short periods. For more details, see appendix G.

TABLE 3.3 Major energy stores in the human body with approximate total caloric value*

Energy source	Major storage form	Total body Calories	Total body kilojoules	Distance covered**
ATP	Tissues	1	4.2	17.5 yards
PCr	Tissues	4	16.8	70 yards
Carbohydrate	Serum glucose	20	88	350 yards
	Liver glycogen	400	1,680	4 miles
	Muscle glycogen	1,500	6,300	15 miles
Fat	Serum-free fatty acids	7	29.2	123 yards
	Serum triglycerides	75	315	0.75 mile
	Muscle triglycerides	2,500	10,500	25 miles
	Adipose tissue triglycerides	80,000	336,000	800 miles
Protein	Muscle protein	30,000	126,000	300 miles

*These values may have extreme variations depending on the size of the individual, amount of body fat, physical fitness level, and diet.
**Running at an energy cost of 100 Calories per mile (1.6 kilometers).

protein. The total amount of energy, represented by Calories, is approximate and may vary considerably between individuals. Carbohydrate is stored in limited amounts as blood (serum) glucose, liver glycogen, and muscle glycogen. The largest amount of energy is stored in the body as fats. Fats are stored as triglycerides in both muscle tissue and adipose (fat) tissue; triglycerides and free fatty acids (FFA) in the blood are a limited supply. The protein of the body tissues, particularly muscle tissue, is a large reservoir of energy but is not used under normal circumstances. Table 3.3 also depicts how far an individual could run using the total of each of these energy sources as the sole supply. The role of each of these macronutrient energy stores during exercise is an important consideration that is discussed briefly in this chapter and more extensively in their respective chapters.

What are the human energy systems?

Why does the human body store chemical energy in a variety of different forms? If we look at human energy needs from an historical perspective, the answer becomes obvious. Sometimes humans needed to produce energy at a rapid rate, such as when sprinting to safety to avoid dangerous animals. Thus, a fast rate of energy production was an important human energy feature that helped ensure survival. At other times, our ancient ancestors may have been deprived of adequate food for long periods, and thus needed a storage capacity for chemical energy that would sustain life throughout these times of deprivation. Hence, the ability to store large amounts of energy was also important for survival. These two factors—rate of energy production and energy capacity—appear to be determining factors in the development of human energy systems.

One need only watch weekend television programming for several weeks to realize the diversity of sports popular throughout the world. Each of these sports imposes certain requirements on humans who want to be successful competitors. For some sports, such as weight lifting, the main requirement is brute strength, while for others such as tennis, quick reactions and hand/eye coordination are important. A major consideration in most sports is the rate of energy production, which can range from the explosive power needed by a shot-putter to the tremendous endurance capacity of an ultramarathoner. The physical performance demands of different sports require specific sources of energy.

As noted above, the body stores energy in a variety of ways—in ATP, PCr, muscle glycogen, and so on. In order for this energy to be used to produce muscular contractions and movement, it must undergo certain biochemical reactions in the muscle. These biochemical reactions serve as a basis for classifying human energy expenditure by three energy, or power,

systems: the ATP-PCr system, the lactic acid system, and the oxygen system.

The **ATP-PCr system** is also known as the phosphagen system because both adenosine triphosphate (ATP) and phosphocreatine (PCr) contain phosphates. ATP is the immediate source of energy for almost all body processes, including muscle contraction. This high-energy compound, stored in the muscles, rapidly releases energy when an electrical impulse arrives in the muscle. No matter what you do, scratch your nose or lift 100 pounds, ATP breakdown makes the movement possible. ATP must be present for the muscles to contract. The body has a limited supply of ATP and must replace it rapidly if muscular work is to continue. See figure 3.7 for a graphical representation of ATP breakdown.

PCr, which is also a high-energy compound found in the muscle, can help form ATP rapidly as ATP is used. Energy released when PCr splits is used to form ATP from ADP and P. PCr is also in short supply and needs to be replenished if used. PCr breakdown to help resynthesize ATP is illustrated in figure 3.8.

The ATP-PCr system is critical to energy production. Because these phosphagens are in short supply, any all-out exercise for 5 to 10 seconds could deplete the supply in a given muscle. Hence, the phosphagens must be replaced, and this is the function of the other energy sources. Although some supplements, such as creatine, dis-

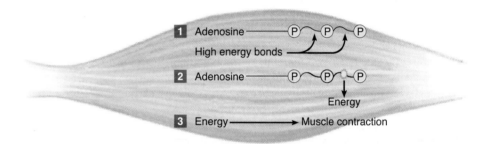

FIGURE 3.7 ATP, adenosine triphosphate. (*1*) ATP is stored in the muscle in limited amounts. (*2*) Splitting of a high-energy bond releases adenosine diphosphate (ADP), inorganic phosphate (P), and energy, which (*3*) can be used for many body processes, including muscular contraction. The ATP stores may be used maximally for fast, all-out bursts of power that last about one second. ATP must be replenished from other sources for muscle contraction to continue.

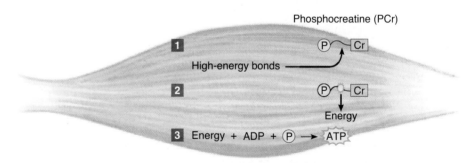

FIGURE 3.8 Phosphocreatine (PCr). (*1*) PCr is stored in the muscle in limited amounts. (*2*) Splitting of the high-energy bond releases energy, which (*3*) can be used to rapidly synthesize ATP from ADP and P. ATP and PCr are called phosphagens and together represent the ATP-PCr energy system. This system is utilized primarily for quick, maximal exercises lasting about 1 to 6 seconds, such as sprinting.

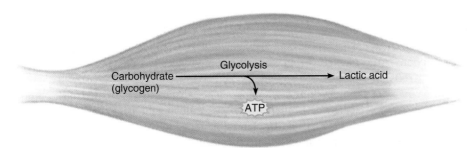

FIGURE 3.9 The lactic acid energy system. Muscle glycogen can break down without the utilization of oxygen. This process is called anaerobic glycolysis. (See appendix G, figure G.1, for more details.) ATP is produced rapidly, but lactic acid is the end product. Lactic acid may be a major cause of fatigue in the muscle. The lactic acid energy system is utilized primarily during exercise bouts of very high intensity, those conducted at maximal rates for about 30 to 120 seconds.

cussed in later chapters are theorized to facilitate ATP or PCr replenishment, we do not eat ATP-PCr per se, but we can produce it from the other nutrients stored in our body. PCr replenishment will not be discussed, but keep in mind that when ATP is being regenerated, so is some PCr. In summary, the value of the ATP-PCr system is its ability to provide energy rapidly, for example, in sport events such as competitive weight lifting or sprinting 100 meters. *Anaerobic power* is a term often associated with the ATP-PCr energy system.

The **lactic acid system** cannot be used directly as a source of energy for muscular contraction, but it can help replace ATP rapidly when necessary. If you are exercising at a high intensity level and need to replenish ATP rapidly, the next best source of energy besides PCr is muscle glycogen. To be used for energy, muscle glycogen must be broken down to glucose, which undergoes a series of reactions to eventually form ATP, a process called **glycolysis.** One of the major factors controlling the metabolic fate of muscle glycogen is the availability of oxygen in the muscle cell. In simple terms, if oxygen is available, a large amount of ATP is formed. This is known as **aerobic glycolysis.** If inadequate oxygen is available to meet the energy demands of the exercise task or to maintain a high level of aerobic glycolysis, then insufficient ATP is formed and lactic acid is a by-product of the process to generate more ATP. This is known as anaerobic (inadequate oxygen) glycolysis; **anaerobic glycolysis** is the scientific term for the lactic acid energy system. The lactic acid system is diagrammed in figure 3.9. It is used in sport events in which energy production is near maximal for 30–120 seconds, such as a 200- or 800-meter run. *Anaerobic capacity* is a term often associated with the lactic acid energy system.

The lactic acid system has the advantage of producing ATP rapidly. Its capacity is limited in comparison to aerobic glycolysis, for only about 5 percent of the total ATP production from muscle glycogen can be released. Moreover, the lactic acid produced as a by-product may be involved in the onset of fatigue. Anaerobic glycolysis releases hydrogen ions, increasing the acidity within the muscle cell and disturbing the normal cell environment. The processes of energy release and muscle contraction in the muscle cell are controlled by enzymes whose functions may be impaired by the increased acidity in the cell. The lactate present after loss of the hydrogen ion still has considerable energy content, which may be used by other tissues for energy or converted back into glucose in the liver.

The third system is the **oxygen system.** It is also known as the aerobic system. *Aerobics* is a term used by Dr. Kenneth Cooper in 1968 to describe a system of exercising that created an exercise revolution in this country. In essence, aerobic exercises are designed to stress the oxygen system and provide benefits for the heart and lungs. Figure 3.10 represents the major physiological processes involved in the oxygen system. The oxygen system, like the lactic acid system, cannot be used directly as a source of energy for muscle contraction, but it does produce ATP in rather large quantities from other energy sources in the body. Muscle glycogen, liver glycogen, blood glucose, muscle triglycerides, blood FFA and triglycerides, adipose cell triglycerides, and body protein all may be ultimate sources of energy for ATP production and subsequent muscle contraction. To do this, glycogen and fats must be present within the muscle cell or must enter the muscle cell as glucose, FFA, or amino acids. Through a complex series of reactions metabolic by-products of carbohydrate, fat, or protein combine with oxygen to produce energy, carbon diox-

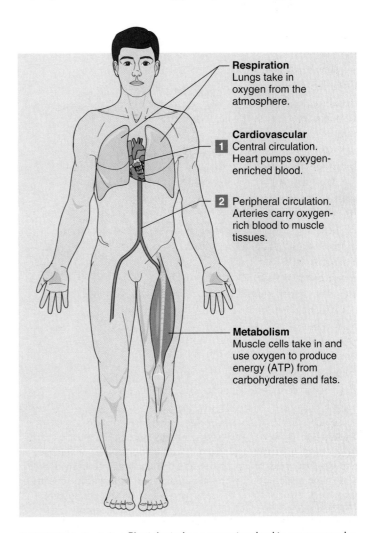

Respiration
Lungs take in oxygen from the atmosphere.

Cardiovascular
1 Central circulation. Heart pumps oxygen-enriched blood.

2 Peripheral circulation. Arteries carry oxygen-rich blood to muscle tissues.

Metabolism
Muscle cells take in and use oxygen to produce energy (ATP) from carbohydrates and fats.

FIGURE 3.10 Physiological processes involved in oxygen uptake.

ide, and water. These reactions occur in the energy powerhouse of the cell, the **mitochondrion.** The whole series of events of oxidative energy production primarily involves aerobic processing of carbohydrates and fats (and small amounts of protein) through the **Krebs cycle** and the **electron transfer system.** The oxygen system is depicted in figure 3.11. The Krebs cycle and the electron transfer system represent a highly structured array of enzymes designed to remove hydrogen, carbon dioxide, and electrons from substrates such as glucose. At different steps in this process, energy is released and ATP is formed, with most of the ATP produced during the electron transfer process. The hydrogen and electrons eventually combine with oxygen to form water (see appendix G).

Although the rate of ATP production is lower, the major advantage of the oxygen system over the other two energy systems is the production of large amounts of energy in the form of ATP. However, oxygen from the air we breathe must be delivered to the mus-

cle cells deep in the body and enter the mitochondria to be used. This process may be adequate to handle mild and moderate levels of exercise but may not be able to meet the demand of very strenuous exercise. The oxygen system is used primarily in sports emphasizing endurance, such as distance runs ranging from 5 kilometers (3.1 miles) to the 26.2-mile marathon and beyond.

Hawley and Hopkins subdivided the oxygen energy system into two systems. The scientific terms for these two subdivisions are aerobic glycolysis, which uses carbohydrates (muscle glycogen and blood glucose) for energy production, and **aerobic lipolysis,** which uses fats (muscle triglycerides, blood FFA). As discussed in the next two chapters, carbohydrate is the more efficient fuel during high-intensity exercise, whereas fat becomes the predominant fuel used at lower levels of exercise intensity. Thus, aerobic glycolysis provides most of the energy in high-intensity aerobic running events such as 5 kilometers (3.1 miles), 10 kilometers (6.2 miles), and even races up to two hours, while aerobic lipolysis may contribute significant amounts of energy in more prolonged aerobic events, such as ultramarathons of 50 to 100 kilometers (31 to 62 miles). Aerobic glycolysis and aerobic lipolysis may respectively be referred to as *aerobic power* and *aerobic capacity*. Details relative to the role of these energy systems during exercise are presented in chapters 4 and 5.

Figure 3.12 presents a simplified schematic reviewing the three human energy systems.

What nutrients are necessary for the operation of the human energy systems?

Although the energy for the formation of ATP is derived from the energy stores in carbohydrate, fat, and sometimes protein, this energy transformation and utilization would not occur without the participation of the other major nutrients—water, vitamins, and minerals. These three classes of nutrients function very closely with protein in the structure and function of numerous enzymes, many of which are active in the muscle-cell energy processes.

Water is used to help break up and transform some energy compounds by a process known as hydrolysis.

Several vitamins are needed for energy to be released from the cell sources. For example, niacin serves an important function in glycolysis, thiamin is needed to convert glycolytic end products to acetyl CoA for entrance into the Krebs cycle, and riboflavin is essential to forming ATP through the Krebs cycle and electron transfer system. A number of other B vitamins are also involved in facets of energy transformation within the cell.

Minerals, too, are essential for cellular energy processes. Iron is one of the more critical compounds. Aside from helping hemoglobin deliver oxygen to the muscle cell, it is also a component of myoglobin and the cytochrome part of the electron transfer system. It is needed for proper utilization of oxygen within the cell itself. Other minerals such as zinc, magnesium, potassium, sodium, and calcium are involved in a variety of ways, either as parts of active enzymes, in energy storage, or in the muscle-contraction process.

Proper utilization of body energy sources requires attention not only to the major energy nutrients but also to the regulatory nutrients—water, vitamins, and minerals. In addition, other nutrients and non-nutrients (such as creatine and caffeine) found in food may affect energy metabolism.

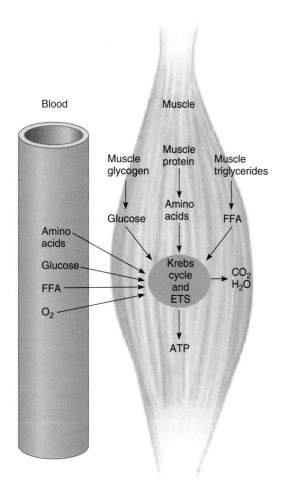

FIGURE 3.11 The oxygen energy system. The muscle stores of glycogen and triglycerides, along with blood supplies of glucose and free fatty acids (FFA), as well as small amounts of muscle protein and amino acids, undergo complex biochemical changes for entrance into the Krebs cycle and the associated electron transfer system (ETS). In this process, in which oxygen is the final acceptor to the electron, large amounts of ATP may be produced. The oxygen energy system is utilized primarily during endurance-type exercises, those lasting longer than 4 or 5 minutes. (See appendix G for more details.)

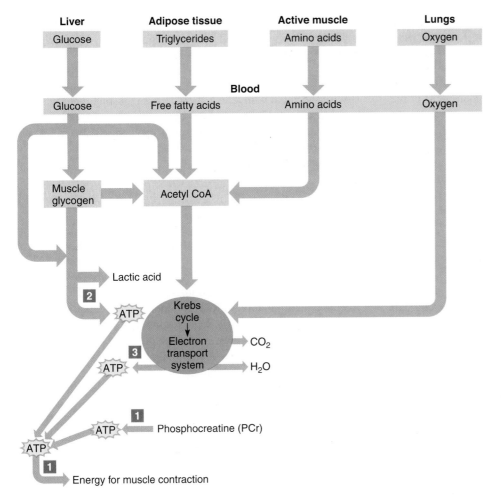

Liver — Glucose
Adipose tissue — Triglycerides
Active muscle — Amino acids
Lungs — Oxygen

Blood

Glucose | Free fatty acids | Amino acids | Oxygen

Muscle glycogen → Acetyl CoA

Lactic acid

2

ATP

Krebs cycle ↓ Electron transport system → CO_2 → H_2O

3 ATP

1 ATP ← Phosphocreatine (PCr)

ATP

1 → Energy for muscle contraction

FIGURE 3.12 Simplified flow diagram of the three energy systems. The major nutrients and oxygen are transported to the cells for energy production. In the muscles, ATP is the immediate source of energy for muscle contraction. *(1)* The ATP-PCr system is represented by muscle stores of ATP and phosphocreatine (PCr); PCr can replenish ATP rapidly. *(2)* Glucose or muscle glycogen can produce ATP rapidly via the lactic acid system. *(3)* The oxygen system can produce large amounts of ATP via the aerobic processes in the Krebs cycle. Numerous other energy pathways exist, and some are described in chapter 4 (carbohydrates), chapter 5 (fats), and chapter 6 (protein).

Key Concept Recap

▶ Carbohydrates and fats are the primary energy nutrients, but protein may also be an energy source. In the human body one gram of carbohydrate = 4 Calories, one gram of fat = 9 Calories, and one gram of protein = 4 Calories. Alcohol is also a source of energy; one gram = 7 Calories.

▶ The potential energy sources in the body include ATP and PCr; serum glucose, glycogen in the liver and muscle; serum free fatty acids (FFA); triglycerides in the muscle and in adipose tissue; and muscle protein.

▶ Three human energy systems have been classified on the basis of their ability to release energy at different rates of speed; they are the ATP-PCr, lactic acid, and oxygen energy systems.

Human Energy Metabolism during Rest

What is metabolism?

Human **metabolism** represents the sum total of all physical and chemical changes that take place within the body. The transformation of food to energy, the formation of new compounds such as hormones and enzymes, the growth of bone and muscle tissue, the destruction of body tissues, and a host of other physiological processes are parts of the metabolic process.

Metabolism involves two fundamental processes, anabolism and catabolism. Anabolism is a building-up process, or constructive metabolism. Complex body components are synthesized from the basic nutrients. For the active individual, this may mean an increased muscle mass through weight training or an increased amount of cellular enzymes to better use oxygen following endurance-type training. Energy is needed for anabolism to occur. Catabolism is the tearing-down process. This involves the disintegration of body compounds into their simpler components. The breakdown of muscle glycogen to glucose and eventually CO_2, H_2O, and energy is an example of a catabolic process. The energy released from some catabolic processes is used to support the energy needs of anabolism.

Metabolism is life. It represents human energy. The metabolic rate reflects how rapidly the body is using its energy stores, and this rate can vary tremendously depending upon a number of factors. For all practical purposes, the **total daily energy expenditure (TDEE)** may be accounted for by three factors: basal energy expenditure, increases due to eating a meal, and physical activity. Basal energy expenditure accounts for the largest component of TDEE, whereas physical activity is the most variable. We shall examine basal energy expenditure and the effect of eating in this section, while the role of physical activity, or exercise, will be covered in the section "Human Energy Metabolism during Exercise."

What factors account for the amount of energy expended during rest?

The body is constantly using energy to build up and tear down substances within the cells. Certain automatic body functions such as contraction of the heart, breathing, secretion of hormones, and the constant activity of the nervous system also are consuming energy.

Basal metabolism, or the **basal metabolic rate (BMR),** represents the energy requirements of the many different cellular and tissue processes that are necessary to continuing physiological activities in a resting, postabsorptive state throughout most of the day. Other than sleeping, it is the lowest rate of energy expenditure. The determination of the BMR is a clinical procedure conducted in a laboratory or hospital setting. The individual fasts for 12 hours. Then, with the subject in a reclining position, the individual's oxygen consumption and carbon dioxide production are measured. Through proper calculations, the BMR is determined. **Basal energy expenditure (BEE)** represents the BMR extrapolated over a 24-hour period.

The **resting metabolic rate (RMR)** is slightly higher than the BMR. It represents the BMR plus small amounts of additional energy expenditure associated with eating and previous muscular activity. According to the National Research Council, the BMR and RMR differ by less than 10 percent. Consequently, although there are some fine differences in the two terms, they are often used interchangeably. Additionally, the National Research Council uses the term **resting energy expenditure (REE)** to account for the energy processes at rest when extrapolated over 24 hours. In general, we shall use REE to also represent RMR.

Although some of the energy released during oxidative processes at rest supports physiological functions, such as pumping activity of the heart muscle, the majority of energy is released as heat, a thermal effect that keeps our body temperature at about 98.6° Fahrenheit (37° Celsius). Eating a meal and exercise are two other factors that induce a thermal effect.

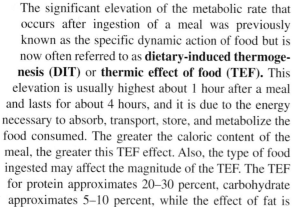

What effect does eating a meal have on the metabolic rate?

The significant elevation of the metabolic rate that occurs after ingestion of a meal was previously known as the specific dynamic action of food but is now often referred to as **dietary-induced thermogenesis (DIT)** or **thermic effect of food (TEF).** This elevation is usually highest about 1 hour after a meal and lasts for about 4 hours, and it is due to the energy necessary to absorb, transport, store, and metabolize the food consumed. The greater the caloric content of the meal, the greater this TEF effect. Also, the type of food ingested may affect the magnitude of the TEF. The TEF for protein approximates 20–30 percent, carbohydrate approximates 5–10 percent, while the effect of fat is minimal (0–5 percent). Crovetti and others noted that a very high protein meal (68% of Calories) elicited a greater TEF for seven hours post-eating than did corresponding diets high in carbohydrate and fat. However, the increased TEF averaged only about six Calories more per hour, not an appreciable amount. Alcohol intake also causes about a 15 percent rise in the REE.

The TEF is expressed as a percent of the energy content of the ingested meal. The normal increase in the BMR due to TEF from a mixed meal of carbohydrate, fat, and protein is about 5–10 per-

cent. A TEF of 10 percent will account for 50 Calories of a 500 Calorie meal. The remaining 450 Calories are available for energy use by other body processes. The TEF effect accounts for approximately 5–10 percent of the total daily energy expenditure.

de Jonge and Bray, in a review of 49 studies, reported that obesity is associated with a decreased TEF, suggesting that the obese are more efficient in storing fat. The composition of some diets for weight-loss purposes has been based upon this TEF effect; this topic is discussed in chapters 10 and 11 concerning diets for weight control.

How can I estimate my daily resting energy expenditure (REE)?

There are several ways to estimate your REE, but whichever method is used, the value obtained is an estimate and will have some error associated with it. To get a truly accurate value you would need a clinical evaluation, such as a standard BMR test. Accurate determination of REE is important for clinicians dealing with obesity patients, for such testing is needed to rule out hypometabolism. However, a number of formula estimates may give you an approximation of your daily REE.

Table 3.4 provides a simple method for calculating the REE of males and females of varying ages. Examples are provided in the table along with calculation of a 10-percent variability. Keep in mind that this is only an estimate of the daily REE, and additional energy would be expended during the day through the TEF effect and the effect of physical activity, as noted later.

A very simple, rough estimate of your REE is one Calorie per kilogram body weight per hour. Using this procedure, the estimated value for the male in table 3.4 is 1,680 Calories per day (1×70 kg $\times 24$ hours) and for the female is 1,320 Calories (1×55 kg $\times 24$ hours), values which are not substantially different from those calculated by the table procedure.

What genetic factors affect my REE?

Your REE is directly related to the amount of metabolically active tissue that you possess. At rest, tissues such as the heart, liver, kidneys, and other internal organs are more metabolically active than muscle tissue, but muscle tissue is more metabolically active than fat. Changes in the proportion of these tissues in your body will therefore cause changes in your REE.

Many factors influencing the REE, such as age, sex, natural hormonal activity, body size and surface area, and to a degree, body composition, are genetically determined. The effect of some of these factors on the REE is generally well known. Because infants have a large proportion of metabolically active tissue and are growing rapidly, their REE is extremely high. The REE declines through childhood, adolescence, and adulthood as full growth and maturation are achieved. Individuals with naturally greater muscle mass in comparison to body fat have a higher REE; the REE of women is about 10–15 percent lower than that of men, mainly because women have a higher proportion of fat to muscle tissue. Genetically lean individuals have a higher REE than do stocky individuals because their body surface area ratio is larger in

TABLE 3.4 Estimation of the daily resting energy expenditure (REE)

Age (years)	Equation
Males	
3–9	$(22.7 \times \text{body weight*}) + 495$
10–17	$(17.5 \times \text{body weight}) + 651$
18–29	$(15.3 \times \text{body weight}) + 679$
30–60	$(11.6 \times \text{body weight}) + 879$
> 60	$(13.5 \times \text{body weight}) + 487$
Example	
154-lb male, age 20	
154 lbs/2.2 = 70 kg	
$(15.3 \times 70) + 679 = 1,750$	
Females	
3–9	$(22.5 \times \text{body weight*}) + 499$
10–17	$(12.2 \times \text{body weight}) + 746$
18–29	$(14.7 \times \text{body weight}) + 496$
30–60	$(8.7 \times \text{body weight}) + 829$
> 60	$(10.5 \times \text{body weight}) + 596$
Example	
121-lb female, age 20	
121 lbs/2.2 = 55 kg	
$(14.7 \times 55) + 496 = 1,304$	

To get a range of values, simply add or subtract a normal 10-percent variation to the RMR estimate.

Male example: 10 percent of 1,750 = 175 Calories
Normal range = 1,575–1,925 Calories/day
Female example: 10 percent of 1,304 = 130 Calories
Normal range = 1,174–1,434 Calories/day

*Body weight is expressed in kilograms (kg).

proportion to their weight (body volume) and they lose more body heat through radiation.

How does body composition affect my REE?

Body composition may be changed so as to alter REE. Losing body weight, including both body fat and muscle tissue, generally lowers the total daily REE. The REE may be decreased significantly in obese individuals who go on a very low-Calorie diet of less than 800 Calories per day. The decrease in the REE, which is greater than would be due to weight loss alone, may be caused by lowered levels of thyroid hormones. In one study, the REE of obese subjects dropped 9.4 percent on a diet containing only 472 Calories per day. This topic is covered in more detail in chapters 10 and 11. The possibility of decreased REE in some athletes who maintain low body weight through exercise, such as female distance runners and male wrestlers, has been the subject of recent debate and will be covered in chapter 10 when we discuss body composition.

On the other hand, maintaining normal body weight while reducing body fat and increasing muscle mass may raise the REE slightly because muscle tissue has a somewhat higher metabolic level than fat tissue or because the ratio of body surface area to body weight is increased. The decline in the REE that occurs with aging may be attributed partially to physical inactivity with a consequent loss of the more metabolically active muscle tissue and an accumulation of body fat. Methods to lose body fat and increase muscle mass are covered in chapters 11 and 12.

What environmental factors may also influence the REE?

Several lifestyle and environmental factors may influence our metabolism. For example, although caffeine is not a food, it is a common ingredient in some of the foods we may eat or drink. Caffeine is a stimulant and may elicit a significant rise in the REE. One study reported that the caffeine in 2–3 cups of regular coffee increased the REE 10–12 percent.

Smoking cigarettes also raises the REE. Apparently the nicotine in tobacco stimulates the metabolism similarly to caffeine. This may be one of the reasons why some individuals gain weight when they stop smoking.

Climatic conditions, especially temperature changes, may also raise the REE. Exposure to the cold may stimulate the secretion of several hormones and muscular shivering, which may stimulate heat production up to 400 percent. Exposure to warm or hot environments will increase energy expenditure through greater cardiovascular demands and the sweating response. Altitude exposure will also increase REE due to increased ventilation.

Many of these factors influencing the REE are important in themselves but may also be important considerations relative to weight control programs and body temperature regulation. Thus, they are discussed further in later chapters.

The most important factor that can increase the metabolic rate in general is exercise. As we shall see in the next section, exercise also may exert some effects upon the REE.

What energy sources are used during rest?

The vast majority of the energy consumed during a resting situation is used to drive the automatic physiological processes in the body. Because the muscles expend little energy during rest, there is no need to produce ATP rapidly. Hence, the oxygen system is able to provide the necessary ATP for resting physiological processes.

The oxygen system can use carbohydrates, fats, and protein as energy sources. However, as noted in chapter 6, protein is not used as a major energy source under normal dietary conditions. Carbohydrates and fats, when combined with oxygen in the cells, are the major energy substrates during rest. Several factors may influence which of the two nutrients is predominantly used. In general, though, on a mixed diet of carbohydrate, protein, and fat, about 40 percent of the REE is derived from carbohydrate and about 60 percent comes from fat. However, eating a diet rich in carbohydrate or fat will increase the percent of the REE derived, respectively, from carbohydrate and fat. Also, when carbohydrate levels are low, such as after an overnight fast, the percentage of the REE derived from fat increases.

Human Energy Metabolism during Exercise

What effect does muscular exercise have on the metabolic rate?

As noted in the previous section, the REE is measured with the subject at rest in a reclining position. Any physical activity will raise metabolic activity above the REE and thus increase energy expenditure. Accounting for changes in physical activity over the day may provide a reasonable, although imprecise, estimate of the total daily energy expenditure. Very light activities such as sitting, standing, playing cards, cooking, and typing all increase energy output above the REE, but we normally do not think of them as exercise as noted later in this chapter. For purposes of this discussion, the **exercise metabolic rate (EMR),** represents the increase in metabolism brought about by moderate or strenuous physical activity such as brisk walking, climbing stairs, cycling, dancing, running, and other such planned exercise activities. The EMR is known more appropriately as the **thermic effect of exercise (TEE).**

Exercise is a stressor to the body, and almost all body systems respond. If the exercise is continued daily, the body systems begin to adapt to the stress of exercise. As noted previously and as we shall see in later chapters, these adaptations may have significant health benefits. The two body systems most involved in exercise are the nervous system and the muscular system. The nervous sys-

tem is needed to activate muscle contraction, but it is in the muscle cell itself that the energetics of exercise occur. Most other body systems are simply designed to serve the needs of the muscle cell during exercise.

The muscle cell, or muscle fiber, is a rather simple machine in design but extremely complex in function. It is a tube-like structure containing filaments that can slide by one another to shorten the total muscle. The shortening of the muscle moves bones, and hence work is accomplished, be it simply the raising of a barbell as in weight training or moving the whole body as in running. Like most other machines, the muscle cell has the capability of producing work at different rates, ranging from very low levels of energy expenditure during sleep to nearly a ninety-fold increase during maximal, short-term anaerobic exercise.

The human body possesses several different types of muscle fibers, and their primary differences are in the ability to produce energy. Type I is called a slow-twitch red fiber, and it can produce energy primarily by aerobic processes, the oxygen system. It is also referred to as the slow-oxidative fiber (SO). Type IIa is known as a fast-twitch red fiber; it also can produce energy by aerobic processes but in addition can produce energy anaerobically via the lactic acid system. It is also known as the fast-oxidative glycolytic fiber (FOG). The third fiber type, IIb, is a fast-twitch white fiber that produces energy primarily by anaerobic processes and is also known as the fast glycolytic fiber (FG). Type II fibers may use the ATP-PCr system at a faster rate than type I fibers.

The most important factor affecting the metabolic rate is the intensity or speed of the exercise. To move faster, your muscles must contract more rapidly, consuming proportionately more energy. Use of type I muscle fibers predominates during low-intensity exercise, and type II fibers are increasingly recruited with more intense exercise. The following represents approximate energy expenditure in Calories per minute for increasing levels of exercise intensity for an average-sized adult male. However, for most of us it would be impossible to sustain the higher levels of energy expenditure for a minute, and the highest level could be sustained for only a second or so.

Level of intensity	Caloric expenditure per minute
Resting metabolic rate	1.0
Sitting and writing	2.0
Walking at 2 mph	3.3
Walking at 3 mph	4.2
Running at 5 mph	9.4
Running at 10 mph	18.8
Running at 15 mph	29.3
Running at 20 mph	38.7
Maximal power weightlift	>90.0

Although the intensity of the exercise is the most important factor affecting the magnitude of the metabolic rate, there are some other important considerations. In some activities the increase in energy expenditure is not directly proportional to speed, for the efficiency of movement will affect caloric expenditure. Very fast walking becomes more inefficient, so the individual burns more

Calories per mile walking briskly compared to more leisurely walking. A beginning swimmer wastes a lot of energy, whereas one who is more accomplished may swim with less effort, saving Calories when swimming a given distance. Swimming and cycling at very high speeds exponentially increase water or air resistance, so caloric expenditure also increases exponentially. Moreover, the individual with a greater body weight will burn more Calories for any given amount of work in which the body has to be moved, as in walking, jogging, or running. It simply costs more total energy to move a heavier load.

How is exercise intensity measured?

The intensity of a given exercise may be measured in two general ways. One way is to measure the actual work output or power of the activity, such as foot-pounds per second, kilojoules per second, or watts. In some cases this is rather easy to do because some machines, such as bicycle ergometers, are designed to provide an accurate measure of work output. However, the actual work output of a basketball player during a game is more difficult to measure, although use of accelerometers and other motion-detection devices help. Data, such as watt production, derived from these techniques may be used to infer the predominant energy system being used.

A second way is to measure the physiological cost of the activity by monitoring the activity of the three human energy systems. Ward-Smith noted that due to accurate measurements of oxygen uptake and carbon dioxide output, the energy contributions from aerobic metabolism are readily quantifiable, while the energy contribution from anaerobic metabolism is far more difficult to determine.

Energy production from the ATP-PCr energy system has been measured by several procedures. One procedure involves a muscle biopsy with subsequent analysis for ATP and PCr levels to determine use following exercise, but the small muscle biopsy may not represent ATP-PCr use in other muscles. ATP and PCr levels may also be determined by computerized imaging procedures, a noninvasive procedure, but the exercise task needs to be confined to specific movements due to the nature of the imaging equipment. Thus, Lange and Bury indicate that it is difficult to obtain precise physiological or biochemical data during common explosive-type exercise tests, such as short sprints.

Laboratory techniques are also available to measure the role of the lactic acid system in exercise, primarily by measuring the concentration of lactic acid in the blood or in muscle tissues. One measure of exercise intensity is the so-called anaerobic threshold, or that point where the metabolism is believed to shift to a greater use of the lactic acid system. This point is often termed the **onset of blood lactic acid (OBLA),** or lactate threshold. The anaerobic threshold may also be referred to as the **steady-state threshold,** indicating that endurance exercise may continue for prolonged periods if you exercise below this threshold value. Exercise physiologists disagree about which is the better term, but all terms may be found in scientific literature. Some sport scientists also use specific measurements to define these terms, such as a certain level of blood lactic acid.

Laboratory tests also are necessary to measure the contribution of the oxygen system during exercise, and this is the most commonly used technique for measuring exercise intensity (see figure 3.3). The most commonly used measurement is the **maximal oxygen uptake,** which represents the highest amount of oxygen that an individual may consume under exercise situations. In essence, the technique consists of monitoring the oxygen uptake of the individual while the exercise intensity is increased in stages. When oxygen uptake does not increase with an increase in workload, the maximal oxygen uptake has been reached. Maximal oxygen uptake is usually expressed as **VO$_2$ max,** which may be stated as liters per minute or milliliters per kilogram body weight per minute. An example is provided in figure 3.13. A commonly used technique to indicate exercise intensity is to report it as a certain percentage of an individual's VO$_2$ max, such as 50 or 75 percent. If blood samples are taken periodically, the percent of VO$_2$ max at which the steady-state threshold occurs may be determined. Additionally, measurement of oxygen during recovery from exercise may be used to calculate the maximal accumulated oxygen deficit (MAOD), an indirect marker for anaerobic contributions to energy expenditure during exercise. Proper training may increase both VO$_2$ max and the steady-state threshold, as illustrated in figure 3.14.

FIGURE 3.13
Maximal oxygen uptake (VO$_2$ max). The best way to express VO$_2$ max is in milliliters of oxygen per kilogram (kg) of body weight per minute (ml O$_2$/kg/min). As noted in the figure, the smaller individual has a lower VO$_2$ max in liters but a higher VO$_2$ max when expressed relative to weight. In this case, the smaller individual has a higher degree of aerobic fitness, at least as measured by VO$_2$ max per unit body weight.

VO$_2$ max: liters/minute	3.6 L (3600 ml)	4.0 L (4000 ml)
kg body weight	60	80
VO$_2$ max: ml O$_2$/kg/minute	60	50

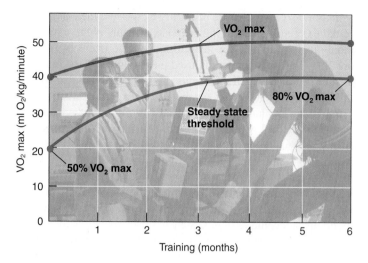

FIGURE 3.14 The effect of training upon VO_2 max and the steady-state threshold. Training increases both your VO_2 max and your steady-state threshold, which is the ability to work at a greater percentage of your VO_2 max without producing excessive lactic acid—a causative factor in fatigue. For example, before training the VO_2 max may be 40 ml while the steady-state threshold is only 20 ml (50% of VO_2 max). After training, VO_2 max may rise to 50 ml, but the steady-state threshold may rise to 40 ml (80% of the VO_2 max).

In summary, measurement of the three energy systems during exercise provides us with a measure of the energy cost of the physical activity.

How is the energy expenditure of exercise metabolism expressed?

A number of research studies have been conducted to determine the energy expenditure of a wide variety of sports and other physical activities.

The energy costs have been reported in a variety of ways, including Calories per minute based upon body weight, kilojoules (kJ), oxygen uptake, and **METS**. The MET is a unit that represents multiples of the resting metabolic rate (see figure 3.15). These concepts are, of course, all interrelated, so an exercise can be expressed in any one of the four terms and converted into the others. For our purposes, we will express energy cost in Calories per minute based upon body weight, as that appears to be the most practical method for this book. However, just in case you see the other values in another book or magazine, here is how you may simplify the conversion. We know the following approximate values:

$$1 \text{ C} = 4 \text{ kJ}$$

$$1 \text{ L O}_2 = 5 \text{ C}$$

$$1 \text{ MET} = 3.5 \text{ ml O}_2/\text{kg body weight/min}$$

(amount of oxygen consumed during rest)

These values are needed for the following calculations:
Example: Exercise cost = 20 kJ/minute
To get Calorie cost, divide kJ by the equivalent value for Calories.

$$20 \text{ kJ/min}/4 = 5 \text{ C/min}$$

Example: Exercise cost = 3 L of O_2/min
To get Calorie cost, multiply liters of O_2 × Calories per liter.

$$\text{Caloric cost} = 3 \times 5 = 15 \text{ C/min}$$

Example: Exercise cost = 25 ml O_2/kg body weight/min
You need body weight in kg, which is weight in pounds divided by 2.2. For this example 154 lbs = 70 kg. Determine total O_2 cost/min by multiplying body weight times O_2 cost/kg/min.

$$70 \times 25 = 1,750 \text{ ml O}_2$$

Convert ml to L: 1,750 ml = 1.75 L

Multiply liters O_2 × Calories per liter

$$\text{Caloric cost} = 1.75 \times 5 = 8.75 \text{ C/min}$$

Example: Exercise cost = 12 METS
You need body weight in kg—for this example, 70 kg.
Multiply total METS times O_2 equivalent of 1 MET.

$$12 \times 3.5 \text{ ml O}_2/\text{kg/min} = 42.0 \text{ ml O}_2/\text{kg/min}$$

Multiply body weight times this result

$$70 \times 42 \text{ ml O}_2/\text{kg/min} = 2,940 \text{ ml O}_2/\text{min}$$

Convert ml to L: 2,940 ml O_2/min = 2.94 L O_2/min

Multiply liters O_2 × Calories per liter

$$\text{Caloric cost} = 2.94 \times 5 = 14.70 \text{ C/min}$$

How can I tell what my metabolic rate is during exercise?

The human body is basically a muscle machine designed for movement. Almost all of the other body systems serve the muscular system. The nervous system causes the muscles to contract. The digestive system supplies nutrients. The cardiovascular system delivers these nutrients along with oxygen in cooperation with the respiratory system. The endocrine system secretes hormones that affect muscle nutrition. The excretory system removes waste products. When humans exercise, almost all body systems increase their activity to accommodate the increased energy demands of the muscle cell. In most types of sustained exercises, however, the major demand of the muscle cells is for oxygen.

As noted previously, the major technique for evaluating metabolic rate is to measure the oxygen consumption of an individual during exercise. Athletes may benefit from such physiological testing. Measurements of VO_2 max, maximal heart rate, and the anaerobic threshold may help in planning an optimal training program, and subsequent testing may illustrate training effects. Such testing is becoming increasingly available at various universities and comprehensive fitness/wellness centers.

Unfortunately, this may not be practical for most of us. However, because of some interesting relationships among exercise intensity, oxygen consumption, and heart rate, the average individ-

	Rest	Slow walk (2 mph)	Fast walk (5 mph)	Run (8 mph)
Liters of oxygen/minute	.25	.5–.75	1.5–1.75	2.5–3.0
Calories/minute	1.25	2.5–3.75	7.5–8.75	12.5–15.0
Kilojoules/minute	5	10–15	30–35	50–60
METS	1	2–3	6–7	10–12

FIGURE 3.15 Energy equivalents in oxygen consumption, Calories, Kilojoules, and METS. This figure depicts four means of expressing energy expenditure during four levels of activity. These approximate values are for an average male of 154 pounds (70 kg). If you weigh more or less, the values will increase or decrease accordingly.

ual may be able to get a relative approximation of the metabolic rate during exercise. A more or less linear relationship exists between exercise intensity and oxygen uptake. As the intensity level of work increases, so does the amount of oxygen consumed. The two systems primarily responsible for delivering the oxygen to the muscles are the cardiovascular and respiratory systems. There is also a fairly linear relationship between their responses and oxygen consumption. In general, maximal heart rate (HRmax) and VO_2 max coincide at the same exercise intensity level. A simplified schematic is presented in figure 3.16.

Because the heart rate (HR) generally is linearly related to oxygen consumption (the main expression of metabolic rate), and because it is easy to measure this physiological response during exercise either at the wrist or neck pulse, it may prove to be a practical guide to your metabolic rate. The higher your heart rate, the greater your metabolic rate. However, a number of factors may influence your specific heart rate response to exercise, such as the type of exercise (running vs. swimming), your level of physical fitness, sex, age, skill efficiency, percentage of body fat, and a number of environmental conditions. Thus, it is difficult to predict your exact metabolic rate from your exercise HR. As we shall see in chapter 11, however, the HR data during exercise may be used as a basis for establishing a personal fitness program for health and weight control.

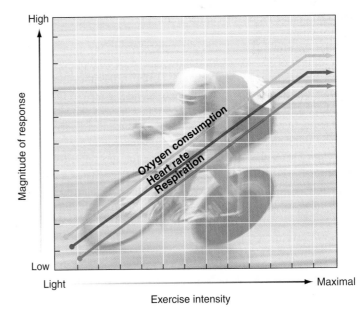

FIGURE 3.16 Relationships between oxygen consumption, heart rate, and respiration responses to increasing exercise rates. In general, as the intensity of exercise continues, there is a rise in oxygen consumption, which is accompanied by proportional increases in heart rate and respiration. VO_2 max and HRmax usually occur at the same exercise intensity.

How can I determine the energy cost of exercise?

To facilitate the determination of the energy cost of a wide variety of physical activities, appendix B has been developed. This is a composite table of a wide variety of individual reports in the literature. When using this appendix, keep the following points in mind.

1. The figures include the REE. Thus, the total cost of the exercise includes not only the energy expended by the exercise itself, but also the amount you would have used anyway during that same period. Suppose you ran for 1 hour and the calculated energy cost was 800 Calories. During that same time at rest you may have expended 75 Calories as your REE. The net cost of the exercise is only 725 Calories.
2. The figures in the table are only for the time you are doing the activity. For example, in an hour of basketball you may exercise strenuously for only 35–40 minutes, as you may take time-outs and rest during foul shots. In general, record only the amount of time that you are actually moving during the activity.
3. The figures may give you some guidelines to total energy expenditure, but actual caloric cost might vary somewhat because of such factors as your skill level, running against the wind or uphill, and so forth.
4. Not all body weights could be listed, but you may approximate by going to the closest weight listed.
5. There may be small differences between men and women, but not enough to make a marked difference in the total caloric value for most exercises.

As one example, suppose we calculate the energy expenditure of a 154-pound individual who ran 5 miles in 30 minutes. You must calculate either the minutes per mile or miles per hour (mph).

1. 30 minutes / 5 miles = 6 min/mile
2. 60 minutes / 6 minutes/mile = 10 mph

Consult appendix B and find the caloric value per minute for a body weight of 155 lbs and a running speed of 10 mph, a value of 18.8 Calories/minute. Multiply this value times the number of minutes of running, and you get the total caloric cost of that exercise. In this example, $30 \times 18.8 = 564$ total Calories expended.

If the activity you do does not appear in appendix B, try to find one you think closely matches the movements found in your activity. Then check the caloric expenditure for the related activity. Additionally, Barbara Ainsworth, from San Diego State University, has compiled a compendium of physical activities, providing the MET value for hundreds of different activities of daily living, specific exercises, and sports. The complete compendium is available at http://prevention.sph.sc.edu/tools/compendium.htm.

What are the best types of activities to increase energy expenditure?

Activities that use the large muscle groups of the body and are performed continuously usually will expend the greatest amount of Calories. Intensity and duration are the two key determinants of total energy expenditure. Activities in which you may be able to exercise continuously at a fairly high intensity for a prolonged period will maximize your total caloric loss. Although this may encompass a wide variety of different physical activities, those that have become increasingly popular include walking, running, swimming, bicycling, and aerobic dance. A few general comments about these common modes of exercising would appear to be in order.

Walking and Running Walking and running are popular exercises because they are so practical to do. All you need is a good pair of shoes. As a general rule, the caloric cost of running a given distance does not depend on the speed. It will take you a longer time to cover the distance at a slower speed, but the total caloric cost will be similar to that expended at a faster speed. However, Biewener and others note that walking is more economical than running, and hence you generally expend fewer Calories for a given distance walking than you do running. A good rule of thumb is that you expend about 1 Calorie per kilogram/body weight per mile walking at a speed for 2–4 miles per hour. Walking uses fewer Calories per mile as compared to running. This does not hold true, however, if you walk vigorously at a high speed. A study by Thomas and Londeree has shown that the caloric cost of jogging at 4.7 mph is only about 5 percent higher than walking at the same speed. At high walking speeds (above 5 mph), you may possibly expend more energy than if you jogged at the same speed. Fast, vigorous walking, known as aerobic walking, can be an effective means to expend Calories. However, as with other exercise activities, it takes practice to become a fast walker.

For a simplified procedure, you may calculate the approximate caloric expenditure for running a given distance by either one of the following formulas based on data from Hall and others:

$$\text{Caloric cost} = 1 \text{ C/kg body weight/kilometer}$$

$$\text{Caloric cost} = 0.74 \text{ C/pound body weight/mile}$$

If you are an average-sized male of about 154 lbs (70 kg), or an average-sized female of about 121 lbs (55 kg), you would burn approximately the following amounts of Calories for a kilometer or a mile.

	Male (165 lbs, 75 kg)	Female (132 lbs, 60 kg)
Kilometer	75	60
Mile	122	98

Slow, leisurely walking would burn about 40 percent fewer Calories per mile.

Climbing stairs, at home, at work, in an athletic stadium, or on step machines, is one means to make walking more vigorous. Skipping is also more vigorous but may lead to injuries.

Many individuals use small weights in conjunction with their walking or running programs either by carrying them or strapping them to the ankles or wrists. The most popular technique is to carry small weights of 1–3 pounds. A number of research studies have reported that this technique, particularly if the arms are swung vigorously through a wide range of motion during walking, may increase the energy expenditure about 5–10 percent or higher above unweighted walking at the same speed. Use of walking poles, similar to ski poles, may increase caloric expenditure by 15 percent. Increases in energy expenditure greater than 30 percent have been reported with vigorous pumping of 1-pound hand weights as compared with just running at the same speed. The heart rate response also increases, and using hand weights with fast walking is an adequate stimulus to promote a training effect on the cardiovascular system. However, use of hand weights exaggerates the blood pressure response, and thus should be used with caution by individuals with blood pressure problems. Since some researchers have noted that simply walking a little faster without weights will have the same effect on energy cost and heart rate response, this may be a good alternative. Nevertheless, at any given walking speed, hand weights will increase energy expenditure. Addition of weights to the ankle also will increase energy expenditure, but it may also change the normal running style and may predispose one to injury.

Swimming   Because of water resistance, swimming takes more energy to cover a given distance than does either walking or running. Although the amount of energy expended depends somewhat on the type of swimming stroke used and the ability of the swimmer, swimming a given distance takes about four times as much energy as running. For example, swimming a quarter-mile is the energy equivalent of running a mile. Water aerobics and water running (doing aerobics or running in waist-deep, chest-deep, or deep water) may be effective exercise regimens that help prevent injuries due to impact.

Cycling   Bicycling takes less energy to cover a given distance in comparison to running on a level surface. The energy cost of bicycling depends on a number of factors such as body weight, the type of bicycle, hills, and body position on the bike (assuming a streamlined position to reduce air resistance). Owing to rapidly increasing air resistance at higher speeds such as 20 mph, the energy cost of bicycling increases at a much faster rate at such speeds. A detailed method for calculating energy expenditure during bicycling is presented in the article by Hagberg and Pena. In general, cycling 1 mile is approximately the energy equivalent of running one-third the distance.

Aerobic Dance   Aerobic dance, as now known, has been a popular form of exercise for over 30 years. There is a variety of styles of aerobic dance varying in intensity and the degree of impact with the floor. Several studies have shown that high-intensity, high-impact aerobic dancing approximates 10 Calories per minute in women, which is indicative of strenuous exercise. Unfortunately, other research has shown that high-impact dancing is more traumatic and may lead to a higher incidence of leg injuries. Thus, the low-impact, or soft-impact, technique in which one foot usually remains in contact with the floor was introduced. Several studies have also shown that if done at a high intensity, low-impact aerobic dance may also use approximately 9–10 Calories per minute and be less likely to induce injuries to the legs. The use of step benches may also increase exercise intensity.

Home Exercise Equipment   Home exercise equipment may also provide a strenuous aerobic workout. Recent research suggests that for any given level of perceived effort, treadmill running burned the most Calories. Exercising on elliptical trainers, cross-country ski machines, rowing ergometers, and stair-climbing apparatus also expended significant amounts of Calories, more so than bicycling apparatus. Many modern pieces of exercise equipment are electronically equipped with small computers to calculate energy cost as Calories per minute and total caloric cost of the exercise.

Table 3.5 provides a classification of some common physical activities based upon rate of energy expenditure. The implications of these types of exercises in weight control programs are discussed in later chapters.

TABLE 3.5   Classification of physical activities based upon rate of energy expenditure*

Light, mild aerobic exercise (< 5 Calories/min)

Archery	Bowling	Horseback riding (walk)
Badminton, social	Dancing, waltz	Swimming (20–25 yards/min)
Baseball	Golf (Cart)	Walking (2–3 mph)
Bicycling (5 mph)		

Moderate aerobic exercise (5–10 Calories/min)

Badminton, competitive	Golf (carrying clubs)	Swimming (30–40 yards/min)
Basketball, recreational	Rope skipping (60 rpm)	Tennis, recreational
Bicycling (10 mph)	Running (5 mph)	Walking (3–4.5 mph)
Dancing, aerobic	Skiing, cross-country (2.5 mph)	Weight training

Moderately heavy to heavy aerobic exercise (> 10 Calories/min)

Bicycling (15–20 mph)	Rope skipping (120–140 rpm)	Swimming (50–70 yards/min)
Calisthenics, vigorous	Running (6–9 mph)	Tennis, competitive
In-line skating (10–15 mph)	Skiing, cross-country (5–6 mph)	Walking (5.0–6.0 mph)

*Calories per minute based upon a body weight of 70 kg, or 154 pounds. Those weighing more or less will expend more or fewer Calories, respectively, but the intensity level of the exercise will be the same. The actual amount of Calories expended may also depend on a number of other factors, depending on the activity. For example, bicycling into or with the wind will increase or decrease, respectively, the energy cost. See appendix B for more details.

Source: Modified from M.H. Williams, *Nutritional Aspects of Human Physical and Athletic Performance*, 1985, Charles C Thomas Publishers, Springfield, IL.

Does exercise affect my resting energy expenditure (REE)?

Exercise not only raises the metabolic rate during exercise but, depending upon the intensity and duration of the activity, will also keep the REE elevated during the recovery period. The increase in body temperature and in the amounts of circulating hormones such as adrenaline (epinephrine) will continue to influence some cellular activity, and some other metabolic processes, such as circulation and respiration, will remain elevated for a limited time. This effect, which has been labeled the **metabolic aftereffects of exercise,** is calculated by monitoring the oxygen consumption for several hours during the recovery period after the exercise task. The amount of oxygen in excess of the preexercise REE, often called excess postexercise oxygen consumption (EPOC), reflects the additional caloric cost of the exercise above and beyond that expended during the exercise task itself.

Some older research noted that the average number of additional Calories expended after each exercise session would be about 45–50. However, in a series of more recent studies with more appropriate controls, although most investigators did report an increased REE following exercise of varying durations and intensities, the magnitude of the response was generally lower. Depending on the intensity and duration of the exercise bout in these studies, the REE during the recovery period ranged from 4–16 percent higher than the preexercise REE, and it remained elevated for only 15–20 minutes in some studies but up to 4–5 hours in others. Both aerobic and resistance-type exercises increase EPOC, with greater increases associated with high-intensity, long duration exercise. Burleson and others reported that when matched for oxygen consumption during exercise, weight training exhibited a greater postexercise oxygen consumption, but the amount was rather small. Using the oxygen consumption values presented in these studies, the additional energy expenditure ranged from 3–30 Calories.

Although the metabolic aftereffects of exercise would not appear to make a significant contribution to weight loss, exercise may help mitigate the decrease in the REE often seen in individuals on very low-Calorie diets. This point is explored further in chapter 11.

Does exercise affect the thermic effect of food (TEF)?

Many studies have been conducted to investigate the effect of exercise on the thermic effect of food (TEF). Unfortunately, no clear answer has been found. Some studies have reported an increase in TEF when subjects exercise either before or after the meal, while others revealed little or no effects. Some research even suggests that exercise training decreases the TEF. Other studies have investigated differences between exercise-trained and untrained individuals relative to TEF, and although some preliminary research noted a decreased TEF in endurance-trained athletes, Tremblay and others also noted that it is still unclear if training causes any significant alterations in TEF. In any case, the increases or decreases noted in the TEF due to either exercise or exercise training were minor, averaging about 5–9 Calories for several hours.

How much energy do I need to consume daily?

The National Academy of Sciences, through the Institute of Medicine, recently released its DRI for energy in conjunction with DRI for carbohydrate, fat, and protein, as noted in chapter 2. Because of possible problems in developing obesity, no RDA or UL were developed for energy. Instead, the Institute of Medicine uses the term **Estimated Energy Requirement (EER),** which it defines as the dietary intake that is predicted to maintain energy balance in a healthy adult of a defined age, gender, weight, height, and level of physical activity consistent with good health. In essence, the EER estimates your REE based on age, gender, weight, and height, and then modifies this value depending on your daily level of physical activity, which we refer to in this book as TEE.

Your total daily energy expenditure (TDEE) is the sum of your BEE, your TEF, and your TEE. Figure 3.17 provides some approximate values for the typical active individual, indicating that BEE accounts for 60–75 percent of the total daily energy expenditure, TEF represents 5–10 percent, and TEE explains 15–30 percent. These values are approximate and may vary tremendously, particularly TEE, which may range from near 0 percent in the totally sedentary individual to 50 percent or more in ultraendurance athletes.

In order to illustrate the effect that physical activity, or TEE, may have on your TDEE, the Institute of Medicine developed four **physical activity level (PAL)** categories, which are presented in Table 3.6. The PAL describes the ratio of the TDEE divided by the BEE over a 24-hour period. The PAL in figure 3.17 is 1.43, or low active. The higher the ratio, the greater the amount of daily physical activity.

The energy expenditure in individuals in the Sedentary category represents their REE, including the TEF, plus various physical activities associated with independent living, such as walking

Category	Physical Activity Level (PAL)	Physical Activity Coefficient (PA) Males/Females
Sedentary	$\geq 1.0 - < 1.4$	1.00/1.00
Low Active	$\geq 1.4 - < 1.6$	1.11/1.12
Active	$\geq 1.6 - < 1.9$	1.25/1.27
Very Active	$\geq 1.9 - < 2.5$	1.48/1.45

TABLE 3.6   The Physical Activity Level Categories

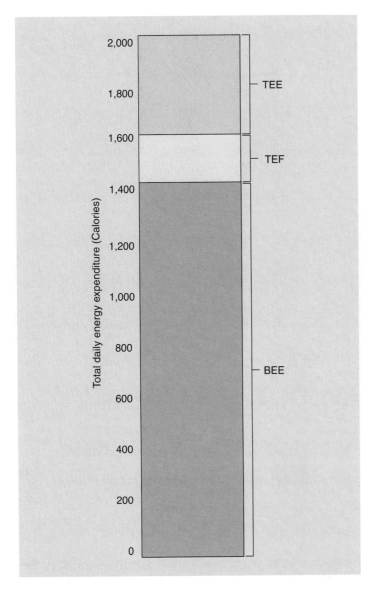

FIGURE 3.17 Total daily energy expenditure. Three major factors account for the total daily energy expenditure. Basal energy expenditure (BEE) accounts for 60–75 percent, the thermic effect of food (TEF) accounts for 5–10 percent, and 15–30 percent is accounted for by the thermic effect of exercise (TEE). However, all of these percentages are variable in different individuals, with exercise being the most modifiable component. In the figure, the BEE is 70 percent, the TEF is 10 percent, and the TEE is 20 percent.

from the house or work to the car, typing, and other forms of very light activity. Levine has coined the term **nonexercise activity thermogenesis (NEAT)** for these very light activities, which represent all the energy we expend daily that is not sleeping, eating, or sports-related exercise. We shall discuss the role of NEAT in weight control in chapter 10.

For the other categories, the Institute of Medicine bases the PAL on the amount of daily physical activity that is the equivalent of walking at a rate of 3–4 miles per hour. For example, an adult male who weighs 154 pounds (70 kg) and who, in addition to the

normal daily activities of independent living, expended the physical activity equivalent of walking 2.2 miles per day would be in the Low Active category, with a PAL of 1.5. To be in the Active category with a PAL of 1.75, he would need to expend the physical activity energy equivalent of walking 7.0 miles per day, and to be in the Very Active category an energy equivalent of 17 miles per day. Keep in mind that you do not need to walk this many miles per day, but simply do a multitude of physical activities, such as climbing stairs, golfing, swimming, and jogging that add up to this energy equivalent. Table 3.5 provides examples of physical activities ranging from light to heavy that may be used to total the required energy equivalents of walking. A more detailed table, based on body weight, is presented in appendix B.

Based on a number of doubly labeled water studies, the Institute of Medicine developed equations for the Estimated Energy Requirement (EER). Here are two:

Males, 19 years and older:

$$EER = 662 - 9.53 \times age + [PA \times (15.91 \times Weight + 539.6 \times Height)]$$

Females, 19 years and older:

$$EER = 354 - 6.91 \times age + [PA \times (9.361 \times Weight + 726 \times Height)]$$

Age: In years.

Weight: In kilograms (kg). To convert weight in pounds to kilograms, multiply by 0.454.

Height: In meters (m). To convert height in inches to meters, multiply by 0.0254.

PA: PA is the physical activity coefficient, which is based on the PAL. Based on mathematical consideration to equate energy expenditure between the various PAL categories, the PA coefficient for the Sedentary category was set at 1.0 and the PA for the other categories adjusted accordingly. The PAs for the four PAL categories are presented for adult males and females in Table 3.6.

Although there may be variances in this estimate of your EER, the estimate may provide you with a ballpark figure of your daily energy needs. Let's look at an example, as depicted in figure 3.18, of the difference that physical activity may have on the daily energy needs of a sedentary and very active adult female. Both are 20 years old, weigh 132 pounds (60 kg), and are 55 inches (1.4 m) tall.

Sedentary:

$$EER = 354 - 6.91 \times 20 + [1.0 \times (9.361 \times 60 + 726 \times 1.4)]$$

$$EER = 354 - 138.2 + [1.0 \times (561.66 + 1016.4)]$$

$$EER = 215.8 + [1578.06] = 1794 \text{ Calories}$$

Very active:

$$EER = 354 - 6.91 \times 20 + [1.45 \times (9.361 \times 60 + 726 \times 1.4)]$$

$$EER = 354 - 138.2 + [1.45 \times (561.66 + 1016.4)]$$

$$EER = 215.8 + [2288.19] = 2504 \text{ Calories}$$

Sedentary lifestyle	Very Active lifestyle
PA = 1.0	PA = 1.45
EER = 1,794 Calories	EER = 2,504 Calories

FIGURE 3.18 Estimated Energy Requirement (EER) for two 20-year-old females. Both weigh 132 pounds (60 kg) and are 55 inches (1.4 m) tall. The sedentary female has a Physical Activity Coefficient (PA) of 1.0, whereas the very active female has a PA of 1.45. Compared to her sedentary counterpart, the very active female needs 700 additional Calories to sustain her physically active lifestyle.

The total caloric difference between the sedentary and very active women approximates 700 Calories per day, which may be important in several ways for the very active female. First, as noted in chapter 1, increased physical activity is an important aspect of a healthy lifestyle to prevent a variety of chronic diseases. Second, this additional 700 Calories of energy expenditure daily could have a significant impact on her body weight over time, approximating a loss of over a pound per week if not compensated for by increased food intake. Third, if she is at an optimal body weight, she may consume an additional 700 Calories per day without gaining weight.

If you are interested in increasing your PAL, then your best bet is to incorporate more light, moderate, and moderately heavy to heavy physical activities into your daily lifestyle. Some additional guidelines for estimating your daily TDEE and EER, particularly in the design of a proper weight control program, are presented in chapter 11. If you are interested in obtaining the full details concerning the EER and PAL, you may do so at the National Academies Press Website, www.nap.edu. Simply type in Dietary Reference Intake for Energy in the search box, and review chapters 5 and 12 which focus on energy and physical activity.

Key Concept Recap

▶ The thermic effect of exercise (TEE), or exercise metabolic rate (EMR), provides us with the most practical means to increase energy expenditure.

▶ The metabolic rate during exercise is directly proportional to the intensity of the exercise, and the exercise heart rate may serve as a general indicator of the metabolic rate.

▶ Activities that use the large muscle groups of the body, such as running, swimming, bicycling, and aerobic dance, facilitate energy expenditure.

▶ The total daily energy expenditure (TDEE) is accounted for by BEE (60–75%), TEF (5–10%), and TEE (15–30%), although these percentages may vary.

▶ The Estimated Energy Requirement (EER) is defined as the dietary intake that is predicted to maintain energy balance in a healthy adult of a defined age, gender, height, weight, and level of physical activity consistent with good health. Changing from a sedentary Physical Activity Level (PAL) to a very active PAL is a very effective means to increase TDEE and EER.

Human Energy Systems and Fatigue during Exercise

What energy systems are used during exercise?

In sport, energy expenditure can vary tremendously. For example, Asker Jeukendrup and his associates recently noted that in one sport, World Class Cycling, events may range in duration from 10 seconds to 3 weeks, involving race distances between 200 meters to 4,000 kilometers. Exercise intensity in a 200-meter event would be extremely high, and much lower during the prolonged event.

The most important factor determining which energy system will be used is the intensity of the exercise, which is the rate, speed, or tempo at which you pursue a given activity. In general, the faster you do something, the higher your rate of energy expenditure and the more rapidly you must produce ATP for muscular contraction. Very rapid muscular movements are characterized by high rates of power production. If you were asked to run 100 meters as fast as you could, you would exert maximal speed for a short time. On the other hand, if you were asked to run 5 miles, you certainly would not run at the same speed as you would for the 100 meters. In the 100-meter run your energy expenditure would be very rapid, characterized by a high-power production. The 5-mile run would be characterized by low-power production, or endurance.

The requirement of energy for exercise is related to a power-endurance continuum. On the power end, we have extremely high rates of energy expenditure that a sprinter might use; on the endurance end, we see lower rates that might be characteristic of a marathon runner. The closer we are to the power end of the contin-

uum, the more rapidly we must produce ATP. As we move toward the endurance end, our rate of ATP production does not need to be as great, but we need the capacity to produce ATP for a longer time.

It should be noted from the outset that all three energy systems—ATP-PCr, lactic acid, and oxygen—are used in one way or another during most athletic activities. (Gastin provides an excellent overview.) However, one system may predominate, depending primarily upon the intensity level of the activity. In this regard, the three human energy systems may be ranked according to several characteristics, which are displayed in table 3.7

Both the ATP-PCr and the lactic acid systems are able to produce ATP rapidly and are used in events characterized by high intensity levels that occur for short periods, because their capacity for total ATP production is limited. Because both of these systems may function without oxygen, they are called anaerobic. Relative to running performance, the ATP-PCr system predominates in short, powerful bursts of muscular activity such as the short dashes like 100 meters, whereas the lactic acid system begins to predominate during the longer sprints and middle distances such as 200, 400 and 800 meters. In any athletic event where maximal power production lasts about 1–10 seconds, the ATP-PCr system is the major energy source. The lactic acid system begins to predominate in events lasting 30–120 seconds, but studies have noted significant elevations in muscle lactic acid in maximal exercise even as brief as 10 seconds.

The oxygen system possesses a lower rate of ATP production than the other two systems, but its capacity for total ATP production is much greater. Although the intensity level of exercise while using the oxygen system is by necessity lower, this does not necessarily mean that an individual cannot perform at a relatively high speed for a long time. The oxygen system can be improved through a physical conditioning program so that ATP production may be able to meet the demands of relatively high-intensity exercise, as discussed previously and highlighted in figure 3.14. Endurance-type activities, such as those that last 5 minutes or more, are dependent primarily upon the oxygen system, but the oxygen system makes a very significant contribution even in events as short as 30–90 seconds, as recently documented by Spencer and Gastin.

In summary, we may simplify this discussion by categorizing the energy sources as either aerobic or anaerobic. Anaerobic sources

TABLE 3.7 Major characteristics of the human energy systems*

	ATP-PCr	Lactic acid	Oxygen	Oxygen
Main energy source	ATP; phosphocreatine	Carbohydrate	Carbohydrate	Fat
Intensity level	Highest	High	Lower	Lowest
Rate of ATP production	Highest	High	Lower	Lowest
Power production	Highest	High	Lower	Lowest
Capacity for total ATP production	Lowest	Low	High	Highest
Endurance capacity	Lowest	Low	High	Highest
Oxygen needed	No	No	Yes	Yes
Anaerobic/aerobic	Anaerobic	Anaerobic	Aerobic	Aerobic
Characteristic track event	100-meter dash	200–800 meters	5,000-meter (5 km) run	Ultradistance
Time factor	1–10 seconds	30–120 seconds	5 minutes or more	Hours

*Keep in mind that during most exercises, all three energy systems will be operating to one degree or another. However, one system may predominate, depending primarily on the intensity of the activity. See text for further explanation.

include both the ATP-PCr and lactic acid systems while the oxygen system is aerobic. Table 3.8 illustrates the approximate percentage contribution of anaerobic and aerobic energy sources, dependent upon the level of maximal intensity that can be sustained for a given time period. Thus, for a 100-meter dash covered in 10 seconds, 85 percent of the energy is derived from anaerobic sources. For a marathoner (26.2 miles) with times of approximately 125–130 minutes in international-level competition, the aerobic energy processes contribute 99 percent. Although Ward-Smith, using a mathematical approach to predict aerobic and anaerobic contributions during running, noted that these percentage values may be modified slightly for elite athletes, the concept is correct. For example, using track athletes as subjects, Spencer and Gastin found that the relative contribution of the aerobic energy system was 29 percent in the 200-meter run and increased progressively to 84 percent in the 1500-meter run, noting that the contribution of the aerobic energy system during track running events is greater than traditionally thought. These values are somewhat higher than the aerobic percentage values presented in table 3.8, but support the concept. The key point is that the longer you exercise, the less your intensity has to be, and the more you rely on your oxygen system for energy production.

What energy sources are used during exercise?

The ATP-PCr system can use only adenosine triphosphate and phosphocreatine, but as noted previously, these energy sources are in short supply and need to be replaced by the other two energy systems.

The lactic acid system uses only carbohydrate, primarily the muscle glycogen stores. At high-intensity exercise levels that may be sustained for 1–2 minutes or less, such as exercising well above your VO_2 max, carbohydrate will supply over 95 percent of the energy. However, the accumulation of lactic acid may be associated with the early onset of fatigue.

On the other hand, the oxygen system can use a variety of different energy sources, including protein, although carbohydrate and fat are the primary ones. The carbohydrate is found as muscle glycogen, liver glycogen, and blood glucose. The fats are stored primarily as triglycerides in the muscle and adipose cells. As we shall see in this section and in chapters 4, 5, and 6, a number of different factors can influence which energy source is used by the oxygen system during exercise, but exercise intensity and duration are the two most important factors.

Under normal conditions, exercise intensity is the key factor determining whether carbohydrate or fat is used. Holloszy and others note that both absolute and relative (i. e., percent of VO_2 max) exercise intensities play important roles in the regulation of substrate metabolism. The absolute work rate determines the total quantity of fuel required, while relative exercise intensity plays a major role in determining the proportions of carbohydrate and fat oxidized by the working muscles. Hoppeler and Weibel noted that as one does mild to moderate exercise, say up to 50 percent of one's VO_2 max, blood glucose and fat may provide much of the needed energy. However, the transfer of glucose and fat from the vascular system to the muscles becomes limited at about 50 percent of VO_2 max. Thus, as you start to exceed 50 percent of your VO_2 max, you begin to rely more on your intramuscular stores of glycogen and triglycerides. As you continue to increase your speed or intensity, you begin to rely more and more on carbohydrate as an energy source. Apparently the biochemical processes for fat metabolism are too slow to meet the increased need for faster production of ATP, and carbohydrate utilization increases. The major source of this carbohydrate is muscle glycogen. The transition from use of fat to carbohydrate as the primary fuel source during increasing intensity of exercise has been referred to as the **crossover concept,** and although the technicalities of specific fuel contributions are the subject of debate, exercise scientists agree that at some specific point in the increase of exercise intensity an individual will begin to derive more energy from carbohydrate than fat. At high levels of energy expenditure, 70–80 percent of VO_2 max, carbohydrates may contribute more than 80 percent of the energy sources. This speaks for the need of adequate muscle glycogen stores when this level of exercise is to be sustained for long periods, say in events lasting over 60–90 minutes.

In events of long duration, when body stores of carbohydrate are nearly depleted, the primary energy source is fat. In the later stages of ultramarathoning events, fat may become the only fuel available. However, protein may become an important energy source in these circumstances; its role is detailed in chapter 6.

Other than exercise intensity and duration, a number of different factors are known to influence the availability and use of human energy sources during exercise. Gender, hormones, state of training, composition of the diet, time of eating prior to competition, nutritional status, nutrient intake during exercise, environmental temperature, and drugs are some of the more important considerations. For example, warm environmental temperatures may increase the use of carbohydrates, whereas fasting may facilitate the use of fats. These considerations will be incorporated in the following chapters where appropriate. For the interested reader, Hargreaves provides an excellent detailed review.

What is fatigue?

Fatigue is a very complex phenomenon. It may be chronic, or it may be acute. Both types may affect the athlete.

Chronic fatigue in the athlete may develop over time, usually in endurance athletes involved in prolonged, intense training that may involve conditions known as overreaching and overtraining. *Over-*

TABLE 3.8 Percentage contribution of anaerobic and aerobic energy sources during different time periods of maximal work

Time	10 sec	I min	2 min	4 min	10 min	30 min	60 min	120 min
Anaerobic	85	70	50	30	15	5	2	I
Aerobic	15	30	50	70	85	95	98	99

*Percentages are approximate and may vary between sedentary individuals and elite athletes.

reaching is a condition of physical and mental stress that may impair physical performance, but may be a planned phase of training in elite athletes followed by short-term recovery with return to previous or improved levels of performance. *Overtraining* is a term often used to characterize a syndrome in athletes involving prolonged periods of fatigue. However, Halson and Jeukendrup note that although some scientific and anecdotal evidence support its existence, there appear to be no clear markers for overtraining and more research is needed to establish its existence with certainty. Some contend the term *overtraining* is misleading, and may actually be related to *underrecovery*, particularly involving inadequate nutrition.

The **chronic fatigue syndrome** is a genuine medical condition characterized by numerous symptoms, the most prevalent being prolonged incapacitating fatigue. For those who exercise, fatigue is disproportionate to the effort. Roy Shephard, the renowned Canadian sport scientist, indicated that overtraining and/or a negative energy balance may be related to the development of the chronic fatigue syndrome. In such cases, training would be adversely affected and performance certainly would suffer. Given the debilitating effects on exercise and sports performance, scientists are attempting to identify the causes, prevention, and treatment of both overtraining and the chronic fatigue syndrome. Some recent research suggests impaired immune functions.

Acute fatigue is experienced by most athletes at one time or another during maximal efforts. As acute fatigue can adversely affect sports performance, it has been the subject of considerable research. In general, sports scientists classify the site of acute fatigue in the body as either central or peripheral (see figure 3.19). Central fatigue involves the brain or spinal cord of the central nervous system (CNS), while peripheral fatigue is associated primarily with the muscles and, under some conditions, other body organs such as the heart or lungs.

Although the cause of acute exercise-induced fatigue has not been determined, numerous hypotheses exist, involving both peripheral and central fatigue. In a symposium chaired by Green, various causes of peripheral fatigue in the muscles, such as disturbance of optimal calcium levels, were presented. Relative to central fatigue, Peters and others indicate that the brain is selfish and will protect its energy supply, mainly glucose, which could inhibit glucose delivery to the muscles during exercise. Most recently, Lambert and others indicated that the actual cause of fatigue appears to be a complex phenomenon induced by both central and peripheral factors. They hypothesized that all changes in peripheral physiological systems, such as substrate (carbohydrate) depletion or metabolite (hydrogen ions) accumulation in the muscles, send signals to the brain that may lead to neutral inhibition of optimal energy production.

The site and cause of exercise-induced fatigue are indeed complex, but appear to be closely related to the intensity and duration of the mental or physical tasks to be accomplished. For example, the site and cause of fatigue are different between maximal performances in powerlifting and marathon running.

For purposes of the present discussion, **fatigue** will be defined as the inability to continue exercising at a desired level of intensity. Relative to this definition, fatigue may be due to a failure of the rate of energy production in the human body to meet the demands of the exercise task. In simple terms, ATP production rates are unable to match ATP utilization rates. This failure may be due to an inability of the central nervous system to adequately stimulate the appropriate

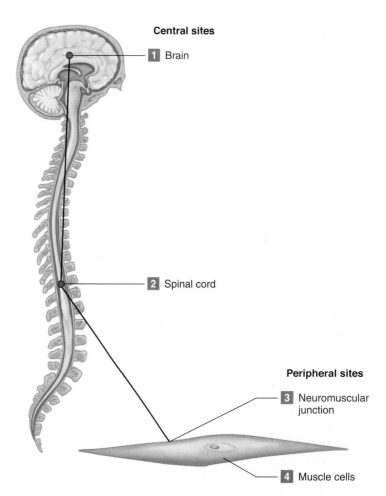

Central sites

1 Brain

2 Spinal cord

Peripheral sites

3 Neuromuscular junction

4 Muscle cells

FIGURE 3.19 Fatigue sites. The causes of fatigue are complex and may involve central sites such as the brain and spinal cord or peripheral sites in the muscles. Hypoglycemia, or low blood sugar, could adversely affect the functioning of the brain, while the acidity associated with the production of lactic acid could possibly interfere with optimal energy production in the muscle cells.

muscles, an insufficient supply of the optimal energy source, a reduced ability to metabolize the energy source in the muscle, or inadequate support from body systems, such as blood flow, to optimize muscle energy production and utilization. In essence, for one or more of these reasons the muscle cannot produce or use ATP rapidly enough to sustain the desired level of exercise intensity. Some possible causes of fatigue during exercise are listed in table 3.9.

How can I delay the onset of fatigue?

The most important factor in the prevention of premature fatigue is proper training, including physiological, psychological, and biomechanical training.

Physiologically, athletes must train specifically the energy system or systems that are inherent to their event. Under the guidance of sport physiologists and coaches, appropriate physiological training for each specific energy system may increase its energy stores, enzymatic activity, and metabolic efficiency, thus enhancing energy production. Physiological training enhances physical power.

Psychologically, athletes must train the mind to tolerate the stresses associated with their specific event. Sport psychologists

TABLE 3.9 Some possible causes of fatigue during exercise

Increased formation of depressant neurotransmitters

Increased serotonin levels

Decreased levels of energy substrates

Decrease in phosphocreatine levels
Depletion of muscle glycogen
Decrease in blood-sugar levels
Decrease in plasma branched-chain amino acids

Disturbed intracellular environment

Impaired calcium recycling

Disturbed acid-base balance

Increase in hydrogen ions due to excess lactic acid production

Decreased oxygen transport

Decreased blood volume due to dehydration

Increased core body temperature resulting in hyperthermia

Decreased cooling effect due to dehydration

Disturbed electrolyte balance

Increased or decreased concentration due to sweat losses and water replacement

---

may help provide the athlete with various mental strategies, such as inducing either a state of relaxation or arousal, whichever may be appropriate for their sport. Physiological training may also confer some psychological advantages, such as tolerating higher levels of pain associated with intense exercise. Psychological training enhances mental strength.

Biomechanically, athletes must maximize the mechanical skills associated with their sport. For any sport, sport biomechanists can analyze the athlete's skill level and recommend modifications in movement patterns or equipment to improve energy production or efficiency. In many cases, modification of the amount of body fat and muscle mass may provide the athlete with a biomechanical advantage. Biomechanical training helps provide a mechanical edge.

Proper physiological, psychological, and biomechanical training represents the best means to help deter premature fatigue. However, what you eat may affect physiological, psychological, and biomechanical aspects of sport performance. Thus, nutrition is an important consideration in delaying the onset of fatigue during sport training and competition.

How is nutrition related to fatigue processes?

As noted in our discussion of the power-endurance continuum, we can exercise at different intensities but the duration of our exercise is inversely related to the intensity. We can exercise at a high intensity for a short time or at a low intensity for a long time. The importance of nutrition to fatigue is determined by this intensity-duration interrelationship.

In very mild aerobic activities, such as distance walking or low-speed running in a trained ultramarathoner, the body can sustain energy production by using fat as the primary fuel when carbohydrate levels diminish. Because the body has large stores of fat, energy

---

TABLE 3.10 Examples of some nutritional ergogenic aids and, theoretically, how they may influence physiological, psychological, or biomechanical processes to delay fatigue

Provide energy substrate

Carbohydrate: Energy substrate for aerobic glycolysis
Creatine: Substrate for formation of phosphocreatine (PCr)

Enhance energy-generating metabolic pathways

B vitamins: Coenzymes in aerobic and anaerobic glycolysis
Carnitine: Enzyme substrate to facilitate fat metabolism

Increase cardiovascular-respiratory function

Iron: Substrate for hemoglobin formation and oxygen transport
Glycerol: Substance to increase blood volume

Increase size or number of energy-generating cells

Arginine and ornithine: Amino acids that stimulate production of human growth hormone, an anabolic hormone
Chromium: Mineral to potentiate activity of insulin, an anabolic hormone

Attenuate fatigue-related metabolic by-products

Aspartate salts: Amino acids that mitigate ammonia production
Sodium bicarbonate: Buffer to reduce effects of lactic acid

Prevent catabolism of energy-generating cells

Antioxidants: Vitamins to prevent unwanted oxidation of cell membranes
HMB: By-product of amino acid metabolism to prevent protein degradation

Ameliorate psychological function

BCAA: Amino acids that favorably modify neurotransmitter production
Choline: Substrate for formation of acetylcholine, a neurotransmitter

Improve mechanical efficiency

Ma huang: Stimulant to increase metabolism for fat loss
Hydroxycitrate (HCA): Supplement to increase fat oxidation for fat loss

Note: These examples as to how nutritional aids may delay fatigue are based on theoretical considerations. As shall be shown in respective chapters, supplementation with most of these nutritional ergogenic aids has not been shown to enhance exercise or sport performance.

supply is not a problem. However, low blood-sugar levels, dehydration, and excessive loss of minerals may lead to the development of both mental and physical fatigue in very prolonged activities.

In moderate to heavy aerobic exercise, the body needs to use more carbohydrate as an energy source and thus will run out of muscle glycogen faster. As we shall see later, carbohydrate is a more efficient fuel than fat, so the athlete will have to reduce the pace of the activity when liver and muscle carbohydrate stores are depleted, such as during endurance-type activities lasting over 90 minutes. Thus, energy supply may be critical. Low blood sugar, changes in blood constituents such as certain amino acids, and dehydration also may be important factors contributing to the development of mental or physical fatigue in this type of endeavor.

In very high-intensity exercise lasting only 1 or 2 minutes, the probable cause of fatigue is the disruption of cellular metabolism caused by the accumulation of hydrogen ions resulting from excess lactic acid production. There is some evidence to suggest that sodium bicarbonate (discussed in chapter 13) may help reduce this disruptive effect of lactic acid to some extent. Furthermore, a very low supply of muscle glycogen in fast-twitch muscle fibers may impair this type of performance.

In extremely intense exercise lasting only 5–10 seconds, a depletion of phosphocreatine (PCr) may be related to the inability to maintain a high force production. Although some nutritional practices, such as phosphate loading or gelatin supplements, have been used in attempts to increase PCr, they have not been regarded to be effective. However, recent research involving creatine supplements has shown some beneficial effects, which are discussed in chapter 6.

In summary, a deficiency of almost every nutrient may be a causative factor in the development of fatigue. A poor diet can hasten the onset of fatigue. Proper nutrition is essential to assure the athlete that an adequate supply of nutrients is available in the diet not only to provide the necessary energy, such as through carbohydrate and fat, but also to ensure optimal metabolism of the energy substrate via protein, vitamins, minerals, and water. The role of specific nutrients relative to fatigue processes will be discussed in later sections of the book where appropriate. Table 3.10 provides some examples of how some nutrients or dietary supplements are thought to delay fatigue.

Key Concept Recap

▶ The ATP-PCr and lactic acid energy systems are used primarily during fast, anaerobic, power-type events, while the oxygen system is used primarily during aerobic, endurance-type events.
▶ Fats serve as the primary source of fuel during mild levels of exercise intensity, but carbohydrates begin to be the preferred fuel as the exercise intensity increases.
▶ A sound training program and proper nutrition are important factors in the prevention of fatigue during exercise.

Check for Yourself

Check the world records in running for 100 meters, 400 meters, 1,500 meters, and the marathon (42,200 meters). Calculate the average speed for each distance. Can you relate your findings to the human energy systems and their relationship to fatigue?

APPLICATION EXERCISE

Borrow, rent, or buy a pedometer or an accelerometer and keep a record of your daily movement (recording the amount every 2 hours). This will provide you with an estimate of your daily physical activity involving movement and will be useful in determining your estimated energy requirement (EER) and maintaining an optimal body weight as discussed in chapter 11.

	Distance logged Sunday	Distance logged Monday	Distance logged Tuesday	Distance logged Wednesday	Distance logged Thursday	Distance logged Friday	Distance logged Saturday
12:00–2:00 A.M.							
2:00–4:00 A.M.							
4:00–6:00 A.M.							
6:00–8:00 A.M.							
8:00–10:00 A.M.							
10:00–12:00 A.M.							
12:00–2:00 P.M.							
2:00–4:00 P.M.							
4:00–6:00 P.M.							
6:00–8:00 P.M.							
8:00–10:00 P.M.							
10:00–12:00 P.M.							

1. Which energy system would predominate in an all-out, high-intensity, 400-meter dash in track?
   (a) ATP-PC
   (b) lactic acid
   (c) oxygen–carbohydrate
   (d) oxygen–fat
   (e) oxygen–protein

2. If a 50 kilogram body-weight athlete was exercising at an oxygen consumption level of 2.45 liters (2,450 ml) per minute, approximately how many METS would she be attaining?
   (a) 8
   (b) 10
   (c) 11
   (d) 12
   (e) 14
   (f) insufficient data to calculate the answer

3. Which of the following classifications of physical activity is rated as light, mild aerobic exercise—because it is likely to burn less than 7 Calories per minute?
   (a) competitive racquetball
   (b) running at a speed of 7 miles per hour
   (c) walking at a speed of 2.0 miles per hour
   (d) competitive singles tennis
   (e) bicycling at a speed of 12 miles per hour

4. Which of the following statements relative to the basal metabolic rate or resting metabolic rate is false?
   (a) The BMR is high in infancy but declines throughout adolescence and adulthood.
   (b) The BMR is higher in women than in men due to the generally higher levels of body fat in women.
   (c) The resting metabolic rate is the equivalent of one MET.
   (d) The resting metabolic rate is higher than the BMR.
   (e) Dietary-induced thermogenesis raises the resting metabolic rate.

5. Which of the following energy sources found in the human body represents the greatest storage of potential energy in the form of total Calories?
   (a) blood glucose
   (b) ATP
   (c) muscle glycogen
   (d) adipose tissue triglycerides
   (e) muscle protein

6. Of the following statements concerning the interrelationships between various forms of energy, which one is false?
   (a) A kilojoule is greater than a kilocalorie.
   (b) A kilogram-meter is equal to 7.23 foot-pounds.
   (c) A gram of fat has more Calories than a gram of carbohydrate.
   (d) A gram of fat has more Calories than a gram of protein.
   (e) A liter of oxygen can release more than one kilocalorie when metabolizing carbohydrate.

7. Approximately how many Calories will a 200-pound individual use while jogging a mile?
   (a) 70 (d) 255
   (b) 145 (e) 440
   (c) 200

8. Which of the following statements relative to exercise and metabolic rate is false?
   (a) The intensity of the exercise is the most important factor to increase the metabolic rate.
   (b) Increased efficiency for swimming a set distance will decrease the energy cost.
   (c) The heavier person will burn more Calories running a mile than a lighter person.
   (d) Oxygen consumption and heart rate are two ways to monitor the metabolic rate.
   (e) Walking a mile slowly or jogging a mile cost the same amount of Calories.

9. Which energy system has the greatest capacity for energy production, i.e., endurance?
   (a) ATP-PCr
   (b) lactic acid
   (c) anaerobic glycolysis
   (d) oxygen
   (e) phosphagens

10. Which of the following is *not* needed to calculate the estimated energy requirement (EER)?
    (a) body fat percentage
    (b) age
    (c) height
    (d) weight
    (e) physical activity level (PAL)

Answers to multiple choice questions:
1. b; 2. e; 3. c; 4. b; 5. d; 6. a; 7. b; 8. e; 9. d; 10. a.

1. If an individual performed 5,000 foot pounds of work in one minute, how many kilojoules of work were accomplished?

2. Name the sources of energy stored in the human body and discuss their role in the three human energy systems.

3. Differentiate between BMR, RMR, BEE, REE, TEF, TEE, EER, and TDEE as defined in this text.

4. Explain the role of the three energy systems during exercise and provide an example using track running events.

5. List the major causes of fatigue during exercise and indicate how various nutritional interventions may help prevent premature fatigue.

Books

Driskell, J., and Wolinsky, I. 1999. *Energy-yielding macronutrients and energy metabolism in sports nutrition.* Boca Raton, FL: CRC Press.

Lee, R., and Nieman, D. 2003. *Nutritional Assessment.* Boston: McGraw-Hill.

National Academy of Sciences. 2002. *Dietary Reference Intakes for Energy, Carbohydrates, Fiber, Fat, Protein, and Amino Acids (Macronutrients).* Washington, DC: National Academy Press.

Welk, G. 2002. *Physical Activity Assessments for Health-Related Research.* Champaign, IL: Human Kinetics.

Review Articles

Ainsworth, B. 2003. The compendium of physical activities. *President's Council on Physical Fitness and Sports Research Digest* 4 (2): 1–8.

Bassett, D. R., and Howley, E. T. 2000. Limiting factors for maximum oxygen uptake and determinants of endurance performance. *Medicine & Science in Sports & Exercise* 32:70–84

Brooks, G. A. 1998. Mammalian fuel utilization during sustained exercise. *Comparative Biochemistry and Physiology: Part B. Biochemistry and Molecular Biology* 120:89–107.

Budgett, R. 1998. Fatigue and underperformance in athletes: The overtraining syndrome. *British Journal of Sports Medicine* 32:107–10.

Burke, L. 2001. Energy needs of athletes. *Canadian Journal of Applied Physiology* 26:S202–19.

Cairns, S., et al. 2005. Evaluation of models used to study neuromuscular fatigue. *Exercise and Sports Sciences Reviews* 33:9–16

Carpenter, W., et al. 1995. Influence of body composition and resting metabolic rate on variation in total energy expenditure: A meta-analysis. *American Journal of Clinical Nutrition* 61: 4–10.

Coggan, A. R. 1997. The glucose crossover concept is not an important new concept in exercise metabolism. *Clinical Experimental Pharmacology and Physiology* 24:896–90.

Conley, K., et al. 2001. Limits to sustainable muscle performance: Interaction between glycolysis and oxidative phosphorylation. *Journal of Experimental Biology* 204:3189–94.

Davis, J. M., et al. 2000. Serotonin and central nervous system fatigue: Nutritional considerations. *American Journal of Clinical Nutrition* 72:573S–78S.

de Jonge, L. and Bray, G. A. 1997. The thermic effect of food and obesity. *Obesity Research* 5:622–31.

Fitts, R. H. 1996. Muscle fatigue: The cellular aspects. *American Journal of Sports Medicine* 24:S9–13.

Gandevia, S. C. 1998. Neural control in human muscle fatigue: Changes in muscle afferents, motoneurones and motorcortical drive. *Acta Physiologica Scandinavica* 162:275–83.

Gastin, P. 2001. Energy system interaction and relative contribution during maximal exercise. *Sports Medicine* 31:725–41.

Goran, M. I. 1997. Genetic influence on human energy expenditure and substrate utilization. *Behavior Genetics* 27:389–99.

Green, H. 2004. Mechanisms and management of fatigue in health and disease: Symposium introduction. *Canadian Journal of Applied Physiology* 29:264–73.

Green, H. J. 1997. Mechanisms of muscle fatigue in intense exercise. *Journal of Sports Sciences* 15:247–56.

Greenhaff, P. L., and Timmons, J. A. 1998. Interaction between aerobic and anaerobic metabolism during intense muscle contraction. *Exercise and Sport Sciences Reviews* 26:1–30.

Hagberg, J., and Pena, N. 1989. Bicycling's exclusive calorie counter. *Bicycling* 30:100–103.

Halson, S., and Jeukendrup, A. 2004. Does overtraining exist? An analysis of overreaching and overtraining research. *Sports Medicine* 34:967–81.

Hargreaves, M. 2000. Skeletal muscle metabolism during exercise in humans. *Clinical and Experimental Pharmacology and Physiology* 27:225–28.

Hawley, J., and Hopkins, W. 1995. Aerobic glycolytic and aerobic lipolytic power systems. *Sports Medicine* 19:240–50.

Holloszy, J. O., et al. 1998. The regulation of carbohydrate and fat metabolism during and after exercise. *Frontiers in Bioscience* 3:D1011–27.

Hoppeler, H., and Weibel, E. 2000. Structural and functional limits for oxygen supply to muscle. *Acta Physiologica Scandinavica* 168:445–56.

International Life Sciences Institute. 2000. Measurement of moderate physical activity: Advances in assessment techniques. *Medicine & Science in Sports & Exercise* 32: S438–516.

Jeukendrup, A., et al. 2000. The bioenergetics of World Class Cycling. *Journal of Science and Medicine in Sport* 3:414–33.

Kearney, J. T., et al. 2000. Measurement of work and power in sport. In *Exercise and Sport Sciences,* eds. W. E. Garrett and D. T. Kirkendall. Philadelphia: Lippincott Williams & Wilkins.

Kirkendall, D. T. 2000. Fatigue from voluntary motor activity. In *Exercise and Sport Sciences,* eds. W. E. Garrett and D. T. Kirkendall. Philadelphia: Lippincott, Williams & Wilkins.

Knuttgen, H. 1995. Force, work, and power in athletic training. *Sports Science Exchange* 8(4):1–6.

Lambert, C., and Flynn, M. 2002. Fatigue during high-intensity intermittent exercise: Application to bodybuilding. *Sports Medicine* 32:511–22.

Lambert, E., et al. 2005. Complex systems model of fatigue: Integrative homeostatic control of peripheral physiological systems during exercise in humans. *British Journal of Sports Medicine* 39:52–62.

Lange, B., and Bury, T. 2001. Physiologic evaluation of explosive force in sports. *Revue Medicale de Liege* 56:233–38.

Levine, J. 2004. Non-exercise activity thermogenesis. *Nutrition Reviews* 62:S82–S97.

Lindstedt, S., and Conley, K. 2001. Human aerobic performance: Too much ado about limits to VO$_2$. *Journal of Experimental Biology* 204:3195–99.

McLester, J. R. 1997. Muscle contraction and fatigue: The role of adenosine 5'-diphosphate and inorganic phosphate. *Sports Medicine* 23:287–305.

McMahon, S., and Jenkins, D. 2002. Factors affecting the rate of phosphocreatine resynthesis following intense exercise. *Sports Medicine* 32:761–84.

Melanson, E., et al. 2004. Commercially available pedometers: Considerations for accurate step counting. *Preventive Medicine* 39:361–68.

Myburgh, K. 2004. Protecting muscle ATP: Positive roles for peripheral defense mechanisms. *Medicine & Science in Sports & Exercise* 37:16–19.

Newsholme, E. 1993. Application of knowledge of metabolic integration to the problem of metabolic limitations in sprints, middle distance and marathon running. In *Principles of Exercise Biochemistry,* ed. J. Poortmans. Basel, Switzerland: Karger.

O'Connor, P., and Puetz, T. 2005. Chronic physical activity and feelings of energy and fatigue. *Medicine & Science in Sports & Exercise* 37:299–305.

Peters, A., et al. 2004. The selfish brain: Competition for energy resources. *Neuroscience and Biobehavior Reviews* 28:143–80.

Richardson, R. 2000. Skeletal muscle: Master or slave of the cardiovascular system? *Medicine & Science in Sports & Exercise* 32:89–93.

Robergs, R., et al. 2004. Biochemistry of exercise-induced acidosis. *American Journal of Physiology. Regulatory, Integrative and Compartive Physiology* 287:R502–16.

Sahlin, K., et al. 1998. Energy supply and muscle fatigue in humans. *Acta Physiologica Scandinavica* 162:261–66.

Shephard, R. 2001. Chronic fatigue syndrome: An update. *Sports Medicine* 31:167–94.

Skinner, J. 2004. Chronic fatigue syndrome. *Physician and Sportsmedicine* 32 (2): 28–32.

Stager, J., et al. 1995. The use of doubly labelled water in quantifying energy expenditure during prolonged activity. *Sports Medicine* 19:166–72.

Thompson, J., et al. 1996. Effects of diet and diet-plus-exercise programs on resting metabolic rate: A meta-analysis. *International Journal of Sport Nutrition* 6:41–61.

Tremblay, A., et al. 1985. The effects of exercise-training on energy balance and adipose tissue morphology and metabolism. *Sports Medicine* 2:223–33.

Walsh, M. 2000. Whole body fatigue and critical power: A physiological interpretation. *Sports Medicine* 29:153–66.

Ward, D., et al. 2005. Accelerometer use in physical activity: Best practices and research recommendations. *Medicine & Science in Sports & Exercise* 37:S582–S588.

Specific Studies

Beets, M., et al. 2005. The accuracy of pedometer steps and time during walking in children. *Medicine & Science in Sports & Exercise* 37:513–20.

Biewener, A., et al. 2004. Muscle mechanical advantage of human walking and running: Implications for energy cost. *Journal of Applied Physiology* 97:2266–74.

Burleson, M. A., et al. 1998. Effect of weight training exercise and treadmill exercise on post-exercise oxygen consumption. *Medicine & Science in Sports & Exercise* 30:518–22.

Cade, R., et al. 1992. Marathon running: Physiological and chemical changes accompanying late race functional deterioration. *European Journal of Applied Physiology* 65:485–91.

Crovetti, R., et al. 1998. The influence of thermic effect of food on satiety. *European Journal of Clinical Nutrition* 52:482–88.

Gillette, C., et al. 1994. Postexercise energy expenditure in response to acute aerobic or resistive exercise. *International Journal of Sport Nutrition* 4:347–60.

Graves, J., et al. 1987. The effect of hand-held weights on the physiological responses to walking exercise. *Medicine & Science in Sports & Exercise* 19:260–65.

Hall, C., et al. 2004. Energy expenditure of walking and running: Comparison of prediction equations. *Medicine & Science in Sports & Exercise* 36:2128–34.

Hargreaves, M., et al. 1998. Muscle metabolites and performance during high-intensity, intermittent exercise. *Journal of Applied Physiology* 84:1687–91.

Leblanc, J. 1992. Mechanisms of adaptation to cold. *International Journal of Sports Medicine* 13 (Supplement 1): S169–178.

Meijer, G. 1992. Physical activity and energy expenditure in lean and obese adult human subjects. *European Journal of Applied Physiology* 65 (6): S25–28.

Melanson, E., et al. 1996. Exercise responses to running and in-line skating at self-selected paces. *Medicine & Science in Sports & Exercise* 28:247–50.

Morgan, D., et al. 1995. Variation in the aerobic demand of running among trained and untrained subjects. *Medicine & Science in Sports & Exercise* 27:404–9.

Nijs, J., et al. 2005. Chronic fatigue syndrome: Exercise performance related to immune dysfunction. *Medicine & Science in Sports & Exercise* 37:1647–54.

Reed, G., and Hill, J. 1996. Measuring the thermic effect of food. *American Journal of Clinical Nutrition* 63:164–69.

Schoeller, D., and Hnilicka, J. 1996. Reliability of the doubly labeled water method for the measurement of total daily energy expenditure in free-living subjects. *Journal of Nutrition* 126:348S–354S.

Segal, K., et al. 1990. Thermic effect of a meal over 3 and 6 hours in lean and obese men. *Metabolism* 39:985–92.

Sjodin, A., et al. 1996. The influence of physical activity on BMR. *Medicine & Science in Sports & Exercise* 28:85–91.

Spencer, M., and Gastin, P. 2001. Energy system contribution during 200- to 1500-m running in highly trained athletes. *Medicine & Science in Sports & Exercise* 33:157–62.

Suter, E., et al. 1993. Muscle fiber type distribution as estimated by Cybex testing and by muscle biopsy. *Medicine & Science in Sports & Exercise* 25:363–70.

Thomas, T., and Londeree, B. 1989. Energy cost during prolonged walking vs jogging exercise. *Physician and Sportsmedicine* 17 (5):93–102.

Thompson, J., and Manore, M. 1996. Predicted and measured resting metabolic rate of male and female endurance athletes. *Journal of the American Dietetic Association* 96:30–34.

Tremblay, A., et al. 1990. Long-term exercise training with constant energy intake. 2: effect of glucose metabolism and resting energy expenditure. *International Journal of Obesity* 14:75–81.

Ward-Smith, A. J. 1999. Aerobic and anaerobic energy conversion during high-intensity exercise. *Medicine & Science in Sports & Exercise* 31:1855–60.

Westerterp, K., et al. 1991. Physical activity and sleeping metabolic rate. *Medicine & Science in Sports & Exercise* 23:166–70.

Williams, J. H., et al. 1998. Functional aspects of skeletal muscle contractile apparatus and sarcoplasmic reticulum after fatigue. *Journal of Applied Physiology* 85:619–26.

Wilmore, J. H., et al. 1998. Alterations in resting metabolic rate as a consequence of 20 wk of endurance training: The HERITAGE Family Study. *American Journal of Clinical Nutrition* 68:66–71.

Zhang, K., et al. 2004. Improving energy expenditure estimation for physical activity. *Medicine & Science in Sports & Exercise* 36:883–89.

Carbohydrates: The Main Energy Food

CHAPTER FOUR

LEARNING OBJECTIVES

After studying this chapter, you should be able to:

1. List the different types of dietary carbohydrates and identify foods typically rich in the different types.

2. Calculate the approximate number of Calories from carbohydrate that should be included in your daily diet.

3. Describe how dietary carbohydrate is absorbed, how it is distributed in the body, and what its major functions are in human metabolism.

4. Explain the role of carbohydrate in human energy systems during exercise.

5. Describe the various mechanisms whereby inadequate amounts of dietary carbohydrate may contribute to fatigue during exercise.

6. Understand the mechanisms whereby various dietary strategies involving carbohydrate intake (amount, type, and timing) before, during, and after exercise may help to optimize training for and competition in sport.

7. Identify athletes for whom carbohydrate loading may be appropriate, and describe the full carbohydrate loading protocol, highlighting dietary intake and exercise training considerations.

8. Evaluate the efficacy of metabolic by-products of carbohydrate metabolism as ergogenic aids.

9. Identify carbohydrate-containing foods that are considered to be more healthful and explain why.

One of the most important nutrients in your diet, from the standpoint of both health and athletic performance, is dietary carbohydrate.

Over the years the reputation of carbohydrate, particularly as a component of a weight-control diet, has seesawed between friend and foe. Most recently, some have dubbed carbohydrate as foe, alleging that high-carbohydrate diets are contributing to the epidemic of obesity within industrialized nations. However, most dietitians and nutrition scientists consider consumption of carbohydrate-rich foods to be one of the most important components of a healthful diet, not only for its potential in preventing certain chronic diseases but also as an integral part of a proper diet to lose excess body fat. The possible health benefits of a diet high in complex carbohydrates and fiber and low in added sugars were introduced in chapter 2 and are explained further in this chapter. The role of carbohydrate foods in a weight-control plan will be addressed in chapter 11 and as we shall see, carbohydrates *per se* do not cause obesity, but excess Calories do.

As noted in chapter 3, the major role of carbohydrate in human nutrition is to provide energy, and scientists have long known that carbohydrate is one of the prime sources of energy during exercise. Of all the nutrients we consume, carbohydrate has received the most research attention in regard to a potential influence upon athletic performance, particularly in exercise tasks characterized by endurance such as long-distance running, cycling, and triathloning. Such research is important to athletes who are concerned about optimal carbohydrate nutrition during training and competition. Indeed, continued research over the past quarter century has enabled sports nutritionists to provide more specific and useful responses to athletes' questions. For example, compared to the first edition of this book published in 1983, readers of this eighth edition will note several significant differences concerning

dietary carbohydrate recommendations to athletes.

In this chapter, we explore the nature of dietary carbohydrates, their metabolic fates and interactions in the human body, their possible influence upon health status, and their potential application to physical performance, including the following: the adverse effects of low-carbohydrate diets; the value of carbohydrate intake before, during, and after exercise; the efficacy of different types of carbohydrates; the role of carbohydrate loading; and carbohydrate foods or compounds, with alleged ergogenic properties. Although the role of sports drinks containing carbohydrate, such as Gatorade and PowerAde, is introduced in this chapter, additional detailed coverage of these beverages and their effect upon performance is presented in chapter 9: Water, Electrolytes, and Temperature Regulation.

Dietary Carbohydrates

What are the different types of dietary carbohydrates?

Carbohydrates represent one of the least expensive forms of Calories and hence are one of the major food supplies for the vast majority of the world's peoples. They are one of the three basic energy nutrients formed when the energy from the sun is harnessed in plants through the process of photosynthesis. Although the energy content of the various forms of carbohydrate varies slightly, each gram of carbohydrate contains approximately 4 Calories.

Carbohydrates are organic compounds that contain carbon, hydrogen, and oxygen in various combinations. A wide variety of different forms exist in nature and in the human body, and novel manufactured carbohydrates, including sports drinks, have been developed for the food industry. In general terms, the major categories of importance to our discussion are simple carbohydrates, complex carbohydrates, and dietary fiber.

Simple carbohydrates, which are usually known as sugars, can be subdivided into two categories: disaccharides and mono-

saccharides. *Saccharide* means "sugar" or "sweet." Think of saccharin, a noncaloric sweetener. The three major **monosaccharides** (single sugars) are **glucose, fructose,** and **galactose.** Glucose and fructose occur widely in nature, primarily in fruits, as free monosaccharides. Glucose is often called dextrose or grape sugar, while fructose is known as levulose or fruit sugar. Galactose is found in milk as part of lactose. Figure 4.1 presents two configurations illustrating the structure of monosaccharides.

The combination of two monosaccharides yields a **disaccharide.** The disaccharides (double sugars) include maltose (malt sugar), lactose (milk sugar), and sucrose (cane sugar or table sugar). Upon digestion these disaccharides yield the monosaccharides as follows:

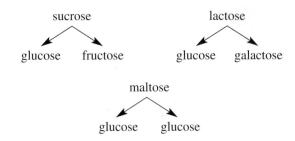

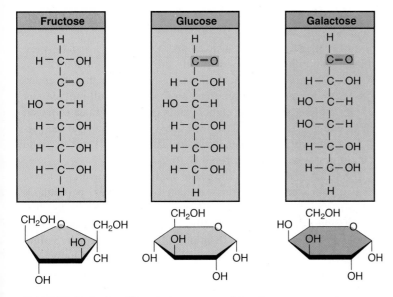

Fructose	Glucose	Galactose

FIGURE 4.1 Chemical structure of the three monosaccharides is depicted in both the linear and ring configurations.

Monosaccharides and disaccharides, such as glucose and sucrose, may be isolated from foods in purified forms known as refined sugars. Trisaccharides and higher saccharides also exist, and may be found in commonly used sweeteners such as corn syrup. For example, high-fructose corn syrup, a common food additive, is a manufactured carbohydrate derived from the conversion of glucose in corn starch to fructose. Other food additives that are primarily sugar include honey, brown sugar, maple syrup, molasses, and fruit juice concentrate.

Complex carbohydrates, commonly known as starches, are generally formed when three or more glucose molecules combine. This combination is known as a **polysaccharide** when more than ten glucose molecules are combined and may contain thousands of linked glucose molecules (figure 4.2). Starches, which exist in a variety of forms such as amylose, amylopectin, and resistant starch, are the storage form of carbohydrates. The vast majority of carbohydrates that exist in the plant world are in polysaccharide form. Of prime interest to us are the plant starches, through which we obtain a good proportion of our daily Calories along with a wide variety of nutrients, and the animal starch, glycogen, about which we shall hear more later in relation to energy for exercise. Additionally, **glucose polymers** are polysaccharides prepared commercially by controlled hydrolysis of starch. Maltodextrins are common glucose polymers used in sports drinks, which are discussed later.

Unfortunately, because of disagreements over the classification of various forms of carbohydrate, the term "complex carbohydrate" does not appear on the Nutrition Facts food label. You may obtain a rough estimate of the complex carbohydrate content by subtracting the grams of sugar from the grams of total carbohydrate. In some cases, the term "other carbohydrates" is used, which could include complex carbohydrates and other forms of carbohydrate as well.

In its recent report on Dietary Reference Intakes, the National Academy of Sciences settled on three terms to define fiber. **Dietary fiber** consists of nondigestible carbohydrates and lignin that are intrinsic and intact in plants; this would include resistant starch. **Functional fiber** consists of isolated, nondigestible carbohydrates that have beneficial physiological effects in humans. **Total fiber** is the sum of dietary fiber and functional fiber. These nondigestible substances, which means that they are not digested and absorbed in the human small intestine, are usually a mixture of polysaccharides found in the plant wall or intracellular structures.

The National Academy of Sciences carefully defines both dietary and functional fiber, particularly as they may impact health. In essence, dietary fiber is consumed as part of intact foods (even if mechanically altered) containing other macronutrients, such as digestible carbohydrate and protein. For example, cereal brans derived from whole grains contain carbohydrate and protein, along with nondigestible fiber. Some examples of dietary fiber are cellulose, hemicellulose, lignin, pectin, and gums. When studying the health effects of dietary fiber, it is difficult to determine if health benefits are attributed to dietary fiber or to other potential healthful substances, such as certain phytochemicals, found in the food. The definition of dietary fiber includes the phytochemicals that come with it.

Functional fibers, on the other hand, may be isolated or extracted from foods by chemical or other means, and may be manufactured synthetically. For example, various gums may be extracted from seeds and used as food ingredients for various purposes. Some examples of functional fiber are pectin, gums, and resistant starch. The specific fiber needs to demonstrate a physiological effect in the body to be classified as a functional fiber, and this effect may be associated with a specific health benefit.

Total fiber is the sum of dietary fiber and functional fiber. A specific fiber may be classified as both dietary fiber and functional fiber. For example, cellulose can be classified as dietary fiber as a natural ingredient of an intact food, or it may be considered to be a functional fiber if extracted from a natural source and added to another food.

Previously, the various components of dietary and functional fiber have been classified on the basis of their solubility in water.

FIGURE 4.2 Glucose polymer. A glucose polymer is a string of glucose molecules. Muscle glycogen is a glucose polymer. Commercial glucose polymers also have been developed for consumption by endurance athletes.

Some fibers have been referred to as water soluble because they have been found to dissolve or swell in water and may be metabolized by bacteria in the large intestine. Others which do not possess these characteristics have been referred to as water-insoluble fibers. Common water-soluble fibers include gums, beta-glucans, and pectins. Common water-insoluble fibers include cellulose, hemicellulose, and lignin. Each of these types of fibers may confer specific health benefits, which will be discussed accordingly.

Sugar substitutes are designed to provide the sweetness of sugars, but with no or fewer Calories. Two of the most commonly used sugar substitutes include aspartame, a derivative of two amino acids, and sucralose, made from sugar.

A summary of the different types of carbohydrates is presented in table 4.1, and the effects of different forms of carbohydrate on physical performance or health are presented later in this chapter.

What are some common foods high in carbohydrate content?

Three of the six Food Exchanges are the primary contributors of carbohydrate in the diet; per serving, the starch exchange contains 15 grams, the fruit exchange 15 grams, and the vegetable exchange 5 grams. Some foods in the meat and milk groups also contain moderate to high amounts of carbohydrate. Dried beans and peas, because their protein content is comparable to meat, may be listed in the meat group. One-third cup of navy beans contains 15 grams of carbohydrate, which is nearly 70 percent of its energy content. A glass of skim milk contains 12 grams of carbohydrate, over 50 percent of its energy content. Table 4.2 shows some foods in the different Food Exchanges that have high carbohydrate content. A more extensive listing is provided in appendix E. Complex-carbohydrate

foods are accentuated, as they are highly recommended in the Prudent Healthy Diet.

Miscellaneous foods such as sodas, fruit ades, candy, pies, cake, and other processed sweets are high in carbohydrates. **Added sugars** is the term applied to refined sugars that are added to foods during production. Reading food labels will provide you with the total amount of carbohydrate in grams, grams of sugar, and grams of fiber. The label will also provide you with the percentage of your recommended Daily Value for total carbohydrate and fiber, as explained on pages 60–63.

As carbohydrates are the major fuel for most exercise tasks, several products have been marketed to athletes, particularly sports drinks, sports gels, and sports bars. Sports drinks, like Gatorade and PowerAde, usually contain about 6–8 percent carbohydrates, or about 14–18 grams of carbohydrate per 8 fluid ounces. The carbohydrate source in each varies, but usually contains a mixture of one of the following: glucose, fructose, sucrose, and glucose polymers. More details on sports drinks are presented in chapter 9. Sports gels, such as ReLode, GU, Power-Gel, and Clif-Shot, contain forms of carbohydrates similar to those used in sports drinks, but in a more solid gel form. They come in small squeeze containers (usually about 1 ounce) and contain roughly 20–30 grams of carbohydrate. Sports bars are also high in carbohydrate, usually with small amounts of protein and fats. The amount and type of carbohydrate per bar varies, the amount generally ranging between 20 to 45 grams. So-called "energy" drinks may contain substantial amounts of carbohydrate, often 30 to 50 or more grams in 8 ounces. Again, Nutrition Facts food labels on sports and "energy" drinks, sports gels, and sports bars provide information on the nutrient content, including amount of total carbohydrate, sugar, and fiber, as well as other ingredients such as caffeine, amino acids, vitamins, and minerals. By careful label reading and price comparisons, you may be able to get a better buy on some products. For example, sports bars are rather expensive, so purchasing lower-cost granola bars that contain similar nutrient value may provide some financial savings.

Foods high in dietary fiber include most vegetables and fruits, foods in the starch exchange made from whole grains, and dried beans and peas in the meat exchange. Wheat products are good sources of insoluble fiber, while oats, beans, dried peas, fruits and vegetables are excellent sources of soluble fiber. Because of the purported health benefits of fiber, cereal manufacturers have released new products containing 13–14 grams of fiber per serving. Psyllium, rich in both soluble and insoluble fiber, is now added to several breakfast cereals. Table 4.3 presents the average fiber content in some common foods, several of which are highlighted in figure 4.3. Food labels also document fiber content

---

TABLE 4.1 Types of dietary carbohydrates

Monosaccharides	Disaccharides	Polysaccharides	Other carbohydrates
Glucose	Sucrose	Plant starch	Sorbitol (sugar alcohol)
Fructose	Maltose	Amylose	Ribose (a five-carbon sugar)
Galactose	Lactose	Amylopectin	
		Resistant starch	
		Animal starch	
		Glycogen	
Dietary fiber	**Functional fiber**	**Dietary/ Functional fiber****	
Hemicellulose	Polydextrin	Beta-glucans	
Resistant starch*	Psyllium	Cellulose	
	Resistant starch*	Gums	
		Pectins	

*Certain forms
**Dietary fiber if found intact in food; Functional fiber if extracted and added to foods.

TABLE 4.2 Foods high in carbohydrate content (grams per serving)

Starch exchange (15 grams)	Fruit exchange (15 grams)	Vegetable exchange (5 grams)	Milk exchange (12 grams)	Meat exchange (15 grams)	Sports drinks/ sports gels/ sports bars (14–52 grams)	Miscellaneous (10–40 grams)
Whole grain	Apples	Asparagus	Ice milk	Kidney beans	Gatorade	Candy
Brown rice	Apricots	Broccoli	Rice milk	Navy beans	Gatorade Energy Drink	Cookies
Corn tortillas	Bananas	Carrots	Skim milk	Split peas	PowerAde	Fruit ades
Granola	Blueberries	Mushrooms	Soy milk	Lentils	ReLode	Soft drinks
Oatmeal	Cantaloupe	Radishes	Yogurt, fruit		GU	
Ready-to-eat cereal*	Cherries	Rutabaga			Power Gel	
Rye crackers	Dried fruits	Squash, summer			Power Bar	
Whole wheat bread	Fruit juices	Tomatoes			Clif Bar	
Enriched	Oranges	Zucchini			PRBar	
Bagels	Peaches					
English muffins	Pineapple					
Pasta	Plums					
Ready-to-eat cereal*	Raspberries					
White bread						
White rice						
Starchy vegetables						
Corn						
Green peas						
Potatoes						

*May be whole wheat or enriched, depending on the brand.

per serving. Currently food labels document total fiber content per serving, but future labels may contain both dietary and functional fiber content.

How much carbohydrate do we need in the diet?

As we shall see, the human body can convert part of dietary protein and fat to carbohydrate. Thus, the National Academy of Sciences indicated that the lower limit of dietary carbohydrate compatible with life apparently is zero, provided that adequate amounts of protein and fat are consumed. Several populations around the world have subsisted on a diet with minimal amounts of carbohydrate without any apparent adverse effects. However, given that a very low carbohydrate diet may be associated with various micronutrient deficiencies and health problems in Western societies, DRIs recently have been developed for carbohydrate and total fiber, and may be found in the DRIs table for macronutrients in the front inside cover.

FIGURE 4.3 Foods high in dietary fiber.

TABLE 4.3 Fiber content in some common foods†

Beans	7–9 grams per 1/2 cup, cooked
Vegetables	3–5 grams per 1/2 cup, cooked
Fruits	1–3 grams per piece
Breads and cereals*	1–3 grams per serving
Nuts and seeds	2–5 grams per ounce

*Fiber content may vary considerably in bran-type cereals, ranging up to 13–14 grams per serving. Select whole-grain products for higher fiber content.
†Check food labels for grams of fiber per serving.

The RDA for carbohydrates is set at 130 grams per day for adults and children, which is based on the average minimum amount of glucose utilized by the brain. The Academy developed an Acceptable Macronutrient Distribution Range (AMDR), recommending that 45–65 percent of the daily energy intake be derived from carbohydrate. The AMDR for individuals has been set for carbohydrate based on scientific evidence suggesting such an intake may play a role in the prevention of increased risk of chronic diseases and may also ensure sufficient intakes of essential nutrients.

Most of us consume carbohydrate within this range and meet the RDA, as men consume an average 200–330 grams per day while women average 180–230 grams per day. The Daily Value (DV) for carbohydrate on the food label is based on a recommendation of 60 percent of the caloric intake. The Daily Value (DV) for a 2,000 Calorie diet is 300 grams of carbohydrate, which represents 60 percent of the daily caloric intake ($4 \times 300 = 1,200$ carbohydrate Calories; $1,200/2,000 = 60$ percent).

The Academy also recommended that no more than 25 percent of total Calories should come from added sugars. This standard was set based on evidence that individuals who exceed this level may not be obtaining adequate amounts of essential micronutrients that are not present in foods and beverages that contain added sugars. It should be stressed that the 25 percent is the maximal amount, not a recommended goal. In fact, the recommendation from most health professionals is to reduce this amount to approximately 10 percent. Current estimates of sugar intake approximate 12–14 percent of daily energy intake.

The Academy recommends an Adequate Intake (AI) for total fiber, being 38 grams for men up to age 50, and 30 grams over 50. The AI set for women is 25 grams up to age 50, and 21 grams over 50. The DV for a 2,000 Calorie diet is 25 grams of fiber, or 12.5 grams per 1,000 Calories. Thus, the DV is in accord with the AI for women but somewhat lower than the AI for men. The current average amount of total fiber intake is approximately 12–14 grams per day, so most individuals are not meeting this recommendation. An increased intake of complex carbohydrates would help meet this recommendation.

Sports nutritionists also recommend a high-carbohydrate diet for individuals engaged in athletic training programs. The general recommendation for most athletes parallels the recommended dietary goals noted above. For an athlete consuming 3,000 Calories per day, 55–60 percent from carbohydrate would be 1,650–1,800 Calories, or about 400–450 grams. However, Melinda Manore, an international authority in sports nutrition, noted that the amount of carbohydrate recommended will depend on the type of sport, level of fitness, and body composition. Thus, the amount of carbohydrate needed by an individual exercising to lose weight will be quite different from the amount needed by an individual in training to run a marathon. These considerations will be discussed later in this chapter and in chapter 11.

Many recent dietary surveys conducted with athletes, including endurance athletes, often reveal a carbohydrate intake significantly lower than these recommendations.

Key Concept Recap

▶ Most foods in the starchy, fruit, and vegetable exchanges contain a high percentage of carbohydrate, primarily complex carbohydrates, which should constitute about 45–65 percent of the daily caloric intake of most individuals and athletes.

▶ The RDA for carbohydrate is 130 grams daily, while the AMDR is 45–65 percent. The AI for total fiber is 38 and 25 grams per day for young men and women, respectively, and somewhat lower amounts for older men and women. However, the Daily Value (DV) for carbohydrate is 300 grams and for dietary fiber is 25 grams, based on a 2,000 Calorie diet.

Check for Yourself

Peruse food labels of some of your favorite foods and check carbohydrate. Pay particular attention to percent of daily value for total carbohydrates, sugars, and fiber.

Metabolism and Function

How do dietary carbohydrates get into the body?

Carbohydrates usually are ingested in the forms of polysaccharides (starches), disaccharides (sucrose, maltose, and lactose), and monosaccharides (glucose and fructose). In addition, special carbohydrate compounds, such as glucose polymers, have been developed for athletes. In order to be useful in the body, these carbohydrates must be digested, absorbed, and transported to appropriate cells for metabolism.

Figure 4.4 represents the digestive system and some of the major associated organs that we will discuss in the following chapters. The digestive tract from the mouth to the anus is also known as the alimentary canal, which includes the mouth, pharynx, esophagus, stomach, small intestine, large intestine (colon), rectum, and anal canal. The most important segments for digestion and absorption include the stomach and the intestines, known as the gastrointestinal tract (GI tract). The major area of the GI tract where most nutrients are absorbed is the intestines, highlighted in figure 4.4.

Digestion is the process by which food is broken down both mechanically and chemically in the digestive tract and converted into absorbable forms. It is not necessary to detail all the intricate steps of the digestive process here, but essentially, specific enzymes break down the polysaccharides and disaccharides to the monosaccharides. The key enzymes and their end products are presented in table 4.4. The primary site of digestion is the small intestine, and the monosaccharides are then absorbed into the blood.

Some substances are absorbed in the stomach and large intestine as noted in figure 4.4, but most absorption of nutrients occurs through the millions of villi lining the small intestine. Some substances are absorbed by diffusion, which may be passive or facili-

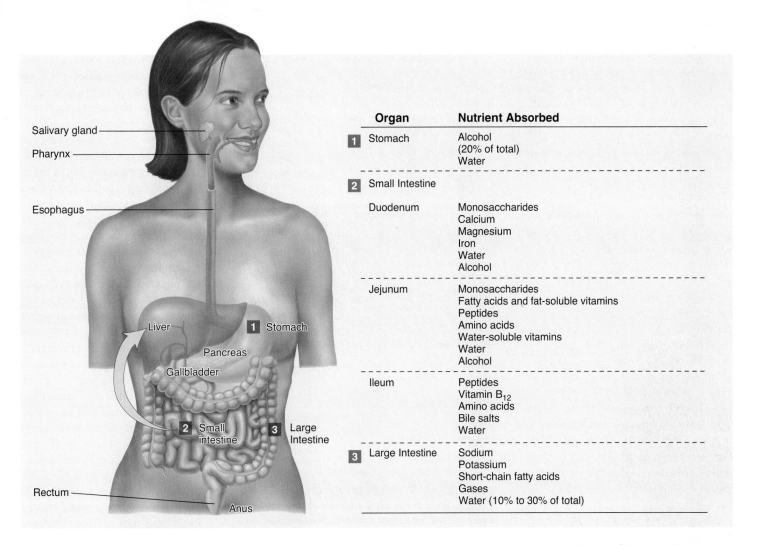

Organ	Nutrient Absorbed
1 Stomach	Alcohol (20% of total) Water
2 Small Intestine	
Duodenum	Monosaccharides Calcium Magnesium Iron Water Alcohol
Jejunum	Monosaccharides Fatty acids and fat-soluble vitamins Peptides Amino acids Water-soluble vitamins Water Alcohol
Ileum	Peptides Vitamin B_{12} Amino acids Bile salts Water
3 Large Intestine	Sodium Potassium Short-chain fatty acids Gases Water (10% to 30% of total)

FIGURE 4.4 The alimentary canal. The alimentary canal includes the mouth, the pharynx, the esophagus, the stomach, the small intestine (duodenum, jejunum, ileum), the large intestine (colon), the rectum, and the anal canal. Various glands and organs including the salivary glands, the gallbladder, and the pancreas secrete enzymes and other constituents into the digestive tract. Most blood draining from the intestines goes to the liver for processing. Note the general sites in the digestive tract where principal nutrients and other substances are absorbed (although there is some overlap in the exact site of absorption). Most absorption of nutrients occurs throughout the small intestine.

TABLE 4.4	Major digestive enzymes involved in carbohydrate digestion	
Enzyme	**Source**	**Effects**
Salivary amylase	Salivary glands	Starts conversion of starch to disaccharides in the mouth
Pancreatic amylase	Pancreas	Converts starch to disaccharides in the small intestine
Sucrase	Intestinal cells	Converts sucrose to glucose and fructose in the small intestine
Maltase	Intestinal cells	Converts maltose to two molecules of glucose in the small intestine
Lactase	Intestinal cells	Converts lactose to glucose and galactose in the small intestine

tated. In passive diffusion the substance simply diffuses across the cell membrane. Osmosis is the passive diffusion of water. In **facilitated diffusion,** a receptor in the cell membrane is needed to transport the substance from the intestine into the cell. No energy is required for diffusion, but other substances need energy supplied by the villi cells in order to be absorbed, a process known as active transport. Figure 4.5 presents a cross section of a villus and highlights some of the key nutrients and the associated process of absorption.

Optimal functioning of the GI tract following carbohydrate intake has been studied extensively because improper functioning may impair athletic performance. For example, although there is very little digestion of carbohydrate in the stomach, the rapidity with which carbohydrate leaves the stomach, and its impact upon the absorption of water, may be important considerations for athletes involved in prolonged exercise under warm environmental conditions. Foods containing carbohydrate and sodium may enhance water absorption via a co-transport mechanism, a topic that is discussed in chapter 9.

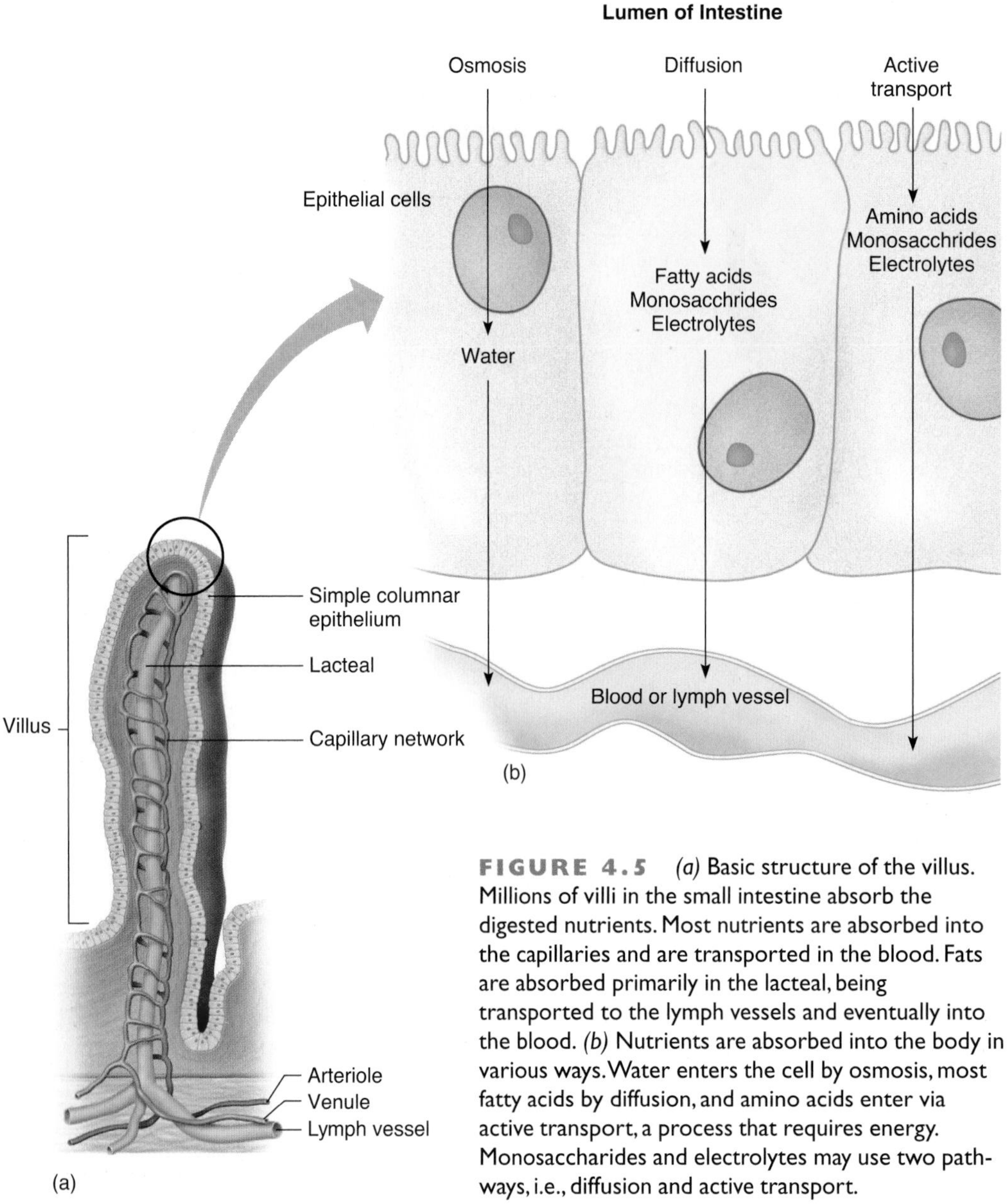

Lumen of Intestine

Osmosis   Diffusion   Active transport

Epithelial cells

Water

Fatty acids
Monosacchrides
Electrolytes

Amino acids
Monosacchrides
Electrolytes

Simple columnar
epithelium

Lacteal

Capillary network

Blood or lymph vessel

(b)

Villus

Arteriole
Venule
Lymph vessel

(a)

FIGURE 4.5 *(a)* Basic structure of the villus. Millions of villi in the small intestine absorb the digested nutrients. Most nutrients are absorbed into the capillaries and are transported in the blood. Fats are absorbed primarily in the lacteal, being transported to the lymph vessels and eventually into the blood. *(b)* Nutrients are absorbed into the body in various ways. Water enters the cell by osmosis, most fatty acids by diffusion, and amino acids enter via active transport, a process that requires energy. Monosaccharides and electrolytes may use two pathways, i.e., diffusion and active transport.

Certain dietary practices may predispose individuals to gastrointestinal distress, which will compromise exercise performance. High concentrations of simple sugars, particularly fructose, may exert a reverse osmotic effect in the intestines, drawing water from the circulatory system into the intestinal lumen. The resulting symptoms are referred to as the dumping syndrome and include weakness, sweating, and diarrhea. Lactose may present a problem to some athletes, and its possible effects are discussed later in the chapter.

What happens to the carbohydrate after it is absorbed into the body?

Of the three monosaccharides, glucose is of most importance to human physiology. Most dietary carbohydrates are broken down to glucose for absorption into the blood, while the majority of the absorbed fructose and galactose are converted to glucose by the liver. Glucose is the blood sugar.

A high-carbohydrate meal will lead to a rather rapid increase in the blood sugar level, usually within an hour. Although its use is controversial, the **glycemic index** represents the effect a particular food has upon the rate and amount of increase in the blood glucose level. Many factors other than its carbohydrate content, such as the physical form (coarse or fine) and serving mode (raw or cooked), may influence the glycemic index of any given food. Moreover, the glycemic index for any given food may vary considerably between individuals, so although some general values of the glycemic index may be given, the effects of different foods should be tested individually in those who are concerned about their blood sugar levels. In general, foods containing high amounts of refined sugars have a high glycemic index because they lead to a rapid rise in the blood sugar, but some starchy foods also have a high glycemic index. On the other hand, foods high in fiber, such as beans, generally have a low glycemic index. Interestingly, fructose has a low glycemic index, which is one of the reasons its use as the primary carbohydrate source in sports drinks had been advocated for endurance athletes. We discuss the role of fructose later in this chapter. Based on various sources in the scientific literature, table 4.5 classifies some common foods according to their glycemic index. Keep in mind, however, that one person's glycemic response to a given food may be very different from someone else's response. Moreover, people do not normally consume carbohydrate foods by themselves, but usually with other foods containing fat and protein such as a hamburger on a bun. The addition of fat and protein will usually reduce the glycemic effect of the carbohydrate, and the term *glycemic load* may be used to quantify the glycemic response.

Normal blood glucose levels (normoglycemia) range between 80–100 milligrams per deciliter of blood (80–100 mg/ml, or 80–100 milligram percent). The maintenance of a normal blood glucose level is very important for proper metabolism. Thus, the human body possesses a variety of mechanisms, primarily hormones, to help keep blood glucose levels under precise control. The rise in blood glucose, also known as serum glucose, stimulates the pancreas to secrete insulin into the blood. **Insulin** is a hormone that facilitates the uptake and utilization of glucose (facilitated diffusion) by various tissues in the body, most notably the muscles and adipose (fat) tissue. Cell membranes contain receptors to transport glucose into the cell. The primary receptors in muscle and fat cell membranes are known as GLUT-4 receptors, which are directly activated by insulin. Exercise also activates these receptors to transport blood glucose into the muscle cell, independently of the effect of insulin. Other hormones, discussed later in this chapter, are also involved in regulating blood glucose. With normal amounts of carbohydrate intake in a mixed meal, blood glucose levels remain normal.

However, foods with a high glycemic index may lead rapidly to high blood glucose levels, possibly **hyperglycemia** (> 140 mg %), which will cause an enhanced secretion of insulin from the pancreas. High serum levels of insulin will then lead to a rapid, and possibly excessive, transport of blood glucose into the tissues. This may lead in turn to **hypoglycemia** (< 40–50 mg %), or low blood glucose level. This insulin response and **reactive hypoglycemia** following carbohydrate intake may be an important consideration for some athletes and is discussed later.

Foods with a low glycemic index, particularly soluble fiber forms, lead to a slower insulin response and a more stable blood glucose level. Consuming a diet based on the glycemic index has been studied as a possible means to enhance health, as well as sports performance, as noted later in this chapter.

The fate of blood glucose is dependent upon a multitude of factors, and exercise is one of the most important. The following points represent the major fates of blood glucose. Figure 4.6 schematically represents these fates.

1. Blood glucose may be used for energy, particularly by the brain and other parts of the nervous system that rely primarily on glucose for their metabolism. Hypoglycemia can impair the normal function of the brain. Although hypoglycemia as a clinical condition is quite rare in the general population, transitory hypoglycemia may occur in very prolonged endurance exercise.

2. Blood glucose may be converted to either liver or muscle glycogen. It is important to note that liver glycogen may later be reconverted to blood glucose. However, this does not occur to any appreciable extent with muscle glycogen. In essence, glucose is locked in the muscle once it enters, owing to the lack of a specific enzyme needed to change its form so it can cross the cell membrane back into the bloodstream. Most of the muscle glycogen is converted to this locked form

TABLE 4.5 Glycemic index of some common foods

The glycemic index is a measure of the rate of digestion and absorption of carbohydrate foods and the resultant effect on the blood sugar level. The baseline is 100, which is based on the response to the oral ingestion of glucose. However, the glycemic index of any food may vary among different individuals.

High glycemic index (> 85)	Medium glycemic index (60–85)	Low glycemic index (< 60)
Bagel	All-Bran cereal	Apple
Bread, white and whole wheat	Baked beans	Applesauce
Candy	Banana	Cherries
Carrots	Corn	Chick-peas
Corn flakes	Grapes	Dates
Corn syrup	Oatmeal	Figs
Crackers	Orange juice	Fructose
Honey	Pasta	Ice cream
Potatoes	Potato chips	Kidney beans
Raisins	Rice	Lentils
Soda, with sugar	Rice, long grain	Milk, skim
Sports drinks with sugar	Spaghetti	Navy beans
Sucrose	Whole-grain rye bread	Peaches
	Yams	Plums
		Tomato soup
		Yogurt

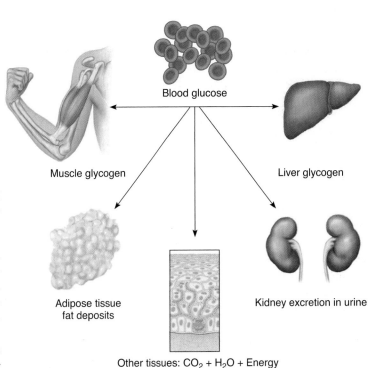

Blood glucose

Muscle glycogen

Liver glycogen

Adipose tissue
fat deposits

Kidney excretion in urine

Other tissues: $CO_2 + H_2O$ + Energy

FIGURE 4.6 Fates of blood glucose. After assimilation into the blood, glucose may be stored in the liver or muscles as glycogen or be utilized as a source of energy by these and other tissues, particularly the nervous system. Excess glucose may be partially excreted by the kidneys, but major excesses are converted to fat and stored in the adipose tissues.

of glucose during the production of energy. Researchers discovered two forms of muscle glycogen, proglycogen and macroglycogen, but in this text we shall use the term glycogen to represent both forms.

3. Blood glucose may be converted to and stored as fat in the adipose tissue. This situation occurs when the dietary carbohydrate, in combination with caloric intake of other nutrients, exceeds the energy demands of the body and the storage capacity of the liver and muscles for glycogen.

4. Some blood glucose also may be excreted in the urine if an excessive amount occurs in the blood because of rapid ingestion of simple sugars.

How much total energy do we store as carbohydrate?

A common method to express the concentration of carbohydrate stored in the body is in millimoles (mmol). A **millimole** is 1/1000 of a mole, which is the term representing gram molecular weight. In essence, a mole represents the weight in grams of a particular substance such as glucose. The chemical formula for glucose is $C_6H_{12}O_6$, so it contains six parts of carbon and oxygen and twelve parts of hydrogen. The atomic weight of carbon is 12, hydrogen is 1, and oxygen, 16. If you multiply the number of parts by the respective atomic weights of each of the elements for glucose $[(6 \times 12) + (12 \times 1) + (6 \times 16)]$, you would get a total of 180. Thus, one mole of glucose is 180 grams, or about 6 ounces. One millimole is 1/1000 of 180 grams, or 180 milligrams. (See figure 4.7.)

As an illustration, the normal glucose concentration is about 5 mmol per liter of blood, or 90 mg/100 ml, (90 mg/dL). To calculate, 5 mmol × 180 mg = 900 mg/liter, which is the same as 90 mg/100 ml. The normal individual has about 5 liters of blood. Thus, this individual would have a total of 25 mmol of glucose in the blood, or a total of 4,500 milligrams (25 × 180), or 4.5 grams.

These calculations have been presented here because this is the means whereby concentrations of glucose, glycogen, and other nutrients are expressed in contemporary scientific literature. A knowledge of these mathematical relationships should help you interpret research more effectively. However, because we are using the Calorie as the measure of energy in this book, and because each gram of carbohydrate equals approximately 4 Calories, an estimate of the energy content of the major human energy sources of carbohydrate may be obtained.

For our purposes, the body has three major energy sources of carbohydrate—blood glucose, liver glycogen, and muscle glycogen. Some glucose (about 10–15 grams) is also found in the lymph and intercellular fluids. Initial stores of blood glucose are rather limited, totaling only about 5 grams, or the equivalent of 20 Calories (C). However, blood glucose stores may be replenished from either liver glycogen or absorption of glucose from the intestine. The liver has the greatest concentration of glycogen in the body. However, because its size is limited, the liver normally contains only about 75–100 g of glycogen, or 300–400 C. One hour of aerobic exercise uses over half of the liver glycogen supply. It is also important to note that the liver glycogen content may be decreased by starvation or increased by a carbohydrate-rich diet. Fifteen hours or more of starvation will deplete the liver glycogen, while certain dietary patterns may nearly double the glycogen content of the liver, a condition that may be useful in certain tasks of physical performance.

The greatest amount of carbohydrate stored in the body is in the form of muscle glycogen. This is because the muscles compose such a large proportion of the body mass as contrasted to the liver. One would expect large differences in total muscle glycogen content between different individuals because of differences in body size. However, for an average-sized, untrained man with about 30 kg of his body weight consisting of muscle tissue, one could expect a total muscle glycogen content of approximately 360 g, or 1,440 C. This would represent a concentration of about 66 mmol, or 12 grams, per kg of muscle tissue. As with liver glycogen, the muscle glycogen stores also may be decreased or increased, with considerable effects on physical performance. For example, a trained endurance athlete may have twice the amount of stored muscle glycogen that an untrained sedentary individual has.

If we calculate the body storage of carbohydrate as blood glucose, liver glycogen, and muscle glycogen, the total is only about 1,800–1,900 C, not an appreciable amount. One full day of starvation could reduce it considerably. Some normal ranges of carbohydrate stores are presented in table 4.6, although these normal ranges may be increased or decreased considerably by diet or exercise.

Can the human body make carbohydrates from protein and fat?

Because the carbohydrate stores in the body are rather limited, and because blood glucose is normally essential for optimal functioning of the central nervous system, it is important to be able to produce glucose internally if the stores are depleted by starvation or a zero-carbohydrate diet. This process in the body is called **gluconeogenesis,** meaning the new formation of glucose. A number of different substrates from each of the three energy nutrients may be used and are depicted graphically in figure 4.8.

Protein may be a significant source of blood glucose. Protein breaks down to amino acids in the body, and certain of these amino acids, notably alanine, may

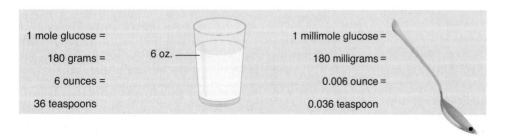

1 mole glucose =		1 millimole glucose =
180 grams =	6 oz.	180 milligrams =
6 ounces =		0.006 ounce =
36 teaspoons		0.036 teaspoon

FIGURE 4.7 The millimole concept. The concentration of some nutrients in the body is often expressed in millimoles. See text for explanation.

TABLE 4.6	Approximate carbohydrate stores in the body of a normal, sedentary adult	
Source	Amount in grams	Equivalent amount in Calories
Blood glucose	5	20
Liver glycogen	75–100	300–400
Muscle glycogen	300–400	1,200–1,600

Through gluconeogenesis, one gram of protein will yield about 0.56 gram of glucose. Triglycerides are about 10 percent glycerol, and each gram of glycerol may be converted to a gram of glucose.

In addition, certain by-products of carbohydrate metabolism, notably pyruvate and lactate, may be converted back to glucose in the liver. Lactic acid, produced in the muscle during intense exercise, may be released into the blood and carried to the liver for reconversion to glucose. The glucose may then return to the muscles to be used as an energy source or stored as glycogen. This is the **Cori cycle.** Figure 4.9 illustrates some of the basic interrelationships among carbohydrate, fat, and protein in human nutrition.

be converted to glucose in the liver. This is referred to as the **glucose-alanine cycle,** which is explained further in chapter 6. A number of other amino acids also are gluconeogenic. Glucose is essential for the brain and several other tissues. If about 130 grams of carbohydrate are not consumed daily, then the body will produce the glucose it needs, primarily from protein in the body.

Fats in the body break down into fatty acids and glycerol. Although there is no mechanism in human cells to convert the fatty acids to glucose, glycerol may be converted to glucose through the process of gluconeogenesis in the liver.

What are the major functions of carbohydrate in human nutrition?

The major function of carbohydrate in human metabolism is to supply energy. Some body cells, such as the nerve cells in the brain and retina and the red blood cells, are normally totally dependent upon glucose for energy and require a constant source. Through a series of biochemical reactions in the body cells, glucose is oxidized, eventually producing water, carbon dioxide, and energy. Zierler notes that although carbohydrate is an excellent source of energy, it is not the major fuel when the body is at rest;

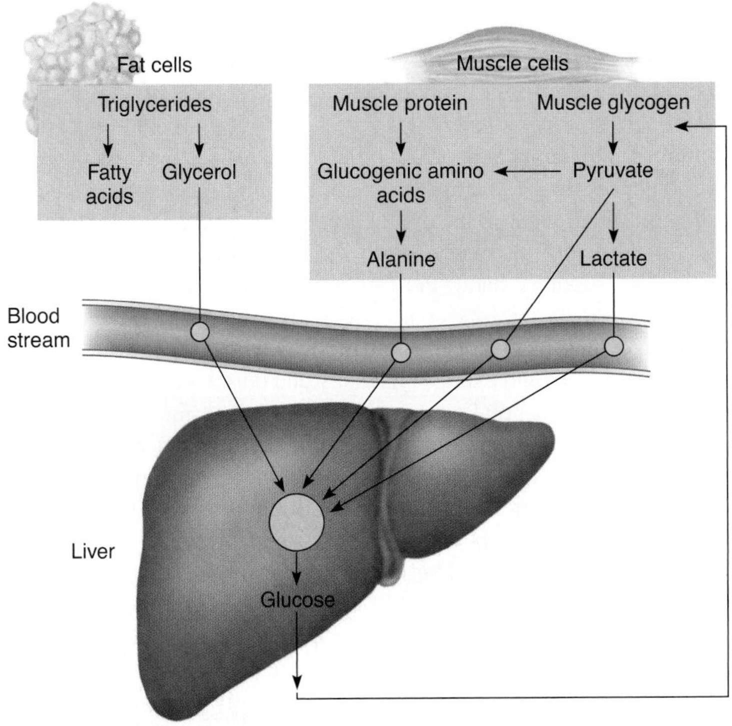

FIGURE 4.8 Gluconeogenesis. The liver is the major site for gluconeogenesis in the body. The breakdown products of fats, protein, and carbohydrate from other parts of the body may be transported to the liver by the blood for eventual reconversion into glucose. Glycerol, glucogenic amino acids, lactate, and pyruvate may be important sources for the new formation of glucose. The Cori cycle involves the transport of lactate to the liver and conversion to glucose, which may then be transported back to the muscle.

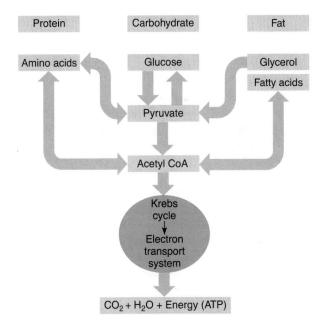

FIGURE 4.9 Interrelationships among carbohydrate, fat, and protein metabolism in humans. All three nutrients may be utilized for energy, although the major energy sources are carbohydrate and fat. Excess carbohydrate may be converted to fat; the carbohydrate structure also may be used to form protein, but nitrogen must be added. Fat cannot be used to generate carbohydrate to any large extent because acetyl CoA cannot be converted to pyruvate. The glycerol component of fat possibly may form very small amounts of carbohydrate. Fats may serve as a basis for the formation of protein, but again nitrogen must be added. Excess protein cannot be stored in the body but can be converted to either carbohydrate or fat.

fats are. Carbohydrate is the main fuel for certain tissues during rest, such as the brain, central nervous system, and red blood cells, but provides only about 15–20 percent of muscle energy needs during rest. Thus, the body conserves its limited carbohydrate stores by using fats as the primary energy source during resting conditions. As noted in chapter 3, carbohydrate can be used to produce energy either aerobically or anaerobically. Recall that in the lactic acid system, ATP is produced rapidly via anaerobic glycolysis, but for this system to continue functioning, the end product of glycolysis, pyruvic acid or pyruvate, must be converted into lactic acid. In the oxygen system, aerobic glycolysis predominates and pyruvic acid is converted into acetyl CoA, which enters into the Krebs cycle and electron transfer system for complete oxidation and the production of relatively large amounts of ATP. For the same amount of carbohydrate, anaerobic metabolism yields only two ATP, whereas aerobic metabolism yields thirty-six to thirty-eight ATP. See appendix G, figures G.1 to G.3, for more detail.

Carbohydrates have some functions in the body other than energy production. Monosaccharides can be used to form other smaller carbohydrate molecules such as trioses and pentoses. These substances may combine with other nutrients and form body chemicals essential to life, such as glycolipids or glycoproteins. Glycoproteins are very important components of cell membranes, serving as receptors to help regulate cell function. Ribose is a key pentose (5-carbon sugar) that is a part of a number of indispensable compounds in the body. One of those compounds is RNA, or ribonucleic acid, which plays an important part in anabolic processes in the cells.

Key Concept Recap

▶ Most ingested carbohydrates are initially converted into blood glucose and used for energy or stored as liver and muscle glycogen, but excess carbohydrates may be converted into fat.

▶ The major function of carbohydrates in human metabolism is to supply energy; blood glucose is essential for optimal functioning of the nervous system, whereas muscle glycogen is essential for both anaerobic and aerobic endurance exercise.

▶ The three sources of carbohydrate in the body of an average adult male are blood glucose (5 grams; 20 Calories), liver glycogen (75–100 grams; 300–400 Calories), and muscle glycogen (350–400 grams; 1,400–1,600 Calories).

▶ The body can make glucose from certain by-products of protein and fat.

Carbohydrates for Exercise

Both hypoglycemia and depleted muscle glycogen may precipitate fatigue, so maintaining optimal levels of blood glucose, liver glycogen, and muscle glycogen is essential in various athletic endeavors, particularly prolonged exercise tasks. Some sports authorities indicate carbohydrate is the master fuel for athletes. Indeed, Kenyan runners, who dominate world competition in endurance running events, subsist on a diet that is about 76.5 percent carbohydrate.

In this section we discuss the role of carbohydrate as an energy source during exercise, the effect of training to enhance carbohydrate use for energy when needed, and various methods to provide adequate carbohydrate nutrition to the athlete before, during, and after competition, and carbohydrate intake during training.

In what types of activities does the body rely heavily on carbohydrate as an energy source?

Carbohydrate supplies approximately 40 percent of the body's total energy needs during rest with about 15–20 percent used by the muscles. During very light exercise fat is an important energy source, but van Loon and others found that muscle glycogen and plasma glucose oxidation rates increased with every increment in exercise intensity. When exercise becomes more intense, such as when a person is working at 65–85 percent of capacity, carbohydrate becomes the preferred energy source; this is the crossover concept discussed in chapter 3. At maximal or supramaximal exercise levels, carbohydrate is used almost exclusively. Thus, carbohydrate may be the prime energy source for high-intensity anaerobic events lasting for less than one minute and high-intensity aerobic events lasting over an hour or two.

As Holloszy and others recently summarized, carbohydrate use, then, is associated with the intensity level of the exercise. The more intense the exercise, the greater the percentage contribution of carbohydrate. Of course, the more intense the exercise, the sooner exhaustion occurs. A fairly well-conditioned person may be able to exercise for many hours at 40–50 percent of VO_2 max, for 1 to 2 hours or so at 70–80 percent of VO_2 max, but only for minutes at maximal or supramaximal levels of VO_2 max. As noted in chapter 3, the fatigue that occurs in very high-intensity exercise of short duration, such as a minute or two, is probably due to the increased acidity associated with the rapid production of lactic acid. On the other hand, the fatigue associated with more prolonged exercise may be connected with inadequate supplies of liver and muscle glycogen, both of which may be affected by dietary practices and exercise intensity and duration.

Carbohydrate intake is most important for prolonged endurance events lasting more than 90–120 minutes. Data from such endurance tasks as the Tour de France, the bicycle Race Across America, and the Ironman Triathlon, illustrate the importance of dietary carbohydrate in sustaining high energy output for prolonged periods. Most of the athletes in these events consumed high-caloric diets rich in carbohydrates both before and during competition. A classic example is the ultradistance runner from Greece, Yannis Kouros, who won the Sydney to Melbourne race in Australia, a distance of approximately 600 miles, in 5 days and 5 hours, or about 114 miles of running per day. He consumed up to 13,400 Calories per day, with up to 98 percent being derived from carbohydrates. Cyclists in major multiday races consume more than 800 grams of carbohydrate daily. Data obtained from exercise tasks of lesser magnitude, such as marathons (26.2 miles; 42.2 kilometers) and ultramarathons (50 kilometers and longer), also provide evidence for the importance of carbohydrate as the prime energy fuel, as evidenced in the recent review by Peters.

Carbohydrate is also an essential energy fuel for prolonged sports involving many intermittent bouts of high-intensity exercise such as soccer, rugby, field hockey, ice hockey, and tennis. Athletes in these sports repeatedly use muscle glycogen stored in their fast-twitch muscle fibers, which may lead to a selective depletion in these fibers. In a recent review, Kirkendall indicates there is overwhelming evidence proving that a diet rich in carbohydrates can fill muscles with glycogen, and glycogen is critical to optimal performance in soccer.

In other reviews, both Burke and Febbraio noted that carbohydrate oxidation, particularly muscle glycogen, is increased during exercise in the heat. Febbraio suggests this may be due to an augmented sympathetic-adrenal response, or to an increased intramuscular temperature. However, some research indicates no adverse effect on the rate of carbohydrate oxidation in subjects who are heat acclimated. Exercise at high altitudes and in very cold temperatures may also increase carbohydrate use as an energy source.

Why is carbohydrate an important energy source for exercise?

Carbohydrate is the most important energy food for exercise. Besides being the only food that can be used for anaerobic energy production in the lactic acid system, it is also the most efficient fuel for the oxygen system. If we look at the caloric value of carbohydrate (1 gram = 4 C) and fat (1 gram = 9 C), we might think that fat is a better source of energy. Indeed, this is so if we just look at Calories per gram. However, more oxygen is needed to metabolize the fat, and if we look at how many Calories we get from one liter of oxygen, we will find that carbohydrate yields about 5.05 Calories and fat gives only 4.69. Thus, carbohydrate appears to be a more efficient fuel than fat, by about 7 percent. The metabolic pathways for carbohydrate are also more efficient than those for fat. In essence, during aerobic glycolysis carbohydrate is able to produce ATP for muscle contraction up to three times more rapidly than fat and even faster during anaerobic glycolysis.

The primary carbohydrate source of energy for physical performance is muscle glycogen, specifically the glycogen in the muscles that are active. As the muscle glycogen is being used during exercise, blood glucose enters the muscles and the energy pathways. In turn, the liver will release some of its glucose to help maintain or elevate blood glucose levels and prevent hypoglycemia. Coyle noted that during moderate exercise, muscle glycogen and liver glycogen contribute equally to carbohydrate oxidation. At higher intensities, muscle glycogen use increases.

Thus, all body stores of carbohydrate—blood glucose, liver glycogen, and muscle glycogen—are important for energy production during various forms of exercise. Proper physical training is essential to optimize carbohydrate utilization during exercise, as is proper carbohydrate nutrition.

What effect does endurance training have on carbohydrate metabolism?

Since carbohydrate is a primary fuel for exercise, as you initiate an endurance exercise program a major proportion of your energy will be derived from your muscle glycogen stores. An acute bout of exercise itself exerts an insulin-type effect by facilitating the transport of blood glucose into the muscle both during and immediately following the exercise bout.

As you continue your endurance exercise program, such as running or bicycling, the physical activity serves as a metabolic stressor to the body, and various tissues begin to adapt to better accommodate the exercise stress. These adaptations have implications for physical performance and the fuels used. Figure 4.10 schematically represents some of these changes at the cellular level. The following have been noted to occur in both males and females, young and old, after several months of endurance training:

1. You will increase your VO_2 max through beneficial changes in your cardiovascular system and the oxygen system in your muscle tissues. This will help your body deliver and utilize more oxygen at the muscle tissue, significantly increasing your endurance capacity.

2. Of equal or greater importance, you will be able to work at a greater percentage of your VO_2 max without fatigue. At the beginning of your training program you may reach your steady-state threshold at about 50 percent of your VO_2 max and start producing lactic acid more rapidly, which may cause an early onset of fatigue. Stallknecht and others noted that training not only decreases lactic acid production during a standardized exercise task, but also increases lactic acid clearance by the liver, heart, and resting and working muscles. Thus, after training you may be able to perform at 70 percent or higher of your VO_2 max without excess lactic acid accumulation. World-class marathoners may operate above 80 percent. You may wish to refer back to figure 3.14.

3. Endurance training improves insulin sensitivity by inducing an increase in the glucose transporter GLUT-4, which enables a more rapid inflow of glucose from the blood into the muscle during exercise, and more rapid replenishment of muscle glycogen during recovery. However, Richter and others noted that although the muscle generates more GLUT-4 transporters, they are not translocated from the interior of the muscle cell to the cell membrane unless needed. Thus, the endurance-trained muscle may use less glucose at low-intensity exercise, but have the capacity to use more during intense, maximal exercise.

4. Endurance-trained muscle has an increased maximal capacity to utilize carbohydrates. Turcotte notes that the mitochondria readily adapt to changes in muscle use and disuse to meet functional demands of the muscle. Muscle cell mitochondria density increases. Also, LeBlanc and others reported that the enzymes that metabolize carbohydrate in the muscle cells will increase, especially oxidative enzymes associated with the Krebs cycle. This allows your muscles to process carbohydrate more efficiently. All muscle fiber types can increase their oxidative capacity to metabolize carbohydrates during exercise.

5. As we shall see in chapter 5, training also enhances the use of fat during exercise. By doing so, there is less reliance on carbohydrate oxidation during submaximal exercise. Recent research by Friedlander and others, from George Brooks' laboratory, reveals that the oxidation of blood glucose decreases

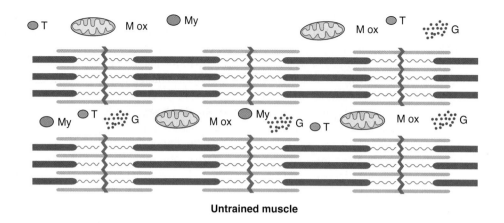

Untrained muscle

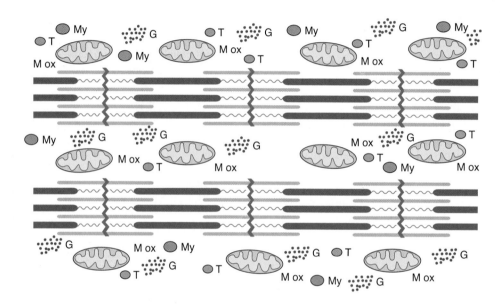

Trained muscle

FIGURE 4.10 Some of the effects of aerobic or endurance training upon skeletal muscle. Increases in glycogen (G) and triglyceride (T) provide a greater energy store, while the increase in mitochondria size and number (M), myoglobin content (My), oxidative enzymes (ox), and slow-twitch muscle fiber size facilitates the use of oxygen for production of energy.

in men during both absolute and relative exercise intensity tasks; but, although noting decreased glucose flux in women during exercise for absolute exercise intensity, they found no changes during relative exercise intensity tasks. In general, these changes are beneficial and may minimize the possibility of hypoglycemia. Other research from Brooks' laboratory suggests that training decreases the use of muscle glycogen during exercise at an absolute intensity level.

6. More glycogen is stored in the muscle. The increase in GLUT-4 receptors is partly responsible for this response, but research also reveals an increased activity of the enzyme that synthesizes glycogen. Synthesis of muscle glycogen may be twofold faster in trained versus untrained individuals.

What do all these changes mean? You may be able to run a 10-kilometer (6.2 miles) road race at a 7-minute-per-mile pace instead of 8 minutes. You can cruise in high gear for longer periods because you have increased your ability to produce energy from

carbohydrates. Also, by reducing your reliance on carbohydrates at lower running speeds, you may compete in more prolonged races, such as marathons, without becoming hypoglycemic.

How is hypoglycemia related to the development of fatigue?

As noted previously, blood glucose is in very short supply, so as it is being used during exercise it must be replenished from liver glycogen stores. A depletion of liver glycogen may lead to hypoglycemia during high-intensity aerobic exercise because gluconeogenesis normally cannot keep pace with glucose utilization by the muscles.

Hypoglycemia is known to impair the functioning of the central nervous system and is often accompanied by acute feelings of dizziness, muscular weakness, and fatigue. The normal blood glucose level usually ranges from 80–100 mg of glucose per 100 ml of blood (4.4–5.5 mmol per liter). As this level gets progressively lower, hypoglycemic symptoms may develop. The point usually used to identify hypoglycemia during research studies with exercise is 45 mg per 100 ml, or 2.5 mmol per liter, although some investigators have used higher levels.

Since hypoglycemia may disrupt functioning of the central nervous system (brain and spinal cord), the body attempts to maintain an optimal blood glucose level. Zierler noted that exercise increases muscle glucose uptake, in part due to increased cell membrane GLUT-4 receptors. Exercise may also increase the sensitivity to insulin, so more glucose is transported into the muscle for the same level of insulin. Thus, insulin levels normally drop during exercise so as to help maintain normal serum glucose. Other hormones—epinephrine (adrenaline), glucagon, and cortisol—also help maintain, and even increase, blood glucose levels during exercise.

Epinephrine is secreted from the adrenal gland during exercise, particularly intense exercise, and stimulates the liver to release glucose; it also accelerates the use of glycogen in the muscle. Glucagon and cortisol levels generally increase during the stress of exercise, cortisol particularly during prolonged exercise. **Glucagon** is released from the pancreas and generally increases the rate of gluconeogenesis in the liver. Kjaer noted that liver gluconeogenesis may contribute substantially during prolonged aerobic exercise when liver glycogen levels decline and gluconeogenic substrate becomes more abundant. **Cortisol** is secreted from the adrenal gland and facilitates the breakdown and release of amino acids from muscle tissue to provide some substrate to the liver for gluconeogenesis. Blood glucose normally increases during the initial stages of exercise and is normally well maintained by these hormonal mechanisms. A summary of hormonal actions in the regulation of blood glucose is presented in table 4.7.

Hypoglycemia may be a concern of athletes in several situations. One possibility is a reactive hypoglycemia following the consumption of a high-carbohydrate meal 30–60 minutes or more prior to an athletic event. If hypoglycemia develops just prior to or during the early stages of the event, the effect could impair performance. This possibility will be covered later in this section.

Hypoglycemia may also develop during prolonged exercise tasks, but it may be dependent upon the intensity level of the exercise. In low-intensity exercise, such as 30–50 percent of VO_2 max, the primary fuel is fat, and hence the use of carbohydrate is minimized. Moreover, at this low intensity level, gluconeogenesis can

help maintain blood glucose above hypoglycemic levels. However, in exercise tasks above 50–60 percent VO_2 max (or higher percentages in highly-trained individuals), muscle glycogen use increases, more blood glucose is used, and gluconeogenesis is not rapid enough to replace that which is used.

During the early part of prolonged moderate- to high-intensity aerobic exercise, muscle glycogen is the major source of energy derived from carbohydrate, although some blood glucose is utilized. However, Weltan and others recently found that as muscle glycogen levels get low in the latter stages of an endurance task, the muscle increases its fat oxidation. Blood glucose now accounts for most of the muscular energy from carbohydrate, the liver glycogen stores become rapidly depleted, and thus the blood glucose levels fall toward hypoglycemia.

Whether hypoglycemia impairs physical performance may depend upon the individual. In a recent study, Utter and others reported that a lower rating of perceived exertion (RPE) during prolonged running was associated with higher blood glucose, suggesting that maintenance of optimal blood glucose levels could help prevent psychological distress. Some earlier research reported that exercise-induced hypoglycemia led to the expected symptoms, including dizziness and partial blackout. However, more contemporary research from three different laboratories has revealed that a number of subjects may become hypoglycemic during the latter stages of a prolonged exercise task to exhaustion at 60–75 percent of their VO_2 max, and yet are able to continue exercising while hypoglycemic, even at levels as low as 25 mg per 100 ml. It appears that the role hypoglycemia plays in the etiology of fatigue in prolonged exercise has not been totally elucidated, although there appears to be individual susceptibility. Nevertheless, prevention of hypoglycemia is one of the major objectives of carbohydrate consumption during prolonged exercise because every individual will eventually suffer ill effects when they reach their minimum blood glucose threshold.

How is low muscle glycogen related to the development of fatigue?

Investigators generally agree that prolonged, moderately high- to high-intensity aerobic exercise is limited by muscle glycogen stores. The depletion of muscle glycogen seems to be a limiting

TABLE 4.7 Major hormones involved in regulation of blood glucose levels

Hormone	Gland	Stimulus	Action
Insulin	Pancreas	Increase in blood glucose	Helps transport glucose into cells; decreases blood glucose levels
Glucagon	Pancreas	Decrease in blood glucose; exercise stress	Promotes gluconeogenesis in liver; helps increase blood glucose levels
Epinephrine	Adrenal	Exercise stress; decrease in blood glucose	Promotes glycogen breakdown and glucose release from the liver; helps increase blood glucose levels
Cortisol	Adrenal	Exercise stress; decrease in blood glucose	Promotes breakdown of protein and resultant gluconeogenesis; helps increase blood glucose levels

factor when exercising at 65–85 percent or higher of VO_2 max. A number of studies have shown that physical exhaustion was correlated with very low muscle glycogen levels, but others have shown some glycogen remaining even though subjects were exhausted. Several mechanisms have been postulated to explain the development of fatigue with low levels of muscle glycogen.

- Location of glycogen. Costill has indicated that performance would be adversely affected only when muscle glycogen levels went below 40 mmol/kg of muscle tissue. It may be that complete depletion of muscle glycogen is not necessary for performance to suffer, for glycolysis may be impaired with lower glycogen levels or the glycogen in the muscle fiber may be located where it is not readily available for glycolysis.
- Rate of energy production. Shulman and Rothman propose a model in which energy is supplied in milliseconds via glycogenolysis, and indicate that one possible mechanism for muscle fatigue is that at low, but nonzero glycogen concentrations, there is not enough glycogen to supply millisecond energy needs.
- Muscle fiber type. The fatigue that develops may be related to the depletion of muscle glycogen from specific muscle fiber types. In prolonged exercise at 60–75 percent of VO_2 max, Type I fibers (red, oxidative slow twitch) and Type IIa fibers (red, oxidative-glycolytic fast twitch) are recruited during the early stages of the task, but as muscle glycogen is depleted, the athlete must recruit Type IIb fibers (white, glycolytic fast twitch) to maintain the same pace. However, it takes more mental effort to recruit the Type IIb fibers, which will be more stressful to the athlete. Type IIb fibers also are more likely to produce lactic acid, increasing the acidity, which may increase the perceived stress of the exercise. In a recent study, Krustrup and others recently reported that glycogen depletion of the slow-twitch muscle fibers, necessitating recruitment of fast-twitch muscle fibers and increased energy demands, is a factor that may predispose to fatigue.
- Use of fat for energy. As muscle glycogen becomes depleted in the slow-twitch muscle fibers, the muscle cell will rely more on fat as the primary energy source. Since fat is a less efficient fuel than carbohydrate, the pace will slow down.
- Role of the brain. Signals sent from peripheral tissues to the brain may regulate energy metabolism. A low glycogen level in exercising muscle may be such a signal, and may invoke neural responses causing fatigue.

Fatigue in very high-intensity, anaerobic-type exercise generally is attributed to the detrimental effects of the acidity in the muscle cell associated with lactic acid production. Research has now shown that maximal high-intensity exercise, lasting only about 60 seconds, is not impaired by a very low muscle glycogen concentration, approximately 30 mmol/kg muscle. However, it is possible that performance in such very high-intensity, short-term exercise tasks may be impaired with extremely low muscle glycogen in the fast-twitch muscle fibers. Moreover, with somewhat longer anaerobic tasks, approximating 3 minutes, one laboratory study reported a reduced performance in the time to exhaustion test after 4 days of a low-carbohydrate, high-fat diet when

compared to a normal, mixed diet and a high-carbohydrate diet. Although muscle glycogen levels were not measured, a logical assumption is that they were lower on the low-carbohydrate diet.

In addition, field research has suggested that slower overall sprint speed, such as in the latter parts of prolonged athletic contests like soccer and ice hockey, may be due to muscle glycogen depletion. Muscle biopsies of these athletes revealed very low glycogen levels, which were attributed not only to the strenuous exercise in the contest but also to the fact that these athletes were consuming diets low in carbohydrates. In support of these field studies, Balsom and others recently reported that low muscle glycogen levels impaired laboratory exercise performance in repeated bouts of very-high-intensity intermittent exercise bouts, 6-second cycle ergometer performance followed by 30 seconds of rest. Also, low muscle glycogen stores may lead to a decrease in exercise intensity during training.

Low muscle glycogen levels, because they are associated with premature fatigue, have been theorized to be a major cause of the overtraining syndrome in endurance athletes. However, in a recent review, Ann Snyder noted that cyclists who met the criteria of short-term overtraining maintained their muscle glycogen levels. Thus, she concluded that some other mechanism than reduced muscle glycogen levels must be responsible for the development of the overtraining syndrome. Carl Foster also ruled out carbohydrate depletion as a likely cause of overtraining syndrome.

In summary, low levels of glycogen in the white, fast-twitch IIb muscle fibers may limit performance in intermittent, anaerobic-type exercise tasks. Both hypoglycemia and low glycogen in the red muscle fiber types, most likely a combination of the two, may be contributing factors to fatigue in prolonged endurance exercise.

How are low endogenous carbohydrate levels related to the central fatigue hypothesis?

As noted above, hypoglycemia and low muscle glycogen levels may impair exercise performance, and one mechanism for each involves adverse effects on brain function. Collectively, they may contribute to central fatigue in a different way.

In the latter stages of prolonged exercise bouts, low muscle glycogen, in combination with decreased blood glucose levels, will stimulate gluconeogenesis from protein. In particular, branched-chain amino acids (BCAA) in the muscle will be catabolized to provide energy. Because BCAA release from the liver may be decreased or uptake by the muscle may increase, blood levels of BCAA decline. The *central fatigue hypothesis* during prolonged exercise suggests that this decline in blood BCAA may contribute to fatigue. In general, fatigue is hypothesized to occur when BCAA levels drop and the concentration of another amino acid—tryptophan—increases in its free form, or free tryptophan (fTRP). BCAA compete with fTRP for similar receptors that facilitate their entry into the brain, so high BCAA levels prevent brain uptake of fTRP. With an increased fTRP: BCAA ratio, entry of fTRP into the brain cells will be facilitated. Increased brain levels of tryptophan may stimulate the formation of serotonin, a neurotransmitter in the brain that may be related to fatigue sensations. Preventing the increase in the fTRP:BCAA ratio is theorized to prevent the premature development of fatigue, and the use of BCAA supplements in this regard will be covered in chapter 6. However, carbohydrate intake during exercise may also be helpful, as discussed later in this section.

Will eating carbohydrate immediately before or during an event improve physical performance?

Because hypoglycemia or muscle glycogen depletion may be causes of fatigue during endurance exercise, supplementation with glucose or other forms of carbohydrate before or during exercise may be theorized to delay the onset of fatigue and improve performance. Thousands of studies have been conducted on this topic ever since carbohydrates were identified as the most efficient energy source for exercise over 80 years ago, and researchers' interest in this topic remains unabated today. In recent years the research designs have usually been highly sophisticated as investigators have attempted to provide specific answers relative to the type, amount, and timing of carbohydrate ingestion before and during performance. Although some problems remain in providing quantitative data, the use of stable isotopes of ingested carbohydrates (referred to as exogenous carbohydrates in comparison to endogenous stores in the body) as detailed by Wolfe and George has enhanced our understanding of their metabolic fate when ingested prior to or during exercise.

However, the reviewer attempting to synthesize the available research is confronted with a difficult task since the experimental designs varied considerably. The amount and type of carbohydrate ingested, the use of liquid or solid forms, the method of administration (oral ingestion or venous infusion), the time prior to or during the exercise that it was taken, the diet of the subject several days prior to the study, the amount of glycogen in the muscle and liver, the intensity and duration of the exercise, the type of exercise task (running, swimming, cycling, etc.), the fitness level of the subjects, the environmental temperature, and the method used to evaluate blood glucose and muscle glycogen utilization are some of the important differences between studies.

Although the results from all of these studies were not similar, some general consistencies have evolved. The role of carbohydrate supplementation on exercise performance has been the subject of numerous reviews, and a number of contemporary reviews may be found in the reference list at the end of this chapter. Based on these reviews and an overall review of specific studies, the following generalizations appear to be logical. More specific information relative to practical recommendations is provided following this discussion.

Initial Endogenous Stores   If the individual has normal liver and muscle glycogen stores, glucose feedings are unnecessary for continuous moderately high-intensity exercise bouts lasting 60–90 minutes or less but may be beneficial for high-intensity exercise tasks of similar duration, as noted below. Since the body can store carbohydrate in the muscles and liver, the usefulness of glucose or other carbohydrate intake before or during exercise depends on the adequacy of those supplies already in the muscle and liver to meet energy needs. For competition, the muscle and liver glycogen stores should be adequate to meet carbohydrate energy needs. The critical point is to consume substantial amounts of carbohydrates a day or two prior to the event and to decrease the duration and intensity of training to assure ample endogenous glycogen supplies.

The available research has shown that the consumption of glucose, fructose, sucrose, maltodextrin (a glucose polymer), or other carbohydrate combinations immediately prior to events of short or moderate duration has a negligible effect upon performance. Adding a gallon of gas to a full tank will not make a car go faster during a short ride. The same is true of sugar to a muscle already filled with glycogen. On the other hand, if muscle glycogen levels are low and the exercise task is somewhat prolonged, then ingestion of carbohydrate prior to the exercise bout may improve performance. It is important to note, however, that in order to enhance performance, the exogenous carbohydrate source must be able to delay the onset of fatigue that might otherwise occur as a result of premature depletion of endogenous carbohydrate sources, a viewpoint also proposed by Tsintzas and Williams in a recent review.

In his review, Ivy indicated that fatigue occurs during exercise intensities between 60–75 percent VO_2 max when there is insufficient muscle glycogen and blood glucose to supply about 40 percent of the total energy requirement at this exercise intensity. Fatigue may occur because of the slower rate of energy production from fat oxidation, or the need to maintain an adequate supply of substrate to the Krebs cycle.

Exercise Intensity and Duration   The potential beneficial effects of carbohydrate supplementation depend on the interaction of exercise intensity and duration, which of course are interrelated. The shorter the duration, the greater the exercise intensity can be. The following time frames are representative of those that have been studied to evaluate the effects of carbohydrate supplementation.

Very high-intensity exercise for less than 30 minutes Research suggests that carbohydrate supplementation will not enhance performance in high-intensity exercise bouts less than 30 minutes in length. For example, Palmer and others recently noted that consuming carbohydrate 10 minutes before competing in a 20-kilometer cycle time trial did not enhance performance in well-trained cyclists. Nevertheless, if carbohydrate supplements could ameliorate a muscle or liver glycogen deficiency, performance might improve. For example, Walberg-Rankin reported that carbohydrate supplementation improved high-intensity anaerobic exercise performance in wrestlers following a drastic weight reduction program with very limited carbohydrate intake. Presumably, the carbohydrate supplement, consumed in a 5-hour period before testing, increased muscle glycogen levels, particularly in fast-twitch fibers, enhancing carbohydrate utilization and subsequent performance.

Very high-intensity resistance exercise training In a recent review, Conley and Stone noted that resistance, or strength, training, may use considerable amounts of muscle glycogen, which can lead to fatigue and strength loss. However, they noted that there are inadequate data to determine whether or not carbohydrate supplements increase performance if consumed before or during training. Subsequent to this review, Dalton and others reported that carbohydrate supplementation did not improve muscular endurance performance as evaluated by the number of repetitions of the bench press and leg extension at 80 percent of 10 repetition maximum, even under conditions of energy restriction.

High-intensity exercise for 30 to 90 minutes Normally, with adequate muscle and liver glycogen, carbohydrate supplements have not been found to improve exercise performance in this time frame. For example, two recent studies found that neither consumption of a 6 percent carbohydrate solution nor infusing glucose at the rate of 1 gram per minute improved performance in a one-hour maximal cycling protocol. However, some recent research has suggested that supplementation may benefit well-trained athletes who may be able to exercise at high intensity for about an hour. For example, Jeukendrup and el-Sayed, with their associates, recently reported that cyclists exercising for about an hour at high intensity significantly improved their performance following ingestion of a carbohydrate supplement, as compared to a placebo. Also, Ball and others reported that carbohydrate intake during a simulated time trial improved performance in a sprint at the end of 50 minutes of high-intensity cycling. In such cases, it is possible that the ingested carbohydrates may help provide glucose to the fast-twitch muscle fibers or prevent premature depletion in the slow-twitch fibers.

Interestingly, simply swishing a carbohydrate (maltodextrin) solution in the mouth periodically during exercise enhanced performance in a 1-hour cycle time trial. Carter and others hypothesized that carbohydrate receptors in the mouth may have increased central nervous system drive or motivation.

Intermittent high-intensity exercise for 60 to 90 minutes Research has shown that individuals engaged in endurance-type contests with intermittent bouts of sprinting, such as soccer, ice hockey, or tennis, may benefit from carbohydrate supplements taken before and during the game. In a recent controlled laboratory protocol representative of a 60-minute intermittent, high-intensity competitive sport such as soccer or field hockey, Welsh and colleagues from Mark Davis's laboratory reported that carbohydrate intake before and during the exercise task resulted in significant improvements in various tests of physical and mental functions performed throughout the experimental trial. Toward the end of the 60-minute period, the carbohydrate trial resulted in faster 20-meter sprint time, longer time to fatigue in a shuttle run, enhanced whole body motor skills, and decreased self-reported perceptions of fatigue. The results suggested a beneficial role of carbohydrate-electrolyte ingestion on physical and mental functions during intermittent exercise similar to that of many competitive team sports. Similar findings were reported by Winnick and others. Other field research studies, although not universally supportive, have shown similar benefits of carbohydrate intake under game conditions. Several reviewers, such as Kirkendall, indicate carbohydrate intake before and during intermittent high-intensity exercise sports may enhance performance.

High- to moderate-intensity exercise greater than 90 minutes Research generally supports a beneficial effect of carbohydrate intake on exercise performance tasks greater than 90 minutes (if the exercise intensity is high enough), particularly so when the task is more prolonged, such as 2 hours or more. For example, Kimber and others reported a significant inverse correlation between the amount of carbohydrate consumed and the finishing time of male triathletes in an Ironman triathlon, suggesting that increasing carbohydrate consumption during such a prolonged event may enhance performance.

Timing of Carbohydrate Intake Athletes may consume diets rich in carbohydrate for several days prior to competition, as discussed later under carbohydrate loading. Most of the studies evaluating the effect of carbohydrate supplements on subsequent exercise performance have used time frames ranging from 4 hours prior to immediately prior to the task, and at various times during the exercise task. Athletes should experiment in training with several of the carbohydrate-intake strategies presented below and find that which works best. For prolonged endurance events, carbohydrate intake several hours before, immediately before, and during the event may be recommended.

Four hours or less before exercise Carbohydrate intake 60–240 minutes prior to prolonged exercise tasks (longer than 90 minutes) may enhance performance. Research has demonstrated improved performance when adequate carbohydrate was consumed either 1, 3, or 4 hours prior to a prolonged exercise task involving simulated racing conditions during the latter stage. Other research revealed no significant differences in 30-kilometer run performance when equal amounts of carbohydrate were supplemented either 4 hours before or during the run, suggesting the ingested carbohydrate was available for energy production using either strategy.

Less than 1 hour before exercise Individuals who may be prone to reactive hypoglycemia should avoid carbohydrate intake, particularly high-glycemic-index foods, 15–60 minutes prior to performance. Simple sugars ingested within this time frame may actually impair physical performance in such individuals because of the adverse effects of reactive hypoglycemia, such as muscular weakness. Moreover, this same insulin response may speed up muscle glycogen utilization. This may be a disadvantage to the marathoner, whose glycogen levels may be depleted too early in the race. Several earlier studies showed that run time to exhaustion was shorter by about 20–25 percent after athletes consumed 2–3 ounces of glucose within an hour before the endurance test.

However, not all individuals experience reactive hypoglycemia. Kuipers and others recently noted that about one-third of well-trained subjects experienced hypoglycemia following the ingestion of 50 grams of glucose after a 4-hour fast. However, the hypoglycemia was transient as blood glucose levels returned to normal after 20 minutes of exercise at 60 percent VO_2 max. No performance data were measured. In a study by John Seifert and others, subjects were given various carbohydrate solutions to raise their insulin levels; when their insulin levels peaked, they undertook an exercise task at 60 percent of VO_2 max for 50 minutes. No hypoglycemia developed, nor were there any adverse sensory or psychological responses.

Other well-controlled studies have reported no adverse effects of glucose, fructose, or maltodextrin ingestion 30–45 minutes prior to prolonged exercise. Compared to placebo conditions with artificially sweetened water, the various carbohydrate solutions elicited no significant differences in muscle glycogen utilization or exercise capacity when subjects were exercising at 55–75 percent of VO₂ max.

For individuals not prone to reactive hypoglycemia, the consumption of carbohydrates within 15–60 minutes prior to performance may confer some benefits. Possible increases in liver and muscle glycogen may offset the reported increase in muscle glycogen utilization.

Immediately before exercise As noted previously, consuming carbohydrate immediately before exercise of short duration, and even exercise tasks less than 90 minutes or so, normally will not enhance performance. For example, Smith and others reported no significant effect on swim time performance of ingesting a 10-percent glucose solution 5 minutes before a 4-kilometer swim of approximately 70 minutes. However, carbohydrate intake immediately prior to (within 5–10 minutes) prolonged endurance exercise tasks of 2 hours or more may help delay the development of fatigue and improve performance if the athlete is exercising at a level greater than 50 percent VO₂ max, such as 60–75 percent. The majority of the studies, including controlled laboratory investigations and field research involving different types of endurance athletes, support this point of view. At this level of exercise intensity, the insulin response to glucose ingestion is suppressed; in addition, the secretion of epinephrine is increased. These two hormonal responses interact to help maintain or elevate the blood glucose level and prevent the hypoglycemic response that typically may occur in reactive individuals if more time elapses between the ingestion of the carbohydrate and the initiation of exercise.

During exercise Carbohydrate ingested during prolonged exercise can help maintain blood glucose levels and reduce the psychological perception of effort, as measured by the ratings of perceived exertion, during the latter stages of an endurance task. As the exercise task continues and the muscle glycogen level falls, the amount of energy derived from the ingested carbohydrates increases. Most research supports the benefits of consuming carbohydrates early in and throughout the exercise task, but even a single carbohydrate feeding late in a prolonged exercise bout may help replenish blood glucose levels, increase carbohydrate oxidation, and delay fatigue.

All major investigators who have published extensive reviews, most recently Mark Hargreaves and Asker Jeukendrup, conclude that carbohydrate intake during prolonged exercise, when contrasted with placebo conditions, will enhance performance. This general finding is supported by both laboratory and field studies and applies to both females and males.

Use of the Ingested Carbohydrate Using labeled carbohydrate sources and analyzing the expired carbon dioxide for radioactivity, investigators have shown that some of the ingested, or exogenous, carbohydrate may be used as an energy source within 5–10 minutes, indicating that it may empty rapidly from the stomach, be absorbed from the small intestine into the blood, and enter into metabolic pathways. Peak use of exogenous carbohydrate appears to occur 75 to 90 minutes after ingestion. A number of studies have shown that the ingested carbohydrate may contribute a significant percentage of the carbohydrate energy source during exercise, ranging from 20–40 percent in some studies, but as much as 60–70 percent during the latter stages of exercise when endogenous liver and muscle glycogen stores become depleted.

Possible Fatigue-Delaying Mechanisms The precise mechanism whereby glucose ingestion helps delay the onset of fatigue during moderate- to high-intensity exercise (i.e., > 65 percent VO₂ max) has not been totally elucidated, but several theories have been studied.

Maintenance of blood glucose levels The available data suggest that the ability of carbohydrate intake to delay fatigue may be related to the maintenance of higher blood glucose levels, possibly by sparing liver glycogen until late in the exercise, and the prevention of hypoglycemia in susceptible individuals; blood glucose would be available to enter the muscle and provide a source of energy for aerobic glycolysis. As noted, exogenous glucose is used increasingly as the exercise task becomes prolonged.

Maintenance of blood BCAA levels In several recent studies carbohydrate supplementation during exercise has been reported to prevent the decrease in serum BCAA during the later stages of prolonged exercise, possibly by mitigating secretion of cortisol. According to the central fatigue hypothesis, preventing an increase in the fTRP:BCAA ratio would deter the onset of fatigue.

Some research has shown that glucose ingestion could make an endurance task psychologically easier and suggested that the physiological effects of the glucose, either in the brain or in the muscles, reduced the stressful effects of exercise. Several studies by Utter and others found that carbohydrate ingestion reduced the ratings of perceived exertion during prolonged running and cycling. For example, they reported that marathoners ingesting carbohydrate compared to placebo beverages were able to run at a higher intensity during a competitive marathon, and yet the ratings of perceived exertion (RPE) were similar in both groups of runners, suggesting the carbohydrate may have permitted them to run at a faster rate with similar psychological effort. However, it has not been determined whether these ergogenic effects may be attributed to the effect of glucose on the central nervous system, either as a direct energy source for brain metabolism or through its effect on BCAA levels, or to its effect in the muscle as an energy source.

Sparing of muscle glycogen Although sparing of muscle glycogen could be another benefit of carbohydrate ingestion before or during moderate- to high-intensity exercise, research findings are equivocal.

In a unique experiment from the University of Texas, subjects received venous glucose infusions to maintain a hyperglycemic state during 2 hours of exercise at 73 percent of VO₂ max, but the net rate of muscle glycogen utilization was not affected compared to control conditions, a recent finding confirmed by Arkinstall and Chryssanthopoulos and their colleagues. Other research has also noted no muscle glycogen sparing effect following carbohydrate supplementation.

On the other hand, Yaspelkis and others, also from the University of Texas, noted that during low-intensity exercise (i.e., <50 percent VO$_2$ max) or during low- to moderate-intensity exercise tasks, carbohydrate supplementation during exercise could spare use of muscle glycogen in slow-twitch muscle fibers and enhance performance. They noted that during low-intensity exercise the serum levels of both glucose and insulin were elevated, which could promote muscle use of serum glucose and sparing of muscle glycogen. Bosch and others, as well as Tsintzas and others, recently reported that carbohydrate intake during prolonged exercise at about 70 percent VO$_2$ max did spare muscle glycogen use, and the Tsintzas group reported the sparing effect occurred in the Type I, slow-twitch muscle fibers, but not in the Type II fast-twitch fibers. Interestingly, Tsintzas and others also found that carbohydrate intake spared the use of PCr in both fiber types. Williams noted that although other reviewers concluded that consuming carbohydrate during exercise did not spare use of muscle glycogen in cyclists, research findings from his laboratory did find glycogen sparing in runners who consumed carbohydrate drinks throughout prolonged exercise, and the glycogen sparing occurred early in the exercise task. Hargreaves noted also that the breakdown of muscle glycogen may be slowed because the supply of blood glucose is improved when carbohydrate is consumed.

Limitations to Prevent Fatigue Although glucose ingestion may help delay fatigue during moderately high-intensity exercise, it cannot totally prevent the onset of fatigue. It appears that a maximum of about 1.5 to 1.7 grams of the ingested carbohydrate may be available each minute, which is much lower than the required energy needs at 65–85 percent of VO$_2$ max. Jeukendrup and Jentjens indicate the intestines and liver may be limiting factors, the intestines being unable to absorb the ingested carbohydrate at a faster rate while the liver may limit the amount of glucose released into the blood. When blood glucose, BCAA, and/or muscle glycogen levels are eventually reduced to a critical level, fatigue occurs.

Optimal Supplementation Protocol Several studies have indicated that although the intake of carbohydrate either before or during exercise may separately enhance performance, the best effect was observed when carbohydrate was consumed both before and during exercise. For example, Chryssanthopoulos and others had subjects run to exhaustion at 70 percent VO$_2$ max and found that although a high-carbohydrate meal 3 hours prior to performance improved endurance time, the combination of the meal and a carbohydrate-electrolyte solution during exercise further improved endurance running capacity.

When, how much, and in what form should carbohydrates be consumed before or during exercise?

The most common athletic events or physical performance activities that may benefit from carbohydrate feedings are those associated with long duration (90–120 minutes or more) at moderate- to high-

intensity levels. Marathon running, cross-country skiing, and endurance cycling are common sports of this kind. Other sports that require intermittent bouts of intensive activity over a prolonged period, such as soccer, may also benefit. However, the individual participating in these activities, particularly under warm or hot environmental conditions, also needs to replenish fluid losses incurred through sweating. In such cases, fluid replenishment is more critical than carbohydrate. The topic of fluid replacement during exercise is covered in more detail in chapter 9, but since carbohydrate is one of the contents in the majority of the sport drinks developed as fluid replacements for athletes, its role is discussed briefly here.

Many studies have been conducted in recent years to determine the best carbohydrate feeding regimen to prevent fatigue during prolonged exercise. A number of different variables have been studied, such as the timing of the feeding and the type, amount, and concentration of carbohydrate.

Again, based on current reviews by the primary investigators regarding carbohydrate supplementation for exercise performance and a careful analysis of individual studies, the following points represent the general conclusions and recommendations for individuals who may be exercising at 60–80 percent of their VO$_2$ max or greater for 1–2 hours or longer. These points may also be applicable to athletes engaged in intermittent high-intensity exercise sports that last an hour or more. But remember, individuals may have varied reactions to carbohydrate intake, so athletes should experiment in training before using these recommendations in actual competition. Table 9.9 on page 345 presents the following recommendations in tabular format.

Pre-exercise: When and How Much The amount of carbohydrate ingested 4 hours prior to performance should be based upon body weight. Several studies have used 4–5 grams/kg (1.8–2.3 grams/pound) with good results. For an athlete who weighs 60 kg (132 pounds), the recommended amount would be 240–300 grams. The carbohydrates could be consumed in any of several forms, including fluids such as juices or glucose polymer solutions, or solid carbohydrates such as fruits or starches. The fiber content should be minimized to prevent possible intestinal problems during exercise. Keep in mind that 300 grams of carbohydrate is about 1,200 Calories, a somewhat substantial meal. You may consult appendix E for an expanded list of foods high in carbohydrate, but use the following for a quick estimate of carbohydrate content:

1 fruit exchange = 15 grams carbohydrate
  1 apple
  1 orange
  1/2 banana
  4 ounces orange juice
1 starch exchange = 15 grams carbohydrate
  1 slice bread
  1/2 cup cereal
  1/4 large bagel
  1/2 cup cooked pasta
  1 small baked potato
Sports drinks: 7–8 ounces = 15 grams carbohydrate
  Gatorade

PowerAde
SportAde
Sports bars = 20–50 grams carbohydrate
    1 PR Bar
    1 Power Bar
Sports gels = 20–30 grams carbohydrate
    1 Power Gel packet
    1 ReLode packet
Energy Drinks: 8 ounces = 25–50 grams carbohydrate
    Gatorade Energy Drink
    SoBe Energy

The guidelines presented on pages 72–76 relative to precompetition meals provide appropriate guidelines.

If carbohydrate is consumed approximately 1 hour prior to performance, about 1–2 grams/kg (60–120 grams for a 60–kg athlete) may be recommended, for these levels have been shown to enhance performance in several studies. One study using only 12 grams 1 hour prior to performance has shown no beneficial effect. Both glucose polymers and foods with a low glycemic index have been used successfully.

If carbohydrates are consumed immediately before exercise, that is, within 10 minutes of the start, about 50–60 grams of a glucose polymer in a 40–50 percent solution has been used effectively in some studies. Dry glucose polymers are available commercially. One tablespoon is about 15 grams. To make a 50 percent solution containing 50 grams of the polymer, put about 3 level tablespoons of the polymer into 100 milliliters (about 3–4 ounces) of water. To make a 7.5 percent solution containing 15 grams, put 1 tablespoon of the polymer into 200 milliliters (about 7 ounces) of water. As noted above, several commercial "energy" drinks contain 25–50 grams of carbohydrate per 8 fluid ounces, which are about 10–20 percent solutions.

During Exercise: When and How Much   During exercise, feedings every 15–30 minutes appear to be a reasonable schedule, but possibly more frequently when attempting to maximize carbohydrate intake or to obtain fluids when exercising under warm or hot environmental conditions. Although you may consume considerable quantities of carbohydrate during exercise, your ability to use this exogenous source for energy is limited. The reason is not known, but as noted previously may be related to insufficient intestinal absorption or impaired delivery from the liver.

In the past, reasonable evidence-based estimates suggested that athletes could use approximately 0.5–1 gram of ingested carbohydrate per minute, or about 30–60 grams of carbohydrate per hour. More recently, studies have shown that ingesting various combinations of carbohydrates could increase this amount to 1.2–1.7 grams per minute, or about 72–102 grams per hour. The rationale is presented in the next section.

Sports drinks averaging 6–10 percent carbohydrate have been found to enhance prolonged endurance performance. A typical serving of a sport drink (8 ounces) would contain about 14–24 grams of carbohydrate, so depending on the concentration, an athlete who wanted to maximize utilizable carbohydrate intake would need to drink about 32–56 ounces to obtain about 100 grams of carbohydrate

per hour. Drinking 8 ounces every 15 minutes would provide 32 ounces (1 quart) over the course of an hour, but consumption would need to be more frequent to obtain 56 ounces. Consuming 56 ounces of fluid over the course of an hour might be difficult, and may pose a potential health risk for some individuals. Although the fluids could provide the desired amount of carbohydrate, excessive fluid consumption could lead to overhydration and a serious medical condition known as hyponatremia, as shall be discussed in chapter 9.

Several other protocols have been effective. One involved consumption of a high concentration (about 1 gram carbohydrate/kg body weight) immediately before or during the first 20 minutes of the exercise, and then use lower concentrations such as found in commercial sports drinks at regular intervals. Other investigators have noted that taking a single more concentrated dose of carbohydrate, such as 100–200 grams total, in the latter stages of prolonged exercise may be beneficial. Additionally, because of the nature of their sport, soccer players and other such athletes may need to consume a high concentration before the game and during halftime, or breaks in the game as they occur.

It should be noted that consumption of carbohydrate solutions above 10 percent during exercise may cause gastrointestinal distress, as may other high concentrations of simple carbohydrates. However, some athletes may learn to tolerate larger concentrations, such as 15–20 percent. Ultradistance athletes, who exercise at a lower intensity, may tolerate even higher concentrations ranging from 20–50 percent.

Type of Carbohydrate   A number of different types of carbohydrates have been studied, including glucose, glucose polymers, fructose, and sucrose, both individually and in various combinations, as well as soluble starch (a very long polymer), high-glycemic-index foods like potatoes, and low-glycemic-index foods such as legumes. In general, there appears to be no difference between these different types of carbohydrates as a means to enhance endurance performance when used appropriately. However, there may be some important considerations relative to the use of various carbohydrate combinations, fructose, solid carbohydrates, and low-glycemic-index foods.

Carbohydrate combinations   Jeukendrup noted studies have shown that a single carbohydrate ingested during exercise will be oxidized at rates up to about 1 gram/minute, even when large amounts of carbohydrate are ingested. However, combinations of carbohydrate, particularly sucrose, glucose and fructose, that use different intestinal transporters for absorption have been shown to result in higher oxidation rates. This seems to be the way to increase exogenous carbohydrate oxidation rates, up to 1.7 grams/minute. Thus, check food labels for ingredients to ensure obtaining a sports drink containing such combinations.

Fructose   Fructose has been theorized to be a better source of carbohydrate than glucose because it is absorbed more slowly from the intestine and hence will not create an insulin response and the potential reactive hypoglycemia. Indeed, research has shown that fructose, compared to glucose, may lead to a more stable blood sugar during the early stages of prolonged exercise when ingested 45 minutes prior to the activity, for most ingested fructose is eventually converted to glucose in the liver. However, when fructose is ingested immediately before or during exercise, its effect on the blood sugar and carbohydrate metabolism appears to be little different than that of glucose.

Most people can tolerate small amounts of fructose. It is found naturally in fruits, and is an ingredient in some sports drinks. However, consuming larger amounts may pose problems. Since fructose is absorbed slowly from the intestinal tract, it can create a significant osmotic effect in the intestines leading to diarrhea and gastrointestinal distress in some individuals. Research has indicated that a 6 percent solution of fructose, when compared to similar solutions of glucose and sucrose, caused significant gastrointestinal distress and an impairment in exercise performance. The athlete should be cautious in using fructose as the sole source of carbohydrate before or during exercise. Sports drinks containing fructose do so in small concentrations.

Additionally, high fructose corn syrup, although rich in fructose, is treated as an added sugar. The health risks of added sugars are covered later in this chapter.

Solid and liquid carbohydrates   In her review, Ellen Coleman noted that solid and liquid forms of carbohydrate were equally effective in maintaining blood glucose levels and enhancing exercise performance. Robergs and others recently confirmed this viewpoint, finding that the ingestion of a solid food containing carbohydrate, protein, and fat with added water produced similar blood glucose, metabolic, and exercise performance responses to those seen with the ingestion of liquid carbohydrate. However, Peters and others noted that triathletes who consumed a liquid form of carbohydrates performed better on a 3-hour cycling-running exercise task when compared to both a placebo trial and a trial in which the triathletes consumed isocaloric semi-solid carbohydrate foods (orange juice, white bread, marmalade, and bananas). The authors did note that the athletes may have had a negative perception toward eating solid foods during performance, which could have adversely affected their performance in that trial.

Although the effects of consuming equivalent amounts of carbohydrate in either liquid or solid form would appear to be minimal (providing adequate fluid intake in each case), more research is desirable to explore this issue, particularly with ultraendurance performance events where many athletes may consume liquid and solid carbohydrate sources.

Low-glycemic-index foods   In a review, Guezennec indicated that a low-glycemic-index meal, such as lentils, consumed prior to prolonged exercise might provide an advantage over a high-glycemic-index meal, such as potatoes. The underlying mechanism might be a slower rate of absorption resulting in a blunted insulin response and maintenance of higher blood glucose levels during prolonged exercise, an effect associated with soluble fiber. Guezennec indicated some preliminary research showed improved performance with low-glycemic-index foods, but recommended verification of these findings.

In general, subsequent research suggests that there are no differences between low-glycemic-index and high-glycemic-index meals relative to their effects on performance. Febbraio and Stewart provided either a low-glycemic-index meal, a high-glycemic-index meal, or a control meal to trained individuals before cycling at 70 percent VO$_2$ max for 2 hours followed by a 15-minute performance ride. Although the high-glycemic-index food increased blood glucose levels and depressed free fatty acid levels during the early stages, there were no differences later in the exercise task and no effects on the rate of muscle glycogen use or exercise performance. Several other well-controlled studies from Febbraio's laboratory, using similar glycemic-index meal and exercise protocols, reported no significant differences between the meals and performance. Other studies support this viewpoint. Most recently, Earnest and others studied the effects of consuming periodically either a low-glycemic-index carbohydrate (honey) versus a high-glycemic-index carbohydrate (dextrose) on performance in a 64-kilometer cycling time trial. Although the results indicated a trend for improved performance with each carbohydrate compared to the placebo trial, there was no difference between the two carbohydrate sources.

The potential role of low-glycemic-index foods is an important consideration for the endurance athlete, and more research is needed to evaluate their effect on prolonged endurance performance. In a recent review, Burke and others noted that although consumption of low-glycemic-index foods exerts some beneficial effects on blood glucose levels in the hours prior to exercise, there is insufficient evidence that athletes who consume low-glycemic-index, high-carbohydrate meals prior to a prolonged event will enhance their performance.

Individuality   Probably the most important recommendation is for the athlete to experiment with different types and amounts of carbohydrate during training before using them in competition. Just as it is important for you to know your optimal race pace for an endurance event, so too must you know how well you can tolerate different amounts and concentrations and types of carbohydrates. Williams noted that the type of event may influence the amount of carbohydrate ingested, as runners may be more prone to gastrointestinal distress than cyclists. "Runner's trots" is a form of diarrhea which may be associated with excess consumption of highly concentrated sugar solutions, such as "energy" drinks.

Just as you train your muscles to learn their capacity, you may also be able to train your digestive system to know its limits. Ron Maughan, an internationally respected authority in sport nutrition, indicated that the optimal strategy relative to carbohydrate utilization is to use your own subjective experience.

What is the importance of carbohydrate replenishment after prolonged exercise?

There are several possible applications of this question. One is the athlete who may be involved in a prolonged exercise bout, have a rest period of 1–4 hours, and then must exercise again, such as athletes who train two or three times daily. Benefits may accrue to anaerobic endurance-, aerobic endurance-, and resistance-trained individuals. A second application is the athlete who trains intensely every day and must have an adequate recovery in the one-day rest interval. A third application, covered in the next section, is the technique of carbohydrate loading.

After prolonged exercise, increased levels of GLUT-4 receptors in the muscle cell membrane help move available blood glucose into the muscle for resynthesis to muscle glycogen. Several studies have shown that ingesting carbohydrate during the rest interval between two prolonged exercise bouts improves performance in the second bout. This finding is comparable to the beneficial effects of carbohydrate intake during prolonged exercise bouts. The carbohydrate can help restore blood glucose levels but may also be used to resynthesize muscle glycogen. In cases such as this, where the rate of muscle glycogen resynthesis is important, high-glycemic-index foods such as potatoes, bread, glucose, or glucose polymers would be the preferred source of carbohydrate, for they apparently lead to a faster restoration of muscle glycogen than does a meal rich in low-glycemic-index foods. For repeat prolonged exercise tasks with about a 4-hour interval, a general recommendation is to consume 1 gram of carbohydrate per kilogram body weight immediately after the first event and again 2 hours prior to the second event. Additional carbohydrate may also be consumed immediately before and during the second event.

Carbohydrate has been combined with other nutrients, particularly protein, in attempts to enhance muscle glycogen resynthesis. Protein and some amino acids, such as arginine, may stimulate the release of insulin which, if added to the effects of carbohydrate-mediated insulin release, could increase the rate at which glucose is transported into the muscle cell. Some earlier studies found that consuming a protein/carbohydrate mixture after exercise would promote glycogen resynthesis more effectively compared to carbohydrate alone. However, these studies simply added protein to the standard amount of carbohydrate provided, and thus provided more total energy. Recent studies, such as those by those by Jentjens, Rotman, van Loon, and their associates, have shown that although adding protein and amino acids to a carbohydrate solution may increase muscle glycogen synthesis after exercise compared to the carbohydrate alone, adding an equivalent amount of carbohydrate for the protein will elicit the same results. However, as shall be noted in chapter 6, consuming some additional protein following strenuous exercise may have some beneficial effects, such as improved muscle protein balance.

John Ivy, an international scholar on carbohydrate metabolism, recently reviewed dietary strategies to promote glycogen synthesis after exercise. He indicated that supplementing at 30-minute intervals at a rate of 1.2–1.5 grams of carbohydrate per kilogram body mass per hour appears to maximize synthesis for a period of 4–5 hours post exercise. Consuming carbohydrate early after completion of exercise may facilitate glycogen synthesis, possibly because of an exercise-induced insulin-like action. Ivy further notes that if a lighter carbohydrate supplement is desired, protein and certain amino acids may be used in place of some of the carbohydrates. A ratio of 3 or 4 grams of carbohydrate for each gram of protein is one recommended protocol; some commercial products that combine high amounts of carbohydrate and protein are available. For example, a PowerBar contains about 40 grams of carbohydrate and 10 grams of protein, but similar amounts may be obtained from natural foods, such as a turkey breast sandwich on a large whole wheat bagel.

If rapid resynthesis of muscle glycogen is not important, it is good to note that studies have shown consumption of adequate amounts of carbohydrate over a 24-hour period will restore muscle glycogen levels to normal. For athletes who train intensely on a daily basis with either resistive or aerobic exercise that leads to muscle glycogen depletion, sport nutritionists normally recommend that approximately 8–10 grams of carbohydrate per kilogram body weight should be consumed daily in order to restore muscle glycogen levels to normal. For an individual who weighs 70 kilograms, this approximates 560–700 grams of carbohydrate, or 2,240–2,800 carbohydrate Calories. This amount of carbohydrate would represent about 65–80 percent of the daily caloric intake of an athlete consuming 3,500 Calories. Over the 24-hour period, the rate of muscle glycogen recovery is approximately 5–7 percent per hour. Sports drinks may be a convenient means to consume carbohydrate immediately after exercise. The remaining carbohydrate should be derived from other natural sources in the diet, including both simple carbohydrates in fruits and complex carbohydrates in grains, potatoes, and other foods with adequate dietary fiber and other nutrients. The inclusion of high-glycemic-index foods in the daily diet will help speed resynthesis of muscle glycogen over the 24-hour period, and may be very compatible with the Prudent Healthy Diet. Regular meals consumed during the 24-hour recovery period should include healthful low-glycemic-index foods with adequate amounts of protein.

Following prolonged, high-intensity competitive exercise performance, such as running a marathon, the resulting muscle damage will limit muscle glycogen replenishment for several days. Rest is important during this time, and muscle glycogen levels may return to normal following seven or more days of high-carbohydrate meals.

Will a high-carbohydrate diet enhance my daily exercise training?

Most scientists and sport nutritionists who study carbohydrate metabolism in athletes recommend a high-carbohydrate diet for most athletes, particularly endurance athletes, because success in athletic competition is contingent upon optimal training, and for the endurance athlete, optimal training may be contingent upon adequate nutrition, primarily the ingestion of sufficient carbohydrate every day. In a recent review Louise Burke, a prominent sports nutritionist, and her associates recommended that athletes in general training should consume daily approximately 5–7 grams of carbohydrate per kilogram body weight, but endurance athletes should consume about 7–10 grams per kilogram. These recommendations are comparable to those of Melinda Manore, another sport nutrition expert. Burke and others noted that most male athletes may be meeting these needs, but many female endurance athletes, particularly those attempting to lose weight for competition, may not. Older athletes may need to insure adequate carbohydrate intake during training. According to Mittendorfer and Klein, aging causes a shift in energy substrate use during exercise with an increased oxidation of glucose and less fat, presumably caused by age-related changes in skeletal muscle.

There are some limited data supporting the concept of enhanced training following a high-carbohydrate diet. A number of field and laboratory studies with athletes have attempted to mimic actual sport conditions. For example, one group of soccer players improved performance on an intermittent exercise task designed to mimic physical activity in a game, while another group improved performance in a standardized intermittent running task and a run to exhaustion. In other studies, runners were able to endure longer on a treadmill run to exhaustion, swimmers were better able to maintain 400-meter swim velocity, while triathletes experienced a significant improvement in treadmill endurance following 30 minutes of swimming, cycling, and running. Based on the available data, Edward Coyle, an international authority in carbohydrate metabolism during exercise, indicated that physical performance seems better maintained with a high versus moderate carbohydrate diet. In general, the normal carbohydrate intake of athletes in training studies was increased from approximately 40–45 percent to 55–70 percent of the daily Calories for varying periods, but usually a week or more. This level of carbohydrate approximates the upper levels of the AMDR for carbohydrate.

Not all athletes, including endurance athletes, may need high-carbohydrate diets all the time. In a recent meta-analysis, Erlenbusch and others indicated that subjects following a high-carbohydrate diet could exercise longer until exhaustion, but this finding applied more so to untrained individuals than trained individuals. As you may recall, aerobic exercise training improves the ability of the muscles to use fat as an energy source, so they may be somewhat less dependent on carbohydrate for a given training protocol. Thus, a moderate-carbohydrate diet may be adequate for trained athletes. For example, obtaining 45 percent of daily energy needs from carbohydrate might be considered moderate, as it is at the lower end of the AMDR. On such a diet, an endurance athlete who consumes 3,000 Calories per day during training would derive 1,350 Calories from carbohydrate (0.45 × 3,000), which is about 340 grams of carbohydrate. For a 60-kilogram athlete, this is about 5.6 grams of carbohydrate per kilogram body weight. Although this is slightly less than that recommended for endurance athletes, research has shown such amounts may be sufficient to maintain training on a daily basis.

However, training may appear more stressful psychologically. In several studies, the psychological status of athletes, as measured by the vigor and fatigue components of the Profile of Mood States (POMS) questionnaire and their rating or perceived exertion (RPE) during exercise, was improved when they switched from moderate to higher carbohydrate diets. In his recent review, Coyle concluded that mood state seems better maintained with a high-versus-moderate carbohydrate diet.

Coyle also indicates that a high-carbohydrate diet may help reduce symptoms of overreaching and, possibly, overtraining. Gleeson and others note that heavy prolonged exertion is associated with numerous hormonal and biochemical changes in the body, many of which may have detrimental effects on immune function. A well-balanced diet helps promote optimal immune function, and consuming carbohydrate during exercise attenuates rises in stress hormones such as cortisol and appears to limit the degree of exercise-induced immunosuppression. An impaired immune response is one possible factor associated with the overtraining syndrome. Carbohydrate intake following exercise also promotes protein synthesis via the insulin effect, which may enhance muscle and overall recovery.

Some nutritionists indicate that many athletes do not eat high carbohydrate diets because it may be impractical for them to do so. Selecting foods high in carbohydrate content, highlighted earlier in this chapter, provides a sound guide to increase the carbohydrate content of the diet, as do some of the recommendations in the following section regarding carbohydrate loading. Chapter 11 will provide additional information specific to daily caloric intake for planning a diet.

In summary, as Coyle notes, athletes don't train hard every day, so they do not require a high intake of carbohydrate every day of training. Nevertheless, a diet rich in healthful carbohydrates not only may have several major health benefits, but may also help guarantee optimal energy sources for daily exercise training. Moreover, as Louise Burke points out, experts in the field of energy metabolism indicate that there is no evidence that diets which are restricted in carbohydrate, such as the "zone" diet discussed in chapters 5 and 6, enhance training. Carbohydrate is the major fuel for most athletes in training.

Key Concept Recap

▶ Carbohydrate is the most important energy source for moderately high- to high-intensity exercise.

▶ Regular training increases the ability of the muscles to store and use carbohydrate for energy production.

▶ Low levels of blood glucose or muscle glycogen may be contributing factors in the premature onset of fatigue in prolonged exercise.

▶ Carbohydrate intake before and during prolonged intermittent high-intensity or continuous exercise may help delay the onset of fatigue, but unless they correct a muscle glycogen deficiency, such practices will not improve performance in most athletic events of shorter duration.

▶ Glucose, sucrose, glucose polymers, and solid carbohydrates appear to be equally effective as a means of enhancing performance, but fructose may be more likely to cause gastrointestinal distress if used alone.

▶ Combinations of carbohydrates, such as sucrose, glucose, and fructose, consumed during exercise appear to optimize the amount of exogenous carbohydrate that can be oxidized.

▶ In order to maintain the quality of training, athletes who train at moderate to high intensity on a daily basis should eat a healthful diet rich in complex carbohydrates, complemented with some high-glycemic-index foods, to replenish muscle glycogen.

▶ Carbohydrates with a high glycemic index may facilitate muscle glycogen replenishment when consumed immediately after exercise and every 2 hours thereafter.

Check for Yourself

Given the recommendation to consume about 1.0 to 1.5 grams of carbohydrate per kilogram body weight per hour for 4–5 hours after exercise in order to rapidly replenish muscle glycogen, calculate how much carbohydrate you would need per hour and list specific foods, and amounts, that you might need to consume each hour.

Carbohydrate Loading

What is carbohydrate, or glycogen, loading?

Because carbohydrate becomes increasingly important as a fuel for muscular exercise as the intensity of the exercise increases, and because the amount of carbohydrate stored in the body is limited, muscle and liver glycogen depletion could be factors that may limit performance capacity in distance events characterized by high levels of energy expenditure for prolonged periods. **Carbohydrate loading,** also called glycogen loading and glycogen supercompensation, is a dietary technique designed to promote a significant increase in the glycogen content in both the liver and the muscles in an attempt to delay the onset of fatigue. It is generally used for 3–7 days in preparation for major athletic competitions.

What type of athlete would benefit from carbohydrate loading?

In general, carbohydrate loading is primarily suited for those individuals who will sustain high levels of continuous energy expenditure for prolonged periods, such as long-distance runners, swimmers, bicyclists, triathletes, cross-country skiers, and similar athletes. In addition, athletes who are involved in prolonged stop-and-go activities, such as soccer, lacrosse, and tournament-play sports like tennis and handball, may benefit. For example, in a recent study Rico-Sanz and others concluded that exhaustion during soccer-specific performance is related to the capacity to use muscle glycogen, underlying the importance of glycogen loading. In essence, carbohydrate loading may be effective for athletes engaged in events that use muscle glycogen as the major energy source and that may lead to a depletion of glycogen in the muscle fibers. Athletes who compete in sports involving high-intensity, short-duration energy expenditure will not benefit from carbohydrate loading. However, bodybuilders have been reported to carbohydrate load in attempts to appear more muscular owing to increased muscle glycogen levels and associated water retention.

Recall from chapter 3 that humans have several different types of skeletal muscle fibers. In general, the slow-twitch red and fast-twitch red fibers are used mainly during long, continuous activities and are aerobic in nature, whereas the fast-twitch white fibers are used for short, fast activities and are anaerobic in nature. Consider the differences between a distance runner and a soccer player. The former may run at a steady pace for hours, whereas the latter will constantly be changing speeds, with many bouts of full speed interspersed with recovery periods of slower running. Research has shown that glycogen depletion patterns of the two different muscle fiber types are related to the type of exercise. Long, continuous exercise depletes glycogen principally in the slow-twitch red and fast-twitch red fibers, whereas fast, intermittent bouts of exercise with periods of rest, actually a form of interval training, primarily deplete glycogen in the fast-twitch white fibers. However, it should be noted that glycogen depletion may occur in all types of fibers in either prolonged continuous or intermittent exercise and may be quite appreciable, depending upon intensity and duration of the exercise bouts.

If carbohydrate loading works for the specific muscle fiber involved, then both types of athletes may benefit. Both should have greater glycogen stores in the latter stages of their respective athletic contests.

How do you carbohydrate load?

As you might suspect, the key to carbohydrate loading is to switch from the normal, balanced diet to one very high in carbohydrate content. The original, classic carbohydrate loading technique, emanating from earlier Scandinavian research, involved a glycogen depletion stage induced by prolonged exercise and a restricted diet. For example, a runner might go for an 18- to 20-mile run to use as much stored glycogen as possible, and then ingest very little carbohydrate in the following 2- to 3-day period. Exercise is continued during this 2- to 3-day period to keep glycogen stores low. Following the depletion stage, the loading stage began. During this phase, carbohydrate may contribute 70 or more percent of the caloric intake. The intensity and duration of exercise during this phase was reduced considerably. The usual case was to rest fully for 2 to 3 days. Thus, the classic carbohydrate loading pattern involved three stages: depletion, carbohydrate deprivation (high-fat/protein diet), and carbohydrate loading. However, this original method may be particularly difficult to tolerate, especially if one tries to exercise at high levels during the depletion phase. The lack of carbohydrate in the diet combined with the exercise bouts may elicit symptoms of hypoglycemia (weakness, lethargy, irritability). Moreover, prolonged exhaustive exercise may lead to muscle trauma, which may actually impair the storage of extra glycogen. This classic, original method is presented in table 4.8.

Although some early research supported this technique, more recent data suggest that this strict routine may be unnecessary, particularly the total program of depletion. For example, in trained runners, research has shown that simply changing to a very high-carbohydrate diet, combined with 1 or 2 days of rest or reduced activity levels (tapering), will effectively increase muscle and liver glycogen. Well-controlled research has revealed that exhaustive running is not necessary to achieve muscle glycogen supercompensation. It appears to be important to continue endurance training, or other high-intensity training specific to the sport, during the 7–14 days prior to competition. Such training will serve to maintain adequate levels of GLUT-4 receptors to transfer blood glucose into the muscle cell and of glycogen synthase, the enzyme in the muscle that synthesizes glycogen from glucose. Evidence also suggests that if the total carbohydrate content is consumed over the entire week, in contrast to concentrating it in 2–3 days, there will be little difference in the muscle glycogen content between the two techniques.

Although there may be a number of variations in the carbohydrate loading protocol, a generally recommended format is also presented in table 4.8. The interested athlete may want to experiment with both techniques, and also make adjustments through experience.

The high-carbohydrate diet should contain about 8–10 grams of carbohydrate per kilogram of body weight, or about 400–700

TABLE 4.8 Different methods for carbohydrate loading

A recommended method		Original, classic method	
1st day:	depletion exercise (optional)	1st day:	depletion exercise
2nd day:	mixed diet, moderate carbohydrate; tapering exercise	2nd day:	high-protein/fat diet; low carbohydrate; tapering exercise
3rd day:	mixed diet, moderate carbohydrate; tapering exercise	3rd day:	high-protein/fat diet; low carbohydrate; tapering exercise
4th day:	mixed diet, moderate carbohydrate; tapering exercise	4th day:	high-protein/fat diet; low carbohydrate; tapering exercise
5th day:	high-carbohydrate diet; tapering exercise	5th day:	high-carbohydrate diet; tapering exercise
6th day:	high-carbohydrate diet; tapering exercise or rest	6th day:	high-carbohydrate diet; tapering exercise or rest
7th day:	high-carbohydrate diet; tapering exercise or rest	7th day:	high-carbohydrate diet; tapering exercise or rest
8th day:	competition	8th day:	competition

High-carbohydrate diet: 400–700 g per day depending on body
weight; about 70–80 percent of dietary Calories should be carbohydrate.

grams per day, depending on the size of the individual, which is not too different from the generally recommended dietary content of carbohydrate for the endurance athlete in regular training. It is important to note that the athlete should not change his or her diet drastically prior to competition. Consuming a high-carbohydrate diet during training will condition the body to metabolize carbohydrate properly during this loading phase. Table 4.9 represents a general dietary plan for carbohydrate loading. The total caloric value and grams of carbohydrate should be adjusted to individual needs. They are dependent upon the size of the individual and daily energy expenditure in exercise. It is important not to consume excess Calories, for they may be converted into body fat if in excess of the maximal storage capacity of the muscle and liver for glycogen.

Some guidelines for replenishment of glycogen were presented earlier. Because glycogen loading for long-distance events occurs over 2 to 3 days, it would be wise to stress complex carbohydrates in the diet because of their higher nutrient content. However, simple carbohydrates may also be used effectively to increase muscle glycogen stores, as can high-carbohydrate sports drinks such as Gatorade Energy Drink. Moreover, the diet should also include the daily requirements for protein and fat. If, for some reason, the athlete cannot carbohydrate load over the 3–7 day period, a rapid protocol may be effective. Fairchild and others found that one day of a high-carbohydrate intake, approximately 10 grams of high-glycemic index carbohydrate per kilogram body mass, nearly doubled the muscle glycogen concentration, from 109 to 198 mmol/kg wet weight muscle. The carbohydrate feeding was preceded by a short bout of near maximal-intensity exercise for 3 minutes. They reported that these muscle glycogen levels were comparable to those achieved over a 2–6 day regimen.

Most prolonged endurance events begin in the morning. The last large meal should be about 15 hours prior to race time, possibly topped off with a simple carbohydrate snack before retiring for the night. Some athletes drink a glucose polymer for the last major meal to avoid the presence of intestinal residue the morning of competition. A carbohydrate breakfast such as orange juice, toast, jelly, or other carbohydrates along with some protein may be eaten 3 to 4 hours prior to competition. This overall dietary regimen should help maximize muscle and liver glycogen stores. The athlete should then follow the guidelines presented previously relative to carbohydrate intake before and during performance.

Will carbohydrate loading increase muscle glycogen concentration?

Most, but not all, studies show that an appropriate carbohydrate loading protocol, compared to normal or low dietary carbohydrate intake, will substantially increase muscle glycogen levels. Although some previous research found that muscle glycogen levels in the early phases of loading did not increase as much in females as in males, more recent, better controlled research by James, Paul, and Tarnopolsky, with their associates, revealed that carbohydrate loading increased muscle glycogen concentration in both men and women provided total energy intake was adequate. No gender differences were noted. In general, carbohydrate intakes of 8 grams or more per kilogram body weight will provide optimal muscle glycogen concentrations for both males and females.

Glycogen content in the muscle has been reported to increase about two to three times beyond normal and liver glycogen content nearly doubled following a carbohydrate loading regimen, and this increase may last at least 3 days in a rested athlete. However, it may be important to taper and rest about 2 days prior to the event. Fogelholm and others reported no increase in muscle glycogen following

TABLE 4.9 Daily food plan for carbohydrate loading

Dietary sources of fats, proteins, and carbohydrates	Amount and Calories	Grams of carbohydrate, protein, and fat
Meat, fish, poultry, eggs, cheese, select low-fat items	6–8 oz Calories: 330–440	0 grams carbohydrate* 42–56 grams protein 18–24 grams fat
Breads, cereals, and grain products	10–20 servings Calories: 800–1,600	150–300 grams carbohydrate 24–60 grams protein
Vegetables, high Calorie (such as corn)	4 servings Calories: 280	60 grams carbohydrate 8 grams protein
Fruits	4 servings Calories: 240	60 grams carbohydrate
Fats and oils	2–4 teaspoons Calories: 90–180	10–20 grams fat
Milk, skim	2 servings Calories: 180	24 grams carbohydrate 16 grams protein
Desserts, like pie	2 servings Calories: 700	102 grams carbohydrate 6 grams protein 30 grams fat
Beverages, naturally sweetened	8–24 ounces Calories: 80–240	20–60 grams carbohydrate
Water	8 or more servings Calories: 0	
TOTAL KCAL	2,700–3,860	

TOTAL GRAMS AND APPROXIMATE % OF DIETARY CALORIES

Carbohydrate	416–606	65%
Protein	96–146	15%
Fat	58–74	20%

Consult table 4.2 for specific high-carbohydrate foods in each of the food sources.

*Beans are listed in the meat group because of their high protein content; however, they are also low in fat and high in carbohydrates, so they are an excellent selection from this food group. Substitution of beans for meat will increase the total grams of carbohydrate and the percentage of dietary Calories from carbohydrate.
Including high-carbohydrate drinks, such as glucose polymers, can add significant amounts of carbohydrate to the diet and may substitute for other foods, such as desserts.
Source: Adapted from M. Forgac, "Carbohydrate Loading: A Review" in *Journal of the American Dietetic Association* 75:42–5, 1979.

the classic loading protocol if athletes continued to train 45–60 minutes per day, even though the training was easy. This finding merits confirmation, as other studies have shown muscle glycogen supercompensation when individuals tapered, although most studies use at least 1 day of rest before the competitive exercise test.

Carbohydrate loading has been shown to increase muscle glycogen stores after exhaustive exercise, but apparently the

process does not work repeatedly within a short time frame. McInerney and others reported that muscle glycogen supercompensation did not occur when subjects attempted to increase muscle glycogen levels repeatedly during a five-day period while performing exhaustive exercise every other day.

In general, the full carbohydrate loading procedure should be used sparingly, mainly in preparation for a peak event. However, athletes should experiment with the procedure, or at least experiment with various forms of carbohydrate to be used, sometime during training before using it in competition.

How do I know if my muscles have increased their glycogen stores?

The most accurate way would be to have a muscle biopsy taken (a needle is inserted into the muscle and a small portion is extracted and analyzed), but this is not very practical. However, keeping an accurate record of your body weight, which should be recorded every morning as you arise and after you urinate, may help you determine the answer to this question. Approximately 3 grams of water are bound to each gram of stored glycogen. If your body stores an additional 300–400 grams of glycogen, along with 900–1,200 grams of water, your body weight will increase about 1,200–1,600 grams, or 2.5–3.5 pounds above your normal training weight during the loading phase. The weight gain would be greater with additional glycogen storage. This is indicative that the carbohydrate loading has been effective, since rapid weight gains from one day to another are usually due to changes in body water content.

Bodybuilders may use carbohydrate loading because the increased muscle water content may hypertrophy the muscles, leading to a more muscular, aesthetic appearance in competition. However, Horowitz and others reported no increase in the girths of seven different muscle groups following a carbohydrate loading regimen in resistance-trained bodybuilders.

Will carbohydrate loading improve exercise performance?

Although athletes in most sports may benefit from an increased carbohydrate content in the diet, the full procedure of carbohydrate loading is not necessary for the vast majority of athletes.

In general, carbohydrate loading has not been found to enhance performance in single high-intensity exercise tasks ranging up to 60 minutes or so. For example, Vandenberghe and others found no effect of muscle glycogen levels (manipulated by carbohydrate loading) on muscle glycolytic rate during very high-intensity exercise (125 percent VO_2 max) or on all-out performance at this exercise intensity, a time approximating 3 minutes. Various other studies have reported that carbohydrate loading does not increase the speed of runners in events ranging from 10 kilometers to the half-marathon or in cycling time-trials up to 60 minutes. However, Pizza and others, using an exercise task consisting of a 15-minute submaximal run followed by a run to exhaustion at 100 percent VO_2 max reported an increase in performance associated with carbohydrate loading. The run to exhaustion approximated 5 minutes. In general, this finding is an exception to the rule, but additional research is warranted.

Carbohydrate loading may benefit athletes involved in prolonged intermittent high-intensity exercise tasks. Akermark and others, using elite Swedish ice hockey players on two competitive teams as subjects, reported that the team that carbohydrate loaded between two games had higher muscle glycogen levels, which were associated with improvement in distance skated, number of shifts skated, and skating speed in the second game.

Carbohydrate loading has been studied most extensively as a means to improve performance in more prolonged aerobic endurance exercise tasks. In general, the results are supportive of an ergogenic effect. Laboratory studies have shown that exercise time to exhaustion is closely associated with the amount of muscle glycogen available or the amount of carbohydrate in the diet. When endurance performance is compared after subjects have been on either a high-fat/high-protein diet, a mixed, balanced diet, or a high-carbohydrate diet for 4–7 days, performance on the high-fat/high-protein diet is worse than on the other two. However, research findings comparing a mixed, balanced diet with a high-carbohydrate diet have been equivocal, with some results favoring the high-carbohydrate diet and others revealing no difference between the two.

A number of studies have shown that carbohydrate loading, as compared to a normal carbohydrate intake, does not enhance endurance performance. However, in many of these studies the performance tests may not have been long enough for the individual to derive the full benefit from carbohydrate loading as the duration was less than two hours. On the other hand, one of the best-designed, placebo-controlled studies also found no beneficial effect of carbohydrate loading. Using a cycling exercise protocol designed to be similar to a competitive 100-km road race (about 2.5 hours), Burke and others found that a 3-day carbohydrate-loading regimen (9 grams carbohydrate/kg), as compared to a moderate carbohydrate diet (6 grams carbohydrate/kg), did not enhance performance even though muscle glycogen content increased significantly. They also provided carbohydrate (1 gram per kilogram body mass) during the exercise test and suggested that the availability of blood glucose during exercise may offset any detrimental effects on performance of lower preexercise muscle and liver glycogen concentrations. Additionally, the authors noted that carbohydrate loading may possibly be effective in prolonged endurance events in which the exercise intensity is relatively more constant. In this study, the exercise task included repeated high-intensity sprints, which are common in cycling races but not in other events, such as marathon running. Additionally, the cyclists consumed over 60 grams of carbohydrate per hour, which although recommended for runners as well, is often more difficult to do in running than cycling. Finally, the investigators also indicated that although the time to finish the 100-km ride (about 1.6 minutes faster with carbohydrate loading) was not statistically significant, such an effect, if real, could make a difference in the finishing order of top cyclists.

On the other hand, a number of studies suggest that carbohydrate loading may be an effective technique to enhance endurance exercise performance. However, it should be noted that most of these studies have not used a true placebo, as was done in the aforementioned study by Burke and others.

Hargreaves and others note that the increased muscle glycogen may be used more readily in exercise tasks approximating 65–70 percent VO_2 max, which might be a reasonable pace for an average runner competing in a marathon. If muscle glycogen were used more rapidly during the early stages of a marathon, theoretically carbohydrate loading would provide no advantage during the latter stages of the race. However, Bosch and others note that although carbohydrate loading may reduce the relative contribution of blood glucose to overall carbohydrate oxidation, the improved performance may be attributed to the initially greater amount of muscle glycogen.

Another supportive study was conducted by Clyde Williams in England. Male and female runners performed a 30-kilometer (18.6 miles) run on a treadmill and then were divided into two groups, one used a carbohydrate loading technique for a week while the other group maintained their normal carbohydrate intake. Although there were no significant differences between the groups for overall performance time in the 30 kilometers, the carbohydrate-loading group ran the last 5 kilometers significantly faster compared to their initial trial.

A study by Rauch and others compared the effects of a 3-day carbohydrate loading protocol (10 grams carbohydrate per kilogram body weight per day, versus a normal mixed diet at 6 grams per kilogram) on performance in a 3-hour cycling task. Endurance-trained cyclists rode 2 hours at 75 percent VO_2 max, interspersed with five 60-second sprints every 20 minutes, and then completed a 60-minute performance ride. The carbohydrate loading regimen significantly increased the distance covered in the performance ride. In another cycling study, Walker and others studied the effect of a carbohydrate-loading and exercise-tapering regimen in well-trained women on performance of a cycling test to exhaustion at 80 percent VO_2 max. The high carbohydrate diet (approximately 78 percent carbohydrate), as compared to the moderate diet (approximately 48 percent carbohydrate), induced a 13 percent greater muscle glycogen content and an 8 percent improvement in cycling time.

Moreover, several field studies with runners and cross-country skiers have shown improved performances with carbohydrate loading. In general, carbohydrate loading, in contrast to a mixed diet, did not enable these athletes to go faster during the early stages of their events, but the high glycogen levels enabled them to perform longer at a given speed. The end result was an overall faster time. Failure to carbohydrate load has also been identified as one of the factors contributing to collapse of runners in an ultramarathon. Indeed, in a recent review, Peters noted that current evidence continues to support high carbohydrate intakes for ultraendurance athletes to increase muscle glycogen stores before the event.

Based on studies published prior to that of Burke and others, several major reviews support the performance-enhancing effectiveness of carbohydrate loading. Clyde Williams reported that an International Consensus Conference on sports nutrition concluded that the most significant influence on performance was the amount of carbohydrate stores in the athlete's body prior to heavy endurance exercise, which is the purpose of carbohydrate loading. Hawley and others concluded that carbohydrate loading would postpone fatigue in endurance events lasting over 90 minutes, and may improve performance in events where a set distance is covered as fast as possible, such as cycling and running, by about 2–3 percent according to some scientists. Given the findings of the recent study by Burke and others, additional research is needed to support these viewpoints.

Although carbohydrate loading may be an effective technique to enhance performance in prolonged aerobic endurance events, research suggests the most effective protocol is to carbohydrate load and use carbohydrate supplements during the event. Kang and others recently noted this method can exert an additional ergogenic effect by preventing a decline in blood glucose levels and maintaining carbohydrate metabolism during the later stages of prolonged aerobic exercise. Given the findings of the recent study by Burke and others, this method appears to be the most appropriate as it will help provide increases in muscle glycogen before exercise as well as replenishment of blood glucose during exercise, two factors that may be associated with enhancement of endurance performance.

Are there any possible detrimental effects relative to carbohydrate loading?

From a performance standpoint, the extra body weight associated with the increased water content may be a disadvantage. In activities where moving the body weight is important, extra energy will be required to lift the extra 2–3 pounds of body water. However, in most performance events for which carbohydrate loading is advocated, the benefits from the energy aspects of the increased glycogen should more than offset the additional water weight. Moreover, if the individual is performing in a hot environment, the extra water could be available as a source of sweat and may be helpful in controlling body temperature during exercise in the heat. Although one study suggested that the water stored with glycogen did not confer any advantage in regulation of body temperature while exercising in heat, the duration of the exercise, only 45 minutes, would not be sufficient to benefit from the increased water levels. Another study conducted in South Africa revealed no beneficial or detrimental effects of carbohydrate loading on body temperature during 2.5 hours of exercise in a moderate environment (70° Fahrenheit; 21° Celsius). However, performance in longer exercise tasks with greater levels of water losses might be benefited.

From a health standpoint there may be some potential hazards to individuals with certain conditions. Although diabetics have been known to carbohydrate load, they should consult their physicians prior to using the technique. Individuals with high blood-lipid or cholesterol levels might avoid the high-fat/high-protein diet phase of the depletion stage if, for some reason, they prefer the original, classic method of carbohydrate loading. Blood serum lipids and cholesterol have been reported to rise significantly during this phase. In addition, these individuals should eat mostly low-glycemic-index carbohydrates during the loading phase because an increased intake of high-glycemic-index carbohydrates may raise blood-lipid levels. Furthermore, hypoglycemia may occur during the high-fat/high-protein phase.

Several laboratory studies and one case study have reported electrocardiographic (ECG) abnormalities in individuals who used the classic carbohydrate loading technique. Although no cause and effect relationship was determined, these investigators speculated that hypoglycemia or glucose intolerance may be involved. On the other hand, other well-controlled research with marathoners and typical joggers revealed no ECG changes following the classic method of carbohydrate loading.

Several investigators theorized that carbohydrate loading could possibly lead to destruction of muscle fibers by excessive glycogen storage, but no data were presented to support their contentions. It appears that the muscle has a maximal capacity to store glycogen, approximately 4 grams/100 grams of muscle, and beyond that level excess carbohydrate would apparently be converted to fat and stored in adipose tissues.

Other potential problems with the high-carbohydrate phase are diarrhea, nausea, and cramping, particularly when the diet is changed drastically or large amounts of simple carbohydrates are consumed. Individuals who wish to carbohydrate load should experiment with such diets during their training and not just before competition.

In general, however, the recommended carbohydrate loading technique presented in table 4.8, which at the most is only a 7-day dietary regimen, poses no significant health hazards to the normally healthy individual.

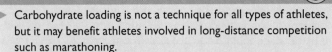
Carbohydrates: Ergogenic Aspects

Throughout this chapter you have learned that carbohydrate intake, in a variety of ways, may be used to enhance physical performance. Truly, carbohydrates represent one of our most important ergogenic nutrients. In this brief section we shall look at several forms of carbohydrate that might possess ergogenic properties. Additionally, numerous carbohydrate-based products, such as the sports "energy" drinks, have been marketed to athletes and many contain purported ergogenic substances, such as caffeine, ephedrine, and amino acids. These specific nutritional ergogenics will be discussed in later chapters where appropriate.

Do the metabolic by-products of carbohydrate exert an ergogenic effect?

Recall that the primary mechanism in the transformation of muscle glycogen into energy is glycolysis. The end product during aerobic metabolism is normally pyruvate. However, glycolysis leading to the formation of pyruvate involves production of a number of metabolic by-products in a chain of about a dozen sequential steps, each step being controlled by an enzyme (see appendix G, figure G.1). One theory of fatigue is that if one of these steps is blocked by inactivation of an enzyme, glycolysis may not continue at an optimal rate since a necessary metabolic by-product may be in short supply. This blocked step could represent a weak link in the chain, possibly reducing the formation of pyruvate and subsequent ATP production. Pyruvate has been studied as a potential ergogenic aid, as have other metabolic by-products of carbohydrate metabolism.

Pyruvate　Pyruvate is a three-carbon metabolic by-product of glycolysis. Although the mechanism of its underlying potential as an ergogenic aid is unknown, pyruvate is theorized to accelerate the Krebs cycle or use glucose more efficiently, both of which could enhance exercise performance. DHAP is a combination of pyruvate and dihydroxyacetone, another three-carbon metabolic by-product of glycolysis.

Pyruvate administered alone has been used in attempts to decrease body fat and increase muscle mass, possibly by speeding up Krebs-cycle activity. In a recent review, Antonio and others reported significantly more body weight and fat loss in obese women following pyruvate supplementation (19 grams/day) as well as in obese males and females with a smaller dose of pyruvate (6 grams/day). Kalman and others reported also a significant decrease in body weight and fat mass in healthy, overweight men and women following 6 weeks of pyruvate supplementation (6 grams per day). No exercise performance data were reported from these studies. Although these findings may be important to the obese, they may not be applicable to the healthy, nonobese, well-trained individual as a means of shedding additional body fat for sports competition.

Research investigating the ergogenic effect of pyruvate supplementation is very limited, and generally has not shown any beneficial effects on exercise performance. For example, in a double-blind, crossover study, Morrison and others found that pyruvate supplementation (7 grams/day for one week) did not enhance cycle time to exhaustion in well-trained male cyclists in an aerobic endurance test. However, some research suggests beneficial effects of DHAP supplementation.

Previous studies with animals have shown that DHAP increases muscle glycogen content, so Ronald Stanko and his associates at the University of Pittsburgh investigated the potential ergogenic effect of DHAP in humans. Two studies were conducted, both using untrained males as subjects. The dosage of DHAP in both studies was 100 grams per day for 7 days; DHAP was prepared in a 3:1 ratio of dihydroxyacetone (75 g) to sodium pyruvate (25 g) and administered either in Jello or artificially sweetened fluids. The placebo in both studies was 100 grams of Polycose, a carbohydrate. The DHAP or Polycose was substituted for a portion of the carbohydrate in the diet. Both studies were well designed, using a double-blind, placebo, repeated-measures crossover approach. In the first study, the diet was standardized at 55 percent carbohydrate of the daily caloric intake. The criterion test was an arm ergometer exercise task to exhaustion at 60 percent VO_2 peak following a week of supplementation. DHAP significantly increased endurance time, attributed primarily to an increased muscle glycogen concentration and increased extraction of blood glucose, both factors providing more glucose to the exercising muscle. In the second experiment, subjects consumed a high-carbohydrate diet (70 percent of the daily caloric intake). The criterion test was a cycle ergometer exercise task to exhaustion at 70 percent VO_2 peak. DHAP improved performance in an identical fashion to the first study, the effect being attributed to an increased blood glucose extraction by the exercising muscle. The results of these two well-controlled studies indicate an ergogenic effect of DHAP with untrained subjects, but confirming data are needed with well-trained athletes.

Lactate Salts　As noted previously, lactic acid is a metabolic by-product of anaerobic glycolysis. We also indicated that although lactic acid is often associated with fatigue, it is the hydrogen ion release that increases the acidity and impairs performance, not the lactate itself. Lactate is actually a small metabolite of glucose; its formula is $C_3H_5O_3$, about half of that of glucose, $C_6H_{12}O_6$. Thus, lactate still possesses considerable energy and, as Van Hall recently noted, may be converted back to pyruvate to enter the energy pathway in the skeletal muscles. Lactate may also be converted back to glucose by the liver.

Various lactate supplements have been studied as a means to enhance endurance performance. Larsen and others investigated the effect of polylactate, a combination of lactate and an amino acid, upon physiological and psychological responses to a 3-hour bicycle ergometer exercise task at 50 percent of VO_2 max. They reported that compared to a sweetened placebo, polylactate can help maintain blood glucose, reduce perceived exertion, and enhance blood buffering capacity (lower blood acidity). No performance data were presented. On the basis of these findings, it would appear polylactate is comparable to other carbohydrate supplements, although the potential effect of the improved blood buffering capacity would appear to have some ergogenic potential. Moreover, Fred Brouns and his colleagues at Maastricht in the Netherlands reported that 3 weeks of supplementation with oral lactate salts did not influence the removal of lactate during and following exercise, suggesting no value to lactate supplementation in this regard. Bryner and others compared the effects of four sports drinks (2 percent lactate; 8 percent carbohydrate; 2 percent lactate/8 percent carbohydrate combination; placebo) on performance in a cycle ergometer exercise test to exhaustion which also incorporated a 30-second Wingate cycle power test. Subjects consumed 100 grams of carbohydrate several hours before the test, and then consumed the sport drinks during the test. There were no significant differences among the sports drinks for endurance time, peak power, glucose, insulin, or blood pH, indicating that lactate supplementation, either alone or in combination with carbohydrate, provided no advantage over carbohydrate alone.

Based on the current data, it would appear that lactate preparations may provide additional energy, somewhat comparable to carbohydrate sources. However, the latter are more readily available and most likely, less expensive.

Ribose   Ribose is a 5-carbon monosaccharide found throughout body cells as part of various compounds, such as RNA (ribonucleic acid) in the cell nucleus. Ribose also comprises the sugar portion of adenosine, the nucleotide found in ATP (adenosine triphosphate). ATP, as you recall, is the immediate source of energy for muscle contraction both in the heart and skeletal muscles.

Although found in nature, very little ribose is consumed in a natural diet. Instead, a specific metabolic pathway (pentose phosphate pathway) produces ribose from glucose to meet our body needs. Recently, ribose supplements (made from corn sugar) have been marketed to physically active individuals as a means to promote faster recovery in heart and skeletal muscles, presumably by facilitating the formation of adenosine, one of the major components of ATP.

Research indicates that strenuous exercise may necessitate rapid recovery of adenosine within muscle cells, which might benefit from adequate ribose. Pliml and others found that ribose ingestion (60 grams daily for 3 days) improved exercise performance time in patients with severe coronary artery disease, while other studies have suggested that ribose, when supplemented, could serve as an energy source and promote adenosine synthesis in various patient groups.

Only limited, preliminary research has been conducted to evaluate the effect of ribose supplementation on exercise performance in healthy subjects. Berardi and Ziegenfuss studied the effect of oral ribose supplementation (32 grams over a 36-hour period) on high-intensity, intermittent, anaerobic cycle ergometer performance; the exercise task consisted of six 10-second sprints with a 60-second recovery. They concluded that ribose supplementation does not have a consistent or substantial effect on anaerobic cycle sprinting as evaluated by peak and mean power output. In a well-designed study, Op 'T Eijnde and others evaluated the effect of oral ribose supplementation (16 grams/day for 6 days) on two maximal knee-extension exercise protocols and ATP recovery. The exercise bouts were separated by a 60-minute rest period. They concluded that oral ribose supplementation had no effect on maximal intermittent exercise performance or ATP recovery. Hellsten and others reported that 3 days of ribose supplementation (based on body weight, approximately 45 grams daily) elicited a greater resynthesis of ATP compared to the placebo. However, the slight increase in ATP availability did not enhance performance, as there were no differences between the placebo and ribose supplement for mean and peak power outputs. The authors note that a small reduction in muscle ATP does not appear to limit high-intensity exercise performance.

Current data are limited and, in general, do not support an ergogenic effect of ribose supplementation. Additional research is warranted.

Multiple carbohydrate by-products   Sports supplements manufacturers often combine multiple nutrients in a single supplement on the theory that each may exhibit an ergogenic effect, but the effect will be amplified with multiple components. Limited research is available with multiple by-products of carbohydrate metabolism, but Brown and others recently investigated the ergogenic potential of a multi-nutrient supplement composed primarily of intermediates of the Krebs cycle, which may be derived from carbohydrate, fat, or protein. Three weeks of supplementation did not improve cycling time to exhaustion at approximately 70–75 percent VO_2 max, nor did it improve the rate of recovery.

Key Concept Recap

▶ Metabolic by-products of carbohydrate metabolism have been tested as ergogenics. Most have been found to be ineffective, although research with physically trained individuals is rather limited.

Check for Yourself

Go to a health food store that sells sports supplements and ask the clerk for carbohydrate products, including metabolites, that may help you train or compete more effectively. Evaluate the supplement fact labels for content and performance claims. What is your judgment?

Dietary Carbohydrates: Health Implications

Although improving somewhat, the diet of the typical American and Canadian still appears to be unbalanced. In general, we consume too many Calories for the level of physical activity we do, we eat too much of the unhealthy fats and carbohydrates. Such a diet may pose several health problems. As we shall see in chapter 5, excessive consumption of total and saturated fat appears to be of major concern relative to the development of several chronic diseases. In this section, we discuss the health aspects of dietary carbohydrates. In general, the health effects associated with various sugars and starches is not in the substances themselves, but rather in the nutrients that accompany them in the foods we eat. For example, sugar in orange juice is little different from sugar in a soda, but the orange juice contains substantial amounts of vitamin C, potassium, and other nutrients, whereas the soda has none unless fortified. Whole grains contain more fiber and more of some micronutrients than refined grains.

In the recent past, low carbohydrate diets have been all the rage. As shall be noted in chapter 10, research has indicated that such diets may have some health benefits, but these health benefits appear to be attributed more to decreased caloric intake than to diet composition. The pendulum, rightfully so, has shifted toward a diet rich in carbohydrate.

Nutritional objectives in *Healthy People 2010* and in the 2005 *Dietary Guidelines for Americans* recommend that we should consume more carbohydrates, particularly complex carbohydrates and fiber-containing foods, often referred to as the *good carbs*. We should also moderate intake of refined carbohydrates and added sugars, often referred to as the *bad carbs*. Although no foods, or carbohydrates, are inherently *good* or *bad,* following these two general guidelines may produce some significant health benefits. Additionally, an appropriate exercise program may have a healthful influence on carbohydrate metabolism.

How do refined sugars and starches affect my health?

As noted previously, sugars may be found naturally in foods, or they may be manufactured from starches, such as high fructose corn syrup, and added to foods. Refined starches are predominant in many foods, such as white bread, pasta, and rice. Consumption of refined sugars and starches in excess may be associated with various health risks, attributed mainly to their high glycemic index.

Dental caries One of the most common health problems that has been associated with dietary sugar is tooth decay, or dental caries. However, the National Institutes of Health in its consensus statement on management of dental caries throughout life noted that effective preventive practice involves a number of factors, including proper oral hygiene (brushing, flossing, use of fluoride) and dietary modifications (use of sugarless products). Tooth decay is not necessarily a matter of how much sugar one eats, but in what form and how often. Dental erosion is increas-

ing and is associated with dietary acids, a major source of which is soft drinks. Sticky, chewy, sugary foods eaten often between meals increase the risk of developing dental caries. Starchy foods that adhere to teeth, like bread, are also cariogenic.

Of particular interest to athletes, von Fraunhofer and Rogers reported far greater enamel dissolution in flavored and energy (sports) drinks than previously noted for water. They noted that sipping sports drinks over long periods of time may erode tooth enamel; therefore, drink quickly. On the other hand, Mathew and others recently reported no relationship between consumption of sports drinks and dental erosion in university athletes. Nevertheless, scientists have developed a prototype sports drink, containing substantial amounts of calcium and maltodextrins, which is alleged to cause less dental enamel erosion than the typical commercial sports drink.

Chronic diseases Over the years, dietary intake of refined sugar has been alleged to contribute to a wide variety of health problems, including obesity, diabetes, heart disease, and cancer, as well as various psychological afflictions such as hyperactivity in children, premenstrual syndrome (PMS), and seasonal affective disorder (SAD). Such allegations have been based mainly on theoretical considerations, but with support from some recent epidemiological studies. For example, an habitual diet rich in high-glycemic index foods theoretically may lead to insulin resistance and high serum triglyceride levels, risk factors for diabetes and heart disease, respectively. This may be especially so in individuals who are obese, and will be discussed in detail in chapter 10. Added sugars can increase caloric intake and predispose to obesity. Additionally, as discussed previously, a high-carbohydrate diet can increase the fTRP:BCAA ratio and facilitate the entry of tryptophan into the brain and the increased formation of the neurotransmitter serotonin. Serotonin may influence mood and behavior associated with PMS and SAD or other psychological states.

However, the National Academy of Sciences in its recent DRI recommendations for carbohydrate noted that given the currently available scientific evidence relative to the effect of dietary sugar on dental caries, psychological behavior, cancer, risk of obesity, and risk of hyperlipidemia, there is insufficient evidence to set a UL for total or added sugar in the diet.

Nevertheless, the Academy noted that the theory linking a high-glycemic index to certain health problems, such as diabetes and CHD, appears to be valid and supported by some studies, but the evidence at this time appears to be insufficient to substantiate the theory. Furthermore, the Academy noted that individuals who consume excess amounts of added sugars may not obtain sufficient amounts of various micronutrients, and that this may lead to adverse health effects. Thus, the Academy set a maximal intake level of 25 percent or less of energy from added sugars.

Given these considerations, and the fact that many health organizations recommend a reduced intake of refined sugars to about 10 percent or less of the daily caloric intake, it appears to be prudent to moderate your consumption of refined sugars and starches.

Suggestions to decrease intake of refined starches and sugars were presented in chapter 2. To reiterate some of these points:

- Eat refined starches and grains sparingly, mainly as a side dish; eat them with added protein or small amounts of healthier fats to reduce the glycemic load.
- Read food labels and select foods low in sugar. Most of the sugar we eat has been added to our foods during commercial processing. Sugar is everywhere. Even "healthy-type" foods such as yogurt and instant oatmeal may contain substantial amounts of sugar.
- Know the different ways in which sugar may appear on a food label. Sugar is sugar. There is no additional nutritional value of added "natural" sugars, such as fruit juice concentrate, compared to ordinary table sugar (sucrose).
- Reduce the sugar in foods prepared at home. Use less sugar at the table.
- Eat more fruits for a naturally occurring source of sugar.
- Decrease intake of soft drinks. A typical regular soft drink contains 10 teaspoons of sugar, about 150 Calories and constitutes the largest source of added sugars in the diet. Drink diet soda, or better yet, water.
- Use other sweeteners, such as cinnamon, nutmeg, ginger, or artificial sweeteners.

Are artificial sweeteners safe?

Artificial sweeteners are products designed to provide sweetness, but fewer or no Calories, as a means for individuals to reduce refined sugar consumption. However, in a recent review Liebman noted that although dietary intake of artificial sweeteners has increased over the past ten years, so too has the consumption of refined sugars. As these products have been used as food additives, their safety has been evaluated.

A number of artificial sweeteners have been produced over the years, and currently several are approved for use in the United States. Saccharin, 300 times as sweet as sucrose, is a noncaloric derivative of coal tar. Aspartame, 180 times as sweet as sucrose, is derived from two amino acids (aspartic acid and phenylalanine) and contains 4 Calories per gram. Neotame, derived from the same amino acids as aspartame, is over 7,000 times as sweet as sugar. Acesulfame K, 200 times as sweet as sucrose, is a naturally occurring potassium salt. Sucralose is produced by altering the sugar molecule, resulting in a product that is about 600 times sweeter than sugar. Sugar alcohols, such as sorbitol, mannitol, and lactitol, are not absorbed, so they are low glycemic and provide no Calories.

Saccharin in extremely large doses has been shown to cause urinary bladder cancer in laboratory animals, and according to the Delaney clause, it should be banned as an additive to food products. However, the United States Congress passed a law exempting saccharin from the Delaney clause, and its use continues. Epidemiological data with humans have not shown any relationship between urinary bladder cancer and saccharin at levels normally consumed by the general population, so it is assumed to be safe and has been removed from the government's list of carcinogens. Weihrauch and Diehl concluded that the risk of artificial sweeteners to induce cancer was negligible.

The safety of aspartame, also known as Equal or NutraSweet, has been questioned because some reports have associated it with headaches, dizziness, or fatigue in some individuals, which may have been an allergic reaction; more recent reports have associated it with brain tumors. However, Butchko and Stargel evaluated the scientific evidence, including anecdotal reports of adverse health effects, and found that the weight of the scientific evidence indicates that aspartame is safe for its intended use as a sweetener and flavor enhancer—even in amounts many times what people typically consume. Moreover, the Food and Drug Administration and other federal health agencies consider aspartame to confer no significant health risks, with the exception of individuals who have phenylketonuria (PKU), a rare genetic disease that limits the ability to metabolize phenylalanine. Such individuals are aware of their condition, and products containing aspartame must carry a warning on the label that the product contains phenylalanine.

In a recent review, the Consumers Union concluded that all artificial sweeteners appear to be safe in small amounts. In particular, studies have raised no safety concerns at all about sucralose. However, the Consumers Union states several caveats. For one, high intakes of sugar alcohols, because they are not absorbed, may cause gastrointestinal distress. For another, individuals who may suffer from headaches or other symptoms from aspartame should avoid it.

Some contend that use of sugar substitutes perpetuate cravings for sweet foods, and do nothing to promote good health. However, artificial sweeteners may be effective in weight-control programs, and their role will be discussed in chapter 11. Nevertheless, one should keep in mind that *sugar free* does not mean low-Calorie; check the food label for Calories per serving.

Why are complex carbohydrates thought to be beneficial to my health?

To increase consumption of total carbohydrate in the diet while reducing the consumption of refined sugars, one must increase the consumption of complex carbohydrates. Some diet plans developed for health, such as the Pritikin program, recommend that 80 percent of the dietary Calories be supplied by carbohydrates, mostly complex and unrefined. A diet rich in complex carbohydrates may reduce the percentage contribution from fats if excessive, which may confer significant health benefits, as noted in chapter 5. Complex carbohydrates are found primarily in starchy vegetables, whole grains, and legumes, but small amounts are also found in fruits.

Current thinking supports the concept that the beneficial health effects of a diet rich in complex carbohydrates, which may be considered to be a low-glycemic-index diet, may be linked to several important attributes of such a diet, including the collective presence of various phytochemicals, vitamins, minerals, and dietary fiber. The health benefits of phytochemicals were discussed in chapter 2, while the benefits of vitamins and minerals will be covered in chapters 7 and 8. Most research relative to the healthful benefits of complex carbohydrates has focused on dietary fiber.

Why should I eat foods rich in fiber?

The National Academy of Sciences, for the first time, recently established dietary recommendations for fiber. The daily AI for total fiber has been set at 38 grams for men and 25 grams for women up to age 50, and slightly lesser amounts thereafter. Recall that total fiber consists of both dietary fiber and functional fiber, and various specific forms of fiber are found in each category; some specific forms of fiber may be classified as both dietary and functional fiber. Although the Academy indicates that specific forms of fibers have properties that result in different physiological effects that may impact health, it did not feel that the evidence was sufficient to establish separate recommendations for each type of fiber. Nevertheless, some feel that the use of the water-solubility classifications system, as discussed previously, might be useful conceptually to illustrate the potential health benefits of certain forms of fiber.

Exactly how dietary fiber may be protective is not known, but several mechanisms have been proposed that may help in the prevention of certain forms of cancer, coronary heart disease, obesity, diabetes, hypertension, and various disorders of the gastrointestinal tract. Here are some of the theories relative to the potential health benefits of total fiber:

1. Water-insoluble fibers are considered to be those with the greatest effect on fecal bulk. Adding bulk to the contents of the large intestine stimulates peristalsis and speeds up the transit time of food through the intestines. The increased bulk has been shown to dilute any possible cancer-causing (carcinogens) that might attack cell walls, while faster transit diminishes the time carcinogens may have to act. Increased bulk—and peristalsis—also decreases the incidence rate of diverticulosis, an inflammatory disorder in the large intestine that may cause rupture, leading to serious complications.

2. Fiber-rich foods are low-glycemic-index foods, and may increase insulin sensitivity and prevention of weight gain. Fiber slows down gastric (stomach) emptying and thereby slows glucose absorption in the small intestine. The high viscosity of soluble fiber also decreases intestinal absorption. These effects may lead to better control of blood sugar and may also lengthen the sensation of fullness or satiety, which may be important to individuals on weight-loss diets. Fiber-rich diets are frequently lower in fat and added sugars, and thus contain fewer Calories. So, high-fiber diets may be useful in the prevention or treatment of obesity and obesity-related chronic diseases such as diabetes and hypertension.

3. Fiber, particularly gummy forms of water-soluble fiber like beta-glucans in oats, may bind with various substances in the gastrointestinal tract. Soluble fiber may bind with carcinogens so that they are excreted by the bowel. Soluble fibers may also bind with and lead to the excretion of bile salts, which contain cholesterol; normally bile salts are reabsorbed into the body, but excretion of bile salts, along with their cholesterol content, may help reduce serum cholesterol levels. This effect may decrease the risk of coronary heart disease. (Lower serum cholesterol levels decrease the risk of atherosclerosis, a major cause of heart disease.)

4. Some water-soluble fibers may be fermented in the large intestine to form short-chain fatty acids (SCFA). SCFA may be absorbed and transported to the liver where they may suppress cholesterol synthesis, possibly helping to decrease serum cholesterol levels and the risk of coronary heart disease, as noted in benefit number 3.

Although it may be illustrative to view the health benefits of fiber based on its water solubility, Joanne Slavin, a scholar on the health effects of dietary fiber, notes that it is difficult to generalize as to the physiological effects of fiber based on this classification system. For example, she notes that rice bran, which is devoid of soluble fiber, has been shown to reduce serum cholesterol, while recent research has also supported the effect of insoluble fiber to reduce the risk of heart disease. Thus, health benefits may be attributable to total fiber.

Numerous studies, including major epidemiological studies and clinical trials, have investigated the effect of total fiber on reducing the risk or incidence of chronic diseases. Based on these studies, the National Academy of Sciences established the AI for total fiber because it may reduce the risk of coronary heart disease, and more recent research supports this concept. Although the Academy cited studies showing a beneficial effect of total fiber and a low-glycemic-index diet on other health problems, particularly in individuals with diabetes or hyperlipidemia, the evidence (in contrast to that for prevention of heart disease) was not enough to merit establishing an RDA or AI for healthy individuals. Scientists have expressed different opinions regarding the use of the glycemic index as a means to design a diet for enhanced health, and the interested reader is referred to the opposing reviews by Pi-Sunyer and Jenkins and his associates.

Given that coronary heart disease is the number one cause of death in Western societies, consuming a fiber-rich diet is certainly prudent dietary behavior. And, although the National Academy of Sciences indicates that the relationship of fiber intake to other health problems is the subject of ongoing investigation and currently unresolved, there appear to be no adverse health effects associated with a fiber-rich diet. Indeed a fiber-rich diet may be useful for other possible health benefits. For example, a recent meta-analysis of 24 studies concluded that increasing the intake of fiber in Western populations, where intake is far below recommended levels, may contribute to the prevention of hypertension. This finding, in addition to lower serum cholesterol levels, may be one of the mechanisms whereby diets rich in dietary fiber reduce the risk of heart disease.

Prevention of colon cancer has been one of the main theories underlying the promotion of a high-fiber diet. However, Martinez notes that although the relationship between intake of dietary fiber and risk of colon cancer has been studied for three decades, the results are still inconclusive. Martinez suggests that some micronutrients or phytochemicals in fiber-rich foods may be important in prevention of colon cancer.

As the different types of fiber appear to convey health benefits in different ways, a balanced intake of total fiber appears to be the best approach. The Academy notes that although the AI are based on total fiber, the greatest health benefits may come from the ingestion of cereal fibers and various viscous fibers, including gums and pectins, which are found in fruits and vegetables. Obtaining 25–38 grams of fiber daily is not difficult, but you have to eat more whole grains, fruits, vegetables, and legumes. Total fiber is listed on food labels. In particular, check food labels on breads and cereals, staples of the daily diet. Cleveland notes that on the average, Americans consume nearly seven servings of grain products per day but that only one of the seven is whole grain. Refined grains contain little or no fiber, whereas whole grains are usually rich in fiber. Some brands of bread contain 3 grams of fiber per slice, and only 50 Calories. Breakfast cereals may also be very high in fiber, some containing 10 or more grams per serving. The following general equivalencies may help you reach your goal:

3 fruits	=	6 grams fiber
3 vegetables	=	9 grams fiber
3 slices of whole-grain bread	=	6 grams fiber
1/2 cup beans	=	7 grams fiber
1 serving bran cereal	=	9 grams fiber
Total	=	37 grams fiber

According to one physician, a good way to see if you are eating enough fiber is to observe the buoyancy of your stool in the toilet. It should float, or at least appear flaky and break apart. If it sinks or does not break apart, you are not eating enough fiber.

There appear to be few or no health disadvantages to a high-fiber diet. As we shall see in chapter 8, there has been some concern that high-fiber diets could lead to increased losses of certain minerals, such as iron and zinc, but research has shown that such concerns are generally unwarranted if one follows the recommendations just given.

Schneeman, discussing development of a scientific consensus on the importance of dietary fiber, notes that fiber serves as a marker for diets rich in plant foods, which provide additional benefits for maintaining health. It is important to recognize that the health benefits attributed to dietary fiber may be associated with the form in which the fiber is consumed—as part of a whole, natural food containing other potential health-promoting nutrients such as vitamins and phytochemicals, rather than by consumption of a purified supplement form. This is in accord with the position stand of the American Dietetic Association on dietary fiber. Get more plant foods in your diet!

What is lactose intolerance?

About one in nine Americans may develop gastrointestinal distress when they consume dairy products containing substantial amounts of lactose, particularly milk. Such individuals lack the enzyme lactase and hence cannot metabolize lactose in the digestive tract. The most common symptoms of **lactose intolerance** are gas, bloating, abdominal pain, and diarrhea, although headache and fatigue may also occur. Levey has noted that lactose intolerance may be the cause of runner's diarrhea that often occurs during exercise.

Individuals may be diagnosed as being lactose intolerant through a lactose tolerance test administered by a physician. One physician suggests, however, that a self-detection technique may be an effective approach. If you experience problems such as gas and diarrhea after consuming milk, abstain from all dairy products for 2 weeks and then evaluate the results. If the symptoms resolve, and then reoccur when you resume dairy food consumption, you may need to reduce the amount of lactose in your diet. Unfortunately, usually this means a reduced intake of dairy foods, which are considered to be the main dietary source of not only lactose, but calcium as well. Di Stefano and others indicated that lactose intolerance may prevent the achievement of adequate peak bone mass in young adults and may, therefore, predispose to severe osteoporosis.

Calcium will be discussed in detail in chapter 8, but here are several strategies lactose-intolerant individuals may use to obtain adequate calcium intake. In some cases, milk may be consumed in small amounts, such as one-half cup, without triggering adverse effects, for the intestinal tract may be able to process smaller amounts. Consuming small amounts of milk over the course of the day may provide significant amounts of calcium. Reduced-lactose milk is available, as are enzyme supplements, such as Lactaid, to help prevent indigestion. Other dairy products which have been fermented, such as yogurt, may be tolerated and provide a good calcium source. Cheese may also be a good source of calcium, although it is high in fat. Dark-green leafy vegetables, tofu, sardines, and salmon are all nondairy sources of calcium. Additionally, calcium supplements may be useful either in tablet form or as added to various foods, such as soy milk, rice milk, or orange juice.

Does exercise exert any beneficial health effects related to carbohydrate metabolism?

As noted in chapter 1, an appropriate exercise program may provide a variety of health benefits. In subsequent chapters, we shall detail the preventive health effects of exercise as related to several major health problems, such as obesity, diabetes, hypertension, and coronary heart disease. Some of these beneficial effects may be attributed to the effect of exercise on carbohydrate metabolism.

Aging is normally associated with impaired glucose tolerance, which is associated with decreased insulin sensitivity. As shall be noted in chapter 10, such effects may contribute to metabolic aberrations associated with the development of coronary heart disease. However, Holloszy and Greiwe noted that these deleterious changes are not inevitable but are most likely related to a sedentary lifestyle and increased body weight. They found that athletic individuals 60 years and older had glucose tolerance and insulin action as good as young athletes nearly half their age.

Exercise may enhance glucose tolerance and insulin sensitivity in several ways. In their review, Borghouts and Keizer noted that both acute and chronic exercise may affect blood glucose and insulin activity favorably. Up to two hours after an acute bout of exercise, glucose uptake is in part elevated due to insulin-independent mechanisms, probably involving an increase in GLUT-4 receptors in the cell membrane induced by exercise. Additionally, an exercise bout can increase insulin sensitivity for up to 16 hours afterwards. Chronic exercise training potentiates the effect of exercise on insulin sensitivity through multiple adaptations in glucose transport and metabolism. Borghouts and Keizer conclude that exercise plays an important, if not essential, role in the prevention and treatment of impaired insulin sensitivity.

Given the epidemic of obesity and type 2 diabetes in the United States and other industrialized nations, these beneficial effects of exercise on carbohydrate metabolism underscore its importance as preventive medicine.

Key Concept Recap

▶ Added sugars should be limited in the diet. The maximal recommended amount is 25 percent of daily energy intake, but some health professionals recommend lower amounts of about 10 percent. Intake of refined starches should also be limited.

▶ An increase in the amount of total fiber to about 25–38 grams per day may be helpful as a protective measure against the development of several chronic diseases.

Check for Yourself

Check the food labels of various breads for fiber content. Do some brands have significantly more than others? What impact could switching breads have on meeting the recommended daily fiber intake of 25 grams for females and 38 grams for males?

APPLICATION EXERCISE

If you are not currently eating enough fiber, try this experiment. Keep a record of your appetite and your bowel movements for a week or so, and then switch to a high fiber diet, consuming fruits and vegetables, whole wheat and whole grain breads, and other high fiber foods as documented by food labels. Record approximate grams of total fiber consumed daily. Also record an increase (↑), decrease (↓), or no change (NC) for appetite, and record the number of daily bowel movements. Compare your appetite and bowel movements to the previous week. Did the high-fiber diet influence either?

Week 1 (Normal Diet)

	Sunday	Monday	Tuesday	Wednesday	Thursday	Friday	Saturday
Breakfast							
Lunch							
Dinner							
Snacks							
Appetite							
Bowel Movement(s)							

Week 2 (High-fiber diet)

	Sunday	Monday	Tuesday	Wednesday	Thursday	Friday	Saturday
Breakfast							
Lunch							
Dinner							
Snacks							
Appetite							
Bowel Movement(s)							

1. Which of the following statements relative to carbohydrate loading is false?
   (a) It is beneficial primarily for athletes involved in prolonged endurance events, such as the typical marathon (26.2 miles).
   (b) It involves the intake of about 500–600 grams of carbohydrate each day for several days prior to competition.
   (c) Research generally supports its effectiveness as a means of improving performance by helping to delay the onset of fatigue in the latter stages of prolonged exercise tasks.
   (d) The major advantage of carbohydrate loading is the increased storage of glycogen in the adipose cells for use during exercise.
   (e) The increase in carbohydrate stores in the body may be detected by the increased body weight attributed to the water-binding effect of stored glycogen.

2. If you were to recommend to a runner a fluid replacement protocol, including carbohydrate content, for use during a marathon, which of the following would you *not* recommend?
   (a) Use a 50–60 percent solution of galactose.
   (b) Provide approximately 10–15 grams per feeding.
   (c) Provide feedings about every 15–20 minutes.
   (d) Limit the amount of fructose in the solution.
   (e) Choose a combination of carbohydrates.

3. Which of the following statements relative to the intake of carbohydrates and physical performance is false?
   (a) If an individual has normal glycogen levels in the muscle and liver, carbohydrate feedings are usually not necessary if the exercise task is only about 60–90 minutes.
   (b) The intake of concentrated sugar solutions may actually impair performance if they lead to osmosis of fluids into the stomach and precipitate the feeling of gastric distress.
   (c) Carbohydrate intake may help delay the onset of fatigue in prolonged exercise by either preventing the early onset of hypoglycemia or delaying the depletion of muscle glycogen levels.
   (d) Carbohydrate intake prior to and during endurance exercise tasks lasting more than 2 hours may be helpful as a means of enhancing performance.
   (e) If consumed during exercise, it takes approximately 60–90 minutes for the carbohydrate to find its way into the muscle and be used as an energy source.

4. Following a meal high in simple carbohydrate, which of the following is most likely to occur in the next 1–2 hours?
   (a) suppression of insulin with a resultant hyperglycemia
   (b) hyperglycemia which stimulates insulin secretion followed by a possible hypoglycemia
   (c) hypoglycemia which stimulates insulin secretion and a return to normal blood glucose levels
   (d) hyperglycemia with a suppression of insulin and movement of blood glucose into the liver and muscle tissues
   (e) no change in blood glucose level

5. Which of the following is *not* one of the potential health benefits of dietary fiber?
   (a) It may increase the bulk in the large intestine and dilute possible carcinogens.
   (b) It may increase the bulk in the large intestine and help speed up intestinal transit.
   (c) It may bind with carcinogens and help to excrete them.
   (d) It may help excrete bile salts and reduce serum cholesterol levels.
   (e) It may bind with certain minerals such as zinc and help to excrete them.

6. Which of the following food exchanges is least likely to be high in dietary fiber?
   (a) vegetable
   (b) starch/bread
   (c) milk
   (d) fruit
   (e) legumes (meat exchange)

7. What two tissues in the body store the most carbohydrate?
   (a) adipose and kidney
   (b) kidney and liver
   (c) liver and muscles
   (d) muscles and kidney
   (e) adipose and muscles

8. Common table sugar is:
   (a) glucose
   (b) dextrose
   (c) fructose
   (d) sucrose
   (e) maltose

9. The total amount of carbohydrate, as a percentage of the daily calories, that represents the Acceptable Macronutrient Distribution Range (AMDR) for Americans and Canadians is:
   (a) 12–15
   (b) 20–30
   (c) 30–45
   (d) 45–65
   (e) 85–90

10. The glycemic index represents:
    (a) the degree to which an athlete suffers from hypoglycemia
    (b) the amount of glucose released into the blood in response to exercise
    (c) the effect a particular food has on the rate and amount of increase in the blood glucose level
    (d) the amount of stored glycogen in the muscle and liver
    (e) the total amount of insulin released in response to food intake

Answers to multiple-choice questions:
1. d; 2. a; 3. e; 4. b; 5. e; 6. c; 7. c; 8. d; 9. d; 10. c.

1. Differentiate between dietary fiber and functional fiber, and contrast the new AI for total fiber with the current Daily Value (DV) used on food labels.
2. You have eaten a high-carbohydrate meal for lunch. Explain the digestion and metabolic fate of this carbohydrate over the next five hours, including an hour of running at the end of this time frame.
3. Explain three possible mechanisms of fatigue due to inadequate carbohydrate intake prior to and during the running of a 26.2 mile marathon.
4. Identify athletes who might benefit from carbohydrate loading and present details of the dietary and exercise training protocol.
5. Discuss the possible health benefits associated with a diet rich in complex carbohydrates and low to moderate in refined carbohydrates.

References

Books

Jeukendrup, A. 1997. *Aspects of Carbohydrate and Fat Metabolism During Exercise.* Haarlem, Netherlands: De Vrieseborch.

Maughan, R., and Murray, R. 2001. *Sports Drinks.* Boca Raton, FL: CRC Press.

National Academy of Sciences. 2002. *Dietary Reference Intakes for Energy, Carbohydrates, Fiber, Fat, Protein and Amino Acids (Macronutrients).* Washington, DC: National Academy Press.

U.S. Department of Health and Human Services Public Health Service. 2000. *Healthy People 2010.* Washington, DC: Government Printing Office.

Reviews

Antinoro, L. 2001. Battling brain diseases: Diet links to Alzheimer's and Parkinson's. *Environmental Nutrition* 24 (4):1, 4.

Antonio, J., et al. 1999. Pyruvate: Ergogenic aid and weight loss supplement. *AMAA Quarterly* 12 (4):13, 18.

Bonci, L. 2002. "Energy" drinks: Help, harm or hype? *Sports Science Exchange* 15 (1):1–4.

Borghouts, L., and Keizer, H. 2000. Exercise and insulin sensitivity: A review. *International Journal of Sports Medicine* 21:1–12.

Brown, L., et al. 1999. Cholesterol-lowering effects of dietary fiber: A meta-analysis. *American Journal of Clinical Nutrition* 69:30–42.

Burke, L., et al. 2004. Carbohydrates and fat for training and recovery. *Journal of Sports Sciences* 22:15–30.

Burke, L., et al. 2001. Guidelines for daily carbohydrate intake: Do athletes achieve them? *Sports Medicine* 31:267–99.

Burke, L. 2001. Nutritional needs for exercise in the heat. *Comparative Biochemistry and Physiology: Part A, Molecular and Integrative Physiology* 128:735–48.

Burke, L. 2001. Nutritional practices of male and female endurance cyclists. *Sports Medicine* 31:521–32.

Burke, L. 2000. Dietary carbohydrates. In *Nutrition in Sport,* ed. R. J. Maughan. Oxford: Blackwell Scientific.

Burke, L., et al. 1998. Glycemic index: A new tool in sport nutrition. *International Journal of Sport Nutrition* 8:401–15.

Butchko, H., and Stargel, W. Aspartame: Scientific evaluation in the postmarketing period. *Regulatory Toxicology and Pharmacology* 34:221–33.

Christ-Roberts, C., and Mandarino, L. 2004. Glycogen synthase: Key effect of exercise on insulin action. *Exercise and Sport Sciences Reviews* 32:90–94.

Coleman, E. 1994. Update on carbohydrate: Solid versus liquid. *International Journal of Sport Nutrition* 4:80–88.

Conley, M., and Stone, M. 1996. Carbohydrate ingestion/supplementation for resistance exercise and training. *Sports Medicine* 21:7–17.

Consumers Union. 2005. Sweeteners can sour your health. *Consumer Reports on Health* 17 (1):8–9.

Consumers Union. 2003. Carbohydrates without fear. *Consumer Reports on Health* 15 (10):1–6.

Coombes, J., and Hamilton, K. 2000. The effectiveness of commercially available sports drinks. *Sports Medicine* 29:181–209.

Costill, D. 1988. Carbohydrates for exercise: Dietary demands for optimal performance. *International Journal of Sports Medicine* 9:1–18.

Coyle, E. 2004. Highs and lows of carbohydrate diets. *Sports Science Exchange* 17 (2):1–6.

Coyle, E. 2000. Physical activity as a metabolic stressor. *American Journal of Clinical Nutrition* 72:512S–20S.

Coyle, E. 1995. Substrate utilization during exercise in active people. *American Journal of Clinical Nutrition* 61 (Supplement): 968S–979S.

Davis, J.M. 1996. Carbohydrates, branched-chain amino acids and endurance: The central fatigue hypothesis. *Sports Science Exchange* 9 (2): 1–6.

Erlenbusch, M., et al. 2005. Effect of high-fat or high-carbohydrate diets on endurance exercise: A meta-analysis. *International Journal of Sport Nutrition and Exercise Metabolism* 15:1–14.

Febbraio, M. 2001. Alterations in energy metabolism during exercise and heat stress. *Sports Medicine* 31:47–59.

Food and Drug Administration. 1996. FDA statement on aspartame. *FDA Talk Paper* T96–75, November 18.

Gleeson, M., et al. 2004. Exercise, nutrition and immune function. *Journal of Sports Sciences* 22:115–25.

Graham, T. 2000. The importance of carbohydrate, fat and protein for the endurance athlete. In *Endurance in Sport,* eds. R.J. Shephard and P.O. Astrand. Oxford: Blackwell Science.

Guezennec, C. 1995. Oxidation rates, complex carbohydrates and exercise. *Sports Medicine* 19:365–72.

Hargreaves, M., et al. 2004. Pre-exercise carbohydrate and fat ingestion: Effects on metabolism and performance. *Journal of Sports Sciences* 22:31–38.

Hargreaves, M. 2000. Carbohydrate metabolism and exercise. In *Exercise and Sport Science,* eds. W. E. Garrett and D. T. Kirkendall. Philadelphia: Lippincott, Williams & Wilkins.

Hargreaves, M. 2000. Carbohydrate replacement during exercise. In *Nutrition in Sport,* ed. R. J. Maughan. Oxford: Blackwell Science.

Hawley, J., and Hopkins, W. 1995. Aerobic glycolytic and aerobic lipolytic power systems. *Sports Medicine* 19:240–50.

Hawley, J., et al. 1997. Carbohydrate-loading and exercise performance: An update. *Sports Medicine* 24:73–81.

Holloszy, J., and Greiwe, J. 2001. Overview of glucose metabolism and aging. *International Journal of Sport Nutrition and Exercise Metabolism* S58–63.

Holloszy, J. O., et al. 1998. The regulation of carbohydrate and fat metabolism during and after exercise. *Frontiers in Science* 3:D1011–27.

Hultman, E., and Greenhaff, P. L. 2000. Carbohydrate metabolism in exercise. In *Nutrition in Sport,* ed. R. J. Maughan. Oxford: Blackwell Scientific.

Ivy, J. 2001. Dietary strategies to promote glycogen synthesis after exercise. *Canadian Journal of Applied Physiology* 26:S236–45.

Ivy, J. L. 2000. Optimization of glycogen stores. In *Nutrition in Sport* Ed. R. J. Maughan. Oxford: Blackwell Scientific.

Jenkins, D., et al. 2002. Glycemic index: Overview of implications in health and disease. *American Journal of Clinical Nutrition* 76:266S–73S.

Jeukendrup, A. 2004. Carbohydrate intake during exercise and performance. *Nutrition* 20:669–77.

Jeukendrup, A., and Jentjens, R. 2000. Oxidation of carbohydrate feedings during prolonged exercise: Current thoughts, guidelines and directions for future research. *Sports Medicine* 29:407–24.

Keim, N. et al. 2006. Carbohydrates. In *Modern Nutrition in Health and Disease,* eds. M. Shils, et al. Philadelphia: Lippincott Williams & Wilkins.

Kirkendall, D. 2004. Creatine, carbs, and fluids: How important in soccer nutrition? *Sports Science Exchange* 17(3):1–6.

Kjaer, M. 1998. Hepatic glucose production during exercise. *Advances in Experimental Medicine and Biology* 441:117–27.

Levey, J. M. 2000. Runner's diarrhea. *AMAA Quarterly* 14 (1): 6–7.

Liebman, B. 2002. Cancer: How to lower your risk. *Nutrition Action Health Letter* 29 (8): 1–8.

Liebman, B. 1998. Sugar: The sweetening of the American diet. *Nutrition Action Health Letter* 25 (9):1–8.

Liu, S., and Manson, J. 2001. Dietary carbohydrates, physical inactivity, obesity, and the 'metabolic syndrome' as predictors of coronary heart disease. *Current Opinion in Lipidology* 12:395–404.

Lupton, J., and Trumbo, P. 2006. Dietary Fiber. In *Modern Nutrition in Health and Disease,* eds. M. Shils, et al. Philadelphia: Lippincott Williams & Wilkins.

Ma, Y., et al. 2005. Association between dietary carbohydrates and body weight. *American Journal of Epidemiology* 161:359–67.

Manore, M. 2002. Carbohydrate: Friend or foe? *ACSM's Health & Fitness Journal* 6 (5):25–27.

Marlett, J., et al. 2002. Position of the American Dietetic Association: Health implications of dietary fiber. *Journal of the American Dietetic Association* 102:993–1010.

Martinez, M. 2005. Primary prevention of colorectal cancer: Lifestyle, nutrition, exercise. *Recent Results in Cancer Research* 166:177–211.

Maughan, R., et al. 1997. Diet composition and the performance of high-intensity exercise. *Journal of Sports Sciences* 15:265–75.

Mittendorfer, B., and Klein, S. 2001. Effect of aging on glucose and lipid metabolism during endurance exercise. *International Journal of Sport Nutrition and Exercise Metabolism* 11:S86–91.

National Institutes of Health. 2001. Diagnosis and management of dental caries throughout life. *NIH Consensus Statement* 18 (1):1–23.

Newsholme, E. 1993. Basic aspects of metabolic regulation and their application to provision of energy in exercise. In *Principles of Exercise Biochemistry,* ed. J. Poortmans. Basel, Switzerland: Karger.

Nieman, D. C., and Pedersen, B. K. 1999. Exercise and immune function: Recent developments. *Sports Medicine* 27:73–80.

Opperman, A., et al. 2004. Meta-analysis of the health effects of using the glycaemic index in meal-planning. *British Journal of Nutrition* 92:367–81.

Perez-Martin, A., et al. 2001. Insulin resistance and associated metabolic abnormalities in muscle: Effects of exercise. *Obesity Research* 2:47–59.

Peters, E. 2003. Nutritional aspects in ultra-endurance exercise. *Current Opinions in Clinical Nutrition and Metabolic Care* 6:427–34.

Pi-Sunyer, F. X. 2002. Glycemic index and disease. *American Journal of Clinical Nutrition* 76:290S–98S.

Rauch, H., et al. 2005. A signalling role for muscle glycogen in the regulation of pace during prolonged exercise. *British Journal of Sports Medicine* 39:34–38.

Reddy, B. S. 1999. Role of dietary fiber in colon cancer: An overview. *American Journal of Medicine* 106:16S–19S.

Richter, E., et al. 2004. Exercise signaling to glucose transport in skeletal muscle. *Proceedings of the Nutrition Society* 63:211–16.

Richter, E., et al. 2001. Regulation of muscle glucose transport during exercise. *International Journal of Sport Nutrition and Exercise Metabolism* 11:S71–77.

Schneeman, B. O. 1999. Building scientific consensus: The importance of dietary fiber. *American Journal of Clinical Nutrition* 69:30–42.

Short, S. 1993. Surveys of dietary intake and nutrition knowledge of athletes and their coaches. In *Nutrition in Exercise and Sport,* eds. I. Wolinsky and J. Hickson. Boca Raton, FL: CRC Press.

Shulman, R., and Rothman, D. 2001. The "glycogen shunt" in exercising muscle: A role of glycogen in muscle energetics and fatigue. *Proceedings of the National Academy of Sciences* 98:457–61.

Silvera S., et al. 2005. Dietary carbohydrates and breast cancer risk: A prospective study of the roles of overall glycemic index and glycemic load. *International Journal of Cancer* 114:653–58.

Slavin, J., et al. 2001. The role of whole grains in disease prevention. *Journal of the American Dietetic Association* 101:780–85.

Snyder, A. C. 1998. Overtraining and glycogen depletion hypothesis. *Medicine & Science in Sports & Exercise* 30:1146–50.

Spriet, L. L. 1998. Regulation of fat/carbohydrate interaction in human skeletal muscle during exercise. *Advances in Experimental Medicine and Biology* 441:249–61.

Stallknecht, B., et al. 1998. Lactate production and clearance in exercise. Effects of training: A mini-review. *Scandinavian Journal of Medicine and Science in Sports* 8:127–31.

Steen, S. N. 1998. Eating on the road: Where are the carbohydrates? *Sports Science Exchange* 11 (4):1–6.

Streppel, M., et al. 2005. Dietary fiber and blood pressure: A meta-analysis of randomized placebo-controlled trials. *Archives of Internal Medicine* 165:150–56.

Tarnopolsky, M. 2000. Gender differences in substrate metabolism during endurance exercise. *Canadian Journal of Applied Physiology* 25:312–27.

Turcotte, L. 2003. Mitochondria: Biogenesis, structure, and function: Symposium introduction. *Medicine & Science in Sports & Exercise* 35:82–85.

Tsintzas, K., and Williams, C. 1998. Human muscle glycogen metabolism during exercise: Effect of carbohydrate supplementation. *Sports Medicine* 25:7–23.

Van Hall, G. 2000. Lactate as fuel for mitochondrial respiration. *Acta Physiologica Scandinavica* 168:643–56.

Walberg-Rankin, J. 2000. Dietary carbohydrate and performance of brief, intense exercise. *Sports Science Exchange* 13(4):1–4.

Weihrauch, M., and Diehl, V. 2004. Artificial sweeteners: Do they bear a carcinogenic risk? *Annals of Oncology* 15:1460–65.

Williams, C. 1998. Diet and sports performance. In *Oxford Textbook of Sports Medicine.* eds. M. Harries, et al. Oxford: Oxford University Press.

Wolfe, R., and George, S. 1993. Stable isotopic tracers as metabolic probes in exercise. *Exercise & Sports Science Reviews* 21:1–31.

Yeaman, S., et al. 2001. Regulation of glycogen synthesis in human muscle cells. *Biochemical Society Transactions* 29:537–41.

Zierler, K. 1999. Whole body glucose metabolism. *American Journal of Physiology* 276:E409–26.

Specific Studies

Abt, G., et al. 1998. The effect of a high-carbohydrate diet on the skill performance of midfield soccer players after intermittent treadmill exercise. *Journal of Science and Medicine in Sport* 1:203–12.

Achten, J., et al. 2004. Higher dietary carbohydrate content during intensified running training results in better maintenance of performance and mood state. *Journal of Applied Physiology* 96:1331–40.

Adamo, K. B., et al. 1998. Dietary carbohydrate and postexercise synthesis of proglycogen and macroglycogen in human skeletal muscle. *American Journal of Physiology* 275:E229–E234.

Akermark, C., et al. 1996. Diet and muscle glycogen concentration in relation to physical performance in Swedish elite ice hockey players. *International Journal of Sport Nutrition* 6:272–84.

Arkinstall, M., et al. 2001. Effect of carbohydrate ingestion on metabolism during running and cycling. *Journal of Applied Physiology* 91:2125–34.

Asp, S., et al. 1999. Muscle glycogen accumulation after a marathon: Roles of fiber type and pro- and macroglycogen. *Journal of Applied Physiology* 86:474–78.

Ball, T., et al. 1995. Periodic carbohydrate replacement during 50 min of high intensity cycling improves subsequent sprint performance. *International Journal of Sport Nutrition* 5:151–58.

Balsom, P. D., et al. 1999. High-intensity exercise and muscle glycogen availability in humans. *Acta Physiologica Scandinavica* 165:337–45.

Below, P., et al. 1995. Fluid and carbohydrate ingestion independently improve performance during 1-h of intense exercise. *Medicine & Science in Sports & Exercise* 27:200–10.

Berardi, J., and Ziegenfuss, T. 2003. Effects of ribose supplementation on repeated sprint performance in men. *Journal of Strength Conditioning Research* 17:47–52.

Blair, S., et al. 1980. Blood lipid and ECG response to carbohydrate loading. *Physician and Sports Medicine* 8:69–75.

Bosch, A., et al. 1994. Influence of carbohydrate ingestion on fuel substrate turnover and oxidation during prolonged exercise. *Journal of Applied Physiology* 76:2364–72.

Brouns, F., et al. 1995. Chronic oral lactate supplementation does not affect lactate disappearance from blood after exercise. *International Journal of Sport Nutrition* 5:117–24.

Brown, A., et al. 2004. Tricarboxylic-acid-cycle intermediates and cycle endurance capacity. *International Journal of Sport Nutrition and Exercise Metabolism* 14:720–29.

Bryner, R. W., et al. 1998. Effect of lactate consumption on exercise performance. *Journal of Sports Medicine and Physical Fitness* 38:116–23.

Burke, L., et al. 2000. Carbohydrate loading failed to improve 100-km cycling performance in a placebo-controlled trial. *Journal of Applied Physiology* 88:1284–90.

Carter, J., et al. 2004. The effect of carbohydrate mouth rinse on 1-h cycle time trial performance. *Medicine & Science in Sports & Exercise* 36:2107–11.

Carter, J., et al. 2004. The effect of glucose infusion on glucose kinetics during a 1-h time trial. *Medicine & Science in Sports & Exercise* 36:1543–50.

Chryssanthopoulos, C., et al. 2002. Influence of a carbohydrate-electrolyte solution ingested during running on muscle glycogen utilization in fed humans. *International Journal of Sports Medicine* 23:279–84.

Chryssanthopoulos, C., et al. 2002. The effect of a high carbohydrate meal on endurance running capacity. *International Journal of Sport Nutrition and Exercise Metabolism* 12:157–71.

Chryssanthopoulos, C., and Williams, C. 1997. Pre-exercise carbohydrate meal and endurance running capacity when carbohydrates are ingested during exercise. *International Journal of Sports Medicine* 18:543–48.

Cleveland, L., et al. 2000. Dietary intake of whole grains. *Journal of the American College of Nutrition* 19:331S–38S.

Dalton, R. A., et al. 1999. Acute carbohydrate consumption does not influence resistance exercise performance during energy restriction. *International Journal of Sport Nutrition* 9:319–32.

Desbrow, B., et al. 2004. Carbohydrate-electrolyte feedings and 1 h time trial cycling performance. *International Journal of Sport Nutrition and Exercise Metabolism* 14:541–49.

Di Stefano, M., et al. 2002. Lactose malabsorption and intolerance and peak bone mass. *Gastroenterology* 122:1793–99.

Earnest, C., et al. 2004. Low vs. high glycemic index carbohydrate gel ingestion during simulated 64-km cycling time trial performance. *Journal of Strength Conditioning Research* 18:466–72.

el-Sayed, M., et al. 1997. Carbohydrate ingestion improves performance during a 1 h simulated cycling trial. *Journal of Sports Sciences* 15:223–30.

Fairchild, T., et al. 2002. Rapid carbohydrate loading after a short bout of near maximal-intensity exercise. *Medicine & Science in Sports & Exercise* 34:980–86.

Febbraio, M., et al. 2000. Effects of carbohydrate ingestion before and during exercise on glucose kinetics and performance. *Journal of Applied Physiology* 89:2220–26.

Febbraio, M., et al. 2000. Pre-exercise carbohydrate ingestion, glucose kinetics, and muscle glycogen use: Effect of the glycemic index. *Journal of Applied Physiology* 89:1845–51.

Febbraio, M., and Stewart, K. 1996. CHO feeding before prolonged exercise: Effect of glycemic index on muscle glycogenolysis and exercise performance. *Journal of Applied Physiology* 81:1115–20.

Ferrauti, A., et al. 1997. Metabolic and ergogenic effects of carbohydrate and caffeine beverages in tennis. *Journal of Sports Medicine and Physical Fitness* 37:258–66.

Fogelholm, M., et al. 1991. Carbohydrate loading in practice: High muscle glycogen concentration is not certain. *British Journal of Sports Medicine* 25:41–44.

Friedlander, A. L., et al. 1999. Training-induced alterations of carbohydrate metabolism in women: Women respond differently from men. *Journal of Applied Physiology* 85:1175–86.

Hargreaves, M., et al. 1995. Influence of muscle glycogen on glycogenolysis and glucose uptake during exercise in humans. *Journal of Applied Physiology* 78:288–92.

Hellsten, Y., et al. 2004. Effect of ribose supplementation on resynthesis of adenine nucleotides after intense intermittent training in humans. *American Journal of Physiology, Regulatory, Integrative, and Comparative Physiology* 286:R182–88.

Horowitz, J., et al. 1989. Effects of carbohydrate loading and exercise on muscle girth. *Medicine & Science in Sports & Exercise* 21:S58.

Jacobs, D. R., et al. 1998. Whole-grain intake and cancer: An expanded review and meta-analysis. *Nutrition and Cancer* 30:85–96.

James, A., et al. 2001. Muscle glycogen supercompensation: Absence of a gender-related difference. *European Journal of Applied Physiology* 85:533–58.

Jensen, M., et al. 2004. Intakes of whole grains, bran, and germ and the risk of coronary heart disease in men. *American Journal of Clinical Nutrition* 80:1492–99.

Jentjens, R., et al. 2001. Addition of protein and amino acids to carbohydrate does not enhance muscle glycogen synthesis. *Journal of Applied Physiology* 91:839–46.

Jeukendrup, A., et al. 1997. Carbohydrate-electrolyte feedings improve 1-h time trial cycling performance. *International Journal of Sports Medicine.* 18:125–29.

Kalman, D., et al. 1999. The effects of pyruvate supplementation on body composition in overweight individuals. *Nutrition* 15:337–40.

Kang, J., et al. 1995. Effect of carbohydrate ingestion subsequent to carbohydrate supercompensation on endurance performance. *International Journal of Sport Nutrition* 5:329–43.

Kavouras, S., et al. 2004. The influence of low versus high carbohydrate diet on a 45-min strenuous cycling exercise. *International Journal of Sport Nutrition and Exercise Metabolism* 14:62–72.

Kimber, N., et al. 2002. Energy balance during an Ironman triathlon in male and female triathletes. *International Journal of Sport Nutrition and Exercise Metabolism* 12:47–62.

Kirwan, J., et al. 2001. Effects of moderate and high glycemic index meals on metabolism and exercise performance. *Metabolism* 50:849–55.

Kreider, R., et al. 2003. Effects of oral D-ribose supplementation on anaerobic capacity and selected metabolic markers in healthy males. *International Journal of Sport Nutrition and Exercise Metabolism* 13:76–86.

Krustrup, P., et al. 2004. Slow-twitch fiber glycogen depletion elevates moderate-exercise fast-twitch fiber activity and O2 uptake. *Medicine & Science in Sports & Exercise* 36:973–82.

Kuipers, H., et al. 1999. Pre-exercise ingestion of carbohydrate and transient hypoglycemia during exercise. *International Journal of Sports Medicine* 20:227–31.

Larsen, J., et al. 1988. Effects of ingesting polylactate during prolonged cycling. Paper presented at Southwest Regional Meeting of the American College of Sports Medicine, Las Vegas, NV. December 1988.

LeBlanc, P., et al. 2004. Effects of aerobic training on pyruvate dehydrogenase and pyruvate dehydrogenase kinase in human skeletal muscle. *Journal of Physiology* 557:559–70.

Mathew, T., et al. 2002. Relationship between sports drinks and dental erosion in 304 university athletes. *Caries Research* 36:281–87.

McConell, G., et al. 1996. Effect of timing of carbohydrate ingestion on endurance exercise performance. *Medicine & Science in Sports & Exercise* 28:1311–20.

McInerney, P., et al. 2005. Failure to repeatedly supercompensate muscle glycogen stores in highly trained men. *Medicine & Science in Sports & Exercise* 37:404–11.

Morrison, M., et al. 2000. Pyruvate ingestion for 7 days does not improve aerobic performance in well-trained individuals. *Journal of Applied Physiology* 89:549–56.

Murray, R., et al. 1989. The effects of glucose, fructose, and sucrose ingestion during exercise. *Medicine & Science in Sports & Exercise* 21:275–82.

Nieman, D., et al. 2001. Cytokine changes after a marathon race. *Journal of Applied Physiology* 91:109–14.

O'Brien, M., et al. 1993. Carbohydrate dependence during marathon running.

Medicine & Science in Sports & Exercise 25:1009–17.

Op 'T Eijnde, B., et al. 2001. No effects of oral ribose supplementation on repeated maximal exercise and de novo ATP resynthesis. *Journal of Applied Physiology* 91:2275–81.

Palmer, G. S., et al. 1998. Carbohydrate ingestion immediately before exercise does not improve 20 km time trial performance in well trained cyclists. *International Journal of Sports Medicine* 19:415–18.

Paul, D., et al. 2001. Carbohydrate during the follicular phase of the menstrual cycle: Effects on muscle glycogen and exercise performance. *International Journal of Sport Nutrition and Exercise Metabolism* 11:430–31.

Peters, H., et al. 1995. Exercise performance as a function of semi-solid and liquid carbohydrate feedings during prolonged exercise. *International Journal of Sports Medicine* 16:105–13.

Pitsiladis, Y. P., and Maughan, R. J. 1999. The effects of alterations in dietary carbohydrate intake on the performance of high-intensity exercise in trained individuals. *European Journal of Applied Physiology* 79:433–42.

Pizza, F., et al. 1995. A carbohydrate loading regimen improves high intensity, short duration exercise performance. *International Journal of Sport Nutrition* 5:110–16.

Pliml, W., et al. 1992. Effects of ribose on exercise-induced ischaemia in stable coronary artery disease. *Lancet* 340:507–10.

Rauch, L., et al. 1995. The effects of carbohydrate loading on muscle glycogen content and cycling performance. *International Journal of Sport Nutrition* 5:25–36.

Rico-Sanz, J., et al. 1999. Muscle glycogen degradation during simulation of a fatiguing soccer match in elite soccer players examined noninvasively by 13C-MRS. *Medicine & Science in Sports & Exercise* 31:1587–93.

Robergs, R. A., et al. 1998. Blood glucose and glucoregulatory hormone responses to solid and liquid carbohydrate ingestion during exercise. *International Journal of Sport Nutrition* 8:70–83.

Rotman, S., et al. 2000. Muscle glycogen recovery after exercise measured by 13C-magnetic resonance spectroscopy in humans: Effect of nutritional solutions. *MAGMA* 11:114–21.

Saris, W. 1989. Study of food intake and energy expenditure during extreme sustained exercise. The Tour de France. *International Journal of Sports Medicine* 10:S26–S31.

Seifert, J., et al. 1994. Glycemic and insulinemic response to preexercise carbohydrate feedings. *International Journal of Sport Nutrition* 4:46–53.

Smith, G., et al. 2002. The effect of preexercise glucose ingestion on performance during prolonged swimming. *International Journal of Sport Nutrition and Exercise Metabolism* 12:136–44.

Stanko, R., et al. 1990. Enhanced leg exercise endurance with a high-carbohydrate diet and dihydroxyacetone and pyruvate. *Journal of Applied Physiology* 69:1651–56.

Stanko, R., et al. 1990. Enhancement of arm exercise endurance capacity with dihydroxyacetone and pyruvate. *Journal of Applied Physiology* 68:119–24.

Tarnopolsky, M., et al. 2001. Gender differences in carbohydrate loading are related to energy intake. *Journal of Applied Physiology* 91:225–30.

Tsintzas, K., et al. 2001. Phosphocreatine degradation in type I and type II muscle fibers during submaximal exercise in man: Effect of carbohydrate ingestion. *Journal of Physiology* 537:305–11.

Tsintzas, O., et al. 1996. Influence of carbohydrate supplementation early in exercise on endurance running capacity. *Medicine & Science in Sports & Exercise* 28:1373–79.

Tsintzas, O., et al. 1995. Influence of carbohydrate-electrolyte drinks on marathon running performance. *European Journal of Applied Physiology* 70:154–60.

Utter, A., et al. 2004. Carbohydrate supplementation and perceived exertion during prolonged running. *Medicine & Science in Sports & Exercise* 36:1036–41.

Utter, A., et al. 2002. Effect of carbohydrate ingestion on ratings of perceived exertion during a marathon. *Medicine & Science in Sports & Exercise* 34:1779–84.

Utter, A. C., et al. 1999. Effect of carbohydrate ingestion and hormonal responses on ratings of perceived exertion during prolonged cycling and running. *European Journal of Applied Physiology* 80:92–99.

Vandenberghe, K., et al. 1995. No effect of glycogen level on glycogen metabolism during high intensity exercise. *Medicine & Science in Sports & Exercise* 27:1278–83.

van Loon, L., et al. 2001. The effects of increasing exercise intensity on muscle fuel utilisation in humans. *Journal of Physiology* 536:295–304.

van Loon, L., et al. 2000. Maximizing postexercise muscle glycogen synthesis: Carbohydrate supplementation and the application of amino acid or protein hydrolysate mixtures. *American Journal of Clinical Nutrition* 72:106–11.

Venables, M., et al. 2005. Erosive effect of a new sports drink on dental enamel during exercise. *Medicine & Science in Sports & Exercise* 37:39–44.

Vergauwen, L., et al. 1998. Carbohydrate supplementation improves stroke performance in tennis. *Medicine & Science in Sports & Exercise* 30:1289–95.

von Fraunhofer, J., and Rogers, M. 2005. Effects of sports drinks and other beverages on dental enamel. *General Dentistry* 53:28–31.

Walberg-Rankin, J., et al. 1996. Effect of weight loss and refeeding diet composition on anaerobic performance in wrestlers. *Medicine & Science in Sports & Exercise* 28:1292–99.

Walker, J., et al. 2000. Dietary carbohydrate, muscle glycogen content, and endurance performance in well-trained women. *Journal of Applied Physiology* 88:2151–58.

Wallis, G., et al. 2005. Oxidation of combined ingestion of maltodextrins and fructose during exercise. *Medicine & Science in Sports & Exercise* 37:426–32.

Welsh, R., et al. 2002. Carbohydrates and physical/mental performance during intermittent exercise to fatigue. *Medicine & Science in Sports & Exercise* 34:723–31.

Weltan, S. M., et al. 1998. Influence of muscle glycogen content on metabolic regulation. *American Journal of Physiology* 274:E72–E82.

Weltan, S. M., et al. 1998. Preexercise muscle glycogen content affects metabolism during exercise despite maintenance of hyperglycemia. *American Journal of Physiology* 274:E83–E88.

Williams, C., et al. 1992. The effect of a high carbohydrate diet on running performance during a 30-km treadmill time trial. *European Journal of Applied Physiology* 65:18–24.

Winnick, J., et al. 2005. Carbohydrate feedings during team sport exercise preserve physical and CNS function. *Medicine & Science in Sports & Exercise* 37:306–15.

Yaspelkis, B. B., and Ivy, J. L. 1999. The effect of a carbohydrate-arginine supplement on postexercise carbohydrate metabolism. *International Journal of Sport Nutrition* 9:241–50.

Zeederberg, C., et al. 1996. The effect of carbohydrate ingestion on the motor skill proficiency of soccer players. *International Journal of Sport Nutrition* 6:348–55.

Zehnder, M., et al. 2001. Resynthesis of muscle glycogen after soccer specific performance examined by 13C-magnetic resonance spectroscopy in elite players. *European Journal of Applied Physiology* 84:443–47.

Fat: An Important Energy Source during Exercise

CHAPTER FIVE

LEARNING OBJECTIVES

After studying this chapter, you should be able to:

1. List the different types of dietary fatty acids and identify general types of foods in which they are found.

2. Calculate the approximate amount, in grams or milligrams, of total fat, saturated fat, and cholesterol that should be included in your daily diet.

3. Describe how dietary fat is absorbed, how it is distributed in the body, and what its major functions are in human metabolism.

4. Explain the role of fat in human energy systems during exercise and how endurance exercise training affects exercise fat metabolism.

5. Explain the theory underlying the role of increased fat oxidation to enhance prolonged aerobic endurance performance.

6. List the various dietary fat strategies and dietary supplements that have been investigated as a means of enhancing exercise performance, and highlight the major findings.

7. Describe the proposed process underlying the development of atherosclerosis and cardiovascular disease, including the role that dietary fat and cholesterol may play in its etiology.

8. List and describe at least 8 of the 10 dietary strategies that are proposed to help treat or prevent the development of atherosclerosis and cardiovascular disease.

9. Explain the role of exercise as a means of helping prevent the development of atherosclerosis and cardiovascular disease.

Introduction

From a health standpoint, dietary fat is the nutrient of greatest concern to a variety of health organizations, such as the American Heart Association and the American Cancer Society, for excessive consumption of certain types of fat has been associated with the development of a host of pathological conditions, including coronary heart disease, cancer, and obesity. Thus, one of the major recommendations advocated in Healthy People 2010 *for a healthier diet is to reduce the amount of dietary fat intake to a reasonable level. Part of the rationale for this recommendation and some general guidelines for implementing it are presented in this chapter, but additional information may also be found in chapters 2 and 11.*

We need some fat in our diet. Despite its potential health hazards when consumed in excess, dietary fat contains several essential nutrients that serve a variety of important functions in human nutrition. The National Academy of Sciences recently set an Acceptable Macronutrient Distribution Range (AMDR) for total fat of 20–35 percent of daily energy intake. Because some types of fat may confer various health benefits, the Academy also set Adequate Intakes (AI) for several fatty acids. Moreover, in their recent position statement regarding nutrition and athletic performance, the American Dietetic Association, Dietitians of Canada, and the American College of Sports Medicine noted that, overall, diets should provide moderate amounts of energy from fat (20 to 25 percent of energy) and that there is no health or performance benefit to consuming a diet containing less than 15 percent energy from fat. For the endurance athlete, one of the most important functions of fat is to provide energy during exercise, and researchers have explored a variety of techniques in attempts to improve endurance performance by increasing the ability of the muscle to use fat as a fuel.

To clarify the role of dietary fat in health and its possible relevance to sports, this chapter presents information on the basic nature of dietary fats and associated lipids, the metabolic fate and physiological functions of fats and cholesterol in the body, the role of fat as an energy source during exercise, the use of various dietary practices or ergogenic aids in attempts to improve fat metabolism and endurance performance, and possible health problems associated with excessive dietary fat.

Dietary Fats

What are the different types of dietary fats?

What we commonly call fat in our diet actually consists of several substances classified as lipids. **Lipids** represent a class of organic substances that are insoluble in water but soluble in certain solvents like alcohol or ether. The three major dietary lipids of importance to humans are triglycerides, cholesterol, and phospholipids. All three have major functions in the body.

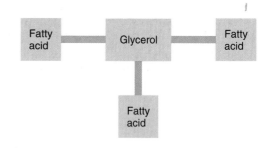

FIGURE 5.1 Structure of a triglyceride. Three fatty acids combine with glycerol to form a triglyceride.

What are triglycerides?

The **triglycerides,** also known as the true fats or the neutral fats, are the principal form in which fats are eaten and stored in the human body. Triglycerides are composed of two different compounds—fatty acids and glycerol. When an acid (fatty acid) and an alcohol (glycerol) combine, an **ester** is formed, the process being known as esterification. (Three fatty acids are attached to each glycerol molecule.) Figure 5.1 is a diagram of a triglyceride. Another term used for triglyceride is *triacylglycerol.* Some triglyc- erides may be modified commercially to contain only two fatty acids, known as diglycerides, or diacylglycerols.

Fatty acids, one of the components of fat, are chains of carbon, oxygen, and hydrogen atoms that vary in length and in the degree of saturation of carbon with hydrogen. Short-chain fatty acids (SCFAs) contain fewer than six carbons, medium-chain fatty acids (MCFAs) have six to twelve carbons, and long-chain fatty acids (LCFAs) have fourteen or more carbons.

Fatty acids may be saturated or unsaturated. A **saturated fatty acid** contains a full quota of hydrogenated ions so that all of its carbon bonds are full; saturated fats such as butter are solid at room temperature. Carbon molecules in unsaturated fatty acids may incorporate more hydrogen because they have some unfilled bonds, or double bonds. These unsaturated fatty acids may be classified as **monounsaturated,** having a single double bond and capable of incorporating two hydrogen ions, and **polyunsaturated,** having two or more double bonds and capable of incorporating four or more hydrogen ions; monounsaturated and polyunsaturated fats as oils are liquid at room temperature.

Polyunsaturated fatty acids are further identified according to the location of the first carbon double bond from the last, or omega, carbon. **Omega-3** and **omega-6** fatty acids are the two major types, and the numeric represents the location of the first double bond. Other terminology to identify these two fatty acids are ω-3 and n-3, and ω-6 and n-6. Adequate amounts of omega-3 and omega-6 fatty acids may confer health benefits, as noted later in the chapter. At room temperature, saturated fats are usually solid, while unsaturated fats are usually liquid. **Partially hydrogenated fats** or oils have been treated by a process that adds hydrogen to some of the unfilled bonds, thereby hardening the fat or oil. In essence, the fat becomes more saturated. During the hydrogenation process, the normal position of hydrogen ions at the double bond is on the "same side" (*cis*). This is known as a *cis* **fatty acid,** and may be partly transposed so that hydrogen ions are on opposite sides of the double bond, resulting in a *trans* **fatty acid.** Figure 5.2 represents the structural difference between a saturated, a monounsaturated, an unsaturated (*cis* and *trans*), and an omega-3 fatty acid. The health implications of these different types of fats are discussed later in this chapter. In general though, excess intake of saturated and *trans* fatty acids is associated with increased health risks, whereas adequate intake of monounsaturated, polyunsaturated, and omega-3 fatty acids may be associated with neutral or some beneficial health effects. Bell and others noted recently that food technology is evolving to create structured triglycerides that may possess health benefits.

Glycerol is an alcohol, a clear, colorless syrupy liquid. It is obtained in the diet as part of triglycerides, but it also may be produced in the body as a by-product of carbohydrate metabolism. On the other hand, glycerol can be converted back to carbohydrate in the process of gluconeogenesis in the liver.

What are some common foods high in fat content?

The fat content in foods can vary from 100 percent, as found in most cooking oils, to minor trace amounts, less than 5–10 percent, as found in most fruits and vegetables. Some foods obviously have a high-fat content: butter, oils, shortening, mayonnaise, margarine, and the visible fat on meat. However, in other foods the fat content may be high but not as obvious. This is known as **hidden fat.** Whole milk, cheese, nuts, desserts, crackers, potato chips, and a wide variety of commercially prepared foods may contain considerable amounts of fat. For example, a 5-ounce baked potato contains 145 Calories with about 3 percent fat, while a 5-ounce serving of potato chips contains 795 Calories, over 60 percent of them from fat. Figure 5.3 presents some examples of hidden fat.

FIGURE 5.2 Structural differences between saturated, monounsaturated, and polyunsaturated fatty acids (including the *cis* and *trans* forms) and the omega-3 fatty acid. Note there is a single double bond between carbon atoms in the monounsaturated fatty acid and two or more in the polyunsaturated fatty acid. In the omega-3 fatty acid, the double bond is located three carbons from the last, or omega, carbon. The R represents the radical, or the presence of many more C—H bonds. In the *trans* configuration, one of the hydrogen ions is moved to the opposite side.

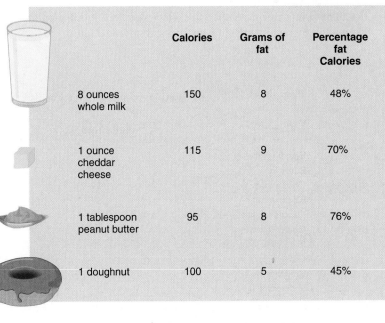

	Calories	Grams of fat	Percentage fat Calories
8 ounces whole milk	150	8	48%
1 ounce cheddar cheese	115	9	70%
1 tablespoon peanut butter	95	8	76%
1 doughnut	100	5	45%

FIGURE 5.3 Hidden fat. Many of the foods we consume may contain significant amounts of Calories in the form of hidden fat.

In general, animal foods found in the meat and milk groups are high in fat, particularly saturated fat. Hamburger meat contributes the most saturated fat to the typical American diet. However, careful selection and preparation of foods in these groups will considerably reduce fat content. The percentage of fat in meat and milk products may vary considerably; beef, pork, and cheese products usually contain considerable amounts of fat, up to 70 percent or more fat Calories. The meat and dairy industries are responding to dietary modifications by many Americans and are making low-fat red meats and low-fat cheeses available to consumers. For example, 3 ounces of beef eye of round or pork tenderloin contain about 140 Calories, 4 grams of total fat, and 1.5 grams of saturated fat; both cuts of meat contain fewer than 30 percent of their Calories as fat. Lean cuts of poultry and fish have much lower levels of fat. Trimming the fat from meats or removing the skin from poultry drastically reduces the fat content. Some fish, such as flounder and tuna, are remarkably low in fat while others, such as salmon and mackerel, are higher in total fat content but contain greater amounts of omega-3 fatty acids. Look for foods in the very lean meat exchange list in appendix E. In the milk group, whole milk contains about 8 grams of fat per cup; skim milk contains about 0.5–1.0 grams, which is much less than whole milk. Low-fat cheese alternatives containing soy or rice are available.

Small amounts of *trans* fatty acids are found naturally in beef, butter, and milk, but deep-fried foods and commercially prepared products, particularly stick margarine and snack foods such as chips, cakes, and cookies, may contain substantial amounts. The health risks associated with *trans* fatty acids are discussed later in this chapter.

Most plant foods, such as vegetables, fruits, beans, and natural whole-grain products, generally are low in fat content, and the fat they do contain is mostly unsaturated. On the other hand, some plant foods, such as nuts, seeds, and avocados, are very high in fat, but again primarily unsaturated fats. However, coconuts and palm kernels are extremely high in both total and saturated fats.

All fats contain a mixture of saturated, monounsaturated, and polyunsaturated fatty acids. Since later in this chapter we discuss some health implications relating to the types of fats we eat, table 5.1 presents an approximate percentage of the amount of saturated, monounsaturated, and polyunsaturated fatty acids found in some common oils and fats. Several high-content sources for each of the three types of fatty acids are noted.

How do I calculate the percentage of fat Calories in a food?

It is important to realize that a product advertised as 95 percent fat free (or only 5 percent fat) may contain a considerably higher percentage of its Calories as fat: The advertised percentage refers to the weight of the product, not its caloric content. The product may contain a considerable amount of water, which contains no Calories. Thus, luncheon meat advertised as 95 percent fat free may actually contain more than 40 percent of its Calories from fat depending upon the water weight. Foods with a high water content contain even higher percentages of fat Calories. A striking example is whole milk, which is only 3.5 percent fat by weight; however, one glass of milk contains about 150 Calories and 8 grams of fat, which accounts for 48 percent of the caloric content ($8 \times 9 = 72$; $72/150 = 48$). Even low-fat milk (2 percent fat) contains about 37 percent fat Calories.

If you want to calculate the percentage of fat calories in most foods you eat, you can get the information you need from the food label, which will include the total Calories and the Calories from fat; additional mandatory information is the total fat, saturated fat, and *trans* fatty acid content. The label optionally may list the Calories from saturated fat and the amounts of polyunsaturated and monounsaturated fat. If you do not have a food label, then you will need to know the Calories and grams of fat for the food. Both of these values can be obtained from a food composition table found in most basic nutrition texts or at www.nal.usda.gov/fnic/foodcomp. Table 5.2 presents the meth-

TABLE 5.1 Approximate percentage of fatty acids in common fats and oils*

Oil/fat	Saturated fat	Monounsaturated fat	Polyunsaturated fat
Beef fat (tallow)	50[+]	43	4
Butterfat	62[+]	30	4
Chicken fat	30	46	22
Coconut oil	87[+]	6	2
Canola oil (rapeseed oil)	6	62[+]	30
Corn oil	13	25	60[+]
Margarine (soft tub)	21	48	31
Olive oil	14	74[+]	9
Safflower oil	9	12	78[+]
Shortening (animal)	44	48	5
Soybean oil	15	24	58[+]
Tuna fat	27	26	37

*May not total 100 percent owing to the presence of other fatty substances
[+] = high-content source

TABLE 5.2 Calculation of the percentage of Calories in foods that are derived from fat

Method A. Data from food label

Amount per serving

Calories = 90
Calories from fat = 30
To calculate percentage of food Calories that consists of fat, simply divide the Calories from fat by the Calories per serving and multiply by 100 to express as a percent.

$$30/90 = 0.33 \qquad 0.33 \times 100 = 33 \text{ percent fat Calories}$$

Method B. Data from food composition table

Amount per serving

Calories = 90
Total fat, grams = 8
Saturated fat, grams = 3
To calculate percentage of food Calories that consists of total fat or saturated fat, use the caloric value for fat of 1 gram = 9 Calories.
Total fat = 8 grams
Total fat Calories = 8 grams × 9 Calories/gram = 72 Calories
Use the same procedure as in Method A.

$$72/90 = 0.80 \qquad 0.80 \times 100 = 80 \text{ percent fat Calories}$$

Saturated fat = 3 grams
Saturated fat Calories = 3 grams × 9 Calories/gram = 27 Calories

$$27/90 = 0.30 \qquad 0.30 \times 100 = 30 \text{ percent saturated fat Calories}$$

ods for calculating the percent of fat Calories and percent of saturated fat Calories from either a food label or food composition table. Table 5.3 represents the percentage of food energy that is derived from fat in some common foods; the percentages are indicated for both total fat and saturated fat. Additional information is presented in chapter 11, where the focus is on reducing high-fat foods in the diet as a means to Calorie control.

What are fat substitutes?

Fat substitutes, or fat replacers, are supposedly designed to provide the taste and texture of fats, but without the Calories (9 Calories per gram), saturated fat, or cholesterol. They are found in many normally high-fat products, such as ice cream, that are marketed as fat free. Fat substitutes may be manufactured from carbohydrate, protein, or fats. Although a number of fat substitutes are under development, the following are commonly used.

Some carbohydrates, such as starches and gums, provide thickness and structure and are useful as fat substitutes. Guar gum, gum arabic, and cellulose gel are examples. Oatrim, made from oats, is being used to replace fat in milk. Depending on the form used, the caloric content may range from 0–4 Calories per gram. Simplesse is manufactured from milk or egg protein by a microparticulation process so that it has the taste and texture of fat.

The caloric value of Simplesse is only 1.3 Calories per gram. The use of Simplesse has been approved by the FDA. Salatrim, which is an acronym for short- and long-chain fatty acid triglyceride molecule, is a modified fat containing only 5 Calories per gram. Olestra is an ester of sucrose with long-chain fatty acids, a structure that cannot be hydrolyzed by digestive enzymes or absorbed by the gastrointestinal tract and therefore supplies no Calories to the body.

The effect of fat substitutes on health is covered later in this chapter, and their use in weight-control programs is detailed in chapter 11.

What is cholesterol?

Cholesterol is one of the lipids known as sterols. It is not a fat, but it is a fat-like pearly substance found in animal tissues. Cholesterol is not an essential nutrient for it is manufactured naturally in the liver of animals from fatty acids and from the breakdown products of carbohydrate and protein—glucose and amino acids.

What foods contain cholesterol?

Cholesterol is found only in animal products and is not found in fruits, vegetables, nuts, grains, or other nonanimal foods. Table 5.4 presents some foods from the meat and milk groups with the cholesterol content in milligrams. Several foods from the bread/cereal group are also included, indicating that the preparation of some bread/cereal products may add cholesterol by including some animal product containing cholesterol, mainly eggs (see figure 5.4).

Some plants contain various products that resemble cholesterol. Plant sterols and stanols may possess some health benefits, as noted later in this chapter.

What are phospholipids?

Chemically, **phospholipids** are somewhat comparable to triglycerides. They have a glycerol base, one or two attached fatty acids, and an additional structure that contains a phosphate group. One of the

FIGURE 5.4 Foods high in cholesterol. Eggs added to flour in some products in manufacturing or preparation (for example, bread and pancake mix) will increase cholesterol content.

TABLE 5.3 Percentage of total fat Calories and saturated fat Calories in some common foods*

Food	% Calories total fat	% Calories saturated fat	Food	% Calories total fat	% Calories saturated fat
Meat group			*Vegetables*		
Bacon	80	30	Asparagus	8	2
Beef, lean and fat (untrimmed)	70	32	Beans, green	7	1.5
			Broccoli	12	1.5
Beef, lean only (trimmed)	35	15	Carrots	4	< 1
			Potatoes	1	< 1
Hamburger, regular	62	29			
Chicken, breast (with skin)	35	11	*Fruits*		
Chicken, breast (without skin)	19	5	Apples	5	< 1
			Bananas	5	2
Luncheon meat (bologna)	82	35	Oranges	4	< 1
Salmon	37	7	*Starches/Breads/Cereals*		
Flounder, tuna	8	2			
Egg, white and yolk	67	22	Bread		
Egg, white	0	0	White	12	2
			Whole wheat	12	2
Milk group			Crackers	30	12
			Doughnuts	43	7
Milk, whole	45	28	Macaroni	5	< 1
Milk, skim	5	2.5	Macaroni and cheese	46	20
Cheese, cheddar	74	47	Oatmeal	13	2
Cheese, mozzarella, part skim	56	35	Pancakes, wheat	30	7
			Spaghetti	5	< 1
Ice cream	49	28			
Ice milk	31	18	*Fats and oils*		
Yogurt, partially skim milk	29	14			
			Butter	99	62
Dried beans and nuts			Lard	99	40
			Margarine	99	21
Beans, dry, navy	4	< 1	Oil, corn	100	13
Beans, navy, canned with pork	28	12	Oil, coconut	100	87
			Salad dressings		
Peanuts	77	17	French	95	15
Peanut butter	76	19	French, special dietary low fat	14	< 1

< 1 = less than 1 percent
*Percentages may vary. See food labels for specific information when available.

most common phospholipids is **lecithin**, whose structure is depicted as a simple diagram in figure 5.5. Phospholipids are not essential nutrients as the body can make them from triglycerides. As discussed later in this chapter, lecithin has been studied as a potential ergogenic aid.

What foods contain phospholipids?

Egg yolks provide substantial amounts of lecithin, and other good sources include liver, wheat germ, and peanuts. However, lecithin may be degraded in the digestive tract to smaller constituents. Your body can make all of the phospholipids it needs. Because dietary phospholipids are not associated with any health risks, there is little concern with dietary intake.

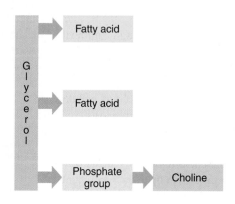

FIGURE 5.5 Simplified diagram of the phospholipid lecithin.

TABLE 5.4 Cholesterol content, in milligrams, for some common foods

	Amount	Cholesterol
Meat group		
Beef, pork, ham	1 oz	25
Poultry	1 oz	23
Fish	1 oz	21
Shrimp	1 oz	45
Lobster	1 oz	25
Eggs	1	220
Liver	1 oz	120
Milk group		
Milk, whole	1 cup	27
Milk, 2%	1 cup	15
Milk, skim	1 cup	7
Butter	1 tsp	12
Margarine	1 tsp	0
Cream cheese	1 tbsp	18
Ice milk	1 cup	10
Ice cream	1 cup	85
Bread/Cereal group		
Bread	1 slice	0
Biscuit	1	17
Pancake	1	40
Sweet roll	1	25
French toast	1 slice	130
Doughnut	1	28
Cereal, cooked	1 cup	0

Fruits, vegetables, grains, and nuts have no cholesterol.

How much fat and cholesterol do we need in the diet?

In a recent review, Jequier indicated that we need dietary fat for three reasons: to meet energy needs; to provide essential fatty acids; and, to provide essential fat-soluble vitamins.

Dietary fats are a concentrated source of energy, and adequate dietary intake is very important during the growth and development years. Dietary fats also provide several essential fatty acids, without which various health problems would develop. Dietary fats also provide the fat-soluble vitamins A, D, E, and K.

These factors, along with possible implications for health, were taken into consideration in the recent development of Dietary Reference Intakes for dietary fats, which may be found in the DRIs table for macronutrients in the front inside cover. For the purpose of developing its DRIs, the National Academy of Sciences classified fat into the following categories:

Total fat
Saturated fatty acids (SFAs)
Cis monounsaturated fatty acids (MUFAs)
Cis polyunsaturated fatty acids (PUFAs)
  n-6 fatty acids (omega-6)
  n-3 fatty acids (omega-3)
Trans fatty acids

The abbreviations for the various fatty acids, as well as the omega classification, will be used interchangeably with the respective fat or fatty acids.

Total Fat The Academy developed an AMDR of 20–35 percent of daily energy intake from total fat, which is an estimate based on adverse effects that may occur from consuming either a low-fat or high-fat diet. Individuals should obtain sufficient but not excessive amounts of dietary fat within this range of energy intake. No RDA, AI, or UL have been developed for total fat because of insufficient evidence, but diets higher than 35 percent dietary fat are not recommended because saturated fat intake may be increased beyond this level. Other health professional groups have recommended 30 percent of daily energy intake as the maximal from fat.

Saturated Fatty Acids and *trans* Fatty Acids The Academy did not develop an RDA, AI, or UL for saturated fat or *trans* fat. However, increased intake of both of these fats is associated with increased risk of coronary heart disease. Although the Academy notes that because most diets contain fats, and because most fats contain a mixture of fatty acids, it is not possible to consume a diet devoid of saturated and *trans* fats. Nevertheless, the prevailing undertone in this DRI report is to minimize the dietary intake of these two types of fat. Other health organizations suggest a maximum of 7–10 percent of the daily energy intake be derived from the combination of saturated and *trans* fats. In the popular media, saturated and *trans* fats are often referred to as *bad* fats.

Cis Monounsaturated Fatty Acids The Academy did not develop an RDA, AI, or UL for monounsaturated fats, indicating that they are not essential fatty acids because they may be synthesized by the body. About 20–40 percent of the fat we consume is monounsaturated, and primarily olive oil. Although no DRI have been set for monounsaturated fat, the Academy notes that they may have some benefit in the prevention of chronic disease. Olive oil is a staple in the Mediterranean diet and its alleged health benefits will be discussed later in this chapter. In the popular media, monounsaturated fats are often referred to as *good* fats.

Cis Polyunsaturated Fatty Acids The Academy developed an AI for polyunsaturated fatty acids because there may be some health benefits associated with such dietary intakes. AI were set for both omega-6 and omega-3 fatty acids. In the popular media, some polyunsaturated fats, particularly omega-3 fatty acids, are often referred to as *good* fats.

Omega-6 fatty acids Linoleic acid, an essential omega-6 polyunsaturated fatty acid, must be supplied in the diet because the body cannot produce it from other fatty acids. The AI for adult males age 19–50 is 17 grams of linoleic acid daily, and 12 grams per day for females. For males and females age 51 and over the AI is 14 and 11 grams daily, respectively. Somewhat smaller AIs have been developed for children and adolescents age 9–18. Linoleic acid is found in vegetable and nut oils—such as corn, sunflower, peanut, and soy oils—that constitute food products such as margarine, salad dressings, and cooking oils. Conjugated linoleic acid, an isomer of linoleic acid, has been suggested to be ergogenic and possess health benefits, which will be discussed in later sections of this chapter.

Omega-3 fatty acids Alpha-linolenic acid, an omega-3 polyunsaturated fatty acid, is also considered to be an essential fatty acid. The AI for adult males age 19 and older is 1.6 grams of alpha-linolenic acid daily, and 1.1 grams per day for females. Somewhat smaller AIs have been developed for children and adolescents age 9–18. Alpha-linoleic acid is found in green leafy vegetables, canola oil, flaxseed oil, soy products, some nuts, and fish. The potential health benefits of omega-3 fatty acids, including several derived from fish oils (eicosapentaenoic acid, EPA; docosahexaenoic acid, DHA), are discussed later in this chapter.

Cholesterol Cholesterol is vital to human physiology in a variety of ways, so the body needs an adequate supply. Because cholesterol may be manufactured in the body from either fats, carbohydrate, or protein, however, there is apparently little need for us to obtain large amounts, if any, in the foods we eat. Also, because a positive relationship has been established between high blood cholesterol levels and coronary heart disease, reduction of dietary cholesterol has been advocated by a number of health-related associations. The American Heart Association, in their set of dietary guidelines, recommends cholesterol intake be less than 300 milligrams per day, or about 100 milligrams of cholesterol for every 1,000 Calories you eat.

Table 5.5 indicates the grams of fat and saturated fat and milligrams of cholesterol that may be consumed daily on a diet containing 30 percent of the Calories as fat and less than 300 milligrams of cholesterol. For the 30 percent recommendation, a very simple method to determine the grams of total fat you may consume on a given caloric diet is to simply drop the zero from the daily caloric total and divide by 3. For example,

2,100 Calorie diet

2,100 = 210

210/3 = 70 grams total fat

For lower percentages of fat Calories, say 20 percent, simply multiply the daily caloric intake by the percentage desired and divide by 9 to get the grams of fat allowed per day. For example, 20 percent of 2,500 Calories would permit 500 Calories from fat, or about 55 grams per day.

As we shall see later in this chapter and in chapter 10, excessive consumption of dietary fat and cholesterol may be linked to a variety of chronic diseases, including heart disease and obesity. In certain individuals with blood lipid abnormalities, the recommended reduction in dietary fats and cholesterol is even greater than the Prudent Healthy Diet, with the total dietary Calories from fat being 20 percent or lower in some diet plans, as in the Ornish diet plan.

Theoretically, high-fat diets may be deleterious to physical performance in several ways. The fat may displace carbohydrate in the diet, may lead to excessive caloric intake and body weight, and may cause gastrointestinal distress if consumed as part of a pregame meal. All of these factors could possibly impair physical performance. On the other hand, some investigators have contended that high-fat diets may enhance exercise performance. These issues will be discussed later in this chapter.

Key Concept Recap

▶ The three major lipids in human nutrition are triglycerides, cholesterol, and phospholipids.

▶ Triglycerides, which consist of fatty acids and glycerol, account for about 98 percent of the lipids we eat. Fatty acids may be saturated or unsaturated. Unsaturated fatty acids may be monounsaturated and polyunsaturated. Polyunsaturated fatty acids may exist in two forms, *cis* and *trans*.

▶ The fat content of foods varies considerably, but generally the fruit, vegetable, and starch food exchanges are good sources of unsaturated fats and are low in total fat, whereas the meat and milk food exchanges contain foods that may have a high total fat and saturated fat content.

▶ The AMDR for dietary fat is 20–35 percent of daily caloric intake. Although some fat is essential in the diet as a source of essential fatty acids (linoleic and alpha-linolenic) and the fat-soluble vitamins (A, D, E, K), these nutrients may be obtained from polyunsaturated fats.

▶ Cholesterol is a nonfat substance vital to human metabolism, and although it may be obtained in the diet only from animal foods, the body can produce its own supply from other dietary nutrients such as saturated fats.

Check for Yourself

Peruse food labels of some of your favorite foods and check the fat content. Pay particular attention to percent of daily value for total fat, saturated fat, and cholesterol. Check also for *trans* fat content, which may be listed; if not, check list of ingredients for partially hydrogenated fats or oils.

TABLE 5.5	Daily allowance for grams of fat and saturated fat, and milligrams of cholesterol*			
Total Calories	**Fat Calories**	**Grams of fat**	**Grams of saturated fat**	**mg of cholesterol**
1,000	300	33	11	100
1,500	450	50	16	150
2,000	600	66	22	200
2,500	750	83	27	250
3,000	900	100	33	300

*Based upon a diet containing 30 percent of Calories as fat with 100 milligrams of cholesterol per 1,000 Calories.

Metabolism and Function

In this section we briefly cover the digestion of dietary lipids, their metabolic disposal in the body, interactions with carbohydrate and protein, the major functions of fats in the body, and energy stores of fat.

How does dietary fat get into the body?

The major dietary sources of lipids are the triglycerides, comprising about 98 percent, while the other 2 percent consists mainly of sterols and phospholipids. Most of the dietary triglycerides contain long-chain fatty acids (14 or more carbons). Lipids are insoluble in water, and therefore their digestion and absorption is somewhat more complicated than that of carbohydrates. As lipids enter the small intestine, they stimulate hormonal secretion by the intestines that culminates in the secretion of bile from the gallbladder and lipases from the pancreas into the intestinal lumen. The bile salts serve as emulsifiers, breaking up the lipid droplets into smaller segments that may be hydrolyzed by the lipid enzymes, pancreatic lipases, and cholesterases. In essence, lipids are hydrolyzed into free fatty acids (FFA), glycerol, cholesterol, and phospholipids, which through an intricate process are then absorbed into the cells of the intestinal mucosa. Here they are combined into a fat droplet called a **chylomicron,** which contains a large amount of triglyceride and smaller amounts of cholesterol, phospholipids, and protein. The chylomicron is one form of a **lipoprotein,** which, by its name, you can see is composed of lipids and protein. A diagram of a lipoprotein is presented in figure 5.6. The chylomicron then leaves the intestinal cell and is absorbed by the lacteal in the villi, where it is eventually transported in the lymphatic system to the blood. A schematic of this process is presented in figure 5.7.

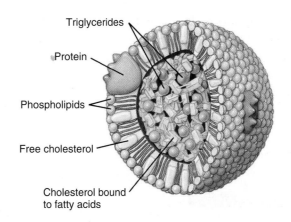

FIGURE 5.6   Schematic of a lipoprotein. Lipoproteins contain a core of triglycerides and cholesterol esters surrounded by a coat of apoproteins, cholesterol, and phospholipids. The proportion of protein, cholesterol, triglycerides, and phospholipids varies between the different types of lipoproteins.

Medium-chain triglycerides (MCTs) release medium-chain fatty acids (MCFAs) with shorter carbon chain lengths (6–12 carbons), enabling them to be absorbed directly into the blood without being converted into chylomicrons. They are transported directly to the liver. Because of this rapid processing, MCTs have been theorized to possess ergogenic potential, and their efficacy in this

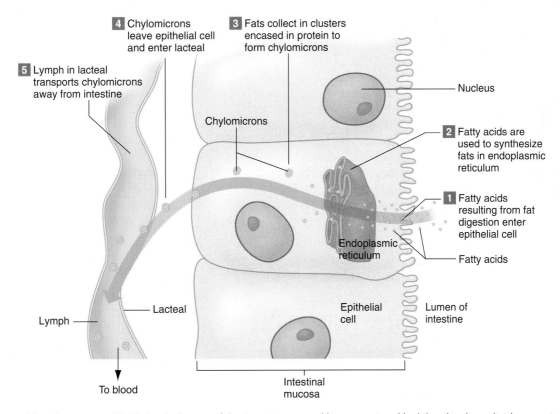

FIGURE 5.7   The absorption of lipids. In the lumen of the intestine, several lipases, assisted by bile salts, digest lipids to various forms of fatty acids, phospholipids, cholesterol, and glycerol, which are absorbed by an intricate process into the epithelial cells of the intestinal mucosa. Here they are combined with protein to form chylomicrons, a form of lipoprotein, which are transported out of the cell and into the lacteal, where the lymph eventually carries them to the blood. Medium chain triglycerides (MCTs) may be absorbed directly into the blood (not depicted).

regard will be discussed in a later section. Short-chain fatty acids (SCFAs) derived from triglycerides are also absorbed like MCFAs.

What happens to the lipid once it gets in the body?

The digestion of lipids into chylomicrons is slow, and the absorption after a high-fat meal can last several hours. As the chylomicron circulates in the blood, it reacts with various cells in the body, particularly cells in the muscle and adipose tissues. Specific proteins in the outer coat of lipoproteins are known as apolipoproteins. **Apolipoproteins** or apoproteins, increase lipid solubility and enable the various lipoproteins to react with specific receptors in cells throughout the body. The apolipoproteins in the chylomicron interact with an enzyme, lipoprotein lipase, which is produced in the muscle and adipose cells and released to the capillary blood vessels surrounding the cells. The lipoprotein lipase releases fatty acids and glycerol from the chylomicron. The fatty acids are absorbed into the cells by simple diffusion and receptors for some LCFAs, while the glycerol is transported primarily to the liver for conversion to glucose. The remains of the chylomicron, the chylomicron remnant, are transported to the liver for disposal.

In the muscle, the fatty acids may either be used as a source of energy or may combine with newly generated glycerol, which is derived as a metabolic by-product of glycolysis, leading to the formation and storage of muscle triglycerides. In the adipose cell, most of the fatty acids combine with glycerol and are stored as adipose cell triglycerides.

The key organ in the body for the metabolism of most nutrients is the liver. It is a clearinghouse in human metabolism. As blood passes through the liver, its cells take the basic nutrients and convert them into other forms. As mentioned in chapter 4, the liver is able to manufacture glucose from a variety of other nutrients, including glycerol. Pertinent to our discussion here is its role in lipid metabolism. As noted above, glycerol and chylomicron remnants, including phospholipids, are transported to the liver, as are the MCFAs and SCFAs directly from the intestinal tract. Adipose cells are metabolically active in the sense that they are constantly releasing fatty acids for use by the body, including the liver. The major role of the liver is to combine these various components (fatty acids, glycerol, cholesterol, and phospholipids), along with protein, into various forms of lipoproteins.

What are the different types of lipoproteins?

After the chylomicrons have been cleared from the blood, which may take several hours, other lipoproteins constitute approximately 95 percent of the serum lipids. The metabolism of lipoproteins is complex, for they are constantly being synthesized and catabolized by the liver and other body tissues. As a result, there is an exchange of protein and lipid components among the different classes of lipoproteins, which can lead to the conversion of one form into another.

The classification of lipoproteins may be determined by several methods. One of the methods is by the type of apolipoprotein pre-

sent and its functions. Lipoproteins have a number of different apoproteins, which enable them to react with different tissues. The letters *A, B, C, D,* and *E,* including subdivisions such as *A-I* and *A-II* are common designations. The second method, most popularly known, is based on the density of the lipoprotein particle. Designations range from high to very low density.

The chylomicron is one form of lipoprotein, but it is relatively short-lived because it is derived from dietary fat intake. For our purposes in this book, the major classifications of lipoproteins along with their suggested composition and function are listed next; a graphical depiction is presented in figure 5.8. However, it should be noted that a wide variety of lipoproteins exist based upon their specific lipid and protein content. Additionally, their metabolism and complete functions have not been totally elucidated.

VLDL (very low-density lipoproteins). **VLDL** consist primarily of triglycerides formed in the liver from endogenous sources, whereas chylomicrons contain triglycerides from exogenous

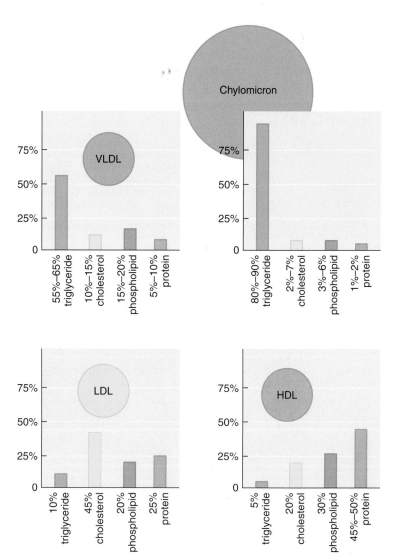

FIGURE 5.8 The approximate content of four different types of lipoproteins.

sources, that is, the diet. Like chylomicrons, VLDL are transported to the tissues to provide fatty acids and glycerol. The loss of some triglycerides to the liver or tissues produces VLDL remnants, referred to as IDL (intermediate-density lipoprotein) or TRL (triglyceride-rich lipoprotein). These remnants are either taken up by the liver or converted to LDL. Apoprotein B is the major apoprotein associated with both VLDL and IDL.

LDL (low-density lipoproteins). **LDL** contain a high proportion of cholesterol and phospholipids, but little triglycerides. LDL are formed after the VLDL and IDL release most of their stores of triglycerides. LDL size may be important. One form of LDL, a small, dense LDL, with important health implications has been identified. LDL, interacting with cell membrane receptors, deliver cholesterol into body cells. Apolipoprotein B is the major apolipoprotein associated with LDL.

HDL (high-density lipoproteins). **HDL** contain a high proportion of protein (about 45–50 percent), moderate amounts of cholesterol and phospholipids, and very little triglycerides. Various HDL are produced in the liver and intestinal tract. Several subclasses of HDL have been identified, most notably HDL_2 and HDL_3. HDL transport cholesterol from peripheral cells to the liver, known as reverse cholesterol transport. Apolipoprotein A is the major apolipoprotein associated with HDL.

Lipoprotein (a). **Lipoprotein (a)** is very similar to the LDL, being in the upper LDL density range. The principal apolipoprotein associated with lipoprotein (a) is apolipoprotein (a).

Other apolipoproteins comprise the structure of lipoproteins. For example, apolipoprotein E is formed in the liver and present in all lipoproteins. These lipoproteins are needed to bind with cell membrane receptors.

A simplified schematic of fat metabolism is presented in figure 5.9.

Can the body make fat from protein and carbohydrate?

You may recall that glycogen is made up of many individual glucose molecules and is a glucose polymer. In essence, fatty acids are polymers of acetyl CoA, the primary substrate for the Krebs cycle.

As noted in figure 4.9, the amino acids of protein may be converted to acetyl CoA, which can then be converted into fat. Carbohydrates also may be converted to fat via acetyl CoA. As recently

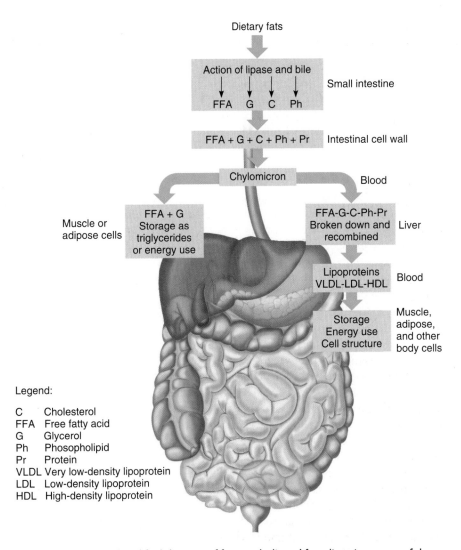

Legend:

C	Cholesterol
FFA	Free fatty acid
G	Glycerol
Ph	Phospholipid
Pr	Protein
VLDL	Very low-density lipoprotein
LDL	Low-density lipoprotein
HDL	High-density lipoprotein

FIGURE 5.9 Simplified diagram of fat metabolism. After digestion, most of the fats are carried in the blood as chylomicrons. Through the metabolic processes in the body, fat may be utilized as a major source of energy, used to help develop cell structure, or stored as a future energy source.

noted by Zierler, this is especially so with excess dietary carbohydrate. It is important to understand that the body will take excess amounts of both carbohydrate and protein and convert them to fat when caloric expenditure is less than caloric intake. Thus, in general, it is not necessarily what you eat, but rather how much, that determines whether or not you gain body fat. However, as discussed in chapters 10 and 11, there is some evidence to suggest that dietary fat may be stored as body fat more readily than carbohydrate or protein, and thus may be a factor in the development of obesity.

It is important to note that although carbohydrates and protein may be converted to fat (primarily fatty acids), fatty acids cannot be converted to carbohydrate or protein. If excess nitrogen is available from protein, it may combine with metabolic by-products of fatty acids to form nonessential amino acids—but fatty acids cannot be converted into protein without this excess nitrogen.

What are the major functions of the body lipids?

The body lipids are derived from the dietary lipids and other carbon sources, namely carbohydrate and protein, but with the exception of linoleic fatty acid and alpha-linolenic fatty acid, all lipids essential to human metabolism may be produced by the liver. The body lipids serve a variety of functions, including all three purposes of food: they form body structures, help regulate metabolism, and provide a source of energy.

Structure The structure of virtually all cell membranes, including the nerve membranes, consists partly of lipids, notably cholesterol and phospholipids. Lipids form myelin, an important component in the sheath covering nerve fibers. The structural fat deposits in the adipose tissues are used as insulators to conserve body heat and shock absorbers to protect various organs.

Metabolic Regulation Various fatty acids interact with proteins, the major metabolic regulators in the body. Essential fatty acids are found in cell membranes and are involved in various intracellular metabolic pathways, including regulation of gene expression. Cholesterol is a component of several hormones, such as testosterone and estrogen, which have diverse effects in the regulation of human metabolism. The majority of cholesterol in the body is used by the liver to produce bile salts, essential for the digestion of fats. Phospholipids are also instrumental for blood clotting.

Some derivatives of the omega-6 and omega-3 fatty acids formed by oxidation have some potent biologic functions in the body. These derivatives—prostaglandins, prostacyclins, thromboxanes, and leukotrienes—are collectively known as **eicosanoids.** These eicosanoids possess local hormone-like properties that influence a number of physiological functions, including several that may have implications for health or physical performance. Several important eicosanoids are derived from omega-3 fatty acids, and the theorized health and performance implications will be discussed in later sections of this chapter.

Energy Source In general, the function of the majority of the body lipids, the triglycerides, is to provide energy to drive metabolic processes. The majority of the triglycerides in the body are stored in the adipose tissue. They break down to free fatty acids (FFA) and glycerol, which are released into the blood, with the FFA being transported to the tissues and the glycerol going to the liver. In the tissues, the FFA are reduced to acetyl CoA and enter the Krebs cycle to produce energy via the oxygen system. The glycerol is used by the liver to form other lipids or glucose. This energy-yielding process is illustrated in figure G.4 on page 540.

During rest, nearly 60 percent of the energy supply is provided by the metabolism of fats when the individual consumes a mixed diet, but may be higher when blood glucose is low, as after an overnight fast. Most of the energy provided is presented to cells as fatty acids, either FFA delivered via the blood or fatty acids from stored intracellular triglycerides. Inside the cell, the metabolism of fatty acids into acetyl CoA (a 2-carbon molecule) is known as **beta-oxidation,** for the beta carbon is the second carbon on the

fatty acid chain. The acetyl-CoA is then processed through the citric acid (Krebs) cycle and associated electron transport system for production of energy as ATP. At rest, a high-fat meal will increase the proportion of energy derived from fat. In general, the greater the amount of fatty acids available in the plasma, the greater their use as a source of energy. For example, the heart muscle may derive 100 percent of its energy needs from fatty acids after a lipid-rich meal.

Ketones, ketoacids that are metabolic by-products of excess fatty acid metabolism, may also serve as an energy source for body cells. Ketones diffuse from the liver into the blood, and are transported to the body tissues where they can eventually be used as a source of energy. The major ketones are acetoacetic acid, beta-hydroxybutyric acid, and acetone. These ketones usually are produced in small amounts, but when the use of fatty acids as an energy source is high (such as with fasting, high-fat diets, and diabetes) ketone levels in the blood will increase. Ketones are an important energy source during fasting or starvation. However, excessive accumulation may lead to acidosis (ketosis) in the blood, a condition which may cause coma and death, such as in uncontrolled diabetes.

How much total energy is stored in the body as fat?

The greatest amount of energy stored in the body is fat in the form of triglycerides. Fat is a very efficient, compact means to store energy for several reasons. First, fat has 9 Calories per gram, more than twice the value of carbohydrate and protein. Also, there is very little water in body fat compared to the 3–4 grams of water stored with each gram of carbohydrate or protein. In essence, body fat is about 5–6 times as efficient an energy store as carbohydrate and protein. If the average 154-pound man had to carry all the potential energy of his fat stores as carbohydrate, he would weigh nearly 300 pounds.

Most of the triglycerides are stored in the adipose tissues, approximately 80,000–100,000 Calories of energy in the average adult male with normal body fat. The triglycerides within and between the muscle cells may provide approximately 2,500–2,800 Calories, while those in the blood provide only about 70–80 Calories. The free fatty acids (FFA) in the blood total about 7–8 Calories. The liver also contains an appreciable store of triglycerides. Thus, you can see that the human body contains a huge reservoir of energy Calories in the form of fat. A summary is presented in table 3.3 on page 87.

Key Concept Recap

▶ Dietary lipids may be utilized as an energy source, stored in the adipose tissue, or used as part of body-cell structure.
By-products of fat metabolism, eicosanoids, may act as local hormones and affect a variety of physiological functions.

▶ Fats are transported in the blood primarily as lipoproteins, but plasma free fatty acids from adipose tissue are a major source of energy during rest.

Fats and Exercise

Are fats used as an energy source during exercise?

The two major energy sources for the production of ATP during exercise are carbohydrates in the form of muscle glycogen and fats in the form of fatty acids, mainly LCFA. In steady-state exercise, both can be converted to acetyl CoA for subsequent oxidation in the citric acid cycle. In general, a mixture of both fuel sources is used during exercise, although the quantitative values may vary depending on a variety of factors, including the intensity and duration of the exercise bout, the diet, and the training status of the individual. The use of fat as an energy source during exercise has been the subject of several recent symposia and reviews, including those by Brouns and van der Vusse, Jacobs and others, Hawley, Jeukendrup, Spriet, Turcotte, and Wolfe, and several key studies, such as those by Romijn and associates. The following discussion represents some of the key findings from these reviews and studies.

Fat Energy Sources The fatty acids used by the muscle cells during exercise may be derived from a variety of sources, including the plasma triglycerides in the chylomicrons and VLDL but these sources are considered to be minor, providing less than 10 percent of fat energy.

The two major energy sources are the plasma FFA and the fatty acids derived from muscle triglycerides. The plasma FFA are in very short supply, so they must be replenished by the vast stores of triglycerides in the adipose tissue. An enzyme in the adipose cells, known as hormone-sensitive lipase (HSL), catabolizes the intracellular triglycerides to FFA and glycerol. The FFA are released into the blood, bound to the protein albumin as a carrier, and transported to the muscle cells or other cells. The FFA enter the cell by diffusion and by specific protein receptors (transporters) in the cell membrane. The FFA are activated in the cell cytoplasm, transported into the mitochondria by an enzyme complex containing the amine, **carnitine,** metabolized to acetyl CoA by beta-oxidation, and produce energy via the citric acid cycle and the associated electron transport system. The muscle triglycerides may also be metabolized to fatty acids and glycerol by an enzyme similar to HSL, and the fatty acids may be transported into the mitochondria. (See figure 5.10.) van Loon indicated that intramuscular triglyceride, also referred to as *intramyocellular triacylglycerol (IMTG),* can function as an important substrate source during exercise and its use is determined by various factors, including exercise intensity and training status.

Use During Exercise During rest, most of the fat energy needs of the body are met by the supply of plasma FFA to the cells. Fatty acids are constantly being mobilized from the adipose tissues to replenish the plasma FFA. Most of the FFA released during rest, about 70 percent, are actually re-esterified back into triglycerides, the remainder being delivered to the body cells for energy.

During exercise, only about 25 percent of these FFA are re-esterified, so this alone provides a substantial increase in FFA delivery to the muscle cells. Additionally, hormones that activate HSL, such as epinephrine, are secreted during exercise, stimulating the breakdown of adipose cell triglycerides and the release of FFA into the blood for transport and entrance to the muscle cell. Glatz and others recently noted that muscle contraction activates fatty acid

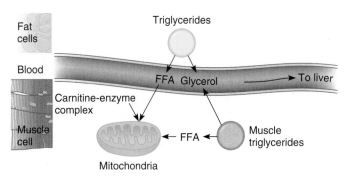

FIGURE 5.10 Fat as an energy source during exercise. Free fatty acids (FFA) are an important energy source during endurance exercise. They may be released by the adipose tissue triglycerides and travel by the blood to the muscle cells, and also may be derived from the muscle cell triglycerides. A carnitine-enzyme complex is needed to transport the FFA into the mitochondria. The glycerol that is released from the triglycerides may be transported to the liver for gluconeogenesis. (See appendix G, figure G.4, for more details.)

transporters in the muscle cell membrane, thus increasing FFA uptake into the muscle cell. Epinephrine also stimulates intramuscular lipases to catabolize muscle triglycerides into FFA. These fatty acids then enter the mitochondria and are degraded to acetyl CoA.

During mild exercise at about 25 percent of VO$_2$ max, 20 percent or less of the total energy cost is derived from carbohydrate while the other 80 percent or more comes from fat. Wolfe indicates that exercise-induced lipolysis normally provides FFA at a rate in excess of that needed during exercise. Thus, the plasma FFA provided by the adipose tissue appear to be the major source of fat energy during mild exercise, but their percentage use decreases and that of muscle triglycerides increases as the exercise intensity increases up to about 65 percent VO$_2$ max. At this point, fats and carbohydrates appear to contribute equally to the energy expenditure, and the plasma FFA and muscle triglycerides contribute equally to the energy derived from fats. Carbohydrate increasingly becomes the predominant fuel as exercise exceeds 65 percent of VO$_2$ max. At high-intensity exercise levels, about 85 percent VO$_2$ max, the percentage contribution from fats (mostly muscle triglycerides) diminishes to 25 percent or less as muscle glycogen becomes the preferential energy source. These percentages are relevant to trained athletes, and will be somewhat lower in untrained individuals. A summary of fat utilization during exercise is presented in table 5.6.

TABLE 5.6 Fat energy sources during exercise

Plasma chylomicrons	Not a major source
Plasma VLDL	Not a major source
Plasma FFA	Major source; Replenished by adipose cell release of FFA; Used in exercise at low to moderate intensity, i.e., 25–65 percent VO$_2$ max; Use decreases as exercise intensity increases toward 65 percent VO$_2$ max
Muscle FFA	Major source; Released from intramuscular triglycerides; Low use during mild exercise; Used increasingly as exercise intensity increases toward 65 percent VO$_2$ max

Note: With high-intensity exercise, 65 percent VO$_2$ max or higher, total fat oxidation falls.

Limiting Factors   In a review, Lange stated that the human being is far from optimally designed for fat oxidation during exercise, noting that fat oxidation alone can sustain a metabolic rate corresponding to only 50–60 percent of VO_2 max. Although reviewers contend that factors limiting fatty acid utilization during high-intensity exercise are largely unknown, several have been suggested. First, inadequate FFA mobilization from adipose tissue may limit FFA delivery to the muscle. Wolfe indicates that fat oxidation is increased significantly at exercise intensities of 85 percent VO_2 max when lipid is infused, but carbohydrate still remains the most significant source of energy. Second, suboptimal intramuscular processes may also limit fat oxidation. For example, Wolfe indicated that the high rate of carbohydrate oxidation during high-intensity exercise may inhibit fatty acid oxidation by limiting transport into the mitochondria, possibly by inhibition of the carnitine-enzyme complex.

In his recent review, Spriet noted that these two factors may limit fat utilization during high-intensity exercise, but other regulatory factors may be involved as well, such as limited transport of fatty acids into the muscle cell and the optimal muscle triglyceride lipase activity. Jeukendrup, in a detailed review of fatty acid metabolism during exercise, indicated that regulation of skeletal muscle fat metabolism is clearly multifactorial, and different mechanisms may dominate in different conditions. As noted by Spriet, research is needed to determine what down-regulates fat use during exercise intensity above 85 percent of VO_2 max.

Dietary Effects   As noted in previous chapters, the amount of energy that may be obtained from muscle and liver glycogen is rather limited. Feeding carbohydrate before and during exercise may affect fat utilization. Achten and Jeukendrup indicated that carbohydrate availability before exercise can increase blood glucose and plasma insulin, which may decrease the rate of adipose tissue lipolysis and concentration of plasma FFA. Research from Wolfe's laboratory suggested that increased glucose flux inhibited fatty acid transport into the mitochondria during exercise. However, Horowitz and others recently reported that although carbohydrate ingestion during moderate-intensity exercise suppressed lipolysis, the lipolytic rate remained in excess of that needed, and thus did not limit fat oxidation until late in the exercise. From a physiological viewpoint, these findings would appear to indicate no negative effect of carbohydrate intake before or during exercise. Although fat oxidation may possibly be reduced, the available carbohydrate would provide a more efficient energy source.

Carbohydrate intake before and during prolonged exercise helps, but within 90–120 minutes or more of high-intensity aerobic exercise, glycogen stores approach very low levels and the body shifts to an increasing usage of FFA, leading to a decrease in the intensity of the exercise. In cases such as prolonged endurance tasks like ultramarathons, FFA may provide nearly 90 percent of the energy in the latter stages of the event.

Use of Ketones   Although ketones may be utilized by the muscle, they do not appear to contribute significantly to energy production during exercise.

Do women use fats more efficiently during exercise than men?

Women possess a greater percentage of body fat than men, and several writers for popular runners' magazines have suggested that women could process this fat more efficiently and thus be more effective in ultramarathon events. Tarnopolsky indicated some theoretical rationale supports this viewpoint as both the muscle lipid content and the maximal activity of a key enzyme in fat metabolism are higher in females. In several studies Tarnopolsky and his associates, using the respiratory exchange ratio to evaluate energy substrate utilization following carbohydrate loading, reported that women oxidized significantly more fat and less carbohydrate than men when exercising at 65 or 75 percent VO_2 max. Similar findings were presented in studies headed by Knechtle and Venables.

However, other studies have shown that the utilization of fat as an energy source by men and women during exercise is similar, particularly when matched for their aerobic capacity. Replicating their previous study with males, Romijn and others recently studied substrate metabolism in well-trained females at 25, 65, and 85 percent of VO_2 max. As with the men, carbohydrate oxidation in women increased progressively with exercise intensity, whereas the highest rate of fat oxidation was during exercise at 65 percent of VO_2 max. They concluded that the patterns of use of carbohydrate and fat during moderate- and high-intensity exercise are similar in trained men and women.

Whether or not women oxidize fat more efficiently than men appears to be debatable, and whether or not it improves performance is also questionable. For example, in one of their studies cited above, Tarnopolsky and others found that although the women oxidized more fat and less carbohydrate than the men, the men improved their performance in the exercise task following carbohydrate loading but the women did not.

What effect does exercise training have on fat metabolism during exercise?

A single bout of exercise influences fat utilization during exercise. Tunstall and others found that a single endurance exercise session led to an increased expression of genes in the skeletal muscle that increase the capacity for fat oxidation, and 9 days of training augmented this effect.

In general, reviewers indicate that trained athletes use more fat than untrained athletes during a standardized exercise task. For example, if you ran an 8-minute mile both before and after a 2-month endurance training program, you would use the same amount of caloric energy each time. However, after training, more of that energy would be derived from fat. Hence, training helps you become a better fat burner, so to speak, which may help spare some of the glycogen in your muscles.

Although all of the exact mechanisms have not been identified, several factors may be involved. Recent reviews, such as those by Brouns and van der Vusse, Horowitz and Klein, and Jeukendrup and his colleagues, indicate multiple mechanisms may be operative, including the following:

- Increased blood flow and capillarization to the muscle, delivering more plasma FFA.
- Increased muscle triglyceride content, possibly associated with increased insulin sensitivity. Insulin regulates movement of FFA into muscle cells. Exercise training may also increase the activity of lipoprotein lipase or fatty acid transporters at the muscle cell membrane.
- Increased sensitivity of both adipose and muscle cells to epinephrine, resulting in increased FFA release to the plasma and within the muscle from triglycerides.
- Increased number of fatty acid transporters in the muscle cell membrane to move fatty acids from the plasma into the muscle cell.
- Improved ability to use ketones as an energy source.
- Increased number and size of mitochondria, and associated oxidative enzymes for processing of activated FFA.
- Increased activation of FFA and transport across the mitochondrial membrane.
- Increased activity of oxidative enzymes.

Overall, according to Martin, the increased content and use of muscle triglycerides may be the primary mechanism underlying the greater capacity of trained muscle to oxidize fatty acids during exercise. Increased utilization of fat during exercise is one of the major effects of training experienced by the endurance athlete.

Although carbohydrate becomes more important as an energy source during high-intensity exercise, Coggan and others found highly trained endurance athletes may be able to use fats more efficiently at exercise intensity levels of 75–80 percent VO_2 max, and in a recent review Pendergast and his associates concluded that fat, particularly intramuscular fat, plays an important role in metabolism at exercise intensities as high as 80 percent of VO_2 max or more in trained endurance athletes. In this regard, Dr. David Costill has noted that some highly trained runners could derive as much as 75 percent of their energy from fat even when they were running at about 70 percent of their VO_2 max. The ability to derive a substantial proportion of the energy demands of intensive exercise from fatty acids is extremely important for athletes such as marathoners who may be able to save some of their muscle glycogen for utilization in the latter stages of the race. The mixture of fatty acids and glycogen for energy will enable them to sustain their pace, whereas the total depletion of muscle glycogen and subsequent reliance on fatty acids as the sole energy supply would force them to slow down. Thus, it is important for the endurance athlete to become a better "fat burner," and a variety of ergogenic aids have been proposed to enhance this effect.

Key Concept Recap

▶ One of the major functions of fat is to provide energy. Although fat may be an important energy source for low- to moderate-intensity exercise, it is not the optimal energy source during high-intensity aerobic or anaerobic exercise.

▶ Endurance exercise training, by enacting multiple mechanisms, enhances the use of fat for energy during aerobic exercise.

Fats: Ergogenic Aspects

Because exercise training leads to an increased utilization of fatty acids as an energy source and improved performance in endurance events (theoretically by sparing muscle glycogen), a variety of dietary practices, dietary supplements, and pharmacological agents have been employed in attempts to facilitate this metabolic process during exercise. In a review of the proposed mechanism, Jeukendrup noted that the increased availability and oxidation of fatty acids would generate more acetyl-CoA, which in turn would inhibit a cascade of events that would essentially inhibit enzymes involved in carbohydrate breakdown. Such an effect could spare the use of muscle glycogen and enhance endurance performance. However, Jeukendrup indicated that although this effect may be operative in light exercise, it might not be during moderate- to high-exercise intensities.

Both acute and chronic dietary strategies have been used to increase the concentration of muscle triglycerides or serum level of FFA. Such strategies include high-fat diets, fasting, and even infusion of lipids into the bloodstream. Dietary supplements and drugs have been used to either increase the supply of oxidizable fats or the rate of fat metabolism. Dietary supplements include medium-chain triglycerides, lecithin, glycerol, and carnitine. Caffeine also has been theorized to enhance fat oxidation, and its role as an ergogenic aid is covered in chapter 13.

What is fat loading?

Dietary strategies designed to increase the supply or metabolism of fat as an energy source during exercise may be referred to as **fat** **loading.** Fat loading may be done on an acute or chronic basis.

Acute fat loading involves dietary strategies immediately before exercise. Because the rate at which FFA are oxidized in the muscle is dependent in part upon their concentration in the blood plasma, several different acute dietary techniques have been tried in attempts to increase plasma FFA levels.

Chronic fat loading involves dietary strategies about a week or so prior to endurance exercise. These strategies are designed to increase lipid metabolism and gene expression in skeletal muscle, resulting in an increased ability of the skeletal muscle to use fat as an energy source during exercise. In a recent study, Helge and others found that consuming a fat-rich diet will increase intramuscular lipid stores, while in their review Brown and Cox noted that intramuscular stores of triglycerides may provide an important fuel during exercise, including high-intensity exercise. Thus, chronic high-fat diets are designed primarily to increase muscle triglyceride stores. Some investigators have also evaluated the effect of chronic fat loading prior to 1–2 days of carbohydrate loading to see if there were any additional benefits associated with this dietary protocol. This latter dietary protocol is similar to the classic carbohydrate-loading protocol discussed in chapter 4.

Acute High-fat Diets Lipid digestion and absorption is slow, so one strategy is to infuse a lipid solution (such as Intralipid) directly into the blood along with heparin, a substance that stimulates lipoprotein lipase activity and increases plasma FFA levels.

Such a strategy increases fat oxidation and reduces carbohydrate oxidation, which may enhance endurance exercise performance. However, after a lipid solution had been used by a national team in the Tour de France, the entire team withdrew from the race allegedly due to adverse reactions. No research has been uncovered that supports this ergogenic technique.

A second strategy is to ingest a high-fat meal prior to exercise performance. In a recent well-designed crossover study, Pitsiladis and others evaluated the effect of a 90 percent fat-content meal, versus a 70 percent carbohydrate-content meal, on cycling time to exhaustion at 75 percent VO_2 max. Subjects were carbohydrate loaded for 3.5 days prior to exercise testing. The meals were consumed four hours prior to testing. Prior to the single high-fat meal, subjects received an infusion of heparin. Performance time was significantly greater after the high-fat meal. However, although the subjects knew the content of the meals, no placebo infusion was given prior to the high-carbohydrate meal, a factor which may have influenced exercise performance. Moreover, the authors indicated that this study was not intended to have immediate application to sports performance because heparin injection to elevate plasma FFA would not represent sound medical practice.

Without using heparin, other studies have not shown any benefits of high-fat diets on exercise performance. For example, in two studies Okano and others reported no significant differences between a high-fat diet (61 percent fat content) and a control or low-fat diet on performance in a cycling test to exhaustion at 78–80 percent VO_2 max following 2 hours of riding at 60–67 percent VO_2 max. Additionally, Rowlands and Hopkins investigated the effect of a high-fat (85 percent fat energy) meal, as compared to a high-carbohydrate (85 percent carbohydrate energy) meal and high-protein (30 percent protein energy) meal consumed 90 minutes before an endurance cycling test, which involved a 1-hour preload at 55 percent VO_2 max, five 10-minute incremental loads from 55–82 percent of peak power, and a 50-kilometer time trial that included several 1-km and 4-km sprints. Subjects consumed a carbohydrate supplement during the cycling protocol. The meal composition had no clear effect on sprint or 50-kilometer cycle performance.

An acute high-fat dietary strategy does not appear to enhance performance, and, in fact, may actually impair performance if it contributes to gastrointestinal distress because of the delayed gastric emptying associated with fats. Research has shown that consuming a high-fat diet for 1 or 2 days, another acute approach, may actually impair performance in high-intensity exercise tasks.

Chronic High-fat Diets Several investigators have challenged the dogma that endurance athletes need high-carbohydrate diets and suggest that endurance performance may benefit from diets containing about 50 percent or more energy from fat. Brown and Cox note that athletes can adapt to such a diet and maintain physical endurance capacity, will increase their muscle triglyceride levels, and may increase the use of fat and decrease use of carbohydrate during exercise. Research has shown that when an individual is placed on a chronic low-carbohydrate and high-fat diet for about a week or more, the body adjusts its metabolism to use fats more efficiently. But, do such changes lead to enhanced endurance exercise performance?

Studies showing ergogenic effect Several studies support an ergogenic effect of chronic fat loading. Pendergast and Horvath, along with their associates, conducted several of the first contemporary studies. Although two studies from their laboratory have shown that adapting to a high-fat diet (38–41 percent fat content) over a 1–4 week period improved treadmill running time to exhaustion, both studies had problems with the experimental design, such as no random assignment of the diet conditions and no counterbalancing of diet order. Moreover, the diets were not exceptionally high in fat content. Muoio and others acknowledged the limitations to experimental design in their prototype study, and the interested reader is referred to the other study by Venkatraman and Pendergast.

More recently, Horvath and others had male and female runners consume diets of 16 and 31 percent fat for four weeks, and then about half the subjects increased their dietary fat intake to 44 percent. All diets were designed to be isocaloric, but the runners actually consumed about 19 percent fewer Calories on the low-fat (16 percent) diet. There were no differences among the diets for VO_2 max, anaerobic power, or body mass, but the endurance run after the low-fat diet was reduced compared to the medium- and high-fat diets. However, it is possible that decreased energy intake may have contributed to this decrease in performance.

Lambert and her colleagues also found some ergogenic effects in several studies. In one study, they placed athletes on a high-fat (70 percent fat Calories) diet or low-fat (12 percent fat Calories) diet for 2 weeks, testing the effects on three performance tests done in consecutive order with 30 minutes rest between each. The three exercise tests included a Wingate high-power test, a high-intensity test to exhaustion at 90 percent VO_2 max, and a moderate-intensity test to exhaustion at 60 percent VO_2 max. Although there were no significant effects between the two diets for performance in the first two exercise tests, the cyclists rode significantly longer on the moderate-intensity test following adaptation to the high-fat diet. The investigators noted that adaptation to the high-fat diet decreased the reliance on carbohydrate as an energy source during exercise, and thus suggested the improved performance was due to muscle-glycogen sparing.

In a subsequent study, Lambert and others evaluated the effect of a 10-day high-fat diet, prior to 3 days of a carbohydrate-loading regimen, on cycling performance in a trial consisting of 150 minutes at 70 percent VO_2 max followed by a 20-kilometer time trial. Compared to their habitual diet with carbohydrate loading, the high-fat diet enabled the endurance cyclists to increase total fat oxidation and reduce carbohydrate oxidation, and significantly improve time trial performance by 1.4 minutes.

Studies showing no ergogenic effect Conversely, other well-controlled research suggests that chronic high-fat diets do not benefit endurance performance. In a well-designed, crossover study, Pogliaghi and Veicsteinas reported no significant effect of a high-fat (55 percent fat) diet versus a normal or low-fat diet on cycle endurance time to exhaustion at 75 percent VO_2 max in untrained individuals. Helge and others had untrained males undertake an endurance training program for 4 weeks while consuming either a high-fat (62 percent fat) or high-carbohydrate (65 percent carbohydrate) diet, and measured performance by time to exhaustion at 80 percent VO_2 max. They reported no significant differences between the two diets. In earlier research, they found that endurance performance was actually lower after 7 weeks adaptation to training and a high-fat diet. Similar findings of impaired endurance and power also were recently reported by Fleming and others. However, in these studies, untrained individuals, not trained athletes, served as subjects.

Several recent studies have shown no effect of chronic fat loading on endurance performance in trained individuals. Brown and Cox, in a randomized study using 32 endurance-trained cyclists, reported no difference in 20-km road time performance over a period of 12 weeks when subjects consumed either a high-fat (47 percent of energy) versus a high-carbohydrate (69 percent of energy) diet. Burke and her associates found no beneficial effects in two studies. In the first study they investigated the effects of a high-fat diet for 5 days, followed by a 1-day high-carbohydrate diet, on an endurance cycling protocol involving cycling at 70 percent VO_2 max for 2 hours followed by an intense time trial. Compared to a high-carbohydrate diet, the high-fat diet induced greater utilization of fat with an associated muscle glycogen sparing, but there was no significant improvement in the cycling time trial, even though performance following the high-fat phase was about 3.4 minutes faster. In a subsequent study using a similar protocol, Burke and her associates reported no significant effect on endurance performance.

In a similar vein, Rowlands and Hopkins compared the effects of three different 14-day dietary regimens on 100-kilometer cycling performance. One of the diets was high-carbohydrate, one was high-fat, and one was high-fat before 2.5 days of carbohydrate loading. Both high-fat diets increased fat oxidation during the cycling trial, and although there were no significant differences between the three trials, the 100-kilometer performance was approximately 3–4 percent faster with the high-fat diets. Interestingly, power output in the last 5 kilometers of the time trial was significantly greater for the high-fat with carbohydrate-loading trial as compared to the high-carbohydrate trial. The authors noted that although the main effects of the study were not significant, there was some evidence for enhanced ultraendurance cycling with a high-fat diet compared to a high-carbohydrate diet. Carey and others compared the effects of two 6-day diets, either high-carbohydrate or high-fat, on a prolonged cycling task involving 4 hours at 65 percent VO_2 peak followed by a 1-hour time trial. In both diets, a high-carbohydrate diet was consumed on the day prior to testing. Similar to other studies, the high-fat diet increased total fat oxidation and reduced carbohydrate oxidation, but there was no effect on cycling performance. However, the power output was 11 percent higher during the time trial after the high-fat diet as compared to the high-carbohydrate condition, but this difference was not statistically significant.

It is interesting to note that in three of these contemporary studies, although the chronic fat-loading protocol was not shown statistically to improve performance, the investigators did note that performance was generally improved compared to the other diets.

Reviews concluding an ergogenic effect Several reviewers from the same research group have concluded that chronic high-fat diets may enhance endurance performance. Venkatraman and others have noted that short-term, high-fat diets may improve endurance exercise performance at 60–80 percent VO_2 max in endurance cyclists and runners. Pendergast and others cited various studies indicating high-fat diets (42–55 percent of energy) that maintained adequate carbohydrate levels have shown increased endurance capacity in both men and women when compared with low-fat diets (10–15 percent of energy).

Reviews concluding no ergogenic effect Conversely, other reviewers concluded chronic high-fat diets are not ergogenic. In her review, Bente Kiens noted that varying periods of fat adaptation followed by a carbohydrate-rich diet, despite an increased fat oxidation and a concomitant decrease in carbohydrate oxidation during submaximal exercise, exerts no beneficial effects on subsequent time trial endurance cycling performance.

In their recent review, Burke and Hawley indicated that endurance athletes who consume chronic high-fat diets, as compared to isocaloric high-carbohydrate diets, may increase fat oxidation and spare use of muscle glycogen during submaximal exercise. They noted that these effects persist even under conditions in which carbohydrate availability is increased, either by consuming a high-carbohydrate meal before exercise and/or ingesting glucose solutions during exercise. Yet, despite marked changes in the patterns of fuel utilization that favor fat oxidation, they conclude that this strategy does not provide clear benefits to the performance of prolonged endurance exercise. Helge reiterates the potential beneficial ergogenic effects of chronic high-fat diets, but indicates that overall the scientific evidence suggests that endurance performance can, at best, only be maintained on such diets when compared with carbohydrate-rich diets, and therefore long-term fat diet usage cannot be recommended as a tool to improve endurance performance, a conclusion also supported by Hargreaves and others.

Given these studies and reviews, the findings appear to be equivocal but generally support the conclusion that chronic high-fat diets for 1–2 weeks are not ergogenic for endurance athletes. Nevertheless, if this dietary regimen could spare the use of muscle glycogen during exercise as noted in several studies, and if indeed muscle glycogen stores represent a limiting factor in the premature development of fatigue, then such a dietary strategy could possibly enhance endurance performance in events that may benefit from preservation of muscle glycogen.

A high-fat diet does not appear to be recommended on a long-term basis. One reason may be possible adverse health effects associated with such diets, as discussed later in this chapter, although athletes involved in intense training may not experience such adverse effects. Another reason may be the quality of training. Helge noted that optimal competitive performance is dependent on several factors, including the quality and quantity of training. Training may be compromised on a fat-rich diet as it compromises glycogen storage in both muscle and liver. Although Stepto and others found that endurance athletes could maintain levels of high-intensity training while adapting to a high-fat diet over a 3-day period, the training sessions were associated with increased ratings of perceived exertion when compared to training with a high-carbohydrate diet. Thus, such diets may make training more psychologically stressful.

Will fasting help improve my performance?

Sherman and Leenders indicate that fasting for 24 hours may increase the plasma FFA availability. Unfortunately, endurance exercise performance is usually impaired because fasting reduces muscle glycogen stores or induces hypoglycemia. For example, in a recent study Gutierrez and others evaluated the effects of a 3-day fast on exercise performance in young men during training. The researchers reported a significantly decreased aerobic endurance physical working capacity based on heart rate responses to a cycling exercise protocol. The effect of fasting on physical performance when athletes attempt to lose body weight for sport competition is covered in chapter 10.

Can the use of medium-chain triglycerides improve endurance performance?

Medium-chain triglycerides (MCTs) have been suggested to be ergogenic, possibly because they are water soluble which may confer two advantages; they can be absorbed by the portal circulation and delivered directly to the liver instead of via the chylomicron route in the lymph and they more readily enter the mitochondria in the muscle cells. MCTs have been marketed commercially. Research has shown that MCTs do not inhibit gastric emptying as common fat does and may be absorbed rapidly in the small intestine. Also, Massicotte and his associates reported exogenous MCTs are oxidized at a rate comparable to exogenous glucose, being oxidized within the first 30 minutes of exercise. Researchers have investigated the ergogenic effect of MCT supplementation by itself and also combined with carbohydrate. Most studies provided the supplements just before and during the exercise task, but one study involved chronic supplementation.

Some early research found that MCT supplementation alone may actually impair exercise endurance exercise performance, whereas an MCT-carbohydrate supplement might be ergogenic. Van Zyl and others, using endurance-trained cyclists, compared the effects of three supplements on an endurance performance task consisting of a 2-hour ride at 60 percent VO_2 max followed by a 40-kilometer performance ride. The three supplements, consumed throughout the performance task, were carbohydrate only, MCTs only, and carbohydrate with MCTs; the MCT dose was about 86 grams. Compared to the carbohydrate supplement, the MCT supplement actually impaired 40-kilometer performance, whereas the combination carbohydrate-MCT supplement improved performance. These investigators suggested that the carbohydrate-MCT supplement improved performance in the 40-kilometer performance ride by decreasing oxidation of muscle glycogen during the preliminary submaximal 2-hour ride, thus sparing the glycogen for the more intense exercise task.

However, most studies have not shown any beneficial effects of MCT supplementation, either alone or combined with carbohydrate, on endurance exercise performance. In several recent studies with his University of Maastricht colleagues in the Netherlands, Jeukendrup investigated similar supplementation protocols and reported very little contribution of ingested MCTs to energy metabolism during exercise. Using a protocol comparable to the Van Zyl research group, but also incorporating a placebo trial and using a 15-minute cycle performance task instead of a 40-kilometer ride, Jeukendrup and colleagues also found that MCT supplementation impaired performance and attributed the impairment to gastrointestinal distress. However, in contrast to the Van Zyl study, they reported no significant differences between the other trials, suggesting the carbohydrate-MCT combination was not an effective ergogenic. Goedecke and others, from Tim Noakes laboratory in South Africa, reported similar findings. Nine endurance-trained cyclists cycled for 2 hours at 63 percent of VO_2 peak, and then completed a 40-kilometer time trial under three conditions: glucose, glucose and low-dose MCTs, and glucose and high-dose MCTs, all in solution. The solutions were ingested immediately before and every 10 minutes during exercise. Although MCT ingestion increased serum FFA concentration, there were no beneficial effects on performance as compared to the glucose trial. In a well-designed crossover study, Angus and others compared the effects of carbohydrate to carbohydrate plus MCT on 100-kilometer cycling time trial in eight endurance-trained males. The beverages were provided during the trial at about every 15 minutes, and consisted of a 6 percent carbohydrate solution with and without a 4.2 percent MCT solution. Compared to the placebo trial, they found that the carbohydrate enhanced 100-kilometer cycling performance, but the addition of MCT did not provide any further performance enhancement. In a similar study with ultraendurance athletes, but with carbohydrate or MCTs provided before an ultra-distance ride, Goedecke and others reported that MCT supplementation actually impaired periodic sprint performance within the event. Using muscle biopsies, Horowitz and others have also shown that a carbohydrate-MCT solution does not spare muscle glycogen during high-intensity aerobic exercise.

Using a chronic MCT feeding protocol, Misell and others had twelve trained male endurance runners consume either corn oil (LCT) or MCT (60 grams) daily for 2 weeks. The runners then performed an endurance treadmill test consisting of a 30-minute run at 85 percent VO_2 max followed by a run to exhaustion at 75 percent VO_2 max. The investigators reported that chronic MCT consumption neither enhances endurance performance nor significantly alters exercise metabolism in trained male runners.

The available evidence suggests that MCT supplementation, by itself, has no ergogenic effect on endurance performance. MCT supplementation may actually impair performance as ingestion of large amounts may lead to gastrointestinal distress. Additionally, consuming a MCT-carbohydrate solution provides no additional benefits compared to the carbohydrate solution by itself.

Is the glycerol portion of triglycerides an effective ergogenic aid?

As you may recall, glycerol is one of the by-products of triglyceride breakdown. Burelle and others have noted that exogenous glycerol can be oxidized during prolonged exercise, presumably following conversion into glucose in the liver. Thus, researchers theorized that it could be an efficient energy source during exercise. However, in well-controlled research, glycerol feedings did not prevent either hypoglycemia or muscle glycogen depletion patterns in several prolonged exercise tasks. Apparently the rate at which the human liver converts glycerol to glucose is not rapid enough to be an effective energy source during strenuous prolonged exercise. However, as noted in chapter 9, glycerol may be used to increase body water stores, including plasma volume, prior to exercise, which may improve cardiovascular functions and help regulate body temperature more effectively, possible ergogenic effects.

How effective are lecithin or choline supplements?

Lecithin is a phospholipid that occurs naturally in a variety of foods, such as beans, eggs, and wheat germ. Because it is an important component of many types of human body tissues, contains choline needed for the synthesis of acetylcholine (an important neurotransmitter), and contains phosphorus, it has been theorized to be ergogenic in nature. Several German studies conducted over 50 years ago reported increases in power and strength following several days of supplementation with 22–83 milligrams of lecithin. However, these early studies have been discredited because of poor experimental design. In a study with better experimental design, Staton reported that 30 grams of lecithin supplementation daily for 2 weeks had no effect upon grip strength.

Although lecithin does not appear to be an effective ergogenic aid, several of its constituents have been theorized to enhance exercise performance. Choline, an amine associated with vitamin-like activity, has been studied independently or as part of lecithin for potential ergogenic effects on endurance performance, and is discussed in chapter 7. Phosphate salts are covered in chapter 8.

Why are omega-3 fatty acids suggested to be ergogenic, and do they work?

Omega-3 fatty acids are theorized to be ergogenic, not because of their energy content, but because they may elicit favorable physiological effects relative to several types of physical performance. One theory is based on the finding that omega-3 fatty acids may be incorporated into the membrane of the red blood cell (RBC), making the RBC less viscous and less resistant to flow. Another theory is based on the role of certain by-products—the eicosanoids mentioned previously—whose production in the body cells is related to omega-3 fatty acid metabolism. In particular, two specific forms of the eicosanoids, prostaglandin E_1 (PGE_1) and prostaglandin I_2 (PGI_2), may elicit a vasodilation effect on the blood vessels and may stimulate the release of human growth hormone. Theoretically, the less viscous RBC and the vasodilative effect should enhance blood flow, facilitating the delivery of blood and oxygen to the muscles during exercise, benefitting the endurance athlete. Additionally, the increased secretion of human growth hormone might stimulate muscle growth and benefit the strength/power athlete and may also facilitate recovery from intense exercise bouts.

Unfortunately, although the ergogenic potential of omega-3 fatty acids is an interesting hypothesis, there are few supportive scientific data. Bucci, in his book discussing nutritional ergogenic aids, cites several studies with Eicomax®, a commercially available blend of fish oils and vegetable oils. The studies were conducted with university football teams and focused on measures of strength and speed, possibly testing the potential anabolic effect of omega-3 fatty acids via stimulated release of human growth hormone. In one of the studies, there was no control group. Bucci notes that both studies reported improved performance with the use of Eicomax®, however, perusal of the cited references reveals that these studies have not appeared in the scientifically reviewed literature, but were published in the training manual of the company that produces Eicomax®. If indeed these are valid findings, they need to be published in the scientific literature and confirmed.

Results from well-controlled, peer-reviewed scientific research indicate omega-3 fatty acids do not benefit aerobic endurance performance. Brilla and Landerholm studied the effect of fish oil supplements containing 4 grams per day of omega-3 fatty acids, either separately or in combination with an aerobic exercise training program, on aerobic fitness as measured by a test of VO_2 max. They reported that although exercise training increased VO_2 max, the omega-3 fatty acids yielded no ergogenic effect when taken without exercise training, nor did they have any additive effect with training. Raastad and others also reported that daily supplementation of 2.6 grams omega-3 fatty acids for 10 weeks did not improve maximal aerobic power or running performance in well-trained male soccer players. In a similar fashion, Oostenbrug and others reported no significant effect of 6.0 grams omega-3 fatty acids for 3 weeks, with or without vitamin E supplementation, on red blood cell characteristics or on bicycle time trial performance approximating 1 hour, while Huffman and others reported that supplementation with 4 grams of omega-3 fatty acids daily for four weeks did not improve performance in a maximal performance test following a 75-minute submaximal treadmill run.

As noted previously, some foods are rich in omega-3 fatty acids. Certain diet plans incorporate such foods, and one plan suggests that such a diet may enhance sport performance. In his best-selling book, *The Zone,* Barry Sears describes his diet plan for health and appearance, mainly weight loss. Basically the diet consists of a set ratio of Calories from carbohydrate (40 percent), fat (30 percent), and protein (30 percent), and is often referred to as the 40:30:30 diet. It is basically a low-carbohydrate, moderate-fat, and high-protein diet.

Sears suggests that certain fats in the "zone" diet may be of value to athletes, and part of the underlying theory may be the eicosanoid-generating fatty acids, particularly the omega-3 fatty acids. Indeed, some companies manufacture food products based on the 40:30:30 ratio and target them at the sport nutrition market. Sports bars including omega-3 fatty acids are one example. However, Cheuvront recently noted that the key eicosanoid reportedly produced in the "zone" diet and responsible for improved muscle oxygenation is not found in skeletal muscle. Several reports in swimming magazines indicated that such a diet was instrumental in the success of the Stanford University swim team, but the data presented were anecdotal rather than scientific. Cheuvront also indicted that based on the best available scientific evidence, the "zone" diet should be considered more ergolytic than ergogenic to performance. As this diet is primarily a high-protein diet, it will be discussed further in the next chapter.

At the present time, there do not appear to be sufficient data to support an ergogenic effect of omega-3 fatty acids.

Can carnitine supplements enhance fat metabolism and physical performance?

Carnitine is a water-soluble, vitamin-like compound that facilitates the transport of long-chain fatty acids into the mitochondria. There are basically two forms of carnitine, L-carnitine and D-carnitine, but other forms are available, such as L-propionylcarnitine. L-carnitine is the physiologically active form in the body, so in the following discussion, carnitine will refer mostly to L-carnitine, but in some studies L-propionylcarnitine has been used.

Carnitine was discovered in 1905 and was considered to be an essential vitamin (B_T) at one time; more recently Kelly labeled it as a conditionally essential amino acid. Although Rebouche has indicated that carnitine is an extremely important catalyst for metabolic reactions in the muscle, carnitine is not an essential dietary nutrient because it may be formed in the liver from other nutrients—principally two amino acids, lysine and methionine. Also, carnitine is found in substantial amounts in animal foods. Meat products, particularly beef and pork, are good sources of carnitine; much less is found in fish and poultry, and even lower amounts in dairy products. Only minimal amounts of carnitine are found in fruits, vegetables, and grains. For example, for similar weights, beef has about 300 times as much carnitine as bread; 3 ounces of beef contains about 60 mg of carnitine. There is no RDA for carnitine. Most individuals consume enough carnitine in the daily diet, and the body also has an effective conservation system. The typical nonvegetarian diet provides about 100–300 milligrams per day. Carnitine deficiencies are very rare. Rebouche indicated that there is no evidence that carnitine deficiency occurs in the general population of strict vegetarians, whose diet generally provides a very minimal amount of carnitine.

Carnitine supplementation has been theorized to enhance physical performance because of several of its metabolic functions in the muscle cell. Approximately 90 percent of the body supply of carnitine is located in the muscle tissues where it is part of an enzyme (carnitine palmitoyl transferase) important for transport of long-chain fatty acids (LCFAs) into the mitochondria for oxidation. Theoretically, supplemental carnitine might facilitate the transport of LCFAs into the mitochondria for oxidation, which would be an important consideration if the oxidation of fatty acids was limited by their transport into the mitochondria. Some research has reported an increase in respiratory chain enzymes in the mitochondria of long-distance runners following carnitine supplementation. Combining these two potential effects, carnitine would theoretically be beneficial for athletes in very prolonged endurance events by increasing the utilization of fatty acids during exercise and sparing the use of muscle glycogen. This is the primary theory underlying carnitine supplementation for endurance athletes.

Given the theory of carnitine supplementation to increase fatty acid oxidation, Villani and others have noted that manufacturers marketed it as a weight loss supplement, either alone or combined with exercise to facilitate fat burning. Inducing a loss of excess body fat could provide a mechanical edge to some athletes.

Carnitine plays other metabolic roles that have been theorized to be ergogenic. Wagenmakers notes that carnitine may facilitate the oxidation of pyruvate, which may possibly enhance the utilization of glucose and reduce the production of lactic acid during exercise, factors that may enhance performance in short-term maximal or supramaximal exercise, such as in a 400-meter or 800-meter run. Wagenmakers also notes that carnitine may increase blood flow both at rest and during exercise, which may enhance delivery of both oxygen and energy substrate to the muscle during exercise, a theoretical ergogenic effect independent of the role of carnitine in the muscle cells.

Conversely, Wagenmakers notes that carnitine may expedite the oxidation of branched-chain amino acids (BCAA), leading to a series of biochemical reactions that could lead to premature fatigue, an ergolytic rather than ergogenic effect.

Carnitine supplementation, particularly L-propionylcarnitine, has been used effectively to improve exercise capability in patients with serious diseases. After carnitine supplementation for several weeks, patients with peripheral vascular disease increased their walking distance before experiencing pain. Several studies have also reported improved exercise capacity in patients with heart and end-stage renal disease following carnitine supplementation.

Although these are logical theories and interesting medical applications, the available scientific evidence is somewhat equivocal, and in general does not appear to support an ergogenic effect of carnitine supplementation. Major reviews regarding the effect of carnitine supplementation on physical performance have been published in recent years, and the following are the key points regarding the ergogenic effects of carnitine supplementation emanating from these reviews and recent studies:

1. Supplementation will increase plasma levels of carnitine, but much of this will be excreted by the kidneys. However, although some previous research has suggested that carnitine supplementation could increase muscle carnitine levels, in a recent review Wagenmakers concluded that carnitine supplements do not increase muscle carnitine concentration. He based this conclusion on research using direct measurements in muscle showing no changes in muscle carnitine concentration after 14 days of supplementation with 4–6 grams of carnitine per day. Most recently, Wacher and others reported no increased muscle carnitine content following supplementation with 4 grams of L-carnitine daily for 3 months.

2. Acute supplementation does not appear to enhance performance. Although acute supplementation was not studied extensively, Colombani and others, in a well-designed, double-blind, placebo, crossover study, reported no significant effect on performance in either a marathon or a 20-kilometer run after supplements of 2 grams of carnitine 2 hours before the events. Such short-term supplementation may not be adequate to increase muscle levels of carnitine.

3. Chronic supplementation, with as much as 6 grams per day for 7 days, has no effect on lactic acid accumulation during high-intensity anaerobic exercise, nor does it increase performance in such exercise tasks. For example, Trappe and others reported no effect of carnitine supplementation on performance in five repeat 100-yard swims with a 2 minute recovery.

4. Recent well-controlled studies, and the conclusions of most reviewers, indicated that chronic carnitine supplementation has no effect on VO_2 max. The effects of carnitine supplementation on aerobic endurance performance have not been studied extensively, but those data that are available, such as the effect on a 70-minute cycling task, cycling to exhaustion at 60 percent of maximal workload, and a 5-kilometer run, have shown no beneficial effect. There are no scientific data showing a beneficial effect of chronic carnitine supplementation on very prolonged aerobic endurance tasks, such as a marathon.

5. The primary theory underlying carnitine supplementation is enhanced fat utilization. However, research by Decombaz and colleagues and Vukovich and colleagues reported no effect of chronic carnitine supplementation on fat oxidation or muscle glycogen sparing under exercise conditions maximizing fatty acid oxidation.

6. Carnitine supplementation has not been shown to reduce body fat in obese individuals, and thus would not appear to be effective in athletes either.

7. D-carnitine may be toxic, as it can deplete L-carnitine, leading to a carnitine deficiency. L-carnitine appears to be a safe supplement, but some reviewers recommend no more than 2–5 grams per day, possibly for only one month at a time.

For a detailed review of carnitine metabolism and its potential ergogenic effect, the interested reader is referred to the excellent critiques by Brass, Heinonen, Kelly, and Wagenmakers. Although interpretation of the scientific data regarding the ergogenic value of carnitine supplementation may vary somewhat, Brass indicates that there is no compelling evidence that carnitine supplementation can improve physical performance in healthy subjects. He does note, however, that additional research is needed because although the data do not allow a conclusion to be drawn that carnitine is beneficial, the negative has not been proven either.

Can hydroxycitrate (HCA) enhance endurance performance?

Hydroxycitric acid is derived from a tropical fruit and marketed as a dietary supplement, hydroxycitrate (HCA). Kriketos and others noted that as a competitive inhibitor of citrate lysase, HCA has been hypothesized to modify citric acid cycle metabolism to promote fatty acid oxidation. Although some studies with mice suggest HCA supplementation may enhance endurance performance, human studies do not support such an ergogenic effect.

Kriketos and others, in an excellent crossover study, reported no significant effect of HCA supplementation (3.0 grams/day for 3 days) on blood serum energy substrates, fat metabolism, or energy expenditure either during rest or during moderately intense exercise. However, the subjects were sedentary males. Using endurance-trained cyclists as subjects, van Loon and others evaluated the effect of HCA supplementation (3.1 ml/kilogram body mass of a 19 percent HCA solution) given twice to the cyclists before and during 2 hours of cycling at 50 percent VO_2 max. They concluded that HCA supplementation, even in large quantities, does not increase total fat oxidation in endurance-trained cyclists.

Thus, the available evidence indicates that HCA supplementation does not modify fat utilization during exercise, much less confer an ergogenic effect.

Can conjugated linoleic acid (CLA) enhance exercise performance?

Conjugated linoleic acid (CLA) has been marketed as a sports dietary supplement to resistance-trained individuals, mainly as a means to promote weight loss and to gain muscle mass. For similar and other reasons, CLA also has been marketed as a means to improve health.

Research regarding its ergogenic effect on exercise-trained individuals is very limited. Using resistance-trained athletes as subjects, Kreider and others investigated the effect of CLA supplementation (6 grams prescribed daily dose; 28 days) on body composition and muscular strength, and reported no significant effects on total body mass, fat mass, fat-free mass, or strength as measured by a single maximal repetition in the bench press and leg press.

Based on limited research, CLA supplementation does not currently appear to be an effective ergogenic aid for trained individuals, but confirming research is needed.

What's the bottom line regarding the ergogenic effects of fat-burning diets or strategies?

As noted in this section, numerous fat-burning strategies have been employed in attempts to enhance prolonged endurance exercise performance. Theoretically, such strategies would increase the oxidation of fat, decrease the utilization of carbohydrate, and thus spare some muscle glycogen for use in the later stages of exercise. As muscle glycogen is a more efficient fuel compared to fats, performance should be enhanced.

However, John Hawley, an international sports science scholar, recently reviewed all such fat-burning strategies and concluded that endurance exercise capacity is not systematically improved with increases in serum FFA availability, even in some studies with substantial muscle glycogen sparing. He noted that for some reason, exercise capacity is remarkably resistant to change. Other studies suggest high-fat diets may impair performance in some events, such as high-intensity surges during a race or sprints to the finish. Moreover, individuals may find that it may be difficult to adhere to a high-fat diet.

In a journal targeted to marathoners and ultramarathoners, Shulman suggests that both high-carbohydrate and high-fat diets may contribute to poor endurance running performance, and indicates the best diet may be somewhere in between. Such a diet should have enough fat to stimulate fat metabolism, but also supply enough carbohydrate to keep the brain and nervous system happy and the liver and muscle glycogen stores filled. She indicates that many sports nutrition experts are recommending a basic diet that supplies 50-percent carbohydrate, 30-percent fat, and 20-percent protein, with additional carbohydrates after hard or long-duration training. Such a diet composition is very reasonable and within guidelines for healthful eating.

Key Concept Recap

▶ Fat-loading practices, either acute or chronic, do not appear to enhance exercise or sport performance.

▶ Various lipid-based dietary supplements theorized to possess ergogenic potential, such as medium-chain triglycerides (MCTs), lecithin, omega-3 fatty acids, carnitine, hydroxycitrate (HCA), and conjugated linoleic acid (CLA), do not appear to enhance exercise or sport performance.

Check for Yourself

Go to a health food store that sells sport supplements and ask the clerk for supplements that will help you burn more fat, primarily as a means to enhance endurance performance. Evaluate the supplement fact labels for content and performance claims and compare them to the text discussion. What is your judgement?

Dietary Fats and Cholesterol: Health Implications

As noted in previous chapters, the etiology of chronic diseases such as cancer and coronary heart disease is complex and involves multiple risk factors. Eliminating or reducing as many risk factors as possible is the best approach to optimize your health. Your diet is one of the most important risk factors that can be modified to promote good health, particularly the amount and composition of fat you eat. In this section we shall focus on the role of dietary fat in the etiology of coronary heart disease (CHD), and in chapter 10 we will discuss the possible role of dietary fat in obesity and related health problems, such as diabetes, high blood pressure, and various forms of cancer.

CHD is still the number one cause of death in industrialized nations. In their recent recommendations for dietary fat, the National Academy of Sciences indicated that although very-high fat diets may predispose to CHD, so too may very-low fat diets. Diets that are rich in refined sugars and starches and low in fiber and fat may modify the metabolic profile in ways that may also be conducive to CHD. Lipid expert Penny Kris-Etherton and her associates recently noted that the main message regarding dietary fat is very simple: Avoid diets that are *very low* and *very high* in fat. The guiding principle is that moderation in total fat is the defining benchmark for a contemporary diet that reduces risk of chronic disease. Moreover, within the range of a moderate-fat diet it is still important to individualize the total fat prescription. Fats are not all equal. Some are better for your health than others, and, as noted, the terms *good* and *bad* fats have been popularized. Remember, however, that even some *bad* fats can fit into a healthy diet. The key is moderation.

Because the available evidence relating dietary lipids to cardiovascular diseases is so compelling, we shall treat this subject in some detail. However, note that the dietary and exercise recommendations advanced later in this chapter for the prevention of cardiovascular disease may also help prevent other chronic diseases, such as obesity and certain forms of cancer.

How does cardiovascular disease develop?

Nearly one out of every two deaths in the United States is due to diseases of the heart and blood vessels. Each year, approximately one million Americans die from some form of cardiovascular disease, including coronary heart disease, stroke, hypertensive disease, rheumatic heart disease, and congenital heart disease.

Coronary heart disease is the major disease of the cardiovascular system; of the million deaths noted previously, it is responsible for over half. Although the total percentage of deaths due to coronary heart disease has been declining in recent years, it is still an epidemic and the number one cause of death among both males and females.

Coronary heart disease (CHD) is also known as **coronary artery disease (CAD)** because obstruction of the blood flow in the coronary arteries is responsible for the pathological effects of the disease. The coronary arteries, which nourish the heart muscle, are illustrated in figure 5.11. The major manifestation of CHD is a heart attack, which results from a stoppage of blood flow to parts of the heart muscle. A decreased blood supply, known as **ischemia,** will deprive the heart of needed oxygen. In some individuals, ischemia results in **angina,** a sharp pain in the chest, jaw, or along the inside of the arm indicative of a mild heart attack. Other terms often associated with a heart attack include **coronary thrombosis,** a blockage of a blood vessel by a clot (thrombus), **coronary occlusion,** which simply means blockage, and **myocardial infarct,** death of heart cells that do not get enough oxygen due to the blocked coronary artery. The major cause of blocked arteries is atherosclerosis.

Arteriosclerosis is a term applied to a number of different pathological conditions wherein the arterial walls thicken and lose their elasticity. It is often defined as hardening of the arteries. **Atherosclerosis,** one form of arteriosclerosis, is characterized by deposits of fat, oxidized LDL cholesterol, cytokines (mediators of inflammation), macrophages (white blood cells that oxidize LDL cholesterol), foam cells, cellular debris, calcium, and fibrin on the inner linings of the arterial wall. These deposits, known as **plaque,** result in a narrowing of the blood channel, making it easier for blood clots to form and eventually resulting in complete blockages of blood flow to vital tissues such as the heart or the brain. Additionally, inflammatory processes precipitated by cytokines are now recognized to play a central role in the pathogenesis of atherosclerosis by interacting with serum cholesterol and serving as an initiating factor in plaque buildup. Figure 5.12 illustrates the gradual, progressive narrowing of the arterial channel. Figure 5.13 presents a schematic of the content of arterial plaque.

Atherosclerosis is a slow, progressive disease that begins in childhood and usually manifests itself later in life. Because of its prevalence in industrialized society, scientists throughout the world have been conducting intensive research to identify the cause or

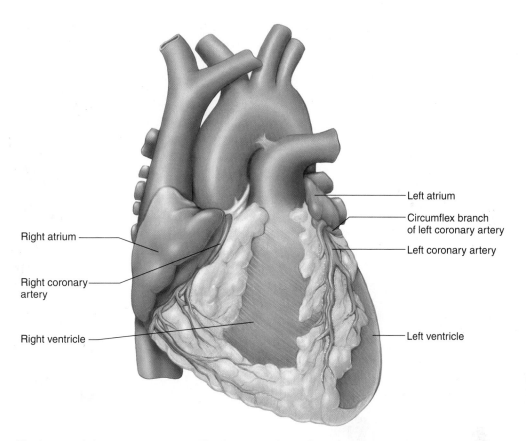

Right atrium

Right coronary
artery

Right ventricle

Left atrium

Circumflex branch
of left coronary artery

Left coronary artery

Left ventricle

FIGURE 5.11 The heart and the coronary arteries. The heart muscle itself receives its blood supply from the coronary arteries. The main coronary arteries are the left coronary artery, one of its branches named the circumflex, and the right coronary artery. Atherosclerosis of these arteries leads to coronary heart disease.

causes of atherosclerosis and coronary heart disease. The actual cause has not yet been completely identified, but considerable evidence has identified factors that may predispose an individual.

As noted previously, a risk factor represents a statistical relationship between two items such as high serum cholesterol and heart attack. This does not mean that a cause and effect relationship exists, although such a relationship is often strongly supported by the available evidence. The three principal risk factors associated with CHD are high blood pressure, high serum cholesterol levels, and cigarette smoking. Several major professional and governmental health organizations also believe that physical inactivity is a fourth principal risk factor. Other interacting risk factors are heredity, diabetes, diet, obesity, age, gender, stress, and several others, particularly several blood markers such as homocysteine and C-reactive protein (CRP). Homocysteine is discussed in chapter 7. CRP is a marker for inflammation. A guide to assessing your risk factor profile may be found on the American Heart Association Website, www.AMHRT.org.

How do the different forms of serum lipids affect the development of atherosclerosis?

In atherosclerosis, the plaque that develops in the arterial walls is composed partly of fats and cholesterol. Hence, high levels of blood lipids (triglycerides and cholesterol) are associated with

increased plaque formation. However, as you recall, triglycerides and cholesterol may be transported in the blood in a variety of ways but primarily as constituents of lipoproteins. Considerable research has been devoted to identifying those specific lipoproteins and other lipid components that may predispose to CHD, and although there is some debate about the meaningfulness of specific serum lipid profiles, some theories prevail.

The major villain appears to be serum cholesterol, as depicted in figure 5.14. Total cholesterol, expressed in milligrams per 100 milliliters of blood, is a significant risk factor. As noted in table 5.7, a cholesterol level below 200 is considered to be desirable, between 200 and 239 is borderline-high, and above 240 is high. However, you should be aware that there is a rather large standard error of measurement involved in some tests of cholesterol, being on the order of 30 milligrams. What this means is that if your blood cholesterol is reported as 220 (borderline-high), it may be possible that you actually have a cholesterol level of 190 (desirable) or 250 (high) if you vary, respectively, one standard error below or above your actual measurement of 220. For this reason, it may be a good idea to have a second test completed if you are concerned with your total cholesterol level.

The form by which cholesterol is transported in your blood may also be related to the development of atherosclerosis. In general, a high level of low-density lipoproteins (LDL) is the major risk factor associated with atherosclerosis. A current theory

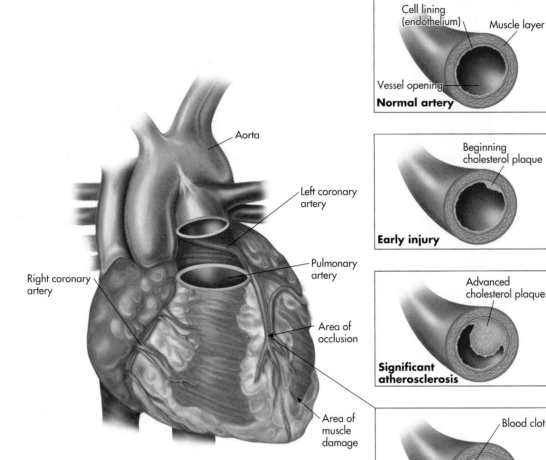

Normal artery
Cell lining (endothelium)
Muscle layer
Vessel opening

Early injury
Beginning cholesterol plaque

Significant atherosclerosis
Advanced cholesterol plaque

Complete blockage
Blood clot

Aorta

Left coronary artery

Right coronary artery

Pulmonary artery

Area of occlusion

Area of muscle damage

FIGURE 5.12 The developmental process of atherosclerosis and thrombosis. Deposits of cholesterol and other debris (plaque) accumulate in the inner lining of the artery, leading to a decrease or cessation of blood flow to the tissues. Atherosclerosis in the coronary arteries is a major cause of heart disease.

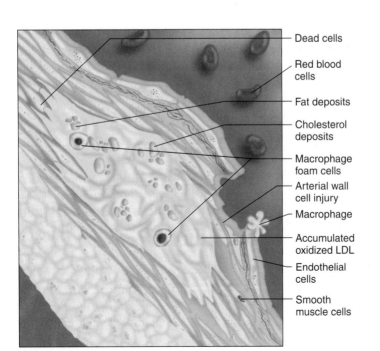

Dead cells

Red blood cells

Fat deposits

Cholesterol deposits

Macrophage foam cells

Arterial wall cell injury

Macrophage

Accumulated oxidized LDL

Endothelial cells

Smooth muscle cells

suggests various forms of LDL, such as small, dense LDL and the variant lipoprotein (a), may be more prone to oxidation by macrophages at an injured site in the arterial epithelium, leading to an influx into the cell wall and the formation of plaque. The presence of oxygen free radicals has been suggested to accelerate this process. Other mechanisms, such as increased clotting ability, may be operative. As noted in table 5.7, LDL levels less than 100 are optimal, while those above 160 pose a high risk and those above 190 a very high risk. Although not normally listed in risk factor tables, lipoprotein (a) values greater than 25–30 milligrams per deciliter of blood are associated with increased risk of CHD. A high level of IDL (which some consider a form of LDL) is also recognized as a risk factor, as is apolipoprotein B, involved in cholesterol transport to the tissues.

FIGURE 5.13 An enlargement of atherosclerotic plaque. Oxidized LDL cholesterol, macrophages, foam cells, fibrous material, and other debris collect beneath the endothelial cells lining the coronary artery. The site of the plaque may be initiated by some form of injury to the cell lining, possibly an ulceration as shown.

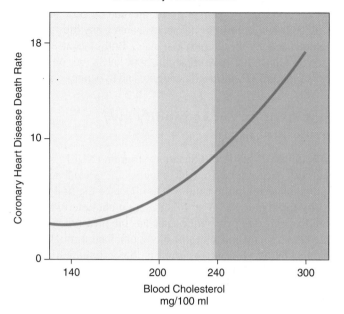

The Relationship of Blood Cholesterol
to Coronary Heart Disease

FIGURE 5.14 A desirable blood cholesterol is below 200 milligrams per deciliter (mg/dl). The rise of coronary heart disease fatalities increases progressively in individuals with borderline-high (200–240 mg/dl) and high blood cholesterol (> 240 mg/dl).

Source: U.S. Department of Health and Human Services, Public Health Service, National Institutes of Health, "So you have high blood cholesterol . . .," in *NIH Publication No. 8972922,* 1989, U.S. Government Printing Office, Washington, D.C.

Conversely, high levels of high-density lipoproteins (HDL), particularly the subfraction HDL_2 and HDL with apolipoprotein A-I, appear to be protective against the development of atherosclerosis, although research is continuing to explore other relationships. Levels of 60 milligrams or more of HDL appear to be protective, but because HDL varies daily, several measurements over time may be required to obtain an accurate reading. Research suggests that HDL interacts with the arterial epithelium, acting as a scavenger by picking up cholesterol from the arterial wall and transporting it to the liver for removal from the body, known as reverse cholesterol transport. HDL may also inhibit LDL oxidation and platelet aggregation. HDL_2 levels are higher in women until menopause and then decrease, with an associated increased risk for CHD.

The Consumers Union notes that although once the subject of controversy, an increased level of serum triglycerides is now firmly established as an independent risk factor for CHD. Also, it is often associated with increased levels of LDL, particularly the small, dense LDL, and decreased levels of HDL. Current guidelines for the National Cholesterol Education Program (NCEP) indicate triglyceride levels below 150 milligrams per deciliter are normal, whereas the risk associated with progressively increasing levels goes from borderline high to very high (see table 5.7). However, the Consumers Union notes that the risk may be greater at lower levels, even at 100 milligrams, in individuals with other risk factors.

A summary of serum lipid factors associated with increased risk of atherosclerosis is presented in table 5.8, representing new guidelines from the National Cholesterol Education Program.

If your total blood cholesterol is borderline or high, a determination of the LDL and HDL levels may be desirable, for they provide additional information relative to your risk. Based on epidemiological data, several ratios have been developed to assess risk of CHD, with the lower the ratio, the lower the risk.

One common comparison is the ratio of total cholesterol (TC) to the HDL level, or TC/HDL. A ratio of about 4.5 is associated with an average risk for CHD. For example, an individual with a total cholesterol of 200 and an HDL of 60 would have a ratio of 3.33 (200/60), or a lower risk, while someone with the same total cholesterol but an HDL of 20 would have a much higher risk with a ratio of 10 (200/20).

Another comparison is the ratio of LDL to HDL, or LDL/HDL. An LDL to HDL ratio of about 3.5 is considered to be an average risk for CHD. Thus, a ratio of 140/60, or 2.3, would be a much lower risk than 140/20, or 7.0.

Additional tests are merited for those at high risk for CHD. Special lipoprotein tests may measure density levels of the various lipoproteins. Tests for other markers of atherosclerosis, such as homocysteine and CRP, will add to the diagnosis. For example, Ridker and others recently noted that high CRP levels may be more effective predictors of heart attacks than high LDL-cholesterol levels, but the greatest risk is when both are high.

Can I reduce my serum lipid levels and possibly reverse atherosclerosis?

Several approaches may help you improve your serum lipid levels and reduce the risk of atherosclerosis. A healthy lifestyle is one, and appropriate drug therapy is another. However, even with a healthy lifestyle some individuals may have poor serum lipid profiles. Certain forms of hypercholesteremia are genetic in nature. In the future, gene therapy may be the treatment of choice for such individuals, possibly manipulating genes to decrease LDL and increase HDL.

TABLE 5.7 Recommended fasting lipoprotein profile* of the National Cholesterol Education Program

Total cholesterol	LDL-cholesterol	HDL-cholesterol	Triglycerides
Less than 200—desirable	Less than 100—optimal	Less than 40—low	Less than 150—normal
200–239—borderline high	100–129—near optimal	60 or above—protective	151–199—borderline high
240 or above—high	130–159—borderline high		200–499—high
	160–189—high		500 and above—very high
	190 and above—very high		

*Fasting levels expressed in mg/dl; testing recommended every 5 years for those over 20

TABLE 5.8 Serum lipid factors associated with increased risk of atherosclerosis

High levels of total cholesterol
High levels of LDL-cholesterol
High levels of dense form of LDL-cholesterol
High levels of IDL-cholesterol
High levels of abnormal lipoprotein, lipoprotein (a)
High levels of apolipoprotein B
High levels of triglycerides
Low levels of HDL-cholesterol
Low levels of HDL$_2$-cholesterol
Low levels of apolipoprotein A-I

Currently, drug therapy may be required to reduce serum lipid levels in genetically predisposed individuals, as well as in those with poor diets. Some drugs stimulate liver degradation and excretion of cholesterol, others increase lipoprotein lipase activity or LDL receptor function to decrease serum triglyceride levels, while still others may bind with bile salts in the intestines so that they are not reabsorbed; because bile salts are derived from cholesterol, it is effectively excreted from the body. Statins, drugs that inhibit an enzyme (HMG-CoA reductase) that regulates cholesterol, have been particularly effective to reduce serum LDL-cholesterol. For more detail on types of drug therapy and their overall effectiveness, the interested reader is referred to the reviews by Hunninghake and Bucher and others.

The National Cholesterol Education Program indicated that individuals at high risk for cardiovascular disease might consider getting their LDL levels as low as possible and could explore with their doctor the possibility of taking lipid-lowering drugs; table 5.9 provides some guidelines. However, even if on drug therapy, individuals should not abandon a healthy lifestyle.

Adopting a healthier lifestyle is the first step in attempts to improve one's serum lipid profile. A healthy lifestyle may not only help to prevent the development of atherosclerosis, but may also lead to regression of coronary artery blockage. In their review, Greg Brown and others noted that the available data support the hypothesis that lowering of serum lipids may lead to the regression of atherosclerotic lesions and elicit improved clinical effects. For those who are interested in preventing the development of atherosclerosis or reversing its progress, an appropriate diet and exercise program, as discussed below, are two key elements of a healthy lifestyle that are recommended by health professionals. Both factors may have favorable effects not only on serum lipid levels, but on other risk factors for CHD as well, such as obesity and hypertension.

What should I eat to modify my serum lipid profile favorably?

The National Cholesterol Education Program (NCEP) was developed with the general goal of reducing the prevalence of high serum cholesterol in the United States. One of the first steps is to identify those individuals with high serum cholesterol by various simplified screening techniques, such as the measurement of total cholesterol by small samples of blood obtained through fingertip capillary blood. If this measure is borderline-high (200–239 mg/dl) or high (> 240 mg/dl), venous blood samples may be taken to determine LDL and HDL levels. If high serum cholesterol levels are detected, dietary modifications and other appropriate lifestyle changes may be recommended.

Figure 5.15 illustrates the composition of the average American diet and the Step 1 diet of the NCEP. Although the differences between the two diets appear to be small, such changes may reduce serum lipids. A sensible plan to reduce serum lipid levels is presented in figure 5.16, and representative results are shown in figure 5.17. If the original dietary plan is not effective after several months, the Step 2 NCEP diet may be recommended, which is essentially the same as the Step 1 diet but with less than 7 percent of the dietary Calories from saturated fat and less than 200 milligrams of cholesterol per day. Two recent meta-analyses revealed that the NCEP diet plan significantly decreased total blood cholesterol, and may have multiple beneficial effects on major cardiovascular risk factors.

Several health organizations, including the American Heart Association, the National Institutes of Health, and the National Heart, Lung, and Blood Institute have recommended a number of dietary guidelines that have been shown to lower serum cholesterol or serum triglycerides.

TABLE 5.9 National Serum Cholesterol Guidelines

Risk Category	Heart Disease Risk Factors	Target LDL in Milligrams/deciliter	Take Drugs if LDL is
Low	Those with zero or one heart diease risk factor	Less than 160	190 or higher
Moderate	Those with two or more risk factors and less than a 10% to 20% risk of heart attack within 10 years	Less than 130	160 or higher
Moderately High	Those with two or more risk factors and a 10% to 20% risk of heart attack within 10 years	Less than 130 (optional goal 100)	130 or higher
High	Those who have heart diease or diabetes, or have two or more risk factors that give them greater than a 20% chance of a heart attack within 10 years	Less than 100 (optional goal 70)	100 or higher

Source: National Cholesterol Education Program Guidelines

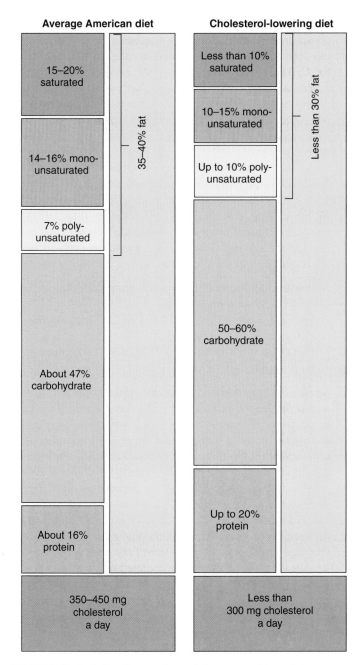

FIGURE 5.15 Comparison of the composition of the average American diet to the National Cholesterol Education Program Step 1 cholesterol-lowering diet.

Source: U.S. Department of Health and Human Services.

Based on the available scientific evidence, the following guidelines appear to be prudent and are consistent with the recent National Academy of Sciences recommendations for dietary fat. Although these guidelines have been developed to help individuals reduce high serum lipid profiles, they will also help to maintain normal levels and thus may be regarded as preventive medicine. As you may note, these recommendations are extensions of some guidelines for the Prudent Healthy Diet. Each guideline may be used to select foods that appeal to personal tastes. King and Gibney noted that individuals are more likely to eat a healthful diet if

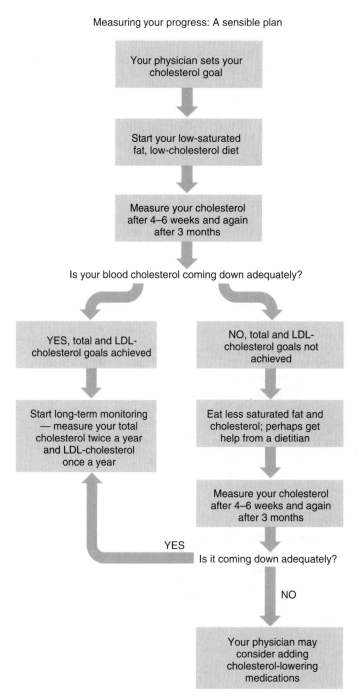

FIGURE 5.16 A sensible plan to monitor the effects of a cholesterol-lowering diet. The initial diet plan may involve the National Cholesterol Education Program Step 1 diet, but if unsuccessful, the Step 2 diet may be implemented. In individuals highly resistant to dietary modifications, drug therapy may be prescribed.

Source: U.S. Department of Health and Human Services.

it includes foods they enjoy. It should be noted that in the near future, the application of nutrigenomics may permit individualized dietary recommendations. Menus may be tailored to the genetic profile of each individual to maximize dietary effects favorable to the lipid profile and prevention of CHD, and prevention of other chronic disease as well.

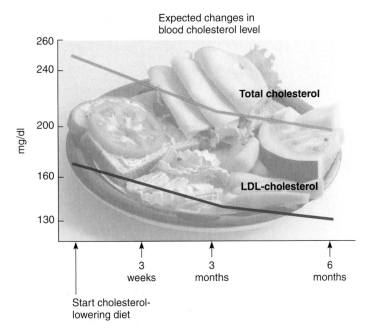

Expected changes in
blood cholesterol level

Total cholesterol

LDL-cholesterol

mg/dl

260

240

200

160

130

3
weeks

3
months

6
months

Start cholesterol-
lowering diet

FIGURE 5.17 Representative expected changes in total serum cholesterol and LDL cholesterol associated with appropriate dietary modifications, such as switching from the typical American diet to the Step 1 diet of the National Cholesterol Education Program (NCEP).

Source: U.S. Department of Health and Human Services.

1. *Adjust caloric intake to achieve and maintain ideal body weight.* One of the most common causes of high triglyceride levels is too much body fat, particularly in the abdominal region. The health risks of obesity are detailed in chapter 10. In many cases, simply losing body weight or reducing caloric intake will reduce these levels.

2. *Reduce the total amount of fats in the diet.* As mentioned previously, eating moderate amounts of fat, less than 30 percent of dietary Calories, is the recommended goal. Reducing the total amount of fat will usually reduce the amount of Calories also, but nutrient content will actually improve. Reducing total fat intake to 20 percent or even 10 percent of total daily Calories will reduce total and LDL-cholesterol even more. However, a very low-fat diet (10 percent fat Calories) may actually cause a negative lipid profile in some individuals. To help prevent this, the carbohydrate Calories that replace the fat Calories should *not* be derived from refined carbohydrates, but rather from complex carbohydrates containing dietary fiber.

   The Consumers Union, summarizing a report by 50 nutrition researchers, indicated fat intake need not be restricted drastically in the diet, as long as you watch the type of fat in your diet (discussion follows) and your total caloric intake.

3. *Reduce the amount of saturated fat to less than 10 percent of dietary Calories.* As a matter of fact, scientists recommend reducing intake of saturated fats as low as possible while consuming a nutritionally adequate diet. The National Academy of Sciences indicated that there is a positive linear trend

between total saturated fatty acid intake and total and LDL cholesterol concentration and increased risk of CHD. Saturated fats may also increase blood clotting, another risk factor for CHD. In two recent meta-analyses, Howell and others found that consumption of saturated fatty acids was the major dietary determinant of plasma cholesterol response to diet, while Clarke and others indicated that reducing the intake of saturated fat produced the most significant benefits regarding the prevention of CHD.

Animal foods may contain significant amounts of saturated fat. The biggest contributor of saturated fat to the American diet is hamburger meat, even if it is labeled lean. However, lean cuts of meat may contain relatively low amounts of fat and saturated fat. Note the following comparison for one serving (4 ounces) of hamburger (ground beef) containing various percentages of fat:

> Regular hamburger (25%) = 331 Calories, 28 grams of fat (10.7 grams saturated fat)
> Lean hamburger (15%) = 243 Calories, 17 grams of fat (6.6 grams saturated fat)
> Extra lean hamburger (5%) = 155 Calories, 5.6 grams of fat (2.5 grams saturated fat)

4. *Reduce the consumption of trans fats and, comparable to saturated fat, keep dietary intake as low as possible.* The combined total of dietary saturated and *trans* fats should not exceed 10 percent of daily caloric intake. In a recent review, Lichtenstein noted that *trans* fats elevate LDL-cholesterol, and at relatively high intakes decrease HDL-cholesterol levels. Some data suggest *trans* fatty acids may also trigger inflammation. The National Academy of Sciences also noted that, like saturated fats, there is a positive linear trend between *trans* fat and CHD. Although some reviewers contend that the adverse effects of *trans* fatty acids are somewhat less than those associated with saturated fatty acids, the Consumers Union recently cited research indicating that they may be as bad, or even worse.

   To decrease *trans* fat intake, you need to know what foods contain it. Although we know that meat and dairy products contain small amounts of *trans* fats, the Consumers Union has referred to *trans* fat as the "stealth" fat because we may not realize it is in the foods we eat. The vast majority of *trans* fat consumed by Americans is in processed foods, particularly margarine; vegetable shortening; white bread; packaged goods such as cookies, crackers, potato chips, and cakes; and fried fast foods such as french fries. The major component of each of these foods that adds *trans* fatty acids is usually partially hydrogenated vegetable oil. *Trans* fatty acid content per serving is now listed in the Nutrition Facts food label.

5. *Substitute monounsaturated fats for saturated fats.* Consume about 10–15 percent of Calories from monounsaturated fats. Although no DRI have been set for monounsaturated fats, the National Academy of Sciences notes that they may have some benefit in the prevention of chronic disease.

The Mediterranean diet is rich in monounsaturated fatty acids. One staple in the Mediterranean diet is olive oil, and Stark and Madar indicated that it may be a healthful functional food. Olive oil is not only rich in monounsaturated fatty acids but is also a good source of various phytochemicals and the antioxidant vitamin E. Mediterranean-type diets have been associated with reductions in total and LDL-cholesterol levels without decreases in HDL-cholesterol, and may also decrease blood clotting, factors that may help prevent CHD. A *qualified* health claim, for use on food labels, has recently been accepted, indicating that eating two tablespoons of olive oil daily may, due to its monounsaturated fat content, reduce the risk of CHD.

These effects may be associated with consuming a MUFA-rich diet, but such diets also tend to be low in saturated fats so it may be that the MUFAs are substituting for the saturated fatty acids. The American Heart Association provided their stamp of approval to diets rich in MUFAs, provided saturated fatty acid intake is limited to a minimum and caloric intake is in balance. Other than olive oil, avocados, nuts, and canola oil are rich sources of MUFAs.

6. *Consume adequate amounts of polyunsaturated fatty acids.* As indicated previously, the National Academy of Sciences developed an AI for both the omega-6 and omega-3 polyunsaturated fatty acids because there may be some health benefits associated with such dietary intakes. Both types of fatty acids help promote healthy skin and are a source of various eicosanoids that may influence health processes. When substituted for saturated fat, polyunsaturated fat may reduce total serum cholesterol, including LDL cholesterol.

Polyunsaturated fatty acids should constitute about 10 percent of the daily caloric intake, and if foods are selected wisely this should provide adequate amounts of both omega-6 and omega-3 fatty acids. The essential omega-6 linoleic fatty acid is found in various vegetable oils that constitute food products such as margarine, salad dressings, and cooking oils. Several sources are listed in table 5.10. The essential omega-3 alpha-linolenic fatty acid is found in green leafy vegetables, canola oil, flaxseed oil, soy products, some nuts, and fish. Some nuts are especially rich in both the omega-3 and omega-6 fatty acids. Although both essential fatty acids may confer separate health benefits, the omega-3 fatty acids are thought to be more important for the prevention of CHD.

The three principal omega-3 fatty acids—alpha-linolenic, EPA (eicosapentaenoic acid), and DHA (docasahexaenoic acid)—are believed to reduce the risk of CHD, but EPA and DHA are believed to be more potent. EPA and DHA may be formed in the body from alpha-linolenic acid, but this process appears to be limited. However, both EPA and DHA are found in substantial quantities in various fish oils, as highlighted in table 5.11. Eggs from chickens fed a special diet may contain DHA in amounts ranging from 0.05–0.15 grams, but the eggs are still high in cholesterol. Fish oil supplements may contain 0.3–0.5 grams.

As mentioned earlier, omega-3 fatty acids have been theorized to be ergogenic in nature because of the production of specific eicosanoids. Omega-3 fatty acids are also being studied for their potential health benefits, which also may be related to specific eicosanoids that are produced. Although the health-related role of omega-3 fatty acids and eicosanoids is complex and has not been totally determined, here is a simple summarization. The cell membrane contains a variety of molecular compounds, including phospholipids and their associated fatty acids. When the diet is high in linoleic acid, one of the main fatty acids in the phospholipids is arachidonic acid, which produces one form of eicosanoids when it is metabolized. When the diet is high in fish oils, EPA and DHA become the major source of eicosanoids, which are different in nature compared to those derived from arachidonic acid. In essence, the different forms of eicosanoids function as local hormones

TABLE 5.10 Alpha-linolenic content of selected oils, nuts, and seeds

Oils, Nuts, and Seeds	Alpha-linolenic content, grams/tablespoon
Olive oil	0.1
Walnuts, English	0.7
Soybean oil	0.9
Canola oil	1.3
Walnut oil	1.4
Flaxseed	2.2
Flaxseed (linseed) oil	8.5

Source: USDA Nutrient Data Laboratory.

TABLE 5.11 Grams of EPA and DHA in fish per 3-ounce edible fish portion and in fish oils per gram of oil

> 1 gram/ 3 ounces	0.5–1.0 gram/ 3 ounces	< 0.5 gram/ 3 ounces
Herring	Halibut	Catfish
Oysters, Pacific	Omega-3 concentrate*	Cod
Salmon, Atlantic, farmed	Salmon, sockeye	Cod liver oil*
Salmon, Atlantic, wild	Trout	Crab
Salmon, chinook	Tuna, fresh	Flounder/Sole
Sardines	Tuna, white, canned in water	Haddock
		Lobster
		Oysters, Eastern
		Scallops
		Shrimp
		Tuna, light, canned in water

*Note: Omega-3 content in fish oils or supplement is per gram of oil. Check supplement labels for content.

Source: Adapted from USDA Nutrient Data Laboratory. Ranges listed are rough estimates because oil content can vary markedly with species, season, diet, and packaging and cooking methods.

in body cells affecting metabolism and gene expression, and the effects associated with omega-3 fatty acid-derived eicosanoids appear to provide some health benefits.

Epidemiological research has suggested populations that consume diets rich in fish products have a lower incidence rate of CHD, and experimental research has suggested a number of possible mechanisms underlying this relationship. Omega-3 fatty acids may reduce serum triglycerides and may increase HDL-cholesterol, although they appear to have no effect on total serum cholesterol. Eicosanoids derived from omega-3 fatty acids may also decrease platelet aggregation and stickiness, possibly helping to prevent clot formation. They may improve vascular tone and decrease blood viscosity. They may optimize blood pressure and decrease abnormal heart rhythms. They may also possess anti-inflammatory activity. Collectively, all of these effects could help prevent CHD. Just as there are good and bad forms of cholesterol, there may be good and bad forms of eicosanoids, at least as related to cardiovascular health. Some preliminary research suggests they may be helpful in preventing the development of type 2 diabetes as well as the dementia (loss of intellectual functions; behavior change) associated with aging. On the other hand, a recent extensive review by MacLean and others concluded that supplementation with omega-3 fatty acids is unlikely to prevent cancer.

Numerous studies have reported the beneficial health effects of omega-3 fatty acids. In a recent meta-analysis, Studer and others concluded that consumption of omega-3 fatty acids were effective as a means of preventing mortality from cardiovascular disease, and the risk ratio was even lower than that for statin drug therapy. A *qualified* health claim was recently passed, indicating that supportive, but not conclusive, research shows that consumption of omega-3 fatty acids may reduce the risk of coronary heart disease.

Based on the available evidence, Kris-Etherton and others provided some dietary guidelines in the American Heart Association Scientific Statement: Fish Consumption, Fish Oil, Omega-3 Fatty Acids, and Cardiovascular Disease. The key points are:

- Eat fish, particularly fatty fish, at least two times a week. Fatty fish like mackerel, lake trout, herring, sardines, albacore tuna, and salmon are high in EPA and DHA.
- Eat plant foods rich in the alpha-linolenic acid, an omega-3 fatty acid that may be converted to EPA and DHA in the body.
- Individuals who have high serum triglycerides may benefit from a fish oil supplement of 2–4 grams of EPA and DHA per day. Patients with CHD may benefit but should consult with their physicians.

Although eating more fish and fish oils is a healthful recommendation, there are some caveats. Some types of fish may contain significant amounts of mercury, which may harm the nervous system if consumed in excess. Some types of fish may also contain environmental contaminants, particularly older, larger predatory fish such as shark and farmed fish such as Atlantic salmon. Based on these health risks, the AHA indicated that the benefits and risks of eating fish depend on a person's stage in life:

- Children and pregnant and nursing women may be at higher risk of exposure to excessive mercury in fish. The FDA indicates that pregnant women and small children should limit the intake of shark, swordfish, king mackerel, and tilefish, and limit consumption of other fish to no more than 12 ounces a week.
- For middle-aged and older men, and women after menopause, the benefits of eating fish far outweigh the risks.

Selecting fresh, local seafood where available, and eating a wide variety of fish will help minimize any potential adverse effects of environmental pollutants. Five of the most commonly eaten fish that are low in mercury are canned light tuna, shrimp, Pollock, catfish, and salmon. With salmon, peel away the skin before cooking it. Select fish oil supplements with care, and be aware that a recent report by ConsumerLab.com indicated that many fish oil supplements contained much less fish oil than indicated on the label. Additionally, excess intake of omega-3 fatty acids may cause excessive bleeding in some individuals. A physician should be consulted if this is a concern.

Conjugated linoleic acid (CLA), a polyunsaturated omega-6 fatty acid found naturally in small amounts in dairy foods and beef, has been studied for its potential to reduce body fat. However, Gaullier and others reported that while CLA supplementation did induce a small weight loss, subjects experienced adverse changes in serum cholesterol markers for heart disease. The role of CLA in weight control will be discussed further in chapter 10, but those at risk for CHD might be advised not to use it.

7. *Limit the amount of dietary cholesterol.* In recent years some have contended that dietary cholesterol does not influence serum cholesterol and the development of CHD. For example, Hasler noted it is now known that there is little if any connection between dietary cholesterol and blood cholesterol levels, and consuming up to one or more eggs per day does not adversely affect blood cholesterol levels. On the other hand, in a meta-analysis covering 17 studies that evaluated cholesterol intake for at least 14 days, Weggemans and others noted that the addition of 100 milligrams of dietary cholesterol per day would increase slightly the ratio of total cholesterol to HDL-cholesterol, an adverse effect on the serum cholesterol profile. They concluded that the advice to limit cholesterol intake by reducing consumption of eggs and other cholesterol-rich foods may still be valid.

Limiting cholesterol intake is particularly important for cholesterol responders, those individuals with a genetic predisposition whose body production of cholesterol does not automatically decrease when the dietary intake increases. The average U.S. daily intake is approximately 400–500 milligrams or more. The American Heart Association recommends that this amount be reduced to 300 milligrams per day or less, or 100 milligrams per 1,000 Calories consumed.

8. *If you consume foods with artificial fats, do so in moderation.* The fat substitutes discussed earlier in this chapter are generally recognized as safe and have been approved by the Food and Drug Administration (FDA). Although Olestra has been approved by the FDA, some contend that its use may interfere with the absorption of several fat-soluble vitamins and beta-carotene. However, the FDA requires that products containing olestra-type fat substitutes be enriched with fat-soluble vitamins to offset potential losses.

Snack foods containing olestra, particularly when consumed in large amounts, may cause intestinal cramps and loose stools. McRorie and others reported that although olestra-containing potato chips induced a gradual stool softening effect after several days of consumption, when consumed in smaller amounts, such as 20–40 grams, there were no objective measures of diarrhea or increased gastrointestinal symptoms. Nevertheless, the Center for Science in the Public Interest noted that the FDA received over 18,000 adverse-reaction reports from people who had eaten olestra-containing foods. Sales of such foods have dropped dramatically.

In its position statement, the American Dietetic Association (ADA) concludes that the majority of fat replacers, when used in moderation by adults, can be safe and useful adjuncts to lowering the fat content of foods and may play a role in decreasing total dietary energy and fat intake. However, the ADA notes that they are effective only if they lower the total caloric content of the food and if the consumer used these foods as part of a balanced meal plan, such as that promoted in the 2005 Dietary Guidelines for Americans.

Some fat is needed in the diet to provide the essential fatty acids and fat-soluble vitamins, and this fat should be obtained easily through natural, wholesome foods such as whole grains, fruits, and vegetables. Following such appropriate guidelines, the American Diabetes Association indicated that foods with fat replacers have the potential to help people with diabetes reduce total and saturated fat intake and may help improve the serum lipid profile. Another possible health benefit of fat substitutes may be their application in weight-loss programs. This topic will be covered in chapter 11.

9. *Reduce intake of refined sugars and increase consumption of foods high in complex carbohydrates and dietary fiber, particularly water-soluble fiber.* Table sugar provokes higher triglyceride concentrations more than complex carbohydrates with fiber do. Again, the value of complex carbohydrates in the diet is stressed, particularly high-fiber foods, as a means to help reduce serum cholesterol. Research has suggested that without adequate amounts of fiber, a diet low in saturated fats and cholesterol has only modest effects on lowering CHD risk. Thus, replace high-fat foods with high-fiber foods. Legumes, such as beans, are an excellent source of carbohydrate and water-soluble fiber. Beans also contain protein, and soy protein, as found in products such as tofu, has been shown to reduce cholesterol in men with both normal and high serum cholesterol. Oat products, such as found in oatmeal, may effectively lower serum cholesterol. Increased consumption of fruits and vegetables is recommended as well, for they may provide substantial amounts of the antioxidant vitamins (C, E, and beta-carotene) that may help to prevent undesired oxidations in the body. Guidelines presented in the preceding chapter are helpful to increase carbohydrate intake, and the role of antioxidant vitamins will be discussed in chapter 7.

Plant foods, such as almonds and oats, may also contain various sterols and stanols, which are known to reduce serum cholesterol. Vanstone and others found that plant sterols and stanols, blended into a butter component, could reduce total and LDL-cholesterol in hypercholesterolemic individuals. Commercial margarines such as Benecol and Take Control contain such plant stanols and sterols, and an Arbor Clinical Nutrition report indicated that a dietary intake of 2–3 grams per day of plant sterols usually produces a 10–15 percent fall in LDL-cholesterol. As noted in chapter 2, a health claim associating a diet rich in plant sterols and stanols may reduce the risk of heart disease. Plant foods also contain several phytochemicals that may reduce serum cholesterol. Many food manufacturers, such as those who produce breakfast cereals, are fortifying their products with sterols, stanols, phytochemicals, and other nutrients, creating functional foods designed to reduce serum cholesterol and provide other health benefits as well.

10. *Nibble food throughout the day.* Interestingly, David Jenkins showed a significant reduction in serum LDL cholesterol if subjects consumed their daily Calories, actually the same food, throughout the day rather than in three concentrated meals at breakfast, lunch, and dinner. Additionally, the Consumers Union recently reported that a single high-fat meal may increase your short-term risk of heart attack, noting that 5 hours after a high-fat meal men had doubled their pre-meal blood levels of triglycerides; and blood flow through their hearts dropped substantially, possibly because of the increase in artery-clogging triglycerides.

In simple practical terms, what do all of these recommendations mean? You should not eliminate all fat from your diet, but simply reduce the amount of fat that you eat. In essence, eat less butter, fatty meats, organ foods such as liver and kidney, egg yolks, whole milk, cheeses, ice cream, gravies, creamed foods, high-fat desserts, and refined sugar. Eat more lean meats, fish, poultry, egg whites, skim and low-fat milk products, fruits and vegetables, beans, and whole-grain products, or the Prudent Healthy Diet. Table 5.11 provides some specifics.

You may have noted that alcohol intake was not one of these recommendations. As detailed in chapter 13, low-risk alcohol intake may provide some protection against CHD for those who do drink. However, most health professionals do not recommend that nondrinkers begin to consume alcohol for its potential health benefits because of other health risks associated with drinking in excess.

TABLE 5.11 Food selections to decrease total dietary fat, saturated fat, and cholesterol

	Choose	Go easy on	Decrease
Meat, poultry, fish and shellfish (up to 6 ounces a day)	Lean cuts of meat with fat trimmed, like: beef—round, sirloin, chuck, loin lamb—leg, arm, loin, rib pork—tenderloin, leg (fresh), shoulder (arm or picnic) veal—all trimmed cuts except ground poultry without skin fish, shellfish		"Prime" grade fatty cuts of meat like: beef—corned beef brisket, regular ground short ribs pork—spareribs, blade roll Goose, domestic duck Organ meats like: liver, kidney, sweetbreads, brain Sausage, bacon, frankfurters, regular luncheon meats Caviar, roe
Dairy products (2 servings a day; 3 servings for women who are pregnant or breast-feeding)	Skim milk, 1% milk, low-fat buttermilk, low-fat evaporated or nonfat milk Low-fat yogurt and low-fat frozen yogurt Low-fat soft cheeses, like: cottage, farmer, pot Cheese labeled no more than 2 to 6 grams of fat an ounce	2% milk Part-skim ricotta Part-skim or imitation hard cheeses, like: part-skim mozzarella "Light" cream cheese "Light" sour cream	Whole milk, like: regular, evaporated, condensed Cream, half-and-half, most nondairy creamers and products, real or nondairy whipped cream Cream cheese, sour cream, ice cream, custard-style yogurt Whole-milk ricotta High-fat cheeses, like: Neufchatel, Brie, Swiss, American, mozzarella, feta, cheddar, Muenster
Eggs (no more than 3 egg yolks a week)	Egg whites Cholesterol-free egg substitutes		Egg yolks
Fats and oils (up to 6 to 8 teaspoons a day)	Unsaturated vegetable oils, like: corn, olive, peanut, rapeseed (canola oil), safflower, sesame, soybean Margarine or shortening made with unsaturated fats listed above: liquid, tub, stick Diet mayonnaise, salad dressings made with unsaturated fats listed above Low-fat dressings	Nuts and seeds Avocados and olives	Butter, coconut oil, palm kernel oil, palm oil, lard, bacon fat Margarine or shortening made with saturated fats listed above Dressings made with egg yolk
Breads, cereals, pasta, rice, dried peas and beans (6 to 11 servings a day)	Breads, like: white, whole wheat, pumpernickel, and rye breads; sandwich buns; dinner rolls; bagels; English muffins; rice cakes Low-fat crackers, like: matzo, pita, bread sticks, rye krisp, saltines, zwieback Hot cereals, most cold dry cereals Pasta, like: plain noodles, spaghetti, macaroni Any grain rice Dried peas and beans, like: split peas, black-eyed peas, chickpeas, kidney beans, navy beans, black beans, lentils, soybeans, soybean curd (tofu)	Store-bought pancakes, waffles, biscuits, muffins, cornbread	Croissants, butter rolls, sweet rolls, Danish pastry, doughnuts Most snack crackers, like: cheese crackers, butter crackers, those made with saturated fats Granola-type cereals made with saturated fats Pasta and rice prepared with cream, butter, or cheese sauces, egg noodles

TABLE 5.11 Continued

	Choose	Go easy on	Decrease
Fruits and vegetables (2 to 4 servings of fruit and 3 to 5 servings of vegetables)	Fresh, frozen, canned, or dried fruits and vegetables		Vegetables prepared in butter, cream, or sauce
Sweets and snacks (avoid too many sweets)	Low-fat frozen desserts, like: sherbet, sorbet, Italian ice, frozen yogurt, popsicles Low-fat cakes, like: angel food cake Low-fat cookies, like: fig bars, gingersnaps Low-fat candy, like: jelly beans, hard candy Low-fat snacks, like: plain popcorn, pretzels Nonfat beverages, like: carbonated drinks, juices, tea, coffee	Frozen desserts, like: ice milk Homemade cakes, cookies, and pies using unsaturated oils sparingly Fruit crisps and cobblers Potato and corn chips prepared with unsaturated vegetable oil	High-fat frozen desserts, like: ice cream, frozen tofu High-fat cakes, like: most store-bought, pound, and frosted cake Store-bought pies, most store-bought cookies Most candy, like: chocolate bars Potato and corn chips prepared with saturated fat Buttered popcorn High-fat beverages, like: frappes, milkshakes, floats, eggnogs
Label ingredients (To avoid much fat, saturated fat, or cholesterol, go easy on products that list first any fat, oil, or ingredients higher in saturated fat or cholesterol. Choose more often those products that contain ingredients lower in fat, saturated fat, and cholesterol.)	Ingredients lower in saturated fat or cholesterol: Carob, cocoa Oils, like: corn, cottonseed, olive, safflower, sesame, soybean, sunflower Nonfat dry milk, nonfat dry milk solids, skim milk		Ingredients higher in saturated fat or cholesterol: Chocolate Animal fat, like: bacon, beef, ham, lamb, meat, pork, chicken or turkey fats, butter, lard Coconut, coconut oil, palm-kernel or palm oil Cream Egg and egg-yolk solids Hardened fat or oil Hydrogenated vegetable oil Shortening or vegetable shortening, unspecified vegetable oil (could be coconut, palm-kernel, palm)

Source: Adapted from "Report of the Expert Panel of Detection, Evaluation, and Treatment of High Blood Cholesterol in Adults." National Heart, Lung, and Blood Institutes of Health.

Can exercise training also elicit favorable changes in the serum lipid profile?

Physical inactivity, or lack of exercise, has been identified as one of the primary risk factors associated with an increased incidence of atherosclerosis and cardiovascular disease. Hence, exercise programs stressing aerobic endurance-type activities have been advocated as a means of reducing the incidence levels of these conditions, possibly via direct beneficial effects on the heart or blood vessels. However, the precise mechanism whereby exercise may help reduce the morbidity and mortality of CHD has not been identified. Therefore, many authorities believe that the beneficial effect may not be due to exercise itself, but rather the possible associated effects such as reductions in body fat and blood pressure. Although some investigators believe endurance exercise may have a preventive function independent of these associated effects, it also exerts a significant beneficial influence on the serum lipid profile, which, like blood pressure, is one of the major risk factors.

An acute bout of exercise may reduce risk factors for CHD. For example, Thompson and others recently noted that acute exercise may reduce blood pressure and serum triglycerides, increase HDL-cholesterol, and improve insulin sensitivity and glucose homeostasis. Thus, some of the beneficial effects of exercise on risk factors for CHD, including the serum lipid profile, may be attributed to recent exercise bouts. However, some of these benefits may become long-lasting with a chronic exercise training program.

Chronic exercise training has been shown to affect favorably the serum lipid profile. Literally hundreds of epidemiological and experimental studies have been conducted over the past several decades to investigate the effects of exercise on serum lipids. Space does not permit a detailed analysis of each, but major reviews of the worldwide literature have been reported by prominent authorities such as Stefanik and Wood, Leon and Sanchez, Durstine, and Williams. Although most of these reviews involved males, similar reviews have evaluated the effects of exercise training on women, such as those by Dowling and the recent meta-analysis by Kelley and others. These reviews have noted a rather consistent pattern relating exercise and blood lipids, and some of the benefits have been associated with concomitant body weight control. In general, increased levels of exercise are associated with lower plasma levels of triglycerides and higher levels of HDL. However, Durstine and others note that exercise training seldom alters total and LDL cholesterol, although some studies have shown small decreases in the latter. Moreover, research has shown that exercise may not improve the lipid profile of some individuals, primarily in those with genetic defects. These individuals may receive other health benefits of exercise, but may need drug therapy to control elevated serum lipid levels.

In an attempt to quantify the serum lipid changes with the amount of exercise, Durstine and his associates conducted a meta-analysis of well-controlled studies. One of the dose-response findings from their analysis indicated that an exercise training volume of 1200–2200 Calories per week is often effective at elevating HDL-C levels from 2–8 mg/dl and lowering triglyceride levels by 5–38 mg/dl. Their analysis also suggests greater increases in HDL-cholesterol can be expected with additional increases in exercise training volume. This amount of physical activity is reasonable and attainable for most individuals and is within the ACSM recommended range for healthy adults. Lifetime aerobic exercise appears to be the key, and moderately intense leisure-time activity, such as brisk walking, may elicit beneficial effects in men, women, children, and adolescents. As noted by Kelley and others, walking favorably affects the adult serum lipid profile independent of changes in body composition.

However, in women, extreme amounts of exercise combined with insufficient energy intake and leading to amenorrhea may reverse these benefits. The effects of exercise-induced amenorrhea will be discussed further in chapters 8 and 10, but it appears that the lower levels of estrogen associated with this condition may lead to lower levels of HDL-cholesterol.

Although the precise biochemical mechanisms underlying the beneficial effects of exercise on serum lipids have not been identified, researchers have found that in physically trained males and females, activity levels of several enzymes, such as hepatic lipase and lipoprotein lipase, are modified in such a way as to promote a more rapid catabolism of triglycerides and a greater production of HDL. The muscle cell membrane may be modified favorably to become more insulin sensitive, helping clear lipids from the blood into the muscle. Exercise may also favorably modify the serum lipid levels by helping the individual lose body fat or influencing changes in other aspects of his or her lifestyle, such as diet.

Research has revealed that the beneficial effects of exercise training are additive to a diet modified in fat content, such as one reduced in total and saturated fat. A low-fat diet will reduce total cholesterol and LDL-cholesterol but may also undesirably, decrease HDL-cholesterol. Exercise may prevent or attenuate the decrease in HDL-cholesterol on such diets, but when combined with omega-3 fatty acid supplementation may actually increase serum HDL-cholesterol as reported in a recent study by Thomas and others. Thus, the combination of both dietary modifications and exercise is the recommended approach to modify favorably serum lipid levels.

Recent research also reveals that highly trained endurance runners who increase their dietary fat to about 40 percent or more of daily caloric intake for 4 weeks do not experience any adverse effects in their blood lipid profiles. Although this type of diet is not recommended on a long-term basis, the review by Brown and Cox illustrates some of the protective effects of exercise training on serum lipid changes associated with short-term increases in dietary fat. They suggest that the strenuous physical training seems to metabolize the increased fat intake for energy and prevents adverse changes in the lipid profile.

APPLICATION EXERCISE

The American Heart Association established its Food Certification Program in 1995 to provide consumers an easy and reliable way to identify heart-healthy foods. Foods that display the distinctive red heart with the white check mark are evaluated to meet the Program's standards.

Go to your local supermarket and look for foods with labels that display the American Heart Association *heart-check mark,* as displayed here. Try to find foods in the different food groups, such as grains, fruits, vegetables, meats, and dairy. Make a list of foods you find in each of the food categories, and visit heartcheckmark.org to review the nutritional criteria these products must meet to be certified.

American Heart Association

Products displaying the heart-check mark meet
American Heart Association food criteria
for saturated fat and cholesterol
for healthy people over age 2.

heartcheckmark.org

Used with permission of the
American Heart Association, Inc.

Review Questions—Multiple Choice

1. If a 2000 Calorie diet contains 100 grams of fat, the percentage of fat Calories in the diet is which of the following?
   (a) 20%
   (b) 25%
   (c) 35%
   (d) 45%
   (e) 60%

2. Which of the following dietary supplements has been proven to increase fat utilization during exercise, spare muscle glycogen, and enhance endurance exercise performance?
   (a) carnitine
   (b) conjugated linoleic acid
   (c) omega-3 fatty acids
   (d) hydroxycitrate
   (e) medium-chain triglycerides
   (f) a and b
   (g) none of the above

3. Which of the following is most conducive to the development of atherosclerosis?
   (a) a total cholesterol of 190 milligrams
   (b) a low level of very low density lipoprotein cholesterol
   (c) a high density lipoprotein cholesterol of 70 milligrams
   (d) a low density lipoprotein cholesterol of 170 milligrams

(e) a total cholesterol/high density lipo-protein cholesterol ratio of less than 3.5

4. Which lipid dietary component appears to be most likely to cause an increase in serum cholesterol and the development of atherosclerosis?
   (a) saturated fats
   (b) polyunsaturated fats
   (c) monounsaturated fats
   (d) omega-3 fatty acids
   (e) phospholipids

5. What compound in the diet cannot be used to form fat if it is consumed in excess?
   (a) fat
   (b) complex carbohydrate
   (c) simple carbohydrate
   (d) protein
   (e) alcohol
   (f) all are capable of forming fat

6. Which compound is not found in plant foods?
   (a) saturated fats
   (b) polyunsaturated fats
   (c) cholesterol

   (d) iron
   (e) complex carbohydrates

7. Which essential fatty acids are needed in the diet?
   (a) linoleic and alpha-linolenic
   (b) oleic and linoleic
   (c) stearic and alpha-linolenic
   (d) palmitic and stearic
   (e) palmitoleic and stearic

8. Which of the following statements relative to fats is false?
   (a) Hydrogenation of fats makes them more saturated.
   (b) Saturated fats are found primarily in animal foods.
   (c) Vegetable fats are primarily unsaturated fats.
   (d) Polyunsaturated fats are theorized to be more healthful than saturated fats.
   (e) Saturated fats appear to help lower blood cholesterol levels.

9. Which of the following is not good advice in attempts to reduce *serum* cholesterol?
   (a) Limit whole egg consumption to about 2–4 per week.

   (b) Eat fish and white poultry meat in place of saturated fat meat.
   (c) Drink skim milk instead of whole milk.
   (d) Use butter instead of soft tub, non-*trans* fatty acid margarine.
   (e) Eat more fruits, vegetables, and whole-grain products.

10. Fats may be a significant source of energy during exercise of low intensity and long duration. What is the main form of fats used for energy production during low-intensity exercise?
    (a) phospholipids derived from the cell membrane
    (b) chylomicrons from the liver
    (c) free fatty acids from the adipose cells and muscle cells
    (d) VLDL from the liver
    (e) cholesterol from the kidney

Answers to multiple choice questions:
1. d; 2. g; 3. d; 4. a; 5. f; 6. c; 7. a; 8. e; 9. d; 10. c.

Review Questions—Essay

1. List the major classes of dietary fatty acids and discuss their relative importance to cardiovascular health. Include in your discussion specific fatty acids as deemed relevant.

2. Describe the role that the blood lipoproteins play in the etiology of atherosclerosis and cardiovascular disease.

3. What is carnitine and how is it theorized to enhance endurance exercise performance? Does research support the theory?

4. Describe the process of chronic fat loading as a strategy to enhance endurance exercise performance, and provide a synthesis of research findings relative to its efficacy.

5. List at least five dietary strategies that may help reduce the risk of atherosclerosis and cardiovascular disease, including specific foods in the diet.

References

Books

Bucci, L. 1993. *Nutrients as Ergogenic Aids for Sports and Exercise.* Boca Raton, FL: CRC Press.

Jeukendrup, A. 1997. *Aspects of Carbohydrate and Fat Metabolism During Exercise.* Haarlem the Netherlands: De Vriesborch.

National Academy of Sciences. 2002. *Dietary Reference Intakes for Energy,*

Carbohydrates, Fiber, Fat, Protein and Amino Acids (Macronutrients). Washington, DC: National Academies Press.

U.S. Department of Health and Human Services Public Health Service. 2000. *Healthy People 2010: National Health Promotion and Disease Prevention Objectives.* Washington, DC: U.S. Government Printing Office.

U.S. Department of Health and Human Services Public Health Service. 2001. *Third Report of the National Cholesterol Education Program of the Expert Panel on Population Strategies for Blood Cholesterol Reduction.* Bethesda, MD: National Institutes of Health.

Wardlaw, G.M., and Kessel, M. 2002. *Perspectives in Nutrition:* McGraw-Hill Companies.

Reviews

Achten, J., and Jeukendrup, A. 2004. Optimizing fat oxidation through exercise and diet. *Nutrition* 20:716–27.

American Dietetic Association: 2005. Position of the American Dietetic Association: Fat replacers. *Journal of the American Dietetic Association* 105:266–75.

American Diabetes Association. 2000. Role of fat replacers in diabetes medical nutrition therapy. *Diabetes Care* 23:S96–97.

American Dietetic Association, et al. 2000. Position of the American Dietetic Association, Dietitians of Canada, and the American College of Sports Medicine: Nutrition and Athletic performance. *Journal of the American Dietetic Association* 100:1543–56.

American Heart Association. 1999. Monounsaturated fatty acids and risk of cardiovascular disease. *Circulation* 1253–8.

American Heart Association. 1996. Dietary guidelines for healthy American adults. *Circulation* 94:1795–1800.

Ascherio, A., et al. 1999. *Trans* fatty acids and coronary heart disease. *New England Journal of Medicine* 340:1994–8.

Bell, S., et al. 1997. The new dietary fats in health and disease. *Journal of the American Dietetic Association.* 97:280–86.

Brass, E. 2004. Carnitine and sports medicine: Use or abuse? *Annals of the New York Academy of Sciences* 1033:67–78.

Brouns, F., and van der Vusse, G. J. 1998. Utilization of lipids during exercise in human subjects: Metabolic and dietary constraints. *British Journal of Nutrition* 79:117–28.

Brown, R., and Cox, C. 2001. Challenging the dogma of dietary carbohydrate requirements for endurance athletes. *American Journal of Medicine & Sports* 3:75–86.

Brown, G., et al. 1993. Lipid lowering and plaque regression: New insights into prevention of plaque disruption and clinical events in coronary disease. *Circulation* 87:1781–89.

Bucher, H. C., et al. 1999. Systematic review on the risk and benefit of different cholesterol-lowering interventions. *Arteriosclerosis, Thrombosis and Vascular Biology* 19:187–95.

Burke, L., and Hawley, J. 2002. Effects of short-term fat adaptation on metabolism and performance of prolonged exercise. *Medicine & Science in Sports & Exercise* 34:1492–98.

Center for Science in the Public Interest. 1999. Olean times at P & G. *Nutrition Action Health Letter* 26 (8):2.

Charkoudian, N., and Joyner, M. 2004. Physiologic considerations for exercise performance in women. *Clinics in Chest Medicine* 25:247–55.

Cheuvront, S. N. 1999. The zone diet and athletic performance. *Sports Medicine* 27:213–28.

Clarke, R., et al. 1997. Dietary lipids and blood cholesterol: Quantitative meta-analysis of metabolic ward studies. *British Medical Journal* 314:112–17.

Consumers Union. 2003. The stealth fat. *Consumer Reports* 68 (3):28–31.

Consumers Union. 2002. Chest pain after eating? *Consumer Reports on Health* 14 (7):3.

Consumers Union. 1998. Do you know your triglycerides? *Consumer Reports on Health* 10 (11):7–8.

Consumers Union. 1998. Finally, a consensus on fat. *Consumer Reports on Health* 10 (8):8.

Consumers Union. 1995. Cutting cholesterol: More vital than ever. *Consumer Reports on Health* 7:13–14.

Craig, W. Y., et al. 1998. Lipoprotein (a) as a risk factor for ischemic heart disease: Meta-analysis of prospective studies. *Clinical Chemistry* 44:2301–6.

Donsmark, M., et al. 2005. Hormone-sensitive lipase as mediator of lipolysis in contracting skeletal muscle. *Exercise and Sport Sciences Reviews* 33:127–33.

Dowling, E. 2001. How exercise affects lipid profiles in women. *Physician and Sportsmedicine* 29 (9):45–52.

Durstine, J., et al. 2001. Blood lipid and lipoprotein adaptations to exercise: A quantitative analysis. *Sports Medicine* 31:1033–62.

Erlenbusch, M., et al. 2004. Effect of high-fat or high-carbohydrate diets on endurance exercise: A meta-analysis. *International Journal of Sport Nutrition and Exercise Metabolism* 15:1–14.

Feldman, E. 2002. The scientific evidence for a beneficial health relationship between walnuts and coronary heart disease. *Journal of Nutrition* 132:1062S–1101S.

Fraser, C. E. 1999. Nut consumption, lipids, and risk of a coronary event. *Clinical Cardiology* 22:III11–15.

Fruchart, J. C., and Duriez, P. 1998. High density lipoproteins and coronary heart disease: Future prospects in gene therapy. *Biochimie* 80:167–72.

German, J., and Dillard, C. 2004. Saturated fats: What dietary intake? *American Journal of Clinical Nutrition* 80:550–59.

Glatz, J., et al. 2002. Exercise and insulin increase muscle fatty acid uptake by recruiting putative fatty acid transporters to the sarcolemma. *Current Opinion in Clinical Nutrition and Metabolic Care* 5:365–70.

Grundy, S. M. 2006. Nutrition in the management of disorders of serum lipids and lipoproteins. In *Modern Nutrition in Health and Disease,* eds. M. Shils, et al. Philadelphia: Lippincott Williams & Wilkins.

Hargreaves, M., et al. 2004. Pre-exercise carbohydrate and fat ingestion: Effects on metabolism and performance. *Journal of Sports Sciences* 22:31–38.

Harris, W. 2004. Are omega-3 fatty acids the most important nutritional modulators of coronary heart disease risk? *Current Atherosclerosis Reports* 6:447–52.

Hasler, C. 2000. The changing face of functional foods. *Journal of the American College of Nutrition* 19:499S–506S.

Hawley, J. 2002. Symposium: Limits to fat oxidation by skeletal muscle during exercise—Introduction. *Medicine & Science in Sports & Exercise* 34:1475–76.

Hawley, J. 2002. Effect of increased fat availability on metabolism and exercise capacity. *Medicine & Science in Sports & Exercise* 34:1485–91.

Hawley, J., and Hopkins, W. 1995. Aerobic glycolytic and aerobic lipolytic power systems. *Sports Medicine* 19:240–50.

Hawley, J. A., et al. 2000. Fat metabolism during exercise. In *Nutrition in Sport,* ed. R. Maughan. Oxford: Blackwell Scientific.

Heinonen, O. 1996. Carnitine and physical exercise. *Sports Medicine* 22:109–32.

Helge, J. 2002. Long-term fat diet adaptation effects on performance, training capacity, and fat utilization. *Medicine & Science in Sports & Exercise* 34:1499–1504.

Horowitz, J., and Klein, S. 2000. Lipid metabolism during endurance exercise. *American Journal of Clinical Nutrition* 72:558S–63S.

Howell, W., et al. 1997. Plasma lipid and lipoprotein responses to dietary fat and cholesterol: A meta-analysis. *American Journal of Clinical Nutrition* 65:1747–64.

Hu, F., et al. 2001. Types of dietary fat and risk of coronary heart disease: A critical review. *Journal of the American College of Nutrition* 20:5–19.

Hulbert, A. 2005. Dietary fats and membrane function: Implications for metabolism and disease. *Biological Reviews of the Cambridge Philosophical Society* 80:155–69.

Hunninghake, D. B. 1999. Pharmacologic management of triglycerides. *Clinical Cardiology* 22:II44–48.

Jacobs, K. A., et al. 2000. Fat metabolism. In *Exercise and Sport Science,* eds. W. E. Garrett and D. T. Kirkendall. Philadelphia: Lippincott Williams & Wilkins.

Jequier, E. 1999. Response to and range of acceptable fat intake in adults. *European Journal of Clinical Nutrition* 53:S84–S88.

Jeukendrup, A., and Aldred, S. 2004. Fat supplementation, health, and endurance performance. *Nutrition* 20:678–88.

Jeukendrup, A. 2002. Regulation of fat metabolism in skeletal muscle. *Annals of the New York Academy of Sciences* 967:217–35.

Jeukendrup, A. E., et al. 1998. Fat metabolism during exercise: A review. Part II: Regulation of metabolism and the effects of training. *International Journal of Sports Medicine* 19:293–302.

Jones, P., and Kubow, S. 2006. Lipids, sterols, and their metabolites. In *Modern Nutrition in Health and Disease,* eds. M. Shils, et al. Philadelphia: Lippincott Williams & Wilkins.

Kelley, G., et al. 2004. Aerobic exercise and lipids and lipoproteins in women: A meta-analysis of randomized controlled trials. *Journal of Women's Health* 13:1148–64.

Kelley, G., et al. 2004. Walking, lipids, and lipoproteins: A meta-analysis of randomized controlled trials. *Preventive Medicine* 38:651–61.

Kelly, G. S. 1998. L-carnitine: Therapeutic applications of a conditionally-essential amino acid. *Alternative Medicine Reviews* 3:345–60.

Kiens, B. 2001. Diet and training in the week before competition. *Canadian Journal of Applied Physiology* 26:S56–63.

Kiens, B., and Helge, J. W. 2000. Adaptations to a high fat diet. In *Nutrition in Sport,* ed. R. Maughan. Oxford: Blackwell Scientific.

Kris-Etherton, P., et al. 2002. AHA Scientific Statement: Fish, fish oils and omega-3 fatty acids. *Circulation* 106:2747–57.

Kris-Etherton, P., et al. 2002. Dietary fat: Assessing the evidence in support of a moderate-fat diet: The benchmark based on lipoprotein metabolism. *Proceedings of the Nutrition Society* 61:287–98.

Lamarche, B., and Desroches, S. 2004. Metabolic syndrome and effects of conjugated linoleic acid in obesity and lipoprotein disorders: The Quebec experience. *American Journal of Clinical Nutrition* 79:1149S–52S.

Lamarche, B., et al. 1999. The small, dense LDL phenotype and the risk of coronary heart disease: Epidemiology, pathophysiology and therapeutic aspects. *Diabetes and Metabolism* 25:199–211.

Lange, K. 2004. Fat metabolism in exercise—With special reference to training and growth hormone administration. *Scandinavian Journal of Medicine and Science in Sports* 14:74–99.

Leon, A., and Sanchez, O. 2001. Response of blood lipids to exercise training alone or combined with dietary interventions. *Medicine & Science in Sports & Exercise* 33:S502–15.

Lichtenstein, A. 2000. Trans fatty acids and cardiovascular disease risk. *Current Opinion in Lipidology* 11:37–42.

Liebman, B. 2005. Fading memories. *Nutrition Action Health Letter* 32 (1):1–7.

Luiken, J., et al. 2001. Skeletal muscle fatty acid transport and transporters. *International Journal of Sport Nutrition and Exercise Metabolism* 11:S92–96.

Martin, W. 1997. Effect of endurance training on fatty acid metabolism during whole body exercise. *Medicine & Science in Sports & Exercise* 29:635–39.

Pendergast, D., et al. 2000. A perspective on fat intake in athletes. *Journal of the American College of Nutrition* 19:345–50.

Pendergast, D., et al. 1996. The role of dietary fat on performance, metabolism, and health. *American Journal of Sports Medicine* 24:S53–S58.

Rados, C. 2004. FDA, EPA revise guidelines on mercury in fish. *FDA Consumer* 38 (3):8–9.

Rebouche, C. J. 2006. Carnitine. In *Modern Nutrition in Health and Disease,* eds. M. Shils, et al. Philadelphia: Lippincott Williams & Wilkins.

Schardt, D. 2005. Weight loss in a bottle? *Nutrition Action Health Letter* 32 (4):10–12.

Sherman, W. M., and Leenders, N. 1995. Fat loading: The next magic bullet? *International Journal of Sport Nutrition* 5:S1–S12.

Shrier, I. 2005. Mediterranean diet for reducing mortality and easing the metabolic syndome. *Physician and Sportsmedicine* 33 (5):8–9.

Shulman, D. 2002. Fuel on fat for the long run. *Marathon & Beyond* 6 (5):128–36.

Spriet, L., and Gibala, M. 2004. Nutritional strategies to influence adaptations to training. *Journal of Sports Sciences* 22:127–41.

Spriet, L. 2002. Regulation of skeletal muscle fat oxidation during exercise in humans. *Medicine & Science in Sports & Exercise* 34:1477–84.

Stark, A., and Madar, Z. 2002. Olive oil as a functional food: Epidemiology and nutritional approaches. *Nutrition Reviews* 60:170–76.

Stefanik, M., and Wood, P. 1994. Physical activity, lipid and lipoprotein metabolism, and lipid transport. In *Physical Activity, Fitness, and Health,* eds. C. Bouchard, et al. Champaign, IL: Human Kinetics.

Stroud, M. 1998. The nutritional demands of very prolonged exercise in man. *Proceedings of the Nutrition Society* 57:55–61.

Studer, M., et al. 2005. Effect of different antilipidemic agents and diets on mortality: A systematic review. *Archives of Internal Medicine* 165:725–30.

Tarnopolsky, M. 2000. Gender differences in substrate metabolism during endurance exercise. *Canadian Journal of Applied Physiology* 25:312–27.

Tarnopolsky, M. A. 2000. Gender differences in metabolism: Nutrition and supplements. *Journal of Science and Medicine in Sport.* 3:287–98.

Thompson, P., et al. 2001. The acute versus the chronic response to exercise. *Medicine & Science in Sports & Exercise* 33:S438–45.

Turcotte, L. P. 2000. Muscle fatty acid uptake during exercise: Possible mechanisms. *Exercise & Sport Sciences Reviews* 28:4–9.

van Loon, L. 2004. Use of intramuscular triacylglycerol as a substrate source during exercise in humans. *Journal of Applied Physiology* 97:1170–87.

Wagenmakers, A. 1998. Carnitine supplementation: Effects on metabolism and performance. *Insider* 6 (1):5–7.

Wagenmakers, A. 1991. L-carnitine supplementation and performance in man. *Medicine and Sport Science: Advances in Nutrition and Top Sport* 32:110–27.

Weggemans, R., et al. 2002. Dietary cholesterol from eggs increases the ratio of total cholesterol to high-density lipoprotein cholesterol in humans: A meta-analysis. *American Journal of Clinical Nutrition* 73:885–91.

Westerterp-Plantenga, M. 2004. Fat intake and energy-balance efforts. *Physiology & Behavior* 83:579–85.

Whitten, P. 1993. Stanford's secret weapon: New nutrition program lifts Cardinal swimmers to record-breaking year. *Swimming World and Junior Swimmer* 34 (March/April): 28–33.

Williams, P. 2001. Health effects resulting from exercise versus those from body fat loss. *Medicine & Science in Sports & Exercise* 33:S611–21.

Winder, W. W. 1998. Intramuscular mechanisms regulating fatty acid oxidation during exercise. *Advances in Experimental Medicine and Biology* 441:239–48.

Wolfe, R. 1998. Fat metabolism in exercise. *Advances in Experimental Medicine and Biology* 441:147–56.

Zierler, K. 1999. Whole body glucose metabolism. *American Journal of Physiology* 276:E409–E426.

Specific Studies

Angus, D., et al. 2000. Effect of carbohydrate or carbohydrate plus medium-chain triglyceride ingestion on cycling time trial performance. *Journal of Applied Physiology* 88:113–19.

Brilla, L., and Landerholm, T. 1990. Effect of fish oil supplementation and exercise on serum lipids and aerobic fitness. *The Journal of Sports Medicine and Physical Fitness* 30:173–80.

Brown, R., and Cox, C. 2000. High-fat versus high-carbohydrate diets: Effect on exercise capacity and performance of endurance trained cyclists. *New Zealand Journal of Sports Medicine* 28:55–59.

Burelle, Y., et al. 2001. Oxidation of [(13)C]-glycerol ingested along with glucose during prolonged exercise. *Journal of Applied Physiology* 90:1685–90.

Burke, L., et al. 2002. Adaptations to short-term high-fat diet persist during exercise despite high carbohydrate availability. *Medicine & Science in Sports & Exercise* 34:83–91.

Burke, L., et al. 2000. Effect of fat adaptation and carbohydrate restoration on metabolism and performance during prolonged cycling. *Journal of Applied Physiology* 89:2413–21.

Carey, A., et al. 2001. Effects of fat adaptation and carbohydrate restoration on prolonged endurance exercise. *Journal of Applied Physiology* 91:115–22.

Coggan, A., et al. 2000. Fat metabolism during high-intensity exercise in endurance-trained and untrained men. *Metabolism* 49:122–28.

Colombani, P., et al. 1996. Effects of L-carnitine supplementation on physical performance and energy metabolism of endurance-trained athletes: A double-blind crossover field study. *European Journal of Applied Physiology* 73:434–39.

Costill, D., et al. 1979. Lipid metabolism in skeletal muscle of endurance trained males and females. *Journal of Applied Physiology* 47:787–91.

Coyle, E., et al. 2001. Low-fat diet alters intramuscular substrates and reduces lipolysis and fat oxidation during exercise. *American Journal of Physiology. Endocrinology and Metabolism* 280:E391–98.

Decombaz, J., et al. 1993. Effect of L-carnitine on submaximal exercise metabolism after depletion of muscle glycogen. *Medicine & Science in Sports & Exercise* 25:733–40.

Eyjolfson, V., et al. 2004. Conjugated linoleic acid improves insulin sensitivity in young, sedentary humans. *Medicine & Science in Sports & Exercise* 36:814–20.

Fleming, J. 2003. Endurance capacity and high-intensity exercise performance responses to a high-fat diet. *International Journal of Sport Nutrition and Exercise Metabolism* 13:466–78.

Friedlander, A. L., et al. 1999. Endurance training increases fatty acid turnover, but not fat oxidation, in young men. *Journal of Applied Physiology* 86:2097–2105.

Gaullier, J., et al. 2004. Conjugated linoleic acid supplementation for 1 y reduces body fat in healthy overweight humans. *American Journal of Clinical Nutrition* 79:1118–25.

Goedecke, J. H., et al. 2005. The effects of medium-chain triacylglycerol and carbohydrate ingestion on ultra-endurance exercise performance. *International Journal of Sport Nutrition and Exercise Metabolism* 15:15–27.

Goedecke, J. H., et al. 1999. Effect of medium-chain triacylglycerol ingested with carbohydrate on metabolism and exercise performance. *International Journal of Sports Medicine* 9:35–47.

Gutierrez, A., et al. 2001. Three days fast in sportsmen decreases physical work capacity but not strength or perception-reaction time. *International Journal of Sport Nutrition and Exercise Metabolism* 11:420–29.

Helge, J. W., et al. 1998. Impact of a fat-rich diet on endurance in man: Role of dietary period. *Medicine & Science in Sports & Exercise* 30:456–61.

Horowitz, J. F., et al. 2000. Preexercise medium-chain triglyceride ingestion does not alter muscle glycogen use during exercise. *Journal of Applied Physiology* 88:219–25.

Horowitz, J. F., et al. 1999. Substrate metabolism when subjects are fed carbohydrates during exercise. *American Journal of Physiology* 276:E825–35.

Horvath, P., et al. 2000. The effect of varying dietary fat on performance and metabolism in trained male and female runners. *Journal of the American College of Nutrition* 19:52–60.

Huffman, D., et al. 2004. Effect of n-3 fatty acids on free tryptophan and exercise fatigue. *European Journal of Applied Physiology* 92:584–91.

Jeukendrup, A. E., et al. 1998. Effect of medium-chain triacylglycerol and carbohydrate ingestion during exercise on substrate utilization and subsequent cycling performance. *American Journal of Clinical Nutrition* 67:397–404.

Jeukendrup, A. E., et al. 1996. Effect of endogenous carbohydrate availability on oral medium-chain triglyceride oxidation during prolonged exercise. *Journal of Applied Physiology* 80:949–54.

King, S., and Gibney, M. 1999. Dietary advice to reduce fat intake is more successful when it does not restrict habitual eating patterns. *Journal of the American Dietetic Association* 99:685–89.

Knechtle, B., et al. 2004. Fat oxidation in men and women endurance athletes in running and cycling. *International Journal of Sports Medicine* 25:38–44.

Kreider, R., et al. 2002. Effects of conjugated linoleic acid supplementation during resistance training on body composition, bone density, strength and selected hematological markers. *Journal of Strength Conditioning Research* 16:325–34.

Kriketos, A., et al. 1999. (-)-Hydroxycitric acid does not affect energy expenditure and substrate oxidation in adult males in a post-absorptive state. *International Journal of Obesity and Related Metabolic Disorders* 23:867–73.

Lambert, E., et al. 2001. High-fat diet versus habitual diet prior to carbohydrate loading: Effects of exercise metabolism and cycling performance. *International Journal of Sport Nutrition and Exercise Metabolism* 11:209–25.

Lambert, E., et al. 1994. Enhanced endurance in trained cyclists during moderate intensity exercise following 2 weeks adaptation to a high fat diet. *European Journal of Applied Physiology* 69:287–93.

MacLean, C., et al. 2006. Effects of omega-3 fatty acids on cancer risk: A systematic review. *JAMA* 295: 403-15.

Manson, J. E. 1999. A prospective study of walking as compared with vigorous exercise in the prevention of coronary heart disease in women. *New England Journal of Medicine* 341:650–58.

Massicotte, D., et al. 1992. Oxidation of exogenous medium-chain free fatty acids during prolonged exercise: Comparison with glucose. *Journal of Applied Physiology* 73:1334–39.

McRorie, J., et al. 2000. Effects of olestra and sorbitol consumption on objective measures of diarrhea: Impact of stool viscosity on common gastrointestinal symptoms. *Regulatory Toxicology and Pharmacology* 31:59–67.

Misell, L., et al. 2001. Chronic medium-chain triacylglycerol consumption and endurance performance in trained runners. *Journal of Sports Medicine and Physical Fitness* 41:210–15.

Moloney, F., et al. 2004. Conjugated linoleic acid supplementation, insulin sensitivity, and lipoprotein metabolism in patients with type 2 diabetes mellitus. *American Journal of Clinical Nutrition* 80:887–95.

Mora-Rodriguez, R., and Coyle, E. 2000. Effects of plasma epinephrine on fat metabolism during exercise: Interactions with exercise intensity. *American Journal of Physiology. Endocrinology and Metabolism* 278:E669–76.

Morgan, S., et al. 1997. A low-fat diet supplemented with monounsaturated fat results in less HDL-C lowering than a very-low-fat diet. *Journal of the American Dietetic Association* 97:151–56.

Muoio, D., et al. 1994. Effect of dietary fat on metabolic adjustments to maximal VO$_2$ and endurance in runners. *Medicine & Science in Sports & Exercise* 26:81–88.

Nagel, D., et al. 1989. Effects of an ultra-long distance (1000 km) race on lipid metabolism. *European Journal of Applied Physiology* 59:16–20.

Okano, G., et al. 1998. Effect of elevated blood FFA levels on endurance performance after a single fat meal ingestion. *Medicine & Science in Sports & Exercise* 30:763–68.

Okano, G., et al. 1996. Effect of 4 h preexercise high carbohydrate and high fat meal ingestion on endurance performance and metabolism. *International Journal of Sports Medicine* 17:530–34.

Oostenbrug, G. S., et al. 1997. Exercise performance, red blood cell deformability, and lipid peroxidation: Effects of fish oil and vitamin E. *Journal of Applied Physiology* 83:746–52.

Pitsiladis, Y. P., et al. 1999. Increased fat availability enhances the capacity of trained individuals to perform prolonged exercise. *Medicine & Science in Sports & Exercise* 31:1570–79.

Pogliaghi, S., and Veicsteinas, A. 1999. Influence of low and high dietary fat on physical performance in untrained males. *Medicine & Science in Sports & Exercise* 31:149–55.

Raastad, T., et al. 1997. Omega-3 fatty acid supplementation does not improve maximal aerobic power, anaerobic threshold and running performance in well-trained soccer players. *Scandinavian Journal of Medicine and Science in Sports* 7:25–31.

Ridker, P. et al. 2002. Comparison of C-reactive protein and low-density-lipoprotein cholesterol levels in the prediction of first cardiovascular events. *New England Journal of Medicine* 347:1557–65.

Romijn, J., et al. 2000. Substrate metabolism during different exercise intensities in endurance-trained women. *Journal of Applied Physiology* 88:1707–14.

Romijn, J., et al. 1993. Regulation of endogenous fat and carbohydrate metabolism in relation to exercise intensity and duration. *American Journal of Physiology* 265:E380–E391.

Rowlands, D., and Hopkins, W. 2002. Effect of high-fat, high-carbohydrate, and high-protein meals on metabolism and performance during endurance cycling. *International Journal of Sport Nutrition and Exercise Metabolism* 12:318–35.

Rowlands, D., and Hopkins, W. 2002. Effects of high-fat and high-carbohydrate diets on metabolism and performance in cycling. *Metabolism* 51:678–90.

Staton, W. 1951. The influence of soya lecithin on muscular strength. *Research Quarterly* 22:201–207.

Stepto, N., et al. 2002. Effect of short-term fat adaptation on high-intensity training. *Medicine & Science in Sports & Exercise* 34:449–55.

Tarnopolsky, M., et al. 1995. Carbohydrate loading and metabolism during exercise in men and women. *Journal of Applied Physiology* 68:302–8.

Thomas, T., et al. 2004. Effects of omega-3 fatty acid supplementation and exercise on low-density lipoprotein and high-density lipoprotein subfractions. *Metabolism* 53:749–54.

Trappe, S., et al. 1994. The effect of L-carnitine supplementation on performance during interval swimming. *International Journal of Sports Medicine* 15:181–85.

Tunstall, R., et al. 2002. Exercise training increases lipid metabolism gene expression in human skeletal muscle. *American Journal of Physiology. Endocrinology and Metabolism* 283:E66–72.

van Loon, L., et al. 2000. Effects of acute (-)-hydroxycitrate supplementation on substrate metabolism at rest and during exercise in humans. *American Journal of Clinical Nutrition* 72:1445–50.

Vanstone, C., et al. 2002. Unesterified plant sterols and stanols lower LDL-cholesterol concentrations equivalently in hypercholesterolemic persons. *American Journal of Clinical Nutrition* 76:1272–78.

Van Zyl, C., et al. 1996. Effects of medium-chain triglyceride ingestion on fuel metabolism and cycling performance. *Journal of Applied Physiology* 80:2217–25.

Venables, M., et al. 2005. Determinants of fat oxidation during exercise in healthy men and women: A cross-sectional study. *Journal of Applied Physiology* 98:160–67.

Venkatraman, J. T., and Pendergast, D. 1998. Effect of the level of dietary fat intake and endurance exercise on plasma cytokines in runners. *Medicine & Science in Sports & Exercise* 30:1198–1204.

Villani, R., et al. 2000. L-carnitine supplementation combined with aerobic training does not promote weight loss in moderately obese women. *International Journal of Sport Nutrition and Exercise Metabolism* 10:199–207.

Vukovich, M., et al. 1994. Carnitine supplementation: Effect on muscle carnitine and glycogen content during exercise. *Medicine & Science in Sports & Exercise* 26:1122–29.

Wacher, S., et al. 2002. Long-term administration of L-carnitine to humans: Effect on skeletal muscle carnitine content and physical performance. *Clinical Chimica Acta* 318:51–61.

Warber, J., et al. 2000. The effects of choline supplementation on physical performance. *International Journal of Sport Nutrition and Exercise Metabolism* 10:170–81.

Wong, W. W., et al. 1998. Cholesterol-lowering effect of soy protein in normocholesterolemic and hypercholesterolemic men. *American Journal of Clinical Nutrition* 68:1385S–1389S.

Zambell, K., et al. 2001. Conjugated linoleic acid supplementation in humans: Effects on fatty acid and glycerol kinetics *Lipids* 36:767–72.

Zderic, T., et al. 2004. High-fat diet elevates resting intramuscular triglyceride concentration and whole body lipolysis during exercise. *American Journal of Physiology. Endocrinology and Metabolism* 286:E217–25.

Protein:
The Tissue Builder

CHAPTER SIX

LEARNING OBJECTIVES

After studying this chapter, you should be able to:

1. Distinguish between complete and incomplete protein and identify foods that may be one or the other.

2. Calculate the approximate grams of protein that should be included in your daily diet.

3. Name the nine essential amino acids.

4. Describe the digestion of protein, its metabolic fate and distribution in the body, and its major functions in human metabolism.

5. Explain the role of protein in human energy systems during exercise.

6. Understand the rationale underlying the judgment of some investigators that both strength and endurance athletes need more dietary protein than the amount provided by the RDA. State general recommendations to various athletes based on grams of protein per kilogram body weight.

7. Based on current research findings, describe the dietary strategies involving protein intake (amount, type, and timing) before and/or after exercise that may help provide the substrate and hormonal milieu conducive to muscle tissue anabolism.

8. Explain the theory underlying the use of protein supplements, various amino acids, and other dietary supplements such as creatine and HMB, as ergogenic aids, and highlight the major research findings relative to their efficacy.

9. Identify the potential health risks associated with either inadequate or excess dietary intake of protein or individual amino acids.

Protein is one of our most essential nutrients. It has a wide variety of physiological functions that are essential to optimal physical performance. For example, protein forms the structural basis of muscle tissue, is the major component of most enzymes in the muscle, and can serve as a source of energy during exercise. Because protein is so important to the development and function of muscle tissue, and because most feats of human physical performance involve strenuous muscular activity in one form or another, it is no wonder that protein has persisted throughout the years as the food of the athlete. Indeed, surveys have revealed that many high school and college athletes believe that athletic performance is improved by a high-protein diet. Protein is one of the best-selling sports supplements. A best-selling diet book suggests protein is the key macronutrient for the athlete, and for health as well.

Companies that market nutritional supplements for athletes have capitalized on this belief. Probably the athletic groups most susceptible to the lure of protein supplements are bodybuilders and strength-type athletes, such as weight lifters and football players. Numerous high-protein products have been developed for these athletes in attempts to exploit the protein-muscle strength relationship. In recent years, specific amino acids have been theorized to maximize muscle mass and strength gains and have been advertised extensively in magazines for bodybuilders. Some advertisements even suggest that certain amino acid mixtures have an effect similar to drugs such as anabolic steroids, which have been used to stimulate muscle development.

Protein supplements are marketed for other types of athletes as well. Although protein is not regarded as a major energy source during exercise, research has suggested that endurance athletes may use some specific amino acids for energy production under certain conditions. Pro-tein supplements, often combined with carbohydrate, are marketed to endurance athletes. Additionally, specific amino acids have been theorized to delay the onset of fatigue during prolonged exercise through their effect on neurotransmitters in the brain.

There is no doubt that an adequate amount of dietary protein and related essential amino acids is required by all individuals. However, the advertisements directed toward athletes imply that additional protein, usually in the form of protein or amino acid supplements, is necessary for optimal performance. Although the National Academy of Sciences has indicated that the Recommended Daily Allowance (RDA) provides sufficient protein to athletes, some investigators recommend that athletes in training need to increase their protein intake. However, these investigators usually recommend that the protein be derived from natural food sources and the amount of protein recommended is well within the Acceptable Macronutrient Dietary Range (AMDR).

Other dietary supplements related to protein or amino acids, such as amines or various metabolic by-products, have become increasingly popular in recent years. One of the current hot sellers is creatine, but other supplements such as inosine and HMB are available. In most cases these dietary supplements have been marketed to strength-trained athletes as a means to foster muscle growth and strength development, but some are intended for use by athletes involved in other sports, such as aerobic endurance events.

Does the physically active individual need more protein or related dietary supplements in the diet? The information presented in this chapter should provide a general answer to this question. Topics to be covered include dietary needs and sources of protein; metabolic fates and functions in the body; the effects of exercise on protein metabolism and dietary requirements; the ergogenic potential of protein, amino acids, or other related supplements; and health aspects of dietary protein.

Dietary Protein

What is protein?

Protein is a complex chemical structure containing carbon, hydrogen, and oxygen—just as carbohydrates and fats do. Protein has one other essential element—nitrogen, which constitutes about 16 percent of most dietary protein. These four elements are combined into a number of different structures called **amino acids,** each one possessing an amino group (NH_2) and an acid group (COOH), with the remainder being different combinations of carbon, hydrogen, oxygen, and in some cases sulfur. There are twenty amino acids, all of which can be combined in a variety of ways to form the proteins necessary for the structure and functions of the human body. The body may also modify the structure of dietary amino acids, such as converting proline to hydroxyproline, to meet its needs. Figure 6.1 depicts the formula of **alanine,** an amino acid discussed later.

Proteins are created when two amino acids link and form a peptide bond; hence, a dipeptide is formed. As more amino acids are added, a polypeptide is formed. Most proteins are polypeptides, combining up to 300 amino acids. Figure 6.2 depicts the building of a protein.

Protein is contained in both animal and plant foods. Humans obtain their supply of amino acids from these two general sources.

Is there a difference between animal and plant protein?

To answer this question, let us first look at a basic difference between two groups of amino acids. Humans can synthesize some amino acids in their bodies but cannot synthesize others. The nine amino acids that cannot be manufactured in the body are called **essential,** or **indispensable, amino acids** and must be supplied in the diet. Those that may be formed in the body are called **nonessential,** or **dispensable, amino acids.** Six of the dispensable amino acids are conditionally indispensable, which means that they must be obtained through the diet when endogenous synthesis cannot meet metabolic demands, such as in severe catabolic states. Although nutrition scientists prefer the terms *indispensable* and *dispensable,* this text uses the terms *essential* and *nonessential* because they are most commonly used.

It should be noted that all twenty amino acids are necessary for protein synthesis in the body and must be present simultaneously for optimal maintenance of body growth and function. The use of the terms *essential* and *indispensable* in relation to amino acids is to distinguish those that must be obtained in the diet. Table 6.1 presents the dietary essential, nonessential, and conditionally essential amino acids.

TABLE 6.1   The dietary amino acids

Essential amino acids	Nonessential amino acids
Histidine	Alanine
Isoleucine*	Arginine**
Leucine*	Asparagine
Lysine	Aspartic acid
Methionine	Cysteine**
Phenylalanine	Glutamic acid
Threonine	Glutamine**
Tryptophan	Glycine**
Valine*	Proline**
	Serine
	Tyrosine**

*Branched-chain amino acids
**Conditionally essential

The National Academy of Sciences indicates that different sources of protein vary widely in their composition and nutritional value. The quality of a source of protein is an expression of its ability to provide the nitrogen and amino acid requirements for growth, maintenance, and repair. The key factors are digestibility and the ability to provide the indispensable amino acids. All natural, unprocessed animal and plant foods contain all twenty amino acids. However, the amount of each amino acid in specific foods varies. Over the years a number of different techniques have been used, usually with animals, to assess the quality of protein in selected foods. One of the most recent is the Protein Digestibility-Corrected Amino Acid Score (PDCAAS), which incorporates real-life variables. Scores can range from 1.0 to 0.0, with 1.0 being the highest quality. We need not go into a detailed discussion of all techniques to evaluate protein quality, but essentially they focus on the concept of **nitrogen balance,** the ability of the body to retain nitrogen. In essence, nitrogen balance is protein balance. In

FIGURE 6.1   The chemical structure of alanine, an amino acid. The amino group (NH_2) contains nitrogen, while the acid group is represented by COOH.

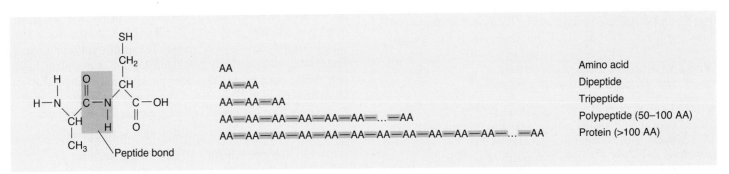

FIGURE 6.2   Formation of peptides and polypeptides from amino acids, with eventual formation of proteins.

positive nitrogen balance the body is retaining protein to adequately support growth and development, while in negative nitrogen balance the body is losing protein, with possible impairment in growth and development. The quality of the protein in foods we eat may affect nitrogen balance.

In general, those foods that contain an adequate content of all nine essential amino acids to support both life and growth are known as **complete proteins,** or high-quality proteins, while those that have a deficiency of one or more essential amino acids and are unable to support life or growth are called **incomplete proteins,** or low-quality proteins. Relative to human requirements, an essential amino acid that is in limited supply in a particular food is labeled a **limiting amino acid.**

The proteins ingested as animal products are generally regarded to be of a higher quality than those found in plants. This is not to say that an amino acid found in a plant is inferior to the same amino acid found in an animal. They are the same. When we look at the distribution of all the amino acids in the two food sources, however, we can then see two major reasons why animal protein is called a high-quality protein, whereas plant protein is of lower quality. The PDCAAS for egg white and meat is, respectively, 1.0 and 0.92, while the score for kidney beans and whole wheat is, respectively, 0.68 and 0.40.

Animal protein is a complete protein because it contains each essential amino acid in the proper proportion to human requirements. As noted, all twenty amino acids must be present simultaneously for the body to synthesize them into necessary body proteins. If one amino acid is in short supply, protein construction may be blocked. Having the proper amount of animal protein in the diet is a good way to ensure receiving a balanced supply of amino acids. Some protein supplements marketed to athletes are made from animal protein, including milk, egg, and whey protein.

Although plant proteins are regarded as being of lower quality than animal proteins, they still may provide you with all the protein and amino acids you need for optimal growth and development. However, proteins usually exist in smaller concentrations in plant foods. For example, 2 ounces of fish contain about 14 grams of protein, while 2 ounces of cooked macaroni only have 2 grams; 2 ounces of beans, which are generally regarded to be good sources of protein, have only 5 grams. In addition, most plant proteins have insufficient amounts of one or more of the essential amino acids, i.e., limiting amino acids. Grain products are usually deficient in lysine, whereas legumes are low in methionine. An exception to this generality is the protein isolated from soybeans, which when processed properly is comparable to animal protein. As noted in chapter 2, if plant foods are eaten in proper combinations over the course of the day, the individual may receive a balanced supply of amino acids. Some populations receive most of their protein from plant sources.

What are some common foods that are good sources of protein?

Animal foods in the milk and meat groups generally have substantial amounts of high-quality protein. One glass of milk or its equivalent contains about 7–8 grams of protein, as does 1 ounce of meat, fish, or poultry. One egg contains 6 grams of high-quality protein, as does one serving of Egg Beaters, but the latter has half the Calories and no fat or cholesterol. **Legumes,** such as dry beans (black,

garbanzo, great northern, kidney, lima, navy, pinto, soybeans), lentils, and peas (black-eyed, split), are relatively good sources of protein. Legumes also are high in carbohydrate and for this reason are currently classified as a starch food exchange. However, because of their relatively high protein content, legumes may be included within the meat and meat substitutes exchange list. One-half cup contains about 7–9 grams of protein. Nuts contain fair amounts of protein but are high in fat. Fruits, vegetables, and grain products all have some protein, but the content varies; generally speaking, the protein content is low, ranging from less than 1 gram to about 3 grams of protein per serving, although some products may contain more, such as protein-enriched pasta. Some sports drinks and sports bars contain significant amounts of protein. Protein supplements targeted to strength-trained individuals may contain substantial amounts of protein, but may also be expensive.

Table 6.2 and figures 6.3 and 6.4 present some common foods in each of several food groups, with the number of grams of protein in each. Notice the effect combination-type foods have on protein content: for example, macaroni and cheese versus plain macaroni. Most food labels today will list the grams of protein per serving.

How much dietary protein do I need?

Humans actually do not need protein per se, but rather an adequate amount of nitrogen and essential amino acids. However, because all nine essential amino acids and almost all dietary nitrogen are derived from dietary protein, it serves as the basis for our daily requirements.

In the United States, the recommended dietary intake of protein is based upon the RDA. The amount of protein necessary in the diet varies in different stages of the life cycle, as may be noted in the Dietary Reference Intakes table for macronutrients in the front inside cover. During the early years of life, children manufacture protein tissue during rapid growth stages, with the rate of growth (and thus the protein needs) varying from infancy through late adolescence. In young adulthood, the protein requirement stabilizes. Throughout the life cycle, however, the protein requirement established in the RDA is based upon the body weight of the individual. As a person passes from infancy to adulthood, the protein RDA per unit body weight decreases, but the absolute amount of protein needed by the body as a whole actually increases because of increases in body weight.

Table 6.3 presents the amount of protein needed per kilogram or per pound of body weight for different age groups. A variety of scientific techniques have been used over the years to determine human protein needs, and more recent research has reaffirmed these estimates for adults and children. The values for the first year of life are AI, while the remainder are RDA. The values in this table are dependent upon adequate daily energy intake (i.e., Calories), for a low-energy diet will increase protein needs. To calculate your requirement, simply determine your body weight in kilograms or pounds and multiply by the appropriate figure for your age group. Recall that one kilogram is equal to 2.2 pounds. As an example, compute the protein requirement for a 154-pound, or 70-kg, average 23-year-old male:

$$0.36 \text{ g protein/pound} \times \text{pounds} = 55.4 \text{ or } 56 \text{ g protein/day}$$

$$0.8 \text{ g protein/kg} \times 70 \text{ kg} = 56 \text{ g protein/day}$$

On a protein-free diet, the average individual loses approximately 0.34 g protein/kg body weight per day, which could be

TABLE 6.2 Protein content in some common foods

Food	Amount	Protein (grams)	Food	Amount	Protein (grams)
Milk list			*Fruit list*		
Milk, whole	1 c	8	Banana	1	1
Milk, skim	1 c	8	Orange	1	1
Cheese, cheddar	1 oz	7	Pear	1	1
Yogurt	1 c	8			
			Starch list		
Meat list			Bread, wheat	1 slice	3
			Bran flakes	1 c	4
Beef, lean	1 oz	8	Doughnuts	1	1
Chicken breast	1 oz	8	Macaroni	1/2 c	3
Luncheon meat	1 oz	5	Macaroni and cheese	1/2 c	9
Fish	1 oz	7	Peas, green	1/2 c	4
Eggs	1	6	Potato, baked	1	3
Navy beans, cooked*	1/2 c	7			
Peanuts, roasted	1/4 c	9	*Sports drinks and bars*		
Peanut butter	1 tbsp	4			
			Gatorade Nutrition Shake	11 oz	18
Vegetable list			Power Bar Protein Plus	1	24
			Endurox4	12 oz	11
Broccoli	1/2 c	2			
Carrots	1	1	*Protein sports supplements*		
			WheyPro	1 oz	22

Protein (grams) may vary slightly from the food exchange lists because these data were derived from food analyses reported by the United States Department of Agriculture.

*Found in both the meat and meat substitutes and starch lists in appendix E.

FIGURE 6.3 Foods high in protein include meats, milk, cheese, eggs, and plants such as wheat and legumes. Some sports bars are also rich in protein.

	1 glass milk	=	8 grams
	1 ounce chicken breast	=	7 grams
	1 slice of bread	=	3 grams
	1/2 cup vegetables	=	2 grams
	1/2 cup navy beans	=	7 grams

FIGURE 6.4 Protein in food.

TABLE 6.3	Grams of protein needed per kilogram or per pound body weight during the life cycle	
Age in years	Grams/kg body weight	Grams/pound body weight
0.0–0.5	1.52	.69
0.5–1.0	1.10	.50
1–3	1.10	.50
4–8	0.95	.43
9–13	0.95	.43
14–18	0.85	.39
19 and up	0.8	.36

TABLE 6.4	RDA for the essential amino acids in an adult male (70 kg)	
	RDA (mg/kg)	Total mg
Histidine	14	980
Isoleucine	19	1,260
Leucine	42	2,940
Lysine	38	2,660
Methionine plus cysteine	19	1,260
Phenylalanine plus tyrosine	33	2,310
Threonine	20	1,400
Tryptophan	5	350
Valine	24	1,680
Total		14,840

replaced by a similar amount of high quality egg protein. However, allowances are made in the RDA for the fact that individual protein needs vary, that the biologic quality of all dietary protein is not as good as egg protein, and that the efficiency of utilization decreases at higher dietary protein-intake levels. Hence, the RDA is adjusted upward to account for these factors.

The RDA for protein, as noted, is based upon body weight of the individual at different ages. If you would take the recommended energy intake in Calories for each age group, say 2,500 C for the average adult male, and calculate the percentage of this value that the RDA for protein supplies, the values approximate 10 percent for each age group. The National Academy of Sciences indicated that the AMDR should not be set below levels for the RDA for protein, which is about 10 percent of energy. Mathematically, 56 grams of protein, at 4 Calories per gram, total 224 Calories, which is about 9 percent of 2,500, or near the lower limit of the AMDR.

As noted in previous chapters, the Acceptable Macronutrient Distribution Ranges (AMDRs) for individuals have been set based on evidence from interventional trials, with support of epidemiological evidence, to suggest a role in the prevention of increased risk of chronic disease and based on ensuring sufficient intakes of essential nutrients. The AMDR for protein is 10–35 percent of energy for adults and 5–20 and 10–30 percent for young and older children, respectively. The health implications of the AMDR will be discussed later in this chapter.

It is important to note, as Millward indicated in a recent review, that protein needs are determined by overall food energy intake. If energy intake is inadequate, such as may be the case in those on weight-loss diets or the elderly, dietary protein may be used for energy instead of its core purpose of building tissue. Thus, some individuals may need more or higher quality protein because their energy intake may be low.

How much of the essential amino acids do I need?

The Academy also established RDA for the nine indispensable amino acids. The amounts for adults age 19 and over are found in table 6.4.

Slightly larger amounts are recommended for children and adolescents. For the average adult, about 25 percent of the total protein requirement should consist of the essential amino acids; this amounts to about 14–15 grams. Phenylalanine is an essential amino acid, whereas tyrosine is normally listed as a nonessential amino acid. The two are of similar chemical structure so that when substantial quantities of tyrosine are contained in the diet, the need for phenylalanine will decrease somewhat. The same holds true for the essential sulfur-containing amino acid methionine and its chemically related counterpart, cysteine. Individuals who obtain the RDA for protein should have no problem obtaining these recommended values.

Fortunately, we do not need to memorize these amino acids and check our food products to see if they are present. A few general rules can help ensure that we receive a balanced supply in our diet.

What are some dietary guidelines to ensure adequate protein intake?

To answer in one sentence: Eat a wide variety of animal and plant foods. The high-quality, complete proteins are obtained primarily from animal foods. Meat, fish, eggs, poultry, milk, and cheese contain the type and amount of the essential amino acids necessary for maintaining life and promoting growth and development. They are high-nutrient-density foods, particularly if fat content is low to moderate. Because animal protein is of high quality, you do not need as much of it to satisfy your RDA. For example, for a male who needs about 56 grams of protein per day, only 45 grams is needed if it is animal protein. One glass of milk, with 8 grams of protein, will provide almost 20 percent of his protein RDA. Two glasses of milk, one egg, and 3 ounces of lean meat, fish, or poultry will provide 100 percent of his RDA. In addition, a substantial proportion of daily vitamin and mineral needs will also be supplied in these foods. As noted in chapter 5, selection of low-fat foods will enhance the nutrient density by reducing Calories.

Plant foods also may provide good sources of protein. Grain products such as wheat, rice, and corn, as well as soybeans, peas, beans, and nuts, have a substantial protein content. However, most plant foods contain incomplete proteins because they lack a sufficient quantity of some essential amino acids. For this reason, the protein RDA for the adult male is 65 grams per day when plant proteins are the primary source. However, the American Dietetic Association, in their position stand on vegetarian diets, states that if certain plant foods are eaten over the course of a day, such as grains and legumes, they may supply all the essential amino acids necessary for human nutrition and be as complete a protein as animal protein.

Some recent research has suggested that if the daily dietary protein is obtained through a mixture of animal and plant foods in a ratio of 30:70, that is 30 percent of the protein from animal foods and 70 from plant foods, the protein quality would be similar to the use of animal foods alone. Mixing animal and plant foods in the same meal is common, and is also healthful and nutritious. Animal foods provide excellent sources of essential minerals, such as iron, zinc, and calcium, while plant foods provide carbohydrate, dietary fiber, and various phytochemicals.

Key Concept Recap

▶ Protein contains nitrogen, an element essential to the formation of twenty different amino acids, the building blocks of all body cells. All twenty amino acids are necessary for protein formation in the body.

▶ Essential, or indispensable, amino acids cannot be adequately synthesized in the body and thus must be obtained through dietary protein, whereas nonessential, or dispensable, amino acids may be synthesized in the body. Conditionally indispensable amino acids may be synthesized from other amino acids under normal conditions, but their synthesis may be limited under certain conditions when insufficient amounts of their precursors are available.

▶ The human body needs a balanced mixture of essential amino acids, and although animal protein provides all of the essential amino acids in the proper blend, a combination of certain plant proteins, such as grains and legumes, will satisfy this dietary requirement.

▶ The RDA for protein is based upon the body weight of the individual, and the amount needed per unit body weight is greater during childhood and adolescence than during adulthood. The adult RDA is 0.8 gram of protein per kilogram body weight, or 0.36 gram per pound body weight.

▶ The Acceptable Macronutrient Dietary Range for protein indicates that dietary intake should be no less than 10 percent nor greater than 35 percent of daily energy needs. Although animal foods in the meat and milk groups have a high protein content, they also may be high in fat. Increasing the proportion of dietary protein intake from plant sources is recommended.

Metabolism and Function

What happens to protein in the human body?

Dietary protein consists of long, complex chains of amino acids. In the digestive process, enzymes (proteases) in the stomach and small intestine break the complex protein down into polypeptides and then into individual amino acids. The amino acids are absorbed through the wall of the small intestine, pass into the blood, and then to the liver via the portal vein. The digestion of protein takes several hours, but once the amino acids enter the blood they are cleared within 5 to 10 minutes. There is a constant interchange of amino acids among the blood, the liver, and the body tissues. The liver is a critical center in amino acid metabolism. It is continually synthesizing a balanced amino acid mixture for the diverse protein requirements of the body. These amino acids are secreted into the blood and carried as free amino acids or as plasma proteins such as albumin. All these functions consume energy, and the thermic effect (TEF) is greater for protein as compared to carbohydrate and fat. Whether or not this plays an important role in weight control is discussed in chapter 10.

The most important metabolic fate of the amino acids is the formation of specific proteins, including the structural proteins such as muscle tissue and the functional proteins such as enzymes. Body cells obtain amino acids from the blood, and the genetic apparatus in the cell nucleus directs the synthesis of proteins specific to the cell needs. The body cells may also use some of the nitrogen from the amino acids to form non-protein nitrogen compounds, such as creatine. For example, the muscle cells will form contractile proteins as well as the enzymes and creatine phosphate necessary for energy production. The body cells will use only the amount of amino acids necessary to meet their protein needs. They cannot store excess amino acids to any significant amount, although the protein formed may be catabolized to release amino acids back to the blood.

Because the human body does not have a mechanism to store excess nitrogen, it cannot store amino acids per se. Through the process of **deamination** the amino group (NH_2) containing the nitrogen is removed from the amino acid, leaving a carbon substrate known as an **alpha-ketoacid.** The excess nitrogen must be excreted from the body. In essence, the liver forms **ammonia** (NH_3) from the excess nitrogen; the ammonia is converted into **urea,** which passes into the blood and is eventually eliminated by the kidneys into the urine.

The alpha-ketoacid that is released may have several fates. For one, this carbon substrate may be oxidized for the release of energy. For another, it may accept another amino group and be reconstituted to an amino acid. It also may be channeled into the metabolic pathways of carbohydrate and fat. The liver is the main organ where this conversion occurs. In essence, some of the amino acids are said to be **glucogenic amino acids,** that is, glucose forming. At various stages of the energy transformations within the liver, the glucogenic amino acids may be converted to glucose. This process is called gluconeogenesis. The **ketogenic amino acids** are metabolized in the liver to acetyl CoA, which may be used for energy production via the Krebs cycle or converted to fat. The glucose and fat produced may be transported to other parts of the body to be used. Thus, although excess protein cannot be stored as amino acids in the body, the energy content is not wasted, for it is converted to either carbohydrate or fat.

Protein turnover represents the process by which all body proteins are being continuously broken down and resynthesized, and it is an ongoing process. The National Academy of Sciences indicates that about 250 grams of body protein turns over daily in an adult, or about 0.5 pound of body mass. Figure 6.5 presents a summary of the fates of protein in human metabolism. See also appendix G, figure G.5.

Can protein be formed from carbohydrates and fats?

Yes, but with some major limitations. Protein has one essential element, nitrogen, which is not possessed by either carbohydrate or fat. However, if the body has an excess of amino acids, the liver

may be able to use the nitrogen-containing amino groups from these excess amino acids and combine them with alpha-ketoacids derived from either carbohydrate or fat metabolism. A key alpha-ketoacid from carbohydrate is pyruvic acid, while fat yields acetoacetic acid. The net result is the formation in the body of some of the nonessential amino acids using carbohydrates and fats as part of the building materials. Keep in mind that nitrogen must be present for this to occur, and its source is through dietary protein.

What are the major functions of protein in human nutrition?

Dietary protein may be utilized to serve all three major functions of food. Through the action of the individual amino acids, protein serves as the structural basis for the vast majority of body tissues, is essential for regulating metabolism, and can be used as an energy source. In one way or another protein is involved in almost all body functions. Its individual roles are beyond the scope of this text, so the following discussion represents just some of its major functions of importance to health and fitness. Table 6.5 highlights the major functions of protein in the body.

Protein is the main nutrient used in the formation of all body tissues. This role is extremely important in periods of rapid growth, such as childhood and adolescence. Athletes who attempt to gain muscle tissue also need an adequate dietary supply of protein to create a positive protein balance. Certain amino acids, such as the branched-chain amino acids (BCAA) leucine, isoleucine, and valine, constitute a significant amount of muscle tissue.

Protein is critical in the regulation of human metabolism. It is used in the formation of almost all enzymes, many hormones, and other compounds that control body functions. Insulin, hemoglobin, and the oxidative enzymes in the mitochondria are all proteins that have important roles in regulating metabolism during exercise. Other metabolic roles of protein include the maintenance of water balance and acid-base balance, regulation of the blood clotting process, prevention of infection, and development of immunity to disease. Proteins also serve as carriers for nutrients in the blood, such as the free fatty acids (FFA) and the lipoproteins, and help transport nutrients into the body cells.

Although protein is not a major energy source for humans at rest, it can serve such a function under several conditions. In nutritional balance, the priority use of dietary protein is to promote synthesis of body proteins essential for optimal structure and function. However, as noted previously, excess dietary protein may be deaminated and used for energy, or may be converted to carbohydrate or fat and then enter metabolic pathways for energy production or storage. On the other hand, during periods of starvation or semistarvation, adequate amounts of dietary or endogenous carbohydrates and dietary fats may not be available. Both dietary protein and the body protein stores are used for energy purposes in such a situation, because energy production takes precedence over tissue building in metabolism. Hence, if the active individual desires to maintain lean body mass, it is essential to have not only adequate protein intake but also sufficient carbohydrate Calories in the diet to provide a **protein-sparing effect.** In other words, carbohydrate Calories will be used for energy production, thus

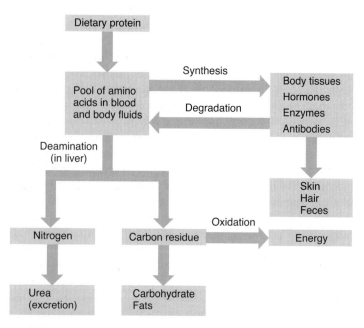

FIGURE 6.5 Simplified diagram of protein metabolism. Following the digestion of dietary proteins, one of the major functions of the amino acids is the synthesis of body tissues, enzymes, hormones, and antibodies. However, protein also is constantly being degraded by the liver. The excess nitrogen is excreted as urea while the carbon residue may be converted into carbohydrate or fat or used to produce energy.

TABLE 6.5 Summary of the functions of proteins and amino acids in human metabolism

1. Structural function	Form vital constituents of all cells in the body, such as contractile muscle proteins
2. Transport function	Transport various substances in the blood, such as the lipoproteins for conveying triglycerides
3. Enzyme function	Form almost all enzymes in the body to regulate numerous diverse physiological processes
4. Hormone and neurotransmitter function	Form various hormones, such as insulin; form various neurotransmitters, or neuropeptides, that function in the central nervous system, such as serotonin
5. Immune function	Form key components of the immune system, such as antibodies
6. Acid-base balance function	Buffer acid and alkaline substances in the blood to maintain optimal pH
7. Fluid balance function	Exert osmotic pressure to maintain optimal fluid balance in body tissues, particularly the blood
8. Energy function	Provide source of energy to the Krebs cycle when deaminated; excess protein may be converted to glucose or fat for subsequent energy production
9. Movement function	Provide movement when structural muscle proteins use energy to contract

sparing utilization of protein as an energy source and allowing it to be used for its more important structural and metabolic functions.

Although body proteins are composed of all twenty amino acids, individual amino acids may have important specific effects in the body. For example, the amino acid glycine is a neurotransmitter substance, tryptophan and tyrosine are important for the formation of several chemical transmitters in the brain, while the branched-chain amino acids (leucine, isoleucine, and valine) are major components of muscle tissue that may provide a source of energy.

Because of the diverse roles of protein and amino acids in the body, athletes have used protein supplements for years in attempts to improve performance. Amino acid supplements have only recently been introduced for this purpose. The effectiveness of such supplements is evaluated in later sections.

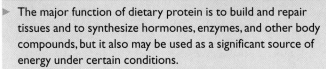

Key Concept Recap

▶ The major function of dietary protein is to build and repair tissues and to synthesize hormones, enzymes, and other body compounds, but it also may be used as a significant source of energy under certain conditions.

Proteins and Exercise

Are proteins used for energy during exercise?

In a recent review, Gibala noted that protein is regarded as a minor source of fuel during rest, usually accounting for less than 5 percent of total daily energy expenditure. However, given its nutritional importance, researchers have attempted to determine the effect of exercise on protein balance and needs.

Scientists have used a variety of techniques to study protein metabolism during exercise. Because urea is a by-product of pro-

tein metabolism, its concentration in the urine, blood, and sweat has been analyzed. Also, the presence in the urine of a marker for muscle protein breakdown known as 3-methylhistidine, a modified amino acid, has been studied to evaluate protein catabolism. The nitrogen balance technique consists of precisely measuring nitrogen intake and excretion to determine whether the individual is in positive or negative protein balance. Finally, labeled isotopes of amino acids have been ingested or injected to study their metabolic fate during exercise, not only in the whole body but also in isolated muscle groups.

Using these techniques, investigators have evaluated the use of protein during both resistance exercise and aerobic endurance exercise. Although both types of exercise affect protein metabolism, the use of protein as an energy source appears to be more prevalent in aerobic exercise, particularly when prolonged.

Resistance Training In a recent review, Rennie and Tipton noted that resistance exercise causes little change in amino acid oxidation, but probably depresses protein synthesis and elevates breakdown acutely. In this regard, Evans suggested that the eccentric muscle contraction associated with resistance training may produce ultrastructural damage that may stimulate this protein turnover. However, Wolfe noted that factors regulating muscle protein breakdown in human subjects are complex and interactive, and proposed that muscle protein breakdown is paradoxically elevated in the anabolic state following resistance exercise. Thus, while it appears that resistance exercise does not increase protein or amino acid oxidation, it may provoke muscle tissue breakdown.

Aerobic Endurance Exercise Poortmans has noted that although protein may be used to produce significant amounts of ATP in the muscle, during aerobic endurance exercise the rate of production is much slower than with carbohydrate and fat, the preferred fuels. On the other hand, Rennie and Tipton noted that sustained dynamic exercise stimulates amino acid oxidation, mainly by activating an enzyme that oxidizes BCAA, and ammonia production in proportion to exercise intensity. If the exercise is intense enough, there is a net loss of muscle protein as a result of decreased protein synthesis, increased catabolism, or both. Some of the amino acids are oxidized as fuel, and the rest provide substrates for gluconeogenesis. In this regard, prolonged exercise may be comparable to a state of starvation. As the endurance athlete depletes the endogenous carbohydrate stores, the body catabolizes some of its protein for energy or eventual conversion to glucose. Protein catabolism has been shown to increase significantly even when muscle glycogen is depleted by only about 33–55 percent.

In general, a brief session of exercise lowers the rate of protein synthesis and speeds protein breakdown. The exact mechanisms of protein metabolism during exercise have not been determined, though several mechanisms have been proposed. Parkhouse has reported that exercise, particularly exercise to exhaustion, activates specific proteolytic enzymes in the muscle that degrade the myofibrillar protein. Fitts and Metzger found elevated levels of proteolytic enzymes in fatigued muscle. In a recent review, Wagenmakers indicated that six amino acids may be metabolized in the muscle, providing the nitrogen needed for the synthesis of ammonia, alanine, and glutamine. During exercise, particularly prolonged aerobic exercise, Graham and MacLean noted significant muscle efflux of ammonia, glutamine, and alanine. These three products carry excess nitrogen from the muscle to other parts of the body, most notably the liver, for recycling or conversion to urea.

Ammonia, a nitrogen by-product of protein catabolism, is an indicator of increased muscle amino acid breakdown. Although no underlying mechanism has been identified, increasing levels of ammonia in the body have been associated with fatigue, somewhat comparable to the accumulation of lactic acid. One theory is that increased ammonia levels in the muscle may impair oxidative processes, thus decreasing energy production, while another theory suggests increased plasma ammonia may impair brain functions and induce central fatigue. Because ammonia is formed in the muscle from the amino group, removal of the amino group by alanine or glutamine may help decrease the production of ammonia and delay the onset of fatigue.

Glutamine release from the muscle also increases during exercise, and it is an important fuel for various cells in the body, particularly those in the immune system. As we shall see later, glutamine supplementation has been studied as a means to enhance immune function in athletes.

Although a number of amino acids may be used as energy substrate during exercise, the major research effort has focused on the fate of leucine. Leucine is the primary branched-chain amino acid in the muscle that is oxidized during exercise. The oxidation of leucine has been shown to increase during exercise. In essence, the amino group of leucine catabolism eventually combines with pyruvate in the muscle cell to form alanine and the residual alpha-ketoacid. The alpha-ketoacid may enter the Krebs cycle and be used for energy production. The alanine is released into the bloodstream and transported to the liver where it is converted into glucose. The glucose may then be released into the blood to be used by the central nervous system and may eventually find its way to the contracting muscle to be used as an energy source. Alanine appears to be the most

important means of transporting the amino group to the liver for excretion as urea. This overall process involving gluconeogenesis, known as the glucose-alanine cycle, is depicted graphically in figure 6.6. Some investigators have noted that during the latter part of endurance exercise, the blood levels of alanine increase, presumably because more is released from the muscle. However, the estimated glucose production approximates only 4 grams per hour, which might be important in mild-intensity exercise but is possibly insignificant during high-intensity exercise when carbohydrate use may approximate 3 grams per minute. Additionally, several investigators have reported an increased release of branched-chain amino acids (BCAA) from the liver during endurance exercise, with subsequent uptake by the muscle cells.

Thus, protein (amino acids) can be utilized during exercise to provide energy directly in the muscle and via glucose produced in the liver, particularly when the body stores of glycogen and glucose are low. In earlier research, Lemon has reported that in the latter stages of prolonged endurance exercise, protein could contribute up to 15 percent of the total energy cost. However, less protein would be used for energy during the early stages of prolonged exercise when carbohydrate is adequate. Thus, Gibala suggested that the contribution of amino acid oxidation to total energy expenditure is negligible during short-term intense exercise and accounts for 3–5 percent of the total energy production during prolonged exercise. In his recent review, Tarnopolsky cited similar figures, indicating that protein oxidation could account for 1 to 6 percent of the energy cost of aerobic exercise.

It is important to note how dietary carbohydrate influences protein as an energy source during exercise. A low-carbohydrate diet leading to decreased muscle glycogen levels will lead to increased dependence on protein as an energy source. On the other hand, adequate carbohydrate intake before and during prolonged exercise will help reduce the use of body protein for this purpose, because the presence of adequate muscle glycogen appears to inhibit enzymes that catabolize muscle protein. Scientists from the

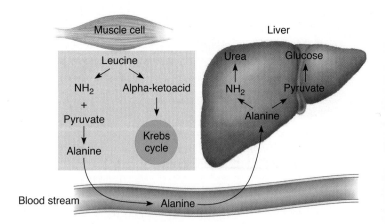

FIGURE 6.6 Glucose-alanine cycle. Alanine may be produced in the muscle tissue from the breakdown of other amino acids, most notably leucine. The alanine is then released into the blood and travels to the liver for eventual conversion to glucose through the process of gluconeogenesis. (See appendix G, figure G.5, for other amino acids that may enter energy pathways.)

University of Maastricht in the Netherlands recently noted that high-carbohydrate diets may have a protein-sparing effect for endurance athletes.

Although the available evidence suggests that metabolism of protein and its use as an energy source are increased during exercise, the magnitude of its contribution may depend on a variety of factors, such as the intensity and duration of exercise and the availability of other fuels, such as glycogen, in the muscle.

Does exercise increase protein losses in other ways?

Exercise has been shown to increase protein losses from the body in several other ways. For one, exercise may cause an elevated level of protein in the urine, a condition known as **proteinuria.** This condition has been observed following competition in a wide variety of sports, including running, football, basketball, and handball. Research suggests that the greater the intensity of the exercise, such as a high-intensity 400-meter sprint versus a lower-intensity 3,000-meter run, the greater the loss of protein in the urine. Prolonged aerobic exercise, such as the triathlon, has also increased urinary protein loss. Yaguchi and others suggested heavy, prolonged exercise, such as a triathlon, may induce some transient kidney damage in some individuals. Such damage may explain the findings of Poortmans, who reported a decreased reabsorption of protein in the kidney tubules following intense exercise. However, the total amount of protein lost in this manner appears to be rather negligible, amounting to less than 3 grams per day.

Protein also may be lost in the sweat. Several investigators have reported the presence of both amino acids and proteins in exercise-induced sweat, with both sweat rate and sweat nitrogen losses increasing with greater exercise intensities. Again, the losses are relatively minor, on the order of 1 gram per liter of sweat in adult males. This avenue could account for 2–4 grams of protein in an endurance athlete training in a warm environment.

As shall be noted in chapter 8, prolonged intense exercise may also increase gastrointestinal losses of iron, which may be bound to blood proteins. Again, however, these protein losses would be relatively minor.

What happens to protein metabolism during recovery after exercise?

Although net protein breakdown occurs during exercise, in general protein synthesis is believed to predominate during the recovery period. In a recent review, Tipton and Wolfe noted that whole body protein breakdown is generally reduced following aerobic endurance exercise, while whole body protein synthesis is either increased or unchanged. However, they note that whole body protein synthesis may not represent changes in specific muscle groups. Muscle groups which have been exercised may experience protein synthesis as they may be especially insulin sensitive after exercise. In another review, Walberg-Rankin notes that although leucine may be oxidized during moderate aerobic exercise, leucine balance returns to normal in 24 hours, indicating a reduced leucine catabolism over this time frame.

Tipton and Wolfe report that resistance exercise induces protein breakdown in the exercised muscles, which may persist in the immediate recovery period. However, over the next 24–48 hours, protein anabolism appears to predominate and the net effect is increased protein synthesis. Wolfe notes that anabolic states appear to be due more to stimulation of synthesis rather than a decrease in breakdown. This is especially so if adequate amino acids are available.

Eccentric exercise, such as lowering weights during resistance exercise or running downhill rapidly, puts tremendous stress on muscle tissue, and often induces muscle soreness in the following days. Tipton and Wolfe note that following eccentric exercise, whole body protein breakdown is increased. Microtears in muscle fibers may impair protein synthesis and delay recovery from such exercise.

What effect does exercise training have upon protein metabolism?

Rennie noted that protein metabolism may also become more efficient as a result of training, noting that the response of muscle protein turnover to habitual exercise is comparable to other metabolic changes in the muscle associated with exercise training. Although an initial bout of exercise may markedly elevate protein breakdown and synthesis in an untrained individual, the effect would be much less in one who has trained habitually. Tarnopolsky indicated that training induces a decreased *activity* in the enzyme that oxidizes BCAA.

As mentioned, protein synthesis appears to predominate in the muscles during recovery. With training, or repeated bouts of exercise on a regular basis, changes in the muscle structure and function are additive. Numerous studies have found that after resistance or endurance exercise, protein balance becomes positive. Trained individuals, during rest, have been shown to experience a preferential oxidation of fat and a sparing of protein, as measured by leucine metabolism and the respiratory quotient. The specific exercise task apparently stimulates the DNA in the muscle cell nucleus to increase the synthesis of protein, and the type of protein that is synthesized is specific to the type of exercise. Aerobic exercise stimulates syntheses of mitochondria and oxidative enzymes, which are composed of protein and are necessary for energy production in the oxygen system. Resistance training promotes synthesis of the contractile muscle proteins. These adaptations are the key factors underlying improved performance.

Other than its beneficial effects in increasing structural and functional protein important to resistance or aerobic endurance exercise, training may influence protein metabolism in other ways to help prevent premature fatigue. You may recall from previous chapters that there is substantial research to support the conclusion that aerobic endurance training improves the ability of the muscle cell to use both carbohydrate and fat as energy sources during exercise. Although extensive evidence is not available, in a recent review, Graham and others noted that following endurance training enzymes in the muscles appear to develop the potential for increased capacity for oxidation of leucine and the other BCAA which are an abundant source of energy in the muscles. Thus, endurance training may increase the capacity of the muscle to derive energy from protein in a fashion similar to the increased utilization of fat, another possible means to spare the use of carbohydrates such as blood glucose and muscle glycogen. Although these changes do not appear to spare the use of muscle protein, they would appear to spare the use of carbohydrate, and thus may help prevent fatigue when carbohydrate levels are decreased during exercise.

Additionally, when exercising at a standardized workload before and after training, training may also decrease the production or accumulation of ammonia. Extrapolating from animal research, some investigators theorize that instead of forming ammonia, the nitrogen is incorporated into other amino acids, such as alanine, for transportation from the muscle to the liver. Theoretically, reduced plasma ammonia levels may be associated with less fatigue.

Training properly may also help prevent muscle injury associated with eccentric exercise. Research shows that physically trained individuals, when compared to untrained individuals, do not experience as much muscle tissue damage during prolonged, eccentric exercise tasks. However, specificity of training is also important, and individuals preparing for a race with a significant downhill component, such as the Boston Marathon, should gradually incorporate increasing intensities of eccentric exercise in their training.

In general, these changes associated with appropriate training appear to represent another means whereby the body adapts to endurance training in an attempt to prevent fatigue. On the other hand, some research indicates that excessive training leading to the overtraining syndrome is associated with a persistent decrease in plasma amino acids, particularly glutamine.

The effect of training in producing a positive nitrogen balance or a positive protein balance, and possibly the effect of preventing the overtraining syndrome, depends on an adequate dietary supply of protein and Calories.

Do individuals in strenuous physical training, including the developing adolescent athlete, need more protein in the diet?

In their recent joint position stand, the American College of Sports Medicine, the American Dietetic Association, and the Dietitians of Canada concluded that protein requirements are higher in very active individuals and suggested that resistance athletes need 1.6–1.7 grams per kilogram body weight while endurance athletes need approximately 1.2–1.4 grams per kilogram. Conversely, in its recent Dietary Reference Intakes for protein, the National Academy of Sciences concluded that in view of the lack of compelling evidence to the contrary, no additional dietary protein is suggested for healthy adults undertaking resistance or endurance exercise. Some investigators even contend that because exercise training increases the ability of the body to retain protein in the recovery period, athletes in training may need less protein than sedentary individuals if they consume enough Calories to maintain body weight.

The following is a brief summary of the divergent viewpoints relative to the protein needs of athletes involved in either strength-type or endurance-type activities, including the special condition of sports anemia.

Strength-Type Activities Individuals involved in strength training, such as weight lifters, bodybuilders, and football players, are usually interested in increasing muscle mass and decreasing body fat, as well as improving strength and power. Other than water, protein is the main component of muscle tissue, so strength-trained individuals have valued dietary protein as a key nutrient for centuries as a means of maximizing muscle protein synthesis.

Unfortunately, there is very little scientific information about the specific protein requirements for the development of lean muscle mass in weight-training programs. Protein balance is usually positive during these programs, and research studies have suggested that weight lifters could retain between 7 and 28 grams of protein per day, a range of about 12–50 percent of the RDA for an adult 70-kilogram male. Although it might be assumed this protein would be assimilated as muscle tissue, this has not been determined. A number of respected investigators have recommended that weight lifters and other athletes training to increase muscle mass and strength, particularly the developing adolescent athlete and those in the early stages of training, consume more protein. Peter Lemon, in a 2000 review, notes that with strength activities there is good evidence that the current RDA for protein (0.8 g/kg/day) will actually limit muscle growth in strength-trained individuals. Optimal intakes appear to be in the range of 1.5 to 1.8 g/kg/day, but he also noted some research supports even higher intakes, particularly when athletes concomitantly use anabolic agents. However, the use of anabolic steroids and other anabolic agents, as discussed in chapter 12, is prohibited by most athletic governing organizations.

In addition to protein, Gail Butterfield recommends strength-trained athletes attempting to increase muscle mass also consume additional energy, about 200 more Calories per day. Carbohydrate is a recommended energy source, as the insulin effect of carbohydrate is also anabolic. This topic is covered in chapter 12.

On the other hand, the National Academy of Sciences notes that although athletes commonly believe they need a higher protein intake to maintain optimum physical performance, few studies have evaluated the protein needs of individuals engaged in strenuous physical activity such as resistance training. The Academy has criticized the available studies and concluded the available data do not support the conclusion that the protein requirement for resistance training individuals is greater than that of nonexercising subjects.

Michael Rennie, an international scholar in protein metabolism, has noted that muscle contractile activity enhances the anabolic response so that habitual training makes individuals more efficient users of dietary protein, suggesting that physically active people probably do not need to eat more protein and could likely manage perfectly adequately on less.

Dietary protein suggestions for strength-trained individuals are presented in chapter 12.

Endurance-Type Activities It is important to reinforce the viewpoint that carbohydrate is the main energy source for endurance-type athletes. Besides its efficiency as a metabolic fuel during exercise, carbohydrate also provide a potent protein-sparing effect. Consuming sufficient carbohydrate will decrease reliance on protein during aerobic endurance exercise, reduce the formation of ammonia, and better maintain normal protein status in the body.

Nevertheless, additional dietary protein has been recommended for endurance athletes because they may utilize protein as an energy source during exercise and may need protein to synthesize oxidative enzymes and mitochondria. Athletes involved in prolonged intermittent high-intensity sports, such as soccer, field or ice hockey, lacrosse, and basketball, may also fall into this category. Additionally, extra protein has been recommended to prevent development of anemia during the early stages of training. In brief, **sports anemia** is thought to occur because the body uses dietary protein for these aforementioned purposes at the expense of hemoglobin formation, leading to anemia.

As with strength-trained individuals, various investigators have also estimated the protein requirement of endurance-trained individuals. In the most recent review based on protein balance studies, Lemon indicated that individuals involved in vigorous aerobic endurance exercise are recommended to consume 1.1 to 1.4 g/kg/day while slightly higher amounts, about 1.4–1.7 grams per kilogram body weight, have been recommended for individuals involved in intermittent high-intensity sports because these include a balance of endurance and power activities.

Some early Japanese studies suggested that 1.5–2.0 grams of protein per kilogram body weight were needed to prevent sports anemia during the early stages of endurance training, but a more contemporary Japanese report indicates that although low protein intake may contribute to the development of sports anemia, it may be prevented by normal protein intake of 1.25 grams per kilogram, which is greater than the current RDA in the United States. Sports anemia also has been associated with iron nutriture and will be discussed in more detail in chapter 8.

Although these considerations could conceivably increase the protein requirements for endurance-type athletes, the National Academy of Sciences believes otherwise. The Academy noted that although studies have reported significant increases in amino acid oxidation during endurance exercise, the increased oxidation was measured around the time of the exercise itself and did not take into account the remaining part of the day. The Academy noted that the amount of protein oxidized, although significant, was small in comparison to the total daily amount of oxidation

Given these divergent opinions, what are some prudent recommendations regarding dietary protein intake for physically active individuals?

What are some general recommendations relative to dietary protein intake for athletes?

In a recent review, Peter Lemon, an international authority on protein metabolism during exercise, stated that it is difficult to make a conclusive protein intake recommendation for those active in vigorous regular exercise because of the complexity of the protein metabolic response to exercise. Nevertheless, recent reviews by some of the most prominent investigators in protein metabolism during exercise provide the basis for some reasonable guidelines. All of the recommendations are consistent with the AMDR for protein.

1. *Obtain the RDA for protein.* All athletes should obtain at least the protein RDA of approximately 0.8–1.0 gram per kilogram body weight daily. As you may recall from our discussion in chapter 2, the RDA contains a safety factor and actually provides more protein than required by most individuals. Although some investigators have suggested trained athletes may actually need less dietary protein because training may have improved their protein efficiency, obtaining at least the RDA appears to be prudent.

2. *Increase the protein RDA by 50 to 100 percent.* Although some research does suggest that athletes need to consume at least the RDA for protein, Lemon has indicated it may be prudent to recommend more. Amounts recommended by various investigators have varied slightly, but are comparable to the recommendations contained in the position stand on nutrition for the athlete recently published by the American College of Sports Medicine, the American Dietetic Association, and Dietitians of Canada. As noted previously, they recommend 1.2–1.4 grams of protein per kilogram body weight for endurance-trained athletes and 1.6–1.7 grams per kilogram for resistance-trained athletes. These recommendations approximate a 50–100 percent increase of the protein RDA, but are well within the AMDR of 10–35 percent of daily energy intake from protein.

The following mathematical presentations are possible scenarios for various athletes who may wish to maintain or increase protein balance. The protein needs are based upon the RDA, a rough estimate of the amount of protein used during strenuous exercise, and additional protein needs for the individual who wants to gain weight.

Let us look first at the young resistance-trained athlete who wants to gain body weight, preferably in the form of muscle tissue, through a weight-training program. The protein RDA for an adolescent male is 0.85 gram per kilogram. At moderate activity levels, the average 70-kg adolescent male would be in protein balance with about 60 grams daily. However, according to the suggested upper recommendation of about 1.7 grams per kilogram, he would need about 119 g daily if involved in a strenuous training program. Is this a reasonable amount?

One pound of muscle tissue is equal to 454 grams, and its composition is approximately 70 percent water, 7 percent lipids, and 22 percent muscle tissue. Hence, 1 pound of muscle contains about 100 grams of protein ($454 \times .22$). If the desired weight gain is 1 pound of lean body mass per week, a reasonable goal, then this young male would need an additional 14 grams of protein per day (100 grams/7 days) to supply the amount in 1 pound of muscle tissue. A gain of 2 pounds per week, although probably more difficult to accomplish, would require 28 additional grams of protein per day. Let us be liberal and estimate an additional 22 grams of protein per day to cover losses due to exercise. In summary, assuming that a portion of these protein needs are not covered by the safety margin incorporated in the RDA, this young athlete would need approximately 110 grams of protein per day (60 + 28 + 22) to gain 2 pounds of lean body tissue per week, or about 1.6 grams of protein per kilogram body weight. This value falls within the recommended range for resistance-trained athletes.

Endurance athletes are not necessarily interested in gaining weight, but they may need to replenish the protein that may serve as an energy source during training. Running 10 miles per day would expend approximately 1,000 Calories. Again, let us be liberal and assume that if 6 percent of this energy cost, or 60 Calories, was derived from protein, then approximately 15 grams of protein (60 Calories/4 Calories per gram of protein) would need to be replaced. With a liberal estimated additional loss of 10 grams of protein in the urine and sweat, the total daily protein requirement for a 70-kg young male, again assuming that these additional needs are not accounted for by the safety margin in the RDA, would be 85 grams (60 + 15 + 10), or 1.2 g/kg. Again, this value falls within the recommended range.

3. *Obtain about 15 percent of daily energy intake from protein.* As do most investigators, Peter Lemon indicates that it is possible to get these recommended amounts from natural food sources in the daily diet. For example, the average caloric intake for a moderately active young male averages 2,500–3,000 C. This caloric intake may be increased through physical training as more Calories are expended. Thus, caloric intake would be increased to approximately 3,500–4,000 C. It is important to note that adequate energy intake, primarily in the form of carbohydrates, will improve protein balance. In essence, an increased energy intake appears to decrease protein requirements somewhat.

If the protein portion of the dietary Calories averaged 12 percent, a general recommended level of protein intake, then the intake of protein would approximate 1.5–1.7 grams per kilogram body weight, which parallels the amounts estimated in the examples cited previously. Currently, the protein content of the average American is 12 to 16 percent, and Walberg-Rankin recently noted that most athletes consume this much or more in their daily diets. Consuming a diet with a protein content of 15 percent could provide a value of 2.0 grams or more per kilogram body weight, and other surveys among strength-type athletes indicate they obtain this amount. These values approach or exceed the higher amounts recommended by some investigators for individuals in training. The calculations are presented in table 6.6.

Some athletes may need to increase the percentage of protein in their daily caloric intake. Athletes in weight-control sports, such as wrestlers and gymnasts, may be in greater need of protein because of low caloric intake. Endurance athletes, particularly ultraendurance athletes, are susceptible to overtraining and chronic fatigue. Such athletes have been found to have depressed plasma levels of amino acids, which Kingsbury and others indicated appeared to be associated with inadequate protein intake. Young athletes have high protein needs to support growth and development. Female endurance athletes may need more protein because of inadequate energy intake, and low dietary protein intake has been associated with amenorrhea, a topic discussed further in chapters 8 and 10.

Increasing the protein percentage of daily energy intake may help such athletes obtain adequate protein. For example, a young wrestler attempting to lose weight to compete in a lower weight category might be on a diet of 1,600 Calories

TABLE 6.6 Calculation of grams protein/kilogram body weight

Body weight: 70 kg
One gram protein = 4 Calories

Daily caloric intake:	3,500–4,000	3,500–4,000
Percent protein:	15	12
Calories in protein:	525–600	420–480
Grams of protein:	131–150	105–120
Grams protein/kg:	1.9–2.1	1.5–1.7

per day. With an RDA of 1.0 gram of protein per kilogram body weight, a 60-kilogram (132 pound) wrestler would need 60 grams of protein to meet the RDA and up to 102 grams to meet the highest recommendation for strength-type athletes. In order to consume 60 grams of protein, the wrestler would need to obtain only 15 percent of daily energy intake from protein, but to obtain 102 grams of protein would need to obtain about 25 percent of daily energy intake from protein. These amounts are well within the AMDR for protein.

Wise selection of high-quality protein foods will provide adequate amounts through a balanced diet to meet bodily needs during the early and continued stages of training. It is not difficult to increase the protein content of the diet. For example, 8 ounces of roasted, skinless chicken breast and two glasses of skim milk, a total of less than 600 Calories, will provide over 70 grams of high-quality protein, the RDA for our typical 70-kg adolescent and more than half of the 125 grams that may be recommended for such an athlete attempting to gain muscle mass. Perusal of table 6.2 and appendix E will help you select high-protein foods. Additional points on this subject are covered in chapter 12 under the topic of gaining weight.

4. *Consume protein, preferably with carbohydrate, before and after workouts.* Eating strategies may also be an important consideration. In a review of protein supplements and exercise, Wolfe noted that amino acid intake after exercise stimulates muscle protein synthesis as a consequence of stimulating amino acid transport into the muscle, and that this stimulatory effect is greater after exercise than at rest. However, questions remain as to the exact composition, amount, and timing of ingestion of the supplement. The timing of protein intake may be important. Lemon indicates that some data suggest the practice of consuming nutrients prior to training may be beneficial, possibly by providing fuel and/or minimizing catabolic processes. Studies from Robert Wolfe's laboratory, using both intravenous and oral administration of amino acids, have suggested that providing an ample supply to the muscle within 1–3 hours following exercise may help to further stimulate protein synthesis. The increased blood flow to the muscle during the immediate recovery period may permit a more effective delivery of the amino acids. In his review, Rennie indicated that muscle protein synthesis appears to be very

sensitive to increased availability of amino acids in the blood and appears to be saturated by a relatively small increase in amino acid availability equivalent to about 3.5–7.0 grams of protein over an hour.

Carbohydrate alone may have some effect on protein synthesis following exercise, as it may help to decrease secretion of cortisol, a hormone that promotes protein catabolism. Moreover, Lemon has noted that the insulin response to dietary carbohydrate has been shown to enhance the already elevated protein synthetic rate in muscle following a strength-training session. However, studies led by Andersen and Børsheim found that postexercise carbohydrate supplementation induces only minor improvements in muscle protein balance as compared to protein supplementation.

Several studies and reviews have suggested that such protein intake soon *after* exercise, possibly combined with carbohydrate, was beneficial. Levenhagen and others recently reported that consuming protein immediately after exercise enhanced accretion of whole body and leg protein as compared to protein consumption several hours later. Rasmussen and others, using three separate techniques (infusion of a labeled amino acid, phenylalanine; femoral arterial and venous blood sampling; muscle biopsies) to study leg muscle protein kinetics, found that supplementation with amino acids plus carbohydrate (6 grams essential amino acids and 35 grams sucrose) stimulated muscle protein anabolism by increasing muscle protein synthesis when ingested 1 or 3 hours after resistance exercise. These findings were supported in recent studies by Koopman and others, who used a protein/carbohydrate solution during exercise and added leucine to a protein/carbohydrate feeding after exercise. Esmarck also found that consumption of protein with carbohydrate soon after exercise also benefits muscle protein synthesis in the elderly as well. Based on available studies, Fielding and Parkington suggested that athletes should consume a diet rich in amino acids and carbohydrate soon after the exercise training bout. In their book entitled *Nutrient Timing,* Ivy and Portman recommended that the carbohydrate: protein ratio should be about 3–4 grams of carbohydrate for each gram of protein, preferably in a highly digestible, liquid form.

On the other hand, in a recent review Wolfe noted that a mixture of essential amino acids and carbohydrate more effectively simulates muscle protein synthesis when taken *before* as opposed to after exercise. Wolfe also noted that exercise and exogenous essential amino acids have an additive effect on muscle protein synthesis, and that you do not need nonessential amino acids.

Some earlier research had noted that consuming protein or amino acids along with a carbohydrate solution would speed muscle glycogen recovery following exercise, which could be important to both resistance-type and endurance-type athletes. However, those studies provided more energy in the protein and carbohydrate solution compared to the carbohydrate solution alone. Studies that balanced the energy intake in the solutions found that carbohydrate alone was just as effective as the carbohydrate-protein combination.

Summarizing these viewpoints, Gibala indicated that consumption of a drink containing about 0.1 gram of essential

amino acids per kilogram of body weight (7 grams for a 70-kilogram athlete) during the first few hours of recovery from heavy resistance exercise will produce a transient, net positive increase in muscle protein balance. Gibala also noted that it is uncertain if ingesting amino acids immediately before exercise or ingesting carbohydrate along with amino acids, either immediately before exercise or during recovery, further enhances the rate of muscle protein buildup during recovery. Some investigators have suggested that it may be helpful to consume, throughout the day, multiple small meals having adequate protein. Gibala indicates that although these strategies will promote a net "anabolic" environment in the body, it remains to be determined if the acute effects of supplementation eventually lead to greater gains in muscle mass following habitual training. For those athletes interested in restoring muscle glycogen rapidly, Gibala concluded if enough carbohydrate is ingested during the first 2–5 hours of recovery, protein supplementation does not further increase muscle glycogen replenishment.

Overall, given these findings, consuming a small amount of protein and carbohydrate, such as a turkey breast sandwich or a protein/carbohydrate energy drink, before or after exercise training may be prudent behavior for many athletes. Adequate carbohydrate, as discussed in chapter 4, is essential for muscle glycogen replenishment.

5. *Be prudent regarding protein intake.* Whether or not athletes in training need additional protein is not clear at this time. Two experts in protein metabolism, Kevin Tipton and Robert Wolfe, noted that given sufficient energy intake, lean body mass can be maintained within a wide range of protein intakes. They note that since a high protein intake is not likely harmful, and since there is a metabolic rationale for the efficacy of an increase in dietary protein if muscle hypertrophy is the goal, a higher protein intake within the context of an athlete's overall dietary requirements may be beneficial. However, they also note that there are few convincing data to indicate that the ingestion of a high amount of protein (2–3 grams per kilogram body weight) is necessary. Based on current literature, they conclude that it may be too simplistic to rely on recommendations of a particular amount of protein per day because the amount depends on energy intake, type of protein, and timing of intake.

Consuming additional protein within the AMDR is both safe and prudent. Table 6.7 presents a summary of some prudent daily protein intakes for sedentary and physically active individuals.

Key Concept Recap

▶ During aerobic endurance exercise, particularly with low carbohydrate stores in the body, muscle protein may supply nearly 5 percent of the energy Calories.

▶ Although protein catabolism may occur during exercise, protein synthesis predominates in the recovery period. The type of protein synthesized is specific to the type of exercise program, such as weight (strength) training or aerobic endurance.

▶ Several recognized authorities have recommended a protein intake of 1.6–1.7 grams per kilogram body weight per day for

- athletes attempting to gain weight, and about 1.2–1.4 grams per kilogram body weight per day for endurance athletes.
- ▶ Although some athletes may benefit from additional protein in the diet, they do not need expensive commercial protein supplements; instead, they should obtain the extra protein they need through the increased caloric intake needed to match energy expenditure.
- ▶ The National Academy of Sciences has indicated that the RDA is sufficient to meet the protein needs of athletes. However, others have suggested that physical training increases the protein requirements, but these recommended increases are well within the AMDR.

Check for Yourself

Using table 6.7 as a guide, calculate how many grams of protein may be recommended for you. If you have not already done so, keep a record of your daily food intake for several days and determine if you are obtaining sufficient dietary protein.

TABLE 6.7 Prudent protein intakes in grams per kilogram body weight for sedentary and physically active individuals

	Grams of protein/kg body weight
Sedentary	0.8
Strength-trained, maintenance	1.2–1.4
Strength-trained, gain muscle mass	1.6–1.7
Endurance-trained	1.2–1.4
Intermittent, high-intensity training	1.4–1.7
Weight-restricted	1.4–1.8

The values presented represent a synthesis of those recommended by leading researchers involved in protein metabolism and exercise. Teenagers should add 10 percent to the calculated values.

To calculate body weight in kilograms, simply multiply your weight in pounds by 0.454. Then, multiply your weight in kilograms by the appropriate value in the grams per kilogram body weight column to determine the range of grams of protein intake per day. Teenagers should increase this amount by 10 percent.

Protein: Ergogenic Aspects

Given the potential importance of protein to optimal physical performance, a wide variety of ergogenic aids associated with protein nutrition have been used in attempts to enhance performance. Such supplements remain popular. As Lawrence and Kirby recently noted, protein, amino acids, and creatine were among the top five most popular sports supplements.

Are high-protein diets or special protein supplements necessary?

As already discussed, some investigators suggest that athletes involved in weight training to gain weight or in strenuous endurance exercise may need somewhat more than the RDA for protein to maintain or increase protein balance, particularly if energy intake (Calories) is not adequate to meet daily energy expenditure.

To provide additional protein to the diet, investigators have used high protein diets, powdered protein sources, canned liquid meals high in protein and energy, sports drinks and bars, or special foods and concoctions high in protein content. However, the protein content is actually derived from natural protein, such as milk, egg, or soy protein. As Bucci has indicated, supplements of intact proteins, such as the proteins found in these products, offer no advantages over protein found in other food sources, since these supplements are in fact derived from natural foods. In addition, many of these protein supplements are expensive when compared to natural protein that may be obtained easily in high-protein foods such as powdered milk, skim milk, eggs, and chicken. Blending powdered milk into a glass of skim milk, with some vanilla or other flavoring, will provide substantial amounts of high-quality protein—your own personal protein supplement. Some comparative costs for different sources of protein are presented in table 6.8.

Nevertheless, commercial supplements may be a convenient means for some busy athletes to secure additional protein in the diet. Many of these products contain high-quality protein, such as milk or egg protein; provide a balanced mixture of protein, carbohydrate, and fat for additional Calories; and may also contain supplemental vitamins and minerals. Although these products do not contain all of the nutrients of natural foods, they may be useful adjuncts to a balanced diet. Certain brands have been available for years, such as Nutrament, but several companies have marketed products specifically for physically active individuals, such as Nitrofuel by Twin Labs and Nutrition Shake by Gatorade. It is important to reemphasize the point that these supplements should be used as an adjunct to an otherwise balanced nutritional plan, not as a substitute.

Whey and colostrum are two forms of protein that are theorized to be ergogenic. Whey proteins are extracted from the liquid whey that is produced during the manufacture of cheese or casein. Whey protein isolates are more than 90 percent protein and contain all essential amino acids, but Walzem and others note that bovine whey may contain other substances, including growth factors. Colostrum, or bovine colostrum, is the first milk secreted by cows. Brinkworth and others indicate that colostrum is a rich source of protein, carbohydrates, vitamins, minerals, and various biologically active components, also including growth factors. Although no mechanism has been identified, one theory involves increased levels of serum insulin-like growth factor (IGF-1), which could be anabolic. However, Kuipers and others provided 60 grams of colosturm daily for 4 weeks to endurance-trained males and found no effect on blood IGF-I or IGF binding protein levels.

Other protein substances such as spirulina (algae), brewer's yeast, specific enzymes, and even DNA and RNA have been advocated as means to improve physical performance. Spirulina and

TABLE 6.8 Costs of protein found in various food sources

Source	Serving size	Grams of protein/serving	Cost per serving	Cost per 8 grams of protein
Powdered milk	23 grams	8	$0.13	$0.13
Egg	1	6	$0.10	$0.13
Turkey breast	4 ounces	28	$0.75	$0.21
Skim milk	8 fluid ounces	8	$0.20	$0.20
Protein capsules	8 capsules	8	$1.20	$1.20
MetRx Bar	3.5-ounce bar	27	$2.50	$0.74
Boost	8 fluid ounces	10	$1.10	$0.88
Avalanche Power Drink	16 fluid ounces	40	$3.00	$0.60
Whey Pro	1 scoop	23	$1.01	$0.34

brewer's yeast are good sources of protein and a variety of vitamins and minerals but convey no magical ergogenic qualities. The enzymes and DNA would be degraded in the digestive process and thus could not be utilized for the purpose for which they were ingested.

Protein/carbohydrate solutions, some marketed as sports drinks, have been theorized to enhance endurance performance above and beyond that provided by carbohydrate alone. As noted in chapter 4, carbohydrate-containing sports drinks may enhance performance in prolonged endurance exercise. However, as noted below, research findings revealing additional benefits of additional protein have been criticized.

Although athletes in training may need more protein, the following sections indicate few data are available to support the viewpoint that high protein diets or protein supplements provide an ergogenic effect to athletes.

Strength-Type Activities Limited research is available regarding the effect of increased dietary protein, including whey and colostrum, on strength-type performance.

High protein diets Several earlier laboratory studies have compared the effect of normal protein intake, about 0.8–1.4 grams per kilogram, to higher levels, such as 1.6–2.8 grams per kilogram, on body composition changes during a weight-training program. In general, these studies revealed that although protein balance could be maintained or even be positive with the consumption of a normal amount of protein, the body protein balance was even more positive with the larger amounts. The additional body weight also appears to be in the form of lean body mass.

Other well-designed studies have not shown any ergogenic effects on strength-type performance. Weideman and others, using nuclear magnetic resonance to measure leg volume, reported no significant increase in leg muscle hypertrophy following 13 weeks of weight training with 2.94 grams of protein per kilogram per day, nor did Lemon and others find increased muscle mass when subjects consumed 2.62 grams of protein per kilogram per day, as compared to 1.35 grams per kilogram. Additionally, neither of these two studies reported a significant effect of the high-protein intake on measures of strength. In a recent review, Garlick and others noted an absence of strong evidence that high-protein diets confer any advantage in terms of strength.

As noted previously, some investigators recommend protein intake immediately following exercise. Several studies have evaluated the effect of protein supplementation on possible muscle damage during training, but the results are contradictory. One study reported that 15 grams of protein consumed immediately after exercise enhanced muscle repair, as measured by changes in enzyme status associated with muscle damage. Conversely, another study, using 37.5 grams of protein, showed no facilitation in recovery from muscle damage, as measured by a strength test. Given the possibility of enhanced muscle repair, consuming some of the recommended daily amount of protein immediately following exercise may be a prudent behavior.

Whey and colostrum The research regarding the ergogenic effect of whey protein to strength-type individuals is very limited. Burke and others studied the effect of whey supplementation (1.2 grams per kilogram per day) as compared to a carbohydrate placebo on body composition and strength in males undergoing resistance training for 6 weeks. Subjects consuming the whey supplement significantly increased lean body mass and performance in some, but not all, strength tests more so than the placebo group. Although this study shows some significant benefits of whey protein, other forms of protein may be just as effective as the placebo contained only carbohydrate. For example, Tipton and others reported that acute ingestion of both whey protein and casein after exercise resulted in similar increases in net muscle protein synthesis even though there were different patterns of blood amino acid responses.

Several studies have evaluated the ergogenic effect of colostrum supplementation, using whey protein as a placebo which could reveal whether colostrum supplementation produced any benefits beyond those attributed to whey protein alone. Hofman and others evaluated the effect of bovine colostrum on body composition and four tests of exercise performance in elite male and female field hockey players. The tests included two shuttle sprints (50 and 300 meters total for time), a shuttle sprint test to exhaustion, and a vertical jump. The subjects consumed 60 grams of colostrum daily for 8 weeks and whey protein served as the placebo. The colostrum had no effect on body composition or three of the four exercise tests, but did appear to improve performance in the 50-meter shuttle sprint test. Antonio and others investigated the effect of 20 grams of bovine colostrum, given daily during 8 weeks of aerobic and heavy-resistance exercise training, on body composition, strength, and aerobic endurance. There were no effects of the colostrum on exercise performance. The whey group significantly increased total body mass, whereas the colostrum group, although not increasing total body mass, did increase lean body mass which was attributed to a slight decrease in body fat. Brinkworth and others, studying the effect of either bovine colostrum or whey protein supplementation (60 grams daily) during 8 weeks of resistance training, found that subjects in the colostrum group increased arm circumference and cross-sectional area, but the increase was due principally to a greater increase in skin and subcutaneous fat.

Although these studies are suggestive of some ergogenic effects, they should be regarded as preliminary. Additional research is merited.

Endurance-Type Activities Although the data are limited, several studies have evaluated the effects of a high-protein diet and various types of protein supplements on endurance exercise performance.

High-protein diet or meal The recent 40:30:30 "zone diet" alluded to in chapter 5 may be considered to be a high-protein diet because 30 percent of the daily Calories are derived from protein (high end of the AMDR), 40 percent are derived from carbohydrate, and 30 percent are derived from fat. The premise underlying the "zone diet" is a change in hormonal activity, resulting in vasoactive eicosanoids that permit greater oxygen delivery to the muscle, a condition referred to as the "zone." In a recent review, Cheuvront criticized the "zone diet" book, noting that the claims of improved sport performance are based on anecdotal reports and selectively quoted research, not on sound scientific evidence. Cheuvront states that, in actuality, reliable and abundant peer-reviewed literature is in opposition to the suggestion that such a diet can support competitive athletic endeavors, much less improve them, and even suggests the "zone diet" may actually be ergolytic in nature. Some evidence does indicate that high-protein diets, at the expense of carbohydrate, may impair endurance performance. Jarvis and others evaluated the effects of a 7-day Zone diet, compared with a normal diet, on body composition and run time to exhaustion in recreational endurance athletes. Daily energy intake was significantly reduced by about 300 Calories on the Zone diet, as was body mass and run time to exhaustion at 80 percent of VO_2 max. These investigators do not recommend the Zone diet for athletes unless future research validates its proposed ability to enhance athletic performance. However, it should be noted that subjects consumed fewer Calories while on the Zone diet, a factor that may have impeded performance.

Nevertheless, for weight-restricted athletes attempting to lose body fat or maintain a low body weight for sports competition, some investigators recommend increased protein intake. With a 1,500-Calorie diet, a 30 percent protein allotment would be 450 Calories, or approximately 112 grams of protein. For a lean athlete, this amount of protein may help insure protein adequacy and may fall in the range of recommended protein intake.

In summary, Lemon notes that although endurance athletes may need a higher protein intake (1.2–1.4 grams per kilogram body weight) than sedentary individuals, these recommendations are based on protein balance studies. Lemon further states that there are no data to indicate that such a protein intake, as compared to the RDA of 0.8 grams per kilogram, will enhance sport performance. Such studies are needed.

Moreover, protein intake might best be restricted within an hour of competition. A recent study by Wiles and others noted an increased oxygen consumption during various exercise intensities (an indicator of impaired efficiency), particularly the more intense levels approaching 100 percent VO_2 max, when protein was consumed 1 hour prior to the exercise task. Ratings of perceived exertion were also higher with the protein diet. The protein meal content was 0.4 gram per kilogram body weight. However, no adverse effects were noticed when the same protein intake was consumed 3 hours prior to the exercise task. These research data appear to be in accord with the dietary recommendations for precompetition meals presented in chapter 2, stressing the importance of carbohydrate.

Colostrum Several recent studies evaluated the effect of colostrum on endurance exercise performance. Brinkworth and others supplemented the daily diet of elite rowers during 9 weeks of training for the world championships with 60 grams of bovine colostrum. Whey protein was used as the placebo. Subjects completed several bouts of a rowing protocol involving both submaximal and a 4-minute maximal test. They found that although the colostrum supplement increased the estimated buffer capacity, it had no effect on rowing performance. Coombes and others evaluated the effect of different colostrum dosages on two tests of aerobic capacity in competitive cyclists. The dosages included 60 grams of colostrum, 20 grams of colostrum plus 40 grams of whey protein, and 60 grams of whey protein, which was the placebo group. The exercise tests included two VO_2 max tests with a 20-minute interval between each, and a cycle time-trial test following 2 hours of cycling at 65 percent of VO_2 max. Although performance in the VO_2 max tests was not improved by colostrum, it did provide a small but significant improvement in the time-trial performance. As with the effects of colostrum on strength-type activities, these too should be considered preliminary data and confirmation with additional research is needed.

Carbohydrate/protein solutions In a placebo-controlled study, Ivy and others compared the effects of adding protein to a carbohydrate solution on aerobic endurance performance. Trained cyclists, consuming 200 milliliters of solution every 20 minutes, exercised for 3 hours at intensities varying from 45 to 75 percent of VO_2 max and then exercised to exhaustion at 85 percent of VO_2 max. The carbohydrate solution (7.75 percent) significantly improved endurance performance compared to the placebo, but the carbohydrate/protein combination (7.75/1.94 percent) enhanced performance even more so than the carbohydrate solution. Saunders and others conducted a similar study and reported comparable findings. In these studies, there were no metabolic, physiological, or psychological differences between the trials, so the reason for the performance enhancement was not evident. In each study, critics note that the carbohydrate/protein beverage contained more energy than the carbohydrate beverage, indicating that the additional energy provided by the protein may have been a contributing factor to the performance enhancement.

Recently, investigators evaluated the effect of a carbohydrate/protein drink, as compared to carbohydrate alone, on muscle protein breakdown induced by a marathon run. They concluded that although no obvious negative metabolic effects occurred, the carbohydrate/protein provided no additional advantage in preventing muscle tissue damage.

Are amino acid, amine, and related nitrogen-containing supplements effective ergogenic aids?

As noted previously, providing all essential amino acids during recovery from exercise may be associated with enhanced muscle protein synthesis, but whether or not this translates into enhanced exercise performance has not been determined. In recent years, however, specific amino acids have become increasingly available and popular in certain athletic circles.

Weight lifters are consuming various amino acids in attempts to stimulate the release of growth hormone from the pituitary gland, hoping that the growth hormone will then stimulate muscle development. Amino acids have also been used to stimulate the release of insulin from the pancreas; insulin is also considered to be an anabolic hormone because it facilitates the uptake of amino acids by the muscle cells. Indeed, certain amino acid mixtures have been advertised to be more potent than anabolic steroids, one of the most popular drugs used by strength and power athletes. Anabolic steroids and related substances are discussed in chapter 12. Other amino acids have been advertised in magazines for endurance athletes, suggesting that they may be utilized as a fuel during training or help prevent fatigue by altering the formation of neurotransmitters in the brain. Still other amino acid mixtures and related compounds such as creatine and inosine have been used in attempts to increase ATP or PCr levels in the muscle or to help athletes lose body weight for competition.

Scientific research has shown that individual amino acid supplements may induce specific physiological responses in the body, particularly the formation of certain chemicals in the brain needed for nerve impulse transmission as well as secretion of hormones.

However, amino acid metabolism is very complex. It depends upon a variety of factors such as the concentration in the blood, competition with other amino acids, feedback control mechanisms, and the presence in the diet of other nutrients. Consumption of specific amino acid mixtures or even high-protein diets may actually lead to nutritional imbalances, as an overload of one amino acid may inhibit the absorption of others into the body.

Because purified amino acids, known as free-form amino acids, amines such as creatine, and other nitrogen-containing substances have become commercially available for athletes, they have been the focus of increased research activity by sports medicine scientists. However, although the number of studies is increasing relative to the effect of amino acid supplementation upon physical performance, with the exception of creatine the data are still somewhat limited. Moreover, some investigators combine several amino acids or use commercial supplements that may contain not only several amino acids but other nutrients as well, which may cloud the possible ergogenic effect of any one specific amino acid. The following discussion highlights some of the current key findings regarding specific amino acids, various combinations of amino acids, amines, and nitrogen-containing compounds that have been studied for their potential ergogenic effect.

Arginine, Lysine, and Ornithine Research has shown that infusing any of a number of amino acids into the blood potentiates the release of **human growth hormone (HGH),** a polypeptide. HGH is released from the pituitary gland into the bloodstream, affecting all tissues. One of its effects is to stimulate the production of another hormone, insulin-like growth factor-1, that spurs growth of tissue, including muscle tissue.

Some amino acids may also stimulate the release of insulin, an anabolic hormone, from the pancreas. Such effects could be ergogenic for strength-trained individuals. Arginine is also a substrate for nitric oxide, a substance secreted by the walls of blood vessels that may decrease resistance and increase blood flow to the muscles, a potential ergogenic effect for endurance-trained individuals. Arginine may also stimulate epinephrine release from the adrenal gland, a stimulant effect that could benefit various athletic endeavors.

Although more than a half-dozen amino acids may stimulate HGH release when infused, the effect of oral supplementation is less clear. However, Jacobson has reported that the oral administration of selected amino acids may lead to HGH release similar to that promoted by infusion. Bucci, in his book on nutritional ergogenics, also notes that oral intake of amino acids, particularly arginine and ornithine, may increase HGH release, while others have suggested lysine may elicit similar effects. Research by Bucci and his colleagues has supported the effect of ornithine to increase serum HGH levels. Using dosages of 40, 100, and 170 milligrams per kilogram body weight, only the highest dose of ornithine increased HGH levels, but it caused intestinal distress (osmotic diarrhea) in many of the subjects, and thus its use at this effective dose may be impractical. Moreover, in a related study, Bucci and others noted ornithine did not increase the secretion of insulin.

Arginine, lysine, and ornithine, separately or in various combinations, have received the most research attention regarding an ergogenic effect for strength/power-type athletes. They have been advertised in bodybuilding magazines as being more powerful than anabolic steroids, potent drugs used by some athletes to increase muscle mass. The advertisers apparently are capitalizing on the potential of these amino acids to enhance HGH release.

Two of the earliest published studies by Elam collectively reported that arginine and ornithine supplementation in conjunction with a weight-training program reduced body fat, increased lean body mass, and increased strength over a 5-week period. The dosage was 2 grams per day (1 gram each of arginine and ornithine), 5 days per week. Unfortunately, both studies have been criticized in the literature on the grounds of the statistical procedure by which the experimental and control groups were compared. A different analysis of the same data revealed no significant difference between the experimental and control groups in the first study. The studies have also been criticized for questionable measurement techniques and for making assumptions without adequate supporting data.

Several studies with better experimental designs have not shown any significant ergogenic effect of arginine and lysine, or other similar amino acid combinations. Lambert and others, using combinations of arginine/lysine and ornithine/tyrosine, reported no significant increases in HGH, while Fogelholm and his associates noted no significant increases in HGH or insulin secretion following supplementation with arginine, ornithine, and lysine in competitive weight lifters. Hawkins and associates, using experienced male weight lifters as subjects, reported no beneficial effects of oral arginine supplementation on various measures of muscle function, including peak torque and endurance. Suminski and others reported that although a bout of weight training would increase HGH levels in noncompetitive weight lifters, supplementation with arginine and lysine provided no additional benefit. Mitchell and others, also using experienced weight lifters, reported that 8 weeks of supplementation with arginine and lysine elicited no significant effect on HGH secretion, body composition, or various strength measures. As discussed in chapter 12, increased HGH may not induce an ergogenic effect in young, resistance-trained males.

In a recent review, Cheng and others reported that oral arginine supplementation may enhance vasodilation, and has been shown to improve exercise ability in CHD patients. Research involving the independent effect of arginine supplementation on the aerobic endurance capacity of healthy athletes has not been uncovered, but a recent study by Buchman and others reported no effect of arginine supplementation on the prevention of intestinal ischemia, and related gastrointestinal distress, in marathon runners. They speculated that arginine supplementation may have induced an ergolytic effect, as the predicted times of the runners receiving arginine were slower than those receiving the placebo.

In their recent review, Chromiak and Antonio indicated that oral doses of arginine, lysine, and ornithine that are great enough to induce significant growth hormone release are likely to cause gastrointestinal discomfort. Moreover, they reported no studies have found that such supplementation augments human growth hormone release, nor do any studies support an ergogenic effect to increase muscle mass and strength to a greater extent than strength training alone. Williams notes that no data support an ergogenic effect of isolated arginine supplementation on aerobic endurance in healthy individuals.

Tryptophan Although tryptophan is one of the amino acids that may increase the release of HGH, its theoretical ergogenic effect is based upon another function. A neurotransmitter in the brain, serotonin (5-hydroxytryptamine), is derived from tryptophan. This neurotransmitter may induce sleepiness and elicit a mellow mood, and Segura and Ventura hypothesize that it may help to decrease the perception of pain. They postulate that individuals who show the best tolerance of or resistance to pain may be able to delay the onset of fatigue, and that tryptophan supplementation therefore might improve exercise performance. In their study, twelve healthy athletes exercised to exhaustion on a treadmill at 80 percent of their VO_2 max under two conditions: A placebo was compared with a dosage of 1,200 milligrams of L-tryptophan consumed in 300-mg doses over the 24 hours prior to testing. They reported no significant improvement in peak oxygen uptake or heart rate response but did note a significant improvement in time to exhaustion (49 percent) and a decreased rating of perceived exertion (RPE) following the L-tryptophan trial. The times to exhaustion were extremely variable among the individual subjects, ranging from 2.5–18 minutes, suggesting some of the individuals may not have been well trained. In another study with untrained individuals, Cunliffe and others reported that tryptophan supplementation (30 mg per kilogram body weight), increased both subjective and objective measures of fatigue. Although tryptophan supplementation had no effect on grip strength, work output on a wrist ergometer increased significantly.

Stensrud and his associates challenged the results of the Segura and Ventura study, indicating a 49 percent increase in performance would be rather phenomenal in trained athletes. Thus, they decided to replicate this study using forty-nine well-trained male runners and better control conditions, although they had their subjects run to exhaustion at 100 percent VO_2 max, not 80 percent. In contrast to the study by Segura and Ventura, they reported no significant effect of tryptophan supplementation on performance. Other research from the University of Maastricht revealed no effect of tryptophan supplementation on endurance performance at 70–75 percent of VO_2 max, and research with horses reported a decrease in endurance performance at 50 percent of VO_2 max.

Based on these limited data, tryptophan does not appear to be an effective ergogenic in either short-term or prolonged exercise tasks in exercise-trained individuals, a finding also supported in the recent review by Anton Wagenmakers. Some adverse health effects have been associated with tryptophan supplementation and are discussed in the next section.

Branched-Chain Amino Acids (BCAA) Branched-chain amino acid (BCAA) supplementation has been theorized to enhance exercise performance in a variety of ways. BCAA could be used as a fuel during exercise to prevent adverse changes in neurotransmitter function, to spare the use of muscle glycogen, and to prevent or decrease the net rate of protein degradation. These effects could influence mental and physical performance, and may also favorably affect body composition, but most research has focused on the central fatigue hypothesis.

Central fatigue hypothesis Eric Newsholme, a biochemist at Oxford University, proposed the central fatigue hypothesis, postulating that high levels of serum free-tryptophan (fTRP) in conjunction with low levels of BCAA, or a high fTRP:BCAA ratio, may be a major factor in the etiology of fatigue during prolonged endurance exercise. Research with animals has shown that a high fTRP:BCAA ratio may lead to an increased production of serotonin. Newsholme suggested that serum BCAA levels eventually decrease in endurance exercise, such as marathon running, because they may be used for energy production. Such an effect would possibly increase the fTRP:BCAA ratio, facilitating the transport of tryptophan into the brain and increasing serotonin production, which could lead to fatigue because increased serotonin levels may depress central nervous system functions. Some, but not all, research with humans supports this finding. Blomstrand and others have shown in several studies that prolonged endurance exercise, such as the 26.2 mile (42.2 kilometer) marathon, increases the fTRP:BCAA ratio, but Conlay and others noted no change in this ratio in experienced runners immediately following completion of the Boston Marathon. Tanaka and others also noted no change in the fTRP:BCAA ratio in a 6-week study designed to induce overtraining.

The central fatigue hypothesis and BCAA supplementation have received considerable research attention since Newsholme proposed his hypothesis in the late 1980s, and these studies have served as the basis for several reviews. Based on these reviews, and research studies published subsequent to these reviews, the following appear to be the key points regarding the central fatigue hypothesis and the effects of nutritional interventions, particularly BCAA and carbohydrate supplementation.

Support for the hypothesis Animal studies support the concept of central fatigue during prolonged exercise tasks. Fatigue appears to be associated with increases in brain serotonin, but fatigue is also correlated to changes in other brain neurotransmitters as well, such as dopamine. Some human data also suggest serotonin may be involved in the development of fatigue. Several drugs, approved for use with humans, may block the removal of serotonin from its active sites, thus magnifying its effects. In several studies involving running or cycling at 70 percent VO$_2$ max, these drugs either impaired performance or increased the psychological perception of effort, both negative findings.

However, J. Mark Davis of the University of South Carolina points out that although the central fatigue hypothesis has some support from experimental data, the underlying mechanism has not been determined. Investigators are studying this issue, looking not only at mechanisms associated with serotonin, but other brain neurotransmitters as well, such as dopamine.

BCAA supplementation and the fTRP:BCAA ratio If serum BCAA fall during prolonged exercise, then BCAA supplementation might be a preventive measure. It is known that BCAA are metabolized primarily in the muscle, not the liver, and thus may provide an energy source during exercise. Some research has shown that oral supplementation with BCAA or leucine will increase the serum levels of BCAA, the BCAA may possibly be used as an energy source during exercise, the BCAA may prevent or decrease the rate of endogenous protein degradation during exercise, and the BCAA may help to maintain a normal fTRP:BCAA ratio during prolonged exercise.

BCAA supplementation and mental performance Several sports, such as tennis and soccer, involve prolonged, high-intensity intermittent bouts of exercise in which mental alertness must be maintained. In such events, the fTRP:BCAA ratio may increase, as documented by Struder and associates in a study involving nationally ranked tennis players involved in 4 hours of continuous tournament tennis.

As evaluated by various tests of cognitive performance, several studies by Blomstrand and her associates reported that BCAA supplementation improved mental performance in national-class soccer players after a game and in runners after a 30-kilometer race. However, other investigators reported no effect of BCAA supplementation on mental acuity following a 40-kilometer cycle performance test. These are interesting field studies, and additional similar research is merited, complemented by well-controlled laboratory studies.

BCAA supplementation and perceived exertion Somewhat related to mental performance is the psychological perception of effort, or how mentally stressful the subject perceives a given exercise task to be. This psychological effort is usually evaluated by Borg's Rating of Perceived Exertion Scale, or RPE. In recent research, Blomstrand and others reported that BCAA supplementation, compared to a placebo trial, reduced the RPE and mental fatigue of endurance-trained cyclists during a 60-minute ride at 70 percent VO$_2$ max followed by another 20 minutes of maximal exercise. The fTRP:BCAA ratio increased in the placebo trial, but remained unchanged or even decreased in the BCAA trial. Conversely, other well-controlled studies have reported no significant effect of BCAA supplementation on RPE during intense exercise, such as during a 40-kilometer cycling performance test and 90 minutes of exercise at a 2-millimole lactate threshold.

BCAA supplementation and physical performance Investigators have studied BCAA supplementation with acute dosages administered to subjects just before and during the exercise task, and chronic dosages provided to the subject for several weeks prior to and during the exercise task. Dosages have varied, ranging from 5–20 grams per day. When provided with liquids, the dosages ranged up to 7 grams per liter.

In one of the first reports of acute supplementation, Blomstrand and her colleagues studied the performance of 193 marathoners, separated into placebo and BCAA supplement groups. Overall, there was no significant difference in marathon performance between the placebo group and the BCAA group. However, using some debatable statistical tactics, they reported that BCAA supplementation significantly improved performance in the "slower" runners in the race (3:05–3:30 hours) but had no effect on the performance of the "faster" runners (<3:05 hours). They suggested that the slower runners may have depleted their muscle glycogen earlier, therefore decreasing their serum BCAA levels earlier in the race and benefiting more from the supplementation. Although this was an interesting field study, it has been criticized by Davis for several problems with experimental methodology.

Most well-controlled laboratory studies and field studies involving acute BCAA supplementation have reported no significant ergogenic effects on exercise performance. In many of these studies, the BCAA supplement was compared to a carbohydrate supplement, usually involving three trials: carbohydrate alone, BCAA alone, and BCAA with carbohydrate. An analysis of about ten studies revealed that acute BCAA supplementation, particularly when compared to carbohydrate solutions, had no effect on time to exhaustion in running or cycling tests ranging in intensities from 70–85 percent VO_2 max, performance cycling tests of 40 kilometers and 100 kilometers, intermittent, prolonged high-intensity 20-second anaerobic running performance, and prolonged shuttle-run performance tasks comparable to energy expenditure in soccer, basketball, and hockey. Even the study by Blomstrand and others that reported decreased RPE and mental fatigue in endurance-trained cyclists did not find any significant improvement in performance as measured by the total work done in the 20-minute maximal test.

An earlier well-controlled study conducted under heat stress conditions did report an ergogenic effect of BCAA supplementation. Mittleman and others, providing BCAA (9.4–15.8 grams) as part of a carbohydrate-free drink before and during exercise, reported an increase of 12 percent in cycle time to exhaustion at 40 percent VO_2 peak. Plasma BCAA levels were elevated, but cardiovascular, thermoregulatory, and psychological data were unchanged compared to the placebo condition. They noted that comparison of this study with others must be made with caution because the environmental stress (95° F), low exercise intensity, and form of BCAA supplement (without glucose) were unique. Moreover, no specific mechanism underlying the improved performance was proposed. A lack of effect on the RPE does not support the central fatigue hypothesis. Two subsequent studies reported no beneficial effect of BCAA supplementation on exercise in the heat. Watson and others had subjects consume BCAA in solution before (12 grams) and during (1.8 grams every 15 minutes) a cycling trial to exhaustion at 50 percent VO_2 max in the heat. They reported no effect in performance time, or on heart rate, core or skin temperature. Cheuvront and others induced muscle glycogen depletion and hypohydration in subjects prior to 60 minutes of cycling at 50 percent of VO_2 peak followed by a 30-minute time trial in the heat. A BCAA/carbohydrate solution was consumed during the trial, and although the plasma BCAA increased 2.5 fold, compared to the carbohydrate solution there was no effect on time-trial performance nor were cognitive performance, mood, perceived exertion, or perceived thermal comfort affected. These studies indicate that BCAA supplementation does not enhance prolonged exercise performance under warm environmental conditions.

Several recent reviews provide conflicting opinions regarding the ergogenic effects of acute BCAA supplementation. Davis indicates that most studies show no effects of BCAA supplementation on performance, and Hargreaves and Snow note that BCAA supplementation does not appear to affect fatigue during prolonged exercise. Conversely, Blomstrand indicates that ingestion of BCAA reduces the perceived exertion and mental fatigue during prolonged exercise and improves cognitive performance after the exercise. She suggests also that in some situations BCAA ingestion may improve physical performance, such as during actual competitive races where central fatigue may be more pronounced than in laboratory experiments. Nevertheless, she also notes that more research is needed.

Research regarding the effects of chronic BCAA supplementation on exercise performance is more limited, but in one study conducted at the University of Virginia, researchers reported an improvement in 40-kilometer cycling performance following 14 days of BCAA supplementation. Several other studies used a commercial supplement containing BCAA along with glutamine and carnitine. In general, these laboratory studies reported no significant effects on total time to complete a simulated half-Ironman triathlon (2-km swim; 90-km bike; 21-km run), prolonged aerobic endurance exercise at 65 percent VO_2 max, or cycle ergometer time to exhaustion at 120 percent VO_2 peak. Although these last three studies have shown no beneficial effect, subjects in the triathlon study ran the last segment 12.8 minutes faster while on the supplement, but this time was not significant due to highly variable performances. This finding, combined with the University of Virginia study, indicates additional research relative to chronic BCAA supplementation and exercise performance is merited.

Importance of carbohydrate Although research with BCAA supplementation is merited to help understand the underlying causes of fatigue in prolonged aerobic endurance exercise, endurance athletes apparently do not need to take BCAA supplements in attempts to enhance performance if carbohydrate is available. In most studies that compared carbohydrate solutions, carbohydrate/BCAA solutions, and placebo solutions, both solutions with carbohydrate improved endurance performance compared to the placebo solution, but there were no differences between the carbohydrate solution and the carbohydrate/BCAA solution. In general, the carbohydrate solution attenuates the increase in the fTRP:BCAA ratio. However, Davis points out that the mechanism whereby carbohydrate supplementation prevents fatigue during prolonged exercise is not clear; it may prevent fatigue centrally by ameliorating brain functions, or it may prevent fatigue peripherally by providing energy substrate for the contracting muscle.

Most recent reviews evaluating exercise and the central fatigue hypothesis have concluded that although the data are equivocal, in general they suggest that BCAA supplementation is neither ergogenic nor ergolytic. Carbohydrate still appears to be the preferential fuel for athletes to consume before and during prolonged intermittent and continuous endurance exercise tasks.

BCAA supplementation and body composition BCAA supplementation has been theorized to decrease muscle protein breakdown during exercise. In a recent review, Williams cited some evidence that chronic BCAA supplementation, as part of a low-Calorie diet, was more effective than three other diets as a means for elite wrestlers to lose body fat over a 19-day period. No changes in muscular strength or aerobic and anaerobic capacities were noted, suggesting that exercise performance was maintained even with the greater body fat losses. Conversely, Williams cited other research noting no significant effect of BCAA supplementation on skeletal muscle characteristics of elderly men involved in cycle training. These findings should be considered as preliminary and merit additional research.

Glutamine   Glutamine, a nonessential amino acid, is the most abundant amino acid in the plasma. Glutamine, like alanine, is synthesized in the muscle tissue, where it is found in high concentrations, and is a major means for removing excess amino groups from the muscle, delivering the amino groups to the liver and kidneys for excretion or reuse of excess nitrogen.

Glutamine supplementation, muscle mass, and strength
Glutamine appears to be involved in the regulation of a number of metabolic processes important to exercise. Oral glutamine supplementation has been shown to increase HGH levels, and glutamine may also stimulate protein synthesis by increasing muscle cell volume. Abcower and Souba noted that patients may be provided nutritional support including glutamine or glutamine precursors to help spare muscle mass. However, several recent studies indicate that neither short-term nor long-term glutamine supplementation has an ergogenic effect on muscle mass or strength performance. In a double-blind, placebo, short-term crossover study, Antonio and others studied the effects of high-glutamine supplementation (0.3 grams per kilogram) or glycine on exercise performance in resistance-trained men. One hour after ingestion, subjects performed four total sets of exercise to fatigue, but the glutamine supplementation had no significant effect on performance. In another well-designed study, Candow and others provided glutamine (0.9 grams/kilogram lean tissue mass) or placebo to two groups undertaking 6 weeks of total body resistance training. Although the training increased lean muscle mass and strength, the glutamine supplementation provided no additional benefits. Additionally, alpha-ketoglutarate, a precursor of glutamine, has been theorized to be anabolic, but no data are available to support this theory.

Glutamine supplementation and muscle glycogen
Glutamine is also gluconeogenic, and is also involved in glycogen synthesis, two factors that could influence energy production from carbohydrate during prolonged aerobic endurance exercise. However, the limited available data are conflicting. In one study, adding glutamine to a glucose drink did not provide any additional benefits on muscle glycogen resynthesis following muscle glycogen depletion. In another study, adding glutamine to a glucose polymer solution appeared to provide an additive effect on total body carbohydrate storage during recovery from prolonged exercise, possibly increasing liver glycogen levels. However, as noted previously, adding protein to carbohydrate may increase glycogen levels during recovery, and although glutamine may stimulate muscle glycogen synthesis, Hargreaves and Snow noted that it provides no advantage over ingestion of adequate carbohydrate alone.

Glutamine supplementation and immune function
Glutamine also is a major fuel for key cells, notably lymphocytes and macrophages, of the immune system. Melis and others indicated glutamine has a major impact on the functionality of the immune system. In sports, a healthy immune system is theorized to prevent overtraining. In a recent review, Abcower and Souba indicated that glutamine may be considered a conditionally essential amino acid because it may be needed in individuals, such as burn patients, suffering a catabolic insult. This might also include athletes undertaking strenuous exercise and inducing microtrauma to the muscles, a possible contributing factor to the overtraining syndrome.

Overtraining, or staleness, in athletes is characterized by a number of signs and symptoms, referred to as the overtraining syndrome. Subjective symptoms such as fatigue, irritability, sleep disturbance, heaviness, and depression are associated with decreases in physical performance. Overtrained athletes are also thought to be more susceptible to various infections, particularly upper respiratory tract infections, possibly because of an impaired immune system.

Several studies have reported a positive association between decreased plasma glutamine levels and overtraining. Parry-Billings and others studied forty overtrained, international-class athletes at the British Olympic Medical Centre; most of the overtrained athletes were involved in endurance-type events. The investigators noted a decreased plasma glutamine level compared to control athletes not regarded as being overtrained. Kingsbury and others reported similar findings for overtrained elite track and field athletes, as compared to other elite athletes without symptoms of overtraining. In a recent review, Williams cited research indicating that plasma glutamine levels are decreased in athletes who participate in sport activities predisposing to overtraining, including marathon running and repeated bouts of intensive training. One research group indicated that plasma glutamine may be useful as an indicator of the overtrained state.

Most research with glutamine supplementation in athletes has focused on its role to affect favorably markers of immune function or to prevent signs and symptoms of overtraining, particularly upper respiratory tract infections. Williams notes that both animal and human studies provide conflicting data regarding beneficial effects of glutamine supplementation before, during, or after exercise. For example, some research revealed a lower incidence of infections during the 7 days following intense exercise bouts in various athletic groups who consumed a glutamine-supplemented drink (81 percent with no infections) compared to those taking a placebo drink (49 percent with no infections) immediately after and 2 hours after the exercise bout. The investigators suggested these effects are possibly associated with an apparent increase in specific lymphocyte cells. However, this same investigative group reported no beneficial effects of glutamine supplementation on lymphocyte distribution following the Brussels Marathon. Additionally, other investigators reported that although glutamine supplementation helped to maintain plasma glutamine levels following prolonged aerobic exercise, no beneficial effects on lymphocyte function were noted.

Although some investigators have suggested that carbohydrate intake may counter glutamine depletion, a well-controlled study by van Hall and others indicated that carbohydrate intake during prolonged exercise (cycling to exhaustion) did not prevent the normal decrease in plasma glutamine concentration during recovery. On the other hand, Gleeson and others indicated that a low-carbohydrate diet over 3 days is associated with a greater fall in plasma glutamine levels during recovery from exercise. Thus, as documented previously, adequate daily carbohydrate intake appears to be a sound dietary strategy for most athletes.

Castell cited some preliminary data indicating that glutamine supplementation may reduce the self-reported incidence of illness in endurance athletes following prolonged exercise. Based on such findings, Antonio and Street speculated that glutamine has potential utility as a dietary supplement for athletes engaged in heavy exercise training. Although such a recommendation may be prudent, confirming data are needed to provide more solid scientific support. In recent reviews, Hargreaves and Snow, along with Nieman, indicated that there is little support from controlled studies to recommend glutamine supplementation for enhanced immune function.

Aspartates Potassium and magnesium aspartate are salts of aspartic acid, a nonessential amino acid. Although the mechanism has not been clearly documented, these substances have been postulated to improve aerobic and anaerobic exercise performance, possibly by enhancing fatty acid metabolism and thereby sparing glycogen, by reducing accumulation of ammonia (metabolic by-product of protein), or simply by improving psychological motivation. The ammonia hypothesis has been tested in several studies since increases in serum ammonia have been associated with muscular fatigue, although, as noted previously, the mechanism is not clear.

Research findings relative to the ergogenic effect of aspartates are equivocal. A number of both early and contemporary studies have reported no beneficial effects of aspartate supplementation. For example, Maughan and Sadler had eight males ride to exhaustion on a bicycle ergometer at 75–80 percent of their VO_2 max following either a placebo or 3,000 milligrams each of potassium and magnesium aspartate consumed in the 24 hours prior to testing. No beneficial effects upon blood concentrations of energy substrates or ammonia were found, nor were any significant effects on physiological or psychological variables important to aerobic exercise performance reported. In an anaerobic exercise task, Tuttle and others reported no significant effect of aspartate supplementation (approximately 10 grams) on plasma ammonia concentrations, ratings of perceived exertion during a resistance training workout, or performance in a bench press repetition test to failure at 65 percent of maximal bench press strength.

On the other hand, an equal number of early and contemporary studies have found some beneficial applications of aspartates. Although several of these studies possessed flaws in experimental design, increases in aerobic endurance of 21–50 percent have been reported. Wesson and others, using a double-blind, placebo protocol, revealed that the ingestion of 10 grams of aspartates over a 24-hour period increased endurance capacity by over 15 percent when subjects exercised at 75 percent of their VO_2 max. These researchers also reported increased blood levels of free fatty acids and decreased levels of blood ammonia.

It appears that additional quality research is needed to evaluate the ability of aspartates to exert an ergogenic effect. Dosage may be a key factor, for dosages of about 10 grams have usually been associated with improved performance.

Glycine Glycine is a nonessential amino acid. Because it is involved in the formation of creatine, and hence phosphocreatine (PCr), it could theoretically be an ergogenic aid. Gelatin, an incomplete protein, is composed of approximately 25 percent glycine, and thus also has been ascribed ergogenic qualities. Several studies conducted over a half-century ago suggested a beneficial effect of glycine or gelatin supplementation on various measures of strength, but the experiments were poorly designed. More contemporary research with proper experimental design and relatively large doses of glycine revealed no beneficial effects upon physical performance. However, although glycine supplementation has not been shown to be ergogenic, direct supplementation with creatine may induce favorable effects, as noted below.

Glycine is the first-listed ingredient in glycine-arginine-alpha-ketoisocaproic acid (GAKIC), which has been theorized to enhance muscle performance by favorably modifying protein metabolism by use of amino acids (glycine, arginine) combined with ketoacids (alpha-ketoisocaproic acid). Previous research has supported its use to increase muscle strength, and a recent well-designed study by Buford and Koch also provides some support for its potential to enhance anaerobic performance. Subjects consumed 11.2 grams of GAKIC prior to five supramaximal 10-second cycle ergometer sprints, separated by 1-minute rest intervals. The GAKIC treatment produced a greater retention of mean power between sprints 1 and 2, but no significant differences were noted among the other trials. The investigators suggested the data supported an ergogenic effect of GAKIC. However, these data should be considered preliminary, and additional research is merited to support these findings.

Chondroitin and Glucosamine Chondroitin and glucosamine are derived from connective tissue, and each has been marketed as a dietary supplement, either separately or in combination, to help promote healthy joints in individuals who exercise. Gelatin, also derived from connective tissue, has also been advertised to promote joint health. Although weight-bearing or resistance exercise training has not been shown to cause excessive wear-and-tear on healthy joints, and may actually improve joint health, some dietary supplement entrepreneurs may suggest otherwise. In a sense, if a dietary supplement could prevent joint pain, and thus promote optimal exercise training, it could be considered an ergogenic.

Both chondroitin and glucosamine may be synthesized in the human body from amino acids and other nutrients, and both are found in human cartilage, one of the main components involved in joint health. Glucosamine is believed to help form compounds, such as proteoglycans, that form the structural basis for cartilage, while chondroitin is part of a protein that gives cartilage its resiliency. Cartilage serves as a kind of shock absorber, and prevents bone-to-bone contact. Excessive wear of cartilage leads to osteoarthritis, a painful joint condition. Dietary supplements of chondroitin are made from cattle cartilage, while those of glucosamine are made from shellfish. Theoretically, such supplements will help maintain normal cartilage levels and prevent development of osteoarthritis.

Over 30 studies have investigated the role of chondroitin and/or glucosamine supplementation on symptoms of arthritic pain. Several recent reviews by the Consumers Union and Tufts University indicated that most of the studies found that chondroitin and/or glucosamine supplementation relieved pain and improved mobility better than a placebo. For example, in one study of Navy Seals in training, who could be considered as fit athletes, a commercial supplement containing both chondroitin and glucosamine relieved knee pain symptoms in a small group of men with arthritic pain. In general, these findings have also been supported in several recent reviews, including a recent meta-analysis of 15 studies by McAlindon and others who concluded that trials of glucosamine and chondroitin preparations for osteoarthritic symptoms demonstrate moderate to large beneficial effects, but research quality issues and publication bias suggest these effects are exaggerated. Brief and others also noted that advocates of these modalities cite research suggestive of reduced joint pain and improved mobility, while critics point out that in the great majority of the relevant clinical trials, sample sizes were small and follow-up was short term.

Subsequent to these reviews, several studies have reported equivocal effects. Hughes and Carr found that glucosamine sulfate (1,500 milligrams daily for 6 months) was no more effective than a placebo in modifying pain symptoms in patients with osteoarthritis of the knee. On the other hand, in a well-controlled, 3-year study using American College of Rheumatology criteria, Pavelka and others evaluated the progression of knee osteoarthritis following either ingestion of glucosamine sulfate (1,500 mg daily) or a placebo. Given some beneficial effects on joint space narrowing and symptoms including pain, function, and stiffness, they concluded that long-term treatment with glucosamine sulfate retarded the progression of knee osteoarthritis. In another 3-year randomized, double-blind controlled study of patients with knee arthritis, Reginster and others found that subjects consuming glucosamine sulfate (1,500 milligrams daily) experienced no significant joint-space loss while those on the placebo experienced a progressive joint-space narrowing. The authors suggested glucosamine sulfate could help modify the disease process in osteoarthritis. These findings suggest some beneficial effects of glucosamine in the treatment of osteoarthritis, but more conclusive data may be forthcoming. The National Institutes of Health funded a large multicenter clinical study called GAIT (Glucosamine/Chondroitin Arthritis Intervention Trial) designed to provide a clearer picture of the role that these dietary supplements, both separately and in combination, may play in the treatment of osteoarthritis. Preliminary results revealed that, overall, glucosamine, chondroitin, or a glucosamine/chondroitin combination did not reduce knee pain in patients with osteoarthritis more so than a placebo. However, the glucosamine/chondroitin combination did provide relief to a subset of patients with moderate-to-severe knee pain, but not to those with mild knee pain.

Other related dietary supplements have been studied as a means to treat osteoarthritis. SAM-e, short for S-adenosylmethionine, is derived from the essential amino acid methionine, and plays some important metabolic functions in the body including serving as a possible anti-inflammatory agent. In a recent meta-analysis of 11 studies, Soeken and others concluded that SAM-e appears to be comparable to NSAIDS for treatment of pain and functional limitations, and less likely to report adverse effects. Schardt reiterated these points, but also noted that doses used were high and could cost as much as twenty dollars daily. Schardt also indicated that the quality of SAM-e dietary supplements available in the United States is variable, with some brands containing less than listed on the label.

Currently, chondroitin, glucosamine, and related supplements are being marketed to those with existing arthritic pain. To our knowledge, there are no data that these supplements will prevent the development of joint pain or osteoarthritis in young, healthy athletes. However, they may be of some benefit to older athletes experiencing joint pain that limits training or competition.

For anyone, particularly those with osteoarthritis, who may want to experiment with chondroitin and glucosamine, Tufts University offers several caveats. First, although these supplements are believed to be safe, they may cause mild side effects, such as bloating or a touch of diarrhea. Second, check with your doctor because there may be some complications. For example, diabetics may react adversely to glucosamine because it may increase insulin resistance. Third, a reasonable dose would be 1,500 milligrams of glucosamine and 1,200 milligrams of chondroitin daily for about 2–4 months. If pain symptoms have not improved, they probably are not going to. Finally, remember as with most dietary supplements, purity, safety, and effectiveness are not guaranteed. You may wish to visit the Website consumerlab.com for a recent analysis of commercial glucosamine and chondroitin preparations.

Creatine Creatine is not an amino acid, but a nitrogen-containing compound known as an amine. Creatine is found in some foods, particularly meat products, and it may be formed in the kidney and liver from glycine and arginine. Creatine may be delivered to the muscle, where it may combine readily with phosphate to form phosphocreatine, a high-energy phosphagen in the ATP-PCr energy system that is stored in the muscle. As you may recall, the ATP-PCr energy system is important for rapid energy production, such as in speed and power events. Sahlin and others recently noted that during very high-intensity exercise, within 10 seconds maximal power output decreases considerably and coincides with depletion of PCr.

Creatine supplements have been marketed to athletes at all levels. They come in various forms (powder, pills, candy, chews, gels, serum, micronized) for both strength and endurance athletes, including products specifically for men (Runners Advantage™ Male), women (Runners Advantage™ Female), and adolescent athletes age 11–19 (Teen Advantage Serum Creatine). Relative to the latter, Metzl and others, in a survey of middle and high school athletes age 10–18 in a New York City suburb, found that creatine is being used by middle and high school athletes at all grades. Use increases with grade level and the prevalence of use by athletes in grades 11 and 12 approaches levels reported among college athletes. The most cited reasons for taking creatine were enhanced performance and appearance. Indeed, creatine continues to be one of the most popular sports supplements of all time.

Although creatine has been known for years to play an important role in energy metabolism, it is only within the past 10 years or so that considerable research has been devoted to evaluate the potential ergogenic effect of creatine supplementation. Numerous studies, several major reviews, and a book focusing on creatine supplementation have been published in recent years, and the following represent some of the key points.

Supplementation protocol, effects on total muscle creatine and phosphocreatine (PCr), and theory The average individual needs to replace about 2 grams of creatine per day to maintain normal total creatine and creatine phosphate (PCr). The normal daily intake of creatine approximates 1 gram for those who consume meat, but may be virtually zero for pure vegetarians. Endogenous formation of creatine helps complement dietary sources to achieve 2 grams, but because of inadequate dietary intake, vegetarians may have lower amounts of total creatine in the body. For example, Lukaszuk and others found that switching from a meat-eating diet to a lactoovovegetarian diet for three weeks significantly reduced muscle total creatine.

Several supplementation strategies have been used in attempts to increase total body creatine stores. One very effective strategy is to consume a total of 20–30 grams of creatine, usually pure creatine monohydrate, in four equal doses (5–7 grams per dose) over the course of the day (morning, noon, afternoon, evening). Significant effects have been observed even after only 2 days of creatine loading. Paul Greenhaff, one of the leading researchers with creatine, noted that this supplementation protocol will enhance muscle creatine storage. Excessive amounts will not be stored but as noted by Burke and others, excesses will be excreted unchanged in the urine. Longer-term supplementation with lower doses, such as 4 weeks at a dose of 3 grams per day, has been shown to be as effective. However, one study providing 2 grams per day for 6 weeks showed no beneficial effects on either muscle creatine stores or PCr levels.

Subjects may be responders or nonresponders. Recent research by Burke and others, in a study with vegetarians, found that individuals with initially low levels of intramuscular creatine are more responsive to supplementation, while Syrotuik and Bell identified several characteristics of nonresponders, such as higher initial levels of creatine and phosphocreatine before loading and fewer Type II muscle fibers. However, Green and others have shown that combining creatine with a simple carbohydrate, such as glucose, will increase creatine transport into the muscle even in subjects with near-normal levels of muscle creatine, possibly via an insulin-mediated effect. The solution used in Green's study consisted of 5 grams of creatine and about 90 grams of simple carbohydrate, consumed 4 times per day. However, Preen and others found that a smaller amount of glucose (1 gram per kilogram body weight) taken with only two of four daily 5-gram creatine doses, increased muscle creatine stores significantly more than creatine supplementation alone. This loading protocol may be useful for those who may want to cut the carbohydrate intake by 50 percent or more. Once creatine is in the muscle, it is locked there and gradually disappears over several weeks.

In general, although not all studies are in agreement, well-controlled research by Greenhaff, Harris, Casey, and their associates has shown that an appropriate creatine-loading protocol will increase total muscle creatine, including free creatine and PCr. In their book, Williams, Kreider, and Branch reviewed over 20 studies, and reported an average 18.5 percent increase in total muscle creatine, and an average 20.7 percent increase in PCr. Preen and others found that, once loaded, total muscle creatine levels could be maintained with creatine doses of 2–5 grams per day.

Most of the creatine in the body is found in the muscles, and Casey and others suggest that any performance benefits may be related to increased creatine within Type II muscle fibers. About 60 percent of the total muscle creatine is PCr, and the remainder is free creatine. Theoretically, according to Casey and Greenhaff, increasing the amount of PCr will provide more substrate for generating ATP during high-intensity exercise, and higher levels of free creatine will help resynthesize PCr. Additionally, Yquel and others, using magnetic resonance to evaluate PCr levels during repeated bouts of maximal plantar flexion exercise, found that creatine supplementation increased muscle power by about 5 percent. They noted that this effect could be attributed to a higher rate of phosphocreatine resynthesis, which would provide more PCr for ATP resynthesis.

Another theory suggests that creatine supplementation may have favorable effects on anabolic hormones, particularly human growth hormone. Schedel found that a large single dose of creatine monohydrate (20 grams) increased growth hormone secretion in the 6-hour period following ingestion, and most of the increases occurred between 2–6 hours after ingestion. However, Op 'T Eijnde and Hespel found that a standard 5-day creatine-loading protocol did not alter the responses of growth hormone, testosterone, or cortisol during the hour following a single bout of heavy resistance exercise. Because exercise itself stimulates human growth hormone release, and because there appears to be no additive effect of creatine supplementation, this theory appears to have little support or value for the athlete in training.

In essence, increased muscle phosphocreatine and free creatine may enhance the potential of the ATP-PCr energy system and provide the athlete with an edge in competitive events involving very high-intensity exercise performance. Moreover, the enhanced ATP-PCr energy system may permit more intensive training. Volek and others found that creatine supplementation appears to be effective for maintaining muscular performance during the initial phase of high-volume resistance training, possibly deterring overreaching and the associated small decrements in performance. Enhanced training should translate into enhanced competitive performance.

Effect on exercise performance Most research has investigated the effect of creatine supplementation on short-term, maximal exercise tasks of less than 30 seconds, those highly dependent on the ATP-PCr energy system, which may be referred to as anaerobic power. Many studies also incorporated repetitive exercise tasks with short recovery intervals, which could evaluate the possible effect of enhanced PCr resynthesis during recovery. However, some research has also investigated the effect of creatine supplementation on exercise performance tasks of somewhat longer duration, including anaerobic endurance, that would be dependent on the lactic acid energy system (anaerobic glycolysis) and aerobic endurance that would be dependent on the oxygen energy system (aerobic glycolysis).

ATP-PCr Energy System Research involving the effects of creatine supplementation on strength and power continues at a steady pace. As with most research evaluating the effectiveness of ergogenic aids, all studies are not in agreement. However, many studies with creatine, conducted at some leading universities throughout the world, have provided some strong evidence supportive of a positive ergogenic effect of creatine supplementation in certain exercise endeavors, primarily those characterized by repetitive high-intensity exercise bouts with brief recovery periods. Using appropriate research methodology, recent studies have shown significant improvement in the following exercise tasks following creatine supplementation.

- Improvement in total and maximal force in repetitive isometric muscle contractions
- Improvement in muscular strength and endurance in isotonic strength tests, including 1-RM tests
- Improvement in muscular force\torque and endurance in isokinetic strength testing
- Improvement in cycle ergometer performance in maximal tests ranging from 6 to 30 seconds

In their book, Williams, Kreider, and Branch note that approximately 75 percent of the studies reported beneficial effects of creatine supplementation on isotonic strength and endurance and cycle ergometer power and endurance, while about 50 percent of the studies revealed ergogenic effects on isometric and isokinetic tests of muscular strength, power, and endurance. All of these test protocols involved laboratory procedures, although some of the isotonic strength tests, such as the bench press, could be analogous to the sport of competitive weightlifting. Most studies involved males, but studies with females also reported improved performance. Studies subsequent to publication of this book continue to provide supportive evidence of the ergogenicity of creatine supplementation.

The effects of creatine supplementation on field performance tests, such as jumping, running, swimming, skating, and other miscellaneous events, are less consistent, but overall still favorable. For example, of seven recent studies evaluating the effect of creatine supplementation on single or repetitive sprint-run or sprint-cycle performance ranging from 5 to 100 meters, creatine supplementation improved performance in five of the trials, but had no effect in the other two. For example, Skare and others, using a standard creatine-loading protocol with well-trained male sprinters as subjects, reported significant improvements in 100-meter sprint velocity and time to complete 6 intermittent 60-meter sprints. Additionally, Preen and others studied the effect of a 5-day creatine-loading protocol on long-term repetitive sprints, doing 10 sets of multiple 6-second bike sprints with varying periods of recovery in an 80-minute time frame. Muscle biopsies revealed increased total creatine and PCr following supplementation, and both peak power and total work production were increased significantly. Conversely, Op 'T Eijnde and others reported no significant improvement in a 70-meter shuttle run sprint power test by well-trained tennis players following a standard 5-day creatine-loading protocol.

Some of these findings have a direct application to sports competition, such as an increased 1-RM performance in weight lifting, faster 50-yard swim times, and faster 100-meter sprint run times. The laboratory findings for other types of exercise performance are also rather strong, and do support a possible application to actual field competitions. For example, Preen and others noted that the findings from their study could suggest improved performance in intermittent high-intensity sports, such as soccer.

In this regard, several investigators have designed laboratory-controlled exercise protocols designed to mimic an actual sport event. Romer and others, in a well-controlled placebo, crossover study with competitive squash players, found that creatine loading for 5 days enhanced performance in an exercise protocol involving high-intensity, intermittent exercise involving 10 sets of simulated positional play to mimic squash. Creatine supplementation improved mean set sprint time by 3.2 percent compared to the placebo condition. The authors concluded that this study provides evidence that oral creatine supplementation improves exercise performance in competitive squash players. In one of the few studies with creatine supplementation conducted with young athletes, Ostojic reported enhanced performance in various soccer-related performance tests, such as sprint-power times and dribble test times, in 16-year-old soccer players. In a related study, Cox and others studied the effects of creatine supplementation on an exercise test protocol designed to simulate match play in soccer. The test involved 5 blocks of 11-minute exercise involving sprint running, agility runs, and a precision ball-kicking drill interspersed with recovery walks, jogs, and runs. Creatine supplementation improved performance in some repeated sprint and agility tasks even though the subjects increased body mass, but the creatine had no effect on ball-kicking accuracy.

Thus, creatine supplementation might improve speed in repetitive sprints, important for many sports, but may not necessarily enhance sports skills. In support of this viewpoint, Op 'T Eijnde and others, in the study cited previously with well-trained tennis players, reported no significant effects of creatine loading on tennis stroke performance as measured by power and precision of their serves.

Kirkendall suggests the available research is not applicable to the actual style of running in soccer and indicates that because so much of the running in soccer is at less than maximal sprinting speed, creatine supplementation likely provides no benefit to match performance. It certainly is difficult to study the effect of nutritional interventions on actual game performance. However, one might rationalize that if additional phosphocreatine could provide a slight advantage in speed at a critical point during a match, it might make the difference in the outcome of the contest.

Available research suggests that prolonged supplementation with maintenance doses of creatine may not provide any additional performance-enhancing advantage compared to a 5-day creatine-loading protocol. Peyrebrune and others reported that five days of creatine loading (20 grams/day) improved performance time of elite swimmers in eight 50-yard repeat swims. Swimmers were then assigned to either a creatine-maintenance dose (3 grams/day) or placebo for 22-27 weeks of additional swim training. Following the training period, all subjects again followed the creatine-loading protocol and repeated the 50-yard swim protocol. There was no statistically significant difference in performance times between the two groups, suggesting the maintenance protocol was not necessary if the athlete undergoes a creatine-loading protocol prior to performance.

Lactic Acid Energy System   Theoretically, increasing muscle PCr concentration could possibly buffer acidity and mitigate the effect of lactic acid production on muscle contraction, thus improving anaerobic endurance performance in events of maximal exercise ranging from about 30 to 150 seconds. Fewer studies are available, but creatine supplementation has been reported to benefit performance in some anaerobic endurance tests, including maximal isometric and isotonic muscular work output, cycle ergometer work output, running performance in 300 meters, and treadmill run to exhaustion at intensities greater than 100 percent VO_2 max. On the other hand, the vast majority of the studies reported no beneficial effect of creatine supplementation on 100-meter swim performance.

Overall, approximately 50 percent of the studies evaluating anaerobic endurance have shown some improvement in performance following creatine supplementation. The results are not as consistent as those shown for anaerobic power, but do provide some evidence that creatine supplementation may be helpful in more prolonged anaerobic endurance events, such as a 400- or 800-meter track race. More research is needed to document this effect.

Oxygen System   There appears to be little theoretical support for a beneficial effect of creatine supplementation on more prolonged exercise endeavors, those lasting over several minutes and depending primarily upon aerobic endurance capacity. However, some investigators have suggested creatine supplementation could modify substrate availability to improve performance, or could benefit athletes who perform repeated sprints during their overall aerobic endurance events, such as cycling sprints during a triathlon.

Several studies have reported ergogenic effects on exercise performance tasks greater than 3 minutes in duration, such as repeat 1,000-meter runs and a 1,000-meter rowing event. However, these tasks may still depend somewhat on anaerobic metabolism, particularly in sprints near the end, and thus performance may be improved as noted previously. Some evidence also indicates creatine supplementation may benefit anaerobic sprint performance within an overall aerobic endurance event, but confirming data are needed.

There is little scientific support that creatine supplementation benefits VO_2 max, energy metabolism when running or cycling at 50–90 percent of VO_2 max, or performance in exercise tasks of longer duration, those that depend primarily on aerobic glycolysis or lipolysis, such as endurance cycling. Moreover, Swedish investigators reported that creatine supplementation did not improve, but actually impaired, performance in a 3.6-kilometer forest terrain run. Of some concern, as noted below, may be a gain in body mass with creatine supplementation. Such an effect could possibly impair performance in sports such as running.

As noted above, creatine supplementation has been shown to improve performance in interval run repeats of 300 and 1,000 meters. If creatine supplementation could help an athlete train more effectively at shorter distances, conceivably performance in longer distances might eventually be improved. However, the available research does not support this hypothesis. In a placebo-controlled study, Syrotuik and others trained competitive rowers for 6 weeks with both rowing and resistance training. The creatine group consumed a standard 5-day loading protocol followed by a 5-week standard maintenance dose. Although the training significantly improved body composition, VO_2 max, repeated power interval performance, and 2,000-meter rowing times in both groups, the creatine provided no additional advantage.

One possible application of creatine loading for the endurance athlete, as reported by Santos and others, is prevention of muscle soreness. Following a typical creatine-loading protocol with experienced marathon runners, they found reduced markers of muscle cell damage and inflammation after a 30-kilometer race. No performance difference between the creatine and control group was noted. Confirmation of these findings is recommended.

Effect on body mass   The effect of creatine supplementation on body mass has been studied on both a short-term and long-term basis. Over 50 studies have shown an increase in body mass during the first week of creatine supplementation, and most of these studies suggest that the gains in body mass may be associated with water retention in the muscles. Increased creatine content in the muscle draws water.

Evaluation of the effects of long-term creatine supplementation on body mass has been conducted primarily with strength-trained individuals, or athletes training specific to their sport. Of approximately 20 studies, 80 percent provided evidence of significant gains in either total body mass or lean body mass. Many of these studies used carbohydrate as the placebo, but Tarnopolsky and others were one of the first to use protein, which may be a more appropriate placebo. They compared a creatine-dextrose supplement (10 grams creatine; 75 grams dextrose) with a protein-dextrose supplement (10 grams casein; 75 grams dextrose) on body mass, body composition, and strength over 8 weeks of resistance training in untrained young men. Both groups increased lean body mass and strength in a similar fashion, but the creatine-dextrose group experienced a significantly greater gain in body mass (4.3 kilograms) compared to the protein-dextrose group (1.9 kilograms). The authors note that the greater body mass gains may have implications for certain sports.

The increase in muscle mass may be associated with a creatine supplementation-induced ability to do more repetitions during training, which may induce favorable genetic adaptations. Willoughby and Rosene studied the effect of 12 weeks of creatine supplementation and resistance training on muscular strength and myosin heavy chain (MHC) mRNA and protein expression. Compared to both a control and placebo group, the creatine group significantly increased fat-free mass and strength. Additionally, they found that in general the MHC mRNA and protein expression were significantly higher in the creatine group compared to the other groups, and suggested that the increased strength and muscle size associated with creatine supplementation may be attributed to increased MHC synthesis. Other research, such as the study by Deldicque and others, indicated that creatine supplementation may favorably affect signaling pathways, such as those involving insulin-like growth factor (IGF), in the muscle. These cellular mechanisms may underline the research finding, as determined by muscle biopsy techniques, that creatine supplementation augments the increases in muscle cell diameter normally found after weeks of resistance training.

Rockwell and others found that during voluntary weight loss, creatine supplementation maintained anaerobic performance better than a placebo. However, in another study, creatine supplementation made it more difficult for weight-control athletes to lose weight for competition. This could produce adverse health effects if athletes would resort to more drastic weight-cutting methods, a topic covered in chapter 10.

Caffeine and creatine In research from Peter Hespel's laboratory in Belgium, Vandenberghe and others have shown that when caffeine, about 2.5 milligrams per kilogram body weight, is consumed with creatine, the caffeine negates the potential ergogenic effect of creatine. In their studies, both creatine and creatine with caffeine increased muscle creatine and PCr stores, but muscular performance improved only with the creatine supplement. In subsequent research, Hespel and others found that caffeine intake prolongs muscle relaxation time following muscle contraction and thus overrides the shortening of the relaxation time due to creatine supplementation. However, some of the early studies that revealed an ergogenic effect of creatine supplementation reportedly used coffee, with naturally occurring caffeine, as the mixing solution to deliver the creatine. Moreover, Doherty and others found that caffeine still provided an ergogenic effect in subjects who had followed a standard creatine-loading protocol and abstained from daily caffeine during the conduct of the study. Subjects performed three treadmill runs to exhaustion at 125 percent of VO_2 max, including a baseline test before creatine supplementation and a placebo and caffeine trial after supplementation. Compared to the baseline and placebo trial, caffeine significantly increased run time to exhaustion, and the rating of perceived exertion was also lower at 90 seconds during the treadmill run, suggesting the ergogenic effects were attributed partly to psychological effects. However, one might note that this exercise protocol primarily involves anaerobic glycolysis, not the ATP-PCr energy system, which might be more dependent on rapid rates of muscle relaxation during very-high-intensity, repetitive exercise tasks.

Because some athletes may take both creatine and caffeine in attempts to enhance performance, these preliminary findings merit additional research to substantiate this possible detrimental effect of caffeine.

Formulation The form of creatine may be important. Most studies reporting performance-enhancing effects in high-intensity exercise have used creatine monohydrate in powder form mixed with various fluids, including high-carbohydrate fluids. As reported by Gill and others, research has not reported any ergogenic benefits from creatine serum, products which may con-

tain less creatine. Moreover, some studies have administered creatine in combination with other possible ergogenic nutrients, such as sodium bicarbonate, magnesium, HMB, ribose, and glutamine. However, in some of these studies the experimental design did not permit the determination of which substance elicited the ergogenic effect.

Safety Given its effectiveness and increasing popularity and widespread use as a sports supplement, the safety of creatine supplementation has been a major concern to various health professional organizations. In a recent scientific roundtable on creatine supplementation, the American College of Sports Medicine (ACSM) noted that although available evidence indicates that creatine supplementation, using recommended protocols, does not pose any serious adverse side effects, the apparent absence of health risks does not necessarily make creatine supplementation safe.

Based mainly on anecdotal reports, the following represent the major health concerns with creatine supplementation and related research findings. The research is somewhat limited, and the ACSM recommends additional research to evaluate the possibility of theoretical health problems.

Kidney and Liver Function The breakdown product of creatine is creatinine, which is excreted by the kidneys. Individuals with impaired kidney function may be at risk, but there appears to be little danger to those with healthy kidneys who follow recommended supplementation protocols. None of the studies using creatine supplements for up to 12 weeks have reported any acute adverse side effects, nor did several long-term studies. Schilling and others evaluated the health effects of creatine supplementation on 3 groups of athletes from various sports. Groups included those who did not use creatine, those who used it about a year, and those who used it more than a year. The mean loading dose was 13.7 grams and the mean maintenance dose was 9.7 grams. All group means for standard clinical examination of complete blood count, 27 blood chemistries, and hormone levels fell within normal clinical range. Mayhew and others recruited 10 American football players who consumed, on an average, about 14 grams of creatine per day for approximately 3 years. They reported no differences in tests of kidney or liver function as compared to a control group of football players, and concluded that long-term creatine supplementation has no detrimental effects on kidney or liver functions in highly trained college athletes. Poortmans and Francaux, in a study that evaluated kidney function in several individuals who consumed creatine over a period of 10 months to 5 years, also reported no adverse effects. Although some individual case studies have associated kidney problems with creatine supplementation, Poortmans noted that these studies did not show definitively that creatine supplementation was the cause. For example, in one case study the individual had a preexisting kidney problem.

In a recent review of twelve reports, Yoshizumi and Tsourounis concluded that creatine supplementation appears to be safe when used by healthy adults at the recommended loading and maintenance doses. However, in people with a history of renal disease or those taking medications that may impair kidney functions, creatine may be associated with an increased risk of renal dysfunction.

Gastrointestinal Distress Creatine supplementation has also been associated with gastrointestinal distress, including nausea, vomiting, and diarrhea. However, most studies do not report such effects with recommended creatine-loading protocols. Creatine is often consumed along with glucose, and high glucose loads can cause gastrointestinal distress. Consuming a large dose of creatine just before an event may also cause problems. It should be noted that there is no need to use such a practice, as it has not been shown to enhance performance.

Dehydration, Muscle Cramps, and Tears Bailes and others suggested that creatine supplementation could contribute to subclinical dehydration and heatstroke in selected individuals. Theoretically, an increase in intramuscular water content could dilute electrolytes, possibly leading to cramps, and a tightened musculature associated with intracellular swelling could predispose to muscle tears. Although some anecdotal reports indicate creatine supplementation may lead to these health problems, most controlled studies do not. For example, Jeff Volek, an expert on creatine metabolism, studied the effect of a 7-day creatine-loading protocol on physiological responses to exercise in the heat and reported no adverse effects on thermoregulatory processes or other heat-related health problems, such as muscle cramping. In their study cited above, Schilling and others also reported that there were no differences in the reported incidence of muscle injury, cramps, or other adverse side effects. Additionally, research conducted with American football players, training under hot environmental conditions, revealed no significant differences between those taking and those not taking creatine supplements in the number of cases of dehydration, muscle cramps, or heat illnesses. Moreover, Kilduff and others found that creatine supplementation, by inducing greater water retention, reduced the heart rate and rectal temperature during prolonged exercise in the heat, resulting in a more efficient thermoregulatory response.

However, Schroeder and others found that creatine supplementation (6 days of loading and 28 days of maintenance) with typical dosages significantly increased anterior compartment pressure in the lower leg after the 6-day loading protocol both at rest and following 20 minutes of running, and these pressures remained elevated during the maintenance period. The authors noted that these pressures were abnormal. Such pressures could impair blood supply to the lower leg muscles and lead to tissue death if not treated in a timely fashion. This could be a significant health problem and merits close attention by those who use creatine supplements.

Overdoses and Contaminants As with any dietary supplement, overdoses can be harmful. In a recent review, Poortmans and Francaux did note that abnormal effects may occur when large amounts are consumed. For example, Poortmans and others recently reported that although short-term, high-dose creatine supplementation (21 grams/day for 14 days) had no effect on kidney function in young, healthy subjects, there was an increased excretion of two cytotoxic compounds. Although both compounds were in the normal range, the investigators recommended that kidney function should be monitored regularly in those consuming creatine supplements. As mentioned previously, once the muscles are saturated with creatine, any excess is simply excreted in the urine so large doses are unnecessary, are a waste of money, and may be dangerous.

Although many creatine dietary supplements on the market contain pure creatine monohydrate or related forms, some may contain contaminants. For example, one manufacturer concealed ephedrine in the supplement, not listing it on the product label. Individuals consuming this product might experience the stimulant effect of the ephedrine and think it is one of the effects of creatine, which could induce them to continue to purchase that product. However, as mentioned previously, ephedrine use is prohibited by most athletic-governing associations. Benzi and Ceci noted that in France sale of creatine-containing products was banned because sarcosine, one of the products from which creatine is synthesized, could originate from bovine tissues, and thus the risk of contamination with products leading to bovine spongiform encephalopathy (Mad-Cow Disease) could not be excluded.

Medical applications The ACSM, in their scientific roundtable, also indicated that creatine may have some clinical uses. In this regard, Persky and Brazeau highlighted the clinical pharmacology of creatine monohydrate and its potential medical application to patients with Huntington's and Parkinson's disease, Duchenne muscular dystrophy, various neuromuscular disorders, and congestive heart failure. Several case studies have shown that creatine supplementation could be helpful. For example, Stout and others found that resistance training with creatine supplementation may promote gains in strength and fat-free mass in patients with myasthenia gravis, while Tarnopolsky and others reported that four months of creatine monohydrate supplementation improved several health characteristics, such as handgrip strength and fat-free mass, of young boys with Duchenne muscular dystrophy. However, Tarnopolsky has noted that creatine supplementation may not provide benefits in some other types of muscular dystrophy. Other studies with standard creatine supplementation protocols have reported improved exercise capacity in patients with heart disease, and enhanced exercise capacity in persons with complete cervical-level spinal cord injury, but research findings are equivocal regarding improvement in patients with amyotrophic lateral sclerosis (ALS). A large multicenter, clinical trial is currently underway to further investigate the efficacy of creatine supplementation in ALS patients.

Creatine supplementation may be useful in rehabilitation from musculoskeletal injury, including athletic injuries. Peter Hespel, a renowned creatine researcher, and his associates evaluated the potential of creatine supplementation during the rehabilitation process for disuse atrophy. In a remarkable double-blind, placebo-controlled study, they casted the right leg of subjects for 2 weeks in order to induce disuse atrophy. The subjects then participated in a 10-week rehabilitation program for knee extension, with some subjects taking creatine and others the placebo. As expected, the casting decreased both the cross-sectional area of the quadriceps muscle and knee extension strength. During the rehabilitation period, the creatine subjects recovered muscle size and strength at a faster rate than the placebo group, suggesting creatine supplementation may be an effective adjunct in various forms of rehabilitative therapy. However, creatine supplementation may not facilitate the rehabilitative process for all injuries; Tyler and others reported no effect on recovery from anterior cruciate ligament (ACL) reconstruction.

Given these overall findings, the role of creatine supplementation as medical therapy appears to hold promise, but additional controlled research is needed to substantiate these preliminary findings.

Summary Several major reviews have appeared in recent years, and most suggest that creatine supplementation may enhance performance in events where the amount of PCr may be a limiting factor. The ergogenic effect of creatine appears to be due to the greater stores of PCr, but may also involve a greater resynthesis of PCr during recovery between exercise bouts. For additional details, the interested reader is referred to the meta-analyses by Branch, the reviews by Kreider, Rawson and Clarkson, Volek and Rawson, and the book by Williams, Kreider, and Branch.

HMB (Beta-Hydroxy-Beta-Methylbutyrate) Beta-hydroxy-beta-methylbutyrate **(HMB)** is not a nutrient per se, but a by-product of leucine metabolism in the human body. The body produces about 0.2–0.4 gram of HMB per day depending on dietary leucine intake. HMB is being marketed as a dietary supplement salt, calcium-HMB, primarily to strength-trained and power-trained athletes. HMB supplementation is theorized to increase lean muscle mass, decrease body fat, and increase muscular strength and power. Although the underlying mechanism is not known, investigators who developed HMB speculate that it may inhibit the breakdown of muscle tissue during strenuous exercise.

Initially, in attempts to increase the nutritional quality of animal meat, research with various farm animals has indicated that HMB supplementation may increase lean muscle mass and decrease body fat. However, knowledge of the effect of HMB supplementation in humans is in its infancy, and only a few studies and one review have been published at this point.

Nissen and others reported that HMB supplementation significantly increased lean body mass and strength in untrained males who initiated a resistance-training program for 3 weeks. Subjects consumed either 0 (placebo), 1.5 grams (low), or 3.0 grams (high) of HMB daily, and although all subjects increased lean muscle mass and strength with the resistance-training program, the HMB groups gained more than the placebo group, and the high group gained more than the low group. As measured by urinary 3-methylhistidine levels, the HMB groups also experienced less muscle tissue catabolism. Also in this same report, HMB supplementation (3.0 grams per day) did not increase total body mass, decrease body fat, or improve performance in two of three strength tests in physically active males who continued resistance training several hours per day over a 50-day period. Although the HMB group experienced favorable changes in lean body mass at various points over the course of the study, there were no significant differences between the placebo and HMB group at the completion of the study. The findings contained in this single report are somewhat inconsistent, showing that HMB supplementation appears to benefit untrained individuals, but not trained ones.

In their year 2000 review of research evaluating claims that HMB supplementation can enhance exercise performance, Slater and Jenkins indicated that at that time there were only two reports published in peer-reviewed journals, and the remaining eight papers were published as abstracts only and had not undergone the peer-review process. Based on these data, they indicated that although there is some support for the claims, at least in young, untrained individuals, the response of resistance-trained individuals is less clear and that there is a need for more tightly controlled, longer duration studies to evaluate the ergogenic effect of HMB supplementation. Peer-reviewed studies published subsequent to their review are equivocal regarding the ergogenic effect of HMB supplementation on exercise performance in untrained individuals, but in general indicate that it does not benefit trained individuals.

Panton and others reported that in untrained individuals, short-term HMB supplementation (3 grams daily for 4 weeks) during resistance training significantly increased upper body strength in both males and females. Vukovich and others reported that older subjects engaged in 8 weeks of resistance training and consuming 3 grams HMB daily experienced a significant decrease in body fat but no significant change in fat-free mass. These changes were similar to those seen in younger men in the study by Nissen and others. Jowko and others, in a placebo-controlled study, compared the effects of HMB (3 grams daily) and creatine (20 grams for 10 days; 10 grams for 14 days), both separately and in combination, on body composition and strength of subjects undergoing resistance training for 3 weeks. All subjects gained body mass and strength with training, but the supplement groups gained more than the placebo group. However, the only significant effect on body mass was that of the creatine group compared to the placebo group. Gallagher and others evaluated the effect of HMB supplementation, at doses of 38 or 76 milligrams per kilogram body weight, on 1-repetition maximum (1-RM) strength performance. College-age males trained for 8 weeks at 80 percent of their 1-RM with ten exercises. Although there were some inconsistent findings on isometric and isokinetic test performance, the major conclusion was that HMB supplementation did not improve 1-RM performance compared to the placebo group. There were no differences in body fat between the groups, but the authors indicated that the 38-milligram group increased lean body mass more so than the other two groups. Although the authors suggested a high dose of HMB may not be as effective as a low dose, the effect on lean body mass could be a chance finding.

Overall these findings with untrained individuals are equivocal, meriting additional research.

Several studies, using resistance-trained individuals as subjects, reported no significant effects of HMB supplementation. In a study by Richard Kreider, a leading authority on sports supplements, 40 experienced strength-trained athletes were matched on training volume and assigned to one of three groups receiving a carbohydrate/protein supplement with either 0, 3, or 6 grams of HMB per day. After 4 weeks of training and supplementation, there was no significant effect of HMB on indicators of muscle tissue breakdown, fat-free body mass, or combined strength gains in the bench press and leg press 1-RM. Slater and others studied the effect of daily HMB supplementation (3 grams in either standard or time-release capsules) on body composition, muscular strength, and markers of muscle damage and muscle protein turnover following 3 and 6 weeks of training. While both the placebo and HMB groups increased lean body mass and strength with the training, the HMB supplementation provided no additional benefits. Two recent well-controlled studies, let by Ransone and Hoffman, reported no significant effects of HMB supplementation (3 grams/day) on body composition, muscular strength, or anaerobic power in conditioned football players.

Thus, the available data indicate that HMB supplementation does not appear to affect muscle strength, body composition, or anaerobic exercise performance belong in resistance-trained subjects.

Given its theorized anti-catabolic effect, investigators have theorized HMB supplementation could help prevent muscle tissue damage during intense training. Paddon-Jones and others provided HMB, at a dose of 40 milligrams per kilogram body weight, for 6 days prior to and 10 days following a bout of 24 maximal isokinetic eccentric muscle contractions designed to induce muscle damage. They reported no significant effects of the HMB supplementation on muscle swelling, soreness, or torque, but noted a longer period of supplementation may be required to provide any benefits. In this regard, Knitter and others evaluated the effect of daily HMB supplementation (3 grams) during 6 months of training on muscle damage following a 20-kilometer run. Using serum levels of several muscle enzymes as markers of muscle damage, the lower serum enzyme levels found in the HMB group suggested supplementation could help prevent exercise-induced muscle damage. However, no performance-enhancing effects were reported. Conversely, in the previously cited studies, Kreider and others reported that HMB supplementation for 4 weeks had no effect on markers of muscle tissue breakdown, while in the 6-week study by Slater and others HMB supplementation had no effect on markers of muscle damage or muscle protein turnover. In general, these findings suggest HMB supplementation has no protective effects against muscle damage during resistance exercise training, but may benefit endurance athletes. Additional research is merited.

At the present time, it would appear there is little evidence to support HMB supplementation as an anabolic agent for strength-trained individuals. Some data suggest that HMB supplementation may decrease muscle tissue breakdown during the first few weeks of training in untrained individuals or in more prolonged training by endurance athletes, but additional research is needed to support these preliminary findings. Although data are scarce relative to the health effects of HMB supplementation, studies by Crowe and Gallagher and their associates reveal that 6–8 weeks of HMB supplementation (3–6 grams/day) had no adverse effects on serum hormones, glucose, lipids, or electrolytes, the immune system, or psychological state.

Tyrosine Tyrosine is a precursor for the catecholamine hormones and neurotransmitters, specifically epinephrine, norepinephrine, and dopamine. Some have suggested that inadequate production of these hormones or transmitters could compromise optimal physical performance. Thus, as a precursor for the formation of these hormones and neurotransmitters, tyrosine has been suggested to be ergogenic.

However, research is very limited. Sutton and others, in a well-designed placebo-controlled, crossover study, had subjects consume tyrosine (150 milligrams/kilogram body weight) 30 minutes prior to taking a series of physical performance tests. Although the tyrosine supplementation significantly increased plasma tyrosine levels, there were no significant ergogenic effects on aerobic endurance, anaerobic power, or muscle strength.

Taurine Taurine is synthesized from amino acids, mainly methionine and cysteine, and is found only in animal foods. Taurine is a vitamin-like compound that has multiple functions in the body, including effects on heart contraction, insulin actions, and antioxidant activity that could be of interest to the athlete. Taurine is an ingredient in several energy drinks, such as Red Bull.

Relative to sports performance, Cuisinier and others reported increased concentrations of urinary taurine following a marathon. Based on these observations, they theorized the increased taurine secretion could be a marker for muscle damage and speculated as to whether taurine supplementation would minimize such changes. Baum and Weiss compared the effects of three drinks on heart function before, during, and after endurance exercise performance. The drinks were Red Bull, which contains taurine and caffeine; a similar drink without taurine but with caffeine; and a placebo drink without taurine or caffeine. They reported that the Red Bull drink may influence cardiac parameters during recovery after exercise, mainly an increased stroke volume. However, the effect of taurine on physical performance was not evaluated in either of these studies.

In a study from Japan, Zhang and others studied the effect of the antioxidant properties of taurine, and reported that 7 days of taurine supplementation may attenuate exercise-induced DNA damage and enhance the capacity of exercise due to its cellular protective properties. They reported significant increases in VO_2 max and exercise time to exhaustion. These preliminary data need to be evaluated with additional research.

Inosine **Inosine** is not an amino acid but is classified as a nucleoside. It is included for discussion here because it is associated with the development of **purines,** nonprotein nitrogen compounds that have important roles in energy metabolism. On the basis of animal research and studies of blood storage techniques, writers in popular magazines have theorized that inosine may be an effective ergogenic aid for a variety of athletes. Advertisements have suggested that inosine may improve ATP production in the muscle and thus be of value to strength-type athletes. Additionally, inosine is thought to enhance oxygen delivery to the muscles, thus being beneficial to aerobic endurance athletes.

There are no data to support these claims. No studies investigating the effect of inosine upon strength or power have been uncovered. Research from our laboratory at Old Dominion University has revealed no ergogenic effect of inosine on aerobic endurance, but on the contrary, a possible decrement in performance. Nine highly trained runners consumed either a placebo or 6 grams of inosine prior to several tests of performance, including a peak oxygen uptake test and a 3-mile run on the treadmill conducted to simulate an all-out race. Although there were no differences in 3-mile run performance, peak oxygen uptake, or a variety of hematological and psychological variables, time to exhaustion during the peak oxygen uptake test was longer in the placebo condition. We speculated that inosine may impair the ability of fast-twitch muscle to function optimally in very high-intensity exercise, which occurs in the latter stages of tests of maximal or peak oxygen uptake. Recent research from Ball State University revealed similar findings. Starling and his colleagues investigated the effect of 5,000 milligrams of inosine daily for 5 days on the performance of competitive male cyclists on three tests: a Wingate bike test, a 30-minute self-paced cycling performance test, and a supramaximal cycling sprint to fatigue. Compared to the placebo trial, they reported no significant effect of inosine supplementation on any performance measures in the three tests, and actually reported an impaired performance in the supramaximal test following inosine supplementation. In the most recent double-blind, placebo, crossover study, McNaughton and others studied the effect of inosine supplementation on cycling performance in highly trained cyclists. The subjects consumed 10 grams of inosine daily for 10 days, with a 6-week washout period between trials. Subjects were tested at baseline, after 5 days, and after 10 days on three cycle-performance tests designed to measure different energy systems. The first test included five repetitions of a 6-second sprint; the second test was a 30-second sprint; and the last test was a 20-minute time trial. Inosine supplementation had no effect on any of the tests. Thus, on the basis of the available data, inosine does not appear to be an effective ergogenic aid.

One of the byproducts of inosine is uric acid, a compound that may accumulate in the joints and cause gout. In both the Starling and McNaughton studies, inosine supplementation increased serum uric acid levels. Individuals predisposed to gout should be aware of this possible complication.

Summary   A balanced diet containing 12–15 percent of the Calories as protein will provide amounts of the individual amino acids more than adequate to obtain the estimated RDA, even for those who exercise extensively. For example, some reports suggest that endurance athletes need more leucine because they may use about 850 mg, or 29 percent of the estimated leucine RDA, in a 2-hour workout. However, one glass of milk contains 950 mg of leucine, while over 5,000 mg are consumed in a normal daily diet. Similar comparisons could be made with other amino acids.

In a recent study, Tipton and others indicated that net muscle protein synthesis following exercise was similar whether amino acids were infused or taken orally. However, we are unaware of any research indicating that amino acid preparations taken orally are, over the course of a day, more effective than amino acids consumed as natural components of protein-rich foods. Nevertheless, companies that market amino acid supplements for athletes indicate that amino acids found in food are liberated slowly in the digestive processes, somewhat like a time-release tablet, and may not elicit similar effects compared to consumption of free-form

amino acids. Whether or not such individual amino acids confer any ergogenic effect is still questionable at best. Although several amino acids have received some research attention, the available reputable scientific data are still somewhat limited. Additional research is merited with several purported ergogenic amino acids, particularly aspartic acid salts and the BCAA. Creatine supplementation appears to be an effective ergogenic aid for repetitive, high-intensity, short-duration exercise tasks, but additional research is needed to evaluate the effectiveness of acute or chronic creatine supplementation as applied to specific sport events. Moreover, more research is needed to explore the effect of creatine supplementation on performance in events characterized by anaerobic and aerobic glycolysis. Research findings regarding the ergogenic effect of HMB are ambiguous. Additional research is needed to study the effect of HMB supplementation on body composition, strength, power, and related sports events. Inosine supplementation appears to an ineffective ergogenic aid.

Key Concept Recap

▶ Although several interesting hypotheses have been proposed, amino acid supplements are not currently considered to be effective as a means of improving physical performance. Valid data are sparse; additional research is needed.

▶ Research suggests creatine may be an effective ergogenic aid, including laboratory-controlled, repetitive short-duration, high-intensity exercise tasks designed to mimic sports competition. Research findings are equivocal regarding the ergogenic effect of other protein-related supplements, such as HMB. Additional research is needed to document an ergogenic effect of creatine in actual sport competition and to help resolve the ambiguity with other related supplements.

Check for Yourself

Using table 6.8 as a guide, go to a health food store that sells sports supplements and check the cost of various protein supplements. Calculate the cost per serving and the average cost per 8 grams of protein. Compare to the table.

Dietary Protein: Health Implications

The Acceptable Macronutrient Distribution Range (AMDR) for individuals has been set for protein based on evidence from interventional trials, with support of epidemiological evidence, to suggest a role in the prevention of increased risk of chronic diseases and based on ensuring sufficient intakes of essential nutrients. As noted previously, the AMDR for protein is 10–35 percent of energy, and slightly lower percentages for children (5–20 percent for young and 10–30 percent for older children). There may be several possible adverse health effects from consuming a diet which is consistently outside the AMDR for protein, either too low or too high. Excess intake of individual amino acids may also pose health risks.

Does a deficiency of dietary protein pose any health risks?

A short-term protein deficiency (several days) is not likely to cause any serious health problems, mainly because body metabolism adjusts to conserve its protein stores. However, because protein is the source of the essential amino acids, and because protein-rich foods also contain an abundance of essential vitamins and minerals, a prolonged deficiency could be expected to cause serious health problems. Such is the case in certain parts of the world where protein intake is inadequate for political, economic, or other reasons. Protein–Calorie malnutrition is one of the major nutritional problems in the world today, particularly for young children. Infections develop because the immune system, which depends on adequate protein, is weakened. Death is common. For children who survive, physical and mental growth may be permanently retarded.

Protein deficiency may also occur in individuals who abuse sound nutritional practices, such as drug addicts, chronic alcoholics, and extreme food faddists, but adults are more likely to recover fully with adequate nutrition. Elderly individuals, those over 65 years, may be more prone to protein undernutrition because they may eat less protein-rich food and may use protein less efficiently. Lesourd indicated protein undernutrition in the elderly may impair immune function, making them more susceptible to infections. Adequate protein also plays an important role in bone development, thereby influencing peak bone mass. Bonjour and others note that low protein intake can be detrimental for both the acquisition of bone mass during growth and its conservation during adulthood. Low protein intake impairs both the production and action of IGF-I, an essential factor for bone longitudinal growth. Protein intake is especially important during childhood but is very important during adulthood as well.

Individuals who are on a low-protein diet plan, or young athletes who are on modified starvation diets to lose weight for such sports as gymnastics, ballet, or wrestling, may experience periods of protein insufficiency. During this time, the individual may be in negative nitrogen balance; that is, more nitrogen is being excreted from the body than is being ingested. Body tissues such as muscles and hemoglobin may be lost with a possible reduction in strength and endurance capacity. Adequate protein intake is essential for proper physiological functioning and health, both in the inactive and active individual.

Several major health problems associated with excessive weight loss, both in nonathletes and athletes, are related to both energy and protein balance. The role of protein in weight control, both weight loss and gain, will be discussed in chapters 10 through 12.

Does excessive protein intake pose any health risks?

Although the National Academy of Sciences did not establish an UL for protein, the upper level of the AMDR is 35 percent of daily energy intake from protein. Recent American and Canadian survey data reveal that adult males consume about 71–100 grams of protein per day, while women consume about 55–62 grams. Protein constitutes approximately 12–16 percent of the daily energy intake, which is within the AMDR for protein. However, some individuals may consume much greater percentages of their caloric intake as protein, particularly athletes and individuals on weight-loss diets. Even though the Academy did not set an UL for protein, it did note that high protein intakes have been implicated in various chronic diseases. The health effects of dietary protein may depend on its source. As noted previously in several chapters, a plant-based diet may confer some health benefits.

Cardiovascular Disease and Cancer The National Academy of Sciences reported that high-protein diets do not appear to increase the risk for CHD, and even suggested that such diets may be more healthful because of possible beneficial effects on blood pressure and lowering of LDL-cholesterol and triglycerides. The Academy also noted that no clear role has emerged for total dietary protein in the development of cancer. However, the Academy did note that the dietary source of protein may be involved. For example, excessive consumption of animal foods such as meat may be a contributing factor to the development of disease, possibly because of a relationship to the potential high total and saturated fat content or the method of preparation, e. g., charring.

In the United States, approximately 70 percent of dietary protein is obtained from animal products, with most coming from meat, fish, and poultry, and smaller amounts from dairy products and eggs. Although such a diet assures adequate protein, it is not in accord with general healthful guidelines to consume less meat and derive more protein from plant foods. This ratio of animal:plant protein of 70:30 might be more healthful if reversed to 30:70.

A reduction in animal-derived dietary protein has been recommended for various reasons. One point to consider is that protein in many animal foods is often accompanied by substantial quantities of saturated fat and cholesterol, which have been associated with an increased risk of atherosclerosis and coronary heart disease. Interestingly, a recent epidemiological study by Hu and others reported that after controlling for specific types of fat in the diet, women consuming high-protein diets did not experience an increase in heart disease risk. Nevertheless, the researchers recommended caution in consuming high-protein diets given the saturated fat/cholesterol connection. Thus, you should be selective in the types of protein foods you eat. For example, a glass of whole milk and a glass of skim milk both have 8 grams of protein, but the whole milk also has 8 grams of fat compared to less than 1 gram in the skim milk. Nutritionally, skim milk is 40 percent protein Calories while the whole milk is 22.5 percent.

As noted in chapter 2, increased consumption of meat, especially prolonged high consumption of red and processed meat, has been associated with increased levels of cancer, mainly colon cancer. In particular, meat that has been charred, as by excessive grilling, produces heterocyclic aromatic amines (HCAs) that may be carcinogenic.

One general recommendation is to obtain a greater proportion of daily protein intake from plant foods, mainly because of the decreased fat and increased phytochemicals. In particular, soy protein has been recommended as a meat substitute. Modern processing techniques, fortifying soybeans with methionine, have helped to make soy a complete protein. Soy products derived from soybeans include tofu, tempeh, miso, soy nuts, soy nut butter, and soy milk. Many of these products have been added to school lunches—as soy-based burgers and hot dogs—to decrease fat intake. For health benefits, the FDA-approved health claim is based on an intake of about 25 grams of soy protein a day.

Other than containing high-quality protein and being virtually free of saturated fat and sodium, soy contains a number or substances that might confer health benefits, including isoflavones, phytosterols, and omega-3 fatty acids. Some have suggested that most health benefits are believed to be due to the isoflavones (genistein and daidzien) as they may function as phytoestrogens, or weak estrogen-like substances, and possibly have protective effects against heart disease. However, as we will see, research indicates that the soy protein and soy isoflavones provide greater benefits when combined than when either occurs alone. Whole soy foods are recommended as they naturally contain about 2 milligrams of isoflavones for every gram of soy protein. Isoflavones may be lost in highly processed foods, and isoflavone supplements may not contain protein. Check the food label; soy should be one of the first three ingredients.

Clarkson noted that dietary soy protein has been shown to have several beneficial effects on cardiovascular health. This viewpoint is supported by Dunn, who cited a meta-analysis concluding that soy protein consumption achieved an average 9.3 percent decrease in total cholesterol, a 12.9 percent decrease in LDL-cholesterol, and a 10.5 percent decrease in triglycerides. Several recent studies have shown that whole soy protein, not the isolated isoflavones, induces the beneficial effects on serum lipids. In a randomized, crossover study, Jenkins and others studied the cholesterol-lowering effect of a soy protein-based diet (about 50 grams daily) that contained either low or high amounts of isoflavones. Although both soy diets reduced total and LDL-cholesterol, the isoflavone content had no effect. Lichtenstein and others found that relatively high levels of soy protein (>50 grams per day) induced a small but significant drop in total and LDL-cholesterol in mildly hypercholesterolemic individuals, but soy-derived isoflavones had little effect. In a recent review of 22 studies, Sacks and others reported a relatively small decrease (3 percent) in LDL-cholesterol relative to the large amount of soy protein consumed, and also noted no effect of isolated isoflavones on serum cholesterol.

In his recent review, Schardt noted that soy products have been marketed as a means of preventing several forms of cancer, most notably breast and prostate cancer. Natural estrogen is believed to contribute to the development of breast cancer. It is thought that isoflavones functioning as phytoestrogens may block this cancer-causing effect. However, Skibola and Smith noted that at high levels, flavonoids may act as mutagens, or prooxidants that generate free radicals. In this regard, Schardt indicated some investigators suggest that adding an estrogen-like compound in excess may act like estrogen and actually cause cancer. He further notes some researchers believe that the isoflavones in soy may be protective prior to menopause when serum estrogens are high, but may become harmful after menopause when serum estrogens are lower. Based on these considerations, some recommend that women who have a family history of estrogen-dependent breast cancer should limit soy food intake to only several servings per week.

In an FDA review Henkel indicated that adverse health concerns focus on specific components of soy, such as the isoflavones, not the whole food or intact soy proteins. This recommendation is supported in a recent American Heart Association Scientific Advisory by Sacks and others, recommending against isoflavone supplements because their efficacy or safety are not established and cautioning against possible adverse effects. For any potential health benefits scientists agree with the general recommendation to incorporate soy foods into the diet in moderation rather than consuming soy or isoflavone supplements. Moreover, investigators note that although those with hypercholesterolemia may benefit slightly from a diet rich in soy protein, they might be better advised to use other therapy to reduce serum cholesterol and the risk of heart disease.

Liver and Kidney Function   As you may recall, the liver is the major organ involved in protein metabolism. Excess dietary protein may be converted to carbohydrate or fat, with the excess nitrogen being converted to urea for excretion from the body via the kidneys. High-protein diets may also lead to excessive production of ketones, which also must be excreted by the kidneys to prevent an increase in blood acidity, known as ketosis. Thus, excess dietary protein would appear to stress the liver and kidney.

Diets containing moderate amounts of protein do not appear to adversely affect liver or kidney function. Although kidney function progressively declines with aging, according to the National Academy of Sciences the protein content of the diet is not responsible for this decline. Some research has also shown that athletes on somewhat high-protein diets might not be adversely affected. For example, in a recent study Poortmans and Dellalieux reported no evidence of kidney damage, as evaluated by renal clearance tests, in male bodybuilders who had protein intakes of less than 2.8 g protein/kg body weight daily.

However, certain individuals should be concerned with the protein content in their diet. Eisenstein and others noted that caution with high-protein diets is recommended in those individuals who may be predisposed to kidney disease, particularly in those with diabetes mellitus. The American Diabetes Association recommends that diabetics consume no more than the daily RDA for protein.

Individuals prone to kidney stones should also moderate protein intake. High-protein diets may lead to more acidic urine—and the more acidic the urine, the greater the excretion of calcium. The Academy notes that the most common form of kidney stones is composed of calcium oxalate, and its formation is promoted by an acidic urine with high concentrations of calcium and oxalate.

Bone and Joint Health   As noted, excess dietary protein may increase urine acidity, which may be attributed to the increased acids in the blood associated with the oxidation of the sulfur amino acids. The National Academy of Sciences indicates that calcium might be absorbed from the bones to help buffer this acidity. If so, excess calcium losses could lead to a decreased bone density. However, the Academy indicates that whether this bone resorption leads to bone loss and osteoporosis is controversial, but does cite recent studies showing no association between protein intake and bone mineral density. The Academy suggests that the diet may be the key.

Studies present conflicting data as to whether or not animal protein, as contrasted to plant protein, decreases bone density with an increased risk of osteoporosis and bone fractures. Protein is needed for bone development at all stages of life, but excessive intake may lead to increased calcium losses. Krall and Dawson-Hughes indicate that over a wide range of protein intake, an average increase in dietary protein of 1 gram leads to the loss of 1 milligram of calcium in the urine. Although this does not seem too substantial a loss given the RDA for calcium, it could be significant for those on a high-protein and low-calcium diet. The Academy notes that inadequate protein intake itself leads to bone loss, but increased protein intake may lead to increased calcium intake and bone loss does not occur if calcium intake is adequate. Dawson-Hughes and Harris reiterate these points, noting that there is currently no consensus on the effect of dietary protein intake on the skeleton. However, they also note that there is some indication that low calcium intakes adversely influence the effect of dietary protein on fracture risk.

The key appears to be getting enough of both protein and calcium. The topic of calcium balance is presented in chapter 8.

Gout, a painful inflammation of the joints, may be aggravated by high-protein diets containing substantial quantities of purines, which are metabolized to uric acid (not the same as urea). The uric acid may accumulate in the joints and cause inflammation.

Heat Illnesses   Because both urea and ketone bodies need to be eliminated by the kidneys, dehydration could occur from excessive fluid losses. Such an effect could compromise the ability to deal with exercise in the heat. Additionally, Johnson and others found that increasing the protein content of the diet from 17 to 31 percent of energy would significantly increase the resting energy expenditure, an effect they suggested could contribute to the development of heat illnesses when exercising under warm environmental conditions. Both of these are possibilities, and the implications are discussed in chapter 9 when we discuss fluid balance and temperature regulation during exercise.

Does the consumption of individual amino acids pose any health risks?

Amino acids do not exist free in foods we eat, but are complexed with other amino acids to form protein. The National Academy of Sciences noted there is no evidence that amino acids derived from usual or even high intakes of protein from foodstuffs present any health risk. Although no UL has been established for amino acids, the Academy indicated that the absence of a UL

means that caution is warranted in using any single amino acid at levels significantly above that normally found in food. Extreme consumption of individual amino acid supplements may pose a health risk.

Free amino acids have been manufactured to serve as a drug, to be given to patients intravenously for adequate protein nutrition. They may also be used as food additives to enhance the protein quality of foods deficient in specific amino acids. They are also marketed as dietary supplements and sold separately, or in combination with other amino acids. As dietary supplements, the purity and safety are not guaranteed. In 1989 a serious epidemic of eosinophilia-myalgia syndrome (EMS), a neuromuscular disorder characterized by weakness, fever, edema, rashes, bone pain, and other symptoms was attributed to an L-tryptophan supplement contaminated during manufacturing.

Slavin and her colleagues have noted that amino acids taken in large doses are essentially drugs with unknown effects. The long-term effects of even moderate doses are also unknown, as noted previously in regard to arginine and its effect on HGH secretion. One problem is that excessive reliance on free-form amino acids, in comparison to dietary protein, may lead to a diet deficient in key vitamins and minerals that are normally found in protein foods, such as iron and zinc in meat, fish, and poultry. Some evidence from human and animal research indicates individual amino acids may interfere with the absorption of other essential amino acids; suppress appetite and food intake; precipitate tissue damage; contribute to kidney failure; lead to osteoporosis; cause gastrointestinal distress such as nausea, vomiting, and diarrhea; or create unfavorable psychological changes.

In a recent review, Barrett and Herbert indicated that the Federation of American Societies for Experimental Biology (FASEB) criticized the widespread use of amino acids in supplements, noting that they were being used as drugs for pharmacologic purposes, not for nutritive purposes. In this regard, FASEB notes that there is little scientific support for the use of amino acid supplements for their stated purposes and that safety levels for amino acid use have not been established.

So what's the bottom line? At the present time there are inadequate scientific data to support either an ergogenic or a health benefit of supplementation with individual amino acids in the healthy individual. Adequate amounts of each amino acid may be obtained in a diet containing protein in amounts consistent with the Prudent Healthy Diet, and because such a diet may confer some benefits relative to physical performance and health, it should be the source of amino acid nutrition. Additional research is needed to evaluate both the ergogenic effectiveness and the health implications of supplementation with individual amino acids.

Key Concept Recap

▶ Dietary deficiencies, as well as dietary excesses, of protein and amino acids may interfere with optimal physiological efficiency, which may lead to impairment of physical performance or health status.

Obtain a supply of creatine monohydrate—about 100 grams, enough to provide 20 grams a day for 5 days. Measure your weight accurately in the morning after arising and your normal bathing routine, but before eating breakfast. Consume 20 grams of creatine per day for the 5 days, taking it in 4 equal doses of 5 grams at breakfast, at lunchtime, late afternoon, and before bed. Weigh yourself again the morning after taking the last dose. Did your body weight change? Record your weight again next week, and the following three weeks. Did your body weight change again? Compare your findings to the text discussion.

Creatine Monohydrate Trial

	Day 1	Day 6	1 Week Later	2 Weeks Later	3 Weeks Later
Morning Weight					

Review Questions—Multiple Choice

1. A HIGH QUALITY protein is best described as one that:
   (a) contains 10 grams of protein per 100 grams of food
   (b) contains all of the essential amino acids in the proper amounts and ratio
   (c) contains all of the nonessential amino acids
   (d) contains adequate amounts of glucose for protein sparing
   (e) contains the amino acids leucine, isoleucine, and valine

2. Which of the following statements involving the interaction of protein and exercise training is false?
   (a) Small amounts of protein may be used as an energy source during endurance exercise but usually account for less than 5 percent of the energy cost of the exercise.
   (b) Small amounts of protein may be lost in the urine and sweat during exercise.
   (c) Resistance weight-training programs usually result in the development of a positive nitrogen balance in most athletes who are attempting to gain body weight in the form of muscle mass.
   (d) Although weight lifters and endurance athletes may need slightly more protein than accounted for by the RDA, such increased protein may be obtained readily and more economically through a planned diet.
   (e) Research has shown conclusively that amino acid supplements and other protein supplements will enhance performance in sports.

3. Which of the following has the least amount of dietary protein?
   (a) one ounce of chicken breast
   (b) one-half cup of baked beans
   (c) one slice of whole wheat bread
   (d) one orange
   (e) one-half glass of skim milk

4. Which of the following statements relative to protein and exercise is false?
   (a) Protein may be catabolized during exercise and used as an energy source, but the contribution is less than 10 percent.
   (b) Carbohydrate intake may exert a protein-sparing effect during exercise.
   (c) Very low levels of protein intake during training may lead to the development of a condition known as sports anemia.
   (d) Research has shown that individuals who are training to gain weight need about 6 to 8 grams of protein per kilogram body weight.
   (e) Research has shown that protein supplementation above the RDA will not improve physiological performance capacity during exercise.

5. In the recommendations for a healthy diet from the National Academy of Sciences, what is the Acceptable Macronutrient Distribution Range for protein as a percent of daily energy intake in Calories?
   (a) 15–20
   (b) 10–35
   (c) 4–6
   (d) 12–14
   (e) 40–65

6. Which of the following statements relative to protein metabolism is false?
   (a) Excess protein may be converted to glucose in the body.
   (b) The liver is a critical center for the control of amino acid metabolism.
   (c) Essential amino acids can be formed in the liver from carbohydrate and nitrogen from nonessential amino acids.
   (d) Excess protein may be converted to fat in the body.
   (e) Urea is a waste product of protein metabolism.

7. Which is most likely to be a complete, high-quality protein food?
   (a) cheddar cheese
   (b) peanut butter
   (c) green peas
   (d) corn
   (e) macaroni

8. Supplementation with some amino acids has been theorized to decrease the

formation of serotonin in the brain and possibly help delay the onset of central nervous system fatigue in prolonged aerobic endurance exercise. Which amino acids are theorized to do this?

(a) leucine, isoleucine, and valine

(b) arginine, ornithine, and inosine

(c) tryptophan, arginine, and creatine

(d) inosine, creatine, and alanine

(e) asparagine, aspartic acid, and glutamine

9. If an adult weighed 176 pounds, the RDA for protein would be what, in grams?

(a) 176

(b) 140.8

(c) 80

(d) 64

(e) 309.7

10. Recent research has suggested that creatine supplementation may enhance performance in which of the following types of physical performance tasks?

(a) an all-out power lift in one second

(b) high intensity exercise lasting 6–30 seconds

(c) 10 kilometer race lasting about 30 minutes

(d) marathon running (26.2 miles)

(e) ultramarathons, such as Ironman-type triathlons

Answers to multiple-choice questions: 1. b; 2. e; 3. d; 4. d; 5. b; 6. c; 7. a; 8. a; 9. d; 10. b.

Review Questions—Essay

1. Differentiate between complete and incomplete proteins as related to essential and nonessential amino acids and indicate several specific foods that are considered to contain either complete or incomplete protein.

2. Describe the process of gluconeogenesis from protein.

3. Explain why some scientists recommend that both strength and endurance athletes may need more dietary protein than the RDA. Provide some recommended values and calculate the recommended grams of protein for a 70-kilogram athlete.

4. Explain the central fatigue hypothesis as related to BCAA supplementation for endurance athletes and summarize the research findings as to the related ergogenic efficacy of BCAA supplementation.

5. Discuss the theory underlying the possible health benefits associated with soy protein and summarize the research findings at this point in time.

References

Books

Bucci, L. 1993. *Nutrients as Ergogenic Aids for Sports and Exercise.* Boca Raton, FL: CRC Press.

Driskell, J. A., and Wolinsky, I. 2000. *Energy-yielding Macronutrients & Energy Metabolism in Sports Nutrition.* Boca Raton, FL: CRC Press.

Ivy, J., and Portman, R. 2004. *Nutrient Timing: The Future of Sports Nutrition.* North Bergen, NJ: Basic Health Publications.

National Academy of Sciences. 2002. *Dietary Reference Intakes for Energy, Carbohydrates, Fiber, Fat, Protein and Amino Acids (Macronutrients).* Washington, DC: National Academies Press.

Williams, M. H., Kreider, R. B., and Branch, J. D. 1999. *Creatine: The Power Supplement.* Champaign, IL: Human Kinetics.

Reviews

Abcouwer, S. F., and Souba, W. W. 1999. Glutamine and arginine. In *Modern Nutrition in Health and Disease,* eds. M. Shils, et al. Baltimore: Williams & Wilkins.

American College of Sports Medicine. 2000. The Physiological and Health Effects of Oral Creatine Supplementation. *Medicine & Science in Sports & Exercise* 32: 706–17.

American Dietetic Association. 1997, Vegetarian Diets: Position of the ADA. *Journal of the American Dietetic Association* 97:1317–21.

Anderson, J., et al. 1995. Meta-analysis of the effects of soy protein intake on serum lipids. *New England Journal of Medicine* 333:276–82.

Antonio, J., and Street C. 1999. Glutamine: A potentially useful supplement for athletes. *Canadian Journal of Applied Physiology* 24:1–14.

Bailes, J., et al. 2002. The neurosurgeon in sport: Awareness of the risks of heatstroke and dietary supplements. *Neurosurgery* 51:283–86.

Barrett, S., and Herbert, V. 1999. Fads, frauds, and quackery. In *Modern Nutrition in Health and Disease,* eds. M. Shils, et al. Baltimore: Williams and Wilkins.

Benzi, G., and Ceci, A. 2001. Creatine as nutritional supplementation and medicinal product. *Journal of Sports Medicine and Physical Fitness* 41:1–10.

Blomstrand, E. 2001. Amino acids and central fatigue. *Amino Acids* 20:25–34.

Bonjour, J., et al. 2000. Protein intake and bone growth. *Canadian Journal of Applied Physiology* 26:S153–66.

Branch, J. D. 2003. Effect of creatine supplementation on body composition and performance: A meta-analysis. *International Journal of Sport Nutrition and Exercise Metabolism* 13:198– 226.

Brief, A., et al. 2001. Use of glucosamine and chondroitin sulfate in the management of osteoarthritis. *Journal of the American Academy of Orthopedic Surgeons* 9:352–53.

Budgett, R., et al. 1998. The overtraining syndrome. In *Oxford Textbook of Sports Medicine,* eds. M. Harries, et al. Oxford: Oxford University Press.

Butterfield, G. 1991. Amino acids and high protein diets. In *Perspectives in Exercise Science and Sports Medicine. Ergogenics: Enhancement of Sports Performance,* eds. D. Lamb and M. Williams. Indianapolis, IN: Benchmark Press.

Casey, A., and Greenhaff, P. 2000. Does dietary creatine supplementation play a role in skeletal muscle metabolism and performance? *American Journal of Clinical Nutrition* 72:607S–17S.

Castell, L. 2003. Glutamine supplementation in vitro and in vivo, in exercise and in immunodepression. *Sports Medicine* 33:323–45.

Cheng, J., et al. 2001. L-arginine in the management of cardiovascular disease. *Annals of Pharmacotherapy* 35:755–64.

Cheuvront, S. N. 1999. The zone diet and athletic performance. *Sports Medicine* 27:213–28.

Chromiak, J., and Antonio, J. 2002. Use of amino acids as growth-hormone releasing agents by athletes. *Nutrition* 18:657–61.

Clarkson, T. 2002. Soy, soy phytoestrogens and cardiovascular disease. *Journal of Nutrition* 132:566S–69S.

Clegg, D., et al. 2006. Glucosamine, chondroitin sulfate, and the two in combination for painful knee arthritis. *New England Journal of Medicine* 354: 795–808

Consumers Union. 2004. Soy: Cutting through the confusion. *Consumer Reports* 69(7):28–31.

Consumers Union. 2001. How much protein is enough? *Consumer Reports on Health* 13(2):8–10.

Consumers Union. 2000. Alternatives for arthritis. *Consumer Reports on Health* 12 (1):6–9.

Cowart, V. 1992. Dietary supplements: Alternatives to anabolic steroids? *Physician and Sportsmedicine* 20 (March): 189–96.

Davis, J. M., et al. 2000. Serotonin and central nervous system fatigue: Nutritional considerations. *American Journal of Clinical Nutrition* 72:573S–78S.

Davis, J. M. 2000. Nutrition, neurotransmitters and central nervous system fatigue. In *Nutrition in Sport,* ed. R. J. Maughan. Oxford: Blackwell Science.

Davis, J.M. 1996. Carbohydrates, branched-chain amino acids and endurance: The central fatigue hypothesis. *Sports Science Exchange* 9 (2): 1–5.

Dawson-Hughes, B., and Harris, S. 2002. Calcium intake influences the association of protein intake with rates of bone loss in elderly men and women. *American Journal of Clinical Nutrition* 75:773–79.

DiPasquale, M. D. 2000. Proteins and amino acids in exercise and sport. In *Energy-yielding Macronutrients & Energy Metabolism in Sports Nutrition,* eds. J. A. Driskell and I. Wolinsky. Boca Raton, FL: CRC Press.

Dunn, A. 2000. Incorporating soy protein into a low-fat, low-cholesterol diet.

Cleveland Clinic Journal of Medicine 67:767–72.

Eisenstein, J., et al. 2002. High-protein weight-loss diets: Are they safe and do they work? A review of the experimental and epidemiologic data. *Nutrition Reviews* 60:189–200.

Evans, W. 2001. Protein nutrition and resistance exercise. *Canadian Journal of Applied Physiology* 26:S141–52.

Fielding, R., and Parkington, J. 2002. What are the dietary protein requirements of physically active individuals? New evidence on the effects of exercise on protein utilization during post-exercise recovery. *Nutrition in Clinical Care* 5:191–96.

Fitts, R., and Metzger, J. 1993. Mechanisms of muscular fatigue. In *Principles of Exercise Biochemistry,* ed. J. Poortmans. Basel, Switzerland: Karger.

Friedman, M., and Brandon, D. 2001. Nutritional and health benefits of soy protein. *Journal of Agricultural and Food Chemistry* 49:1069–86.

Garlick, P. J., et al. 1999. Adaptation of protein metabolism in relation to limits to high dietary protein intake. *European Journal of Clinical Nutrition* 53:S34–S43.

Gibala, M. 2002. Dietary protein, amino acid supplements, and recovery from exercise. *Sports Science Exchange* 15 (4):1–4.

Gibala, M. 2001. Regulation of skeletal muscle amino acid metabolism during exercise. *International Journal of Sport Nutrition and Exercise Metabolism* 11:87–108.

Graham, T. E., and MacLean, D. A. 1998. Ammonia and amino acid metabolism in skeletal muscle: Human, rodent and canine models. *Medicine & Science in Sports & Exercise* 30:34–46.

Graham, T., et al. 1997. Effect of endurance training on ammonia and amino acid metabolism in humans. *Medicine & Science in Sports & Exercise* 29:646–53.

Greenhaff, P. 1997. Creatine supplementation and implications for exercise performance. In *Advances in Training and Nutrition for Endurance Sports,* eds. A. Jeukendrup, M. Brouns, and F. Brouns. Maastricht, the Netherlands: Novartis Nutrition Research Unit.

Hargreaves, M., and Snow, R. 2001. Amino acids and endurance exercise. *International Journal of Sport Nutrition and Exercise Metabolism* 11:133–45.

Henkel, J. 2000. Soy: Health claims for soy protein, questions about other components. *FDA Consumer* 34 (3):13–20.

Jacobson, B. 1990. Effect of amino acids on growth hormone release. *Physician and Sportsmedicine* 18 (January): 63–70.

Kirkendall, D. 2004. Creatine, carbs, and fluids: How important in soccer nutrition? *Sports Science Exchange* 17(3):1–6.

Krall, E. A., and Dawson-Hughes, B. 1999. Osteoporosis. In *Modern Nutrition in Health and Disease,* eds. M. Shils, et al. Baltimore: Williams and Wilkins.

Kreider, R. 2003. Effects of creatine supplementation on performance and training adaptations. *Molecular and Cellular Biochemistry* 244:89–94.

Kreider, R., et al. 1993. Amino acid supplementation and exercise performance: Analysis of the proposed ergogenic value. *Sports Medicine* 16:190–209.

Lawrence, M., and Kirby, D. 2002. Nutrition and sports supplements: Fact or fiction? *Journal of Clinical Gastroenterology* 35:299–306.

Lemon, P. W. 2000. Protein metabolism during exercise. In *Exercise and Sport Science,* eds. W. E. Garrett and D. T. Kirkendall. Philadelphia: Lippincott Williams & Wilkins.

Lemon, P. W. 2000. Effects of exercise on protein metabolism. In *Nutrition in Sport,* ed. R. J. Maughan. Oxford: Blackwell Science.

Lemon, P. W. 1998. Effects of exercise on dietary protein requirements. *International Journal of Sport Nutrition,* 8:426–47.

Lesourd, B. 1995. Protein undernutrition as the major cause of decreased immune function in the elderly: Clinical and functional implications. *Nutrition Reviews* 53:S86–S94.

Matthews, D. E. 2006. Proteins and amino acids. In *Modern Nutrition in Health and Disease,* eds. M. Shils, et al. Philadelphia: Lippincott Williams & Wilkins.

McAlindon, T.E., et al. 2000. Glucosamine and chondroitin for treatment of osteoarthritis: A systematic quality assessment and meta-analysis. *JAMA* 283: 1469–75.

Melis, G., et al. 2004. Glutamine: Recent developments in research on the clinical significance of glutamine. *Current Opinion in Clinical Nutrition and Metabolic Care* 7:59–79.

Messina, M., et al. 2002. Gaining insight into the health effects of soy but a long way still to go: Commentary on the fourth International Symposium on the Role of Soy in Preventing and Treating Chronic Disease. *Journal of Nutrition* 132:547S–51S.

Messina, V. K., and Burke, K. I. 1997. Position of the American Dietetic Association: Vegetarian diets. *Journal of the American Dietetic Association* 97:1317–21.

Millward, D. 2004. Macronutrient intakes as determinants of dietary protein and amino acid adequacy. *Journal of Nutrition* 134:1588S–96S.

Newsholme, E., et al. 1992. Physical and mental fatigue: Metabolic mechanisms and importance of plasma amino acids. *British Medical Bulletin* 48:477–95.

Newsholme, E. A., and Castell, L. M. 2000. Amino acids, fatigue and immunodepression in exercise. In *Nutrition in Sport,* ed. R. J. Maughan. Oxford: Blackwell Science.

Nieman, D. 2001. Exercise immunology: Nutrition countermeasures. *Canadian Journal of Applied Physiology* 26:S45–55.

Parkhouse, W. 1988. Regulation of skeletal muscle myofibrillar protein degradation: Relationships to fatigue and exercise. *International Journal of Biochemistry* 20:769–75.

Peeters, P., et al. 2003. Phytoestrogens and breast cancer risk. Review of the epidemiological evidence. *Breast Cancer Research and Treatment* 77:171–83.

Persky, A., and Brazeau, G. 2001. Clinical pharmacology of the dietary supplement creatine monohydrate. *Pharmacology Reviews* 53:161–76.

Phillips, S. 2004. Protein requirements and supplementation in strength sports. *Nutrition* 20:689–95.

Poortmans, J., and Francaux, M. 2000. Adverse effects of creatine supplementation: Fact or fiction. *Sports Medicine* 30:155–70.

Poortmans, J. 1993. Protein metabolism. In *Principles of Exercise Biochemistry,* ed. J. Poortmans. Basel, Switzerland: Karger.

Rawson, E., and Clarkson, P. 2003. Scientifically debatable: Is creatine worth its weight? *Sports Science Exchange* 16(4):1–6.

Rennie, M. 2001. Control of muscle protein synthesis as a result of contractile activity and amino acid availability: Implications for protein requirements. *International Journal of Sport Nutrition and Exercise Metabolism* 11:S170–76.

Rennie, M., and Tipton, K. 2000. Protein and amino acid metabolism during and after exercise and the effects of nutrition. *Annual Review of Nutrition* 20:457–83.

Sacks, F., et al. 2006. Soy protein, isoflavones, and cardiovascular health: An American Heart Association Science Advisory for professionals from the Nutrition Committee. *Circulation* January 17 [Epub ahead of print].

Sahlin, K., et al. 1998. Energy supply and muscle fatigue in humans. *Acta Physiologica Scandinavica* 162:261–66.

Schardt, D. 2002. Got soy? *Nutrition Action Health Letter* 29 (9):8–11.

Schardt, D. 2001. Sam-e so-so. *Nutrition Action Health Letter* 28 (2):10–11.

Skibola, C., and Smith, M. 2000. Potential health impacts of excessive flavonoid intake. *Free Radical Biology & Medicine* 29:375–83.

Slater, G., and Jenkins, D. 2000. Beta-hydroxy-beta-methylbutyrate (HMB) supplementation and the promotion of muscle growth and strength. *Sports Medicine* 30:105–16.

Slavin, J., et al. 1988. Amino acid supplements: Beneficial or risky? *Physician and Sportsmedicine* 16 (March): 221–24.

Snow, R., and Murphy, R. 2003. Factors influencing creatine loading into human skeletal muscle. *Exercise and Sport Sciences Reviews* 31:154–58.

Soeken, K., et al. 2002. Safety and efficacy of S-adenosylmethionine (SAMe) for osteoarthritis. *Journal of Family Practice* 51:425–30.

St Jeor, S., et al. 2001. Dietary protein and weight reduction: A statement for healthcare professionals from the Nutrition Committee of the Council on Nutrition, Physical Activity, and Metabolism of the American Heart Association. *Circulation* 104:1869–74.

Tarnopolsky, M. 2004. Protein requirements for endurance athletes. *Nutrition* 20:662–68.

Tarnopolsky, M., et al. 2004. Creatine monohydrate enhances strength and body composition in Duchenne muscular dystrophy. *Neurology* 62:1771–77.

Tipton, K., and Wolfe, R. 2004. Protein and amino acids for athletes. *Journal of Sports Sciences* 22:65–79.

Tipton, K., and Wolfe, R. R. 1998. Exercise-induced changes in protein metabolism. *Acta Physiologica Scandinavica* 162:377–87.

Tufts University. 2000. A look at glucosamine and chondroitin for easing arthritis pain. *Tufts University Health & Nutrition Letter* 17 (11):4–5.

Volek, J., and Rawson, E. 2004. Scientific basis and practical aspects of creatine supplementation for athletes. *Nutrition* 20:609–14.

Wagenmakers, A. 2000. Amino acid metabolism in exercise. In *Nutrition in Sport,* ed. R. J. Maughan. Oxford: Blackwell Science.

Wagenmakers, A. 1999. Amino acid supplements to improve athletic performance. *Current Opinion in Clinical Nutrition and Metabolic Care* 2:539–44.

Wagenmakers, A. 1997. Branched-chain amino acids and endurance performance. In *The Clinical Pharmacology of Sport and Exercise,* eds. T. Reilly and M. Orme. Amsterdam: Elsevier Science BV.

Walberg-Rankin, J. W. 1999. Role of protein in exercise. *Clinics in Sports Medicine* 18:499–511.

Walzem, R., et al. 2002. Whey components: Millennia of evolution create functionalities for mammalian nutrition. What we know and what we may be overlooking. *Critical Reviews in Food Science and Nutrition* 42:353–75.

Williams, M. H. 1999. Facts and fallacies of purported ergogenic amino acid supplements. *Clinics in Sports Medicine* 18:633–49.

Wolfe, R. 2001. Effects of amino acid intake on anabolic processes. *Canadian Journal of Applied Physiology* 26:S220–27.

Wolfe, R. 2001. Control of muscle protein breakdown: Effects of activity and nutritional states. *International Journal of Sport Nutrition and Exercise Metabolism* 11:S164–69.

Wolfe, R. 2000. Protein supplements and exercise. *American Journal of Clinical Nutrition* 72:551S–557S.

Yoshimura, H. 1970. Anemia during physical training (sports anemia). *Nutrition Review* 28:251–53.

Yoshizumi, W., and Tsourounis, C. 2004. Effects of creatine supplementation on renal function. *Journal of Herbal Pharmacotherapy* 4:1–7.

Specific Studies

Andersen, L., et al. 2005. The effect of resistance training combined with timed ingestion of protein on muscle fiber size and muscle strength. *Metabolism* 54:151–56.

Antonio, J., et al. 2002. The effects of high-dose glutamine ingestion on weightlifting performance. *Journal of Strength and Conditioning Research* 16:157–60.

Antonio, J., et al. 2001. The effects of bovine colostrum supplementation on body composition and exercise performance in active men and women. *Nutrition* 17:243–47.

Baum, M., and Weiss, M. The influence of a taurine containing drink on cardiac parameters before and after exercise measured by echocardiography. *Amino Acids* 20:75–82.

Bednarz, B., et al. 2004. L-arginine supplementation prolongs exercise capacity in congestive heart failure. *Kardiologia Polska* 60:348–53.

Blomstrand, E., et al. 1997. Influence of ingesting a solution of branched-chain amino acids on perceived exertion during exercise. *Acta Physiologica Scandinavica* 159:41–49.

Blomstrand, E., et al. 1995. Effect of branched-chain amino acid and carbohydrate supplementation on the exercise-induced change in plasma and muscle concentration of amino acids in human subjects. *Acta Physiologica Scandinavica* 153:87–96.

Blomstrand, E., et al. 1991. Administration of branched-chain amino acids during sustained exercise—Effects on performance and on plasma concentration of some amino acids. *European Journal of Applied Physiology* 65:83–88.

Blomstrand, E., et al. 1991. Effect of branched-chain amino acid supplementation on mental performance. *Acta Physiologica Scandinavica* 143:225–26.

Børsheim, E., et al. 2004. Effect of an amino acid, protein, and carbohydrate mixture on net muscle protein balance after resistance exercise. *International Journal of Sport Nutrition and Exercise Metabolism* 14:255–71.

Børsheim, E., et al. 2004. Effect of carbohydrate intake on net muscle protein synthesis during recovery from resistance exercise. *Journal of Applied Physiology* 96:674–78.

Brinkworth, G., et al. 2004. Effect of bovine colostrum supplementation on the composition of resistance trained and untrained limbs in healthy young men. *European Journal of Applied Physiology* 91:53–60.

Brinkworth, G., et al. 2002. Oral bovine colostrum supplementation enhances buffer capacity, but not rowing performance in elite female rowers. *International Journal of Sport Nutrition and Exercise Metabolism* 12:349–63.

Bucci, L., et al. 1992. Ornithine supplementation and insulin release in bodybuilders. *International Journal of Sport Nutrition* 2:287–91.

Bucci, L., et al. 1990. Ornithine ingestion and growth hormone release in bodybuilders. *Nutrition Research* 10:239–45.

Buchman, A. L., et al. 1999. The effect of arginine or glycine supplementation on gastrointestinal function, muscle injury, serum amino acid concentrations and performance during a marathon run. *International Journal of Sports Medicine* 20:315–21.

Buford, B., and Koch, A. 2004. Glycine-arginine-alpha-ketoisocaproic acid improves performance of repeated cycling sprints. *Medicine & Science in Sports & Exercise* 36:583–87.

Burke, D., et al. 2003. Effect of creatine and weight training on muscle creatine and performance in vegetarians. *Medicine & Science in Sports & Exercise* 36:1946–55.

Burke, D., et al. 2001. The effect of 7 days of creatine supplementation on 24-hour urinary creatine excretion. *Journal of Strength and Conditioning Research* 15:59–62.

Burke, D., et al. 2001. The effect of whey protein supplementation with and without creatine monohydrate combined with resistance training on lean tissue mass and muscle strength. *International Journal of Sport Nutrition and Exercise Metabolism* 11:349–64.

Candow, D., et al. 2001. Effect of glutamine supplementation combined with resistance training in young adults. *European Journal of Applied Physiology* 86:142–49.

Casey, A., et al. 1996. Creatine ingestion favorably affects performance and muscle metabolism during maximal exercise in humans. *American Journal of Physiology* 271:E31–E37.

Chao, A., et al. 2005. Meat consumption and risk of colorectal cancer. *JAMA* 293:172–82.

Cheuvront, S., et al. 2004. Branched-chain amino acid supplementation and human performance when hypohydrated in the heat. *Journal of Applied Physiology* 97:1275–82.

Coombes, J., et al. 2002. Dose effects of oral bovine colostrum on physical work capacity in cyclists. *Medicine & Science in Sports & Exercise* 34:1184–88.

Cox, G., et al. 2002. Acute creatine supplementation and performance during a field test simulating match play in elite soccer players. *International Journal of Sport Nutrition and Exercise Metabolism* 12:33–46.

Crowe, M., et al. 2003. The effects of beta-hydroxy-beta-methylbutyrate (HMB) and HMB/creatine supplementation on indices of health in highly trained athletes. *International Journal of Sport Nutrition and Exercise Metabolism* 13:184–97.

Cuisinier, C., et al. 2001. Changes in plasma and urinary taurine and amino acids in runners immediately and 24h after a marathon. *Amino Acids* 20:13–23.

Cunliffe, A., et al. 1998. A placebo controlled investigation of the effects of tryptophan or placebo on subjective and objective measures of fatigue. *European Journal of Clinical Nutrition* 52:425–30.

Dawson-Hughes, B., and Harris, S. 2002. Calcium intake influences the association of protein intake with rates of bone loss in elderly men and women. *American Journal of Clinical Nutrition* 75:773–79.

Davis, J. M., et al. 1999. Effects of branched-chain amino acids and carbohydrate on fatigue during intermittent, high-intensity running. *International Journal of Sports Medicine* 20:309–14.

Deldicque, L., et al. 2005. Increased IGF mRNA in human skeletal muscle after creatine supplementation. *Medicine & Science in Sports & Exercise* 37:731–36.

Doherty, M., et al. 2002. Caffeine is ergogenic after supplementation of oral creatine monohydrate. *Medicine & Science in Sports & Exercise* 34:1785–92.

Elam, R. 1988. Morphological changes in adult males from resistance exercise and amino acid supplementation. *Journal of Sports Medicine and Physical Fitness* 28:35–39.

Elam, R., et al. 1989. Effects of arginine and ornithine on strength, lean body mass and urinary hydroxyproline in adult males. *Journal of Sports Medicine and Physical Fitness* 29:52–56.

Esmarck, B. 2001. Timing of postexercise protein intake is important for muscle hypertrophy with resistance training in elderly humans. *Journal of Physiology* 535:301–11.

Finn, J., et al. 2001. Effect of creatine supplementation on metabolism and performance in humans during intermittent sprint cycling. *European Journal of Applied Physiology* 84:238–43.

Fogelholm, G. M., et al. 1993. Low-dose amino acid supplementation: No effects on serum human growth hormone and insulin in male weightlifters. *International Journal of Sport Nutrition* 3:290–97.

Gallagher, P. M., et al. 2000. β-hydroxy-β-methylbutyrate ingestion, Part I: Effects on strength and fat-free mass. *Medicine & Science in Sports & Exercise* 32:2109–15.

Gallagher, P. M., et al. 2000. β-hydroxy-β-methylbutyrate ingestion, Part II: Effects on hematology, hepatic and liver function. *Medicine & Science in Sports & Exercise.* 32:2116–19.

Gill, N., et al. 2004. Creatine serum is not as effective as creatine powder for improving cycle sprint performance in competitive male team-sport athletes. *Journal of Strength and Conditioning Research* 18:272–75.

Gleeson, M., et al. 1998. Effect of low- and high-carbohydrate diets on the plasma glutamine and circulating leukocyte responses to exercise. *International Journal of Sport Nutrition* 8:45–59.

Green, A., et al. 1996. Carbohydrate ingestion augments creatine retention during creatine feeding in humans. *Acta Physiologica Scandinavica* 158:195–202.

Greenhaff, P., et al. 1994. Effect of oral creatine supplementation on skeletal muscle phosphocreatine resynthesis. *American Journal of Physiology* 266:E725–E730.

Harris, R., et al. 1993. The effect of oral creatine supplementation on running performance during maximal short term exercise in man. *Journal of Physiology* 467:74P.

Harris, R., et al. 1992. Elevation of creatine in resting and exercised muscle on normal subjects by creatine supplementation. *Clinical Science* 83:367–74.

Hassmen, P., et al. 1994. Branched-chain amino acid supplementation during 30-km competitive run: Mood and cognitive performance. *Nutrition* 10:405–10.

Hawkins, C., et al. 1991. Oral arginine does not affect body composition or muscle function in male weight lifters. *Medicine & Science in Sports & Exercise* 23:S15.

Hefler, S., et al. 1995. Branched-chain amino acid (BCAA) supplementation improves endurance performance in competitive cyclists. *Medicine & Science in Sports & Exercise* 27:S149.

Hernandez, M., et al. 1996. The protein efficiency ratios of 30:70 mixtures of animal:vegetable protein are similar or higher than those of the animal foods alone. *Journal of Nutrition* 126:574–81.

Hespel, P., et al. 2002. Opposite actions of caffeine and creatine on muscle relaxation time in humans. *Journal of Applied Physiology* 92:513–18.

Hespel, P., et al. 2001. Oral creatine supplementation facilitates the rehabilitation of disuse atrophy and alters the expression of muscle myogenic factors in humans. *Journal of Physiology* 536:625–33.

Hoffman, J., et al. 2004. Effects of beta-hydroxy-beta-methylbutyrate on power performance and indices of muscle damage and stress during high-intensity training. *Journal of Strength and Conditioning Research* 18:747–52.

Hofman, Z., et al. 2002. The effect of bovine colostrum supplementation on exercise performance in elite field hockey players. *International Journal of Sport Nutrition and Exercise Metabolism* 12:461–69.

Hu, F. B., et al. 1999. Dietary protein and risk of ischemic heart disease in women. *American Journal of Clinical Nutrition* 70:221–27.

Hughes, R., and Carr, A. 2002. A randomized, double-blind, placebo-controlled trial of glucosamine sulfate as an analgesic in osteoarthritis of the knee. *Rheumatology* 41:279–84.

Hultman, E., et al. 1996. Muscle creatine loading in men. *Journal of Applied Physiology* 81:232–37.

Ivy, J., et al. 2003. Effect of a carbohydrate-protein supplement on endurance performance during exercise of varying intensity. *International Journal of Sport Nutrition and Exercise Metabolism* 13:382–95.

Izquierdo, M., et al. 2002. Effects of creatine supplementation on muscle power, endurance, and sprint performance. *Medicine & Science in Sports & Exercise* 34:332–43.

Jacobs, P., et al. 2002. Oral creatine supplementation enhances upper extremity work capacity in persons with cervical-level spinal cord injury. *Archives of Physical Medicine and Rehabilitation* 83:19–23.

Jacobson, B., et al. 2001. Nutrition practices and knowledge of college varsity athletes: A follow-up. *Journal of Strength and Conditioning Research* 15:63–68.

Jarvis, M., et al. 2002. The acute 1-week effects of the Zone diet on body composition, blood lipid levels, and performance in recreational endurance athletes. *Journal of Strength and Conditioning Research* 16:50–57.

Jenkins, D., et al. 2002. Effects of high- and low-isoflavone soy foods on blood lipids, oxidized LDL, homocysteine, and blood pressure in hyperlipidemic men and women. *American Journal of Clinical Nutrition* 76:365–72.

Johnson, C., et al. 2002. Postprandial thermogenesis is increased 100% on high-protein, low-fat diet versus a high-carbohydrate, low-fat diet in healthy, young women. *Journal of the American College of Nutrition* 21:55–61.

Jowko, E., et al. 2001. Creatine and beta-hydroxy-beta-methylbutyrate (HMB) additively increase lean body mass and muscle strength during a weight-training program. *Nutrition* 17:558–66.

Kilduff, L., et al. 2004. The effects of creatine supplementation on cardiovascular, metabolic, and thermoregulatory responses during exercise in the heat in endurance-trained humans. *International Journal of Sport Nutrition and Exercise Metabolism* 14:443–60.

Kingsbury, K. J., et al. 1998. Contrasting plasma free amino acid patterns in elite athletes. *British Journal of Sports Medicine* 32:25–32.

Knitter, A., et al. 2000. Effects of beta-hydroxy-beta-methylbutyrate on muscle damage after a prolonged run. *Journal of Applied Physiology* 89:1340–44.

Koopman, E., et al. 2004. Combined ingestion of protein and carbohydrate improves protein balance during ultra-endurance exercise. *American Journal of Physiology. Endocrinology and Metabolism* 287:E712–20.

Koopman, R., et al. 2005. Combined ingestion of protein and free leucine with carbohydrate increases postexercise muscle protein synthesis in vivo in male subjects. *American Journal of Physiology. Endocrinology and Metabolism* 288:E645–53.

Kreider, R., et al. 1999. Effects of calcium beta-hydroxy-beta-methylbutyrate (HMB) supplementation during resistance-training on markers of catabolism, body composition, and strength. *International Journal of Sports Medicine* 20:503–9.

Kreider, R., et al. 1996. Effects of ingesting supplements designed to promote lean tissue accretion on body composition during resistance training. *International Journal of Sport Nutrition* 6:234–46.

Kuipers, H., et al. 2002. Effects of oral bovine colostrum supplementation on serum insulin-like growth factor-I levels. *Nutrition* 18:566–67.

Lambert, M., et al. 1993. Failure of commercial oral amino acid supplements to increase serum growth hormone concentrations in male bodybuilders. *International Journal of Sport Nutrition* 3:298–305.

Lemon, P., et al. 1992. Protein requirements and muscle mass/strength changes during intensive training in novice bodybuilders. *Journal of Applied Physiology* 73:767–75.

Levenhagen, D., et al. 2001. Postexercise nutrient intake timing in humans is critical to recovery of leg glucose and protein homeostasis. *American Journal of Physiology. Endocrinology and Metabolism* 280:E982–93.

Levenhagen, D., et al. 2002. Postexercise protein intake enhances whole-body and leg protein accretion in humans. *Medicine & Science in Sports & Exercise* 34:828–37.

Liappis, N., et al. 1979. Quantitative study of free amino acids in human eccrine sweat excreted from the forearms of healthy trained and untrained men during exercise. *European Journal of Applied Physiology* 42:227–34.

Lichtenstein, A., et al. 2002. Lipoprotein response to diets high in soy or animal protein with and without isoflavones in moderately hypercholesterolemic subjects. *Arteriosclerosis, Thrombosis, and Vascular Biology* 22:1852–58.

Lukaszuk, J., et al. 2002. Effect of creatine supplementation and a lactoovovegetarian diet on muscle creatine concentration. *International Journal of Sport Nutrition and Exercise Metabolism* 12:336–48.

Madsen, K., et al. 1996. Effects of glucose, glucose plus branched-chain amino acids, or placebo on bike performance over 100 km. *Journal of Applied Physiology* 81:2644–50.

Maughan, R., and Sadler, D. 1983. The effects of oral administration of salts of aspartic acid on the metabolic response to prolonged exhausting exercise in man. *International Journal of Sports Medicine* 4:119–23.

Mayhew, D., et al. 2002. Effects of long-term creatine supplementation on liver and kidney functions in American college football players. *International Journal of Sport Nutrition and Exercise Metabolism* 12:453–60.

Mazzini, L., et al. 2001. Effects of creatine supplementation on exercise performance and muscular strength in amyotrophic lateral sclerosis: Preliminary results. *Journal of the Neurological Sciences* 191:139–44.

McGuine, T., et al. 2001. Creatine supplementation in high school football players. *Clinical Journal of Sport Medicine* 11:247–53.

McNaughton, L., et al. 1999. Inosine supplementation has no effect on aerobic or anaerobic cycling performance. *International Journal of Sport Nutrition* 9:333–44.

Metzl, J., et al. 2001. Creatine use among young athletes. *Pediatrics* 108:421–25.

Mitchell, M., et al. 1993. Effects of supplementation with arginine and lysine on body composition, strength and growth hormone levels in weightlifters. *Medicine & Science in Sports & Exercise* 25:S25.

Mittleman, K. D., et al. 1998. Branched-chain amino acids prolong exercise during heat stress in men and women. *Medicine & Science in Sports & Exercise* 30:83–91.

Mujika, I., et al. 2000. Creatine supplementation and sprint performance in soccer players. *Medicine & Science in Sports & Exercise* 32:518–25.

Newman, J., et al. 2003. Effect of creatine ingestion on glucose tolerance and insulin sensitivity in men. *Medicine & Science in Sports & Exercise* 35:69–74.

Newsholme, E., and Blomstrand, E. 1996. The plasma level of some amino acids and physical and mental fatigue. *Experientia* 52:413–15.

Nissen, S., et al. 1996. Effect of leucine metabolite β-hydroxy-β-methylbutyrate on muscle metabolism during resistance-exercise training. *Journal of Applied Physiology* 81:2095–2104.

Op 'T Eijnde, B., and Hespel, P. 2001. Short-term creatine supplementation does not alter the hormonal response to resistance training. *Medicine & Science in Sports & Exercise* 33:449–53.

Op 'T Eijnde, B., et al. 2001. Creatine loading does not impact on stroke performance in tennis. *International Journal of Sports Medicine* 22:76–80.

Ostojic, S. 2004. Creatine supplementation in young soccer players. *International Journal of Sport Nutrition and Exercise Metabolism* 14:95–103.

Paddon-Jones, D., et al. 2001. Short-term beta-hydroxy-beta-methylbutyrate supplementation does not reduce symptoms of eccentric muscle damage. *International Journal of Sport Nutrition and Exercise Metabolism* 11:442–50.

Panton, L., et al. 2000. Nutritional supplementation of the leucine metabolite beta-hydroxy-beta-methylbutyrate (HMB) during resistance training. *Nutrition* 16:734–39.

Parry-Billings, M., et al. 1992. Plasma amino acid concentrations in the overtraining syndrome: Possible effects on the immune system. *Medicine & Science in Sports & Exercise* 24:1353–58.

Pavelka, K., et al. 2002. Glucosamine sulfate use and delay of progression of knee osteoarthritis: A 3-year, randomized, placebo-controlled, double-blind study. *Archives of Internal Medicine* 162:2113–23.

Peyrebrune, M., et al. 2005. Effect of creatine supplementation on training for competition in elite swimmers. *Medicine & Science in Sports & Exercise* 37:2140–47.

Poortmans, J., et al. 2005. Effect of oral creatine supplementation on urinary methylamine, formaldehyde and formate. *Medicine & Science in Sports & Exercise* 37:1717–20.

Poortmans, J. R., and Dellalieux, O. 2000. Do regular high protein diets have potential health risks on kidney function in athletes? *International Journal of Sport Nutrition and Exercise Metabolism* 10:28–38.

Poortmans, J. R., and Francaux, M. 1999. Long-term oral creatine supplementation does not impair renal function in healthy athletes. *Medicine & Science in Sports & Exercise* 31:1108–10.

Poortmans, J. R., et al. 1997. Evidence of differential renal dysfunctions during exercise in man. *European Journal of Applied Physiology* 76:88–91.

Poortmans, J., et al. 1996. Postexercise proteinuria in childhood and adolescence. *International Journal of Sports Medicine* 17:448–51.

Preen, D., et al. 2003. Creatine supplementation: A comparison of loading and maintenance protocols on creatine uptake by human skeletal muscle. *International Journal of Sport Nutrition and Metabolism* 13:97–111.

Preen, D., et al. 2001. Effect of creatine loading on long-term sprint exercise performance and metabolism. *Medicine & Science in Sports & Exercise* 33:814–21.

Ransone, J., et al. 2003. The effect of beta-hydroxy-beta-methylbutyrate on muscular strength and body composition in collegiate football players. *Journal of Strength and Conditioning Research* 17:34–39.

Rasmussen, B., et al. 2000. An oral essential amino acid-carbohydrate supplement enhances muscle protein anabolism after resistance exercise. *Journal of Applied Physiology* 88:386–92.

Reginster, J., et al. 2001. Long term effects of glucosamine sulfate on osteoarthritis progression: A randomised, placebo-controlled clinical trial. *Lancet* 357:251–56.

Rockwell, J. A., et al. 2001. Creatine supplementation affects muscle creatine during energy restriction. *Medicine & Science in Sports & Exercise* 33:61–68.

Romer, L., et al. 2001. Effects of oral creatine supplementation on high intensity, intermittent exercise performance in competitive squash players. *International Journal of Sports Medicine* 22:546–52.

Roy, B.D., et al. 2000. Macronutrient intake and whole body protein metabolism following resistance exercise. *Medicine & Science in Sports & Exercise* 32:1412–18.

Santos, R., et al. 2004. The effect of creatine supplementation upon inflammatory and muscle soreness markers after a 30km race. *Life Sciences* 75: 1917–24.

Saunders, M., et al. 2004. Effects of a carbohydrate-protein beverage on cycling endurance and muscle damage. *Medicine & Science in Sports & Exercise* 36:1233–38.

Schedel, J., et al. 2000. Acute creatine loading enhances human growth hormone secretion. *Journal of Sports Medicine and Physical Fitness* 40:336–42.

Schilling, B., et al. 2001. Creatine supplementation and health variables: A retrospective study. *Medicine & Science in Sports & Exercise* 33:183–88.

Schroeder, C., et al. 2001. The effects of creatine dietary supplementation on anterior compartment pressure in the lower leg during rest and following exercise. *Clinical Journal of Sport Medicine* 11:87–95.

Segura, R., and Ventura, J. 1988. Effect of L-tryptophan supplementation on exercise performance. *International Journal of Sports Medicine* 9:301–5.

Shomrat, A., et al. 2000. Effect of creatine feeding on maximal exercise performance in vegetarians. *European Journal of Applied Physiology* 82:321–25.

Skare, O., et al. 2001. Creatine supplementation improves sprint performance in male sprinters. *Scandinavian Journal of Medicine & Science in Sports* 11:96–102.

Slater, G., et al. 2001. Beta-hydroxy-beta-methylbutyrate (HMB) supplementation does not affect changes in strength or body composition during resistive training in trained men. *International Journal of Sport Nutrition and Exercise Metabolism* 11:384–96.

Starling, R., et al. 1996. Effect of inosine supplementation on aerobic and anaerobic cycling performance. *Medicine & Science in Sports & Exercise* 28:1193–98.

Stensrund, T., et al. 1992. L-tryptophan supplementation does not improve running performance. *International Journal of Sports Medicine* 13:481–85.

Stout, J., et al. 2001. Effects of resistance exercise and creatine supplementation on myasthenia gravis: A case study. *Medicine & Science in Sports & Exercise* 33:869–72.

Struder, H. K., et al. 1998. Influence of paroxetine, branched-chain amino acids and tyrosine on neuroendocrine system responses and fatigue in humans. *Hormone and Metabolic Research* 30:188–94.

Suminski, R., et al. 1997. Acute effect of amino acid ingestion and resistance exercise on plasma growth hormone concentration in young men. *International Journal of Sport Nutrition* 7:48–60.

Sutton, E., et al. 2005. Ingestion of tyrosine: Effects on endurance, muscle strength, and anaerobic performance. *International Journal of Sport Nutrition and Exercise Metabolism* 15:173–85.

Syrotuik, D., and Bell, G. 2004. Acute creatine monohydrate supplementation: A descriptive physiological profile of responders vs. nonresponders. *Journal of Strength and Conditioning Research* 18:610–17.

Syrotuik, D., et al. 2001. Effects of creatine monohydrate supplementation during combined strength and high intensity rowing training on performance. *Canadian Journal of Applied Physiology* 26:527–42.

Tanaka, H., et al. 1997. Changes in plasma tryptophan/branched-chain amino acid ratio in responses to training volume variation. *International Journal of Sports Medicine* 18:270–5.

Tarnopolsky, M., et al. 2001. Creatine-dextrose and protein-dextrose induce similar strength gains during training. *Medicine & Science in Sports & Exercise* 33:2944–52.

Tarnopolsky, M., et al. 1992. Evaluation of protein requirements for trained strength athletes. *Journal of Applied Physiology* 73:1986–95.

Tipton, K. D., et al. 2004. Ingestion of casein and whey proteins result in muscle anabolism after resistance exercise. *Medicine & Science in Sports & Exercise* 36:2073–81.

Tipton, K. D., et al. 1999. Postexercise net protein synthesis in human muscle from orally administered amino acids. *American Journal of Physiology* 276:E628–E634.

Tuttle, J., et al. 1995. Effect of acute potassium-magnesium aspartate supplementation on ammonia concentrations during and after resistance training. *International Journal of Sport Nutrition* 5:102–9.

Tyler, T., et al. 2004. The effect of creatine supplementation on strength recovery after anterior cruciate ligament (ACL) reconstruction: A randomized, placebo-controlled, double-blind trial. *American Journal of Sports Medicine* 32:383–88.

Vandenberghe, K., et al. 1997. Inhibition of muscle phosphocreatine resynthesis by caffeine after creatine loading. *Medicine & Science in Sports & Exercise* 29:S249.

Vandenberghe, K., et al. 1996. Caffeine counteracts the ergogenic action of muscle creatine loading. *Journal of Applied Physiology* 80:452–57.

van Hall, G., et al. 1998. Effect of carbohydrate supplementation on plasma glutamine during prolonged exercise and recovery. *International Journal of Sports Medicine* 19:82–86.

van Hall, G., et al. 1995. Ingestion of branched-chain amino acids and tryptophan during sustained exercise in man: Failure to affect performance. *Journal of Physiology* 486:789–94.

van Loon, L., et al. 2003. Effects of creatine loading and prolonged creatine supplementation on body composition, fuel selection, sprint and endurance performance in humans. *Clinical Science* 104:153–62.

Volek, J. S., et al. 2004. The effects of creatine supplementation on muscular performance and body composition responses to short-term resistance training overreaching. *European Journal of Applied Physiology* 91:628–37.

Volek, J. S., et al. 2001. Physiological responses to short-term exercise in the heat after creatine loading. *Medicine & Science in Sports & Exercise* 33:1101–8.

Volek, J. S., et al. 2000. No effect of heavy resistance training and creatine supplementation on blood lipids. *International Journal of Sport Nutrition and Exercise Metabolism* 10:144–56.

Vukovich, M., et al. 2001. Body composition in 70-year-old adults responds to dietary beta-hydroxy-beta-methylbutyrate similarly to that of young adults. *Journal of Nutrition* 131:2049–52.

Watson, P., et al. 2004. The effect of acute branched-chain amino acid supplementation on prolonged exercise capacity in a warm environment. *European Journal of Applied Physiology* 93:306–14.

Weideman, C., et al. 1990. Effects of increased protein intake on muscle hypertrophy and strength following 13 weeks of resistance training. *Medicine & Science in Sports & Exercise* 22:S37.

Wesson, M., et al. 1988. Effects of oral administration of aspartic acid salts on the endurance capacity of trained athletes. *Research Quarterly for Exercise and Sport* 59:234–39.

Wiles, J., et al. 1991. Effect of pre-exercise protein ingestion upon VO_2, R, and perceived exertion during treadmill running. *British Journal of Sports Medicine* 25:26–30.

Williams, B. D., et al. 1998. Alanine and glutamine kinetics at rest and during exercise in humans. *Medicine & Science in Sports & Exercise* 30:1053–58.

Williams, M., et al. 1990. Effect of oral inosine supplementation on 3-mile treadmill run performance and VO_2 peak. *Medicine & Science in Sports & Exercise* 22:517–22.

Willoughby, D., and Rosene, J. 2001. Effects of oral creatine and resistance training on myosin heavy chain expression. *Medicine & Science in Sports & Exercise* 33:1674–81.

Yaguchi, H., et al. 1998. The effect of triathlon on urinary excretion of enzymes and proteins. *International Urology and Nephrology* 30:107–12.

Yquel, R., et al. 2002. Effect of creatine supplementation on phosphocreatine resynthesis, inorganic phosphate accumulation and pH during intermittent maximal exercise. *Journal of Sports Sciences* 20:427–37.

Zhang, M., et al. 2004. Role of taurine supplementation to prevent exercise-induced oxidative stress in healthy young men. *Amino Acids* 26:203–207.

Ziegenfuss, T., et al. 2002. Effect of creatine loading on anaerobic performance and skeletal muscle volume in NCAA Division I athletes. *Nutrition* 18:397–402.

Vitamins: The Organic Regulators

CHAPTER SEVEN

LEARNING OBJECTIVES

After studying this chapter, you should be able to:

1. Describe the various means whereby vitamins may carry out their functions in the human body.

2. Name the essential vitamins, state the RDA or AI for each, and identify several foods rich in each vitamin.

3. Describe the metabolic roles in the human body of each of the thirteen essential vitamins and choline.

4. Explain the potential effects on health and sport performance associated with a deficiency of each essential vitamin and choline.

5. Identify those fat-soluble and water-soluble vitamins that are most likely to cause health risks if consumed in excess. Indicate at what doses adverse health effects may be observed, and determine how likely such a dose may be obtained by consuming daily vitamin supplements and fortified foods.

6. Explain the theory as to how supplementation with each vitamin, and choline, may enhance sport performance, and highlight the research findings regarding the ergogenic efficacy of each.

7. Explain the theory as to how vitamin-like compounds may enhance sport performance, and highlight the research findings regarding the ergogenic efficacy of each.

8. Understand why health professionals recommend that we should obtain our vitamins through natural foods, such as fruits and vegetables, and why some health professionals recommend that most adults also take a daily multivitamin supplement.

Vitamins are a diverse class of thirteen known specific nutrients that are involved in almost every metabolic process in the human body. We need only minute amounts of vitamins in our daily diet, so they are classified as micronutrients. Nevertheless, they are one of our most critical nutrients. Noticeable symptoms of a deficiency may appear in 2 to 4 weeks for several of the vitamins, and major debilitating diseases may occur with prolonged deficiencies. Vitamin deficiencies appear to be widespread in many developing countries, and according to Bouis, they affect a greater number of people in the world than does protein-energy malnutrition. Hopefully, plant breeding of commonly eaten food crops, such as wheat, rice, and corn, to fortify them with vitamins and minerals may help alleviate this major health problem.

Major vitamin deficiencies are rare in industrialized societies because a wide variety of food products are available, many of them fortified with vitamins. However, Fairfield and Fletcher, the lead authors in two reports recently published by the American Medical Association, have noted that some individuals, such as the elderly, vegans, women of childbearing age, and those at risk for cardiovascular disease, may not be obtaining adequate amounts of various vitamins. Moreover, they note that most people do not consume an optimal amount of vitamins by diet alone. Pending strong evidence of effectiveness from randomized trials, they indicate that it appears *prudent* for all adults to take vitamin supplements.

In general, most studies reveal that athletes are obtaining adequate vitamin nutrition, probably because of the additional food energy intake associated with the increased energy expenditure of exercise. Additionally, many athletes take vitamin supplements. For example, Jacobson and others recently reported that vitamin/mineral pills were the most commonly used dietary supplement by female NCAA Division I collegiate athletes. However, like members of the general population, many athletes may not be obtaining optimal levels of vitamins from the diet. Moreover, certain athletic groups, particularly those who are on weight-reduction programs to qualify for competition or to enhance performance, may not receive adequate vitamin nutrition. Furthermore, individual athletes in generally well-nourished athletic groups may have a suboptimal vitamin intake.

As noted throughout this chapter, adequate vitamin nutrition is essential for both optimal health and athletic performance. But, if you do not obtain the RDA for a specific vitamin or vitamins, will your health or physical performance suffer? Will vitamin supplements above and beyond the RDA improve your health or performance? A major purpose of this chapter is to provide you with factual data, based upon the available research, to help answer these two very general questions.

A slightly different approach is used in this chapter and in chapter 8. The first section provides some basic facts about the general role of vitamins in the human body. The next two sections cover the fat-soluble and water-soluble vitamins, respectively, with each individual vitamin discussed in terms of its Dietary Reference Intake (DRI), either its Recommended Dietary Allowance (RDA) or Adequate Intake (AI); food sources that provide ample amounts; metabolic functions in the body with particular reference to health and the physically active individual; and the findings of research relative to the impact of deficiencies and supplementation. The fourth section focuses on ergogenic aspects of special vitamin or vitamin-like preparations, while the final section highlights some health implications of vitamin supplementation.

Basic Facts

What are vitamins and how do they work?

Vitamins are a class of complex organic compounds that are found in small amounts in most foods. They are essential for the optimal functioning of many different physiological processes in the human body. The activity levels of many of these physiological processes are increased greatly during exercise, and an adequate bodily supply of vitamins must be present for these processes to function best.

Coenzyme Functions For the fundamental physiological processes of the body to proceed in an orderly, controlled fashion, a number of complex chemicals known as **enzymes** are necessary to regulate the diverse reactions involved. Hundreds of enzymes have been identified in the human body. Enzymes are necessary to digest our foods, to make our muscles contract, to release the energy stores in our bodies, to help us transport body gases such as carbon dioxide, to help us grow, to help clot our blood, and so on. Enzymes serve as catalysts; that is, they are capable of inducing changes in other substances without changing themselves.

Enzymes are chemicals that generally consist of two parts. One part is a protein molecule and to it is attached the second part, a **coenzyme.** For the enzyme to function properly, both parts must be present. The coenzyme often contains a vitamin or some related compound (figure 7.1). The enzyme is not used up in the chemical process that it initiates or in which it participates, but enzymes may deteriorate with time. Coenzymes also may be degraded through body metabolism. It is now known that the B complex vitamins are essential in human nutrition because of their role in the activation of enzymes, and thus a fresh supply of these water-soluble vitamins is constantly needed.

Antioxidant Functions Various oxidative reactions in the body produce substances called free radicals. **Free radicals** are chemical substances that contain a lone, unpaired electron in the outer orbit. The superoxide radical ($O_2^{\bullet-}$) and hydroxyl radical ($OH^{\bullet}$) are true free radicals. Two other related substances, referred to as non-radical oxygen species, are hydrogen peroxide (H_2O_2) and singlet oxygen ($^1O_2$). These substances are known as reactive oxygen species (ROS), and the interested reader is referred to the recent review by Ji for a detailed discussion. For the purpose of our discussion, we shall refer to them collectively as free radicals.

Free radicals are unstable compounds that possess an unbalanced magnetic field that affects molecular structure and chemical reactions in the body. Free radicals may be very reactive with body tissues. Although oxidative processes are essential to life, some oxidations may cause cellular damage by oxidation of unsaturated fats in cellular and subcellular membranes. Free radicals may cause such undesirable oxidations. Halliwell indicated that free radicals may damage DNA, lipids, proteins, and other molecules, and may be involved in the development of cancer, cardiovascular disease, and possibly neurodegenerative disease. Fortunately, although free radicals are formed naturally in the body, body cells produce a number of antioxidant enzymes, such as superoxide dismutase, glutathione peroxidase, and catalase, to help neutralize free radicals and prevent cellular damage. To function properly, these enzymes, often referred to as free radical-scavenging enzymes, must contain certain nutrients such as copper, zinc, and selenium. Comparable to these enzymes, as depicted in figure 7.2, vitamins E, C, and beta-carotene possess antioxidant properties. These antioxidant vitamins have received recent research attention relative to effects on health and physical performance and are discussed at appropriate points later in this chapter.

Hormone Functions Although vitamin D exists in vitamin form, it undergoes several conversions in the body and, in its active form, functions as a hormone. After being produced in the kidney, vitamin D circulates in the blood like other hormones and exerts its functions on various tissues to promote bone metabolism. Other

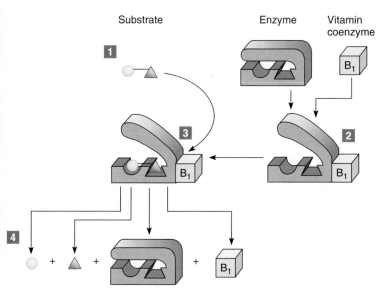

FIGURE 7.1 Role of vitamin as coenzyme. (1) Substrates, such as pyruvate, need enzymes to be converted into more usable compounds. However, many enzymes need to be activated before a reaction occurs. Note that the enzyme is in a closed position. (2) An enzyme and a vitamin coenzyme (B₁) combine to form an activated complex, in essence opening up the enzyme. (3) The open, activated enzyme accepts the substrate and (4) splits it into two compounds while releasing the enzyme and coenzyme.

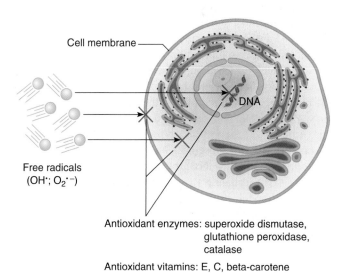

FIGURE 7.2 The antioxidant role of vitamins. To protect against the destructive nature of free radicals such as hydroxyl radicals and superoxides, the cells contain a number of different enzymes (superoxide dismutase, glutathione peroxidase, catalase) to help neutralize them, thus helping to prevent disintegration of cell membranes or the genetic material within the cell. Additionally, several vitamins (E, C, beta-carotene) may serve as antioxidants. Such vitamins are theorized to be protective against cancer, heart disease, and adverse effects of aging.

vitamins, such as A and K, may be produced in the liver and intestines, respectively, and exert functions in other parts of the body, but they are normally not referred to as hormones. Some vitamins may be critical in the formation of various hormones—such as the role vitamin C plays in the formation of epinephrine—but are not classified as hormones. Only vitamin D is assigned hormonal status in its active form.

Energy Although vitamins are indispensable for regulating many body functions and for the maintenance of optimal health, they are not a source of energy. They do not have any caloric value. Moreover, they make no significant contribution to the structure of the body, as do protein and some minerals.

What vitamins are essential to human nutrition?

The existence of vitamins was deduced from their physiological actions before their chemical structures had been identified. In assigning names to vitamins, the alphabet was used in order of their time of discovery. In some cases, a large time gap existed between the discovery of the vitamin and determination of its chemical structure. In others, the chemical nature was discovered rapidly, and the chemical name came into early use.

An essential vitamin is one that cannot be synthesized in the body in sufficient quantity, causes deficiency symptoms when dietary intake is inadequate, and alleviates deficiency symptoms when added back to the diet. At present the human body is known to need an adequate supply of thirteen different vitamins. Choline is a water-soluble essential nutrient, and although it is listed with the DRI alongside the B vitamins, at this time it has not been classified as a vitamin. A well-balanced diet will satisfy all the vitamin requirements of most individuals. Four of these vitamins are soluble in fat and are obtained primarily from the fat in our diet, while the other nine water-soluble vitamins are distributed rather widely in a variety of foods. Although most vitamins must be obtained from the food we eat, several of them may be formed in the body from other ingested nutrients, by the action of ultraviolet rays from sunlight on our skin, or by the activity of some intestinal bacteria.

A number of other substances have been mistakenly classified as vitamins. Included in this group are inositol, para-amino benzoic acid (PABA), vitamin B_{15} or pangamic acid, and vitamin B_{17} or laetrile. Although it has been suggested that these substances have vitamin activity, their essentiality in the diet has not been established. Other substances have been attributed vitamin-like activity and professed to enhance health or physical performance, such as bee pollen, coenzyme Q_{10} (CoQ_{10}), and ginkgo, but these also are not essential vitamins.

Table 7.1 presents an overview of the thirteen essential vitamins and choline with commonly used interchangeable synonyms, major food sources, major functions in the body, and symptoms associated with deficiencies or excessive consumption. The table also presents the RDA or AI for adults aged 19–50, as well as the Daily Value (DV). Note that the DV, which is based on older daily dietary recommendations, may vary considerably with current

RDA or AI. The DV was originally set high enough to cover just about anyone but has not been updated to match current recommendations. RDA and AI values for other age groups may be found in DRI tables on the inside front cover, and the UL may be found on the inside back cover. The health and performance effects of the essential vitamins and selected vitamin-like substances are covered in the following sections.

Only very small amounts of vitamins are required daily. RDA or AI are usually given in milligrams (mg) or micrograms (mcg). Several vitamins come in various forms and thus the RDA may be given as activity equivalents. For example, vitamin A comes preformed as retinol, or may be derived from the conversion of beta-carotene. Thus, vitamin A requirements are technically known as retinol activity equivalents (RAE). The International Unit (IU) is an older measure of vitamin activity that may still be seen on food labels and vitamin supplements. However, it is gradually being replaced with more appropriate terminology. Because IU is still commonly used, we will include it in our discussion where relevant.

In general, how do deficiencies or excesses of vitamins influence health or physical performance?

Whether or not a vitamin deficiency affects one's health or physical performance may depend on the magnitude of the deficiency. Four stages of vitamin deficiency associated with the duration of undernourishment and inadequate vitamin intake have been described. These same four stages may apply to mineral deficiency diseases discussed in the next chapter.

1. *A preliminary stage* is associated with inadequate amount or availability of the vitamin in the diet. For example, a drastic change in the diet may influence vitamin **bioavailability** (the amount of a nutrient that the body absorbs), whereas pregnancy may increase the need for several vitamins.
2. *Biochemical deficiency.* In this stage, the body's pool of the vitamin is decreased. For a number of vitamins, biochemical deficiency can be identified by blood or tissue tests. For example, deficiencies of riboflavin may be detected by the activity of an enzyme in the red blood cells.
3. *Physiologic deficiency* is associated with the appearance of unspecific symptoms such as loss of appetite, weakness, or physical fatigue.

    These first three stages are known as latent or marginal vitamin deficiency, or **subclinical malnutrition.** Whether or not these stages impair physical performance may depend upon the nature of the sport, but weakness or physical fatigue would certainly be counterproductive to optimal performance.
4. *Clinically manifest vitamin deficiency.* In this final stage, specific clinical symptoms are observed. For example, anemia is a clinical symptom associated with a deficiency of several vitamins, such as folic acid and vitamin B_6. Both health and performance would be adversely affected with a clinically manifest vitamin deficiency.

In the past, RDA for vitamins have been established to prevent vitamin-deficiency diseases. However, recommendations are beginning to incorporate the role of vitamins in health promotion. For example, as noted later, the new Adequate Intake (AI) for vitamin D has been modified to help prevent osteoporosis, while the folic acid RDA is designed to prevent damage to the nervous system of the unborn child during pregnancy. When scientific evidence is deemed sufficient, vitamin recommendations may be modified to help prevent chronic diseases such as cancer and cardiovascular diseases. If the RDA for some vitamins are increased as a possible means of achieving health promotion objectives, the most likely recommendation will be to obtain the increased amounts from natural foods. However, food fortification or supplementation may be recommended for a few vitamins, such as folic acid. Moreover, Challem suggests that the definition of essential micronutrients be broadened to include other vitamin-like substances such as flavonoids and coenzyme Q10.

Except for consumption of large amounts of certain foods, such as cod liver oil, it is very difficult to obtain excessive amounts of vitamins through the diet to the point that health or performance is impaired. Even when supplements are taken, the body may rapidly excrete several vitamins, keeping body functions normal. However, **hypervitaminosis** may occur when vitamins are not excreted effectively and accumulate in the tissues, beginning to function as a drug instead of a nutrient. Toxic reactions specific to the vitamin overdose may occur.

Key Concept Recap

▶ Vitamins are complex organic compounds that function in the body in a variety of ways. Some act as coenzymes to help regulate metabolic processes; others are antioxidants that protect cell membranes; and one is even classified as a hormone.

▶ Vitamins do not contain energy *per se*, such as Calories, but they do help regulate energy processes in the body.

▶ The RDA for vitamins have been established to prevent vitamin-deficiency diseases like scurvy, but the new vitamin DRI may be modified to help prevent chronic diseases, such as osteoporosis, cancer, and coronary heart disease, or excessive intake and associated adverse health effects.

▶ There may be four stages in a vitamin deficiency: the preliminary stage, the biochemical deficiency stage, the physiologic deficiency stage, and the clinically manifest deficiency stage.

Check for Yourself

Check the food labels for various foods you have in the cupboard to see what vitamins are listed. If the DV is provided, compare the amount of the vitamin provided and its DV with the current RDA or AI. Relate your findings to the text discussion.

Fat-Soluble Vitamins

The four fat-soluble vitamins are A, D, E, and K. Because they are soluble in fat but not in water, dietary sources include foods that have some fat content. The body may contain appreciable stores of each fat-soluble vitamin, and several of them may be manufactured by the body, so deficiencies are relatively rare in industrialized societies. On the other hand, excessive intake may be toxic. With the exception of vitamin E, very little research has been conducted relative to deficiency or supplementation effects upon physical performance.

Vitamin A (retinol)

Vitamin A is a fat-soluble, unsaturated alcohol. The physiologically active form of vitamin A is known as **retinol.** The human body is capable of forming retinol from provitamins known as carotenoids, primarily **beta-carotene.** Both preformed vitamin A, or retinol, and carotenoids are found in the foods we eat.

DRI The RDA for vitamin A may be obtained by consuming retinol, beta-carotene and other carotenoids, or a combination of the two. The RDA may be expressed in several ways, usually as **retinol equivalents (RE), retinol activity equivalents (RAE)** as a combination of retinol and carotenoids, or as international units. In brief, 1 RAE equals 1 microgram of retinol, or 12 micrograms of beta-carotene, or about 3.3 IU. The RDA is 900 RAE, or 3,000 IU for adult males and 700 RAE, or 2,300 IU for adult females. See the DRI table on the inside cover for more details on vitamin A requirements derived from either retinol or the carotenoids. The Daily Value (DV) for use on food labels is 5,000 IU, but should be set at 3,000. The UL for adults is 3 milligrams/day from retinol, or 10,000 IU; no UL has been established for carotenoids. See the UL table on the inside of the back cover for more details.

Food Sources Preformed vitamin A is found in substantial amounts in some animal foods such as liver, butter, cheese, egg yolks, fish liver oils, and fortified milk. Provitamin A, as beta-carotene, is found in dark-green leafy and yellow-orange vegetables as well as in some fruits such as oranges, limes, pineapples, prunes, and cantaloupes. Fortified margarine also contains beta-carotene. One glass of milk provides about 15 percent of the RDA, while one medium carrot will supply nearly 200 percent and a serving of liver a whopping 1,000 percent or more of the RDA.

Major Functions Vitamin A is essential for maintenance of the epithelial cells, those cells covering the outside of the body and lining the body cavities. It is also essential for proper visual function, such as night vision and peripheral vision. Vitamin A also has a variety of other physiological roles in the body that are not well understood, although it is considered essential in proper bone development and for maintaining optimal function of the immune system. Palace and others note that vitamin A and beta-carotene may function as antioxidants and have been theorized to confer some health benefits.

Deficiency: Health and Physical Performance Vitamin A is stored in the body in relatively large amounts. However, an inadequate intake of vitamin A could have serious health implications if prolonged. The gradual loss of night vision is one of the first symptoms of vitamin A deficiency. Other symptoms of mild

TABLE 7.1   Essential vitamins*

Vitamin name (Other terms)	RDA or AI for adults age 19–50*; Daily Value (DV)	Major sources
Fat-soluble vitamins		
Vitamin A (retinol: provitamin carotenoids) RDA	900 RAE ♂ 700 RAE ♀ (RAE = retinol activity equivalents) DV = 1,000 RAE	Retinol in animal foods: liver, whole milk, fortified milk, cheese. Carotenoids in plant foods: carrots, green leafy vegetables, sweet potatoes, fortified margarine from vegetable oils
Vitamin D (cholecalciferol) AI	200 IU or 5 mcg DV = 400 IU	Vitamin-D fortified foods like dairy products and margarine, fish oils; action of sunlight on the skin
Vitamin E (tocopherol) RDA	15 mg d-alpha Tocopherol DV = 30 IU	Vegetable oils, margarine, green leafy vegetables, wheat germ, whole-grain products, egg yolks
Vitamin K (phylloquinone; menoquinone) RDA	120 mcg ♂ 90 mcg ♀ DV = 80 mcg	Pork and beef liver, eggs, spinach, cauliflower; formation in the human intestine by bacteria
Water-soluble vitamins		
Thiamin (vitamin B_1) RDA	1.2 mg ♂ 1.1 mg ♀ DV = 1.5 mg	Ham, pork, lean meat, liver, whole-grain products, enriched breads and cereals, legumes
Riboflavin (vitamin B_2) RDA	1.3 mg ♂ 1.1 mg ♀ DV = 1.7 mg	Milk and dairy products, meat, eggs, enriched grain products, green leafy vegetables, beans
Niacin (nicotinamide, nicotinic acid) RDA	16 mg ♂ 14 mg ♀ DV = 20 mg	Lean meats, fish, poultry, whole-grain products, beans; may be formed in the body from tryptophan, an essential amino acid
Vitamin B_6 (pyridoxal, pyridoxine, pyridoxamine) RDA	1.3 mg DV = 2 mg	Protein foods: liver, lean meats, fish, poultry, legumes; green leafy vegetables, baked potatoes, bananas
Vitamin B_{12} (cobalamin; cyanocobalamin) RDA	2.4 mcg DV = 6 mcg	Animal foods only: meat, fish, poultry, milk, eggs
Folate (folic acid) RDA	400 DFE (DFE = dietary folate equivalents) DV = 400 DFE	Liver, green leafy vegetables, legumes, nuts, fortified cereals
Biotin AI	30 mcg DV = 300 mg	Meats, legumes, milk, egg yolk, whole-grain products, most vegetables
Pantothenic acid AI	5 mg DV = 300 mg	Beef and pork liver, lean meats, milk, eggs, legumes, whole-grain products, most vegetables
Choline**	550 mg ♂ 425 mg ♀ DV = None	Milk, liver, eggs, peanuts; found in most foods as part of cell membranes
Vitamin C (ascorbic acid)) RDA	90 mg ♂ 75 mg ♀ DV = 60 mg	Citrus fruits, green leafy vegetables, broccoli, peppers, strawberries, potatoes

Major functions in the body	Deficiency symptoms	Symptoms of excessive consumption*
Fat-soluble vitamins		
Maintains epithelial tissue in skin and mucous membranes; forms visual purple for night vision; promotes bone development	Night blindness, intestinal infections, impaired growth, xerophthalmia	UL is 3 milligrams/day. Nausea, headache, fatigue, liver and spleen damage, skin peeling, pain in the joints
Acts as a hormone to increase intestinal absorption of calcium and promote bone and tooth formation	Rare; rickets in children and osteomalacia in adults	UL is 50 micrograms/day. Loss of appetite, nausea, irritability, joint pain, calcium deposits in soft tissues such as the kidney
Functions as an antioxidant to protect cell membranes from destruction by oxidation	Extremely rare; disruption of red blood cell membranes; anemia	UL is 1000 milligrams/day. General lack of toxicity with doses up to 400 mg. Some reports of headache, fatigue, or diarrhea with megadoses
Essential for blood coagulation processes	Increased bleeding and hemorrhage	No UL set. Possible clot formation (thrombosis), vomiting
Water-soluble vitamins		
Serves as a coenzyme for energy production from carbohydrate; essential for normal functioning of the central nervous system	Poor appetite, apathy, mental depression, pain in calf muscles, beriberi	No UL set. General lack of toxicity
Functions as a coenzyme involved in energy production from carbohydrates and fats; maintenance of healthy skin	Dermatitis, cracks at the corners of the mouth, sores on the tongue, damage to the cornea	No UL set. General lack of toxicity
Functions as a coenzyme for the aerobic and anaerobic production of energy from carbohydrate; helps synthesize fat and blocks release of FFA; needed for healthy skin	Loss of appetite, weakness, skin lesions, gastrointestinal problems, pellagra	UL is 35 milligrams/day. Nicotinic acid causes headache, nausea, burning and itching skin, flushing of face, liver damage.
Functions as a coenzyme in protein metabolism; necessary for formation of hemoglobin and red blood cells; needed for glycogenolysis and gluconeogenesis	Nervous irritability, convulsions, dermatitis, sores on tongue, anemia	UL is 100 milligrams/day. Loss of nerve sensation, impaired gait
Functions as a coenzyme for formation of DNA, RBC development, and maintenance of nerve tissue	Pernicious anemia, nerve damage resulting in paralysis	No UL set. General lack of toxicity
Functions as coenzyme for DNA formation and RBC development	Fatigue, gastrointestinal disorders, diarrhea, anemia, neural tube defects in newborns	UL is 1,000 micrograms/day. May prevent detection of pernicious anemia caused by B_{12} deficiency
Functions as coenzyme in the metabolism of carbohydrates, fats, and protein	Rare; may be caused by excessive intake of raw egg whites: fatigue, nausea, skin rashes	No UL set. General lack of toxicity
Functions as part of coenzyme A in energy metabolism	Rare; produced only clinically: fatigue, nausea, loss of appetite, mental depression	No UL set. General lack of toxicity
Functions as a precursor for lecithin, a phospholipid in cell membranes	Rare; liver damage	UL is 3.5 grams/day. May lead to fishy body odor, gastrointestinal distress, vomiting, low blood pressure
Forms collagen essential for connective tissue development; aids in absorption of iron; helps form epinephrine; serves as antioxidant	Weakness, rough skin, slow wound healing, bleeding gums, scurvy	UL is 2,000 milligrams/day. Diarrhea, possible kidney stones, rebound scurvy

*RDA, AI, and UL values for all age groups may be found on the inside of the front and back covers of this text.   **Not classified as a vitamin.
mg = milligrams; mcg = micrograms

deficiencies include increased susceptibility to infection and skin lesions. Epidemiological research also has suggested that a deficient intake of beta-carotene could predispose the individual to the development of cancer in the epithelial tissues such as the skin, lungs, breasts, and intestinal lining. Although severe deficiencies are not common in industrialized nations, they do occur in some parts of the world and lead to blindness through destruction of the cornea of the eye, a condition known as **xerophthalmia.** Vitamin A deficiency has been associated with higher mortality rates in children of developing countries, with several million childhood deaths annually. Some, but not all, studies have shown that vitamin A supplementation to such children may decrease the death rate, possibly by strengthening the immune system.

Theoretically, vitamin A deficiency could affect physical performance. Some investigators have suggested that a deficiency may impair the process of gluconeogenesis in the liver, which may be an important consideration for the endurance athlete in the latter stages of competition. Others have implied a reduction in the synthesis of muscle protein and impaired vision, which could negatively affect strength athletes or those involved in sports requiring eye alertness. Very little research is available to support these theoretical views.

Supplementation: Health and Physical Performance   Vitamin A in supplements can come from retinol (vitamin A palmitate or acetate) or beta-carotene, or both. Check the label; it may or may not list the separate components. The UL is set at 10,000 IU, and although companies are reformulating their products, supplements containing 25,000 IU may still be on the shelves. In general, supplements of vitamin A as retinol are not recommended unless under the guidance of a health professional. Excessive amounts of vitamin A, generally caused by self-medication with megadoses, can cause a condition known as hypervitaminosis A. Symptoms may include weakness, headache, loss of appetite, nausea, pain in the joints, and peeling of skin. Similar symptoms were reported in a young soccer player who took about 100,000 IU daily for 2 months in an attempt to improve performance. The symptoms were relieved when he stopped taking the supplements. Excess vitamin A may also weaken the bones. Binkley and Krueger reported that excess vitamin A stimulates bone resorption and inhibits bone formation, leading to bone loss and contributing to osteoporosis. In a recent study, Feskanich and others found that women with the highest intake of vitamin A as retinol, greater than 3,000 micrograms daily, had double the risk of hip fractures compared to women with the lowest intake, less than 1250 micrograms per day. As noted by Ross, excessive vitamin A during pregnancy may be teratogenic, causing deformities in the developing embryo or fetus. Recent research by Rothman and others has indicated that vitamin A doses as low as four times the RDA can markedly increase a pregnant woman's chances of having a baby with birth defects, such as a cleft palate, heart defects, or other problems. Although this amount would not be consumed with a normal diet, it could be obtained by someone who takes a daily supplement, drinks substantial amounts of milk, eats liver, and has several servings of fortified cereals. Additionally, Zachman and Grummer indicated that consuming alcohol during pregnancy may worsen these teratogenic effects of vitamin A. Finally, extremely large doses of vitamin A may lead to severe liver damage, especially with concomitant alcohol intake, and may be fatal.

Beta-carotene supplements are not believed to be toxic but may cause harmless yellowing of the skin when taken in excess because the beta-carotene may accumulate in the fat tissues. The supplements may also cause adverse health effects in some individuals, particularly smokers, discussed later in this chapter.

There appears to be little theoretical value to use vitamin A supplementation for ergogenic purposes, and no scientific evidence supports its use as a means to enhance physical performance. However, beta-carotene has been combined with other antioxidants in an attempt to prevent muscle damage during exercise and this research is discussed later.

Prudent Recommendations   In summary, vitamin A supplementation to the diet of the active individual does not have a sound theoretical basis. Moreover, the research conducted with vitamin A and physical performance has shown no beneficial effect. Hence, there appears to be no advantage for the active individual to supplement the diet with vitamin A, particularly not with megadoses that may have undesirable effects. The advisability of beta-carotene supplementation for its antioxidant properties is discussed in the later sections of this chapter dealing with ergogenic and health issues. As shall be noted, individuals should not consume high doses of beta-carotene.

Vitamin D (cholecalciferol)

 **Vitamin D,** a term representing a number of compounds, has been classified as both a fat-soluble vitamin and as a hormone. The physiologically active form is calcitriol, which is the hormone of this vitamin. In brief, the ultraviolet rays from sunshine convert a compound found in the skin (ergocalciferol; vitamin D_2) into **cholecalciferol (vitamin D_3),** a prohormone, which is released into the blood and is eventually converted by the liver and kidneys into the active hormone, calcitriol.

DRI   The Adequate Intake (AI) for vitamin D is given in micrograms of cholecalciferol or as IU. One microgram of cholecalciferol is the equivalent of 40 IU. In the absence of adequate sunlight, the AI for children and adults to age 50 is 5 micrograms, or 200 IU per day. Given the potential role of vitamin D to optimize bone health, the National Academy of Sciences recently updated the AI to 400 IU for those aged 51–70 and to 600 IU for those over age 70. The DV is 400 IU. The UL for adults age 19–50 is 2,000 IU, or 50 micrograms daily. See the DRI tables on the inside of the front and back covers for more details.

Food Sources   Most foods do not contain any vitamin D. Fish liver oils are good sources, and small amounts are found in eggs, tuna, and salmon. Several foods are fortified with vitamin D, such as milk, margarine, and some breakfast cereals. One glass of fortified milk will provide 100 IU, which is 25 percent of the DV, but 50 percent of the RDA for children and adults to age 50.

The Consumers Union notes that we normally get about 90 percent of our vitamin D from sunlight and the remaining 10 percent from food. The RDA for vitamin D may be obtained by exposing the hands, arms, and face to 10–20 minutes of summer sunshine about 2–3 times per week. The ultraviolet-B (UV-B) radiation waves promote vitamin D formation in the skin, but UV-B waves also cause wrinkles and skin cancer. Total sunblocking agents prevent vitamin D formation, but their use by individuals concerned with skin cancer due to sun exposure is still recommended because even very small amounts of sunshine will promote vitamin D formation. Longer periods of exposure may be necessary in the winter, and it may be difficult to obtain adequate vitamin D by sunlight in northern latitudes. Vieth and Fraser indicated this was especially true for the northern latitudes of Canada during winter, and it may also apply to the northern parts of the United States. Aging also decreases the formation of vitamin D from sunlight.

Major Functions Vitamin D plays a central role in bone metabolism through its effect on calcium and phosphorus, whose roles in bone metabolism are discussed in the next chapter. It works in conjunction with several other hormones, particularly parathormone secreted by the parathyroid gland. In particular, vitamin D helps to absorb calcium from the intestinal tract and the kidneys, helping to maintain normal serum calcium levels and proper bone metabolism. Vitamin D also helps regulate phosphorus metabolism, another mineral essential in bone formation. Verhaar and others note that besides the classical actions of vitamin D in bone metabolism, it also appears to be important for muscle function. Vitamin D is also involved in the development of the skin and has been used in the treatment of psoriasis, a chronic skin disorder, and other dermatological problems. For a detailed review of vitamin D metabolism, the interested reader is referred to the recent review by Holick.

Deficiency: Health and Physical Performance Deficiencies of vitamin D are unusual in most temperate climates because the body possesses adequate stores in the liver and can manufacture it through exposure to the sun. Children normally get adequate sun exposure if they play outdoors during daylight. However, deficiencies may occur in individuals who have little exposure to sunshine, such as elderly people who are homebound. Many elderly are more concerned with health, and are more likely to wear more clothing and use sunscreen lotions, possibly blocking vitamin D formation. Vegans who avoid sunlight may also be at risk for vitamin D deficiency.

Vitamin D deficiency may be related to a variety of health problems. In particular, a deficiency leads to increased serum levels of parathyroid hormone, which removes calcium from bones. Thus, deficiencies may lead to inadequate calcium metabolism and bone deformities known as rickets, especially in children. This was a major concern years ago, but it has nearly been eradicated through the use of vitamin D-fortified foods, primarily milk. However, in a recent interview, Holick indicated that adults do not drink much milk and many are not getting enough vitamin D to satisfy their body requirements, predisposing them to bone loss. Loss of bone tissue may occur in adults, leading to **osteomalacia,**

or a softening of the bones, accompanied by muscular weakness. The muscle weakness has been theoretically linked with an impairment of calcium metabolism in the muscle, possibly due to inadequate activation of vitamin D receptors in muscle. Some research notes a decrease in muscle strength in institutionalized elderly patients who are deficient in vitamin D. Although muscle weakness associated with a vitamin D deficiency could certainly impair physical performance, there appear to be no data to indicate that this is a problem with healthy athletes.

Vitamin D may help inhibit cell proliferation, so a deficiency could lead to increased cell proliferation, a key characteristic in cancer growth. John and others recently reported a decreased risk of breast cancer in women who lived in regions of the United States with high solar radiation. Dietary intake of vitamin D was also associated with a decreased risk of breast cancer. They hypothesized that vitamin D, obtained either via sunlight or dietary intake, may decrease the risk of breast cancer. The Consumers Union in their review also indicated those living in the South experience lower levels of other cancers, such as colon, ovary, and prostate, and note that some researchers believe this is related to sunlight exposure. Additional research is needed to confirm these preliminary epidemiological data.

Chiu and others reported that a low level of vitamin D in the blood is associated with insulin resistance and increased risk of diabetes. Additionally, vitamin D deficiency may lead to an increased production of renin by the kidney, which could lead to an increased blood pressure.

Supplementation: Health and Physical Performance Although Vieth indicates high levels of vitamin D supplementation may not be toxic, in general, vitamin D supplements in amounts greater than the RDA are not recommended. Because vitamin D is fat soluble, megadoses may lead to increased storage in the body, and pathological results have been reported. Hypervitaminosis D may lead to vomiting, diarrhea, weight loss, loss of muscle tone, and possible damage to soft tissues such as the kidney, heart, and blood vessels due to deposits of calcium. Although adequate amounts of vitamin D are needed for prevention of osteomalacia and osteoporosis, Moon and others hypothesized that chronic excess intake may induce osteoporosis and also exacerbate atherosclerosis by increasing the calcium content in plaque. Adequate exposure to the sun and a balanced diet, unless the food is improperly fortified, will not lead to hypervitaminosis D, but supplements may.

For various health reasons, vitamin D supplementation is receiving considerable research attention. Calvo and others indicated that vitamin D fortification practices in the United States and Canada are not effective in preventing hypovitaminosus D in various groups, such as those living in northern latitudes. Infants who breastfeed may also be deficient if their mothers have inadequate vitamin D. Thus, Raiten and Picciano recently noted that there is a reemergence of vitamin-D-deficient rickets in young children. On the other end of the age spectrum, researchers have indicated that vitamin D supplementation, possibly by increasing muscle strength, reaction time, and balance, may help prevent falls and debilitating hip fractures in older individuals.

Recommended doses of vitamin D supplementation vary. Bischoff-Ferrari and others indicate that oral vitamin D supplementation between 700 to 800 IU daily appears to reduce the risk of hip and some other fractures in elderly persons. However, Weaver and Fleet indicate that in order to achieve optimum serum D concentrations, some individuals may need amounts of vitamin D supplementation greater than the UL of 2,000 IU daily. For example, Harris indicated that doses of 2,000 IU and higher daily may have a strong protective effect in children at risk for type I diabetes. In a recent review, Holick suggested an UL of 4,000 IU may be more reasonable for individuals after the first year of life.

There is very little theoretical basis for athletes to take vitamin D supplements. For this reason, only a few studies have been conducted with vitamin D supplementation and physical performance, and they revealed no beneficial effect, either through single megadoses or supplementation over a 2-year period. Some recent research has revealed that weight training increases the serum concentration of vitamin D, and the investigators theorized this could be related to the increased bone mass which is developed through exercise. Others indicate that the exercising elderly need to obtain adequate vitamin D. However, these studies do not suggest that vitamin D supplementation would be ergogenic in those with normal vitamin D status.

Prudent Recommendations   There appear to be sound medical reasons for most healthy individuals not to use vitamin D supplements. However, those at risk for vitamin D deficiency, such as the elderly and those not exposed to adequate sunshine, including young children, may benefit from supplementation with fortified foods or vitamin pills.

Vitamin E (alpha-tocopherol)

Vitamin E is a fat-soluble vitamin. It is a complex family of eight compounds including tocopherols and tocotrienols, both with alpha, beta, gamma, and delta forms. The two major forms are **RRR-alpha-tocopherol** and **RRR-gamma-tocopherol.**

DRI   The RDA for vitamin E is 15 mg of natural and other forms of alpha-tocopherol, although you might see the RDA expressed as IU. One mg RRR-alpha-tocopherol is equivalent to about 1.5 IU. The RDA is slightly less for children. See the DRI table on the inside of the front cover for more details. The DV is 30 IU. The UL for adults is 1,000 mg/day, which is equal to 1,500 IU.

Food Sources   Vitamin E is found primarily in the small fat content in various vegetables. The most common dietary sources are polyunsaturated vegetable oils such as corn, soybean, and safflower oils, and margarines made from these oils; one tablespoon contains about 3–5 IU. Other good sources of vitamin E include fortified ready-to-eat cereals, whole-grain products, wheat germ oil, and eggs. One ounce of a fortified cereal may include about 10–45 IU of vitamin E, while a tablespoon of wheat germ oil contains about 40 IU. Moderate to small amounts are found in meats, dairy products, fruits, and vegetables, particularly sweet potatoes and dark-green leafy vegetables. Four spears of asparagus contain 2 IU. The fat substitute, Olestra, may retard the absorption of vitamin E found in natural foods but the FDA has mandated that foods containing Olestra should be fortified with vitamin E. The RDA for vitamin E actually increases as the amount of polyunsaturated oils in the diet increases. Fish oil supplements may be contraindicated in this regard since they are high in polyunsaturated fatty acids, but low in vitamin E unless fortified. Vitamin E supplements may contain natural or synthetic sources. The form should be listed on the food label. Unlike other vitamins, synthetic vitamin E is not the same as the natural source. Synthetic vitamin E is a form of alpha-tocopherol different from that found in natural sources, and is less likely to contain other forms of vitamin E, such as gamma-tocopherol. Both forms are appropriate, but you need to take about 40–50 percent more of the synthetic form to get the potency of the natural form.

Major Functions   Traber notes that the total function of vitamin E in human nutrition is unclear, stating that for over 80 years it is still a vitamin looking for a disease. Its principal role is to serve as an antioxidant in the cell membrane. Vitamin E works in concert with other antioxidants, such as the aqueous vitamin C, to maintain its ability to help prevent the oxidation of unsaturated fatty acids in cell membrane phospholipids, thereby protecting the cell from damage. It may also help prevent the oxidation of vitamin A. Other claims, extrapolated from research with animals, have suggested that vitamin E may also play a key role in the synthesis of hemoglobin or serve a pro-oxidant effect by activating enzymes in the mitochondria to improve cellular oxygen utilization, but these claims are not well documented in humans. Some of the vitamin E antioxidant effects are theorized to help prevent the development of several chronic diseases. The related mechanisms are discussed later in this chapter.

Deficiency: Health and Physical Performance   Because vitamin E is rather widely distributed in foods, and because it is also stored in the body, a true vitamin E deficiency in humans is rare. In one experiment prisoners were fed a vitamin E-deficient diet for 13 months and evidenced no symptoms of a deficiency. However, certain individuals with genetic diseases, such as the inability to absorb fat, do experience a deficiency. Others on very-low-fat diets may not obtain enough dietary vitamin E. In such cases, anemia may occur because the membranes of the red blood cells (RBC) are oxidized and release their hemoglobin. Deficiency symptoms noted in animals include nutritional muscular dystrophy and damage to the heart and blood vessels. Because of its role in preventing cellular damage from free radical oxidation, a deficiency of vitamin E has been theorized to contribute to the development of heart disease and cancer in humans. For example, vitamin E may help prevent the oxidation of LDL-cholesterol which, as noted in chapter 5, is associated with atherosclerosis and coronary heart disease. Some studies have suggested that a deficiency will lead to premature aging and decreased fertility.

Although vitamin E deficiency is rare in humans, several authors have used the data from research with animals and those humans with genetic defects to support the need for supplementation by athletes. They suggest that a vitamin E deficiency may lead to impaired oxygen transport due to RBC damage and to reduced oxidative capacity within the muscle cell. These effects would reduce VO_2 max and lead to a decrease in aerobic endurance capacity.

Supplementation: Health and Physical Performance
Vitamin E supplementation, based on the potential antioxidant effects, has been studied extensively as a means of enhancing health and physical performance. Vitamin E has often been combined with other antioxidants to evaluate the effects on disease processes or muscle damage during exercise, and these topics are discussed later in the chapter. Vitamin E supplementation has also been studied as a means to enhance aerobic endurance capacity, possibly by maintaining integrity of the red blood cells and oxygen delivery.

Over a dozen studies have been conducted to investigate the effect of vitamin E supplementation upon physical performance, especially VO_2 max and aerobic endurance capacity. Some of the early studies showed a beneficial effect, particularly at higher altitudes, but the experiments were poorly designed. However, one very well-planned experiment by Kobayashi, using a double-blind, placebo protocol, found that 1,200 IU of vitamin E supplements daily for 6 weeks improved VO_2 max, reduced blood lactic acid during submaximal exercise, and increased aerobic endurance at altitudes of 5,000 and 15,000 feet. The vitamin E was theorized to prevent the increased rate of oxidation of the RBC membrane that might occur while exercising at altitude. Although this was a well-designed study, the subjects were sedentary and were not in a state of training, so it may not be applicable to athletes. More recent research by Simon-Schnass and Pabst has supported these earlier findings. These researchers reported that 400 milligrams of vitamin E given to high-altitude mountain climbers over a 10-week period improved the anaerobic (lactate) threshold. Additional research would appear to be warranted with athletes at altitude.

Moreover, one investigator has noted a similar situation may exist with athletes exercising in high-smog areas, where some of the pollutants in the air could damage the RBC. With the magnitude of sports conducted in cities with poor air quality, this topic also might benefit from such research. Given these findings, and the possible effects of vitamin E on exercise-induced muscle damage (discussed later in this chapter), Simon-Schnass noted in a recent review that athletes should consume 100–200 IU daily and that it would be bordering on malpractice not to point out the benefits of such supplementation to athletes.

On the other hand, the majority of the recent well-designed studies, using doses from 400–1,200 IU and using athletes in training as subjects, revealed no significant effect upon physiological functions such as VO_2 max, tests of aerobic endurance when performed at sea level, or even performance in running a marathon, or an Ironman-distance triathlon. One possible reason for this finding is that the plasma level of vitamin E appears to rise significantly during intense exercise, as reported by Pincemail and others. But even when 5 months of vitamin E supplementation, as compared to a placebo treatment, significantly increased serum vitamin E levels in national class racing cyclists, Rokitzki and others noted no improvement in VO_2 max and other cycling performance measures.

Although the potential ergogenic effect of vitamin E supplementation at altitude needs additional research, Tiidus and Houston recently reviewed the scientific literature and concluded that while supplementation may increase tissue or serum vitamin E concentration, there is currently a lack of conclusive evidence that exercise performance or recovery in either elite or recreational athletes would benefit in any significant way.

Prudent Recommendations
As a means of enhancing physical performance, vitamin E supplements are not recommended. However, as noted later in this chapter, although most health professionals recommend increased attention to foods rich in vitamin E, others may recommend supplements for possible prevention of various chronic diseases.

Vitamin K (phylloquinone; menoquinone)

Vitamin K is a fat-soluble vitamin. It is often called the blood coagulation vitamin or antihemorrhagic vitamin. Vitamin K was discovered in Denmark, and K is derived from *koagulation*, the Danish word for coagulation. Vitamin K is the generic term for menadione, or vitamin K_3.

DRI
The AI is 120 and 90 micrograms/day for adult males and females, respectively. The DV is 80 micrograms. No UL has been established.

Food Sources
Vitamin K is found in a variety of plant and animal foods. **Phylloquinone (K_1)** is the plant form of vitamin K, while **menoquinone (MK)** is the animal form, formerly known as K_2. Good plant sources include vegetable oils (soybean, olive); green and leafy vegetables such as kale, peas, broccoli, and spinach; while meats and milk contain much lower amounts. Phylloquinone is the major dietary source of vitamin K; three ounces of spinach contain 380 micrograms, whereas three ounces of meat contain less than one microgram. The typical American diet contains about 100–150 micrograms per day. Additionally, vitamin MK (menoquinone) is also formed in the intestines by bacteria, so a deficiency is unlikely. The RDA is usually met easily by a combination of dietary intake and endogenous synthesis.

Major Functions
Vitamin K is needed for the formation of four compounds that are essential in two steps of the blood-clotting process. In addition, vitamin K appears to enhance the function of osteocalcin, a protein that plays an important role in strengthening bones. Suttie has provided a recent review of the role of vitamin K in human nutrition.

Deficiency: Health and Physical Performance
A deficiency of vitamin K is uncommon in healthy adults, but may occur with very-low vitamin K diets and in some individuals when antibiotic medications kill the intestinal bacteria that produce the vitamin. Deficiencies may impair blood clotting and lead to hemorrhage. Zittermann noted that some epidemiological studies have shown an association between low vitamin K intake and increased risk of osteoporotic bone fractures.

There are no data indicating deficiency states in physically active individuals or related effects on physical performance.

Supplementation: Health and Physical Performance Recent studies have suggested that vitamin K supplementation may have positive effects on bone health. Zittermann indicated that studies with very high pharmacological doses of MK may enhance bone mineralization in individuals with osteoporosis, but the effect of dietary supplements is less clear. However, Weber noted that there is emerging evidence in human intervention studies that vitamin K_1 supplementation may benefit bone health, in particular when coadministered with vitamin D. Moreover, Liebman and Hurley, citing research involving the effect of vitamin K to prevent hip fracture, noted that doses ranging from 150–250 micrograms daily were effective. However, Suttie recently noted that the relationship of vitamin K to bone health needs substantially more study.

No supplementation studies are available to evaluate the effect of vitamin K on physical performance because it does not appear to play an important role in this regard. However, as related to bone health, Craciun and others reported an increased index of bone formation markers in female elite athletes following vitamin K supplementation (10 mg/day) for one month. Some of the athletes were vitamin-K deficient prior to the supplementation protocol. Conversely, in a 2-year clinical study, Braam and others failed to find any effect of supplementary vitamin K on the rate of bone loss in female endurance athletes. The importance of bone health in young female athletes is discussed further in chapter 8.

The National Academy of Sciences has noted that, unlike vitamins A and D, vitamin K as phylloquinone is not very toxic when consumed in large doses. However, Weber notes that individuals taking anticoagulant drugs should consult with their physicians about diet and supplements. As vitamin K promotes clotting, the prescription may need to be adjusted.

Prudent Recommendations There is no evidence available that supports vitamin K supplementation as a means to improve the health status of the average individual or to improve performance in athletes. Therefore, vitamin K supplements are not recommended unless under the guidance of a physician.

Key Concept Recap

▶ The fat-soluble vitamins are A, D, E, and K.

▶ Although most vitamins must be obtained from the food we eat, several may be manufactured in the body. Vitamin A may be produced from dietary beta-carotene, vitamin D from exposure to sunlight, and vitamin K from intestinal bacterial activity.

▶ Fat-soluble vitamin deficiencies are rare in developed countries. Supplementation is not generally recommended, except for vitamin D in the elderly who have very limited sunshine exposure. The UL for vitamins A and D is relatively low, so excess intake may pose various health risks.

▶ Supplementation with fat-soluble vitamins has not been shown to enhance sports performance.

Water-Soluble Vitamins

There are nine water-soluble vitamins, including eight in the vitamin B complex and vitamin C (ascorbic acid). The B complex vitamins include thiamin, riboflavin, niacin, B_6, B_{12}, folate, biotin, and pantothenic acid. Choline, although included in the DRI for the B vitamins, has not been classified as a vitamin at this time. Being water soluble they are not, with a few exceptions, stored to any significant extent in the body. The effects of a deficiency may be noted in 2–4 weeks for some of these vitamins, often reducing physical performance capacity. Excess supplements of these vitamins are usually excreted in the urine and are generally considered to be relatively harmless. However, there are some exceptions.

Because several of the B vitamins work closely together in energy metabolism, many studies have investigated the effect of a deficiency or supplementation of multiple vitamins from the B complex. A summary of this research follows a discussion of each individual vitamin.

Figure 7.3 provides a broad perspective on the major sites of activity of the water-soluble vitamins, highlighting sites for vitamin E and other antioxidants as well.

Thiamin (vitamin B₁)

Thiamin, also known as **vitamin B_1,** is a water-soluble vitamin and is also known as the antiberiberi or antineuritic vitamin. It was one of the first vitamins discovered.

DRI The RDA for thiamin varies according to the intake of Calories, being approximately 0.5 mg per 1,000 Calories. The average adult male needs approximately 1.2 mg/day, while the adult female needs about 1.1 mg/day. See the DRI table on the inside front cover for more details. The DV is 1.5 mg. No UL has been established.

Food Sources Thiamin is widely distributed in both plant and animal tissues. Excellent sources include whole-grain cereals, beans, and pork. One lean pork chop contains over 50 percent of the RDA. Several fortified ready-to-eat cereals contain 100 percent of the RDA for thiamin, as well as most of the other B vitamins.

Major Functions Thiamin has a central role in the metabolism of glucose. It is part of a coenzyme known as thiamin pyrophosphate, which is needed to convert pyruvate to acetyl CoA for entrance into the Krebs cycle. Thiamin is essential for the normal functioning of the nervous system and energy derivation from glycogen in the muscles.

Deficiency: Health and Physical Performance Deficiency symptoms may occur in several weeks, and may include loss of appetite, mental confusion, muscular weakness, and pain in the calf muscles. Prolonged deficiencies lead to beriberi, a serious disease involving damage to the nervous system and the heart. Fortunately, thiamin deficiency is not very common, although it may be rather prevalent among the homeless, alcoholics, and other special groups.

Of importance to the athlete, two factors that increase the need for thiamin are exercise and high-carbohydrate intake. A deficiency of thiamin could prove to be detrimental to the active individual who might rely on high levels of carbohydrate metabolism

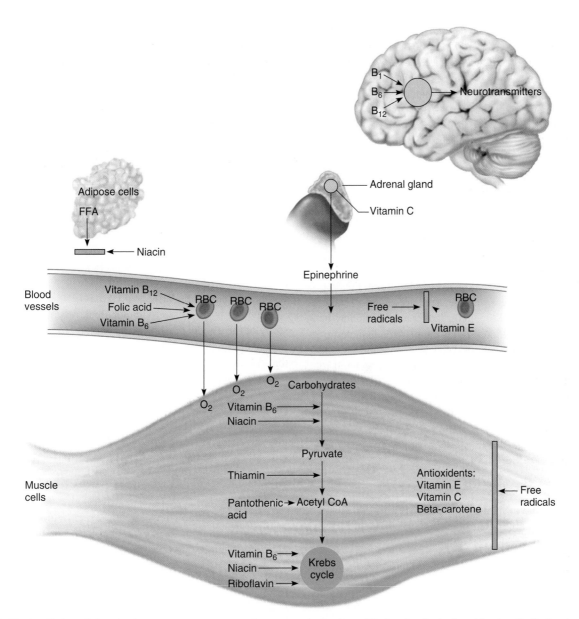

FIGURE 7.3 Roles of vitamins important to sports performance. A number of B vitamins, including thiamin, riboflavin, niacin, B_6, and pantothenic acid are essential for the conversion of carbohydrate into energy for muscular contraction. Vitamin B_{12} and folic acid are essential for the development of the red blood cells (RBC), which deliver oxygen to the muscle cell. Vitamin E helps protect the RBC membrane from destruction by free radicals. Vitamin E and other antioxidant vitamins are theorized to prevent free radical damage in muscle cells during exercise. Vitamin C is needed for the formation of epinephrine (adrenaline), a key hormone during strenuous exercise. Niacin may actually block the release of free fatty acids from the adipose tissue, which could be a disadvantage for ultraendurance athletes. Finally, several of the B vitamins are also involved in the formation of neurotransmitters in the brain, which may induce a relaxation effect.

for aerobic energy production during exercise, such as endurance athletes. Indeed, some well-controlled research conducted during World War II to evaluate military nutrition needs in combat noted decreased endurance capacity after several weeks of a thiamin-deficient diet. More contemporary research has also investigated the role of thiamin deficiency upon exercise performance but in conjunction with riboflavin and niacin deficiencies. These reports are discussed under vitamin B complex.

Supplementation: Health and Physical Performance
Thiamin supplementation apparently has no health benefits for a well-nourished individual. Tanphaichitr indicates there is no evi-

dence of thiamin toxicity with oral administration as the excess will be excreted in the urine. No UL has been set for thiamin.

No contemporary research appears to exist relative to the effect of thiamin supplementation upon physical performance, although results from a number of studies conducted more than 50 years ago are available. Following a careful review of these studies, many with problems in establishing a proper experimental design, there appears to be no conclusive evidence to support the contention that vitamin B_1 intake above and beyond the normal RDA will enhance performance.

Although not using thiamine, Doyle and others recently reported that 5 days of supplementation with allithiamine, a thiamin derivative, did not improve muscular strength and endurance. In several well-controlled studies, Michael Webster reported no significant effects of thiamin derivatives on metabolic, physiologic, or psychologic responses to various cycling exercise tasks in well-trained cyclists. In both studies, performance time in a 2000-meter time trial (in one study after a 50-kilometer ride) was not affected by the thiamine derivatives.

Thiamin, as indicated, is important for normal neurological functions. In a recent study from Japan, Suzuki and Itokawa reported that 100 milligrams of thiamine for 3 days increased serum thiamin levels and reduced subjective complaints of fatigue from subjects following a strenuous exercise task. As noted later under the B-complex section, thiamin was one of the vitamins proposed to improve neurological function in pistol shooting. These are interesting observations and merit additional research.

As noted above, physical activity, particularly high-intensity, endurance-type activity, increases the need for thiamin in the diet; this exercise training also increases the need for caloric intake. With proper selection of foods, the increased thiamin need may be met by the content in the additional foods eaten. An adequate thiamin intake is one of the reasons physically active individuals need to select foods that are dense in nutrients, and in general to avoid those foods that provide Calories but few nutrients.

Prudent Recommendations Thiamin supplements are not needed by the individual who is consuming an adequate diet, and they do not appear to enhance exercise performance.

Riboflavin (vitamin B₂)

Riboflavin is also known as **vitamin B₂.** It is a water-soluble vitamin and is a component of the B complex.

DRI The RDA for riboflavin is 1.3 mg for the adult male and 1.1 mg for the adult female. The DRI table on the inside front cover contains the RDA for other age groups. The DV is currently 1.7 mg and no UL has been established.

Food Sources Riboflavin is distributed widely in foods. A major source is milk and other dairy products; one glass of milk contains 20 percent of the RDA. Other good sources include liver, eggs, dark-green leafy vegetables, wheat germ, yeast, whole-grain products, and enriched breads and cereals.

Major Functions Riboflavin is important for the formation of several oxidative enzymes known as flavoproteins, which are involved in energy production from carbohydrate and fats in the body cells. It is also involved in protein metabolism and maintenance of healthy skin tissue.

Deficiency: Health and Physical Performance Deficiencies are very rare but have been seen in alcoholics and those adhering to various fad diets. Early signs of deficiency may include glossitis (an inflammation of the tongue), cracks at the corners of the mouth, and dry, scaly skin at the corners of the nose, symptoms common in individuals who experience multiple nutrient deficits.

Although the effect of a riboflavin deficiency upon physical performance has not been studied directly, research from Cornell University suggests that physically untrained women who initiate an aerobic training program may need a higher intake of riboflavin to synthesize more flavoproteins in the muscles. Using a blood test, the investigators determined that the RDA did not maintain proper riboflavin status in the early stages of training, but they suggested a value of about 1.1 mg per 1,000 Calories would be sufficient. It should be noted that no data were reported relative to the effect of this deficiency upon performance. Haralambie also reported a possible deficiency in trained athletes but did not relate it to performance.

Supplementation: Health and Physical Performance Riboflavin supplementation apparently has no health benefits for a well-nourished individual. McCormick indicates that toxicity for excess riboflavin intake is doubtful. Excesses will not be stored but will be excreted in the urine. No UL has been set for riboflavin.

Reviews by Keith and van der Beek reveal only one reputable study of the effects of riboflavin supplementation on physical performance. Tremblay and others, studying elite swimmers, reported that 60 mg of riboflavin daily for 16 to 20 days did not improve VO₂ max, anaerobic (lactate) threshold, or swim performance.

Prudent Recommendations Considering the available research data and the absence of riboflavin deficiency in most individuals, one must conclude that riboflavin supplementation will not enhance health or physical performance.

Niacin

Niacin is also known as nicotinic acid, nicotinamide, or the antipellagra vitamin. It is a water-soluble vitamin in the B complex and is sometimes erroneously referred to as vitamin B₃.

DRI Niacin is found naturally in many foods, but it also may be formed in the body from excess amounts of dietary tryptophan, an essential amino acid. Therefore, the RDA is expressed in **niacin equivalents,** or **NE.** One NE equals 1 mg of niacin or 60 mg of tryptophan, because 1 mg of niacin can be produced from that amount of tryptophan. The RDA for niacin is 16 NE for adult males and 14 NE for adult females. The requirement is different for other age groups, and specific values may be obtained from the DRI table on the inside front cover. The DV is 20 mg. As excess niacin intake may cause some health problems, as we will note, an UL of 35 mg/day has been set for adults, and even lesser amounts for younger individuals.

Food Sources Niacin is found in foods that have a high protein content. It is most abundant in lean meats, organ meats, fish, poultry, whole-grain cereal products, legumes such as beans and peanuts, and enriched foods. Milk and eggs contain small amounts of niacin, but they contain sufficient tryptophan. One-half of a chicken breast contains over 60 percent of the RDA of niacin.

Major Functions Niacin serves as a component of two coenzymes concerned with energy processes within the cell. One of these coenzymes is important in the process of glycolysis, which is the means by which muscle glycogen produces energy both aerobically and anaerobically. The other coenzyme is involved in fat metabolism by promoting fat synthesis in the body.

Deficiency: Health and Physical Performance Although niacin deficiency was prevalent in the past, the enrichment of foods with niacin has nearly eliminated this problem. Deficiency symptoms include loss of appetite, skin rashes, mental confusion, lack of energy, and muscular weakness. Serious deficiencies lead to pellagra, a disease characterized by severe dermatitis, diarrhea, and symptoms of mental illness.

In theory, physical performance would be impaired by a niacin deficiency because the production of energy from carbohydrate could be impaired. Both aerobic- and anaerobic-type performances could be affected. However, no research has been uncovered that has directly studied the effects of niacin deficiency alone on exercise performance.

Supplementation: Health and Physical Performance Megadoses of niacin have been used in attempts to treat several health problems, being relatively ineffective in the treatment of mental disease and somewhat successful in reducing high serum lipid levels. McKenney noted that niacin favorably affects all components of the lipid profile to a significant degree, as it has consistently been shown to significantly reduce levels of total cholesterol, LDL-cholesterol, triglycerides, and lipoprotein (a); in particular, niacin has a very potent effect to increase HDL-cholesterol. Ito also noted that niacin, when combined with statin drugs, may enhance the effectiveness of the treatment of dyslipidemia. In several recent reviews of clinical studies, Hunninghake and Bourgeis revealed that niacin, either alone or combined with other agents, can result in regression of atherosclerosis and reduce patient mortality. Some health professionals consider niacin the drug of first choice in the treatment of high blood cholesterol, but with cautions as noted below.

Although niacin is generally considered to be nontoxic, large doses in the form of nicotinic acid may cause flushing, with burning and tingling sensations around the face, neck, and hands occurring within 15 to 20 minutes after ingestion (i.e., the histamine-like effect). Taken over long periods, niacin may contribute to liver problems such as hepatitis and peptic ulcers. Pieper noted that niacin comes in three formulations, immediate-release, sustained-release, and extended-release. The latter appears to minimize the flushing effects seen with the immediate-release form and the hepatotoxic effects seen with the sustained-release form. The Center for Science in the Public Interest recommends that no one take niacin to lower blood cholesterol without guidance from a physician.

Because of the role of niacin in energy metabolism, a number of experiments have been conducted relative to niacin supplementation and physical performance capacity. However, several recent reviews concluded that niacin supplementation has not been shown to be an effective ergogenic aid for well-nourished athletes, having no effect on various exercise endeavors, including performance in a 10-mile run and in a 3.5-mile cycle time trial following 2 hours of cycling.

As a matter of fact, niacin supplementation is not recommended for most athletes, particularly those involved in endurance-type exercise such as marathon running because excessive niacin intake (3–9 grams/day) influences fat metabolism, blocking the release of

FFA from the adipose tissue. This will decrease the supply of FFA to the muscle, which may lead to an increased dependence on carbohydrate as an energy source during exercise, as shown by Heath and others. This could lead to a more rapid depletion of muscle glycogen, an important energy source during exercise. As noted by Bulow, niacin supplements may reduce endurance capacity.

Niacin supplements may also increase blood flow to the skin due to a histamine-like effect. In one experiment, Kolka and Stephenson found that such an effect could lower the sweat rate and decrease body heat storage during exercise. These effects could possibly be ergogenic to athletes exercising in the heat, but further investigation is needed.

Prudent Recommendations Unless recommended under the treatment of a physician, niacin supplements are not recommended for a physically active individual on a balanced diet. Excessive intake may actually impair certain types of athletic performance and elicit adverse health effects.

Vitamin B₆ (pyridoxine)

Vitamin B$_6$ is a collective term for three naturally occurring substances that are all metabolically and functionally related. They are pyridoxine, pyridoxal, and pyridoxamine. Pyridoxine is most often used as a synonym. Vitamin B$_6$ is water soluble.

DRI The adult RDA for vitamin B$_6$ is 1.3 mg/day for ages 19 to 50, and then increases to 1.7 mg for males and 1.5 for females above age 51. Slightly different amounts are needed at different age levels. Consult the DRI table on the inside front cover for specific RDA. Actually, the RDA for vitamin B$_6$ is based on protein intake, so requirements may increase with high-protein diets. The DV is 2 mg. As excess B$_6$ intake may cause some health problems, as noted in this section, a UL of 100 mg/day has been set for adults, and even lesser amounts for younger individuals.

Food Sources Vitamin B$_6$ is widely distributed in foods. The most reliable sources are protein foods such as meats, poultry, fish, wheat germ, whole-grain products, brown rice, and eggs. One-half of a chicken breast contains over 25 percent of the RDA.

Major Functions In its coenzyme form (primarily pyridoxal phosphate), vitamin B$_6$ is critically involved in the metabolism of protein, but it is also involved in carbohydrate and fat metabolism. It functions with more than sixty enzymes in such processes as the synthesis of dispensable amino acids, the conversion of tryptophan to niacin, the formation of neurotransmitters in the nervous system, and the incorporation of amino acids into body proteins such as hemoglobin, myoglobin, and oxidative enzymes. It is also involved in the breakdown of muscle glycogen as well as gluconeogenesis in the liver. Interested readers are directed to the review by Melinda Manore for more details on the metabolic functions of vitamin B$_6$.

Deficiency: Health and Physical Performance Vitamin B$_6$ deficiency is not considered to be a major health problem. The average American diet appears to provide an adequate amount of the vitamin, but poor diets do not. The use of diuretics and oral contraceptives has been associated with deficiencies. Most studies report that male athletes have adequate dietary intakes of vitamin B_6, whereas some females, especially those with low energy intakes, appear to have low vitamin B_6 intakes. Deficiency symptoms include nausea, impaired immune function, skin disorders, mouth sores, weakness, mental depression, anemia, and epileptic-like convulsions.

Theoretically, a B_6 deficiency could adversely affect endurance activities dependent upon oxygen, for it is involved in the formation of protein compounds such as hemoglobin that are essential to oxidative processes. Its role in carbohydrate metabolism, particularly muscle glycogen utilization, is also important to the endurance athlete. Its role in the formation of neurotransmitters could be important to athletes engaged in fine motor control sports, such as archery and riflery. In addition, the requirement for B_6 increases with protein intake, which may have some implications for those athletes who may be on high-protein diets. However, since B_6 is found in protein products, it should be easily obtainable in such a diet.

No research has been uncovered that has directly studied the effect of a B_6 deficiency upon physical performance. One report did suggest that runners who covered 5 to 10 miles per day appear to use more B_6 than their sedentary counterparts, but these investigators also noted that exercise may actually promote storage of the vitamin in the athlete, thus helping to prevent a deficiency state. Serum levels of B_6 actually increase during exercise. Hoffman and others noted the source of serum B_6 remains to be identified, but it may be derived from the B_6-dependent enzyme phosphorylase, which breaks down muscle glycogen.

In general, exercise does not appear to cause excessive losses of vitamin B_6 from the body. For example, Rokitzki and others estimated a loss of only 1 milligram over the course of a marathon, an amount that could easily be replaced in the diet. On the other hand, Leonard and Leklem recently found that plasma pyridoxal phosphate levels fell following a 50-kilometer ultramarathon, results that are not consistent with those reported in previous studies involving shorter length endurance tasks. However, whether or not ultraendurance athletes are at risk for vitamin B_6 deficiency has not been determined.

Supplementation: Health and Physical Performance Vitamin B_6 supplementation has been used to treat the nausea of pregnancy, mental depression associated with the use of oral contraceptives, and premenstrual syndrome (PMS), but its effectiveness for these purposes has received mixed reviews. For example, in a recent systematic review, Wyatt and others found that conclusions are limited due to the poor quality of most studies, but doses of 100 mg per day of B_6 (which coincides with the UL) are likely to benefit in the treatment of PMS symptoms. As discussed later, folate supplementation may decrease plasma homocysteine levels, possibly reducing the risk of CHD. McKinley and others noted that although not as effective as folate, low doses of B_6 (1.6 milligrams/day) may provide additional homocysteine-lowering benefits to elderly individuals who have adequate intake of the other B vitamins.

Several reports relative to the effect of B_6 supplementation upon physical performance are available. Although the muscle may store B_6, Coburn and others recently noted that B_6 supplementation did not markedly increase muscle stores. Moreover, in general, the studies reveal no significant effect upon metabolic functions during exercise or the capacity to do more work. One investigator suggested B_6 may actually be detrimental to endurance athletes because it may facilitate the use of muscle glycogen and lead to an earlier depletion in prolonged events. However, in a recent study from the laboratory at Oregon State University, Virk and others reported that B_6 supplementation (20 g/day for 9 days) did not influence, either positively or negatively, performance of trained males in an exhaustive aerobic endurance exercise task just under 2 hours in duration.

There appears to be little or no toxicity associated with moderate doses, but Bender noted that at high levels, B_6 supplementation can cause peripheral nerve damage, evidenced by such problems as loss of natural sensation from the limbs and an impaired gait. The National Research Council noted neurological symptoms with smaller dosages, averaging 117 mg per day for 6 months to 5 years.

Prudent Recommendations Vitamin B_6 supplementation does not appear to be warranted for the physically active individual, and may be associated with some health risks if consumed in large doses for prolonged periods.

Vitamin B_{12} (cobalamin)

Vitamin B_{12} (cobalamin) is a water-soluble vitamin. It is part of the B complex and is the latest vitamin to be discovered.

DRI The adult RDA for B_{12} is 2.4 micrograms per day. The average diet contains about 5–15 micrograms. Slightly different allowances are made for other age groups; see the DRI table on the inside front cover. The DV is 6 micrograms. No UL is available.

Food Sources Vitamin B_{12} is found in good supply only in animal foods such as meat, fish, poultry, cheese, eggs, and milk. One glass of milk contains nearly 30 percent of the RDA. It is not found in natural plant foods such as fruits, vegetables, beans, and grains, but may be an excellent source in vitamin-fortified cereals. However, it is present in microorganisms such as bacteria and yeast, which may be found in some plant foods, but the bioavailability of B_{12} from these sources is uncertain. Although B_{12} may be produced by microorganisms in the human bowel, the site of production is below the point of absorption.

Major Functions Vitamin B_{12} is a part of coenzymes present in all body cells and is essential in the synthesis of DNA. It works closely with folic acid, and both have important roles in the development of red blood cells. Vitamin B_{12} is also essential for the formation of the protective sheath around nerve fibers (the myelin sheath) and for the metabolism of homocysteine.

Deficiency: Health and Physical Performance Deficiency of vitamin B_{12} in humans due to inadequate dietary intake is rare. Even strict vegetarians appear to receive enough in their diet, either through the consumption of microorganisms or the use of fortified products. The body also stores a considerable amount in the liver, which may last for years; the body contains about 2,500 micrograms, but loses only about one microgram daily. A deficiency normally is caused by the inability to release cobalamin from food or a deficiency of intestinal absorption due to decreased transport proteins. The major symptoms are a severe form of anemia, known as pernicious anemia, and nerve damage that may cause paralysis. Pregnant women, particularly vegans, need to obtain adequate B_{12} because a deficit may impair myelination and cause birth defects in the newborn. Aging affects the absorption of B_{12} when it is present in food and bound to protein.

Because of its role in the formation of RBC, a deficiency of B_{12} resulting in pernicious anemia would be theorized to decrease aerobic endurance capacity. No research is available relative to the effect of a vitamin B_{12} deficiency upon performance, but other types of anemia have been shown to impair exercise performance.

Supplementation: Health and Physical Performance B_{12} megadoses may be an effective medical treatment for pernicious anemia, but do not appear to benefit the active individual on a balanced diet. However, as noted below, lower-dose supplements may be recommended for some individuals.

Relative to sports, vitamin B_{12} is one of the most abused vitamins in the athletic world, with some reports of athletes receiving large amounts by injection just prior to competition. The belief probably exists that if a little vitamin B_{12} can prevent anemia, then a lot of it will do something magical to increase performance capacity. However, several well-controlled studies have been conducted with B_{12} supplementation with the general conclusion that it will not help to increase metabolic functions, such as VO_2 max, or endurance performance. B_{12} supplements appear to be safe, but do not appear to benefit the active individual on a balanced diet.

Prudent Recommendations Individuals who consume animal products normally do not need vitamin B_{12} supplements, and there are no sound data that supplementation will enhance sport performance. However, vegans should consume food products fortified with vitamin B_{12}. Additionally, individuals over age 50, including senior athletes, may have decreased intrinsic factor and limited B_{12} absorption from natural B_{12} food sources, so they are advised to get about 2.4 mcg of B_{12} from fortified food products, such as cereals, or supplements. One serving of B_{12}-fortified cereal contains about 1.5 mcg, while a senior multivitamin usually contains 25 mcg.

Folate (folic acid)

Folate, or **folic acid,** is a water-soluble vitamin. It is part of the B complex. Folate is found naturally in some foods, but folic acid is a synthetic form found in fortified foods and dietary supplements.

DRI The RDA for folate is given as micrograms of **dietary folate equivalents (DFE).** One DFE equals 1 microgram of food folate, 0.6 microgram of folic acid in fortified foods, or 0.5 microgram of folic acid supplements taken on an empty stomach. One microgram of folic acid in fortified foods equals 1.7 DFE, while one microgram folic acid in a supplement equals 2 DFE, because these forms are better absorbed. The RDA for folate is 400 micrograms of DFE/day. During pregnancy the RDA is increased to 600 micrograms of DFE per day, and it is 500 micrograms DFE during the early stages of lactation. The DV is 400 micrograms of DFE. An UL of 1,000 micrograms DFE/day has been set for adults, and even lesser amounts for younger individuals.

Food Sources Folate derives its name from foliage because it is found in green leafy vegetables like spinach. Other good sources include organ meats such as liver and kidney, dry beans, whole-grain products, and some fruits like oranges and bananas. One cup of cooked black or navy beans contains about 60–75 percent of the folate RDA. One banana provides almost 10 percent of the RDA. Currently, all cereal and grain product in the United States are fortified with folic acid to reduce the occurrence of neural tube defects. The average fortification is 140 micrograms per 100 grams of food product. Studies indicate that such fortification has increased daily dietary folic acid intake by 100 micrograms or more.

Major Functions Folate serves as part of a coenzyme that plays a critical role in the metabolism of methionine, an essential amino acid. In this regard, folic acid is critical to the formation of DNA, the genetic material that regulates cell division. It is essential for maintaining normal production of RBC, one of the most rapidly dividing cells in the body. Folate is also critical during the very early stages of pregnancy when cells in the fetus divide rapidly. Researchers indicate during periods of rapid cell division large amounts of folate are needed to make DNA.

Deficiency: Health and Physical Performance One national survey has reported folate intakes below the RDA for some Americans. Individuals who consume large quantities of alcohol and women who take oral contraceptives may experience deficiencies in folic acid, as these drugs may impair absorption of the vitamin. A folic acid deficiency may impair DNA formation, or lead to an increase in homocysteine, a metabolic product of methionine metabolism.

Due to its effect on DNA synthesis, one of the major effects of folate deficiency is anemia, attributed to inadequate RBC regeneration. Anemia could impair delivery of oxygen and significantly impair performance in aerobic endurance events.

DNA and chromosomal damage caused by folic acid deficiency has been suggested to increase the risk of cancer. For example, in a recent Tufts University review, a low level of folate in large intestine cells was associated with an increased risk of colon cancer, a finding one of the authors reported to be consistent with the results of 20 other epidemiologic studies which have found that people who eat the most folic acid are the least likely to get colon cancer. Zhang and others also reported that for women who consume alcohol, those with the lowest dietary folic acid intake were at the highest risk for developing breast cancer.

Either due to DNA damage or the adverse neural effects of homocysteine, women who are folate-deficient and become pregnant may give birth to children with neural tube defects (NTD) such as spina bifida, an incomplete closure of the tissue surrounding the spinal cord. Such defects may cause paralysis and severe disabling conditions in the child. Approximately 2,500 infants in the United States are affected each year.

Elevated plasma levels of homocysteine are thought to damage the lining of the blood vessels or initiate growth of cells that form the framework of plaque, increasing the risk for several vascular diseases, including coronary heart disease (CHD), stroke, peripheral vascular disease (PVD), and Alzheimer's disease. Seman and others noted that studies suggest homocysteine, although associated with other CHD risk factors, may be considered to be an independent risk factor. In a recent review, Andreotti and others reported that the risk of CHD increases directly with increases in plasma concentration of homocysteine, a finding reported previously in a meta-analysis by Boushey. However, some researchers speculate that homocysteine may not be the cause of artery damage but rather the result of damage already done.

Supplementation: Health and Physical Performance   In a recent review, Law indicated there is irrefutable evidence that adequate folic acid helps prevent neural tube defects. All women who have the potential to become pregnant should consume 400 micrograms of synthetic folic acid daily. The 400 micrograms should be consumed as folic acid in fortified foods or dietary supplements, in addition to normal food folate intake. When pregnancy is confirmed, the RDA is increased to 600 micrograms DFE. Currently, only 1 in 3 women consume 400 micrograms DFE daily, so many women need to increase their intake of folic acid-fortified foods or dietary supplements, a recommendation of many health professionals. Carmel indicates adequate folic acid intake clearly prevents birth defects. Some researchers suggest that women at high risk for neural tube defects should take 4,000 micrograms daily, but only in consultation with their physicians.

Law also indicated good evidence exists that folic acid supplementation will help lower homocysteine, which may help reduce the risk of several diseases. Krishnaswamy and Madhavan Nair noted that 350 micrograms folic acid may maintain normal homocysteine levels, but higher doses, such as 650 micrograms, may be needed to lower elevated plasma homocysteine levels.

In their review, Andreotti and others indicated that folic acid supplementation increases plasma folate levels and may decrease plasma homocysteine levels by 25 percent. However, although this effect may be important, they also indicated that randomized controlled studies are needed to determine whether or not a reduction in plasma homocysteine levels results in a reduced rate of CHD or other vascular diseases. One recent study suggests not, at least in individuals who have already survived a first heart attack. Such individuals received either folate supplements or placebo for 3.5 years, and although the supplementation significantly reduced homocysteine levels, there was no significant effect on the occurrence of a second heart attack. However, in one epidemiological study, women who consumed a dietary total of at least 1,000 micrograms of folate daily, through diet and supplements, had a lower risk of high blood pressure, which is a major risk factor for

CHD. Overall, however, Carmel notes that the benefits of folic acid in preventing heart disease and cancer remain unproven.

A UL of 1,000 micrograms/day has been established for folic acid from fortified foods or supplements because megadoses could mask a vitamin B_{12} deficiency by preventing the development of anemia that would otherwise be discovered by a blood test. Unfortunately, folic acid does not prevent nerve damage, so the B_{12} deficiency may lead to paralysis if not detected. Rothenberg indicated that this may be a problem associated with the mandatory folic acid fortification of grain products. Thus, individuals who may be prone to a vitamin B_{12} deficiency are advised to take a B_{12} supplement or consume B_{12}-fortified foods.

One advocate of vitamin supplementation to athletes has reported that runners need additional folic acid to replace RBC that may be destroyed in heavy training programs. Unfortunately, no evidence is available to support this theory, nor are there any data that folic acid supplements will benefit physical performance. Only one study has been uncovered related to folate supplementation to athletes. Matter and her colleagues provided folate therapy (5 mg/day for 11 weeks) to female marathon runners who were diagnosed as being folate deficient. Although the folate therapy restored serum folate levels to normal, no improvements were noted in VO_2 max, maximum treadmill running time, peak lactate levels, or running speed at the lactate anaerobic threshold.

To be sure, anemia resulting from a folate deficiency could have serious consequences for endurance performance, but a balanced diet including fortified grain products should prevent this condition from developing.

Prudent Recommendations   All individuals should increase their intake of folate-rich foods, particularly vegetable sources, not only to obtain adequate folate but other healthful nutrients as well. Women in their childbearing years should obtain 400 micrograms DFE daily from a supplement to complement natural dietary sources, a recommendation approved by the American Academy of Pediatrics. Given the importance of adequate DFE, the National Academy of Sciences, in establishing the new RDA, indicated that women should get folic acid from fortified foods or supplements. Relative to the risk of vascular diseases, 400 micrograms DFE again appears to be a reasonable amount that may be obtained through the diet, particularly with folic acid-fortified cereals, or with the use of a daily supplement.

Pantothenic acid

Pantothenic acid is a water-soluble vitamin. It is a factor in the B complex. Pantothenate is a salt of pantothenic acid.

DRI   The adult AI for pantothenic acid is 5 mg, with lesser amounts for younger age groups and greater amounts during pregnancy and lactation. The DV is 10 mg and no UL has been established.

Food Sources   Pantothenic acid is distributed widely in foods. It is found in all natural animal and plant products, but best sources include organ meats, eggs, legumes, yeasts, and whole grains. It should also be noted that highly refined, processed foods have lost most of the pantothenate content.

Major Functions   Pantothenic acid is an essential component of coenzyme A (CoA), which plays a central role in energy metabolism. You may recall acetyl CoA, which may be derived from carbohydrate, fat, and protein metabolism, is the principal substrate for the Krebs cycle. Pantothenic acid is also involved in gluconeogenesis, in the synthesis and breakdown of fatty acids, modification of proteins, and in the synthesis of acetylcholine, a chemical released by the motor neuron to initiate muscle contraction.

Deficiency: Health and Physical Performance   Except under experimentally induced conditions, deficiencies are not seen in humans. In such cases deficiencies have been reported to cause a variety of symptoms, including fatigue, muscle cramping, and impairment of motor coordination.

On a theoretical basis, pantothenic acid appears crucial to the active individual because it has an important function at the center of energy pathways. Several investigators have suggested that a deficiency would decrease the availability of acetyl CoA for the Krebs cycle and thus shift energy production to anaerobic glycolysis, which is less efficient. Because deficiencies of pantothenic acid have not been observed, such effects upon physical performance have not been studied.

Supplementation: Health and Physical Performance   Pantothenic acid supplementation apparently has no health benefits for a well-nourished individual. Liebman, in her review on how to select a multivitamin, indicated you can ignore it on the label.

Research findings regarding the effect of pantothenic acid supplementation on physical performance are equivocal. Data from one well-designed study with supplements of pantothenic acid—2 grams per day for 14 days—suggested a beneficial effect by reducing oxygen consumption and lactate production during a submaximal exercise task at 75 percent VO_2 max for 40 minutes. This would suggest that pantothenic acid increased the efficiency of the exercise task. No data on maximal performance were provided. Unfortunately this report was available only as a brief abstract and very few details were presented. Conversely, another well-designed study revealed that 1 gram of pantothenic acid given daily for 2 weeks had no effect upon various blood measures or maximal performance in highly trained distance runners. Most recently Webster, using 6 highly trained cyclists, reported no significant effects of pantothenic acid supplementation (1.8 grams per day for 7 days, combined with allithiamin) on a 2000-meter time trial following a 50-kilometer steady-state ride. There also were no significant metabolic, physiologic, or psychologic effects.

Supplements of pantothenic acid appear to be relatively nontoxic. However, large doses of 10 to 20 grams have been known to cause diarrhea.

Prudent Recommendations   Given the fact that pantothenic acid deficiency is rather nonexistent and there is little research to support a beneficial effect on health or physical performance at this time, supplementation is not recommended. A balanced diet should provide adequate pantothenic acid for the healthy, physically active individual.

Biotin

Biotin is a water-soluble vitamin in the B complex.

DRI   The adult AI for biotin is 30 micrograms, with somewhat lesser amounts for younger age groups, and greater amounts during lactation. The DV is 300 micrograms, and no UL is available.

Food Sources   Good dietary sources of biotin include organ meats such as liver, egg yolk, legumes such as peas and beans, and dark-green leafy vegetables. It is also synthesized in significant amounts in the intestines by bacteria.

Major Functions   McMahon noted recent research suggests that biotin may be involved in the regulation of gene expression, which may be related to its role as a coenzyme for a variety of enzymes involved in amino acid metabolism. Biotin is also involved in the synthesis of glucose and fatty acids. Because biotin is an important coenzyme for gluconeogenesis, it may have some implications relative to endurance performance.

Deficiency: Health and Physical Performance   Deficiency states are rare but may occur when the diet contains large amounts of raw egg whites; a protein in the raw egg white binds biotin and prevents its absorption into the body. In such cases symptoms include loss of appetite, mental depression, dermatitis, and muscle pain. For athletes who consume eggs for their protein content, it may be important to know that cooking the egg white eliminates this problem while providing the same amount of high-quality protein. It should also be mentioned in passing that raw eggs pose a risk of salmonella, a type of bacteria associated with food poisoning.

Although a biotin deficiency could impair physical performance, no data are available to support this hypothesis.

Supplementation: Health and Physical Performance   No research into the effects of biotin supplementation on health or physical performance has been uncovered. Thus, there is no evidence that biotin supplementation improves health or increases physical performance capacity. Supplements of biotin appear to be harmless, as Mock reports no adverse effects in doses ranging up to 200 mg daily.

Prudent Recommendations   It would appear that biotin supplements are unnecessary for the physically active individual.

Choline

Choline, an amine, is a water-soluble essential nutrient listed in the DRI report with the B vitamins, but has not been classified as a vitamin. Commercial choline products are available as lecithin or choline salts, but the actual choline content may vary. Check the labels for actual choline content. Choline is also marketed as a powder with carbohydrate and electrolytes to make a sports drink for athletes.

DRI   An AI has recently been set at 550 and 425 milligrams/day for male and female adults, respectively. Lesser amounts have been established for adolescents and children. No DV has been established. The UL is 3.5 grams/day.

Food Sources   Choline is found in most foods, particularly as lecithin (phosphotidylcholine) in animal foods and free choline in plants. Milk, liver, and eggs are good animal sources, while good plant sources include vegetables, legumes, nuts, seeds, and wheat germ. Zeisel and Niculescu note that normal diets deliver sufficient choline.

Major Functions   Choline functions as a precursor for lecithin, a phospholipid in cell membranes. Choline is also involved in the formation of acetylcholine, an important neurotransmitter in the central nervous system.

Deficiency: Health and Physical Performance   As choline is found in most foods as part of cell membranes, choline deficiency is very rare. The only research available, involving individuals fed a choline-deficient solution, revealed the development of fatty livers and liver damage. Plasma choline levels have been reported to be significantly reduced following exhaustive exercise such as marathon running, and thus a possible reduction in acetylcholine levels in the nervous system may be theorized to be a contributing factor to the development of fatigue. However, exercise performance was not evaluated in these reports.

Supplementation: Health and Physical Performance   As choline deficiency is very rare, the effects of choline supplementation on health status has received little research attention. On the other hand, its effects on exercise performance has been the focus of several studies in recent years. According to Zeisel and Niculescu, several reports indicate that choline administration accelerated synthesis and release of acetylcholine by neurons.

Research has shown that choline supplementation, either as choline salts or lecithin preparations, will increase blood choline levels at rest and during prolonged exercise. Some preliminary field and laboratory research has suggested increased plasma choline levels are associated with a significantly decreased time to run 20 miles and improved mood states of cyclists 40 minutes after completion of a cycle ergometer ride to exhaustion. On the other hand, well-controlled laboratory research has revealed that choline supplementation, although increasing plasma choline levels, exerted no effect on either brief, high-intensity anaerobic cycling tests lasting about 2 minutes, or on more prolonged aerobic exercise tasks lasting about 70 minutes.

Based on these equivocal findings, several reviewers recommended more research with choline supplementation, particularly controlled laboratory research involving prolonged aerobic endurance exercise tasks greater than 2 hours duration. In this regard, Warber and others, in a double-blind, placebo-controlled, crossover study, recently evaluated the effect of choline supplementation (6 g total free choline) on performance of trained Army Rangers during and after 4 hours of strenuous exercise. Although choline supplementation increased plasma choline levels by 128 percent, there were no significant effects on any exercise performance measure, including a treadmill run to exhaustion following the 4-hour treadmill exercise protocol. In a short-term supplementation field study, Buchman and others had 12 marathoners consume either a lecithin supplement or placebo one day prior to the Houston marathon. The lecithin supplement provided approximately 1.1 grams of choline on a daily basis, or 2.2 grams total. Although the lecithin supplementation increased plasma choline concentration while the placebo group experienced a significant decrease, there were no significant differences between marathon running times.

Excessive choline intake may lead to a fishy body odor, gastrointestinal distress, vomiting, and low blood pressure. A UL of 3.5 grams/day has been set for adults, and smaller amounts have been set for adolescents and children.

Prudent Recommendations   Given the evidence that choline deficiency states are very rare, and that supplementation does not appear to enhance health or exercise performance, choline supplementation is not recommended. A balanced diet will provide adequate choline.

Vitamin B complex

Because several of the vitamins in the B complex work together in energy metabolism, a number of studies have investigated the effect of either a deficiency or supplement of more than one vitamin upon physical performance. Several of these studies were well-controlled experiments during World War II, but contemporary evidence is also available. The Consumers Union has also indicated a growing body of research has investigated the role of various B vitamins, particularly folate and B_6, as a means to help prevent heart disease and other serious cardiovascular problems.

Deficiency: Health and Physical Performance   As noted previously, a deficiency of folate has been associated with elevated homocysteine levels. Deficiencies in several other B vitamins, vitamin B_6 and B_{12}, have also been associated with increased plasma homocysteine. The Consumers Union cited a recent analysis of 72 studies concluding that very high levels of homocysteine can predict heart attack and stroke.

As might be expected from evidence presented on deficiencies of individual vitamins, a deficiency of several B vitamins together would negatively affect physical performance. This theory has been supported by those studies in which daily intake was reduced to less than 50 percent of the RDA. Several studies detailed by van der Beek in his review from the Netherlands have shown that a daily intake of less than one-third of the Dutch RDA for several of the B vitamins (B_1, B_2, B_6) and vitamin C leads to a dramatic decrease of VO_2 max and the anaerobic threshold in less than 4 weeks. The reduction in performance occurred even when other vitamins in the diet were supplemented at twice the RDA. In the most recent study VO_2 max decreased by 10 percent and the onset of blood lactate accumulation (anaerobic threshold) decreased approximately 20 percent after 8 weeks of a deficient diet. The findings support earlier research showing a significant decrease in endurance capacity with a B complex deficiency.

Supplementation: Health and Physical Performance

Some research has found that folic acid supplementation (5 mg/day), along with vitamin B_6 supplementation (250 mg/day), over a 2-year time span could lower blood pressure in clinically healthy individuals. Combined with other beneficial findings from their laboratory, van Dijk and others suggested such supplementation is associated with a decreased risk of CHD. However, results from experimental studies are not promising. In the largest clinical trial, the Vitamin Intervention for Stroke Prevention (VISP) study, B vitamin supplementation (folic acid, 2 mg; vitamin B_6, 400 mcg; vitamin B_{12}, 400 mcg) modestly lowered serum homocysteine levels, but had no effect on recurrent stroke, coronary events, or death. Furthermore, in a study with heart attack survivors, those taking a combination of folic acid (800 mcg) and vitamin B_6 (40 mg) actually had an increased risk of heart attack and stroke. However, Schwammenthal and Tanne noted that the VISP study had some limitations, and both studies involved individuals with cardiovascular disease. Additional research is merited with healthy adults.

In general, research supports the idea that individuals who obtain adequate vitamins through a balanced diet will not improve performance through the use of B complex supplements. However, a number of studies, several with children, have shown that when a deficiency state is corrected by vitamin supplements, physical performance is restored to normal. Moreover, some research with large dosages of B_1, B_6, and B_{12} (about 60–200 times the RDA) has shown increases in fine motor control and performance in pistol shooting. Bonke suggested the beneficial effect was related to the role of these vitamins in promoting the development of neurotransmitters that induce relaxation. Additional research is needed to confirm this finding.

Several of the principal Dutch investigators in this area, such as van Erp-Baart and Saris, suggest that B complex supplementation may be useful in sports with a high energy expenditure if these athletes consume large amounts of foods with empty Calories—high-sugar and high-fat foods. This again stresses the importance of eating foods that are high in nutrient value.

Prudent Recommendations

Vitamin B complex supplementation does not appear to be needed for the individual consuming a balanced diet of wholesome, natural foods. However, consuming fortified foods or supplements to provide adequate amounts of all B vitamins for potential health benefits may be prudent. Moreover, athletes involved in intensive training for endurance-type sports and consuming highly processed foods may benefit from a B complex supplement.

Vitamin C (ascorbic acid)

Vitamin C, or **ascorbic acid,** is a water-soluble vitamin. Its alleged effects upon health and physical performance have been the subject of much controversy.

DRI The vitamin C RDA for adult males is 90 mg/day and 75 mg/day for adult females. Slightly lower amounts are recommended for children, while somewhat larger amounts are recommended during pregnancy and lactation. The DV is only 60 mg, while the UL has been set at 2,000 mg/day for adults and lower amounts for children and adolescents. For current DRI, see the tables on the inside front and back covers.

Food Sources The best food sources of vitamin C are fruits and vegetables, primarily the citrus fruits and the leafy parts of green vegetables. Excellent sources include oranges, grapefruit, broccoli, and salad greens. Other good sources are green peppers, potatoes, strawberries, and tomatoes. One orange contains the RDA. Milk, meats, and grain products are low in vitamin C. Some products are fortified with vitamin C. Keep in mind when reading food labels that the DV is only 60 milligrams, while the RDA is 75 and 90 for adult females and males, respectively. A food label indicating one serving is 100 percent of the vitamin C RDA would contain only about 67 percent of the current RDA for males.

Major Functions Although vitamin C does not directly participate in enzyme-catalyzed conversions of substrate to product, Jacob suggests it modifies mineral ions in the enzymes to make them active. Vitamin C has a number of different functions in the body, some of which have important implications for the physically active individual. Its principal role is in the synthesis of collagen, which is necessary for the formation and maintenance of the connective tissues of the body such as cartilage, tendon, and bone. Vitamin C is also involved in the formation of certain hormones and neurotransmitters, such as epinephrine (adrenaline), which are secreted during stressful situations like exercise. It helps absorb some forms of iron from the intestinal tract—about a two to fourfold increased absorption—and is involved in the synthesis of RBC. Vitamin C helps regulate the metabolism of folic acid, cholesterol, and amino acids. It is also important in the healing of wounds through the development of scar tissue. Finally, vitamin C is a powerful antioxidant.

Deficiency: Health and Physical Performance Serious deficiencies of vitamin C are rare in industrialized societies because fresh or frozen fruits and vegetables are abundant. Also, the human body has a pool of vitamin C ranging from 1.5–3.0 grams. However, smoking, aspirin, oral contraceptives, and stress may increase the need for this vitamin, and a recent study by Johnston and others reported marginal vitamin C status in 12–16 percent of college students. The major deficiency disease is scurvy, a disintegration of the connective tissue in the gums, skin, tendons, and cartilage that may develop in a month on a vitamin C-free diet. Typical symptoms include bleeding gums, rupture of blood vessels in the skin, impaired wound healing, muscle cramps, and weakness. Anemia also may develop.

Observations by Ness and others indicate that adequate vitamin C intake is associated with increased serum HDL-cholesterol levels, reduced serum triglycerides, and lower blood pressure. Adequate vitamin C is also needed to maintain optimal antioxidant functions. Thus, inadequate vitamin C may increase the risk for various chronic diseases. Some epidemiological research has indicated that individuals with low plasma levels of vitamin C, most often associated with a vitamin deficiency, had a higher incidence of CHD and stroke. For example, Kurl and others evaluated the effect of serum levels of vitamin C on the incidence of stroke over a 12-year period, and found that those with the lowest levels had a 2.4-fold greater risk of stroke than those with the highest levels, especially among hypertensive and overweight men. Additionally, the Consumers Union noted that men with the lowest levels of plasma vitamin C had a 57 percent higher risk of dying from any cause, and a 62 percent higher risk of cancer death, than men with the highest levels. The effects were not seen in women, possibly because they had far more hormone-sensitive cancers, which seem to be unaffected by the vitamin. However, other research from Japan has shown similar benefits, and the vitamin C was consumed mainly from foods, not supplements. Thus, the Consumers Union indicated the health benefits may be from other substances in foods that accompany vitamin C.

It is obvious that many of the symptoms of a vitamin C deficiency we have cited would impair physical performance. Sensations of weakness could adversely affect all types of performance, whereas anemia would hamper aerobic endurance. Data available from several studies with vitamin C–deficient subjects do suggest such an effect, particularly the widely known Minnesota starvation experiments during World War II, directed by Ancel Keys.

Supplementation: Health and Physical Performance Vitamin C supplementation has been claimed to have significant health benefits, most notably the prevention of CHD and cancer. Because vitamin C is an antioxidant, and because many related supplementation studies have included other antioxidant vitamins (beta-carotene and vitamin E), we will discuss its effects on chronic disease and prevention of muscle tissue damage in physically active individuals later in this chapter.

There is some debate regarding the safety of megadoses of vitamin C. Several investigators have found that excessive amounts of vitamin C, such as 5–10 grams daily, may produce some undesirable side effects such as diarrhea; destruction of vitamin B_{12} in the diet; excessive excretion of vitamin B_6; decreased copper bioavailability; predisposition to gout, creating pain in the joints; and formation of kidney stones from oxalate salts, one of the breakdown products of vitamin C. Although for some individuals, increased iron absorption is a beneficial effect of vitamin C, it may be a major health problem for individuals prone to iron-storage disease, discussed in the next chapter. Moreover, one study reported increased markers of oxidative DNA damage in some subjects when vitamin C and iron supplements were taken together. Excess vitamin C may potentiate the oxidative effects of iron. Excessive amounts of vitamin C also may interfere with the correct interpretation of certain blood and urine tests. Finally, several case studies revealed the development of a condition known as rebound scurvy when the individual stopped taking the supplements. The researchers suggested a mechanism whereby the increased activity of an enzyme in the body that destroys excess vitamin C during the supplement stages continued after the supplements were stopped, leading to a deficiency and symptoms of scurvy.

Conversely, others have reported megadoses to be relatively harmless because excessive amounts are excreted by the kidneys. They criticize the research upon which claims of adverse effects are based, noting that some of the conclusions rest on isolated case studies. Others support a middle viewpoint, noting that larger doses may be harmless to many, but certain individuals may be prone to problems, such as those who have a family history of kidney stones. For example, in a recent highly-controlled supplementation study, Levine and others saw evidence of oxalates appearing in the urine when subjects were supplemented with 1,000 milligrams of vitamin C per day. This was a short-term study and no observations of kidney stones were detected, but increased oxalates could lead to stone formation over time in those at risk. However, in a longer prospective study involving men between the ages of 40 and 75 with no history of kidney stones, Curhan and others found that after 6 years of follow-up there was no association between vitamin C intake—up to levels of 250–1,500 milligrams per day—and kidney stone formation. Nevertheless, Gerster notes that those at risk for kidney stones should restrict daily vitamin C intake to about 100 mg. The National Academy of Sciences recommends against the routine use of large supplements. Megadose supplementation with vitamin C remains controversial, and the interested reader is referred to the opposing viewpoints presented by Herbert and Enstrom.

The effect of vitamin C supplementation upon physical performance has received considerable attention, mainly because it is one of the vitamins that athletes consume in rather substantial quantities. Both early and contemporary research have shown that vitamin C supplementation improves physical performance in subjects who were vitamin C-deficient, but a thorough analysis of these studies supports the general conclusion that vitamin C supplementation does not increase physical performance capacity in subjects who are not vitamin deficient. Bell and others found that vitamin C, 500 milligrams daily for 30 days, did not increase VO_2 max or cardiac output in either young or older men. No solid experimental evidence supports the use of megadoses of 5–10 grams that some athletes take. The interested reader may consult the reviews by Gerster, Keith, and Peake.

On the other hand, because exercise is a stressor, some investigators have recommended that the active individual may need slightly more vitamin C than the RDA, for example, 200–300 milligrams per day. Some research with runners doing 5–10 miles a day does not support this viewpoint; in any case, this amount could easily be obtained by wise selection of foods high in vitamin C content. Keith also suggests vitamin C supplementation may be beneficial to heat acclimation, a topic that merits additional research with trained athletes.

Although exercise normally promotes health benefits, Nieman notes that in contrast to moderate levels of physical activity, prolonged and intensive exertion, such as running an ultramarathon, causes numerous changes in the human immune system that may predispose to certain illnesses, such as upper respiratory tract infections (URTI). Large doses of vitamin C have been claimed to strengthen the immune system and prevent URTI. Some early research suggests the antihistamine effects of vitamin C may decrease the severity of some symptoms of a cold. For example, Peters and others reported 600 milligrams of vitamin C supplementation for 21 days prior to an ultramarathon reduced symptoms of respiratory tract infections. However, recent research revealed that 200 milligrams of vitamin C daily will lead to full saturation of plasma and white blood cells, which should optimize immune functions associated with vitamin C. It may be possible that smaller amounts of vitamin C, such as 200 milligrams, may provide effects comparable to those seen with larger doses.

In general, although the duration of the symptoms may be reduced slightly, a recent review and meta-analysis indicated that vitamin C (>200 milligrams per day) supplementation had no effect on developing a cold or its severity. Moreover, vitamin C supplementation does not appear to benefit immune function, even in ultraendurance athletes. David Nieman, an international expert in exercise and immune function, along with his colleagues recently reported no effect of 7 days of vitamin C supplementation (1500 mg/day) on oxidative and immune responses in runners both during and after a competitive ultramarathon race. In a recent review of his own and other research, Nieman indicated that vitamin C supplementation, as well as combined antioxidant vitamin supplementation, is not an effective countermeasure to exercise-induced immunosuppression.

Prudent Recommendations A recent review by Weber and others suggests that adequate vitamin C intake may be associated with various health benefits for certain individuals. The amounts recommended approximate 200 milligrams per day, an amount easily obtained in the diet. Currently, the Consumers Union indicates it is premature to recommend vitamin C supplements, but it does recommend a diet rich in fruits and vegetables, which as previously noted, contain not only substantial amounts of vitamin C but other healthful substances as well. Eating the recommended 5–9 fruits and vegetables daily should supply about 200–350 milligrams of vitamin C. This is a solid recommendation for both the sedentary and physically active individual.

Key Concept Recap

▶ The water-soluble vitamins consist of those in the B complex and vitamin C. Choline is also a water-soluble nutrient for which DRI have been established.

▶ Water-soluble vitamin deficiencies are rare in developed countries. However, supplements may be advised for some individuals. Women of childbearing age should consume 400 micrograms of folic acid daily in order to prevent the possibility of birth defects in the newborn. Elderly individuals should obtain adequate vitamin B_{12} through fortified foods or vitamin supplements.

▶ In general, water-soluble vitamins are not toxic in excess. However, excess niacin may interfere with proper liver function and excess vitamin B_6 has been associated with neurological problems.

▶ A water-soluble vitamin deficiency may impair physical performance, usually by interfering with some phase of the energy-producing process. In some cases, impairment may be seen in 2–4 weeks on a deficient diet.

▶ Supplementation with water-soluble vitamins has not been shown to enhance sports performance.

Vitamin Supplements: Ergogenic Aspects

Like the general population, the vast majority of athletes receive the RDA for most vitamins in their daily diet. It is true that some studies report that certain groups of athletes receive less than the RDA for some vitamins or even have indicators of a biochemical deficiency, but other studies, such as that by Ziegler and others involving athletes in weight-control sports with low energy intake, find that biochemical indexes of nutritional status are usually within normal limits. Sarah Short of Syracuse University, in her exhaustive review of dietary surveys with athletes, and Larry Armstrong and Carl Maresh in their review, found that vitamin deficiency symptoms rarely are reported. Moreover, in his review, Michael Fogelholm reported that, at least in developed countries, dietary vitamin intake by athletes is more than required for maximal exercise performance. Nevertheless, elite endurance athletes, such as Tour de France cyclists, and the majority of both high school and college athletes believe vitamins are essential for success, and it is a matter of fact that many consume vitamin supplements either as nutritional insurance or in the hope of improving performance. For example, in a review of over fifty-one studies involving data on more than ten thousand male and female athletes in fifteen sports, Sobol and Marquart reported that the overall mean prevalence of athletes' supplement use was 46 percent, a finding supported in a recent survey by Krumbach and others. Elite athletes use supplements more than college or high school athletes, and women more often than men. Athletes appear to use supplements more than the general population, and some take high doses that may lead to nutritional problems.

In recent years some vitamin manufacturers have turned their attention to the physically active individual, including older athletes, suggesting through advertisements that their special product enhances athletic performance. In her review, Priscilla Clarkson of the University of Massachusetts suggested such advertisements were a major reason for the use of vitamin supplements by athletes.

Should physically active individuals take vitamin supplements?

There may be some good reasons for physically active individuals to take vitamin supplements. For example, in certain types of athletic activity such as wrestling, gymnastics, and ballet, participants may undertake prolonged semi-starvation or starvation diets. As discussed in chapter 10, this is not a recommended procedure, but some athletes may do it to obtain or maintain an optimal body weight for competition. In such cases, when the energy intake may be well below 1,200–1,600 Calories per day, many surveys have shown that the athlete may not be receiving enough vitamins. Research suggests that vitamin depletion, mainly the water-soluble vitamins, can occur rapidly in humans on low-Calorie diets and that these vitamins should be replaced daily. Athletes may also need vitamin supplementation if they are subsisting on poor diets, as discussed in the next section. Moreover, some vitamin requirements are increased in pregnant women and the elderly, so those who exercise need to consume vitamin-rich diets.

Sacheck and Roubenoff recommended vitamin supplements for elderly athletes when adequate dietary intakes cannot be obtained. In general, however, individuals should consult appropriate health professionals before self-prescribing vitamin supplements, particularly megadoses of individual vitamins.

As is obvious from the evidence presented in this chapter, the athlete who is on a balanced diet has no need for vitamin supplementation to improve performance. Nevertheless, some interesting hypotheses suggest antioxidant vitamin supplements may help prevent muscle tissue damage during training, and a variety of special vitamin-like compounds have been marketed specifically for athletes.

Can the antioxidant vitamins prevent muscle damage during training?

As noted previously, individual supplementation with either vitamin C or E has not been shown to enhance exercise performance, with the possible exception of vitamin E at altitude. Overall, recent reviews by Powers and Sen and their colleagues concluded that antioxidants, including antioxidant cocktails containing several vitamins, have not been shown to reliably improve physical performance.

It has been known for years that certain forms of physical training for sports, particularly intense training, can induce muscle damage and soreness. Eccentric muscle contractions, such as those incurred in the quadriceps muscle when running downhill, may cause mechanical trauma to the muscle and connective tissue resulting in soreness during the following days. Sen indicates that although an *acute* bout of exercise increases the activity of antioxidant enzymes in the body, strenuous exercise may generate reactive oxygen species (ROS) to a level to overwhelm tissue antioxidant defense systems. The result is oxidative stress. The magnitude of the stress depends on the ability of the tissues to detoxify ROS. Excessive production of free radicals may induce lipid peroxidation, possibly damaging the integrity of cellular and subcellular membranes in the muscles, leading to muscle soreness. For example, Child and others reported an increase in total antioxidant capacity (TAC) during a half-marathon (13.1 mile) run, but the increase in TAC did not prevent exercise-induced lipid peroxidation and muscle damage.

Recent reviews by Ji and Powers and others noted that *chronic* exercise training increased the activity of several antioxidant enzymes, including superoxide dismutase and glutathione peroxidase, most notably the latter which is proposed to be the most important to muscle cell survival during increased oxidative stress, as during exercise. These endogenous antioxidant enzymes help prevent exercise-induced muscle damage.

Theoretically, prevention of muscle tissue damage may enable the athlete to train more effectively, the desired result being improvement in competition. Some endurance athletes will train at altitude in attempts to enhance their oxygen-delivery ability, and as noted earlier in this chapter, vitamin E supplements may convey some benefits when exercising at altitude. Additionally, older individuals may be more susceptible to oxidative stress during exercise, for optimal functioning of the free radical-scavenging enzymes appears to decline with the aging process. Millions of older individuals perform aerobic exercise for the related health benefits and often become involved in various forms of athletic competition, including local, national, and international competition for athletes over age 40. Companies are now marketing *Super Antioxidants* to speed recovery in athletes during sport trainnig. Do they help?

Numerous studies have been conducted to evaluate the effect of antioxidant supplements on exercise-induced muscle damage and, in some studies, on performance. The designs of these studies have varied, including differences in subjects (animals versus humans, young and old), methods to induce muscle soreness (e.g., downhill running versus level running; resistance exercise), the type and amount of supplement given, and the biochemical markers used to assess muscle damage. The most common supplements used were vitamins E and C, and beta-carotene, but coenzyme Q10, selenium, and other substances have also been used. Some studies used "antioxidant cocktails" consisting of approximately 800 IU of vitamin E, 1,000 milligrams of vitamin C, and 10–30 milligrams of beta-carotene. The markers of muscle tissue damage include serum enzymes that may leak from the muscle such as creatine kinase (CK) and lactic acid dehydrogenase (LDH), end products of lipid peroxidation such as malondialdehyde (MDA), myoglobin leakage from the muscle tissue, and others.

Overall, the results of these studies may be regarded as promising. A number of studies such as the recent report by Itoh and others, have shown some beneficial effects of antioxidant supplementation, that is, reduced markers of muscle tissue damage when compared to the placebo treatment. Benefits have been reported for both young and old physically active individuals. Most studies used multiple markers of muscle tissue damage, and in some cases one marker of muscle damage would be improved by the antioxidant supplements but another would be unaffected. Some studies compared different antioxidants, for example, C versus E, reporting a beneficial effect of one but not the other.

On the other hand, other recent studies, such as those led by Avery, Dawson, and Thompson, have reported no significant benefits of antioxidant supplementation to prevent muscle tissue damage during exercise. Moreover, Nieman and others found that vitamin E supplementation actually promoted lipid peroxidation and inflammation during an Ironman-distance triathlon.

The role of antioxidants to prevent exercise-induced muscle tissue damage was the subject of several recent reviews, and the opinions are mixed regarding their efficacy. Adams and Best indicated that although animal studies have shown some promising effects of antioxidant supplementation to lessen exercise-induced oxidative stress damage, studies with humans are less convincing. Relative to vitamin E, Jackson and others concluded that supplements are unlikely to reliably reduce the severity of muscle damage. Viitala and Newhouse also concluded that vitamin E supplementation does not appear to decrease exercise-induced lipid peroxidation in humans. Clarkson and Thompson noted that whether the body's own natural antioxidant defense system is sufficient to combat oxidative stress during prolonged exercise or whether antioxidant supplements are needed is unknown, but trained athletes who received antioxidant supplements have shown evidence of reduced oxidative stress. Ji notes that the aging process lessens the exercise training-induced improvement in natural antioxidant enzymes and suggests exercise training in older athletes might be assisted with antioxidant supplementation in attempts to optimize antioxidant defense. Sacheck and Blumberg concluded that the use of dietary antioxidants like vitamin E to reduce exercise-induced muscle injury have met with mixed success, which seems to be the prevailing viewpoint. All reviewers indicate more research is needed to address this issue and to provide guidelines for recommendations to athletes.

Prudent Recommendations In a recent review, Sen noted that universal recommendations specifying types and dosages of antioxidants are difficult to make. Some reviewers suggest there are no clear guidelines regarding optimal dietary intake of antioxidant vitamins beyond those provided by the RDA. However, others note that the prudent use of antioxidant supplementation can provide insurance against a suboptimal diet and/or the elevated demands of intense physical activity, and thus may be recommended to limit the effects of oxidative stress in individuals performing regular, heavy exercise. For example, Takanami and others are convinced that vitamin E contributes to preventing exercise-induced lipid peroxidation and possible muscle tissue damage, and recommend that athletes supplement with 100–200 milligrams of vitamin E daily to help prevent exercise-induced oxidative damage.

Most experts in this area recommend physically active individuals obtain antioxidant vitamins naturally from food. Increasing the consumption of fruits, fruit juices, and vegetables will enable athletes to obtain the recommended amounts of beta-carotene (10–30 milligrams) and vitamin C (250–1,000 milligrams) but it would be difficult to obtain 100–200 IU of vitamin E through natural dietary sources. Watson and others indicate that there seems no valid reason to recommend antioxidant supplements to most athletes, except in those known to be consuming a low-antioxidant diet for prolonged periods. For the athlete who wants to supplement vitamin E, inexpensive over-the-counter preparations are available in 100 and 200 IU capsules. For health benefits, remember that most research documents beneficial effects when these vitamins, along with other phytochemicals, are obtained through natural foods, primarily fruits and vegetables.

How effective are the special vitamin supplements marketed for athletes?

Special athletic vitamin packs have been appearing on the market—even in single packets at your local convenience store—that have been advertised as a means for the athlete to increase energy and reach peak performance. Many of these have simply been multivitamin-mineral supplements, while others have been special concoctions like bee pollen and ginseng. Three such products will be highlighted.

Multivitamin-Mineral Supplements Because in human metabolism vitamins often work together, and often in conjunction with minerals, the ergogenic potential of multivitamin-mineral compounds has been studied for half a century. In a review of the older research, Williams reported that although results of a number of studies suggested ergogenic effects, the experimental designs

were usually poorly controlled. In contrast, contemporary research indicates that such supplements, consumed for substantial periods, are not ergogenic for the athlete on a balanced diet. From Timothy Noakes' laboratory in South Africa, Weight conducted a thorough 9-month double-blind, placebo, crossover study. Although multivitamin-mineral supplements did raise blood levels of some vitamins, the authors reported that 3 months of supplementation did not improve maximal oxygen uptake, the anaerobic (lactate) threshold, treadmill run time to exhaustion, or running performance in a 15-kilometer time trial. Anita Singh and her colleagues provided either a high-potency multivitamin-mineral supplement or a placebo to 22 healthy, physically active males for 90 days. The vitamin dosages ranged from 300 to 6,000 percent of the RDA. Although serum levels of many of the vitamins increased, there were no significant effects on physiological variables during a 90-minute run, nor were there any effects on maximal heart rate, VO_2 max, or time to exhaustion. Finally, Richard Telford, and his colleagues matched 82 nationally ranked Australian athletes in training at the Australian Institute of Sport and assigned them to either a supplement or placebo treatment. The supplement contained an assortment of vitamins and minerals, ranging from about 100 to 5,000 percent of the RDA. The supplement was taken for approximately 7–8 months, and the subjects were tested on a variety of sport specific tests (e.g., swim bench) as well as common tests of strength (torque), anaerobic power (400-meter run), and aerobic endurance (12-minute run and VO_2 max). These investigators reported no significant effect of the supplement on any measure of physical performance when compared with athletes whose vitamin and mineral RDA were met by dietary intake.

Thus, all of the current reputable research refutes an ergogenic effect of multivitamin-mineral supplements in adequately nourished athletes.

Prudent recommendations Although multivitamin-mineral supplements may not enhance athletic performance in well-nourished athletes, those involved in weight-control sports with limited caloric intake might consider taking a simple one-a-day supplement with no more than 100 percent of the RDA for the essential vitamins and minerals.

Bee Pollen **Bee pollen** has been marketed almost specifically for athletes, primarily runners, as a means to improve performance. Chemical analysis of bee pollen reveals it is a mixture of vitamins, minerals, amino acids, and other nutrients. Although no specific physiological effects of bee pollen have been documented, theoretical ergogenic effects are based on some of the roles that vitamins have in the body. Advertising claims for bee pollen cite questionable research: a field study showing faster recovery rates in athletes who took pollen supplements. However, six well-designed studies using double-blind placebo protocols revealed that supplementation with bee pollen had no significant effect upon VO_2 max, other physiological responses to exercise, endurance capacity, or rate of recovery from exhausting exercise.

Prudent recommendations Bee pollen supplements are not recommended for physically active individuals. Moreover, caution is necessary as some individuals may experience an allergic reaction.

CoQ₁₀ The compound **CoQ₁₀,** also known as coenzyme Q_{10} and ubiquinone, is actually a lipid but has characteristics common to vitamins; its chemical structure is similar to vitamin K. CoQ_{10} is found in the mitochondria of all mammalian tissues, but concentrations are relatively high in the heart and other organs in humans. It plays an important role in oxidative metabolism within the mitochondria, facilitating the aerobic generation of ATP as part of the electron transfer system. CoQ_{10} also functions as an antioxidant. It has been used therapeutically for treatment of cardiovascular disease since 1965 because it may protect heart tissue from damage associated with inadequate oxygen, although Webb recently noted that not all scientists agree it has shown beneficial applications. Tran and others noted that if used therapeutically, coenzyme Q_{10} should be used only in conjunction with other drugs and not relied on by itself for the treatment of any cardiovascular health problem.

Because some studies have shown that CoQ_{10} may improve heart function, maximal oxygen uptake, and exercise performance in cardiac patients, it has been theorized to be ergogenic for athletes. Moreover, Bucci has cited a number of studies indicating that CoQ_{10} levels are lower in trained athletes compared to sedentary controls and that oral supplementation with CoQ_{10} will increase tissue levels, two factors providing theoretical support for its role as an ergogenic. Theoretically, CoQ_{10} should benefit endurance performance because of its role in aerobic metabolism. However, Demopoulous and others suggest CoQ_{10} might actually be ergolytic, indicating that when taken orally it may actually auto-oxidize, producing free radicals and damaging the mitochondria.

Are CoQ_{10} supplements ergogenic? In his book on nutritional ergogenics, Bucci cites results from six studies with sedentary young men, sedentary middle-aged women, aerobically trained volleyball players, male professional basketball players, and endurance runners supporting an ergogenic effect of CoQ_{10}, noting improvements in one or more of the following: VO_2 max, exercise performance, indicators of enhanced aerobic capacity, and improved antioxidant function. Most of these studies were presented in a book entitled *Biomedical and Clinical Aspects of Coenzyme Q* and do not appear to have been published in refereed scientific journals. Moreover, a careful review of these studies indicated each suffered one or more flaws in proper experimental design, including no control group, no placebo, no randomization of order in which CoQ_{10} or placebo was given, and use of a submaximal heart rate exercise task to predict maximal oxygen uptake.

To be effective, the CoQ_{10} must get into the muscle and mitochondria. However, Svensson and others reported that although CoQ_{10} supplementation significantly increase CoQ_{10} plasma concentrations, there was no corresponding increase in the skeletal muscle or mitochondria.

There are several published studies regarding the effect of CoQ_{10} on exercise performance, but most that are available do not support its effectiveness as an ergogenic. For example, Weston and others, using 1 milligram of CoQ_{10} per kilogram body weight daily for 28 days, reported no beneficial effects on oxygen uptake, substrate use, or cycle ergometer exercise time to exhaustion in trained male cyclists and triathletes. Although serum CoQ_{10} levels were increased, Braun and others reported no effect of 100 milligrams daily for 8 weeks on submaximal physiological indicators of enhanced aerobic capacity, VO_2 max, time to exhaustion on a bicycle ergometer, or lipid peroxidation, indicating no effect on either aerobic metabolism or antioxidant function. Bonetti and others also found no effect of CoQ_{10} supplementation for 8 weeks on the aerobic power, including VO_2 peak and anaerobic threshold, of trained middle-aged cyclists. In a well-designed, double-blind, placebo, crossover study, Laaksonen and others supplemented both young and old physically trained males with 120 milligrams of CoQ_{10} per day for 6 weeks, and reported no significant effect on maximal oxygen uptake or on time to exhaus-tion in a progressive cycling task following 60 minutes of submaximal cycling. Actually, performance time in the placebo trial was significantly greater than the CoQ_{10} trial. Additionally, there were no effects of the CoQ_{10} supplement on MDA, a marker of lipid peroxidation. In yet another study from the Karolinska Institute in Sweden, Malm and others reported that CoQ_{10} supplementation (120 milligrams per day for 20 days) exerted no effect on fifteen high-intensity, anaerobic 10-second sprint tests on a cycle ergometer with 50 seconds recovery between each sprint. These investigators noted that, compared to the placebo groups, subjects taking the CoQ_{10} supplement showed evidence of muscle tissue damage. In actuality, the placebo group improved their performance in the cycle sprints, but the supplement group did not, suggesting that CoQ_{10} might be ergolytic. On the other hand, Ylikoski and others reported that CoQ_{10} supplementation (90 mg/day) improved several measures of performance, such as VO_2 max, in Finnish cross-country skiers, but they did not evaluate its effect on actual exercise performance.

CoQ_{10} is also one of the ingredients in a supplement (also containing vitamin E, inosine, and cytochrome C) widely advertised for endurance athletes, particularly triathletes. In a recent double-blind, placebo, crossover study, Snider and others reported that 4 weeks of supplementation with this commercial product had no ergogenic effect on an endurance task that consisted of a 90-minute treadmill run at 70 percent VO_2 max followed by a cycling test to exhaustion at 70 percent VO_2 max. In another study, Kaikkonen and others found that supplementation with both CoQ_{10} and vitamin E to marathon runners for three weeks had no beneficial effects on lipid peroxidation or muscle damage induced by running the marathon.

At the present time, the most contemporary published well-designed studies do not support an ergogenic effect of CoQ_{10} supplementation.

Prudent recommendations Given these findings, CoQ_{10} supplementation is not recommended for the physically active individual.

What's the bottom line regarding vitamin supplements for athletes?

Given the available scientific data, there does not appear to be a very strong case supporting an ergogenic effect of any single vitamin, vitamin-mineral combinations, or the various vitamin-like compounds. As noted, additional research is warranted for those that have some limited support as an ergogenic, for example, the effect of vitamin E on performance at altitude.

At the present time, the recommended advice is to obtain adequate vitamin nutrition through a well-planned diet. For example,

Melinda Manore noted that athletes involved in heavy training may need more of several vitamins, such as thiamin, riboflavin, and B₆ because they are involved in energy production, but the amount needed is only about twice the RDA and that may be easily obtained through the increased food intake associated with heavy training.

However, in a recent scientific roundtable exchange, Dan Benardot and three other sport nutrition experts indicated that some athletes may be at risk for a vitamin deficiency, such as those in weight-control sports and those who for one reason or another do not eat a well-balanced diet. Thus, some health professionals recommend vitamin supplementation, not only to prevent a deficiency that may impair sport performance, but also for beneficial health reasons as noted in the next section.

Key Concept Recap

▶ Although research findings regarding the ability of antioxidant vitamin supplements to prevent muscle tissue damage following intense exercise are equivocal, such supplements have not been shown to enhance sport or exercise performance.

▶ Results from well-controlled research generally indicated that multivitamin/mineral supplements and vitamin-like compounds, such as coenzyme Q₁₀, are not effective ergogenic aids.

Check for Yourself

Use a search engine on the Internet, such as www.google.com, and search for "vitamins." Check out the advertisements and claims, and compare to the text discussion.

Vitamin Supplements: Health Aspects

Vitamins are big business, being the most popular of all the dietary supplements. They are marketed to all segments of the population, from infant formulas to geriatric preparations, and for a wide variety of health reasons, ranging from combating the stress of everyday life to helping prevent heart disease and cancer. Surveys indicate that vitamin-supplement users have strong health beliefs about their effectiveness, and this is evident in the multibillion-dollar sales annually by the vitamin industry.

In the preceding sections, we have already covered each individual vitamin and the possible effects of deficiencies and supplementation upon health (review table 7.1 for a broad overview). This section summarizes prudent dietary recommendations for overall optimal vitamin nutrition, including the possible use of supplements, relative to health.

Can I obtain the vitamins I need through my diet?

Some advertisements for vitamin supplements may leave you with the impression that it is difficult, if not impossible, to obtain adequate vitamin nutrition through the typical American diet. In contrast, most health professional organizations focusing on nutrition,

such as the American Dietetic Association (ADA), support the view that a balanced diet will satisfy all nutrient needs of the healthy individual. There is some truth to both positions, for the typical diet of some individuals may not be a balanced diet. Our selection, storage, and preparation of food may lead to poor vitamin intake.

Vitamin intake may be inadequate for several reasons. First, the refining process of many foods removes vitamins. For example, the preparation of flour for white bread removes many of the vitamins found in the outer parts of the grain. Although some of these vitamins are returned by an enrichment process, not all are restored. Thus, many processed foods may be lower in total vitamin content than their natural counterparts. In some cases, however, processing actually increases the vitamin content of foods. Examples include the fortification of milk with vitamins A and D, grain products with folic acid, and the use of vitamin C as an antioxidant preservative in some foods. Second, improper storage of foods may lead to vitamin losses. Once fruits and vegetables are harvested, the vitamin content begins to diminish. In general, such foods should be refrigerated or frozen in airtight containers as applicable and stored in dark places to minimize vitamin losses caused by exposure to air, heat, and light. Third, improper preparation may also lead to significant vitamin losses from foods. Prolonged cooking, excessive heat, and cooking vegetables in water should be avoided. Steaming, microwave cooking, and the use of boiling bags and waterless cookware will help retain the natural vitamin content of foods. Thus, the individual who consumes a diet high in processed foods with empty Calories and does not store or prepare foods properly may receive less than the RDA for several vitamins.

The key to adequate vitamin nutrition is to consume a balanced diet of natural foods that have a high nutrient density. Buy foods in their natural state and store them properly as soon as possible. Prepare them to eat so as to minimize vitamin losses.

The position of the ADA is that the best nutritional strategy for promoting optimal health and reducing the risk of chronic disease is to obtain essential nutrients through a wide variety of foods. In this way, other nutrients, particularly minerals, will be obtained at the same time, as they also are natural constituents of the food we eat. Vitamins often work in conjunction with minerals, such as vitamin D and calcium, vitamin B₆ and magnesium, and vitamin E and selenium. By obtaining vitamins through the selection of a balanced diet containing wholesome, natural foods, we may be assured of receiving sufficient amounts of other nutrients necessary for optimal physiological functioning, in addition to various phytochemicals that may also confer some health benefits. Moreover, it is recommended that the active individual be selective in choosing foods. The stress of exercise can increase the utilization of some water-soluble and antioxidant vitamins, but these can be replaced easily if the extra Calories expended during exercise are replaced by foods with high nutrient density, that is, foods rich in vitamins and minerals. Table 7.2 presents a quick overview of foods containing substantial amounts of the major vitamins, while table 7.3 presents a list of ten foods, totaling approximately 1,200 Calories, that will provide at least 100 percent of the RDA for every vitamin, assuming adequate sunlight for vitamin D and intestinal synthesis of biotin and vitamin K.

TABLE 7.2 High-vitamin-content foods

Vitamin A	Folate
Beef liver, fish liver oils, egg yolks Milk, butter, cheese, fortified margarine Orange vegetables (carrots, sweet potatoes) Green vegetables (spinach, collards)	Meats, liver, eggs Milk Legumes Whole wheat products Green leafy vegetables

Thiamin (Vitamin B_1)	Vitamin B_{12} (Cobalamin)
Pork, legumes (dried peas and beans) Milk Nuts Whole-grain and enriched cereal products (bread) All vegetables Fruits	Meats, poultry, fish, eggs Milk, cheese, butter Not found in plant foods

Riboflavin (Vitamin B_2)	Biotin
Meats, liver, kidneys, eggs Milk, cheese Whole-grain and enriched cereal products Wheat germ Green leafy vegetables	Meats, liver, egg yolks Legumes, nuts Vegetables

Niacin	Vitamin C
Lean meats, organ meats (liver), poultry Legumes, peanuts, peanut butter Whole-grain and enriched cereal products	Citrus fruits, oranges, grapefruit, melons, berries, tomatoes Broccoli, brussels sprouts, cabbage, salad greens, green peppers, cauliflower

Vitamin B_6 (Pyridoxine)	Vitamin D
Meat, poultry, fish Whole-grain cereals, seeds Vegetables	Liver, tuna, salmon, cod liver oil, eggs Fortified milk and margarine

Pantothenic acid	Vitamin E
Meats, poultry, fish Milk, cheese Legumes Whole-grain products	Legumes, nuts, seeds Margarine, salad oils, wheat germ oil Green leafy vegetables

	Vitamin K
	Pork, liver, meats Green leafy vegetables, cauliflower, spinach, cabbage

Why are vitamin supplements often recommended?

Several recent reviews, most notably those by Fairfield and Fletcher, have indicated that there are many bona fide reasons for vitamin supplementation. In her review, Manore also indicated vitamin supplementation may be important for various groups of physically active individuals. Moreover, although still supporting the view that we should obtain our vitamins through healthful foods, the ADA in its recent position statement noted that additional vitamins and minerals from fortified foods and/or supplements can help some people meet their nutritional needs as specified by such standards as the DRI. Based on these and other reviews, the following groups of individuals may possibly benefit from supplementation.

- Women who are pregnant or lactating have an increased RDA or AI for most vitamins, so many physicians recommend a general vitamin supplement, particularly one containing adequate folic acid. Folic acid supplements are also recommended for all women of childbearing age.
- Individuals with certain diseases or disorders may have an increased need for a specific vitamin supplement. For example, supplements of folic acid and other B vitamins may be recommended for those at high risk for CHD and stroke. Additionally, an impaired ability to absorb fat decreases the availability of the fat-soluble vitamins, while a lack of the intrinsic factor necessitates provision of B_{12}.
- Individuals taking drugs to prevent various illnesses may experience a vitamin deficiency. For example, antibiotics kill

TABLE 7.3	1,200 Calorie diet containing at least 100% of the RDA or AI for each vitamin	
Food	**Amount**
Milk, skim, fortified with vitamins A and D	2 cups
Carrot	1 medium
Orange	1 average
Bread, whole wheat	4 slices
Chicken breast, roasted	3 ounces
Broccoli	1 stalk
Margarine	1 tablespoon
Cereal, Grape-Nuts	2 ounces
Tuna fish, in water	3 ounces
Cauliflower	1/2 cup

intestinal bacteria and decrease the production of vitamin K. In such cases, specific vitamins are prescribed by physicians. Use of social drugs, such as smoking nicotine cigarettes and drinking alcohol, may also increase vitamin needs.

- Elderly individuals have a greater RDA or AI for certain vitamins, such as B_6 and D, and may benefit from the synthetic form of vitamin B_{12} because of difficulty in absorbing the natural form.
- Vegans who abstain from foods fortified with vitamin B_{12} may need to take this specific vitamin supplement.
- Individuals who restrict energy intake for weight loss or maintenance of a low body weight, particularly under 1,200 Calories daily, may need a supplement to obtain the RDA.
- Physically active individuals who do not eat enough to maintain body weight during periods of high energy expenditure may also benefit from supplementation.
- Individuals who are intolerant to or purposely avoid certain foods, such as dairy products, may limit the intake of certain vitamins, such as riboflavin and vitamin D.
- Individuals who consume enough energy but, because of poor dietary choices, do not obtain the needed vitamins and minerals, will benefit from vitamin-mineral supplementation. This would be the case if one eats mainly highly processed foods or if one restricts one or more food groups (such as dairy products) in their diet.

Based on these viewpoints, Fletcher and Fairfield noted that most people do not consume an optimal amount of vitamins by diet alone. Pending strong evidence of effectiveness from randomized trials, they indicate that it appears *prudent* for all adults to take vitamin supplements.

If an individual feels he or she is not receiving a balanced diet for some reason—most medical authorities agree that a simple, balanced vitamin supplement containing 50–150 percent of the RDA or AI will not do any harm. There are a number of preparations on the market that contain the daily RDA or AI of most vitamins. However, the American Dietetic Association recommends low levels that do not exceed the RDA or AI for those who chose to use supplements, and the American Medical Association suggests that use of larger amounts be under medical supervision. Nevertheless, millions of Americans consume vitamin megadoses without such supervision.

Why do individuals take vitamin megadoses?

We have all heard of the adage "if a little bit is good, more is better." As already noted, vitamin nutrition for optimal health can be obtained from a proper diet, but foods must be selected wisely. Excluding choline, the adult male RDA or AI for all thirteen vitamins totals approximately 130 milligrams, yet some individuals are consuming prodigious amounts of vitamins—thousands of milligrams—via supplements, for a variety of health reasons, particularly to help deter the effects of aging and the development of various chronic diseases. For example, as discussed previously, niacin supplements in high doses may be useful therapy for reducing serum cholesterol levels. In general, however, Kim and others reported no increase in longevity among vitamin and mineral supplement users in the United States. Nevertheless, vitamins C and E are the two most popular supplements, and many individuals are taking beta-carotene supplements probably because all three possess antioxidant properties. Although most authorities indicate that much needs to be learned, they also note that some interesting data are emerging in relation to the health aspects of antioxidants as found naturally in foods and as dietary supplements.

Do foods rich in antioxidant vitamins help deter disease?

As discussed on page 239, free radicals may be very reactive with body tissues, causing cellular damage by oxidation of unsaturated fats in cellular and subcellular membranes. Free radicals are theorized to contribute to the aging process and to the development of more than sixty diseases, including cardiovascular disease and cancer. Discussing the free radical theory of aging, Koltover estimated that our life span could be 250 years but for the damages due to free radicals. Various antioxidant enzymes in the cells counteract undesirable effects of free radicals, but there is increasing evidence that what we eat may also help to prevent certain adverse health effects associated with free radicals.

Fruits and vegetables, along with whole grains, nuts, and seeds, are rich in antioxidants, including vitamins C and E and carotenoids (beta-carotene, lycopene, lutein, zeaxanthin), as well as other micronutrients and phytochemicals. Mehta indicated that there is no doubt that antioxidants and other micronutrients, taken in their proper form in vegetables and fruits, confer a number of overall health benefits. Prevention of cancer and cardiovascular disease appear to be the two major health benefits. Several recent reviews, including those by Lee, Gaziano and Hennekens, and by Steinmetz and Potter indicated that the evidence for a protective effect of increased consumption of vegetables and fruits, foods rich in antioxidant vitamins, is consistent for cancers of the stomach, esophagus, lung, endometrium, pancreas, and colon, and that the most effective are raw vegetables. The precise mechanism underlying this possible protective effect is not known, although phytochemicals found in some vegetables may block tumor formation. Other investigators believe the antioxidant vitamins (vitamin C, vitamin E, beta-carotene) found naturally in vegetables and fruits may confer the protective effect, for various epidemiologic studies have shown that high serum levels of some antioxidant vitamins are associated with a decreased risk of cancer. In a review, Gladys Block presented biochemical data suggesting that optimal antioxidant intake may protect against environmental factors, such as cigarette smoke and polluted air, that may generate free radicals and subsequent cancer. Antioxidant vitamins may also strengthen the immune system, a major defense against cancer, particularly as we grow older. Meydani indicated cells of the immune system have a very high content of polyunsaturated fatty acids, which makes them susceptible to oxidative damage. When oxidized, polyunsaturated fats may produce PGE_2, an eicosanoid that may suppress immune function by interfering with several major functions, such as the activity of T cells. Dietary antioxidant vitamins may help prevent this undesirable oxidation.

Research also suggests that dietary antioxidant vitamins may help to prevent cardiovascular disease. Several epidemiologic studies indicated high intakes of vitamin E are associated with a reduced risk for coronary heart disease. Rimm and others reported a reduced risk in men, while Kushi and Stampfer, with their associates, reported a reduced risk in women. Prevention of oxidation of LDL-cholesterol and the subsequent formation of atherosclerosis is theorized to be the primary underlying mechanism. Antioxidants may also reduce factors that may lead to blood clot formation, including platelet aggregation and coagulability.

Universally, all reviewers recommend diets rich in fruits, vegetables, whole grains, and other vitamin-rich foods as the best means of obtaining the antioxidant vitamins, and along with other potential health-promoting phytochemicals, as the most effective dietary strategy to promote health and prevent disease. In this regard, the National Cancer Institute has sponsored a campaign called "Five a Day for Better Health," meaning to eat at least five servings of fruits and vegetables daily. The point is stressed that five is the minimum number of servings and more should be consumed, hopefully five servings *each* of fruits and vegetables.

However, the health benefits of a diet rich in antioxidant-containing nutrients presented here are based on epidemiological studies. Such diets appear to protect against CHD and other chronic diseases, but the underlying mechanism is not known. Fruits and vegetables are rich in various vitamins that may exert beneficial health effects, such as the antioxidant vitamins, folate, and vitamins B_6 and B_{12}, and these vitamins may individually or collectively account for such positive health effects. As noted, these foods also contain other micronutrients and phytochemicals, and vitamins may interact with them, either individually or collectively, to provide the apparent health benefits. Thus, controlled randomized studies have been conducted in attempts to determine the health-promoting nutrient.

Do antioxidant vitamin supplements help deter disease?

If the epidemiological evidence suggests that vitamin antioxidants in fruits and vegetables may provide some protection against the development of chronic diseases, such as cancer and heart disease, will supplements provide any additional benefit? Scientists have used a variety of research techniques to evaluate the effect of antioxidant supplementation to prevent disease.

Basic research studies, using *in vitro* techniques or animal models, have evaluated the effects of antioxidants on underlying mechanisms of disease. These studies provide evidence in relation to the theory underlying the beneficial effects of supplementation.

Both retrospective and prospective epidemiological studies of various populations have compared differences in the incidence of disease between supplement users and nonusers. These studies provide evidence of a relationship between supplement use and disease, but do not establish a cause-and-effect relationship. Moreover, as Patterson and others have noted, vitamin supplement users are more likely to engage in other healthy behaviors, such as exercising regularly, that may confound the relationship.

Randomized, clinical intervention studies with humans, providing antioxidant supplements to some and placebos to others for years, have evaluated the effect of supplementation on disease. These trials provide cause-and-effect evidence and are considered to be the strongest research approach.

Nevertheless, as mentioned previously, results from a single study are insufficient to support or refute a theory. The totality of evidence needs to be considered. Based on recent individual randomized, controlled clinical studies and several major reviews, the following represents a generalized summary regarding the effects of antioxidant supplementation, both separately and in combination with other antioxidant vitamins or minerals, on several diseases. Most research has focused on CHD.

Cardiovascular Disease and Stroke Basic research using *in vitro* techniques and biomarkers of oxidation appears to support the theoretical mechanisms underlying the beneficial effects of antioxidant supplementation on cardiovascular disease. In a recent review, Diplock indicated that there is substantial basic research evidence that vitamin E may prevent undesirable free radical oxidation associated with the development of disease processes. In support of this point, Devaraj and Jialal cite several studies showing that vitamin E decreases the susceptibility of LDL to oxidation, and by becoming part of cell membranes, vitamin E may also inhibit other factors, such as platelet adhesion and resultant clotting, that contribute to atherosclerosis. However, Meagher and others questioned whether vitamin E does prevent lipid oxidation in healthy individuals, as they reported no significant effect of 8 weeks supplementation (200, 400, 600, 800, or 1,000 IU/day) on three indices of lipid peroxidation.

Diplock notes that there is also a large body of epidemiological evidence suggesting that the incidence of cardiovascular disease is lower in populations having a high level of antioxidants, even those taking supplements. However, these effects may be specific to vitamin E. Mayne concluded that beta-carotene supplements do not prevent cardiovascular disease. In addition, Rimm and Stampfer noted that epidemiological data do not support a cardiovascular benefit from vitamin C. However, they did note that in several large prospective studies the greatest reduction in cardiovascular risk was associated with those groups of subjects who took vitamin E supplements, usually in doses greater than 100 IU daily. Epidemiological research has also found that vitamin E supplementation may also help to prevent stroke. In a longitudinal study, Paganini-Hill and others found that individuals who took antioxidant vitamin supplements decreased the risk of cerebral occlusion. It should be noted that not all epidemiological studies reveal positive findings. For example, Ascherio and others, in a recent study covering 8 years, found that neither vitamin C, nor vitamin E, nor beta-carotene prevented stroke.

Tufts University notes that about a decade ago, the scientific community was flush with findings from large population studies that diets high in antioxidants, vitamin E in particular, could help stave off heart disease. But those studies, while they included tens of thousands of people, were simply observations of the way people ate and lived. Although these epidemiological studies are persuasive, recent large clinical trials do not appear to support the role of antioxidant supplements in the prevention of cardiovascular disease mortality. Collectively, these clinical trials involved tens of thousands of subjects taking large doses of antioxidant supplements for prolonged periods, such as 400–666 IU of vitamin E for three to six years. Some trials experimented with combined antioxidants, such as vitamins E and C.

In a recent review of the major clinical trials, Kritharides and Stocker noted that some of the studies with smaller populations and shorter duration of follow-up have shown some positive effects of vitamin E. However, the larger randomized studies have indicated no benefits of supplementation with vitamin E or other antioxidant vitamins in the prevention of CHD. There were no adverse effects of vitamin E.

However, some research suggests that antioxidant supplementation to heart disease patients may be harmful. Miller and others, in a meta-analysis of 19 clinical trials involving vitamin E alone or combined with other antioxidants, reported an increased risk of all-cause mortality with dosages greater than 150 IU/day, and concluded that high-dosage vitamin E supplements (equal to or greater than 400 IU daily) may increase all-cause mortality and should be avoided. The increased mortality may be due to heart failure, as reported in a recent study by Lonn and others.

Some critics of these recent negative findings contend that antioxidants, notably vitamin E, may still play a role in the prevention of heart disease. Webb, interviewing vitamin E experts, notes that the major clinical studies tested vitamin E in people already at high risk or with a history of heart disease, a limitation Miller and others noted in their meta-analysis revealing increased all-cause mortality from high-dose vitamin E supplementation; they also noted the generalizability of these findings to healthy adults is uncertain. Webb contends that vitamin E may not be helpful in treating heart disease but may help prevent clogged arteries in healthy people, suggesting vitamin E supplementation is not a cure, but rather prevention.

In a recent review, Futterman and Lemberg make an excellent point. They note that even if antioxidants prove to be effective, their place on the therapeutic ladder of cardiovascular disease prevention should be low. Modifying other risk factors, such as treating hypertension and achieving a normal body weight, should have a higher priority.

Cancer Antioxidants are theorized to prevent cancer in several ways, primarily by preventing DNA damage and strengthening the immune system, as noted previously.

In a recent review, Prasad and others noted that extensive *in vitro* studies and some *in vivo* studies have revealed that individual antioxidants may affect animal and human cancer cells by complex mechanisms, and that multiple antioxidant-vitamin supplementation, together with other lifestyle modifications, may improve the efficacy of cancer therapies.

Epidemiological data suggest antioxidant supplementation, particularly vitamin E, may help in the fight against cancer. Gridley and others indicated that individuals who took supplements of individual vitamins, such as C and E, had a significantly lower risk of oral and pharyngeal cancer, whereas Losonczy and others reported that vitamin E supplementation was associated with about a 50 percent reduction in overall cancer mortality. However, in a recent review of the relationship between vitamin E and breast cancer, Kimmick and others noted that the epidemiologic study results have been inconsistent.

Experimental studies do not appear to support a cancer-protective effect of antioxidant supplementation. Lonn and others reported that long-term vitamin E supplementation does not prevent cancer in patients with vascular disease or diabetes. In a meta-analysis of 14 randomized trials, European investigators could find no evidence that vitamin E and other antioxidant supplements can prevent various gastrointestinal cancers (esophageal, gastric, colorectal, pancreatic, liver) and similar to the findings of Miller and others, indicated supplements seemed to increase overall mortality.

Nevertheless, some intervention data with vitamin E also show promise. Improved immune functions may help prevent prostate cancer. Heinonen and others found that vitamin E supplementation (50 mg daily for 5–8 years) significantly reduced the incidence of and mortality from prostate cancer. Currently, a large clinical trial called SELECT (Selenium and Vitamin E Cancer Prevention Trial) is underway to detect possible prevention of prostate cancer. The antioxidant effects of selenium are discussed in chapter 8.

Beta-carotene supplements do not appear to prevent cancer. Pryor and others noted that three large clinical trials found supplemental beta-carotene had no effect in the prevention of lung cancer, and two of the trials actually found a higher risk for lung cancer in those who took the supplements compared to those taking the placebo. Those who smoke were particularly at risk. Moreover, in a recent international review, Vainio and Rautalahti indicated that there is little evidence that vitamin A intake, including supplementation interventions, has any substantial cancer-preventive effects.

Eye Health According to Christen, basic research studies suggest that oxidative mechanisms may play an important role in the pathogenesis of cataract and age-related macular degeneration (ARMD), the two most important causes of visual impairment in older adults. In the United States, over 1.3 million cataract extractions are performed annually. Jacques theorized that these eye problems may be prevented by optimal antioxidant nutrition, particularly vitamin E. Johnson also noted that the carotenoids, including lycopene and lutein, particularly from natural foods, may play a role in prevention of macular degeneration.

Christen notes that findings from several epidemiological studies are generally compatible with a possible protective effect of antioxidant vitamins, but the data are inconsistent. In general, the results from clinical intervention studies, as reported by Smith and Teikari and their associates, do not show any benefit of beta-carotene, vitamin C, or vitamin E in the prevention of ARMD. However, Tufts University recently noted some positive effects from a very large study coordinated by the National Institutes of Health. Various dietary regimens were tested over a 6-year period to evaluate their effects on macular degeneration. Tufts notes that the results are very promising. In fact, the investigators recommend that those who are in the intermediate stages of the disease take 400 IU vitamin E daily, along with 500 milligrams of vitamin C, 15 milligrams of beta-carotene, 80 milligrams of zinc, and 2 milligrams of copper. Note that this recommendation is for those who already have ARMD, not for the general public. The Consumers Union recommends individuals taking such supplements do so under a doctor's supervision. As shall be noted in the next chapter, the recommended zinc intake exceeds the UL.

Mental Health Brain cells are also susceptible to oxidative damage, which may contribute to neurologic disease such as Alzheimer's, a devastating disease developing primarily in the elderly. In an epidemiological study, Morris and others found that of individuals 65 years of age and older who used vitamin C or vitamin E supplements, none developed Alzheimer's disease during a 4.3 year follow-up, whereas several cases developed in nonusers. The authors suggested that the use of these antioxidant supplements may lower the risk of Alzheimer's disease. In a more recent study, Englehart and others also found that high dietary intake of vitamin C and vitamin E may lower the risk of Alzheimer's disease. However, in a subsequent study, Morris and others reported that vitamin E from food, but not other antioxidants, may be associated with a reduced risk of Alzheimer's disease. Both of these latter studies followed healthy older adults, aged 55 or 65 and above for a period of 4–7 years. In one intervention study, using 2,000 IU vitamin E daily for 2 years, the onset of the major debilitating effects associated with Alzheimer's disease was delayed by 7 months.

Although research findings are still considered preliminary, several recent reviews suggest vitamin E supplementation may be useful in the prevention and treatment of Alzheimer's disease. Munoz and others indicate that vitamin E may decrease the vascular damage caused by peptides involved in development of Alzheimer's, while Berman and Brodaty suggest current clinical practice favors its use during treatment.

General Health The theory of a health-protective effect of antioxidant supplementation is enticing, but the available scientific data are somewhat indecisive. In their review of the epidemiological studies and recent intervention clinical trials, Adams and Best noted that although epidemiological studies have shown some protective effects of antioxidants against chronic diseases such as CHD and cancer, most recent well-controlled clinical trials have not. They note that antioxidant recommendations for the prevention of disease are complex. Consumers Union also indicated that the picture is less clear than it seemed only several years ago, but the positive findings from many epidemiological studies cannot easily be dismissed. Because of these conflicting data, most reviewers recommend more study. In this regard, Tufts University indicates that the research is not over. Several large-scale clinical trials with vitamin E, along with other antioxidants, are currently under way and will help clarify their role in the prevention of CHD, cancer, and other chronic diseases. It is hoped that future data from these long-term clinical trials will provide us with information as to whether or not antioxidant vitamin supplementation confers any significant health benefits above and beyond those associated with the Prudent Healthy Diet.

In the meantime, as noted previously, most health professionals recommend we obtain our antioxidants from healthful foods. The Consumers Union recently reported preliminary findings suggesting that the gamma form of vitamin E, which is prevalent in food, may offer better protection against heart disease and prostate cancer than the alpha form, which is prevalent in supplements. However, that does not mean gamma supplements are more effective. Again, it may be the whole food and its array of nutrients, rather than a single isolated nutrient, that provides health benefits. In an American Heart Association scientific advisory based on its analysis of clinical trials, Kris-Etherton and others concluded that antioxidant supplements do not have the same heart-protective effects of a healthy diet rich in fruits, vegetables, whole grains, and legumes.

Although many health professionals that once touted and recommended antioxidant supplementation to prevent chronic disease have reversed their recommendation, some contend that antioxidant supplements may still be appropriate for healthy people. They indicate that antioxidants cannot reverse damage already done by the diease, but may help prevent the development of disease in the first place. For example, Schutte and others recently reported that supplementation with vitamins C (1,000 mg) and E (800 mg), along with 10 milligrams of folate, had some potential health benefits for the cardiovascular system, such as decreased blood pressure, in young healthy subjects. Moreover, in a recent review by experts in the field of antioxidant supplementation, Hathcock and others concluded from clinical trial evidence that vitamin E supplements appear safe for most adults in amounts equal to or less than 1,600 IU, and that vitamin C supplements of equal to or less than 2,000 milligrams daily are safe for most adults. These values appoximate the UL for vitamins C and E developed by the National Academy of Sciences.

How much of a vitamin supplement is too much?

As noted throughout this chapter, vitamins play some very important roles in helping us maintain our health. They are the most popular of all the dietary supplements. However, can we get too much of a good thing? Based on possible adverse health effects of excess vitamin intake, the National Academy of Sciences has established the UL, which is the highest level of a vitamin that can be safely taken without any risk of adverse effects. In general, the higher above the UL, the greater the risk. Exceeding the UL on an occasional basis may not pose any significant health risks, but doing so on a daily basis eventually will. An UL has been set for choline and for seven of the thirteen vitamins for which DRI have been developed. These data can be found on the inside of the back cover of this book. For some vitamins, such as niacin and folate, the UL is only about twice the RDA, whereas for others, such as vitamins C and E, the UL is about 20–60 times greater than the RDA.

In general, it is difficult to exceed the UL for any given vitamin by eating natural, wholesome foods. However, consuming large amounts of fortified foods may provide daily amounts of vitamins that exceed the UL. For example, the adult UL for niacin is 35 milligrams, but only synthetic niacin derived from fortified foods or supplements and not from niacin in non-fortified foods. Some breakfast cereals may be fortified with 100 percent of the DV for various vitamins, which for niacin would be 20 milligrams, or nearly half the UL. Consumption of other fortified foods could easily lead to excess niacin intake.

If the vitamin content of the body is adequate, excessive vitamin intake serves no useful purpose and may even be harmful in certain situations. As noted previously, vitamins function primarily as coenzymes. When a vitamin enters the body, it travels through the bloodstream to a particular body cell and then forms part of the enzyme complex within that cell. The cell has a limited capacity to produce these enzymes, and when that capacity is reached, the vitamin cannot be used for its basic purpose. It may now have other fates. It may be excreted from the body if in excess, particularly if it is a water-soluble vitamin; it may be stored in some body tissue, particularly if it is a fat-soluble vitamin; or it may begin to function in uncharacteristic ways, as a drug instead of a nutrient.

Although research findings regarding the potential health benefits of the antioxidant vitamins are equivocal, most investigators note that additional research is needed before specific doses may be recommended. There may be an appropriate balance between free radicals and antioxidants in the body, and upsetting this balance may elicit negative effects. Dreosti and others noted that the point may be reached where the beneficial effects of antioxidant vitamins inhibiting deleterious free-radical reactions are outweighed by the adverse effects on essential reactions. For example, Omenn noted that beta-carotene may become a pro-oxidant under conditions of high oxygen pressure, such as in the lungs, producing derivatives that might lead to carcinogenic effects, especially in smokers or others exposed to second-hand smoke. Omenn also notes that in the early 1980s, beta-carotene was a promising agent against common cancers when the National Cancer Institute initiated several major clinical intervention studies. These studies not only showed no benefit, but those receiving high-dose beta-carotene experienced significant increases in lung-cancer incidence. Vitamins C and E appear to be relatively safe, but as discussed previously under the supplementation section for each vitamin, some health problems may be associated

with excessive intake of each. For example, vitamin E supplements may aggravate bleeding tendency in individuals taking anticoagulation drugs.

As noted throughout this chapter, megadoses of several vitamins may be pathological, particularly A, D, niacin, and B_6, when not taken under medical supervision. There are more than 4,000 cases of vitamin/mineral overdose in the United States each year, resulting in about thirty fatalities. Although most of these cases occur in children, the literature contains some case reports of serious health problems with adults, including athletes taking vitamin megadoses in attempts to improve athletic performance. A good review of possible adverse effects of excessive vitamin supplementation is presented by Hathcock.

If I want to take a vitamin-mineral supplement, what are some prudent guidelines?

Unfortunately, scientific data are not available to provide specific guidelines relative to the amounts of each particular vitamin or mineral needed to promote optimal health. Although individual vitamin and mineral supplements are available, in general, health professionals who do recommend such supplements suggest multivitamin/mineral combinations. Minerals are covered in detail in the next chapter, but because they are found in most multivitamin/mineral preparations, it was deemed appropriate to include them in this discussion. For those who desire to take vitamin supplements, the American Dietetic Association recommends low levels that do not exceed the RDA or AI. To reiterate, excess amounts of some vitamins (A, D, niacin, and B_6) can be toxic, as can excess amounts of some minerals (calcium, phosphorus, iron, chromium, selenium, and zinc) as discussed in the next chapter. However, other organizations, such as the Center for Science in the Public Interest (CSPI), used an educated guess approach to offer some prudent guidelines. The following are the highlights of the CSPI recommendations, as reported in an article written by Bonnie Liebman, with some modifications based on advice from the Consumers Union, publishers of *Consumer Reports on Health,* and other nutrition health professionals.

General Points

1. Check the Daily Value (DV). The amounts of vitamins and minerals listed on food and dietary supplement labels are based on the Daily Value (DV) for each nutrient, a value based on the RDA that has not been changed since the 1970s. For example, the DV for vitamin C is 60 milligrams, and yet the new RDA for adult males is 90 milligrams. For zinc, the DV is set at 15 milligrams, yet the new RDA for adult males is 11 milligrams. Thus, supplements that contain 100 percent of the DV may contain less than the current RDA, in the case of vitamin C, or more than the current RDA, as in the case for zinc. In general, these differences are not substantial, but may be for certain vitamins. For example, the DV for vitamin A is 5,000 IU, while the UL is only twice this amount, or 10,000 IU.

2. Buy the inexpensive house brand of vitamins that contains about 100 percent of the DV for most vitamins and minerals. There usually is no need to buy special brands, such as those labeled with catchy terms, such as *High Potency*. The best buys may be at major drug stores and warehouse stores. Most companies that market vitamins buy their vitamins from the same manufacturers, so the contents in national brands and house brands are similar. Look for labels with USP (United States Pharmacopeia), or better yet, USP-Verified, which means the product meets standards for quality and purity. In a recent evaluation of vitamin supplements, the Consumers Union and CSPI recommended that if you decide to take vitamins, including antioxidants, go for the bargain price.

Fat-soluble Vitamins

1. Buy a supplement low in vitamin A, particularly one with preformed retinol. CSPI recommends limiting vitamin A to no more than 3,000 IU of retinol, preferably less. Select supplements containing vitamin A from beta-carotene. If the supplement is beta-carotene, 15,000 IU is a recommended limit. Obtain most of your vitamin A as beta-carotene in fruits and vegetables, a recommendation especially important to smokers.

2. Buy a supplement with 400–600 IU of vitamin D if you are elderly, a vegan, or a postmenopausal woman, particularly if you do not drink adequate amounts of vitamin D-fortified milk or do not get enough sunshine. Look for supplements with vitamin D_3, which is more effective than D_2.

3. Buy a supplement containing at least the DV for vitamin E, which is 30 IU. The Consumers Union states you should not take vitamin E to prevent chronic disease; doses of 400 IU or more per day may cause harm. Daily intake of 100–200 IU would appear to pose little risk to most healthy adults. Given the current research data, it may be prudent to limit intake of high-dose vitamin E supplements.

4. Buy a supplement that contains vitamin K. Not all supplements include vitamin K, so check the label. The AI for an adult male is 120 micrograms, but the DV is only 80 micrograms. Multivitamins contain about 25 micrograms.

Water-soluble Vitamins

1. Buy a supplement that contains 100–200 percent of thiamin, riboflavin, niacin, folic acid, B_6 and B_{12}. You can ignore biotin and pantothenic acid. Check the label to ensure that the supplement contains at least 200–400 micrograms of folic acid, which should complement the diet to provide about 400–600 micrograms per day.

2. Buy a B_{12} supplement that contains 6 micrograms of vitamin B_{12} if you are a vegan, and 25 micrograms if you are elderly. The DV for B_{12} is 6 micrograms, so many supplements contain this amount. Some preparations for seniors may contain the 25 micrograms.

3. Buy a supplement that contains 100–200 percent of vitamin C. The RDA for an adult male is 90 milligrams, yet the DV is only 60 milligrams. The supplement should complement vitamin C intake from a variety of fruits and vegetables.

Minerals

1. Buy a supplement with calcium if you are female or elderly and do not consume adequate dietary calcium. Most multivitamin/mineral tablets contain about 200–300 milligrams of calcium, which can substitute for a serving of low-fat milk. If you consume no dairy products and few calcium-rich foods, you may consider buying a separate calcium supplement.

2. Buy a supplement limited in iron, copper, and zinc, with no more than 100 percent of the RDA for each. The DV for iron is 18 milligrams, while the RDA for young women is 15–18 milligrams. The RDA for adult males and women over age 50 is only 8 milligrams, so men and postmenopausal women may want to select supplements without iron since the diet should provide ample amounts.

3. Buy a supplement that provides no more than 100 milligrams of magnesium and is limited in phosphorus. Magnesium should be obtained primarily from foods, and we normally consume too much phosphorus from foods already.

4. Buy a supplement containing 100 percent of the RDA for chromium and selenium. For those concerned with prostate cancer, one recommendation is to consume 200 micrograms of selenium daily, along with 400 IU of vitamin E. This amount of selenium is about half of the UL, so caution is warranted to prevent excess intake.

Think food first! Although the CSPI published these recommendations, they, along with most investigators researching the health implications of vitamin supplementation, note there is no guarantee of improved health. Almost all health professionals note we should obtain our vitamin nutrition through consumption of a wide variety of healthful, natural foods, particularly fruits and vegetables. Remember, vitamin supplements do not supply all of the nutrients and other substances, such as phytochemicals, present in foods that are believed to be important to health.

Key Concept Recap

▶ Although several national surveys have reported that some Americans and Canadians are receiving less than the RDA for several vitamins, actual vitamin deficiencies resulting in disease are rare.

▶ Vitamins certainly are essential for good health, but most health professionals recommend that vitamins should be obtained through their natural sources—fruits, vegetables, and other wholesome, natural foods. Such foods also provide other nonessential nutrients that may possess health benefits.

▶ In general, health professionals indicate that vitamin supplements are not necessary for the individual on a well-balanced diet, but they may be recommended for certain individuals, such as the elderly, vegans, and women of childbearing age. Moreover, some health professionals note that most people do not consume an optimal amount of vitamins by diet alone and indicate that it appears *prudent* for all adults to take vitamin supplements.

- Epidemiologic data strongly suggest that diets rich in fruits and vegetables are associated with lower risks of certain chronic diseases, such as heart disease and cancer, and that some of this effect may be due to the antioxidant vitamin and phytochemical content of fruits and vegetables.
- Antioxidant vitamin supplementation has been theorized to provide multiple health benefits, but more research is needed before specific recommendations may be offered.

- Megadoses of some vitamins are potentially harmful.

APPLICATION EXERCISE

Construct a brief, one-page survey regarding vitamin supplements, and other supplements as well, if you like. For example, you might use some of the following questions:

1. Do you take a vitamin supplement?
   __ Yes __ No
2. What type of supplement do you take?
   __ Multivitamin
   __ Multivitamin/mineral
   __ Vitamin B Complex
   __ Vitamin E
   __ Other

3. How often do you take the supplement?
   __ Two or more times a day
   __ Daily
   __ Several times a week
   __ Once a week
   __ Several times a month
   __ Once a month
   __ Never
4. Why do you take the vitamin supplement?
   __ To help guarantee good health
   __ To enhance my sport or exercise performance
   __ Other

Once your survey is developed, get permission to administer it to some physically active individuals or athletes, such as participants in recreational sports activities or sports at your school, members of a local cycling or running club, or members of a commercial fitness facility. Share the findings with your class.

Review Questions—Multiple Choice

1. Vitamin A toxicity is most likely to occur from:
   (a) consuming too many dark green and deep orange vegetables
   (b) eating liver more than once per week
   (c) consuming high-dosage vitamin A supplements
   (d) drinking too much vitamin A fortified milk
   (e) eating rabbit meat two days per week
2. The task of acquiring enough vitamin B_{12} may pose a problem to vegans because:
   (a) Fibers in vegetables inhibit its absorption.
   (b) Vegans lack the intrinsic factor.
   (c) B_{12} is found only in animal products.
   (d) A deficiency may occur from excess intake of soy products.
   (e) Folacin retards its absorption.

3. Which of the following statements is not true about vitamin B_6?
   (a) The term vitamin B_6 refers to a family of compounds: pyridoxine, pyridoxal, and pyridoxamine.
   (b) As a coenzyme, it acts in the conversion of the amino acid tryptophan to one of the essential vitamins.
   (c) It is fat soluble and therefore can be stored in the body.
   (d) Foods containing it should be included in the diet daily.
   (e) The richest food sources are meats, liver, vegetables, and whole grains.
4. A deficiency of either of these two vitamins produces a similar anemia:
   (a) thiamin and riboflavin
   (b) riboflavin and niacin
   (c) thiamin and vitamin B_2

   (d) pantothenic acid and biotin
   (e) vitamin B_{12} and folate
5. If an individual is on a well-balanced diet, which of the following vitamin supplements will increase physical performance at sea level competition?
   (a) thiamin
   (b) niacin
   (c) vitamin C
   (d) vitamin E
   (e) none will
6. Most of the B vitamins function in human metabolism as
   (a) coenzymes
   (b) hormones
   (c) antioxidants
   (d) a source of Calories
   (e) activators of mineral metabolism

7. Although athletes on weight reduction diets normally may not need vitamin supplementation, which athletes, based on the nature of their sport, may be best advised to take a supplement?
   (a) swimmers
   (b) wrestlers
   (c) baseball players
   (d) field hockey players
   (e) sprinters
8. Which of the following are fat-soluble vitamins?
   (a) vitamins B, C, D, niacin
   (b) vitamin E, niacin, thiamin, riboflavin
   (c) vitamins A, D, E, K
   (d) vitamins A, B, C, D
   (e) vitamins B_1, B_2, B_6, C
9. Which of the following are true B vitamins? (1) inositol (2) choline (3) biotin (4) lipoic acid (5) PABA (6) niacin (7) bioflavinoids (8) ubiquinone (9) vitamin B_6 (10) thiamin (11) laetrile (12) pantothenic acid (13) vitamin B_{15} (14) vitamin P (15) vitamin B_{17}
   (a) 1, 2, 3, 5, 7
   (b) 2, 4, 7, 8, 9
   (c) 3, 6, 9, 10, 12
   (d) 5, 9, 11, 13, 15
   (e) 7, 11, 12, 14, 15
10. The main function of vitamin E in the body is to act as a(n):
   (a) antioxidant
   (b) superoxide
   (c) free radical
   (d) hormone
   (e) source of energy

Answers to multiple choice questions:
1. c; 2. c; 3. c; 4. e; 5. e; 6. a; 7. b; 8. c; 9. c; 10. a.

Review Questions—Essay

1. Explain at least three ways whereby vitamins function in metabolic processes in the human body.
2. Name the four fat-soluble vitamins and describe the metabolic function of each in the human body.
3. Name the nine water-soluble vitamins, and, along with choline, describe their major metabolic functions in the human body.
4. What is coenzyme Q_{10}, why is it purported to be an ergogenic aid, and does research support its efficacy as an ergogenic?
5. Would you consider taking antioxidant vitamin supplements, such as beta-carotene, E, and C. If so, why so? If not, why not?

References

Books
Bucci, L. 1993. *Nutrients as Ergogenic Aids for Sports and Exercise.* Boca Raton, FL: CRC Press.

Keys, A. 1950. *Human Starvation.* Minneapolis, MN: West.

National Academy of Sciences. 2002. *Dietary Reference Intakes for Vitamin A, Vitamin K, Arsenic, Boron, Chromium, Copper, Iodine, Iron, Manganese, Molybdenum, Nickel, Silicon, Vanadium, and Zinc.* Washington, DC: National Academy Press.

National Academy of Sciences. 2000. *Dietary Reference Intakes for Vitamin C, Vitamin E, Selenium, and Carotenoids.* Washington, DC: National Academy Press.

National Academy of Sciences. 2000. *Dietary Reference Intakes for Thiamin, Riboflavin, Niacin, Vitamin B6, Folate, Vitamin B12, Pantothenic Acid, Biotin, and Choline.* Washington, DC: National Academy Press.

National Academy of Sciences. 1999. *Dietary Reference Intakes for Calcium, Phosphorus, Magnesium, Vitamin D, and Fluoride.* Washington, DC: National Academy Press.

National Research Council. 1989. *Diet and Health: Implications for Reducing Chronic Disease Risk.* Washington, DC: National Academy Press.

Shils, M., et al. 2006. *Modern Nutrition in Health and Disease.* Philadelphia: Lippincott Williams & Wilkins.

Walter, P., et al. eds. 1989. Elevated dosages of vitamins: Benefits and hazards. *International Journal for Vitamin and Nutrition Research,* Supplement 30.

Wolinsky, I., and Driskell, J. 1996. *Sports Nutrition: Vitamins and Trace Elements.* Boca Raton, FL: CRC Press.

Reviews
Adams, A., and Best, T. 2002. The role of antioxidants in exercise and disease prevention. *Physician and Sportsmedicine* 30 (5):37–44.

American Academy of Pediatrics. 1999. Folic acid for the prevention of neural tube defects. *Pediatrics* 104:325–27.

American Dietetic Association. 2001. Position of the American Dietetic Association; Food fortification and dietary supplements. *Journal of the American Dietetic Association* 101:115–25.

American Dietetic Association. 1996. Position of the American Dietetic Association: Vitamin and mineral supplementation. *Journal of the American Dietetic Association* 96:73–77.

Armstrong, L., and Maresh, C. 1996. Vitamin and mineral supplements as nutritional aids to exercise performance and health. *Nutrition Reviews* 54:S148–S158.

Andreotti, F., et al. 1999. Homocysteine and arterial occlusive disease: A concise review. *Cardiologia* 44:341–45.

Benardot, D., et al. 2001. Can vitamin supplements improve sport performance? *Sports Science Exchange Roundtable* 12 (3): 1–4.

Bender, D. A. 1999. Non-nutritional uses of vitamin B6. *British Journal of Nutrition* 81:7–20.

Berman, K., and Brodaty, H. 2004. Tocopherol (vitamin E) in Alzheimer's disease and other neurodegenerative disorders. *CNS Drugs* 18:807–25.

Binkley, N., and Krueger, D. 2000. Hypervit-aminosis A and bone. *Nutrition Reviews* 58:138–44.

Birjmohun, R., et al. 2005. Efficacy and safety of high-density lipoprotein cholesterol-increasing compounds: A meta-analysis of randomized controlled trials. *Journal of the American College of Cardiology* 45:185–97.

Bischoff-Ferrari, H., et al. 2005. Effect of vitamin D on falls: A meta-analysis. *JAMA* 291:1999–2006.

Bischoff-Ferrari, H., et al. 2005. Fracture prevention with vitamin D supplementation: A meta-analysis of randomized controlled trials. *JAMA* 293:2257–64.

Bjelakovic, G., et al. 2004. Antioxidant supplements for prevention of gastrointestinal cancers: A systematic review and meta-analysis. *Lancet* 364:1219–28.

Block, G. 1992. The data support a role for antioxidants in reducing cancer risk. *Nutrition Reviews* 50:207–13.

Bouis, H. 1996. Enrichment of food staples through plant breeding: A new strategy for fighting micronutrient malnutrition. *Nutrition Reviews* 54:131–37.

Bourgeois, C., et al. 2006. Niacin. In *Modern Nutrition in Health and Disease,* eds. M. Shils, et al. Philadelphia: Lippincott Williams & Wilkins.

Boushey, C., et al. 1995. A quantitative assessment of plasma homocysteine as a risk factor for vascular disease: Probable benefits of increasing folic acid intakes. *Journal of the American Medical Association* 274:1049–57.

Bulow, J. 1993. Lipid metabolism and utilization. In *Principles of Exercise Biochemistry,* ed. J. Poortmans. Basel, Switzerland: Karger.

Calvo, M., et al. 2004. Vitamin D fortification in the United States and Canada: Current status and data needs. *American Journal of Clinical Nutrition* 80:1710S–16S.

Carmel, R. 2006. Folic acid. In *Modern Nutrition in Health and Disease,* eds. M. Shils, et al. Philadelphia: Lippincott Williams & Wilkins.

Challem, J. J. 1999. Toward a new definition of essential nutrients: Is it now time for a third 'vitamin' paradigm? *Medical Hypotheses* 52:417–22.

Chen, J. 2000. Vitamins: Effects of exercise on requirements. In *Nutrition in Sport,* ed. R. J. Maughan. Oxford: Blackwell Science.

Christen, W. G. 1999. Antioxidant vitamins and age-related eye disease. *Proceedings of the Association of American Physicians* 111:16–21.

Clarkson, P., and Thompson, H. 2000. Antioxidants: What role do they play in physical activity and health? *American Journal of Clinical Nutrition* 72:637S–46S.

Clarkson, P. 1991. Vitamins, iron and trace minerals. In *Perspectives in Exercise Science and Sports Medicine. Ergogenics: The Enhancement of Sports Performance,* eds. D. Lamb and M. Williams. Indianapolis, IN: Benchmark.

Consumers Union. 2005. Vitamin E pills: What to do now? *Consumer Reports on Health* 17 (7):3.

Consumers Union. 2004. Disease-fighting B vitamins. *Consumer Reports on Health* 16 (1):10.

Consumers Union. 2003. A better vitamin E? *Consumer Reports on Health* 15 (4):12.

Consumers Union. 2002. Do you need more vitamin D? *Consumer Reports on Health* 14 (11):1, 4–5.

Consumers Union. 2001. Surprising health risk from low vitamin C? *Consumer Reports on Health* 13 (5):7.

Consumers Union. 2001. Vitamin A: How much is too much? *Consumer Reports on Health* 13 (10):1, 4–5.

Consumers Union. 1996. Is E for you? *Consumer Reports on Health* 8:121–24.

Demopoulous, H., et al. 1986. Free radical pathology: Rationale and toxicology of antioxidants and other supplements in sports medicine and exercise science. In *Sport, Health and Nutrition,* ed. F. Katch. Champaign, IL: Human Kinetics.

Devaraj, S., and Jialal, I. 1998. The effects of alpha-tocopherol on critical cells in atherogenesis. *Current Opinion in Lipidology* 9:11–15.

Diplock, A. T. 1997. Will the 'good fairies' please prove to us that vitamin E lessens human degenerative disease? *Free Radical Research* 26:565–83.

Douglas, R., et al. 2004. Vitamin C for preventing and treating the common cold. *Cochrane Database of Systematic Reviews* 18:CD000980.

Dreosti, I., et al. 1998. How best to ensure daily intake of antioxidants (from the diet and supplements) that is optimal for life span, disease, and general health. *Annals of the New York Academy of Sciences* 854:463–76.

Enstrom, J. 1993. Counterpoint: Vitamin C and mortality. *Nutrition Today* 28 (May/June):39–42.

Fairfield, K., and Fletcher, R. 2002. Vitamins for chronic disease prevention in adults: Scientific review. *JAMA* 287:3116–26.

Fletcher, R., and Fairfield, K. 2002. Vitamins for chronic disease prevention in adults: Clinical applications. *JAMA* 287:3127–29.

Fogelholm, M. 2000. Vitamins: Metabolic functions. In *Nutrition in Sport,* ed. R. J. Maughan. Oxford: Blackwell Science.

Futterman, L. G., and Lemberg, L. 1999. The use of antioxidants in retarding atherosclerosis: Fact or fiction? *American Journal of Critical Care* 8:130–33.

Gaziano, J., and Hennekens, C. 1996. Update on dietary antioxidants and cancer. *Pathological Biology* 44:42–45.

Gerster, H. 1997. No contribution of ascorbic acid to renal calcium oxalate stones. *Annals of Nutrition and Metabolism* 41:269–82.

Gerster, H. 1989. Review: The role of vitamin C in athletic performance. *Journal of the American College of Nutrition* 8:636–43.

Giovannucci, E. 2002. A review of epidemiologic studies of tomatoes, lycopene, and prostate cancer. *Experimental Biology and Medicine* 227:852–59.

Halliwell, B. 1996. Oxidative stress, nutrition and health: Experimental strategies for optimization of nutritional antioxidant intake in humans. *Free Radical Research* 25:57–74.

Harris, S. 2005. Vitamin D in type 1 diabetes prevention. *Journal of Nutrition* 135:323–25.

Hathcock, J., et al. 2005. Vitamins E and C are safe across a broad range of intakes. *American Journal of Clinical Nutrition* 81:736–45.

Hathcock, J. 1997. Vitamins and minerals: Efficacy and safety. *American Journal of Clinical Nutrition* 66:427–37.

Hawley, J., et al. 1995. Nutritional practices of athletes: Are they sub-optimal? *Journal of Sports Sciences* 13:S75–S87.

Hemila, H. 2004. Vitamin C supplementation and respiratory infections: A systematic review. *Military Medicine* 169:920–25.

Herbert, V. 1993. Viewpoint: Does mega-C do more good than harm, or more harm than good? *Nutrition Today* 28 (January/February): 28–32.

Holick, M. F. 2006. Vitamin D. In *Modern Nutrition in Health and Disease,* eds. M. Shils, et al. Philadelphia: Lippincott Williams & Wilkins.

Hunninghake, D. B. 1999. Pharmacologic management of triglycerides. *Clinical Cardiology* II44–II48.

Ito, M. 2002. Niacin-based therapy for dyslipidemia: Past evidence and future advances. *American Journal of Management Care* 8:S315–22.

Jackson, M., et al. 2004. Vitamin E and the oxidative stress of exercise. *Annals of the New York Academy of Sciences* 1031:158–68.

Jacob, R. A. 1999. Vitamin C. In *Modern Nutrition in Health and Disease*, eds. M. Shils, et al. Baltimore: Williams & Wilkins.

Jacques, P. F. 1999. The potential preventive effects of vitamins for cataract and age-related macular degeneration. *International Journal of Vitamin and Nutrition Research* 69:198–205.

Ji, L. 2002. Exercise-induced modulation of antioxidant defense. *New York Academy of Sciences* 959:82–92.

Ji, L. 2000. Free radicals and antioxidants in exercise and sports. In *Exercise and Sport Science*, eds. W. E. Garrett and D. T. Kirkendall. Philadelphia: Lippincott Williams & Wilkins.

Johnson, E. 2002. The role of carotenoids in human health. *Nutrition in Clinical Care* 5:56–65.

Keith, R. 1994. Vitamins and physical activity. In *Nutrition in Exercise and Sport*, eds. I. Wolinsky and J. Hickson. Boca Raton, FL: CRC Press.

Kimmick, G., et al. 1997. Vitamin E and breast cancer: A review. *Nutrition and Cancer* 27:109–17.

Knip, M., et al. 2000. Safety of high-dose nicotinamide; A review. *Diabetologia* 43:1337–45.

Koltover, V. 1992. Free radical theory of aging: View against the reliability theory. *EXS* 62:11–19.

Kontush, K., and Schekatolina, S. 2004. Vitamin E in neurodegenerative disorders: Alzheimer's disease. *Annals of the New York Academy of Sciences* 1031:249–62.

Kris-Etherton, P., et al. 2004. Antioxidant vitamin supplements and cardiovascular disease. *Circulation* 110:637–41.

Krishnaswamy, K., and Madhavan Nair, K. 2001. Importance of folate in human nutrition. *British Journal of Nutrition* 85:S115–24.

Kritharides, L., and Stocker, R. 2002. The use of antioxidant supplements in coronary heart disease. *Atherosclerosis* 164:211–19.

Lachance, P. A. 1998. Overview of key nutrients: Micronutrient aspects. *Nutrition Reviews* 56:S34–S39.

Lachance, P. 1996. Future vitamin and antioxidant RDAs for health promotion. *Preventive Medicine* 25:46–47.

Law, M. 2000. Fortifying food with folic acid. *Seminars in Thrombosis and Hemostasis* 26:349–52.

Lee, I. M. 1999. Antioxidant vitamins in the prevention of cancer. *Proceedings of the American Association of Physicians* 111:10–15.

Levine, M., et al. 2006. Vitamin C. In *Modern Nutrition in Health and Disease*, eds. M. Shils, et al. Philadelphia: Lippincott Williams & Wilkins.

Levine, M., et al. 1999. Criteria and recommendations for vitamin C intake. *Journal of the American Medical Association* 281:1415–23.

Liebman, B. 2004. Eye wise: Seeing into the future. *Nutrition Action Health Letter* 31 (9)1–7.

Liebman, B. 2003. Spin the bottle: How to pick a multivitamin. *Nutrition Action Health Letter* 30 (1):1–9.

Liebman, B. 2002. Antioxidants: No magic bullets. *Nutrition Action Health Letter* 29 (3):1–8.

Liebman, B. 2000. 10 vitamin tricks. *Nutrition Action Health Letter* 27 (3):5–13.

Liebman, B., and Hurley, J. 2002. Vegetables: Vitamin K weighs in. *Nutrition Action Health Letter* 29 (6):13–15.

Lou, Y., et al. 2004. The role of vitamin D3 metabolism in prostate cancer. *Journal of Steroid Biochemistry and Molecular Biology* 92:317–25.

Lucock, M., and Yates, Z. 2004. Folic acid: Vitamin and panacea or genetic time bomb? *Nature Reviews. Genetics* 6:235–40.

Lukaski, H. 2004. Vitamin and mineral status: Effects on physical performance. *Nutrition* 20:632–44.

Manore, M. 2001. Vitamins and minerals: Part I. How much do I need? *ACSM's Health & Fitness Journal* 5 (3):33–35.

Manore, M. 2001. Vitamins and minerals: Part II. Who needs to supplement? *ACSM's Health & Fitness Journal* 5 (4):30–34.

Manore, M. 2001. Vitamins and minerals: Part III. Can you get too much? *ACSM's Health & Fitness Journal* 5 (5):26–28.

Manore, M. 1994. Vitamin B6 and exercise. *International Journal of Sport Nutrition* 4:89–103.

Mansfield, L., and Goldstein, G. 1981. Anaphylactic reaction after ingestion of local bee pollen. *Annals of Allergy* 47:154–56.

Mayne, S. 1996. Beta-carotene, carotenoids, and disease prevention in humans. *FASEB Journal* 10:690–701.

McCormick, D. B. 2006. Riboflavin. In *Modern Nutrition in Health and Disease*, eds. M. Shils, et al. Philadelphia: Lippincott Williams & Wilkins.

McKenney, J. 2004. New perspectives on the use of niacin in the treatment of lipid disorders. *Archives of Internal Medicine* 164:697–705.

McMahon, R. 2002. Biotin in metabolism and molecular biology. *Annual Review of Nutrition* 22:221–39.

Mehta, J. 1999. Antioxidants are useful in preventing cardiovascular disease: A debate. Con antioxidants. *Canadian Journal of Cardiology* 15:26B–28B.

Miller, E., et al. 2005. Meta-analysis: High-dosage vitamin E supplementation may increase all-cause mortality. *Annals of Internal Medicine* 142:37–46.

Mock, D. M. 2006. Biotin. In *Modern Nutrition in Health and Disease*, eds. M. Shils, et al. Philadelphia: Lippincott Williams & Wilkins.

Moon, J., et al. 1992. Hypothesis: Etiology of atherosclerosis and osteoporosis: Are imbalances in the calciferol endocrine system implicated? *Journal of the American College of Nutrition* 11:567–83.

Munoz, F., et al. 2005. The protective effect of vitamin E in vascular amyloid beta-mediated damage. *Subcellular Biochemistry* 38:147–65.

Ness, A. R., et al. 1997. Vitamin C and blood pressure: An overview. *Journal of Human Hypertension* 11:342–50.

Nieman, D. 2001. Exercise immunology: Nutritional countermeasures. *Canadian Journal of Applied Physiology* 26:S45–55.

Omenn, G. S. 1998. An assessment of the scientific basis for attempting to define the Dietary Reference Intake for beta-carotene. *Journal of the American Dietetic Association* 98:1406–9.

Omenn, G. S. 1998. Chemoprevention of lung cancer: The rise and demise of beta-carotene. *Annual Review of Public Health* 19:73–99.

Palace, V. P., et al. 1999. Antioxidant potentials of vitamin A and carotenoids and their relevance to heart disease. *Free Radical Biology and Medicine* 26:746–61.

Peake, J. 2003. Vitamin C: Effects of exercise and requirements with training. *International Journal of Sport Nutrition and Exercise Metabolism* 13:125–51.

Pieper, J. 2002. Understanding niacin formulations. *American Journal of Management Care* 8:S308–14.

Powers, S., et al. 2004. Dietary antioxidants and exercise. *Journal of Sports Sciences* 22:81–94.

Prasad, K., et al. 1999. High doses of multiple antioxidant vitamins: Essential ingredients in improving the efficacy of standard cancer therapy. *Journal of the American College of Nutrition* 18:13–25.

Pryor, W., et al. 2000. Beta carotene: From biochemistry to clinical trials. *Nutrition Reviews* 58:39–53.

Pryor, W. 2000. Vitamin E and heart disease: Basic science to clinical intervention trials. *Free Radicals Biology & Medicine* 28:141–64.

Raiten, D., and Picciano, M. 2004. Vitamin D and health in the 21st century: Bone and beyond. *American Journal of Clinical Nutrition* 80:1673S–77S.

Rimm, E., and Stampfer, M. J. 1997. The role of antioxidants in preventive cardiology. *Current Opinion in Cardiology* 12:188–94.

Ross, A. C. 2006. Vitamin A and retinoids. In *Modern Nutrition in Health and Disease,* eds. M. Shils, et al. Philadelphia: Lippincott Williams & Wilkins.

Rothenberg, S. 1999. Increasing the dietary intake of folate: Pros and cons. *Seminars in Hematology* 36:65–74.

Sacheck, J., and Blumberg, J. 2001. Role of vitamin E and oxidative stress in exercise. *Nutrition* 17:809–14.

Sacheck, J., and Roubenoff, R. 1999. Nutrition in the exercising elderly. *Clinics in Sports Medicine* 18:565–84.

Schneider, C. 2005. Chemistry and biology of vitamin E. *Molecular Nutrition & Food Research* 49:7–30.

Schwammenthal, Y., and Tanne, D. 2004. Homocysteine B-vitamin supplementation, and stroke prevention: From observational to interventional trials. *Lancet Neurology* 3:493–95.

Seman, L., et al. 1999. Lipoprotein (a), homocysteine, and remnantlike particles: Emerging risk factors. *Current Opinion in Cardiology* 14:186–91.

Sen, C. 2001. Antioxidants in exercise nutrition. *Sports Medicine* 31:891–908.

Sen, C., et al. 2000. Exercise-induced oxidative stress and antioxidant nutrients. In *Nutrition in Sport,* ed. R. J. Maughan. Oxford: Blackwell Science.

Short, S. 1994. Surveys of dietary intake and nutrition knowledge of athletes and their coaches. In *Nutrition in Exercise and Sport,* eds. I. Wolinsky and J. Hickson. Boca Raton, FL: CRC Press.

Simon-Schnass, I. 1993. Vitamin requirements for increased physical activity: Vitamin E. In *Nutrition and Fitness for Athletes* 71:144–53, eds. A. Simopoulos and K. Pavlou. Basel, Switzerland: Karger.

Sobol, J., and Marquart, L. 1994. Vitamin/mineral supplement use among athletes: A review of the literature. *International Journal of Sport Nutrition* 4:320–34.

Steinmetz, K., and Potter, J. 1996. Vegetables, fruit, and cancer prevention: A review. *Journal of the American Dietetic Association* 96:1027–39.

Stipanuk, M. 2006. Homocysteine, cysteine and taurine. In *Modern Nutrition in Health and Disease,* eds. M. Shils, et al. Philadelphia: Lippincott Williams & Wilkins.

Suttie, J. 2006. Vitamin K. In *Modern Nutrition in Health and Disease,* eds. M. Shils, et al. Philadelphia: Lippincott Williams & Wilkins.

Takanami, Y., et al. 2000. Vitamin E supplementation and endurance exercise: Are there benefits? *Sports Medicine* 29:73–83.

Tanphaichitr, V. 1999. Thiamin. In *Modern Nutrition in Health and Disease,* eds. M. Shils, et al. Philadelphia: Lippincott Williams & Wilkins.

Tiidus, P., and Houston, M. 1995. Vitamin E status and response to exercise training. *Sports Medicine* 20:12–23.

Traber, M. G. 2006. Vitamin E. In *Modern Nutrition in Health and Disease,* eds. M. Shils, et al. Philadelphia: Lippincott Williams & Wilkins.

Tran, M., et al. 2001. Role of coenzyme Q10 in chronic heart failure, angina, and hypertension. *Pharmacotherapy* 21:797–806.

Tufts University. 2002. Antioxidant supplements lose promise as disease preventers. *Tufts University Health & Nutrition Letter* 20 (1):4–5.

Tufts University. 2002. Eating for eye health. *Tufts University Health & Nutrition Letter* 19 (11):4–5.

Vainio, H., and Rautalahti, M. 1999. An international evaluation of the cancer preventive potential of vitamin A. *Cancer Epidemiology, Biomarkers and Prevention* 8:107–9.

van der Beek, E. 1991. Vitamin supplementation and physical exercise performance. *Journal of Sports Sciences* 92:77–79.

Vieth, R., and Fraser, D. 2002. Vitamin D insufficiency: No recommended dietary allowance exists for this nutrient. *Canadian Medical Association Journal* 166:1541–42.

Vieth, R. 1999. Vitamin D supplementation, 25-hydroxyvitamin D concentrations, and safety. *American Journal of Clinical Nutrition* 69:842–56.

Viitala, P., and Newhouse, I. 2004. Vitamin E supplementation, exercise and lipid peroxidation in human participants. *European Journal of Applied Physiology* 93:108–15.

Weaver, C., and Fleet, J. 2005. Vitamin D requirements: Current and future. *American Journal of Clinical Nutrition* 80:1735S–39S.

Webb, D. 2002. From starring role to bit part: Has the curtain come down on vitamin E? *Environmental Nutrition* 25 (5):1, 4.

Webb, D. 1997. Coenzyme Q_{10}: Miracle nutrient or merely promising? *Environmental Nutrition* 20 (11): 1, 4.

Weber, P. 2001. Vitamin K and bone health. *Nutrition* 17:880–87.

Weber, P. 1996. Vitamin C and human health: A review of recent data relevant to human requirements. *International Journal of Vitamin and Nutrition Research* 66:19–30.

Williams, M. 1989. Vitamin supplementation and athletic performance. *International Journal for Vitamin and Nutrition Research,* Supplement 30:161–91.

Zachman, R. D., and Grummer, M. A. 1998. The interaction of ethanol and vitamin A as a potential mechanism for the pathogenesis of Fetal Alcohol Syndrome. *Alcoholism, Clinical and Experimental Research* 22:1544–56.

Zeisel, S., and Niculescu, M. 2006. Choline and phosphatidylcholine. In *Modern Nutrition in Health and Disease,* eds. M. Shils, et al. Philadelphia: Lippincott Williams & Wilkins

Zittermann, A. 2001. Effects of vitamin K on calcium and bone metabolism. *Current Opinion in Clinical Nutrition and Metabolic Care* 4:483–87.

Specific Studies

Ascherio, A., et al. 1999. Relation of consumption of vitamin E, vitamin C, and carotenoids to risk for stroke among men in the United States. *Annals of Internal Medicine* 130:963–70.

Avery, N., et al. 2003. Effects of vitamin E supplementation on recovery from repeated bouts of resistance exercise. *Journal of Strength and Conditioning Research* 17:801–09.

Bell, C., et al. 2005. Ascorbic acid does not affect the age-associated reduction in maximal cardiac output and oxygen consumption in healthy adults. *Journal of Applied Physiology* 98:845–49.

Bonetti, A., et al. 2000. Effect of ubidecarenone oral treatment on aerobic power in middle-aged trained subjects. *Journal of Sports Medicine and Physical Fitness* 40:51–57.

Bonke, D. 1986. Influence of vitamin B_1, B_6 and B_{12} on the control of fine motoric movements. *Bibliotheca Nutritio et Dieta* 38:104–9.

Braam, L., et al. 2003. Factors affecting bone loss in female endurance athletes: A two-year follow-up study. *American Journal of Sports Medicine* 31:889–95.

Braun, B., et al. 1991. The effect of coenzyme Q10 supplementation on exercise performance, VO$_2$max, and lipid peroxidation in trained cyclists. *International Journal of Sport Nutrition* 1:353–65.

Bryant, R., et al. 2003. Effects of vitamin E and C supplementation either alone or in combination on exercise-induced lipid peroxidation in trained cyclists. *Journal of Strength and Conditioning Research* 17:792–800.

Buchman, A., et al. 2000. The effect of lecithin supplementation on plasma choline concentrations during a marathon. *Journal of the American College of Nutrition* 19:768–70.

Chandler, J., and Hawkins, J. 1984. The effect of bee pollen on physiological performance. *International Journal of Biosocial Research* 6:107–14.

Child, R. B., et al. 1998. Elevated serum antioxidant capacity and plasma malondialdehyde concentration in response to a simulated half-marathon run. *Medicine & Science in Sports & Exercise* 30:1603–7.

Chiu, K., et al. 2004. Hypovitaminosis D is associated with insulin resistance and β cell dysfunction. *American Journal of Clinical Nutrition* 79:820–25.

Coburn, S., et al. 1990. Effect of vitamin B$_6$ intake on the vitamin content of human muscle. *FASEB Journal* 4:A365.

Craciun, A. M., et al. 1998. Improved bone metabolism in female elite athletes after vitamin K supplementation. *International Journal of Sports Medicine* 19:479–84.

Curhan, G., et al. 1996. A prospective study of the intake of vitamin C and B$_6$, and the risk of kidney stones in men. *Journal of Urology* 155:1847–51.

Dawson, B., et al. 2002. Effect of vitamin C and E supplementation on biochemical and ultrastructural indices of muscle damage after a 21-km run. *International Journal of Sports Medicine* 23:10–15.

Dhesi, J., et al. 2004. Vitamin D supplementation improves neuromuscular function in older people who fall. *Age and Ageing* 33:589–95.

Doyle, M., et al. 1997. Allithiamine ingestion does not enhance isokinetic parameters of muscle performance. *International Journal of Sport Nutrition* 7:39–47.

Englehart, M., et al. 2002. Dietary intake of antioxidants and risk of Alzheimer disease. *JAMA* 287:3223–29.

Feskanich, D., et al. 2002. Vitamin A intake and hip fractures among postmenopausal women. *JAMA* 287:47–54.

Forman, J., et al. 2005. Folate intake and the risk of incident hypertension among US women. *JAMA* 293:320–29.

Gridley, G., et al. 1992. Vitamin supplement use and reduced risk of oral and pharyngeal cancer. *American Journal of Epidemiology* 135:1083–92.

Haralambie, G. 1976. Vitamin B$_2$ status in athletes and the influence of riboflavin administration on neuromuscular irritability. *Nutrition and Metabolism* 20:1–8.

Heath, E., et al. 1993. Effect of nicotinic acid on respiratory exchange ratio and substrate levels during exercise. *Medicine & Science in Sport & Exercise* 25:1018–23.

Heinonen, O. P., et al. 1998. Prostate cancer and supplementation with alpha-tocopherol and beta-carotene: Incidence and mortality in a controlled trial. *Journal of the National Cancer Institute* 90:440–6.

Hoffman, A., et al. 1989. Plasma pyridoxal phosphate concentrations in response to ingesting water or glucose polymer during a two hour run. *Medicine & Science in Sport & Exercise* 21:S59.

Itoh, H., et al. 2000. Vitamin E supplementation attenuates leakage of enzymes following 6 successive days of running training. *International Journal of Sport Medicine* 21:369–74.

Jacobson, B., et al. 2001. Nutrition practices and knowledge of college varsity athletes: A follow-up. *Journal of Strength and Conditioning Research* 15:63–68.

John, E. M., et al. 1999. Vitamin D and breast cancer risk: The NHANES I epidemiologic follow-up study, 1971–75 to 1992. *Cancer Epidemiology, Biomarkers and Prevention* 8:399–406.

Johnston, C., et al. 1998. Vitamin C status of a campus population: College students get a C minus. *Journal of the American College of Health* 46:209–13.

Kaikkonen, J., et al. 1998. Effect of combined coenzyme Q$_{10}$ and d-alpha-tocopheryl acetate supplementation on exercise-induced lipid peroxidation and muscular damage: A placebo-controlled double-blind study in marathon runners. *Free Radical Research* 29:85–92.

Kim, I., et al. 1993. Vitamin and mineral supplement use and mortality in a U.S. cohort. *American Journal of Public Health* 83:546–50.

Kobayashi, Y. 1974. Effect of vitamin E on aerobic work performance in man during acute exposure to hypoxic hypoxia. Unpublished doctoral dissertation. University of New Mexico.

Kolka, M., and Stephenson, l. 1990. Skin blood flow during exercise after niacin ingestion. *FASEB Journal* 4:A279.

Krumbach, C. J., et al. 1999. A report of vitamin and mineral supplement use among university athletes in a Division I institution. *International Journal of Sport Nutrition* 9:416–25.

Kurl, S., et al. 2002. Plasma vitamin C modifies the association between hypertension and risk of stroke. *Stroke* 33:1568–73.

Kushi, L., et al. 1996. Dietary antioxidant vitamins and death from coronary heart disease in postmenopausal women. *New England Journal of Medicine* 334:1156–62.

Laaksonen, R., et al. 1995. Ubiquinone supplementation and exercise capacity in trained young and older men. *European Journal of Applied Physiology* 72:95–100.

Lee, B., et al. 2004. Folic acid and vitamin B$_{12}$ are more effective than vitamin B$_6$ in lowering fasting plasma homocysteine concentration in patients with coronary artery disease. *European Journal of Clinical Nutrition* 58:481–87.

Leonard, S., and Leklem, J. 2000. Plasma B-6 vitamer changes following a 50-km ultra-marathon. *International Journal of Sport Nutrition and Exercise Metabolism* 10:302–14.

Lonn, E., et al. 2005. Effects of long-term vitamin E supplementation on cardiovascular events and cancer: A randomized controlled trial. *JAMA* 293:1338–47.

Losonczy, K., et al. 1996. Vitamin E and vitamin C supplement use and risk of all cause and coronary heart disease mortality in older persons: The Established Populations for Epidemiologic Studies of the Elderly. *American Journal of Clinical Nutrition* 64:190–96.

Malm, C., et al. 1996. Supplementation with ubiquinone-10 causes cellular damage during intense exercise. *Acta Physiologica Scandinavica* 157:511–12.

Matter, M., et al. 1987. The effect of iron and folate therapy on maximal exercise performance in female marathon runners with iron and folate deficiency. *Clinical Science* 72:415–22.

McKinley, M., et al. 2001. Low-dose vitamin B-6 effectively lowers fasting plasma homocysteine in healthy elderly persons who are folate and riboflavin replete. *American Journal of Clinical Nutrition* 73:759–64.

Meagher, E., et al. 2001. Effects of vitamin E on lipid peroxidation in healthy persons. *JAMA* 285:1178–82.

Morris, M. C., et al. 2002. Dietary intake of antioxidant nutrients and the risk of incident Alzheimer disease in a biracial community study. *JAMA* 287:3230–37.

Morris, M. C., et al. 1998. Vitamin E and vitamin C supplement use and risk of incident Alzheimer disease. *Alzheimer Disease and Associated Disorders* 12:121–26.

Murray, R., et al. 1995. Physiological and performance responses to nicotinic-acid ingestion during exercise. *Medicine & Science in Sport & Exercise* 27:1057–62.

Nielsen, A. N., et al. 1999. No effect of antioxidant supplementation in triathletes on maximal oxygen uptake, 31P-NMRS detected muscle energy metabolism and muscle fatigue. *International Journal of Sports Medicine* 20:154–58.

Nieman, D., et al. 2004. Vitamin E and immunity after the Kona Triathlon World Championship. *Medicine & Science in Sports & Exercise* 36:1328–35.

Nieman, D., et al. 2002. Influence of vitamin C supplementation on oxidative and immune changes after an ultramarathon. *Journal of Applied Physiology* 92:1970–77.

Paganini-Hill, A., and Perez Barreto, M. 2001. Stroke risk in older men and women: Aspirin, estrogen, exercise, vitamins, and other factors. *Journal of Gender-Specific Medicine* 4:18–28.

Patterson, R. E., et al. 1998. Cancer-related behavior of vitamin supplement users. *Cancer Epidemiology, Biomarkers and Prevention* 7:79–81.

Peters, E., et al. 1993. Vitamin C supplementation reduces the incidence of postrace symptoms of upper-respiratory-tract infection in ultramarathon runners. *American Journal of Clinical Nutrition* 57:170–74.

Pincemail, J., et al. 1988. Tocopherol mobilization during intensive exercise. *European Journal of Applied Physiology* 57:188–91.

Racek, J., et al. 2005. The influence of folate and antioxidants on homocysteine levels and oxidative stress in patients with hyperlipidemia and hyperhomocysteinemia. *Physiological Research* 54:87–95.

Rimm, E., et al. 1993. Vitamin E consumption and the risk of coronary heart disease in man. *New England Journal of Medicine* 328:1450–56.

Rokitzki, L., et al. 1994. Acute changes in vitamin B_6 status in endurance athletes before and after a marathon. *International Journal of Sport Nutrition* 4:154–65.

Rokitzki, L., et al. 1994. α-tocopherol supplementation in racing cyclists during extreme endurance training. *International Journal of Sport Nutrition* 4:253–64.

Rothman, K., et al. 1995. Teratogenicity of high vitamin A intake. *New England Journal of Medicine* 333:1369–73.

Salonen, R., et al. 2003. Six-year effect of combined C and E supplementation on atherosclerotic progression: The Antioxidant Supplementation in Atherosclerosis Prevention (ASAP) Study. *Circulation* 107:947–53.

Schutte, A., et al. 2004. Cardiovascular effect of oral supplementation of vitamin C, E and folic acid in young healthy males. *International Journal of Vitamin Nutrition Research* 74:285–93.

Simon-Schnass, I., and Pabst, H. 1988. Influence of vitamin E on physical performance. *International Journal for Vitamin and Nutrition Research* 58:49–54.

Singh, A., et al. 1992. Chronic multivitamin-mineral supplementation does not enhance physical performance. *Medicine & Science in Sport & Exercise* 24:726–32.

Smith, W., et al. 1999. Dietary antioxidants and age-related maculopathy: The Blue Mountains Eye Study. *Ophthalmology* 106:761–67.

Snider, I., et al. 1992. Effects of coenzyme athletic performance system as an ergogenic aid on endurance performance to exhaustion. *International Journal of Sport Nutrition* 2:272–86.

Stampfer, M., et al. 1993. Vitamin E consumption and the risk of coronary heart disease in women. *New England Journal of Medicine* 328:1444–49.

Suzuki, M., and Itokawa, Y. 1996. Effects of thiamine supplementation on exercise-induced fatigue. *Metabolism in Brain Diseases* 11:95–106.

Svensson, M., et al. 1999. Effect of Q_{10} supplementation on tissue Q_{10} levels and adenine nucleotide catabolism during high-intensity exercise. *International Journal of Sport Nutrition* 9:166–80.

Teikari, J. M., et al. 1998. Six-year supplementation with alpha-tocopherol and beta-carotene and age-related maculopathy. *Acta Ophthalmologica Scandinavica* 76:224–29.

Telford, R., et al. 1992. The effect of 7 to 8 months of vitamin/mineral supplementation on athletic performance. *International Journal of Sport Nutrition* 2:135–53.

Telford, R., et al. 1992. The effect of 7 to 8 months of vitamin/mineral supplementation on the vitamin and mineral status of athletes. *International Journal of Sport Nutrition* 2:123–34.

Thompson, D., et al. 2004. Prolonged vitamin C supplementation and recovery from eccentric exercise. *European Journal of Applied Physiology* 92:133–38.

Tremblay, A., et al. 1984. The effects of a riboflavin supplementation on the nutritional status and performance of elite swimmers. *Nutrition Research* 4:201.

Troppman, L., et al. 2002. Supplement use: Is there any nutritional benefit? *Journal of the American Dietetic Association* 102:818–25.

van Dijk, R., et al. 2001. Long-term homocysteine-lowering treatment with folic acid plus pyridoxine is associated with decreased blood pressure but not with improved brachial artery endothelium-dependent vasodilation or carotid artery stiffness: A 2-year, randomized, placebo-controlled trial. *Arteriosclerosis, Thrombosis, and Vascular Biology* 21:2072–79.

van Erp-Baart, A., et al. 1989. Nationwide survey on nutritional habits in elite athletes. *International Journal of Sports Medicine* 10 (Suppl 1): S11–S16.

Verhaar, H., et al. 2000. Muscle strength, functional mobility and vitamin D in older women. *Aging* 12:455–60.

Virk, R. S., et al. 1999. Effect of vitamin B-6 supplementation on fuels, catecholamines, and amino acids during exercise in men. *Medicine & Science in Sports & Exercise* 31:400–8.

Warber, J., et al. 2000. The effects of choline supplementation on physical performance. *International Journal of*

Sport Nutrition and Exercise Metabolism 10:170–81.

Watson, T., et al. 2005. Antioxidant restriction and oxidative stress in short-duration exhaustive exercise. *Medicine & Science in Sports & Exercise* 37:63–71.

Webster, M. J. 1998. Physiological and performance responses to supplementation with thiamin and pantothenic acid derivatives. *European Journal of Applied Physiology* 77:486–91.

Webster, M. J., et al. 1997. The effect of a thiamin derivative on exercise performance. *European Journal of Applied Physiology* 75:520–24.

Weight, L., et al. 1988. Vitamin and mineral supplementation: Effect on the running performance of trained athletes. *American Journal of Clinical Nutrition* 47:192–95.

Weston, S., et al. 1997. Does exogenous coenzyme Q_{10} affect aerobic capacity in endurance athletes? *International Journal of Sport Nutrition* 7:197–206.

Wyatt, K. M., et al. 1999. Efficacy of vitamin B-6 in the treatment of premenstrual syndrome: Systematic review. *British Medical Journal* 318:1375–81.

Ylikoski, T., et al. 1997. The effect of coenzyme Q_{10} on the exercise performance of cross-country skiers. *Molecular Aspects of Medicine* 18:S283–S290.

Zhang, S., et al. 1999. A prospective study of folate intake and the risk of breast cancer. *Journal of the American Medical Association* 281:1632–37.

Ziegler, P., et al. 2002. Nutritional status of teenage female competitive figure skaters. *Journal of the American Dietetic Association* 102:374–79.

Minerals: The Inorganic Regulators

CHAPTER EIGHT

LEARNING OBJECTIVES

After studying this chapter, you should be able to:

1. Describe the various means whereby minerals may carry out their functions in the human body.

2. Name the essential minerals, state the RDA or AI for each, and identify several foods rich in each mineral.

3. Describe the metabolic roles in the human body of calcium, phosphorus, magnesium, iron, copper, zinc, chromium, selenium, fluoride, and iodine.

4. Explain the role of calcium in bone metabolism and identify the factors that may contribute to bone health and those that may contribute to osteoporosis.

5. Explain the theory as to how phosphate salt supplementation may enhance sport performance, and highlight the research findings regarding its ergogenic efficacy.

6. Explain the potential effects on health and sport performance associated with a deficiency of each trace mineral.

7. Explain the theory as to how iron, zinc, chromium, selenium, boron, and vanadium may enhance sport performance, and highlight the research findings regarding the ergogenic efficacy of each.

8. Understand why health professionals may recommend mineral supplements under certain circumstances to improve the health of some individuals.

You may recall the periodic table of the elements hanging on the wall in your high school or college chemistry class. At latest count there were 116 known elements, seventy-eight of them occurring naturally and the remainder being synthetic. Many of the natural elements, including a wide variety of minerals, are essential to human bodily structure and function.

Much research attention is currently being devoted to the role of mineral nutrition in health and disease, including both epidemiological and laboratory research. For example, using the RDA as a basis for comparison, national surveys among the general population have revealed that either an inadequate dietary intake of some minerals or an excessive dietary intake of others in certain small segments of the population may be contributing to several health problems. Laboratory studies using either animals or humans as subjects have explored the roles of both deficiencies and supplementation of minerals on human health and disease processes.

An increasing number of research studies have been conducted with athletes to evaluate the effect of mineral nutrition on physical performance and the converse—the effect of exercise on mineral metabolism. Because some minerals function similarly to vitamins, a deficiency state could adversely affect performance. Moreover, exercise in itself may be a contributing factor to mineral deficiencies or impaired mineral metabolism in some types of athletes. Additionally, several mineral supplements are being marketed specifically for physically active individuals.

This chapter is especially important to all females and young athletes because it addresses two of their major dietary concerns, obtaining sufficient calcium and obtaining sufficient iron. These key minerals are of particular interest to females who participate in sports or are otherwise physically active. The female athlete triad—disordered eating, amenorrhea, and osteoporosis—is introduced in this chapter with the major focus on osteoporosis because of its relationship to calcium metabolism. An expanded discussion of eating disorders is presented in chapter 10. Female endurance athletes also need to obtain adequate dietary iron intake because of its important role in the oxygen energy system.

The major purpose of this chapter is to analyze the available data relative to the effect of mineral nutrition on physical performance and health. The first section discusses some basic facts about the general role of those minerals that are essential to human nutrition. The second and third sections cover, respectively, the major minerals and the trace minerals. In these two sections, each of the minerals is discussed in terms of its Dietary Reference Intake (DRI), good dietary sources, metabolic functions in the body with particular reference to the physically active individual, an evaluation of the research pertaining to the effects of deficiencies or supplementation on health or exercise performance, and prudent recommendations. The last section summarizes dietary mineral nutrition guidelines for those who exercise for health or sport.

Basic Facts

What are minerals, and what is their importance to humans?

A **mineral** is an inorganic element found in nature, and the term is usually reserved for those elements that are solid. Hence, a mineral is an element, but an element is not necessarily a mineral. For example, oxygen is an element, but it is not classified as a mineral. In nutrition, the term *mineral* is usually used to classify those dietary elements essential to life processes.

Minerals are found in the soil and are eventually incorporated in growing plants. Animals get their mineral nutrition from the plants they eat, whereas humans obtain their supply from both plant and animal food. Drinking water also may be a good source of several minerals. As minerals are excreted daily from the body in sweat, urine, or feces, they must be replaced.

Minerals serve two of the three basic functions of nutrients in foods. First, many are used as the building blocks for body tissues such as bones, teeth, muscles, and other organic structures. Second, a number of minerals are components of enzymes known as **metalloenzymes,** which are involved in the regulation of metabolism. Several other minerals exist as **ions,** or **electrolytes,** which are small particles carrying electrical charges. They are important components or activators of several enzymes and hormones. Speich and others recently reviewed the physiological roles of minerals important to athletes, noting that minerals are involved in muscle contraction, normal heart rhythm, nerve impulse conduction, oxygen transport, oxidative phosphorylation, enzyme activation, immune functions, antioxidant activity, bone health, acid-base balance of the blood, and maintenance of body water supplies. Minerals do not provide a source of caloric energy, which is the third function of nutrients.

Inadequate mineral nutrition has been associated with impairment of normal physiological functions, as well as with a variety of human diseases, including anemia, high blood pressure, diabetes, cancer, tooth decay, and osteoporosis. Thus, proper dietary intake of essential minerals is necessary for optimal health and physical performance.

What minerals are essential to human nutrition?

Of all the elements in the periodic table, only twenty-five are currently known to be, or presumed to be, essential in humans. Five of these elements, which make up the carbohydrate, fat, and protein that we eat and the water we drink, constitute over 96 percent of the body weight. In varying combinations, hydrogen, oxygen, carbon, sulfur, and nitrogen are the components of the body water, protein, fat, and carbohydrate stores. The remaining twenty minerals compose less than 4 percent of the body weight but are equally important.

Table 8.1 lists those minerals for which the National Academy of Sciences (NAS) has established a DRI or other recommenda-

tion. The DRIs include the Recommended Dietary Allowance (RDA), the Adequate Intake (AI), and the Tolerable Upper Intake Level (UL). The NAS has recently established the RDA or AI for most minerals, discussed in this chapter, and for sodium, chloride, and potassium, elements that are discussed in the next chapter. Sulfur is found in the diet mainly as a component of the sulfur-containing amino acids (methionine and cysteine), and body needs are satisfied by the RDA for these amino acids.

Other minerals such as boron, nickel, silicon, and vanadium, among others, are found in animal tissues and also may be important to human nutrition, but their roles have not yet been completely elucidated and thus no RDA or AI have yet been established, but UL have been set for nickel and vanadium.

In general, how do deficiencies or excesses of minerals influence health or physical performance?

Similar to vitamin deficiencies, mineral deficiencies may occur in several stages. The first three stages (preliminary, biochemical deficiency, and physiological deficiency) may be termed subclinical

TABLE 8.1 Mineral Dietary Reference Intakes for adults aged 19–50*

Mineral	Symbol	RDA or AI (mg)		UL (mg)	Amount in adult body (g)
Calcium (2)	Ca	1,000 ♂	1,000 ♀	2,500	1,500
Phosphorus (1)	P	700 ♂	700 ♀	4,000	850
Potassium (2)	K	4,700 ♂	4,700 ♀	ND	180
Chloride (2)	Cl	2,300 ♂	2,300 ♀	3,500	75
Sodium (2)	Na	1,500 ♂	1,500 ♀	2,300	65
Magnesium (1)	Mg	420 ♂	320 ♀	350	25
Iron (1)	Fe	8 ♂	18 ♀	45	5
Fluoride (2)	F	4 ♂	3.0 ♀	10	2.5
Zinc (1)	Zn	11 ♂	8 ♀	40	2
Copper (1)	Cu	0.9 ♂	0.9 ♀	10	0.1
Selenium (1)	Se	0.055 ♂	0.055 ♀	0.4	0.013
Manganese (2)	Mn	2.3 ♂	1.8 ♀	11	0.012
Iodine (1)	I	0.15 ♂	0.15 ♀	1.1	0.011
Molybdenum (1)	Mo	0.045 ♂	0.045 ♀	2	0.009
Chromium (2)	Cr	0.035 ♂	0.025 ♀	ND	0.006

*Different terms are used to quantify the recommended dietary intake of minerals: (1) Recommended Dietary Allowance (RDA); (2) Adequate Intake (AI). The UL listed is for adult males; lower values are set for females and other age groups. See the DRI tables on the inside of the front and back covers for more details. Arsenic, boron, nickel, silicon, and vanadium are also covered in the DRI reports, but no RDA or AI have been established. A UL has been set for nickel and vanadium.
ND=not determined

malnutrition and may or may not have significant effects on health or physical performance. In the clinically manifest deficiency state, however, health and performance most likely will suffer.

The interaction of exercise and mineral nutrition may pose some special health problems, as we shall see in later sections of this chapter. In regard to the preliminary stage, some athletes may reduce their mineral intake as they shift toward a low-Calorie diet. Changes in food selection may also be important, for the bioavailability of many minerals is markedly influenced by the form in which they are consumed. In general, most minerals are poorly absorbed from the intestine. For example, the RDA for iron is ten times the amount actually needed by the body, because only about 10 percent of dietary iron from the average American diet is absorbed. Moreover, mineral absorption may be inhibited by certain compounds in foods, and supplementation with one mineral may impair the absorption of another. In athletes, factors that lower intake and absorption may be compounded because athletic activity may raise some mineral requirements. Additional minerals may be needed for the synthesis of new tissues associated with physical training, or to replace losses in the sweat, urine, and feces often observed during and following intense exercise training.

Sports nutritionists are becoming concerned that the presence of these factors during the preliminary stage of a mineral deficiency could lead to the subsequent stages of subclinical malnutrition or even to a clinical deficiency. Based on dietary surveys and clinical studies with biochemical measures of mineral status, Pennington reported there is some concern for adequate calcium, iron, and zinc nutrition in some segments of the United States population. Most dietary surveys indicate athletes, particularly males, are obtaining the RDA for all minerals. However, a number of studies have reported athletes with inadequate dietary intake and biochemical deficiencies of several minerals, predominately athletes involved in weight-control sports such as gymnastics, figure skating, and wrestling. Switching to a vegetarian diet for 1 year also decreased plasma levels of several minerals. Experts disagree about the potential adverse effects of such dietary or biochemical deficiencies, but certain physiologic and clinically manifest mineral deficiencies are known to have impaired physical performance.

The human body possesses a very effective control system for some minerals. When a deficiency occurs, the body absorbs more of the mineral from the food in the intestine and excretes less via routes such as the urine. When an excess is consumed, the opposite is true; less is absorbed and more is excreted. On the other hand, the body has a limited ability to excrete certain minerals, so excessive consumption may override these natural control systems and cause a number of health problems, even in relatively small dosages. Additionally, a few minerals not important to human nutrition, such as lead, mercury, cadmium, arsenic, and some industrial forms of chromium, may be extremely toxic to the human body. For example, as discussed in chapter 5, mercury in polluted waterways may accumulate in fish which if eaten may damage the nervous system of unborn or young children.

Let us now detail the role of various macrominerals and trace minerals in health and exercise performance.

Key Concept Recap

▶ Minerals perform two of the three major functions of food, including the formation of several body tissues and the regulation of numerous physiological processes. Minerals do not contain energy per se, such as Calories, but they do help regulate energy processes in the body.

▶ RDA or AI have been established for 15 different minerals. UL have also been established for most minerals, including several for which no RDA or AI have been established. Like vitamins, the mineral DRI have been modified to help prevent chronic diseases, such as osteoporosis.

▶ Mineral deficiencies or excess may have adverse effects on both health and sports performance.

Check for Yourself

Check the food labels for various foods you have in the cupboard to see what minerals are listed. If the DV is provided, compare the amount of the mineral provided and its DV with the current RDA or AI. Relate your findings to the text discussion.

Macrominerals

The seven **macrominerals** (major minerals) are calcium, phosphorus, magnesium, potassium, sodium, chloride, and sulfur. Minerals are classified as macrominerals if the RDA or AI is greater than 100 mg per day or the body contains more than 5 grams. In general, the human body maintains a proper balance of these minerals through precise hormonal control mechanisms, but deficiencies or excesses may occur and disturb normal physiological functions, thus impairing health or physical performance. Sulfur, an integral component of several amino acids and vitamins, is not discussed here because its functions are associated with those nutrients. Because potassium, sodium, and chloride are the major electrolytes in sweat, and in some sports drinks, they are covered in the following chapter dealing with water and temperature regulation.

Calcium (Ca)

Calcium, a silver-white metallic element, is the most abundant mineral in the body, representing almost 2 percent of the body weight.

DRI The AI for calcium is intended to provide optimal amounts for health, particularly for bone health and the prevention of osteoporosis. The daily recommendations, in parentheses, are given for several selected age groups: children 1–3 years (500 mg); youths 4–8 years (800 mg); youth and adolescents 9–18 years (1,300 mg); adults 19–50 (1,000 mg); adults 50 and older (1,200 mg). Pregnant and breast-feeding women should get the amount recommended for their age group. The DV is 1,000 mg. The Tolerable Upper Intake Level (UL) is 2,500 mg per day.

Food Sources Calcium content is highest in dairy products. One 8-ounce glass of skim milk, which contains about 300 mg of calcium, supplies about one-third of the RDA for an adult and one-fourth for adolescents and adults 50 and over. It is used as the basis of comparison for other foods. Other equivalent dairy foods are $1\frac{1}{2}$ ounces of cheese, 1 cup of yogurt, and $1\frac{3}{4}$ cups of ice cream. Other good sources are fish with small bones such as sardines and canned salmon, dark-green leafy vegetables (particularly broccoli, kale, and turnip greens), calcium-set tofu, legumes, and nuts. Incorporation of milk or cheese into foods such as soups, pasta dishes, and pizza is an excellent way to obtain dietary calcium. For individuals with lactose intolerance, the use of yogurt, lactase enzymes, or smaller portions of milk may be helpful. Calcium is also used as a preservative in some foods, such as breads, which may provide small amounts. Additionally, some food products such as orange juice and cereals are now being fortified with calcium; one serving of orange juice may contain 300–350 milligrams while one brand of cereal contains 100 percent of the calcium DV. Foods high in calcium are listed in table 8.2.

Calcium is one of the key nutrients listed on food labels, and although the food label does not indicate the milligrams of calcium per serving, you can calculate the amount fairly easily. The Daily Value (DV) for calcium is 1,000 milligrams, and the label will provide you with the percentage of the calcium DV contained in one serving. All you need to do is multiply the percentage, as a decimal, times 1,000 milligrams. For example, if a glass of calcium-fortified orange juice provides you with 30 percent of the DV, then it contains 300 milligrams of calcium ($0.30 \times 1,000$ milligrams = 300 milligrams). Both the United States and Canada

have approved food label health claims for calcium if one serving contains 20 percent of the Daily Value, or 200 milligrams.

Some nutrients in food may influence calcium absorption or excretion. The calcium in milk appears to be absorbed more readily because vitamin D and lactose in milk facilitate absorption. Calcium absorption from broccoli, cabbage, and kale is good, but the calcium content per serving is much less than that for milk. Phytates (phytic acid compounds) found in legumes and oxalates in spinach may diminish somewhat the absorption of calcium from those foods. Dietary fiber may reduce calcium absorption, although the effect is rather variable and presumably small. Dietary phosphorus may also decrease calcium absorption, but decreases its excretion by the kidney as well, so its effect on calcium balance is somewhat neutral. Excess sodium intake increases calcium excretion. Dawson-Hughes indicates that for every 500-mg increase in urinary sodium excretion, there is about a 10-mg increase in urinary calcium loss. As mentioned in chapter 6, excessive protein intake may lead to calcium excretion, an estimate cited by the National Dairy Council being 1 milligram of calcium lost for every gram of protein consumed. However, as also noted, adequate protein intake is needed to optimize calcium bone metabolism.

Overall, however, calcium balance in the body is attributed mostly to adequate calcium intake. Although certain food constituents may impair the absorption of calcium, the effect is not as great as once believed. In general, the amounts of protein, phosphorus, fiber, phytates, and oxalates found in the average North American diet do not appear to pose a problem for calcium absorption. For example, research has revealed that vegetarian diets provide adequate calcium nutrition as measured by body

TABLE 8.2 Major minerals: calcium, phosphorus, and magnesium

Major mineral	Major food sources	Major body functions	Deficiency symptoms	Symptoms of excessive consumption
Calcium (Ca)	All dairy products: milk, cheese, ice cream, yogurt; egg yolk; dried beans and peas; dark-green leafy vegetables; soy milk; calcium-fortified food products	Bone formation; enzyme activation; nerve impulse transmission; muscle contraction; cell membrane potential	Osteoporosis; rickets; impaired muscle contraction; muscle cramps	Constipation; inhibition of trace mineral absorption. In susceptible individuals: heart arrhythmias; kidney stones; calcification of soft tissues
Phosphorus (P)	All protein products: meat, poultry, fish, eggs, milk, cheese, dried beans and peas; whole-grain products; soft drinks	Bone formation; acid-base balance; cell membrane structure; B vitamin activation; organic compound component, e.g., ATP-PCr, 2, 3-DPG	Rare. Deficiency symptoms parallel calcium deficiency. Muscular weakness	Rare. Impaired calcium metabolism; gastrointestinal distress from phosphate salts
Magnesium (Mg)	Milk and yogurt; dried beans; nuts; whole-grain products; fruits and vegetables, especially green leafy vegetables	Protein synthesis; metalloenzyme; 2, 3-DPG formation; glucose metabolism; smooth muscle contraction; bone component	Rare. Muscle weakness; apathy; muscle twitching; muscle cramps; cardiac arrhythmias	Nausea; vomiting; diarrhea

stores. Nevertheless, non-lactovegetarian females should be sure to include calcium-rich foods in their diet. High intakes of coffee and alcohol may increase calcium loss from the body, although studies have shown that up to five cups of coffee and moderate alcohol consumption appear to have little effect on calcium balance.

As we shall see, the major factor underlying calcium deficiency is inadequate calcium intake, and although some of these other dietary factors may adversely influence calcium balance if taken to excess, their effect is lessened if calcium intake is adequate.

Major Functions The vast majority of body calcium, 98 percent, is found in the skeleton, where it gives strength by the formation of salts such as calcium phosphate. One percent is used for tooth formation. The remainder, which exists in an ionic state or in combination with certain proteins, exerts considerable influence over human metabolism. Calcium ions (Ca^{2+}) are involved in all types of muscle contraction, including that of the heart, skeletal muscle, and smooth muscle found in blood vessels such as the arteries. Calcium activates a number of enzymes; in this capacity it plays a central role in both the synthesis and breakdown of muscle glycogen and liver glycogen. Calcium also helps regulate nerve impulse transmission, blood clotting, and secretion of hormones. It should be noted that the skeletal content of calcium is not inert. The physiological functions of calcium, such as nerve cell transmission, take precedence over formation of bone tissue. If the diet is low in calcium for a short time, the body can mobilize some from the skeleton through the action of hormones, such as

parathormone and calcitriol (hormonal form of vitamin D), to maintain an adequate amount in ionic form.

Deficiency: Health and Physical Performance Calcium balance in the human body is rather complex. Figure 8.1 depicts the fate of an intake of 1,000 mg. Only 400 mg (about 40 percent) is absorbed while the remaining 600 mg is excreted in the feces. The calcium that is absorbed into the blood interacts with the current body stores, the net result being the excretion of 400 mg through the intestines, kidneys, and sweat to balance the amount originally absorbed. Calcium deficiency may develop from inadequate dietary intake or increased excretion.

Nationwide surveys have revealed that many Americans, particularly females, are not obtaining adequate dietary calcium. Recent data indicate that 75 percent of women do not consume the AI for calcium and more than 50 percent don't even consume half of the new AI. However, surveys with athletic groups reveal some athletes are getting well above the recommended amount, particularly males. Nevertheless, Clarkson and Haymes indicated many female athletes are also consuming less than the AI, and in a Canadian study, Webster and Barr noted that although the mean value of calcium intake for a group of gymnasts met the Canadian recommendations, many individual gymnasts within the group consumed considerably less. Many athletes trying to obtain a low body weight for competition, such as female gymnasts, long-distance runners, and figure skaters, have substandard intakes.

Exercise may increase sweat or urinary loss of calcium. Bullen and others noted that moderate exercise (80 percent HR_{max} for 45

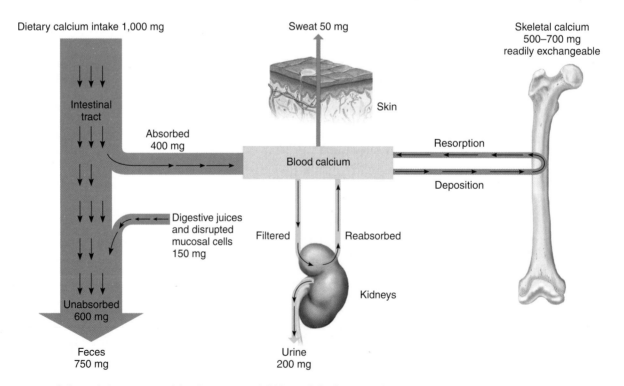

FIGURE 8.1 Calcium balance in an adult who requires 1,000 mg daily. On an intake of 1,000 mg, only about 400 mg are absorbed into the body, the remaining 600 mg being excreted in the feces. To maintain calcium balance, 400 mg are excreted including an additional 150 mg in the feces, 200 mg through the kidneys to the urine, and 50 mg in sweat. See text for further discussion.

minutes in a warm environment) induced a loss of 45 mg calcium via sweating. More strenuous exercise may also increase sweat losses of calcium. In another study, Klesges and others, studying primarily African American basketball players, reported losses of greater than 400 milligrams of calcium per daily training session. Such a loss would match or exceed the amount normally absorbed from the daily diet. Dressendorfer and others examined the effect of 10-week intense endurance training, including volume, interval, and tapering phases, on serum and urinary minerals levels. The training did not affect magnesium, iron, zinc, or copper metabolism, but urinary calcium increased and serum calcium decreased below the clinical norm following the high-intensity interval phase. However, these changes were reversed following the tapering phase. Thus, it appears that calcium excretion may be increased with high-intensity training.

Relative to health, an inadequate dietary intake or increased excretion of calcium has been associated with several health problems, most notably colon cancer, high blood pressure, and osteoporosis.

Some evidence indicates that low levels of dietary calcium may contribute to the development of cancer of the colon. Calcium is believed to combine with bile salts or fatty acids, forming an insoluble complex and helping to excrete them in the feces, thereby reducing their potential carcinogenic effect on the walls of the colon, something akin to the role of dietary fiber. However, in a recent review, Bostick reported it is unlikely that calcium supplementation can substantially decrease the proliferation of colonic epithelial cells. Moreover, Martinez and Willett, evaluating the results from over twenty published studies, suggested that calcium intake is not associated with a substantially lower risk of colorectal cancer. Nevertheless, Baron and others recently noted that calcium supplementation significantly, though moderately, reduced the recurrence of colorectal adenomas. Thus, researchers recommend additional research, particularly evaluating the combined effects of both calcium and vitamin D deficiency in the development of cancer.

One theory also suggests that calcium deficiency is involved in the development of high blood pressure through the mechanism of contraction of the smooth muscles in the arterioles. However, the National Academy of Sciences reports that the relationship of dietary calcium to high blood pressure is weak and the data are inconclusive. Somewhat supportive of this viewpoint, Sacks and others recently reported that calcium supplementation (1,200 mg for 16 weeks), provided to women with low calcium intakes and normal blood pressure, had no significant effect.

The major health problems associated with impaired calcium metabolism involve diseases of the bones. A number of factors are involved in the formation, or mineralization, of bone tissue including mechanical stresses such as exercise; hormones such as parathormone, calcitonin, vitamin D (calcitriol), and estrogen; and dietary calcium. An imbalance in any one of these factors could lead to bone demineralization, resulting in the development of rickets in children and osteoporosis in adults.

Osteoporosis (thinning and weakening of the bones related to loss of calcium stores) is a debilitating disease that is primarily age- and gender-related. A National Institutes of Health consensus panel noted that although prevalent in white postmenopausal women, osteoporosis occurs in all populations and at all ages and has significant physical, psychosocial, and financial consequences.

A positive family history, or heredity, and low levels of estrogen are the two primary risk factors in women. Caucasian and Asian women are at higher risk for osteoporosis than women of African ancestry. Following menopause, estrogen production is diminished. Estrogen is a hormone essential for optimal calcium balance in women. Bone receptors for estrogen have been identified, indicating an active role in bone metabolism. In general, reduced levels of estrogen lead to negative calcium balance and a rapid onset of bone demineralization. This softening of the bones predisposes to fractures, particularly in the spine, the end of the radius in the forearm, and the neck of the femur at the hip joint, as illustrated in figure 8.2. These latter two fractures may be completely debilitating to the older individual. The spinal fracture is more common since the vertebrae are composed of **trabecular bone,** a spongy type of bone more susceptible to calcium loss than the more dense compact bone. However, both types of bone may be lost during osteoporosis, as depicted in figure 8.3.

The FDA indicated that during their lifetimes half of Americans older than 50 will be at risk of fractures from thinning bones. Each year, osteoporosis causes 1.5 million fractures, including 300,000 hip and 700,000 vertebral fractures. Although more common in women, more than two million American men suffer from osteoporosis, and millions more are at risk. Each year 80,000 men suffer a hip fracture. Osteoporosis is known as the silent killer. The disease itself causes no pain, but following a serious bone fracture nearly a third or more of women and men die due to accompanying illnesses within a year.

Although heredity and estrogen status are strong risk factors for osteoporosis, some lifestyle factors may impair optimal bone

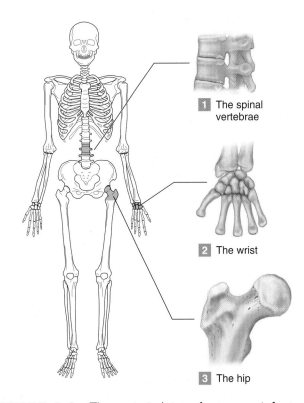

1　The spinal vertebrae

2　The wrist

3　The hip

FIGURE 8.2　Three principal sites of osteoporosis fractures.

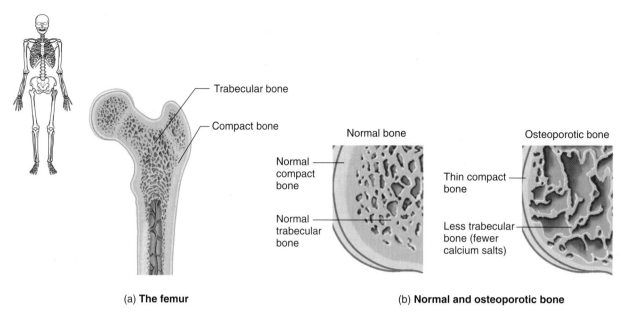

(a) **The femur**

(b) **Normal and osteoporotic bone**

FIGURE 8.3   In osteoporosis, impaired calcium metabolism may decrease the external compact bone thickness and the strength of the internal trabecular bone lattice network.

metabolism. Both physical inactivity and inadequate dietary intake of calcium are risk factors for osteoporosis, and so too are cigarette smoking, excess consumption of coffee and alcohol, stress, and various medications. Table 8.3 highlights the risk factors for osteoporosis. All these factors may influence **peak bone mass** (the highest bone mass in young adulthood). Modifying your lifestyle to increase your peak bone mass is like putting money in the bank for later in life. However, Modlesky and Lewis note that although the idea that the growing years are an opportune time to

optimize bone mass and strength certainly has merit, the importance of these gains depends largely on their permanence. Thus, you need to continue to practice good dietary and exercise habits to maintain optimal bone health.

Relative to physical performance, the effect of a calcium deficiency depends on whether calcium levels are low in the blood or in the bones. Serum calcium levels are usually regulated by several hormones in the average individual. The body can adapt to low dietary intake by increasing the rate of absorption from the intestines and decreasing the rate of excretion by the kidneys. Because the skeleton is a large reservoir of body calcium, low serum levels are rare. When they do occur, it usually is because of hormonal imbalances rather than dietary deficiencies.

Nevertheless, owing to the diverse physiological roles of calcium, a low serum level reflecting low calcium concentration in the tissues could be expected to cause a number of problems. For the athlete, impaired muscular contraction would certainly affect sport performance. One symptom may be muscle cramping due to an imbalance of calcium in the muscle and in the surrounding body fluids. Fortunately, serious deficiencies of serum calcium are rare in athletes because hormones may extract calcium from the bone as needed.

Supplementation: Health and Physical Performance
Although genetic factors are involved in optimal bone health, so too are lifestyle factors. Most of the research regarding calcium supplementation and health has focused on prevention or treatment of osteoporosis. The National Institutes of Health consensus panel on osteoporosis indicated that supplementation with calcium, along with vitamin D, may be necessary in persons not achieving the recommended dietary intake. The NIH panel also indicated regular exercise—especially resistance and high-impact activities—contributes to development of maximal peak bone mass. Additionally, the panel noted that gonadal steroid hormones are important determinants of peak and lifetime bone mass in men,

TABLE 8.3	Risk factors for osteoporosis
Heredity	Positive family history
Race	White or Asian
Gender	Female
Menstrual status	Postmenopausal; amenorrheic
Age	Advanced age
Exercise	Physical inactivity; bed rest
Diet	Inadequate calcium; inadequate vitamin D; excessive coffee; excessive alcohol
Tobacco	Cigarette smoking
Alcohol	Excessive use
Stress	Excessive stress; anxiety
Medications	Certain medications increase calcium losses
Hormonal status	Low estrogen; low testosterone

women, and children. The role of vitamin D in bone health was discussed in the preceding chapter. This discussion will focus on calcium supplements, exercise, and hormone replacement or non-hormonal drug therapy.

Calcium supplements Calcium supplements come in a variety of forms, such as calcium carbonate, calcium citrate, calcium lactate, and calcium gluconate, and are found in certain antacids, such as Tums. The Consumers Union indicates that calcium citrate may offer a few advantages over calcium carbonate because the body appears to absorb it better and it is less likely to cause gastrointestinal side effects, but also notes that the absorption difference is small so most people should look for calcium supplements that deliver calcium at the lowest price. The Consumers Union also suggests that people over age 50 may do better with a chewable calcium-carbonate supplement, such as *Caltrate Plus Chewables,* or calcium-antacid tablets like *Rolaids Calcium Rich* and *Tums.* Be sure to check the label for the calcium content per tablet, which may range from 50–600 mg depending on the brand. Be aware that some forms of calcium supplements are contaminated with lead, particularly calcium from oyster shells, bone meal, and dolomite.

For those who desire to take a calcium supplement, it may be wise to take a tablet with about 200 mg with snacks and small meals three times a day, rather than one tablet with 600 mg, since it appears more calcium is absorbed when the intake is spread throughout the day. Moreover, when the supplement is combined with meals, gastric acidity and slower transit time in the gut promote calcium absorption. A daily total supplement of 600 mg calcium, combined with a dietary intake of 500–600 mg, should provide adequate calcium nutrition for most individuals. Multivitamin/mineral tablets normally contain about 200 milligrams of calcium, or 20 percent of the AI. However, three tablets are needed to provide 600 milligrams of calcium and may not be the best means to obtain calcium as the three tablets may provide excess amounts of other nutrients, such as vitamin A. However, the point should be stressed that careful selection of foods will provide all of the calcium you need from the daily diet, thus eliminating the need for supplements.

Weaver and Heaney note that hypercalcemia essentially never occurs from ingestion of natural food sources, but only with supplements. Although supplements up to 600 mg per day do not appear to pose much danger, excessive amounts may contribute to abnormal heart contractions, constipation, and the development of kidney stones in susceptible individuals, particularly those with a family history of kidney problems. For those susceptible to kidney stones, data from the Nurses' Health Study revealed that dietary calcium does not contribute to kidney stone formation because it reduces the absorption of oxalate in foods, preventing the formation of calcium oxalates, or kidney stones. However, calcium supplements taken without food do not retard oxalate absorption, and thus may contribute to kidney stone formation. Moreover, excessive dietary calcium or calcium supplements may interfere with the absorption of other key minerals, notably iron and zinc. The calcium AI for some age groups (1,000–1,300 milligrams) may require supplementation for some individuals, but the National Academy of Sciences recommends against supplementation to a total much above the AI. The UL is 2,500 mg, which may be exceeded if one takes supplements and consumes too many calcium-fortified foods. Some health professionals recommend there is no need to exceed 1,500 milligrams of calcium per day, as excess calcium may promote prostate cancer by interfering with the ability of vitamin D to prevent cell proliferation in the prostate.

Calcium supplementation has also been theorized to promote weight loss. Zemel and Miller indicated that low-calcium diets cause an increase in calcitriol, the vitamin D hormone, which can affect adipose cell metabolism promoting fat accumulation. Zemel and others have shown that supplementing a reduced-Calorie diet with calcium, in particular calcium derived from dairy products, led to greater weight loss compared to placebo groups. However, more recent studies led by Gunther and Thompson, with the latter study being conducted at the Mayo Clinic, reported no significant effect of a high-dairy diet with a calcium intake of about 1,300–1,400 milligrams daily for about a year, on body weight changes. The control groups consumed approximately 800 milligrams of calcium daily. Whether or not a high-dairy, calcium-rich diet will help with weight loss is questionable, although current well-controlled studies suggest not. However, there certainly are other healthy benefits that may accrue from a calcium-rich diet, including one derived from low-fat dairy products or other dietary sources of calcium.

Although the use of calcium supplements alone in the treatment of osteoporosis has been the subject of debate, several recent studies and reviews provide some positive data. Teegarden and Weaver cited a meta-analysis of studies examining the relationship between calcium intake and bone density in adults, indicating a significant positive correlation with a stronger relationship in premenopausal than in postmenopausal women. In their review, they also cited research that calcium supplementation may increase bone mineral density and content in adolescent girls as well.

One of the key purposes of calcium supplementation is to prevent fractures. In a recent meta-analysis, Bendich and others concluded that daily calcium supplements are a cost-effective means of preventing hip fractures in the elderly, while Meunier noted that they are particularly effective when calcium and vitamin D supplements are combined. Dawson-Hughes indicated that supplemental calcium may reduce bone loss, in premenopausal and postmenopausal women, but noted that its effect on the risk of fractures is uncertain, a finding also supported in a review by Shea and others of calcium supplementation in postmenopausal women.

As a potential side benefit to females, recent well-controlled research by Thys-Jacobs and others has indicated that a daily 1,200-mg calcium supplement significantly decreased some adverse side effects of the premenstrual syndrome (PMS), including psychological symptoms, food craving, and water retention.

Exercise Exercise places a mechanical stress on the bone, facilitating its development and the deposition of calcium salts. In a recent review of exercise regimens to increase bone strength, Turner and Robling indicated that mechanical loading through exercise will add bone, and a small amount of added new bone results in dramatic increases in bone strength because the location of the new bone through exercise is where mechanical stresses in the bone will cause fracture. However, they note that not all exercises are equally effective. Dynamic exercise, as compared to static exercise, creates a unique stress on the bone to stimulate bone strength gains. Dynamic, high-impact exercise, such as running and jumping, may stimulate bone growth more so than low-impact exercise. Studies find that female athletes in high-impact sports have greater bone mineral density than athletes in low-impact sports.

Age is an important consideration in optimizing bone mass with exercise, and youth is the age of opportunity. Turner and Robling also indicate that although exercise has clear benefits for the skeleton, engaging in exercise during skeletal growth is clearly more osteogenic than exercise during skeletal maturity. Periosteal expansion occurs predominantly during growth, and consequently, the childhood and adolescent years provide a window of opportunity to enhance periosteal growth with exercise. As Bloomfield notes, you should get bone in your bone bank by age 30. Exercise is an important means of doing so, and Bloomfield also notes that you should engage in multiple brief bouts of activity during the day, focusing on weight-bearing activities and a variety of movements. However, you also need adequate calcium intake in order to reap the benefits of exercise. Weaver notes that during the development of peak bone mass, calcium intakes of less than a gram per day are associated with lower bone mineral density.

Although adult bone health is dependent on maximal attainment of peak bone mass in youth and the prevention of bone loss during young adulthood, whether or not exercise prevents bone loss after menopause appears to be debatable. Numerous studies have indicated that resistance strength training can increase bone density in postmenopausal women. Such findings were reported in a recent study by Cussler and others, and they also noted that the increase in bone mineral density in the femur at the hip was linearly related to the amount of weight lifted in the leg squat exercise. Miller and others, in a review of 13 studies, concluded the findings provide support for regular aerobic activity in postmenopausal women as a means to offset age-related declines in bone mineral density. Additionally, in a meta-analysis of 18 randomized controlled trials, Bonaiuti and others concluded that aerobics, weight-bearing, and resistance exercises are all effective in increasing the bone mineral density of the spine in postmenopausal women, and walking is also effective on the hip.

However, others suggest exercise provides minimal, if any, benefits. Turner and Robling note that in elderly adults with low bone mass, exercise constitutes only a moderately effective bone-building therapy and may elicit only minor reductions in bone mineral density loss per year. The American College of Sports Medicine (ACSM), in a position statement on physical activity and bone health, indicated that although physical activity for optimal bone health is important across the age spectrum, currently there is no strong evidence that even vigorous physical activity attenuates the menopause-related loss of bone mineral in women.

Adequate calcium intake may be the answer to these varying viewpoints as it may be needed to complement the effects of exercise. Weaver has found that in studies of postmenopausal women, calcium intakes of one gram or more appear to be necessary to effect a positive impact of exercise on bone mineral density in the spine.

The current position statement by the ACSM, complemented by recent reviews, offer the following points relative to exercise and prevention of osteoporosis.

1. Dynamic exercises, such as resistance training through a range of motion and high-impact weight-bearing aerobic exercise are effective means to stimulate development of bone.

2. Development of peak bone mass through exercise is best achieved during the developmental years of youth; high-impact exercises are more effective.

3. Exercise may increase bone mass slightly in adulthood, but the primary benefit of exercise at this time of life may be the avoidance of further loss of bone that occurs with inactivity.

4. The optimal program for older women would include moderate- to high-impact activities that improve strength, flexibility, and coordination that may increase postural stability and decrease the incidence of osteoporotic fractures by lessening the likelihood of falling.

5. Exercise will stimulate bone development, but optimal calcium intake approximating 1,000 milligrams or more daily appears to be equally important.

Although the ACSM does recommend exercise throughout the life span for bone health, it also indicates that pharmacologic therapy for the prevention of osteoporosis may be indicated even for those postmenopausal women who are habitually physically active.

Hormone replacement or nonhormonal drug therapy In the past, hormone replacement therapy (HRT) involving estrogen, possibly combined with progesterone, was commonly used for prevention and treatment of osteoporosis and, as noted by the Consumers Union, a host of other health benefits. However, in a recent report from the National Institutes of Health Women's Health Initiative, the biggest hormone study ever done, women on estrogen-progestin therapy were at increased risk for breast cancer, heart attacks, and strokes as compared to women not taking these hormones. Following this report, Bern highlighted the updated FDA recommendations for postmenopausal women and the use of estrogen-containing drugs. The recommendations vary depending on the health condition, and if a woman and her health care provider decide that estrogen-containing products are appropriate, they should be used at the lowest doses for the shortest duration to reach treatment goals. Research is under way to provide more precise recommendations which will be provided as they become available.

The FDA recommended that when estrogen was being taken primarily for the prevention of postmenopausal osteoporosis, estrogen and combined estrogen-progestin products should be considered only for women with significant risk of osteoporosis, a risk that outweighs the risks of the drug. The FDA recommended that women should carefully consider using approved non-estrogen treatments. In a recent Canadian review, Brown and Josse noted that some drugs, (bisphosphonates and raloxifene) are first-line therapies in the prevention and treatment of osteoporosis. Bisphosphonates (alendronate) are nonhormonal agents with a high affinity for bone mineral. One common brand is Fosamax. Bisphosphonates inhibit bone resorption, but do not inhibit bone mineralization, thus preventing bone loss and possibly increasing bone mineral density. Raloxifene (brand name Evista), a selective estrogen receptor modulator, appears to act like estrogen on the skeleton but blocks estrogen's effect on the breast, and may actually decrease the risk of breast cancer. Calcitonin, a hormone secreted by the thyroid gland, helps deposit calcium in the bone and may be useful as a means of deterring bone loss. Nasal calcitonin is available. Teriparatide, marketed under the brand name Forteo, stimulates the activity of osteoblasts, the cells that build bone, but is recommended for use only in cases of severe osteoporosis. Ibandronate, marketed as Boniva, has been approved for postmenopausal osteoporosis, and may be taken just once monthly. Hansen and Tho indicate that androgens (male sex hormones) may also be useful as an adjunct to hormone replacement therapy. Moreover, phytoestrogens in soy foods may also reduce bone loss through their estrogen-like activity.

Osteoporosis in sports Although osteoporosis occurs primarily in older individuals, investigators are expressing serious concern regarding disturbed calcium metabolism in young female athletes, particularly endurance athletes and those involved in weight-control sports. The **female athlete triad**—disordered eating, amenorrhea, osteoporosis—has been reported in numerous studies. As noted previously, a properly planned exercise program may actually help to prevent osteoporosis and is one of the three major components of a treatment program. However, when research first began to show that amenorrhea and osteoporosis were associated with excessive exercise, such as in female distance runners, exercise was thought to be one of the causative factors.

However, other theories prevail today. Although the exact cause has not been identified, the underlying behavior appears to be disordered eating, as will be discussed in chapter 10. Females who attempt to lose body weight in order to improve their appearance or competitive ability in sports may modify their diets, decreasing energy and protein intake. They may also exercise excessively to burn Calories. Restrictive diets and excessive exercise regimens may affect hormone status in various ways, including disturbed functioning of the hypothalamus and pituitary gland, two glands that significantly influence overall hormone status in the body including female reproductive hormones, and decreased levels of body fat, which may lead to a reduced production of estrone, a form of estrogen. **Secondary amenorrhea** (cessation of menses for prolonged periods) is a classic sign of disturbed hormonal status associated with disordered eating in postpubertal females, as seen in patients with anorexia nervosa. When observed in athletic females, secondary amenorrhea is often referred to as **athletic amenorrhea** and it may involve oligomenorrhea, or intermittent periods of amenorrhea. In young female athletes, athletic amenorrhea is often associated with osteoporosis.

Sophisticated techniques have been used to assess bone density, or bone mineral content. In a number of these studies, amenorrheic and oligomenorrheic athletes were found to have significantly less bone mineral content in the spine and other bones, including the femur, than sedentary women and athletes who were menstruating normally. For example, Gremion and others recently reported that long-distance runners with oligomenorrhea had greater decreases in bone mineral density in the spine than in the femur, even though they had similar energy, calcium, and protein intakes compared to eumenorrheic runners. Moreover, these young, amenorrheic athletes had a higher incidence of stress fractures. As with postmenopausal

women, the decreased estrogen is believed to be the causative factor in loss of bone density. However, Zanker and Swaine evaluated the effect of energy restriction during running, and reported significant decreases in IGF-1 when compared to normal energy intake. They suggested lower levels of IGF-1 could be associated with decreased bone density that has been observed in some male and female distance runners. Some evidence suggests that when amenorrheic athletes resume normal menstruation, bone mineral content increases. On the other hand, Warren and Stiehl indicated that some bone loss in amenorrheic athletes is irreversible.

Although these premenopausal athletes do not need any more exercise, one investigator recommended a daily intake of 1,200–1,500 milligrams of calcium as a possible means of helping to prevent osteoporosis. For premenopausal athletes who become amenorrheic and estrogen depleted, oral contraceptive pills have been suggested as a practical means of getting additional estrogen. However, the medical treatment suggested for this condition depends on the point of view of the individual endocrinologist, and may include individualized hormone/drug therapy. An appropriate physician, such as a sports-oriented gynecologist, should be consulted.

Males are at less risk for developing osteoporosis than females; however, recent reviews by Seeman and by Bennell and others noted that low calcium intake, weight loss, low body fat, and excess alcohol intake, along with other risk factors, may adversely affect bone density in males. Low levels of testosterone, the male sex hormone, are also associated with decreased bone density in males. Interestingly, Bilanin and Ormerod, along with their colleagues, reported decreased spinal bone mass in male long-distance runners, suggesting the decreased levels of testosterone or increased levels of cortisol often seen in endurance runners could be the cause. Klesges and others also recently reported a decrease in total-body bone mineral content in male basketball players involved in intense training from preseason to midseason. However, these investigators also reported that calcium supplementation was associated with significant increases in bone mineral content. Androgen therapy may also be recommended.

Although calcium supplementation may be useful to help maintain bone mass in some female and male athletes, research regarding the effect of calcium supplementation on physical performance is almost nonexistent. Low serum levels may impair neuromuscular functions, but such conditions are rare because the body will draw from calcium reserves in the skeleton to restore serum levels.

Prudent Recommendations Adequate daily calcium intake and weight-bearing exercise is very important during the developmental years of childhood and adolescence to maximize peak bone mass, and such practices should be continued throughout adult life .

To help prevent osteoporosis, postmenopausal women and elderly men should obtain about 1,300 milligrams of calcium per day, along with adequate vitamin D (200–600 IU). Both weight-bearing aerobic and resistance strength-training exercises are recommended. Postmenopausal women should consult with their physicians relative to hormone replacement or drug therapy. Older men should also obtain adequate calcium, exercise, and consult their physicians for appropriate drug therapy if warranted.

For younger, premenopausal women, the nonpharmacological approach is recommended. The key with younger women, and men as well, is prevention. They need to develop peak bone mass, the optimal amount within genetic limitations, prior to age 25–30, and attempt to keep the bone mass high in the advancing years. Anderson and others note that because evidence suggests osteoporosis is easier to prevent than to treat, initiating sound health behaviors early in life and continuing them throughout life is the best approach. As the venerable Fred Astaire once noted, "Old age is like everything else. To make a success of it, you've got to start young." Thus, it would appear prudent for young women to develop a lifetime exercise program and obtain the AI of 1,000–1,300 milligrams for calcium in the diet. The earlier the better, for research has suggested a greater increase in bone mass when calcium supplements are given to prepubertal children, but adequate calcium intake is critical for adolescents as well. Weight-bearing exercises, such as walking or jogging, promote bone mineralization by stressing the hips and spine, while resistance strength training and modified push-ups are also excellent for the spine and for the radial bone at the wrist joint.

Dairy products often are not consumed because they are believed to be high in fat and Calories. However, research with young girls has shown that a low-Calorie, calcium-rich diet mainly from dairy products, can promote bone health and is not necessarily associated with excess weight gain. Although some dairy products may contain significant amounts of fat, four glasses of skim milk provide 1,200 mg of calcium. In addition, the milk (or its equivalent) would provide 32 grams of protein, which is about 80 percent of the protein RDA for the average woman, and a variety of other vitamins and minerals in less than 400 Calories.

It should also be noted that a balanced intake of multiple nutrients is needed for optimal bone health. Ilich and Kerstetter note that although approximately 80–90 percent of bone is comprised of calcium and phosphorus, other nutrients such as protein, magnesium, zinc, copper, iron, fluoride, and vitamins A, C, D, and K are also required for bone metabolism.

Because coffee, alcohol, and tobacco use are secondary risk factors associated with the development of osteoporosis, moderation or abstinence is advocated.

The Consumers Union recommends a bone density test for women at risk, indicating women over age 65 should be tested every two years. For younger women, whether or not to be tested depends on individual risks, such a family history, being underweight, low calcium intake, little weight-bearing physical activity, and cigarette smoking. Amenorrheac athletes may also be at risk. Men over age 65 should also be tested. A dual energy x-ray absorptiometry (DEXA) test is recommended, not the ultrasound of the heel at your local drugstore.

Phosphorus (P)

Phosphorus is a nonmetallic element and is the second most abundant mineral in the body after calcium.

DRI The adult RDA is 700 mg for both men and women. Higher amounts are needed between ages 9 and 18. Specific values for different age groups may be found in the DRI table on the inside of the front cover. The DV is 1,000 mg. The UL for adults is 4 grams, but only 3 grams between ages 1–8 and over 70.

Food Sources As noted earlier in table 8.2, phosphorus is distributed widely in foods, mainly as phosphate salts in conjunction with animal protein. Excellent sources include seafood, meat, eggs, milk, cheese, nuts, dried beans and peas, grain products, and a wide variety of vegetables. Phosphate is a common food additive, and soft drinks have a relatively high phosphate content. In some foods, phosphorus is also a part of phytate, which may diminish the absorption of minerals like calcium, iron, zinc, and copper by forming insoluble phosphate salts in the intestine. However, as noted previously, this is not a major problem with the typical North American diet.

Most Americans consume more than the RDA for phosphorus, and as noted previously, too little calcium. The recommended calcium:phosphorus ratio is about 1:1, that is equal amounts of each. In a recent review, Anderson and Barrett indicated too much dietary phosphorus, which may occur because of phosphate additives in food, may impair calcium metabolism and predispose to osteoporosis. Too much phosphorus may also stimulate the release of parathyroid hormone. Anderson and Barrett noted that a ratio of up to 1:1.6 may be compatible with bone health, but ratios of 1:4 may be associated with osteoporosis. Conversely, Heaney and Nordin found that high intakes of dietary calcium may impair phosphorus absorption and eventually lead to phosphorus insufficiency and osteoporosis. A high dietary calcium:phosphorus ratio can occur with the use of calcium supplements and calcium-fortified foods.

Major Functions Knochel notes that phosphorus is a critically important element in every cell in the body. In the human body, phosphorus occurs only as the salt phosphate, which exists as inorganic phosphate or is coupled with other minerals or organic compounds. Phosphates are extremely important in human metabolism. About 80–90 percent of the phosphorus in the body combines to form calcium phosphate, which is used for the development of bones and teeth. As with calcium, the bones represent a sizable store of phosphate salts. Other phosphate salts, such as sodium phosphate, are involved in acid-base balance.

The remainder of the body phosphates are found in a variety of organic forms, including the phospholipids, which help form cell membranes, and DNA. Several other organic phosphates are of prime importance to the active individual. For example, organic phosphates are essential to the normal function of most of the B vitamins involved in the energy processes within the cell. They are also part of the high-energy compounds found in the muscle cell, such as ATP and PCr, which are needed for muscle contraction. Glucose also needs to be phosphorylated in order to proceed through glycolysis. Organic phosphates also are a part of a compound in the RBC known as 2,3-DPG (2,3-diphosphoglycerate), which facilitates the release of oxygen to the muscle tissues.

Deficiency: Health and Physical Performance Because phosphorus is distributed so widely in foods and because hormonal control is very effective, deficiency states are rare. They have been known to occur in hospital patients with serious illnesses, recovering alcoholics, and in those who use antacid compounds for long periods, as the antacid decreases the absorption of phosphorus. Symptoms parallel those of calcium deficiency, such as loss of bone material resulting in rickets or osteomalacia. Other symptoms include muscular weakness. Extreme muscular exercise may increase phosphorus excretion in the urine but has not been reported to cause a deficiency state. Phosphorus deficiency could theoretically impair physical performance, but it has not been the subject of study because such deficiencies are rare.

Supplementation: Health and Physical Performance

Although various health problems, most notably osteoporosis, could occur with a phosphate deficiency, supplementation for health-related benefits has not received research attention because deficiency states are rare. However, phosphate salt supplementation has been studied as a means of enhancing exercise performance.

Phosphate salt supplements, such as sodium phosphate and potassium phosphate, were reported to relieve fatigue in German soldiers during World War I. Other research in Germany during the 1930s suggested phosphate salts could improve physical performance. Over 50 years ago one reviewer discredited much of this early research, but he did note that phosphates probably could increase human work output when consumed in quantities exceeding the amounts found in the normal diet. Indeed, they still are advertised today in some European sports-medicine journals and continue to be a favorite among European athletes. They have also been marketed as an ergogenic aid in the United States, most recently as the main ingredient in PhosFuel. Although phosphate salt supplementation may influence various physiological processes associated with physical performance, its effects to increase 2,3-DPG and related oxygen dynamics during aerobic endurance exercise has received most research attention. Bremner and others found that a 7-day phosphate loading protocol would increase erythrocyte phosphate pools and 2,3-DPG.

The results of contemporary research relative to the ergogenic effect of phosphate supplementation are somewhat equivocal. A number of studies, using appropriate experimental methods and the recommended phosphate dosages, have shown no effects of phosphate supplementation on a variety of performance variables. For example, Mannix and others reported that although phosphate supplementation did increase 2,3-DPG levels, it did not improve cardiovascular function or oxygen efficiency in subjects exercising at 60 percent of VO_2 max. These investigators generally concluded that phosphate salts were not ergogenic in nature, at least in relation to the type of performance tested in their studies.

In contrast, the results of other contemporary, well-designed studies suggest that phosphate salts may enhance exercise performance. One of the first studies reported was conducted by Robert Cade and his associates at the University of Florida. In a double-blind, placebo, crossover study, highly trained runners took 1 gram of sodium phosphate four times a day during the experimental phase. The phosphate salts increased the 2,3-DPG in the RBC, which related very closely to an increase in VO_2 max. The amount of lactate produced at a standard exercise workload decreased, suggesting more efficient oxygen delivery to the muscles. Although no performance data were presented, the authors did report that the subjects ran longer on the treadmill during the phosphate trials. This University of Florida research group also noted a reduced sensation of psychological stress while exercising at a standard workload.

Other investigators, using a protocol similar to that of Cade and his associates, have also revealed ergogenic effects. Richard Kreider and his colleagues, using highly trained cross-country runners as subjects, found that 4 grams of trisodium phosphate for 6 days produced a significant increase in VO_2 max, approximately 10 percent—very similar to the improvement noted in Cade's study. Changes in 2, 3-DPG were not the mechanism for this increase, however, since these values did not increase. However, performance in a 5-mile competitive run on a treadmill did not improve. Ian Stewart and his associates from Australia, using trained cyclists, reported that 3.6 grams of sodium phosphate for 3 days did significantly increase 2,3-DPG levels and also increased VO_2 max by 11 percent and time to exhaustion on a progressive workload test on a bicycle ergometer by nearly 16 percent. In a follow-up to his previous study, Kreider looked at the effect of 4 grams of trisodium phosphate, 1 gram four times daily for 3–4 days, on physiological and performance factors during a maximal cycling test and a 40-kilometer bike race on a Velodyne. The study followed a double-blind, placebo, crossover protocol. Kreider and his colleagues noted a significant 9 percent increase in VO_2 max, a significantly faster 40-km time (improving from 45.75 to 42.25 minutes), and enhanced myocardial efficiency as monitored by echocardiographic techniques. These investigators suggested that phosphate salt supplementation could possess ergogenic qualities. However, Tremblay and others addressed methodological differences between studies (e.g., calcium versus sodium phosphate supplements) that could contribute to the equivocal results and also recommended additional research employing rigorous methodological control. These viewpoints have been reiterated in subsequent reviews by Horswill and Clarkson, although Clarkson did indicate several studies have documented ergogenic effects and the degree to which performance improved was similar among the studies.

Studies with phosphate supplementation conducted following these reviews revealed equivocal effects. Goss and others examined the effect of potassium phosphate supplementation (4000 mg/day for 2 days) on ratings of perceived exertion (RPE) and physiological responses during a maximal graded exercise test in highly trained endurance runners. They found that although the phosphate supplementation did not affect physiological responses during exercise, the RPE was lower, suggesting that phosphate supplementation may have a beneficial effect on perceived exertion during moderately intense exercise at about 70–80 percent VO_2 max. Galloway and others provided an acute dose (22.2 grams) of calcium phosphate to trained cyclists and untrained subjects 90 minutes prior to a submaximal cycle test followed by a maximal exercise test, and reported no significant effects on heart rate, ventilation, oxygen uptake, or time to exhaustion. In another study, Kraemer and others had recreationally trained cyclists and untrained subjects consume a commercial product (PhosFuel) for 3.5 days and evaluated its effect on anaerobic performance in four 30-second cycle Wingate tests with 2 minutes rest between. The supplement provided no advantage over the placebo relative to peak power or mean power. However, these studies employed procedures (acute dose and calcium or potassium phosphate; commercial supplement and anaerobic performance) unlike those studies reporting beneficial effects, which used sodium phosphate, a more prolonged supplementation protocol, and more aerobic exercise performance tests.

The effect of 5–6 days of sodium phosphate supplementation on aerobic performance merits additional research.

Adenosine triphosphate (ATP), as you may recall, is the immediate source of energy for muscle contraction. Although some entrepreneurs have marketed ATP supplements for athletes, there is no available evidence that they enhance physical performance. Jordan and others studied the effect of 14 days of low dose (150 milligrams) or high dose (225 milligrams) oral ATP supplementation on indices of anaerobic capacity as measured by a 30-second Wingate power test and muscular strength. Although the investigators noted within-group differences in the high ATP group suggesting some small ergogenic effects on muscular strength, the finding of no differences between groups supports the conclusion that the ATP supplementation did not enhance performance.

Creatine phosphate is used to replenish ATP rapidly as a component of the ATP-PCr energy system. As noted in chapter 6, recent research with oral creatine supplementation has suggested some ergogenic effects on muscular strength and running speed. In a recent study with patients over 60 years of age who experienced muscular atrophy following fracture of the femur, creatine phosphate supplements, as compared to a placebo, significantly increased muscle mass during a rehabilitation program. As noted in chapter 6, similar benefits have been associated with creatine supplementation alone.

Excesses of phosphorus in the body are excreted by the kidneys. Phosphorus excess per se does not appear to pose any problems, with the exception of individuals with limited kidney function. Subjects consuming phosphate supplements may experience gastrointestinal distress, which may be alleviated by mixing the salts in a liquid and consuming with a meal. Excessive amounts of phosphate over time may impair calcium metabolism and balance.

Prudent Recommendations   Phosphate supplements are not recommended on a long-term basis as they may create calcium imbalances, possibly leading to osteoporosis. Some evidence suggests sodium phosphate salt supplementation may enhance aerobic endurance performance. An accepted protocol appears to be a total of 4 grams of trisodium phosphate per day, consumed in 1-gram portions with food and drink, for 5–6 days. If you decide to experiment with phosphate supplementation, do so in training before using it in conjunction with competition. Given the association with possible calcium imbalances, this procedure should be used sparingly. Currently, the International Olympic Committee does not prohibit the use of phosphate salts.

Magnesium (Mg)

Magnesium is the fourth most abundant mineral found in the body; it is a positive ion and is related to calcium and phosphorus.

DRI   The adult RDA for magnesium is 400–420 mg for men and 310–320 mg for women. Slightly different amounts, found in the DRI table on the inside front cover, are required by children and adolescents. The DV is 400 mg. The UL of 350 mg for magnesium applies only to pharmacological forms of magnesium, as in supplements and fortified foods. There are no restrictions in obtaining magnesium via natural food sources.

Food Sources   Magnesium is widely distributed in foods, particularly nuts, seafood, green leafy vegetables, other fruits and vegetables, black beans, and whole-grain products. One-half cup of shrimp or cooked spinach contains about 20 percent of the RDA, and a glass of skim milk has 10 percent. Many other foods contain about 2–10 percent of the RDA per serving. Areas with hard water may contain up to 20 mg of magnesium per liter, and some bottled waters may have over 100 mg per liter. About 25–60 percent of dietary magnesium is absorbed, depending on the amount consumed. See table 8.2.

Major Functions   The body stores about 50–60 percent of its magnesium in the skeletal system, which may serve as a reserve during short periods of dietary deficiency. Sojka and Weaver indicate magnesium influences bone metabolism and helps prevent bone fragility. A small percentage is in the serum, but the remainder is found in soft tissues such as muscle, where it is a component of over 300 enzymes. As such, magnesium plays a key role in a variety of physiological processes, many of which are important to the physically active individual, including neuromuscular, cardiovascular, and hormonal functions. For example, as a part of ATPase it is involved in muscle contraction and all body functions involving ATP as an energy source. Magnesium helps regulate the synthesis of protein and other compounds, such as 2,3-DPG, which may be essential for optimal oxygen metabolism, and glutathione, an antioxidant. It is a part of an enzyme that facilitates the metabolism of glucose in the muscle and is involved in gluconeogenesis. It is required in lipid metabolism. Magnesium also helps block some of the actions of calcium in the body, such as contraction in both the skeletal and smooth muscles.

Deficiency: Health and Physical Performance   In a recent review, Antinoro noted that almost three of every four Americans fail to get the RDA of magnesium. The mean magnesium intake for males and females is 323 and 228 milligrams daily, respectively, which is about 100 milligrams less than the RDA. However, the National Academy of Sciences has reported that magnesium deficiency is rare. No purely dietary magnesium deficiency has been reported in people consuming normal diets, probably because of its wide availability in a variety of foods, an effective system of conservation by the kidneys and intestines, and a substantial storage in the bone tissue. However, certain health conditions such as kidney malfunction and prolonged diarrhea, as well as the use of diuretics and excessive alcohol, may contribute to a deficiency state. Durlach and others note that primary magnesium deficiency is due to inadequate magnesium intake, and certain athletic groups may have diets deficient in magnesium. Henry Lukaski reported that dietary survey findings were somewhat mixed; some studies indicated that although most male athletes equaled or exceeded the RDA for magnesium, many female athletes were obtaining only about 60–65 percent of the RDA while athletes in weight-control sports were getting only 30–35 percent. In a recent study, Nuviala and others reported that no group of female athletes in their survey consumed the RDA for magnesium. Over time, such low dietary intakes may lead to a magnesium deficiency.

Deficiency symptoms include apathy, muscle weakness, muscle twitching and tremor, muscle cramps (particularly in the feet), and cardiac arrhythmias. The muscular symptoms may occur because the low levels of magnesium are not able to block the stimulating effect of calcium on muscle contraction. In this sense, magnesium deficiency may be related to high blood pressure because excessive calcium may cause the muscles in the arterioles to constrict. Indeed, in a recent review, Mizushima and others suggested that a low dietary intake of magnesium is associated with increased blood pressure. Additionally, Lima and others note low serum magnesium is associated with type 2 diabetes. Given the possible relationship of magnesium deficiency to cardiac arrhythmias, high blood pressure, and type 2 diabetes, Durlach and others suggested magnesium deficiency may be a cardiovascular disease risk factor. Some epidemiological research from Europe and the United States has indicated that males who consume hard drinking water, which is high in magnesium, experience fewer deaths from myocardial infarction. Rubenowitz and others reported a 35 percent reduction in death for those who consumed the most magnesium from municipal water supplies.

Exercise appears to influence magnesium metabolism, but in an unknown way. Deuster has noted that one of the most common research observations is a decrease in plasma levels of magnesium following exercise, a recent finding confirmed by Buchman and others who measured magnesium levels following a marathon run. It is thought that magnesium enters the tissues in response to exercise-related requirements, for example, of the muscle tissue for energy metabolism and the adipose tissue for lipolysis. Some investigators also suggested that prolonged exercise increases magnesium losses from the body via urine and sweat. However, the reported sweat losses of 4–15 mg per liter are relatively small in comparison to body stores and daily intake. Casoni and others reported significantly lower serum magnesium levels in Italian endurance athletes as compared with sedentary individuals, but the serum values were well within the normal range. One study reported a correlation between plasma levels of magnesium and VO_2 max in trained individuals, but this finding has not been replicated. Other research suggests magnesium deficiency may be associated with an impaired immune function and chronic fatigue syndrome, characterized by unexplained fatigue or easy fatigability lasting longer than 6 months. On the basis of some of these findings, several reports have recommended that individuals undergoing prolonged, intensive physical training should increase their daily intake of magnesium, but these recommendations are within range of the new RDA. The extra Calories consumed when energy expenditure increases during exercise should provide the additional magnesium.

Lukaski indicates that a magnesium deficiency increases oxygen requirements to complete submaximal exercise and reduces endurance performance. Although there is little evidence showing a magnesium deficiency in athletes severe enough to impair physical performance, such could be the case with athletes on strict diets in weight-control sports.

Supplementation: Health and Physical Performance
Relative to health, Antinoro noted that magnesium may help reduce blood pressure, but usually as part of a healthful diet, such as the DASH (Dietary Approaches to Stop Hypertension) diet discussed in the next chapter. Magnesium may be helpful for healthy bones as well. Although magnesium supplementation may benefit individuals with deficiencies, there appears to be little research to support health benefits of magnesium supplementation in well-nourished individuals.

In an earlier review, McDonald and Keen indicated they are not aware of any data showing a positive effect of magnesium supplementation on exercise performance in individuals who are in adequate magnesium status. However, several studies published subsequent to their review have provided some preliminary data, although the results are equivocal. For example, relative to aerobic endurance, Brilla and Gunter reported magnesium enhanced running economy at 90 percent VO_2 max because the oxygen cost of running was lower compared to a placebo condition. However, magnesium did not significantly increase run time to exhaustion in this study. Additionally, Terblanche and others, matching twenty marathon runners into two groups based on performance time, provided either a placebo or 365 milligrams of magnesium per day to the subjects 4 weeks prior to and 6 weeks after running a marathon. Their dependent variables were marathon performance and several tests of quadriceps muscular strength and fatigue during the recovery phase after the marathon. They reported no significant effects of magnesium supplementation on muscle or serum levels of magnesium, marathon performance, muscle function, or muscle recovery. They suggested excess magnesium in the diet may not be absorbed in those with normal levels in the body. More recently, Weller and others confirmed these findings. In a double-blind, placebo-controlled study, athletes who received 500 mg magnesium oxide for 3 weeks experienced no significant increase in serum or muscle magnesium levels, nor did the athletes improve performance on three exercise protocols (cycle ergometer; arm ergometer; treadmill run) to exhaustion.

These three studies appear to be well designed, and, in general, indicate magnesium supplements were not helpful. Indeed, in their recent meta-analysis of human supplementation studies, Newhouse and Finstad noted that the strength of the evidence favors those studies finding no effect of magnesium supplementation on any form of exercise performance, including aerobic, anaerobic-lactic acid, and strength activities. However, it may be possible that if a magnesium deficiency is corrected, exercise performance may be improved. For example, Lukaski noted that some earlier studies have shown that magnesium supplementation improved strength and cardiorespiratory function in healthy persons and athletes, but also noted it is unclear as to whether these observations related to improvement of an impaired nutritional status or a pharmacologic effect. In a case study, magnesium supplementation also helped resolve muscle cramps in a tennis player, which may be part of the reason some sport drinks contain magnesium.

However, at the present time the data are too limited to support an ergogenic effect of magnesium supplementation, and additional well-controlled research is justified.

As noted, an UL of 350 mg has been established for magnesium supplements or fortified foods. Mildly excessive intakes of magnesium may cause nausea, vomiting, and diarrhea. In individuals with kidney disorders who cannot excrete the excess, increased serum levels of magnesium may lead to coma and death.

Prudent Recommendations Physically active individuals should obtain adequate magnesium from a balanced diet containing foods rich in magnesium. For those trying to lose body weight for competition, dietary magnesium may be compromised. In particular, Newhouse and Finstad indicate that female athletes are at risk for magnesium deficiency. In such cases, magnesium from supplements and/or fortified foods is recommended, but not to exceed 350 milligrams daily. There is no need for larger doses as they may be associated with some adverse effects.

Key Concept Recap

▶ Calcium is most prevalent in the milk food group.

▶ In particular, children, adolescents, and all women should obtain adequate dietary calcium.

▶ Although calcium supplements are not necessary for the average individual, calcium-fortified foods and supplements may be recommended for some females and older individuals, including athletes.

▶ Two keys to the prevention of osteoporosis are weight-bearing or resistance exercise and adequate calcium in the diet. Appropriate hormone/drug therapy may be recommended for some women.

▶ Phosphate salts have been used for more than 70 years in attempts to improve athletic performance, but the research is equivocal. Recent studies supporting ergogenic effects need confirmation by additional research.

▶ A deficiency of magnesium may be associated with muscle cramps. At the present time, the data are too limited to support an ergogenic effect from magnesium supplementation.

Trace Minerals

The **trace minerals** (trace elements) are those needed in quantities less than 100 mg per day. These minerals are often known as microminerals. For several the body needs only extremely minute amounts, such as a few micrograms (millionth of a gram) per day. The term *ultratrace* is applied to these minerals.

Iron (Fe)

Iron is a metallic element that exists in two general forms, ferrous (Fe^{2+}) and ferric (Fe^{3+}).

DRI Depending upon age and sex, the average individual needs to replace about 1.0–1.5 mg of iron that is lost from the body daily.

However, because the bioavailability of iron is very low, with only about 10 percent of food iron being absorbed, the RDA is ten times the need. Currently the RDA is 8 mg for men, 11 mg for males age 14–18, and 15 mg for female teenagers and 18 mg for female adults. Slightly different amounts are needed by other age groups and may be found in the DRI table on the inside front cover. Pregnant women need 27 mg, while postmenopausal women need only 8 mg. The current DV is 18 mg. The UL range is 40–45 mg/day.

Food Sources Dietary iron comes in two forms. **Heme iron** is associated with hemoglobin and myoglobin and thus is found only in animal foods, such as meat, chicken, and fish. About 35–55 percent of the iron found in meat is heme iron, the percentage being somewhat higher in beef as compared to chicken and fish. Nonheme iron is found in both animal and plant foods. About 20–70 percent of the iron in animal foods and 100 percent in plant foods is in the nonheme form. Heme iron has greater bioavailability, for about 10–35 percent of it is absorbed from the intestines compared to only 2–10 percent for nonheme iron. The percent absorbed depends on the iron needs of the individual. Those with higher needs will absorb more and those with lower needs will absorb less.

Excellent animal sources of dietary iron include liver, heart, lean meats, oysters, clams, and dark poultry meat. One ounce of lean meat provides about 1 mg of heme iron. Good sources of nonheme iron include dried fruits such as apricots, prunes, and raisins; vegetables such as broccoli and peas; legumes; and whole-grain products. Six dried apricot halves or one-half cup of beans provides about 3 mg of nonheme iron, and some breakfast cereals are fortified to provide 100 percent of the RDA. Cooking in iron pots or skillets also contributes some iron to the diet. On a balanced diet, about 6 mg of iron is provided in every 1,000 Calories ingested. See table 8.4 for foods high in iron.

Certain factors in food may affect the amount of iron absorbed into the body. A muscle protein factor found in meat, fish, poultry, is an unknown agent that facilitates the absorption of both heme and nonheme iron. The existence of such a factor is suggested by the fact that small amounts of meat added to vegetable or grain products enhance nonheme absorption. Certain peptides in meat may cause this increased absorption. For example, iron absorption from beans is almost doubled when mixed with small amounts of meat, as in dishes such as chili. Baech and others even found that small amounts of meat significantly increase nonheme iron absorption in a meal low in vitamin C and rich in phytates, two factors that would limit iron absorption. Vitamin C prevents the oxidation of ferrous iron to the ferric form (ferrous iron is more readily absorbed) and thus facilitates nonheme iron absorption, but it has no effect on absorption of heme iron. Thus, for breakfast, drinking orange juice improves the bioavailability of iron in toast.

On the other hand, substances found naturally in some foods, such as tannins in tea, phytic acid in grains, oxalic acid in vegetables, and excessive fiber may decrease the bioavailability of nonheme iron by forming insoluble salts (phytates, oxalates) or by promoting rapid transport and excretion through the intestines. Tea, for example, which is high in tannins, decreases iron absorption by 60 percent. However, if the diet is balanced these factors should not

TABLE 8.4 Trace minerals: iron, copper, zinc, chromium, selenium

Trace mineral	Major food sources	Major body functions	Deficiency symptoms	Symptoms of excessive consumption
Iron (Fe)	Organ meats such as liver; meat, fish, and poultry; shellfish, especially oysters; dried beans and peas; whole-grain products; green leafy vegetables; spinach; broccoli; dried apricots, dates, figs, raisins; iron cookware	Hemoglobin and myoglobin formation; electron transfer; essential in oxidative processes	Fatigue; anemia; impaired temperature regulation; decreased resistance to infection	Hemochromatosis; liver damage
Copper (Cu)	Organ meats such as liver; meat, fish, and poultry; shellfish; nuts; eggs; whole-grain breads; bran cereals; avocado; broccoli; banana	Proper use of iron and hemoglobin in the body; metalloenzyme involved in connective tissue formation and oxidations	Rare; anemia	Rare; nausea; vomiting
Zinc (Zn)	Organ meats; meat, fish, poultry; shellfish, especially oysters; dairy products; nuts; whole-grain products; vegetables, asparagus, spinach	Cofactor of many enzymes involved in energy metabolism, protein synthesis, immune function, sexual maturation, and sensations of taste and smell	Depressed immune function; impaired wound healing; depressed appetite; failure to grow; skin inflammation	Increased LDL- and decreased HDL-cholesterol; impaired immune system; nausea; vomiting; impaired copper absorption
Chromium (Cr)	Organ meats such as liver; meats; oysters; cheese; whole-grain products; asparagus; beer	Enhances insulin function as glucose tolerance factor	Glucose intolerance; impaired lipid metabolism	Rare from dietary sources
Selenium (Se)	Meat, fish, poultry; organ meats such as kidney, liver; seafood; whole grains and nuts from selenium-rich soil	Cofactor of glutathione peroxidase, an antioxidant enzyme	Rare; cardiac muscle damage	Nausea; vomiting; abdominal pain; hair loss

pose a major problem for adequate iron nutrition. Certain mineral supplements, particularly calcium, and even the calcium in milk, when taken with a meal, may impair absorption of nonheme iron. This effect may be lessened by ingestion of vitamin C with the meal. Conversely, iron supplements may decrease the bioavailability of other minerals, such as zinc.

Major Functions   The major function of iron in the body is the formation of compounds essential to the transportation and utilization of oxygen. The vast majority is used to form hemoglobin, a protein-iron compound in the RBC that transports oxygen from the lungs to the body tissues. Other iron compounds include myoglobin, the cytochromes, and several Krebs-cycle metalloenzymes, which help use oxygen at the cellular level. The remainder of the body iron is stored in the tissues, principally as protein compounds called **ferritins.** The iron in the blood, serum ferritin, is used as an index of the body iron stores, as are a number of other markers such as transferrin, protoporphyrin, and hemoglobin. Other major storage sites include the liver, spleen, and bone marrow. When ferritin

levels become excessive in the liver, the iron is stored as hemosiderin, an insoluble form. Approximately 30 percent of the body iron is in storage form, while the remaining 70 percent is involved in oxygen metabolism. Because iron is so critical to oxygen use in humans, it is essential that those individuals engaged in aerobic endurance-type exercises have an adequate dietary intake. Figure 8.4 represents a brief outline of iron metabolism in humans. For a comprehensive review of iron metabolism and regulation, the interested reader is referred to the review by Fairbanks.

Deficiency: Health and Physical Performance   According to Fairbanks, other than hunger iron deficiency is the most common nutrient deficiency in the world. Iron is one of the few nutrients commonly found to be slightly deficient in the diet of many Americans, particularly women and teenagers. The body normally loses very little iron through such routes as the skin, gastrointestinal tract, hair, and sweat. About 8 mg of dietary iron daily will replace these losses. Females also lose some additional iron in the blood flow during menstruation. They need about 15–18 mg of dietary iron per day to replace their total losses. Adolescent boys need about 11 mg as they are increasing muscle tissue and blood volume during this rapid period of growth. With 6 mg of iron per 1,000 Calories, the adult male has no problem meeting his requirement of 8 mg per day. With a normal intake of 2,900 Calories, he will receive 17.4 mg. With 2,200 Calories, the average intake for females, only 13.2 mg iron would be provided. This is somewhat short of the 15–18 mg needed.

Wood and Ronnenberg estimate that iron deficiency affects more than 30 percent of the world's population, and the Centers for Disease Control and Prevention noted that it is the most common form of nutritional deficiency mainly among females. The main factor underlying iron deficiency in Western diets is inadequate dietary intake. Fairbanks indicates that the diet has evolved so that many individuals consume iron-poor diets, such as snack foods, white bread, and soft drinks. However, most females have normal hemoglobin and serum ferritin status. Because the normal loss of iron from the body is relatively low, and because excessive amounts in the body may be harmful, the intestine limits the amount absorbed from the diet. On the other hand, when an individual becomes iron deficient, the intestines may increase the amount of dietary iron absorbed to above 30 percent. Nevertheless, in a recent study, Looker and others reported that iron deficiency and iron deficiency anemia are still relatively common in adolescent girls and women of childbearing age. The National Academy of Sciences has reported that the frequency of iron deficiency without anemia is much greater than that of iron-deficiency anemia. Nevertheless, about 3–5 percent of the female population has iron-deficiency anemia, a common nutrient-deficiency disorder in the United States and Canada.

Deficiency stages Iron deficiency occurs in stages. The first stage involves depletion of the bone marrow stores and a decrease in serum ferritin. It is referred to as the stage of iron depletion. The second stage involves a further decrease in serum ferritin and less iron in the hemoglobin, or less circulating iron. Other markers are used to evaluate iron stores in this stage, including free erythrocyte protoporphyrin (FEP), which is used to form hemoglobin. FEP in the blood increases when adequate iron is not available. Serum transferrin, a protein that carries iron in the blood, also increases. This is the stage referred to as iron-deficiency erythropoiesis. In these first two stages the hemoglobin concentration in

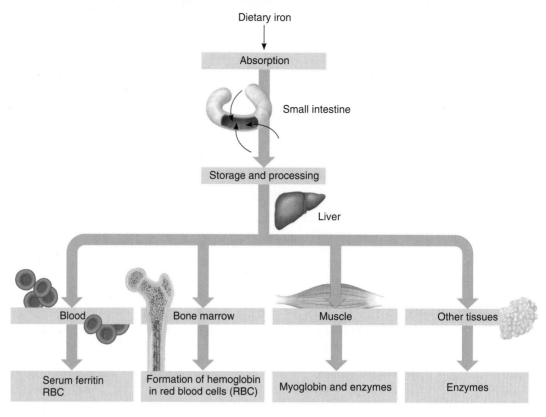

FIGURE 8.4 Simplified diagram of iron metabolism in humans. After digestion, iron is used in the formation of hemoglobin, myoglobin, and certain cellular enzymes, all of which are essential for transportation of oxygen in the body.

the blood is still normal. Collectively, these stages are often alluded to as **iron deficiency without anemia.** The third stage consists of a very low level of serum ferritin and decreased hemoglobin concentration, or **iron-deficiency anemia.** Symptoms of iron-deficiency anemia include paleness, tiredness, and low vitality, and impaired ability to regulate body temperature in a cold environment. Most notably, iron-deficiency anemia impairs muscular performance. In their review of 29 research reports, Haas and Brownlie noted a strong causal effect of iron-deficiency anemia to impaired work capacity in both humans and animals.

Deficiency in athletes Because iron is so critical to the oxygen energy system, it is essential for endurance athletes to have adequate iron in the diet to maintain optimal body supplies. There are some differences of opinion about the magnitude of iron deficiency in athletes. A substantial number of studies, using serum ferritin levels as a basis of iron status, revealed that 50–80 percent of female athletes, particularly gymnasts and endurance runners, were at risk of iron deficiency. Serum ferritin levels in the range of 20–30 nanograms per milliliter have been considered markers of iron deficiency. However, the National Research Council has stated that there is currently no single biochemical indicator available to reliably assess iron adequacy, so several markers should be used. But then, Newhouse and Clement reported wide variations in these markers. In her review, Emily Haymes estimated the prevalence of iron depletion in runners to be about 30 percent.

Although iron deficiency appears not to be a problem in most male athletes, several studies, including one using a bone biopsy to measure marrow iron stores, have reported poor iron status in about

15–30 percent of male distance runners while Constantini and others reported low serum ferritin levels in a high percentage of adolescent male gymnasts.

After reviewing the literature, Priscilla Clarkson reported that iron deficiency to the point of decreased RBC and hemoglobin production does not appear to be prevalent in the athletic population. Some studies have reported iron-deficiency anemia occurs in female athletes at the same rate as in the general U.S. female population (about 3–5 percent) or at a higher rate. However, in a recent review, Beard and Tobin indicated that the prevalence of iron-deficiency anemia is likely to be higher in athletic groups, especially younger female athletes, than in healthy sedentary individuals. One recent study reported iron-deficiency anemia in 14 percent of female national basketball team players, and 3 percent of male players.

The normal hemoglobin level is 14–16 grams per deciliter (100 ml) of blood for males and 12–14 grams for females. Males have been classified as anemic with less than 13 grams, whereas values less than 11 grams, and in some cases 12 grams, have been used as the criterion for anemia in females. Randy Eichner, a hematologist involved in sports medicine, poses the interesting question of whether an athlete whose usual hemoglobin is 16 grams per deciliter is anemic if his level decreases to 14 grams.

Although there may be some debate about the magnitude of the problem of iron deficiency in athletes, most investigators concede that it may be important to monitor the diet and iron status of certain athletes, particularly if performance begins to suffer without any obvious explanation. One report noted that Greg Lemond was struggling in the first stages of the Tour of Italy until his trainer suggested iron therapy. Following several injections, Lemond finished strong in the Tour, winning the last trial race. A month later he won the Tour de France in a remarkable finish.

The International Center for Sports Nutrition and the Sports Medicine and Science Division of the United States Olympic Committee recommend screening for hemoglobin and hematocrit twice yearly. Other tests of iron stores might be recommended for menstruating female athletes. Some, but not all, NCAA Division I-A schools screen for iron deficiency in female athletes.

Causes of deficiency in athletes There may be a number of causes for the low iron or hemoglobin levels found in some athletes. Although adult male athletes appear to obtain sufficient dietary iron, numerous studies have revealed that dietary intake of iron may be inadequate in female and adolescent male athletes. The type of dietary iron may also be important. Ann Snyder and her colleagues noted that although female athletes on a normal mixed diet or a modified vegetarian diet had the same iron intake (14 mg/day), the modified vegetarian diet was associated with significantly lower iron stores in the body, suggestive of a beneficial effect of heme iron. In a study by Wilson and Ball of male Australian athletes, although vegetarians consumed more iron than omnivores, their serum ferritin levels were significantly lower. Other studies, such as by Weight and Lyle, and their colleagues, have confirmed the value of meat to help prevent decreases in iron stores during training, while Telford also stresses the value of dietary protein. Three ounces of beef per day were effective. Vege-

tarian athletes should be aware of the need to incorporate plant foods with high iron content in their diets, a viewpoint supported by the American Dietetic Association in their position stand on vegetarian diets. Athletes who begin to train at altitude will need to ensure adequate dietary iron intake, since the increased production of red blood cells at altitude will draw upon the body reserves.

Exercise, particularly running, may contribute to iron loss in both sexes for a variety of reasons. In their review, Jones and Newhouse report a common condition often seen in distance runners, **hematuria,** the presence of hemoglobin or myoglobin in the urine. This may be caused by repeated foot contact with the ground, rupturing some RBC and releasing hemoglobin (a process called **hemolysis**), some of which may be excreted by the kidneys. For example, in a recent study Jones and others examined the effect of intense training in middle distance track athletes on urine markers of hematuria over a 4-week period. Hematuria was reported after 45 percent of the workouts observed, and 90 percent of the athletes experienced post-workout hematuria at least once. The highest incidence of hematuria was observed after interval workouts run at high intensity over distances ranging from 400–3,000 meters. Moreover, Schumacher and others compared blood markers of iron status among various male athletic groups and found a marker in endurance runners, as compared to endurance cyclists, that suggested runners may experience more hemolysis due to foot impact.

Prolonged running may also lead to ruptured muscle cells, releasing myoglobin, which may have the same fate. An irritation of the inner lining of the urinary bladder may also be a source of RBC loss. Even nonimpact athletes like rowers and weight lifters have experienced hemolysis possibly due to the mechanical stress developed in the muscles or hand-grip hemolysis, similar to foot-strike hemolysis in runners. Several studies also have revealed increased loss of blood in the feces of endurance runners and endurance cyclists. Horn and Feller indicated that intense prolonged endurance exercise may shunt blood flow from the gastrointestinal track to the skin and muscles, which may cause inflammation and bleeding in the GI tract. They cite several studies with marathon runners indicating hemoglobin found in the feces after races. Another contributing factor may be bleeding caused by the use of aspirin or other anti-inflammatory drugs to control pain. Athletes who detect blood loss in the urine or feces should see a physician, since there may be other causes that may need medical treatment.

An additional source of iron loss is the sweat. Although one study has shown that sweat losses of iron are relatively low when induced by sauna (0.02 mg per liter), according to a recent study by Waller and Haymes the total amount of iron lost in sweat increases during exercise, more so in males than in females. This may be related to the fact that serum iron may actually increase during an exercise session and may be partially excreted in the sweat. Earlier studies suggested that approximately 0.3–0.4 mg of iron is lost per liter of sweat during exercise. In a recent study, DeRuisseau and others measured iron sweat losses during a 2-hour exercise bout under temperate climate conditions. Sweat iron losses were higher during the first 60 minutes, approximating 0.18–0.20 mg per liter of sweat, but were reduced almost by half during the second 60 minutes. These do not appear to be substantial iron losses, but if an athlete loses 2 liters of sweat in a heavy workout, and if we use a value of 0.20 milligrams of iron per liter, then 0.4 milligrams of iron would be lost. At a 10 percent rate of absorption, it would take 4 milligrams of iron to replace these sweat iron losses, which is 50 percent of the adult male RDA.

In summary, athletes in training may lose more iron than nonathletes. In a recent review, Weaver and Rajaram noted that when compared to the reference value of sedentary individuals, iron losses in the feces, urine, and sweat may be 75 percent greater in male athletes (1.75 versus 1.0 milligrams) and about 65 percent greater in female athletes (2.3 versus 1.4 milligrams). In less-athletic women engaging in a moderate exercise training program for 6 months, Rajaram and others found that training at 60–75 percent of the heart rate reserve had little effect on serum ferritin levels, although they remained below normal from the beginning to the end of the study.

Sports anemia   As would be expected, the problem of concern to the endurance athlete is the development of iron-deficiency anemia. A number of studies have shown that anemia causes a significant reduction in the ability to perform prolonged high-level exercise. The donation of blood causes a drop in hemoglobin, which may also decrease performance capacity. This is, of course, related to the decreased ability to transport and use oxygen in the body.

One form of anemia associated with endurance training is sports anemia, mentioned previously in chapter 6. Sports anemia is not a true anemia. Although the hemoglobin concentration is toward the lower end of the normal range, the other indices of iron status are normal. Whether sports anemia is a beneficial physiological response to endurance exercise or a condition that will hinder performance is not known. Short-term sports anemia appears to develop in some individuals during the early phases of training or when the magnitude of training increases drastically. One of the effects of endurance training is to increase both the plasma volume and the number of RBC. However, the plasma expansion appears to be greater, so there is a dilution of the RBC and a lowering of the hemoglobin concentration. This effect is believed to be beneficial to the athlete, however, because it reduces the viscosity, or thickness, of the blood and allows it to flow more easily. In many athletes the hemoglobin concentration returns to normal after the first month or so of training. Long-term sports anemia is often seen in highly trained endurance athletes. One theory proposes that the production of RBC by the bone marrow is decreased in endurance athletes because the RBC become so efficient in releasing oxygen to the tissues. The authors of this theory suggest that sports anemia is not due to poor iron status. Moreover, in a recent review relating hematological factors to aerobic power, Norman Gledhill and his associates indicated that an increase in blood volume can compensate for a moderate reduction in hemoglobin concentration.

In recent reviews, Eichner noted that the term *sports anemia* is a pseudoanemia, or a false anemia in athletes who are aerobically fit. Weight also indicated the term is misleading and its use should be discouraged because athletes who develop anemia do so not because of exercise, but for the same reasons that nonathletes do, primarily inadequate dietary iron.

Iron deficiency without anemia   As reinforced in a recent study at the Australian Institute of Sport, rigorous physical training may lead to a decreased iron status, but not to the point of anemia. The effect of iron deficiency without anemia on physical performance is controversial and still under study. Lukaski and others had eleven females live in a metabolic ward for 80–100 days to induce iron deficiency without anemia. They observed a decreased rate of oxygen uptake and reduced energy production during exercise. Other research with iron-deficient, nonanemic human subjects revealed an increased lactate production during maximal exercise, indicative of reduced oxygen utilization in the muscle cells. More recent research by Khaled and others indicates that a mild iron deficiency in elite athletes could be associated with an increased subjective feeling of exercise overload. Based on his review, Lukaski indicated that iron deficiency without anemia impairs muscle function and limits exercise capacity.

On the other hand, research has shown that it is possible to maintain VO_2 max, endurance capacity, and maximal functioning of the muscle oxidative enzymes even when the body iron stores are severely diminished or depleted. Swedish investigators, as cited by Celsing, withdrew blood over a 4-week period to create an iron deficiency. They then infused the blood back into the subjects so that they were in a condition of iron deficiency without anemia. Even though the iron status was poor, physiological functioning and endurance performance were not impaired. These investigators noted that low serum ferritin levels may not reflect low iron levels in the muscles.

One might speculate that differences between these studies, that is, poor iron status due to diet versus blood withdrawal, could influence the results. As many athletes may be iron deficient, yet nonanemic, this continues to be an important research topic.

Supplementation: Health and Physical Performance   The importance of iron to oxygen transport and endurance capacity and the possibility that many athletes, particularly females, may be iron deficient have led a number of investigators in the area of sport nutrition to recommend that more athletes take dietary iron or supplements. Others discourage the indiscriminate use of iron supplements by athletes.

Does iron supplementation improve physical performance? Many studies have been conducted in attempts to answer this question, and the answer appears to be dependent upon the iron status of the individual.

Iron-deficiency anemia   If the individual suffers from iron-deficiency anemia, iron therapy could help correct this condition and concomitantly increase performance capacity.

Iron deficiency without anemia   The effect on exercise performance of iron supplementation to iron-deficient, nonanemic individuals is somewhat more controversial.

Several studies have shown beneficial effects. In some cases small increases in hemoglobin levels have been associated with an increased VO_2 max. For example, Magazanik and others reported that 160 mg of a daily oral iron supplement to young women in training had a more favorable effect on hemoglobin status and VO_2 max during the first 21 days of training, but there were no differences between the supplemented and placebo group after 42 days of training. Beneficial effects on exercise performance have also been observed in several well-designed studies with iron deficient, nonanemic subjects. One double-blind, placebo study did note an improvement in running performance when iron-deficient, yet nonanemic, female high school distance runners were treated with iron supplements for 1 month. Hudgins and others found that 65 milligrams of iron per day improved the 5-kilometer performance of twelve female cross-country runners. Rowland and associates reported significant improvements in treadmill endurance time in competitive runners following 4 weeks of ferrous sulfate supplementation. Compared to a placebo group, Hinton and others from Cornell University reported a significantly improved 15-kilometer cycle ergometer performance in iron-deficient females who received 100 milligrams ferrous sulfate daily during six weeks of strenuous exercise training. In a similarly designed follow-up study from the Cornell University research group, Brownlie and others reported that untrained, iron-depleted, nonanemic women who received an iron supplement had significantly greater increases in VO_2 max as compared to the placebo group. Based on these two studies the investigators suggested that iron deficiency without anemia impairs favorable adaptation to aerobic exercise.

Conversely, most research with iron-deficient, nonanemic subjects has shown that iron supplementation may improve iron status, for example by increasing serum ferritin, but appears to have little effect upon maximal physiological functioning as measured by VO_2 max. Additionally, other researchers have observed no beneficial effect of iron supplementation on physical performance in subjects who had iron deficiency without anemia. Lamanca and Haymes revealed a 38 percent improvement in an endurance task following iron supplementation as compared with a 1 percent decrease in the control group; although this difference is impressive, it was not statistically significant. Matter and her associates found no improvement in the treadmill endurance performance of female marathon runners following either 1 week or 10 weeks of iron supplementation, which was combined with a folate supplement. Also, Newhouse and others reported no improvement in performance on a variety of exercise tests, both aerobic and anaerobic, in physically active females following 8 weeks of oral iron supplementation. In a single-blind, placebo, crossover study, Powell and Tucker provided a placebo or 130 mg of elemental iron per day for 2 weeks to ten highly trained female cross-country runners. The supplementation had no significant effect on metabolic variables related to running performance, but the authors noted that serum iron indices were also unaffected by the supplements. Fogelholm and others studied the effect of 100 mg iron daily for 8 weeks, versus a placebo, on a bicycle ergometer ride to exhaustion in two groups of female athletes. The supplement did increase serum ferritin levels but had no effect on performance. Klingshirn and others matched eighteen distance runners on endurance time, giving half of them 100 mg elemental iron per day and the other half a placebo for 8 weeks. The supplement improved serum iron status but did not enhance endurance capacity in a treadmill run to exhaustion, nor did it improve VO_2 max. Similar findings were reported in a recent study by Karamizrak and others, who supplemented both male and female athletes with iron for 3 weeks.

Thus, the research relative to the beneficial effects of iron supplementation to those athletes who are iron deficient, yet nonanemic, is contradictory, but the majority of the studies indicate that although iron supplementation will improve iron status, performance does not appear to be enhanced. Indeed, in a critical review of the scientific evidence relating low iron stores to endurance performance, Garza and others concluded that although iron supplementation can raise serum ferritin levels, increases in ferritin concentration unaccompanied by increases in hemoglobin concentration have not been shown to improve endurance performance. Nevertheless, although Nielsen and Nachtigall agree with this finding, they note that many of the studies reporting no benefit of iron supplementation did not meet the general recommendations for the optimal clinical management of iron deficiency, and recommend that more research with appropriate supplementation protocols is needed to resolve this issue.

Iron saturated Iron supplementation offers no benefits to individuals with normal hemoglobin and iron status. Some well-controlled research on highly active, nonanemic, females with normal iron status has shown no effect of iron supplementation on hemoglobin concentration or exercise performance.

However, endurance athletes with normal hemoglobin status who attempt to increase their red blood cells (RBC) and hemoglobin levels may benefit from iron supplementation. Increased hemoglobin levels increase the ability to transport oxygen to the muscles, with the goal of enhancing performance. Previously, athletes used blood doping techniques (reinfusion of one's own blood previously drawn or from a blood-matched donor) or injection of recombinant erythropoietin (rEPO), a hormone that stimulates RBC and hemoglobin production. However, both blood doping and rEPO have been prohibited by the International Olympic Committee not only because they may provide an unfair advantage, but also because their use may be lethal.

The technique of "Live high, train low" may be an effective alternative. When one ascends to altitude, such as 2,500 meters (8,225 feet) or so, the atmospheric oxygen pressure decreases, leading to lower oxygen pressure in the blood. The body immediately begins to adapt. The kidneys produce natural EPO, which stimulates the bone marrow to produce more RBC. Over time, the RBC and hemoglobin concentration are elevated. This is the benefit of "Live high." However, given the decreased oxygen pressure, athletes may not train as intensely at altitude, and thus may not train optimally as they could at sea level, the "Train low" component. Some athletes may reside in geographical locations where it is possible to live high and train low by driving an hour or so to a lower altitude. Such is not the case for most athletes, so scientists have constructed houses at sea level whose inside atmosphere has been manipulated to resemble one of high altitude. Thus, the athlete can "Live high" in the house and produce EPO naturally, but can also step outside and "Train low" at sea level atmosphere. Recent research by Saunders and others has shown that elite distance runners using this technique for 20 days improved running economy by over 3 percent. *Runner's World* magazine recently reported that many elite athletes have been reported to use such methods, including the women's world record holder in the marathon, Paula Radcliffe, and multiple Tour de France champion Lance Armstrong. Such a strategy has been considered legal, although a commission within the International Olympic Committee has endorsed a position of not allowing the use of such strategies. Systems are available commercially to adapt rooms or sleeping chambers to high atmospheric conditions.

For athletes who use this strategy, iron supplementation may be necessary to provide substrate for hemoglobin synthesis. Interestingly, two recent studies reported that elite and professional cyclists were found to have abnormally high serum ferritin levels, suggestive of an excessive intake of iron. Such excess supplementation with iron may be dangerous over time.

Excess Iron   Iron is both an essential nutrient and a potentially harmful toxicant to cells. If you plan to take iron supplements, you should have your serum ferritin checked, since some danger may be associated with iron supplements if they lead to excessive iron in the body. Prolonged consumption of large amounts can cause a disturbance in iron metabolism in susceptible individuals. Iron then tends to accumulate in the liver as hemosiderin, which in excess can cause **hemochromatosis** in those genetically predisposed. This condition causes cirrhosis and may lead to the ultimate destruction of the liver. Of every 1,000 Americans, approximately two to three have a genetic predisposition to hemochromatosis. Other health problems associated with excessive iron intake have been detailed by Emery, and some preliminary epidemiological data reported by Wurzelmann and others suggest that high levels of iron intake may confer an increased risk for colon cancer. High iron intakes may interfere with the absorption of other essential minerals, such as copper. Excessive iron may be fatal to young children; more than thirty deaths occur each year from overdoses of iron obtained by eating large amounts of candy-flavored vitamin tablets with iron.

In their recent review, deValk and Marx indicate there is growing epidemiologic evidence for a relationship between iron levels and cardiovascular disease. One hypothesis suggests that inflammatory processes in the coronary arteries provoke increased numbers of white blood cells, which may release iron. Iron is a pro-oxidant, and may possibly oxidize LDL-cholesterol, a reaction believed to be one of the causes of atherosclerosis. Other observations have suggested a link between serum iron and coronary heart disease; for example, females have lower serum iron levels due to menstruation and also have lower incidence rates of heart attack compared to men, and aspirin reduces the risk of heart attack, possibly because it causes gastrointestinal bleeding and increased loss of iron.

However, Derstine and others, using a controlled diet for 4 to 8 weeks to vary iron status in the blood, reported no relationship between iron status and LDL-oxidative susceptibility, a possible risk factor for CHD. Moreover, a recent meta-analysis by Danesh and Appleby, based on 12 prospective studies, indicated that there is no good evidence supporting an association between iron status and cardiovascular disease. Individuals who may be concerned about high serum levels of iron should consult a physician for advice.

Prudent Recommendations   In summary, it would be wise for developing adolescent males and females of all ages to be aware of the iron content in their diets. This concern is especially important to endurance athletes, although it would appear that the extra Calories they eat to meet the additional energy requirements of training would provide the necessary iron. All active males and females should be aware of heme iron-rich foods, such as lean red meat, and be sure to include them in the daily diet, or at least two to three times a week. Mixing small amounts of meat with iron-rich plant foods, such as lean beef and chili beans, will enhance iron nutrition. Eating foods rich in vitamin C with nonheme iron-containing foods and using iron cookware also will increase iron bioavailability. Heath and others found that an intensive 16-week dietary program, one that includes an increased intake of meat, heme iron, vitamin C, and foods cooked using cast-iron cookware, along with decreased phytate and calcium intakes, could significantly increase serum ferritin in women with iron deficiency, but the increase was less than that in women who took a 50-milligram iron supplement daily.

Iron supplementation by commercial preparations may be recommended for certain individuals who have or who are at high risk of having low serum ferritin levels, including female distance runners, some vegetarian athletes, those who experience heavy menstrual blood flow, athletes who initiate altitude training, and athletes who are on restricted caloric intake. Although the iron content in multivitamin/mineral products may soon be reduced, currently the typical multivitamin with iron contains about 18 mg iron, which is 100 percent of the RDA for adult females and 120 percent for adolescent girls. One tablet a day may be advisable for these individuals, and it should be consumed on an empty stomach to minimize adverse effects of some foods on absorption. According to Schmid and others, ingestion of iron together with physical exercise increased serum iron concentrations more so than supplementation and rest. The individual with iron-deficiency anemia should consult a physician for iron therapy, which may consist of 100–200 mg of elemental iron per day until the condition is corrected. It is important to reemphasize that iron supplementation should not be done indiscriminately, but preferably only after determination of one's iron status. Health professionals indicate that iron supplements should be given to athletes only by prescription, primarily only in cases of iron-deficiency anemia.

Copper (Cu)

Copper is an essential mineral whose function is closely associated with the function of iron.

DRI   The RDA for copper is 900 micrograms, or 0.90 mg, for adults age 19–50, but amounts vary for other age groups and may be found in the DRI table on the inside of the front cover. The DV is 2 mg, or about twice the amount of the RDA. The UL for adults is 10 milligrams/day.

Food Sources   Copper is widely distributed in foods and is high in seafoods, meats, nuts, beans, and whole-grain products. One cup of whole-grain cereal contains about 8 percent of the DV, or nearly 18 percent of the adult RDA. Copper also may be found in drinking water, particularly soft water, which leaches it from copper pipes.

Some good food sources are listed in table 8.4. About 30–40 percent of dietary copper is absorbed, but this percentage may increase or decrease depending on body copper stores.

Major Functions   Copper functions in the body as a metalloenzyme and works closely with iron in oxygen metabolism. It is needed for the absorption of iron from the intestinal tract, helps in the formation of hemoglobin, and is involved in the activity of a specific cytochrome, an oxidative enzyme in the mitochondria. Copper is also a component of ceruloplasmin, a glycoprotein in the plasma, and is in superoxide dismutase (SOD), an enzyme that functions as an antioxidant to quench free radicals. Lowe and others indicate that copper is also involved in bone formation, being an essential cofactor in enzymes involved in the synthesis of various bone matrix constituents.

Deficiency: Health and Physical Performance   Copper deficiency due to inadequate dietary intake is not known to exist in humans, although a deficiency has occurred in some patients receiving prolonged intravenous feeding of a copper-free solution and in malnourished infants. The major deficiency symptom is anemia, but osteoporosis, neurological defects, and heart disease may also develop.

Available surveys indicate that most athletes consume ample amounts of copper. The effects of exercise or exercise training on serum copper levels are variable, with studies showing increases, decreases, or no changes. Several studies have reported decreases in serum copper in athletes involved in prolonged training or after an endurance exercise task. The authors theorized that the decreased levels were due to sweat or fecal losses. However, no deficiency symptoms were noted. In his review, Lukaski indicated that physical training does increase the copper-containing SOD, and normal body stores of copper are apparently adequate to support the increase of this antioxidant enzyme.

Supplementation: Health and Physical Performance   No research is available relative to copper supplementation and health or physical performance. Supplements are not recommended because excessive copper intake, even 5–10 milligrams, may cause nausea and vomiting. The National Academy of Sciences reports that toxicity from dietary sources is rare. However, Turnlund indicates copper poisoning can result from excess intake via supplements.

Prudent Recommendations   Copper supplements are not recommended for the physically active individual.

Zinc (Zn)

Zinc is a blue-white metal that is an essential nutrient for humans.

DRI   The RDA for zinc is 11 mg per day for adult males and 8 mg per day for adult females. The DV is 15 mg per day. The UL for adults is 40 mg per day.

Food Sources   Good sources of zinc are found in animal protein, such as meat, milk, and seafood, particularly oysters. Three ounces of meat contain approximately 30–50 percent of the RDA, whereas only one oyster will provide over 70 percent. Whole-grain products also contain significant amounts of zinc, but the phytate and fiber content will slightly decrease its bioavailability. Zinc is lost in the milling process of wheat, but some breakfast cereals are fortified to 25–100 percent of the RDA. In general, if you receive enough protein in the diet you will obtain the RDA for zinc. The MPF enhances zinc absorption. About 20–50 percent of dietary zinc is absorbed. Table 8.4 presents foods high in zinc.

Major Functions   Zinc is found in virtually all tissues in the body and, according to Micheletti and others, is required for the activity of more than 300 enzymes. Several of these enzymes are involved in the major pathways of energy metabolism, including lactic acid dehydrogenase (LDH), which is important for the lactic acid energy system. Zinc also is involved in a wide variety of other body functions such as protein synthesis, the growth process, bone formation, and wound healing. Zinc is also associated with immune functions, including optimal functioning of white blood cells and the lymphatic system.

Deficiency: Health and Physical Performance   Helen Lane has noted that zinc nutritional status appears to be well maintained in the average U.S. population, even with marginal intakes. For example, Hunt and others reported that although some vegetarians have both decreased dietary zinc and zinc absorption, the inclusion of whole grains and legumes in the diet helps them maintain normal zinc balance. However, several zinc researchers have indicated that a mild dietary zinc deficiency is not uncommon in the United States, particularly in areas where animal protein intake is relatively low and consumption of grain products is high. King and Cousins note that zinc deficiency states have been observed in young children with symptoms of impaired wound healing, depressed appetite, and failure to grow properly.

Most research indicates that athletes who obtain sufficient dietary Calories generally meet the RDA for zinc, but Micheletti and others indicated that endurance athletes who adopt a diet rich in carbohydrate, but low in protein and fat, may decrease zinc intake which over time may lead to a zinc deficiency with loss of body weight, latent fatigue, decreased endurance, and increased risk of osteoporosis. Female athletes are more likely to have inadequate zinc intake as compared to males. Zinc deficiency could be a problem for certain athletes, particularly young athletes in sports that stress weight loss for optimal performance or competition. Very low-Calorie or starvation-type diets may induce significant zinc losses. In addition, sweat also may contain substantial amounts of zinc. DeRuisseau and others measured sweat losses of zinc during a 2-hour exercise bout under temperate climate conditions. Sweat zinc losses were higher during the first 60 minutes, approximating 0.8–1.0 mg per liter of sweat, but were reduced by about 40 percent the second 60 minutes. The authors indicated the zinc sweat losses approximated 9 percent and 8 percent of the RDA for men and women, respectively.

Although few experimental data are available, young wrestlers and gymnasts who use both dieting and sweating techniques to induce weight loss may be at risk for zinc deficiency and possible impairment of optimal growth, as suggested by Brun and others. Several studies also have reported a low serum zinc level in endurance runners, triathletes, and other athletes, and the cause was attributed to high sweat losses, increased urinary excretion, or low-Calorie diets. Low dietary zinc intake has been shown to depress testosterone levels, which may be related to the decreased serum testosterone often observed in endurance athletes and wrestlers. Zinc deficiency may also depress immune functions. However, no zinc deficiency symptoms were noted in these athletes or wrestlers; the authors suggested that low serum levels do not necessarily reflect low levels of zinc in the muscles. In this regard, Hambidge noted that there is a lack of ideal biomarkers for mild zinc deficiency states. Following her review of the available literature, which is limited, Lane noted that, in general, there is no evidence that exercise causes a poor zinc status or that a marginal deficiency impairs performance. A more recent review by Lukaski supports this viewpoint.

Supplementation: Health and Physical Performance   In a meta-analysis of 33 randomized, intervention controlled trials, Brown and others concluded that zinc supplementation produced highly significant, positive responses in height and weight increments in prepubertal children. They note that interventions to improve children's zinc nutriture should be considered in populations at risk for zinc deficiency.

Zinc supplementation has been advocated as a means of enhancing immune functions, particularly treatment of the common cold, a health problem that could impair exercise training. Nearly a dozen clinical studies have evaluated the effect of zinc lozenges as a means to reduce the duration of symptoms of the common cold, but a recent review by Nieman and a meta-analysis by Jackson and others concluded that evidence supporting its effectiveness in this regard is still lacking. Diets rich in zinc may be associated with a decreased risk of macular degeneration, and clinical trials are underway to evaluate the effect of zinc supplementation combined with several other micronutrients.

Given the potential ergogenic importance of zinc, it is unusual that only limited research has been uncovered that has investigated the effect of zinc supplementation upon physical performance. In a recent study, Van Loan and others used a zinc-deficient diet (0.3 mg zinc for 33–41 days) to induce a zinc deficiency in apparently untrained males, and reported a significant decrease in muscular endurance in some, but not all, muscle groups. However, the zinc deficiency had no effect on peak muscle force. Following three weeks of zinc repletion, muscular endurance did not return to normal even though serum zinc levels did. In the most cited study by Krotkiewski and others, subjects were untrained women with an average age of 35 years. In a series of tests for both isometric and isokinetic strength and endurance, zinc supplements improved performance in isometric endurance and in isokinetic strength at one speed. However, performance was not affected in isokinetic endurance or in isokinetic strength at two other speeds of muscle contraction. Although the authors reported a beneficial effect of zinc supplementation and theorized it helped optimize the function of LDH in the muscle during fast contractions, it would appear additional research is needed to confirm this finding. Both of these studies provide some important data, but the findings are somewhat equivocal. In his review, Lukaski noted that study designs limit our ability to provide recommendations regarding zinc supplementation to athletes. Zinc supplementation studies are needed, particularly using physically trained subjects.

Small amounts of zinc supplements do not appear to pose any major problems to the healthy individual, but larger doses may. Research has shown that zinc supplements, even 25–50 mg per day, may impair the absorption of other essential minerals, such as copper and iron. Supplements over 100 mg/day may increase the amount of LDL-cholesterol and decrease the HDL-cholesterol level, increasing the risk of coronary artery disease. Anemia may also result from such doses. Higher doses may impair the immune system and cause nausea and vomiting; they may even be fatal.

Prudent Recommendations   On the basis of available evidence, zinc supplementation is not warranted for most athletes. Foods rich in zinc, similar to the animal protein rich in iron, should be selected to replace the increased Calories expended through exercise. However, athletes such as wrestlers and others incurring weight losses, as well as older endurance athletes whose immune system normally declines, should be exceptionally aware of high-zinc foods. Zinc-fortified foods may provide the RDA for zinc. Check the food label. If a supplement for these athletes is recommended, it should not exceed the RDA. Keep in mind that the current DV used on food labels is 15 milligrams, or nearly twice the RDA for females and almost 40 percent higher than the RDA for males.

Chromium (Cr)

Chromium is a very hard metal essential in human nutrition.

DRI   The AI for chromium is 35 and 25 micrograms per day, respectively, for adult males and females. The DV is 120 micrograms. Thus, a vitamin pill containing 100 percent of the DV for chromium will provide about 3 to 5 times the RDA for adult males and females. No UL is currently available.

Food Sources   Good sources of chromium include brewer's yeast, whole grains, baked beans, nuts, molasses, cheese, mushrooms, and asparagus. Beer also contains some chromium. One slice of whole wheat bread provides approximately 15 percent of the daily requirement of chromium. Cooking acidic foods in stainless steel cookware provides negligible additional chromium. Chromium is poorly absorbed from the intestinal tract, less than 1 percent being absorbed with intakes in the AI range. At lower dietary intakes, absorption is somewhat increased.

Major Functions   Chromium is considered to be an essential component of the glucose-tolerance factor associated with insulin in the proper metabolism of blood glucose. In her review, Stoecker notes that chromium potentiates the activity of insulin and thus may also influence lipid and protein metabolism. In addition to maintenance of blood glucose levels, it may be involved in the formation of glycogen in muscle tissue and may facilitate the transport of amino acids into the muscles. Chromium may also affect cholesterol metabolism.

Deficiency: Health and Physical Performance Clinically manifest deficiencies of chromium are rare, but abnormally high blood glucose levels have been reported in hospital patients receiving prolonged intravenous nutrition containing no chromium. Richard Anderson, one of the principal investigators in chromium metabolism, observed that the average American intake of chromium may not be optimal and also noted that the role of chromium in the development of diabetes is currently being studied.

Chromium deficiency could be a problem with both endurance- and strength-type athletes. Impairment in carbohydrate metabolism would not be conducive to optimal performance in endurance events, whereas decreased amino acid transport into the muscle could limit the benefits from a weight-training program. On the basis of animal experiments, Anderson has linked chromium to carbohydrate and protein metabolism during exercise, noting, for example, that chromium-deficient rats use muscle glycogen at a faster rate. Anderson believes that strenuous exercise may increase the need for chromium in humans. He noted that chromium losses are associated with stress, such as exercise, and reported increased excretion of chromium in the urine following a strenuous run. Lefavi speculated that athletes may incur a negative chromium balance under various conditions. One, increased intensity and duration of exercise may increase chromium excretion. Two, athletes who consume substantial amounts of carbohydrates may need more chromium to process glucose. And three, athletes who lose weight for competition may decrease dietary intake of chromium.

Supplementation: Health and Physical Performance Given the potential role of chromium in glucose metabolism, supplementation has been studied for possible benefits on blood sugar and glucose tolerance. In a recent meta-analysis of 20 randomized, controlled trials, Althuis and others noted that although some studies have shown that chromium supplementation reduced serum glucose and insulin concentrations in diabetics, other studies have not and thus the data should be regarded as inconclusive at this time. Moreover, they noted that chromium supplementation has no effect on serum glucose and insulin concentrations in healthy, nondiabetic individuals.

Other research has suggested that chromium may help lower total cholesterol and LDL-cholesterol while raising HDL-cholesterol in individuals with unhealthy serum cholesterol levels. Grant and others did find that chromium nicotinate supplementation, when combined with exercise training, significantly reduced body weight in young, obese women and improved their glucose tolerance, but that chromium picolinate supplementation actually increased body weight in similar subjects. However, Anderson has noted that chromium supplements can correct only that part of a health problem which is associated with a deficiency. In other words, individuals who have a health problem in which chromium deficiency plays a part will benefit if the deficiency is corrected,

just like any nutrient-deficiency-related health problem. Anderson noted that chromium acts as a nutrient, not a therapeutic agent. Unfortunately, there is currently no reliable measure of chromium status in the body. Thus, individuals who are chromium deficient and who might benefit from chromium supplementation cannot be identified.

Theoretically, chromium supplementation might benefit the endurance athlete by improving insulin sensitivity and carbohydrate metabolism during exercise. Also, because chromium may enhance the anabolic effect of insulin, it may increase amino acid uptake into the muscle and modify the body composition, hopefully increasing muscle mass and decreasing body fat. Given the potential commercial application of this latter theoretical possibility to both athletes and the general population, most of the research to date has focused on the effect of chromium supplementation on body composition, but several recent studies have evaluated its effect on strength. Most studies have used chromium picolinate.

In the first published report of the effects of chromium supplementation on body composition, Gary Evans, a chemistry professor at Bemidji State University in Minnesota, used chromium picolinate as an adjunct to a weight-training program to investigate its effect upon body composition. Picolinate is a natural derivative of tryptophan, an amino acid, and apparently facilitates the absorption of chromium into the body. In a review article, Evans described two of his studies. In the first study, ten male volunteers from a weight-training class were assigned to either a placebo or a chromium supplement group. The chromium dosage was 200 micrograms. Body fat and lean body mass were determined by skinfold and girth measurements. The subjects trained with weights for 40 days, and at the conclusion Evans found that the chromium group had increased their body weight by 2.2 kilograms, mostly as lean body mass. The placebo group had also increased their body weight slightly, but Evans noted this increase was due almost totally to body fat. The second study was similar to the first, but thirty-two football players at Bemidji State University served as subjects. After a 42-day training period, the chromium group actually lost body weight, but most of it was fat so their proportion of lean body mass increased. The placebo group also lost body weight, but their lean body mass increased only slightly. In both studies, Evans noted that the results were statistically significant, suggesting that chromium picolinate supplementation enhanced body composition by decreasing body fat and increasing lean body mass. The findings of this report are certainly interesting, but it should be noted that the studies were reported in a review article on the health benefits of chromium and do not appear to have been published previously in a refereed scientific journal.

Following the publicity associated with this report, chromium picolinate was billed in certain muscle magazines as the alternative to anabolic steroids. The advertisers suggesting that chromium's insulin-like effects may elicit significant anabolic hormone effects in the body. Advertisements also appeared in magazines targeted for the general population, suggesting chromium picolinate would facilitate the loss of body fat.

However, well-controlled research does not support these advertisement claims. For example, Hallmark and others conducted a study with sixteen untrained males, matching the subjects based on initial levels of strength and giving half of them a placebo and the other half 200 micrograms chromium picolinate daily for 12 weeks of progressive resistance training. Dependent variables included measures of body composition as determined by underwater weighing, and strength. The authors reported no significant effects of chromium picolinate supplementation on lean body mass, body fat, or strength. Clancy and others randomly placed twenty-one football players into either a placebo group or an experimental group receiving 200 micrograms chromium picolinate daily while involved in intensive resistance training over a 9-week period. A number of dependent variables were studied, including body composition determined by underwater weighing, anthropometrical measurements such as muscle girth, and strength. Chromium picolinate supplementation had no effect on lean body mass, body fat percentage, or strength. The studies by Hallmark and Clancy and their associates paralleled those conducted by Evans, yet the results were diametrically opposite.

Other studies have not found any significant effect of chromium supplementation on body composition. Lukaski and others compared the effects of two different types of chromium supplements, chromium chloride and chromium picolinate (about 200 micrograms each), with a placebo on body composition changes during 8 weeks of supplementation and controlled resistance strength training. Using several measures of body composition, they found no significant effects of the chromium supplements on body fat or lean muscle mass. Trent and Thieding-Cancel also reported no significant effects of chromium picolinate (400 micrograms for 16 weeks) on body weight, body fat, or lean muscle mass in either men or women engaging in aerobic exercise for 30 minutes three times a week. Compared to a placebo group, Volpe and others reported that chromium picolinate supplementation (400 micrograms/day) during a 12-week walking and resistance exercise program had no effect on body composition, resting metabolic rate, blood glucose and insulin concentrations, and other related factors in moderately obese women aged 27 to 51. In a similar fashion, Campbell and others found no significant effect of high-dose chromium picolinate supplementation (924 micrograms/day) on strength or body composition of older women (54 to 71 years) following 12 weeks of resistance training. In a recent review, Vincent noted that over a decade of human studies with chromium picolinate indicate that the supplement has not demonstrated effects on the body composition of healthy individuals, even when taken in combination with an exercise training program. In general, these studies did not use athletes as subjects.

Several recent studies evaluated the effect of chromium picolinate on performance of highly trained athletes and physically active individuals. In a very well-designed study, Walker and others reported no beneficial effects of chromium supplementation (200 mg chromium picolinate for 14 weeks) on body composition, or on neuromuscular or metabolic performance, in highly trained NCAA Division-I wrestlers. In a placebo, randomized study, Livolsi and others reported no significant ergogenic effect of chromium picolinate supplementation (500 micrograms/day) on muscular strength and body composition in fifteen female softball players during 6 weeks of resistance training. In a well-designed, crossover study with physically active males, Davis and others evaluated the effects of adding chromium to a carbohydrate-electrolyte sports drink on prolonged intermittent high-intensity exercise to fatigue, and found that the chromium picolinate provided no additional advantage above that provided by the carbohydrate.

Contemporary well-designed studies have not shown any beneficial effects of chromium picolinate supplementation on lean body mass, body fat, strength, or intermittent, high-intensity, prolonged endurance performance in athletes or untrained individuals involved in exercise training programs. These findings argue against an ergogenic effect of chromium supplementation.

The safety of chromium picolinate has been questioned. In its recent review, the Institute of Medicine reported that no consistent, frequent adverse events were evident from human studies, but also noted that most of these studies were not long-term. Vincent noted that recent *in vitro* cell culture and *in vivo* animal studies have indicated that chromium picolinate probably generates oxidative damage of DNA and is mutagenic, but the significance of these results on humans taking the supplement for prolonged periods of time is unknown. The Institute of Medicine does note that there is a lack of information on the long-term effects of chronic chromium picolinate supplementation at the recommended doses, and does recommend additional research to resolve any uncertainties. Current data suggest that using up to 200 micrograms of chromium picolinate daily for 3 to 6 months appear to be safe. Several case studies have shown that using larger doses (1,200–2,400 mg) of chromium picolinate for several months could lead to liver damage and other health problems.

Prudent Recommendations   In a recent review of chromium supplementation by Schardt and Schmidt, the Center for Science in the Public Interest provided a bottom-line recommendation, which appears to be in accord with this presentation of the scientific data. If you are glucose intolerant or a type 2 diabetic, consult your physician about chromium supplementation. In general, chromium supplementation will not help you lose weight or gain muscle. If you insist on taking a chromium supplement, it should not exceed 200 micrograms and might best be taken as part of an inexpensive multivitamin-mineral tablet containing the other essential vitamins and minerals. Keep in mind, however, that the best sources of chromium are whole grains, fruits, and vegetables.

Selenium (Se)

Selenium is a chemical element resembling sulfur.

DRI   The RDA for selenium is 55 micrograms per day for males and females, with lower amounts for children. The DV currently is 70 micrograms. The UL has been set at 400 micrograms/day for adults, but somewhat lower levels for children and adolescents.

Food Sources   Most selenium found in nature is a part of protein. Foods rich in selenium include seafoods, organ meats like kidney and liver, other meats, and grains grown in soil abundant in selenium. About 3 ounces of meat contains over 30 micrograms of selenium, as does 3 ounces of wheat bread.

Major Functions Selenium, as a part of selenoproteins in the body, is essential for the functioning of numerous enzymes, particularly glutathione peroxidase, an enzyme that helps catabolize free radicals and prevent damage to cellular structures, such as the membranes of RBC. As mentioned in the last chapter, selenium works with vitamin E as an antioxidant. Selenium is also involved in thyroid hormone metabolism and immune functions and has been theorized to be important in the prevention of cancer.

Deficiency: Health and Physical Performance The selenium content of plants depends on the selenium content of the soil. Selenium deficiency is rare in industrialized countries because foods in the diet are obtained from diverse geographical areas. For example, Burk notes that in the United States more than 99 percent of subjects are selenium replete. Estimates of daily intake approximate 80 micrograms. However, deficiency diseases may be noted in geographical areas where the selenium content in the soil is low. Keshan disease, a cardiomyopathy, is evident in parts of China because the primary sources of food are plants grown locally in selenium-depleted soil. Other possible health effects of selenium deficiency include heart disease, possibly because of a diminished ability to prevent oxidation of LDL-cholesterol. Selenium deficiency has also been linked to an impaired immune system and to cancer. Rayman and Rayman cite studies showing that those with the lowest consumption of selenium, as compared to those with the highest dietary intake, were almost five times more likely to develop prostate cancer. The interested reader is referred to the review by Burk and Levander.

For the athlete, selenium deficiency may impair antioxidant functions during intense exercise, possibly leading to muscle tissue or mitochondrial damage, thus impairing physical performance.

Supplementation: Health and Physical Performance Intervention trials in China have shown that selenium supplementation may help prevent Keshan disease by preventing a deficiency. But, can selenium supplementation help prevent cardiovascular disease or cancer in Western populations with better nutritional status? In theory, selenium supplementation may help protect cell membranes from peroxidation. Preventing LDL oxidation may help prevent cardiovascular disease, but in a recent review Neve indicated that the therapeutic benefit of selenium administration in the prevention and treatment of cardiovascular diseases still remains insufficiently documented.

Selenium, as an antioxidant, may also be theorized to prevent cancer. Recent reviews by Combs and Bjelakovic suggested that selenium can play a role in cancer prevention, particularly cancers of the gastrointestinal tract. In a long-term (4.5 years) study, Clark and others found that selenium supplementation (200 micrograms/day) reduced prostate cancer by 63 percent. However, subsequent reviews of the data from this study, as reported by Burk and Levander, suggested some uncertainty in the findings. Thus, current investigators indicate that the role of selenium supplementation in cancer prevention is unclear, and recommend additional research.

In this regard, the National Cancer Institute is conducting a long-term study (SELECT; Selenium and Vitamin E Cancer Prevention Trial) to evaluate the effect of selenium supplementation (200 micrograms/day), separately and in combination with vitamin E, on the development of prostate cancer. The study is scheduled to end in 2013.

As noted in the previous chapter, selenium was often combined with vitamin antioxidants as a combined antioxidant supplement to evaluate the effect on muscle tissue damage. The effects of selenium supplementation by itself on physical performance has received only limited research attention. Although antioxidant supplements have not universally been shown to prevent peroxidation of lipids in cell membranes and other cell structures, some studies by Tessier and his associates have shown that selenium supplementation will enhance glutathione peroxidase status and reduce lipid peroxidation during prolonged aerobic exercise. Although these findings are intriguing, selenium supplementation did not improve actual physical performance, as evaluated by VO_2 max or running performance of an aerobic/anaerobic nature. In a subsequent study, Margaritis and others reported that selenium supplementation (180 micrograms/day) had no effect on muscle antioxidant capacity or exercise performance during 10 weeks of endurance training.

Selenium supplements within RDA levels under 100 micrograms appear to be safe, and investigators in the United States using supplements up to 200 micrograms saw no problems. However, Vinceti and others noted that dietary intake of around 300 micrograms of selenium daily could lead to adverse health effects, such as impaired synthesis of thyroid hormones. Accidental intakes of large amounts (over 25 milligrams per day) have been associated with nausea, vomiting, abdominal pain, hair loss, and unusual fatigue.

Prudent Recommendations Adequate selenium may be obtained on a healthful, balanced diet containing substantial amounts of grain products. In the United States and Canada, most grains are produced in the upper Great Plains, where the soil is rich in selenium. Selenium in foods is present in an organic form, which may be more effectively used by the body than inorganic selenium salt supplements. Selenium supplements do not appear to enhance exercise training or performance, but if you decide to take a selenium supplement, note that most experts agree such a supplement, or a multivitamin-mineral supplement, should not exceed 200 micrograms. Larger doses are not recommended at the present time; 200 micrograms is adequate. In fact, some experts suggest that consuming 200 micrograms of selenium a day may help lower the risk of prostate, lung, and colorectal cancer.

Boron (B)

Boron is a nonmetallic element.

DRI Although boron is an essential nutrient for plants, no RDA or AI has been established. However, some scientists suggest it is of nutritional and clinical importance and most likely is an essential nutrient for humans. In a recent review, Nielsen indicated that establishment of a DRI for boron is justified, and he indicated an acceptable safe range for adults could well be 1–13 mg/day. A UL of 20 mg/day has been set for adults.

Food Sources Boron is found naturally in many plant foods, particularly dried fruits, nuts, peanut butter, legumes, fresh vegetables, apple sauce, milk and dairy products, grape juice, and wine. One ounce of almonds contains about 0.75 milligram of boron. Five servings of fruits and vegetables, along with legumes and some nuts, could easily provide 3 milligrams.

Major Functions Boron is believed to influence cell membrane structure and function in some unknown way to influence mineral metabolism, and to be involved in the metabolism of steroid hormones, such as estrogen. Nielsen indicated that the effects of boron on calcium and estrogen metabolism could favorably affect bone development. Some investigators indicate that boron may also influence testosterone metabolism.

Deficiency: Health and Physical Performance Barr and others recently noted that evidence on boron deficiency is scanty. Rainey and others recently noted that the mean boron intake by Americans approximates 1.0–1.5 mg per day. Because the mean represents 50 percent of the population, Nielsen indicates that a significant number of Americans do not consistently consume this amount. However, Rainey and others concluded that we need more data to determine whether our daily intake of boron is adequate. Although boron deficiency has been studied in relation to bone metabolism—possibly because of its potential role in estrogen metabolism—its role is poorly understood.

If a boron deficiency would impair testosterone production, muscle development could be compromised.

Supplementation: Health and Physical Performance Boron supplementation may not increase body stores. Hunt and others reported that a boron supplement of 3 milligrams did not accumulate in the body. Recent research indicates that increases in dietary boron intake are rapidly excreted by the kidney, suggesting that the human body maintains a stable boron level.

In his review, Nielsen presents an excellent example of how the results of a single study may be distorted by nutritional supplement entrepreneurs to market new products. In their study, Nielsen and his colleagues designed a diet for twelve postmenopausal women to deprive them of adequate dietary boron for nearly 4 months, and then fed them the same diet for 48 days but supplemented with 3 milligrams of boron daily, an amount found in a diet high in fruits and vegetables. The authors reported that the boron supplements reduced the plasma concentration of calcium and the urinary excretion of calcium and magnesium, at the same time elevating the serum concentration of one form of estrogen and testosterone. The authors concluded that correcting a boron deficiency with boron supplements elicits physiological effects associated with the prevention of calcium loss and bone demineralization, suggesting dietary boron may play an important nutritional role in the prevention of osteoporosis. The major focus of this study was on the effects of boron deprivation and deficiency, not boron supplementation. The authors simply created a boron deficiency to see its physiological effects, and then restored normal dietary boron to evaluate its effects.

Nielsen notes that these findings were completely misinterpreted, the media reporting erroneously that boron could end bone disease. Commercial enterprises immediately began marketing boron supplements for prevention of osteoporosis. In his review, Nielsen negates the sensational claims the media propagated, but did indicate that boron may be one of a number of nutrients that may play a role in the prevention of osteoporosis.

One of the other findings of this study, the elevated serum testosterone levels in these postmenopausal women, was also sensationalized. Advertisements began to appear in muscle magazines indicating that boron supplements could act pharmacologically like anabolic steroids. However, Nielsen indicated that this was an erroneous extrapolation of the research data, noting that boron supplementation increased serum testosterone only after these postmenopausal women had been deprived of boron for nearly 4 months; continuation of boron supplementation did not further elevate serum testosterone levels. Moreover, Nielsen conducted other studies with males and reported no significant changes in serum testosterone levels when dietary boron intake was modified. Nevertheless, although noting more research is needed, Naghii recently indicated that boron supplementation could increase serum testosterone, suggesting it could be used safely as an ergogenic aid by athletes.

Limited research data are available relative to the ergogenic efficacy of boron supplementation. Ferrando and Green randomly assigned nineteen nonsteroid-using, male bodybuilders to receive either a placebo or 2.5 milligrams of a commercial boron supplement daily for 7 weeks. The bodybuilders maintained their normal diets and consumed no other supplements. The authors found that although boron supplements increased serum boron levels, there were no significant effects on total and free testosterone, lean body mass, or strength. In his recent review, Kreider concluded that currently there is no evidence that boron supplementation promotes muscle growth during resistance training. These limited findings indicate that boron supplements are not ergogenic, but additional research is desirable.

Nielsen notes that 10 milligrams per day may possibly be obtained in the diet, and that this amount is probably not too high. However, he cautions that an intake of 50 milligrams per day may be toxic.

Prudent Recommendations Based on the available scientific evidence, boron supplementation does not enhance athletic performance and is not recommended. However, a leading expert on boron indicated that boron deprivation for 3 weeks or more may have a negative impact on the ability to exercise. A balanced diet containing adequate amounts of plant foods will provide sufficient dietary boron, so physically active individuals who consume a typical diet should have no problem with boron deprivation.

Vanadium (V)

Vanadium is a light gray metallic element.

DRI No RDA or AI has been established for vanadium because it has not been deemed essential for human metabolism. Nevertheless, based on some animal research, Nielsen estimated about 10 micrograms per day would meet any postulated requirement. An UL of 1.8 mg/day has been set for adults.

Food Sources   Good sources of vanadium include shellfish, grain products, parsley, mushrooms, and black pepper. The average North American diet supplies 15–30 micrograms of vanadium daily, and approximately 5 percent of that is absorbed into the body.

Major Functions   Research with animals suggests vanadium may be involved in several enzymatic reactions in the body, including the metabolism of carbohydrate and lipids. Nielsen noted that the action of vanadium receiving the most attention is its insulin-like effect on glucose and protein metabolism.

Deficiency: Health and Physical Performance   Nielsen indicated that a vanadium deficiency has not been detected in humans. However, if vanadium does induce an insulin-like effect, a deficiency could impair glucose metabolism.

Supplementation: Health and Physical Performance   Vanadium supplements are available as vanadyl salts, primarily vanadyl sulfate, and in various organic vanadium complexes that are regarded as being more readily absorbed, more effective, and safer. Verma and others indicated that there is a growing body of experimental and clinical research indicating that vanadium, when supplemented in pharmacological doses, may exert a potent insulin-like effect and improve glucose status in humans with noninsulin-dependent diabetes mellitus. However, similar effects may not occur in healthy individuals. Jentjens and Jeukendrup recently evaluated the effect of vanadyl sulfate supplementation (100 milligrams for 6 days) on insulin sensitivity in healthy adults, and reported no significant effects of vanadyl sulfate supplementation on plasma glucose and insulin concentrations, indicating no significant effects on insulin sensitivity.

Vanadyl salts have been marketed to athletes as a means to favorably modify body composition, comparable to the proposed effects of chromium supplementation. However, there are very limited research data with vanadium supplementation. In a well-controlled study, Fawcett and others found that supplementation with 0.5 milligrams per kilogram body weight (about 40 milligrams daily) of vanadyl sulfate to subjects undertaking strength training for 12 weeks had no effect on body fat or lean muscle mass. The investigators also studied strength gains in four tasks, a 1-repetition and 10-repetition maximal test for both the bench press and leg extension. There were no significant effects of vanadyl sulfate on three of the tests. Although subjects taking vanadyl sulfate did gain more strength on the 1-repetition maximal leg extension test during the first 4 weeks of the study, the investigators suggested this may be attributed to low scores on the pretest. The investigators concluded that vanadyl sulfate supplementation was ineffective in changing body composition, and any modest performance-enhancing effect requires further investigation.

Although Jentjens and Jeukendrup noted that short-term supplementation with vanadyl sulfate resulted in no adverse side effects, they indicated that long-term safety studies are needed. The National Academy of Sciences set the UL for vanadium at 1.8 milligrams/day for adults. Vanadium constitutes about one-third of the atomic weight of vanadyl sulfate, so it could constitute 33 milligrams in a 100 milligram tablet, and thus greatly exceed the UL.

Adverse side effects of vanadyl salt supplementation when taken in milligram doses may include gastrointestinal distress, primarily diarrhea. Excess supplementation may also cause damage to both the liver and kidney.

Prudent Recommendations   Type 2 diabetics should consult with their physicians regarding the use of vanadyl salt as a therapeutic agent to control blood glucose. Vanadyl salt supplementation is not recommended for the physically active individual, as it has not been found to enhance either body composition or physical performance. Moreover, excess amounts may be toxic.

Other Trace Minerals

A number of other trace minerals have physiological roles that may have important implications for health or physical performance. Food sources, RDA or AI, major physiological functions, and the effects of deficiencies or excesses are summarized in table 8.5. Only trace minerals for which an RDA or AI have been developed are included. Other elements, such as nickel, tin, silicon, and arsenic may prove to be essential. It should be noted that deficiencies and excesses due to dietary sources for most of these nutrients are extremely rare. However, to help prevent a deficiency it is important to consume unprocessed foods because many of the trace elements that are removed during processing are not returned. For example, as already noted, one slice of whole wheat bread provides about 15 percent of the daily requirement of chromium, whereas a slice of white bread contains only 1 percent. Excesses may occur with use of supplements or through industrial exposure, and an UL has been set for nickel.

Two of these trace elements deserve mention for they have been shown to prevent health problems in humans.

Fluoride   A fluoride AI has been established, ranging from about 1 to 4 mg/day from childhood through adulthood. Featherstone indicates that fluoride may prevent dental caries, possibly by inhibiting bacterial enzymes and demineralization of the tooth. In its recent position stand regarding the impact of fluoride on health, the American Dietetic Association (ADA) noted that the use of systemic and topical fluoride for oral health has resulted in major reductions in dental caries. Thus, fluoridation of public water supplies has been endorsed by over ninety professional health organizations as the most effective dental public health measure in existence. Brushing teeth with fluoride toothpaste may also be beneficial, as may sucking on fluoride-containing tablets or lozenges. In these cases the fluoride is applied topically, mixing in the saliva and around the teeth. Excess fluoride use may contribute to fluorosis, or varying shades of whiteness (known as mottling) in the outer tooth enamel. Although the underlying mechanism is not known, DenBesten indicates that fluorosis may occur when excess fluoride interferes in some way with the maturation of dental enamel. Ismail

TABLE 8.5 Trace minerals: cobalt, fluoride, iodine, manganese, molybdenum

Trace mineral	RDA or AI*	Major food sources	Major body functions	Deficiency symptoms	Symptoms of excessive consumption	Recommended as dietary supplement
Cobalt (Co)	**	Meat, liver, milk	Component of vitamin B_{12}; promotes development of red blood cells	Not found in humans	Nausea, vomiting, death	No
Fluoride (F)	3.0–4.0 mg	Milk, egg yolks, drinking water, seafood	Helps form bones and teeth	Higher incidence of dental cavities	Discolored teeth	No
Iodine (I)	150 micrograms	Iodized salt, seafood, vegetables	Helps in formation of thyroid hormones	Goiter, an enlarged thyroid gland	Depressed thyroid gland activity	No
Manganese (Mn)	1.8–2.3 mg	Whole-grain products, dried peas and beans, leafy vegetables, bananas	Many enzymes involved in energy metabolism; bone formation; fat synthesis	Poor growth	Weakness; nervous system problems; mental confusion	No
Molybdenum (Mo)	45 micrograms	Liver, organ meats, whole-grain products, dried beans and peas	Works with riboflavin in enzymes involved in carbohydrate and fat metabolism	Not found in humans	Rare	No

* For adults. RDA or AI for other age groups may be found in the DRI table on the inside front cover.
** Essential as part of vitamin B_{12}.

and Bandekar, using a meta-analysis, concluded that children in non-fluoridated communities who use fluorine supplements during childhood are an increased risk of developing dental fluorosis. In such communities, dental health professionals should be consulted for appropriate advice on use of fluoride supplements.

Fluoride may possess other health benefits as it is believed to work with calcium and other minerals in bone mineralization. The ADA notes that although fluoride plays a role in bone health, the role of high doses of fluoride for prevention of osteoporosis is undergoing active study and thus should be considered experimental at this point. Osteoporotic patients should consult with their physicians regarding use of fluoride supplements.

Iodine Iodine is used in the formation of thyroxine and triiodothyronine, two hormones produced in the thyroid gland. Decreased production of these hormones would lower the body's metabolism, a possible contributing factor to the development of obesity. The use of iodized salt has nearly eliminated iodine deficiency in the United States and has thereby greatly reduced the incidence of goiter, a serious iodine-deficiency disease. However, iodine deficiency is a major problem worldwide, with nearly 750 million people suffering from goiter. Iodized salts could help.

Research literature relative to the effect of exercise on the metabolic fates of these trace nutrients is almost nonexistent, nor are there any studies available regarding the effects of supplements on performance. This may be understandable, as deficiencies are rare.

Key Concept Recap

▶ Iron deficiency, particularly among women and young children, is a major nutritional health concern, so iron-rich foods such as lean meats and beans should be stressed in the diet.

▶ Iron supplementation may be recommended for certain individuals, particularly female endurance athletes and those on low-Calorie diets.

▶ Iron supplementation may improve performance in individuals with iron-deficiency anemia, but not in individuals with normal iron status. Although individuals who have iron deficiency without anemia may experience less favorable responses to aerobic training, findings from studies are equivocal as to the efficacy of iron supplementation to improve performance, and investigators recommend additional research.

▶ Zinc deficiency has been shown to impair the growth process in children, so it may be a problem for young athletes who incur heavy sweat losses and are on low-Calorie diets, such as wrestlers, dancers, or gymnasts.

▶ Chromium supplements have been marketed to increase muscle mass and decrease body fat, but research does not support these claims.

▶ There does not appear to be much valid scientific evidence to support an ergogenic effect of trace mineral supplementation including zinc, copper, boron, selenium, and vanadium.

Mineral Supplements: Exercise and Health

Following her extensive review of dietary surveys, Sarah Short noted that both athletes and health professionals are becoming more concerned with mineral deficiencies. Perusal of athletic and health magazines marketed for the general public reveals a variety of articles and advertisements suggesting that supplementation of certain minerals will enhance athletic performance or health. As the foregoing discussion indicates, individuals who have a mineral deficiency may experience improved health or physical performance if that deficiency is corrected. In general, however, supplementation has little effect on the individual whose mineral status is adequate. This last section summarizes some key points relative to mineral nutrition, focusing on the need for supplementation.

Does exercise increase my need for minerals?

Exercise may induce mineral losses from the body by several mechanisms. Many minerals appear to be mobilized into the circulation during exercise, probably being released from body stores in the muscles or elsewhere. As they circulate, some may be removed by the kidneys and excreted in the urine, whereas others may appear in the sweat, particularly in a warm environment. Losses from the gastrointestinal tract may also occur during exercise, although the mechanism is not totally understood.

Other body changes mediated by exercise may influence mineral requirements. The female athlete who develops secondary amenorrhea may need additional calcium, as might the male endurance athlete in whom trabecular bone mass is decreased. The need for iron in the female athlete may decrease somewhat with the cessation of menses in secondary amenorrhea.

Because of potential mineral losses, at least one investigator in sport nutrition has suggested that mineral supplementation should be considered for athletes. Although supplementation may be helpful for some, the first concern should be to educate the athlete about obtaining adequate mineral nutrition through dietary means.

Can I obtain the minerals I need through my diet?

As many dietary surveys have shown, many Americans are not obtaining the RDA or AI for a variety of minerals, including iron, zinc, calcium, and chromium. Similar dietary deficiencies have been noted in surveys with athletes, but mainly with athletes who participate in activities such as wrestling, distance running, ballet, and gymnastics, where weight control is a concern. Let us briefly highlight the dietary recommendations that will help ensure adequate amounts of nutrients in the diet.

In general, as with all other nutrients, a balanced diet is essential. Select a wide variety of foods from all the food groups and within each group. Table 8.6 presents the percentage of the DV provided by servings of different foods from several food groups. Keep in mind that the DV, the value used on food labels, may vary with the RDA and AI, being higher for some minerals and lower for others. But the purpose of this table is simply to support the value of eating a wide variety of foods to obtain adequate mineral nutrition.

Note that the percentage values for the minerals differ not only between food groups but also for some minerals in foods within the same group. For example, note that calcium is high in dairy

---

TABLE 8.6 Approximate percentages of the DV in various foods for selected minerals

Food	Serving	Calories	Ca	P	Mg	Fe	Cu	Zn
Milk, skim	1 glass	90	30	25	7	1	2	7
Cheese, cheddar	1 ounce	114	21	15	2	1	0	6
Oyster	1 ounce	20	1	4	4	11	40	166
Liver, beef	3 ounces	150	1	34	4	32	150	35
Beef, lean sirloin	3 ounces	230	1	18	6	13	7	33
Potato, baked	medium	220	2	11	14	15	15	4
Broccoli	1/2 cup	25	4	5	5	4	2	2
Bread, whole wheat	1 slice	70	2	5	5	4	14	3
Bread, enriched white	1 slice	70	2	2	2	4	6	1

foods but low in meats. On the other hand, iron is high in meats but low in dairy products. Also, in the meat group, an oyster is high in copper, but lean beef is relatively low, even more so if you consider the caloric value of each. It is also important to eat foods in their natural state as much as possible. The milling of flour removes many minerals, but only iron is replaced in the enrichment process. Note the differences between whole wheat and enriched white bread in table 8.6. Some food products rich in other healthful nutrients, such as orange juice and whole-grain cereal, are fortified with minerals and may be an effective means to ensure adequate mineral nutrition.

A basic principle of mineral nutrition is to eat natural foods that are rich in calcium and iron. If you select a diet to provide your RDA for these two minerals, you will receive adequate amounts of the other major and trace minerals at the same time. Dairy products and meats are excellent sources of these minerals, but other foods such as legumes and dark-green leafy vegetables also may provide significant amounts if selected wisely. Note the foods rich in calcium and iron in tables 8.2 and 8.4, and compare the similarity to the foods listed for the other minerals in these two tables and table 8.5.

Are mineral megadoses harmful?

One of the generally accepted facts relative to mineral nutrition in the healthy individual is that the levels associated with toxicity can normally be obtained only through the use of supplements or fortified foods, not through natural dietary sources. Because they hope to improve health or physical performance, many individuals purchase supplements containing minerals. However, surveys indicate the most common preparations purchased contain the RDA or less, which should pose no health problems to the healthy individual. Unfortunately, as indicated in the last chapter, many individuals self-prescribe and may consume more than the recommended daily dosage. Although the toxicity and possible health problems associated with excessive intake of several minerals, such as calcium, iron, zinc, and copper, are fairly well documented, the level of safety for intake of a variety of other minerals, particularly some of the trace minerals suggested to be therapeutic in nature, has been more difficult to document. Nevertheless, the National Academy of Sciences has noted that all trace minerals are toxic if consumed at high doses for a long enough time.

Several nonessential minerals may be consumed inadvertently and cause significant health problems, even in small amounts. Lead can displace other minerals, such as calcium and zinc, in various enzymes and thus interfere with intracellular processes involving protein and gene expression. Industrial chromium is regarded as a carcinogen. Of recent concern is mercury, which may be found in foods that we normally think of as healthy. Fish!

Methylmercury, an industrial waste product, has been dumped into the seas where it may be consumed by fish. As noted on page 182, high levels of mercury may accumulate more in larger, older, predatory fish, such as shark, swordfish, king mackerel, and tilefish; tuna may contain somewhat less mercury. Too much mercury may damage the nervous system, especially the brain during its formative years prior to birth and the first 7 years of life. Thus, the FDA advises women who are or who can become pregnant and small children should not eat any shark, swordfish, king mackerel, or tilefish. The FDA advisory does not apply to men or to women who are not pregnant or who cannot become pregnant.

Should physically active individuals take mineral supplements?

In general, the answer to this question for most athletes is *no*—for several reasons. First, contrary to advertising claims of mineral-supplement manufacturers, you can obtain adequate mineral nutrition from the diet if you adhere to some of the guidelines presented throughout this chapter. Second, although some athletes may not be obtaining the recommended amounts of several minerals, such as zinc and calcium, mineral deficiencies to the point of impairing physical performance are rare. Very few data are available on this topic, but the evidence that is available with most minerals suggests that though serum levels may be low, physical performance is not affected. An exception may be low levels of serum iron for, as noted previously, supplementation, although controversial, has been helpful to some athletes. Third, many minerals may be harmful when taken in excess. As noted throughout this chapter, the absorption rate for most minerals is relatively low. Only 40 percent of calcium is absorbed from the intestinal tract, while the percentages for iron and chromium are, respectively, 10 and 1–2 percent. Also, a high dietary intake of several minerals that are easily absorbed increases their excretion rate by the kidney. Thus, a low absorption or high excretion rate prevents the accumulation of excess amounts of minerals in the body, which may interfere with normal metabolism. Large supplemental doses may overload the body and cause numerous health problems, and as noted for several minerals, may be fatal.

However, it is recognized that certain athletes may not be obtaining adequate mineral nutrition from their diets and may possibly benefit from supplementation. As noted previously, athletes who are attempting to lose weight for performance are at most risk for developing a mineral deficiency. Because many of the dietary surveys of these athletes have reported intakes lower than the RDA for iron and calcium, it may be assumed that their diets are also low in other trace minerals.

If there is concern for the nutritional status of the athlete, the ideal situation would be to consult a sport nutritionist or nutritionally oriented physician. Unfortunately, this approach does not appear to be common among athletes who may be in need of nutritional counseling, although the situation is improving. Some elite athletes take medically prescribed iron supplements, and dieticians with specialties in exercise physiology and sport nutrition are becoming increasingly available.

For athletes who cannot or will not seek professional advice, it may be prudent to recommend a one-a-day vitamin-mineral supplement to those who are known to have poor nutritional habits.

The tablet should contain no more than 50–100 percent of the RDA for any mineral. Additionally, the point should be made to the athlete that the supplement is being recommended to help prevent a deficiency, not for any ergogenic purposes. As noted in chapter 7, large doses of multivitamin-mineral supplements taken over prolonged periods of time have not been shown to enhance physical performance. In the meantime, efforts should be undertaken to educate the athlete concerning sound nutritional practices.

For those considering mineral supplementation for health reasons, the new DRI being developed by the National Academy of Sciences reflect a new paradigm in which the determination of nutrient requirements include consideration of the total health effects of nutrients, not just their roles in preventing deficiency pathology. For example, the recently updated AI for calcium and vitamin D as a possible means to prevent osteoporosis reflect this new paradigm. Although much research is needed before concrete recommendations may be made relative to mineral supplementation and purported health benefits, the recommendations presented on page 270 may be useful guidelines for healthy sedentary and physically active individuals to use in the meantime.

Key Concept Recap

▶ Health professionals recommend that individuals obtain their mineral needs from healthful foods. A diet that provides the RDA for iron, calcium, and Calories from a balanced selection of foods throughout the different food groups will provide adequate amounts of both the major and trace minerals.

▶ Mineral supplements may be recommended for some individuals as a means to improve health or sports performance, but excessive intake is not recommended because of potential health problems.

Check for Yourself

Calcium and iron are two of our key nutrients for health and sport performance. If you obtain adequate amounts of each through natural dietary sources, you should obtain adequate amounts of most other essential minerals. Using food labels or computerized dietary analyses, calculate the calcium and iron intake of your typical daily diet to determine if you are obtaining the RDA for your gender and age.

APPLICATION EXERCISE

Your municipal water supply may contain a variety of minerals, such as calcium, magnesium, fluoride, and sodium. Contact the appropriate governmental authorities in your community to see if you may obtain a detailed water quality report highlighting the mineral content of city drinking water. Calculate the amount of various minerals you consume with each quart of water.

Mineral Content of Municipal Drinking Water

Minerals	Calcium	Magnesium	Fluoride	Sodium	Other	Other
Mineral content in 1 quart of water						

Review Questions—Multiple Choice

1. Which statement does *not* describe the role of major minerals in the body?
   (a) They give teeth and bone their rigidity and strength.
   (b) They regulate body processes.
   (c) They are constituents of soft tissues.
   (d) They provide energy.
   (e) They help to maintain the acid-base balance.

2. Who has the lesser need for iron as specified by the RDA?
   (a) adolescent boys
   (b) adolescent girls
   (c) young adult females
   (d) adult males
   (e) female distance runners

3. In order to help prevent the development of osteoporosis in later life, females should consume adequate quantities of which nutrient during the years in which they are developing peak bone mass?
   (a) calcium
   (b) iron
   (c) retinol
   (d) vitamin E
   (e) ascorbic acid

4. Which mineral may be an effective ergogenic aid for runners since it may possibly increase the delivery of oxygen to the muscle cell by facilitating its release from hemoglobin?
   - (a) calcium
   - (b) phosphorus
   - (c) zinc
   - (d) magnesium
   - (e) chromium

5. Excessive intake of iron can lead to a condition called hemachromatosis, which is damage to which organ in the body?
   - (a) arterial walls
   - (b) kidney
   - (c) heart
   - (d) liver
   - (e) lungs

6. Approximately how much calcium is found in one glass (8 ounces) of skim milk?
   - (a) 50 milligrams
   - (b) 100 milligrams
   - (c) 300 milligrams
   - (d) 800 milligrams
   - (e) 1200 milligrams

7. Which of the following would not contain heme iron?
   - (a) liver
   - (b) dried beans
   - (c) fish
   - (d) chicken
   - (e) beef

8. Which of the following contains the least amount of calcium?
   - (a) milk
   - (b) meat
   - (c) dried beans
   - (d) dark-green leafy vegetables
   - (e) cheese

9. Which food exchange is the best source of zinc, iron, and copper in regards to the concept of bioavailability?
   - (a) milk
   - (b) meat
   - (c) starch/bread
   - (d) fruit
   - (e) vegetable

10. Which of the following statements concerning trace minerals is false?
    - (a) Copper and iron are needed for optimal functioning of the red blood cell.
    - (b) Selenium works as an antioxidant with one of the vitamins.
    - (c) Chromium appears to be essential in the use of blood glucose.
    - (d) Zinc is a part of numerous metalloenzymes.
    - (e) Mercury is essential for carbohydrate metabolism.

Answers to multiple-choice questions: 1. d; 2. d; 3. a; 4. b; 5. d; 6. c; 7. b; 8. b; 9. b; 10. e.

Review Questions—Essay

1. Explain several ways whereby minerals function in metabolic processes in the human body.
2. Name three macrominerals and at least five trace minerals and describe the metabolic function of each in the human body.
3. Osteoporosis is a significant health problem in the United States and Canada. Discuss the risk factors for osteoporosis and provide specifics as to how lifestyle behaviors may help prevent its development.
4. Discuss the role that iron supplementation may play if provided to an athlete under three conditions: (a) normal iron and hemoglobin status; (b) iron deficiency without anemia; (c) iron-deficiency anemia
5. Several minerals have been alleged to possess ergogenic potential. Select two of the following, explain the theoretical rationale underlying their purported ergogenic effects, and highlight the current research findings regarding their efficacy:

   chromium   phosphate salts
   boron   vanadium

References

Books

Celsing, F. 1987. *Influence of Iron Deficiency and Changes in Hemoglobin Concentration on Exercise Capacity in Man.* Stockholm: Repro Print.

Emery, T. 1991. *Iron and your Health.* Boca Raton, FL: CRC Press.

Institute of Medicine. 2005. *Dietary Supplements: A Framework for Evaluating Safety.* Washington, DC: National Academies Press.

National Academy of Sciences. 2002. *Dietary Reference Intakes for Vitamin A, Vitamin K, Arsenic, Boron, Chromium, Copper, Iodine, Iron, Manganese, Molybdenum,* *Nickel, Silicon, Vanadium, and Zinc.* Washington, DC: National Academy Press.

National Academy of Sciences. 2000. *Dietary Reference Intakes for Vitamin C, Vitamin E, Selenium and Carotenoids.* Washington, DC: National Academy Press.

National Academy of Sciences. 1999. *Dietary Reference Intakes for Calcium, Phosphorus, Magnesium, Vitamin D, and Fluoride.* Washington, DC: National Academy Press.

National Research Council. 1989. *Diet and Health: Implications for Reducing Chronic Disease Risk.* Washington, DC: National Academy Press.

Nelson, M. 2005. *Strong Women, Strong Bones.* New York: Penguin Putnam.

Reviews

Althuis, M., et al. 2002. Glucose and insulin responses to dietary chromium supplements: A meta-analysis. *American Journal of Clinical Nutrition* 76:148–55.

American College of Sports Medicine. 2004. Physical activity and bone health. *Medicine & Science in Sports & Exercise* 36:1985–96.

American Dietetic Association. 2000. Position of the American Dietetic Association: The impact of fluoride on health. *Journal of the American Dietetic Association* 100:1208–13.

American Dietetic Association. 1997. Position of the American Dietetic Association: Vegetarian diets. *Journal of the American Dietetic Association* 97:1317–21.

Anderson, J., and Barrett, C. 1994. Dietary phosphorus: The benefits and the problems. *Nutrition Today* 29 (2): 29–34.

Anderson, R. A. 1998. Chromium, glucose intolerance and diabetes. *Journal of the American College of Nutrition* 17:548–55.

Anderson, R. A. 1998. Effects of chromium on body composition and weight loss. *Nutrition Reviews* 56:266–70.

Anderson, R. 1988. Selenium, chromium, and manganese. (B) Chromium. In *Modern Nutrition in Health and Disease,* eds. M. Shils and V. Young. Philadelphia: Lea and Febiger.

Antinoro, L. 2002. Marvelous magnesium offers health benefits: From heart to bones. *Environmental Nutrition* 25 (9):1, 6.

Beard, J., and Tobin, B. 2000. Iron status and exercise. *American Journal of Clinical Nutrition.* 72:594S–97S.

Bendich, A., et al. 1999. Supplemental calcium for the prevention of hip fracture: Potential health-economic benefits. *Clinical Therapeutics* 21:1058–72.

Bennell, K., et al. 1996. Effect of altered reproductive function and lowered testosterone levels on bone density in male endurance athletes. *British Journal of Sports Medicine* 30:205–8.

Bern, L. 2003. The estrogen and progestin dilemma: New advice, labeling guidelines. *FDA Consumer* 37 (2):10–11.

Bjelakovic, G., et al. 2004. Antioxidant supplements for prevention of gastrointestinal cancers: A systematic review and meta-analysis. *Lancet* 364:1219–28.

Bloomfield, S. 2001. Optimizing bone health: Impact of nutrition, exercise, and hormones. *Sports Science Exchange* 14 (3):1–4.

Bonaiuti, D., et al. 2002. Exercise for preventing and treating osteoporosis in postmenopausal women. *Cochrane Database of System Reviews* 3:CD000333.

Bostick, R. M. 1997. Human studies of calcium supplementation and colorectal epithelial cell proliferation. *Cancer Epidemiology, Biomarkers, and Prevention* 6:971–80.

Brilla, L. R., and Lombardi, V. P. 1999. Magnesium in exercise and sport. In *Macroelements, Water, and Electrolytes in Sports Nutrition,* eds. J. A. Driskell and I. Wolinsky. Boca Raton, FL:CRC Press.

Brown, J., and Josse, R. 2002. 2002 clinical practice guidelines for the diagnosis and management of osteoporosis in Canada. *Canadian Medical Association Journal* 167:S1–S34.

Brown, K., and Arthur, J. 2001. Selenium, selenoproteins and human health: A review. *Public Health Nutrition* 4:593–99.

Brown, K., et al. 2002. Effect of supplemental zinc on the growth and serum zinc concentrations of prepubertal children: A meta-analysis of randomized controlled trials. *American Journal of Clinical Nutrition* 75:1062–71.

Burk, R. 2002. Selenium, an antioxidant nutrient. *Nutrition in Clinical Care* 5:75–79.

Burk, R. F., and Levander, O. A. 2006. Selenium. In *Modern Nutrition in Health and Disease,* eds. M. Shils, et al. Philadelphia: Lippincott Williams & Wilkins.

Centers for Disease Control and Prevention. 1998. Recommendations to prevent and control iron deficiency in the United States. *MMWR-Morbidity and Mortality Weekly Report* 47 (April 3):1–29.

Clarkson, P. M. 1997. Effects of exercise on chromium levels. Is supplementation required? *Sports Medicine* 23:341–49.

Clarkson, P. 1996. Nutrition for improved sports performance. *Sports Medicine* 21:393–401.

Clarkson, P., and Haymes, E. 1995. Exercise and mineral status of athletes: Calcium, magnesium, phosphorus, and iron. *Medicine & Science in Sports & Exercise* 27:831–45.

Combs, G. 2005. Current evidence and research needs to support a health claim for selenium and cancer prevention. *Journal of Nutrition* 135:343–47.

Consumers Union. 2004. Stronger bones without the hype. *Consumer Reports on Health* 16 (5):1, 4–5.

Consumers Union. 2002. Raising the bar on hormones. *Consumer Reports on Health* 14 (12):2.

Consumers Union. 2001. What's best for your bones? *Consumer Reports on Health* 13 (7):1, 4–6

Danesh, J., and Appleby, P. 1999. Coronary heart disease and iron status: Meta-analysis of prospective studies. *Circulation* 99:852–54.

Dawson-Hughes, B. 2006. Osteoporosis. In *Modern Nutrition in Health and Disease,* eds. M. Shils, et al. Philadelphia: Lippincott Williams & Wilkins.

DenBesten, P. K. 1999. Biological mechanisms of dental fluorosis relevant to the use of fluoride supplements. *Commu-*

nity Dentistry and Oral Epidemiology 27:41–47.

Deuster, P. 1989. Magnesium in sports medicine. *Journal of the American College of Nutrition* 8:462.

DeValk, B., and Marx, J. J. 1999. Iron, atherosclerosis, and ischemic heart disease. *Archives of Internal Medicine* 159:1542–48.

Durlach, J., et al. 1999. Cardiovasoprotective foods and nutrients: Possible importance of magnesium intake. *Magnesium Research* 12:57–61.

Eichner, E. R. 2001. Anemia and blood boosting. *Sports Science Exchange* 14 (2). 1–4.

Eichner, E.R. 1992. Sports anemia, iron supplements, and blood doping. *Medicine & Science in Sports & Exercise* 24:S315–S318.

Evans, G. 1989. The effect of chromium picolinate on insulin controlled parameters in humans. *International Journal of Biosocial and Medical Research* 11:163–80.

Fairbanks, V. F. 1999. Iron in medicine and nutrition. In *Modern Nutrition in Health and Disease,* eds. M. Shils, et al. Baltimore: Williams and Wilkins.

Featherstone, J. D. 1999. Prevention and reversal of dental caries: Role of low-level fluoride. *Community Dentistry and Oral Epidemiology* 27:31–40.

Food and Drug Administration. 2005. Americans over 50 at risk of bone fractures. *FDA Consumer* 39 (1):10–11.

Garza, D., et al. 1997. The clinical value of serum ferritin tests in endurance athletes. *Clinics in Sport Medicine* 7:46–53.

Gledhill, N., et al. 1999. Haemoglobin, blood volume, cardiac function, and aerobic power. *Canadian Journal of Applied Physiology* 24:54–65.

Haas, J., and Brownlie, T. 2001. Iron deficiency and reduced work capacity: A critical review of the research to determine a causal relationship. *Journal of Nutrition* 131:676S–88S.

Hambidge, M. 2000. Human zinc deficiency. *Journal of Nutrition* 130:1344S–49S.

Hansen, K. A., and Tho, S. P. 1998. Androgens and bone health. *Seminars in Reproductive Endocrinology* 16:129–34.

Haymes, E. 1993. Dietary iron needs in exercising women: A rational plan to follow in evaluating iron status. *Medicine, Exercise, Nutrition, and Health* 2:203–12.

Horn, S., and Feller, E. 2003. Gastrointestinal (GI) bleeding in endurance runners. *AMAA Journal* 16 (1):5–6, 11.

Horswill, C. 1995. Effects of bicarbonate, citrate, and phosphate loading on performance. *International Journal of Sport Nutrition* 5:S111–S119.

Ilich, J., and Kerstetter, J. 2000. Nutrition in bone health revisited: A story beyond calcium. *Journal of the American College of Nutrition* 19:715–37.

Ismail, A. I., and Bandekar, R. R. 1999. Fluoride supplements and fluorosis: A meta-analysis. *Community Dentistry and Oral Epidemiology* 27:48–56.

Jackson, J. L., et al. 2000. Zinc and the common cold: A meta-analysis revisited. *Journal of Nutrition* 130:1512S–1515S.

Jones, G. R., and Newhouse, I. 1997. Sport-related hematuria: A review. *Clinical Journal of Sports Medicine* 7:119–25.

King, J. C., and Cousins, R. J. 2006. Zinc. In *Modern Nutrition in Health and Disease,* eds. M. Shils, et al. Philadelphia: Lippincott Williams & Wilkins.

Knochel, J. P. 2006. Phosphorus. In *Modern Nutrition in Health and Disease,* eds. M. Shils, et al. Philadelphia: Lippincott Williams & Wilkins.

Kreider, R. B. 1999. Dietary supplements and the promotion of muscle growth with resistance exercise. *Sports Medicine* 27:97–110.

Lane, H. 1989. Some trace elements related to physical activity: Zinc, copper, selenium, chromium, and iodine. In *Nutrition in Exercise and Sport,* eds. J. Hickson and I. Wolinsky. Boca Raton, FL:CRC Press.

Lefavi, R. 1992. Efficacy of chromium supplementation in athletes: Emphasis on anabolism. *International Journal of Sport Nutrition* 2:111–22.

Lowe, N., et al. 2002. Is there a potential therapeutic value of copper and zinc for osteoporosis? *Proceedings of the Nutrition Society* 61:181–85.

Lukaski, H. 2004. Vitamin and mineral status: Effects on physical performance. *Nutrition* 20:632–44.

Lukaski, H. 2001. Magnesium, zinc, and chromium nutrition and athletic performance. *Canadian Journal of Applied Physiology* 26:S13–22.

Lukaski, H. C. 1999. Chromium as a supplement. *Annual Reviews in Nutrition* 19:279–302.

Lukaski, H. 1995. Micronutrients (magnesium, zinc, and copper): Are mineral supplements needed for athletes? *International Journal of Sport Nutrition* 5:S74–S83.

Manore, M. 2001. Vitamins and minerals: How much do you need? *ACSM's Health & Fitness Journal* 5 (1):33–35.

Martinez, M. E., and Willett, W. C. 1998. Calcium, vitamin D, and colorectal cancer: A review of the epidemiologic evidence. *Cancer Epidemiology, Biomarkers and Prevention* 7:163–68.

McDonald, R., and Keen, C. 1988. Iron, zinc and magnesium nutrition and athletic performance. *Sports Medicine* 5:171–84.

Meunier, P. J. 1999. Evidence-based medicine and osteoporosis: A comparison of fracture risk reduction data from osteoporosis randomized clinical trials. *International Journal of Clinical Practice* 53:122–29.

Micheletti, A., et al. 2001. Zinc status in athletes: Relation to diet and exercise. *Sports Medicine* 31:577–82.

Miller, L., et al. 2004. Bone mineral density in postmenopausal women. *Physician and Sportsmedicine* 32 (2):18–24.

Mizushima, S., et al. 1998. Dietary magnesium intake and blood pressure: A qualitative overview of the observational studies. *Journal of Human Hypertension* 12:447–53.

Modlesky, C., and Lewis, R. 2002. Does exercise during growth have a long-term effect on bone health? *Exercise and Sport Sciences Reviews* 30:171–76.

Naghii, M. R. 1999. The significance of dietary boron, with particular reference to athletes. *Nutrition and Health* 13:31–37.

New, S. 2001. Exercise, bone and nutrition. *Proceedings of the Nutrition Society* 60:265–74.

Newhouse, I., and Finstad, E. 2000. The effects of magnesium supplementation on exercise performance. *Clinical Journal of Sport Medicine* 10:195–200.

Newhouse, I., and Clement, D. 1988. Iron status in athletes: An update. *Sports Medicine* 5:337–52.

Nielsen, F. 1996. How should dietary guidance be given for mineral elements with beneficial actions or suspected of being essential? *Journal of Nutrition* 126:2377S–2385S.

Nielsen, F. 1992. Facts and fallacies about boron. *Nutrition Today* 27:6–12.

Nielsen, F. H. 1999. Ultratrace minerals. In *Modern Nutrition in Health and Disease,* eds. M. Shils, et al. Philadelphia: Lippincott Williams & Wilkins.

Nielsen, F. H. 1998. The justification for providing dietary guidance for the nutritional intake of boron. *Biological Trace Element Research* 66:319–30.

Nielsen, P., and Nachtigall, D. 1998. Iron supplementation to athletes: Current recommendations. *Sports Medicine* 26:207–16.

Nieman, D. 2001. Exercise immunology: Nutritional countermeasures. *Canadian Journal of Applied Physiology* 26:S45–S55.

NIH Consensus Development Panel on Osteoporosis Prevention, Diagnosis, and Therapy. 2001. Osteoporosis prevention, diagnosis, and therapy. *JAMA* 285:785–95.

Pennington, J. 1996. Intakes of minerals from diets and foods: Is there a need for concern? *Journal of Nutrition* 126:2304S–2308S.

Peterlik, M., and Cross, H. 2005. Vitamin D and calcium deficits predispose for multiple chronic diseases. *European Journal of Clinical Investigation* 35:290–304.

Pittler, M., et al. 2003. Chromium picolinate for reducing body weight: Meta-analysis of randomized trials. *International Journal of Obesity and Related Metabolic Disorders* 27:522–29.

Rayman, M., and Rayman, M. 2002. The argument for increasing selenium intake. *Proceedings of the Nutrition Society* 61:203–15.

Root, A. 2002. Bone strength and the adolescent. *Adolescent Medicine* 13:53–72.

Rude, R., and Gruber, H. 2004. Magnesium deficiency and osteoporosis: Animal and human observations. *Journal of Nutritional Biochemistry* 15:710–16.

Rude, R., and Shils, M. E. 2006. Magnesium. In *Modern Nutrition in Health and Disease,* eds. M. Shils, et al. Philadelphia: Lippincott Williams & Wilkins.

Runner's World. 2003. Live high, train low. *Runner's World* 38 (1):64

Schardt, D., and Schmidt, S. 1996. Chromium. *Nutrition Action Healthletter* 23 (4):10–11.

Seeman, E. 1999. The structural basis of bone fragility in men. *Bone* 25:143–47

Sharman, I. 1984. Need for micro-nutrient supplementation with regard to physical performance. *International Journal of Sports Medicine* 5 (Suppl): 22–24.

Shaskey, D., and Green, G. 2000. Sports haematology. *Sports Medicine* 29:27–38.

Shea, B., et al. 2004. Calcium supplementation on bone loss in postmenopausal women. *Cochrane Database of Systematic Reviews* 1:CD004526.

Short, S. 1994. Dietary surveys and nutrition knowledge. In *Nutrition in Exercise and Sport,* eds. I. Wolinsky and J. Hickson. Boca Raton, FL: CRC Press.

Sojka, J., and Weaver, C. 1995. Magnesium supplementation and osteoporosis. *Nutrition Reviews* 53:71–80.

Speich, M., et al. 2001. Minerals, trace elements and related biological variables in athletes and during physical activity. *Clinical Chimica Acta* 312:1–11.

Stearns, D., et al. 1995. A prediction of chromium (III) accumulation in humans from chromium dietary supplements. *FASEB Journal* 9:1650–57.

Stoecker, B. J. 2006. Chromium. In *Modern Nutrition in Health and Disease,* eds. M. Shils, et al. Philadelphia: Lippincott Williams & Wilkins.

Teegarden, D., and Weaver, C. 1994. Calcium supplementation increases bone density in adolescent girls. *Nutrition Reviews* 52:171–73.

Tremblay, M., et al. 1994. Ergogenic effects of phosphate loading: Physiological fact or methodological fiction? *Canadian Journal of Applied Physiology* 19:1–11.

Turner, C., and Robling, A. 2003. Designing exercise regimens to increase bone strength. *Exercise and Sport Sciences Reviews* 31:45–50.

Turnlund, J. R. 2006. Copper. In *Modern Nutrition in Health and Disease,* eds. M. Shils, et al. Philadelphia: Lippincott Williams & Wilkins.

Verma, S., et al. 1998. Nutritional factors that can favorably influence the glucose/insulin system: Vanadium. *Journal of the American College of Nutrition* 17:11–18.

Vincent, J. 2003. The potential value and toxicity of chromium picolinate as a nutritional supplement, weight loss agent and muscle development agent. *Sports Medicine* 33:213–30.

Vinceti, M., et al. 2001. Adverse effects of selenium in humans. *Reviews on Environmental Health* 16:233–51.

Warren, M. P., and Stiehl, A. L. 1999: Exercise and female adolescents: Effects on the reproductive and skeletal systems. *Journal of the American Medical Women's Association* 54:115–20.

Weaver, C. 2000. Calcium requirements of physically active people. *American Journal of Clinical Nutrition* 72:579S–84S.

Weaver, C. M., and Heaney, R. P. 2006. Calcium. In *Modern Nutrition in Health and Disease,* eds. M. Shils, et al. Philadelphia: Lippincott Williams & Wilkins.

Weaver, C., and Rajaram, S. 1992. Exercise and iron status. *Journal of Nutrition* 122:782–87.

Weight, L. 1993. 'Sports anemia' Does it exist? *Sports Medicine* 16:1–4.

Wood, R., and Ronnenberg, A. 2006. Iron. In *Modern Nutrition in Health and Disease,* eds. M. Shils, et al. Philadelphia: Lippincott Williams & Wilkens.

Wurzelmann, J., et al. 1996. Iron intake and the risk of colorectal cancer. *Cancer Epidemiology and Biomarkers of Prevention* 5:503–7.

Zemel, M., and Miller, S. 2004. Dietary calcium and dairy modulation of adiposity and obesity risk. *Nutrition Reviews* 62:125–31.

Specific Studies

Anderson, R., et al. 1995. Acute exercise effects on urinary losses and serum concentrations of copper and zinc of moderately trained and untrained men consuming a controlled diet. *Analyst* 120:867–70.

Baech, S., et al. 2003. Nonheme-iron absorption from a phytate-rich meal is increased by the addition of small amounts of pork meat. *American Journal of Clinical Nutrition* 77:173–79.

Baron, J., et al. 1999. Calcium supplements for the prevention of colorectal adenomas. *New England Journal of Medicine* 340:101–7.

Barr, S. I., et al. 1998. Spinal bone mineral density in premenopausal vegetarian and nonvegetarian women: Cross-sectional and prospective comparisons. *Journal of the American Dietetic Association* 98: 760–5.

Bilanin, J., et al. 1989. Lower vertebral bone density in male long distance runners. *Medicine & Science in Sports & Exercise* 21:66–70.

Bremner, K., et al. 2002. The effect of phosphate loading on erythrocyte 2,3-bisphosphoglycerate levels. *Clinical Chimica Acta* 323:111–14.

Brilla, L., and Gunter, K., 1994. Magnesium ameliorates aerobic contribution at high intensity. *Medicine & Science in Sports & Exercise* 26:S53.

Brownlie, T., et al. 2002. Marginal iron deficiency without anemia impairs aerobic adaptation among previously untrained women. *American Journal of Clinical Nutrition* 75:734–42.

Brun, J., et al. 1995. Serum zinc in highly trained adolescent gymnasts. *Biological Trace Element Research* 47:273–78.

Buchman, A. L., et al. 1998. The effect of a marathon run on plasma and urine mineral and metal concentrations. *Journal of the American College of Nutrition* 17:124–27.

Bullen, D. B., et al. 1999. Calcium losses resulting from an acute bout of moderate-intensity exercise. *International Journal of Sport Nutrition* 9:275–84.

Cade, R., et al. 1984. Effects of phosphate loading on 2, 3-diphosphoglycerate and maximal oxygen uptake. *Medicine & Science in Sports & Exercise* 16:263–68.

Campbell, W., et al. 2002. Effects of resistive training and chromium picolinate on body composition and skeletal muscle size in older women. *International Journal of Sport Nutrition and Exercise Metabolism* 12:125–35.

Casoni, I., et al. 1990. Changes in magnesium concentrations in endurance athletes. *International Journal of Sports Medicine* 11:234–37.

Clancy, S., et al. 1994. Effects of chromium picolinate supplementation on body composition, strength, and urinary chromium loss in football players. *International Journal of Sport Nutrition* 4:142–53.

Clark, L. C., et al. 1998. Decreased incidence of prostate cancer with selenium supplementation: Results of a double-blind cancer prevention trial. *British Journal of Urology* 81:730–34.

Constantini, N. W., et al. 2000. Iron status of highly active adolescents: Evidence of depleted stores in gymnasts. *International Journal of Sport Nutrition and Exercise Metabolism* 10:62–70.

Cussler, E., et al. 2003. Weight lifted in strength training predicts bone change in postmenopausal women. *Medicine & Science in Sports & Exercise* 35:10–17.

Davis, J., et al. 2000. Effects of carbohydrate and chromium ingestion during intermittent high-intensity exercise to fatigue. *International Journal of Sport Nutrition and Exercise Metabolism* 10:476–85.

Dawson-Hughes, B., and Harris, S. 2002. Calcium intake influences the association of protein intake with rates of bone loss in elderly men and women. *American Journal of Clinical Nutrition* 75:773–79.

Derstine, J., et al. 2003. Iron status in association with cardiovascular disease risk in 3 controlled feeding studies. *American Journal of Clinical Nutrition* 77:55–62.

DeRuisseau, K., et al. 2002. Sweat iron and zinc losses during prolonged exercise. *International Journal of Sport Nutrition and Exercise Metabolism* 12:428–37.

Deugnier, Y., et al. 2002. Increased body iron stores in elite road cyclists. *Medicine & Science in Sports & Exercise* 34:876–80.

Dressendorfer, R., et al. 2002. Mineral metabolism in male cyclists during high-intensity endurance training. *International Journal of Sport Nutrition and Exercise Metabolism* 12:63–72.

Dubnov, G., and Constantini, N. 2004. Prevalence of iron depletion and anemia in top-level basketball players. *International Journal of Sport Nutrition and Exercise Metabolism* 14:30–37.

Fawcett, J., et al. 1996. The effect of oral vanadyl sulfate on body composition and performance in weight-training athletes. *International Journal of Sport Nutrition* 6:382–90.

Ferrando, A., and Green, N. 1993. The effect of boron supplementation on lean body mass, plasma testosterone levels, and strength in male bodybuilders. *International Journal of Sport Nutrition* 3:140–49.

Fogelholm, M., et al. 1992. Effect of iron supplementation in female athletes with low serum ferritin concentration. *International Journal of Sports Medicine* 13:158–62.

Galloway, S., et al. 1996. The effects of acute phosphate supplementation in subjects of different aerobic fitness levels. *European Journal of Applied Physiology* 72:224–30.

Goss, F., et al. 2001. Effect of potassium phosphate supplementation on perceptual and physiological responses to maximal graded exercise. *International Journal of Sport Nutrition and Exercise Metabolism* 11:53–62.

Grant, K. E., et al. 1997. Chromium and exercise training: Effect on obese women. *Medicine & Science in Sport & Exercise* 29:992–98.

Gremion, G., et al. 2001. Oligo-amenorrheic long-distance runners may lose more bone in spine than in femur. *Medicine & Science in Sports & Exercise* 33:15–21.

Gunther, C., et al. 2005. Dairy products do not lead to alterations in body weight or fat mass in young women in a 1-y intervention. *American Journal of Clinical Nutrition* 81:751–56.

Hallmark, M., et al. 1996. Effects of chromium and resistive training on muscle strength and body composition. *Medicine & Science in Sports & Exercise* 28:139–44.

Heaney, R., and Nordin, B. 2002. Calcium effects on phosphorus absorption: Implications for the prevention and co-therapy of osteoporosis. *Journal of the American College of Nutrition* 21:239–44

Heath, A., et al. 2001. Can dietary treatment of non-anemic iron deficiency improve iron status? *Journal of the American College of Nutrition* 20:477–84.

Hinton, P. S., et al. 2000. Iron supplementation improves endurance after training in iron-depleted, nonanemic women. *Journal of Applied Physiology* 88:1103–11.

Hudgins, P., et al. 1990. Effects of iron supplementation on hematologic profile and performance in female endurance athletes. *FASEB Journal* 4:A1197.

Hunt, J. R., et al. 1998. Zinc absorption, mineral balance, and blood lipids in women consuming controlled lactoovovegetarian and omnivorous diets for 8 weeks. *American Journal of Clinical Nutrition* 67:421–30.

Jentjens, R., and Jeukendrup, A. 2002. Effect of acute and short-term administration of vanadyl sulphate on insulin sensitivity in healthy active humans. *International Journal of Sport Nutrition and Exercise Metabolism* 12:470–79.

Jones, G., et al. 2001. The incidence of hematuria in middle distance track running. *Canadian Journal of Applied Physiology* 26:336–49.

Jordan, A., et al. 2004. Effects of oral ATP supplementation on anaerobic power and muscular strength. *Medicine & Science in Sports & Exercise* 36:983–90.

Karamizrak, S., et al. 1996. Evaluation of iron metabolism indices and their relation with physical work capacity in athletes. *British Journal of Sports Medicine* 30:15–19.

Khaled, S., et al. 1998. Increased blood viscosity in iron-depleted elite athletes. *Clinical Hemorheology and Microcirculation* 18:309–18.

Klesges, R., et al. 1996. Changes in bone mineral content in male athletes. *Journal of the American Medical Association* 276:226–30.

Klingshirn, L., et al. 1992. Effect of iron supplementation on endurance capacity in iron-depleted female runners. *Medicine & Science in Sports & Exercise* 24:819–24.

Kraemer, W., et al. 1995. Effects of multibuffer supplementation on acid-base balance and 2,3-diphosphoglycerate following repetitive anaerobic exercise. *International Journal of Sport Nutrition* 5:300–314.

Kreider, R., et al. 1992. Effects of phosphate loading on metabolic and myocardial responses to maximal and endurance exercise. *International Journal of Sport Nutrition* 2:20–47.

Kreider, R., et al. 1990. Effects of phosphate loading on oxygen uptake, ventilatory anaerobic threshold, and run performance. *Medicine & Science in Sports & Exercise* 22:250–56.

Krotkiewski, M., et al. 1982. Zinc and muscle strength and endurance. *Acta Physiologica Scandinavica* 116:309–11.

Lamanca, J., and Haymes, E. 1993. Effects of iron repletion on VO₂max, endurance, and blood lactate in women. *Medicine & Science in Sports & Exercise* 25:1386–92.

Lappe, J., et al. 2004. Girls on a high-calcium diet gain weight at the same rate as girls on a normal diet: A pilot study. *Journal of the American Dietetic Association* 104:1361–67.

Lima, M., et al. 1998. The effect of magnesium supplementation in increasing doses on the control of type 2 diabetes. *Diabetes Care* 21:682–86.

Liu, I., et al. 1983. Hypomagnesemia in a tennis player. *Physician and Sportsmedicine* 11 (May): 79–80.

Livolsi, J., et al. 2001. The effect of chromium picolinate on muscular strength and body composition in women athletes. *Journal of Strength and Conditioning Research* 15:161–66.

Looker, A., et al. 1997. Prevalence of iron deficiency in the United States. *Journal of the American Medical Association* 277:973–76.

Lukaski, H., et al. 1996. Chromium supplementation and resistance training: Effects on body composition, strength, and trace element status of men. *American Journal of Clinical Nutrition* 63:954–65.

Lukaski, H., et al. 1991. Altered metabolic response of iron deficient women during graded, maximal exercises. *European Journal of Applied Physiology* 63:140–45.

Lyle, R., et al. 1992. Iron status in exercising women: The effect of oral iron therapy vs increased consumption of muscle foods. *American Journal of Clinical Nutrition* 56:1049–55

Magazanik, A., et al. 1991. Effect of an iron supplement on body iron status and aerobic capacity of young training women. *European Journal of Applied Physiology* 62:317–23.

Mannix, E., et al. 1990. Oxygen delivery and cardiac output during exercise following oral phosphate-glucose. *Medicine & Science in Sports & Exercise* 22:341–47.

Margaritis, I., et al. 1997. Effects of endurance training on skeletal muscle oxidative capacities with and without selenium supplementation. *Journal of Trace Elements in Medicine and Biology* 11:37–43.

Matter, M., et al. 1987. The effect of iron and folate therapy on maximal exercise performance in female marathon runners with iron and folate deficiency. *Clinical Science* 72:415–22.

Newhouse, I., et al. 1993. Effects of iron supplementation and discontinuation on serum copper, zinc, calcium, and magnesium levels in women. *Medicine & Science in Sports & Exercise* 25:562–71.

Nuviala, R. J., et al. 1999. Magnesium, zinc, and copper status in women involved in different sports. *International Journal of Sport Nutrition* 9:295–309.

Ormerod, S., et al. 1990. The relationship between weekly mileage and bone density in male runners. *Medicine & Science in Sports & Exercise* 22:562.

Powell, P., and Tucker, A. 1991. Iron supplementation and running performance in female cross-country runners. *International Journal of Sports Medicine* 12:462–67.

Rainey, C. J., et al. 1999. Daily boron intake from the American Diet. *Journal of the American Dietetic Association* 99:335–40.

Rajaram, S., et al. 1995. Effects of long-term moderate exercise on iron status in young women. *Medicine & Science in Sports & Exercise* 27:1105–10.

Rowland, T., et al. 1988. The effect of iron therapy on the exercise capacity of nonanemic iron-deficient adolescent runners. *American Journal of Diseases in Children* 142:165–69.

Rubenowitz, E., et al. 1996. Magnesium in drinking water and death from acute myocardial infarction. *American Journal of Epidemiology* 143:456–62.

Sacks, F. M., et al. 1998. Effect on blood pressure of potassium, calcium, and magnesium in women with low habitual intake. *Hypertension* 31:131–38.

Saunders, P., et al. 2004. Improved running economy in elite runners after 20 days of simulated moderate-altitude exposure. *Journal of Applied Physiology* 96:931–37.

Schmid, A., et al. 1996. Effect of physical exercise and vitamin C on absorption of ferric sodium citrate. *Medicine & Science in Sports & Exercise* 28:1470–73.

Schumacher, Y., et al. 2002. Hematological indices and iron status in athletes of various sports and performances. *Medicine & Science in Sports & Exercise* 34:869–75.

Snyder, A., et al. 1989. Influence of dietary iron source on measures of iron status among female runners. *Medicine & Science in Sports & Exercise* 21:7–10.

Stewart, I., et al. 1990. Phosphate loading and the effects on VO_2max in trained cyclists. *Research Quarterly for Exercise and Sport* 61:80–84.

Telford, R., et al. 1993. Iron status and diet in athletes. *Medicine & Science in Sports & Exercise* 25:796–800.

Terblanche, S., et al. 1992. Failure of magnesium supplementation to influence marathon running performance or recovery in magnesium-replete subjects. *International Journal of Sport Nutrition* 2:154–64.

Tessier, F., et al. 1995. Selenium and training effects on the glutathione system and aerobic performance. *Medicine & Science in Sports & Exercise* 27:390–96.

Thompson, W., et al. 2005. Effect of energy-reduced diets high in dairy products and fiber on weight loss in obese adults. *Obesity Research* 13:1344–53.

Thys-Jacobs, S., et al. 1998. Calcium carbonate and the premenstrual syndrome. *American Journal of Obstetrics and Gynecology* 179:444–52.

Torstveit, M., and Sundgot-Borgen, J. 2005. Low bone mineral density is two to three times more prevalent in non-athletic premenopausal women than in elite athletes: A comprehensive controlled study. *British Journal of Sports Medicine* 39:282–87.

Trent, L., and Thieding-Cancel, D. 1995. Effects of chromium picolinate on body composition. *Journal of Sports Medicine and Physical Fitness* 35:273–80.

Turner, C., and Robling, A. 2003. Designing exercise regimens to increase bone strength. *Exercise and Sport Sciences Reviews* 31:45–50.

Van Loan, M. D., et al. 1999. The effects of zinc depletion on peak force and total work of knee and shoulder extensor and flexor muscles. *International Journal of Sport Nutrition* 9:125–35.

Volpe, S., et al. 2001. Effect of chromium supplementation and exercise on body composition, resting metabolic rate and selected biochemical parameters in moderately obese women following an exercise program. *Journal of the American College of Nutrition* 20:293–306.

Walker, L. S., et al. 1998. Chromium picolinate effects on body composition and muscular performance in wrestlers. *Medicine & Science in Sports & Exercise* 30:1730–37.

Waller, M., and Haymes, E. 1996. The effects of heat and exercise on sweat iron loss. *Medicine & Science in Sports & Exercise* 28:197–203.

Webster, B., and Barr, S. 1995. Calcium intake of adolescent female gymnasts and speed skaters: Lack of association with dieting behavior. *International Journal of Sport Nutrition* 5:2–12.

Weight, L., et al. 1992. Dietary iron deficiency and sports anaemia. *British Journal of Nutrition* 68:253–60.

Weller, E., et al. 1998. Lack of effect of oral Mg-supplementation on Mg in serum, blood cells, and calf muscle. *Medicine & Science in Sports & Exercise* 30:1584–91.

Wilson, A. K., and Ball, M. J. 1999. Nutrient intake and iron status of Australian male vegetarians. *European Journal of Clinical Nutrition* 53:189–94.

Zanker, C., and Swaine, I. 2000. Responses of bone turnover markers to repeated endurance running in humans under conditions of energy balance or energy restriction. *European Journal of Applied Physiology* 83:434–40.

Zemel, M. 2005. Dairy augmentation of total and central fat loss in obese subjects. *International Journal of Obesity and Related Metabolic Disorders* 29:391–97.

Ziegler, P., et al. 2002. Nutritional status of teenage female competitive figure skaters. *Journal of the American Dietetic Association* 102:374–79.

Zotter, H., et al. 2004. Abnormally high serum ferritin levels among professional road cyclists. *British Journal of Sports Medicine* 38:704–08.

Water, Electrolytes, and Temperature Regulation

CHAPTER NINE

LEARNING OBJECTIVES

After studying this chapter, you should be able to:

1. Identify the principal water compartments in the body, describe the general function of each, and explain how your body maintains overall water balance.

2. Identify foods that are high or low in sodium and potassium, and explain the physiological responses of your body to restore normal serum sodium levels following a high salt intake.

3. List the four (4) components of environmental heat stress recorded by the Wet Bulb Globe Temperature (WBGT), and explain how each may impact the heat balance equation during exercise under hot, humid environmental conditions.

4. Describe how exercise in the heat may impair endurance performance as compared to exercise in a cooler environment, and explain the physiological responses your body would make in order to promote heat loss.

5. Outline the key guidelines for consuming water, electrolytes, and carbohydrate before, during, and after exercise under warm or hot environmental conditions, and offer general recommendations to athletes participating in such events.

6. Describe the theory underlying the use of glycerol as an ergogenic aid, and understand the current research findings regarding its efficacy in enhancing exercise performance.

7. Learn various strategies to reduce the risk of heat illness while exercising in a hot environment, but also be able to identify the various heat illnesses along with their causes, clinical findings, and appropriate treatment.

8. Understand the meaning of high blood pressure and associated health risks, and describe the role that diet and exercise may play in the its prevention and treatment.

Water is a clear, tasteless, odorless fluid. It is a rather simple compound composed of two parts hydrogen and one part oxygen (H_2O). Of all the nutrients essential in the chemistry and functioning of living forms, it is the most important. Although humans may survive about 7 days without water under optimal conditions, rapid losses of body water through dehydration may prove fatal in a relatively short time, even within hours when young children with diarrhea lose large amounts of water and electrolytes.

Water provides no food energy, but most of the other nutrients essential to life can be used by the human body only because of their reaction with water. Water constitutes most of the body weight and provides the medium within which the other nutrients may function. Water has a number of diverse functions in human metabolism; one of the most important, particularly for the athletic individual, is the regulation of body temperature. In a review of food and drink in sport, Macdonald noted that fluid is still the priority constituent that needs to be monitored.

When the body loses fluids by any route, it not only loses water but electrolytes as well. Electrolytes, particularly those discussed in this chapter (sodium, chloride, and potassium), are involved in numerous physiological functions, such as muscle contraction. Sodium is particularly involved in fluid balance, a major determinant of blood pressure. An abnormal electrolyte status may adversely affect both health and physical performance.

Proper fluid replacement is important for both health and sport. To help decrease mortality from diarrhea, a major health problem associated with cholera in undeveloped countries, medical scientists developed oral rehydration therapy (ORT) solutions to help replace lost fluids rapidly. Today, the standard ORT solution contains sodium chloride, potassium chloride, trisodium citrate, glucose, and water, and its application has effectively decreased mortality during epidemics of cholera. In the 1950s and 1960s, heat illnesses were widespread among military personnel and athletes, primarily because of regulations that restricted fluid intake. Research by sports medicine scientists during this time helped to identify risk factors associated with exercise under warm or hot environmental conditions, and with application of appropriate guidelines, the incidence of heat injuries declined. During these studies, scientists also noted that endurance-exercise performance declined with excessive exercise-induced sweating and fluid loss, and research into sport ORT as a means of helping delay fatigue due to fluid losses increased dramatically, leading to our sports drinks of today.

Of the factors that may influence physical performance on any given day, one of the major concerns is the environmental temperature. Anyone who is physically active for prolonged periods is probably aware of the effect that temperature changes have on performance ability. In particular, as the temperature increases, the combination of the environmental heat and the increased body heat from exercise metabolism may disturb body-water supplies, electrolyte status, and temperature regulation, which at the least may prove detrimental to endurance capacity and at the extreme may have fatal consequences.

Given the seriousness of this topic, the primary focus of this chapter will be upon those problems that may confront you when exercising in the heat and how you may prevent or correct them. Topics covered include the role of water and selected electrolytes in human metabolism, the regulation of body temperature, the effect of fluid and electrolyte losses upon performance, methods of fluid and electrolyte replacement, ergogenic aids, and health-related problems such as heat illnesses and high blood pressure (hypertension).

Water

How much water do you need per day?

Manz and others note that water is recognized as the most essential nutrient, and an AI for total water from beverages and food has recently been established. The requirement for body water depends on the body weight of the individual. The requirement varies in different stages of the life cycle. Under normal environmental temperatures and activity levels, the AI for adult males and females age 19 and over is, respectively, 3.7 and 2.7 liters (3.9 and 2.9 quarts). Some-what lesser AI have been established for teenagers and children. Water requirements may be increased substantially during exercise, particularly under warm environmental conditions, and will be discussed later in this chapter.

Body-water balance is maintained when the output of body fluids is matched by the input of water. A small amount of water is lost in the feces and through the exhaled air in breathing. **Insensible perspiration** on the skin, which is not visible, is almost pure water and accounts for about 30 percent of body-water losses. Perspiration, or sweat, losses may be increased considerably during exercise and/or hot environmental conditions. Urinary output is the main avenue for water loss. It may increase somewhat through the use of diuretics, including alcohol and caffeine. Stookey indicates we lose about 1 milliliter of water for every milligram of caffeine, and 10 milliliters for every gram of alcohol. Also, use of a high-protein diet produces urea, which needs to be excreted by the kidneys and may increase urine output.

Fluid intake of beverages, such as water, soda, milk, juice, coffee, and tea, provides about 80 percent of total water needed to replenish losses. Valtin notes that we obtain significant amounts of fluid from caffeinated and alcoholic beverages, such as coffee and beer. Although both beverages contain diuretics, the Consumers Union recently noted that if you are used to drinking caffeinated or alcoholic beverages, the diuretic effect of each may be offset by the amount of fluid in the beverage and you probably gain more fluid from beverages, such as colas, coffee and beer, than you lose. About 20 percent of our daily total water intake comes from the foods we eat. Solid foods also contribute as a water source, and in two different ways. First, food contains water in varying amounts; certain foods such as lettuce, celery, melons, and most fruits contain about 80–90 percent water; meats and seafood contain about 60–70 percent water; even bread, an apparently dry food, contains 36 percent water. Second, the metabolism of foods for energy also produces water. Fat, carbohydrate, and protein all produce water when broken down for energy. You may recall the reaction when glucose is metabolized to produce energy, with one of the by-products being **metabolic water:**

$$C_6H_{12}O_6 + 6O_2 \rightarrow Energy + 6CO_2 + 6H_2O$$

Table 9.1 summarizes the daily water loss and intake for the maintenance of water balance for an adult female. Amounts would be greater for an adult male. As shall be seen later, however, these amounts may change drastically under certain conditions.

What else is in the water we drink?

In general, the tap water we drink daily is safe. However, it should be noted that most of the water we drink contains more than just water, including substances added from natural geological formations, discharge or runoff from industry or farming, water processing, and pipes in our homes. In some areas, water may contain substantial amounts of various minerals, including calcium, sodium, magnesium, iron, zinc, arsenic, and lead. Some minerals, like excess sodium, arsenic, and lead, may lead to various health problems, whereas others, such as calcium and magnesium, may be beneficial. Other substances find their way into our water supply as well. Lefferts reported that more than 700 contaminants have been found in public drinking water, including organic chemicals like pesticides. Under the Safe Drinking Water Act, the Environmental Protection Agency (EPA) has set maximum contaminant levels for the most harmful substances, and most, but not all, municipal water treatment facilities conform to these standards. The Consumers Union notes that, in general, most community water systems meet federal health-based standards, but also notes that some contaminants found in water systems may not be appropriate for vulnerable populations, such as pregnant women, infants, and the elderly.

If you are concerned about your tap water, know that some health professionals suggest the best alternative is a water filter. Water filters

TABLE 9.1	Daily water loss and intake for water balance in a sedentary adult female (60kg)
Water loss	
Urine output	1,500 ml
Water in feces	130 ml
Lungs (exhaled air)	270 ml
Skin (insensible perspiration)	800 ml
Total	2,700 ml
Water intake	
Fluids	2,200 ml
Water in food	350 ml
Metabolic water	150 ml
Total	2,700 ml

added to your tap may help remove unwanted substances, such as chlorine or chlorinated by-products; some water filters are designed to eliminate lead and mercury, and others can even trap parasites. Many types of water filters are on the market, so, if interested, have your water analyzed and then seek an appropriate filter to help purify your tap water. To get information on the quality of your water supply, you may contact the EPA at www.epa.gov/safewater and click on *local drinking water.* Or, contact your local water utility and ask for the latest water quality or Consumer Confidence Report.

Bottled water is the current rage. Not only do we have artesian, spring or purified water, we also have vitamin water, herbal water, nutraceutical water, oxygen water, and fitness water, to name a few of the specialty beverages available. The Food and Drug Administration (FDA) has set guidelines for defining bottled waters. Artesian water is drawn from a well that taps a confined aquifer; mineral water comes from a protected underground source and must contain minerals distinguishing it from other waters; spring water flows naturally from an underground source; purified water is produced by distillation or some comparable process. Bottled waters must conform to the same safety standards as municipal water supplies. About 85 percent of bottled-water manufacturers belong to the International Bottled Water Association (IBWA), which sets even tougher standards for its members than the FDA. Individuals who drink bottled water should be aware that approximately 25 percent is simply tap water that has undergone a purification process. The nation's best-selling bottled water is purified municipal water, which would cost you a penny per liter from the tap, but nearly a dollar per liter at the supermarket. Also, surveys have shown that most bottled waters do not contain fluoride. For example, Lalumandier and Ayers reported that only 5 percent of 57 samples of bottled water contained fluoride within the recommended range. Check bottled water labels for mineral content. The

FDA is also seeking legislation requiring that bottled water manufacturers list contaminant levels on bottle labels.

Bottled water isn't cheap, especially the specialty waters. A bottle of vitamin water may cost over a dollar, whereas a glass of water with an inexpensive multivitamin/mineral tablet will provide the same benefits but cost ten times less. The Consumers Union indicates that you do not need any of the specialty waters to replenish fluids, but if their taste encourages you to drink more, they may be worthwhile, especially if you normally do not drink adequate fluids.

Where is water stored in the body?

Water is stored in several body compartments but moves constantly between compartments. About 65 percent of body water is stored inside body cells as **intracellular water.** The remaining 35 percent is outside the cells and is termed **extracellular water.** The extracellular water is further subdivided into the **intercellular (interstitial) water** between or surrounding the cells, the **intravascular water** within the blood vessels, and miscellaneous water compartments such as the cerebrospinal fluid. Figure 9.1 represents the distribution of water in the body.

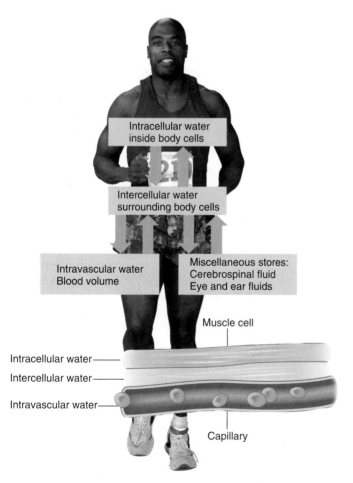

FIGURE 9.1 Body-water compartments. There is a constant interchange among the different body-water compartments. The water inside the body cells, the intracellular water, is important for cell functions. The other three compartments (intercellular, intravascular, and miscellaneous) are known collectively as the extracellular water. Decreases in blood volume may adversely affect endurance capacity.

Water is held in the body in conjunction with protein, carbohydrate, and electrolytes. The protein content in the muscles, blood, and other tissues helps bind water to those tissues. As discussed in chapter 4, muscle glycogen has considerable amounts of water bound to it (about 3 grams of water per gram of glycogen), which may prove to be an advantage when exercising in the heat. In essence, the metabolism of 350 grams of carbohydrate during exercise will provide nearly 1 liter of water for body functions, as recently documented by Rogers and others. The sodium in the extracellular fluid, including sodium in the circulatory system, attracts water.

Proper water and electrolyte balance within these compartments is of extreme importance to the athletic individual. Fluid shifts such as decreases in blood volume and cellular dehydration, both of which may develop during exercise in the heat, could contribute to the onset of fatigue or heat illness.

Water comprises about 60 percent of the body weight in the average adult male and 50 percent in the adult female, but this percentage may be as low as 40 percent in obese individuals and as high as 70 percent or more in muscular individuals. The reason is that fat tissue is low in water content and muscle tissue is high in water content.

How is body water regulated?

Body water is maintained at a normal level through kidney function. Normal body-water level is called **normohydration,** or **euhydration. Dehydration,** the loss of body water, results in a state of **hypohydration,** or low body-water level. **Hyperhydration** represents a condition in which the body retains excess body fluids. Normal kidneys function very effectively to eliminate excess water during hyperhydration and conserve water during hypohydration.

Because water is so essential to life, it is indeed fortunate that the body possesses an efficient mechanism to maintain proper water balance. **Homeostasis** is the term used to describe the maintenance of a normal internal environment so that the body has the proper distribution and use of water, electrolytes, hormones, and other substances essential for life processes. Homeostatic mechanisms are extremely complex, and a full discussion is beyond the scope of this book. However, in essence, all homeostatic mechanisms work by a series of feedback devices. If these feedback devices are functioning properly, the body usually has no problem in maintaining the normal physical and chemical composition of its fluid compartments.

The main feedback device for the control of body water is the osmolality of the various body fluids. **Osmolality** refers to the amount, or concentration, of dissolved substances, known as solute, in a solution. In the body a number of different substances affect osmolality, including glucose, protein, and several electrolytes, most notably sodium. These substances are dissolved in the body water. One mole of a nonionic substance, such as glucose, dissolved in a liter of water is one osmole. One millimole (1/1,000 mole) is one milliosmole. However, a mole of a substance that can dissociate into two ions, such as sodium chloride, is equivalent to two osmoles. One millimole of sodium chloride would be two milliosmoles (mOsm).

A term often used in conjunction with osmolality is **tonicity,** which means tension or pressure. When two solutions have the same osmotic pressure they are said to be isosmotic or, more commonly, isotonic. Iso means "same." When two solutions with different solute concentrations are compared, the one with the higher osmotic pressure is called hypertonic and the other is hypotonic.

When two solutions with different solute concentrations are separated by a permeable membrane, as in the human body between the fluid compartments, a potential pressure difference may develop between the solutions that will allow for water movement. This pressure is known as osmotic pressure. Water moves across the membrane from the hypotonic solution (low solute concentration and high water content) to the hypertonic solution (high solute concentration and low water content). In essence, high solute concentrations create high osmotic pressures and tend to draw water into their compartments. Figure 9.2 depicts this mechanism between the blood and the body cells.

To briefly illustrate the feedback mechanism for control of body water, let us look at what happens when you become dehydrated owing to excessive body-water losses or lowered water intake. The blood then becomes more concentrated, or hypertonic. Because maintenance of a normal blood volume is of prime importance, the blood tends to draw water from the body cells. Certain cells in the hypothalamus, called osmoreceptors, are sensitive to changes in osmotic pressure. These cells react to the more concentrated body fluids by stimulating the release of a hormone from the pituitary gland, the so-called master gland of the body. This hormone is called the **antidiuretic hormone (ADH).** The ADH travels by the blood to the kidneys and directs them to reabsorb more water. Hence, urinary output of water is diminished considerably. Figure 9.3 illustrates this feedback process that helps conserve body water and blood volume. During hyperhydration, which would produce a hypotonic condition in the body fluids, a reverse process would occur leading to increased water excretion. As we shall see, other hormones that influence sodium balance in the body also help regulate water balance.

Osmoreceptors and other mechanisms also may stimulate the sensation of thirst, which is usually a good guide to body-water needs

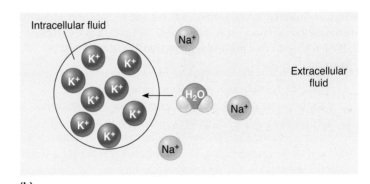

(a)

(b)

FIGURE 9.2 Osmosis and tonicity. *(a)* When the extracellular fluid contains more electrolytes or other osmotic substances, it is hypertonic to the intracellular fluid. In this case water will flow from the interior of the cell to the outside, or to an area of greater osmotic pressure. *(b)* When the intracellular fluid contains more electrolytes or greater osmotic pressure, water will flow into the cell from the extracellular fluid.

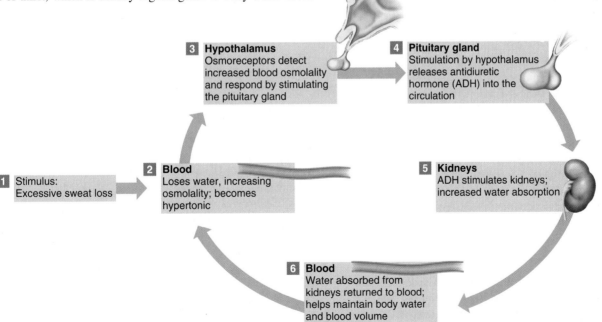

FIGURE 9.3 One feedback mechanism for homeostatic control of body water and blood volume. Other feedback mechanisms operate concurrently. For example, the hypothalamus also stimulates the thirst response to increase fluid intake.

and is effective in restoring body water to normal on a day-to-day basis. However, thirst may not be an accurate indicator of the need for water replacement during exercise in a hot environment. One of the best guides to indicate a state of normohydration is the color of your urine. In general, it should be a clear, pale yellow. A deeply colored urine, usually excreted in small amounts, is indicative of a state of hypohydration. However, vitamin supplements containing riboflavin (B_2) may also cause the urine to appear yellow and suggest a state of dehydration when the individual is euhydrated.

What are the major functions of water in the body?

Water is essential if the other nutrients are to function properly within the human body; it is the solvent for life. It has a number of diverse functions that may be summarized as follows:

1. Water provides the essential building material for cell protoplasm, the fundamental component of all living matter.
2. Because water cannot be compressed, it serves to protect key body tissues such as the spinal cord and brain.
3. Water is essential in the control of the osmotic pressure in the body, or the maintenance of a proper balance between water and the electrolytes. Any major changes in the electrolyte concentration may adversely affect cellular function. A serious departure from normal osmotic pressure cannot be tolerated by the body for long.
4. Water is the main constituent of blood, the major transportation mechanism in the body for conveying oxygen, nutrients, hormones, and other compounds to the cells for their use, and for carrying waste products of metabolism away from the cells to organs such as the lungs and kidneys for excretion from the body.
5. Water is essential for the proper functioning of our senses. Hearing waves are transmitted by fluid in the inner ear. Fluid in the eye is involved in the reflection of light for proper vision. For the taste and smelling senses to function, the foods and odors need to be dissolved in water.
6. Of primary importance to the active individual is the role that water plays in the regulation of body temperature. Water is the major constituent of sweat, and through its evaporation from the surface of the skin, it can help dissipate excess body heat. Of all the nutrients, water is the most important to the physically active person and is one of several that may have beneficial effects on performance when used in supplemental amounts before or during exercise. Hence, the athletic individual should know what is necessary to help maintain proper fluid balance, a topic covered in detail later in this chapter.

Can drinking more water confer any health benefits?

Although the major functions of water have been long known, nutrition scientists now theorize that drinking enough water may have specific health benefits. For example, Michaud and others found that men who consumed the most water had a decreased risk of bladder cancer, while the Consumers Union indicated a similar rela-

tionship between water intake and colon cancer. Theoretically, increased water intake could flush carcinogens from the bladder and colon. Some dietitians indicated that increased water intake may help one reduce excess fat in a body-weight control program by increasing the sensation of fullness and suppressing hunger. Recent research suggests this may be the case, as de Castro reported subjects consumed fewer Calories, at least on a short-term basis, when eating foods with high water content; as discussed in chapter 11, high-volume, low-energy foods may be an integral part of a weight-control diet. Other benefits might include less chance of kidney stones, fewer asthma attacks, and better oral health, all of which are attributed to better hydration. Although you can consume water in a variety of beverages, such as juices, soda, or coffee, scientists recommend water itself. It is cheap and Calorie free.

Key Concept Recap

▶ The average adult, who needs 2 to 3 quarts of water per day, maintains fluid balance primarily by drinking liquids, but substantial amounts of water also are obtained from solid foods in the diet. Caffeine is not as potent a diuretic as once thought and fluids containing caffeine, such as coffee and cola sodas, may augment daily fluid intake.

▶ Normal water levels in the various body fluid compartments are maintained by a feedback mechanism involving specific receptors for osmotic pressure, the antidiuretic hormone (ADH), and the kidneys.

▶ Water has a number of functions in the body. One of its most important benefits for people who exercise is the control of body temperature.

Check for Yourself

Use a measuring cup and accurately measure the amount of fluids you drink for a day.

Electrolytes

What is an electrolyte?

An **electrolyte** is defined as a substance which, in solution, conducts an electric current. The solution itself may be referred to as an electrolyte solution. Acids, bases, and salts are common electrolytes, and they usually dissociate into ions, particles carrying either a positive (cation) or a negative (anion) electric charge. The major electrolytes in the body fluids are sodium, potassium, chloride, bicarbonate, sulfate, magnesium, and calcium. Electrolytes can act at the cell membrane and generate electrical current, such as in a nerve impulse. Electrolytes can also function in other ways, activating enzymes to control a variety of metabolic activities in the cell. In the last chapter we covered some of the important metabolic functions of calcium, phosphorus, and magnesium; in this chapter the focus is on sodium, chloride, and potassium because of their presence in sports drinks, popular beverages used to replace fluid losses in physically active people.

In later sections we shall look at the interaction of these electrolytes with exercise in warm environmental conditions and their role in the etiology of high blood pressure. But first, let us briefly cover the function of each of these electrolytes in the human body.

Sodium (Na)

Sodium is a mineral element also known as natrium, from which the symbol *Na* is derived. It is one of the principal positive ions, or electrolytes, in the body fluids.

DRI The National Academy of Sciences (NAS) recently set an AI for sodium at 1.5 grams (1,500 milligrams) for males and females age 9 to 50, and somewhat lower amounts for young children and older adults. There is no evidence that higher intakes confer any additional health benefits. However, this AI contains no allowance for large sodium losses through exercise-induced sweating. Common table salt (sodium chloride) is about 40 percent sodium, so only about 3.8 grams (3,800 milligrams) is needed to supply the minimum requirement. The NAS also established a UL at 2.3 grams, or the equivalent of about 5.8 grams of salt. Currently, the amount used as the Daily Value for food labels is 2.4 grams (2,400 milligrams), which is higher than the UL. Keep this in mind when purchasing foods if you are attempting to limit sodium intake. Most American males consume about 3,100 to 4,700 milligrams of sodium daily, while the corresponding amount for females is about 2,300 to 3,100 milligrams.

Food Sources Sodium is distributed widely in nature but is found in rather small amounts in most natural foods. However, significant amounts of salt, and hence sodium, are usually added from the salt shaker for flavor. One teaspoon of salt contains about 2,000 milligrams of sodium. Moreover, processing techniques add significant amounts of salt to the foods we buy. For example, a serving of fresh or frozen green peas contains only 2 milligrams of sodium, but increases to 240 milligrams in the canning process. In general, natural foods are low in sodium whereas processed foods are relatively high. Because of health concerns for some individuals with high-sodium diets, food manufacturers have been reducing the salt content in some of their products. For example, canned soups may contain over 1,300 milligrams of sodium per serving, but some brands are available that contain much less, only 40–60 milligrams of sodium per serving. Nevertheless, researchers have reported that the average American consumes about 10–12 grams of salt (4–4.8 grams of sodium) per day, approximately 3 grams from basic foods such as milk and bread, 3–5 grams from processed foods, and 4 grams from the salt shaker. Table 9.2 highlights the sodium content in several foods within the major food groups. Note the difference in sodium content between fresh and processed foods. In one recent study, subjects obtained nearly 80 percent of their daily sodium intake from processed foods. To help reduce sodium intake from this source, read nutrition labels. Food labels must list the sodium content, both in milligrams and in percent of the Daily Value. Check the label for salt content; remember "sodium free" means less than 5

TABLE 9.2 Sodium content of common foods

Food exchange item	Amount	Sodium (mg)
Milk		
Low-fat milk	1 c	120
Cottage cheese		
Creamed	1/2 c	320
Unsalted	1/2 c	30
Cheese, American	1 oz	445
Vegetables		
Beans, cooked fresh	1 oz	5
Beans, canned	1 oz	150
Pickles, dill	1 medium	900
Potato, baked	1 medium	6
Fruits		
Banana	1 medium	1
Orange	1 medium	1
Starch		
Bread, whole wheat	1 slice	130
Bran flakes	3/4 c	340
Oatmeal, cooked	1 c	175
Pretzels	1 oz	890
Meat		
Luncheon meats	1 oz	450
Frankfurter	1 medium	495
Chicken	3 oz	40
Beef, steak	3 oz	70
Tuna, low sodium	3 oz	35
Tuna, in oil	3 oz	800
Fish (cod, flounder)	3 oz	100
Deviled crab, frozen	1 c	2,085
Fats		
Butter, salted	1 tsp	50
Margarine, salted	1 tsp	50
Canned foods and prepared entrees		
Chop suey, canned	1 c	1,050
Spaghetti, canned	1 c	1,220
Turkey dinner, frozen	1	1,735
Chicken noodle soup	5 oz	655
Chicken noodle soup, low sodium	5 oz	120
Condiments		
Mustard	1 tbsp	195
Tomato catsup	1 tbsp	155
Soy sauce	1 tbsp	1,320

As you can see in this table, the sodium content of foods can vary greatly. In general, canned and processed foods have a much higher sodium content than do fresh foods. Eat fresh meats, fruits, vegetables, and bread products whenever possible and prepare them with little or no salt. Avoid highly salted foods like pickles, pretzels, soy sauce, and others. Look for "sodium free" or "low sodium" labels when shopping for canned foods.

Source: U.S. Department of Agriculture.

FIGURE 9.4 Foods with high salt (sodium) content should be reduced in the diet. Be aware of foods that have large amounts of hidden sodium.

milligrams per serving, "very low sodium" means less than 40 milligrams, and "low sodium" means less than 140 milligrams. With some canned vegetables, draining and rinsing the product with fresh water removes some of the sodium. Some processed foods high in sodium are shown in figure 9.4.

Major Functions   Sodium is an important element in a number of body functions. As the principal electrolyte in the extracellular fluids, it serves primarily to help maintain normal body-fluid balance and osmotic pressure. In this regard it is essential in the control of normal blood pressure through its effect on the blood volume. The role of sodium in the etiology of high blood pressure is discussed in a later section.

In conjunction with several other electrolytes, sodium is critical for nerve impulse transmission and muscle contraction. It is also a component of several compounds, such as sodium bicarbonate, that help maintain normal acid-base balance and, as noted in chap-

ter 13, may be an effective ergogenic aid. An overview of sodium is presented in table 9.3.

Deficiency and Excess   Because the maintenance of normal blood pressure is critical to life, the body has an effective regulatory feedback mechanism allowing for a wide range of dietary sodium intake. The hypothalamus helps regulate sodium as well as water balance in the body. If the sodium concentration decreases in the blood, a series of complex reactions leads to the secretion of **aldosterone,** a hormone produced in the adrenal gland, which stimulates the kidneys to retain more sodium. On the other hand, excesses of serum sodium will lead to decreased aldosterone production and increased excretion of sodium by the kidneys in the urine. Other hormones, notably ADH via its effect on water absorption in the kidneys, help maintain normal sodium equilibrium in the body fluids. During exercise, particularly intense exercise, sodium concentration increases in the blood, which helps to maintain blood volume. Exercise also leads to increased secretion of ADH and aldosterone, which helps conserve body water and sodium supplies.

Because this regulatory mechanism is so effective, deficiency states due to inadequate dietary intake are not common. Indeed, humans even have a natural appetite for salt, assuring adequate sodium intake and sodium balance over time. On the other hand, excessive losses of sodium from the body, usually induced by prolonged sweating while exercising in the heat, may lead to short-term deficiencies that may be debilitating to the athletic individual. These problems are discussed later in this chapter in the sections on fluid and electrolyte replacement and health aspects.

Chloride (Cl)

Chloride is the major negative ion in the extracellular fluids.

DRI   The chloride AI for individuals age 9–50 is 2.3 grams, or the equivalent of about 3.8 grams of salt. The UL is 3.5 grams, or 5.8 grams of salt. The DV for food label use is 3,500 milligrams, which is the UL.

TABLE 9.3 Major electrolytes: sodium, chloride, and potassium*				
Major electrolyte	**Adequate intake**	**Major functions in the body**	**Deficiency symptoms**	**Symptoms of excess consumption**
Sodium	1,500 milligrams	Primary positive ion in extracellular fluid; nerve impulse conduction; muscle contraction; acid-base balance; blood volume homeostasis	Hyponatremia; muscle cramps; nausea; vomiting; loss of appetite; dizziness; seizures; shock; coma	Hypertension (high blood pressure) in susceptible individuals
Chloride	2,300 milligrams	Primary negative ion in extracellular fluid; nerve impulse conduction; hydrochloric acid formation in stomach	Rare; may be caused by excess vomiting and loss of hydrochloric acid; convulsions	Hypertension, in conjunction with excess sodium
Potassium	4,700 milligrams	Primary positive ion in intracellular fluid; same functions as sodium, but intracellular; glucose transport into cell	Hypokalemia; loss of appetite; muscle cramps; apathy; irregular heartbeat	Hyperkalemia; inhibited heart function

*Food sources for sodium and potassium may be found in tables 9.2 and 9.4, respectively; food sources for chloride are similar to those for sodium.

Food Sources Chloride is distributed in a variety of foods. Its dietary intake is closely associated with that of sodium, notably in the form of common table salt, which is 60 percent chloride.

Major Functions Chloride ions have a variety of functions in the human body. They work with sodium in the regulation of body-water balance and electrical potentials across cell membranes. They also are involved in the formation of hydrochloric acid in the stomach, which is necessary for certain digestive processes.

Deficiency Under normal circumstances chloride deficiency is rather rare. However, because the losses of sodium and chloride in sweat are directly proportional, the symptoms of chloride loss during excessive dehydration through sweating parallel those of sodium loss. The effects of electrolyte losses and replacement, including chloride, on physical performance and health are covered in later sections of this chapter. An overview of chloride is presented in table 9.3.

Potassium (K)

Potassium is a mineral element also known as kalium, from which the symbol *K* is derived. It is a positive ion.

DRI The potassium AI for individuals age 14 and above is 4.7 grams (4,700 milligrams), and somewhat less for children. No UL has been established for potassium from foods. Supplements are not recommended. The DV used for food labels is 3.5 grams, which is less than the AI. American adults take in much less, only about 2,500 milligrams a day.

Food Sources Potassium is found in most foods and is especially abundant in bananas, citrus fruits, fresh vegetables, milk, meat, and fish. Table 9.4 provides some data on the potassium content of several common foods in the major food groups.

Major Functions As the major electrolyte inside the body cells, potassium works in close association with sodium and chloride in the maintenance of body fluids and in the generation of electrical impulses in the nerves and the muscles, including the heart muscle. Potassium also plays an important role in the energy processes in the muscle; it helps in the transport of glucose into the muscle cells, the storage of glycogen, and the production of high-energy compounds.

Deficiency and Excess Potassium balance, like sodium balance, is regulated by aldosterone but in a reverse way. A high serum potassium level stimulates the release of aldosterone from the adrenal cortex, leading to an increased excretion of potassium by the kidneys into the urine. A decrease in serum potassium levels elicits a drop in aldosterone secretion and hence a greater conservation of potassium by the kidneys. Because a potassium imbalance in the body may have serious health consequences, potassium regulation is quite precise. Deficiencies or excessive accumulation are extremely rare under normal circumstances.

Although potassium deficiencies are rare, they may occur under certain conditions such as during fasting, diarrhea, and the use of diuretics. In such cases **hypokalemia,** or low serum potassium levels,

TABLE 9.4 Potassium content in some common foods in the major food exchanges

Food	Amount	Milligrams of potassium
Milk		
Skim milk	8 oz glass	410
Yogurt, low-fat	1 c	530
Cheese, cheddar	1 oz	28
Meat		
Chicken breast	1 oz	70
Beef, lean	1 oz	100
Fish, flounder	1 oz	160
Starch		
Bread, whole wheat	1 slice	65
Cereal, Cheerios	1 oz	110
Fruit		
Banana	1 medium	460
Orange	1 avg	260
Apple	1 avg	35
Vegetables		
Potato, baked	1 avg	780
Broccoli	1 stalk	270
Carrot	1 medium	275

could lead to muscular weakness and even cardiac arrest due to a decreased ability to generate nerve impulses and an irregular heartbeat. Several deaths of individuals on unbalanced liquid-protein fasting diets several years ago were associated with potassium deficiencies.

Excessive body potassium stores also are not very common, occurring mainly in conjunction with several disease states or in individuals who overdose on potassium supplements. **Hyperkalemia,** or excessive potassium in the blood, may disturb electrical impulses, causing cardiac arrhythmias and possible death. Parisi and others reported a case study of a young soccer player who suffered from premature ventricular arrhythmia while consuming a supplement giving him about 5 grams of potassium daily. The hyperkalemia and arrhythmia resolved when he stopped using the supplements. More than 18,000 milligrams may cause a heart attack. For this reason, individuals should never take potassium supplements in large doses without the consent of a physician. An overview of potassium is presented in table 9.3.

In theory, a potassium deficiency could adversely affect physical performance capacity. The effect of exercise on potassium losses and the need for potassium supplementation in athletic individuals have therefore been studied by several investigators. The role of potassium in the etiology of high blood pressure has also been studied. The results of this research are presented in later sections of this chapter.

Regulation of Body Temperature

What is the normal body temperature?

The temperature of different body parts may vary considerably. The skin may be very cold but the body internally is much warmer. When we speak of body temperature, we mean the internal, or **core temperature,** and not the external shell temperature. **Shell temperature,** which represents the temperature of the skin and the tissues directly under it, varies considerably depending upon the surrounding environmental temperature.

In humans, normal body temperature is approximately 98.6°F (37°C). This core temperature may be measured in a variety of ways. The two most common methods are orally and rectally. For research purposes, a thermocouple is inserted through the nose down into the esophagus to provide a more precise measure of core temperature. Capsules, containing miniature electronic thermometers, may be swallowed and transmit core temperatures during rest or exercise. Normal body temperature at rest varies and may range from 97–99°F (36.1–37.2°C). At rest the rectal temperature is normally about 0.5–1.0°F higher than the oral temperature; however, assessing temperature following a road race one study reported that the rectal temperature was 5.5°F higher than the oral temperature, suggesting that an oral reading may not be an accurate reflection of the true body temperature in an assessment of heat injury. Shell temperatures may be measured by adhesive thermometer pads attached to the skin.

Humans can survive a range of core temperatures for a short time, but optimal physiological functioning usually occurs within a range of 97–104°F (36.1–40.0°C). A variety of factors may affect body temperature. Here we are concerned with the effect exercise has on the core temperature and how our body adjusts to help maintain heat balance.

What are the major factors that influence body temperature?

Humans are warm-blooded animals and are able to maintain a constant body temperature under varying environmental temperatures. To do this, the body must constantly make adjustments to either gain or lose heat.

Humans are heat-producing machines. The basal metabolic heat production is provided through normal burning (oxidation) of the three basic foodstuffs in the body—carbohydrate, fat, and protein. A higher basal metabolic rate, infectious diseases, shivering, and exercise are several factors that might increase heat production.

The human body also has a variety of means to lose heat. Heat loss is governed by four physical means—conduction, convection, radiation, and evaporation.

Conduction—Heat is transferred from the body by direct physical contact, as when you sit on a cold seat.
Convection—Heat is transferred by movement of air or water over the body.
Radiation—Heat energy radiates from the body into the surrounding air.
Evaporation—Heat is lost from the body when it is used to convert sweat to a vapor, known as the heat of vaporization. The lungs also help to dissipate heat through evaporation.

During rest and under normal environmental temperatures, body heat is transported from the core to the shell by way of conduction and convection, the blood being the main carrier of the heat. The vast majority of the heat escapes from the body by radiation and convection, with a smaller amount being carried away by the evaporation of insensible perspiration. A cooler environment, increased air movement such as a cool wind, increased blood circulation to the skin, or an increased radiation surface would facilitate heat loss.

On the other hand, under certain environmental conditions, such as exercising in the sunlight on a hot day, some of these processes may be reversed with the body gaining heat instead of losing it. For example, radiant energy from the sun could add heat to the body.

The well-known **heat-balance equation** may be used to illustrate these interrelationships:

$$H = M \pm W \pm C \pm R - E$$

where H = heat balance, M = resting metabolic rate, W = work done (exercise), C = conduction and convection, R = radiation, E = evaporation.

If any of these factors governing heat production or heat loss are not balanced by an opposite reaction, heat balance will be lost and the body will deviate from its normal value. During exercise, W increases heat production. Hence, compensating adjustments in C, R, and E must be made to dissipate the extra heat. Figure 9.5 illustrates heat stress factors and mechanisms of heat loss during exercise.

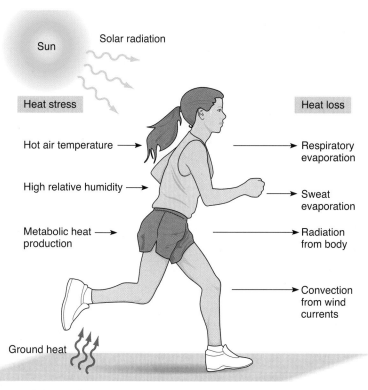

FIGURE 9.5 Sources of heat gain and heat loss to the body during exercise. See text for details.

How does the body regulate its own temperature?

Body temperature is controlled by the autonomic division of the central nervous system. The hypothalamus is an important structure in the brain that is involved in the control of a wide variety of physiological functions, including body temperature. The hypothalamus is thought to function pretty much like the thermostat in your house. If your house gets too cold, the heat comes on; if it gets too warm, the air conditioning system starts. The human body makes similar adjustments.

The temperature-regulating center in the hypothalamus receives input from several sources. First, receptors in the skin can detect temperature changes and send impulses to the hypothalamus. Second, the temperature of the blood can directly affect the hypothalamus as it flows through that structure.

In general, if the skin receptors detect a warmer temperature or the blood temperature rises, the body will make adjustments in an attempt to lose heat. Two major adjustments may occur. First, the blood will be channeled closer to the skin so that the heat from within may get closer to the outside and radiate away more easily. Second, sweating will begin and evaporation of the sweat will carry heat away from the body.

If the skin receptors detect a colder temperature or the blood temperature is lowered, then the body will react to conserve heat or increase heat production. First, the blood will be shunted away from the skin to the central core of the body. This decreases heat loss by radiation and helps keep the vital organs at the proper temperature. Second, shivering may begin. Shivering is nothing more

than the contraction of muscles, which produces extra heat by increasing the metabolic rate. Figure 9.6 is a simplified schematic of body temperature control.

The hypothalamus is usually very effective in controlling body temperature. However, certain conditions may threaten temperature control. For example, an individual who falls into cold water will lose body heat rapidly, for water is an excellent conductor of heat. Such a situation may lead to **hypothermia** (low body temperature) and a rapid loss of temperature control. Hypothermia may also develop in slower runners during the latter part of a road race under cold, wet, and windy environmental conditions when heat is lost more rapidly than it is produced through exercise. Muscular incoordination and mental confusion are early signs of hypothermia.

On the other hand, the most prevalent threat to the athletic individual is **hyperthermia,** or the increased body temperature that occurs with exercise in a warm or hot environment. Hyperthermia is one of the major factors limiting physical performance and one of the most dangerous.

What environmental conditions may predispose an athletic individual to hyperthermia?

The interaction of four environmental factors are important determinants of the heat stress imposed on an active individual:

1. Air temperature. Caution should be advised when the air temperature is 80°F (27°C) or above. However, if the relative humidity and solar radiation are high, lower air temperatures, even 70°F, may pose a risk of heat stress during exercise.
2. Relative humidity. As the water content in the air increases, the relative humidity rises. The increased humidity impairs the ability of sweat to evaporate and thus may restrict the effectiveness of the body's main cooling system when exercising. With humidity levels from 90–100 percent, heat loss via evaporation nears zero. Caution should be used when the relative humidity exceeds 50–60 percent, especially when accompanied by warmer temperatures.
3. Air movement. Still air limits heat carried away by convection. Even a small breeze may help keep body temperature near normal by moving heat away from the skin surface.
4. Radiation. Radiant heat from the sun may create an additional heat load.

Some useful guidelines have been developed taking these four factors into consideration. The wet-bulb globe temperature (WBGT) thermometer, illustrated in figure 9.7, measures all four. Small hand-held WBGT thermometers are available. The dry-bulb thermometer (DB) measures air temperature, the globe thermometer (G) measures radiant heat, and the wet-bulb thermometer (WB) evaluates relative humidity and air movement as they influence air temperature. The **WBGT Index** is computed as follows:

$$\text{WBGT Index} = 0.7\,\text{WB} + 0.2\,\text{G} + 0.1\,\text{DB}$$

For example, if the WB reads 70, the G is 100, and the DB is 80, then the WBGT = $(0.7 \times 70) + (0.2 \times 100) + (0.1 \times 80) = 77°F$.

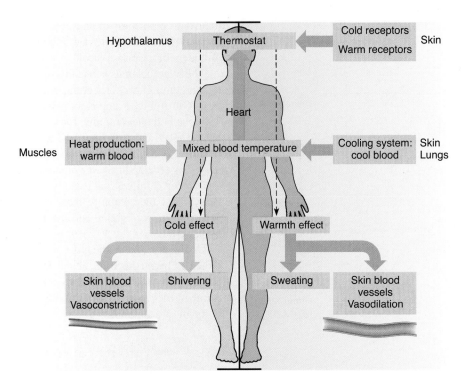

FIGURE 9.6 Simplified schematic of body temperature control. The temperature of the blood returning from the muscles and the skin stimulates the temperature regulation center (thermostat) in the hypothalamus, as do nerve impulses from the warmth and cold receptors in the skin. An overall cold effect will elicit a constriction of the blood vessels near the body surface and muscular shivering, thus helping to conserve body heat. An overall warmth effect will elicit a dilation of blood vessels near the skin and sweating, thus increasing the loss of body heat.

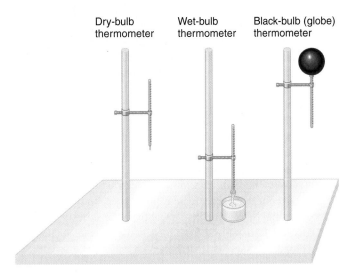

FIGURE 9.7 A typical setup for measurement of the wet-bulb globe temperature index (WBGT). The dry bulb measures air temperature, the wet bulb indirectly measures humidity, and the black bulb measures the radiant heat from the sun. Computerized commercial devices that measure the WBGT rapidly are also available.

Another indicator of heat stress is the **heat index** (table 9.5), which combines the air temperature and relative humidity to determine the apparent temperature, or how hot it feels. Table 9.5 also contains some temperature levels predisposing to heat disorders based on the heat index.

The American College of Sports Medicine (ACSM) has published a position statement with guidelines for the prevention of heat, and cold, illnesses during distance running. These guidelines, which also are applicable to other athletes exercising in the heat, are incorporated in the last section of this chapter. A modified version of the ACSM warnings based on the WBGT is presented in table 9.6.

Other models incorporate physiological variables of interest to assess heat stress. For example, the Predicted Heat Strain model incorporates core temperature, skin temperature, and sweat rate, and may take into consideration the effect of movement and clothing.

How does exercise affect body temperature?

As noted in chapter 3, exercise increases the metabolic rate and the production of energy. Under a normal mechanical efficiency ratio of 20–25 percent, the remaining 75–80 percent of energy is released as heat. The total amount of heat produced in the body depends on the intensity and duration of the exercise. A more intense exercise will produce heat faster, while the longer the exercise lasts the more total heat is produced.

For illustrative purposes only, let us look at a hypothetical example of the body temperature changes that might occur in an exercising individual who was unable to dissipate heat. A physically conditioned person may be able to perform in a steady state for prolonged periods. If a normal-sized male, 154 lbs or 70 kg, were to jog for about an hour, he could expend approximately 900 Calories. Assuming a mechanical efficiency rate of 20 percent, 80 percent, or 720 Calories (0.80 × 900), would be released in the body as heat.

TABLE 9.5 Possible heat disorders in runners and other high-risk groups based on the heat index (air temperature and relative humidity versus apparent temperature)

Relative humidity (%)

Air temperature (°F)	0	5	10	15	20	25	30	35	40	45	50	55	60	65	70	75	80	85	90	95	100
140	125																				
135	120	128																			
130	117	122	131																		
125	111	116	123	131	141																
120	107	111	116	123	130	139	148														
115	103	107	111	115	120	127	135	143	151												
110	99	102	105	108	112	117	123	130	137	143	150										
105	95	97	100	102	105	109	113	118	123	129	135	142	149								
100	91	93	95	97	99	101	104	107	110	115	120	126	132	138	144						
95	87	88	90	91	93	94	96	98	101	104	107	110	114	119	124	130	136				
90	83	84	85	86	87	88	90	91	93	95	96	98	100	102	106	109	113	117	122		
85	78	79	80	81	82	83	84	85	86	87	88	89	90	91	93	95	97	99	102	105	108
80	73	74	75	76	77	77	78	79	79	80	81	81	82	83	85	86	86	87	88	89	91
75	69	69	70	71	72	72	73	73	74	74	75	75	76	76	77	77	78	78	79	79	80
70	64	64	65	65	66	66	67	67	68	68	69	69	70	70	70	70	71	71	71	71	72

Heat index (or apparent temperature)

Heat index	Possible heat disorders for people in higher risk groups
130° or higher	Heatstroke/sunstroke highly likely with continued exposure
105°–129°	Sunstroke, heat cramps, or heat exhaustion likely, and heatstroke possible with prolonged exposure and/or physical activity
90°–104°	Sunstroke, heat cramps, and heat exhaustion possible with prolonged exposure and/or physical activity
80°–89°	Fatigue possible with prolonged exposure and/or physical activity

Source: Adapted from U.S. Department of Commerce. National Oceanic and Atmospheric Administration.

Specific heat is defined as the heat in Calories required to raise the temperature of 1 kilogram of a substance by 1 degree Celsius. Because the specific heat of the body is 0.83, that is, 0.83 Calorie will raise 1 kg of the body 1°C, then 58 Calories (70 kg × 0.83) would raise the body temperature 1°C in this person. Thus, if this excess heat were not dissipated, his body temperature would increase over 12.4°C (720/58), or over 22°F, resulting in a body temperature of 120°F, a fatal condition. Although the core temperature does rise during exercise, it rarely hits these extreme levels. The average core temperature during exercise, even during moderately warm temperatures, may reach about 102.2–104.0°F (39–40°C). This is because of the body's cooling system.

How is body heat dissipated during exercise?

During exercise in a cold or cool environment, body heat is lost mainly through radiation and convection via the air movement around the body. Some evaporation of sweat and evaporative heat loss from the lungs may also contribute to maintenance of heat balance.

TABLE 9.6 Guidelines for preventing heat illness in runners and other athletes

Flag color/WBGT	Risk	Warnings*
Green/below 64°F (18°C)	Low	Although the risk is low, heat injury still can occur; caution still needed.
Yellow/64–72°F (18–22°C)	Moderate	Runners should closely monitor for signs of impending heat injury and slow pace if necessary; in long races, heat stress may increase during the course of the race if run in morning to early afternoon.
Red/73–82°F (23–28°C)	High	Runner must slow running pace and be very aware of warning signs of heat injury. Do not run if unfit, ill, unacclimatized, or sensitive to heat and humidity.
Black/above 82°F (28°C)	Very high	Even with considerable slowing of pace, great discomfort will be experienced. Races should be postponed or cancelled under these conditions.

WBGT = Wet-bulb globe temperature

These precautions should be noted for safety, not only by the active individual but also by those who conduct physical training sessions or athletic competition. Flag colors may be used to inform athletes of prevailing heat stress conditions. Commercial devices are available to quickly and accurately measure the WBGT and should be used to help assess environmental heat stress and modify training or competition as recommended. For those who wish to construct an inexpensive WBGT device, consult the reference cited for Spickard at the end of this chapter.

*Although these warnings are expressed in regard to running, they are also relevant to other sports involving prolonged exercise in the heat, such as soccer, field hockey, and football. Wearing additional clothing or equipment may increase the heat stress.

However, when the environmental temperature rises, the evaporation of sweat becomes the main means of controlling an excessive rise in the core temperature. For example, evaporation of sweat may account for about 20 percent of total heat loss when exercising in an ambient temperature of 50°F (10°C), but increases to about 45 percent at 68°F (20°C) and 70 percent at 86°F (30°C). Although variable, the maximal evaporation rate is about 30 milliliters of sweat per minute, or 1.8 liters per hour. However, greater sweat rates may occur when sweat drops off the skin without vaporizing. Only sweat that evaporates has a cooling effect. One liter of sweat, if perfectly evaporated, will dissipate about 580 C. In our example above, the evaporation of 1.24 liters of sweat (720/580) would prevent a rise in the core temperature. However, the evaporation of sweat from the body is not perfect, as sweat can drip off the body and not carry away body heat, so more than 1.24 liters may be lost. If we assume that 2.0 liters were lost, then this individual would have lost 4.4 lbs of body fluids during the 1-hour run; 1 liter of sweat weighs 1 kg or 2.2 lbs. It should be noted that sweat rates may vary considerably between individuals. Ron Maughan, an environmental physiologist from England, studied two marathoners who completed a race in the same time and had the same fluid intake; one lost only 1 percent of his body weight while the other lost 6 percent.

Under most warm environmental circumstances, the evaporative mechanisms and the body's natural warning signals are able to keep the core temperature during exercise below 104°F (40°C) and prevent heat injuries. However, an excessive rise in the core temperature, above 104°F, or excessive fluid and electrolyte losses, may lead to diminished performance or serious thermal injury.

Key Concept Recap

▶ Our core body temperature is about 98.6° F (37° C). One degree Celsius (C) equals 1.8 degrees Fahrenheit (F). The freezing points of F and C, respectively, are 32° and 0°. Convert C to F by the formula [(C × 1.8°) + 32°]. Convert F to C by the formula [(F − 32°)/1.8°].

▶ Humans are heat producers and their body temperature, regulated by the brain's hypothalamus, is dependent upon the amount of heat they produce and how much they gain or lose from the environment.

▶ High environmental temperatures, high relative humidity, or radiant heat from the sun can impose a severe heat stress on those who exercise under such conditions.

▶ Exercise can produce significant amounts of heat, but the body temperature usually can be regulated quite effectively by activation of heat-loss mechanisms. Body heat is lost mainly by radiation, conduction, and convection, but evaporation of sweat is a major avenue of heat loss during exercise in the heat.

Check for Yourself

Calculate how much heat you would generate if you ran for 60 minutes. Assume you are running at 20 percent mechanical efficiency. How much sweat would you have to evaporate to keep your body temperature at the same level? Assume you do not lose any heat from other avenues such as radiation and convection.

Fluid and Electrolyte Losses

Not all types of physical performance are impaired when performed under warm or hot environmental conditions, but some are. Heat stress itself may contribute to impaired performance, but so too can fluid and electrolyte losses over time.

How does environmental heat affect physical performance?

Performance in strength, power, or speed events that last less than a minute does not appear to be affected adversely by warm environmental conditions. However, performance in more prolonged aerobic endurance activities is normally worse when compared to performance in cooler temperatures. In recent reviews, Febbraio, Hargreaves and Febbraio, and Maughan noted that the cause of fatigue during prolonged exercise in the heat has not been clearly established, but changes in brain function, blood circulation, skeletal muscle function, hyperthermia, and dehydration, either separately or collectively, could impair performance. Much of the research evaluating the effect of heat on endurance performance has been conducted with runners. In this regard, McCann and Adams reported a significant linear relationship between the WBGT and decreased performance in endurance events such as the 10,000-meter run.

The brain appears to play an important role in the development of fatigue during exercise in the heat. Cheung and Sleivert suggest that fatigue occurs when the brain reaches a critical core temperature. Subjects exercising in the heat seem to reach the point of voluntary fatigue at similar and consistent core body temperatures despite various experimental manipulations. In essence, the elevated brain temperature impairs central arousal of voluntary activation of muscle. Moreover, Tucker and others reported reductions in both neuromuscular stimulation and power output during exercise in the heat before there was any abnormal increase in rectal temperature, heart rate, or perception of effort; in other words, the brain apparently anticipates heat stress and reduces heat production (by decreasing muscle contraction) accordingly. Theoretically, this may be the reason Drust and others reported a decrease in mean power output during five 15-second maximal cycle ergometer sprints when exercising in the heat as compared to exercising in normal temperature. These investigators note than an elevated muscle temperature normally is expected to improve sprint performance.

However, Cheung and Sleivert noted other factors may also inhibit performance in the heat, such as high levels of cardiovascular strain. For example, in a 5-kilometer race the runner will be performing at a rather high metabolic rate and thus will be producing heat rapidly. To prevent hyperthermia blood flow to the skin will increase so as to dissipate heat to the environment. This shifting of blood to the skin will result in a lesser proportion of blood, and hence oxygen, being delivered to the active musculature. Young found that under these conditions cellular metabolism changes somewhat, with greater accumulation of lactic acid if the athlete attempts to maintain the pace normally done in a cooler environment. Yaspelkis and others reported similar lactate findings but found no increase in muscle glycogen utilization. They speculated that

the increased lactic acid could be associated with decreased clearance by the liver. Nevertheless, increased lactic acid could be associated with a greater sensation of stress. In some individuals, the circulatory adjustments may not be adequate and the body temperature will rise rapidly, leading to hyperthermia and symptoms of weakness. Because of these changes, and possibly others not yet identified, the runner normally must slow the pace.

In two recent reviews, Mark Febbraio indicated that exercise in the heat may adversely affect muscle metabolism with possible reduction in physical performance. He indicated that exercising in the heat appears to shift energy metabolism toward increased carbohydrate use and decreased fat use. In particular, muscle glycogen use is accelerated, possibly due to an augmented sympatho-adrenal response and intramuscular temperature increases. A more rapid depletion of muscle glycogen could impair prolonged endurance performance. Febbraio also indicated that increased intramuscular temperature may in some way lead to dysfunction of skeletal muscle contraction, which could decrease performance capacity. Supportive of this viewpoint is the review by Marino, who notes that precooling the body prior to exercise, such as by taking a cold shower or bath to lower the body temperature, may be beneficial for endurance exercise tasks up to 30–40 minutes.

Dehydration may also impair exercise performance. Although the 5-kilometer runner will sweat heavily, the duration of the event is usually short, so an excessive loss of body fluids does not occur. However, in more prolonged events, athletes may suffer the problems noted above plus the adverse effects of dehydration. Marathoners may lose 5 percent or more of their body weight (mostly water) during a race, which may not only deteriorate performance but have serious health consequences as well.

How do dehydration and hypohydration affect physical performance?

The effect of dehydration on physical performance has been studied from two different viewpoints. Voluntary dehydration is often used by athletes such as wrestlers and boxers to qualify for lower weight classes prior to competition. In other athletes, dehydration occurs involuntarily during training or competition as the body attempts to maintain temperature homeostasis. Dehydration leads to hypohydration.

Hypohydration may affect numerous physiological processes that may impair physical performance. Michael Sawka and others noted that hypohydration may lead to decreases in both intracellular and extracellular fluid volumes (particularly blood volume) with associated decreases in stroke volume and cardiac output. Body heat storage may increase by reducing sweating rate and skin blood flow responses. Kenefick and others found that hypohydration induced an earlier onset of the lactate threshold during exercise, an adverse effect relative to aerobic endurance performance. Hypohydration could also lead to electrolyte imbalances in the muscle, with subsequent adverse effects. Moreover, Naghii notes that hypohydration also affects mental functioning.

Voluntary Dehydration Voluntary dehydration techniques used by wrestlers have included exercise-induced sweating, thermal-induced sweating such as the use of saunas, diuretics to increase urine losses, and decreased intake of fluids and food.

Much of the research with voluntary dehydration has been conducted with wrestlers. Evaluation criteria have emphasized factors such as strength, power, local muscular endurance, and performance of anaerobic exercise tasks designed to mimic wrestling. In a recent review, Barr noted that the effects of hypohydration on muscle strength and endurance are not consistent and require further study. Many studies conducted in this area suggest that hypohydration, even up to levels of 8 percent of the body weight, will not affect these physical performance factors in events involving brief, intense muscular effort. For example, Greiwe and others recently reported that 4 percent reduction in body weight had no effect on isometric muscle strength or endurance. On the other hand, Schoffstall and others reported that passive dehydration resulting in approximately 1.5 percent loss of body mass adversely affected bench press 1-repetition maximal performance, but these adverse effects seem to be overcome by a 2-hour rest period and water consumption. Other studies have reported significant impairments in such tasks with body weight losses of 4 percent or higher. The adverse effects on strength are not consistent, but anaerobic muscular endurance tasks lasting longer than 20–30 seconds have been impaired when subjects were hypohydrated. For example, Montain and others recently reported that a 4 percent decrease in body weight decreased knee-extension endurance by 15 percent. Suggested mechanisms of impairment include loss of potassium from the muscle and higher muscle temperatures during exercise. It should also be noted that there is no evidence that hypohydration improves performance in these exercise tasks.

Involuntary Dehydration Involuntary dehydration is most common during prolonged physical activity, particularly under warm, humid environmental conditions. The adverse effects of involuntary dehydration are most severe on aerobic endurance performance. In a recent review, Edward Coyle indicates that athletes might tolerate body water losses amounting to 2 percent of body weight without significant risk to physical well-being or performance when the environment is cold or temperate, but may suffer performance impairment and possible heat illness when exercising in a hot environment (>30° C). Magal and others recently reported that a relatively modest hypohydration of 2.7 percent significantly slowed repetitive 5- and 10-meter sprint performance in highly trained male tennis players. The decrease in performance also appears to be proportional to the degree of hypohydration, with greater fluid losses leading to greater impairment. In several major reviews, Michael Sawka, Kent Pandolf, and John Greenleaf have suggested that the deterioration in aerobic endurance performance appears to be related to adverse effects on cardiovascular functions and temperature regulation. They noted that hypohydration would significantly decrease maximal aerobic power by 4–8 percent with a 3 percent weight loss during exercise in a neutral environment, but the impairment would be even greater in a hot environment. Also, a reduction in the plasma volume may reduce cardiac output and blood flow to the skin and the muscles. Reductions in skin blood flow have

been shown to lower the sweat rate and raise the core temperature. In his review, Coyle reported some of the effects of dehydration in endurance-trained cyclists. In general, he reported that skin blood flow decreased with dehydration and that the greater the level of dehydration, the greater the rise in the core temperature and heart rate and the greater the decrease in the stroke volume (amount of blood pumped by the heart per beat). Montain and others recently noted that hypohydration decreased cardiac output, and the greater the intensity of the exercise, the greater the decrease. The effects of dehydration on cardiovascular dynamics are depicted in figure 9.8.

Dehydration may also be a major factor in the onset of gastrointestinal (GI) distress, according to Nancy Rehrer and her associates. GI symptoms include nausea, vomiting, bloating, GI cramps, flatulence, diarrhea, and GI bleeding, many of which could impair performance if severe enough. However, Peters and others contend that the causes of GI distress during exercise are currently unknown and may vary depending on the individual.

Other factors associated with hypohydration may also contribute to suboptimal performance. Disturbed fluid and electrolyte balance in the muscle cells may affect energy processes, while adverse effects of hyperthermia upon mental processes may contribute to central fatigue. Armstrong and Epstein indicated cognitive functions may be impaired at 1–2 percent dehydration.

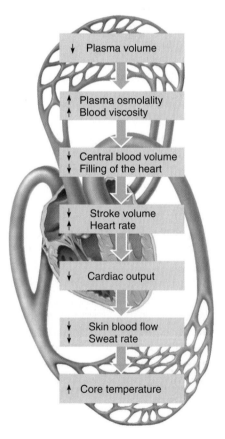

FIGURE 9.8 Some physiological effects of dehydration. The decreased blood volume and increased core temperature may contribute to premature fatigue and heat illness.

How fast may an individual dehydrate while exercising?

Because the maximal sweat rate for a trained athlete is about 2–3 liters per hour, it will not take long to incur a 2–3 percent decrease in body weight. Two liters of sweat is the equivalent of 4.4 pounds (1 liter = 1 kg = 2.2 pounds), so a 150-pound runner could experience a loss of 3 percent body weight in 1 hour (4.4/150 = .03; .03 × 100 = 3%), which could cause premature fatigue as illustrated in figure 9.9. Research has shown that some athletes, like football players, may lose up to 10 kg (22 pounds) over a day with multiple daily workouts.

There may be some gender and age differences in sweating. White and others report significantly greater sweat losses, almost twofold greater, per unit body mass in male compared to female athletes. Meyer and Bar-Or indicate that while children may sweat somewhat less than adults, they still may reach hypohydration levels comparable to adults. Young tennis players may lose 1–2 liters of sweat per hour in tournament play, and some older adolescents as much as 3 liters per hour. Excessive dehydration may not only impair one's physical performance, but possibly also one's health, as discussed later in this chapter.

How can I determine my sweat rate?

The rate of sweating varies among different individuals, so some may be more prone to dehydration than others. Cheuvront and others, studying sweat losses in women running under warm environmental conditions, found that body weight losses, adjusted for fluid intake and urine losses, provided a good esti-

FIGURE 9.9 Body-water loss can be very rapid during exercise in warm or hot weather, leading to dehydration and premature fatigue and heat illness.

mate of total sweat losses. The Gatorade Sports Science Institute has presented a method to calculate the sweat rate during exercise. To do so, one must accurately measure body weight before and after exercise, measure the amount of fluid consumed during exercise, and the amount of urine excreted, if any, during exercise. You may use the following examples as a guide to calculate your own sweat rate during exercise (See the Application Exercise on page 357). The sweat rate for athlete A is calculated in the metric measurement system and for athlete B in the English system. Remember, 1 gram equals about 1 milliliter, and 1 pound equals 16 ounces.

		Athlete A	Athlete B
A.	Body weight before exercise	70.5 kg	180 lbs
B.	Body weight after exercise	68.9 kg	174 lbs
C.	Change in body weight	–1.6 kg 1600 g	–6 lbs 96 oz
D.	Drink volume	+300 ml	16 oz
E.	Urine volume	–100 ml	0 oz
F.	Sweat loss (C + D – E)	1800 ml	112 oz
G.	Exercise time	60 min	90 min
H.	Sweat rate (F ÷ G)	30 ml/min	1.25 oz/min

What is the composition of sweat?

The human body contains two different types of sweat glands. The apocrine sweat glands are located in hairy areas of the body, such as the armpits, and secrete an oily mixture to decrease friction. We are all aware of the odor that may be generated from these sweat glands under certain conditions. Our concern here is with the eccrine sweat glands, about 2–3 million over the surface of the body, which are primarily involved in temperature regulation.

Sweat is mostly water (about 99 percent), but a number of major electrolytes and other nutrients may be found in varying amounts. Sweat is hypotonic in comparison to the fluids in the body. This means that the concentration of electrolytes is lower in sweat than in the body fluids.

The composition of sweat may vary somewhat from individual to individual and will even be different in the same individual when acclimatized to the heat, as contrasted to the unacclimatized state. The major differences are the concentrations of the solid matter in the sweat, the electrolytes or salts.

The major electrolytes found in sweat are sodium and chloride since sweat is derived from the extracellular fluids, such as the plasma and intercellular fluids, which are high in these electrolytes. You may actually note the formation of dried salt on your skin or clothing after prolonged sweating. Carl Gisolfi has reported that the concentration of salt in sweat is variable but averages 2.6 grams (45 mEq) per liter of sweat during exercise with sweat losses of about 1–1.5 liters per hour.

Other minerals lost in small amounts include potassium, magnesium, calcium, iron, copper, and zinc. As noted in chapter 8, certain athletes, especially those who lose large amounts of sweat, may need to increase their dietary intake of certain trace minerals, such as iron and zinc, to replace losses during exercise.

Small quantities of nitrogen (N), amino acids, and some of the water-soluble vitamins also are present in sweat, but these amounts are easily restored by consuming a balanced diet.

Is excessive sweating likely to create an electrolyte deficiency?

There are two ways to look at this question. What happens to electrolyte balance during exercise? And, what happens during the recovery period on a day-to-day basis?

The concentration of electrolytes in the blood during exercise with excessive sweating has been studied under laboratory conditions as well as immediately after endurance events such as the Ironman triathlon and a marathon run. In general, exercise raises the concentration of several electrolytes in the blood. Sodium and potassium concentrations are elevated; the sodium increase may be due to greater body-water loss than sodium loss, so a concentration effect occurs. The potassium may leak from the muscle tissue to the blood, thereby increasing the blood concentration of this ion. Chloride and calcium ion concentrations remain relatively unchanged during exercise. Magnesium levels usually fall, possibly because the active muscle cells and other tissues need this ion during exercise and it passes from the blood into the tissues. During acute, prolonged bouts of exercise then, even in marathon running, it appears that an electrolyte deficiency will not occur.

This is not to say that electrolyte replacement is not important. As we shall see in the next section, an electrolyte imbalance may occur in the body during extremely prolonged endurance events, such as ultramarathoning and Ironman-type triathlons, if proper fluid replacement techniques are not used. Moreover, what happens during the recovery period after excessive sweating may contribute to an electrolyte deficiency. Prolonged sweating has been shown to decrease the body content of sodium and chloride by 5–7 percent and potassium by about 1 percent. If these electrolytes are not replaced daily, an electrolyte deficiency may occur over time. The next section deals with the need for water and electrolyte replacement.

Key Concept Recap

▶ Both hyperthermia and dehydration may impair endurance capacity.

▶ Sweat consists mainly of water and some minerals, primarily sodium and chloride. It is hypotonic compared to the body fluids.

Fluid, Carbohydrate, and Electrolyte Replacement

Which is most important to replace during exercise in the heat—water, carbohydrate, or electrolytes?

In the 1960s Robert Cade, a scientist-physician working at the University of Florida, developed an oral fluid replacement for athletes that was designed to restore some of the nutrients lost in sweat. This product was eventually marketed as Gatorade (Gator

is the nickname for University of Florida athletes) and was the first of many **glucose-electrolyte solutions (GES)** and, later, **glucose-polymer solutions (GPS)** to appear as a sports drink in the athletic marketplace. The three main ingredients in sports drinks, which Maughan classifies as a functional food for athletes, are water, carbohydrates, and electrolytes.

GES were the first commercial fluid-replacement preparations designed to replace both fluid and carbohydrate. Common brands today include Accelerade, All-Sport, Gatorade, and PowerAde. Other than water, the major ingredients in these solutions are carbohydrates usually in various combinations of glucose, glucose polymers, sucrose, or fructose, and some of the major electrolytes. The sugar content ranges from about 5–10 percent depending on the brand. The caloric values range from about 6–12 Calories per ounce. The major electrolytes include sodium, chloride, potassium, and phosphorus. These ions are found in varying amounts in different brands. Some brands may also include a variety of other substances, including vitamins (B vitamins and C), minerals (calcium and magnesium), amino acids (BCAA), drugs (caffeine), herbals (ginseng), and artificial coloring and flavoring. Do not confuse the standard sports drinks with the newer "Energy" or "Sports Energy" drinks in the marketplace, which contain considerably more carbohydrate and numerous other ingredients.

GPS are designed to provide carbohydrate while decreasing the osmotic concentration of the solution, thus helping to minimize the effect upon gastric emptying. Maltodextrin is a common glucose polymer used in sports drinks, and is the main ingredient in a few commercial brands, such as Ultima. Other sports drinks combine maltodextrins with sucrose, glucose and fructose, as recommended in chapter 4. The European Union sets standards for contents, carbohydrate, sodium and osmolality. The contents of selected ingredients for several GES and GPS are presented in table 9.7.

Each of the components of GES and GPS may be important to the athlete, depending on the circumstances. When dehydration or hyperthermia is the major threat to performance, water replacement is the primary consideration. In prolonged endurance events, where muscle glycogen and blood glucose are the primary energy sources, carbohydrate replacement, as noted in chapter 4, may help improve performance. In very prolonged exercise in the heat with heavy sweat losses, such as ultramarathons, electrolyte replacement may be essential to prevent heat injury. Although the beneficial effects of carbohydrate intake during exercise were covered in chapter 4, the role of carbohydrate as a component of the GES and GPS is stressed in this chapter.

The following questions focus on the importance and mechanisms of water, carbohydrate, and electrolyte replacement for the individual incurring sweat losses while exercising under heat stress conditions.

What are some sound guidelines for maintaining water (fluid) balance during exercise?

Proper hydration is probably the most important nutritional strategy an athlete can use in training and competition. As compared to hypohydration, adequate hydration will help decrease fluid loss, reduce cardiovascular strain,

TABLE 9.7 Fluid replacement and high-carbohydrate* beverage comparison chart per 8 oz. serving

Beverage	Carbohydrate ingredient	Carbohydrate (% concentration)	(grams)	Sodium (mg)	Potassium (mg)
Gatorade Thirst Quencher (Gatorade Company)	Sucrose, Glucose, Fructose	6	14	110	25
Gatorade Endurance Formula	Sucrose, Glucose, Fructose	6	14	200	90
Accelerade (Pacific Health Laboratories)	Sucrose, Fructose, Maltodextrin	7	17	127	40
PowerAde (The Coca-Cola Company)	High-fructose corn syrup, Maltodextrin	8	19	55	30
All Sport (Monarch Beverages)	High-fructose corn syrup	9	21	55	55
Ultima (Ultima Replenisher)	Maltodextrin	1.7	4	8	16
MetRx (MetRx, Inc.)	Fructose, Glucose	8	19	125	40
Cytomax (Cytosport)	Fructose corn syrup, Sucrose	8	19	10	150
Coca-Cola	High-fructose corn syrup, Sucrose	11	26	9.2	Trace
Diet Soft Drinks	None	0	0	0–25	Low
Orange Juice	Fructose, Sucrose	11	26	2.7	510
Water	None	0	0	Low	Low
Gatorade Energy Drink (Gatorade Company)	Maltodextrin, Glucose, Fructose	23	53	133	70
Carboflex* (Unipro, Inc.)	Maltodextrin	24	55	0	0
Ultra Fuel* (Twin Labs)	Maltodextrin, Glucose, Fructose	21	50	0	0

Compiled from product labels and sources provided by the Gatorade Company.

enhance performance, and prevent some heat illnesses. Athletes have used several strategies to help prevent hypohydration and excessive increases in body temperature associated with certain types of sport competition. Depending on the sport, three commonly used practices are skin wetting, hyperhydration, and rehydration.

Skin Wetting Skin wetting techniques, such as sponging the head and torso with cold water or using a water spray have been shown to decrease sweat loss. This could be an important consideration in a long run, as body-water supplies may be depleted less rapidly. These techniques also cool the skin and offer an immediate sense of psychological relief from the heat stress, which may help to improve performance. On the other hand, skin wetting techniques as they may be used in athletic competition have not been shown to cause any major reductions in core temperature or cardiovascular responses. Moreover, some researchers have theorized that skin wetting techniques may be potentially harmful: the psychological sense of relief may encourage athletes to accelerate their pace, increasing heat production without providing for control of the body temperature. If the core temperature increases, heat illness may occur. Although some scientists suggest that skin wetting is not beneficial, many endurance athletes claim that it helps. Additional research appears to be warranted.

Hyperhydration Hyperhydration, also known as superhydration, is simply an increase in body fluids by the voluntary ingestion of water or other beverages. It is an attempt to assure that the body-water level is high before exercising in a hot environment. In a recent review of hyperhydration strategies, Lamb and Shehata noted that increasing body water above normal by drinking fluids before exercise is likely to improve cardiovascular functions and temperature regulation when it is impossible to ingest sufficient fluids during exercise. Although these effects would appear to help prevent fatigue, Lamb and Shehata also indicated that there was insufficient evidence to support the claim that preexercise hyperhydration improves exercise performance. Sawka and others support this viewpoint, noting that hyperhydration provides no advantages over euhydration regarding thermoregulation and exercise performance in the heat.

However, given its potential benefits, the American College of Sports Medicine recommends that hyperhydration be used prior to exercise in heat stress environments. If you plan to compete or do any prolonged exercise in the heat, it may be wise for you to hyperhydrate. Be sure you are euhydrated by drinking a pint (16 ounces) of fluid when you arise in the morning, and another pint an hour before exercising. Then consume a third pint about 15–30 minutes before exercising. Either cold water or a GES may be used to hyperhydrate, although the GES will provide some carbohydrate and sodium that may be helpful.

Glycerol supplementation may help retain more water with hyperhydration, an effect which has been theorized to improve endurance performance. The ergogenic effects of glycerol-induced hyperhydration are discussed later in this chapter.

Rehydration Of the various techniques used, research has shown that rehydration is the most effective to enhance performance. Rehydration techniques have been used to replenish fluid loss associated with both voluntary and involuntary dehydration in sports such as wrestling and distance running, respectively.

One laboratory research approach to evaluate the effects of rehydration is related to the sport of wrestling, in which athletes dehydrate to qualify for a weight class and then attempt to rehydrate rapidly prior to competition. In this approach, subjects performed some exercise or mental task, such as a measure of strength, power, anaerobic endurance, or cognitive function, were then dehydrated and tested again, and finally were rehydrated and tested one more time to see if rehydration could improve performance back to the predehydration level. The results of such research are mixed. In some studies, no effect of rehydration was found, probably because as some studies have shown, dehydration may not impair strength, power, or local muscular endurance. Thus, rehydration would not improve performance as measured by these criteria beyond that usually seen in normohydration. However, some studies reported a partial improvement in endurance performance after rehydration, but usually not all the way back to normal. In one study rehydration returned cognitive functions to normal. Because rehydration may possibly bring about performance improvements beyond the dehydrated level, it is therefore recommended for wrestlers when feasible.

A second approach in studying rehydration is to have subjects ingest fluids during prolonged endurance exercise, particularly in warm environments. Rehydration has been shown to minimize the rise in core temperature, to reduce stress on the cardiovascular system by minimizing the decrease in blood volume, and to help maintain an optimal race pace for a longer period. This beneficial effect is usually attributed to decreased dehydration and the maintenance of a better water balance in the blood and other fluid compartments. Rehydration techniques, both with water alone or with GES solutions, have been shown to improve performance in exercise tasks of 1 hour or more in the heat. Although not all studies have shown improved performance with rehydration, Jeukendrup and Martin, in their review of techniques to improve cycling performance, indicate that carbohydrate-electrolyte drinks may decrease 40-kilometer (25-mile) cycling time by 32–42 seconds. Hargreaves and others also reported that water intake may help reduce muscle glycogen use in prolonged exercise, another benefit.

If fluid replacement is to be effective, water has to be absorbed into the circulating blood so that the reduction in blood volume and sweat production that occurs during prolonged endurance exercise will be minimized. Research in which water was labeled with radionuclides showed that water ingested during exercise may appear in plasma and sweat within 10–20 minutes. However, the amount of the ingested fluid that enters the circulation to benefit the athlete depends on two factors: gastric emptying and intestinal absorption.

What factors influence gastric emptying and intestinal absorption?

In a later section we will discuss factors, such as palatability, that may influence how much fluid you drink during exercise. For any fluid to be of benefit during exercise it must first empty from the stomach and then be absorbed into the bloodstream from the intestines.

Gastric Emptying A number of factors may influence the gastric emptying rate, including volume, solute or caloric density, osmolality, drink temperature, exercise intensity, mode of exercise, and dehydration.

Volume is one of the most important factors affecting gastric emptying. In a recent review, Gisolfi noted that the larger the volume of fluid ingested, up to approximately 700 milliliters, the greater the rate of gastric emptying. However, large volumes consumed during exercise may cause discomfort to the athlete because of abdominal distention.

Although some preliminary data by Murray and others indicated that an 8 percent GES, as compared to 0, 4, and 6 percent GES, decreased gastric emptying, the decrease was only 6 ounces over 90 minutes. Other studies have shown that GES up to 8 percent carbohydrate had no adverse affect on gastric emptying of fluids, a finding in accord with the ACSM position stand on fluid replacement during exercise. Thus, 6 to 8 percent carbohydrate solutions may provide the athlete with the best of both worlds, water and carbohydrate. However, solutions with higher concentrations, particularly above 10 percent, may impair gastric emptying. The mechanism is not known, but may be related to the effects of carbohydrate on osmolality.

Fluids with a higher osmolality generally inhibit gastric emptying. Adding electrolytes and carbohydrates to fluids increases their osmolality, and Gisolfi indicated this effect may be attributed mostly to the carbohydrate content. Although glucose polymers have a lesser effect on osmolality than glucose, some investigators have observed little difference in gastric emptying of fluids that had marked differences in osmotic pressure created by adding electrolytes, glucose, or glucose polymers. On the other hand, more recent research has found that some hypotonic glucose polymers emptied from the stomach more rapidly than hypertonic solutions, about 80 percent faster in the first 10 minutes. In general, cold fluids empty rapidly and may also help cool the body core.

Moderate exercise intensity facilitates emptying, whereas intense exercise greater than 70–75 percent VO_2 max has been reported to exert an inhibitory effect. Little difference is noted in gastric emptying between cycling and running during the first hour even at an exercise intensity of 75 percent VO_2 max, but some research suggests that more fluids appear to be emptied during the later stages of prolonged cycling.

Ryan and others recently noted that hypohydration to approximately 3 percent of body weight does not impair gastric emptying. However, excessive dehydration may inhibit gastric emptying, and may be associated with gastric discomfort experienced by some athletes who consume large amounts of fluids during prolonged exercise in warm environmental conditions.

Intestinal Absorption   Factors affecting intestinal absorption of ingested fluids during exercise have not been studied as extensively as gastric emptying, but several important findings have been presented by key investigators in this area, particularly Carl Gisolfi and Ron Maughan.

Gisolfi recently indicated that the absorptive capacity of the intestines is not likely to limit the effectiveness of an oral rehydration solution. Water is absorbed fairly readily by passive diffusion, and theoretically water absorption may actually be helped by concurrent absorption of glucose and sodium. As highlighted in figure 9.10(a), glucose and sodium interact in the intestinal wall; glucose stimulates sodium absorption, and sodium is necessary for glucose absorption. When glucose and sodium are absorbed, these solutes tend to pull fluid with them via an osmotic effect, thus facilitating the absorption of water from the intestine into the circulation. However, research by Hargreaves and others noted that beverage sodium content of either 0, 25, or 50 mmol per liter had no effect on plasma glucose levels during exercise. Gisolfi indicated that the intestines themselves contain enough sodium from body fluids, so that adding sodium to the rehydration solution provides no additional benefits. Gisolfi and others also recently noted no difference in intestinal fluid absorption or plasma volume changes during exercise when consuming either a hypotonic or isotonic 6 percent carbohydrate beverage with or without sodium. Research by Shi and others, from Gisolfi's laboratory, has shown that when compared to a single form of carbohydrate, using multiple, different forms such as glucose, fructose, and polymers, enhanced intestinal absorption of water. Each form of carbohydrate may have its own receptor for absorption and pull water with it.

However, as discussed in chapter 4, excess carbohydrate in the intestine may cause a reverse osmotic effect, as depicted in figure 9.10(b), leading to gastrointestinal distress with symptoms such as abdominal cramping and diarrhea. In her review, Leslie Bonci notes that this may be one of the problems associated with some of the "energy" drinks available, as they may be too highly concentrated with simple sugars.

Whether exercise impairs intestinal absorption is controversial. High-intensity exercise may compromise blood flow to the intestine, which might impair absorption. Gisolfi, in his review, noted some of the methodological difficulties in studying this problem, citing studies showing that exercise either reduced or had no effect on intestinal absorption.

It should be noted that individual differences in both gastric emptying and intestinal absorption may be significant. In reviewing studies of gastric emptying, Costill noted some subjects could empty 80–90 percent of the ingested solution in 15–20 minutes,

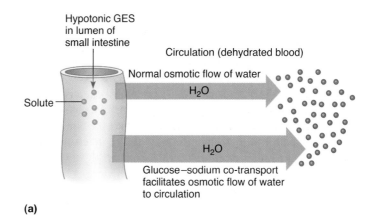

(a)

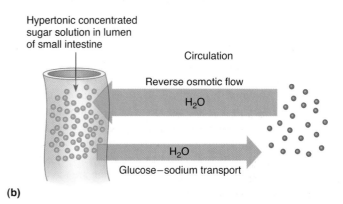

(b)

FIGURE 9.10   *(a)* Water normally diffuses from the intestine to the circulation via osmosis. Glucose and sodium in a GES enhance osmosis, as shown by the larger arrow. *(b)* A hypertonic solution may actually reverse osmosis, moving fluid from the circulatory system to the intestines, possibly leading to gastrointestinal distress symptoms such as diarrhea.

whereas others emptied only 10 percent. As noted above, some subjects may also develop diarrhea caused by ineffective intestinal absorption of fluids. Training to drink during exercise is recommended as a possible means of enhancing tolerance to consuming larger amounts of fluids.

How should carbohydrate be replaced during exercise in the heat?

The value of carbohydrate intake during exercise as a means to improve performance was detailed in chapter 4, primarily in relationship to performance in a cool environment. Keep in mind that carbohydrate intake may be useful primarily in prolonged exercise, under conditions where one is exercising at a high level of intensity for an hour or more. Carbohydrate is the primary fuel during such exercise tasks, and research suggests that warm environmental conditions may accelerate the use of muscle glycogen. Thus, carbohydrate intake may also improve performance during exercise in the heat, but if temperature regulation is of prime importance, water replacement should receive top priority. Hence, one of the goals of researchers has been to develop a fluid that will help replace carbohydrate during exercise in the heat without affecting water absorption. As discussed previously, glucose-electrolyte solutions (GES) and glucose-polymer solutions (GPS) have been developed for this purpose.

Research indicates that an appropriate amount of carbohydrate in solution may maintain body temperature as effectively as water and may enhance performance during prolonged exercise. Water and carbohydrate complement each other to improve physical performance. In a recent unique study, Fritzsche and others, from Coyle's laboratory at the University of Texas, investigated the individual and combined effects of water and carbohydrate intake on power, thermoregulation, cardiovascular function, and metabolism in endurance-trained cyclists exercising for 2 hours in a hot environment. They found that although water alone attenuated the decline in power, ingestion of water with carbohydrate was even more effective. Similar findings have been reported for exercise tests of about an hour duration. Below and others found that water alone and carbohydrate alone improved 1-hour cycling performance in the heat, but the beneficial effects were additive when both were consumed. Mindy Millard-Stafford also reported that a carbohydrate solution, in comparison to water alone, improved performance in highly-trained runners in a 15-kilometer run.

Scores of studies have compared the effectiveness of different carbohydrate combinations and concentrations in enhancing physical performance during prolonged endurance tasks. Most of this research is discussed in chapter 4. The following are the pertinent general findings relative to GES and GPS intake during prolonged exercise under warm environmental conditions.

In general, GES and GPS solutions between 5 to 10 percent seem to empty from the stomach as effectively as water during prolonged exercise in a hot environment, a finding recently supported by Rogers and others. They may possibly also be absorbed more readily from the intestinal tract. No significant adverse effects of these solutions upon plasma volume, sweat rate, or temperature regulation, when compared to water ingestion, have been observed. Actually, they may help maintain plasma volume, liver glycogen, and blood glucose levels during prolonged exercise, and, as noted, most investigators report that carbohydrate intake during exercise enhances endurance capacity in a variety of prolonged tasks in the heat. Recent research by Jeukendrup and his associates suggests about 1.5–1.7 grams of carbohydrate per minute may be oxidized if a mixture of carbohydrates, such as glucose, fructose and sucrose, is used. Additionally, Rowlands and others noted that although hypotonic glucose polymers are reported to empty from the stomach faster than hypertonic solutions, there is no effect on glucose oxidation rates.

Although higher concentrations of carbohydrates deliver more glucose to the intestine, solutions higher than 10–12 percent may significantly delay gastric emptying, decrease intestinal absorption, and possibly cause gastrointestinal distress. Peters and others indicated that excess carbohydrate may pass on to the colon, where bacterial fermentation may lead to excess gas production, flatulence, the urge to defecate, and gastrointestinal cramps, more so in runners than in cyclists. High concentrations of fructose in some fruit juices or juice blends may be particularly debilitating. However, ultraendurance athletes may experiment with higher concentrations of carbohydrate in training and may adapt to such concentrated solutions for use during competition. In a recent case study, Alice Lindeman noted that one cyclist involved in the Race Across America (RAAM) consumed a 23 percent carbohydrate solution with no gastrointestinal problems. In such competitions, where cyclists may ride 20 hours or more a day, such high carbohydrate concentrations may be necessary to meet the high energy demands.

In summary, a recent consensus statement by leading researchers, chaired by Ronald Maughan, indicated that sports drinks containing carbohydrate as an energy source are more effective than plain water in improving prolonged endurance performance. Water is the essential nutrient that needs to be replenished during prolonged exercise in the heat, for it will help deter some of the adverse responses to dehydration. When carbohydrate replenishment is desired, the current evidence suggests that a 5–10 percent solution of multiple carbohydrate sources would be recommended. Louise Burke concludes that although carbohydrate ingestion may not enhance the performance of all events undertaken in hot weather, there are no disadvantages to the consumption of beverages containing recommended amounts of carbohydrate and electrolytes.

Table 9.8 calculates the amount of fluid you must consume, for a given concentration, in order to obtain 30–100 grams of carbohydrate. For example, if you wanted to get 60 grams of carbohydrate per hour, you would need to drink 1 liter (1,000 ml) of a 6 percent solution, but only one-half liter (500 ml) of a 12 percent solution. Strategies for carbohydrate intake before and after exercise are presented in chapter 4.

How should electrolytes be replaced during or following exercise?

Because the major solid component of sweat consists of electrolytes, considerable research has been conducted relative to the need for replacement of these lost nutrients, primarily sodium and potassium. We shall look at this question from two points of view, one dealing with the need for replacement during exercise and the other involving daily replacement.

During exercise Because sweat is hypotonic to the body fluids, the concentration of electrolytes in the blood and other body fluids actually increases during exercise and makes the body fluids hypertonic. Thus, electrolyte replacement during moderately prolonged exercise is not necessary. In a recent study of cyclists who exercised 90 minutes at 60 percent VO_2 max, Sanders and others concluded that a 40 millimole sodium solution, compared to plain water, may not be of much advantage to athletes who practice normal fluid replacement during such exercise tasks. Several studies have reported that even during strenuous prolonged exercise with high levels of sweat losses, like marathon running for several hours, water alone is the recommended fluid replacement to help maintain electrolyte balance, although added carbohydrate may provide some needed energy.

However, electrolyte replacement, particularly sodium, may be necessary for some athletes participating in very prolonged bouts of physical activity, such as marathons, ultramarathons, Ironman-type triathlons, or tennis tournaments where one might play off and on all day. A number of medical case studies following such events have reported complications resulting from a condition known as hyponatremia.

TABLE 9.8 Fluid consumption (milliliters) at a given percent carbohydrate concentration to obtain desired grams of carbohydrate

Percent concentration	Grams of carbohydrate delivered							
	30	40	50	60	70	80	90	100
2%	1,500	2,000	2,500	3,000	3,500	4,000	4,500	5,000
4%	750	1,000	1,250	1,500	1,750	2,000	2,250	2,500
6%	500	666	833	1,000	1,166	1,333	1,500	1,666
8%	375	500	625	750	875	1,000	1,125	1,250
10%	300	400	500	600	700	800	900	1,000
12%	250	333	417	500	583	667	750	833
15%	225	300	375	450	525	600	675	750
20%	150	200	250	300	350	400	450	500

Hyponatremia is a condition of subnormal levels of sodium in the blood. It can occur at rest simply by consuming too much water, and may also be known as *water intoxication.* Hyponatremia can also occur following prolonged exercise, in which case it may be known as *exercise-associated hyponatremia (EAH).* An international consensus conference on EAH defined it as a serum sodium concentration below the normal reference range, or less than 135 mmol/liter. Milder forms are 130–134 mmol/liter and may be asymptomatic, but not always. Signs and symptoms, such as bloating, puffiness of hands and feet, nausea, vomiting, and headache usually occur when serum sodium goes below 130 mmol/liter. Severe cases, below 120 mmol/liter, may cause massive brain swelling, which may be associated with seizures, coma, respiratory arrest, permanent brain damage, and death. In a study from a recent Boston marathon, Almond and others tested 488 runners following the race; 13 percent, or one in eight, had a serious fluid and salt imbalance from drinking too much water or sports drinks, and one 28-year-old woman died from hyponatremia. Treatment of individuals with symptomatic hyponatremia is a medical emergency, and transportation to a hospital is essential. Infusion of hypertonic solutions may be necessary.

Various risk factors have been identified that predispose individuals to development of EAH in marathons and other endurance events, including the following:

- Excessive drinking of fluids before, during, and after the event
- Considerable weight gain over the course of the event
- Slower finishers
- Females
- Low body weight
- Heat-unacclimatized, poorly trained competitors
- High sweat sodium losses
- Race inexperience
- NSAID use; altered kidney functions to excrete fluids

Hyponatremia may be caused by water dilution, excess sodium losses, or both. The EAH consensus conference committee indi-

cated that dilutional hyponatremia, caused by an increase in total body water relative to the amount of total body sodium, is the current etiology of EAH. Factors that normally control body water balance, mainly hormones and the kidney, may malfunction. Nonsteroidal anti-inflammatory drugs (NSAID) interfere with normal kidney function.

Many of these factors may interact to contribute to the development of EAH. For example, females may be of lower body weight, generally run slower marathon times than males, may be more conscientious about consuming fluids given the old adage *to drink as much as you can,* and thus have more time to consume more fluids and gain proportionately more weight. The weight gain is water, which dilutes the serum sodium concentration.

To help prevent hyponatremia USA Track & Field (USATF), following guidelines recently developed by the International Marathon Medical Directors Association, noted that it is neither correct nor safe to provide a blanket recommendation for fluid intake for all athletes during exercise. Athletes should determine their own sweat rate in order to individualize fluid replacement during exercise. USATF recommends that athletes should attempt to replace fluids on a 1:1 ratio, drinking sufficient fluids to match sweat losses.

The EAH consensus committee notes that ingesting sports drinks does not prevent the development of EAH in athletes who drink to excess because all such drinks are hypotonic. Indeed, sports drinks are constituted to be palatable so athletes will drink more. In a recent study, Passe and others reported that exercising individuals consumed more fluid as sport drinks as compared to water and orange juice. However, the EAH consensus committee did note some studies have shown that consuming sports drinks can decrease the severity of EAH.

USATF notes that consumption of sports drinks containing sodium and other electrolytes is preferred as a possible means to prevent hyponatremia. Twenty milliequivalents (20 mEq; 20 mmol/liter) of sodium may be found in some commercial sports drinks, but research by Barr and others suggests this amount may be inadequate to prevent a decrease in plasma sodium during prolonged exercise in the heat. Higher amounts approaching the salt content of sweat (about 30–50 mEq per liter) have been suggested by Nancy Rehrer. In a recent study, Twerenbold and others reported that consuming sodium, in a solution approximating 30 mEq (680 milligrams/liter), minimized hyponatremia in female endurance athletes running for 4 hours; two athletes in the water control trial developed hyponatremia (<130 mmol serum sodium). Some commercial sports drinks may contain higher amounts of sodium. For example, the Gatorade Endurance Hydration Formula contains over 800 milligrams of sodium per liter, or about 35 mEq. The point should be stressed, however, that although sports drinks may help replace some lost sodium, drinking to excess may still lead to hyponatremia.

Individual differences may dictate who may be prone to developing hyponatremia during prolonged exercise, but given the current evidence it appears that athletes involved in ultraendurance events should consume adequate salt in their diet the days before competition to help assure normal serum sodium levels and consume fluids with added sodium during the event. More research is needed to help refine current recommendations. In the meantime, experiment with salty solutions during practice. You can carry some fluids with you in competition, and in others you may have personal beverages located at specific aid stations on the course.

Daily replacement   In general, heavy daily sweat losses do not lead to an electrolyte deficiency. If body levels of sodium and potassium begin to decrease, the kidneys begin to reabsorb more of these minerals and less are excreted in the urine. Research has shown that water alone, in combination with a balanced diet, will adequately maintain proper body electrolyte levels from day to day, even when an individual is exercising and is losing large amounts of sweat.

However, if electrolytes are not adequately replaced because of poor dietary intake, a deficit may occur over 4–7 days of very hard training, especially in hot environmental conditions where fluid losses will tend to be high. Thus, in a recent review, Maughan noted that exercising individuals who experience heavy daily sweat losses need both adequate fluids and sodium to ensure adequate rehydration. For such individuals, adding salt to meals and drinks may help. Ray and others recently reported that consuming high sodium foods, such as chicken broth or chicken noodle soup, improved fluid retention following dehydration. The sodium is needed in the body to help retain water and maintain normal osmotic pressures.

A good method of checking on the adequacy of fluid replenishment on a day-to-day basis is to check your body weight in the morning; it should be nearly the same every day. If you weigh several pounds less from one day to the next, it is likely you are hypohydrated. Conversely, if you weigh several pounds more, you may be overhydrated.

Are salt tablets or potassium supplements necessary?

In general, the use of salt tablets to replace lost electrolytes, primarily sodium, is not necessary. As noted, an adequate diet will replace, on a daily basis, electrolytes lost in sweat.

The concentrations of salt in sweat may vary; we have noted previously that the average may be about 2.6 grams of salt per liter, although there are reports as high as 4.5 grams per liter in unacclimatized individuals and as low as 1.75 grams per liter in the heat-acclimatized individual. Because salt is 40 percent sodium and 60 percent chloride, the sodium content in 2.6 grams of salt is 1 gram, in 4.5 grams of salt is 1.8 grams, and in 1.75 grams of salt is 0.7 grams. If an athlete would lose about 8–9 pounds of body fluids during an exercise period, a total of 4 liters of fluid (about 4 quarts) would be lost because a liter weighs 2.2 pounds. Four liters of sweat would contain, at the most, 7.2 grams of sodium in the unacclimatized individual, but less than 3 grams in one who was acclimatized. Because the average meal contains about 2–3 grams of sodium if well salted, three meals a day would offer 6–9 grams, about enough to just cover the losses in the sweat. However, sodium is lost through other means, primarily in the urine; thus, a slight increase in sodium intake may be reasonable for the unacclimatized athlete. Doug Hiller, a physician who has worked extensively with endurance athletes, suggests that during the week or two of acclimatization to exercising in the heat, athletes should consume about 10–25 grams of salt daily, or 4–10 grams of sodium. Consuming more high-sodium foods or a more liberal salting of the food should provide an adequate amount; 1 teaspoon of salt contains about 5 grams of salt, or 2 grams of sodium. Although this recommendation is much greater than the UL of 2.3 grams recommended by the National Academy of Sciences, that recommendation is based on the sedentary individual, not an athlete losing copious amounts of sodium during a period of acclimatization.

Common salt tablets contain only sodium and chloride. They are not necessary to replace lost sodium but may be recommended for unacclimatized athletes who do not replace sodium through normal dietary means in the early stages of an acclimatization program. Salt tablets should be taken only if the athlete loses substantial amounts of weight via sweat losses during a workout. Checking the body weight before and after a workout provides a good estimate of sweat loss. If we switch to the English system, 1 quart of sweat equals 2 pounds; one-half quart, or a pint, is 1 pound. One recommendation is that salt tablets should be taken only if the athlete needs to drink more than 4 quarts of fluid per day to replace that lost during sweating; that is, an 8-pound weight loss. The general rule is to take two salt tablets with each additional quart of fluid beyond the 4 quarts; this would be equal to 1 gram of sodium (the average tablet has one-half gram of sodium) per quart. Another way to look at it is to take one pint of water with every salt tablet. The use of salt tablets should be discontinued after the athlete is acclimatized, usually about 6–9 days.

Potassium supplements are not recommended—for several reasons. First, research by David Costill and his associates has revealed that a deficiency of potassium is rare, even with large sweat losses and a diet low in potassium. Second, as noted previously, excessive potassium may be lethal as it can disturb the electrical rhythm of the heart. The moderate use of substitutes, such as potassium chloride for common table salt, may be helpful in assuring potassium replacement, but investigators recommended particular attention to the diet, citing citrus fruits and bananas as two of the many foods high in potassium. For example, a large glass of orange juice will replace the potassium lost in 2 liters of sweat.

What are some prudent guidelines relative to fluid replacement while exercising under warm or hot environmental conditions?

In sport nutrition, no other area has received as much research attention as the objective of determining the optimal formulation of an oral rehydration solution (sports drink) for individuals doing prolonged exercise under warm or hot environmental conditions. This may be so because water and carbohydrates are two nutrients that may enhance performance in such events, and water and electrolytes may also help to prevent heat-related illnesses. As discussed above in relation to the need for fluid, carbohydrate, or electrolytes, a number of factors—in particular, the intensity and duration of the exercise task, the prevailing environmental conditions, and individual differences in sweat rate, gastric emptying, and intestinal absorption—may influence the desired composition of the sports drink. Given these considerations, most of the leading investigators in this area, including Louise Burke, Edward Coyle, Carl Gisolfi, Ronald Maughan, and Timothy Noakes have all indicated there currently is no general agreement on the optimal formulation of an oral rehydration solution for all individuals who engage in prolonged exercise tasks.

However, through their concerted research efforts, these and other investigators have provided us with enough information to offer some guidelines that may be regarded as prudent—that is, they are likely to do some good and do no harm. The following guidelines for maintaining body fluid balance, improving performance in the heat, and preventing heat-related illnesses appear to be prudent as based on the current scientific knowledge. These guidelines are related to exercising under warm or hot environmental conditions and are in accord with the American College of Sports Medicine (ACSM) position stand on exercise and fluid replacement (see www.mhhe.com/williams).

Before Competition and Practice

1. Be well trained for the competition and, as discussed later in this chapter, be well acclimated to exercise in the heat.
2. Be sure that you are adequately hydrated the day before and the morning of the competition. Your urine should be a clear pale yellow before competition or practice. Then, hyperhydrate with 10–17 ounces (300–500 milliliters) of cold fluid about 15–30 minutes before exercising. If the exercise task is prolonged, carbohydrate may be added. A concentration of 6–8 percent is advisable, but concentrations of 20 percent and higher have been used by some individuals without adverse effects. As noted in chapter 4, carbohydrate intake may help optimize glycogen stores for prolonged endurance events, and if muscle glycogen levels are low, the intake of carbohydrate before endurance events less than 50–60 minutes may be helpful.
3. Minimize consumption of alcoholic beverages the night before competition, for they may lead to hypohydration in the morning. Avoid drinking caffeinated beverages 1–4 hours

before competition as caffeine may increase urine production during rest. Caffeinated beverages do provide fluids, but you may retain more from noncaffeinated beverages. An expanded discussion of alcohol and caffeine is presented in chapter 13.

During Competition and Practice

1. Cold water, about 40–50°F (4.4–10°C) is effective when carbohydrate intake is of little or no concern, for example, in endurance events less than 50–60 minutes.
2. For longer duration events, carbohydrate may provide an important source of energy. If carbohydrate is desired in the drink, the concentration should not be excessive. As discussed above, a 6–8 percent solution appears to be effective in maintaining fluid balance while supplying carbohydrates. Studies have also shown that concentrations up to 10 percent may also be helpful, but concentrations greater than 10–12 percent may retard gastric emptying. It might be helpful to consume a carbohydrate drink that has multiple forms of carbohydrate, such as glucose, sucrose, fructose, and glucose polymers. Check the food label for ingredients.
3. The fluid should contain small amounts of electrolytes. Gisolfi recommends 460–690 milligrams of sodium per liter (20–30 mmol) and 200–400 milligrams of potassium per liter (about 5–10 mmol) of solution. However, for athletes involved in very prolonged endurance events under warm environmental conditions, some recommend a range of about 700–1,150 milligrams of sodium per liter (approximately 30–50 mmol per liter) and 120–225 milligrams of potassium per liter (approximately 3–6 mmol per liter). Some commercial sports drinks contain electrolytes within this range; check the food label. For example, per each 8-ounce serving, Gatorade Endurance Formula contains 200 milligrams of sodium and 90 milligrams of potassium, which is over 800 milligrams of sodium and 360 milligrams of potassium per liter.
4. The fluid should be palatable and not interfere with normal gastrointestinal functions. Research has shown that the voluntary intake of fluids increases when they are tasty. Being cold and sweet enhances palatability. Carbonated beverages do not appear to inhibit gastric emptying, nor does the use of aspartame (an artificial sweetener), but Zachwieja and others noted that certain flavorings, such as citric acid, may impair gastric emptying by as much as 25 percent. Other research from Costill's laboratory has shown no difference between carbonated and noncarbonated beverages on temperature regulation while exercising submaximally in the heat. However, Lambert and others noted that subjects exercising in the heat consumed less fluid when it was carbonated, suggesting a lower palatability compared to noncarbonated beverages. Caffeinated drinks do not appear to have any detrimental effect when consumed during exercise. Van Nieuwenhoven and others found that sports drinks with caffeine (150 milligrams per liter) had no effect on gastrointestinal function during exercise. The amount of caffeine in sports drinks, although small, may enhance exercise performance. Cox and others recently found that consumption

of a small amount of caffeine (approximately 1.5 mg/kg from Coca-Cola) during exercise enhanced performance in a cycling time trial following 2 hours of steady-state riding. They also reported ergogenic effects following consumption of 6 mg caffeine/kg during a similar cycling protocol. Consult chapter 13 for a more detailed discussion regarding the effect of caffeine on exercise performance.

5. Rehydrate with 6–8 ounces (180–240 milliliters) of cold fluid during exercise at 10- to 15-minute intervals. (A good rule of thumb to remember is that one normal mouthful or swallow equals about 1 ounce.) Such amounts can total to about 1 liter per hour, which could be enough to maintain fluid balance with mild to moderate sweating. It is important to realize that during periods of heavy sweating, it is very difficult to consume enough fluids to replace all of those lost. Costill has noted that, per minute, 50 milliliters of fluid may be lost through sweating (3 liters per hour), but only 20–30 milliliters per minute may be absorbed from the intestines. The sweating rate in this case is simply greater than the ability of the stomach to empty the fluid into the small intestine for absorption to occur. Although some dehydration will occur, rehydration will help maintain circulatory stability and heat balance thereby delaying deterioration in endurance capacity. Cheuvront and Haymes reported that replacing about 60–70 percent of sweat losses helps to maintain thermoregulatory responses during hot and warm weather conditions. If possible, try to replace actual sweat losses, as this may be the best way to maintain blood volume. By calculating your typical sweat losses, as discussed on page 335 and determined in the Application Exercise on page 357, you may be able to determine how much fluid you should consume per hour.

6. It is important to start rehydrating early in endurance events because thirst does not develop until about 1–2 percent of body weight has been dehydrated, by which time performance may have begun to deteriorate. Moreover, research by sport scientists at the University of Maastricht in the Netherlands has shown that dehydration may impair gastric emptying and may be related to a higher rate of gastrointestinal distress.

After Competition and Practice

1. Shirreffs and Maughan state that the key point in restoring fluid balance after exercise is to consume a volume of fluid greater than that lost in sweat and replacement of electrolyte losses, particularly sodium. During recovery, consume enough fluids to regain your body-weight losses. As some of the fluid ingested during recovery may stimulate urine production and be lost, scientists recommend you consume about 150 percent of the body-weight loss, or 24 ounces of fluid for every 16 ounces lost. If you have depleted much of your endogenous carbohydrate stores, consume fluids with a high carbohydrate content. Fruit juices and sports drinks are helpful when you need to replenish both fluids and carbohydrates. Be sure to consume enough sodium as well, using sports drinks or putting additional salt on your food. Rehrer notes that sodium is necessary in the recovery period to reduce the urinary output and increase the rate of restoration of fluid balance. Avoid caffeinated beverages; Brouns and others indicated they can significantly increase electrolyte losses during recovery. Also, Shirreffs and Maughan noted that drinks containing 4 percent alcohol or more, such as beer, tend to delay the recovery process as measured by restoration of blood and plasma volume. Weigh yourself each morning to see that your weight remains stable, a good indication of proper fluid balance.

2. To rehydrate rapidly, research suggests it is best to consume about 120–150 percent of sweat losses, and to consume that amount within 2–3 hours following dehydration. Carbohydrate and salt should also be consumed during this time frame. Rapid restoration of fluids and carbohydrates may be important for certain athletes, such as tennis players, who may have to compete in two or more events daily with a short recovery period. Such a strategy is also important for athletes who may train twice daily. Some recent research supports this protocol. In a recent study, Bilzon and others concluded that provided adequate hydration status is maintained, inclusion of carbohydrate within an oral rehydration solution will delay the onset of fatigue during a subsequent bout of prolonged submaximal running in a warm environment.

In Training

1. Practice consuming fluids while you train. Use a trial and error approach. Some research indicates that consuming GES during training, particularly high-intensity training, may result in a more effective workout, which could lead to better performance in competition. By consuming various formulations while you train, particularly during training comparable to the intensity and duration experienced in competition, you will be able to determine what fluids work specifically for you. Consuming fluids during training may help you overcome some of the factors that inhibit fluid intake during exercise, such as the uncomfortable sensation of fluid in the stomach, and lead to increased fluid intake during competition. This is especially important for older athletes, who tend to drink less than their younger counterparts.

2. If you sip sports drinks throughout the day to stay hydrated, be sure to practice sound dental hygiene. As noted in chapter 4, sports drinks may exert significant eroding effects on dental enamel.

A summary of guidelines for fluid, carbohydrate, and electrolyte replacement during exercise under warm environmental conditions is presented in table 9.9. In brief, Louise Burke cites three key points to prevent hypohydration during exercise. Hydrate well before the exercise task; drink as much as is comfortable and practical during exercise; and, rehydrate aggressively afterwards in preparation for future exercise bouts. Use of sports drinks may be helpful. In their review, Coombes and Hamilton concluded that in studies where a practical protocol has been used along with a currently available sports beverage (less than 10 percent carbohydrate solutions), there is evidence to suggest that consuming a sports drink will improve performance compared with consuming a placebo beverage. For additional information, consult the ACSM position stand on exercise and fluid replacement or the review by Bob Murray.

TABLE 9.9 Summary of guidelines for fluid, carbohydrate, and electrolyte replacement during exercise in warm environmental conditions

Type of event	Timing of consumption	Amount and type of beverage
Sports or exercise less than 60 minutes:	*Before:*	
10-kilometer (6.2 miles) run	1–2 hours	16 ounces (500 ml) cold water or GES (5–10% carbohydrate)
25-kilometer (15.5 miles) bike race	15–30 minutes	10–16 ounces (300–500 ml) cold water or GES (5–10% carbohydrate)
		Beverage may contain carbohydrate (6–10% solution) if there is a possibility of low muscle glycogen levels
	During:	
	Every 10–15 minutes	6–8 ounces (180–240 ml) cold water or GES (6–10% carbohydrate)
	Recovery:	
	Over next 24 hours	Adequate fluid to replace body losses
Sports or exercise from 1 to 4 hours duration:	*Before:*	
Marathon (42.2 kilometers; 26.2 miles)	1–2 hours	16 ounces (500 ml) GES (6–10% carbohydrate)
Triathlon (1-mile swim, 25-mile bike, 6.2-mile run)	15–30 minutes	10–16 ounces (300–500 ml) GES (6–10% carbohydrate)
	During:	
Soccer game	Every 10–15 minutes	6–8 ounces (180–240 ml) GES (6–10% carbohydrate)
Field hockey game	*Recovery:*	
Tennis match	Immediately after and every 2 hours for 6–8 hours	GES or GPS to provide 1 gram carbohydrate per kilogram body weight, i.e., 50–70 grams carbohydrate. Solid carbohydrates also may be used. Ensure adequate sodium intake.
Sports or exercise greater than 4 hours:	*Before:*	
Ultraendurance runs (50 miles or more)	1–2 hours	16 ounces (500 ml) GES (6–10% carbohydrate)
Century bike race (100 miles)	15–30 minutes	10–16 ounces (300–500 ml) GES (6–10% carbohydrate)
Ironman-type triathlons (2.4-mile swim, 112-mile bike, 26.2-mile run)		Higher concentrations (20–50% carbohydrate) may be used with experience
	During:	
	Every 10–15 minutes	6–8 ounces (180–240 ml) GES (6–10% carbohydrate) and 20–50 milliequivalents of sodium; higher concentrations (20–50% carbohydrate) may be used with experience.
	Recovery:	
	Immediately after and every 2 hours for 6–8 hours	GES or GPS to provide 1 gram carbohydrate per kilogram body weight, i.e., 50–70 grams carbohydrate. Solid carbohydrates also may be used. Ensure adequate sodium intake.

These guidelines are approximations and may be modified based on individual preferences derived through personal experience in both training and competition. Body weight should be back to normal the day after training or competition. See text for additional guidelines.

- Hyperhydration before exercise is important, but rehydration is the most important nutritional consideration when exercising in the heat. An effective rehydration solution is one that optimizes gastric emptying and intestinal absorption of fluid.
- Rehydration with cold water is effective in moderating body temperature during exercise in the heat, but carbohydrate solutions may be equally effective and also provide a source of energy for more prolonged endurance exercise.
- Electrolyte replacement generally is not needed during exercise but may be helpful in very prolonged exercise tasks. Water alone, in combination with a balanced diet including adequate sodium and potassium, will adequately restore normal electrolyte levels in the body on a day-to-day basis.
- Excessive water consumption during very prolonged exercise, coupled with inadequate salt intake, may contribute to hyponatremia, a potentially dangerous condition.
- Individuals who desire to rehydrate rapidly following exercise should consume about 120–150 percent of the fluids lost. Added salt will help the body retain the ingested fluids.
- Current research suggests that a 5–10 percent solution of glucose, fructose, glucose polymers, or combinations of these different carbohydrates may be effective for athletes who need carbohydrate replacement during exercise.

Ergogenic Aspects

If preventing or correcting a nutrient deficiency is seen as an ergogenic technique, then certainly water could be construed to be an ergogenic aid. Compared to taking in no fluid before or during exercise, both hyperhydration and rehydration have been shown to enhance temperature regulation or exercise performance by optimizing hydration status. On the other hand, some athletes have attempted to lose body water for ergogenic purposes. Although we have seen that hypohydration generally does not improve performance, and indeed may actually impair performance in endurance-type events, certain athletes such as high jumpers may use drugs like diuretics to lose weight rapidly without losses in power. Research has shown that diuretic-induced weight losses may improve vertical jumping ability because the athlete can develop the same power to move a lower body weight. Detailed coverage of these drugs is beyond the scope of this text. Moreover, the use of diuretics is banned by most athletic governing bodies, such as the United States Olympic Committee and the National Collegiate Athletic Association.

Oxygen water, or water oxygenated before bottling, has been marketed by some companies as a means of enhancing energy and boosting athletic performance. However, there is the question as to whether or not oxygen bound in water would actually be absorbed into the blood stream for delivery to the muscles. Peer-reviewed research does not support marketing claims that oxygen water enhances energy and boosts athletic performance. For example,

Hampson and others reported no effect of oxygenated water on oxygen consumption during exercise, and noted that the amount of oxygen contained in the bottle would last only about two seconds in an individual doing moderate exercise.

Pre-cooling may be an effective ergogenic strategy for some athletes competing in the heat. Although not all studies have shown beneficial effects, several have. The most recent, by Webster and others, evaluated the effect of a light-weight cooling vest on endurance running performance. The subjects wore the cooling vest during stretching and warm-up, but not during the running tests. The vest cooled the body core temperature by 0.5° Celsius and decreased sweat rate by approximately 10–23 percent during a 30-minute run at 70 percent of VO_2 max, and also improved endurance time by 49 seconds when running at 95 percent of VO_2 max. Several marathon runners used cooling vests prior to the 2004 Athens Olympic marathon race.

An electrolyte deficiency could impair physical performance, but supplements above and beyond normal electrolyte nutrition have not been recommended for ergogenic purposes. However, sodium concentration is one of the main determinants of blood volume, acting like a sponge to attract water into the circulatory system. As Gledhill and others note, an increased blood volume may increase VO_2 max. In this regard, Luetkemeier and others noted that ingestion, or infusion, of a saline solution before exercise may expand the plasma volume, leading to cardiovascular responses that could benefit exercise performance, but they also noted such advantages have yet to be reported.

One ergogenic aid will be discussed in this section. Glycerol supplementation has been studied in attempts to enhance endurance performance in warm environments, and the theory underlying its potential ergogenic effect is related to increased blood volume.

Does glycerol supplementation enhance endurance performance during exercise under warm environmental conditions?

As discussed in chapter 5, glycerol is an alcohol that combines with fatty acids to form a triglyceride. Glycerol has been studied as an ergogenic aid because it may serve as substrate for gluconeogenesis (new formation of glucose), but results of these studies have not supported an ergogenic effect. More recently, however, glycerol has been combined with water during hyperhydration prior to exercise to study its potential ergogenic effects on performance in prolonged endurance events, often under warm environmental conditions. Theoretically, glycerol-induced hyperhydration will increase osmotic pressure in the body fluids, helping to retain more total body water and also possibly increase the plasma volume, factors that could enhance temperature regulation and exercise performance.

Various techniques have been used to hyperhydrate subjects with glycerol. The amount used was based on either the subject's body weight, lean body mass, or body-water content. On average, for each kilogram body weight, subjects consumed 1 gram of glycerol combined with about 20–25 milliliters of water. Thus, a 70-kilogram male would consume 70 grams of glycerol in about

1.4–1.75 liters of water or similar fluid. In some studies, glycerol was also provided with carbohydrate solutions. Glycerol-induced hyperhydration protocols were normally compared to water-induced hyperhydration techniques.

Research data are equivocal regarding the effects of glycerol-induced hyperhydration, compared to water-induced hyperhydration, on body-water levels. Freund and his associates from the U.S. Army Research Institute of Environmental Medicine found that glycerol-induced hyperhydration as compared to water hyperhydration resulted in a greater retention of fluids in the body. The investigators noted that the glycerol helped to maintain the osmolality of the blood, leading to better preservation of serum ADH levels, which they suggested may have contributed to the lower urinary output of water. Compared to water hyperhydration, Lyons and others reported that glycerol-induced hyperhydration increased body-water stores by about 700 milliliters, while Hitchins and others reported an expanded body water by approximately 600 milliliters. Conversely, using similar hyperhydration protocols, two reports by Latzka and others have not shown any advantage of glycerol-induced hyperhydration over water-induced hyperhydration on total body water. Inder and others also reported no beneficial effect of glycerol supplementation on body-water stores, but the amount of water ingested was much less than that used in other studies.

Research data regarding the effects of glycerol-induced hyperhydration on temperature regulation and on performance are also equivocal. Lyons and others found that glycerol-induced hyperhydration was more effective than water-induced hyperhydration in reducing the thermal stress of moderate exercise in the heat. Montner and others reported that glycerol-induced hyperhydration significantly improved performance in a cycling endurance test to exhaustion at 65 percent VO_2 max in a neutral laboratory environment. The authors also noted a lower heart rate and rectal temperature response during the glycerol trial and speculated the benefits were due to an increased plasma volume. Scheett and others found that, compared to water alone, glycerol hyperhydration significantly increased plasma volume restoration following dehydration and increased cycle exercise time to exhaustion in the heat. Anderson and others, using a standard glycerol hyperhydration protocol, studied its effects on a 15-minute cycling test following 1 hour of steady-state cycling in the heat at 98 percent of the lactate threshold. Compared to the placebo hyperhydration, the glycerol hyperhydration resulted in greater fluid retention, a lower heart rate, and a lower rectal temperature during the steady-state ride, and a significantly improved cycle test performance. The authors suggested the improved performance resulted from reducing cardiovascular strain and enhancing thermoregulation. In a field study involving a crossover protocol, Coutts and others studied the effects of glycerol hyperhydration on competitive Olympic distance triathlon performance. The triathlon was conducted outdoors. The weather on the day of the first competitive triathlon was classified as hot (WBGT, 30.5°), while on the day of the second triathlon it was classified as warm (WBGT, 25.4°). The glycerol hyperhydration induced a significantly greater plasma expansion compared to the placebo, and the increase in the triathlon completion time between the hot and warm conditions was significantly less than the placebo trial. Based on this finding, the authors suggested that glycerol hyperhydration prior to triathlon competition in high ambient temperatures may provide some protection against the negative performance effect of competing in the heat. Although competitive field studies such as this one are important, the rather substantial temperature difference on the two days of competition may have confounded the results.

On the other hand, Latzka and others reported that glycerol-induced hyperhydration did not affect sweating dynamics, body temperature, or physiological responses during exercise in two studies. In one of these studies, they reported that although glycerol-induced hyperhydration did improve exercise performance in the heat at 55 percent VO_2 max compared to control conditions, the improvement was not significantly greater than that noted in the water-induced hyperhydration trial. Inder and others also reported no beneficial effects of glycerol supplementation on exercise time to exhaustion. In a well-designed crossover study, Magal and others evaluated the effect of glycerol hyperhydration, as compared to water hyperhydration, on tennis-related performance in highly skilled male tennis players. Each trial consisted of three phases: hyperhydration with or without glycerol over 150 minutes; 120 minutes of exercise-induced dehydration; and, rehydration with or without glycerol over 90 minutes. After each phase subjects performed various tests, including short sprints, repeated agility drills, and tennis skills. Compared to the placebo trial, the glycerol hyperhydration protocol provided a better hydration status and greater plasma volume after both the initial hydration phase and the rehydration phase, but no performance benefits were observed. Wingo and others reported that although glycerol hyperhydration resulted in less dehydration and post-race thirst during a 30-mile mountain-bike race in the heat, there was no significant difference in final race time even though the cyclists completed the final 10-mile loop five minutes faster during the glycerol trial. Compared to water hyperhydration, Marino and others also reported no significant effect of a standard glycerol-hyperhydration protocol on a 60-minute cycling time trial under hot, humid conditions.

The ergogenic effect of glycerol-induced hyperhydration has been the subject of several recent reviews, and even the conclusions of these reviewers are somewhat equivocal. Robergs and Griffen concluded that despite the small number of studies available, glycerol-induced hyperhydration appears to be an effective method of improving tolerance to exercise. Contrariwise, Lamb and Shehata conclude that the addition of glycerol to hyperhydration beverages usually is ineffective and should be avoided. Latzka and Sawka also noted that if euhydration is maintained during exercise-heat stress, then hyperhydration appears to have no meaningful advantage. Taking another viewpoint, Wagner indicates that the results of glycerol-induced hyperhydration research are equivocal, most likely because of methodologic differences between studies, such as variations in the intensity of exercise, environmental conditions, and the concentration or dose of glycerol used.

Wagner's viewpoint is reasonable. Although some of these studies suggest that glycerol may be an effective ergogenic aid, the research data are clearly ambivalent. However, several magazines targeted to cyclists and runners have already suggested that glycerol may be an effective ergogenic. Additionally, articles in body-building magazines suggest glycerol-induced hyperhydration may enhance vascularity during judged competition, providing a "cut" appearance for aesthetic purposes.

There may be several caveats for individuals who use glycerol supplements, including health and performance issues. Although the dosages used in these studies appear to be safe, researchers indicate that if larger doses are used there may be some concern with the possibility of excess fluid being retained in the intracellular spaces, leading to abnormal pressures and possible tissue damage. Some investigators suggest glycerol-induced hyperhydration may predispose individuals to hyponatremia. Additionally, reviewers indicate that glycerol supplementation may cause nausea, vomiting, and headaches in some subjects, all of which are symptoms of hyponatremia.

For some athletes, glycerol supplementation may be ergolytic, not ergogenic. Studies showing ergogenic effects of glycerol-induced hyperhydration have used cycling protocols. Although hyperhydration may be ergogenic for cyclists, who need not be too concerned with the additional body weight associated with water retention, runners may be at a slight disadvantage because they need to expend energy to move the extra water weight. If the potential benefits of hyperhydration do not counteract the potential adverse effects of the extra weight, exercise performance may not be improved and may be impaired. However, a recent report in *Runner's World* magazine indicated that several elite U.S. marathon runners used glycerol in some of their best marathons run in the heat.

For those who want to experiment with glycerol, a commercial product, Glycerate, is available with appropriate instructions. A sports drink, Pro Hydrator, also contains glycerol. Glycerine, sold in drug stores, is glycerol. It is not to be taken internally as sold, but should be diluted. One recommendation presented in *FitNews,* a publication of the American Running and Fitness Association, is to mix 36 milliliters of glycerol with 955 milliliters of water for each 100 pounds of body weight. This recommendation is in accord with amounts used in research. Roughly, this would be about 1.25 ounces of glycerol per quart of water. Thus, a 150-pound runner would need to consume 1.5 quarts of this concoction to hyperhydrate prior to performance.

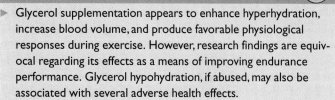

Key Concept Recap

▶ Glycerol supplementation appears to enhance hyperhydration, increase blood volume, and produce favorable physiological responses during exercise. However, research findings are equivocal regarding its effects as a means of improving endurance performance. Glycerol hypohydration, if abused, may also be associated with several adverse health effects.

Health Aspects

For athletes or people who exercise primarily to improve their health, there are two major health considerations related to water and electrolyte balance. We have already noted some of the potential adverse effects of hypohydration and electrolyte losses on physical performance and certain health conditions, such as

hyponatremia. This section concentrates on heat injuries, or heat illnesses, that may confront the physically active individual in a warm or hot environment. We shall also discuss high blood pressure, a health problem that may be aggravated by salt ingestion but ameliorated by proper diet and exercise training.

Heat Injuries

What are the potential health hazards of excessive heat stress imposed on the body?

One of the most serious threats to the performance and health of the physically active individual is heat injury, or heat illness. Barrow and Clark indicated heat-related illnesses caused 240 deaths annually, often in athletes. Any athlete who exercises in a warm environment is susceptible to heat injury, but the increasing popularity of road racing has generated concern for runners who are not prepared for strenuous exercise in the heat, or who participate in races that are poorly organized in regard to preventing and treating heat injuries.

The individual who exercises unwisely under conditions of environmental heat stress may experience one or several of a variety of heat injuries. Three factors may contribute to these injuries: increased core temperature, loss of body fluids, and loss of electrolytes. However, other factors may also be involved, as Noakes noted that several of the heat illnesses, such as muscle cramps, also occur during exercise in cold environments.

Figure 9.11 represents a simple flow chart of heat disorders. When a combination of exercise and environmental heat stress is imposed on the body, vasodilation and sweating increase as the body tries to cool itself. When these two adjustments begin to falter, problems develop. In essence, the circulation is attempting to

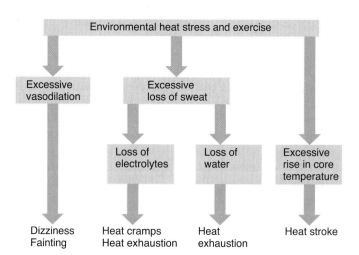

FIGURE 9.11 Basic flow chart for heat illnesses. The combination of environmental heat and exercise may cause an excessive vasodilation or pooling of blood. These conditions may decrease blood return to the heart and brain, causing dizziness and fainting. Excessive loss of sweat may cause significant losses of body water and electrolytes, leading to various heat illnesses. See text for details.

regulate both body temperature and blood pressure at the same time, and when stressed excessively, control of blood pressure wins and body temperature regulation is impaired. In addition, if the exercise metabolic load is very great, heat injuries may develop independent of circulatory and sweating inadequacies.

Excessive vasodilation may contribute to circulatory instability. The blood vessels expand and have a much greater capacity. Owing to a decreased relative blood volume and fall in blood pressure, dizziness and fainting may occur. This condition is called **heat syncope.**

Although no conclusive evidence is available, **heat cramps** may be caused by excessive loss of sodium, potassium, calcium, or magnesium through profuse sweating. Schwellnus indicated that the cause of muscle cramps may be due to abnormal spinal nerve control of the muscles. Possibly normal neural activity may be disturbed by an electrolyte imbalance. Bergeron notes that over time, sodium deficits can lead to muscle cramps. Thus, cramps usually appear late in the day following ingestion of large amounts of plain water, which can dilute electrolyte concentrations, and usually involve the muscles in the calf or the abdomen. To help prevent cramps, Bergeron recommends that at the first sign of subtle muscle twitching, which usually is about 20–30 minutes before full-blown cramps, the athlete should consume a salt solution, such as half a teaspoon of salt in 16 ounces of a sport drink. The athlete should then continue to drink small amounts of a similar solution (the same amount of salt in 32 ounces of a sports drink) at regular intervals for the remainder of the exercise session. Several case studies with tennis players who consistently experienced heat cramps have shown that increased intake of either sodium or magnesium, along with adequate fluids, was effective in preventing muscle cramping during exercise.

Several electrolyte products have been developed for athletes who are prone to muscle cramps. Products such as EnduroLyte and GatorLYTES contain sodium, potassium, calcium and magnesium, all of which may be helpful in the prevention of muscle cramping. However, Sulzer and others, studying triathletes who were either prone to muscle cramping or not, reported that serum electrolytes (sodium, chloride, potassium, and magnesium) did not appear to be associated with muscle cramps. The cause of muscle cramping still remains a mystery.

Water-depletion heat exhaustion is a common heat injury. It resembles heat syncope and is caused by inadequate circulation to the brain. Fatigue and nausea are common symptoms, and the individual is usually lying down but conscious. The skin is usually pale, cool, and covered with sweat. The rectal temperature is usually below 104°F (40°C). Heat exhaustion may incapacitate the individual for a few hours but is usually responsive to body-cooling treatments.

Anhidrotic heat exhaustion resembles water-depletion heat exhaustion, except that sweating has ceased. The skin is dry. Otherwise, the symptoms and treatment are comparable to those for water-depletion heat exhaustion. If the individual continues to exercise when sweating stops, the core temperature may rise rapidly, leading to heat stroke.

Salt-depletion heat exhaustion occurs most frequently in individuals who are not acclimatized to work in the heat and do not replace the salt they have lost over a period of several days.

Symptoms are similar to water-depletion heat exhaustion, although there may be a decrease in the sweat rate. Fatigue is common, and cramps may develop.

Heat stroke is the most dangerous heat injury, as it may be fatal. It usually is preceded by mental changes ranging from disorientation to unconsciousness, as characterized in figure 9.12. The skin is usually warm and red, and sweating may or may not be present. A rectal temperature over 105° F (40.5° C) is a characteristic sign. Heat stroke occurs primarily in the elderly and very young but may also occur in healthy, physically fit athletes. In such cases, it is classified as **exertional heat stroke.** Randy Eichner, a prominent sports medicine physician, indicated that heat stroke in sport is caused by a combination of hot environment, strenuous exercise, clothing that limits evaporation of sweat, inadequate adaptation to the heat, too much body fat, and/or lack of fitness, but it may also occur after excessive loss of body water. Several recent deaths of professional and collegiate athletes have been associated with such circumstances, and one involved the use of ephedrine, which as noted in chapter 13 can stimulate metabolism and heat production and predispose to heat stress. Exertional heat stroke may lead to rhabdomyolysis, damaged muscle tissue that leaks its contents into the blood, eventually leading to kidney damage and possible death.

What are the symptoms and treatment of heat injuries?

The symptoms of impending heat injury are variable. Among those reported are weakness, feeling of chills, pilo-erection (goose pimples) on the chest and upper arms, tingling arms, nausea, headache, faintness, disorientation, muscle cramping, and cessation of sweating. Continuing to exercise in a warm environment when experiencing any of these symptoms may lead to heat injury. Table 9.10 presents the major heat injuries along with principal causes, clinical findings, and treatment.

In particular, heat stroke is a medical emergency and requires immediate medical attention. The life-saving protocol is to cool the body rapidly and then transport to a medical facility as soon as possible. If possible, submerge the torso of the body in cool water. If not, place ice or cold towels or pour cold water over the body.

For collapsed athletes, Sallis indicates it is essential to check vital signs (especially rectal temperature if heat stroke is suspected), assess fluids status (dehydrated versus fluid overload) and perform laboratory tests when needed. He notes that the most common cause of collapse is low blood pressure due to blood pooling in the legs after cessation of exercise, which is benign and resolves upon rest. However, both hyponatremia, mentioned previously, and heat stroke are serious medical problems and need prompt medical attention.

Do some individuals have problems tolerating exercise in the heat?

A number of predisposing factors have been associated with heat injury, including gender, level of physical fitness, age, body composition, previous history of heat injury, and degree of acclimatization.

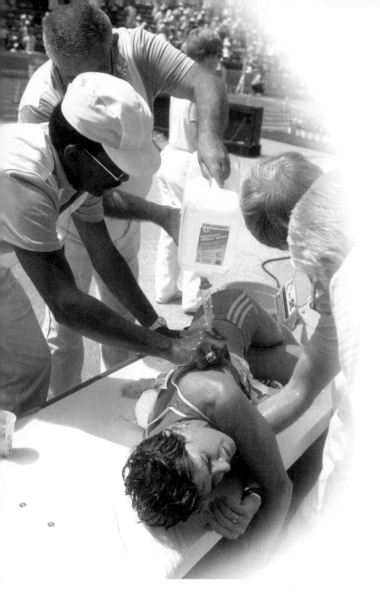

FIGURE 9.12 Heat stroke may be caused by exercising in the heat without taking proper precautions.

One of the major factors contributing to exertional heat illness is poor physical fitness. For example, in a recent study of Marine Corps recruits in training, Gardner and others found that one of the major predictors of exertional heat illness was poor aerobic fitness as measured by 1.5-mile run performance. In general, the better the physical fitness, the better tolerance to a given heat stress. However, even highly trained athletes may experience heat illnesses when using unsafe training practices. NCAA Division I wrestlers have died from heat stroke or related causes in attempts to reduce body weight for competition through exercise-induced sweating in a hot environment. For example, one of the wrestlers was wearing a rubber suit while riding a stationary bicycle in a steam-filled shower.

In earlier studies, investigators found that female subjects tolerated exercise in the heat less well than males. These findings may have been related to the higher percentage of body fat and the generally lower level of physical fitness of women in those studies. More recent studies, such as one by Arngrimsson and others, using subjects with comparable levels of physical fitness found that female responses to heat stress are similar to those

found in males. Kaciuba-Uscilko and Grucza note that while women's sweating response to heat stress is smaller than that of men, they are able to maintain their core body temperature on a similar level to that of men as a result of greater evaporative efficiency of sweating. On the other hand, Marsh and Jenkins indicated that increased progesterone levels during the luteal phase of the menstrual cycle cause increases in both core and skin temperatures and alter the temperature at which sweating begins, factors that could place females at an increased risk of developing heat illness during this time. Cheung and others found that female athletes not using oral contraceptives are at a thermoregulatory disadvantage during the luteal phase of the mensural cycle, suggesting that the use of oral contraceptives eliminates any differences in heat tolerance throughout the menstrual cycle.

Individuals at both ends of the age spectrum may have problems exercising in the heat. The American Academy of Pediatrics (AAP) noted that when compared to adults, young children may produce more metabolic heat during exercise in comparison to their body size, do not have as great a sweating capacity, and have a reduced capacity to convey heat from the core to the skin. These factors would increase the chances of heat injury. The American College of Sports Medicine, in a recent consensus statement, indicated that sports such as youth football may pose increased risks. The AAP recently outlined new recommendations for preventing heat illnesses in children, which are in accord with the recommendations provided in the next section.

At high levels of heat stress, tolerance to the heat is decreased in older individuals, possibly because they sweat less. Reduced heat toleration in the elderly may also be related to fitness levels. As more and more people become and remain physically active throughout middle age and advanced years, we may see the older person tolerating exercise in the heat as well as younger adults. Although Kenney and Chiu have found that during exercise in a warm environment older adults exhibit decreased thirst sensation and reduce fluid intake, Baker found that when exercising intermittingly in the heat, older men and women consumed adequate fluids to rehydrate and consumed more when sports drinks were available compared to water. Nevertheless, older athletes need to be especially diligent in following recommended hydration strategies before, during, and after exercise.

Obese individuals not only have high amounts of body fat to deter heat losses, but also generate more heat during exercise because of a low level of fitness; thus they are more susceptible to heat injuries. In the Marine Corps study cited previously, another major predictor of exertional heat illness was a higher body weight in relation to height.

Individuals who have experienced previous heat injury may be less tolerant to exercise in the heat. Many individuals do regain heat tolerance 8–12 weeks after heat injury. Others lose some of the ability for the circulatory system to adjust to heat stress, possibly because temperature-regulating centers in the brain are irreversibly damaged. The transfer of heat from the core to the skin becomes impaired and the body temperature rises faster.

One of the more important factors determining an individual's response to exercise in the heat is degree of acclimatization, which is discussed on the following pages. Although some individuals may be susceptible to heat illnesses, all individuals who exercise

TABLE 9.10   Heat injuries: causes, clinical findings, and treatment

Heat injury	Causes	Clinical findings	Treatment*
Heat syncope	Excessive vasodilation; pooling of blood in the skin	Fainting Weakness Fatigue	Place on back in cool environment; give cool fluids
Heat cramps	Excessive loss of electrolytes in sweat; inadequate salt intake	Cramps	Rest in cool environment; oral ingestion of salt drinks; salt foods daily; medical treatment in severe cases
Salt-depletion heat exhaustion	Excessive loss of electrolytes in sweat; inadequate salt intake	Nausea Fatigue Fainting Cramps	Rest in cool environment; replace fluids and salt by mouth; medical treatment in severe cases
Water-depletion heat exhaustion	Excessive loss of sweat; inadequate fluid intake	Fatigue Nausea Cool, pale skin Active sweating Rectal temperature lower than 104°F	Rest in cool environment; drink cool fluids; cool body with water; medical treatment if serious
Anhidrotic heat exhaustion	Same as water-depletion heat exhaustion	Nausea Sweating stopped Dry skin Rectal temperature lower than 104°F	Same as water-depletion heat exhaustion
Heat stroke	Excessive body temperature	Headache Vomiting Disorientation Unconsciousness Rectal temperature greater than 105°F	Cool body immediately to 102°F (38.9°C) with ice packs, ice, or cold water; give cool drinks with glucose if conscious; administer intravenous fluids if available; get medical help immediately

*Begin treatment as soon as possible. In cases of suspected heat stroke, begin immediately.

under warm or hot environmental conditions may benefit from the following recommendations.

How can I reduce the hazards associated with exercise in a hot environment?

In a recent review, Eichner indicated that the best treatment for heat illness is prevention. The following list represents a number of guidelines, which, if followed, will reduce considerably your chances of suffering heat injury. For additional information, you may contact the Gatorade Sports Science Institute at www.gssiweb.com.

1. Check the temperature and humidity conditions before exercising. Even if the dry temperature is only 65–75°F, a high humidity will increase the heat stress. Warm, humid conditions cause fatigue sooner, so slow your pace or shorten your exercise session.
2. Exercise in the cool of the morning or evening to avoid the heat of the day.
3. Exercise in the shade, if possible, to avoid radiation from the sun. If you run in the sun, wear an appropriate sunscreen to prevent sun damage to the skin.
4. Wear minimal clothing that is loose to allow air circulation, white or a light color to reflect radiant heat, and porous to permit evaporation. Do not wear a hat if running in the shade, but wear a loose hat if running in the sun.
5. If you are running and there is a breeze, plan your route so that you are running into the wind during the last part of your run. The breeze will help cool you more effectively at the time you need it most.
6. Drink cold fluids periodically. For a long training run, plan your route so that it passes some watering holes, such as gas stations or other sources of water. Alternatively, you may purchase a special water-bottle belt or backpack that will help you carry your own water supply. Take frequent water breaks, consuming about 6–8 ounces of water every 15 minutes or so. During exercise, thirst is not an adequate stimulus to replace water losses, so you should drink before you get thirsty.

7. Replenish your water daily. Keep a record of your body weight. For each pound you lose, drink about 20–24 ounces of fluid. Your body weight should be back to normal before your next workout.

8. Hyperhydrate if you plan to perform prolonged, strenuous exercise in the heat. In essence, drink about 16 or more ounces of fluid 30–60 minutes prior to exercising.

9. Replenish lost electrolytes (salt) if you have sweated excessively. Put a little extra salt on your meals and eat foods high in potassium, such as bananas and citrus fruits.

10. Avoid excessive intake of protein, as extra heat is produced in the body when protein is metabolized. This may contribute slightly to the heat stress.

11. Avoid dietary supplements containing ephedrine. Ephedrine is a potent stimulant that can increase metabolism and heat production, leading to an increased body temperature during exercise in warm environmental conditions and predisposing to heat illness.

12. Avoid consuming dietary supplements or beverages with caffeine several hours before exercising. Caffeine may increase the stress in two ways. First, it is a diuretic and may increase body-water losses. Although caffeinated beverages do provide fluids, noncaffeinated beverages may be preferable as there would be no caffeine-induced body-water losses. Second, caffeine will increase metabolic heat production at rest, which will raise the body temperature prior to exercise.

13. Because alcohol is a diuretic, excess amounts should be avoided the night before competition or prolonged exercise in the heat.

14. If you are sedentary, overweight, or aged, you are less likely to tolerate exercise in the heat and should therefore use extra caution.

15. Be aware of the signs and symptoms of heat exhaustion and heat stroke, as well as the treatment for each. Chills, goose pimples, tingling arms, dizziness, weakness, fatigue, mental disorientation, nausea, and headaches are some symptoms that may signify the onset of heat illness. Stop activity, get to a cool place, and consume some cool fluids.

16. Do not exercise if you have been ill or have had a fever within the last few days.

17. If you plan to compete in a sport held under hot environmental conditions, you must become acclimatized to exercise in the heat.

How can I become acclimatized to exercise in the heat?

It is a well-established fact that **acclimatization** to the heat will help increase performance in warm environments as compared with an unacclimatized state. Simply living in a hot environment confers a small amount of acclimatization. Physical training, in and of itself, provides a significant amount of acclimatization, possibly up to 50 percent of that which can be expected, and also increases body-water levels. However, neither of these two adjustments, either singly or together, can prevent the deterioration of exercise performance in the heat by an unacclimatized individual.

Thus, a period of active acclimatization is necessary to optimize performance when exercising in the heat.

The technique of acclimatization is relatively simple. Simply cut back on the intensity or duration of your normal activity. When the hot weather begins, moderate your activity. Do not avoid exercise in the heat completely, but after an initial reduction in your activity level, increase it gradually. For example, if you were running five miles a day, cut your distance back to two to three miles in the heat; if you need to do five a day, do the remaining miles in the evening. Eventually build up to three, four, and five miles. The acclimatization process usually takes about one to two weeks to complete. However, even when acclimatized, an athlete's endurance capacity in the heat, particularly with high humidity, still will be less than under cooler conditions.

If you live in a cool climate, like New England, and want to compete in a marathon in Florida in January, how do you become acclimatized? Exercising indoors at a warmer temperature will help. Extra layers of clothes can help prevent evaporation and build a hot, humid microclimate around your body. Research has shown that this technique can provide a degree of acclimatization. However, this is advisable only in cool weather and should not be attempted under hot conditions. Wearing a sweat suit or rubberized suit while exercising in the heat may precipitate heat illness. Moreover, even in a cool environment this technique may cause heat injury. Again, be wary of the symptoms of impending heat illness.

Nielsen indicated that repeated exposure to a high core temperature during exercise helps the body make the following important adjustments during acclimatization to the heat. In a recent review, Kent Pandolf indicated that most of the following adjustments occur in 4–6 days, but full acclimatization may take 7–14 days or more. Bar-Or notes that heat acclimatization in children takes several weeks.

1. The plasma volume expands considerably to increase the total blood volume. This occurs because the blood vessels conserve more protein and sodium, which tend to hold water.

2. The increased blood volume allows the heart to pump more blood per beat, so the stress on the heart is reduced.

3. When volume increases, more blood flows to the muscles and skin. The muscles receive more oxygen and skin cooling increases, improving endurance performance.

4. Less muscle glycogen may be used as an energy source at a given rate of exercise, sparing this energy source in endurance events.

5. The sweat glands hypertrophy and secrete about 30 percent more sweat, allowing for greater evaporative heat loss.

6. The amount of salt in the sweat decreases by about 60 percent; evaporation becomes more efficient and electrolytes are conserved.

7. Sweating starts at a lower core temperature, leading to earlier cooling.

8. The core temperature will not rise as high or as rapidly as in the unacclimatized state.

9. The psychological feeling of stress is reduced at a given exercise rate.

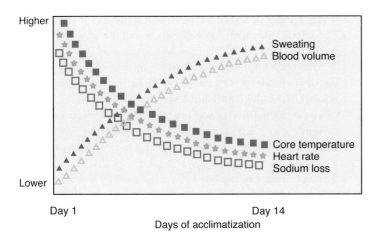

FIGURE 9.13 Changes with acclimatization. Acclimatization to the heat for 7 to 14 days will lead to an increase in the blood volume and the ability to sweat. For a standardized exercise task in the heat, these changes will lead to a lower heart rate, less sodium loss, and a lower core temperature. These changes will lead to improved exercise performance in the heat.

In essence, as illustrated in figure 9.13, these changes increase the ability of the body to dissipate heat with less stress on the cardiovascular system. The end result is a more effective body-temperature control and improved performance when exercising in the heat. These adaptations may be maintained by exercising in the heat several days per week but are lost in about 7–10 days in a cool environment. If you are interested in learning more about acclimatization, consult the review by Maughan and Shirreffs.

High Blood Pressure

What is high blood pressure, or hypertension?

Everybody has blood pressure. Without it we would not be able to sustain body metabolism. Simply speaking, blood pressure is the force that the blood exerts against the blood vessel walls. Although pressure is present in all types of blood vessels, the arterial blood pressure is the one most commonly measured and most important to our health. Blood pressure is usually measured by a sphygmomanometer, which records the pressure in millimeters of mercury (mmHg). Blood pressure readings are given in two numbers, for example 120/80 mmHg. The higher number represents the *systolic* phase, when the heart is pumping blood through the arteries. The lower number represents the *diastolic* phase, when the heart is resting between beats and blood is flowing back into it. Two important determinants of blood pressure are the volume of blood in the circulation and the resistance to blood flow, known as peripheral vascular resistance.

High blood pressure, also known as **hypertension** (hyper = high; tension = pressure), is known as a silent disease. At least 65 million individuals in the United States have hypertension. The Consumers Union recently referred to high blood pressure as an uncontrolled epidemic, noting that most individuals with hypertension do not have it under control. One reason is that nearly a third do not even know they are hypertensive, mainly because it has no outstanding symptoms. Some general symptoms include headaches, dizziness, and fatigue, but since they can be caused by a multitude of other factors, they may not be recognized as symptoms of high blood pressure. Although a great deal of research about the cause of high blood pressure has been conducted, the exact cause is unknown in about 90 percent of all cases. In these cases, the condition is known as essential hypertension, which cannot be cured, although lifestyle changes or medications can lower the pressure by reducing the blood volume or decreasing the peripheral vascular resistance.

High blood pressure is dangerous for several reasons. The heart must work much harder to pump the extra blood volume or to overcome the peripheral vascular resistance. This normally leads to an enlarged heart. Over time the increase in heart size becomes excessive and the efficiency of the heart actually decreases, making it more prone to a heart attack. Second, high blood pressure may directly damage the arterial walls. It is thought to be a major contributing factor in the development of atherosclerosis and a predisposing factor to coronary disease and stroke. High blood pressure is itself a disease and is also involved in the etiology of other diseases. It is one of the primary risk factors for heart disease.

The National Research Council has noted that any definition of high blood pressure is arbitrary. Traditionally, physicians have used elevations in diastolic blood pressure as the basis for their diagnosis, but the Joint National Committee on Detection, Evaluation, and Treatment of High Blood Pressure (JNCDET) of the National Institutes of Health, in its recent classification of blood pressure for adults age 18 years and older, includes both systolic and diastolic pressures. The classification system is presented in table 9.11.

How is high blood pressure treated?

Many individuals with essential hypertension need to take medications to control their blood pressure. A variety of drugs are available to treat hypertension, including diuretics, beta-blockers, angiotensin-converting enzymes (ACE) inhibitors, and calcium-channel blockers. The Consumers Union recommends that if your blood pressure is elevated, you and your doctor need to take aggressive action. If drug therapy is recommended, you may need to experiment with your physician as to type and dose of medicine

TABLE 9.11 Classification of blood pressure for adults age 18 years and older

Category	Systolic (mmHg)	Diastolic (mmHg)
Normal	<120	<80
Pre-hypertension	120–139	80–89
Hypertension		
Stage 1	140–159	90–99
Stage 2	>160	>100

Source: National Heart, Lung, and Blood Institute.

to use. This is especially important for athletic individuals. Niedfeldt suggests using drugs that are less likely to have adverse effects on exercise performance. For example, diuretics and beta-blockers may impair aerobic endurance performance. Physicians should also be aware that use of beta-blockers is prohibited for competition in some sports. Tanji and Batt provide a detailed discussion of the pharmacological treatment of hypertension in physically active individuals.

Other than impairment of aerobic endurance capacity, blood-pressure drugs may cause other adverse health effects. Thus, a nonpharmacologic approach is often a first choice of treatment in cases of mild to moderate hypertension. In recent reviews, Campbell, summarizing the recommendations of the Canadian Consensus Conference dealing with high blood pressure prevention and control, and Appel indicated that a variety of lifestyle changes may be important in the nonpharmacological treatment of hypertension, including several dietary practices and exercise.

What dietary modifications may help reduce or prevent hypertension?

How much and what you eat may influence your blood pressure. The following are the key points to help reduce or prevent hypertension.

1. *Achieve and maintain a healthy body weight.* Numerous studies have shown that reducing body weight, even as little as 10 pounds, will reduce blood pressure in overweight, hypertensive individuals. Maintaining a healthy body weight may be one of the most effective preventive measures. Thus, restriction of caloric intake to either lose or maintain body weight may be a helpful dietary strategy.

2. *Reduce or moderate sodium intake.* This is one of the most controversial recommendations, but it may be a prudent behavior for most individuals. Several recent reviews have indicated only modest reductions in blood pressure following decreased sodium intake. For example, in a meta-analysis of intervention trials, Luft reported a 2-mmHg blood pressure decrease in normotensive individuals. Fodor, presenting the viewpoint of the Canadian Consensus Conference, indicated that restrictions of salt intake for the normotensive population is not recommended at present. On the other hand, in the same meta-analysis Luft reported a 5-mmHg blood pressure decrease in hypertensive patients, and Fodor noted that salt intake should be moderately restricted in hypertensive patients. De Wardener and MacGregor contend that the human race is genetically programmed to consume less than 1 gram of salt per day, but in most societies the diet contains 6–12 grams of salt per day. The result is that blood pressure rises with age, which contributes to increased incidence of heart disease and strokes. In general, current scientific evidence indicates salt restriction may be beneficial for hypertensive individuals but not necessary for normotensive individuals although some

health professionals recommend reduced intakes for everyone. The interested reader may wish to consult the opposing viewpoints presented by Kaplan and McCarron.

Why then might it be prudent for most normotensive individuals to moderate salt intake? It is true that most individuals possess physiological control systems that effectively maintain a proper balance of sodium in the body. It is also true that current medical and scientific evidence does not support the concept that a normal intake of salt in amounts common to the U.S. diet causes hypertension in persons with normal blood pressure. This finding has been supported by a recent meta-analysis—by Midgley and others—of 56 research trials involving dietary sodium intake and blood pressure. However, many individuals are sodium-sensitive, or salt-sensitive, in that their blood pressure may increase with excessive consumption of salt. Possibly because of a defect in excretion, sodium accumulates in the body and holds fluids, particularly blood, thereby raising the blood pressure. In their review, McCarron and Reusser report that salt sensitivity is present in about 30 percent of normotensive and 50 percent of hypertensive persons, and is more prevalent among African Americans and older individuals. That being so, and since many individuals do not know their blood pressure, millions of Americans may benefit from the recommendation to moderate salt intake. Moreover, the American Institute for Cancer Research viewpoint on sodium in the diet is that there appears to be no harm in reducing the amount of salt you eat, and there may be some benefits as well. For example, you may lower your risk for stomach cancer even if it's unclear whether your blood pressure will drop.

The current prudent medical recommendation for dietary prevention or treatment of hypertension is to decrease sodium consumption simply by eating a wide variety of foods in their natural state. Avoid highly salted foods, restrict intake of processed foods, and hide your salt shakers. The recommended upper limit is somewhat less than 6 grams of salt per day, just a little over 1 teaspoon, the equivalent of about 2.3 grams of sodium. The AI, based on potential healthful effects on blood pressure, is only 1.5 grams, or less than 4 grams of salt daily.

It should be noted that decreasing salt and sodium intake poses some practical difficulties. Most salt we eat comes from the packaged foods we buy. Salt is also high in most restaurant foods; some single servings of fast food have over 1,000 milligrams of sodium, some up to nearly 5,000 milligrams. Thus, one might have to buy most foods in their natural state and prepare and cook them at home, from scratch. For those with hypertension, it may be a challenge—but worth it.

3. *Consume a diet rich in fruits, vegetables, and low-fat dairy foods and with reduced saturated and total fat.* McCarron and Reusser note that large-scale studies have shown that whereas manipulation of single nutrients may have beneficial health effects for some individuals, it is improving the total dietary profile that will consistently provide health benefits, such as reducing high blood pressure. The **DASH**

(Dietary Approaches to Stop Hypertension) **diet** emphasizes fruits and vegetables, nuts, low-fat dairy foods, fish and chicken instead of red meat, low-sugar and low-refined carbohydrate foods, and reduced saturated and total fat. The DASH eating plan for a 2,000 Calorie diet is presented in table 9.12. The number of servings may be modified to meet other caloric requirements. For a detailed DASH eating plan, visit www.nhlbi.nih.gov, and click on Heart/Vascular and then "Facts about the DASH eating plan."

In a recent review of his and other studies, Appel indicated that the DASH diet reduced blood pressure in both normotensive and hypertensive adults. The DASH diet is rich in potassium, magnesium, calcium, and fiber, which have been suggested to help prevent high blood pressure. The JNCDET, in its sixth report, particularly recommends increased consumption of potassium, which is abundant in fruits and vegetables. Other studies have reported that DASH-type diets decreased blood pressure and the risk of stroke, but also induced other health benefits, such as improved bone mineral status. The DASH diet is also rich in numerous phytochemicals, which may be associated with multiple health benefits.

For those with hypertension, and even normotensive individuals, some health professionals recommend the DASH diet and the extra effort to cut back to 1,500 milligrams of sodium per day. In a recent randomized, controlled trial, Sacks and others found that the DASH diet for 30 days resulted in significant reductions in both systolic and diastolic blood pressure. All individuals in this study were also randomly assigned to three different levels of salt intake for a 30-day period, and the decrease in blood pressure was greatest when subjects consumed the diet with the lowest amount of salt, only 1,500 milligrams per day.

TABLE 9.12 The DASH Eating Plan

Food Group	Servings	Serving Sizes	Examples and Notes	Significance to the DASH Eating Plan
Grains and grain products	7–8 per day	1 slice bread 1 oz dry cereal $^1/_2$ cup cooked rice, pasta, or cereal	Whole wheat bread, English muffin, pita bread, bagel, cereals, oatmeal, unsalted pretzels, popcorn	Major sources of energy and fiber
Vegetables	4–5 per day	1 cup raw leafy vegetable $^1/_2$ cup cooked vegetable 6 oz vegetable juice	Tomatoes, potatoes, carrots, green peas, broccoli, kale, spinach, lima beans, sweet potatoes	Rich sources of potassium, magnesium, and fiber
Fruits	4–5 per day	6 oz fruit juice 1 medium fruit $^1/_4$ cup dried fruit	Apricots, bananas, dates, grapes, oranges, orange juice, melons, peaches pineapples, raisins, strawberries	Important sources of potassium, magnesium, and fiber
Lowfat or fat free dairy foods	2–3 per day	8 oz milk 1 cup yogurt $1^1/_2$ oz cheese	Fat free (skim) milk, fat free or lowfat regular or frozen yogurt, lowfat and fat free cheese	Major sources of calcium and protein
Meats, poultry and fish	2 or less per day	3 oz cooked meats, poultry, or fish	Select only lean; trim away visible fats; broil, roast, or boil, instead of frying; remove skin from poultry	Rich sources of protein and magnesium
Nuts, seeds, and dry beans	4–5 per week	$^1/_3$ cup or $1^1/_2$ oz nuts 2 Tbsp or $^1/_2$ oz seeds $^1/_2$ cup cooked dry beans or peas	Almonds, mixed nuts, peanuts, walnuts, sunflower seeds, kidney beans	Rich sources of energy, magnesium, potassium, protein, and fiber
Fats and oils	2–3 per day	1 tsp soft margarine 1 Tbsp lowfat mayonnaise 2 Tbsp light salad dressing 1 tsp vegetable oil	Soft margarine, lowfat mayonnaise, light salad dressing, vegetable oil (olive, corn, canola)	DASH has 27 percent of Calories as fat, including fat in or added to foods. 1 Tbsp fat free dressing equals 0 servings
Sweets	5 per week	1 Tbsp sugar 1 Tbsp jelly or jam $^1/_2$ oz jelly beans	Sugar, jelly, jam, jelly beans, hard candy, sorbet, ices	

Adapted from The DASH Eating Plan. National Heart, Lung, and Blood Institute. For more details, go to www.nhlbi.nih.gov/health/public/heart/hbp/dash.

4. *Moderate alcohol consumption.* As noted in chapter 4, moderate alcohol consumption may actually confer some health benefits, particularly the prevention of cardiovascular disease. However, excess alcohol intake may increase the heart disease risk, possibly because it is linked to high blood pressure.

As you probably noticed, all of these recommendations are in accord with the Prudent Healthy Diet. The more of these recommendations you follow, the better. In one study, subjects who lost weight, increased physical activity, and reduced sodium and alcohol intake experienced significant reductions in blood pressure, but subjects who also adhered to the DASH diet experienced the greatest reduction.

Can exercise help prevent or treat hypertension?

Regular mild- to moderate-intensity aerobic exercise, such as jogging, brisk walking, swimming, cycling, and aerobic dancing, has also been recommended to reduce high blood pressure. Since exercise may be an effective means of losing excess body fat, it may exert a beneficial effect through this avenue. However, the exact role or mechanism of exercise as an independent factor in lowering blood pressure has not been totally resolved. Kramer and others theorize that exercise may exert favorable effects on the hypothalamus, inducing favorable neural control to decrease constriction of blood vessels, one factor contributing to elevated blood pressure.

Although a number of studies have shown that exercise training helps decrease resting systolic blood pressure in those who are hypertensive and may even elicit a slight decrease in those with normal blood pressure, not all studies are in agreement. Not all individuals will experience a decrease in blood pressure from an exercise program; they may be exercise-insensitive, or nonresponders. Nevertheless, most health professionals find the available information sufficient to justify an aerobic exercise program as a useful adjunct for the treatment of high blood pressure.

Most research has focused on the chronic effect of exercise training on blood pressure. Most recent reviews and meta-analyses report significant reductions in both diastolic and systolic blood pressure, more so in hypertensive than normotensive individuals. However, the magnitudes of the reductions vary, ranging from a 2.4–18.0 mmHg reduction in diastolic blood pressure, and 3.4–13.0 mmHg reduction in systolic blood pressure.

The American College of Sports Medicine, in its recent position stand on exercise and hypertension, stated that exercise is the cornerstone therapy for the primary prevention, treatment, and control of hypertension. These are some of the major points of the position stand.

- Exercise programs that involve endurance activities, such as walking, jogging, running, or cycling, coupled with resistance training, help to prevent the development of hypertension and to lower blood pressure in adults.

- Exercise should be done daily for 30 minutes or more at a moderate level.
- A higher level of physical activity and fitness resulting from long-term exercise training has a protective effect against hypertension; fitter people with hypertension will have lower blood pressure than those who are less fit.
- Even a single session (acute) exercise bout provides an immediate reduction in blood pressure, which can last for a major portion of the day. Promoting the benefits of lowering blood pressure through single bouts of exercise may help motivate people to exercise.

Special considerations for exercise with hypertension include the following:

- Individuals with controlled hypertension and no cardiovascular or kidney disease may participate in an exercise program.
- Overweight adults should use exercise to lose weight.
- People on medications, such as beta-blockers, should be cautious of developing heat illness when exercising.
- Adults with hypertension should extend the cool-down period of the workout; some medications may cause blood pressure to lower too much after abruptly ending exercise.

Individuals who have high blood pressure and who have concerns about exercising should consult with their physicians about mode and intensity of exercise. Although aerobic exercise may help reduce blood pressure at rest and may evoke a lessened blood pressure rise during exercise, a protective effect, other exercises may be harmful. For example, high-intensity anaerobic exercise and activities that require intense straining, lifting, or hanging, such as isometric exercises, weight lifting, or pull-ups might be inappropriate for some individuals. The use of hand-held weights in aerobic exercises may also be a concern. These activities may create a physiological response that rapidly raises the blood pressure to rather high levels. This increase may be hazardous to someone whose resting blood pressure is already at an elevated level.

Key Concept Recap

▶ Heat injuries, of which heat stroke is potentially the most dangerous, may be due to increased body core temperature, loss of body fluids, or loss of electrolytes. Some individuals, such as the obese, are more susceptible to heat injury.

▶ The general treatment for heat-stress illnesses is to rest, drink cool liquids, and cool the body. Rapid body cooling is essential in suspected cases of heat stroke.

▶ If you exercise in the heat, you should be aware of signs of impending heat injury, such as chills, dizziness, and weakness. You should also be aware of methods to reduce heat gain to the body and methods to facilitate heat loss.

▶ Acclimatization to exercise in the heat takes about 1–2 weeks, but endurance capacity in the heat is still limited somewhat even when one is fully acclimatized.

> Lifestyle practices to help prevent or treat high blood pressure include maintaining an optimal body weight, aerobic exercise, moderation in salt and sodium intake, moderation in alcohol consumption, and increased intake of fruits, vegetables, whole grains, low-fat dairy products, and foods rich in potassium, magnesium, and calcium.

Check for Yourself

Have your blood pressure checked at rest. If possible, have it checked immediately after both an aerobic-type and resistance-type exercise.

APPLICATION EXERCISE

Determine your body temperature response and sweating rate.

First, measure your body temperature accurately before exercise. An oral thermometer is acceptable, but keep your mouth closed tightly during all measurements. Also, weigh yourself exactly in a pair of dry sports shorts.

Second, exercise for about 30–60 minutes, preferably under warm environmental conditions, either indoors or outdoors. Record exactly the amount of fluid you consume during exercise.

Third, immediately after exercise, record your body temperature. Then, immediately towel dry and weigh yourself in the same dry pair of sport shorts. Calculate your body temperature increase from the difference between the preexercise and postexercise recordings. Calculate your sweat loss by subtracting your postexercise weight from your initial weight and adding to this amount the number of ounces of fluid you consumed. This will provide you with your sweat rate for the time you exercised, which you can then calculate to sweat rate per hour.

If feasible, conduct this little self-experiment before and after acclimatization to exercise in the heat and compare the responses. What might you expect to find?

Body Temperature Response and Sweating Rate

Step 1		Step 2	Step 3	
Preexercise temperature		Fluid consumed during exercise	Postexercise temperature	
Preexercise weight			Postexercise weight	

Determination of body temperature response and sweating rate to exercise

Sweating rate

A. Enter your preexercise body weight (nearest 0.25 pound). _____

B. Enter your postexercise body weight in pounds (nearest 0.25 pound). _____

C. Subtract B from A. _____

D. Convert C to ounces (1 pound = 16 fluid ounces). _____

E. Enter the amount of fluid (in ounces) you consumed during the run. _____

F. Add E to D. _____

G. Divide F by the number of minutes of exercise to calculate sweat rate per minute. _____

H. Multiply G by 60 to obtain sweat rate per hour. _____

The final figure is the approximate number of ounces you need to consume per hour to remain well hydrated.

Body temperature response

A. Enter your preexercise body temperature in degrees Fahrenheit or Celsius. ____

B. Enter your postexercise body temperature in degrees Fahrenheit or Celsius. ____

C. Subtract B from A. ____

The final figure represents your core body temperature increase for the intensity and duration of exercise and for the given environmental conditions (air temperature, humidity, solar radiation).

Review Questions—Multiple Choice

1. Which of the following blood pressure values for adults 18 years of age and older represents the minimal blood pressure for the first stage of hypertension (mild)? The values listed are systolic and diastolic, in that order.
   (a) 130 and 80
   (b) 130 and 90
   (c) 140 and 90
   (d) 160 and 100
   (e) 210 and 120

2. Which of the following does *not* occur in acclimatization to exercise in the heat?
   (a) increased sweat production during exercise
   (b) increased blood volume
   (c) a lower rise in the core temperature during exercise
   (d) a lesser rise in the heart rate response to exercise

(e) an increased sodium loss in each liter of sweat

3. Which of the following statements is false?
   (a) The maximal sweat rate appears to be about 2–3 liters per hour.
   (b) Dehydration as low as 2 percent of the body weight may lead to a decrease in aerobic endurance performance.
   (c) Sweat is mainly water.
   (d) The major electrolytes found in sweat are calcium and potassium.

4. Which of the following is most limited in the DASH diet?
   (a) calcium
   (b) fiber
   (c) magnesium
   (d) sodium
   (e) potassium
   (f) phytonutrients

5. Excessive loss of sweat during exercise in the heat will lead to a condition in the body known as
   (a) hyperhydration
   (b) hypohydration
   (c) homeostasis
   (d) normohydration
   (e) euhydration

6. Which of the following is not one of the physical means whereby heat is lost from the human body?
   (a) condensation
   (b) conduction
   (c) evaporation
   (d) convection
   (e) radiation

7. A high relative humidity and sunshine impose a heat stress during exercise by their adverse effects on the body, respectively, as:
   (a) increased condensation of sweat and decreased radiant heat to the body
   (b) increased convection heat loss and decreased radiant heat to the body
   (c) decreased evaporation of sweat and increased radiant heat to the body
   (d) decreased condensation of sweat and decreased convection of heat to the body
   (e) increased evaporation of sweat and increased convection of heat to the body

8. Calculate the increase in the body temperature, in degrees Celsius, that would occur if an individual was unable to dissipate heat and was exercising at an intensity of 3 liters of oxygen per minute for 20 minutes. The athlete weighs 60 KG, her mechanical efficiency is 20 percent, and the specific heat of her body is 0.83.
   (a) 2.2
   (b) 4.8
   (c) 10.2

   (d) 6.0
   (e) 9.4

9. Which of the following statements regarding bottled water is false?
   (a) Bottled water is normally much more expensive than municipal water supplies.
   (b) Bottled water must conform to the same safety standards as municipal water supplies.
   (c) Some bottled waters are simply municipal water that has undergone purification.
   (d) Bottled water normally contains more fluoride than fluoridated municipal water supplies.

10. During prolonged endurance exercise in the heat, excessive intake of water and inadequate intake of salt may lead to a dangerous health condition known as
    (a) hypercalcemia
    (b) hypotension
    (c) hypohydration
    (d) hyponatremia
    (e) hyperkalemia

Answers to multiple-choice questions:
1. c; 2. e; 3. d; 4. d; 5. b; 6. a; 7. c; 8. b; 9. d; 10. d.

Review Questions—Essay Questions

1. Discuss the means whereby your body maintains normal water balance. Include in your discussion the role of the blood, hypothalamus, pituitary gland, antidiuretic hormone, and kidney.

2. Name the four components of heat stress that are recorded by the Wet Bulb Globe Temperature thermometer, and discuss how each factor may contribute to heat stress during exercise under warm environmental conditions.

3. Your friend is going to run a marathon. The projected weather forecast is sunny, warm, and humid. What advice would you offer regarding consumption of fluids, including carbohydrate and electrolytes, before and during the race?

4. List and discuss five strategies to help reduce the hazards associated with exercise in a hot environment.

5. What is high blood pressure? Why is it dangerous to your health? What lifestyle behaviors may help in its prevention or treatment?

References

Books

Armstrong, L. 2003. *Exertional Heat Illnesses.* Champaign, IL: Human Kinetics.

Buskirk, E., and Puhl, S. 1996. *Body Fluid Balance: Exercise and Sport.* Boca Raton, FL: CRC Press.

Driskell, J. A., and Wolinsky, I. 1999. *Macroelements, Water, and Electrolytes in Sports Nutrition.* Boca Raton, FL: CRC Press.

National Academy of Sciences. Institute of Medicine, Food and Nutrition Board. 2004. *Dietary Reference Intakes for Water, Potas-*

sium, Sodium, Chloride, and Sulfate. Washington, DC: National Academy Press.

National Research Council. 1989. *Diet and Health: Implications for Reducing Chronic Disease Risk.* Washington, DC: National Academy Press.

Noakes, T. 2003. *Lore of Running.* Champaign, IL: Human Kinetics.

Reviews

American Academy of Pediatrics. 2000. Climatic heat stress and the exercising child and adolescent. *Pediatrics* 106:158–59.

American College of Sports Medicine. 2005. Youth football: Heat stress and injury risk. *Medicine & Science in Sports & Exercise* 37:1421–30.

American College of Sports Medicine. 2004. American College of Sports Medicine position stand: Exercise and hypertension. *Medicine & Science in Sports & Exercise* 36:533–53.

American College of Sports Medicine. 1996. American College of Sports Medicine position stand: Exercise and fluid replacement. *Medicine & Science in Sports & Exercise* 28 (1): i–vii.

American College of Sports Medicine. 1996. American College of Sports Medicine position stand: Heat and cold illnesses during distance running. *Medicine & Science in Sports & Exercise* 28 (12): i–x.

American Institute for Cancer Research. 1999. Your best bet is to limit salt. *American Institute for Cancer Research Newsletter* 63 (Spring):8.

American Running and Fitness Association. 1996. Glycerol helps fluid balance. *FitNews* 14 (6): 1.

Appel, L. J. 1999. Nonpharmacologic therapies that reduce blood pressure: A fresh approach. *Clinical Cardiology* 22:III1–III5.

Armstrong, L. E., and Epstein, Y. 1999. Fluid-electrolyte balance during labor and exercise: Concepts and misconceptions. *International Journal of Sport Nutrition* 9:1–12.

Bar-Or, O. 1994. Children's responses to exercise in hot climates: Implications for performance and health. *Sports Science Exchange* 7 (2):1–4.

Bar-Or, O., and Wilk, B. 1996. Water and electrolyte replenishment in the exercising child. *International Journal of Sport Nutrition* 6:93–99.

Barr, S. I. 1999. Effects of dehydration on exercise performance. *Canadian Journal of Applied Physiology* 24:164–72.

Barrow, M. W., and Clark, K. A. 1998. Heat-related illnesses. *American Family Physician* 58:749–56.

Bergeron, M. 2002. Averting muscle cramps. *Physician and Sportsmedicine* 30 (11):14.

Bergeron, M. F. 2000. Sodium: The forgotten nutrient. *Sports Science Exchange* 13(3):1–4.

Bonci, L. 2002. "Energy" drinks: Help, harm, or hype? *Sports Science Exchange* 15 (1):1–4.

Brennan, F., and O'Conner, F. 2005. Emergency triage of collapsed endurance athletes. *Physician and Sportsmedicine* 33 (3):28–35.

Burfoot, A. 2004. Should you run naked? *Runner's World* 39 (9):47–48.

Burfoot, A. 2003. Drink to your health. *Runner's World.* 38 (7):52–59.

Burke, L. 2001. Nutritional needs for exercise in the heat. Comparative *Biochemistry and Physiology. Part A. Molecular & Integrative Physiology* 128:735–48.

Campbell, N. R., et al. 1999. Lifestyle modifications to prevent and control hypertension. 1. Methods and an overview of the Canadian recommendations. *Canadian Medical Association Journal* 160:S1–S6.

Cheung, S., and Sleivert, G. 2004. Multiple triggers for hyperthermic fatigue and exhaustion. *Exercise and Sports Sciences Reviews* 32:100–06.

Consumers Union. 2003. Clear choices for clean drinking water. *Consumers Reports* 68 (1):33–38.

Consumers Union. 2002. Blood-pressure perils. *Consumer Reports on Health* 14 (9):1, 4–6.

Consumers Union. 2002. High blood pressure: The uncontrolled epidemic. *Consumer Reports on Health* 14 (10):6–8.

Consumers Union. 1999. Do you drink enough water? *Consumer Reports on Health* 11 (11):8–10.

Coombes, J., and Hamilton, K. 2000. The effectiveness of commercially available sports drinks. *Sports Medicine* 29:181–209.

Costill, D. 1990. Gastric emptying of fluids during exercise. In *Perspectives in Exercise Science and Sports Medicine. Fluid Homeostasis During Exercise,* eds. C. Gisolfi and D. Lamb. Indianapolis, IN: Benchmark.

Costill, D. 1977. Sweating: Its composition and effects on body fluids. *Annals of the New York Academy of Sciences* 301:160–74.

Coyle, E. 2004. Fluid and fuel intake during exercise. *Journal of Sports Sciences* 22:39–55.

Coyle, E. 1994. Fluid and carbohydrate replacement during exercise: How much and why? *Sports Science Exchange* 7 (3):1–6.

Denton, D., et al. 1996. Hypothalamic integration of body fluid regulation. *Proceedings of the National Academy of Sciences* 93:7397–7404.

De Wardener, H., and MacGregor, G. 2002. Sodium and blood pressure. *Current Opinion in Cardiology* 17:360–67.

Doyle, L., and Cashman, K. 2004. The DASH diet may have beneficial effects on bone health. *Nutrition Reviews* 62:215–20.

Eichner, E. 2002. Heat stroke in sports: Causes, prevention, and treatment. *Sports Science Exchange* 15 (3):1–4.

Eichner, E. R. 1998. Treatment of suspected heat illness. *International Journal of Sports Medicine* 19:S150–S153.

Fagard, R. 2001. Exercise characteristics and the blood pressure response to dynamic physical training. *Medicine & Science in Sports & Exercise* 33:S484–S492.

Febbraio, M. 2001. Alterations in energy metabolism during exercise and heat stress. *Sports Medicine* 31:47–59.

Febbraio, M.A. 2000. Does muscle function and metabolism affect exercise performance in the heat? *Exercise and Sport Sciences Reviews* 28:171–76.

Fodor, J. G., et al. 1999. Lifestyle modifications to prevent and control hypertension. 5. Recommendations on dietary salt. *Canadian Medical Association Journal* 160:S29–S34.

Gardner, J. 2002. Death by water intoxication. *Military Medicine* 167:432–34.

Gisolfi, C. 1996. Fluid balance for optimal performance. *Nutrition Reviews* 54:S159–S168.

Gledhill, N. 1999. Haemoglobin, blood volume, cardiac function, and aerobic power. *Canadian Journal of Applied Physiology* 24:54–65.

Hargreaves, M., and Febbraio, M. 1998. Limits to exercise performance in the heat. *International Journal of Sports Medicine* 19:S115–S116.

Hew-Butler, T., et al. 2005. Consensus statement of the 1st International Exercise-Associated Hyponatremia Consensus Development Conference. *Clinical Journal of Sports Medicine* 15:208–13.

Hiller, D. 1989. Dehydration and hyponatremia during triathlons. *Medicine & Science in Sports & Exercise* 21:S219–S221.

Horswill, C. 1991. Does rapid weight loss by dehydration adversely affect high-power performance? *Sports Science Exchange* 3 (30):1–4.

Hsieh, M. 2004. Recommendations for treatment of hyponatremia at endurance events. *Sports Medicine* 34:231–38.

Jeukendrup, A., and Martin, J. 2001. Improving cycling performance: How should we spend our time and money? *Sports Medicine* 31:559–69.

Joint National Committee on Prevention, Detection, Evaluation and Treatment of High Blood Pressure. 1997. The Sixth Report of the Joint National Committee on Prevention, Detection, Evaluation and Treatment of High Blood Pressure. *Archives of Internal Medicine* 157:2413–46.

Kaciuba-Uscilko, H., and Grucza, R. 2001. Gender differences in thermoregulation. *Current Opinion in Clinical Nutrition and Metabolic Care* 4:533–36.

Kaplan, N. 2000. The dietary guideline for sodium: Should we shake it up? No. *American Journal of Clinical Nutrition* 71:1020–26.

Kenney, W. L. 2004. Dietary water and sodium requirements for active adults. *Sports Science Exchange* 17 (1):1–6.

Kramer, J., et al. 2002. Exercise and hypertension: A model for central neural plasticity. *Clinical and Experimental Pharmacology & Physiology* 29:122–26.

Lamb, D. R., and Shehata, A. 1999. Benefits and limitations to prehydration. *Sports Science Exchange* 12 (2):1–6.

Latzka, W., and Sawka, M. 2000. Hyperhydration and glycerol: Thermoregulatory effects during exercise in hot environments. *Canadian Journal of Applied Physiology* 25:536–45.

Lefferts, L. 1990. Water: Treat it right. *Nutrition Action Health Letter* 17:5–7.

Liebman, B. 2005. Pressure cooker: The scoop on salt. *Nutrition Action Health Letter* 32 (6):1–9.

Luetkemeier, M. J., et al. 1997. Dietary sodium and plasma volume levels with exercise. *Sports Medicine* 23:279–86.

Luft, F. C. 1998. Salt and hypertension at the close of the millennium. *Wiener Klinische Wochenschrift* 110:459–66.

Macdonald, I. 1992. Food and drink in sport. *British Medical Journal* 48:605–14.

Manz, F., et al. 2002. The most essential nutrient: Defining the adequate intake of water. *Journal of Pediatrics* 141:587–92.

Marino, F. 2002. Methods, advantages, and limitations of body cooling for exercise performance. *British Journal of Sports Medicine* 36:89–94.

Marsh, S., and Jenkins, D. 2002. Physiological responses to the menstrual cycle:

Implications for the development of heat illness in female athletes. *Sports Medicine* 32:601–14.

Maughan, R., et al. 1993. Fluid replacement in sport and exercise. A consensus statement. *British Journal of Sports Medicine* 27:34–35.

Maughan, R. J. 2000. Water and electrolyte loss and replacement in exercise. In *Nutrition in Sport,* ed. R. J. Maughan. Oxford: Blackwell Science.

Maughan, R. J. 1999. Exercise in the heat: Limitations to performance and the impact of fluid replacement strategies. Introduction to the symposium. *Canadian Journal of Applied Physiology* 24:149–51.

Maughan, R. J. 1998. The sports drink as a functional food: Formulations for successful performance. *Proceedings of the Nutrition Society* 57:15–23.

Maughan, R. J., and Nadel, E. R. 2000. Temperature regulation and fluid and electrolyte balance. In *Nutrition in Sport,* ed. R. J. Maughan. Oxford: Blackwell Science.

McCann, D. J., and Adams, W. C. 1997. Wet bulb globe temperature index and performance in competitive distance runners. *Medicine & Science in Sports & Exercise* 29:955–61.

McCarron, D. 2000. The dietary guideline for sodium: Should we shake it up? Yes. *American Journal of Clinical Nutrition* 71:1013–19.

McCarron, D., and Reusser, M. 2000. The power of food to improve multiple cardiovascular risk factors. *Current Atherosclerosis Reports* 2:482–86.

Meyer, F., and Bar-Or, O. 1994. Fluid and electrolyte loss during exercise: The pediatric angle. *Sports Medicine* 18:4–9.

Midgley, J., et al. 1996. Effect of reduced dietary sodium on blood pressure: A meta-analysis of randomized controlled trials. *Journal of the American Medical Association* 275:1590–97.

Murray, R. 1997. Drink. More! Advice from a world-class expert. *ACSM's Fitness Journal* 1 (1):19–23.

Naghii, M. 2000. The significance of water in sport and weight control. *Nutrition and Health* 14:127–32.

Niedfeldt, M. 2002. Managing hypertension in athletes and physically active patients. *American Family Physician* 66:445–52.

Nielsen, B. 1998. Heat acclimation: Mechanisms of adaptation to exercise in the heat. *International Journal of Sports Medicine* 19:S154–S156.

Noakes, T. 1993. Fluid replacement during exercise. *Exercise and Sport Sciences Reviews* 21:297–330.

Noakes, T. 1992. The hyponatremia of exercise. *International Journal of Sport Nutrition* 2:205–28.

Noakes, T. D. 1998. Fluid and electrolyte disturbances in heat illness. *International Journal of Sports Medicine* 19:S146–S149.

Pandolf, K. 1998. Time course of heat acclimation and its decay. *International Journal of Sports Medicine* 19:S157–S160.

Peters, H., et al. 1995. Gastrointestinal symptoms during exercise: The effect of fluid supplementation. *Sports Medicine* 20:65–76.

Rehrer, N. 2001. Fluid and electrolyte balance in ultra-endurance sport. *Sports Medicine* 31:701–15.

Robergs, R. A., and Griffin S. E. 1998. Glycerol: Biochemistry, pharmacokinetics and clinical and practical applications. *Sports Medicine* 26:145–67.

Sallis, R. 2004. Collapse in the endurance athlete. *Sports Science Exchange* 17 (4):1–6.

Sawka, M., et al. 2001. Hydration effects on thermoregulation and performance in the heat. *Comparative Biochemistry and Physiology. Part A. Molecular and Integrative Physiology* 128:679–90.

Sawka, M., et al. 2000. Effects of dehydration and rehydration on performance. In *Nutrition in Sport,* ed. R. J. Maughan. Oxford: Blackwell Science.

Sawka, M., and Greenleaf, J. 1992. Current concepts concerning thirst, dehydration, and fluid replacement: Overview. *Medicine & Science in Sports & Exercise* 24:643–44.

Sawka, M., and Pandolf, K. 1990. Effects of body water loss on physiological function and exercise performance. In *Perspectives in Exercise Science and Sports Medicine. Fluid Homeostasis During Exercise,* eds. C. Gisolfi and D. Lamb. Indianapolis, IN: Benchmark.

Schwellnus, M. P. 1999. Skeletal muscle cramps during exercise. *Physician and Sportsmedicine* 27 (12):109–15.

Shirreffs, S. M., and Maughan, R. J. 2000. Rehydration and recovery of fluid balance after exercise. *Exercise and Sport Sciences Reviews* 28:27–32.

Spickard, A. 1968. Heat stroke in college football and suggestions for prevention. *Southern Medical Journal* 61:791–96.

Streppel, M., et al. 2005. Dietary fiber and blood pressure: A meta-analysis of randomized placebo-controlled trials. *Archives of Internal Medicine* 165:150–56.

Tanji, J., and Batt, M. 1995. Management of hypertension: Adapting new guidelines for active patients. *Physician and Sportsmedicine* 23 (2): 47–55.

Tufts University. 2000. Purified bottled water . . . from public water supplies. *Health & Nutrition Letter* 18 (1):1.

Valtin, H. 2002. "Drink at least eight glasses of water a day." Really? Is there scientific evidence for "8 × 8"? *American Journal of Physiology. Regulatory Integrative and Comparative Physiology* 283:R993-1004.

Von Duvillard, S., et al. 2004. Fluids and hydration in prolonged endurance performance. *Nutrition* 20:651–56.

Wagner, D. R. 1999. Hyperhydrating with glycerol: Implications for athletic performance. *Journal of the American Dietetic Association* 99:207–12.

Young, A. 1990. Energy substrate utilization during exercise in extreme environments. *Exercise and Sport Sciences Reviews* 18:65–118.

Specific Studies

Almond, C., et al. 2005. Hyponatremia among runners in the Boston Marathon. *New England Journal of Medicine* 352:1550–56.

Anderson, M., et al. 2001. Effect of glycerol-induced hyperhydration on thermoregulation and metabolism during exercise in heat. *International Journal of Sport Nutrition and Exercise Metabolism* 11:315–33.

Appel, L., et al. 1997. A clinical trial of the effects of dietary patterns on blood pressure. *New England Journal of Medicine* 336:1117–24.

Armstrong, L., et al. 2005. Fluid, electrolyte, and renal indices of hydration during 11 days of controlled caffeine consumption. *International Journal of Sport Nutrition and Exercise Metabolism* 15:252–65.

Arngrimsson, S., et al. 2004. Hyperthermia and maximal oxygen uptake in men and women. *European Journal of Applied Physiology* 92:524–32.

Baker, L., et al. 2005. Sex differences in voluntary fluid intake by older adults during exercise. *Medicine & Science in Sports & Exercise* 37:789–96.

Barr, S., et al. 1991. Fluid replacement during prolonged exercise: Effects of water, saline, and no fluid. *Medicine & Science in Sports & Exercise* 23:811–17.

Below, P., et al. 1995. Fluid and carbohydrate ingestion independently improve performance during 1 h of intense exercise. *Medicine & Science in Sports & Exercise* 27:200–210.

Bilzon, J. et al. 2000. Short-term recovery from prolonged constant pace running in a warm environment: The effectiveness of a carbohydrate-electrolyte solution.

European Journal of Applied Physiology 82:305–12.

Brouns, F., et al. 1998. The effect of different rehydration drinks on post-exercise electrolyte excretion in trained athletes. *International Journal of Sports Medicine* 19:56–60.

Cheuvront, S., and Haymes, E. 2001. Ad libitum fluid intakes and thermoregulatory responses of female distance runners in three environments. *Journal of Sport Sciences* 19:845–54.

Cheuvront, S., et al. 2002. Comparison of sweat loss estimates for women during prolonged high-intensity running. *Medicine & Science in Sports & Exercise* 34:1344–50.

Costill, D., et al. 1982. Dietary potassium and heavy exercise: Effects on muscle water and electrolytes. *American Journal of Clinical Nutrition* 36:266–75.

Coutts, A., et al. 2002. The effect of glycerol hyperhydration on Olympic distance triathlon performance in high ambient temperatures. *International Journal of Sport Nutrition and Exercise Metabolism* 12:105–19.

Cox, G. R., et al. 2002. Effect of different protocols of caffeine intake on metabolism and endurance performance. *Journal of Applied Physiology* 93:990–99.

de Castro, J. 2005. Stomach filling may mediate the influence of dietary energy density on the food intake of free-living humans. *Physiology & Behavior* 86:32–45.

Drust, B., et al. 2005. Elevations in core and muscle temperature impairs repeated sprint performance. *Acta Physiologica Scandinavica* 183:181–90.

Freund, B. J., et al. 1995. Glycerol hyperhydration: Hormonal, renal, and vascular fluid responses. *Journal of Applied Physiology* 79:2069–77.

Fritzsche, R., et al. 2000. Water and carbohydrate ingestion during prolonged exercise increase maximal neuromuscular power. *Journal of Applied Physiology* 88:730–37.

Gardner, J., et al. 1996. Risk factors predicting exertional heat illness in male Marine Corps recruits. *Medicine & Science in Sports & Exercise* 28:939–44.

Gisolfi, C., et al. 2001. Intestinal fluid absorption during exercise: Role of sport drink osmolality and [Na$^+$]. *Medicine & Science in Sports & Exercise* 33:907–15.

Gisolfi, C. V., et al. 1998. Effect of beverage osmolality on intestinal fluid absorption during exercise. *Journal of Applied Physiology* 85:1941–48.

Godek, S., et al. 2005. Sweat rate and fluid turnover in American football players

compared with runners in a hot and humid environment. *British Journal of Sports Medicine* 39:205–11.

Greiwe, J. S., et al. 1998. Effect of dehydration on isometric muscular strength and endurance. *Medicine & Science in Sports & Exercise* 30:284–88.

Hampson, N., et al. 2003. Oxygenated water and athletic performance. *JAMA* 290:2408–09.

Hargreaves, M., et al. 1996. Effect of fluid ingestion on muscle metabolism during prolonged exercise. *Journal of Applied Physiology* 80:363–66.

Hargreaves, M., et al. 1994. Influence of sodium on glucose bioavailability during exercise. *Medicine & Science in Sports & Exercise* 26:365–68.

Hitchins, S., et al. 1999. Glycerol hyperhydration improves cycle time trial performance in hot humid conditions. *European Journal of Applied Physiology* 80:494–501.

Inder, W. J., et al. 1998. The effect of glycerol and desmopressin on exercise performance and hydration in triathletes. *Medicine & Science in Sports & Exercise* 30:1263–69.

Kenefick, R., et al. 2002. Hypohydration adversely affects lactate threshold in endurance athletes. *Journal of Strength and Conditioning Research* 16:38–43.

Kenney, W., and Chiu, P. 2001. Influence of age on thirst and fluid intake. *Medicine & Science in Sports & Exercise* 33:1524–32.

Lalumandier, J., and Ayers, L. 2000. Flouride and bacterial content of bottled water vs tap water. *Archives of Family Medicine* 9:246–50.

Lambert, G., et al. 1993. Effects of carbonated and noncarbonated beverages at specific intervals during treadmill running in the heat. *International Journal of Sport Nutrition* 3:177–93.

Latzka, W. A., et al. 1998. Hyperhydration: Tolerance and cardiovascular effect during uncompensable exercise-heat stress. *Journal of Applied Physiology* 84:1858–64.

Latzka, W. A., et al. 1997. Hyperhydration: Thermoregulatory effects during compensable exercise-heat stress. *Journal of Applied Physiology* 83:860–66.

Lindeman, A. 1991. Nutrient intake of an ultraendurance cyclist. *International Journal of Sport Nutrition* 1:79–85.

Lyons, T., et al. 1990. Effects of glycerol-induced hyperhydration prior to exercise in the heat on sweating and core temperature. *Medicine & Science in Sports & Exercise* 22:477–83.

Magal, M., et al. 2003. Comparison of glycerol and water hydration regimens on tennis-related performance. *Medicine & Science in Sports & Exercise* 35:150–56.

Marino, F., et al. 2003. Glycerol hyperhydration fails to improve endurance performance and thermoregulation in humans in a warm humid environment. *Pflugers Archiv* 446:455–62.

Maughan, R., et al. 2005. Fluid and electrolyte balance in elite male football (soccer) players training in a cool environment. *Journal of Sports Sciences* 23:72–79.

McGuire, H., et al. 2004. Comprehensive lifestyle modification and blood pressure control: A review of the PREMIER trial. *Journal of Clinical Hypertension* 6:383–90.

Michaud, D. S., et al. 1999. Fluid intake and the risk of bladder cancer in men. *New England Journal of Medicine* 340:1390–97.

Millard-Stafford, M., et al. 2005. Should carbohydrate concentration of a sports drink be less than 8% during exercise in the heat? *International Journal of Sport Nutrition and Exercise Metabolism* 15:117–30.

Millard-Stafford, M. 1997. Water versus carbohydrate-electrolyte ingestion before and during a 15-km run in the heat. *International Journal of Sport Nutrition* 7:26–38.

Montain, S. J., et al. 1998. Hypohydration effects on skeletal muscle performance and metabolism: A 31P-MRS study. *Journal of Applied Physiology* 84:1889–94.

Montain, S. J., et al. 1998. Thermal and cardiovascular strain from hypohydration: Influence of exercise intensity. *International Journal of Sports Medicine* 19:87–91.

Montner, P., et al. 1996. Pre-exercise glycerol hydration improves cycling endurance time. *International Journal of Sports Medicine* 17:27–33.

Murray, R., et al. 1999. A comparison of the gastric emptying characteristics of selected sports drinks. *International Journal of Sport Nutrition* 9:263–74.

Parisi, A., et al. 2002. Complex ventricular arrhythmia induced by overuse of potassium supplementation in a young male football player. Case report. *Journal of Sports Medicine and Physical Fitness* 42:214–16.

Passe, D., et al. 2004. Palatability and voluntary intake of sports beverages, diluted orange juice, and water during exercise. *International Journal of Sport Nutrition and Exercise Metabolism* 14:272–84.

Ray, M. L., et al. 1998. Effect of sodium in a rehydration beverage when consumed as a fluid or meal. *Journal of Applied Physiology* 85:1329–36.

Rehrer, N., et al. 1992. Gastrointestinal complaints in relation to dietary intake in triathletes. *International Journal of Sport Nutrition* 2:48–59.

Rogers, G., et al. 1997. Water budget during ultra-endurance exercise. *Medicine & Science in Sports & Exercise* 29:1477–81.

Rogers, J., et al. 2005. Gastric emptying and intestinal absorption of a low-carbohydrate sport drink during exercise. *International Journal of Sport Nutrition and Exercise Metabolism* 15:220–35.

Rowlands, D., et al. 2005. Glucose polymer molecular weight does not affect exogenous carbohydrate oxidation. *Medicine & Science in Sports & Exercise* 37:1510–16.

Ryan, A. J., et al. 1998. Effect of hypohydration on gastric emptying and intestinal absorption during exercise. *Journal of Applied Physiology* 84:1581–88.

Sacks, F., et al. 2001. Effects on blood pressure of reduced dietary sodium and the Dietary Approaches to Stop Hypertension (DASH) diet. *New England Journal of Medicine* 344:3–10.

Sanders, B., et al. 1999. Water and electrolyte shifts with partial fluid replacement during exercise. *European Journal of Applied Physiology* 80:318–23.

Scheett, T.P., et al. 2001. Effectiveness of glycerol as a rehydrating agent. *International Journal of Sport Nutrition and Exercise Metabolism* 11:63–71.

Schoffstall, J., et al. 2001. Effects of dehydration and rehydration on the one-repetition maximum bench press of weight-trained males. *Journal of Strength and Conditioning Research* 15:102–8.

Shi, X., et al. 1995. Effects of carbohydrate type and concentration and solution osmolality on water absorption. *Medicine & Science in Sports & Exercise* 27:1607–15.

Shirreffs, S., et al. 2005. The sweating response of elite professional soccer players to training in the heat. *International Journal of Sports Medicine* 26:90–95.

Speedy, D., et al. 2002. Oral salt supplementation during ultradistance exercise. *Clinical Journal of Sport Medicine* 12:279–84.

Speedy, D., et al. 2000. Exercise-induced hyponatremia in ultradistance triathletes is caused by inappropriate fluid retention. *Clinical Journal of Sport Medicine* 10:272–78.

Stookey, J. 1999. The diuretic effects of alcohol and caffeine and total water intake misclassification. *European Journal of Epidemiology* 15:181–88.

Sulzer, N., et al. 2005. Serum electrolytes in Ironman triathletes with exercise-associated muscle cramping. *Medicine & Science in Sports & Exercise* 37:1081–85.

Tucker, R., et al. 2004. Impaired exercise performance in the heat is associated with an anticipatory reduction in skeletal muscle recruitment. *Pflugers Archiv* 448:422–30.

Twerenbold, R., et al. 2003. Effects of different sodium concentrations in replacement fluids during prolonged exercise in women. *British Journal of Sports Medicine* 37:300–03.

Van Nieuwenhoven, M., et al. 2000. Gastrointestinal function during exercise: Comparison of water, sports drink, and sports drink with caffeine. *Journal of Applied Physiology* 89:1075–89.

Verde, T., et al. 1982. Sweat composition in exercise and in heat. *Journal of Applied Physiology* 53:1540–45.

von Fraunhofer, J., and Rogers, M. 2005. Effects of sports drinks and other beverages on dental enamel. *General Dentistry* 53:28–31.

Watson, P., et al. 2005. Blood-brain barrier integrity may be threatened by exercise in a warm environment. *American Journal of Physiology. Regulatory, Integrative, and Comparative Physiology* 288:R1689–94.

Webster, J., et al. 2005. A light-weight vest enhances performance of athletes in the heat. *Ergonomics* 48:821–37.

Wemple, R. D. 1997. Caffeine vs caffeine-free sports drinks: Effects on urine production at rest and during prolonged exercise. *International Journal of Sports Medicine* 18:40–46.

White, J. A., et al. 1998. Fluid replacement needs of well-trained male and female athletes during indoor and outdoor steady state running. *Journal of Science and Medicine in Sport* 1:131–42.

Wingo, J., et al. 2004. Influence of a pre-exercise glycerol hydration beverage on performance and physiologic function during mountain-bike races in the heat. *Journal of Athletic Training* 39:169–75.

Yaspelkis, B., et al. 1993. Carbohydrate metabolism during exercise in hot and thermoneutral environments. *International Journal of Sports Medicine* 14:13–19.

Zachwieja, J., et al. 1992. The effects of a carbonated carbohydrate drink on gastric emptying, gastrointestinal distress, and exercise performance. *International Journal of Sport Nutrition* 2:239–50.

Body Weight and Composition for Health and Sport

CHAPTER TEN

LEARNING OBJECTIVES

After studying this chapter, you should be able to:

1. List the various components that comprise human body composition.

2. Describe the various techniques used to assess body composition and discuss the general uses and limitations of such techniques.

3. Identify Body Mass Index and body fat values associated with overweight and degrees of obesity.

4. Explain the mechanisms whereby the human body regulates body weight, including the role of the central nervous system and feedback from peripheral organs and tissues.

5. List and explain the various genetic and environmental factors that may affect the normal regulation of body weight, particularly factors that may predispose to the development of overweight and obesity.

6. Outline the health problems that are associated with obesity in both adults and youth.

7. Describe the health problems associated with excessive weight loss involving the use of drugs, very-low-Calorie diets, and various eating disorders.

8. Understand the potential health problems associated with the female athlete triad.

9. Understand how either excess or insufficient body weight may impair sport or physical performance.

The human body is a remarkable machine. In most cases it may consume nearly a ton of food, nearly one million Calories, over a year and not change its weight by a single pound. Individuals are constantly harnessing and expending energy through the intricacies of their bodily metabolism in order to remain in energy balance. To maintain a given body weight, energy input must balance energy output. However, sometimes the energy-balance equation becomes unbalanced, and the normal body weight will either increase or decrease.

The term **body image** refers to the mental image we have of our own physical appearance, and it can be influenced by a variety of factors, including how much we weigh or how that weight is distributed. Body weight appears to be a major concern of many Americans. Research has revealed that about 40 percent of adult men and 55 percent of adult women are dissatisfied with their current body weight. Similar findings have been reported at the high school and even the elementary school level, primarily with female students, and some research has found that 85 percent of both male and female first-year college students desire to change their body weight. The primary cause of this concern is the value that society, in general, assigns to physical appearance. Being overweight is viewed by many as a handicap to both personal and professional fulfillment, and the term "fattism" has been coined to reflect society's prejudice toward the obese. Thinness is currently an attribute that females desire highly. Males generally desire muscularity, which is also becoming increasingly popular among women. Most individuals who are dissatisfied with their physical appearance feel that they are overweight, and federal surveys have shown that about two-thirds of American adults are trying to lose weight or keep from gaining weight and spending a lot of money to do so. The Federal Trade Commission noted that consumers spend about $35 billion annually on weight-loss products, the majority of whose advertised claims are false and misleading.

Obesity is a worldwide epidemic in Western and Westernizing countries, and is also associated with poverty in developing countries. In a recent feature article in *National Geographic,* Newman noted that, in an historical first, there are now as many overnourished people as undernourished around the world.

Recent U.S. government reports indicate that sixty-five percent, or about two out of every three U.S. adults aged 20 years and older are overweight or obese. About 16 percent of U.S. children and adolescents ages 6–19 and more than 10 percent of children aged 2–5 are overweight. Over the past 40 years in the United States, the weight of the average adult male and female age 40–49 increased by about 25–27 pounds, while the body weight of 10-year-old boys and girls increased by about 10–11 pounds. Extreme obesity in the United States is growing at an alarming rate, from 1 in 200 adults in 1986 to 1 in 50 today.

Being overweight or obese may have a significant effect upon health and physical performance. Excessive body weight, particularly in the form of body fat, has been associated with a wide variety of health problems. Obesity is one of the most prominent medical concerns in industrialized societies today, with estimated annual health costs approaching $100 billion. The Public Health Service has stated in *Healthy People 2010* that one of the major health objectives for the year 2010 is to decrease the proportion of adults and children who are significantly overweight or obese. Some contend that obesity should be targeted for reduction as aggressively as cigarette smoking has been. For some athletes, simply being a little overweight may prove to be detrimental to physical performance because it costs energy to move the extra body mass. On the other hand, increased body weight, provided it is of the right composition, may be advantageous to other athletes.

At the other end of the body-weight continuum, weight losses leading to excessive thinness also may have an impact upon health and physical performance. Anorexia nervosa and bulimia are two serious health disorders associated with obsessive concern about body weight. Although losing excess body fat may improve performance in some sports, excessive weight losses may have a negative impact upon athletic performance.

The major focus of this chapter is on the basic nature of body composition and its effect on health and physical performance. The following two chapters deal with weight-control methods used to maintain or modify body composition.

Body Weight and Composition

What is the ideal body weight?

We all have heard at one time or another that there is an ideal body weight for our particular height. But ideal in terms of what? Health? Appearance? Physical performance? There appears to be no sound evidence to suggest a specific ideal weight for a given individual, but some general guidelines have been proposed relative to health and physical performance, the major focus of this chapter.

Most of us have our own images of how we would like to look, and indeed most individuals who attempt to attain an ideal body weight do so to enhance their appearance. An enhanced physical appearance may improve one's body image and self-esteem, factors important to psychological health. An enhanced physical appearance may also influence performance in certain sports that involve judging of aesthetic movements, such as gymnastics and diving. Although society may create a perception of an ideal body weight for appearance, this perceived ideal body weight may or may not be in accord with optimal health and physical performance.

Most research efforts have attempted to find an ideal body weight for good health. For example, data collected during the past century, mainly by life insurance companies, have been compiled into normal or desirable ranges of body weight for a given height and age. These height-weight charts represent the ideal weights at which Americans can expect to live the longest. The terminology of ideal weight has changed over the years, today being referred to as a healthy body weight. Although height-weight charts have been used to screen for normal body weight in the past, the Body Mass Index (BMI) is the current standard.

The **Body Mass Index (BMI),** also known as Quetelet's Index, is a weight:height ratio. Using the metric system, the formula is

$$\frac{\text{Body weight in kilograms}}{(\text{Height in meters})^2}$$

An individual who weighs 70 kg (154 pounds) and is 1.78 meters (70 inches) in height would have a BMI of 22.1 ($70 \div [1.78^2]$). If you want to use pounds and inches, the formula is

$$\frac{(\text{Body weight in pounds}) \times 705}{(\text{Height in inches})^2}$$

For the same example using pounds and inches, the BMI is also 22.1 ($154 \times 705 \div [70^2]$). In general, a BMI range of 18.5–25 is considered to be normal. You may calculate your BMI using method A in appendix D.

What are the values and limitations of the BMI?

In relation to determining whether an individual possesses normal body weight for a given height, the BMI may be a useful screening device for health problems. The Consumers Union indicates that a low BMI may be a symptom of a serious disease, while a high BMI may be indicative of obesity. Specific BMI values related to potential health status are presented later.

However, the BMI reveals nothing to us about our body composition. The BMI value does not represent percent body fat, as some mistakenly think. Two individuals may be exactly the same height and weight and have the same BMI, but the distribution of their body weight might be so different that one individual could possibly be considered obese while the other might be considered very muscular. For example, a higher BMI could represent muscle mass developed through a strength training program or it could be body fat resulting from a sedentary lifestyle. A recent study, using BMI data, reported that 56 percent of National Football League players were obese, with a BMI greater than 30. However, the study was criticized because it used data obtained from the Internet, not actual measurements. Some NFL players may be obese, but most with high BMI values are extremely muscular.

Although the BMI is not perfect and may be inappropriate for use with very muscular individuals, it is a good guide that the average person may use to think about a healthier body weight. However, other methods are needed to evaluate actual body composition.

What is the composition of the body?

The human body contains many of the elements of the earth, twenty-five of which appear to be essential for normal physiological functioning. Most of the human body, about 96 percent, consists of four elements (carbon, hydrogen, oxygen, and nitrogen) in various combinations. These four elements are the structural basis for body protein, carbohydrate, fat, and water. The remaining 4 percent of our body is composed of minerals, primarily calcium and phosphorus in the bones, but also including others such as iron, potassium, sodium, chloride, and magnesium. Figure 10.1 illustrates some normal percentages for carbohydrate, fat, protein, water, and bone minerals.

Because body composition may have a significant impact on health and physical performance, scientists have developed a variety of techniques to measure various body components. Wang and others noted that, depending on the purpose, body composition may be evaluated at the atomic, molecular, cellular, tissue-system, and whole-body levels. Of major interest to body composition scientists are four major body components: total body fat, fat-free mass, bone mineral, and body water. Each of these components has a different density. Density represents mass divided by volume, and in body composition, analysis is usually expressed as grams per milliliter (g/ml) or grams per cubic centimeter (g/cc^3). The standard for comparison is water, which has a density of 1.0, or 1 g/ml. Corresponding densities for the other components are approximately 1.3–1.4 for bone, 1.1 for fat-free protein tissue, and 0.9 for fat. The density of the human body as a whole may have a wide range, approximately 1.020 to 1.100. The body-density value may be used to determine the body-fat percentage; a higher density represents a greater amount of fat-free mass and a lower amount of body fat.

Depending on the purpose, body composition is usually analyzed as two, three, or all four components. The two components most commonly measured are total body fat and fat-free mass; bone mineral content and body water may be measured with

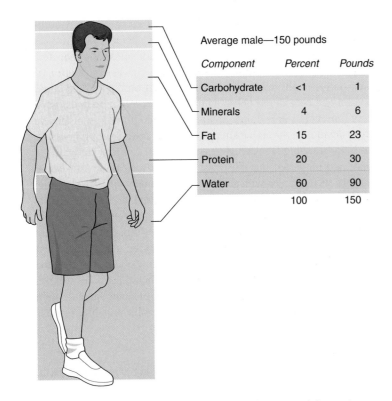

Average male—150 pounds		
Component	Percent	Pounds
Carbohydrate	<1	1
Minerals	4	6
Fat	15	23
Protein	20	30
Water	60	90
	100	150

FIGURE 10.1 Body weight is primarily water, while varying amounts of fat, protein, minerals, and carbohydrate make up the solid tissues. Body-weight losses or gains may be related to changes in any of these components.

more elaborate techniques. Wang and others also introduced a six-component model, which in addition to these four components adds measurement of soft-tissue minerals and glycogen.

Total Body Fat   The total body fat in the body consists of both essential fat and storage fat. **Essential fat** is necessary for proper functioning of certain body structures such as the brain, nerve tissue, bone marrow, heart tissue, and cell membranes. Essential fat in adult males represents about 3 percent of the body weight. Adult females also have additional essential fat associated with their reproductive processes. This additional 9–12 percent of sex-specific fat gives them a total of 12–15 percent essential fat, although this amount may vary considerably among individuals. **Storage fat** is simply a depot for excess energy, and the quantity of body fat in this form also may vary considerably.

Some storage fat is found around body organs for protection, but over 50 percent of total body fat is found just under the skin and is known as **subcutaneous fat.** When this latter type of fat is separated by connective tissue into small compartments that extrude into the dermis, it gives a dimpled, quilt-like look to the skin and is popularly known as **cellulite.** Cellulite is primarily fat, but may contain high concentrations of glycoproteins, particles that can attract water and possibly give cellulite skin that waffle-like appearance. The appearance of cellulite is much more common in women than in men. Other storage fat is located deep in the body, particularly in the abdominal area. This deep fat is referred to as **visceral fat,** which as noted below is associated with increased health risks.

Fat-Free Mass   **Fat-free mass** primarily consists of protein and water, with smaller amounts of minerals and glycogen. The tissue of skeletal muscles is the main component of fat-free mass, but the heart, liver, kidneys, and other organs are included also. A more common term often used interchangeably with fat-free mass is **lean body mass;** technically, however, lean body mass includes essential fat. In a two-component body composition analysis, fat-free or lean body mass complements total body fat. An individual who has 20 percent body fat has 80 percent fat-free mass.

Bone Mineral   Bone gives structure to our body, but it is also involved in a variety of metabolic processes. Bone consists of about 50 percent water and 50 percent solid matter, including protein and minerals. Although total bone weight, including water and protein, may be 12–15 percent of the total body weight, the mineral content is only 3–4 percent of total body weight.

Body Water   The average adult body weight is approximately 60 percent water, the remaining 40 percent consisting of dry weight materials that exist in this internal water environment. Some tissues, like the blood, have a high water content, whereas others, like adipose tissue, are relatively dry. The fat-free mass is about 70 percent water, while adipose fat tissue is less than 10 percent. Under normal conditions the water concentration of a given tissue is regulated quite nicely relative to its needs. When we look at the percentage of the body weight that may be attributed to a given body tissue, the weight of that tissue includes its normal water content.

Although the amount of fat, lean tissue, bone, and water may vary widely in individuals, the following might represent a normal distribution in a young adult male: 60 percent body water and 40 percent solid matter subdivided into 14 percent fat, 22 percent protein, and 4 percent bone minerals.

Body composition may be influenced by a number of factors such as age, sex, diet, and level of physical activity. Age effects are significant during the developmental years as muscle and other body tissues are being formed. Also, during adulthood, muscle mass may decrease, probably because the level of physical activity declines. There are some minor differences in body composition between boys and girls up to the age of puberty, but at this age the differences become fairly great. In general, girls deposit more fat beginning with puberty, while boys develop more muscle tissue. Diet can affect body composition over the short haul, such as during acute water restriction and starvation, but the main effects are seen over the long haul. For example, chronic overeating may lead to increased body-fat stores. Physical activity may also be very influential, with a sound exercise program helping to build muscle and lose fat.

What techniques are available to measure body composition and how accurate are they?

The measurement of body fat has become very popular in recent years. Many high school and university athletic departments routinely analyze the body composition of their athletes in attempts to predict an optimal weight for competition. In some sports, such as wrestling, measurement of body composition may be mandated by various state or national sport associations. Fitness and wellness centers also usually include a body-fat analysis as one of their services. Unfortunately, some of the individuals who analyze body composition in these situations are unaware of the limitations of the tests they employ.

The only direct, accurate method of analyzing body composition is by chemical extraction of all fat from body tissues, obviously not appropriate with living humans. Thus, a variety of indirect methods have been developed to assess body composition. Some are relatively simple, such as visual observation by an experienced judge, and others are rather complex, such as nuclear magnetic resonance imaging, using multimillion dollar machines. Indirect methods are used to measure body fat, lean body mass, bone mineral content, and body water. Some techniques are also used to measure fat in specific locations of the body.

Before continuing this discussion, it must be emphasized that measurement of body composition is not an exact science. All techniques, even technologically sophisticated ones, currently used to predict body density or percentage of body fat are only estimates and are prone to error, particularly when used to determine the body fat of a given individual. Such errors usually are expressed statistically as standard errors of measurement or estimate, which can be used to show the accuracy of the body-fat measurement. Without going into the statistics of standard errors, look at the following example. Let us suppose that a formula using skinfold techniques predicts your body fat at 17 percent, yet the formula has a standard error of 3 percent. What this means is that your true body fat percentage is probably (about 70 percent probability) somewhere between one standard error of the predicted value, or somewhere between 14–20 percent. It may even be lower than 14 and higher than 20 percent, but less likely so. Thus, you should not think of body-fat determinations as precise measures, but consider them as a possible range associated with the error of measurement. A number of body composition measurement techniques are highlighted in table 10.1, but only the more commonly used or promising techniques will be discussed.

When determining changes in body composition of an individual over time, such as in a weight-loss program, it is important to

TABLE 10.1	Methods used to determine body composition
Anthropometry	Measures body segment girths to predict body fat
Bioelectrical impedance analysis (BIA)	Measures resistance to electric current to predict body-water content, lean body mass, and body fat
Body plethysmography	Whole-body plethysmograph measures air displacement and calculates body density; comparable to water displacement protocol used in underwater weighing
Computed tomography (CT)	X-ray scanning technique to image body tissues; useful in determining subcutaneous and deep fat to predict body-fat percentage; used to calculate bone mass
Dual energy X-ray absorptiometry (DEXA; DXA)	X-ray technique at two energy levels to image body fat; used to calculate bone mass
Dual photon absorptiometry (DPA)	Beam of photons passes through tissues, differentiating soft tissues and bone tissues; used to predict body fat and calculate bone mass
Infrared interactance	Infrared light passes through tissues, and interaction with tissue components used to predict body fat
Magnetic resonance imaging (MRI)	Magnetic-field and radio-frequency waves are used to image body tissues similar to CT scan; very useful for imaging deep abdominal fat
Neutron activation analysis	Beam of neutrons passes through the tissues, permitting analysis of nitrogen and other mineral content in the body; used to predict lean body mass
Skinfold thicknesses	Measures subcutaneous fat folds to predict body-fat content and lean body mass
Total body electrical conductivity (TOBEC)	Measures total electrical conductivity in the body, predicting water and electrolyte content to estimate body fat and lean body mass
Total body potassium	Measures total body potassium, the main intracellular ion, to predict lean body mass and body fat
Total body water	Measures total body water by isotope dilution techniques to predict lean body mass and body fat
Ultrasound	High frequency ultrasound waves pass through tissues to image subcutaneous fat and predict body-fat content
Underwater weighing (Hydrodensitometry)	Underwater-weighing technique based on Archimedes' principle to predict body density, body fat, and lean body mass

use the same method throughout the testing to help minimize errors that may occur when using different methods. For example, if you select the skinfold procedure, it should be used consistently throughout, not interspersed with other techniques such as BIA.

Underwater Weighing One of the most common research techniques for determining body density is **underwater weighing,** also known as hydrodensitometry. The technique is based on Archimedes' principle that a body immersed in a fluid is acted upon by a buoyancy force in relation to the amount of fluid the body displaces (see figure 10.2). Since fat is less dense and bone and muscle tissue are more dense than water, a given weight of fat will displace a larger volume of water and exhibit a greater buoyant effect than the corresponding weight of bone and muscle tissue. Different formulas are recommended for determination of body density, depending upon the age and sex of the individual. Although this technique is often referred to as the "gold standard" in body-composition analysis and is still one of the most commonly used methods for research purposes, it has its weaknesses. For example, the assumption that the density of the fat-free protein tissue is 1.10 g/cc^3 may not be valid for all individuals, such as athletes and older persons. The standard error is still about 2–2.5 percent. Thus, Wagner and Heyward recently noted that underwater weighing should not be regarded as the "gold standard" because of these errors. Because the underwater-weighing technique is rather time consuming and difficult for some individuals, other techniques have been developed either for research purposes or practical applications. The interested reader is referred to the reviews by Forbes, Ellis, and Wagner and Heyward for more details, including new techniques such as three-dimensional photon scanning and whole-body tomography.

Air Displacement Plethysmography (APD) A new technique is **air displacement plethysmography (APD),** sometimes referred to as body plethysmography. Subjects enter a dual-chamber plethysmograph designed to measure the amount of air they displace, somewhat comparable to the water displacement technique of underwater weighing. One commercial product available is called the Bod Pod (see figure 10.3). It is portable, easy to operate, requires little time, and eliminates the necessity of going underwater, several clear advantages compared to underwater weighing. Several reviews, including one by Wagner and Heyward, have noted that it may be more valid and reliable than hydrodensitometry for certain individuals, such as those who fear underwater submersion, but has similar limitations. In this regard, Fields noted that the ADP and underwater weighing agree within 1 percent of body fat for adults and children, but when compared to multicomponent models ADP generally underestimated body fat by 2–3 percent. Several studies recently compared the Bod Pod to DEXA and reached different conclusions. A study with men reported a 2.2 percent difference in body fat between the two methods, whereas a study with women reported no significant differences. Overall, ADP appears to be a useful method to use in tracking changes in body composition in individuals over time.

Skinfolds The **skinfold technique** is designed to measure the subcutaneous fat (see figure 10.4). It appears to be the most common procedure for nonresearch purposes. The values obtained are inserted into an appropriate formula to calculate the body-fat percentage. The formula chosen should be specific to the sex, age, and ethnicity of the individual. Some formulas also have been developed for specific athletic groups. To improve the accuracy of this technique, skinfold measures should be obtained from a variety of body sites, because using a single skinfold site may be unrepresentative of total storage fat. The test also should be administered with an acceptable pair of skinfold calipers by an experienced tester. Ultrasound techniques are also available to assess skinfold thicknesses, but these are more expensive than calipers. Orphanidou and others found that measurements of subcutaneous body fat with

FIGURE 10.2 Underwater weighing is one of the more accurate means for determining body composition. However, all current techniques for estimating percent body fat are subject to error. See text for discussion.

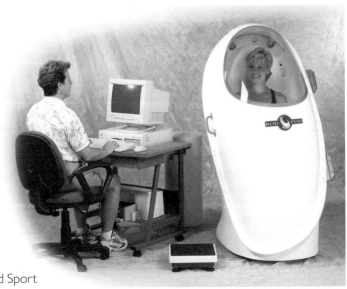

FIGURE 10.3 The Bod Pod. A new application of total body plethysmography, an air displacement technique, to evaluate body composition.
Photo courtesy of Life Measurement Instruments.

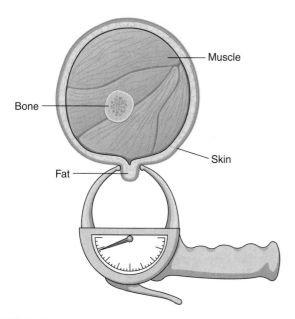

FIGURE 10.4 A schematic drawing showing the skinfold of fat that is pinched up away from the underlying muscle tissue.

skinfold techniques were comparable to those obtained by ultrasound and computed tomography, suggesting the use of skinfold calipers in the clinical setting is appropriate.

Because this method involves some measurement error, and because the formulas are usually based upon the underwater-weighing technique, the standard error for the skinfold technique is about 3–4 percent, which should be kept in mind when using this method to estimate body fat. Nevertheless, Lohman and others indicated the skinfold technique is one of the best practical methods to measure body composition, and Wagner and Heyward noted that it can provide accurate results for lean subjects, such as athletes. For example, Clark and others validated the NCAA skinfold technique as a means to predict minimal weight classes for wrestlers. For those who have access to a good skinfold caliper, generalized equations for the calculation of body fat may be found in appendix D for males and females of several ages.

Bioelectrical Impedance Analysis (BIA)   A more expensive, practical technique is **bioelectrical impedance analysis (BIA).** BIA is based on the principle of resistance to an electrical current that is applied to the body. The less the recorded resistance, the greater the water content, and hence the greater the body density. Early research with BIA revealed large standard errors in predicting lean body mass, so it was not considered to be very valid. However, body composition researchers have developed newer techniques and prediction equations with lower standard errors (3–4 percent), comparable to skinfold techniques. Lohman and others recently noted that BIA is a good practical method to assess body composition. Nevertheless, several problems still appear to exist, including the application to the very obese, the lean athlete, and the elderly. BIA may not accurately predict lean body mass in those with abnormal body-water supplies; it may underestimate lean body mass in athletes and overestimate it in the obese. Pichard and others recently reported valid BIA formulas for

female runners, but recommended research to validate formulas for other athletes. Wagner and Heyward cite recent advancements in BIA, such as use of body segments instead of whole body resistance, that may make BIA a more valid tool.

Dual Energy X-Ray Absorptiometry (DXA; DEXA) **Dual energy X-ray absorptiometry (DXA or DEXA)** is a computerized X-ray technique used to image body tissues and has been used to assess bone mineral content, fat-free mass, and body fat concurrently. DEXA may also be used to assess deep visceral fat, as can other sophisticated techniques such as magnetic resonance imaging (MRI) and computed tomography (CT).

However, Kohrt indicated that although DEXA is the method of choice for measuring bone mass, its use has been associated with errors in measuring fat content. Elowsson and others reported that the amount of water in lean body mass significantly affects the estimation of body fat by DEXA. There are different DEXA models, data collection modes, and software, and each may be a source of error. For example, Van Loan and others reported differences in body composition measurements when two different software packages were used. Although DEXA, and other sophisticated techniques such as MRI and CT, may provide us with valuable information on the composition of specific tissues in the body, overall they do not appear to be any more effective than underwater weighing to predict body-fat percentage.

Nevertheless, DEXA is a valuable technique because it uses only one measurement session to evaluate body fat, fat-free mass, and bone tissue. As new DEXA techniques are developed and validated, it may become the method of choice for body composition evaluations that include bone density. Although expensive, mass utilization may decrease the cost of DEXA analysis.

Infrared Interactance   Another device marketed commercially is based upon infrared interactance. In essence, infrared light passes through the tissues, and its interaction with tissue components is used to predict body fat. One commercial model is the Futrex 5000. Wagner and Heyward reported somewhat higher standard errors of measurement with infrared interactance, greater than 3.5 percent.

Anthropometry   Anthropometry, or measurement of body parts, is an inexpensive, practical method to assess body composition. Body measurements include girths such as the neck and abdomen, and bone diameters such as the hip, shoulders, elbow, and wrist. Girth and bone diameter measurements may be incorporated into various formulas to predict body fat and lean body mass.

Girth measurements of the abdomen, hips, buttocks, thigh, and other body parts, may be important indicators of **regional fat distribution,** which is a concept representing the anatomical distribution of fat over the body. As discussed later, regional fat distribution may be associated with several major health problems. The principal measure of regional fat distribution is the **waist circumference,** the abdominal or waist girth measured by a flexible tape at the narrowest section of the waist as seen from the front. The waist circumference is a good screening technique for regional fat distribution, but does not provide an accurate measure of deep visceral fat, such as provided by CT or MRI techniques.

Multicomponent Models The multicomponent model uses several methods, such as hydrodensitometry, total body water, and DEXA to reduce the errors associated with any single method and to provide information on body fat, body water, bone mass, and lean body mass. Wagner and Heyward note that the multicomponent model is now regarded as the "gold standard" in body composition assessment and should be used when feasible.

What problems may be associated with rigid adherence to body fat percentages in sport?

Table 10.1 lists most of the methods used to estimate body composition. Several recent studies have attempted to validate these techniques, usually against the underwater-weighing method, and have shown some significant differences. In one study comparing four different methods, some individuals were estimated to have body-fat percentages that ranged as much as 10 percent depending on the method used, while another study using four different prediction equations with the BIA reported predicted body-fat percentages ranging from 12.2 to 22.8 in gymnasts. In addition, Stout and others cross-validated sixteen skinfold formulas for prediction of body fat in wrestlers, and reported error values of almost 5 percent. Given the fact that the wrestlers in this study averaged 10.8 percent fat, the researchers concluded that this level of accuracy is not acceptable. More recently, however, Clark and others found that the NCAA skinfold equation is a valid predictor of body fat, and support the NCAA method of estimating body fat in college wrestlers for establishment of minimum weight. Oppliger and others recently developed new infrared interactance equations to predict body fat in high school wrestlers and noted they are comparable to skinfold equations currently used. However, given the problems with assumptions underlying the various methods of body composition determination, estimates of body-fat percentages are approximations only.

The rigid use of body-fat percentages in weight-control sports, such as gymnastics and wrestling, may lead to excessive weight loss. For example, suppose you are a wrestler and your college coach requires you to reach the minimal permitted—5 percent body-fat level. Using a skinfold caliper technique, he finds that you are at 8 percent body fat and suggests that you lose 3 percent more body fat. However, given the standard error of 3–4 percent, you may already be at 5 percent. Losing extra weight may be very difficult because you are already near minimal body-fat levels, so additional weight loss may include muscle tissue that may lead to possible decreases in performance. In young athletes, such practices may also lead to disordered eating and, possibly, clinical eating disorders.

For one of the best resources to select a body composition formula for individuals of different ages, ranging from children to the aged, and with varying physical activity levels, the interested reader is referred to the book by Heyward and Stolarzyk. The review by Wagner and Heyward is also very informative.

Gilbert Forbes, probably the leading expert in body composition analysis over several decades, has noted that each technique used to assess body fat is prone to errors, so the goal of developing a highly precise method for estimating body composition may never be achieved. In any case, most of us do not need a highly accurate assessment of body composition. The critical question probably should be, "How can I tell if I am too fat?" Jean Mayer, an internationally renowned nutritionist, has suggested the use of the mirror test to answer this question. He suggests you look at yourself, nude, from the front and from the side in a full-length mirror. This is usually all the evidence we need if we study ourselves objectively. We probably have a pretty good idea of how we would like our bodies to look, and this test offers us a guide to our desirable physical appearance, at least as far as body-weight distribution is concerned. Exceptions to this suggestion are individuals who are obsessed with thinness and believe they are always too fat, no matter how thin they get. This topic is covered later in this chapter.

How much should I weigh or how much body fat should I have?

That is a complex question, and the response depends on whether you are concerned primarily about appearance, health, or physical performance. From the perspective of physical appearance, you are the best judge of how you wish to look. However, a distorted image may lead to serious health problems or impairment in physical performance. Already thin individuals who desire to be even thinner may be prone to eating disorders, while muscular bodybuilders who perceive themselves as not sufficiently muscular may suffer psychologically.

The effect of body weight and body fat on physical performance is discussed in a later section, although some general guidelines are presented here. The effect of body weight and fat on health has received considerable research attention. Although being underweight may impair health, most of the focus has been on excess body weight and fat, particularly the relationship of obesity to health. By medical definition, **obesity** is simply an accumulation of fat in the adipose tissue. Obesity is also referred to as a disease or disorder and is the most common nutritional health problem in North America. The actual measurement and determination of clinical obesity is a controversial issue. Several approaches have been used to define the point at which a person is classified as clinically obese.

Unfortunately, our present level of knowledge does not provide us with the ability to predict precisely what the optimal weight or percent body fat should be for health in any given individual. However, some general guidelines have been developed by various professional and health organizations.

Body Mass Index As a screening method for health, you may calculate your BMI to assess your body weight. See appendix D for details. The following are some general guidelines presented by the National Institutes of Health regarding the relationship of BMI to health risks. Keep in mind that these are BMI values, not body-fat percentages, which are discussed in the next section.

Below 18.5: May signal malnutrition or serious disease
18.5–24.9: Healthy weight range that carries little health risk
25–29.9: Overweight; at increased risk for health problems, especially if you have one or two weight-related medical conditions
Above 30: Obesity, more than 20 percent over healthy body weight; poses high risk to your health

These values are in accordance with figures presented by the National Academy of Sciences. Additionally, the Food and Agriculture Organization has proposed the use of a BMI less than 18.5 as a criterion for starvation. Other investigators indicate that a BMI greater than 35 or 40 is classified as severe, clinical, or **morbid obesity.** An expanded BMI health risk table, in association with waist circumference, is presented later.

Body Fat Percentage   As noted previously, the use of the BMI height-weight relationship does not evaluate body composition. Thus, health professionals note that there are exceptions to these BMI classifications, indicating that a low BMI may be a symptom of a serious disease, not a cause, and that muscular people may have a high BMI and not be obese.

For health purposes, the body has a need for the essential fat described previously. At a minimum essential fat approximates 3 percent for males and 12–15 percent for females. Several authorities have included additional levels of storage fat and suggested that minimal levels of total body fat for health range from 5–10 percent for males and 15–18 percent for females. The average percentages of body fat for U.S. males and females are, respectively, approximately 15–18 and 22–25 percent.

Lower levels of body fat may be required for optimal performance in certain types of athletic events. Certain male athletes such as wrestlers and gymnasts may function effectively at 5–7 percent body fat. Recommendations have been made for females who compete in distance running to have no more than 10 percent body fat. However, some athletes have performed very successfully even though their body-fat percentage was higher than the recommended values.

Although different levels of body-fat percentages have been cited as the criterion for obesity, the American Dietetic Association and the National Research Council set the value at 25 percent for males and 30 percent for females. The National Academy of Sciences, in its new DRI on energy intake, also published criteria for obesity setting the level at 25 percent body fat for males but 37 percent for females; the NAS noted that over 31 percent and 42 percent body fat in males and females, respectively, was indicative of clinical obesity. A proposed rating scale is presented in table 10.2, keeping in mind that the athletic category is associated with athletes competing in weight-control sports or sports where excess body fat may be a disadvantage. Also, as noted below, although obesity generally increases health risks, some individuals with higher body-fat percentages may not develop obesity-related health problems if they are otherwise physically fit and consume a healthful diet. For example, Lohman and his colleagues recently presented new percent-fat fitness standards for physically active men and women, suggesting a slight increase in fat content as we age. Their recommended body-fat ranges are 5–15 percent for active young men, 7–18 percent for middle-aged men, and 9–18 percent for elderly men; female ranges are 16–28 percent for young women, 20–33 percent for middle-aged women, and 20–33 percent for elderly women.

Waist Circumference   It may not be how much fat you have that affects your health but where that fat is located. The health implications of regional fat distribution are discussed below, but you may use method C in appendix D to calculate your waist cir-

TABLE 10.2   Ratings of body-fat percentage levels for males and females age 18–30

Rating	Males	Females
Athletic	6–10	10–15
Good	11–14	16–23
Acceptable	15–20	24–30
Overweight	21–24	31–36
Obese	25 or over	37 or over

Note: Keep in mind that these are approximate values. The athletic category may apply particularly to athletes who compete in events where excess body fat may be a disadvantage. See text for additional information.

cumference and evaluate associated health risks. As a screening measure for deep visceral fat, increased health risks are associated with waist circumferences greater than 35 inches in females and 40 inches in males. However, as discussed later, lower waist circumferences may be associated with increased risks if accompanied by other conditions, such as high blood pressure. Table 10.3 highlights the risk of chronic disease associated with the BMI and waist size.

Key Concept Recap

▶ The Body Mass Index does not measure body composition, but it may be useful as a screening device to determine whether one is overweight or obese. *Overweight* and *obesity* are not synonymous terms.

▶ The body consists of four components: body fat, protein, minerals, and water.

▶ For practical purposes, body composition may be classified as consisting of two components: fat-free weight, which is about 70 percent water, and body fat.

▶ The body needs a certain amount of fat content, the so-called essential fat, but excessive body fat may contribute to several major health problems and may also impair athletic performance.

▶ All techniques that are currently used to measure body composition, primarily body fat, are prone to error; even the underwater-weighing technique, supposedly the most accurate technique, may be in error by 2–2.5 percent.

▶ Our present level of knowledge does not provide us with the ability to predict precisely what the optimal body composition should be for health or physical performance. However, BMI and body-fat levels higher than normal are associated with increased health risks.

Check for Yourself

Using appendix D, calculate both your Body Mass Index (BMI) and your waist circumference. Compare your findings to the rating scale in table 10.3.

TABLE 10.3 Risk of associated disease according to BMI and waist size

BMI		*Waist less than or equal to 40 in. (men) or 35 in. (women)	*Waist greater than 40 in. (men) or 35 in. (women)
18.5 or less	Underweight	—	N/A
18.5–24.9	Normal	—	N/A
25.0–29.9	Overweight	Increased	High
30.0–34.9	Obese	High	Very High
35.0–39.9	Obese	Very High	Very High
40 or greater	Extremely Obese	Extremely High	Extremely High

Source: www.consumer.gov/weightloss.bmi.htm

*Note: Recent research suggests waist sizes greater than 37 inches in men and 31.5 inches in women may increase health risks when accompanied by other conditions, such as high blood pressure.

Regulation of Body Weight and Composition

How does the human body normally control its own weight?

As noted previously, you may eat over a ton of food—nearly a million Calories—a year and yet not gain one pound of body weight. For this to occur, your body must possess an intricate regulatory system that helps to balance energy intake and output both on a short-term and a long-term basis. The regulation of human energy balance is complex, involving numerous feedback loops to help control energy balance. At the present time we do not know all the exact physiological mechanisms whereby body weight is maintained relatively constant over short or long periods, but some information is available relative to both energy intake and energy expenditure.

Energy Intake George Bray, an international authority on weight control, indicates that food intake is a regulated system. The central nervous system, the brain in particular, is the center for appetite control, either creating a sensation of satiety or stimulating food-seeking behavior. However, its activity is dependent upon a complex array of afferent signals from various body systems. The interaction of the brain with these afferent signals helps regulate the appetite on a short-term (daily) basis, or on a long-term basis, as in keeping the body weight constant for a year.

The forebrain is involved in the conscious selection of foods we eat, while the brainstem controls the motor aspects of eating, such as chewing and swallowing. Between these two structures lies the hypothalamus, a small substructure that appears to be the center for appetite control. You may recall from the last chapter that the hypothalamus is also involved in body-temperature control, involving neural receptors that function as a thermostat to either stimulate energy (heat) production or loss. In a similar fashion, the hypothalamus may contain neural centers that help regulate appetite, often referred to as an **appestat.** In general, the appestat may contain a **hunger center** that may stimulate eating behavior, and a **satiety center** which when stimulated will inhibit the hunger center. As a means of controlling energy intake, specific neural receptors within the appestat monitor various afferent stimuli that may stimulate or inhibit the appetite.

As depicted in figure 10.5, various stimuli may influence the appetite, including blood levels of various nutrients, metabolites, hormones, neural stimuli from other parts of the body, and environmental cues. Some factors may function to control body weight on a short-term basis while others may exert long-term effects. The following afferent stimuli may be involved in body-weight control in one way or another.

- *Senses.* Stimulation of several senses like sight, sound, and smell may influence neural or hormonal activity to stimulate or depress our appetites, even before food is ingested. The sense of taste also has a significant impact on appetite and energy intake.
- *Stomach fullness.* An empty or full stomach may influence mechanical stretch receptors in the stomach walls that generate neural activity. An empty stomach may stimulate the hunger center by various neural pathways, whereas a full stomach may stimulate the satiety center.
- *Blood nutrient levels.* Nutrient levels in the blood may be able to influence receptors in the hypothalamus. Receptors in the hypothalamus, liver, or elsewhere may be able to monitor blood levels of various nutrients. In regard to this, three theories center on the three energy nutrients. The **glucostatic theory** suggests that food intake is related to changes in the levels of blood glucose. A fall will stimulate glucose-sensitive neurons in the hypothalamus and increase appetite whereas an increased blood glucose level will decrease appetite. The **lipostatic theory** suggests a similar mechanism for fats as does the **aminostatic theory** for amino acids, or protein. In essence, by-products of carbohydrate, fat, and protein metabolism may influence production of neurotransmitters that influence appetite, such as serotonin and norepinephrine, in the hypothalamus.
- *Body temperature.* A thermostat in the hypothalamus may respond to changes in body temperature and influence the feeding center. For example, an increase in body temperature inhibits the appetite.
- *Hormones and neurotransmitters.* A number of different hormones in the body have been shown to affect feeding behavior, including insulin, cortisol, thyroxine, and a number of peptides. As discussed later, some hormones may function on a short-term basis to help control meal size, whereas other hormones may be involved in long-term regulation of body weight.

Energy Expenditure Although all of the above may be involved in the physiological regulation of food intake, the other

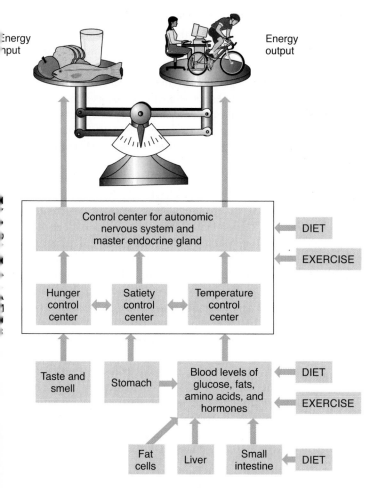

Energy input

Energy output

Control center for autonomic nervous system and master endocrine gland

DIET

EXERCISE

Hunger control center

Satiety control center

Temperature control center

Taste and smell

Stomach

Blood levels of glucose, fats, amino acids, and hormones

DIET

EXERCISE

Fat cells

Liver

Small intestine

DIET

FIGURE 10.5 Basic control mechanisms for body weight. Although other parts of the brain are involved, the control of food intake (energy intake) and resting metabolism (energy output) is governed primarily by the hypothalamus in the brain. The numerous control centers in the hypothalamus are influenced by feedback from the body, such as the blood concentrations of glucose and other nutrients. In turn, food intake and energy expenditure may influence the hypothalamus. For example, exercise will stimulate the hypothalamus, leading to the secretion of several hormones by the endocrine glands in the body. The effects of exercise will also influence the temperature control center and the blood levels of several nutrients, which will in turn influence the hypothalamus. See the text for an expanded discussion.

side of the energy-balance equation is energy expenditure, or metabolism. Although exercise is one way to increase energy expenditure, the vast majority of the energy that is expended by the body on a daily basis is accounted for by the basal energy expenditure (BEE) or resting energy expenditure (REE), as was detailed in chapter 3. Changes in the REE may be involved in the regulation of body weight. Several mechanisms of body-weight regulation have been proposed.

- *Brown fat.* **Brown fat,** which is distinct from the white fat that comprises most fat tissue in the body, is found in small amounts around the neck, back, and chest areas. It has a high rate of metabolism and releases energy in the form of heat without

ATP production. Basically, uncoupling proteins (UCP) in brown fat uncouple respiration from oxidative phosphorylation and convert fuel to heat without producing ATP. Activity of the brown fat tissue may be increased or decreased under certain conditions, such as after a meal or exposure to the cold. This activity is referred to as nonshivering thermogenesis. Research with rats has indicated low levels of brown fat are associated with a higher incidence of dietary-induced obesity. The amount of brown fat in humans appears to be small (about 1 percent of body fat or less) but Stock indicates that as little as 50 grams (about 2 ounces) could make a contribution of 10–15 percent energy turnover in humans. Its role in the etiology of human obesity is controversial and is being researched.

- *White fat tissue and muscle tissue.* UCP are also found in other tissues. In a recent review, Melby and others noted that both white adipose tissue and muscle tissue may also experience thermogenesis without ATP production under conditions of high energy intake, particularly as dietary fat.

- *Hormones.* Levels of hormones from the thyroid and adrenal glands may rise or fall and affect energy metabolism accordingly. Triiodothyronine and thyroxine, hormones from the thyroid gland, may be involved in the stimulation of brown adipose tissue. Hormones, such as epinephrine, also may increase the activity of certain enzymes resulting in increased energy expenditure. Decreases in such hormonal activity may depress energy metabolism. Other hormones may stimulate or depress thermogenesis in adipose or muscle tissues.

- *Nonexercise activity thermogenesis (NEAT).* Levine indicates that nonexercise activity thermogensis (NEAT) is the energy expended for everything we do that is not sleeping, eating or sports-like exercise. Varying levels of NEAT could have a significant impact on daily energy expenditure.

Feedback Control of Energy Intake and Expenditure As noted in an earlier chapter, the human body has developed a number of physiological systems, called feedback systems, to regulate most body processes. Temperature control is a good example. Feedback systems controlling body weight may operate on both a short-term (daily) and long-term (yearly) basis.

On a short-term basis, for example, as the stomach expands while eating a meal, nerve impulses are sent from receptors in the stomach wall to the hypothalamus to help suppress food intake, helping to maintain overall energy balance. Body stores of carbohydrate, protein, and fat are also regulated on a short-term basis. The human body has a limited capacity to store excess carbohydrate and protein, so changes in blood glucose and amino acid levels help regulate carbohydrate and protein intake. Although the human body possesses a high capacity to store fat, blood lipids and other factors help maintain body-fat balance on a short-term basis. However, Stubbs indicated that although dietary protein and carbohydrate exert potent effects on satiety, dietary fat is less satiating and may lead to excess energy intake.

On a long-term basis, the **set-point theory** of weight control is a proposed feedback mechanism. This theory proposes that your body is programmed to be a certain weight, or a set point, something comparable to a set body temperature of 98.6° F. If you begin to deviate from this set point, your body will make metabolic adjustments to return you to normal. This is often referred to as adaptive thermogenesis, which can either increase or decrease energy production to generate heat. Although developed primarily with rats and still only a theory, the set-point concept does involve the interaction of those factors cited above, particularly the lipostatic theory, which may influence energy intake and expenditure in humans. Keesey and Hirvonen indicate that the hypothalamus appears to play the primary role in establishing the set point for body weight.

In his recent review, Levin noted that the brain has special sensing neurons which are involved in the control of energy homeostasis. In particular, Levin notes that neuropeptide Y (NPY) neurons in the hypothalamus represent an example of a neuron capable of sensing both glucose and a host of other peripheral metabolic signals, such as leptin.

Leptin is a regulating peptide hormone encoded and produced by the OB gene in the adipose cells and appears to be involved in the long-term control of body weight. Long-term imbalances in body weight are usually reflected by changes in body-fat stores. Schwartz and Seeley indicate that the more body fat you have, the more leptin you produce; conversely, less leptin is produced when body-fat stores are low. When leptin is released into the blood, it circulates to the hypothalamus and is believed to inhibit the production of NPY (see figure 10.6). NPY is a potent stimulant of food intake and also acts to reduce energy expenditure by decreasing the REE. Thus, as you begin to accumulate body fat your fat cells produce more leptin, which then circulates to the hypothalamus and depresses the formation of NPY. Because NPY stimulates food intake and depresses energy expenditure, decreased levels of NPY will suppress hunger and reduce voluntary food intake, and may also stimulate increases in REE by activating thermogenesis in adipose and muscle tissues. Thus, your body reacts to the increased body fat by decreasing energy intake and increasing energy expenditure. Conversely, if you decrease body fat rapidly via dieting, leptin production is decreased, reducing the inhibitory effect on NPY

production. Increased levels of NPY stimulate hunger and reduce energy expenditure, thus resisting the effect of the diet and promoting restoration of the lost weight. Gomez-Merino and others reported that prolonged, strenuous military-exercise maneuvers, which induced an energy deficit, reduced serum leptin levels to about one-third normal. Baile notes that leptin and its receptors provide the molecular basis for the lipostatic theory of energy-balance regulation proposed 40 years ago, namely that circulating factors generated in proportion to body-fat stores act as signals to the brain and elicit changes in energy intake and expenditure.

Other factors have also been recently identified. **Ghrelin** is a peptide hormone released by the stomach, mainly before mealtime when the stomach is relatively empty. Ghrelin acts on the hypothalamus to stimulate the appetite. When obese individuals lose weight, ghrelin levels appear to be higher all the time. This appears to be one way your body fights against weight loss. Another peptide (PYY3-36) is secreted by the small intestines in proportion to the amount of food digested, and its natural function is to make you stop eating by inducing a sense of fullness, an effect directly opposite that of ghrelin. Other peptide hormones, such as adiponectin and obestatin, may also be involved in energy balance.

Less research has been conducted relative to feedback control of physical activity, but Rowland proposed an **activity-stat,** a center in the brain that functions as a set-point to increase or decrease physical activity. If substantiated, such a center could also support the set-point theory of body-weight control.

Although the set point is a theory, it may help explain why many people maintain a normal body weight throughout life.

What is the cause of obesity?

A recent National Geographic cover story asked the question, *Why are we so fat?* The answer is simple, but the devil is in the details. Energy processes in the human body, like those of other machines, are governed by the laws of thermodynamics. If the human body consumes less energy in the form of food Calories than it expends in metabolic processes, then a negative energy balance will occur and the individual will lose body weight. Conversely, a greater caloric intake in comparison to energy expenditure will result in a positive energy balance and a gain in body weight. In simple terms, obesity is caused by this latter condition of energy imbalance.

Although the first law of thermodynamics provides the basic answer as to how we get fat, it does not provide any insight relative to the specific mechanisms. Claude Bouchard, a prominent international authority on obesity and weight control, noted that at this time there is no common agreement on the specific determinants of obesity, stressing that numerous factors are correlated with body-fat content. In general, most leading obesity scientists, such as Grundy, support a multicausal theory involving the interaction of a number of genetic and environmental factors.

Genetic Factors Heredity appears to be a very important factor in the etiology of obesity, particularly morbid obesity. For example, several genetic diseases result in clinical obesity. Also, studies of adopted children, including both fraternal and identical

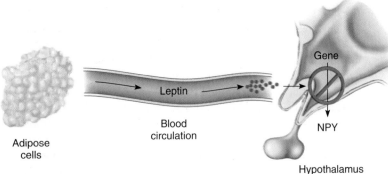

FIGURE 10.6 One possible mechanism of the set-point theory. Leptin is produced in proportion to body-fat stores. When body fat increases, more leptin is released into the bloodstream, circulates to the hypothalamus, and inhibits the formation or release of neuropeptide Y (NPY). NPY is a potent stimulator of food intake and may also decrease energy expenditure.

twins who were separated and adopted by different families, have shown a greater relationship of the body composition between the children and their biological parents as compared to the adoptive parents. For a review of two meticulous studies of the genetic role in obesity, the interested reader is referred to the reports by Bouchard and others on long-term overfeeding of identical twins, and by Stunkard and others on the Body Mass Index of twins who were raised apart. Based on his and others' research, Bouchard indicated that genetic heritability of obesity approximates 25–40 percent. It appears heredity may determine those internal factors in the body that may predispose one to gain weight.

Research into the genetics of obesity has been progressing at a rapid pace. Hirsch and Leibel note several obesity genes have already been identified, which in some persons may maintain an unhealthful set-point. Levin cites one possibility, suggesting that individuals with a genetic susceptibility to obesity may be predisposed to abnormalities in neural function. They establish neural circuits that are not easily abolished. In essence, obesity genes influence appetite to increase energy intake or affect metabolism to decrease energy expenditure. For example, genes in the hypothalamus may decrease the number of protein receptors for leptin, thus preventing leptin from inhibiting the formation of NPY. NPY may then stimulate the appetite. Also, as noted previously, a protein known as the uncoupling protein (UCP) is believed to activate thermogenesis; UCP1 activates thermogenesis in brown fat, whereas UCP2 activates thermogenesis in white fat and muscle tissue. Defects in UCP genes may decrease resting energy expenditure.

Over 340 genes may be involved in weight control. Genetic factors that have been implicated in the development of obesity include the following:

- a predisposition to sweet, high-fat foods
- impaired function of hormones such as insulin and cortisol
- decreased levels of human growth hormone
- low plasma leptin concentrations
- inability of nutrients or hormones in the blood to suppress the appetite control center
- a greater number of fat cells
- an enhanced metabolic efficiency in storing fat
- a lower REE
- a decreased TEF
- low rates of fat oxidation
- lower levels of spontaneous physical activity, or NEAT, during the day
- lower levels of energy expenditure during light exercise

Some scientists have coined the term the "thrifty gene" to indicate an increased efficiency in the obese to conserve energy, and they consider obesity a metabolic disease.

Environmental Factors Although heredity may predispose one to obesity, environmental factors are also highly involved. Capturing the role of environmental factors in a nutshell, Wadden and others indicated that the marked increase in obesity worldwide appears to be attributable to a society that explicitly encourages the consumption of supersized portions of high-fat, high-sugar foods while implicitly discouraging physical activity.

High-fat, high-Calorie foods Excess Calories, or overfeeding, may lead to obesity. For example, Pearcey and de Castro evaluated eating behavior and activity levels of weight-gaining and weight-stable men and women, and found that the basic difference was that the weight-gaining individuals consumed about 400 more Calories per day during the period of active weight gain. Although an excess of caloric input over output will lead to a weight gain, researchers suggest that the main culprit in the diet that leads to obesity is dietary fat. For various reasons, the National Academy of Sciences concluded that higher fat intakes are accompanied with increased energy intake and therefore increased risk for weight gain in populations that are already disposed to being overweight and obesity, such as that of North America. Obesity researchers have postulated several of these reasons. First, dietary fat is highly palatable to most individuals, stimulating hedonistic responses and encouraging overconsumption. Dietary fat contains more Calories per gram, and may not provide the same satiety as carbohydrate and protein. Gibbs noted that the body systems respond quickly to protein and carbohydrates but slowly to fat, too slowly to stop ingestion of a high-fat meal before the body has had too much. Green and Blundell also note that high-fat foods give rise to higher energy intake during a meal than do carbohydrate foods, and Calorie for Calorie are less effective in suppressing subsequent food intake. In support of this point, Shah and Garg reported that spontaneous energy intake is higher on an unrestricted high-fat diet compared to a high-carbohydrate diet. Second, dietary fat may be stored as fat more efficiently compared to carbohydrate and protein. It takes some energy to synthesize fat and store it in the adipose tissue, but Dattilo noted that in comparison to dietary fat, it may cost up to three or four times more energy to convert carbohydrate and protein to body fat. Third, other investigators indicate that chronic intake of a high-fat diet will produce resistance in the hypothalamus to various factors that normally suppress appetite, such as leptin, the end result being increased energy intake and body-fat deposition. The interested student is referred to the reviews by Dattilo, Tso and Liu, and Rolls and Shide regarding the relationship of dietary fat to body weight.

Low-fat, high-Calorie foods Although excess dietary fat, for reasons cited, may be a major culprit in the etiology of obesity, researchers such as Lichtenstein and Willett have noted that the prevalence of obesity in the United States has increased dramatically over the past two decades even though the energy derived from dietary fat has actually decreased, both in absolute terms and in percent of total dietary energy. One reason for this apparent inconsistency may be an increased daily Calorie intake. Fat-free does not mean Calorie-free. Kelly Brownell, an obesity expert from Yale University, indicated that our society promotes eating, mainly fast foods, to excess. Appetizing low-fat, but high-Calorie food is everywhere, and in supersize proportions which significantly increase caloric content. At latest count there are over 300,000 packaged foods available, and a large supermarket may carry 50,000 or more. Portion sizes have increased dramatically; what was once small, is now large. For example, the average soft drink is over 50 percent larger compared to past years.

With excess dietary Calories, Melby and Hill indicate that it is possible for an individual to become obese on a low-fat diet because the body rapidly adjusts to oxidizing excess dietary carbohydrate and protein to meet its energy needs, sparing the use of body-fat stores. Jacobs and others also indicate that significant amounts of body fat may be generated from excess dietary carbohydrate. Recent research by Ma and others indicates that a high-glycemic index diet is associated with increased body weight, but confirming data are needed. The CDC recently reported that compared to 30 years ago, the average American female consumes 335 more Calories daily; the figure for men is 168 Calories. These additional Calories are derived mainly from carbohydrates, such as cookies and soda. An additional 335 Calories daily would lead to a weight gain of about one pound in 10 days.

Physical inactivity and NEAT   As noted, the prevalence of obesity is increasing despite a decrease in consumption of dietary fat. Astrup labels this the American Paradox. Other than the explanation that this observation is attributable to an increased consumption of low-fat, high-Calorie foods, Astrup suggests it also may be explained by concomitantly decreasing levels of physical activity. Modern technology is wonderful, helping to make our lives more comfortable and enjoyable in numerous ways. However, technology may also exert a negative effect on our health, as the development of television, computers, and other labor-saving devices may decrease levels of physical activity. In a recent review, DiPietro noted that the influence of regular physical activity on body composition is complex. However, although there are some methodological problems with the epidemiological research, DiPietro indicated that several cross-sectional studies have reported an inverse relationship between physical activity and body weight; that is, those who were physically inactive weighed more. DiPietro and other reviewers, such as Saris, noted that physical activity and exercise is an important factor in the prevention of overweight or obesity. Furthermore, de Groot and van Staveren indicate that once an individual becomes obese, physical activity decreases, setting up a vicious cycle of increasing body weight and even less physical activity.

Levine contends that the variability in total daily energy expenditure is attributed mainly to nonexercise activity thermogenesis (NEAT). Technology has decreased the amount of energy we normally expend via NEAT each day, such as walking, standing, and even fidgeting, which may lead to an energy imbalance and weight gain. Researchers followed lean and mildly obese people for 10 days, reporting those who were mildly obese stayed seated for about 2.5 hours longer per day than the lean individuals; they indicated that this could amount to 350 fewer Calories expended daily. Watching television or other such sedentary seated behaviors decrease NEAT, which Levine indicates may be of profound importance in the development of obesity.

Other environmental factors   Other environmental factors may predispose to weight gain. Reduced amounts of sleep are associated with overweight and obesity. Vorona and others indicate that lack of sleep may cause one to be more tired and less likely to exercise, and being awake longer will provide more chances to eat.

Emotional stress may also lead to weight gain. Stress may trigger the release of various hormones, particularly cortisol. Dallman and others indicate that cortisol has a major stimulatory effect on caloric intake, and also may redistribute stored energy preponderantly into intraabdominal fat depots. In essence, the body perceives stress as an emergency and responds by attempting to conserve energy by eating more and storing fat.

Certain drugs may increase body weight. For example, asthmatics may use oral corticosteroids, whose use is associated with weight gain. Two important factors may be the use of social drugs, alcohol and nicotine.

Alcohol is rich in Calories. At 7 Calories per gram, it is comparable to a gram of fat, which contains 9 Calories. The National Academy of Sciences has noted that if the energy derived from alcohol is not utilized, the excess is stored as fat. Moreover, Tremblay and others reported that concurrent alcohol intake does not suppress the appetite nor does it suppress fat intake. Thus, the Calories in alcohol are additive and may lead to an energy surplus and weight gain.

Nicotine in cigarettes is a stimulant that may inhibit the appetite and increase REE. Froom and others reported that smokers who quit gained weight (about 11–13 pounds), mostly in a 2-year period immediately following smoking cessation. It is interesting to note that teenagers concerned with weight control and dieting are more likely to start smoking. Although it may be helpful in weight control, smoking carries major health risks itself and there are healthier, more effective methods available.

Interaction of Genetics and Environment   Perusse and Bouchard indicated that genetic factors play an important role in weight control. Although this is so, Grundy noted that the rapid increase in obesity in the United States over the past 20 years cannot be attributed to genetic changes over such a short time frame, indicating that the environment is more important in the development of moderate obesity. Peters and others support this viewpoint, noting that human physiology developed to function within an environment where high levels of physical activity were needed in daily life and food was inconsistently available. The current environment is characterized by a situation whereby minimal physical activity is required for daily life and food is abundant, inexpensive, high in energy density, and widely available.

Many individuals who have maintained a normal body weight during childhood and adolescence begin to put on weight gradually in young adulthood (ages 20–40). The basic cause of this creeping obesity, as depicted in figure 10.7, is usually an increased consumption of Calories, particularly fat Calories, and a decreased level of physical activity, or a combination of the two. In a major epidemiologic study, Simoes and others reported that dietary fat intake and physical activity were strongly and inversely associated, meaning those who ate the most fat had the least physical activity. For young college students, weight gain may be more rapid due to lifestyle changes (i.e., a high-fat, high-Calorie diet and decreased physical activity) during the first year of college life, with some students gaining 10–15 pounds, the proverbial "freshman fifteen." Also, several studies have shown that the risk of developing obesity is directly related to the amount of time

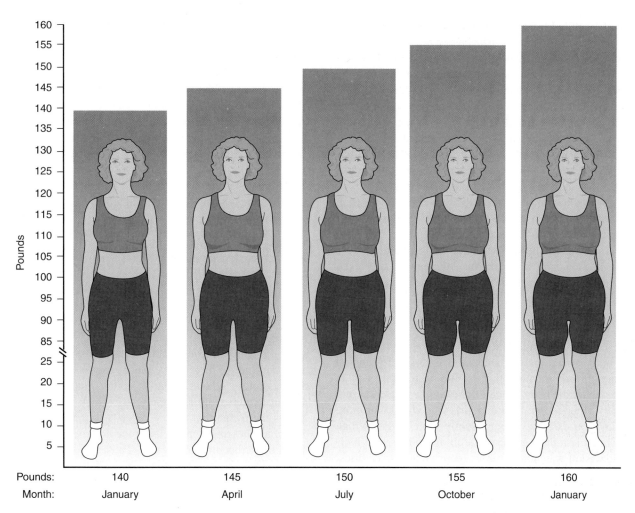

FIGURE 10.7 Adult-onset obesity is often referred to as creeping obesity, for it creeps up on adults slowly. As little as 200 additional Calories per day above normal requirements would result in a gain of approximately 20 pounds of body fat in 1 year.

spent watching television, a sedentary activity usually accompanied by consumption of high-Calorie snack foods.

If the set-point theory is valid, why do some people attain and maintain body weights higher than their set point? Keesey and Hirvonen indicate that an individual's set-point is apparently adjustable, possibly shifting with changes in the hypothalamus. Some investigators have proposed a new theory, the "settling-point" theory. The **settling-point theory** suggests that the set point may be modified, and in the case of weight gain, set at a higher level. Gibbs indicates that whatever genes we have that make us susceptible to obesity settle into a happy equilibrium with our environment. For example, a chronic high-fat diet may modify our genes, possibly increasing leptin resistance, and our body weight rises to a new level. Gibbs provides an example of the Pima Indians living in the United States and Mexico. Both groups have similar genetic backgrounds, yet the Pima Indians living in the United States who consume a high-fat diet are generally obese, while the Pima Indians living in Mexico who consume a grain/vegetable-based diet are generally normal weight. On the other hand, a weight-loss diet may lower the set point to help maintain body weight at a lower level.

Weinsier and others found that caloric restriction in obese women induced a transient decrease in REE, which would be counterproductive to weight loss. However, metabolism returned to normal at the completion of the weight-loss program when energy intake was then adequate to maintain the reduced body weight, suggesting that the set point may settle to a lower level over time. Changes in environmental conditions, such as the diet, may help change neural circuits involved in weight control. Clearly, genetics and environment interact to influence body weight and composition.

Childhood obesity: Time for prevention Once an individual is obese, treatment is not very effective. Levin notes that neural circuits predisposing to obesity are not easily abolished. Most scientists agree that prevention of obesity is of prime importance, particularly in childhood. Gibbs speculates that there must be a window of opportunity in childhood where the environment influences the set point. However, the role of diet and physical activity in the development of obesity during childhood, when the most severe cases of obesity begin to develop, is not totally clear. Of the two, an improper diet appears to be the major problem.

There may be a familial factor involved here, as the child may be raised in a family where high-fat meals and overeating are common, as suggested in a recent study by Fisher and Birch. Also, the supermarket diet of today makes it easy for children to consume large amounts of Calories. Sugar and fat are found in a wide variety of foods that we eat and constitute about 50 percent of our daily caloric intake. In particular, Ludwig and others found that consumption of sugar-sweetened drinks is associated with obesity in children. Bowman also reported fast-food consumption has increased fivefold among children since 1970, noting that children who ate fast food on a regular basis consumed 187 more daily Calories, which total up to about six pounds more per year. Although some studies have shown that obese children do not consume more Calories than their nonobese peers, the data were not collected during the period when the obese children were gaining weight. Studies in which the investigators actually lived with the children suggest that the obese child does eat more, and also eats faster.

Bar-Or and others, in a recent meeting of experts on physical activity and obesity in children, indicated that physical inactivity may be one cause of juvenile obesity. In children, studies have shown that body weight and the amount of time spent watching television are directly related; that is, the more television is watched the greater the body weight. For example, Andersen and others recently reported that boys and girls who watch 4 or more hours of television daily have significantly more body fat than those who watch less than 2 hours. Caroli and others also indicated that television watching replaces more vigorous activities, and noted there is a positive correlation between time spent watching television and being overweight or obese in populations of different ages. However, Marshall and others indicated that relationships between sedentary behavior and youth obesity are unlikely to be explained using single markers of inactivity, such as TV viewing. Thus, watching television per se may not contribute to obesity because any sedentary activity over the same amount of time would produce similar effects. Being physically active during this time frame would burn Calories and help deter weight gain. The role of physical inactivity in the etiology of childhood obesity does not appear to be as important as that of diet, but the effects of physical inactivity and diet may be intertwined. For example, Caroli and others reported that children are exposed to a large number of unhealthy stimulations in terms of food intake when watching television; food commercials have increased, especially for junk food in all of its forms. Bar-Or recently noted that an important effect of television watching is that children snack excessively.

In general, studies show that obese children are just as physically active as nonobese children. This may not be surprising in that typical nonobese American children are not very physically active either. These comments should not be construed as suggesting that exercise is unimportant in the prevention and treatment of obesity, for Russell Pate, an expert in youth fitness, recently noted the true potential for preventing obesity through physical activity is not known, and some data suggest physical activity and body fatness are moderately and inversely related in youngsters. Recent research by Bernard Gutin has shown that exercise, independent of diet, may lead to weight loss in obese children. Exercise is important for weight control, as will be documented in the next chapter.

Individuals with a genetic tendency to obesity do not necessarily have to become obese. Individuals with a weak predisposition to obesity may become obese. Although genetics plays an important role in the etiology of obesity, a desirable body weight may be achieved and maintained in those individuals so predisposed. It may be more difficult and may involve a lifetime of vigilance, but it can be done with an appropriate program of diet and exercise, and the time to start is during childhood.

How is fat deposited in the body?

The actual deposition of fat in the human body may occur in two ways: **hyperplasia** (an increase in the number of fat cells), or **hypertrophy** (an increase in the amount of fat in each cell). Earlier research appeared to support the theory that hyperplasia is a major cause in the development of childhood obesity whereas hypertrophy is the primary cause in adulthood. However, Pi-Sunyer recently noted that in humans, fat cell number may continue to increase as long as excess energy intake occurs. Existing fat cells apparently have a maximal size potential (about 1 microgram of fat per cell), which when exceeded stimulates the formation of new fat cells or the accumulation of fat in preadipocytes, small cells in the adipose tissue that have the potential to become adipocytes. Thus, although a genetic predisposition to inherit a greater number of fat cells, thereby facilitating the development of obesity, may exist, individuals without this genetic predisposition may still become obese with a positive energy balance stored as fat. Interestingly, Pi-Sunyer indicated that once fat cells are formed, the number seems to remain fixed even if weight is lost. To lose body fat, one must reduce the amount of fat in the adipose cells to normal, or even below normal.

Key Concept Recap

▶ The brain's hypothalamus appears to be the central control mechanism in appetite regulation, which involves a complex interaction of physiological and psychological factors. Neural and hormonal feedback from the senses, gastrointestinal tract, and other body organs helps to drive hunger or signal satiety.

▶ Although the ultimate cause of obesity is a positive energy balance, the underlying cause is not known but probably involves the interaction of many genetic and environmental factors.

Check for Yourself

As you go about your normal activities for a day, pay particular attention to environmental conditions that may be conducive to consuming high-Calorie foods and discouraging physical activity. Compare your results with those of your classmates.

Weight Gain, Obesity, and Health

George Bray, an international authority on obesity and health, noted that obesity is an epidemic disease in itself, and related health problems are caused by two factors. First the increased mass of adipose tissue places extra strain on body systems, such as the heart and the joints. Second, the enlarged fat cells secrete numerous substances, referred to as **adipokines,** into the blood stream which may affect metabolic processes; some of these effects are pathogenic, such as increased insulin resistance and inflammation in the blood vessels.

What health problems are associated with overweight and obesity?

Recent reviews have listed numerous health problems and associated risk factors associated with obesity. Some of these listed health problems are associated with the strain of the increased body mass, some with the metabolic effects of adipokines, and some with the combination of the two factors.

Asthma
Cancer
Cardiovascular disease
Diabetes (type 2)
Dyslipidemia
Gallstones
Gastrointestinal reflux disease
Gout
Hypertension
Insulin resistance
Low self-image and self-esteem
Osteoarthritis
Respiratory dysfunction
Sleep apnea
Social disabilities
Stroke
Vertebral disk herniation

According to the Centers for Disease Control and Prevention, the health costs of obesity parallel those associated with smoking-related disease. The American College of Sports Medicine noted that an estimated $100 billion, or 5–10 percent of health care costs, is spent on obesity-related conditions annually. The majority of these health care costs appear to be associated with the two main chronic diseases associated with obesity, namely cardiovascular disease and cancer.

Cardiovascular Disease and Related Health Risks The primary health condition associated with excess body fat is coronary heart disease (CHD). Eckel and Krauss reported that the American Heart Association recently classified obesity as a major risk factor for CHD. Quantifying this risk, Kolotkin and others reported that for every one-point increase in the BMI, heart failure risk increased 5 percent in men and 7 percent in women, and indicated that obesity is, in and by itself, a risk factor for heart failure. Excess body fat also increases the risk of developing high blood pressure, hypercho-

lesterolemia, and diabetes, all of which are risk factors leading to the development of CHD.

In particular, obesity increases the risk of Type 2 diabetes, whose rate has increased dramatically over the past decade in concert with the parallel increase in obesity. *Shape Up America,* a non-profit organization that promotes a healthy body weight, has coined the term *Diabesity*™ to highlight the relationship between the two. Trayhurn and Beattie report that adipose tissue secretes a substance called resistin, which is reported to induce insulin resistance, linking diabetes to obesity. The greater the amount of adipose tissue, the greater potential for diabetes. Gibbs reports that obesity increases the risk of Type 2 diabetes by an astonishing 1,480 percent with a BMI of 27–29, 2,660 percent with a BMI of 29–31, 3,930 percent with a BMI of 31–33, and 5,300 percent with a BMI of 33–35. The detrimental effects of obesity relative to the development of chronic disease occur when it persists for 10 years or more. This may be a serious health problem in the near future as McGill and others recently reported that obesity is associated with accelerated coronary atherosclerosis in adolescent and young adult men. Those with a BMI greater than 30 already had fatty streaks and lesions in the coronary arteries.

Cancer Obesity has been regarded as a risk factor for certain cancers for some time, but a large, recent study by Calle and others from the American Cancer Society revealed that obesity plays a much bigger role in causing cancer than previously believed. They estimated that 90,000 Americans die each year by cancer caused primarily by being overweight, accounting for 14 percent of cancer in men and 20 percent in women. Those with the highest BMI (40 or over) were at greatest risk. In women, obesity plays a role in breast, uterine, cervical, pancreatic, esophageal, renal, and gallbladder cancer, while in men it was involved in liver, pancreatic, colorectal, stomach, and gallbladder cancer.

Obesity may influence the development of cancer in various ways. For example, fat tissue leads to an overproduction of estrogen and other steroid hormones. In women, an increased serum level of estrogen is associated with an increased incidence of breast cancer. Carmichael and Bates reported that most large epidemiological studies have found that overweight or obese women are at increased risk of developing postmenopausal breast cancer, and also indicated that all treatment modalities for breast cancer may be adversely affected by the presence of obesity. Obesity also leads to excess production of insulin and insulin-like growth factor receptors, which have been associated with various cancers. Other factors are also involved.

Mortality, Morbidity, and Quality of Life Obesity shortens life. Even in ancient Greece, Hippocrates recognized that persons who are naturally fat are apt to die sooner than slender individuals. However, a recent analysis by Flegal and others from the Centers for Disease Control (CDC) indicated that body *overweight,* with a BMI of 25.0–29.9, was not associated with increased mortality, or death. These findings have been supported in an independent meta-analysis of 25 observational studies by McGee, who also reported no increase in morality in individuals classified as *overweight.* Flegal and others suggested that improvements in medical care, such as better control of blood pressure and serum cholesterol with medications, along with less cigarette smoking, may have decreased deaths from cardiovascular disease in individuals who were classified as *overweight.*

Critics countered that actual deaths from overweight and obesity are only part of the picture. Excess fat contributes to morbidity, or the increase in various diseases such as diabetes and its associated disabilities. Those who are overweight and have such health problems may experience significant impairments in their quality of life. Moreover, critics note that being overweight is the path to obesity, as over time the overweight become obese.

In the same analysis, the CDC indicated that individuals classified as being *obese,* with a BMI of 30–35, were at a high risk for death, and those with a BMI greater than 35 accounted for the largest majority of deaths. Similar findings were reported in the meta-analysis by McGee. Bren, writing for the Food and Drug Administration, noted that excess weight and physical inactivity account for more than 300,000 premature deaths each year in the United States. Fontaine and others calculated the years of life lost due to obesity and found that those who are obese during young adulthood are at substantial risk for premature death. For example, using data from the National Health and Nutrition Epidemiologic Follow-Up Study, they calculated that white men and women aged 20–30 with severe levels of obesity may lose 13 and 8 years of life, respectively; corresponding years lost for black men and women are 20 and 5, respectively. In general, thinner individuals live longer.

Epidemiological research clearly indicates that being obese increases one's health risks. The greater the BMI, particularly above 30, the greater the health risk. The location of the fat in the body is also an important contributing factor underlying these health risks.

How does the location of fat in the body affect health?

Classifications of different types of obesity based upon regional fat distribution have been proposed, the most popular differentiation being the android versus the gynoid types. **Android-type** (male-type) **obesity** is characterized by accumulation in the abdominal region—particularly the intraabdominal region—of deep, visceral fat, but also of subcutaneous fat. Android-type obesity is also known by other terms, such as abdominal, central, upper body, or lower trunk obesity, and is sometimes referred to as the apple-shape obesity. Although its cause is unknown, researchers have discovered an enzyme in the fat cells of mice that when activated triggers an overproduction of the hormone cortisol, which tends to facilitate the deposition of fat in the abdominal region. **Gynoid-type** (female-type) **obesity** is characterized by fat accumulation in the gluteal-femoral region—the hips, buttocks, and thighs. It is also known as lower body obesity, and is often referred to as pear-shape obesity (see figure 10.8). Bouchard has noted that both types of obesity have a strong genetic component. As mentioned earlier, waist measurement may be an appropriate screening technique for android-type or gynoid-type obesity. The procedure for determin-

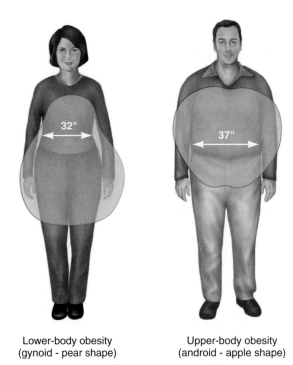

Lower-body obesity
(gynoid - pear shape)

Upper-body obesity
(android - apple shape)

FIGURE 10.8 Android (apple-shape) obesity is associated with a greater risk for chronic diseases, such as diabetes and heart disease, than is gynoid (pear-shape) obesity.

ing waist circumference is described in appendix D and the increase in health risk associated with an increased circumference and various BMI levels is presented in table 10.3.

Android-type obesity is increasingly being recognized as causing a greater health risk than obesity itself. It appears that android-type and gynoid-type fat cells possess dissimilar biochemical functions because of differences in the activity of lipoprotein lipase, an enzyme that regulates fat metabolism. Fat cells in the deep visceral depots are large and highly metabolically active. They readily release free fatty acids into the blood when stimulated by epinephrine, and thus may contribute to abnormalities in glucose and lipid metabolism, particularly in individuals under psychological stress. Data from animal studies have provided direct evidence that the interaction of insulin and fat cell metabolism varies in different fat regions. This finding may be related to humans, for epidemiological data have shown that android-type obesity is associated with certain metabolic disorders, including hyperinsulinemia, insulin resistance, impaired glucose tolerance, hypertriglyceridemia, increased small, dense LDL-cholesterol, decreased HDL-cholesterol, hypertension, and increased plasma fibrinogen and related blood clotting. Reaven has called this cluster of symptoms the **metabolic syndrome,** or syndrome X. Many of these symptoms are risk factors for CHD and type 2 diabetes, and Lamarche indicated that abdominal obesity predicts CHD and type 2 diabetes better than obesity alone.

The metabolic syndrome appears to increase with age, but it may also appear in those with relatively modest BMI levels. Ford and others, from the Centers for Disease Control and Prevention, reported that over 20 percent of Americans aged 20 years and older have the metabolic syndrome. The percentage is less than 7 percent in those aged 20–29 but increases to more than 40 percent of individuals over age 60. Relative to body weight, you may not need to be obese to develop the metabolic syndrome. Janssen and others recently reported that individuals with a normal BMI (18.5–24.9) and overweight BMI (25.0–29.9) who had a high waist circumference were increasingly likely to have hypertension, diabetes, dyslipidemia, and the metabolic syndrome compared with those with normal waist circumference values.

The full metabolic syndrome certainly increases health risks, but Trevisan and others indicated that only a small part of the population possess the full cluster of symptoms in the metabolic syndrome, and we must not forget the proven health risks of individual risk factors, such as LDL-cholesterol, within the syndrome.

In an attempt to provide some standardization, Alberti and others recently convened an international conference to determine a worldwide definition of the metabolic syndrome. Although there are some minor differences among various nations, the presence of the metabolic syndrome in an individual was dependent on waist circumference and having two or more of four metabolic abnormalities. The following apply to North America and Europe:

	Men	Women
Waist circumference (inches (cm))	37 (94)	31.5 (80)
Elevated serum triglycerides (mg/dL)	> 150	> 150
Subnormal HDL-cholesterol (mg/dL)	< 40	< 50
Elevated blood pressure (mmHg)	130/85	130/85
Elevated fasting blood sugar (mg/dL)	100	100

As noted in table 10.3, a waist circumference of 40 inches (102 cm) in men and 35 inches (86 cm) in women has been associated with increased health risks. This new definition lowers the waist circumference to 37 inches (94 cm) for men and 31.5 inches (80 cm) for women. These lower values are in accord with a recent study by Wang and others who reported an increased risk of type 2 diabetes in men with waist sizes greater than 37 inches.

Studies show that android-type obesity is a major risk factor for mortality in both men and women. In a recent study, Bigaard and others found that waist circumference, even when accounting for total body fat, remained strongly and directly associated with all-cause mortality in middle-aged men and women, suggesting that the increased mortality risk related to excess body fat is mainly due to abdominal adiposity. The increased mortality appears to be due primarily to myocardial infarction.

Although abdominal obesity appears to increase health risks, Busetto noted that because of the relatively high rate of visceral fat mobilization, it is a good target for interventions aimed at reducing cardiovascular risk factors. Several recent studies in men, women, and adolescents have shown that weight loss via dieting and exercise will preferentially decrease fat from the abdominal area and, concomitantly, improve the serum lipid profile.

Gynoid-type fat cells appear to store fat more readily and tend to lose it less readily, and thus the health risks do not appear to be as great as those associated with android-type obesity. A combined diet-exercise program may help to reduce gynoid-type obesity, but the pear-shape figure appears to be more resistant to change compared to the apple type.

Does being obese increase health risks in youth?

Childhood obesity is a rapidly emerging epidemic worldwide. Some of the major adverse health effects of excess body fat during childhood and adolescence appear to be social and psychological rather than medical. Because personality development occurs primarily during childhood and adolescence, excessive body fat may contribute more greatly to social-emotional problems at this time than during adult-onset obesity. The Nutrition Committee of the Canadian Pediatric Society noted that obesity interferes with the development of a satisfying self-image and social status, thereby impairing psychological development. Obese children often are rejected and ridiculed by their peers, superiors, and even parents, resulting in a negative self-image, low self-esteem, and even serious psychological illness. In essence, their quality of life suffers.

A contributing factor to the development of psychological problems may be the adverse effect of excessive body fat on physical fitness and athletic performance. Southern indicates that obese children respond differently emotionally to exercise than do normal-weight children, and thus may experience negative consequences to participation in physical activities. A child who is unsuccessful in play activities probably will not participate, and thus will miss the socializing aspects of play. When used in conjunction with appropriate dietary prescriptions and consistent behavior modification, exercise serves as a promising modality that may reverse obese conditions during childhood and, perhaps, prevent the onset of adult obesity.

Obesity can also cause other health problems in children and adolescents. In particular, type 2 diabetes is epidemic among obese youngsters. Although children may not experience the debilitating effects of diabetes early in life, in general children who are overweight and diabetic are likely to stay that way into adulthood. Epidemiological research has shown recently that obese adolescents are at greater risk for chronic disease in adulthood and all-cause mortality compared to their nonobese peers.

Does being physically fit negate the adverse health effects associated with being overweight?

In general, research findings documenting increased health risks associated with obesity have been derived from the general population, and have been based primarily on BMI values. Some investigators have challenged these data, suggesting that a slightly elevated BMI may not be associated with increased health risks in some individuals, particularly those who are physically fit.

As noted previously, the BMI does not evaluate body composition. Although it may be useful in determining health risks in the general population because a high BMI is usually associated with excess body fat, it does not apply to muscular individuals. A high BMI may be associated with the development of various diseases if it does represent obesity and increases various risk factors, such as high serum cholesterol levels and high blood pressure. Glenn Gaesser, an exercise physiologist at the University of Virginia, in his book *Big Fat Lies,* indicated that being overweight is not necessarily associated with increased health risks. Lifestyle may be an important moderating factor. For example, research from the Cooper Institute for Aerobics Research indicates that overweight individuals who have moderate and high levels of physical fitness have a lower risk of mortality than their low-fit peers, even those of normal body weight. In general, these scientists suggest that being overweight does not increase mortality unless it is associated with adverse effects on blood pressure, glucose tolerance, serum cholesterol levels, and physical fitness. Thus, some have proposed use of the term "healthy weight" for overweight individuals who are otherwise healthy.

The *Health at Any Size* movement, as advocated by Jonas, promotes physical activity for the obese individual, suggesting that exercise, even though it may not result in weight loss, may confer health benefits. In support of this contention, Miller and Dunstan found that physical activity intervention for the treatment of type 2 diabetes can lead to small but clinically meaningful improvements in glycemic control, even in the absence of weight loss. Borghouts and Keizer noted that both acute and chronic exercise may affect blood glucose and insulin activity favorably. Up to 2 hours after an acute bout of exercise, glucose uptake is in part elevated due to insulin independent mechanisms, probably involving an increase in GLUT-4 receptors in the muscle cell membrane induced by exercise. Additionally, an exercise bout can increase insulin sensitivity for up to 16 hours afterwards. Chronic exercise training potentiates the effect of exercise on insulin sensitivity through multiple adaptations in glucose transport and metabolism.

Carroll and Dudfield stated that exercise training should be considered an essential part of a therapeutic lifestyle change that may improve the entire cluster of risk factors associated with the metabolic syndrome, but indicated exercise works best when coupled with weight loss. The combination of exercise and weight loss has been shown to produce numerous health effects, including decreased blood pressure, improved serum lipid status, reduced blood glucose, increased self-esteem, improved psychological health, and increased longevity.

Stevens and others examined the effects of both fitness (*fit, unfit*) and fatness (*fat, not fat*) on mortality from all causes and from cardiovascular disease. They found that *fit and not fat* individuals had the lowest mortality rates, those who were *fit and fat* or *unfit and not fat* had mortality rates about 30–40 percent higher, while *fat and unfit* individuals had the highest mortality rates. Hu and others recently reported similar findings in a study with women, noting that those who were lean (BMI < 25) and physically active (3.5 or more hours exercise/week) had much lower relative risk of mortality compared to the other groups. Women who were obese and inactive had the highest mortality rate. These investigators concluded that being fit does not reverse the increased health risks associated with excess adiposity. Although being *fit and fat* appears to be better healthwise than being *unfit and fat*, losing weight to become *fit and unfat* may confer additional health benefits.

Prevention of obesity is the key because once individuals become obese, treatment is difficult. When used in conjunction with appropriate dietary prescriptions and consistent behavior modification, exercise serves as a promising modality not only to prevent obesity in the first place, but perhaps also to help reverse it both during childhood and adulthood. The earlier one begins to exercise, the better. For those who are overweight, an excellent government program is *Active at Any Size,* which can be accessed at www.win.niddk.nhi.gov; click on "Publications for the Public."

Researchers are looking for clues such as genetic, metabolic, or anthropometric markers that can predict which children will become obese so that appropriate interventions may be enacted earlier in life when chances of success may be greater. In the meantime, some successful programs incorporating both diet and exercise for the prevention and treatment of obesity have been developed, and appropriate guidelines are presented in the next chapter.

Key Concept Recap

▶ Excessive body fat is associated with a variety of chronic diseases and impaired health conditions, including coronary heart disease, diabetes, high blood pressure, and arthritis.

▶ For children and adolescents, the major adverse health effects of excessive body fat appear to be social and psychological, but in future years, they may be more prone to chronic diseases than their nonobese peers. However, overweight and obese children are at high risk for diabetes even while young.

▶ Although being obese increases health risks, the deposition of fat in the abdominal area exacerbates these risks. Referred to as android-type, or male-type, obesity, increased abdominal fat is associated with the metabolic syndrome and risk factors for heart disease and diabetes.

▶ Being physically fit and eating a healthful diet may help reduce some of the health risks associated with being overweight. One can be overweight, yet fit, but it appears the greatest health benefits are associated with being fit and not fat.

Check for Yourself

Conduct an observational study. Learn to use the "eyeball" technique to determine if a child is overweight. One afternoon sit outside a secondary public school in your community and as the students exit, make a check in a notebook as to how many out of the first 50 or 100 you would classify as being overweight. Compare your findings to the text discussion and to the findings of classmates who may also undertake this small observational study.

Excessive Weight Loss and Health

Losing excess body fat, even only 5–10 percent of body weight, and attaining a desirable body weight may confer some significant health benefits by counteracting the adverse effects of obesity. However, many individuals attempt to lose weight for other reasons. Slimness is currently very fashionable, particularly among females of all ages. It is desired not only for attractiveness but also for psychological undertones of independence, achievement, and self-control. Also, both male and female athletes, such as distance runners, gymnasts, wrestlers, jockeys, and dancers, practice weight control to improve their performance. Losing body weight for improved performance may also provide some health benefits, for Paul Williams theorized that the elevated HDL-cholesterol concentrations of long-distance runners are primarily a result of reduced adiposity. However, excessive weight loss may actually lead to deterioration of health.

What health problems are associated with improper weight-loss programs and excessive weight losses?

As shall be noted in the next chapter, a well-designed diet and proper exercise are the cornerstones of a sound weight-control program. However, some individuals may establish unrealistically low body-weight goals, which may lead to pathogenic weight-control behaviors. Such techniques as complete starvation, self-induced vomiting, or the use of drugs, diet pills, laxatives, and diuretics may initially be employed to achieve rapid weight losses but may evolve into serious medical disorders, even death, if prolonged. The general effects of excessive rapid and long-term weight losses on health are highlighted here. Rapid weight losses over a week or two usually are achieved by dehydration techniques, drugs, or by starvation-type diets characterized by very low energy intake, whereas long-term weight losses may be associated with eating disorders or problems in young athletes.

Dehydration Dehydration may be induced by exercise, exposure to the heat (as with a sauna), or the use of diuretics and laxatives. The effect of dehydration upon one's health, particularly in relation to heat illnesses, was detailed in the previous chapter. The use of diuretics and laxatives may increase potassium losses from the body, which may lead to electrolyte imbalances and disturbed neurological function, including heart function. For example, in a recent case study Sturmi and Rutecki reported life-threatening hyperkalemia associated with ECG changes and indicators of muscle and kidney damage in a bodybuilder who used diuretics and potassium supplements, along with dietary restrictions, in preparation for competition. Vigorous potassium-lowering maneuvers helped resolve these problems, but the patient's symptoms resembled those of another professional bodybuilder who died after employing similar drug and diet strategies. Disturbed kidney function has also been observed following severe dehydration. The recent deaths of three young collegiate wrestlers have been associated with excessive dehydration.

Weight-Loss Drugs and Supplements Various drugs have been developed to stimulate weight loss and generally are prescribed for the obese, not for those individuals who want to lose a few pounds. Nevertheless, it appears that individuals across the weight spectrum, including physically active individuals and athletes, are using drugs for weight-control purposes. Some drugs are available without prescription, while others need to be used with medical supervision.

Drugs may help reduce body weight by several mechanisms. Some drugs are designed to suppress the appetite by either enhancing or inhibiting the production or activity of various neurotransmitters in the hypothalamus—such as the depressant serotonin, the adrenergic stimulant norepinephrine, or neuropeptide Y (NPY)—involved in appetite control. Increasing serotonin and norepinephrine and decreasing NPY will suppress the appetite. The diet drug sibutramine (Meridia) inhibits the reuptake of serotonin and norepinephrine, thus reducing hunger. Other drugs may be used to increase energy expenditure (thermogenesis) in the peripheral tissues, particularly agents designed to increase resting energy expenditure (REE) by stimulating special receptors (Beta-3 receptors) in brown fat and abdominal adipose tissue, and possibly muscle tissue. Sibutramine also stimulates thermogenesis. Still other drugs, such as orlistat, may be used to block intestinal absorption of dietary fat. Currently, only two prescription drugs, sibutramine and orlistat, are approved for long-term weight loss in the United States, and in a recent review Padwal and others found that both were moderately effective in promoting long-term weight loss. Some research indicates use of nicotine gum or patches may be useful to increase the success rate in smoking cessation and may prevent weight gain. Table 10.4 highlights some common weight-control drugs.

Research shows that many of these drugs may be effective, but the lost weight is regained upon cessation of use of the drug if lifestyle is not changed. The Food and Drug Administration (FDA) recommends that weight-control drugs be used only on a short-term basis in conjunction with an education program stressing proper diet, exercise, and behavior modification. A recent one-year study by Wadden and others found that subjects taking Meridia who also exercised and consumed a low-Calorie diet lost 27 pounds, more than twice as much as those who took Meridia

TABLE 10.4 Examples of some common weight-control drugs
Adrenergic agents
Ephedrine: Inhibits appetite via adrenergic effects comparable to norepinephrine; may also elicit thermogenic effect and increase resting energy expenditure
Serotonin agents
Fluoxetine (Prozac): Blocks reuptake of serotonin in nerve endings; prescribed for antidepressant effects, but some individuals may use it for weight control
Combined agents
Sibutramine: Increases levels of both serotonin and noradrenaline to help suppress appetite; stimulates thermogenesis; brand name Meridia
Fat-absorption blocking agents
Orlistat: Inhibits pancreatic lipase in the intestines, decreasing the digestion and absorption of fat; brand name Xenical

without exercising or dieting. They concluded that the results underscore the importance of prescribing weight-loss medications in combination with, rather than in lieu of, lifestyle modification.

Long-term use of such drugs has been associated with adverse side effects in some individuals, including tremor, seizures, psychoses, heart arrhythmias, pulmonary hypertension, habituation, addiction, and death. Kolanowski recently noted that the prolonged use of all weight-loss drugs may induce serious and life-threatening complications. Indeed, in the 1990s the popular drug dexfenfluramine (Redux) and fenfluramine were pulled from the market because their use was associated with pulmonary hypertension and heart valve problems. These drugs were replaced by sibutramine, but its use also has been associated with various health problems, such as increased blood pressure, heart-rhythm abnormalities, and heart attacks. Orlistat, given its effect on intestinal fat absorption, may cause severe gastrointestinal discomfort.

Numerous over-the-counter (OTC) nonprescription drugs or dietary supplements are also marketed as weight-loss agents. Saper and others note that more than 50 individual dietary supplements and more than 150 combination products are available for weight loss. However, three recent reviews concluded that, overall, various herbal products and dietary supplements promoted for weight loss lack sufficient scientific support, and concluded that none of those reviewed could be recommended. Included in the list were chromium, guar gum, chitosan, conjugated linoleic acid (CLA), ginseng, green tea, hydroxycitric acid, carnitine, psyllium, pyruvate, and St. John's wort. Lenz and Hamilton noted that although CLA and pyruvate have the best supporting evidence, larger and better-controlled trials are needed before these agents should be recommended for weight loss. Saper and others cited evidence of modest weight loss with use of ephedra/caffeine supplements, but they may not be recommended because of potential health risks. Sale of ephedra was banned by the FDA in 2004, but a federal judge overruled the ban in 2005 and currently its return to the marketplace is under litigation. Check chapter 13 for more details on ephedra and caffeine.

Some scientists contend that obesity is an incurable disease, somewhat comparable to type 1 diabetes. Type 1 diabetics need to take insulin daily to control their disease. It is hoped that continued research into the neural mechanisms underlying the etiology of obesity will eventually provide the data base for pharmaceutical companies to develop more effective and safe drugs to prevent and treat obesity. For example, a new hormone, obestatin, has been discovered in some animals. Obestatin is derived from the same prohormone as ghrelin, but has the opposite effects; obestatin actually depresses the appetite and thus may serve as the basis for developing an effective and safe weight-loss drug.

Very-Low-Calorie Diets Starvation-type diets may involve either complete fasting or **very-low-Calorie diets (VLCD)** (< 800 Calories/day), often referred to as modified fasts. These diet plans are most often used with inpatient programs in hospitals. The National Task Force on the Prevention and Treatment of Obesity indicated such diets, under proper medical supervision, are generally regarded as safe and have been effective in inducing rapid weight loss in very obese patients. In their meta-analysis, Anderson and others found that successful VLCDs were associated with significantly greater weight-loss maintenance than other successful low-Calorie balanced diets. However, Astrup and Rossner stressed the point that a very-low-Calorie diet should be considered as just the first step of a weight-management program and is successful only when it is followed by a maintenance program consisting of lifestyle interventions involving behavior modification, dietary changes, and increased physical activity.

Apparently little or no harm is caused by a 1- or 2-day fast, and some authorities have reported that a healthy man or woman can fast completely for 2 weeks and suffer no permanent ill effect. Although VLCD may be safe and effective for promoting short-term weight loss, they are not very satisfactory in long-term maintenance of weight loss and fare no better than other dietary approaches. Atkinson notes, moreover, that there may be some contraindications to their use and they should be used only after a thorough medical examination. A variety of complications may arise with the use of VLCD, including fatigue, weakness, headaches, nausea, constipation, loss of libido, kidney stones, gallbladder disease, decreased HDL-cholesterol, impaired phagocytic function of the white blood cells, inflammation of the intestines and pancreas, decreases in blood volume, decreases in heart muscle tissue, low blood pressure, cardiac arrhythmias, and even death. Thus, medical supervision is highly recommended for those undertaking VLCD.

Weight Cycling Grodner suggested that the chronic dieting syndrome, characterized by intervals of high-Calorie diets and VLCD, may be counterproductive as it may lead to **weight cycling** (yo-yo syndrome), a vicious cycle involving repeated bouts of weight loss followed by weight gain. Research has revealed that VLCD may lead to a decreased lean body mass, a decreased thermic effect of food (TEF), a decreased resting energy expenditure (REE), and an enhanced food efficiency (less energy wasted in processing dietary Calories). In essence, your body recognizes that it is being starved and will attempt to conserve body stores of energy by reducing energy output. When you resume normal eating, these energy-conservation mechanisms may continue to function for some time, so you regain the lost weight and possibly more. It is possible that a good proportion of the weight lost during the fasting state is protein, primarily from muscle tissue, which is used to produce glucose for the central nervous system. When you resume eating, the protein tissue is not readily replaced, so the extra Calories may be converted to fat. Moreover, resumption of normal dietary habits may lead to binge eating, episodes in which large amounts of Calories are consumed. Earlier research had suggested that weight cycling would lead to increased amounts of body fat at the same body weight. For example, an individual who started out at 200 pounds with 30 percent body fat would, after several cycles, eventually return to the same weight, but at 35 percent fat. Judith Rodin and her associates at Yale found that weight-cycling women are more prone to deposit fat in the abdominal area, thereby developing an android-type obesity and increased health risks.

However, more current research with both animals and humans suggests that weight cycling may not be associated with any adverse effects on body composition or health, as long as the weight regain does not exceed the weight lost. Recent studies by McCargar and others reported that chronic dieting does not result in a sustained reduction in REE, while Simkin-Silverman and others found no adverse psychological effects in women who had a history of weight cycling. Moreover, a detailed meta-analysis by the National Task Force on the Prevention and Treatment of Obesity revealed that weight cycling does not exert any adverse effect on body composition, metabolism, risk factors for cardiovascular disease, or on the effectiveness of future efforts to lose weight. The Task Force noted that although the evidence currently available indicates weight cycling does not affect morbidity and mortality, conclusive data regarding its long-term health effects are lacking. Currently, the Task Force indicates that obese individuals should not allow any perceived risks of weight cycling deter them from attempts to lose weight, but the Task Force also notes such individuals should commit to lifelong changes in behavior, diet, and exercise.

Some investigators believe the issue of weight cycling and health is still open for debate. Brownell and Rodin have suggested that while there has been no consistent demonstration that, as was first thought, weight cycling makes subsequent weight loss more difficult or regain more rapid, it is possible that this does occur under some conditions or in particular individuals. Although the mechanisms are not clear at present, they also note stronger and more consistent links between body-weight variability and negative health outcomes. In support of this point, Field and others, in the large Nurses' Health Study, reported that weight cycling was associated with a higher prevalence of binge eating, lower levels of physical activity, and greater weight gain. Given these varying viewpoints there is a clear need for further research on the effects of weight cycling on behavior, metabolism, and health—a viewpoint more recently supported by Foster and others.

Young Athletes One of the major medical concerns is the effect that severe weight restriction over a longer period may have upon children who are still in the growth and development stages of life. For example, young athletes are at a critical age as far as nutritional needs are concerned, yet the importance of making weight for certain sports often outweighs consideration of a balanced diet, adequate fluid intake, and a minimum caloric requirement. Hence they may go for months without adequate intake of essential nutrients like protein, iron, zinc, and calcium. Although numerous studies have revealed nutrient deficiencies and pathogenic weight-control behaviors in young athletes such as wrestlers and ballet dancers, unfortunately we have very few data on the long-range effects of such practices. Benardot and Czerwinski, comparing the height:age and weight:age percentiles for female gymnasts between the ages of 7 and 10 versus 11 and 14, suggested that the decreased percentiles in the older gymnasts could be attributed to nutritional deficits, sport-specific selection factors favoring retention of small muscular gymnasts, or a combination of the two. In a recent prospective study, Theintz and others studied the growth rate of adolescent female gymnasts and swimmers over a 2- to 3-year period and observed that the growth velocity of the gymnasts was lower than the swimmers. They theorized growth rate was impaired by heavy training (> 18 hours/week), possibly combined with the metabolic effects of dieting, leading to inhibition of the hypothalamus and pituitary gland with resultant suppression of proper sexual development. In their review, Daly and others concluded that adolescent athletes may be at risk of delayed maturation and restricted growth when intense training is combined with insufficient energy intake, but catch-up growth commonly occurs when training is reduced or ceases, so final adult stature is unlikely to be compromised. The American College of Sports Medicine also concluded that participation in high school wrestling, which normally involves weight cycling, does not adversely affect normal growth patterns. However, Daly and others indicated that in athletes who have long-term, clinically delayed maturation, catch-up growth may be incomplete, and recently reported a high frequency of reduced growth velocity in some, but not all, female gymnasts.

Within the past 30 years there has been increasing concern over the development of chronic dieting problems, that is, eating disorders in children, adolescents, and young adults that could have serious adverse health consequences.

What are the major eating disorders?

An obsession with having a low body weight may lead to a number of different **eating disorders,** which may become serious health problems. Currently, the American Psychiatric Association, in their *Diagnostic and Statistical Manual of Mental Disorders,* recognizes two clinical eating disorders, anorexia nervosa and bulimia nervosa. In a recent review, Neumark-Sztainer indicated that dieting itself is not necessarily a harmless behavior and has been shown to be a risk for developing an eating disorder. Davis and others also found that excessive exercise may play a role in the pathogenesis of some eating disorders. Weltzin and others indicated that women with eating disorders, particularly bulimia nervosa, may show signs of reduced serotonin activity, which may be related to other psychopathology seen with eating disorders, such as depression, anxiety, and thoughts of suicide. The American Dietetic Association, in their position stand on treatment of eating disorders, reported that more than 5 million Americans suffer from eating disorders, including 5 percent of females and 1 percent of males.

Anorexia nervosa is a complex disorder that is not completely understood but is thought to be a sign of other psychological problems. Research has suggested that anorexics possess characteristics that underlie compulsive personality disorders, and the prevalence of anorexia nervosa is greatest in groups that abuse psychoactive substances. Genes linked to anorexia nervosa have been identified, possibly some involved in appetite control. The diagnostic criteria for anorexia nervosa, as developed by the American Psychiatric Association, are summarized below:

1. Refusal to maintain the body weight over a minimal normal weight for age and height. A weight loss leading to maintenance of body weight less than 85 percent of that expected, including the expected weight gain during the period of growth.
2. An intense fear of gaining weight or becoming fat, even though underweight.

3. A disturbance in the way one's body weight or shape is perceived.
4. Amenorrhea, or the absence of at least three consecutive menstrual cycles in normally menstruating females.

Individuals with anorexia nervosa may be the binge-eating/purging type, engaging in binge eating or purging behavior, such as self-induced vomiting or the misuse of laxatives, diuretics, and enemas. The restricting type does not engage in such behaviors.

The prevalence of anorexia nervosa is relatively low, about 1 percent or less in the general population, but reported to be as high as 2 percent in college students. Anorexia nervosa is generally found in adolescent women, and about 85–95 percent of those affected are young females, usually under the age of 25. Multiple factors underlie the development of anorexia nervosa, but it prevails more in societies that savor the thin physique and consider dieting normal behavior. It appears that the person with the highest probability of developing anorexia nervosa is a perfectionistic and self-critical individual who comes from an upper-middle socioeconomic status, possibly being raised in an overprotective home environment. Susceptible individuals desire to have control over something in their lives. Chronic low self-esteem has been identified as a strong risk factor. Although most anorexics are female, male anorexics possess similar characteristics.

Medical consequences of anorexia nervosa can be very serious, including hormonal imbalances, anemia, decreased heart muscle mass, heart beat arrhythmias attributed to electrolyte imbalances, and even death. Treatment involves an interdisciplinary team consisting of professionals from medical, nursing, nutritional, and mental health disciplines, and is generally prolonged for several years and primarily involves psychological therapy. Steinhausen, in a review of 119 studies, found that the outcome for individuals with anorexia nervosa improved little over the last half of the twentieth century. Mortality is still high, and of those who survive about one-third improved while 20 percent remained chronically ill.

The term **bulimia nervosa** means *morbid hunger*, and the disorder involves a loss of control over the impulse to binge. The bulimic individual repeatedly ingests large quantities of food within a discrete period of time, such as 2 hours, but follows this by self-induced vomiting and other measures to avoid weight gain; this is the binge-purge syndrome. Bulimics may use other techniques, such as fasting or excessive exercise, to compensate for the binge. The American Psychiatric Association criteria for bulimia nervosa include the following:

1. Recurrent episodes of binge eating, at least two per week for 3 months.
2. Lack of control over eating during the binge.
3. Regular use of self-induced vomiting, laxatives, diuretics, fasting, or excessive exercise to control body weight.
4. Persistent concern with body weight and body shape.

Bulimia nervosa is more common than anorexia nervosa, the prevalence in the general population being about 2–3 percent. However, the prevalence among college students may be much higher. Haller indicated up to 10 percent of college students may be bulimic. As with anorexia nervosa, certain characteristics may underlie the development of bulimia nervosa, including the desire for thinness and chronic low self-esteem.

Although McGilley and Pryor noted that serious medical complications of bulimia nervosa are not common, reported adverse health effects of bulimia nervosa include erosion of tooth enamel, tears in the esophagus, aspiration pneumonia, electrolyte imbalances, and heart failure, all of which may be vomiting-induced. As with anorexics, bulimics are in need of psychological counseling by qualified medical professionals. Prozac, a drug that helps increase serotonin levels, has recently been approved for medically supervised use in treating bulimia nervosa.

Wilson and Eldredge noted that although an estimated 30–60 percent of young females in the United States currently diet to influence body weight and shape, the prevalence of full-blown eating disorders, such as anorexia nervosa and bulimia nervosa, in the general population is only about 1–3 percent. However, Brownell and Rodin reported that the number of people who experience eating problems associated with body-weight concerns, but do not meet the strict criteria of the American Psychiatric Association for an eating disorder, is much higher. Research has also suggested that such eating problems may be more prevalent in certain professions or personal pursuits, one in particular being sports.

What eating problems are associated with sports?

Depending on the nature of the sport, the loss of excess body weight may enable an athlete to compete in a lower weight class or improve appearance and/or biomechanics and enhance the potential for success. Examples of such sports include wrestling, gymnastics, ballet, cheerleading, bodybuilding, figure skating, diving, lightweight football, lightweight rowing, and distance running. To lose weight, athletes in these sports, particularly athletes with perfectionistic tendencies, may exhibit some, but not all, of the characteristics associated with eating disorders. Because they may not have a fully diagnosed eating disorder, a more appropriate term may be "disordered eating."

The American Psychiatric Association lists a category, Eating Disorders Not Otherwise Specified, for individuals who do not meet the criteria for anorexia nervosa or bulimia nervosa. Included in this category is anorexia athletica. In recent years the term **anorexia athletica** has been applied to those athletes who become overly concerned with their weight and exhibit some of the diagnostic criteria associated with anorexia nervosa or bulimia nervosa. According to Jorunn Sundgot-Borgen, an international authority on eating disorders in athletes, individuals must meet five criteria for anorexia athletica:

1. Excessive fear of becoming obese
2. Restriction of caloric intake
3. Weight loss
4. No medical disorder to explain leanness
5. Gastrointestinal complaints

In addition, they must meet one or more of these related criteria:

1. Disturbance in body image
2. Compulsive exercising
3. Binge eating
4. Use of purging methods

5. Delayed puberty
6. Menstrual dysfunction

Although male athletes, particularly those in bodybuilding, distance running, and wrestling, may be at risk for disordered eating, Beals and Manore note that it is difficult to obtain a good estimate of the number of male athletes with eating disorders as most studies have focused on female athletes. Although Putukian indicated that females in all sports are subject to disordered eating, Smolak and others, in a meta-analysis of 34 studies, found that elite athletes in sports emphasizing thinness are particularly at risk. This finding is supported by several recent studies by Torstveit and Sundgot-Borgen, but they also noted that a significant proportion of nonathletes were at risk for behaviors associated with the female athlete triad.

In a study conducted by the National Collegiate Athletic Association (NCAA), Dick indicated that at least one documented case of an eating disorder in athletes was reported in 70 percent of the member institutions surveyed. Studies have revealed that approximately 20–40 percent of female athletes may exhibit such criteria, and rates from 50–74 percent have been reported for certain sports, such as gymnastics, distance running, and competitive bodybuilding, sports that emphasize leanness or a specific body weight. In general, this condition improves when the athletic season is completed and the athlete resumes normal dietary habits. For example, O'Conner and others reported that symptoms of eating disorders in female college gymnasts abated after their retirement from the sport. However, what begins as a means to control weight for athletic competition on a short-term basis may develop into a long-term medical problem. Anderson proposed the notion that the development of an eating disorder is analogous to the process whereby an individual gets into a canoe some distance above Niagara Falls. When paddling downstream, the person is in control, but there reaches a point where the current of the falls takes over and the individual loses control. Indeed, in a recent NCAA study with Division I athletes, Johnson and others reported that 13 percent reported clinical signs of eating disorders, about 10 percent with bulimia and 3 percent with anorexia nervosa.

Female Athlete Triad The female athlete triad—disordered eating, amenorrhea, and osteoporosis—was introduced in chapter 8, with the primary focus being on calcium balance and osteoporosis. In this section, we shall consider the role of disordered eating and negative energy balance in the etiology of amenorrhea in female athletes. For a more detailed discussion, the interested reader is referred to the American College of Sports Medicine position stand on the female athlete triad. Also, a joint United States Olympic Committee/ACSM report is available at the ACSM website, www.acsm.org.

The second component of the female athlete triad is amenorrhea, and when it occurs in athletes or those who exercise, it is often known as athletic amenorrhea. Benson and others noted female athletes may go without menstruation for 3–6 months. Although the precise cause of this form of secondary amenorrhea has not been identified, the most common theories involve nutrition and exercise issues. In a recent review by one of the experts in this area of study, Melinda Manore indicated that the most common nutrition issues are poor energy intake and poor food selection, which can lead to inadequate intakes of caloric energy, protein, carbohydrate, and essential fatty acids. Inadequate intakes of any of these may interfere with menstrual function. Although excessive exercise intensity and duration has been theorized to be one of the causes of menstrual dysfunction, Anne Loucks, another expert, has indicated that evidence is continuing to accumulate that exercise has no suppressive effect on the reproductive system beyond the impact of its energy cost on energy availability. Loucks notes that reproductive disruption appears to occur when energy availability falls below a threshold level; the athlete is not consuming sufficient energy to maintain body weight. Collectively, Manore notes that the interaction of diet and exercise involve a number of factors, such as energy balance, exercise intensity and training practices, bodyweight and composition, disordered eating behaviors, and physical and emotional stress levels, that may contribute to the development of athletic menstrual dysfunction. She also notes that there appears to be wide individual variation in response to these factors.

The current focus of research is upon how these factors affect the hypothalamus-pituitary-gonad axis and resultant hormonal activity that governs menstruation. The hypothalamus may be influenced by all of these factors, and since the hypothalamus helps to regulate the pituitary gland, it may affect pituitary hormone secretions. The pituitary hormones, in turn, affect the gonadal secretion of sex hormones, such as the estrogens. Other hormones may also be involved, such as cortisol and epinephrine.

One of the prominent hypotheses underlying the development of athletic amenorrhea is related to excessive loss of body fat. Although no specific body-fat percentage has been associated with the development of athletic amenorrhea, the available evidence suggests that decreased fat levels may lead to a decreased production of one form of estrogen. As noted in chapter 8, estrogen helps to regulate bone metabolism. During estrogen deficiency, the bone is more sensitive to parathyroid hormone, which gradually extracts calcium from the bone. In essence, decreased estrogen levels will impair bone tissue formation, leading to loss of bone mass and the development of osteoporosis. Although exercise is generally advocated as a means to prevent osteoporosis, it does not appear to counteract the adverse effects associated with decreased estrogen levels in athletic amenorrhea. A number of studies have shown that amenorrheic athletes have lower bone-density levels in nonweight-bearing bones such as the spine. Recent research by Myburgh and others also revealed decreased density in appendicular bones, such as the femur, although other research indicates that athletes involved in high-impact sports, such as gymnastics, may have increased bone mass. In general, amenorrheic athletes are more prone to musculoskeletal injuries, such as stress fractures, than athletes who have normal menstruation. Scoliosis, an abnormal lateral curvature of the spine, may also develop. Warren and Stiehl indicated that these low-bone mass health problems may be irreversible. Other hormonal changes in athletic amenorrhea may reduce the resting metabolic rate. These problems are currently the focus of some extensive research, but unfortunately, studies with humans are difficult to control since the cause of athletic amenorrhea itself is not known. However, DeCree recently noted that amenorrhea in athletes is not necessarily harmful as long as attention is paid to preventing osteoporosis or stress fractures which may result from prolonged low-estrogen levels. On the other hand, the USOC/ACSM report suggests each stage of the female athlete triad carries health risks.

Unfortunately, imprecise measurement of body composition may be a predisposing factor to the development of eating disorders in athletes. As noted previously, prediction of body fat may vary considerably, so an athlete who may predict to be 10 percent by one method or prediction equation may predict to be 15–20 percent by others. If, for some reason, a coach believed that an athlete should achieve a set body-fat percentage (e.g., 8 percent), it would be wise to use a variety of techniques to predict body-fat percentages and use the lowest value predicted. This might be the safest approach to help prevent an excessive target loss of body fat that might lead to disordered eating.

Local dietitians and psychologists are excellent contacts if assistance is needed in dealing with eating disorders and may provide addresses for national help groups, such as the American Anorexia/Bulimia Association, whose website is listed on www.mhhe.com/williams. Many hospitals have eating disorder programs and may be able to provide questionnaires to help detect an eating disorder. The NCAA also offers brochures and videotapes to help develop awareness among athletes of the potential health risks associated with these disorders. A local college or university athletic department should be able to provide information about how to contact the NCAA.

The treatment of athletic amenorrhea involves two simple moves, exercise somewhat less and eat a little more. In some athletes, simply decreasing the amount of weekly exercise by 10 percent or so will help return normal menses, while others may resolve the problem by gaining several pounds, usually less than five. Dietary changes should include additional Calories and increased amounts of dietary protein, possibly including small amounts of meat several times per week. Increased protein and calcium from milk and other dairy products are also recommended. Some case studies with amenorrheic athletes suggest that a sport nutritional supplement may improve energy balance and nutritional status. Additionally, Warren and Stiehl indicate oral contraceptive therapy, under guidance of a health professional, may be helpful. Nevertheless, Sudi notes that effective methods of treatment of anorexia athletica are scarce and similar to treatment of eating disorders.

Prevention of eating disorders in young athletes should receive more attention. Several investigators have suggested that special attention should be devoted to young female athletes, particularly those involved in such sports as gymnastics and ballet, because they may meet the age, sex, and socioeconomic-status criteria that may predispose to anorexia nervosa. Coaches and others should look for unexplained weight losses, frequent weight fluctuations, sudden increases in training volume, obsession with exercise, excessive concern with body weight and appearance, and evidence of bizarre eating practices. A summary of warning signs is presented in table 10.5. Some athletic organizations are attempting to prevent excessive weight loss in young athletes. The National Federation of State High School Associations (NFHS), with a focus on prevention of dangerous dehydration practices in wrestling, recently approved rules setting limits on a wrestler's

TABLE 10.5	National Collegiate Athletic Association warning signs for anorexia nervosa and bulimia nervosa
Warning Signs for Anorexia Nervosa	
Dramatic loss in weight	
A preoccupation with food, Calories, and weight	
Wearing baggy or layered clothing	
Relentless, excessive exercise	
Mood swings	
Avoiding food-related social activities	
Warning Signs for Bulimia Nervosa	
A noticeable weight loss or gain	
Excessive concern about weight	
Bathroom visits after meals	
Depressive moods	
Strict dieting followed by eating binges	
Increasing criticism of one's body	

National Collegiate Athletic Association. Reprinted by permission.

hydration level and body-fat percentage, and also limited how much weight could be lost weekly. At the collegiate level, the NCAA has already adopted a similar program for wrestling.

Key Concept Recap

▶ Excessive weight losses, usually associated with behaviors characteristic of eating disorders, may result in health problems ranging from mild to severe and may also have a negative impact upon physical performance.

▶ Drugs and very-low-Calorie diets may be very effective for weight loss under medical supervision, but they may be associated with a variety of health risks if not used properly.

▶ Disordered eating in female athletes, usually excessive dieting and exercise to control body weight, may lead to amenorrhea and osteoporosis.

Check for Yourself

Go to a local health food store and ask the clerk for weight-loss products. Check those available and determine the active ingredient in each. How many contain ephedrine and/or caffeine? Alternatively, ask only for those with ephedrine or ephedrine with caffeine (guarana), and inquire about the safety of each. Compare your findings to the text discussion.

Body Composition and Physical Performance

What effect does excess body weight have on physical performance?

In some sports, extra body weight might prove to be an advantage, especially in football, ice hockey, sumo wrestling, and other sports in which body contact may occur or in which maintaining body stability is important. The effect of the extra weight may be neutralized, however, if the individual loses a corresponding amount of speed. Hence, increases in body weight for sports competition should maximize muscle mass and minimize body-fat gains. In rare instances, such as long-distance swimming in cold water, extra body fat may be helpful for its insulation and buoyancy effects.

On the other hand, there are a variety of sports where excess body weight may be disadvantageous. Whenever the body has to be moved rapidly or efficiently, excess weight in the form of body fat serves only as a burden. Take a good look at high jumpers, long jumpers, ballet dancers, gymnasts, sprinters, and long-distance runners. The amount of musculature may vary in each, but the body-fat percentage is extremely low. Research has also shown that even some professional football players have relatively low percentages of body fat.

According to basic principles of physics, body fat in excess of the amount necessary for optimal functioning will impair physical performance. Body fat increases the mass, or inertia, of the individual but does not contribute directly to energy production, so excess fat will detract from performance in events in which the body must be moved. For example, a high jumper can develop only so much power through muscular force when taking off. Basic laws of physics tell us that an extra 5 pounds of body fat would decrease the height to which the body center of gravity could be raised, thus decreasing the height that could probably be cleared. Extra poundage on a distance runner could add a considerable energy cost. Adding body fat would slow the running pace. In essence, the body becomes a less efficient machine when it must transport extra weight that has no useful purpose. That extra weight is usually excess body fat. Losing excess fat will not influence the total VO_2 max, but will increase VO_2 max when expressed in milliliters per kilogram body weight. For example, Craig Dean, a physician writing for *Running Times*, indicates there is a 1 percent increase in running-speed capacity for every 1 percent reduction in total body weight, provided it is primarily fat loss and not lean muscle mass. Thus, if your current running speed for a 10-kilometer (6.2-mile) race is 8:00 per mile and you lose 5 percent of your body weight as fat, your running speed would then approximate 7:36 per mile (8:00 min × 0.05 = 0:24 sec; 8:00 − 0:24 = 7:36). Similar percentage time savings are associated with other running distances, such as the marathon. These beneficial effects are most relevant for those runners who have excess body fat to lose, and may not be applicable to runners at their optimal body weight.

For a number of reasons it is difficult to predict with certainty a precise percentage of body fat for a given athlete that will result in optimal performance. Nevertheless, studies with elite athletes have given us some general guidelines. Male sprinters, long-distance runners, wrestlers, gymnasts, basketball players, soccer players, swimmers, bodybuilders, and football backs have functioned effectively with 5–10 percent body fat. Other male athletes such as baseball players, football linemen, tennis players, weight lifters, and weight men in track and field may average 11–15 percent, or just below the average for the nonathletic individual. Several authorities have suggested that female athletes should carry no more than 20 percent fat while others note it should be below 15 percent. Female gymnasts and distance runners have been recorded well below 15 percent; some gymnasts were even below 10 percent. Most other female athletes range between 15 and 20 percent, with some of the strength-type athletes, such as discus throwers, recording values of 25 percent or greater. Although these are some general guidelines, it should be noted that body-fat percentage is only one of many factors that may influence physical performance, and athletes may perform well even though their body fat is above these levels. However, everything else being equal, excess body fat is a disadvantage when energy efficiency of body movement in sport is an important consideration.

Care should be taken in advising athletes to lose body weight to achieve an arbitrary predetermined goal, that is, 5 percent body fat. First, recall that the measurement techniques for body composition have a 2–4 percent error rate or higher for estimating body fat. Second, the nature of the athlete's body composition may make it impossible to achieve that low level. And third, as suggested by Benardot and Thompson, excessive weight losses may actually lead to a decrease in physical performance, just the opposite of the desired goal.

Does excessive weight loss impair physical performance?

In 1998 the National Collegiate Athletic Association adopted a rule mandating testing to establish a minimum wrestling weight for each wrestler. Several reports, including that by Davis and others, have found that the Wrestling Weight Certification Program appears to be effective and is reducing extreme weight loss. However, recent studies found that a significant percent of the high school, college, and international-style wrestlers still used potentially harmful weight-loss methods.

Weight-reduction programs used by wrestlers and other athletes have been condemned by sports medicine groups, not only for health reasons but also because these practices may impair physical performance. In its position stand on weight loss in wrestlers, the American College of Sports Medicine noted that the practice of "weight cutting" involving food restriction, fluid deprivation, and dehydration could not only affect physical health and growth and development, but also impair competitive performance. This impairment in performance may be attributed to decreased blood volume, decreased testosterone levels, impaired cardiovascular function, decreased ability to regulate body temperature, hypoglycemia, or depletion of muscle and liver glycogen stores. However, the ultimate effect upon performance may be dependent upon the technique used—dehydration or starvation—and the time over which the weight is lost.

The effect of rapid weight loss by voluntary dehydration upon physical performance was covered in chapter 9. In general, events characterized by power, strength, and speed may not be adversely affected by short-term dehydration, whereas performance in aerobic and anaerobic endurance events is likely to deteriorate, particularly if exercising under warm environmental conditions.

Starvation and semistarvation studies have been conducted over periods ranging from 1 day to 1 year. Short-term starvation, involving rapid weight loss, may impair physical performance if blood glucose and muscle glycogen levels are lowered substantially. Although strength and VO$_2$ max generally are not affected by acute starvation, recent studies using a 24-hour fast have shown that anaerobic and aerobic endurance performance will suffer if dependent upon muscle glycogen or normal blood glucose levels. Long-term semistarvation may lead to significant losses of lean muscle tissue and decreased performance in almost all fitness components. For example, Roemmich and Sinning compared body composition and strength measures of adolescent wrestlers with controls over the course of a wrestling season, and found that the wrestlers decreased body weight, body fat, and various measures of strength and power from pre-season to late-season. The wrestlers failed to gain lean tissue during this time frame, which the authors associated with the decrease in strength and power. However, body weight, strength, and power returned to normal during the post-season. Also, wrestlers who weight cycle during the competitive season do not experience sustained decreases in resting energy expenditure, according to a recent study by Schmidt and others who followed wrestlers over two seasons.

It was interesting to note that in some semistarvation studies in which fewer than 1,000 Calories were consumed daily, vigorous exercise programs were maintained even though the subjects were losing substantial amounts of body weight. In general, the authors noted that the key point was to prevent hypoglycemia, dehydration, and excessive loss of lean muscle mass. If these goals could be achieved, physical performance need not deteriorate on weight-loss programs. Nevertheless, Horswill and others found that performance on a high-intensity arm exercise task decreased significantly after subjects lost 6 percent of their body weight by either a hypocaloric low-carbohydrate diet or a hypocaloric high-carbohydrate diet. However, the impairment was less with the high-carbohydrate diet, suggesting that athletes undergoing weight loss for competition should increase the carbohydrate proportion of the hypocaloric diet. Walberg-Rankin and others also reported that although weight loss by Calorie restriction significantly reduced anaerobic performance in wrestlers, those on a high-carbohydrate refeeding diet tended to recover their performance while those on a moderate carbohydrate diet did not. Maffulli, in a case study of two elite Sumo wrestlers, noted that an 8 percent loss of body weight over a 22-day period had no effect on aerobic power (VO$_2$ max) and maximal isometric strength, but prolonged anaerobic exercise performance was impaired. Other recent studies have shown impairment in physical performance with rapid weight-loss techniques. Gutierrez and others studied the effect of 3-day fast on young men during training, and found that fasting decreased both body fat and muscle mass, had no effect on hand-grip strength or perception-reaction time, but significantly decreased physical working capacity based on heart rate responses to a cycling exercise protocol. Hall and Lane reported an impaired performance, as evaluated by four 2-minute circuit exercise sessions, in experienced amateur boxers who reduced their body weight to their championship weight over one week. The boxers also experienced increased anger, fatigue, and tension, and reduced vigor. Filaire and others also reported significant impairment in strength and 30-second jumping performance in judo athletes who lost weight rapidly via food restriction over 7 days. Conversely, Fogelholm and others found that body-weight losses approximating 5 percent of body weight, either done rapidly in about 2 days or gradually over 3 weeks, did not impair anaerobic performance in experienced wrestlers and judo athletes.

In a unique study of NCAA wrestlers, Scott and Horswill and their associates found that on the average, wrestlers gained approximately 10 pounds between the time of the weigh-in and NCAA championship competition 20 hours later, and that the average difference in weight between opponents on the mat was only about 3 pounds. They also reported that neither acute weight gain after the weigh-in or the weight discrepancy between opponents in the first round influenced success in this national tournament. It appears that collegiate wrestlers are employing similar weight-loss and weight-regain protocols eliminating any potential competitive advantage on the mat. Conversely, Wroble and Moxley reported that high school wrestlers who competed below their recommended minimum wrestling weight had greater wrestling success in post-season state championship qualifying tournaments when compared to wrestlers who competed above the minimum wrestling weight.

It is difficult to predict the specific body weight at which physical performance will begin to deteriorate for a given individual. For those athletes who are on a weight-loss program, it may be wise to monitor performance through certain standardized tests appropriate for their sport. Some examples include basic fitness tests with measures of strength, local muscular endurance, and cardiovascular endurance. A decrease in performance may be indicative that the weight loss is excessive. Personality changes, excessive tiredness, weakness, and lack of enthusiasm may also be telltale clues.

In a recent review, Fogelholm indicated that although various forms of physical performance were adversely affected by rapid weight loss, a gradual weight loss was less likely to impair performance. In support of this viewpoint, Zachwieja and others reported that 2 weeks of moderate dietary energy restriction (750 Calories less per day) induced a weight loss of about 3 pounds in physically fit young men and women, but had no effect on muscle strength and endurance, anaerobic capacity as evaluated by the Wingate test, or aerobic endurance as measured by a 5-mile run. Weight losses have the potential to either improve or diminish performance. The key is to lose weight properly, primarily body fat. The basic guidelines for the development of such a program to improve physical performance, or health, are presented in the next chapter.

Key Concept Recap

▶ Although the average body-fat percentages for young men and women are, respectively, 15–20 percent and 23–30 percent, those involved in athletic competition may be advised to reduce these levels.

▶ Excessive loss of body weight may impair sport performance. Young athletes who exercise and diet excessively may experience a decrease in growth rate.

Have your body-fat percentage measured with as wide a variety of techniques as possible, such as skinfolds, bioelectrical impedance analysis, air displacement plethysmography, and others. Compare the differences and relate to the text discussion.

If access to a variety of techniques is not available, have four or five individuals measure your skinfolds and calculate your body fat according to the directions in appendix D. Compare the differences and compare to the text discussion.

Body-Fat Percentage Measurements

	Skinfold analysis	Bioelectrical impedance	Air displacement plethysmography	Other	Other
Body-fat percentage					

Skinfold Measurements

	Measurement 1	Measurement 2	Measurement 3	Measurement 4	Measurement 5
Skinfold measurement					

Review Questions—Multiple Choice

1. Which of the following best describes the role of leptin in the human body?
   (a) It is secreted by the hypothalamus and stimulates lipolysis in adipose cells.
   (b) It is secreted by the liver and inhibits the digestion of fats.
   (c) It is secreted by the adipose cells and inhibits hunger.
   (d) It is secreted by the stomach and stimulates appetite.
   (e) It is secreted by the intestines and stimulates appetite.

2. Which of the following statements regarding android/gynoid obesity is false?
   (a) Gynoid obesity is associated with a higher incidence of certain diseases, such as hypertension.
   (b) Android obesity is characterized by excess accumulation of fat deposits in the abdominal area.
   (c) Android obesity is seen more often in men, while gynoid obesity is more prevalent in women.
   (d) Gynoid-type fat deposits are more resistant to weight loss compared to android obesity.
   (e) Development of both types of obesity is influence by heredity.

3. If a skinfold technique for body composition has a standard error of estimate of 3%, you can have 70% confidence that for a person who has a predicted body fat of 18%, the actual value is within a range of
   (a) 6–18%
   (b) 18–21%
   (c) 12–24%
   (d) 15–21%
   (e) 18–30%

4. Which of the following ranges of the Body Mass Indexes (BMI) is indicative of a normal height to weight relationship?
   (a) 5–8
   (b) 10–12
   (c) 15–17
   (d) 20–22
   (e) 27–28

5. In which sports might the condition of "anorexia athletica" appear to be more prevalent?
   (a) football and basketball
   (b) swimming and baseball
   (c) wrestling and field hockey
   (d) ballet and gymnastics
   (e) tennis and golf

6. The set-point theory of weight control is based upon a feedback system, suggesting that the individual is programmed to be a certain body weight and that the body will always attempt to maintain that weight by regulating hunger and metabolism. What part of the body is believed to be the regulatory center for the control of the various feedback mechanisms?
   (a) liver receptors
   (b) stomach receptors
   (c) blood receptors in the kidney
   (d) receptors in the hypothalamus in the brain
   (e) receptors in the small intestine where absorption takes place

7. The disorder of bulimia, which is often characterized by the binge-purge syndrome, is found
   (a) only in those with anorexia nervosa
   (b) only in extremely underweight individuals
   (c) only in normal weight individuals
   (d) only in moderately or morbidly obese individuals
   (e) in individuals across the body-weight spectrum

8. Which of the following is mainly an environmental rather than a possible hereditarial factor in the multicausal etiology of obesity?
   (a) a sedentary lifestyle
   (b) hormonal imbalance
   (c) disorder in the brain's hunger and satiety centers
   (d) lower basal metabolic rate
   (e) a higher "set point"

9. Obesity has been associated as a potential risk factor in all the following diseases or health problems except which one?
    (a) coronary heart disease
    (b) anemia
    (c) hyperlidemia
    (d) diabetes
    (e) hypertension

10. Protein consumed during a starvation-type diet most likely will be:
    (a) used to rebuild muscle tissue
    (b) used to replace worn-out cells
    (c) converted to glucose for energy
    (d) used to stabilize fluid balance
    (e) stored as fat

Answers to multiple choice questions:
1. c; 2. a; 3. d; 4. d; 5. d; 6. d; 7. e; 8. a; 9. b; 10. c.

Review Questions—Essay

1. List and describe five different techniques used to evaluate body composition, and highlight at least one value of each.

2. Discuss the set-point theory of body-weight control and relate it to body-fat levels, leptin, and neuropeptide Y.

3. List the various genetic and environmental factors that may be involved in the etiology of obesity. Highlight two of each and explain their possible role.

4. Explain the metabolic syndrome and associated health risks.

5. List the three components of the female athlete triad. Discuss the underlying theories regarding its etiology, the potential effects on hormonal status, and subsequent serious health problems.

References

Books

American Psychiatric Association. 1994. *Diagnostic and Statistical Manual of Mental Disorders DSM IV.* Washington, DC: American Psychiatric Association.

Heymsfield, S., et al. 2005. *Human Body Composition.* Champaign, IL: Human Kinetics.

Heyward, V., and Stolarzyk, L. 1996. *Applied Body Composition Assessment.* Champaign, IL: Human Kinetics.

National Academy of Sciences. 2002. *Dietary Reference Intakes for Energy, Carbohydrates, Fiber, Fat, Protein and Amino Acids (Macronutrients).* Washington, DC: National Academy Press.

National Research Council. 1989. *Diet and Health: Implications for Reducing Chronic Disease Risk.* Washington, DC: National Academy Press.

Shils, M., et al., eds. 2006. *Modern Nutrition in Health and Disease.* Philadelphia: Lippincott Williams & Wilkins.

U.S. Department of Health and Human Services Public Health Service. 2000. *Healthy People 2010.* Washington, DC: U.S. Government Printing Office.

Reviews

Alberti, K., et al. 2005. The metabolic syndrome: A new worldwide definition. *Lancet* 366:1059–62.

American College of Sports Medicine. 2001. ACSM Position Stand on the Appropriate Intervention Strategies for Weight Loss and Prevention of Weight Regain for Adults. *Medicine & Science in Sports & Exercise* 33:2145–56.

American College of Sports Medicine. 1997. Position stand: The female athlete triad. *Medicine & Science in Sports & Exercise.* 29 (5): i–ix.

American College of Sports Medicine. 1996. American College of Sports Medicine Position Stand: Weight loss in wrestlers. *Medicine & Science in Sports & Exercise* 28 (6): ix–xii.

American Dietetic Association. 2001. Position of the American Dietetic Association: Nutrition intervention in the treatment of anorexia nervosa, bulimia nervosa, and eating disorders not otherwise specified (EDNOS). *Journal of the American Dietetic Association* 101:810–19.

Anderson, A. 1990. A proposed mechanism underlying eating disorders and other disorders of motivated behavior. In *Males with Eating Disorders,* ed. A. Anderson. New York: Brunners/Mazel.

Anderson, J., et al. 2001. Long-term weight-loss maintenance: A meta-analysis of US studies. *American Journal of Clinical Nutrition* 74:579–84.

Astrup, A., et al. 2002. Low-fat diets and energy balance: How does the evidence stand in 2002? *Proceedings of the Nutrition Society* 61:299–309.

Astrup, A. 2001. The role of dietary fat in the prevention and treatment of obesity. Efficacy and safety of low-fat diets. *International Journal of Obesity and Related Metabolic Disorders* 25:S46–S50.

Astrup, A., and Rossner, S. 2000. Lessons from obesity management programmes: Greater initial weight loss improves long-term maintenance. *Obesity Reviews* 1:17–19.

Atkinson, R. 1989. Low and very low calorie diets. *Medical Clinics of North America* 73:203–16.

Badman, M., and Flier, J. 2005. The gut and energy balance: Visceral allies in the obesity war. *Science* 307:1909–14.

Baile, C. 2000. Regulation of metabolism and body mass by leptin. *Annual Reviews in Nutrition* 20:105–27.

Bar-Or, O. 2000. Juvenile obesity, physical activity, and lifestyle changes. *Physician and Sportsmedicine* 28 (11): 51–58.

Bar-Or, O., et al. 1998. Physical activity, genetic, and nutritional considerations in childhood weight management. *Medicine & Science in Sports & Exercise* 30:2–10.

Benardot, D. 2000. Gymnastics. In *Nutrition in Sport,* ed. R. J. Maughan. Oxford: Blackwell Science.

Benardot, D., and Thompson, W. R. 1999. Energy from food for physical activity: Enough and on time. *ACSM's Health & Fitness Journal* 3 (4):14–18.

Benson, J., et al. 1996. Nutritional aspects of amenorrhea in the female athlete triad. *International Journal of Sport Nutrition* 6:134–45.

Bouchard, C. 1997. Genetic determinants of regional fat distribution. *Human Reproduction* 12 (Supplement 1):1–5.

Bouchard, C. 1991. Heredity and the path to overweight and obesity. *Medicine & Science in Sports & Exercise* 23:285–91.

Bray, G. 2004. How do we get fat? An epidemiologic and metabolic approach. *Clinics in Dermatology* 22:281–88.

Bray, G. 2004. Medical consequences of obesity. *Journal of Clinical Endocrinology and Metabolism* 89:2583–89.

Bray, G. 2000. Afferent signals regulating food intake. *Proceedings of the Nutrition Society* 59:373–84.

Bren, L. 2002. Losing weight: More than just counting calories. *FDA Consumer* 36 (1):18–25.

Brownell, K. 1998. The pressure to eat. *Nutrition Action Health Letter* 25 (6):3–5.

Brownell, K., and Rodin, J. 1994. Medical, metabolic, and psychological effects of weight cycling. *Archives of Internal Medicine* 154:1325–29.

Brownell, K., and Rodin, J. 1992. Prevalence of eating disorders in athletes. In *Eating, Body Weight and Performance in Athletes: Disorders of Modern Society,* eds. K. Brownell, et al. Philadelphia: Lea and Febiger.

Busetto, L. 2001. Visceral obesity and the metabolic syndrome: Effects of weight loss. *Nutrition, Metabolism and Cardiovascular Disease* 11:195–204.

Carmichael, A., and Bates, T. 2004. Obesity and breast cancer: A review of the literature. *Breast* 13:85–92.

Caroli, M., et al. 2004. Role of television in childhood obesity prevention. *International Journal of Obesity and Related Metabolic Disorders* 28 (Supplement 3):S104–08.

Carroll, S., and Dudfield, M. 2004. What is the relationship between exercise and metabolic abnormalities? A review of the metabolic syndrome. *Sports Medicine* 34:371–78.

Consumers Union. 2004. Outwitting your appetite. *Consumer Reports on Health* 16 (9):8–10.

Coughlin, J., and Guarda, A. 2006. Behavioral disorders affecting food intake: Eating disorders and other psychiatric conditions. In *Modern Nutrition in Health and Disease,* eds. M. Shils, et al. Philadelphia: Lippincott Williams & Wilkins.

Dallman, M., et al. 2004. Minireview: Glucocorticoids—food intake, abdominal obesity, and wealthy nations in 2004. *Endocrinology* 145:2633–38.

Daly, R., et al. 2002. Does training affect growth? *Physician and Sportsmedicine* 30 (10):21–29.

Dattilo, A. 1992. Dietary fat and its relationship to body weight. *Nutrition Today* 27 (January/February): 13–19.

Davey, R., 2004. The obesity epidemic: Too much food for thought? *British Journal of Sports Medicine* 38:360–63.

Dean, C. 1994. Less weight, more speed. *Running Times* (April): 18–19.

DeCree, C. 1998. Sex steroid metabolism and menstrual irregularities in the exercising female: A review. *Sports Medicine* 25:369–406.

de Groot, L., and van Staveren, W. 1995. Reduced physical activity and its association with obesity. *Nutrition Reviews* 53:11–12.

Dietz, W. 2006. Childhood obesity. In *Modern Nutrition in Health and Disease,* eds. M. Shils, et al. Philadelphia: Lippincott Williams & Wilkins.

DiPietro, L. 1995. Physical activity, overweight, and adiposity: An epidemiologic perspective. *Exercise and Sport Sciences Reviews* 23:275–303.

Eckel, R. H., and Krauss, R. M. 1998. American Heart Association call to action: Obesity as a major risk factor for coronary heart disease. *Circulation* 97:2099–2100.

Ellis, K. 2001. Selected body composition methods can be used in field studies. *Journal of Nutrition* 131:1589S–95S.

Fields, D., et al. 2002. Body-composition assessment via air-displacement plethysmography in adults and children: A review. *American Journal of Clinical Nutrition* 75:453–67.

Fogelholm, M. 1994. Effects of bodyweight reduction on sports performance. *Sports Medicine* 18:249–67.

Forbes, G. 2002. Perspectives on body composition. *Current Opinion in Clinical Nutrition and Metabolic Care* 5:25–30.

Forbes, G. B. 1999. Body composition: Influence of nutrition, physical activity, growth, and aging. In *Modern Nutrition in Health and Disease,* eds. M. Shils, et al. Baltimore: Williams & Wilkins.

Foster, G. D., et al. 1997. Psychological effects of weight cycling in obese persons: A review and research agenda. *Obesity Research* 5:474–88.

Froom, P., et al. 1998. Smoking cessation and weight gain. *Journal of Family Practice* 46:460–64.

Gaesser, G. A. 1999. Thinness and weight loss: Beneficial or detrimental to longevity? *Medicine & Science in Sports & Exercise* 31:1118–28.

Gibbs, W. 1996. Gaining on fat. *Scientific American* 275 (August): 88–94.

Grodner, M. 1992. Forever dieting: Chronic dieting syndrome. *Journal of Nutrition Education* 24:207–10.

Grundy, S. M. 1999. Hypertriglyceridemia, insulin resistance, and the metabolic syndrome. *American Journal of Cardiology* 83:25F–29F.

Grundy, S. M. 1998. Multifactorial causation of obesity: Implications for prevention. *American Journal of Clinical Nutrition* 67:563S–572S.

Gutin, B., and Humphries, M. 1998. Exercise, body composition, and health in children. In *Exercise, Nutrition, and Weight Control,* eds. D. Lamb and R. Murray. Carmel, IN: Cooper Publishing Group.

Haller, E. 1992. Eating disorders. A review and update. *Western Journal of Medicine* 157:658–62.

Heymsfield, S., and Baumgartner, R. 2006. Body composition and anthropometry. In *Modern Nutrition in Health and Disease,* eds. M. Shils, et al. Philadelphia: Lippincott Williams & Wilkins.

Hill, J., et al. 2006. Obesity: Etiology. In *Modern Nutrition in Health and Disease,* eds. M. Shils, et al. Philadelphia: Lippincott Williams & Wilkins.

Hirsh, J., and Leibel, R. L. 1998. The genetics of obesity. *Hospital Practice (Office Edition)* 33:55–70.

Jacobs, K. A., et al. 2000. Fat metabolism. In *Exercise and Sport Science,* eds. Garrett, W. E., and Kirkendall, D. T. Philadelphia: Lippincott Williams & Wilkins.

Jequier, E. 2002. Leptin signaling, adiposity, and energy balance. *New York Academy of Sciences* 967:379–88.

Jonas, S. 2001. Weighing in on the obesity epidemic: What do we do now? *ACSM's Health & Fitness Journal* 5 (5):710.

Keesey, R. E., and Hirvonen, M. D. 1997. Body weight set-points: Determination and adjustment. *Journal of Nutrition* 127:1875S–1883S.

King, P. 2005. The hypothalamus and obesity. *Current Drug Targets* 6:225–40.

Kohrt, W. 1995. Body composition by DXA: Tried and true? *Medicine & Science in Sports & Exercise* 27:1349–53.

Kojima, M., and Kangawa, K. 2005. Ghrelin: Structure and function. *Physiological Reviews* 85:495–522.

Kolanowski, J. 1999. A risk-benefit assessment of anti-obesity drugs. *Drug Safety* 20:119–31.

Kolotkin, R., et al. 2001. Quality of life and obesity. *Obesity Reviews* 2:219–29.

Lafontan, M. 2005. Fat cells: Afferent and efferent messages define new approaches to treat obesity. *Annual Review of Pharmacology and Toxicology* 45:119–46.

Lamarche, B. 1998. Abdominal obesity and its metabolic complications: Implications for the risk of ischaemic heart disease. *Coronary Artery Disease* 9:473–81.

Lenz, T., and Hamilton, W. 2004. Supplemental products used for weight loss. *Journal of the American Pharmaceutical Association* 44:59–67.

Levin, B. 2002. Metabolic sensors: Viewing glucosensing neurons from a broader perspective. *Physiology & Behavior* 76:387–401.

Levin, B. 2000. Metabolic imprinting on genetically predisposed neural circuits perpetuates obesity. *Nutrition* 16:909–15.

Levine, J. 2004. Non-exercise activity thermogenesis. *Nutrition Reviews* 62:S82–S97.

Lohman, T., et al. 1997. Body fat measurement goes high-tech: Not all are created equal. *ACSM's Health & Fitness Journal* 1 (1): 30–35.

Loucks, A. 2004. Energy balance and body composition in sports and exercise. *Journal of Sports Sciences* 22:1–14.

Loucks, A. 2003. Energy availability, not body fatness, regulates reproductive function in women. *Exercise and Sports Sciences Reviews* 31:144–48.

Loucks, A. 2001. Physical health of the female athlete: Observations, effects, and causes of reproductive disorders. *Canadian Journal of Applied Physiology* 26:S176–85.

Manore, M. 2002. Dietary recommendations and athletic menstrual dysfunction. *Sports Medicine* 32:887–901.

Manore, M. M. 2000. The overweight athlete. In *Nutrition in Sport,* ed. R. J. Maughan. Oxford: Blackwell Science.

Marshall, S., et al. 2004. Relationships between media use, body fatness and physical activity in children and youth: A meta-analysis. *International Journal of Obesity and Related Metabolic Disorders* 28:1238–46.

McGee, D. 2005. Body mass index and mortality: A meta-analysis based on person-level data from twenty-six observational studies. *Annals of Epidemiology* 15:87–97.

McGilley, B. M., and Pryor, T. L. 1998. Assessment and treatment of bulimia nervosa. *American Family Physician* 57:2743–50.

Melby, C., et al. 1998. Exercise, macronutrient balance, and weight control. In *Exercise, Nutrition, and Weight Control,* eds.

D. Lamb and R. Murray. Carmel, IN: Cooper Publishing Group.

Melby, C. L., and Hill, J. O. 1999. Exercise, macronutrient balance, and body weight regulation. *Sports Science Exchange* 12 (1):1–6.

Miller, Y., and Dunstan, D. 2004. The effectiveness of physical activity interventions for the treatment of overweight and obesity and type 2 diabetes. *Journal of Science and Medicine in Sport* 7:52–59.

National Task Force on the Prevention and Treatment of Obesity. 1996. Long-term pharmacotherapy in the management of obesity. *Journal of the American Medical Association* 276:1907–15.

National Task Force on the Prevention and Treatment of Obesity. 1994. Weight cycling. *Journal of the American Medical Association* 272:1196–1202.

National Task Force on the Prevention and Treatment of Obesity. 1993. Very-low-Calorie diets. *Journal of the American Medical Association* 270:967–74.

Neumark-Sztainer, D. 1995. Excessive weight preoccupation: Normative but not harmless. *Nutrition Today* 30 (2): 68–74.

Newman, C. 2004. Why are we so fat? *National Geographic* 206 (2):48–61.

Padwal, R., et al. 2004. Long-term pharmacotheraphy for obesity and overweight. *Cochrane Database of Systematic Reviews* (3):CD004094.

Pate, R. 1993. Physical activity in children and youth: Relation to obesity. *Contemporary Nutrition* 18 (2): 1–2.

Perusse, L,, and Bouchard, C. 1999. Genotype-environment interaction in human obesity. *Nutrition Reviews* 57:S31–S37.

Peters, J., et al. 2002. From instinct to intellect: The challenge of maintaining healthy weight in the modern world. *Obesity Reviews* 3:69–74.

Pi-Sunyer, F. X. 2002. The medical risks of obesity. *Obesity Surgery* 12:6S–11S.

Pi-Sunyer, F. X. 1999. Obesity. In *Modern Nutrition in Health and Disease,* eds. M. Shils, et al. Baltimore: Williams & Wilkins.

Pittler, M., and Ernst, E. 2004. Dietary supplements for body-weight reduction: A systematic review. *American Journal of Clinical Nutrition* 79:529–36.

Putukian, M. 1998. The female athlete triad. *Clinics in Sports Medicine* 17:675–96.

Reaven, G. 2006. Metabolic syndrome: Definition, relationship to insulin resistance, and clinical utility. In *Modern Nutrition in Health and Disease,* eds. M. Shils, et al. Philadelphia: Lippincott Williams & Wilkins.

Robinson, T. 2001. Television viewing and childhood obesity. *Pediatric Clinics of North America* 48:1017–25.

Rolls, B., and Shide, D. 1992. The influence of dietary fat on food intake and body weight. *Nutrition Reviews* 50:283–90.

Rowland, T. W. 1998. The biological basis of physical activity. *Medicine & Science in Sports & Exercise* 30:392–99.

Saper, R., et al. 2004. Common dietary supplements for weight loss. *American Family Physician* 70:1731–38.

Saris, W. H. 1998. Fit and fat free: The metabolic aspects of weight control. *International Journal of Obesity and Related Metabolic Disorders* 22:S15–S21.

Scheen, A. 2004. Management of the metabolic syndome. *Minerva Endocrinologica* 29:31–45.

Schnirring, L. 2005. NFHS finalizes weight cutting rules for wrestlers. *Physician and Sportsmedicine* 33 (7):9–12.

Schwartz, M., and Seeley, R. 1997. The new biology of body weight regulation. *Journal of the American Dietetic Association* 97:54–58.

Sell, H., et al. 2004. The brown adipocyte: Update on its metabolic role. *International Journal of Biochemistry & Cell Biology* 36:2098–2104.

Shah, M., and Garg, A. 1996. High-fat and high-carbohydrate diets and energy balance. *Diabetes Care* 19:1142–52.

Smith, G. 2006. Controls of food intake. In *Modern Nutrition Health and Disease,* eds. M. Shils, et al. Philadelphia: Lippincott Williams & Wilkins.

Smolak, L., et al. 2000. Female athletes and eating problems: A meta-analysis. *International Journal of Eating Disorders* 27:371–80.

Speakman, J. 2004. Obesity: The integrated roles of environment and genetics. *Journal of Nutrition* 134:2090S–2105S.

Steinhausen, H. 2002. The outcome of anorexia nervosa in the 20th century. *American Journal of Psychiatry* 159:1284–93.

Stock, M. 1989. Thermogenesis and brown fat: Relevance to human obesity. *Infusiontherapie* 16:282–84.

Stubbs, R. J. 1999. Peripheral signals affecting food intake. *Nutrition* 15:614–25.

Sudi, K., et al. 2004. Anoerxia athletica. *Nutrition* 20:657–61.

Sundgot-Borgen, J. 2000. Eating disorders in athletes. In *Nutrition in Sport,* ed. R. J. Maughan. Oxford: Blackwell Science.

Trayhurn, P., and Beattie, J. 2001. Physiological role of adipose tissue: White adipose tissue as an endocrine and secretory organ. *Proceedings of the Nutrition Society* 60:329–39.

Tso, P., and Liu, M. 2004. Ingested fat and satiety. *Physiology & Behavior* 81:275–87.

Wadden, T., et al. 2006. Obesity: Management. In *Modern Nutrition in Health and Disease,* eds. M. Shils, et al. Philadephia: Lippincott Williams & Wilkins.

Wadden, T., et al. 2002. Obesity: Responding to the global epidemic. *Journal of Consulting and Clinical Psychology* 70:510–25.

Wagner, D. R., and Heyward, V. H. 1999. Techniques of body composition assessment: A review of laboratory and field methods. *Research Quarterly for Exercise and Sport* 70:135–49.

Wang, L., et al. 1992. The five-level model: A new approach to organizing body-composition research. *American Journal of Clinical Nutrition* 56:19–28.

Warren, M. P., and Stiehl, A. L. 1999. Exercise and female adolescents: Effects on the reproductive and skeletal system. *Journal of the American Medical Women's Association* 54:115–20.

Weinsier, R. L., et al. 1998. The etiology of obesity: Relative contribution of metabolic factors, diet, and physical activity. *American Journal of Medicine* 105:145–50.

Weltzin, T., et al. 1994. Serotonin and bulimia nervosa. *Nutrition Reviews* 52:399–408.

Willett, W. 2002. Dietary fat plays a major role in obesity: No. *Obesity Reviews* 3:59–68.

Wilmore, J. H. 2000. Weight category sports. In *Nutrition in Sport,* ed. R. J. Maughan. Oxford: Blackwell Science.

Wilson, G., and Eldredge, K. 1992. Pathology and development of eating disorders: Implications for athletes. In *Eating, Body Weight and Performance in Athletes: Disorders of Modern Society,* eds. K. Brownell, et al. Philadelphia: Lea and Febiger.

Specific Studies

Alderman, B., et al. 2004. Factors related to rapid weight-loss practices among international-style wrestlers. *Medicine & Science in Sports & Exercise* 36:249–52.

Andersen, R. E., et al. 1998. Relationship of physical activity and television watching with body weight and level of fatness among children. *Journal of the American Medical Association* 279:938–42.

Angelopoulos, T., et al. 2002. Significant enhancements in glucose tolerance and insulin action in centrally obese subjects following ten days of training. *Clinical Journal of Sport Medicine* 12:113–18.

Ball, S., and Altena, T. 2004. Comparison of the Bod Pod and dual energy x-ray absorptiometry in men. *Physiological Measurement* 25:671–78.

Ballard, T., et al. 2004. Comparison of Bod Pod and DXA in female collegiate athletes. *Medicine & Science in Sports & Exercise* 36:731–35.

Batterham, R., et al. 2003. Inhibition of food intake in obese subjects by peptide YY_{3-36}. *New England Journal of Medicine* 349:941–48.

Beals, K., and Manore, M. 2000. Behavioral, psychological, and physical characteristics of female athletes with subclinical eating disorders. *International Journal of Sport Nutrition and Exercise Metabolism* 10:128–43.

Benardot, D., and Czerwinski, C. 1991. Selected body composition and growth measures of junior elite gymnasts. *Journal of the American Dietetic Association* 91:29–33.

Bigaard, J., et al. 2005. Waist circumference and body composition in relation to all-cause mortality in middle-aged men and women. *International Journal of Obesity and Related Metabolic Disorders.* 29:778–84.

Bouchard, C., et al. 1990. The response to long-term overfeeding in identical twins. *New England Journal of Medicine* 322:1477–82.

Bowman, S., et al. 2004. Effects of fast-food consumption on energy intake and diet quality among children in a national household survey. *Pediatrics* 113:112–18.

Calle, E., et al. 2003. Overweight, obesity, and mortality from cancer in a prospectively studied cohort of U.S. adults. *New England Journal of Medicine* 348:1625–38.

Clark, R., et al. 2004. Minimum weight prediction methods cross-validated by the four-component model. *Medicine & Science in Sports & Exercise* 36:639–47.

Clark, R., et al. 2002. Cross-validation of the NCAA method to predict body fat for minimum weight in collegiate wrestlers. *Clinical Journal of Sport Medicine* 12:285–90.

Daly, R., et al. 2005. Growth of highly versus moderately trained competitive female artistic gymnasts. *Medicine & Science in Sports & Exercise* 37:1053–60.

Davis, C., et al. 1997. The prevalence of high-level exercise in the eating disorders: Etiological implications. *Comprehensive Psychiatry* 38:321–6.

Davis, S., et al. 2002. Preliminary investigation: The impact of the NCAA Wrestling Weight Certification Program on weight cutting. *Journal of Strength and Conditioning Research* 16:305–7.

Dick, R. 1993. Eating disorders in NCAA athletics programs: Replication of a 1990 study. *NCAA Sports Sciences* 3 (Spring).

Elowsson, P., et al. 1998. An evaluation of dual-energy X-Ray absorptiometry and underwater weighing to estimate body composition by means of carcass analysis in piglets. *Journal of Nutrition* 128:1543–49.

Field, A., et al. 2004. Association of weight change, weight control practices, and weight cycling among women in the Nurses' Health Study II. *International Journal of Obesity and Related Metabolic Disorders* 28:1134–42.

Filaire, E., et al. 2001. Food restriction, performance, psychological state and lipid values in judo athletes. *International Journal of Sports Medicine* 22:454–59.

Fisher, J., and Birch, L. 1995. Fat preferences and fat consumption of 3- to 5-year-old children are related to parental adiposity. *Journal of the American Dietetic Association* 95:759–64.

Flegal, K., et al. 2005. Excess deaths associated with underweight, overweight, and obesity. *JAMA* 293:1861–67.

Fogelholm, G.M., et al. 1993. Gradual and rapid weight loss: Effects on nutrition and performance in male athletes. *Medicine & Science in Sports & Exercise* 25:371–77.

Fontaine, K., et al. 2003. Years of life lost due to obesity. *JAMA* 289:187–93.

Ford, E., et al. 2002. Prevalence of the metabolic syndrome among US adults: Findings from the third National Health and Nutrition Examinations Survey. *JAMA* 287:356–59.

Frisch, R., et al. 1989. Lower prevalence of nonreproductive system cancers among female former college athletes. *Medicine & Science in Sports & Exercise* 21:250–53.

Gomez-Merino, D., et al. 2002. Decrease in serum leptin after prolonged physical activity in men. *Medicine & Science in Sports & Exercise* 34:1594–99.

Green, S., and Blundell, J. 1996. Effect of fat- and sucrose-containing foods on the size of eating episodes and energy intake in lean dietary restrained and unrestrained females: Potential for causing overconsumption. *European Journal of Clinical Nutrition* 50:625–35.

Gutierrez, A., et al. 2001. Three days fast in sportsmen decreases physical work capacity but not strength or perception-reaction time. *International Journal of Sport Nutrition and Exercise Metabolism* 11:420–29.

Hall, C., and Lane, A. 2001. Effects of rapid weight loss on mood and performance among amateur boxers. *British Journal of Sports Medicine* 35:390–95.

Harp, J., and Hecht, L. 2005. Obesity in the National Football League. *JAMA* 293:1061–62.

Horswill, C., et al. 1994. Influence of rapid weight gain after the weigh-in on success in collegiate wrestlers. *Medicine & Science in Sports & Exercise* 26:1290–94.

Hu, F., et al. 2004. Adiposity as compared with physical activity in predicting mortality among women. *New England Journal of Medicine* 351:2694–703.

Janssen, I., et al. 2002. Body mass index, waist circumference, and health risk: Evidence in support of current National Institutes of Health guidelines. *Archives of Internal Medicine* 162:2074–79.

Johnson, C., et al. 1999. Athletes and eating disorders: The National Collegiate Athletic Association Study. *International Journal of Eating Disorders* 26:179–88.

Kajioka, T., et al. 2002. Effects of intentional weight cycling on non-obese young women. *Metabolism* 51:149–54.

Kiningham, R., and Gorenflo, W. 2001. Weight loss methods of high school wrestlers. *Medicine & Science in Sports & Exercise* 33:810–13.

Lotti, T., et al. 1990. Proteoglycans in so-called cellulite. *International Journal of Dermatology* 29:272–74.

Ludwig, D., et al. 2001. Relation between consumption of sugar-sweetened drinks and childhood obesity: A prospective, observational analysis. *Lancet* 357:505–8.

Ma, Y., et al. 2005. Association between dietary carbohydrates and body weight. *American Journal of Epidemiology* 161:359–67.

Maffulli, N. 1992. Making weight: A case study of two elite wrestlers. *British Journal of Sports Medicine* 26:107–10.

McCargar, L., et al. 1996. Chronic dieting does not result in a sustained reduction in resting metabolic rate in overweight women. *Journal of the American Dietetic Association* 96:1175–77.

McGill, H., et al. 2002. Obesity accelerates the progression of coronary atherosclerosis in young men. *Circulation* 105:2712–18.

Moore, J., et al. 2002. Weight management and weight loss strategies of professional jockeys. *International Journal of Sport Nutrition and Exercise Metabolism* 12:1–13.

Myburgh, K., et al. 1993. Low bone mineral density at axial and appendicular sites in amenorrheic athletes. *Medicine & Science in Sports & Exercise* 25:1197–1202.

Nikols-Richardson, S. M., et al. 2000. Premenarcheal gymnasts possess higher bone mineral density than controls. *Medicine & Science in Sports & Exercise* 32:63–69.

O'Conner, P., et al. 1996. Eating disorder symptoms in former female college gymnasts: Relations with body composition. *American Journal of Clinical Nutrition* 64:840–43.

Oppliger, R., et al. 2003. Weight loss practices of wrestlers. *International Journal of Sport Nutrition and Exercise Metabolism* 13:29–46.

Orphanidou, C., et al. 1994. Accuracy of subcutaneous fat measurement: Comparison of skinfold calipers, ultrasound, and computed tomography. *Journal of the American Dietetic Association* 94:855–58.

Pate, R., et al. 1989. Relationship between skinfold thickness and performance of health related fitness test items. *Research Quarterly for Exercise and Sport* 60:183–88.

Pearcey, S., and de Castro, J. 2002. Food intake and meal patterns of weight-stable and weight-gaining persons. *American Journal of Clinical Nutrition* 76:107–12.

Pichard, C., et al. 1997. Body composition by x-ray absorptiometry and bioelectrical impedance in female runners. *Medicine & Science in Sports & Exercise* 29:1527–34.

Rodin, J., et al. 1990. Weight cycling and fat distribution. *International Journal of Obesity* 14:303–10.

Roemmich, J., and Sinning, W. 1996. Sport-seasonal changes in body composition, growth, power and strength of adolescent wrestlers. *International Journal of Sports Medicine* 17:92–99.

Rosenbaum, M., et al. 1998. An exploratory investigation of the morphology and biochemistry of cellulite. *Plastic and Reconstructive Surgery* 101:1934–39.

Schmidt, W., et al. 1993. Two seasons of weight cycling does not lower resting metabolic rate in collegiate wrestlers. *Medicine & Science in Sports & Exercise* 25:613–19.

Scott, J., et al. 1994. Acute weight gain in collegiate wrestlers following a tournament weigh-in. *Medicine & Science in Sports & Exercise* 26:1181–85.

Simkin-Silverman, L. R., et al. 1998. Lifetime weight cycling and psychological health in normal-weight and overweight women. *International Journal of Eating Disorders* 24:175–83.

Simoes, E., et al. 1995. The association between leisure-time physical activity and dietary fat in American adults. *American Journal of Public Health* 85:240–44.

Stevens, J., et al. 2002. Fitness and fatness as predictors of mortality from all causes and from cardiovascular disease in men and women in the Lipid Research Clinics Study. *American Journal of Epidemiology* 156:832–41.

Stout, J., et al. 1995. Validity of skinfold equations for estimating body density in youth wrestlers. *Medicine & Science in Sports & Exercise* 27:1321–25.

Stunkard, A., et al. 1990. The body-mass index of twins who have been reared apart. *New England Journal of Medicine* 322:1483–87.

Sturmi, J., and Rutecki, G. 1995. When competitive body builders collapse. *Physician and Sportsmedicine* 23 (11): 49–53.

Theintz, G., et al. 1993. Evidence for a reduction of growth potential in adolescent female gymnasts. *Journal of Pediatrics* 122:306–13.

Torstveit, M., and Sundgot-Borgen, J. 2005. The female athlete triad exists in both elite athletes and controls. *Medicine & Science in Sports & Exercise* 37:1449–59.

Torstveit, M., and Sundgot-Borgen, J. 2005. Participation in leanness sports but not training volume is associated with menstrual dysfunction: A national survey of 1276 elite athletes and controls. *British Journal of Sports Medicine* 39:141–47.

Torstveit, M., and Sundgot-Borgen, J. 2005. The female athlete triad: Are elite athletes at increased risk? *Medicine & Science in Sports & Exercise* 37:184–93.

Tremblay, A., et al. 1995. Alcohol and a high-fat diet: A combination favoring overfeeding. *American Journal of Clinical Nutrition* 62:639–44.

Trevisan, M., et al. 1998. Syndrome X and mortality: A population-based study. *American Journal of Epidemiology* 148:958–66.

Van Loan, M., et al. 1995. Evaluation of body composition by dual energy x-ray absorptiometry and two different software packages. *Medicine & Science in Sports & Exercise* 27:587–91.

Vorona, R., et al. 2005. Overweight and obese patients in a primary care population report less sleep than patients with a normal body mass index. *Archives of Internal Medicine* 165:25–30.

Wadden, T., et al. 2005. Randomized trial of lifestyle modification and pharmacotherapy for obesity. *New England Journal of Medicine* 353:2111–20.

Wagner, D. R., et al. 2000. Validation of air displacement plethysmography for assessing body composition. *Medicine & Science in Sports & Exercise* 32:1339–44.

Walberg-Rankin, J., et al. 1996. Effect of weight loss and refeeding diet composition on anaerobic performance in wrestlers. *Medicine & Science in Sports & Exercise* 28:1292–99.

Wang, Y., et al. 2005. Comparison of abdominal adiposity and overall obesity in predicting risk of type 2 diabetes among men. *American Journal of Clinical Nutrition* 81:555–63.

Wang, Z. M., et al. 1998. Six-compartment body composition model: Inter-method comparisons of total body fat measurement. *International Journal of Obesity and Related Metabolic Disorders* 22:329–37.

Webster, B., and Barr, S. 1993. Body composition analysis of female adolescent athletes: Comparing six regression equations. *Medicine & Science in Sports & Exercise* 25:648–53.

Weinsier, R., et al. 2000. Do adaptive changes in metabolic rate favor weight regain in weight-reduced individuals? An examination of the set-point theory. *American Journal of Clinical Nutrition* 73:1088–94.

Williams, P. 1990. Weight set-point theory and the high-density lipoprotein concentrations of long-distance runners. *Metabolism* 39:460–67.

Wroble, R. R., and Moxley, D. P. 1998. Weight loss patterns and success rates in high school wrestlers. *Medicine & Science in Sports & Exercise* 30:625–28.

Yusuf, S., et al. 2005. Obesity and the risk of myocardial infarction in 27,000 participants from 52 countries: A case-control study. *Lancet* 366:1640–49.

Zachwieja, J., et al. 2001. Short-term dietary energy restriction reduces lean body mass but not performance in physically active men and women. *International Journal of Sports Medicine* 22:310–16.

Zhang, J., et al. 2005. Obestatin, a peptide encoded by the ghrelin gene, opposes effects on food intake. *Science* 310:996–99.

Weight Maintenance and Loss through Proper Nutrition and Exercise

LEARNING OBJECTIVES

After studying this chapter, you should be able to:

1. Determine how many Calories per day are needed to maintain one's current body weight with either a sedentary or physically active lifestyle.

2. Calculate the amount of weight loss needed to attain a healthier BMI or body-fat percentage.

3. Identify behavior modification techniques that are appropriate to incorporate into a recommended weight-loss program.

4. Determine the number of daily Calories needed to lose body fat by diet alone, or with a combination diet-exercise program.

5. State the key principles underlying a weight-control diet designed to maintain a healthy body weight for a lifetime.

6. Use the Food Exchange System to plan a healthy, balanced diet containing sufficient Calories to meet one's daily energy needs for weight loss or weight maintenance.

7. Describe the value of exercise, including type, intensity, duration, and frequency, in a comprehensive weight-loss or weight-maintenance program.

8. Use heart rate responses as a guide to appropriate aerobic exercise intensity.

9. Design a progressive exercise program that will increase caloric expenditure to 300–500 Calories per day as part of a comprehensive weight-loss or weight-maintenance program.

10. Understand how diet and exercise complement each other to help lose or maintain body weight, citing the benefits of each that help compensate for the possible deficiencies of the other.

Introduction

Given the obsession we have with slimness and the fact that millions of Americans and Canadians are overweight, it is no wonder that a multibillion-dollar weight-control industry has developed. Weight-loss centers and health and fitness spas cater to this obsession and promise us new bodies just in time for the swimsuit season. Pharmaceutical companies produce drugs, both prescription and over-the-counter types, to help us lose fat the easy way. Food manufacturers market convenient, low-Calorie, prepackaged—but expensive—meals. Newspaper and magazine advertisements claim you can "Lose weight while you sleep" or "Lose 30 pounds in just 30 days." Each year at least one diet book on the best-seller list is advertised as the last diet we will ever need.

A variety of techniques, some useful and some not, are used in attempts to stimulate weight loss. Drugs are used to depress the appetite or increase metabolism. Creams are applied to specific body parts to shrink local fat deposits. Surgical techniques include intestinal bypasses, removal of or stapling part of the stomach, excision or suction removal of subcutaneous fat tissue, and wiring the jaw shut. Weight-loss diets involve almost every possible manipulation, including the high-fat diet, the high-protein diet, the chocolate diet, the grapefruit diet, the starvation diet, and even the "no diet" diet. Advertisements claim specially designed clothing worn during exercise can help you lose inches of fat in hours. Psychological techniques such as hypnosis or behavior modification are designed to change your eating habits.

The Committee to Develop Criteria for Evaluating the Outcomes of Approaches to Prevent and Treat Obesity identified three types of programs and approaches to treat obesity or overweight: clinical programs, nonclinical programs, and do-it-yourself programs. No matter which program an individual selects to lose weight, the committee recommended consultation with one's primary health care provider before engaging in a weight-loss program.

In severe cases of clinical obesity, treatment usually is administered in a *clinical program* under medical supervision and may involve a combination of many techniques, including surgery, hormone therapy, drugs, and starvation-type diets. An individualized, medically supervised weight-control program is very important for the clinically obese because so many health risks are related to obesity. Unfortunately, clinical obesity is very resistant to treatment and over 95 percent of those individuals who lose weight regain it within 1–5 years and may do this repeatedly. As noted in chapter 10, these fluctuations in body weight, known as weight cycling, may not exert deleterious effects on metabolism and health and should not deter obese individuals from attempts to lose weight. The National Institute of Health notes that other groups may need medically supervised weight-loss programs, including children, pregnant women, persons over the age of 65, and individuals with medical conditions that could be exacerbated by weight loss.

Nonclinical programs for the treatment of obesity are primarily commercial franchises, using packaged materials provided by counselors who are not professional health care providers; an example is Weight Watchers. *Do-it-yourself programs* include any effort by the individual to lose weight by himself or herself or through community-based and work-site programs. These treatment programs may be well suited for individuals who have accumulated excess body fat through environmental conditions, such as excessive eating and decreased physical activity. Such programs may be beneficial to the typical adult, for substantial amounts of body fat appear to accumulate between the ages of 25 and 35. The prevalence of overweight individuals, as measured by the Body Mass Index (BMI), in the United States has increased in the past quarter-century in both children and adults. The latest government reports state that nearly two-thirds of American adults and over half of Canadian adults are overweight, and future projections indicate 9 out of 10 Americans will be overweight while 1 in 3 will be obese.

Because the majority of obese people who lose weight put it back on, most weight-control experts indicate the focus should be on prevention and maintenance. Prevention of excess weight gain is more effective than treatment. Prevention should be a lifelong lifestyle, beginning in childhood and continuing through adulthood. Preventive techniques may be especially helpful during the first 2 years of college, when young females typically gain 10–15 pounds. As noted in a study of twins by Newman and others, prevention may also curtail the weight gain in those genetically predisposed. Many overweight individuals often note that the hard part is not losing weight, it's keeping it off, but that may not necessarily be so. Maintenance of a healthy body weight is a simple form of prevention; preventing weight regain is comparable to preventing weight gain in the first place.

This chapter centers on some basic questions relative to the construction, implementation, and maintenance of a sound weight-control program using the *do-it-yourself* approach. The principles and suggestions advanced here apply to the overweight individual who wants to lose excess body fat and also to the person with normal body weight who may want to maintain that weight level or even lose additional poundage in order to improve physical performance. For individuals interested in participating in *nonclinical* or *clinical programs,* some guidelines are offered later in this chapter.

A comprehensive weight-control program involves three components: (1) a dietary regimen stressing balanced nutrition but with reduced caloric intake; (2) an aerobic and resistance exercise program to increase caloric expenditure and maintain lean body mass; and (3) a behavior modification program to facilitate the implementation of the first two components. These components are emphasized in this chapter.

Basics of Weight Control

How many Calories are in a pound of body fat?

One pound is equivalent to 454 grams. Because we know that 1 gram of fat is equal to 9 Calories, it would appear that a pound of body fat would equal about 4,086 Calories (9 × 454). However, the fat stored in adipose tissue contains small amounts of protein, minerals, and water, which reduces the caloric content of 1 pound of body fat to approximately 3,500 Calories.

Is the caloric concept of weight control valid?

The caloric concept of weight control is relatively simple. As illustrated in figure 11.1, if you take in more Calories than you expend, you will gain weight, a positive energy balance. If you expend more than you take in, you lose weight, a negative energy balance. To maintain your body weight, caloric input and output must be equal. As far as we know, human energy systems are governed by the same laws of physics that rule all energy transformations. The First Law of Thermodynamics is as pertinent to us in the conservation and expenditure of our energy sources as it is to any other machine. Because a Calorie is a unit of energy, and because energy can neither be created nor destroyed, those Calories that we eat must either be expended in some way or conserved in the body. No substantial evidence is available to disprove the caloric theory. It is still the physical basis for body-weight control.

Keep in mind, however, that the total body weight is made up of different components, those notable in weight-control programs being body water, protein in the fat-free mass, small amounts of carbohydrate, and fat stores. Changes in these components may bring about daily body-weight fluctuations of 3–5 pounds that would appear to be contrary to the caloric concept since protein and carbohydrate contain only 4 Calories per gram and water contains no Calories. You may gain water weight by consuming a high-salt diet for a day, or by menstrual cycle changes. You may lose 5 pounds in an hour, but it will be mostly water weight. Starvation techniques may lead to rapid weight losses, but some of the weight loss will be in glycogen stores, body-protein stores such as muscle mass, and the water associated with glycogen and protein stores. In programs to lose body weight, we usually desire to lose excess body fat, and certain dietary and exercise techniques may help to maximize fat losses while minimizing protein losses.

The metabolism of human energy sources is complex, and although the caloric theory is valid relative to body-weight control, one must be aware that weight changes will not always be exactly in line with caloric input and output, and that weight losses may not be due to body fat loss alone. Also keep in mind one of the concepts advanced in the last chapter relative to individual variability in metabolic rates; two individuals with the same body weight may consume the same amount of Calories, yet one may gain while the other may maintain or even lose weight. Other than differences in metabolism, this possibility also may be

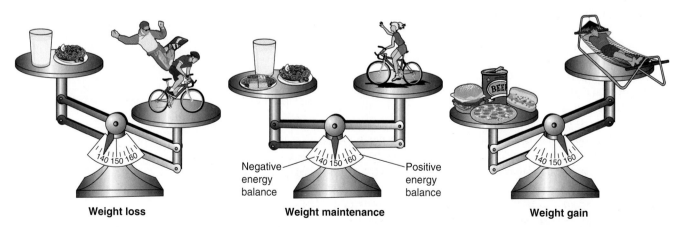

Weight loss Negative energy balance **Weight maintenance** Positive energy balance **Weight gain**

FIGURE 11.1   Weight control is based upon energy balance. Too much food input or too little exercise output can result in a positive energy balance or weight gain. Decreased food intake or increased physical activity can result in a negative caloric balance or weight loss.

related to the type of Calories in the diet; research has suggested that the body may store dietary fat Calories in the adipose tissue more efficiently than carbohydrate or protein Calories. In essence, compared to dietary fat, it may take more energy to convert dietary carbohydrate and protein into body fat. These concepts are explored further in this chapter.

How many Calories do I need per day to maintain my body weight?

This depends on a number of factors, notably age, body weight, sex, resting energy expenditure (REE), the thermic effect of feeding (TEF), and physical activity levels.

The caloric requirement per kilogram of body weight is very high during the early years of life when a child is developing and adding large amounts of body tissue. The Calorie/kilogram requirement decreases throughout the years from birth to old age, with exceptions during pregnancy and lactation.

Body weight influences the total amount of daily Calories you need, but not the Calorie/kilogram level. The large individual simply needs more total Calories to maintain body weight. Body weight is the most significant factor determining daily caloric intake necessary to maintain weight, although body composition also may be important.

Up to the age of 11 or 12, the caloric needs of boys and girls are similar in terms of Calories/kilogram body weight. After puberty, however, males need slightly more Calories/kilogram, probably because of their greater percentage of muscle tissue in comparison to females.

Individual variations in REE may either increase or decrease daily caloric needs, depending on whether the REE is above or below normal. Individual variations may vary 10–20 percent from normal. An extended discussion of the REE was presented in chapter 3.

The TEF effect may also vary among individuals. The TEF is also covered in more detail in chapter 3.

Physical activity levels above resting may have a very significant impact upon caloric needs. Some activities, like bowling, may increase energy needs only slightly, while others, such as running for an hour or more, may add 1,000–1,500 or more Calories to the daily energy requirement. You may wish to review chapter 3 regarding the caloric cost of exercise.

All of these factors make it difficult to make an exact recommendation relative to daily caloric needs. As noted in chapter 3, the doubly labeled water (DLW) technique may provide a fairly accurate measure of total daily energy expenditure (TDEE). However, it is rather expensive and not readily available to most individuals. Several other methods are available to help you determine the amount of Calories you need to consume daily in order to maintain a stable body weight. Some are more detailed than others, but keep in mind that all are estimates that may contain some degree of error.

Estimated Energy Requirement (EER) Technique   In chapter 3 we introduced the concept of Estimated Energy Requirement (EER) as presented by the National Academy of Sciences (NAS) in their recent document focusing on DRI for energy. The EER is defined as the dietary energy intake that is predicted to maintain energy balance in a healthy individual of a defined age, gender, weight, height, and level of physical activity consistent with good health. As you may recall, your total daily energy expenditure (TDEE) includes your resting energy expenditure (REE), the thermic effect of food (TEF), and the thermic effect of exercise (TEE). The EER formulae for gender and different age categories are presented in table 11.1. As noted, the formulae require age, height, weight, and physical activity quotient (PA). You can easily determine the first three criteria, which is all you need to obtain an estimate of your energy requirements if you are sedentary, but determination of your PA requires some effort.

To calculate your EER, you should first determine your energy needs for a sedentary lifestyle. Select the appropriate formula for your gender and age category from table 11.1 and use the value of 1.0 as the PA. For example, a 20-year-old sedentary male weighing 175 pounds (80 kilograms) who is 71 inches (1.8 meters) tall would have a daily EER of 2,715 Calories.

$$EER = 662 - 9.53 \times 20 + [1.0 \times (15.91 \times 80 + 539.6 \times 1.8)]$$
$$= 2,715$$

As you may recall from chapter 3, the PA is based on your physical activity level (PAL), which is the ratio of your TDEE to your BEE, or TDEE:BEE, over a 24-hour period. The NAS indicates that physical activity is the most variable component of TDEE, and also notes that the assessment of physical activity-induced increments in TDEE is fraught with considerable uncertainties. Nevertheless, they have developed four categories of PAL: Sedentary, Low Active, Active, and Very Active. If you would like to calculate

TABLE 11.1	Estimated Energy Requirement (EER) Formulae

Females age 19 and over:

EER = 354 – 6.91 × Age + [PA × (9.361 × Weight + 726 × Height)]

Males age 19 and over:

EER = 662 – 9.53 × Age + [PA × (15.91 × Weight + 539.6 × Height)]

Females age 9–18:

EER = 135.3 – 30.8 × Age + [PA × (10.0 × Weight + 934 × Height)] + 25 (Calories/day for energy deposition)

Males age 9–18:

EER = 88.5 – 61.9 × Age + [PA × (26.7 × Weight + 903 × Height] + 25 (Calories/day for energy deposition)

Age: In years.
Weight: In kilograms (kg). To convert weight in pounds to kilograms, multiply by 0.454.
Height: In meters (m). To convert height in inches to meters, multiply by 0.0254.

Adapted from National Academy of Sciences. 2002. *Dietary Reference Intakes for Energy, Carbohydrates, Fiber, Fat, Protein and Amino Acids* (Macronutrients). Washington, DC. National Academy Press.

your PAL and resultant PA based on the NAS protocol, you may go to www.nap.edu, type in Dietary Reference Intakes for Energy, and then peruse chapters 5 and 12 for details of the procedure.

However, we will use a modified approach to estimate your EER based on your daily record of physical activities and associated caloric expenditure as calculated from appendix B. The correlation between the NAS procedure and our estimates of exercise caloric expenditure are not exact because different calculations are used. However, both provide reasonable values for the energy cost of daily physical activity.

The NAS bases the PAL on the amount of daily physical activity that is the equivalent of walking at a rate of 3–4 miles per hour. To reach a specific PAL category, you are required to expend the energy equivalent of walking a set number of miles. Although the NAS bases the PAL on an energy equivalent of walking, keep in mind that you do not need to walk the required miles to attain a specific PAL category. You may do a multitude of physical activities, such as golfing, swimming, and jogging that add up to this energy equivalent. William Roberts, a past president of the ACSM, suggests that 15 minutes of moderate physical activity other than walking, such as in-line skating or cycling, may approximate one mile of walking.

Here is a brief summary of the amount of physical activity needed for each PAL category. Table 11.2 complements this discussion. Some guidelines based on the energy expenditure equivalents of walking (3–4 mph) or jogging are presented.

Sedentary category   The energy expenditure of individuals in the Sedentary category represents their REE, including the TEF, plus various physical activities associated with independent living, such as walking from the house or work to the car, walking your dog, typing, daily household tasks, and other forms of very light activity. If you engage in no daily physical activity, your PAL will range from 1.00–1.39, but your PA for the formula is set at a baseline of 1.0. Individuals who walk less than 30 minutes daily generally fall in this category.

Low Active category   In addition to the normal daily activities of independent living, you need to expend the physical activity equivalent of walking about 2.2 miles per day in order to be in the Low Active category. Your PAL for the Low Active category will range from 1.40–1.59, but the PA for the formula is set at 1.11–1.16 depending on gender and stage of life. Individuals who walk 30–40 minutes, or jog 10–15 minutes, daily generally fit this category.

Active category   In addition to the normal daily activities of independent living, you need to expend the physical activity equivalent of walking about 7 miles per day in order to be in the Active category. Your PAL for the Active category will range from 1.60–1.89, but the PA for the formula is set at 1.25–1.31 depending on gender and stage of life. Individuals who walk 1.75 hours, or jog 40–45 minutes, daily generally fall in this category.

Very Active category   In addition to the normal daily activities of independent living, you need to expend the physical activity equivalent of walking about 17 miles per day in order to be in the Very Active category. Your PAL for the Very Active category will range from 1.90–2.50, but the PA for the formula is set at 1.42–1.56 depending on gender and stage of life. Individuals who walk 4.25 hours, or jog 1.5 hours, daily generally fit this category.

Let us continue with the example of our 20-year-old male and determine the number of Calories he would need to expend to move from the Sedentary category (2,715 Calories) into each of the active categories. If we consult table 11.2 we see that the PAs for the Low Active, Active, and Very Active categories are, respectively, 1.11, 1.25 and 1.48.

Low Active:

$$EER = 662 - 9.53 \times 20 + [1.11 \times (15.91 \times 80 + 539.6 \times 1.8)]$$
$$= 2,962 \text{ Calories}$$

Active:

$$EER = 662 - 9.53 \times 20 + [1.25 \times (15.91 \times 80 + 539.6 \times 1.8)]$$
$$= 3,276 \text{ Calories}$$

Very Active:

$$EER = 662 - 9.53 \times 20 + [1.48 \times (15.91 \times 80 + 539.6 \times 1.8)]$$
$$= 3,793 \text{ Calories}$$

As his EER for the Sedentary category is 2,715 Calories, he would need to expend about 247, 561, or 1,078 Calories through physical activity to attain, respectively, the Low Active, Active, and Very Active PAL categories.

We will talk more about exercise later in this chapter. In chapter 3 we introduced you to appendix B and explained how you might calculate your daily energy expenditure through physical activity. You may wish to review that discussion on page 98. In brief, record the number of minutes of each type of physical activity you do daily. Then, consult appendix B, find your body weight in the top margin, and determine how many Calories you expend per minute doing each activity.

TABLE 11.2   The Physical Activity Level Categories

PAL Category	Physical Activity Level (PAL)	Physical Activity Coefficient (PA)			
		Males	Females	Boys	Girls
Sedentary	≥ 1.0 –< 1.4	1.00	1.00	1.00	1.00
Low Active	≥ 1.4 –< 1.6	1.11	1.12	1.13	1.16
Active	≥ 1.6 –< 1.9	1.25	1.27	1.26	1.31
Very Active	≥ 1.9 –< 2.5	1.48	1.45	1.42	1.56

Adapted from National Academy of Sciences. 2002. *Dietary Reference Intakes for Energy, Carbohydrates, Fiber, Fat, Protein and Amino Acids (Macronutrients)*. Washington, DC. National Academy Press.

Let's apply this procedure and complete the example of our 20-year-old male. Let us assume that he has engaged in the following physical activities over the course of a week, has calculated his energy expenditure from appendix B, totaled his weekly energy expenditure, and then figured his daily average caloric expenditure.

Day	Physical Activity	Duration	Calories/min	Total Calories
Monday	Tennis, singles	40 min	8.8	352
	Walking, 3 mph	20 min	4.8	96
Tuesday	Running, 7 mph	40 min	14.9	596
Wednesday	Tennis, singles	40 min	8.8	352
	Walking, 3 mph	20 min	4.8	96
Thursday	Running, 8 mph	30 min	17.1	513
Friday	Tennis, singles	40 min	8.8	352
	Bowling	30 min	4.9	147
Saturday	Golf, carry clubs	180 min	4.8	864
Sunday	Running, 7 mph	40 min	14.9	596
Total weekly Calories				3964
Daily average caloric expenditure (3700 Calories/7days)				566

Thus, with an average daily energy expenditure through physical activity totaling 566 Calories, he is in the Active PAL category and can use that formula to calculate his EER. Alternatively, he may simply add the 566 Calories to his Sedentary EER to determine the number of Calories needed to maintain his body weight if it has been stable. Using the formula for the Active category, his EER as noted would total 3,276 Calories. Adding the 566 Calories to his Sedentary category EER of 2,715 would total 3,281 Calories. The difference between the two estimates is negligible in this case, but may vary some in other cases.

Using this same procedure, you may calculate your EER to maintain your normal body weight. Use the formula in table 11.1 that is appropriate for your gender and age and, using the appropriate PA values from table 11.2, calculate your EER for each of the four PAL categories. Next, as per the example above, record the type and amount of time devoted to various physical activities over the course of a week and calculate your average daily physical activity energy expenditure; you may then either add this amount to your Sedentary EER or use the appropriate formula to estimate your total daily EER.

Alternatively, you may go to www.MyPyramid.gov, click on MyTracker, and enter in the average physical activity you do daily. For example, if you jog 45 minutes four days per week, this totals 180 minutes per week, or an average 26 minutes daily. Enter the physical activity you do, and click on Energy Balance. Disregard the food input message, and you will be provided with your EER. If a computerized dietary analysis program accompanies this text, you may also use it to calculate your daily energy requirement.

Calorie Counting Technique If your body weight has been stable, keeping track of the Calories you eat for 3–7 days may provide you with a good estimate of your daily energy requirement. Eat your normal diet, but record everything you consume. Some guidelines for measuring, recording, and calculating your daily caloric intake are presented on pages 414–417. Computerized dietary analysis programs are available to facilitate this task. For example, you may analyze your diet for Calories and other nutritional values at the Center for Nutrition Policy Promotion Website, www.usda.gov/cnpp or at www.MyPyramid.gov.

Simplified Technique The American Heart Association has provided some guidelines for the approximate daily caloric intake needed to maintain a desirable body weight. For example, if you are sedentary, you need about 14 Calories per pound of body weight to maintain your current weight. If you weighed 175 pounds, you would need about 2,450 Calories per day (175 × 14) simply to maintain your weight. Note that this estimate is somewhat less than that estimated by the EER procedure for the Sedentary category. To lose or gain weight, the caloric intake must be adjusted downward or upward. Table 11.3 represents some figures from the American Heart Association for other levels of physical activity which are different than the PAL categories developed by the NAS.

Keep in mind that no matter which procedure you follow, your actual daily caloric needs may vary somewhat from the estimate obtained. In the section of this chapter on dietary modifications, we will discuss how many Calories you may need in your diet if you desire to lose weight. If that is the case, you may wish to estimate your daily energy needs by several techniques and use the lowest value obtained in order to optimize the caloric deficit needed for weight loss, as long as it meets the recommendations presented for safe weight loss.

TABLE 11.3 Approximate daily caloric intake needed to maintain desirable body weight

Activity level	Calories per pound	Calories per kilogram
1. Very sedentary (movement restricted such as patient confined to house)	13	29
2. Sedentary (most Americans, office job, light work)	14	31
3. Moderate activity (weekend recreation)	15	33
4. Very active (meet ACSM standards for vigorous exercise three times/week)	16	35
5. Competitive athlete (daily vigorous activity in high-energy sport)	17+	38+

How much weight can I lose safely per week?

If you decide to lose weight without medical supervision, keep in mind that the recommended maximal weight loss is 2 pounds per week. Because there are 3,500 Calories in a pound of body fat, this would necessitate a deficit of 7,000 Calories for the week, or 1,000 Calories per day. For growing children who carry excess fat, the general recommendation is about 1 pound per week, or a daily 500-Calorie deficit. Keep in mind that these are *maximal* recommended weight-loss values for medically unsupervised programs. Lower weight-loss goals, such as 1 pound per week for adults and one-half pound per week for children and adolescents, may be more appropriate, realizable goals. These recommendations are in line with guidelines presented by health professionals, such as the American College of Sports Medicine.

As we shall see later in this chapter, weight losses may not parallel the caloric deficit we incur during early stages of a weight-reduction program, and the 2-pound limit may be adjusted during this time period. In addition, as mentioned previously, we want our weight loss to be body-fat tissue, not lean body mass. A loss of 10 pounds of body weight may help improve physical performance, but if 5 pounds is muscle tissue, then performance could possibly deteriorate. Thus, you should monitor your weight loss not only with a scale but also with skinfolds and girth measures to help ensure that you are losing body fat, and in the right places.

How can I determine the amount of body weight I need to lose?

As noted in the last chapter, individuals desire to lose weight for one of three reasons—to improve appearance, health, or physical performance. As for your appearance, you are the judge, but consult with your physician or other health professional. You do not want your weight-loss program to induce an eating disorder. Losing excess body fat for health is a good reason. Check with your physician, who can also monitor health risks, such as blood pressure, serum lipids, blood glucose, and regional adiposity, associated with excess body weight. A loss of 5–10 percent body weight or 2–4 inches off the waist, easily achieved in 3–4 months, may help reduce several health risk factors. Losing weight in attempts to enhance physical performance should involve interactions between the athlete, coach, and team physician, and in the case of young athletes parents should be involved. Janet Walberg-Rankin noted that body-weight goals for athletes should be based on current body composition, time remaining until the competitive season, body-weight history, and sport-specific rules.

In a recent review, Brownell and Rodin indicated that weight-loss goals should account for how much weight an individual can reasonably lose and should not be determined solely by health standards. The same reasoning applies for appearance and physical performance standards. They note that pursuit of an unrealistic ideal may lead to various health problems.

Using the body mass index (BMI) as a guide, you will need to calculate your current BMI and determine your target BMI. Calculation of the BMI was presented on page 365 and a healthy BMI range is approximately 18.5–25. The formula to calculate your desired body weight in kilograms is

$$\text{Target body weight (kg)} = \text{Target BMI} \times \text{height in meters}^2$$

As an example, if you are 5′7″ (1.70 meters) tall and weigh 170 pounds (77.2 kilograms), then you have a BMI of 26.7 ($77.2/1.70^2$). If you want to achieve a healthier BMI of 23, simply multiply 23 by 1.70^2 to determine your body-weight goal; 23 by 2.89 equals 66.5 kilograms, or 146 pounds. The desired weight loss would be 24 pounds (170 − 146), which represents a 14 percent reduction in total body weight ($24/170 = 0.14$; $0.14 \times 100\% = 14\%$).

If you want to use body-fat percentage as the guide to weight loss, you will need to measure your current body-fat percentage and determine your target goal. Methods of determining body-fat percentage are presented on pages 519–523 in appendix D. If you are an athlete with 20 percent body fat but desire to get down to 15 percent, you may use the following formula:

$$\text{Target body weight} = \frac{\text{Lean body mass in pounds}}{1.00 - \text{desired body-fat percentage}}$$

As an example, an athlete who weighs 150 pounds and is 20 percent body fat has 30 pounds of body fat, and the remaining 120 pounds (150 − 30) is lean body mass. Substituting in the formula provides the following data:

$$\frac{120}{1.00 - 0.15} = \frac{120}{0.85} = 141 \text{ pounds}$$

Thus, this athlete would need to lose 9 pounds of body fat (150 − 141) to achieve a 15 percent body-fat percentage. If proper methods of weight loss are used as discussed later in this chapter, the losses will be in body fat, not lean body mass.

Key Concept Recap

▶ A comprehensive weight-control program involves a balanced reduced-Calorie diet, an aerobic and resistance exercise program, and appropriate behavior modification.

▶ The caloric deficit, which represents caloric intake minus caloric expenditure, may be useful as a means to predict body-weight losses on a long-term basis, because 3,500 Calories equals approximately 1 pound of body fat.

▶ The average sedentary adult female should be able to maintain her body weight with a daily average of approximately 14 Calories per pound of body weight, while sedentary males need about 15 Calories per pound of body weight. Slightly higher amounts of Calories per unit body weight are needed by sedentary children and adolescents. Daily caloric energy needs increase in direct proportion to daily levels of physical activity.

▶ For the overweight individual who desires to lose weight without the guidance of a physician, the recommended maximal weight loss is 2 pounds per week.

Check for Yourself

Based on your age, gender, height, and weight, calculate your Estimated Energy Expenditure (EER) for a sedentary lifestyle based on the formula in table 11.1. Use a PA value of 1.0.

Behavior Modification

What is behavior modification?

One of the key components of a successful weight-control program is the need to identify and modify those behaviors that contribute to the weight problem. The subject of human behavior development and change is very complex, but psychologists note that three factors are generally involved—the physical environment, the social environment, and the personal environment. For the person with a weight problem, a refrigerator brimming with food (physical environment), a family that consumes high-Calorie snack foods around the house (social environment), and an acquired taste for high-fat or sweet foods (personal environment) may trigger behaviors that make it very difficult to maintain a proper body weight.

A model often used to explain the development or modification of health behaviors, such as a proper diet and exercise program for weight control, involves three steps—knowledge, values, and behavior. First, proper knowledge is essential. A considerable amount of misinformation relative to the roles of nutrition and exercise in weight control exists, so you need to possess accurate information. Second, the health implications of this knowledge may help you develop a set of personal values, or attitudes, toward a specific health behavior. If you perceive excess body fat as a threat to your personal physical or psychological health, you are more likely to initiate behavioral changes. Third, your health behavior should then reflect the knowledge you acquired and the values you developed.

Behavior modification is a technique often used in psychological therapy to elicit desirable behavioral changes. The rationale underlying behavior modification is that many behavioral patterns are learned via stimulus-response conditioning; for example, a stimulus in your environment such as a commercial break in a television program elicits a response of a mad dash to the refrigerator. Because such responses are learned, they also may be unlearned. For a discussion of a comprehensive program conducted by a behavioral psychologist, the reader is referred to the review by Brownell and Kramer.

Relative to a self-designed program of weight control, behavior modification is used primarily to reduce or eliminate physical or social stimuli that may lead to excessive caloric intake or decreased physical activity. George Bray, an international authority on obesity treatment, noted that the most important component of any weight-control program is the associated behavior modification through which the individual learns new ways to deal with old problems. In a recent study stressing the importance of behavior modification, Haus and others recommended that potential weight-program participants should learn and practice the weight-maintenance behavior of reduced dietary fat and regular exercise, independent of and before any weight-reduction attempts. The Consumers Union notes that exercising more and switching to a leaner, healthier diet will yield innumerable health benefits even if you don't lose a single pound.

How do I apply behavior-modification techniques in my weight-control program?

When breaking any well-established habit, self-discipline, or will power, is the key. The most important component of a weight-control program is you. You must want to lose weight, and you must take the major responsibility for achieving your goals. You need to face the fact that being overweight and sedentary is dangerous to your health. You must be convinced that reduced body weight will enhance your life, and you must establish this goal as a high priority. You must be able to tolerate some discomfort as you make lifestyle changes. Data from the National Weight Control Registry, which consists of people who have lost at least 30 pounds and kept it off, indicate the key factor is to do it for yourself. Your desire to lose weight must become more important than the desire to overeat or to not exercise.

Both long-range and short-range realistic goals need to be established. Several experts in weight control, such as Tremblay and Wadden, indicated that for overweight individuals a 10–15 percent weight loss is a reasonable goal over 4–6 months. Thus, a long-range goal may be to lose 30 pounds over 6 months, whereas a short-range goal would be to lose about 1–2 pounds per week. Losing 30 pounds may seem like a daunting task, but setting small goals, a few pounds at a time, is one of the keys to success indicated by the National Weight Control Registry. A long-range goal may also include a large number of behavioral changes to achieve the 30-pound weight loss, but the number of changes would be phased in gradually on a short-term basis. Do not expect to make all recommended behavioral changes overnight. (See figure 11.2.)

As the saying goes, nothing breeds success like success, so it is extremely important to set short-term goals that may be attainable in a reasonable length of time so that you may experience multiple successes in pursuit of your long-term goal. When you achieve your first short-term goal, a new short-term goal should be established as you progress toward your long-term goal. It is also important to remember that no initial short-term goal is too small, nor is any new short-term goal too small in the progress toward your long-term goal. You may go to www.smallstep.gov for more information on how to incorporate small changes into your daily lifestyle, and 120 small steps to a healthier diet and increased physical activity is presented in appendix H. As you achieve each short-term goal, you should reward yourself with something appropriate to the occasion; a reward will provide you with positive feedback to your commitment to your weight-loss program.

One of the first steps in a behavior modification program is to identify those physical and social environmental factors that may lead to problem behaviors. Keeping a diary of your daily activities in your daily planner for a week or two may help you identify some behavioral patterns that may contribute to overeating and extra body weight. The following are some of the factors that might be recorded each time you eat, along with a brief explanation of their possible importance. You should also record your daily physical activity.

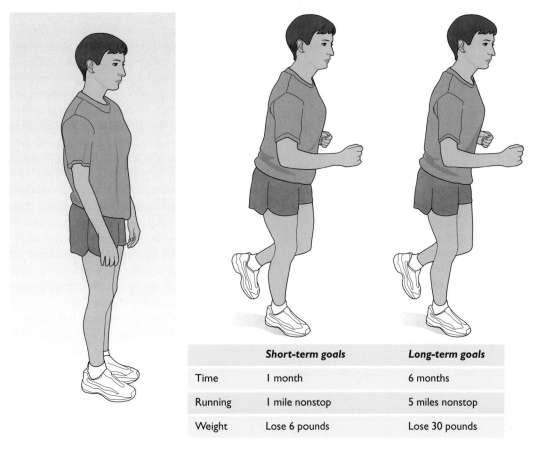

	Short-term goals	Long-term goals
Time	1 month	6 months
Running	1 mile nonstop	5 miles nonstop
Weight	Lose 6 pounds	Lose 30 pounds

FIGURE 11.2 Goal setting is an important factor in an exercise program.

Type of food and amount This may be related to the other factors. For example, do you eat a high-Calorie food during your snacks?

Meal or snack You may find yourself snacking four or five times a day.

Time of day Do you eat at regular hours or have a full meal just before retiring at night?

Degree of hunger How hungry were you when you ate—very hungry or not hungry at all? You may be snacking when not hungry.

Activity What were you doing while eating? You may find TV watching and eating snack foods are related.

Location Where do you eat? The office or school cafeteria may be the place you eat a high-Calorie meal.

Persons involved With whom do you eat? Do you eat more when alone or with others? Being with certain people may trigger overeating.

Emotional feelings How do you feel when eating? You might eat more when depressed than when happy, or vice versa.

Exercise How much walking, stair climbing, or regular aerobic exercise do you get? Do you ride when you could possibly walk? How much time do you just sit?

Recording this information may make you more aware of the physical and social circumstances under which you tend to overeat or be physically inactive. This awareness may be useful to help implement behavioral changes that may make weight control easier. The following suggestions are often helpful:

Self-discipline and self-control:
1. Establish weight loss as a high priority.
2. Think about this priority before eating.
3. Take small helpings deliberately as a means to control your weight.
4. Check your body weight and shape on a daily basis. Use this as a motivational tool.

Foods to eat:
1. Use low-Calorie healthful foods for snacks.
2. Plan low-Calorie, high-nutrient meals.
3. Plan your food intake for the entire day.
4. Eat only foods that have had minimal or no processing.
5. Allow yourself very small amounts of high-Calorie foods that you like, but stay within daily caloric limitations.
6. Know the Food Exchange System, particularly high-fat foods.

Food purchasing:
1. Do not shop when hungry.
2. Prepare a shopping list and do not deviate from it.
3. Buy only foods that are low in Calories and high in nutrient value. Read and compare food labels to limit fat and sugar content.
4. Buy natural foods as much as possible.

Food storage:

1. Keep high-Calorie food out of sight and in sealed containers or cupboards.
2. Have low-Calorie snacks like carrots and radishes readily available.

Food preparation and serving:

1. Buy only foods that need preparation of some type.
2. Do not add fats or sugar in preparation, if possible.
3. Prepare only small amounts. Be able to visualize one serving size for any given food.
4. Do not use serving bowls on the table.
5. Put the food on the plate, preferably a small one.

Location:

1. Eat in only one place, such as the kitchen or dining area.
2. Avoid food areas such as the kitchen or snack table at a party.
3. Avoid restaurants where you are most likely to buy high-Calorie items.

Restaurant eating:

1. When eating out, select the low-Calorie items.
2. Request your meals be prepared without fat.
3. Have condiments like butter, mayonnaise, and salad dressing served on the side; use sparingly.
4. Order water, not a high-Calorie beverage.

Methods of eating:

1. Eat slowly; chew food thoroughly or drink water between bites.
2. Eat with someone, for conversation can slow down the eating process.
3. Cut food into small pieces.
4. Do not do anything else while eating, such as watching TV.
5. Relax and enjoy the meal.
6. Eat only at specified times.
7. Eat only until pleasantly satisfied, not stuffed.
8. Spread your Calories over the day, eating small amounts more often.

Activity:

1. Walk more. Park the car or get off the bus some distance from work. Briskly walk the dog.
2. Use the stairs instead of the elevator when possible.
3. Take a brisk 10-minute walk instead of a coffee-donut break. Do this several times a day.
4. Get involved in activities with other people, preferably physical activities that will burn Calories.
5. Avoid sedentary night routines.
6. Start a regular exercise program, including both aerobic and resistance exercises.
7. Schedule exercise as an appointment in your daily planner.

Mental attitude:

1. Recognize that you are not perfect and lapses may occur.
2. Deal positively with your lapse; put it behind you and get back on your program.
3. Put reminders on the refrigerator door at home or on your telephone at work.
4. Reward yourself for sticking to your plans.

For the interested reader, the books by Dusek and Miller provide an in-depth coverage of behavior modification for weight-control purposes. Many of the commercial, medically oriented weight-loss centers as well as organizations such as Weight Watchers International also may be sources of information. Self-taught, self-administered weight-loss programs may also be very effective, as indicated in the study by Wayne Miller and his associates.

Stress reduction techniques may also be important in a weight-control program. The Consumers Union indicates that emotional stress can hinder weight control by triggering the release of cortisol into the blood, which conserves fat and increases hunger. Exercise in itself may help reduce emotional stress, as may various relaxation techniques such as meditation and yoga.

Individuals with clinical obesity may need professional assistance from health counselors to implement a behavior modification program for weight control. However, others with less severe weight problems may be able to initiate their own program if they have adequate accurate information.

Research has shown that most individuals initiating a weight-loss program do use acceptable strategies, such as exercising and eating a low-fat, low-Calorie diet, but use of these strategies becomes inconsistent in subsequent years, resulting in weight regain. In a recent position statement, the American Dietetic Association resolved that successful weight management requires a lifelong commitment to healthful lifestyle behaviors emphasizing eating practices and daily physical activities that are attainable and enjoyable. The remainder of this chapter focuses on the development of a proper lifelong diet and exercise program for losing weight safely and keeping it off.

Key Concept Recap

▶ Behavior modification is a very important part of a weight-control program. In order for weight control to be effective over a lifetime, dietary and exercise behaviors may need adjustments in order to curtail caloric intake and increase energy expenditure.

▶ Keeping a record of your daily eating habits will help you identify behavioral patterns relative to overeating and may be used as a basis for the elimination of cues that trigger eating.

Check for Yourself

Using information presented in the text, keep a record of your dietary and physical activity behaviors for a period of 3–7 days. Compare your findings to the text discussion regarding dietary and physical activity behaviors that may help you maintain a healthy body weight.

Dietary Modifications

How can I determine the number of Calories needed in a diet to lose weight?

To answer this question you need to provide two figures. First, you need to provide an estimate of how many Calories you need to consume daily to maintain your current body weight. As noted previously on pages 402–404, several techniques are available, so you should select one to provide an estimate of the number of Calories you may need to consume daily to maintain your current body weight. Second, you need to provide an estimate of the amount of weight that you want to lose, as discussed on page 405, and then determine how much you want to lose per week. One pound is the preferable goal, but you may lose up to 2 pounds safely. Some computerized dietary analysis programs will calculate your estimated energy intake needed to lose about 1–2 pounds per week.

For our purposes, we will use the value of 3,500 Calories to represent 1 pound of body-fat, or body-weight, loss. To lose 1 pound of body fat, you must create a 3,500 Calorie deficit. To lose 1 pound per week, your daily caloric deficit should be 500 (3,500/7). To lose 2 pounds per week, the recommended maximum unless under medical supervision, the daily caloric deficit should be 1,000 (7,000/7).

Once you calculate your daily energy needs to maintain your current body weight, simply subtract your daily caloric deficit from it; the result will be your recommended daily caloric intake. An example is presented below:

Example: 35-year-old sedentary woman who weighs 140 pounds desires to lose 1 pound per week.

1. From table 11.3, Calories/lb needed to maintain body weight: 14
2. Predicted total number of Calories to maintain body weight:

$$14 \times 140 = 1,960 \text{ Calories/day}$$

3. Recommended daily caloric deficit = 500 Calories/day
4. Recommended daily caloric intake = 1,460 Calories

(1,960 − 500 = 1,460 Calories/day)

Another technique that has been recommended simply multiplies the body weight in pounds by 10 Calories. This technique is based upon the premise that the body weight may not be maintained at this level of caloric intake. For our example above, the recommended daily caloric intake would be 1,400 (10 × 140).

However, it is important to note that most health professionals do not recommend weight-loss diets lower than 1,000 Calories unless medically supervised.

How can I predict my body-weight loss through dieting alone?

As mentioned in the last chapter, the human body is composed of different components, most commonly compartmentalized into body fat and lean body mass; lean body mass is about 70 percent water. On a dietary program, weight loss may reflect decreases in body fat, body water, or muscle mass, all of which present different caloric values. For example, 1 pound of body fat equals about 3,500 Calories, while an equivalent weight of water contains no Calories. Because of this fact, it is difficult to predict exactly how much body weight one will lose on any given diet, but an approximate value of the time it will take to lose excess body fat may be obtained.

The key point is the caloric deficit. The number of days it takes for this daily deficit to reach 3,500 is how long it will take you to lose 1 pound.

Table 11.4 illustrates the importance of the caloric deficit in determining the rapidity of weight loss by dieting. The higher the deficit, the faster you lose weight. However, rapid weight-loss programs are not usually desirable, and the dieter should realize that a moderate caloric deficit, say 500 Calories/day, may effectively reduce weight in time and yet provide a satisfying diet.

This table is based upon the value of 3,500 Calories for a pound of body fat. There is one precaution, however. Once you lose 5 pounds and every succeeding 5 pounds thereafter, you must adjust the number of Calories it takes to maintain your body weight, for now you are 5 pounds lighter. In our example of the woman who needed 14 Calories/lb to maintain a stable body weight, for every 5-pound loss the woman would need to reduce about 70 Calories (5 × 14 = 70 Calories) from her diet to keep the caloric deficit at 500 Calories/day.

Although these prediction methods are good for the long run, daily body-weight changes may not coincide with daily caloric deficits.

TABLE 11.4 Approximate number of days required to lose weight for a given caloric deficit

Daily caloric deficit	To lose 5 pounds	To lose 10 pounds	To lose 15 pounds	To lose 20 pounds	To lose 25 pounds
100	175	350	525	700	875
200	87	175	262	350	438
300	58	116	175	232	292
400	44	88	131	176	219
500	35	70	105	140	175
600	29	58	87	116	146
700	25	50	75	100	125
800	22	44	66	88	109
900	19	39	58	78	97
1,000	17	35	52	70	88
1,250*	14	28	42	56	70
1,500*	12	23	35	46	58

See text for explanation.   *Note Weight loss greater than 2 pounds per week generally not recommended.

It is very important to note that although we are discussing dieting alone to create a daily caloric deficit, exercise also may be used to increase this deficit. When starting a weight-loss program, the National Institute of Health recommends that most of the 500–1,000 daily Calorie deficit be achieved by eating less food. However, 100–200 Calories of this deficit is achievable through daily exercise, such as walking for 30 minutes or so. Using exercise to contribute to your daily caloric deficit means your food caloric deficit may be reduced accordingly.

Why does a person usually lose the most weight during the first week on a reducing diet?

If you start a diet with a significant caloric deficit, say 1,000 Calories/day, it would normally take you about 3.5 days to lose 1 pound of body fat. However, body-weight loss would be more rapid than this during the first several days, possibly totaling as much as 3–4 pounds. A large percentage of this weight loss would be due to a decrease in body carbohydrate and associated water stores. When you restrict your food intake, the body would then draw on its reserves to meet its energy needs. These reserves consist of both fat and carbohydrate stores, but much of the carbohydrate, stored as liver and muscle glycogen, could be used up in several days, particularly with low-carbohydrate intake, such as the Atkins diet. Because 1 gram of glycogen is stored with about 3 grams of water, a significant weight loss could occur. For example, 300 grams of glycogen, along with 900 grams of water stored with it, would account for a loss of 1,200 grams, or 1.2 kilograms; this would equal over 2.5 pounds alone. About 70 percent of the weight loss during the first few days of a reduced-Caloric diet is due to body-water losses. About 25 percent comes from body-fat stores and 5 percent from protein tissue. As body protein is used for energy, the excess nitrogen needs to be excreted, and this increases water output, about 4–5 grams of water per gram of protein. As noted later, very-low-Calorie diets may lead to greater protein losses, but slower weight losses, such as with a daily 500-Calorie deficit, will help conserve body protein.

If you desired to lose a maximal amount of weight during a 2- to 3-day period, water restriction would cause an even greater weight loss. However, this practice is not recommended, as you would only be decreasing body-water levels. They would return to normal when you returned to normal water intake. There is one additional point relative to body water. At the conclusion of your diet, if you return to a normal caloric diet to maintain your new body weight, you may experience a rapid weight gain of 2 or 3 pounds. This may represent a replenishment of your body glycogen stores with the accompanying water weight. It is important to keep in mind that rather large fluctuations in daily body weight, say in the order of 2 to 3 pounds, are not due to rapid changes in body fat or lean body mass; these fluctuations are due primarily to body-water changes accompanying carbohydrate and protein losses.

Why does it become more difficult to lose weight after several weeks or months on a diet program?

Weight loss may be rapid during the first few days on a diet, primarily because of water loss. Because water contains no Calories, our caloric loss does not need to total 3,500 in order to lose 1 pound of weight. We may lose 1 pound of body weight with a deficit of only about 1,200 Calories, because 70 percent of the weight loss is water. The 1,200 Calories are mostly from fat with a small amount of protein. However, by the end of the second week of dieting, water loss may account for only about 20 percent of body-weight loss; one pound of weight loss will now cost us approximately 2,800 Calories. At the end of the third week, water losses are minimal. The energy deficit to lose 1 pound of body weight now approximates 3,500 Calories. In essence, as you continue your diet, weight losses cost you more Calories because less body water is being lost. At the end of three weeks, you still can be losing weight, but at a much slower rate than during the early stages.

Another factor also slows down the rate of weight loss. As you lose weight, you need fewer Calories to maintain your new body weight. Let's take an example. Suppose you are an athlete who weighs 200 pounds and from table 11.3 you see that you need 17 Calories/pound body weight to maintain your weight. At 200 pounds this would represent 3,400 Calories/day (200×17). However, if your weight drops to 180 pounds after dieting for 10 weeks, you now need only 3,060 Calories/day (180×17), a difference of 340 Calories per day. If you want to continue to have a standard caloric deficit, then you will have to adjust your caloric intake as you lose weight. Suppose our 200-pounder wanted to have a daily caloric deficit of 1,000 Calories. His initial diet should then contain about 2,400 Calories/day (3,400–1,000). However, once he is down to 180 pounds, his diet should now include only 2,060 Calories/day (3,060–1,000). If he did not adjust his diet from 2,400 Calories, then the daily deficit would only be 660 Calories/day (3,060–2,400), not the standard 1,000 he wanted. Weight loss would continue, but at a slower rate.

You should realize that the rate of weight loss will slow as a natural consequence of your diet, but the weight you are losing at that point is primarily body fat. Keeping a standard caloric deficit may also require an additional reduction in caloric intake as you progress on your diet. Knowledge of these factors may help you through the latter stages of a diet designed to attain a set weight goal. Other factors associated with very-low-Calorie diets and exercise, discussed later, may also influence the magnitude of the caloric intake necessary to sustain a given rate of weight loss.

What are the major characteristics of a sound diet for weight control?

As you probably are aware, literally hundreds of different diet plans are available to help you lose weight. Hardly a month goes by without a new miracle diet being revealed in a leading magazine or Sunday newspaper supplement. Recently, three diet books were in the top best-seller list at the same time. These diet plans are recycled over the years and simply represent variations of different themes.

Some of these plans may be highly recommended, for they satisfy the criteria for a safe and effective weight-reduction diet. On the other hand, many of these diets may be nutritionally deficient or even potentially hazardous to your health. For example, an analysis of eleven popular diets revealed deficiencies in one or more of several key nutrients, containing less than 70 percent of the recommended dietary intake for several of the B vitamins, calcium, iron, or zinc. Moreover, one of the diets contained 70 percent of the Calories as fat, and such a high content of fat and/or cholesterol may increase cardiovascular disease risk factors in certain individuals.

Certain types of fad diets should be avoided. Diets that restrict or eliminate various foods, including one-food diets such as the rice diet or the bananas-and-milk diet, may be deficient in certain key nutrients. Avoid miracle diets that are advertised to contain a special weight-reducing formula or fat-burning enzymes, for such compounds simply do not exist or are not effective. In general, you should avoid diets that promise fast and easy weight losses. There is no fast and easy dietary method to lose excess body fat.

Carbohydrate, fat, and protein, and alcohol for those who drink, are the only dietary sources of Calories. Alcohol is not an essential nutrient, but as noted later may play a significant role in weight gain. The majority of our dietary Calories come from carbohydrate and fat with smaller amounts from protein. As you may recall, the National Academy of Sciences has published an Acceptable Macronutrients Distribution Range (AMDR) for carbohydrate, fat, and protein, which represents the percent of dietary Calories that should be derived from each. The AMDR for carbohydrate, fat, and protein is, respectively, 45–65, 20–35, and 10–35 percent. Most popular weight-control diets have focused on limiting intake of either fat or carbohydrate, while some have stressed increased protein intake. Data comparing the caloric and macronutrient content of some popular diets are presented in table 11.5.

Riley has placed popular self-help weight-loss diets on a continuum of themes ranging from antifat to anticarbohydrate. The benefits and drawbacks of both the high-carbohydrate, low-fat (antifat) and low-carbohydrate, high-fat (anticarbohydrate) diets, along with diets somewhere between the two extremes, have been the subject of detailed reviews. In general, these reviews indicate that weight loss can be achieved with a variety of diet interventions, and that it is unlikely that one diet is optimal for all overweight or obese persons. Both low-fat and low-carbohydrate diets have been shown to induce weight loss and reduce obesity-related comorbidities. Reducing caloric intake is the key to the success of any diet. For example, in a recent one-year study, Dansinger and others compared the effects of the Atkins, Ornish, Weight Watchers, and Zone diets, and reported that each popular diet modestly reduced body weight and decreased several markers for coronary heart disease, but there were no differences among the diets. All reduced-Calorie diets were successful in inducing modest weight loss. The interested reader is referred to the reviews by the Consumers Union, Klein, Liebman, and Volek.

Low-fat, High-carbohydrate Weight-loss Diets At the antifat end of Riley's continuum are diets such as those proposed by Dean Ornish and Nathan Pritikin that recommend only 10–15 percent of dietary Calories be derived from fat, which is lower than the AMDR.

Reducing fat in the diet is a sound strategy to lose weight. The American College of Sports Medicine notes that a 10 percent reduction in fat intake can have a significant impact on energy balance and body weight over the long term. Astrup and others assessed the role of macronutrient content of diets on weight loss. They noted that four meta-analyses of weight change occurring on *ad libitum* low-fat diets in intervention trials consistently demonstrate a highly significant weight loss, and concluded that the evidence strongly supports the low-fat diet as the optimal choice for the prevention of weight gain and obesity. However, they also noted that the nonfat macronutrient composition of the diet is also important.

Not all carbohydrates are equal when it comes to weight loss, and some diets have focused on the glycemic index as the key to carbohydrate intake, as highlighted in such books as *The GI Diet* and *Good Carbs, Bad Carbs*. Roberts indicates that consumption of high-glycemic index carbohydrates may increase hunger and promote overeating as compared to consumption of items with a lower glycemic index. In this regard, Astrup and others report that several intervention studies show that sugar in drinks is more likely to produce weight gain than solid sugar in foods, which Ludwig and others found to be especially true in the etiology of obesity in children.

As noted in chapter 4, healthier carbohydrates are rich in dietary fiber, which may play an important role in weight-loss diets. For example, Howarth and others reported that increasing dietary fiber in the diet, by as little as 14 additional grams per day, is associated with a 10 percent decrease in energy intake and significant weight loss over time. Going from the average intake of 15 grams per day up to the recommended 25–38 grams may be an effective part of a total overall weight-control program. Fiber increases the volume of food you eat, which can suppress hunger, the principal underlying

Diet plan	Average Daily Calories	% Carbohydrates	% Fat	% Protein
Weight watchers	1,450	56	24	20
Atkins	1,520	11	60	29
South Beach	1,340	38	39	23
Volumtetrics	1,500	55	23	22
Jenny Craig	1,520	62	18	20
Zone	1,660	40	30	30
Ornish	1,520	77	6	17

TABLE 11.5 Calorie and macronutrient content of popular diets.

Adapted from Consumers Union, Rating the diets. *Consumer Reports* 70 (6):21, 2005.

popular diet books such as *The Volumetrics Eating Plan* and *Eat More, Weigh Less.*

Most members in the National Weight Control Registry consume a high-carbohydrate diet, with about 225 grams for a 1,500–Calorie plan, or about 60 percent of Calories from carbohydrate. A low-fat, high-carbohydrate weight-loss diet may be effective, but selection of nutrient-dense carbohydrates is the key. As will be noted, the protein content of such a diet is also important.

Low-carbohydrate, High-fat Weight-loss Diets   On Riley's anticarbohydrate end of the continuum are diets such as *Dr. Atkins' New Diet Revolution.* The Atkins diet has various phases, starting off as low as 20 grams of carbohydrate a day, mainly from nutrient-dense foods such as leafy green salads. The heart of the diet contains foods high in fat and protein, such as poultry, fish, red meat, and eggs, but gradually progresses to other stages with increasing amounts of carbohydrates, but much lower than AMDR levels. Such diets are also referred to as low-carbohydrate, high-fat, and high-protein weight-loss diets. The South Beach Diet, by Agatston, limits saturated fats and focuses on healthier carbohydrates, which health professionals indicated appears to be a healthier version of the Atkins diet.

Research suggests such diets may be effective. Liebman indicated the Atkins diet may work because it virtually eliminates a whole category of food—carbohydrates, while a Tufts University report indicates that individuals who adopt the Atkins diet generally cut an average of 1,000 Calories per day from their diet, which is most likely the reason underlying its success. Correspondingly, Bravata and others recently reviewed 109 studies involving the use of low-carbohydrate diets and concluded that participant weight loss was principally associated with decreased caloric intake.

One of the criticisms of the Atkins diet was the possible adverse effects on the serum lipid profile and predisposition to cardiovascular disease. However, reviewers such as Volek and Sharman also noted that low-carbohydrate diets had no significant adverse effect on serum lipids, fasting serum glucose, fasting serum insulin levels, or blood pressure. The Consumers Union notes that if you have a healthy serum lipid profile, you most likely will do no harm to your health by adopting the Atkins diet plan for 12 weeks to jump start your weight-loss program.

Weight loss may be rapid at first, primarily due to body fluid losses associated with decreased carbohydrate intake and the resultant decrease in muscle glycogen and associated bound water. Westman and others found that a very-low-carbohydrate diet (less than 25 grams of carbohydrate per day) led to sustained weight loss during a 6-month period. Subjects lost slightly more than 10 percent of body weight, but only about 3 percent of that was body fat, indicating a significant loss of lean body mass. Preferably, a weight-loss diet should induce body-fat losses, not lean body mass such as muscle. Foster and others also recently found that such a diet, as compared to a conventional low-fat diet, induced significantly greater weight losses over 3–6 months, but there were no differences in weight loss at the end of a year. Adherence was poor and attrition was high in both diet groups, suggesting neither is an appropriate lifelong diet.

Based on their comprehensive review, Bravata and others concluded that there is insufficient evidence to make recommendations for or against the use of low-carbohydrate diets. However, although the Atkins diet may be successful, it is not well represented among those in the National Weight Control Registry. Only 8 percent of registry members adhered to a diet containing 90 grams or less of carbohydrate per day. Moreover, although the Atkins diet had a brief revival in popularity, the parent company recently filed for bankruptcy due to decreasing sales.

High-protein Weight-loss Diets   Some diets, such as the *Zone* diet, recommend that protein should account for 30 percent or more of energy, and are marketed as high-protein diets. Although this recommendation falls within the AMDR for protein (10–35 percent), it is generally regarded as high because it may be twice the typical protein intake of 12–15 percent. However, other diets such as Atkins and South Beach, also may be regarded as somewhat high in protein.

High-protein weight-loss diets have been recommended for several reasons. Eisenstein and others note that in short-term studies, dietary protein may reduce energy intake by inducing a sensation of satiety and may also increase total energy expenditure by increasing the TEF. The National Academy of Sciences noted some divergent effects of high-protein diets, reporting some epidemiological studies showing a positive correlation between protein intake and body fatness, but also reporting that replacing carbohydrate with protein on a reduced-fat diet improved weight loss in a 6-month intervention trial. Some recommend that weight-loss diets contain 20–30 percent of energy content from protein. In a most recent study with normal-weight individuals who were not on a weight-loss diet, Weigle and others found that increasing dietary protein content from 15 to 30 percent of energy intake, while keeping carbohydrate content constant, produced a sustained decrease in caloric intake. They suggested that the additional protein may reduce the appetite by enhancing the effect of leptin.

St. Jeor and others, representing the Nutrition Committee of the American Heart Association, noted that high-protein diets may not be harmful for most healthy people for a short period of time, but there are no long-term scientific studies to support their overall efficacy and safety. Friedman indicated there is no clear kidney-related contraindication to high-protein diets in individuals with healthy kidney function, but individuals at risk for chronic kidney disease should be screened for serum creatinine and proteinuria before the initiation of such a diet. Another health concern with high-protein diets is increased calcium losses, but Johnston and others reported no adverse effects of such diets on calcium balance. Although diets containing 20–30 percent protein may be marketed as high-protein, such diets are actually within the AMDR of 10–35 percent of energy from protein. Nevertheless, individuals who have any health concerns should check with their health professionals before initiating such dietary changes.

Balanced Weight-loss Diets   In the middle of Riley's continuum of popular weight-loss diets are mainly those recommended by most professional health organizations, such as the American Heart Association and the American Dietetic and American Diabetes Associations' Food Exchange System Diet, which is the basis of the diet plan advocated in this text.

Highly recommended diets are based upon sound nutritional principles and also are designed to satisfy the individual's personal food tastes. Research with dieters has shown that any weight-reduction diet, to be safe, effective, and realistic, should adhere to the following principles:

1. It should be reduced in Calories and yet supply all nutrients essential to normal body functions. It is important to stress the importance of dietary Calories. Dich and others purposely overfed normal young men, about 1,200 additional Calories per day, with either a carbohydrate-rich or a fat-rich diet for 21 days. They found that the increase in body weight and fat mass was no different between the two diets. Excess dietary Calories lead to weight gain and this study indicates that it does not matter if they come from carbohydrate or fat.

2. It should contain a wide variety of foods that appeal to your taste and help prevent hunger sensations between meals. Low-glycemic-index diets with dietary fiber and moderate amounts of protein and fat may help to suppress the appetite. With respect to weight control, Kris-Etherton and others suggest that a moderate-fat diet can be as, or even more, effective than a lower-fat diet, because of advantages with long-term adherence and potentially favorable effects on lipids and lipoproteins. However, they also note that because fat is energy dense, moderation in fat intake is essential for weight control.

3. It should be suited to your current lifestyle and personal preferences, being easily obtainable whether you eat most of your meals at home or you dine out frequently.

4. It should provide for a slow rate of weight loss, about 1–2 pounds per week.

5. It should be a lifelong diet, one that will satisfy the first three principles once you attain your desired weight.

Based on these principles, several popular diet plans may be recommended. The Consumers Union noted that Weight Watchers, a balanced, low-fat diet that includes weekly meetings, had the highest long-term adherence of any diet. Liebman indicates that the South Beach diet, although the initial phase has some shortcomings, is a healthy diet focusing on seafood, lean meats, low-fat dairy products, most vegetables, most fruits, whole grains, nuts and beans that may be part of a lifelong diet.

In any diet plan, foods should be selected that adhere to the principles of healthful eating. This information was summarized in chapter 2, but for now the major concern is with Calories.

Is it a good idea to count Calories when attempting to lose body weight?

There are both pros and cons to counting Calories. On the con side, counting Calories may not be practical for many who are too busy to plan a daily menu designed around a caloric limit. How many Calories are in the lunch or dinner you eat out daily? And how about serving sizes? Can you picture 3 ounces of roast beef or an ounce of cheese? Also, it may be difficult to calculate the exact amount of Calories consumed, as the caloric content in foods may vary somewhat. For example, certain slices of bread are larger than others and

may have a correspondingly higher caloric content. Although these problems are not difficult to solve, it does take some effort.

On the pro side, counting Calories may be very helpful during the early stages of a diet. Knowledge of the food exchange lists and use of Nutrition Facts on food labels will enable you to substitute one low-Calorie food for another in your daily menu. Additionally, research suggests that recording everything you eat when you start dieting, including the caloric content, can help you stick with your weight-loss program. As you become familiar with the caloric content of various foods, it becomes easier to select those that are low in Calories but high in nutrient value, and to avoid those foods just the opposite, high in Calories and low in nutrients. It will require a little effort in the beginning phases of a diet to learn the Calories in a given quantity of a certain food, but once learned and incorporated into your lifestyle this knowledge is a valuable asset to possess not only when trying to lose weight but also when maintaining a healthy weight over a lifetime. As you incorporate low-Calorie, high-nutrient foods into your diet, as depicted in figure 11.3, it will eventually become second nature to you, and you may eliminate the need to count Calories.

The key to keeping track of Calories is to keep track of dietary fat and sugar. With knowledge of the Food Exchange System and the new food labels, you should be able to determine the grams of fat that you consume daily. Less than 30 percent of your dietary Calories should be derived from fat. On a diet of 1,800 Calories per day, less than 540 Calories should come from fat ($1,800 \times 0.30$), which is the equivalent of 60 grams of fat because 1 gram of fat contains 9 Calories (540/9). Diets containing only 20 percent fat Calories may also be recommended. Less than 10 percent of your dietary Calories should come from sugar. On this 1,800-Calorie diet, that would be less than 180 Calories (45 grams) from sugar.

Once you have attained your desired weight, a good set of scales would be most helpful. Keeping track of your weight on a day-to-day or weekly basis will enable you to decrease your caloric intake for several days once you notice your weight beginning to increase again. Individuals in the National Weight Control Registry who have lost weight and kept it off weigh themselves daily once their weight goal is reached, noting it is easier to deal with a gain of a few pounds rather than 10 or 20. Short-term prevention is more effective than long-term treatment. The dietary habits you acquire during the Calorie-counting phase of your diet will help you during these short-term prevention periods.

What is the Food Exchange System?

At this time it is important to expand our discussion of the Food Exchange System, which was introduced in chapter 2. The Food Exchange System was developed by a group of health organizations, including the American Dietetic Association, as a means of advising patients about healthy eating. In essence, six food groups were established, and foods were assigned to these groups on the basis of similar caloric content and nutritional value. For our purposes at this time, we will concentrate upon the caloric value, but you may also want to refresh your memory on the grams of fat per food exchange.

The six food exchange lists may be found in appendix E. You should study these lists and get an idea of the types and amounts of

FIGURE 11.3 A key dietary principle is to select foods high in nutrients but low in Calories.

foods in each that constitute one exchange. Memorizing the caloric value of each food exchange is instrumental in determining the number of Calories you consume daily and also in planning a healthful, low-Calorie diet. In a recent study, Benezra and others found that the intake of most nutrients can remain at recommended levels when the Food Exchange System is used to plan a weight-loss program. The caloric content and grams of fat of one serving from each of the six exchanges are listed below and expressed in figure 11.4.

1 vegetable exchange	=	25 Calories; 0 g fat
1 fruit exchange	=	60 Calories; 0 g fat
1 fat exchange	=	45 Calories; 5 g fat
1 starch exchange	=	80 Calories; 0–1 g fat
1 meat exchange	=	35–100 Calories
Very lean	=	35 Calories; 0–1 g fat
Lean	=	55 Calories; 3 g fat
Medium fat	=	75 Calories; 5 g fat
High fat	=	100 Calories; 8 g fat
1 milk exchange	=	90–150 Calories
Skim	=	90 Calories; 0–3 g fat
Low fat	=	120 Calories; 5 g fat
Whole	=	150 Calories; 8 g fat

Table 11.6 presents a breakdown of the carbohydrate, fat, protein, and Calorie content of each food exchange.

How can I determine the number of Calories I eat daily?

Simply keep an accurate daily record of what you eat and then determine the caloric value from your food labels or appendix E. Food intake should be recorded over a 3–7 day period, as one single day may give a biased value. Experiments have shown that this method may provide relatively accurate accounts of caloric intake if the amounts of food ingested are measured accurately. The main problem for most people is determining what and how much has been eaten. An 8-ounce glass of skim milk is easy to record, and

Milk	1 cup skim milk	=	90 calories
Meat	1 ounce very lean meat	=	35 calories
Fat	1 tablespoon oil or butter	=	45 calories
Fruit	1 medium piece	=	60 calories
Vegetable	½ cup	=	25 calories
Starch	1 slice bread	=	80 calories

FIGURE 11.4 Knowledge of the various food exchanges and their caloric values can be very helpful in planning a diet. With a little effort, you can learn to estimate the caloric value of most basic foods. See appendix E for other food examples and serving sizes.

the caloric value from the food label or from appendix E is rather precise. However, how many Calories are in a slice of pizza at your favorite Italian restaurant? How big was the piece? What is the caloric content of the cheese, green peppers, pepperoni, and mushrooms? When we deal with complex food combinations such as this, our estimates of caloric content are not as precise. However, some estimates are presented in appendix E in the section on combination foods. For example, one-quarter of a 10-inch cheese pizza with thin crust contains two starch, two medium-fat meat, and one fat exchange, or the equivalent of 355 Calories.

Although you may wish to use a ruler, a small measuring scale, and a measuring cup at home to accurately record the amount of food you eat, they are not practical for many dining situations. Some common objects in everyday life may serve as representative portion sizes for various foods, and some examples are presented in figure 11.5. The following may serve as guidelines for you to record the type and amount of food you eat:

1. Keep a small notepad with you. Record the foods you have eaten as soon as possible, noting the kind of food and the amount. Keep in mind that many servings today are supersized so that one of these servings may actually contain the Calories of 2–3 regular servings. Learn to visualize proper portion sizes and the associated Calorie content in various foods.

TABLE 11.6 Carbohydrate, fat, protein, and Calories in the six food exchanges

Food exchange	Carbohydrate	Fat	Protein	Calories	Average serving size*
Vegetables	5	0	2	25	½ cup cooked; 1 cup raw
Fruits	15	0	0	60	½ cup fresh fruit or juice
Fat	0	5	0	45	1 teaspoon (5 grams)
Meat and meat substitutes					1 ounce
Very lean	0	0–1	7	35	
Lean	0	3	7	55	
Medium fat	0	5	7	75	
High fat	0	8	7	100	
Starch	15	0–1	3	80	⅓–½ cup cereal or pasta; 1 slice of bread
Milk					1 cup (8 fluid ounces)
Skim and very low fat	12	0–3	8	90–110	
Low fat	12	5	8	120	
Whole	12	8	8	150	

Carbohydrate, fat, and protein in grams.
1 g carbohydrate = 4 Calories
1 g fat = 9 Calories
1 g protein = 4 Calories

*See appendix E for specific foods.

Source: *Exchange Lists for Meal Planning*, American Diabetes Association and American Dietetic Association, Chicago, ADA, 1995.

2. Check the labels of the foods you eat. Most commercial products today have nutritional information listed, including the number of Calories per serving. Record these data when available.

3. Calories for most fluids are given in relationship to ounces. For fluids, remember that 1 cup or regular glass is about 8 ounces, but many glasses now hold 12–16 ounces. Most regular canned drinks contain 12 ounces, although smaller and larger sizes are available.

4. Calories for meat, poultry, fish, and other related products are usually given by ounces. To get an idea of how many ounces are in these products, you could purchase a set weight of meat, say 16 ounces, and cut it into four equal pieces. Each would weigh approximately 4 ounces, or about the visual size of a deck of playing cards. For cheese, one ounce is about the size of a ping pong ball. Get a mental picture of these sizes and use them as a guide to portion sizes.

5. For fruits and vegetables the caloric values are usually expressed relative to ½ cup or a small-sized piece. At home, measure ½ cup of vegetables or fruit and place it in a bowl or on a plate. Again, make a mental picture of this serving size and use it as a reference. Compare the sizes of different fruits and notice the difference between a small, medium, and large piece. A medium piece fruit is about the size of a tennis ball, while a medium potato is about the size of a computer mouse.

6. For starch products, the Calories are most often expressed per serving, such as an average-size slice of bread or a dinner roll.

In these cases it is relatively easy to determine quantity. Depending on the type of cereal, pasta, grain, or starchy vegetable, the measure for one exchange is usually ⅓ or ½ cup, but some serving sizes are larger, such as puffed cereals. See appendix E. Use a measuring cup and the mental picture concept again to estimate quantities. A cup of cold cereal is about the size of a large handful, whereas ½ cup of hot cereal is about the size of a tennis ball. A 2-ounce bagel is the size of a yo-yo.

7. For substances such as sugar, jams, jellies, nondairy creamers, and related products, make a mental picture of a teaspoon and tablespoon. These are common means whereby Calories are given. A teaspoon of butter or margarine is about the size of a postage stamp. One level teaspoon of sugar is about 20 Calories; jams and jellies contain similar amounts. Caloric values of other products may be obtained from nutrition labels.

8. Some combination foods, such as a homemade casserole, are included in appendix E. However, for combination foods not listed, you will need to list the ingredients separately to calculate the caloric content. Labels on most food products list caloric content per serving.

9. Caloric values for many fast-food restaurant items may be found in appendix F. Most fast-food restaurants provide fact sheets detailing information on the nutrient content of their products, but you need to ask for it.

Working with the Food Exchange System helps you learn the portion size and caloric content of various foods. Through experience

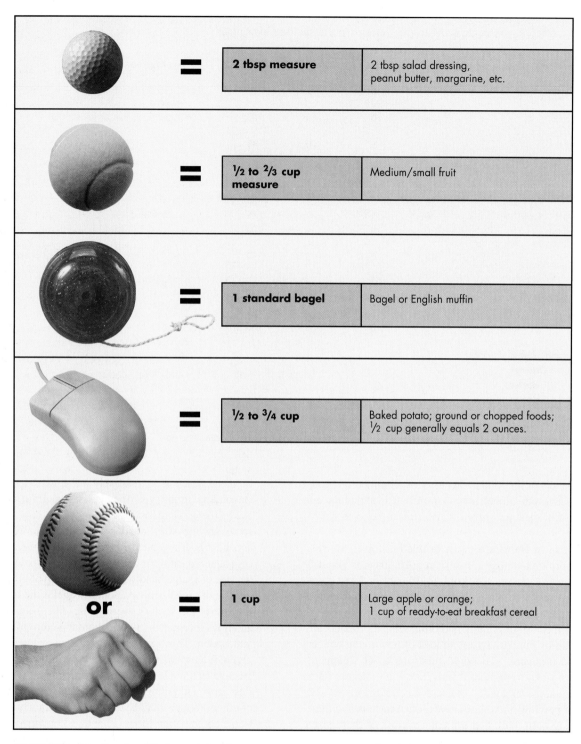

(golf ball)	=	**2 tbsp measure**	2 tbsp salad dressing, peanut butter, margarine, etc.
(tennis ball)	=	**½ to ⅔ cup measure**	Medium/small fruit
(yo-yo)	=	**1 standard bagel**	Bagel or English muffin
(computer mouse)	=	**½ to ¾ cup**	Baked potato; ground or chopped foods; ½ cup generally equals 2 ounces.
(baseball) **or** (fist)	=	**1 cup**	Large apple or orange; 1 cup of ready-to-eat breakfast cereal

FIGURE 11.5 A golf ball, tennis ball, large yo-yo, computer mouse, baseball, and fist make convenient guides to judge MyPyramid serving sizes. Additional handy guides include:

thumb = 1 oz of cheese;
4 stacked dice = 1 oz cheese;
thumb tip to first joint = 1 tsp;
matchbox = 1 oz meat;
bar of soap or deck of
  cards = 3 oz meat;

palm of hand = 3 oz
1 ice cream scoop = 1/2 cup
handful = 1 or 2 oz of a
  snack food; and
ping-pong ball = 2 tbsp.

you should be able to readily identify, within a small error range, the quantities of food you eat. This is not only helpful for determining your caloric intake but may also serve as a motivational device to restrict portion sizes when you are on a weight-loss diet.

The following represents an example of how you might record one meal and calculate the caloric intake from appendix E or food labels.

Breakfast Food	Quantity	Calories
Milk, skim	1 glass, 8 ounces	90
Eggs	2, poached	150
Toast, whole wheat	2 slices	160
with butter	2 pats	90
with jelly	1 tablespoon	60
Orange juice	1 glass, 8 ounces	120
Coffee	1 cup, 8 ounces	0
with sugar	1 teaspoon	20
TOTAL		690

Computer programs are available to calculate caloric intake as well as nutrient content, and appropriate software is provided with your purchase of this textbook at www.mhhe.com/williams. Other dietary analysis programs are also available on the Internet (www.MyPyramid.gov and www.usda.gov/cnpp) or from commercial software retailers.

Knowledge, however, is not the total answer; your behavior should reflect your knowledge. For example, you may know that whole milk contains about 60 more Calories per glass than skim milk, but if you cannot develop a taste for skim milk then the advantage of your knowledge is lost in this instance.

What are some general guidelines I can use in the selection and preparation of foods to reduce caloric intake?

In general, you have to eat less than you are currently eating, or shift your eating habits. The following recommendations, which are based on the Food Exchange System, may help you initiate and maintain a healthful, lifelong diet to achieve and maintain a healthy body weight.

1. *Decrease caloric intake.* You need to decrease the number of Calories you consume daily. The key principle is to select foods, in appropriate portion sizes, and with high-nutrient density from across the six food exchanges or the food groups in the MyPyramid. Avoid energy-dense foods and drinks, such as bagels, soft pretzels, energy bars, smoothies, special coffees, and cocktails, all of which may be loaded with Calories. If you do buy convenience meals, select those that are low in Calories and fat. Check the label for total fat and total Calories from fat and sugar. This you can easily do by reading the label.

2. *Eat foods that make you feel full.* Barbara Rolls, a renowned diet expert at Penn State University, based her excellent book, *The Volumetrics Eating Plan*, on this principle. High-volume, low-Calorie foods, such as salads, soups, vegetables, and whole grains, are rich in dietary fiber and water, and help provide a sensation of fullness that curbs hunger.

3. *Restrict portion sizes.* Although the intake of high-volume, low-Calorie foods like vegetables will help curtail hunger and promote weight loss, one of the major problems contributing to the increasing obesity in the United States is the consumption of large volumes of high-Calorie foods. Most fast-food eateries and convenience stores have increased portion sizes dramatically to give customers their *money's worth.* As examples, years ago a *family* bottle of cola soda was 32 ounces, and now single servings of cola drinks may total up to 64 ounces, with free refills; a McDonald's meal of a single hamburger, small fries, and cola had totalled 600 Calories, but today a supersize meal with the same basic foods may total 1,800 Calories; a small bagel that once contained 200 Calories has been supersized to 500–600 Calories or more. Even manufacturers of "healthy" foods for dieters advertise "heartier" portions that weigh 50 percent more than the original version and contain more Calories. Decreasing the volume of high-Calorie foods is one of the most important dietary means to reduced body fat.

4. *Eat less fat.* Although restricting dietary Calories is most important, and some research indicates the source of caloric intake is irrelevant to weight gain, according to Jequier dietary fat appears to play several roles in the development and maintenance of obesity. First, it is rich in Calories—more than double the amount of Calories per gram as compared to carbohydrate and protein. In a recent study, Rolls and Bell found that when individuals were fed diets varying in caloric density (fat content) and could eat as much as they liked, they ate the same amount of food by weight, so the caloric intake varied directly with the caloric density of the food. Second, dietary fat is appetizing and does not appear to rapidly suppress the appetite, leading to a greater intake of Calories as recently suggested by Blundell and Green. Third, dietary fat has a lower TEF, or higher metabolic efficiency, than carbohydrate and protein. Melby and Hill indicated that dietary fat appears to be stored as fat more efficiently than either carbohydrate or protein, even if the caloric intake is similar; this is especially true in individuals who have lost weight and may be one of the most important reasons why they regain weight so readily. Fourth, dietary fat may also be stored preferentially in the abdominal region, which may increase health risks. Miller and his colleagues found that lean subjects obtained a lower percentage of their dietary Calories from fat compared with obese subjects, and other research has shown that obese subjects maintain their weight by consuming foods of high-caloric density. In a recent major 7-year study of over 48,000 women, Howard and others reported that weight loss was greatest among women who decreased their percentage of energy intake from fat.

To reduce the amount of fat in your diet, you may wish to count the total grams of fat you eat each day. As mentioned above, a general recommendation is to keep your daily total fat intake to 30 percent or less of your total caloric intake. To calculate the total grams of fat you may eat per day, simply multiply your caloric intake by 30 percent and divide by 9 (the Calories per gram of fat). You may wish to get the fat content to a lower percentage, such as 20 percent. Table 11.7

TABLE 11.7 Calculation of daily fat intake in grams

To use this table, determine the number of Calories per day in your diet and the percent of dietary Calories you want from fat, and then find the grams of fat you may consume daily. For example, if your diet contains 2,200 Calories and you desire to consume only 20 percent of your daily Calories as fat, then you could consume 49 grams of fat. The formula is: % fat x Daily Calories ÷ 9 Calories per fat gram = Daily fat grams [0.20 × 2,200 ÷ 9 = 49]

Daily caloric intake	30% fat Calories (maximal grams)	20% fat Calories (maximal grams)	10% fat Calories (maximal grams)
1,000	33	22	11
1,200	40	26	13
1,500	50	33	16
1,800	60	40	20
2,000	66	44	22
2,200	73	49	24
2,500	83	55	28

presents the formula and some calculations for different caloric intake levels and percentages of dietary fat intake.

The recent development of fat substitutes may be helpful in reducing fat intake. Many fat-free products are currently available and may decrease total fat and caloric intake if used judiciously within a healthful diet. The American Dietetic Association, in their position statement on fat replacers authored by Mattes, indicated that they can be used effectively to reduce fat and Calorie intake. The American Heart Association also recently noted that use of fat substitutes may be associated with reduced fat and Calorie intake compared with nonuse of any fat-modified products, and also noted that when used appropriately, fat substitutes may provide some flexibility with diet planning. However, Miller and Groziak noted that although fat substitutes may help decrease dietary fat intake and percentage of caloric intake from fat, many individuals will compensate by increasing their consumption of other macronutrients, primarily carbohydrate. Research by Shide and Rolls supports this point, indicating individuals eat more food at a given meal if they know some of the meal consists of low-fat items. Additionally, fat-free does not mean Calorie-free, and Manore indicated that some fat-free foods may have similar amounts of Calories as the original. Again, check the food label. Cotton and others suggest you gradually blend fat substitutes into your diet; making many changes at one time may lead to overconsumption of other foods, and hence your overall caloric intake may remain the same, or even increase. Fat substitutes can be part of an overall healthful diet for

weight loss, provided you do not compensate for the saved Calories by ingesting other Calorie-rich foods. Remember that you need some fat in your diet for essential fatty acids and fat-soluble vitamins, which you may be able to obtain in a diet containing 10 percent fat Calories. Do not eliminate all fat from your diet, but consume mainly the so-called good fats, such as olive oil and fats in walnuts and almonds.

Several modified fats have been proposed to facilitate weight loss. Diglycerides are components of a new oil to replace the traditional triglycerides. Although the caloric content of the two oils is the same, diglycerides are theorized to increase fat oxidation and not be stored as body fat as readily as triglycerides. However, research with this new oil is limited and health professionals currently recommend that its potential minor effects on weight loss do not justify its price; they recommend olive or canola oils, while limiting intake of other fats and oils. Another modified fat, conjugated linoleic acid (CLA), is theorized to inhibit the ability of fat cells to accrue fat or to promote its removal from fat cells. Some studies have shown small losses of body fat with CLA supplementation, but subjects also experienced adverse changes in serum cholesterol markers of heart disease. Experts currently indicate the benefits of CLA are questionable and some risks have been identified, and thus do not advise taking CLA until additional research clarifies these issues.

Other suggestions for reducing dietary fat are included in the following guidelines, but you may wish to review chapter 5 for additional information. Once individuals adapt to a low-fat diet, they may prefer it because high-fat meals are digested more slowly, possibly leading to indigestion and some gastrointestinal distress.

5. *Eat fewer and smaller amounts of refined sugar.* This may be accomplished by restricting the amount of sugar added directly to foods and limiting the consumption of highly processed foods that may add substantial amounts of sweeteners. Artificial sweeteners may be helpful. For example, Raben and others found that overweight individuals who consumed large amounts of sucrose in their daily diets, mostly as beverages, had increased energy intake, body weight, and fat mass after 10 weeks, but these effects were not seen in a similar group that consumed artificial sweeteners. Pi-Sunyer noted that substitution of artificial sweeteners, such as aspartame, for sugar has been shown to reduce caloric intake without leading to an increased consumption of other foods. Drewnowski also reported that some short-term studies and one long-term study have shown that artificial sweeteners could decrease caloric intake and increase weight loss, but more long-term research is recommended. Again, like fat substitutes, sugar substitutes may be an effective part of a healthful weight-loss diet, but individuals must be cautious not to compensate and eat more food later.

6. *Reduce the intake of both fat and sugar.* In many cases, simply reducing the fat and sugar content in the diet will save substantial numbers of Calories and may be all that is needed. Did you know that fat and sugar together account for nearly 50 percent of the Calories in the average American diet? That represents 5 out of every 10 Calories. Table 11.8 provides some examples

TABLE 11.8 Simple food substitutions to save Calories

Instead of	Select	To save this many Calories
I croissant	I whole wheat bagel	80
I whole egg	2 egg whites	50
I ounce cheddar cheese	I ounce mozzarella (skim)	30
I ounce regular bacon	I ounce Canadian bacon	100
3 ounces tuna in oil	3 ounces tuna in water	60
Cream of mushroom soup	Black bean soup	90
I cup regular ice cream	I cup fat-free frozen dessert	150
I ounce turkey bologna	I ounce turkey breast	50
I McDonald's Big Mac	I McDonald's grilled chicken	120
I cup whole milk	I cup skim milk	60
French fried potatoes	Baked potato	100
I ounce potato chips	I ounce pretzels	90
I tablespoon mayonnaise	I tablespoon fat-free mayonnaise	90
I can regular cola	I can diet cola	150

of how to save Calories via simple substitutions for comparable foods containing fat or sugar. We often unwittingly consume high-fat, high-sugar items when we dine out. Did you know that some appetizers may contain several thousand Calories? For example, a fried whole onion with dipping sauce contains about 2,100 Calories. Even supposedly healthy fast foods, such as salads, can contain as much fat and Calories as the burgers on the menu, mainly because large amounts of fat are added with the dressing; one popular salad contains over 800 Calories, with over 70 percent fat Calories. Ask your waiter if a list of restaurant items with nutritional values, including Calories, is available either at the restaurant or on the Internet. Most national chains provide such information.

7. *Eat more low-fat dairy products.* As noted previously, increased protein intake may help suppress the appetite more so than equivalent amounts of carbohydrate or fat. Milk exchange products are excellent sources of protein but may contain excessive Calories unless the fat is removed. Use skim milk, low-fat cottage cheese, low-fat yogurt, and nonfat dried milk instead of their high-fat counterparts like whole milk, sour cream, and powdered creamers.

8. *Eat more low-fat meat and meat substitutes.* The meat and meat substitute exchange products also are sources of high-quality protein and many other nutrients but also may contain excessive fat Calories. Select very-lean and lean meat exchanges, including meat substitutes such as legumes. Per one ounce serving, very-lean meat and meat substitutes contain only 35 Calories and less than 1 gram of fat. Examples include the white meat of chicken and turkey, 99 percent fat-free ground turkey, tuna fresh or canned in water, shrimp, fat-free cheese, egg whites, and egg substitutes. See appendix E for other sources. If you enjoy beef and pork, use leaner cuts such as beef eye of round, flank steak, pork tenderloin, and 96 percent fat-free hamburger. Trim away excess fat; broil or bake your meats to let the fat drip away. If you eat in fast-food restaurants, select foods that are low in fat, such as grilled chicken, lean meats, and salads. Avoid the high-fat foods, which normally contain 40–60 percent fat Calories. Also be aware that serving sizes have increased dramatically in recent years. That large hamburger deluxe may have triple or more the Calories of a regular hamburger. Select legumes as an excellent meat substitute.

9. *Eat healthier carbohydrates.* The starch exchange contains healthy carbohydrates and is high in vitamins, minerals, and fiber. Eating a low-glycemic, high-fiber diet increases the gastric volume, which might help suppress appetite. Use whole-grain breads and cereals, brown rice, oatmeal, beans, bran products, and starchy vegetables for dietary fiber. Limit the use of processed grain products that add fat and sugar. Substitute products low in fat, such as standard-size whole wheat bagels, for those high in fat, like croissants.

10. *Eat more fruits.* Foods in the fruit exchange are high in vitamins and fiber. Select fresh, whole fruits or those canned or frozen in their own juices. Avoid those in heavy sugar syrups. Limit the intake of dried fruits, which are high in Calories. Eat at least one citrus fruit daily.

11. *Eat more veggies.* The vegetable exchange foods are low in Calories yet high in vitamins, minerals, and fiber. Select dark-green leafy and yellow-orange vegetables daily. Low-Calorie items like carrots, radishes, and celery are highly nutritious snacks for munching. Many of these vegetables are listed as free exchanges in appendix E because they contain fewer than 20 Calories per serving. Fruits and vegetables may provide bulk to the diet and a sensation of fullness without excessive amounts of Calories.

12. *Consumer fewer high-Calorie fat exchanges.* Use smaller amounts of high-Calorie fat exchanges. Many salad dressings, butter, margarine, and cooking oils are pure fat. If necessary, substitute low-Calorie or fat-free dietary versions instead. Fat-free mayonnaise tastes good and has 90 fewer Calories than a serving of regular mayonnaise. Do not prepare foods in fats, such as with frying. Use nonstick cooking utensils or nonfat cooking sprays.

13. *Reduce liquid Calories.* Beverages other than milk and juices should have no Calories. High-Calorie liquids, such as sodas and alcoholic beverages, may be especially harmful in weight-loss programs because they not only add Calories to the diet

but they also do not appear to suppress the appetite as well as similar amounts of Calories in solid foods. Fluid intake should remain high, for it helps create a sensation of satiety during a meal. Water is the recommended fluid, although diet drinks and unsweetened coffee and tea may be used. Consult the free-food list in appendix E.

14. *Limit your intake of alcohol.* It is high in Calories and zero in nutrient value. One gram of alcohol is equal to 7 Calories, almost twice the value of protein and carbohydrate. For 100 Calories in a shot of gin you receive zero nutrient value, but for the same amount of Calories in approximately 2 ounces of chicken breast you get nearly one-third of your RDA in protein plus substantial amounts of iron, zinc, niacin, and other vitamins. Research indicates that consuming alcohol with a meal does not substitute for other foods, so the total caloric intake of the meal is increased. Additionally, excess alcohol Calories are stored as body fat. If you desire alcohol, select the light varieties of wine and beer. Substitution of a light beer for a regular beer will save about 50 Calories. You may wish to try the nonalcoholic wines and beers, which may contain even fewer Calories.

15. *Limit salt intake.* Salt intake should be limited to that which occurs naturally in foods. Try to use dry herbs, spices, and other nonsalt seasonings as substitutes to flavor your food. Salt may increase the appetite or thirst for Calorie-containing beverages.

16. *Eat slowly.* Slowing down the process of eating, by taking time to smell the aromas from your food and chewing slowly, will provide time to help curb your appetite. The Consumers Union notes that it takes about 20–25 minutes for your brain to receive signals from your stomach and intestines that you are satisfied. Eat a salad or soup as an appetizer, which may help curb your appetite for the main course.

17. *Nibble, don't gorge.* Instead of gorging on two or three large meals a day, eat five or six smaller ones. Although Bellisle and others reported no difference between gorging and nibbling on daily energy expenditure, they indicated that any effects of nibbling on the regulation of body weight are likely to be mediated through effects on food intake. Use low-Calorie, nutrient-dense foods for snacks. Research has shown that nibbling may help control sensations of hunger between meals by helping maintain normal blood glucose levels, Nibbling may help in other ways, possibly by minimizing the release of insulin, which assists in the storage of fat in the body.

18. *Eat breakfast.* About 80 percent of individuals in the National Weight Control Registry eat breakfast. A hearty breakfast may help curb hunger throughout the morning hours. One study has shown that when more Calories were eaten in the morning, caloric intake for the entire day was less as compared to eating most daily Calories in the evening; researchers suggested the appetite may be suppressed easier in the morning than in the evening.

19. *Learn to cook!* Microwaves and electric grills make cooking easy. Microwave cooking needs no fat for preparation, while electric grilling helps remove fat from meats. Cook and serve small portions of food for meals. The temptation to overeat may be removed.

20. *Learn low-Calorie foods.* Learn what foods are low in Calories in each of the six food exchanges and incorporate those palatable to you in your diet. Learn to substitute low-Calorie foods for high-Calorie ones. The key to a lifelong weight-maintenance diet is your knowledge of sound nutritional principles and the application of this knowledge to the design of your personal diet.

How can I plan a nutritionally balanced, low-Calorie diet?

The key to a sound diet for weight loss is nutrient density, or the selection of low-Calorie, high-nutrient foods. The twenty points addressed in the previous section represent important guidelines to implement such a diet. Table 11.9 presents a suggested meal pattern based upon the Food Exchange System. The foods should be selected from the food exchange lists found in appendix E. You may use the form below as a guide.

Calories: _____

Meal	Number of servings	Calories per serving	Total Calories	Foods selected
Breakfast				
Milk, skim		90		
Meat, very lean		35		
Fruit		60		
Vegetable		25		
Starch		80		
Fat		45		
Beverage		0		
Lunch				
Milk, skim		90		
Meat, very lean		35		
Fruit		60		
Vegetable		25		
Salad		20		
Starch		80		
Fat		45		
Beverage		0		
Dinner				
Milk, skim		90		
Meat, very lean		35		
Fruit		60		
Vegetable		25		
Salad		20		
Starch		80		
Fat		45		
Beverage		0		

TABLE 11.9 Suggested daily meal pattern based on the Food Exchange System

	Approximate daily caloric intake						
	1,000	**1,200**	**1,500**	**1,800**	**2,000**	**2,200**	**2,500**
Breakfast							
Milk, skim	1	1	1	1	1	1	1
Meat, very lean	1	1	2	2	2	3	3
Starch	1	2	2	3	3	3	3
Fruit	1	1	1	1	2	2	2
Fat	0	0	1	1	1	2	2
Beverage	1	1	1	1	1	1	1
Lunch							
Milk, skim	1	1	1	1	1	1	2
Meat, very lean	2	2	2	3	3	3	4
Starch	2	2	2	2	2	3	3
Vegetable	1	1	2	2	2	2	2
Salad	1	1	1	1	1	1	1
Fruit	1	2	2	2	2	2	2
Fat	½	½	1	2	2	2	2
Beverage	1	1	1	1	1	1	1
Dinner							
Milk, skim	0	0	0	1	1	1	1
Meat, very lean	2	2	3	3	3	4	4
Starch	2	2	3	3	4	4	5
Vegetable	1	2	2	2	2	2	3
Salad	1	1	1	1	1	1	1
Fruit	0	0	1	2	2	2	3
Fat	½	1	1	1	2	2	2
Beverage	1	1	1	1	1	1	1
Totals							
Milk, skim	2	2	2	3	3	3	4
Meat, very lean	5	5	7	8	8	10	11
Starch	5	6	7	8	9	10	11
Vegetable	2	3	4	4	4	4	5
Salad	2	2	2	2	2	2	2
Fruit	2	3	4	5	6	6	7
Fat	1	2	3	4	5	6	6
Beverage	3	3	3	3	3	3	3

Key points
1. Caloric values:
   Milk exchange, skim = 90
   Meat exchange, very lean = 35
   Fruit exchange = 60
   Vegetable exchange = 25
   Starch exchange = 80
   Fat exchange = 45
   Beverage = 0
   Salad = 20
2. See appendix E for a listing of foods in each exchange. Note the following:
   a. Foods other than milk, such as yogurt, are included in the milk exchange.
   b. The meat list includes foods such as eggs, cheese, fish, and poultry; low-fat legumes, like beans and peas, may be considered as meat substitutes.
   c. Some starchy vegetables are included in the bread list.
3. Foods should not be fried or prepared in fat unless you count the added fat as a fat exchange. Broil or bake foods instead.
4. Low-Calorie vegetables like lettuce and radishes should be used in the salads. Use only small amounts of very-low-Calorie salad dressing.
5. Beverages should contain no Calories.

The total caloric values are close approximations for a three-meal pattern. If you decide to include snacks in your diet, such as a fruit or vegetable, then remove each snack from one of the main meals. The salads should contain vegetables with negligible Calories, such as lettuce and radishes. Note that under the exchange system, starchy vegetables such as potatoes are included in the starch group because their caloric content is similar. The beverages, other than milk and fruit juice, should contain no Calories. Although you may drink as many noncaloric beverages as you wish over the course of the day, drinking at least one at each meal will help provide a feeling of satiation and may help suppress the appetite somewhat.

Although only seven levels of caloric intake are presented in table 11.9, you may adjust it according to your needs by simply adding or subtracting appropriate food exchanges. For example, if you wanted a 1,700-Calorie diet, you could subtract one starch exchange and one-half fat exchange (about 100 Calories) from the 1,800–Calorie diet.

After you have determined the number of Calories you need daily, select the appropriate diet plan from table 11.9. To help implement your diet plan and to keep day-to-day track of the food exchanges you eat, you should design a 3″ × 5″ card similar to the model below for the number of food exchanges in your daily diet. As you consume an exchange at each meal, simply cross it off on the card. Make a new card for each day. The model shown is for 1,500 Calories. The total exchanges are summed from table 11.9.

Daily meal plan		1,500 Calories
Milk exchange, skim	(2)	1 2
Meat exchange, very lean	(7)	1 2 3 4 5 6 7
Starch exchange	(6)	1 2 3 4 5 6
Vegetable exchange	(3)	1 2 3
Salads	(2)	1 2
Fruit exchange	(4)	1 2 3 4
Fat exchange	(2)	1 2
Beverages	(3)	1 2 3

Keep in mind that this is not a rigid diet plan. At a minimum you should have 2 skim milk exchanges, 5 very lean meat exchanges, 5 starch exchanges, 2–3 vegetable exchanges and 2–3 fruit exchanges. Once you have guaranteed these minimum requirements, you may do some substitution between the various exchanges so long as you keep the total caloric content within range of your goals. For example, you may delete 2 starch exchanges (160 Calories) in the model and substitute 1 skim milk and 2 very lean meat exchanges (160 Calories). You may also shift a limited number of the exchanges from one meal to another. If you prefer a more substantial breakfast and a lighter lunch, simply shift some of the exchanges from lunch to breakfast.

It may be a good idea to take a little time and construct a diet for yourself, using the following guidelines for your calculations. Use the form on page 420.

1. Calculate the number of Calories you want per day. See pages 408–410 for guidelines.
2. Use table 11.9 to determine how many servings you need from each food exchange.
3. Multiply the number of servings by the Calories per serving to get the total Calories. Add the total Calories column to get total daily intake.

4. Select appropriate foods from the exchange list in appendix E.

One final point: If your diet contains less than 1,600 Calories, it would be wise to take a daily vitamin/mineral supplement with the RDA for all essential vitamins and key minerals such as iron and zinc.

Table 11.10 presents an example of a 1,500–Calorie diet based on the Food Exchange System. You can also obtain a personalized diet at www.MyPyramid.gov; an example of a 2000-Calorie diet is presented in appendix I.

Are very-low-Calorie diets effective and desirable as a means to lose body weight?

As noted in chapter 10, very-low-Calorie diets (VLCD) are defined technically as containing less than 800 Calories per day and are often referred to as modified fasts. In some medical institutions, total fasting programs are used. Under proper medical supervision, such diets are generally regarded as safe and have been effective in inducing rapid weight losses in very obese patients. However, VLCD are not recommended for the individual who wants to lose 10–20 pounds or for the individual who is not under medical supervision, not only because of the possible adverse health consequences as noted in chapter 10, but also because VLCD may be counterproductive to the ultimate goal of long-term weight loss. They do not satisfy the criteria for a recommended weight-loss program for individuals who are not medically supervised and they often lead to weight cycling.

It is recommended that any individual contemplating the use of VLCD should consult a physician and a dietitian.

Is it harmful to overeat occasionally?

Most of us occasionally overindulge in food, particularly on holidays and other festive occasions or when we dine at all-you-can-eat restaurants. Eating is a pleasurable activity, and an occasional pig-out is not harmful, as long as it does not become a habit. After a very large meal, you may step on the scale the next day and find that you have gained 5 pounds or more. Not to worry. Most of that weight is water, which may be bound to the increased carbohydrate (glycogen stores) in your body. Additionally, if the meal was high in sodium, your extracellular water stores will also increase. Going back to your regular diet and exercise program will reduce these water stores in a day or so, and your body weight will return to normal.

Key Concept Recap

▶ Rapid loss of body weight, which may occur during the early stages of dieting, is due primarily to body-water changes. The rate at which weight loss occurs will slow down as your body weight decreases, for then body-fat stores are the prime source of weight loss.

▶ Numerous weight-loss diet plans are available, and all may be effective if the daily caloric energy intake is less than the daily caloric energy expenditure.

TABLE 11.10 A 1,500-Calorie diet based on the Food Exchange System

Exchange	Number of servings	Calories per exchange	Total Calories	Foods selected
Breakfast				
Meat, very lean	2	35	70	1 ounce very lean ham and
Fat	1	45	45	1 ounce low-fat cheese melted on
Starch	2	80	160	2 pieces whole-grain toasted bread
Fruit	1	60	60	4 ounces orange juice
Beverage	1	0	0	1 cup coffee with noncaloric sweetener
Lunch				
Milk, low-fat	1	120	120	8 ounces plain, low-fat yogurt
Fruit	1	60	60	with cut-up fresh fruit (1/2 banana)
Meat, very lean	2	35	70	2 ounces turkey breast on
Starch	2	80	160	whole-grain bun
Vegetable	1	25	25	1 carrot
Salad	1	20	20	lettuce with
Fat	1	45	45	low-Calorie dressing
Beverage	1	0	0	diet cola
Dinner				
Milk, skim	1	90	90	1/2 cup ice milk
Meat, very lean	3	35	105	3 ounces broiled fish
Starch	3	80	240	1 baked potato and 1 slice whole wheat bread
Vegetable	3	25	75	1 1/2 cups steamed broccoli and cauliflower
Salad	1	20	20	cucumbers
Fat	1	45	45	small amount of margarine for potato and low-Calorie dressing for salad
Fruit	2	60	120	1 banana cut up on ice milk
Beverage	1	0	0	iced tea
TOTAL			1,530	

▶ The key principle of dieting is to select from among the six food exchanges low-Calorie, high-nutrient foods that appeal to your taste and are easily incorporated into your daily lifestyle.

▶ Counting Calories and grams of fat may be a useful technique during the early stages of a diet, for the more knowledge you have about the caloric and nutrient content of foods, the better equipped you are to make wise selections.

▶ Very-low-Calorie diets (VLCD) may be effective for weight loss under strict medical supervision but are not recommended for the average individual trying to lose excess pounds.

Check for Yourself

Using the Food Exchange System, plan a balanced, healthy diet of 1,600 Calories for an individual who needs to consume this much to lose excess body fat.

Exercise Programs

What role does exercise play in weight reduction and weight maintenance?

Humans are meticulously designed for physical activity, and yet our modern mechanical age has eliminated many of the opportunities that our ancient ancestors had to incorporate moderate physical activity as a natural part of daily living. The regulation of our food intake has not adapted to the highly mechanized conditions in today's society. As discussed in chapter 10, physical inactivity may be one of major contributing factors to the development and maintenance of obesity. For example, a sedentary lifestyle, principally TV watching, has been significantly associated with obesity in adolescents and adults. In a study of identical and fraternal twins, Samaras and others found that the physically active twin had significantly less fat than the physically inactive twin. After controlling for genetic and environmental factors, the influence of physical activity on body fat was greater than the other environmental factors, including dietary intake. Indeed, the late Dr. Jean Mayer, an international authority on weight control, reported that no single factor is more frequently responsible for obesity than lack of physical exercise.

There are basically two ways you can become more physically active and increase your total daily energy expenditure. First, decrease the amount of time that you are physically inactive, particularly time watching television. In a recent review, Robinson noted that most studies support the suggestion that reducing television viewing may help to reduce the risk for obesity or help promote weight loss in obese children. The same thinking applies to adults as well. In general, you want to increase your level of nonexercise activity themogenesis (NEAT). Keep moving throughout the day; walk rather than ride, don't sit when you can stand, and keep moving, or fidget, when you have to sit. In one study, researchers followed lean and mildly obese people for 10 days, and found that the obese subjects remained seated for about 2.5 hours longer per day than the lean individuals, suggesting this could result in more than 300 fewer Calories expended daily.

Second, start a planned exercise program, which is the main focus of this section. Wim Saris, an internationally respected authority on obesity, noted that although there is some uncertainty regarding the role of exercise in the treatment of obesity, a considerable amount of knowledge substantiates the point that exercise can help reduce and control body weight and should be included in a weight-loss or maintenance program. Indeed the Consumers Union recently noted that to slim down permanently, you need to make a lifelong commitment to regular exercise, including not only aerobic exercise to burn Calories, but strength (resistance) training to build or at least preserve muscle. In addition to the physiological effects upon energy expenditure, Miller notes that exercise consistently shows beneficial effects in medical, psychological, and behavioral outcomes.

Resistance Exercise Training

Resistance-training, or weight-training, programs are detailed in the next chapter in relation to gaining body weight as muscle mass, but such programs may also be very helpful during weight-loss programs. One possibility, as suggested by the American College of Sports Medicine, is that increased strength through resistance training may lead to a more active lifestyle in sedentary overweight and obese individuals, thus leading to health benefits that may include weight loss and prevention of weight regain. Another possibility is maintenance of REE during weight loss. In their recent review, Poehlman and Melby noted that although resistance training may increase the metabolic rate during exercise, its effects on regulation of body weight appear to be mediated primarily by its effects on body composition rather than by the direct energy costs of the resistance exercise. Indeed, recent research by Bryner and his associates has revealed that resistance training may help preserve lean body mass and maintain normal REE during weight loss, even on a very-low-Calorie diet of 800 Calories. Recall that protein tissue, primarily muscle, may be lost along with body fat during a weight-reduction program. However, resistance training may stimulate muscular development and help prevent significant decreases in lean body

FIGURE 11.6 Exercise can be an effective means of increasing energy expenditure and losing excess Calories.

mass. Such an effect may also help prevent decreases in the REE. Additionally, as is noted in the next chapter, dynamic circuit-type resistance-training programs may also be used to burn additional Calories.

Aerobic Exercise

Exercise burns Calories (figure 11.6). The primary function of aerobic exercise in a weight-control program is simply to increase the level of energy expenditure and help tip the caloric equation so that energy output is greater than energy input. As mentioned in chapter 3, the metabolic rate may be increased tremendously during aerobic exercise. For example, while the average person may expend only 60–70 Calories per hour during rest, this value may approach 1,000 Calories per hour during a sustained high-level activity such as rapid walking, running, swimming, or bicycling. Athletes involved in extreme endurance events, such as the Tour de France, and ultradistance runners, such as Yannis Kouros, have been reported to consume between 6,000 and 13,000 Calories per day.

If you are overweight, the same amount of aerobic weight-bearing exercise will cost you more Calories than your leaner counterpart. Because you have more weight to move, you will expend more energy and lose more body fat in the long run. For example, the energy cost of jogging 1 mile would be 70 Calories for the 100-pound individual and 140 Calories for someone twice that weight. Figure 11.7 depicts this concept graphically for one type of exercise—walking.

One major misconception may deter many individuals from initiating an exercise program for weight control. They believe that exercise is a poor means to lose body weight because it expends so few Calories. For example, they have heard that you have to jog about 35 miles to lose a pound of body fat. Because the

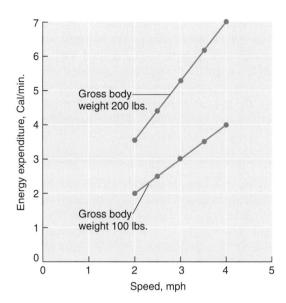

FIGURE 11.7 Effect of speed (mph) and gross body weight (lbs) on energy expenditure (Calories/minute) of walking. The heavier the individual, the greater the expenditure of Calories for any given speed of walking. The same would be true for running and other physical activities in which the body must be moved by foot.

From *Textbook of Work Physiology* by P.O. Astrand and K. Rodahl. Copyright © 1977 McGraw-Hill Book Company. Used with the permission of McGraw-Hill Book Company.

average-sized male uses approximately 100 Calories per mile of jogging, and because 1 pound of body fat contains about 3,500 Calories, there is some truth to that statement. However, you must look at the **long-haul concept** of weight control (figure 11.8). Jogging about 2 miles a day will expend about 6,000 Calories in a month, accounting for almost 2 pounds of body fat. Over 6 to 8 months or longer, the weight loss may be substantial provided the individual does not compensate by consuming more Calories. In a recent review, Ross and others cited recent evidence suggesting that exercise alone is an effective strategy for reducing obesity.

In addition to the direct effect of increased energy output during exercise, exercise has been theorized to facilitate weight loss by other means. As noted in chapter 3, exercise may increase the REE during the period immediately following the exercise bout and may also increase the thermic effect of food (TEF) if you exercise after eating a meal. Unfortunately, the magnitude of this increased REE or TEF is relatively minor and not considered to be of any practical importance in a weight-loss program. Related to the TEF, it does not matter if you exercise before or after a light meal, although as noted below, exercise before a meal may help curb the appetite.

However, like resistance exercise, aerobic exercise may have a beneficial effect on the REE, but to a lesser degree. Although aerobic exercise will not totally prevent the decrease in the REE normally seen with weight loss, particularly with large weight losses,

FIGURE 11.8 To lose body fat by exercising, you must look at the long-haul concept of weight control. The average-weight individual needs to jog about 35 miles to burn off 1 pound of body fat. This would be nearly impossible for most of us to do in 1 day. At 2 miles per day, however, it could be done in about 2 1/2 weeks—and at 5 miles per day, in only 1 week. Even though it takes time, an exercise program is a very effective approach to reducing excess body fat.

some studies suggest that it may help minimize the decrease, thereby helping maintain energy expenditure near normal levels during rest. However, not all research supports this finding. The interested reader is referred to the review by Hill and others.

Moreover, during aerobic exercise, the body mobilizes its fat cells to supply energy to the muscle cells. Hence, body-fat stores are reduced. In the long run, this change in body composition may actually favor a slight increase in the REE because muscle tissue is more active metabolically than fat tissue. Recall that in dieting alone, some lean muscle mass may be lost. In a recent study comparing the effects of either dieting or exercise on loss of body fat and lean tissue, Pritchard and others reported that 40 percent of the weight loss in dieters was lean tissue, while exercisers lost only 20 percent lean tissue, because most of their weight loss was fat.

It should be noted that some research suggests aerobic exercise may decrease the REE in individuals who are already lean, suggesting that the body is attempting to preserve its energy reserves. This may be particularly true among elite endurance athletes, as noted by Sjodin and others. Although this does not appear to be of any concern to overweight individuals who desire to lose weight, it may pose a problem to the lean athlete attempting to shed a few additional pounds for competition.

In addition to the physiological effects upon energy expenditure, exercise may also confer significant psychological and medical benefits, even without any weight loss. As the fitness level and body composition improve, the individual may experience improvements in mood, energy levels, body image, and self-esteem. Exercise may also be the psychological catalyst that helps individuals to improve their nutritional habits and other health-related behaviors.

Exercise may render other significant health benefits. For example, as documented in the recent *Surgeon General's Report on Physical Activity and Health,* exercise, as a form of physical activity, is becoming increasingly important as a means to help prevent, and even treat, many chronic diseases, such as cardiovascular disease, diabetes, and osteoporosis. Mayo and others reported that exercise-induced weight losses in the obese are derived mainly from the abdominal fat depots, which may help reduce symptoms associated with the metabolic syndrome. Many of the health benefits of exercise are related to weight loss and were discussed in chapters 1 and 10. For a detailed review, the interested reader is referred to the American College of Sports Medicine Roundtable on Physical Activity in the Prevention and Treatment of Obesity and its Comorbidities chaired by Claude Bouchard and Steven Blair.

For individuals with normal body weight, exercise is highly recommended for its preventive role, not only to prevent weight gain in the first place, but also to prevent weight regain in those who have lost weight and are on a weight-maintenance program. It is generally recognized that prevention of obesity or excess body weight is more effective than treatment. Epstein and others noted that exercise is an important adjunctive treatment for childhood and adolescent obesity, but indicated it may be of even greater benefit in the prevention of obesity. Moreover, the National Research Council noted that the long-term well-being of our children may depend on increased physical activity. Most people do not become overweight overnight, but rather accumulate an extra 75–150 Calories per day, which over time will lead to excessive

fat tissue. A daily exercise program could easily counteract the effect of these additional Calories and is a key component of a weight-maintenance program. Jakicic and Gallagher recently noted that although exercise may have a modest impact on initial short-term weight loss, it may have its greatest effect on long-term weight loss and prevention of weight regain. For those who like to eat but not gain weight, exercise is the intelligent alternative.

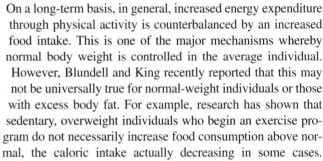

Does exercise affect the appetite?

On a long-term basis, in general, increased energy expenditure through physical activity is counterbalanced by an increased food intake. This is one of the major mechanisms whereby normal body weight is controlled in the average individual. However, Blundell and King recently reported that this may not be universally true for normal-weight individuals or those with excess body fat. For example, research has shown that sedentary, overweight individuals who begin an exercise program do not necessarily increase food consumption above normal, the caloric intake actually decreasing in some cases. Indeed, King recently noted that on a short-term basis, energy intake may not increase to match the increased energy expenditure through exercise, but King also indicated that the individual's psychological strategies underlying dietary restraint and reasons for exercising are important factors regulating the appetite.

An important concern for the athletic individual is the fact that the appetite may not normally decrease with a decreased activity level, as recently reported by Stubbs. If you are physically active, but then must curtail your activity because of an injury or some other reason, your appetite may remain elevated above what you need to maintain body weight at your reduced energy levels. Body fat will increase. Hence, you must reduce your food intake to balance the caloric equation or suffer the consequences.

As will be discussed later, a combined diet and exercise program would be most effective as a means to body-weight control. In this regard, exercise, particularly intense exercise, may be used to curb the appetite on a short-term basis at an appropriate time. Thompson and others found that low-intensity exercise did not suppress hunger, but high-intensity exercise (68 percent VO_2 max) did. Research has related the appetite-suppressing effect of exercise to increased body temperature. The close anatomical relationship of the temperature and hunger centers in the hypothalamus may provide a rationale for the inhibition of the hunger center. Both exercise and the TEF will increase the core temperature of the body, so the body simply may be attempting to protect itself against an excessive rise in core temperature by suppressing the appetite to avoid the TEF. Exercise also will stimulate the secretion of several hormones in the body, notably epinephrine, which may also depress the appetite by affecting the hypothalamus or by increasing serum levels of both glucose and free fatty acids.

If you exercise before a meal, your food intake may be reduced considerably. Try it and see if it works for you. If you have the facilities available, a good half-hour of intense exercise may be an effective substitute for a large lunch. You may lose Calories two ways, expending them through exercise and replacing the large lunch with a low-Calorie, nutritious snack. However, in a recent review King and others noted that although intense exercise may be an effective means of suppressing the appetite, the effects are brief. Thus, while intense exercise may help to curb your appetite at lunch, unless you are cautious you may increase your caloric intake above normal at dinner. In one study, Pomerleau and others reported that neither low-intensity nor high-intensity exercise affected appetite, but women in the high-intensity group tended to consume more Calories.

Does exercise affect the set point?

As you may recall from chapter 10, the set-point theory suggests each individual possesses an inborn mechanism that attempts to maintain a certain level of energy balance, or body weight, by modifying energy intake or energy expenditure. In simple terms, the settling-point theory, another theory, suggests the set point may be adjusted to a new level. In a recent review, James Hill and Renee Commerford indicated that physical activity has a significant impact on the settling point, or that level of body weight and body fatness at which a steady-state is reached. They suggested that physical activity will increase total energy expenditure and fat oxidation, which can lead to an overall energy imbalance if there is not complete compensation in terms of increased energy intake and fat intake, and possibly decreased spontaneous daily activities. In essence, Hill and Commerford indicated that physical activity can help individuals reach fat and energy balances at lower levels of body fatness than would have been achieved with lower levels of physical activity. Body weight and fat should decrease until a new steady-state is achieved. Nevertheless, there may be a limit to lowering the set point. Foster-Schubert and others reported that exercise-induced weight loss over one year resulted in an increase in plasma ghrelin, which you may recall stimulates the appetite. Unless the hypothalamus becomes less sensitive to ghrelin, the appetite will be stimulated to help deter additional weight loss.

What types of exercise programs are most effective for losing body fat?

As you are probably well aware, a number of different exercise programs designed to reduce body weight are available. Perusal of the daily newspaper reveals numerous advertisements for weight-reduction programs sponsored by various commercial fitness centers. Weight training with sophisticated equipment, Slimnastics exercises, aerobic dancing, and special exercise apparatus are a few of the approaches often advertised as the best means to lose body fat fast. The truth is that you do not need any special apparatus or any specially designed program. You can design your own program once you know a few basic principles about exercise and energy expenditure.

Although resistance exercise may play an important role in weight control, the best type of exercise program for losing body fat involves aerobic exercises, those that utilize the oxygen energy system (figure 11.9). This type of exercise program is also the one that conveys the most significant health benefits. The key points of an aerobic exercise program are as follows:

FIGURE 11.9 Aerobic-mode exercises—such as running, bicycling, or swimming—must involve large muscle groups.

1. The mode of exercise must involve large muscle groups. The muscles of the legs comprise a good portion of the total body mass, as do the muscles of the arms. Many people do not realize that the major muscles in the chest and back are attached to the upper arm and are actively involved in almost all arm movements. Walking, jogging, hiking, stair climbing, running, in-line skating, and bicycling primarily involve the legs while swimming primarily stresses the arms. The use of hand-held weights in walking incorporates arm action with the legs. Cross-country skiing, rowing, and rope jumping use both the arms and legs, as does a good aerobic dance routine. These are good large-muscle activities, although there are a host of others.

2. The second factor is the intensity level. The higher the **exercise intensity,** the more Calories you expend per unit of time, and so the less time you need to burn a given amount of Calories. Normal walking uses fewer Calories than easy jogging, which uses fewer Calories than fast running. Simply put, it costs you more energy to move your body weight at a faster pace. However, there is an optimal intensity level for each person depending on how long the exercise will last. You can run at a very high intensity for 50 yards, but you certainly could not maintain that same fast pace for 2 miles. Intensity and duration are interrelated, but for burning the most total Calories, duration becomes more important, and the intensity must be adapted for the amount of time you plan to exercise.

   To get an idea of exercises with high intensity, check appendix B for Calorie cost per minute relative to your body weight. It is a composite table of a wide variety of individual reports in the literature. When using this appendix, keep these points in mind.

   a. The figures are approximate and include the resting metabolic rate. Thus, the total cost of the exercise includes not only the energy expended by the exercise itself, but also the amount you would have used anyway during the same period. Suppose you ran for 1 hour and the calculated energy cost was 800 Calories. During that same time at rest you may have expended 75 Calories, so the net cost of the exercise is 725 Calories.

   b. The figures in the table are only for the time you are performing the activity. For example, in an hour of basketball, you may exercise strenuously only for 35–40 minutes, as you may take time-outs and may rest during foul shots. In general, record only the amount of time that you are actually moving during the activity.

   c. The figures may give you some guidelines to total energy expenditure, but actual caloric costs might vary somewhat according to such factors as skill level, environmental factors (running against the wind or up hills), and so forth.

   d. Not all body weights could be listed, but you can approximate by going to the closest weight listed.

   e. There may be small differences between men and women, but not enough to make a marked difference in the total caloric value for most exercises.

   Appendix B or table 3.5 on page 99 may be useful to determine which types of activities may be of the appropriate intensity for your weight-control program. Listing those activities with higher caloric expenditure per minute may suggest several that you could blend into your lifestyle.

3. Probably the most important factor in total energy expenditure is the duration of the exercise. In swimming, bicycling, running, or walking, distance is the key. For example, running a mile will cost the average-sized individual about 100 Calories. Five miles would approximate 500 Calories. An individual running 1 mile a day would take over 1 month to lose 1 pound of fat, whereas running 5 miles a day would shorten the time span to about 1 week. Thus, if the purpose of the exercise program is to lose weight, the individual should stress the **duration concept.**

   One of the key points about the duration concept is the notion of distance traveled rather than time. For example, tennis and running are both good exercises. However, the runner will expend considerably more Calories in an hour than the tennis player because the activity involved in running is continuous. The tennis player has a number of rest periods in which the energy expenditure is lower. Consequently, at the end of an hour's activity, the runner may have expended two to three times as many Calories as the tennis player. A similar comparison can be made between runners and walkers.

   If you cannot find a big block of time, such as 40 minutes, to do your exercise, then try to incorporate more frequent short bouts of exercise throughout the day. Several recent studies by Jakicic and Murphy and their associates reported that exercising in multiple short bouts per day, such as four 10-minute bouts was just as effective as a single 40-minute bout in producing weight loss and improving cardiovascular fitness over a 20-week period. If your day is filled with other activities, try to squeeze in some short exercise bouts such as brisk walking, possibly before breakfast, during morning and afternoon work breaks, and before or after lunch and dinner. Andersen has indicated this strategy may increase adherence to your exercise program, and it may also help your study or work productivity by providing a psychological pick-me-up during the day.

   A major reason many adults do not use exercise as a weight-loss mechanism is that their level of physical fitness is so low they cannot sustain a moderate level of exercise intensity for very long. However, keep in mind that as you continue to train, your body will begin to adapt so that in time you will be able to exercise for longer and longer periods.

   Additionally, intensity and duration are interrelated, and if balanced, will result in equal weight losses. Melanson and others found that compared to a sedentary day, expending 400 Calories during exercise intensities of 40 and 70 percent of VO_2 max increased 24-hour energy expenditure, but there was no difference attributed to exercise intensity. Grediagin and others also found no significant difference in body-fat losses when women engaged in either high-intensity or low-intensity exercise, provided the total caloric expenditure per exercise session was the same. In both cases it simply took the low-intensity exercise group longer to expend the same amount of

Calories. As you improve your fitness level, Hunter recommends incorporating some higher-intensity exercise in your program, not only because it burns Calories more rapidly, but also because it will make your moderate-intensity workouts seem much easier.

4. **Exercise frequency** complements duration and intensity. Frequency of exercise refers to how often each week you participate. As would appear obvious, the more often you exercise, the greater the total weekly caloric expenditure. In general, three to four times per week would be satisfactory, provided duration and intensity were adequate, but six to seven times would just about double your caloric output. A daily exercise program is recommended if weight control is the primary goal.

5. An important factor is enjoyment of the exercise. For an activity to be effective in the long run, it should be one that you enjoy, yet one that will help expend Calories because it has a recommended intensity level, can be performed for a long time, or both. For example, you may not enjoy jogging or running, so other activities may be substituted. Fast walking with vigorous arm action, golf (pulling a cart), swimming, bicycling, tennis, handball, racquetball, and a variety of other activities may produce a greater feeling of enjoyment and still burn a considerable number of Calories. Even leisure activities and home chores done vigorously such as gardening, yard work, washing the car, and home repairs may be useful in burning Calories and developing fitness. Exercise need not be unpleasant. Enjoy your exercise. Try to make it a lifelong habit by viewing it as play. Next time you vacuum the house or mow the lawn, try to think about it as a good workout rather than work.

6. Practicality is another important factor. You may enjoy swimming, tennis, racquetball, and a variety of other sports, but lack of facilities, poor weather conditions, or high costs may limit your ability to participate. For the active person who travels, this may be a major concern. You probably have noticed by now that an underlying bias toward walking and running exists throughout this book. It is probably because, to me, they satisfy all the previously mentioned criteria necessary for maintaining proper body weight. Moreover, they are very practical activities. All you need is a good pair of shoes and proper clothes for the weather, so nothing short of an injury should deter you from your daily exercise routine. Walking, jogging, or running can be very practical substitutes on those days when you cannot participate in your regular physical activity. Peter Wood, an esteemed researcher at Stanford University, indicated brisk walking is perhaps the best single exercise in regard to energy expenditure, feasibility, and acceptability to a large proportion of the population; for those who are physically unfit, overweight, or elderly, it is probably the best choice of exercise.

Indoor exercise equipment is also very practical for a number of reasons. For example, it can be used while watching children, avoiding inclement weather, or doing two things at one time such as reading or watching television news. This is a highly recommended way to watch television. Numerous types of indoor exercise equipment are available, such as bicycling apparatus, cross-country skiing simulators, rowing machines, stair-steppers, and treadmills. All can provide an aerobic workout, but in a recent study Zeni and others reported that the treadmill is the optimal indoor exercise machine for enhancing energy expenditure at a set rating of perceived exertion. Resistance- or strength-training indoor equipment is also available. *Consumer Reports* magazine offers periodic analyses of various types of indoor exercise equipment.

7. Versatility is also an important factor. Learn and engage in a variety of physical activities, such as running, cycling, swimming, rowing on stationary machines, stair climbing, aerobic dancing, and aerobic walking. By cross-training, such as running 3 days per week, cycling 2 days, and swimming 2 days, you are less likely to become bored with exercise or to sustain overuse injuries. Also, if you plan to exercise for an hour daily, one-half hour each of running and cycling, or some other combination of exercises, is also an effective way to cross-train. Moreover, if you become injured and cannot do your favorite type of exercise, you may be able to expend Calories and maintain fitness by using alternative exercises until you heal. For example, if weight-bearing activities such as jogging bother you, do nonweight-bearing activities such as cycling or swimming, or water-jogging wearing a buoyancy vest.

If I am inactive now, should I see a physician before I initiate an exercise program?

Various medical groups, such as the American College of Sports Medicine and the American Heart Association, have developed guidelines to determine who should receive a medical exam prior to initiating an exercise program. A thorough review of these guidelines is not presented here because they are extensive and beyond the scope of this text. However, the following points represent a synthesis of these guidelines.

1. Before initiating any exercise program, you should be aware of any personal medical problems that possibly could be aggravated. If you have concern about any facet of your health, check with your physician before starting an exercise program. This is especially important in weight-reduction exercise programs where the main stress is placed on the heart and blood vessels, the cardiovascular system.

2. No matter what your age, if you have any of the coronary heart disease risk factors noted in table 11.11, you should have a medical examination. You may also wish to assess your cardiac risk profile at the American Heart Association's website, www.amhrt.org.

3. If you are young (twenties or early thirties), healthy, and have no risk factors, it is probably safe to initiate an exercise program.

4. The older you are, the better the idea to get a medical examination. In fact, it is prudent for those over forty to have an examination.

TABLE 11.11	Major and predisposing risk factors associated with coronary heart disease
1.	High blood pressure
2.	Cigarette smoking
3.	High serum cholesterol
4.	Impaired fasting blood glucose
5.	Obesity
6.	Family history of coronary heart disease
7.	Sedentary lifestyle/physical inactivity

Sources: Data from American College of Sports Medicine, ACSM's *Guidelines for Exercise Testing and Prescription*, 6th ed., 2000.

What other precautions would be advisable before I start an exercise program?

Your initial level of physical fitness is an important determinant of the intensity of exercise during the early stages of the program. If you are completely unconditioned, you should start at a lower intensity level—walk before you jog, for example. Keep in mind that it took time for you to gain weight and become unconditioned, so it will also take time to reverse the process. A gradual progression is the key point. Examples are presented later.

Other general precautions involve safety factors, timing of meals, environmental hazards, and equipment. The individual should adhere to safety principles for the activity selected, particularly swimming, bicycling, and pedestrian safety. Strenuous exercise should not be undertaken within 2 or 3 hours of a heavy meal, but may be done earlier with a light meal or just liquids. As noted in chapter 9, a hot environment poses the most serious threat to the person in training. Be aware of signs of heat stress such as dizziness, nausea, and weakness. If these occur, stop exercising and find a means to help cool your body. Proper equipment should be selected for the chosen activity. For example, of critical importance to the jogger or walker is a well-designed pair of shoes. They may help prevent certain medical problems, such as tendinitis and shin splints, which may occur during the early stages of training.

What is the general design of exercise programs for weight reduction?

Both resistance- and aerobic-exercise training are recommended components of a weight-loss program. Resistance training is covered in the next chapter.

In essence, aerobic-exercise programs to reduce body fat or to help maintain an optimal weight are based on the same principles that underlie exercise programs to improve the efficiency of the cardiovascular system. The total exercise program is based on a balance of exercise intensity, duration, and frequency. However, each daily exercise bout is usually subdivided into three phases—warm-up, stimulus, and warm-down, in that order (figure 11.10).

A proper warm-up and warm-down are important components of the aerobic-exercise prescription. Both may help prevent excessive strain on the heart and may also be helpful in the prevention of muscular soreness or injuries.

The **warm-up** precedes the stimulus period and may be done in several ways. It may be general in nature, such as calisthenics, or specific to the type of exercise you plan to do, such as initially exercising at a lower level of intensity of the actual mode of exercise. Some gentle stretching exercises are also helpful in the warm-up period.

For most aerobic-type exercise, it is probably better to warm up the specific muscles to be used. For example, if you plan to use jogging as your mode of aerobic exercise, you should stretch your leg muscles gently at first and then jog at a slower than normal pace for several minutes. Breaking into a sweat is a good external sign that you have sufficiently elevated your body temperature; by using a specific type of warm-up, the temperature of your exercising muscles will also be increased.

The **warm-down** phase follows the stimulus period and is designed primarily to help restore the cardiovascular system to normal. If one stops exercising abruptly, blood may possibly pool in the exercised body parts, thereby decreasing return of blood to the heart. With less blood to the heart, less will be pumped to the brain and hence dizziness may result. When the warm-down occurs gradually after strenuous exercise—by walking or jogging after a strenuous run, for example—the muscles help massage the blood through the veins back to the heart. Research indicating that abrupt cessation of exercise may increase certain blood hormone levels, which may cause abnormal rhythm of the heart, emphasizes the importance of a gradual warm-down. Complete your warm-down by stretching. Since the muscles are now warm from the exercise they are easier to stretch, which may help prevent muscle stiffness.

The warm-up and warm-down are important components of the daily exercise bout, but most of the Calories are expended during the stimulus period.

What is the stimulus period of exercise?

The **stimulus period** is the most important phase of the daily exercise bout. By modifying the intensity and duration of the exercise, the individual achieves the level of stimulus necessary to elicit a conditioning effect. As illustrated in figure 11.11, several important physiological and psychological measures increase in proportion to the exercise intensity.

The two major components of the stimulus period are intensity and duration of exercise. In any exercise session, these two components are usually inversely related. In other words, if intensity is high, duration is short, and if intensity is low, duration is long. Frequency (the number of exercise sessions per week) is also an important part of the exercise prescription. A number of medical groups, including the American Heart Association (AHA) and the American College of Sports Medicine (ACSM), have made specific recommendations concerning the quality and quantity of exercise for developing and maintaining cardiorespiratory fitness in adults. The recommendations from these groups are slightly different, but the differences are very minor.

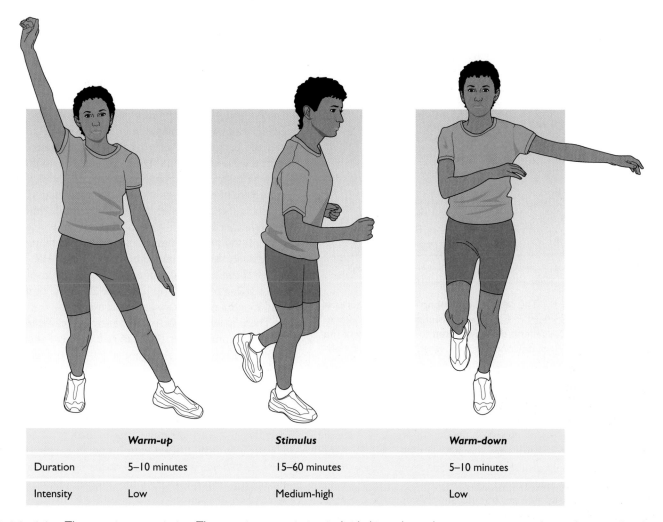

	Warm-up	Stimulus	Warm-down
Duration	5–10 minutes	15–60 minutes	5–10 minutes
Intensity	Low	Medium-high	Low

FIGURE 11.10   The exercise prescription. The exercise prescription is divided into three phases: warm-up period, stimulus period, and warm-down period. The stimulus period is the key to burning Calories.

The recommendations of the ACSM, as presented in their position stand on the recommended quantity and quality of exercise for developing and maintaining cardiorespiratory and muscular fitness in healthy adults (see www.mhhe.com/williams), are based on an exhaustive review of the pertinent research. The most recent ACSM recommendations will be used as the basis for developing an aerobic fitness program here, although they may be modified somewhat under certain circumstances. Such modifications will be noted where appropriate, particularly as related to weight control.

1. Intensity of training: 55/65–90 percent of maximum heart rate (HR max) or 40/50–85 percent of maximum oxygen uptake reserve (VO₂ max reserve) or HR max reserve (see definition on page 432). The lower levels of intensity are for individuals who are quite unfit.
2. Duration of training: 20–60 minutes of continuous or intermittent (minimum of 10-minute bouts) aerobic activity. Duration is dependent on the exercise intensity, as previously discussed.
3. Frequency of training: 3–5 days per week

What is an appropriate level of exercise intensity?

The intensity of exercise is a very important component of the stimulus period; in order to receive the optimal benefits from the exercise program, you must attain a certain **threshold stimulus,** the minimal stimulus intensity that will produce a training effect. The intensity of exercise can be expressed in a number of different ways, such as percentage of VO₂ max, Calories/minute, or heart rate. In general, there is a high degree of relationship among these variables during exercise at a steady state. For example, the heart rate may reflect a certain level of oxygen consumption or caloric expenditure. Because the heart rate is easily obtained, it is usually used to determine the threshold level of exercise intensity. Another means to judge exercise intensity is the **rating of perceived exertion (RPE),** your perception of how strenuous the exercise is.

How do you determine your threshold level? Let's look at two ways—the heart rate and RPE. To obtain the heart rate, press lightly with the index and middle fingers on the carotid artery, located just under the jawbone and beside the Adam's apple. Do not use the thumb as it also has a pulse, and do not press hard on

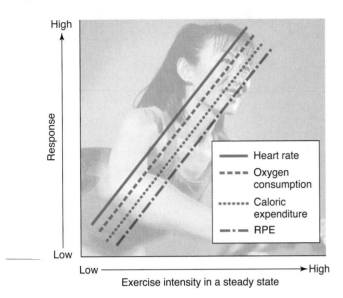

FIGURE 11.11 The relationship among various measures of energy expenditure. Heart rate, oxygen consumption, caloric expenditure, and RPE are, in general, directly related to the intensity of the exercise under steady-state conditions, i.e., when the oxygen supply is adequate for the energy cost of the exercise.

the carotid artery, for it may cause a reflex slowing of the beat in some persons. The radial artery pulse is obtained by placing your fingers on the inside of the wrist on the thumb side. These are the two most common locations for monitoring pulse rate, but other locations (the temple, inside the upper arm, and directly over the heart) may be used (see figure 11.12).

To obtain the heart rate per minute, simply count the pulse rate for 6 seconds and add a zero. Resting and recovery heart rates are easily obtainable, as they may be taken while you are motionless, but it is difficult to manually monitor the heart rate while exercising. Research has shown that the exercise heart rate correlates very highly with the heart rate during the early stages of recovery. Hence, to monitor exercise heart rate, secure the pulse *immediately* upon cessation of exercise and count the beats for 6 seconds. This provides a reliable measure of exercise heart rate, although it may be slightly lower due to the beginning of the recovery effect. If it is difficult for you to monitor your heart rate for 6 seconds, then use a 10-second period and multiply the count by six to obtain your heart rate per minute. You probably should use 30 seconds to determine your resting heart rate; multiply your results by two. It may also be better to measure your resting pulse early in the morning, just after rising. Additionally, for the calculations to follow, you should take your resting heart rate in the position in which you will exercise, for example lying down if you swim, seated if you cycle, or standing if you walk or run.

One of the most prevalent techniques to determine the threshold stimulus for exercise is based upon the **maximal heart rate reserve (HR max reserve)**, the difference between the resting heart rate and the maximum heart rate. You may determine your resting heart rate shortly after you arise in the morning. If you have not been physically active in some time, it may not be advis-

able for you to engage in strenuous physical activity in order to determine your actual maximal heart rate (HR max), but there are ways to predict it based upon your age. Although there are individual variations, the traditional formula (A) for the prediction of HR max in women and untrained men is 220 minus the person's age. More recently, based on a meta-analysis of 352 studies Tanaka and others derived a new formula (B), 208 minus 0.7 × age. For physically trained men, the formula (C) 205 minus one-half the person's age may be more appropriate, while for obese individuals, the formula (D) 200 minus one-half the person's age may be best. Based upon the traditional formula A, a 40-year-old untrained individual would have a predicted HR max of 180, which is the same value predicted by the formula B. Using the formula C, a trained 40-year-old male would have a predicted HR max of 185. Keep in mind, however, that there is considerable individual variation relative to predicted HR max no matter which formula is used. For example, a 40-year-old man may predict a HR max of 180, yet it may be 200, 160, or much lower if he was a victim of coronary heart disease.

There is rather widespread general agreement that in order to obtain a training effect, the heart rate response should be increased above the resting level by about 50–85 percent of the HR max reserve. Recent research has revealed that lower levels, 40–45 percent, may also be effective, particularly in individuals with poor levels of physical fitness.

Continuing with our example of the 40-year-old man, we can calculate the heart rate range needed to elicit a training effect. This is called the **target heart rate range,** or **target HR.** To complete the calculations, we need to know the age-predicted HR max and the resting heart rate (RHR); the latter should be determined under relaxed circumstances. If we assume a RHR of 70 and a HR max of 180, the following formula would give us the target range:

$$\text{Target HR} = X\% \ (\text{HR max} - \text{RHR}) + \text{RHR}$$

For the 50 percent threshold level, the target heart rate for our example would be calculated as follows:

$$.5 \ (180 - 70) + 70 =$$
$$.5 (110) + 70 = 55 + 70 = 125$$

For the 85 percent level, the target heart rate would be

$$.85(180 - 70) + 70 =$$
$$.85(110) + 70 = 93 + 70 = 163$$

Thus, in order to achieve a training effect, our 40-year-old man needs to train within a target HR range of 125–163.

If you wish to bypass the calculations, table 11.12 presents the target HR ranges for various age groups with RHR between 45 and 90 beats/minute. Simply find your age group and RHR in the headings and locate your target HR range. The table is based on a predicted HR max of 220 – age. If you prefer to use one of the other formulae to predict HR max, you may calculate your target HR range using the formula presented.

In general, this table is a useful guide to the threshold heart rate and target HR range. However, there is considerable variability in

HR max among individuals, particularly in the older age groups. If your true HR max is below the predicted value (220 – age), the target HR range in the table would be higher than the recommended level. If your true HR max is higher than the predicted value, the target HR range in the table is lower than the recommended level. Although the target HR range might vary by a few beats, if your actual HR max is slightly higher or lower than the predicted value, you will still receive a good training effect—assuming you are in the middle of the range.

Once you have been training for a month or so, you may desire to determine your HR max in the specific activity you do. You may use the procedures described below, that is, running on a track at different speeds until you reach your maximal level, modifying the test dependent upon your aerobic exercise. For example, research has revealed that HR max is lower in swimming, possibly as much as ten to fifteen beats per minute, so the target heart rate may be slightly lower if this mode of exercise is used. William McArdle of Queens College recommends use of the formula 205 minus age to predict maximal heart rate while swimming.

Although the target heart rate approach is a sound means for monitoring exercise intensity, you may also wish to use the RPE scale developed by Gunnar Borg. This scale was originally designed to reflect heart rate responses by adding a zero to the rating. You simply rate the perceived difficulty or strenuousness of the exercise task according to the scale in table 11.13. If you are running, how do your legs feel? Do they feel light and easy to move, or are they heavy, or possibly beginning to ache or burn? How is your breathing? Are you breathing easily and able to carry on a conversation, or are your sentences shortened to a few words? In general, how does your total body feel? Is the exercise too easy, or are you working too hard? A new ten-point perceived-exertion rating scale has been developed by Borg, but the American College of Sports Medicine uses the original one because it is based on the heart rate response to exercise.

When you determine your exercise heart rate, it is a good idea to associate an appropriate RPE value with it, so that you individualize the RPE to your specific exercise program. For example, at an exercise heart rate of 150 you might make a mental note of the exercise difficulty and assign a value of 15, or hard, to that level of exercise intensity. Research has shown that the RPE can be an effective means to measure exercise intensity in healthy individuals, particularly at heart rates above 150 beats/minute.

Another possible way to monitor your exercise effort, recently validated by Persinger and others, is associated with breathing and is often referred to as the *talk test.* Adam Bean, an editor for

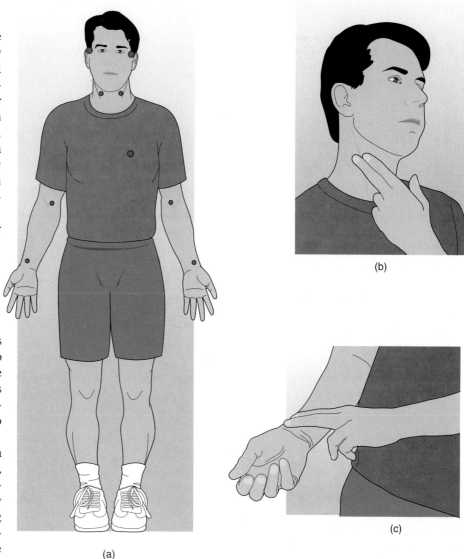

(a)

(b)

(c)

FIGURE 11.12   Palpation of the heart rate. The pulse rate may be taken at a variety of body locations (a), but the two most common locations are (b) the neck (carotid artery) and (c) the wrist (radial artery).

Runner's World, cited research indicating that when you can first hear yourself breathing during exercise, you are entering the lower range of your heart rate zone. When you have difficulty talking, you are near the upper range. A general rule of thumb is: If you cannot maintain a conversation while exercising, you are probably exercising too hard, unless you are training for sports competition.

How can I determine the exercise intensity needed to achieve my target HR range?

To determine the exercise intensity necessary to reach your target HR range, all you need is a stopwatch. You may record your heart rate manually as explained previously, but use of a heart rate monitor would facilitate this task and probably increase the accuracy. Where distances are involved, such as with running, swimming, or cycling, an accurate measure is needed. An ideal situation for

TABLE 11.12 Target heart rate zones

RHR	Age											
	15–19	20–24	25–29	30–34	35–39	40–44	45–49	50–54	55–59	60–64	65–69	70–74
45–49	125–180	123–175	120–171	118–167	115–163	113–158	110–154	108–150	105–146	103–141	100–137	98–133
50–54	127–181	125–176	122–172	120–168	117–164	115–159	112–155	110–151	107–147	105–142	102–138	100–134
55–59	130–181	128–176	125–172	123–168	120–164	118–159	115–155	113–151	110–147	108–142	105–138	103–134
60–64	132–182	130–177	127–173	125–169	122–165	120–160	117–156	115–152	112–148	110–143	107–139	105–135
65–69	135–183	133–178	130–174	128–170	125–166	123–161	120–157	118–153	115–149	113–144	110–140	107–136
70–74	137–184	135–179	132–175	130–171	127–167	125–162	122–158	120–154	117–150	115–145	112–141	110–137
75–79	140–184	138–180	135–176	133–172	130–168	128–163	125–159	123–155	120–151	118–146	115–142	113–138
80–84	142–185	140–181	137–177	135–173	132–169	130–164	127–160	125–156	122–152	120–147	117–143	115–139
85–89	145–186	143–181	140–177	138–173	135–169	133–164	130–160	128–156	125–152	123–147	120–143	118–139

The target zone (50–85 percent threshold) is based upon the median figure for each age range and resting heart rate range.

TABLE 11.13 The RPE scale

6	14
7 very, very light	15 hard
8	16
9 very light	17 very hard
10	18
11 fairly light	19 very, very hard
12	20
13 somewhat hard	

walking or running would be a quarter-mile (400 meters) high school or college track.

A steady-state HR response may be obtained in 3 to 5 minutes of evenly paced activity. A sound method for walking, jogging, or running follows, but this system may be adapted easily to other activities such as swimming, cycling, calisthenics, and aerobic dance.

Mark a one-half mile course. Two laps on a quarter-mile track would be ideal, but you can pace out a quarter-mile on the sidewalks near your home. Measure your resting HR. Walk until you have an even pace and then time yourself for the one-half mile. Immediately record your HR at the conclusion of the exercise.

During your walk, mentally record the RPE. Did you reach the target HR? Was your RPE related to your HR? If the HR response was in the target range or the RPE was not too strenuous, you are at a level to begin your training program. If the HR response was not in the target range, rest until your HR returns close to normal and then take the test at a faster pace. Repeat this procedure until you have a plot of the HR, RPE, and time for the one-half mile. Keep a record of this as it will be useful in evaluating the effects of your conditioning program.

For example, suppose you recorded the following data on the one-half mile test on four trials (figure 11.13).

Test	Time	RPE	HR	Minutes/Mile
1	8:00	11	108	16:00
2	7:10	13	132	14:20
3	6:30	15	156	13:00
4	6:00	18	180	12:00

As your speed increases, both RPE and HR naturally increase. If your predicted HR max is 200, and your resting HR is 70, the 50–85 percent target range approximates 135–180. Test 1 does not provide adequate stimulus intensity, Test 2 is just below the minimum target HR, Test 3 is in the middle of the range, while Test 4 is at your upper limit. Thus, your training intensity should be between 12 and 14 minutes per mile. The RPE may offer a means of judging the intensity of the exercise when you do not have a set distance and watch.

To determine your speed for these tests, simply double the time for the half-mile and you have the time per mile. The last trial was 12 minutes per mile. The caloric expenditure could be obtained from appendix B.

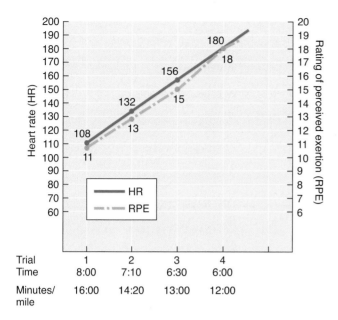

FIGURE 11.13 Plot of heart rate and RPE following a half-mile walk in determination of the threshold heart rate.

How can I design my own exercise program?

The exercise program that you design should not only be safe and effective, but it should be one to which you will adhere for a lifetime. Unfortunately, over 50 percent of the individuals who begin an exercise program to lose excess body weight drop out within a short time. Research with successful exercisers has revealed several clues that increase the likelihood of staying with an exercise program.

1. Do not exceed your abilities during the early stages of the program. Start slowly and progress gradually. If you are overweight, it might be a good idea to start with low-impact activities, such as walking, cycling, or swimming.

2. Set both short-term and long-term goals. A short-term goal may be to walk a mile in 15 minutes, while a long-term goal may be the completion of a local 10-kilometer (6.2-mile) road race.

3. Keep a record of your exercise. This will allow you to evaluate your progress toward your goals. Buy a pedometer. Tudor-Locke indicates that the pedometer, a seemingly insignificant gadget, may be of practical importance in the war on obesity. It will help you document your daily physical activity in an objective way, evaluate your progress over time, and serve as a cue to remind you to be active that may motivate you to exercise more.

4. You must have time available to exercise. Most of us are busy with work, school, family, and friends, so finding the time to exercise is often difficult. Block out time in your daily schedule just as you do for other activities. Exercising before breakfast, at lunch, or immediately after work are some of the strategies used by busy individuals. Doing two things at once, such as running on a treadmill while watching the evening news is another useful strategy.

5. A place to exercise must be convenient. You are more likely to find an excuse not to exercise if you have to travel 5 miles in heavy traffic to a health club. Find a convenient location.

6. Self-motivation is probably the most important determinant of adherence to an exercise program. Enjoying your exercise program, being capable at the exercise task, and knowing that it will help you attain your goals will improve your motivation and hopefully make daily exercise a lifetime habit.

Although diverse modes of aerobic exercise may be used to lose body weight and to help condition the cardiovascular system, the major focus here will be on walk-jog-run programs. This is because they satisfy many of the criteria that may encourage adherence to an exercise program.

Former U. S. Surgeon General C. Everett Koop indicated that walking for exercise should be elevated to a national priority. Walking may be the ideal exercise program for many individuals. Compared to jogging and running there is less stress on the legs due to impact because one foot is always on the ground supporting the body weight. However, leisurely walking usually will not provide an adequate stimulus to achieve the target HR, so the walking pace must be brisk. Walking at a faster-than-normal pace is often called **aerobic walking,** and if done properly can expend Calories at about the same rate as jogging or running. Vigorous arm action is needed, and the length of the stride as well as the step rate must be increased. Also, using hand weights will increase the energy expenditure by about 5–10 percent and also will help tone the arm muscles if used vigorously. Adding 3 pounds to each wrist will increase energy output about 1 Calorie per minute. Carrying the weights in the hands tends to increase the blood pressure more, so it may be helpful to use weights that strap around the wrist. However, you may expend similar amounts of Calories by simply walking faster or longer without hand weights.

A wide variety of methods may be used to initiate an aerobic exercise program of walking, jogging, or running. The key is to begin slowly, gradually increasing the exercise intensity as you become better conditioned. Once you determine the intensity of exercise necessary to achieve the target HR, it becomes a relatively simple matter to individualize the exercise program. The two tables presented on pages 436–437 include exercise programs for individuals who have been sedentary and have low levels of physical fitness. Use your target HR guidelines throughout the 12- to 15-week program.

In the early weeks you should attempt to exercise only at the 50–60 percent target HR range. However, if you find that the exercise intensity needed to achieve this level is too strenuous, reduce it to 40 percent of your calculated heart-rate reserve. As you become more fit, gradually increase your target HR to the 50–85 percent level.

Table 11.14 presents a sample aerobic walking program. It is designed to progress you gradually through 12 weeks to a point where the exercise intensity and duration may make a significant contribution to weight loss over time. If you feel fit you may progress more rapidly than the table indicates, but stay within your target HR range and do not become unduly fatigued.

TABLE 11.14 Sample aerobic walking program

	Warm-up	Target zone exercising	Warm-down	Total time
Week 1*	Walk slowly 5 minutes	Walk briskly 5 minutes	Walk slowly 5 minutes	15 minutes
Week 2	Walk slowly 5 minutes	Walk briskly 7 minutes	Walk slowly 5 minutes	17 minutes
Week 3	Walk slowly 5 minutes	Walk briskly 9 minutes	Walk slowly 5 minutes	19 minutes
Week 4	Walk slowly 5 minutes	Walk briskly 11 minutes	Walk slowly 5 minutes	21 minutes
Week 5	Walk slowly 5 minutes	Walk briskly 13 minutes	Walk slowly 5 minutes	23 minutes
Week 6	Walk slowly 5 minutes	Walk briskly 15 minutes	Walk slowly 5 minutes	25 minutes
Week 7	Walk slowly 5 minutes	Walk briskly 18 minutes	Walk slowly 5 minutes	28 minutes
Week 8	Walk slowly 5 minutes	Walk briskly 20 minutes	Walk slowly 5 minutes	30 minutes
Week 9	Walk slowly 5 minutes	Walk briskly 23 minutes	Walk slowly 5 minutes	33 minutes
Week 10	Walk slowly 5 minutes	Walk briskly 26 minutes	Walk slowly 5 minutes	36 minutes
Week 11	Walk slowly 5 minutes	Walk briskly 28 minutes	Walk slowly 5 minutes	38 minutes
Week 12	Walk slowly 5 minutes	Walk briskly 30 minutes	Walk slowly 5 minutes	40 minutes

From week 13 on, check your pulse periodically to see if you are exercising within your target heart rate range. As you become more fit, walk faster to increase your heart rate toward the upper levels of your target range. Follow the principle of progression. Note: If you find a particular week's pattern tiring, repeat it before going on to the next pattern. *You do not have to complete the walking program in 12 weeks.* Remember that your goal is to continue getting the benefits you are seeking—and to enjoy your activity. Listen to your body and progress less rapidly, if necessary.

*Program should include at *least* three exercise sessions per week.

Source: U.S. Department of Health and Human Services.

Table 11.15 presents an exercise program with a rapid progression to jogging, using an interval-training approach. **Interval training** alternates periods of rest and exercise. Again, the target HR method should be used during this exercise program. As compared to walking, jogging or running may expend 2–3 times the amount of Calories per unit of time. Thus, it may be worthwhile to interject short bouts of more intense exercise into a workout, such as jogging one block out of every three or four when walking. Moreover, research has indicated that more intense exercise may confer additional health benefits. Swain and Franklin concluded that exercise performed at a vigorous intensity appears to convey greater cardioprotective benefits than exercise of moderate intensity, while Franco and others reported that although moderate levels of physical activity increased life expectancy, the gains were twice as large, about two additional years, with higher activity levels.

Whatever mode of exercise you select, the target HR should be maintained for 20–30 minutes. This may be continuous or intermittent. If 30 minutes is the allotted time, the target HR should be achieved for 30 continuous minutes or three 10-minute intervals of exercise with several minutes of rest in between.

The frequency of exercise should be daily or at least three to five times per week. The American College of Sports Medicine has documented a number of studies that support a frequency level of at least three times per week as being necessary to develop and maintain cardiovascular health. During the early stages, however, it may be advisable to exercise daily in order to form sound habits. The exercise intensity at this time may not be too severe, such as walking, and hence daily exercise bouts may be undertaken without serious muscle soreness or related injury patterns. If you switch to jogging or running, decrease the frequency to three or four times per week to avoid overuse injuries. The frequency per week may be increased as you become better physically conditioned.

For weight-control purposes, duration and frequency of exercise are key elements. The longer and more often you exercise, the greater will be the total amount of energy expended. Aerobic walking for 5 miles on a daily basis is the equivalent of approximately 1 pound of body fat per week.

There are a number of other excellent conditioning programs available for the unconditioned individual. Probably the most popular is the aerobics program developed by Dr. Kenneth Cooper. Although dated, his programs may be found in *The Aerobics Program for Total Well Being,* a highly recommended paperback found in most bookstores. Also, books on initiating walking and other aerobic exercise programs are available at your library or local bookstores. An excellent program may be found on the Internet at www.americaonthemove.org.

TABLE 11.15 Sample aerobic jogging program (interval training)

	Warm-up	Target zone exercising	Warm-down	Total time
Week 1*	Stretch and limber up 5 minutes	Walk (nonstop) 10 minutes	Walk slowly 3 minutes; stretch 2 minutes	20 minutes
Week 2	Stretch and limber up 5 minutes	Walk 5 minutes; jog 1 minute; walk 5 minutes; jog 1 minute	Walk slowly 3 minutes; stretch 2 minutes	22 minutes
Week 3	Stretch and limber up 5 minutes	Walk 5 minutes; jog 3 minutes; walk 5 minutes; jog 3 minutes	Walk slowly 3 minutes; stretch 2 minutes	26 minutes
Week 4	Stretch and limber up 5 minutes	Walk 5 minutes; jog 4 minutes; walk 5 minutes; jog 4 minutes	Walk slowly 3 minutes; stretch 2 minutes	28 minutes
Week 5	Stretch and limber up 5 minutes	Walk 4 minutes; jog 5 minutes; walk 4 minutes; jog 5 minutes	Walk slowly 3 minutes; stretch 2 minutes	28 minutes
Week 6	Stretch and limber up 5 minutes	Walk 4 minutes; jog 6 minutes; walk 4 minutes; jog 6 minutes	Walk slowly 3 minutes; stretch 2 minutes	30 minutes
Week 7	Stretch and limber up 5 minutes	Walk 4 minutes; jog 7 minutes; walk 4 minutes; jog 7 minutes	Walk slowly 3 minutes; stretch 2 minutes	32 minutes
Week 8	Stretch and limber up 5 minutes	Walk 4 minutes; jog 8 minutes; walk 4 minutes; jog 8 minutes	Walk slowly 3 minutes; stretch 2 minutes	34 minutes
Week 9	Stretch and limber up 5 minutes	Walk 4 minutes; jog 9 minutes; walk 4 minutes; jog 9 minutes	Walk slowly 3 minutes; stretch 2 minutes	36 minutes
Week 10	Stretch and limber up 5 minutes	Walk 4 minutes; jog 13 minutes	Walk slowly 3 minutes; stretch 2 minutes	27 minutes
Week 11	Stretch and limber up 5 minutes	Walk 4 minutes; jog 15 minutes	Walk slowly 3 minutes; stretch 2 minutes	29 minutes
Week 12	Stretch and limber up 5 minutes	Walk 4 minutes; jog 17 minutes	Walk slowly 3 minutes; stretch 2 minutes	31 minutes
Week 13	Stretch and limber up 5 minutes	Walk 2 minutes; jog slowly 2 minutes; jog 17 minutes	Walk slowly 3 minutes; stretch 2 minutes	31 minutes
Week 14	Stretch and limber up 5 minutes	Walk 1 minute; jog slowly 3 minutes; jog 17 minutes	Walk slowly 3 minutes; stretch 2 minutes	31 minutes
Week 15	Stretch and limber up 5 minutes	Jog slowly 3 minutes; jog 17 minutes	Walk slowly 3 minutes; stretch 2 minutes	30 minutes

From week 16 on, check your pulse periodically to see if you are exercising within your target zone. As you become more fit, try exercising within the upper range of your target zone.

Note: If you find a particular week's pattern tiring, repeat it before going on to the next pattern. *You do not have to complete the jogging program in 15 weeks.* Remember that your goal is to continue getting the benefits you are seeking—and to enjoy your activity.

*Program should include at least three exercise sessions per week.

Source: U.S. Department of Health and Human Services.

How much exercise is needed to lose weight?

Although a properly planned exercise program may produce significant health benefits even without weight loss, most individuals use exercise to decrease body fat. Although weight loss depends on both a balance of energy expenditure through exercise and energy intake through your diet, some guidelines are available from professional and governmental health organizations.

Jakicic and Gallagher recently noted that the magnitude of exercise required to facilitate successful long-term weight loss may be greater than what is necessary to elicit significant improvements in health. For example, the American College of Sports Medicine indicates a threshold (for a 165-pound individual) exercise energy expenditure approximating 250–300 Calories each session at least three days a week, or four 200-Calorie exercise sessions per week may improve health status. This level of activity expends approximately 800–900 Calories per week. However, the ACSM notes that if the primary purpose of the exercise program is for weight loss, then greater duration and frequency of exercise are necessary. In its position stand on weight control, the ACSM indicates that approximately 4.5 hours of moderate-intensity exercise that results in an energy expenditure of at least 2,000 calories per week, in combination with reduced caloric intake, will produce desirable weight-loss results. In their review, Rippe and others indicated that successful weight-loss programs incorporated exercise programs that increased energy expenditure by about 1,500–2,000 Calories per week, which would be in accord with the latter viewpoint of the ACSM. Successful weight losers in the National Weight Control Registry exercised about 1 hour per day, which included walking a total of 10 miles per week, aerobics, resistance training, and other physical activities. Collectively, this amount of physical activity would approximate 1,500–2,000 Calories weekly.

Finally, the Institute of Medicine of the National Academy of Sciences indicates that 30 minutes per day of regular activity is insufficient to maintain body weight within the recommended body mass index range, and hence recommends 60 minutes of daily moderate-intensity physical activity. Walking or jogging at 4–5 MPH is recommended, in addition to the activities required by a sedentary lifestyle. This amount of physical activity leads to an active lifestyle, corresponding to physical activity levels (PAL) greater than 1.6, and is appropriate for both children and adults. Such an activity level for 6–7 days a week would approximate 2,000 Calories or more of energy expenditure.

Collectively, the optimal exercise energy-expenditure goal appears to be 1,500–2,000 Calories per week, or about 200–300 Calories per day. For walkers, this approximates 10,000 steps daily. The average person walks about 5,000 steps a day, and studies have shown that such individuals are overweight as compared to those who walk 10,000 or more steps daily. Gradually adding about 5,000 or 6,000 steps of brisk walking per day to a sedentary routine would approximate 200–300 additional Calories expended, or about 1,500–2,000 per week. Use of a good pedometer will help you keep track of daily steps, and will also serve as a motivation device to encourage you to walk.

From what parts of the body does the weight loss occur during an exercise weight-reduction program?

As mentioned previously, weight loss may come from any one of three body sources—body water, lean tissue such as muscle, and body-fat stores. A diet program, especially one very low in Calories, will cause a rapid weight loss due to decreases in body water and lean tissue. Body-fat losses are moderate at first but may increase in later stages of the diet. On the other hand, weight lost through an exercise program alone is lost at a much slower rate. Body water levels remain relatively normal after replacement of water lost through exercise. The lean tissues, particularly muscle, might actually increase in amount from the stimulating effect of exercise on muscle development. Because a good proportion of the energy demand for exercise is met by the oxidation of fat, most of the body-weight reduction comes from the body-fat stores, particularly in the abdominal area (figure 11.14). As we learned previously, the caloric cost of 1 pound of fat is much higher than that of water or lean muscle tissue.

Should I do low-intensity exercises to burn more fat?

A myth that is circulating contends that in order to burn fat, you must exercise at a lower percentage of your VO_2 max. As noted in chapters 3, 4, and 5, and recently confirmed in a study by Thompson and others, it is true that the *percentage* of energy obtained from fat is greater at lower exercise intensities (e.g., 50 percent VO_2 max) than at higher exercise intensities (e.g., 70 percent VO_2 max). However, at the higher energy intensity, you will derive a lower percentage of your energy output from fat, but the total energy expenditure will be greater, and you will still burn about the same amount of fat Calories as you would exercising at the lower intensity providing you are exercising for the same amount of time. If you want to burn Calories to lose body fat, your objective should be to burn the greatest total Calories possible within the time frame you have to exercise. As an example, suppose a female had 30 minutes to exercise and exercised at 50 percent VO_2 max, running 10-minute miles and deriving 50 percent of her energy from fat. She would cover 3 miles, expending 300 total Calories at an energy cost of about 100 Calories per mile, 150 (.50 × 300) of which would be fat Calories. If she was able to run at 75 percent VO_2 max, running 7.5-minute miles and deriving 33 percent of her energy from fat, she would cover 4.5 miles, expending 450 total Calories, of which 150 (.33 × 450) would still be fat Calories. However, she has expended a total of 450 versus 300 Calories at the higher exercise intensity, which will lead to a greater weight loss or permit her to consume an additional 150 Calories in her daily diet. But, if she has unlimited time, she may be able to exercise longer at the lower exercise intensity and eventually burn more total Calories including more fat Calories. Keep in mind, as noted in chapters 4 and 5, as you become highly trained in aerobic endurance exercise, you become a better fat burner and will be able to oxidize fat at higher exercise intensities. For example, Romijn and others have found that in endurance-trained men and women, the highest rate of fat oxidation was during exercise at 65 percent of maximal oxygen uptake. If you want to burn 500 Calories per day by running 5 miles, it does not matter how fast you run. For weight-control purposes, the total distance covered, which translates into total Calories expended, is the key point. As noted in chapter 3, you may estimate the energy it costs you to run 1 mile by simply multiplying your body weight in pounds by 0.73 Calories.

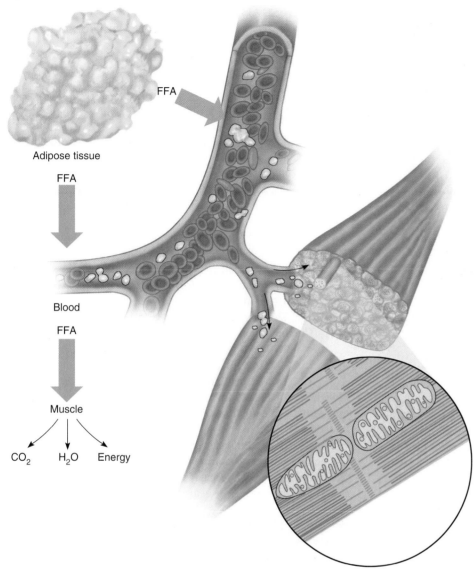

FIGURE 11.14 Exercise helps to release fat (free fatty acids) from the adipose tissues. The fat then travels by way of the bloodstream to the muscles where the free fatty acids are oxidized to provide the energy for exercise. Thus, exercise is an effective measure of reducing body fat.

Is spot reducing effective?

Spot reducing uses isolated exercises in an attempt to deplete local fat deposits in specific body areas. These techniques do not appear to be effective. In one study the fat tissue was biopsied to determine whether sit-ups would reduce fat in the abdominal area. Subjects did a total of 5,000 sit-ups over a 27-day period, but this localized exercise did not preferentially reduce the adipose cell size in the abdominal area.

In their recent review, Smith and Zachwieja indicated that the current view suggests that the reduction of fat in body areas is most likely to occur where fat deposits are the most conspicuous (usually the abdominal area), regardless of the weight-loss format,

including exercise. However, some areas of the body are somewhat resistant to change, particularly the gynoid-type fat distribution around the hips and thighs. Although both large-muscle activities and local isolated-muscle exercises may be beneficial in reducing fat stores, the former are recommended because the total caloric expenditure will be larger.

Is it possible to exercise and still not lose body weight?

Many individuals are disappointed during the early stages of an exercise program because they do not lose weight very rapidly. Unless they understand what is happening in their bodies, the results on the scale may convince them that exercise is not an effective means of reducing weight, and they may quit exercising altogether. There are several reasons why an individual may not lose weight during the early stages of a weight-reduction program, and also why losing weight becomes more difficult after weight loss has occurred.

When a sedentary individual begins a daily exercise program, the body reacts to the exercise stress and changes so it can more easily handle the demands of exercise (figure 11.15):

1. The muscles may increase in size because of hypertrophy of the muscle cells. The increased protein will hold water.
2. Certain structures within the muscle cell that process oxygen, along with numerous enzymes involved in oxygen use, will increase in quantity.
3. Energy substances in the cell will increase, particularly glycogen, which binds water.
4. The connective tissue will toughen and thicken.
5. The total blood volume may increase. An increase of approximately 500 milliliters, or about a pound, has been recorded in 1 week.

At the same time, however, body-fat stores will begin to diminish somewhat as fat is used as a source of energy for exercise. Overall, there may be an increase in body water and lean body mass, particularly the muscle tissues, and a decrease in body fat. These changes may counterbalance each other, and the individual may not lose any weight. However, although little or no weight is lost during those early phases, the body composition changes are favorable. Body fat is being lost.

Once these adaptive changes have occurred, which may take about a month, body weight should decrease in relationship to the

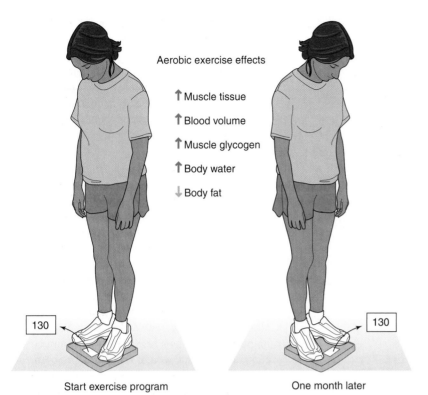

Aerobic exercise effects

↑ Muscle tissue

↑ Blood volume

↑ Muscle glycogen

↑ Body water

↓ Body fat

130

130

Start exercise program   One month later

FIGURE 11.15 Body weight may not change much during the beginning phases of an aerobic exercise program. However, body composition may change. The exercise stimulates an increase in muscle tissue, blood volume, and muscle glycogen stores, which tend to increase weight. Body fat is reduced, but the increases in the other components can balance out the fat losses with no net loss of body weight. Eventually, body weight, particularly abdominal fat, begins to drop as the exercise program is continued.

number of Calories lost through exercise. Keep in mind that weight loss will be slow on an exercise program, but if you can build up to an exercise energy expenditure of about 300 Calories per day, then about 3 pounds per month will be exercised away provided you do not compensate by eating more.

After several months you may begin to notice that your body weight has stabilized even though you continue to exercise and have not reached your weight goal. Part of the reason may be your lower body weight. If you look at appendix B, you can see that the less you weigh, the fewer Calories you burn for any given exercise. If you have been doing the same amount of exercise all along, you may now be at the body weight where your energy output is matched by your energy input in food and your body weight has stabilized. In theory, you have reached your settling point. In addition, you may become more skilled, and hence more efficient, in your physical activity. Fewer Calories may then be expended for any given amount of time. However, this is usually true only of activities that involve a skill factor. It can be highly significant in swimming, but not as great in jogging.

In summary, your body weight may not change during the early stages of an exercise program; it may then begin to drop during a second stage, and then plateau at the third stage. If you are aware of these possible stages, your adherence to an exercise program may be

enhanced. Also, during the third stage, if you desire to lose more weight by exercise, the amount of exercise will need to be increased.

What about the five or six pounds a person may lose during an hour of exercise?

A rapid weight loss may occur during exercise. Some individuals have lost as much as 10–12 pounds in an hour or so. As you probably suspect, this weight loss may be attributed to body-water losses. This is particularly evident while exercising in warm or hot weather. The weight loss is temporary, and under normal food and water intake the body-water content will return to normal. Each pound of weight lost this way is 1 pint of fluid, or 16 ounces. A 2.2-pound weight loss would be the equivalent of 1 liter.

In the heat of summer, you may occasionally see an individual training with heavy sweat clothes or a rubberized suit. The reason often given is to lose more body weight. The individual will lose more body weight, but again it will be body water which will be regained as soon as he or she drinks fluids. In this regard, the technique is worthless. Moreover, it may predispose the individual to an unusually high heat stress, causing severe medical problems. Remember, only sweat that actually evaporates will help reduce the heat stress on the body.

Any water lost through dehydration should be replaced before the next exercise session, especially when exercising in warm environments. The importance of rehydration and problems associated with exercise in the heat were covered in chapter 9.

Key Concept Recap

▶ Aerobic exercise can increase energy expenditure considerably, but in order to lose body fat through exercise one should think in terms of months, not days.

▶ Aerobic weight-reduction exercises need to involve large muscle masses, such as the legs in jogging or bicycling or the arms and legs in swimming. Brisk walking is a highly recommended exercise program.

▶ The general design of the aerobic weight-reduction exercise program involves three phases: warm-up, exercise stimulus, and warm-down.

▶ An effective means of monitoring aerobic exercise intensity is the exercise heart rate (HR). The exercise target HR varies depending upon age and level of conditioning. Ratings of perceived exertion (RPE) may also be used to gauge exercise intensity.

▶ A slow, steady progression in exercise intensity is important in preventing excess stress and injuries.

▶ The minimum aerobic exercise goals for losing weight are an intensity of 40/50–85 percent maximal HR reserve, a duration of 20–60 minutes, and a frequency of 3–5 times per week; however, duration and frequency of exercise are more important than intensity for losing weight.

Check for Yourself

Using several different types of physical activity that you enjoy, use appendix B and calculate how much time you would need to allocate to each in order to burn 500 Calories per day.

Comprehensive Weight-Control Programs

In a recent review, Wayne Miller reported that although a 3–4 month diet or diet-and-exercise program may induce significant weight loss, long-term follow-up data, although limited, suggest almost complete relapse in 3–5 years. Accordingly, in a conference relative to methods for voluntary weight loss and control, the National Institutes of Health indicated that the most important feature of a successful weight-loss or weight-control program is maintenance of the stable or reduced body weight. The NIH noted that the fundamental principle of weight loss and control is a commitment to a change in lifestyle, a viewpoint shared by the American Dietetic Association in their recent position statement on weight management. Behavioral modification incorporating properly designed diets and exercise programs, as detailed in this chapter, may be sufficient to induce and sustain weight losses in the individual with mild obesity, but those with more severe cases may need additional education and skills, social support, medical therapy, and continued professional assistance in order to maintain a stable, healthy body weight. Whatever the case, Miller emphasizes the point that any intervention strategy to decrease body weight should be one that would promote the development of healthy lifestyle behaviors and involve a maintenance plan designed to develop skills necessary to maintain these newly developed behaviors.

Which is more effective for weight control—dieting or exercise?

In a recent review, Grundy and others indicated that curtailment of energy intake and increased physical activity are both necessary to cope with the epidemic of overweight and obesity. Dieting alone or exercise alone may be effective means to reduce body fat, but each technique has certain advantages and disadvantages. However, it appears that the advantages of one technique help counterbalance the disadvantages of the other. Dieting will contribute to a negative caloric balance and may help bring about a rapid weight reduction early in the program but may lead to decreases in lean body mass and REE. Exercise usually results in a slower rate of weight loss but may help develop and maintain the lean body mass and prevent the decrease in REE. Thompson and others used a meta-analysis of twenty-two studies to compare the effect of diet and diet-plus-exercise programs on the resting metabolic rate and concluded that the addition of exercise to dietary restriction appears to prevent some of the decrease in the REE. Garfinkel and Coscina noted that weight lost by dieting is about 75 percent fat and 25 percent protein, but combining exercise and dieting reduces the protein loss to only 5 percent. Other studies have reported that dieting alone may result in lean tissue loss as high as 40 percent of the total weight loss. Resistance training (covered in the next chapter) added to a weight-reduction program may also be very effective in helping to maintain lean body mass. Preferably, both aerobic and resistance exercise should be part of a comprehensive weight-control program. A recent study by Kraemer and others found that the combination of aerobic endurance training and resistance training, compared to dieting alone, exerted more favorable effects on body composition and health-related fitness measures. Dolezal and Potteiger indicated that combining aerobic and resistance exercise provides the beneficial effects of both types of exercise. In a recent excellent review, Hill and others noted that the benefits of exercise alone on body weight, body composition, and energy expenditure are preserved when added to a weight-loss diet.

Hence, a comprehensive weight-reduction program involving both a dietary and an exercise regimen, along with supportive behavioral modification techniques, is highly recommended by major health-related organizations such as the American Dietetic Association and the American College of Sports Medicine. The principles of developing such a program have been presented in the preceding three sections of this chapter.

Research also has been conducted with individuals who have successfully lost weight and maintained their desired level. In essence, during the weight-loss phase they assumed responsibility for their need to lose weight and planned their own program. They did not necessarily diet per se, but simply decreased the amount of fat and sugar in their diet, ate less between meals, and often skipped meals. They also initiated a reasonable exercise program. Wing and Hill summarized three key points of successful weight-loss maintenance by members of the National Weight Control Registry. They eat a diet low in fat, they monitor their body weight and food intake frequently, and they engage in high levels of regular physical activity.

Consider the following. A dietary reduction of 500 Calories per day, along with an exercise energy expenditure of 500 Calories per day, could lead to approximately 2 pounds of weight loss per week, about the maximal amount recommended unless under medical supervision. The removal of 500 Calories from the diet could be done immediately by simply reducing the amount of sugar and fat in the daily diet and using some of the behavioral modification techniques cited earlier. You should review those suggestions given earlier relative to the substitution of nutrient-dense foods for high-Caloric ones. Relative to exercise it may take a month or more before you may be able to use 500 Calories daily, but by following the progressive plans outlined earlier in this chapter you should be able to reach that level safely. In the meantime, change your usual behavior by climbing stairs and walking more to add to your daily caloric expenditure.

Once the excess body fat has been lost, continued exercise appears to be important for maintenance of a stable, healthy body weight. Some preliminary reports from the National Weight Control Registry of individuals who have lost at least 30 pounds and have kept it off indicate that exercise is very important; walking was the most popular activity and the average weekly energy expenditure was 2,667 Calories for women and 3,489 Calories for men. Schoeller and others recently reported that daily exercise of approximately 5 Calories per pound body weight helped to optimize weight maintenance after weight loss. Numerous reviews have indicated that exercise exerted a strong influence on long-term preservation of weight loss, a finding also echoed by the Consumers Union.

Although exercise is important for weight loss and maintenance, Tremblay and Doucet indicated that it is also important to monitor food habits to prevent excessive energy intake that could negate the energy expenditure through exercise. In this regard, Shick and others indicated that the consumption of a low-fat, low-Calorie diet may be necessary for long-term weight control, a viewpoint also advocated by Hill. However, Hill also noted that adopting a strategy to eat less in order to lose weight is designed to fail in the long run. Although some can do it, they are few in number. Many can do it for a limited time frame to reach a healthy body weight, but then may revert back to old eating habits. Exercise, by expending Calories daily, enables the individual to eat more during the maintenance phase and may help promote adherence to a healthy body weight for a lifetime. Thus, both a properly designed exercise program and a healthful, adequate-Calorie diet go hand in hand in helping to lose excess body fat and maintain a healthy body weight.

If I want to lose weight through a national or local weight-loss program, what should I look for?

The weight-loss industry is a multibillion dollar business. National programs, such as Weight Watchers and the Jenny Craig plan, may charge about $100 per week or more for their comprehensive programs. Unfortunately, there is little governmental control over many of these programs, and while the national programs may be well designed, others may not provide appropriate programs for safe and effective long-term weight loss.

What do authorities recommend you should receive for your money if you want to enroll in a commercial weight-loss program? The following points are adapted and summarized from the report of a task force to establish weight-loss guidelines for the state of Michigan, and from other health professional sources, such as Partnership for Healthy Weight Management.

1. The staff should be well trained in their specialty, preferably having appropriate educational backgrounds, such as a physician, nurse, dietician, or exercise physiologist.
2. You should receive a medical screening, verifying you have no medical or psychological condition that might be exacerbated by weight loss through dieting or exercise.
3. A reasonable weight goal should be established given your weight history.
4. The rate of weight loss, after the first 2 weeks, should not exceed 2 pounds per week.
5. You should receive an individualized treatment plan based on your weight-loss goal. You should also obtain an itemized list of costs.
6. The program should disclose in writing all health risks and benefits associated with the program, and you should have the opportunity to read them and sign an informed consent form.
7. The diet should be one that
   a. contains no less than 1,000–1,500 Calories per day
   b. is between 10–30 percent fat Calories
   c. has at least 100 grams of carbohydrate per day
   d. provides at least 100 percent of the RDA; supplements, if used, should not exceed 100 percent of the RDA
   e. if under medical supervision, contains at least 600 Calories and 50 grams of carbohydrate per day
8. The program should have a nutrition-education component that stresses permanent lifestyle changes in your eating habits.
9. Both aerobic and resistance exercise should be a component in the program. The focus should be on aerobic exercise, following the standards relative to mode, intensity, duration, and frequency discussed earlier in this chapter. It should be an exercise program you can live with for a lifetime. Guidelines for resistance exercise are presented in the next chapter.
10. Behavior-modification techniques should be individualized to help you incorporate sound dietary and exercise habits into your personal lifestyle.
11. There should be a weight-maintenance phase in the program once you have achieved your weight-loss goal. This should be a high priority to help you maintain your healthy body weight.

Tsai and Wadden conducted a systematic review of major commercial weight-loss programs in the United States, and indicated that all programs can work to induce weight loss. The major problem is getting people to stick with the program. The greater the compliance, such as in programs like Weight Watchers, the greater the success.

Guidelines similar to those just given should be used if you want to join a health or fitness club facility, particularly the qualifications of the staff and the availability of a variety of safe exercise equipment. Personal trainers should be certified by reputable professional organizations, such as the American Council on Exercise (www.acefitness.org) and the American College of Sports Medicine (www.acsm.org). A personal trainer may help you plan an effective exercise program, including both aerobic and resistance exercise, to help you lose excess body weight. You can check with local fitness-oriented organizations, such as the YMCA, for a list of personal trainers, their certification, and their fees. You may also check the Website of the two organizations above for trainers in your area.

Although some individuals may need the structure of such programs, many successful individuals have lost excess body fat and kept it off with programs they designed by themselves.

What type of weight-reduction program is advisable for young athletes?

In general, athletes who desire to lose weight to enhance performance must rely primarily on dietary modifications because they are already exercising intensely. Excessive weight loss, especially in young athletes, is a major concern in sports.

In sports in which athletes compete in weight classes, such as wrestling, or in those where excess body fat may hinder performance, such as gymnastics, most competitors and their coaches believe that it is best to attain the lowest weight possible to increase chances of success. Although most of the concern in the past was devoted to the sport of wrestling, there is increasing concern about this practice in a variety of other sports.

As noted in the preceding chapter, potentially acute health problems may arise when the youngster sets an unrealistically low body-weight goal and uses nonrecommended techniques, such as starvation, diuretics, laxatives, appetite-suppressing drugs, and dehydration. Previous research had shown that athletes, such as wrestlers, who lose and gain weight repeatedly throughout the season may find it more difficult to lose weight because their metabolism may slow down to conserve energy. However, more recent studies, such as those by Schmidt and others and McCargar and Crawford, noted that the decrease in the RMR is transient or returns to normal pre-season values following completion of the competitive wrestling season. There is also some concern by medical personnel that weight loss during the growth and development years may have adverse long-term effects. For example, as noted in chapter 10, some preliminary research suggests that dieting may retard the growth rate in young gymnasts. On the other hand, many coaches and athletes still remain unconvinced that current weight-control practices pose any immediate or future health hazard. In a questionnaire survey comparing former college wrestlers with other nonwrestling athletes who attended the University of Wisconsin–Madison between 1950 and 1988, Nitzke and others reported no significant differences between the wrestlers and other athletes in the Body Mass Index, weight gained, current exercise practices, or incidence of chronic diseases, even when comparisons were made for all those athletes over the age of 40. Unfortunately, the available scientific data are very limited, and this general area is in dire need of long-term research.

Nevertheless, on the basis of the data that are available, organizations such as the National Collegiate Athletic Association, the American Medical Association, and the American College of Sports Medicine have made some general recommendations to help alleviate potential problems and make weight-control practices in sports as safe as possible.

1. Weight should be lost gradually. A comprehensive program involving a balanced diet of 1,500–2,400 Calories and exercise should be used in the pre-season to lose most of the body weight. With appropriate carbohydrate, protein, minerals, and vitamins in the diet, a limited number of Calories possibly may enable a wrestler or other athlete to lose body weight effectively and yet still maintain high levels of aerobic and anaerobic activity in training. Year-round conditioning and nutrition programs to help maintain a stable, healthy body weight are more desirable than rapid weight loss practices during the season.

2. Dehydration techniques such as rubber suits, saunas, steam baths, hot rooms, laxatives, and diuretics should be prohibited.

3. In the sport of wrestling, having the weigh-in immediately prior to performance may discourage rapid dehydration and weight-gain techniques. Also, suggestions have been made to allow more intermediate weight classes because there are more boys at these weight levels.

4. Encourage methods to predict a minimum body-fat percentage or body weight as currently employed by the National Federation of State High School Associations and the NCAA nationwide.

What is the importance of prevention in a weight-control program?

Health practices designed to prevent the development of chronic diseases currently are being promoted heavily by several major health organizations, and many have focused on the adverse health effects of obesity. For example, the Canadian Task Force on Preventive Health Care has recommended that obesity prevention be a high priority for health professionals. Changing your diet by reducing caloric intake, saturated fats, and cholesterol, and eating more nutritious foods (quality Calories), and concurrently initiating and continuing a good aerobic- and resistance-type exercise program are considered to be two steps toward positive health and the prevention of obesity. James Hill, founder of the obesity-prevention program *America on the Move,* indicated that walking an extra 2,000 steps a day and eating 100 fewer Calories will help prevent the average weight gain of 1–3 pounds per year. You may access the program at www.americaonthemove.org. If you like to eat, additional exercise may help you burn these Calories and maintain your body weight (figure 11.16).

Although most of this chapter has focused on treatment programs for the reduction of excess body fat, the same guidelines may be applied to a prevention program. Obesity in our society is a serious medical problem of epidemic proportions. Although treatment programs for the clinically obese may be successful on a short-term basis, unfortunately much of the weight loss is regained by the vast majority of those treated. As noted by Levin, the formation of neural circuits in the brain that help perpetuate

200 Calorie milkshake =   3 mile leisurely walk at 3 mph   or   30 minutes of easy tennis   or   5 miles of leisurely bicycling at 5 mph

FIGURE 11.16   It is very easy to consume 200 additional Calories per day, which can lead to an increase of about 2 pounds of body fat per month. However, increased physical activity may help to expend these Calories.

maintenance of excess body weight are not easily abolished. We need to have strong prevention programs, particularly for children and adolescents, for this appears to be the time of life when chronic cases of obesity develop.

Prevention of obesity on a large scale necessitates a multipronged effort involving various groups. Some examples are listed.

- Government can set standards for food advertisements to children.
- Food manufacturers could produce healthier products. One example is Fun Fruits, containing a variety of fruits and marketed specifically to kids.
- Communities could plan more bike paths, playgrounds, and recreation centers.
- Schools could schedule daily physical education classes and provide opportunities for students to participate in intramural sports and physical activity clubs after school. Schools could also provide healthier products in vending machines.
- Parents could provide healthy foods and limit sedentary behaviors such as TV and computer time.

Various Websites to obtain helpful information relative to the prevention of obesity have been listed throughout this chapter. An additional excellent source of information is the Weight-Control Information Network (WIN), which may be accessed at www.win.niddk.nih.gov.

It is incumbent upon those involved with the food habits and physical activity of our youth, notably parents and health and physical educators, to instruct and motivate them toward sound health habits. According to the American Medical Association, prevention is the treatment of choice in dealing with obesity. The bottom line is, *we need to eat less and move more.*

Key Concept Recap

▶ Although diet and exercise may each be effective in losing body weight, a combination of the two would be even more beneficial.
▶ Prevention of obesity is more effective than treatment, and appropriate programs should be developed early for children and adolescents.

Albert is overweight by 25 pounds and is very serious about reducing his body weight from 200 pounds down to 175 and a healthier BMI of 22. He is currently sedentary, is consuming an average 3,600 Calories per day, and is still gaining weight. You may assume he needs 15 Calories per pound body weight to maintain his current weight. Using information presented in the text, develop a weight-loss program for Albert. Calculate an appropriate rate of weight loss per week. Based on your calculation, determine the daily caloric deficit needed to achieve his goal. The caloric deficit should incorporate reduced caloric energy intake and increased caloric energy expenditure through your recommended energy program. Once Albert is at his desired body weight and is involved in your exercise program, how many Calories may he consume daily to maintain that weight?

Albert's Weight Status

	Weight	Calorie intake	Maintenance Calories
Current status			
Goal status			

Albert's Weight-Loss Plan

1. Desired weight loss per week:
2. Caloric energy intake reduction:
3. Caloric energy expenditure increase:
4. Total daily caloric deficit:
5. Maintenance Calories at goal weight:

1. If you were to design an aerobic training program for a 30-year-old individual and wanted that person to maintain an exercise intensity of 70–90 percent of the predicted HR max (traditional method) as the target heart rate range, what exercise heart rate range would you recommend?
   (a) 123–156
   (b) 133–171
   (c) 140–180
   (d) 154–198
   (e) 180–220

2. Which of the following statements relative to an exercise program for weight maintenance or loss is true?
   (a) The mode of exercise should involve large muscle groups that are activated in rhythmic, continuous type movement.
   (b) The higher the intensity of aerobic exercise that the individual can sustain, the better, because the greater the intensity, the greater the number of Calories burned per minute.
   (c) The greater the duration of activity, the better.
   (d) The more frequent the exercise during the week, the better.
   (e) All of the above statements are true.

3. Which of the following has the least amount of Calories as per the food exchange system developed by the American Dietetic Association and the American Diabetes Association?
   (a) three servings of skim milk
   (b) four servings of lean meat such as turkey
   (c) five servings of vegetables
   (d) four servings of fruit
   (e) one serving of whole milk

4. Aerobic-type exercise may be an effective part of a comprehensive weight control program for all of the following reasons except which one?
   (a) It increases the metabolic rate.
   (b) It mobilizes and utilizes free fatty acids from the adipose tissues.
   (c) It helps reduce body water stores.
   (d) It will increase the resting metabolic rate for several hours after the exercise period.
   (e) It may help to curb the appetite in some individuals if done prior to mealtime.

5. Suppose a young sedentary woman wanted to lose 10 pounds of body fat in a period of 5 weeks' time. She now weighs 150 pounds and her activity level is so low that she needs only 15 Calories per pound of body weight to maintain her weight. Calculate the number of Calories she may consume daily in order to lose the 10 pounds by diet only.
   (a) 800
   (b) 1250
   (c) 1500
   (d) 1750
   (e) 1900

6. In the exchange lists, high-fat foods are usually found in which two exchanges?
   (a) fruit and vegetables
   (b) starch/bread and lean meat
   (c) whole milk and starch/bread
   (d) fat and vegetable
   (e) medium fat meat and whole milk

7. Research with effective dieters has shown that in order to be successful, a diet

should follow all the following principles except which?

(a) be low in Calories

(b) supply all essential nutrients

(c) contain bland foods to curb the intake of Calories

(d) be able to be accommodated within one's current lifestyle

(e) be a lifelong diet

8. The rate of weight loss on an appropriate low-Calorie diet may be rapid at first, but then may slow down. This decreased rate of weight loss is most likely due to:

(a) an increased BMR and increased use of body-protein stores

(b) a decrease in body weight and increased use of body-fat stores

(c) an increased use of carbohydrate stores and retention of body water

(d) a decreased BMR and an increased loss of body-water stores

(e) an increased BMR and decreased use of body-fat stores

9. Which of the following substitutes would not save Calories in a diet plan?

(a) skim milk in place of whole milk

(b) regular hard-stick margarine in place of butter

(c) plain yogurt in place of sour cream on a baked potato

(d) nonalcoholic beer in place of regular beer

(e) air-popped popcorn in place of potato chips

10. An example of a behavior-modification program for a weight-loss program is

(a) Feel guilty after you overeat.

(b) Eat fast so there is no visible food to tempt you to eat more.

(c) Keep a record of your eating habits so you can see what situations cause you to overeat.

(d) Always clean your plate when you eat.

(e) Always wait until you are hungry to go food shopping.

Answers to multiple choice questions:
1. b; 2. e; 3. c; 4. c; 5. b; 6. e; 7. c; 8. b; 9. b; 10. c.

Review Questions—Essay

1. Melinda wants to lose 30 pounds by summer, which is 20 weeks away. She currently weighs 150 pounds and is maintaining her body weight with an energy intake of 14 Calories per pound body weight. Based on dietary changes only, calculate her daily energy needs during the first week of the diet if she wants to lose weight at a steady level over the 20-week period.

2. Explain the concept of behavior modification in a weight-loss program, and describe some of the strategies one might employ to help change undesirable behaviors.

3. Discuss the positives and negatives of the high-carbohydrate, low-fat diet and the high-protein, high-fat, low-carbohydrate diet. What appears to be the key factor underlying the potential success of each on a short-term basis?

4. Discuss the importance of mode, intensity, duration, and frequency of exercise in a weight-loss program, and provide an example of an appropriate program incorporating each for a physically fit individual who wanted to lose one pound per week through exercise alone.

5. Both dieting and exercise may be helpful in a weight-loss program, but each may possess some drawbacks. Explain how the benefits of exercise may help counteract the possible drawbacks of dieting, and vice versa.

References

Books

Agatston, A. 2003. *The South Beach Diet.* Emmaus, PA: Rodale Press.

American Diabetes Association and American Dietetic Association. 1995. *Exchange Lists for Meal Planning.* Chicago: American Dietetic Association and American Diabetes Association.

Atkins, R. C. 1999. *Dr. Atkins' New Diet Revolution: Revised and Updated.* New York: M. Evans.

Cooper, K. 1982. *The Aerobics Program for Total Well-Being.* New York: M. Evans.

Dusek, D. 1989. *Weight Management: The Fitness Way.* Boston: Jones and Bartlett.

Institute of Medicine. 1994. *Weighing the Options: Criteria for Evaluating Weight Management Programs.* Washington, DC: National Academy Press.

Kirby, J. 1998. *Dieting for Dummies.* Foster City, CA: IDG Books.

Mayer, J. 1968. *Overweight: Causes, Cost and Control.* Englewood Cliffs, NJ: Prentice-Hall.

Miller, W. 1998. *Negotiated Peace. How to Win the War Over Weight.* Boston: Allyn and Bacon.

National Academy of Sciences. 2002. *Dietary Reference Intakes for Energy, Carbohydrates, Fiber, Fat, Protein and Amino Acids (Macronutrients).* Washington, DC: National Academy Press.

National Research Council. 1989. *Recommended Dietary Allowances.* Washington, DC: National Academy Press.

Pritikin, R. 2000. *The Pritikin Principle.* Alexandria, VA: Time-Life Books.

Rolls, B. 2005. *The Volumetrics Eating Plan.* New York: HarperCollins.

Sears, B. 1995. *The Zone.* New York: Regan Books.

Shils, M., et al. 2006. *Modern Nutrition in Health and Disease.* Philadelphia: Lippincott Williams & Wilkins.

U.S. Department of Health and Human Services. Public Health Service. 1996. *The Surgeon General's Report on Physical Activity and Health.* Washington, DC: U.S. Government Printing Office.

Reviews

American College of Sports Medicine. 2001. ACSM Position Stand on the Appropriate Intervention Strategies for Weight Loss and Prevention of Weight Regain for Adults. *Medicine & Science in Sports & Exercise* 33:2145–56.

American College of Sports Medicine. 1998. The recommended quantity and quality of exercise for developing and maintaining cardiorespiratory and muscular fitness and flexibility in healthy adults. *Medicine & Science in Sports & Exercise* 30:975–91.

American Diabetes Association. 2000. Role of fat replacers in diabetes medical nutrition therapy. *Diabetes Care* 23:S96–S97.

American Dietetic Association. 2002. Position of the American Dietetic Association: Weight management. *Journal of the American Dietetic Association* 102:1145–545.

American Dietetic Association. 1997. Position of the American Dietetic Association: Weight management. *Journal of the American Dietetic Association* 97:71–74.

American Heart Association. 2000. American Heart Association Dietary Guidelines. *Circulation* 102:2284–99.

American Heart Association Scientific Council. 1992. Position statement on exercise. Benefits and recommendations for physical activity programs for all Americans. *Circulation* 86:340–44.

Andersen, R. E. 1999. Exercise, an active lifestyle, and obesity. *Physician and Sportsmedicine* 27(10):41–50.

Astrup, A. 2001. The role of dietary fat in the prevention and treatment of obesity. Efficacy and safety of low-fat diets. *International Journal of Obesity and Related Metabolic Disorders* 25:S46–S50.

Astrup, A., et al. 2002. Low-fat diets and energy balance: How does the evidence stand in 2002? *Proceedings of the Nutrition Society* 61:299–309.

Atkinson, R. 1989. Low and very low calorie diets. *Medical Clinics of North America* 73:203–16.

Avenell, A., 2004. What interventions should we add to weight reducing diets in adults with obesity? A systematic review of randomized controlled trials of adding drug therapy, exercise, behavior therapy or combinations of these interventions. *Journal of Human Nutrition and Dietetics* 17:293–316.

Bean, A. 1997. A new way to monitor effort. *Runners World* 32 (9):22.

Bellisle, F., et al. 1997. Meal frequency and energy balance. *British Journal of Nutrition* 77 (Supplement): S57–S70.

Blundell, J., and Green, S. 1997. Effect of sucrose and sweeteners on appetite and energy intake. *International Journal of Obesity and Related Metabolic Disorders* 20 (Supplement 2): S12–S17.

Blundell, J. E., and King, N. A. 1998. Effects of exercise on appetite control: Loose coupling between energy expenditure and energy intake. *International Journal of Obesity and Related Metabolic Disorders* 22 (Supplement 2):S22–S29.

Borg, G. 1973. Perceived exertion: A note on "history" and methods. *Medicine & Science in Sports* 5:90–93.

Bouchard, C., and Blair, S. 1999. Introductory comments for the consensus on physical activity and obesity. *Medicine & Science in Sports & Exercise* 31:S498–S501.

Bravata, D., et al. 2003. Efficacy and safety of low-carbohydrate diets: A systematic review. *JAMA* 289:1837–50.

Bray, G. 1990. Exercise and obesity. In *Exercise, Fitness and Health,* eds. C. Bouchard, et al. Champaign, IL: Human Kinetics.

Bren, L. 2002. Losing weight: More than just counting calories. *FDA Consumer* 36 (1):18–25.

Brownell, K., and Kramer, F. 1989. Behavioral management of obesity. *Medical Clinics of North America* 73:185–202.

Brownell, K., and Rodin, J. 1994. The dieting maelstrom: Is it possible and advisable to lose weight? *American Psychologist* 49:781–91.

Committee to Develop Criteria for Evaluating the Outcomes of Approaches to Prevent and Treat Obesity. 1995. Summary: Weighing the options—Criteria for evaluating weight-management programs. *Journal of the American Dietetic Association* 95:96–105.

Consumers Union. 2005. 7 steps to a stable weight. *Consumer Reports on Health* 17 (8):8–9.

Consumers Union. 2005. Rating the diets. *Consumer Reports* 70 (6)1818–22.

Consumers Union. 2004. Outwitting your appetite. *Consumer Reports on Health* 16 (9):8–10.

Consumers Union. 2003. Eat more without gaining weight. *Consumer Reports on Health* 15 (6):8–9.

Consumers Union. 2000. Secrets of successful losers. *Consumer Reports on Health* 12 (1):1–4.

Consumers Union. 1998. Exercise: Special section. *Consumer Reports* 63:20–29.

Consumers Union. 1996. Health clubs: The right choice for you. *Consumer Reports* 61:27–30.

Convertino, V. 1991. Blood volume: Its adaptation to endurance training. *Medicine & Science in Sports & Exercise* 23:1338–48.

Corbin, C., et al. 2002. Making sense of multiple physical activity recommendations. *President's Council on Physical Fitness and Sports Research Digest* 3 (19):1–8

Davey, R. 2004. The obesity epidemic: Too much food for thought? *British Journal of Sports Medicine* 38:360–63.

Drewnowski, A. 1995. Intense sweeteners and the control of appetite. *Nutrition Reviews* 53:1–7.

Eisenstein, J., et al. 2002. High-protein weight-loss diets: Are they safe and do they work: A review of the experimental and epidemiologic data. *Nutrition Reviews* 60:189–200.

Epstein, L., et al. 1996. Exercise in treating obesity in children and adolescents. *Medicine & Science in Sports & Exercise* 28:428–35.

Friedman, A. 2004. High protein diets: Potential effects on the kidney in renal health and disease. *American Journal of Kidney Disease* 44:950–62.

Gaesser, G. A. 1999. Thinness and weight loss: Beneficial or detrimental to longevity? *Medicine & Science in Sports & Exercise* 31:1118–28.

Garfinkel, P., and Coscina, D. 1990. Discussion: Exercise and obesity. In *Exercise, Fitness, and Health,* eds. C. Bouchard, et al. Champaign, IL: Human Kinetics.

Grundy, S. M., et al. 1999. Physical activity in the prevention and treatment of obesity and its comorbidities. *Medicine & Science in Sports & Exercise* 31:S502–S509.

Hill, J., and Commerford, R. 1996. Physical activity, fat balance, and energy balance. *International Journal of Sport Nutrition* 6:80–92.

Hill, J., et al. 1994. Physical activity, fitness, and moderate obesity. In *Physical Activity, Fitness, and Health,* eds. C. Bouchard, et al. Champaign, IL: Human Kinetics.

Howarth, N., et al. 2001. Dietary fiber and weight regulation. *Nutrition Reviews* 59:129–39.

Hunter, G. R., et al. 1998. A role for high intensity exercise on energy balance and weight control. *International Journal of Obesity and Related Metabolic Disorders* 22:489–93.

Hurley, J., and Liebman, B. 2005. Fast food in '05. *Nutrition Action Health Letter* 32 (2):12–15.

Jakicic, J., and Gallagher, K. 2003. Exercise considerations for the sedentary, over-weight adult. *Exercise and Sport Sciences Reviews* 31:91–95.

Jequier, E. 2000. Pathways to obesity. *International Journal of Obesity and Related Metabolic Disorders* 26:S12–S17.

Jeukendrup, A., and Aldred, S. 2004. Fat supplementation, health, and endurance performance. *Nutrition* 20:678–88.

King, N. A. 1999. What processes are involved in the appetite response to moderate increases in exercise-induced energy expenditure? *Proceedings of the Nutrition Society* 58:107–13.

King, N., et al. 1997. Effects of exercise on appetite control: Implications for energy balance. *Medicine & Science in Sports & Exercise* 29:1076–89.

Klein, S. 2004. Clinical trial experience with fat-restricted vs. carbohydrate-restricted weight-loss diets. *Obesity Research* 12:141S–44S.

Kris-Etherton, P., et al. 2002. Dietary fat: Assessing the evidence in support of a moderate-fat diet; The benchmark based on lipoprotein metabolism. *Proceedings of the Nutrition Society* 61:287–98.

Lamarche, B., and Desroches, S. 2004. Metabolic syndrome and effects of conjugated linoleic acid in obesity and lipoprotein disorders: The Quebec experience. *American Journal of Clinical Nutrition* 79:1149S–52S.

Levin, B. 2002. Metabolic sensors: Viewing glucosensing neurons from a broader perspective. *Physiology & Behavior* 76:387–401.

Levine, J., and Kotz, C. 2005. NEAT–non-exercise activity thermogenesis—egocentric & geocentric environmental factors vs. biological regulation. *Acta Physiologica Scandinavica* 184:309–18.

Liebman, B. 2005. Bigger meals: Smaller waists. *Nutrition Action Health Letter* 32 (5):1–7.

Liebman, B. 2004. Weighing the diet books. *Nutrition Action Health Letter* 31 (1):3–8.

Lohman, T., et al. 2004. Seeing ourselves through the obesity epidemic. *President's Council on Physical Fitness and Sports Research Digest* 5 (3):1–8.

Manore, M. M. 1999. Low-fat foods and weight loss. *ACSM's Health & Fitness Journal* 3 (3):37–39.

Mattes, R. D. 1998. Position of the American Dietetic Association: Fat replacers. *Journal of the American Dietetic Association* 98:463–68.

Melby, C. L., and Hill, J. O. 1999. Exercise, macronutrient balance, and body weight regulation. *Sports Science Exchange* 12 (1):1–6.

Miller, G., and Groziak, S. 1996. Impact of fat substitutes on fat intake. *Lipids* 31:S293–S296.

Miller, W. 2001. Effective diet and exercise treatments for overweight and recommendations for intervention. *Sports Medicine* 31:717–24.

Miller, W. 1999. How effective are traditional dietary and exercise interventions for weight loss? *Medicine & Science in Sports & Exercise* 31:1129–34.

National Institutes of Health. 1992. Methods for voluntary weight loss and control. Technology Assessment Conference Statement. *Nutrition Today* 50 (July/August): 27–33.

Pi-Sunyer, F. X. 1999. Obesity. In *Modern Nutrition in Health and Disease,* eds. M. Shils, et al. Baltimore: Williams & Wilkins.

Pi-Sunyer, F. X. 1990. Effect of the composition of the diet on energy intake. *Nutrition Reviews* 48:94–105.

Poehlman, E. T., and Melby, C. 1998. Resistance training and energy balance. *International Journal of Sport Nutrition* 8:143–59.

Riley, R. E. 1999. Popular weight loss diets. *Clinics in Sports Medicine* 18:691–701.

Rippe, J. M., et al. 1998. Obesity as a chronic disease: Modern medical and lifestyle management. *Journal of the American Dietetic Association* 98 (Supplement 2):S9–S15.

Roberts, S. 2000. High-glycemic index foods, hunger, and obesity: Is there a connection? *Nutrition Reviews* 58:163–69.

Robinson, T. 2001. Television viewing and childhood obesity. *Pediatric Clinics of North America* 48:1017–25.

Rolls, B. J., and Bell, E. A. 1999. Intake of fat and carbohydrate: Role of energy density. *European Journal of Clinical Nutrition* 53:S166–S173.

Ross, R., et al. 2000. Exercise alone is an effective strategy for reducing obesity and related comorbidities. *Exercise and Sport Sciences Reviews* 28: 165–70.

Saris, W. 1993. The role of exercise in the dietary treatment of obesity. *International Journal of Obesity* 17(1): S17–S21.

Schardt, D. 2005. Weight loss in a bottle? *Nutrition Action Health Letter* 32 (4):10–12.

Smith, S. R., and Zachwieja, J. J. 1999. Visceral adipose tissue: A critical review of intervention strategies. *International Journal of Obesity and Related Metabolic Disorders* 23:329–35.

St. Jeor, S., et al. 2001. Dietary protein and weight reduction: A statement for health-care professionals from the Nutrition Committee of the Council on Nutrition, Physical Activity, and Metabolism of the American Heart Association. *Circulation* 104:1869–74.

Swain, D., and Franklin, B. 2006. Comparison of cardioprotective benefits of vigorous versus moderate intensity aerobic exercise. *American Journal of Cardiology* 97:141–47.

Thompson, J., et al. 1996. Effects of diet and diet-plus-exercise programs on resting metabolic rate: A meta-analysis. *International Journal of Sport Nutrition* 6:41–61.

Tremblay, A., et al. 1999. Physical activity and weight maintenance. *International Journal of Obesity and Related Metabolic Disorders* 23 (Supplement 3):S50–S54.

Tremblay, A., and Doucet, E. 1999. Influence of intense physical activity on energy balance and body fatness. *Proceedings of the Nutrition Society* 58:99–105.

Tsai, A., and Wadden, T. 2005. Systematic review: An evaluation of major commercial weight loss programs in the United States. *Annals of Internal Medicine* 142:56–66.

Tudor-Locke, C., and Bassett, D. 2004. How many steps/day are enough? Preliminary pedometer indices for public health. *Sports Medicine* 34:1–8.

Volek, J., et al. 2005. Diet and exercise for weight loss: A review of current issues. *Sports Medicine* 35:1–9.

Volek, J., and Sharman, M. 2004. Cardiovascular and hormonal aspects of very-low-carbohydrate ketogenic diets. *Obesity Research* 12:115S–23S.

Wadden, T., et al. 2004. Efficacy of lifestyle modification for long-term weight control. *Obesity Research* 12:151S–62S.

Walberg-Rankin, J. 2000. Forfeit the fat, leave the lean: Optimizing weight loss for athletes. *Sports Science Exchange* 13 (1):1–4.

Westerterp-Plantenga, M. 2004. Fat intake and energy-balance efforts. *Physiology & Behavior* 83:579–85.

Wing, R., and Hill, J. 2001. Successful weight loss maintenance. *Annual Reviews in Nutrition* 21:323–41.

Wood, P. 1996. Clinical applications of diet and physical activity in weight loss. *Nutrition Reviews* 54:S131–S135.

Wylie-Rosett, J., et al. 2004. Carbohydrates and increases in obesity: Does the type of carbohydrate make a difference? *Obesity Research* 12:124S–29S.

Specific Studies

Benezra, L., et al. 2001. Intakes of most nutrients remain at acceptable levels during a weight management program using the food exchange system. *Journal of the American Dietetic Association* 101:554–61.

Bryner, R. W., et al. 1999. Effects of resistance vs aerobic training combined with an 800 calorie liquid diet on lean body mass and resting metabolic rate. *Journal of the American College of Nutrition* 18:115–21.

Cotton, J., et al. 1996. Replacement of dietary fat with sucrose polyester: Effects on energy intake and appetite control in nonobese males. *American Journal of Clinical Nutrition* 63:891–96.

Dansinger, M., et al. 2005. Comparison of the Atkins, Ornish, Watchers, and Zone diets for weight loss and heart disease risk reduction: A randomized trial. *JAMA* 293:43–53.

Dich, J., et al. 2000. Effects of excessive isocaloric intake of either carbohydrate or fat on body composition, fat mass, de novo lipogenesis and energy expenditure in normal young men. *Ugeskrift for Laeger* 162:4794–99.

DiPietro, L., et al. 2004. Estimated change in physical activity level (PAL) and prediction of 5-year weight change in men: The Aerobics Center Longitudinal Study. *International Journal of Obesity and Related Metabolic Disorders* 28:1541–47.

Dolezal, B. A., and Potteiger, J. A. 1998. Concurrent resistance and endurance training influence basal metabolic rate in nondieting individuals. *Journal of Applied Physiology* 85:695–700.

Foster, G., et al. 2003. A randomized trial of a low-carbohydrate diet for obesity. *New England Journal of Medicine* 348:2082–90.

Foster-Schubert, K., et al. 2005. Human plasma ghrelin levels increase during a one-year exercise program. *Journal of Clinical Endocrinology and Metabolism* 90:820–25.

Franco, O., et al. 2005. Effects of physical activity on life expectancy with cardiovascular diseases. *Archives of Internal Medicine* 165:2355–60.

Gaullier, J., et al. 2004. Conjugated linoleic acid supplementatin for 1 y reduces body fat in healthy overweight humans. *American Journal of Clinical Nutrition* 79:1118–25.

Grediagin, M., et al. 1995. Exercise intensity does not effect body composition change in untrained, moderately overfat women. *Journal of the American Dietetic Association* 95:661–65.

Hall, C., et al. 2004. Energy expenditure of walking and running: Comparison with prediction equations. *Medicine & Science in Sports & Exercise* 36:2128–34.

Haus, G., et al. 1994. Key modifiable factors in weight maintenance: fat intake, exercise, and weight cycling. *Journal of the American Diebetic* Association 94:409–13.

Howard, B., et al. 2006. Low-fat dietary pattern and weight change over 7 years: The Women's Health Initiative Dietary Modification Trial. *JAMA* 295:39–49.

Hultquist, C., et al. 2005. Comparison of walking recommendations in previously inactive women. *Medicine & Science in Sports & Exercise* 37:676–83.

Jakicic, J., et al. 1995. Prescribing exercise in multiple short bouts versus one continuous bout: Effects on adherence, cardiorespiratory fitness, and weight loss in overweight women. *International Journal of Obesity and Related Metabolic Disorders* 19:893–901.

Johnston, C., et al. 2004. High-protein, low-fat diets are effective for weight loss and favorably alter biomarkers in healthy adults. *Journal of Nutrition* 134:586–91.

Johnston, C., et al. 2002. Postprandial thermogenesis is increased 100% on high-protein, low-fat diet versus a high-carbohydrate, low-fat diet in healthy, young women. *Journal of the American College of Nutrition* 21:55–61.

Knight, E., et al. 2003. The impact of protein intake on renal function decline in women with normal renal function or mild renal insufficiency. *Annals of Internal Medicine* 138:460–67.

Kraemer, W. J., et al. 1999. Influence of exercise training on physiological and performance changes with weight loss in men. *Medicine & Science in Sports & Exercise* 31:1320–29.

Kruger, J., et al. 2005. Physical activity profiles of U.S. adults trying to lose weight: NHIS 1998. *Medicine & Science in Sports & Exercise* 37:364–68.

Ludwig, D., et al. 2001. Relation between consumption of sugar-sweetened drinks and childhood obesity: A prospective, observational analysis. *Lancet* 357:505–8.

Mayo, M., et al. 2003. Exercise-induced weight loss preferentially reduces abdominal fat. *Medicine & Science in Sports & Exercise* 35:207–13.

McCargar, L., and Crawford, S. 1992. Metabolic and anthropometric changes with weight cycling in wrestlers. *Medicine & Science in Sports & Exercise* 24:1270–75.

Melanson, E., et al. 2002. Resistance and aerobic exercise have similar effects on 24-h nutrient oxidation. *Medicine & Science in Sports & Exercise* 34:1783–1800.

Melanson, E., et al. 2002. Effect of exercise intensity on 24-h energy expenditure and nutrient oxidation. *Journal of Applied Physiology* 92:1045–52.

Miller, W., et al. 1993. Cardiovascular risk reduction in a self-taught, self-administered weight loss program called the nondiet diet. *Medicine & Science in Sports & Exercise* 25:218–23.

Miller, W., et al. 1990. Diet composition, energy intake, and exercise in relation to body fat in men and women. *American Journal of Clinical Nutrition* 52:426–30.

Moloney, F., et al. 2004. Conjugated linoleic acid supplementation, insulin sensitivity, and lipoprotein metabolism in patients with type 2 diabetes mellitus. *American Journal of Clinical Nutrition* 80:887–95.

Murphy, M., et al. 2002. Accumulating brisk walking for fitness, cardiovascular risk, and psychological health. *Medicine & Science in Sports & Exercise* 34:1468–74.

Newman, B., et al. 1990. Nongenetic influences of obesity on other cardiovascular disease risk factors: An analysis of identical twins. *American Journal of Public Health* 80:675–78.

Nitzke, S., et al. 1992. Weight cycling practices and long-term health conditions in a sample of former wrestlers and other collegiate athletes. *Journal of Athletic Training* 27:257–61.

Persinger, R., et al. 2004. Consistency of the Talk Test for exercise prescription. *Medicine & Science in Sports & Exercise* 36:1632–36.

Pomerleau, M., et al. 2004. Effects of exercise intensity on food intake and appetite in women. *American Journal of Clinical Nutrition* 80:1230–36.

Pritchard, J., et al. 1997. A worksite program for overweight middle-aged men achieves lesser weight loss with exercise than with dietary change. *Journal of the American Dietetic Association* 97:37–42.

Raben, A., et al. 2002. Sucrose compared with artificial sweeteners: Different effects on ad libitum food intake and body weight after 10 wk of supplementation in overweight subjects. *American Journal of Clinical Nutrition* 76:721–29.

Romijn, J., et al. 2000. Substrate metabolism during different exercise intensities in endurance-trained women. *Journal of Applied Physiology* 88:1707–14.

Samaras, K., et al. Genetic and environmental influences on total-body and central abdominal fat: The effect of physical activity in female twins. *Annals of Internal Medicine* 130:873–82.

Shick, S. M., et al. 1998. Persons successful at long-term weight loss and maintenance continue to consume a low-energy, low-fat diet. *Journal of the American Dietetic Association* 98:408–13.

Schmidt, W., et al. 1993. Two competitive seasons of weight cycling does not lower resting metabolic rate in college wrestlers. *Medicine & Science in Sports & Exercise* 25:613–19.

Schoeller, D., et al. 1997. How much physical activity is needed to minimize weight gain in previously obese women? *American Journal of Clinical Nutrition* 66:551–56.

Sedlock, D., et al. 1989. Effect of exercise intensity and duration on postexercise energy expenditure. *Medicine & Science in Sports & Exercise* 21:662–66.

Shide, D., and Rolls, B. 1995. Information about the fat content of preloads influences energy intake in healthy women. *Journal of the American Dietetic Association* 95:993–98.

Sjodin, A., et al. 1996. The influence of physical activity on BMR. *Medicine & Science in Sports & Exercise* 28:85–91.

Stubbs, R., et al. 2004. A decrease in physical activity affects appetite, energy, and nutrient balance in lean men feeding ad libitum. *American Journal of Clinical Nutrition* 79:62–69.

Tanaka, H., et al. 2001. Age-predicted maximal heart rate revisited. *Journal of the American College of Cardiology* 37:153–56.

Thompson, D., et al. 2004. Relationship between accumulated walking and body composition in middle-aged women. *Medicine & Science in Sports & Exercise* 36:911–14.

Thompson, D., et al. 1988. Acute effects of exercise intensity on appetite in young men. *Medicine & Science in Sports & Exercise* 20:222–27.

Utter, A., et al. 2004. Validation of the adult OMNI scale of perceived exertion for walking/running exercise. *Medicine & Science in Sports & Exercise* 36:1776–80.

Weigle, D., et al. 2005. A high-protein diet induces sustained reductions in appetite, ad libitum caloric intake, and body weight despite compensatory changes in diurnal plasma leptin and ghrelin concentrations. *American Journal of Clinical Nutrition* 82:41–48.

Westman, E., et al. 2002. Effect of a 6-month adherence to a very low carbohydrate diet program. *American Journal of Medicine* 113:30–36.

Zeni, A., et al. 1996. Energy expenditure with indoor exercise machines. *Journal of the American Medical Association* 275:1424–27.

Weight Gaining through Proper Nutrition and Exercise

CHAPTER TWELVE

LEARNING OBJECTIVES

After studying this chapter, you should be able to:

1. Describe the steps an individual might take in order to gain body weight, mainly as muscle mass.

2. List and explain the five principles of resistance training.

3. Understand the basic differences among resistance-training programs for muscular hypertrophy, muscular strength and power, and muscular endurance.

4. Design a total-body resistance-training program for an individual who desires to gain body weight as muscle mass.

5. Identify the potential health benefits of resistance exercise and compare them to the health benefits associated with aerobic endurance exercise, noting similarities and differences.

6. Plan a diet for an individual who desires to gain muscle mass in concert with a resistance-training program, focusing on recommended caloric intake and foods compatible with the Prudent Healthy Diet.

7. Identify dietary supplements used by physically active individuals to stimulate muscle building and body-fat loss, and list those, if any, which may be effective.

As noted in the previous chapter, there are basically three reasons why individuals attempt to lose excess body weight—to improve appearance, health, or athletic performance. Some individuals may also wish to gain weight for the same three reasons, and may use resistance training, also known as weight training or strength training, as a means to stimulate weight gain.

For those who wish to improve appearance, resistance training will increase muscularity, a desired physical attribute among many males and an increasing number of females. Resistance training is becoming increasingly popular, particularly among women. Based on epidemiological studies, Galuska and others recently estimated that almost 9 percent of American adults age 17 and over engage in regular weight training, nearly 13 percent of males and 5 percent of females.

Gaining weight, particularly muscle mass stimulated by resistance training, may also be associated with some health benefits. An increased muscularity that improves physical appearance and body image may help elevate self-esteem, contributing to positive psychological health. Additionally, resistance training is recommended for several other health benefits, such as increased bone mineral density, and has been recommended by the American Heart Association and the American College of Sports Medicine as an effective means to promote overall good health. Resistance training is particularly recommended for older adults to help prevent the muscle wasting, and associated health problems, seen with aging. A popular book, *Quick Weight-Gain Program* by Dr. David Reuben has been designed to provide sound medical advice for the 26 million Americans who need to gain weight for a variety of medical and cosmetic reasons.

Increased body weight, particularly increased muscle mass, may be associated with improvements in strength and power, two performance factors important for a wide variety of sports. Most colleges and universities, as well as many high schools, have strength-training programs for their athletes, both males and females. At the elite level, sport-specific resistance-training programs are tailored to the individual athlete.

No matter what the reason for gaining body weight, you should be concerned about where the extra pounds will be stored. The energy-balance equation works equally as well for gaining weight as it does for losing weight, but excess body fat in general will not improve physical appearance, health, or athletic performance. On the contrary, it may detract from all three. To put on body weight, you have to concentrate on means to increase the fat-free mass, particularly muscle tissue, with little or no increase in body-fat stores.

Rasmussen and Phillips note that resistance exercise and nutritional provision are two independent and major stimuli of muscle protein synthesis and overall muscle growth, and numerous related approaches have been employed to increase muscle mass. Specialized exercise equipment or exercise techniques are advertised as the most effective methods available to build muscles. Protein supplements have been a favorite among weight lifters for years, but today athletes can buy numerous dietary supplements that are advertised to produce an anabolic, or muscle-building, effect. Some athletes and nonathletes even use drugs to gain weight for enhanced performance or appearance, a topic that is discussed in chapter 13. Although resistance training may confer significant health benefits, Pope and others indicated some very muscular individuals have a distorted body image, perceiving themselves as too thin or not sufficiently muscular. This condition, which they labeled as muscle dysmorphia or the Adonis Complex, may lead to unhealthful practices, such as the use of drugs, to enhance muscularity. Interestingly, Pickett and others reported that muscle dysmorphia is not confined to competitive bodybuilders, but is also found in noncompetitive weight trainers and even physically active men who do not train with weights.

Like weight-loss programs, weight-gaining programs may be safe and effective or they can be potentially harmful to your health. Although gaining weight, particularly as muscle mass, is difficult for some individuals, the purpose of this chapter is to present basic information on the type of exercise and diet program that is most likely to be effective as a means to put on weight without compromising your health.

Basic Considerations

Why are some individuals underweight?

Being significantly under a healthy body weight may be due to several factors. Heredity may be an important factor, as genetic factors may predispose some individuals to leanness. For example, a lean body frame or high basal metabolic rate may have been acquired through your parents. Medical problems such as heartburn, infections, or cancer could adversely affect food intake and digestion, so a physician should be consulted to rule out nutritional problems caused by organic disease, hormonal imbalance, or inadequate absorption of nutrients. Social pressures, such as the strong desire of a teenage girl to have a slender body, could lead to undernutrition; an extreme example is anorexia nervosa, discussed in chapter 10. Emotional problems also may affect food intake. In many cases, food intake is increased during periods of emotional crisis, but the appetite may also be depressed in some individuals for long periods. Economic hardships may reduce food purchasing power, so some individuals simply may sacrifice food intake for other life necessities.

Being considerably underweight, such as a Body Mass Index below 18.5, may be considered a symptom of malnutrition or undernutrition. It is important to determine the cause before prescribing a treatment. Our concern here is the individual who does not have any of these medical, psychological, social, or economic problems but who simply cannot create a positive energy balance because of excess energy expenditure or insufficient energy (Calorie) intake. Caloric intake has to be increased, and the output has to be modified somewhat.

What steps should I take if I want to gain weight?

The following guidelines may help you develop an effective program to maximize your gains in muscle mass and keep body-fat increases relatively low.

1. Have an acceptable purpose for the weight gain. The desire for an improved physical appearance and body image may be reason enough. For athletes, increased muscle mass may be important for a variety of sports, particularly if strength and power are improved. However, you do not want to gain weight at the expense of speed if speed is important to your sport.
2. Calculate your average energy needs daily as discussed in chapter 11. For a weight-gain program, you may wish to use several techniques to estimate your daily energy needs and select the highest value.
3. Keep a 3- to 7-day record of what you normally eat. See pages 414–417 for guidelines to determine your average daily caloric intake. If the obtained value is less than your energy needs calculated under item 2 in this list, this may be a reason why you are not gaining weight.
4. Check your living habits. Do you get enough rest and sleep? If not, you are burning more energy than the estimate in point 2 of this list. Smoking increases your metabolic rate almost 10 percent and may account for approximately 200 Calories per day. Caffeine in coffee and soft drinks also increases the metabolic rate for several hours. Getting enough rest and sleep and eliminating smoking and caffeine will help decrease your energy output.
5. Set a reasonable goal within a certain time period. Weight gain may be rapid at first but then tapers off as one nears his or her genetic potential. Peter Lemon, an expert in resistance training and protein metabolism, recently indicated that someone starting a resistance-training program may increase

body mass by 20 percent in the first year. After that, gains are somewhat less, possibly only 1–3 percent per year. In general, about 0.5–1 pound per week is a sound approach for a novice, but weight gaining is difficult for some individuals and may occur at a slower rate. Specific goals may also include muscular hypertrophy in various parts of the body.

6. Increase your caloric intake. A properly designed diet should include adequate Calories and protein and not violate the principles of healthful nutrition.
7. Start a resistance-training exercise program. This type of exercise program will serve as a stimulus to build muscle tissue.
8. Use a good cloth or steel tape to take body measurements before and during your weight-gaining program. Be sure you measure at the same points about once a week. Those body parts measured should include the neck, upper and lower arm, chest, abdomen, hips, thigh, and calf. This is to ensure that body-weight gains are proportionately distributed. You should look for good gains in the chest and limbs; the abdominal and hip girth increase should be kept low because that is where fat is more likely to be stored. If available, skinfold calipers may be used to measure subcutaneous fat skinfolds at multiple sites over the body. Fat skinfold thicknesses should remain the same or decrease to ensure that the weight gain is muscle not fat.

In summary, adequate rest, increased caloric intake, and a proper resistance-training program may be very effective as a means to gain the right kind of body weight.

Key Concept Recap

▶ There may be a variety of reasons why an individual is underweight, and the cause should be determined before a treatment is prescribed.
▶ For those who want to gain weight, a weekly increase of 0.5–1 pound is a sound approach, but the weight gain should be primarily muscle tissue and not body fat.
▶ In essence, adequate rest and sleep, increased caloric intake, and a proper resistance-training program should be effective in helping to increase lean body mass.

Exercise Considerations

In the last chapter we discussed the design of an aerobic exercise program for the loss of excess body fat but also mentioned that a resistance-training program could be helpful, for it might help prevent the loss of lean body mass and maintain normal resting-energy expenditure. In this chapter the focus is upon resistance training, sometimes called weight training, as a means to increase lean body mass and body weight. Before we discuss the principles underlying the design of a proper resistance-training program, let us introduce some basic terminology.

Repetition simply means the number of times you do a specific exercise. *Intensity* is determined by the weight, or resistance, that is lifted. A term used to describe the interrelationship between repetitions and intensity in weight training is **repetition maximum (RM).** If you perform an exercise such as a bench press and lift 150 pounds once, but you cannot do a second repetition, you have done one repetition maximum, or 1RM. If you bench press a lighter weight, say 120 pounds, for five repetitions but cannot do a sixth, you have done five repetition maximum, or 5RM. A *set* is any particular number of repetitions, such as five or ten. The total volume of work you do in a single workout is the product of sets, repetitions, and resistance. For example, if you bench press three sets of five repetitions with a resistance of 100 pounds, your total volume of work is 1,500 pounds ($3 \times 5 \times 100$). The *recovery period* may represent the rest intervals between sets in a single workout or the rest interval between workouts during the week.

What are the primary purposes of resistance training?

As is probably obvious to you, there is an inverse relationship between the amount of weight you can lift and the number of repetitions you can do. If your 1RM in the bench press is 150 pounds, you can do more repetitions with 100 pounds than you can with 140. The **strength-endurance continuum** is a training concept that focuses upon the interrelationship between resistance and repetitions. As depicted in figure 12.1, to train for strength you must combine high resistance with a low number of repetitions. Conversely, to train for endurance, you must combine a low resistance with a high number of repetitions.

Resistance-training programs may be designed to train all three of the human energy systems. The ATP-PCr energy system predominates in strength and power activities, the lactic acid energy system is primarily involved in anaerobic endurance, and the oxygen system is involved in aerobic endurance activities. Thus, resistance-training programs may be developed for various purposes.

The American College of Sports Medicine (ACSM) has developed two position stands dealing with resistance exercise. One focuses on resistance training as a component of an overall exercise program to improve muscular strength and endurance in healthy adults. The second deals with progression, or the gradual increase in overload placed on the body during training, and is more appropriate for the individual training to maximize muscular size and strength for bodybuilding or sport competition. These position stands highlight the following purposes of resistance training, along with the recommended type of program.

Training for Muscular Hypertrophy Higher volume, multiple-set programs are recommended for maximizing muscle hypertrophy. Emphasize a range of 6–12 RM per set.

Training for Strength and Power Multiple sets with fewer repetitions are recommended to maximize strength and power.

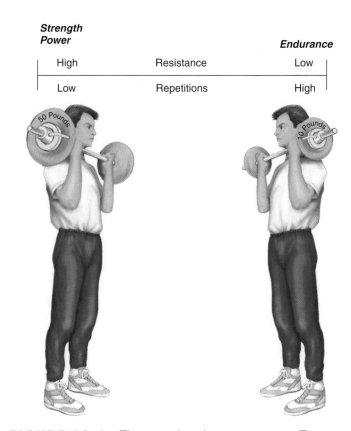

Strength Power		Endurance
High	Resistance	Low
Low	Repetitions	High

FIGURE 12.1 The strength-endurance continuum. To gain strength, you need to train on the strength end of the continuum; to gain endurance, you need to train on the endurance end of the continuum.

Emphasize a range of 4–6 RM per set. Also, incorporate multiple sets of light loads (30–60 percent of 1 RM) at a fast contraction velocity.

Training for Local Muscular Endurance Multiple sets with more repetitions and light to moderate loads, such as 15 or more repetitions at 40–60 percent of 1 RM, are recommended. Use a short recovery period between sets.

Using the two ACSM position stands as the foundation, let us look at the basic principles of resistance-training programs and how they are related to gains in body weight and muscle mass and possible health benefits as well.

What are the basic principles of resistance training?

The following five principles are not restricted to resistance training but apply to all forms of training, even aerobic exercise training programs as introduced in chapter 11. For example, intensity of exercise is simply another way of phrasing the overload principle.

The **principle of overload** is the most important principle in all resistance-training programs. The use of weights places a greater than normal stress on the muscle cell. This overload stress stimulates the muscle to grow—to become stronger—in effect to overcome the increased resistance imposed by the weights (see figure 12.2).

To overload the muscle you must increase the volume of work it must do. There are basically two ways to do this. One is to increase the amount of resistance or weight that you use; the other way is to increase the number of repetitions and sets you do. For beginners, a single set of 8 to 10 exercises will help increase muscle mass and strength gains. Wolfe and others conducted a meta-analysis of available studies, and reported that single-set programs for an initial short training period in untrained individuals result in similar strength gains as multiple-set programs. If you know your 1RM, you should be able to do 8 to 12 RM if you use 60 to 80 percent of your 1RM value. For example, if your bench press 1RM is 150 pounds, you should be able to do at least 8RM with 70 percent of that value, or 105 pounds ($.70 \times 150$).

As the muscle continues to get stronger during your training program, you must increase the amount of resistance, the overload, to continue to get the proper stimulus for sustained muscle growth. This is known as **principle of progressive resistance exercise (PRE),** another basic principle of resistance training.

In their meta-analysis, Wolfe and others noted that as progression occurs and higher gains are desired, multiple-set programs are more effective. Following a learning period, a recommended program for beginners is three to five sets and the ACSM recommends novices should use loads corresponding to 8–12 RM. The first step is to determine the maximum amount of weight that you can lift for eight repetitions. If you can do more than eight repetitions, the weight is too light and you need to add more poundage. As you get stronger during the succeeding weeks, you will be able to lift the original weight more easily. When you can perform twelve repetitions, add more weight to force you back down to eight repetitions; this is the progressive resistance principle. Over several months' time, the weight will probably need to be increased several times as you continue to get stronger. Such a transition is illustrated in figure 12.3. The ACSM recommends that as you become an intermediate or advanced lifter, you should emphasize loads of 1–6 RM and progress when you can do about 1–2 more repetitions than the upper limit of the range. For example, if you are using the 6 RM protocol, you might add resistance when you can do 8 repetitions.

The **principle of specificity** is a broad training principle with many implications for resistance training, including specificity for various sports movements, strength gains, endurance gains, and body-weight gains. For example, a swimmer who wants to gain strength and endurance for a stroke should attempt to find a resistance-weight training program that exercises the specific muscles in a way as close as possible to the form used in that stroke. If you want to gain muscle mass in a certain part of the body, those muscles must be exercised.

Your exercise routine should be based upon the **principle of exercise sequence.** This means that if you have ten exercises in your routine, they should be arranged in logical order so that fatigue does not limit your lifting ability. For example, the first exercise in a sequence of ten might stress the biceps muscle, the second the abdominals, the third the quadriceps, and so forth. After you perform one full set of each of the ten exercises, you

FIGURE 12.2 Lifting heavy weights illustrates the principle of overload in action with weight training. If improvement in strength is to continue, weights must be increased.

then do a complete second set, followed by the third set. This approach may be best for beginners and is the sequence for the eight exercises presented in this chapter.

Another popular option is to do three sets of the same exercise with a rest between sets; then do three sets of the second exercise, and so on. This approach may be a little more fatiguing because you are using the same muscle group in three successive sets, but it appears to be very effective. The ACSM also provides some guidelines on exercise sequence, recommending that you do multiple joint exercises before single joint exercises, large muscle group exercises before small muscle group exercises, and higher intensity before lower intensity exercises.

Resistance training, if done properly to achieve the greatest gains, imposes a rather severe stress on the muscles, requiring a period of recovery both during the workout and between workouts. Research has shown that high-intensity resistance exercise can lead to rapid depletion of ATP and PCr, the high energy phosphates stored in the muscles; however, most of these high energy compounds may be restored in about 2 to 3 minutes of recovery. This is the **principle of recuperation.** Thus, several minutes should intervene between sets if you are using the same exercise. Additionally, for beginners, resistance training should generally be done about

Week:	1	4	7	10	13	16
Weight:	50	50	60	60	70	70
Repetitions:	5	10	5	10	5	10
Sets:	4	4	4	4	4	4

FIGURE 12.3 The principle of progressive resistance exercise (PRE) states that as you get stronger, you need to progressively increase the resistance in order to continue to gain strength and muscle. In this example, the individual increases the resistance when she can complete ten repetitions with a given weight, but then doing only five repetitions with the increased weight.

3 days per week, with a rest or recuperation day in between. This day of rest allows sufficient time for your muscle to repair itself and to synthesize new protein as it continues to grow, for research has shown that muscle protein synthesis occurs for up to 24 hours after a single bout of heavy resistance exercise. The ACSM indicates that advanced lifters could train 4–5 days per week.

These general principles should serve as guidelines during the beginning phase of your resistance-training program and should be used to guide your progress during the first 3 months of the basic resistance-training program described next.

What is an example of a resistance-training program that may help me to gain body weight as lean muscle mass?

If your goal is to gain significant amounts of muscle mass, you may wish to use the **bulk-up method.** This method involves the use of six to ten different exercises that stress the major muscle groups of the body. About three to five sets of each exercise are done. For those with limited time, one set may also provide signif-

icant increases in strength and muscle mass, as recently documented by Starkey and others. You should work up to 8–12 repetitions. The PRE concept is used, starting with resistance you can handle for eight repetitions and progressively increasing the repetitions to twelve. After you reach twelve repetitions, increase the resistance until you must come back to eight repetitions.

The bulk-up method should be used for several months to increase your weight. You may then wish to shape that bulk, a technique that bodybuilders call razoring or "cutting up." This technique uses a wide variety of exercises done with lighter weights and many repetitions at high speed; you are exercising on the endurance end of the continuum. Once you have achieved your desired body weight, you may alternate the bulk-up and razoring techniques to maintain your weight and shape.

The adolescent and adult beginner should adhere to the following procedure using the basic resistance-training program.

1. Learn the proper technique for each exercise with a light weight, possibly only the bar itself, for 2 weeks. Do eight to twelve repetitions of each exercise to develop form. Do not strain during this initial learning phase.
2. For each exercise, determine the maximum weight that you can lift for eight repetitions after the 2-week learning phase.
3. A weekly record form, similar to the one presented in table 12.1, should be used to keep track of your progress.
4. Do one set of the eight exercises shown in figures 12.4 to 12.11. The sequence of exercises should be
   a. Bench press: chest muscles
   b. Lat machine pulldown or bent-arm pullover: back muscles
   c. Half squat: thigh muscles
   d. Standing lateral raise: shoulder muscles
   e. Heel raise: calf muscles
   f. Standing curl: front upper arm muscles
   g. Seated overhead press: back upper arm muscles
   h. Curl-up: abdominal muscles
5. Because the exercise sequence is designed to stress different muscle groups in order, not much recuperation is necessary between exercises—possibly only 30 seconds or so.
6. Do three to five complete sets. You may wish to rest 2 to 3 minutes between sets.
7. Exercise 3 days per week; in each succeeding day try to do as many repetitions as possible for each exercise in each set. When you can do twelve repetitions each after a month or so, add more weight so you can do only eight repetitions.
8. Repeat step 7 as you progressively increase your strength.

Because barbells and dumbbells appear to be the most common means of doing resistance training, this is the method utilized. However, other apparatus such as the Nautilus, Hammer, and others can also be used effectively to gain weight and strength (see figure 12.12). Most of the exercises described here using barbells or dumbbells have similar counterparts on other apparatus.

Note that muscles seldom operate alone, and that most resistance-training exercises stress more than one muscle group. Thus, keep in mind that although an exercise may be listed specifically for the chest muscles, it may also stress the arm and

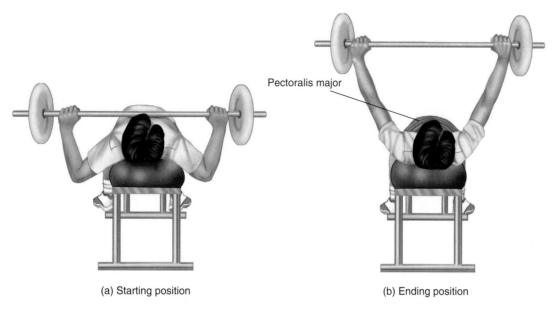

Pectoralis major

(a) Starting position   (b) Ending position

Chest	
Exercise	Bench press
Chest muscles	Pectoralis major
Other muscles	Deltoid, triceps
Sets	3–5
Repetitions	8–12, PRE concept
Safety	Have spotter stand behind bar to assist as fatigue sets in.
Equipment	Bench with support for weight, or two spotters to hand weight to you.
Description	Lie supine on bench. Use wide grip for chest development. Secure bar and lower *slowly* to chest. Press bar straight up to full extension. Do not arch back.

FIGURE 12.4 The bench press. The bench press primarily develops the pectoralis major muscle group in the chest; it also develops the deltoids in the shoulder and the triceps at the back of the arm.

shoulder muscles. The exercises described in this section generally stress more than one body area, although their main effect is on the area noted.

These eight exercises stress most of the major muscle groups in the body and thus provide an adequate stimulus for gaining body weight and strength through an increase in muscle mass. Literally hundreds of different resistance-training exercises and techniques to train are available; if you become interested in diversifying your program (such as using the razoring technique), consult a book specific to resistance training. Several may be found in the reference list at the end of this chapter. For example, nearly thirty different types of programs are presented in the classic text by Fleck and Kraemer, *Designing Resistance Training Programs.*

How does the body gain weight with a resistance-training program?

Muscle hypertrophy simply means increased muscle size. Figure 12.13 depicts the microstructure of muscle tissue. Resistance-training exercises place a heavy overload on the muscle cell, in some way stimulating the DNA within the multiple nuclei found in muscle cells. Carson indicated that the first stage of muscle hypertrophy, at the onset of overload, is associated with increased RNA activity and protein synthesis. Various hormones, such as testosterone and insulin, play important roles in stimulating muscle growth.

Over time the muscle cell tends to adapt to such stress by increasing its size. It may do so in several possible ways. First,

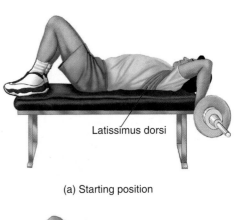

(a) Starting position

(b) Ending position

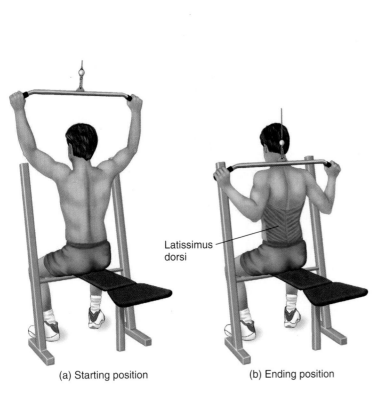

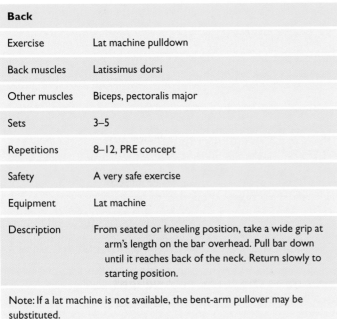

(a) Starting position

(b) Ending position

Back	
Exercise	Lat machine pulldown
Back muscles	Latissimus dorsi
Other muscles	Biceps, pectoralis major
Sets	3–5
Repetitions	8–12, PRE concept
Safety	A very safe exercise
Equipment	Lat machine
Description	From seated or kneeling position, take a wide grip at arm's length on the bar overhead. Pull bar down until it reaches back of the neck. Return slowly to starting position.

Note: If a lat machine is not available, the bent-arm pullover may be substituted.

FIGURE 12.5A The lat machine pulldown. The lat machine pulldown trains the latissimus dorsi in the back and side of the upper body, and it also develops the biceps on the front of the upper arm and the pectoralis major in the chest.

Back	
Alternate exercise	Bent-arm pullover
Back muscles	Latissimus dorsi
Other muscles	Pectoralis major
Sets	3–5
Repetitions	8–12, PRE concept
Safety	Do not arch back. Start with light weights when learning the technique.
Equipment	Bench
Description	Lie supine on bench, entire back in contact with the bench, feet on the bench, knees bent. Hold weight on chest with elbows bent. Swing weight over head, just brushing hair, and lower as far as possible without taking back off the bench. Keeping elbows in, return the weight to the chest.

FIGURE 12.5B The bent-arm pullover. The bent-arm pullover trains the latissimus dorsi and develops the pectoralis major.

Quadriceps

Hamstrings

(a) Starting position

(b) Ending position

Thigh	
Exercise	Half-squat or parallel squat
Thigh muscles	Quadriceps (front), hamstrings (back)
Other muscles	Gluteus maximus
Sets	3–5
Repetitions	8–12, PRE concept
Safety	Have two spotters to assist if using free weights. Keep back straight. Drop weight behind you if you lose balance. Do not squat more than halfway down.
Equipment	Squat rack if available. Pad the bar with towels if necessary.
Description	In standing position, take bar from squat rack or spotters and rest on the shoulders behind the head. Squat until thighs are parallel to ground or until buttocks touch a chair at this parallel position. Do not squat beyond halfway. Keep back as straight as possible. Return to standing position.

FIGURE 12.6 The half-squat or parallel squat. The half-squat develops the quadriceps muscle group on the front of the thigh and the hamstrings on the back of the thigh.

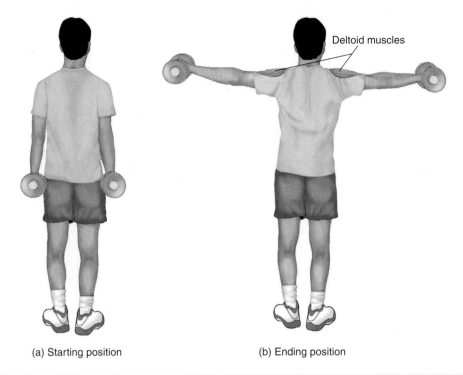

(a) Starting position (b) Ending position

Shoulders	
Exercise	Standing lateral raise
Shoulder muscles	Deltoid
Other muscles	Trapezius
Sets	3–5
Repetitions	8–12, PRE concept
Safety	Do not arch back.
Equipment	Dumbbells
Description	Stand with dumbbells in hands at sides. With palms down, raise straight arms sideways to shoulder level. Bend elbows slightly. Return slowly to starting position.

FIGURE 12.7 Standing lateral raise. The standing lateral raise primarily develops the deltoid muscles in the shoulder; the trapezius in the upper back and neck area is also trained.

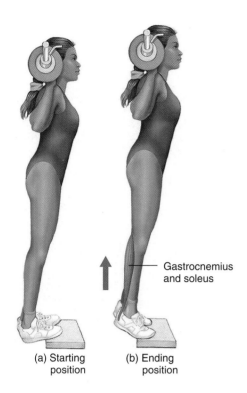

(a) Starting position

(b) Ending position

Gastrocnemius and soleus

Calf	
Exercise	Heel raise
Calf muscles	Gastrocnemius, soleus
Other muscles	Deep calf muscles
Sets	3–5
Repetitions	8–12, PRE concept
Safety	Have two spotters if you use free weights.
Equipment	Squat rack if available. Pad the bar with a towel if necessary.
Description	Place bar on back of shoulders as in squat exercise. Raise up on your toes as high as possible and then return to standing position. Place the toes on a board so heels can drop down lower than normal. Point toes in, out and straight ahead during different sets to work the muscles from different angles.

FIGURE 12.8   Heel raise. The heel raise develops the two major calf muscles—the gastrocnemius and the soleus.

Biceps

(a) Starting position

(b) Ending position

Front of arm	
Exercise	Standing curl
Arm muscle	Biceps
Other muscles	Several elbow flexors
Sets	3–5
Repetitions	8–12, PRE concept
Safety	Do not arch back. Place back against wall to control arching motion.
Equipment	Curl bar if available
Description	Stand with weight held in front of body, palms forward. Place back against wall. Bend the elbows and bring the weight to the chest. Lower it slowly.

FIGURE 12.9   The standing curl. The standing curl strengthens the biceps muscle in the front of the upper arm as well as several other muscles in the region that bend the elbow.

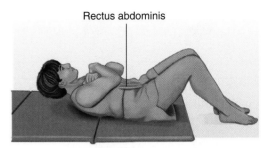

Rectus abdominis

(a) Starting position

(b) Ending position

Triceps

(a) Starting position   (b) Ending position

Back of arm	
Exercise	Seated overhead press
Arm muscle	Triceps
Other muscles	Trapezius, deltoids
Sets	3–5
Repetitions	8–12, PRE concept
Safety	Do not arch back excessively. Have spotter available as fatigue sets in.
Equipment	Bench or chair
Description	Sit on bench with weight held behind the head near the neck. Hands should be close together, elbows bent. Straighten elbows and press weight over head to arm's length. Lower weight slowly to starting position.

FIGURE 12.10 The seated overhead press. The seated overhead press primarily develops the triceps muscle on the back of the upper arm; the exercise also trains the trapezius in the upper back and neck and the deltoids in the shoulder.

Abdominal area	
Exercise	Curl-up
Abdominal muscles	Rectus abdominis
Other muscles	Oblique abdominis muscles
Sets	3–5
Repetitions	8–12, PRE concept
Safety	Develop sufficient abdominal strength before using weights with this exercise. Do not arch back when exercising.
Equipment	Free-weight plates; incline sit-up bench if available.
Description	Lie on back, knees bent with heels close to buttocks. Hands should hold weights on chest. Curl up about a third to half way. Return to starting position slowly.

Note: This exercise may be done without weights but with an increased number of repetitions.

FIGURE 12.11 The curl-up. The curl-up trains the rectus abdominis and the oblique abdominis muscles.

TABLE 12.1   Weekly resistance-training record, basic eight exercises

	Chest (Bench Press)		Back (Lat Pulldown)		Thigh (Half Squat)		Shoulder (Lateral Raise)		Calf (Heel Raise)		Front arm (Curls)		Back arm (Seated Press)		Abdominal area (Curl-ups)	
	Wt	Reps	Wt	Reps	Wt	Reps	Wt	Reps	Wt	Reps	Wt	Reps	Wt	Reps	Wt	Reps
Date _____																
Set 1																
Set 2																
Set 3																
Set 4																
Set 5																
Date _____																
Set 1																
Set 2																
Set 3																
Set 4																
Set 5																
Date _____																
Set 1																
Set 2																
Set 3																
Set 4																
Set 5																
Date _____																
Set 1																
Set 2																
Set 3																
Set 4																
Set 5																

FIGURE 12.12 Machines such as Nautilus provide an alternative to free weights for development of muscular strength and endurance.

the individual muscle cells and myofibrils may simply increase their size by incorporating more protein. Second, the myofibrils in each cell may multiply, which will increase the size of each muscle fiber. Third, the amount of connective tissue around each muscle fiber and around each bundle of muscle may increase and thicken, leading to an overall increase in the size of the total muscle. Fourth, the cell may increase its content of enzymes and energy storage, particularly ATP and glycogen. The increased muscle glycogen, along with increased muscle protein, binds additional water which contributes to an increased body weight. Finally, the muscle fibers themselves may increase in number (hyperplasia), but current evidence suggests this is much less likely to occur compared with the other four means to induce muscle hypertrophy. In addition to the effects on the muscle cell, although not all studies are in agreement, research data indicate that resistance-training exercises may increase bone mineral content, possibly owing to increased muscle tension effects on the bone, which might provide a slight increase in total body weight.

Resistance training may be an effective means to increase muscle size and mass. Such increases help improve muscular strength and endurance and may be important components in weight-control programs. Traditionally, in research studies females did not normally experience the same amount of hypertrophy that males did, although they did experience proportional gains in muscular strength and endurance. However, more recent research revealed a significant increase in muscle cell size when women engaged in an intense, concentrated resistance-training program. Moreover, in a recent study O'Hagan and others found that when exposed to the same short-term resistance-training program, muscle size increased similarly in women and men.

Is any one type of resistance-training program or equipment more effective than others for gaining body weight?

There are a variety of methods for resistance training. **Isometric methods** involve a muscle contraction against an immovable object, such as trying to pull a telephone pole out of the ground. However, if you succeed in moving the object, then you are doing an isotonic exercise. **Isotonic methods** are of two types. The **concentric method** means the muscle is shortening, as the biceps does in the up phase of a pull-up. The **eccentric method** means the muscle is lengthening even though it is trying to shorten. In the down phase of the pull-up the biceps is now contracting eccentrically as it slows your rate of descent. Gravity is attempting to pull you down, but your biceps is resisting it. Finally, the **isokinetic method** uses machines or other devices to regulate the speed at which you can shorten your muscles. For example, you may try to move your arm as fast as possible, but you will be able to move only as fast as the setting on the isokinetic machine. Isokinetic exercise is also known as accommodating-resistance exercise because the resistance automatically adjusts to the force exerted, thus controlling the speed of movement.

Several different resistance-training apparatuses are available, such as Nautilus, Hammer, Cybex, Hydra-Gym, Soloflex, and other similar machines. Depending upon the model, they are designed to utilize one or more of the training methods cited above.

A number of research studies have been conducted to determine which of these methods or machines is best, particularly in relation to strength and power gains. Research suggests that at the present time it is probably safe to say that isotonic and isokinetic programs are comparable in their ability to produce gains in muscle size and strength. Also, other than possible safety considerations, research suggests that the use of specialized machines and resistance-training devices does not appear to have any advantage over the use of free weights, such as barbells and dumbbells. All methods may be effective in increasing body weight provided the basic principles of resistance training, particularly the principle of overload, are followed. The ACSM recommends that your exercise program should include both concentric and eccentric exercise, which are incorporated in most machines and free weights. If you use machines, be sure to exercise all major muscles areas. Free weights are relatively inexpensive and can be used for a wide variety of exercises. They also may be constructed at home, using pipe or solid broomstick handles for the bar and different-sized tin cans filled with cement for the weights.

There may be some specific training programs that are better suited for specific purposes, such as specific sport performance enhancement or injury rehabilitation. These topics are beyond the scope of this text, so the interested reader is referred to more detailed resources, such as the text by Fleck and Kraemer.

If exercise burns Calories, won't I lose weight on a resistance-training program?

Although exercise does cost Calories, the amount expended during resistance training is relatively small compared to more active

Are there any contraindications to resistance training?

There are several health conditions that may be aggravated by resistance training, primarily by the increased pressures that occur within the body when you strain to lift heavy weights and hold your breath at the same time. Because the blood pressure can increase rapidly and excessively during weight lifting, to 300 mmHg or higher, individuals with resting blood pressures over 90 mmHg diastolic and 140 mmHg systolic should refrain from heavy lifting, for they may be exposed to an increased risk of blood vessel rupture and a possible stroke. Lifting with the arms and straining exercises also increase the stress on the heart and thus should be avoided by individuals who have heart problems. Individuals with a hernia (a weakness in the musculature of the abdominal wall) also should refrain from strenuous weight lifting because the increased pressure may cause a rupture. Low back problems also may be aggravated by improper weight lifting techniques. Some individuals may suffer peripheral nerve injuries, such as carpal tunnel syndrome, involving weakness and numbness in the hand due to compressed nerves from improper lifting techniques. Individuals with these types of health problems should seek medical advice and be cleared by a physician before initiating or continuing with a resistance-training program.

There has been some concern about the advisability of prepubescent youth lifting weights. Damage to the growth plate in the bones may occur when children try to lift weights in excess of their ability. However, the American Academy of Pediatrics endorsed the concept of resistance training for youngsters, provided proper techniques were taught and the program was supervised. In this regard, Faigenbaum and others suggested that higher repetitions with moderate loads should be used in the adaptation period. In a meta-analysis of twenty-eight studies, Payne and others found that well-designed resistance-training programs appear to enhance muscular endurance and strength in children and youth, including prepubescent children, while Guy and Micheli concluded that young athletes participating in resistance training do not appear to be at any greater risk of injury than young athletes who have not undergone such training. In his recent review, Faigenbaum indicated that resistance training may also confer some health benefits to youth, such as increased bone density.

Resistance training may be a very effective means of increasing strength in the elderly as well; research has shown that even those in their nineties may experience significant strength gains with

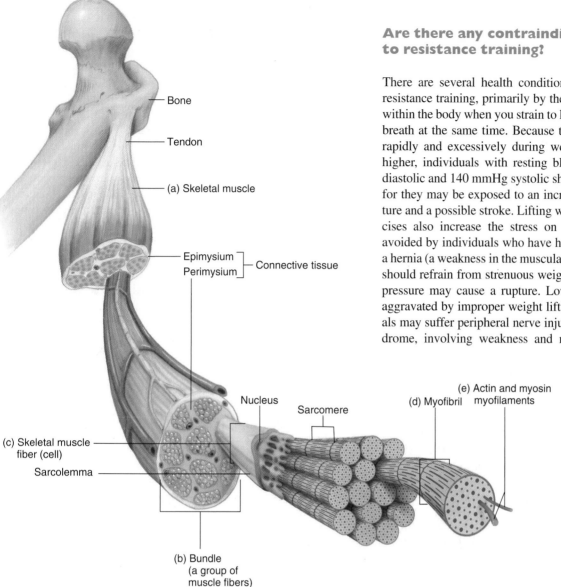

FIGURE 12.13 Muscle structure. The whole muscle is composed of separate bundles of individual muscle fibers. Each fiber is composed of numerous myofibrils, each of which contains thin protein filaments arranged so that they can slide by each other to cause muscle shortening or lengthening. Several layers of connective tissue surround the muscle fibers, bundles, and whole muscles, which eventually band together to form the tendon.

aerobic exercise. Resistance training can be a high-intensity exercise, but the time spent actually lifting during a typical workout is usually short, therefore limiting the number of Calories used. For example, in an hour workout, only about 15 minutes may be involved in actual exercise, the remaining time being recovery between each exercise. Based upon metabolic data collected in research studies, the average-sized male uses about 200 Calories in a typical workout, while the average-sized female uses about 150 (see figure 12.14). However, Melanson and others indicated that circuit resistance training, as discussed later, may lead to a total daily energy expenditure comparable to aerobic cycling exercise. Resistance exercise may have a greater effect on post-exercise REE, as suggested by Schuenke and others.

1 hour = 600–800 Calories   1 hour = 150–200 Calories

FIGURE 12.14 All modes of exercise increase caloric expenditure. However, an hour of regular weight training expends only about one-third to one-fourth as many Calories as vigorous aerobic activity. Combining aerobic exercises with weight training (circuit aerobics) helps burn more Calories than weight training alone; it also provides cardiovascular health benefits while increasing muscular strength and endurance.

appropriately designed resistance-training programs. However, although resistance training helps stimulate muscle hypertrophy and weight gain in the aged, the increase is less than that observed in younger individuals.

Resistance training is generally regarded as a relatively safe sport, particularly if appropriate safety precautions are taken. The following guidelines should be incorporated into all resistance-training programs.

1. Learn to breathe properly. During the most strenuous part of the exercise you are likely to hold your breath. This is a natural response; it helps to stabilize your chest cavity to provide a more stable base for your muscles to function. Usually the breath hold is short and no problems occur. However, if prolonged, it may increase the chances of suffering some of the problems noted previously, such as a hernia.

    Also associated with prolonged breath holding is a response known as the **Valsalva phenomenon** (Valsalva maneuver), which may lead to a possible blackout. Here is what happens. As you reach a sticking point in your lift and strain to overcome it, you normally hold your breath; this causes your glottis to close over your windpipe and the pressure in your chest and abdominal area to rise rapidly. The pressure creates resistance to blood flow, reducing the return of blood to the heart, and eventually leading to decreased blood flow to the brain and a possible blackout. Additionally,

the Valsalva maneuver exaggerates the increase in blood pressure during resistance exercises, and although a brief Valsalva maneuver is unavoidable when doing near maximal exercises, its effect may be minimized by proper breathing.

A recommended breathing pattern that will help minimize these adverse effects is to breathe out while lifting the weight and breathe in while lowering it. You should breathe through both your mouth and nose while exercising. Practice proper breathing when you learn new resistance-training exercises.

2. When using free weights, use spotters when doing exercises that may be potentially dangerous, such as the bench press. If you are doing a bench press alone and reach a sticking point in your lift, the Valsalva phenomenon may lead to serious consequences if you lose control of the weight directly above your head. The use of machines such as Nautilus helps eliminate the need for spotters.

3. If using free weights, place lock collars on the bar ends so the plates do not fall off and cause injury to the feet. Again, the use of machines eliminates this safety hazard. However, do not attempt to change weight plates on machines while they are being used. Your fingers may get caught between the weights.

4. Warm up with proper stretching exercises.

5. Use light weights to learn the proper technique of a given exercise so that you do not strain yourself if you do the exercise incorrectly. Learn to lift smoothly. Do not use jerking motions. When the proper technique is mastered, the weights may be increased. Using proper technique ensures that the desired muscle group is being exercised.

6. Avoid exercises that may cause or aggravate low back problems. Try to prevent an excessive forward motion or stress in the lower back region. Figure 12.15 illustrates some positions that should be avoided.

7. Lower weights slowly. If you lower them rapidly, your muscles have to contract rapidly to slow the weights down as you reach the starting position. This necessitates the development of a large amount of force that may tear some connective tissue and cause muscle soreness.

Are there any health benefits associated with resistance training?

Although resistance training has been recommended mainly as a means of gaining muscle mass, body weight, and strength, its use normally was not associated with any health benefits. However, increasing research efforts focusing on the health implications of resistance training have suggested several favorable effects. Some of the health benefits are associated with increases in lean body mass and strength, but Kraemer and others revealed that resistance training affects a number of systems in the body, not only the neuromuscular system, but also the connective tissue, cardiovascular, and endocrine systems. In this regard, Deschenes and Kraemer indicated that resistance training may confer some additional physiological benefits conducive to good health to individuals of all ages. In recent reviews Pollock, Layne and Nelson, Kell and others, and

(a)   (b)   (c)

FIGURE 12.15 Avoid exercises or body positions that place excessive stress on the low-back region. Poor form in exercises like (a) the bench press and (b) the curl exaggerates the lumbar curve. Be sure to keep the lower back as flat as possible. Exercises similar to (c) the bent-over row place tremendous forces on the lower back because the weight or resistance is so far in front of the body.

Winett and Carpinelli, as well as the American College of Sports Medicine in its position stand on exercise and diabetes, reported multiple health benefits associated with resistance training, benefits which, along with those cited in other reports, include the following:

1. Increased lean body mass to help maintain resting energy expenditure and prevent obesity (The prevention of **sarcopenia** [loss of muscle mass] as one ages is a major health benefit.)
2. Increased strength to prevent falls and injury as one ages
3. Decreased pain in chronic low-back-pain patients to improve mobility
4. Increased bone mineral density to help prevent osteoporosis, particularly in females
5. Improved glucose metabolism and insulin sensitivity to help prevent diabetes or improve glucose control in diabetics
6. Improved serum lipid profiles, such as increased HDL-cholesterol and decreased LDL-cholesterol, to help prevent atherosclerosis and coronary heart disease
7. Improved ability to complete activities of daily living and enhance the quality of life in older individuals
8. Improved mood, body image, self concept, and psychological health in children, adolescents, and adults.

These findings are contrary to the belief that resistance training does not confer any health benefits comparable to aerobic exercise. It is also notable that many cardiac rehabilitation programs now incorporate resistance-training exercises. Indeed, the American Heart Association, the American College of Sports Medicine, and the recent Surgeon General's report on physical activity and health all have recognized the importance of resistance training as

an important component of health. Although 2–3 sets of resistance exercise may be recommended to optimize weight gain as muscle mass, Feigenbaum and Pollock indicated that health benefits may occur using a single set of 8–10 different exercises with 8–15 repetitions of each.

Nevertheless, it still appears to be prudent health behavior to incorporate some aerobic exercise into your lifestyle, even when trying to gain body weight. Although the American College of Sports Medicine has added resistance training to its recommended exercise program for healthy adults, it is designed to complement aerobic exercise, not to substitute for it. (See www.mhhe.com/williams.) Aerobic exercise programs do consume more Calories, so you would have to balance the expenditure with increased food intake. However, the energy expenditure does not need to be excessive to provide a beneficial training effect. For example, running 2 to 3 miles about 4 days per week would provide you with an adequate aerobic-exercise training effect for your heart, but it would cost you only about 200–300 Calories a day. This 200- to 300-Calorie expenditure could be replaced easily by consuming two glasses of orange juice or similar small amounts of food.

Can I combine aerobic and resistance-training exercises into one program?

Although the principles underlying the development of an aerobic-training program and a resistance-training program are similar, the purposes of the two programs are rather different. An aerobic exercise program is designed to improve the efficiency of the cardiovascular system; the basic purpose of a resistance-training program is to increase muscle size, strength, and body weight.

One form of resistance training that has been used to provide some moderate benefits to the cardiovascular system is **circuit weight training,** a method in which the individual moves rapidly from one exercise to the next. Generally, this type of program uses lighter weights with greater numbers of repetitions, thus increasing the aerobic component of training. Research reported energy expenditure of approximately 10 Calories per minute for males and 7 Calories per minute for females. Circuit weight training can improve strength, but Harber and others indicated strength gains are attributed more to neural adaptations because the relatively low resistance loads do not induce appreciable muscle hypertrophy.

A newer version of this method is **circuit aerobics.** Circuit aerobics may be done in a variety of ways, but basically it involves an integration of aerobic and resistance-training exercises. It is actually a form of interval aerobic training, but instead of resting or doing a lower level of aerobic activity during the recovery interval, you do resistance-training exercises. Circuit aerobics may offer multiple health and performance benefits such as improved cardiovascular fitness, increased caloric expenditure for loss of body fat, improved muscular strength and endurance, and increased muscle tone in body areas not normally stressed by aerobic exercise alone.

However, if the main purpose of your resistance-training program is to gain body weight as muscle mass, then you need to train near the strength end of the strength-endurance continuum. For athletes who need to maximize gains in lean body mass, strength, and especially power, in a recent Gatorade Sports Science Institute review Michael Stone recommends that aerobic training should be markedly reduced if not eliminated, indicating that aerobic endurance training does not create a physiological environment compatible to such gains.

Key Concept Recap

- ▶ A basic principle underlying all resistance-training programs is the overload principle, which simply means the muscles should be stressed beyond normal daily levels.
- ▶ Progressive resistance is also a basic principle of resistance training, for as you get stronger through use of the overload principle, you must progressively increase the resistance.
- ▶ To increase muscle mass and body weight, you should exercise near the strength end of the strength-endurance continuum.
- ▶ Your resistance-training program should exercise all major muscle groups in the body.
- ▶ A variety of methods and apparatus are available for resistance training, but research suggests that they are equally effective as a means of gaining strength and muscle mass if the basic principles of resistance training are followed.
- ▶ Resistance training is generally regarded as a safe form of exercise, but it may be contraindicated in some individuals, for example, those with high blood pressure and hernias.

▶ Although resistance-training programs may confer some significant health benefits, it is also highly recommended that one add an aerobic exercise program to help condition the cardiovascular system.

Check for Yourself

Do this after 2–3 weeks of resistance training. Using free weights or an appropriate weight-training machine, such as Nautilus, determine your one repetition maximum (1RM) for a given exercise, such as the bench press. Start out with a light weight that you know you can easily lift one time, and then gradually add on amounts until you reach your limit. You should need only 3–4 attempts. Record the weight of the last successful attempt.

Nutritional Considerations

How many Calories are needed to form one pound of muscle?

Muscle tissue consists of about 70 percent water, 22 percent protein, and the remainder is fat, carbohydrate, and minerals. Because the vast majority of muscle tissue is water, which has no caloric value, the total caloric value is only about 700–800 Calories per pound. However, extra energy is needed to help synthesize the muscle tissue.

It is not known exactly how many additional Calories are necessary to form 1 pound of muscle tissue in human beings, nor is it known in what form these Calories have to be consumed. The National Research Council notes that 5 Calories are needed to support the addition of 1 gram of tissue during growth, while Forbes cites a value of 8 Calories per gram in adults. Because 1 pound equals 454 grams, a range of 2,300–3,500 additional Calories appears to be a reasonable amount. With a recommended weight gain of 1 pound per week, about 400–500 Calories above your daily needs would provide an amount in the suggested range, 2,800–3,500 Calories per week. A study by Robert Bartels and his associates at Ohio State University revealed that an additional 500 Calories per day resulted in nearly a 1-pound increase in lean body weight per week during a resistance-training program.

How can I determine the amount of Calories I need daily to gain one pound per week?

First, review the techniques presented in chapter 11 to determine the number of Calories needed simply to maintain your current body weight. Then add the Calories that you expend during exercise and the additional amount needed to synthesize the muscle tissue. Table 12.2 presents an example of a 154-pound 18-year-old male who desires to gain a pound per week. You may modify the figures according to your own needs. Remember, a weight gain of 0.5–1.0 pound muscle mass per week is a reasonable goal during the early stages of resistance training. If you are maintaining your weight with your current dietary intake, adding 500–1,000 Calories per day may also be an acceptable approach.

TABLE 12.2	Caloric intake for a 154-pound 18-year-old male to gain one pound per week	
Energy expenditure		**Daily Calories needed**
Recommended caloric intake to maintain current weight 19 Calories/pound		2,468
Resistance training 200 Calories per session 4 sessions per week 800/7		115
Aerobic exercise 300 Calories per session 4 sessions per week 1,200/7		170
Muscle tissue synthesis 3,500 Calories per pound 3,500/7		500
Total daily caloric intake		3,253

Increased caloric intake is the key dietary principle, along with adequate protein intake, to gain muscle mass during resistance training, as noted in a recent Gatorade Sports Science Institute review of weight-gain strategies in athletes by leading experts in the area, Gail Butterfield, Susan Kleiner, Peter Lemon, and Michael Stone.

Is protein supplementation necessary during a weight-gaining program?

Gilbert Forbes indicates we need adequate amounts of protein to support increases in lean body mass. One pound of muscle is equal to 454 grams, but only about 22 percent of this tissue, or about 100 grams, is protein. If we divide 100 grams by 7 days, we would need approximately 14 grams of protein per day above our normal protein requirements to gain one pound of muscle per week if we are in protein balance. However, the average American diet already contains extra protein beyond the RDA, so this need probably is satisfied. Incidentally, 14 grams of protein could be obtained in such small amounts of food as 2 glasses of milk, 2 ounces of cheese, 2 scrambled eggs, or 2 ounces of meat, fish, or poultry (see figure 12.16).

Although the daily RDA for protein is about 1 gram per kilogram body weight, some authorities in sports nutrition have recommended up to 1.6–1.7 grams per kilogram for the athlete who is training to increase muscle mass. As noted in chapter 6, a slight increase in the protein content of the typical American daily diet would meet even this recommendation. A brief review of the mathematics in table 6.6 and the related discussion on pages 205–207 will help substantiate this statement.

Supplementation by expensive protein powders or amino acids is not necessary. The average American diet provides sufficient high-quality protein to meet the needs of a weight-gaining program, even more so if a high-Calorie diet is used as recommended below. It is important to note that dietary protein in excess of needs will be converted to fat unless resistance training is used to stimulate muscle growth.

However, as discussed in chapter 6, the timing of food intake may be an important consideration. Muscle protein synthesis is accelerated in the recovery period following resistance exercise, and in a recent review Houston indicated that consuming the additional dietary protein during recovery, along with carbohydrates, will create a hormonal response to further increase protein synthesis. Research by Kraemer and others also suggests consuming protein and carbohydrate prior to exercise creates a similar hormonal milieu. However, in a recent review Kevin Tipton and Robert Wolfe, two experts on protein metabolism, have concluded that it has yet to be determined if these transient hormonal responses result in an appreciable increase in muscle mass over a prolonged training period. They suggested the possibility that these transient increases in anabolism add nothing to the normal anabolic responses that would result from meals ingested in the 24 hours following an appropriate resistance exercise workout. Phillips also recently concluded that strength-trained athletes should consume protein consistent with general population guidelines, or 12–15 percent of energy from protein.

Nevertheless, although additional research is needed to support a more positive recommendation, consuming a protein-carbohydrate mixture before and after resistance training may be prudent, as it may do some good and is unlikely to do any harm. Jeff Volek, a predominant strength researcher, indicated that to date one of the most promising strategies to augment gains in muscle size appears to be consumption of protein/carbohydrate Calories before and after resistance exercise. Recent studies by

1 pound of muscle tissue/week = Additional 400 Calories/day + Additional 14 grams protein/day

FIGURE 12.16 To add a pound of muscle tissue per week, you need to consume approximately 400 additional Calories and 14 grams of additional protein per day. A weight-training program is an essential part of a muscle-building program. One glass of skim milk, three slices of whole wheat bread, and two hard-boiled egg whites provide the necessary Calories and about 23 grams of protein.

Andersen and Børsheim support this viewpoint. A tasty post-workout carbohydrate protein drink, with a ratio of 3–4 grams of carbohydrate for each gram of protein, has been recommended by Ivy and Portman. Both the carbohydrate and the protein will stimulate insulin secretion, which will help move both glucose and amino acids into the muscle to facilitate recovery and support muscle protein synthesis.

Are dietary supplements necessary during a weight-gaining program?

Robert Keith, a sport nutrition professor at Auburn University, and his colleagues reported that the nutrient intakes of individuals, such as bodybuilders, attempting to gain muscle mass were well above recommended levels, indicating there probably would not be any advantage for these subjects to take nutrient supplements. However, dietary supplements appear to be very popular among athletes and others attempting to increase muscle mass and strength, if we can use advertisements as evidence to support this contention. For example, in a survey of only five magazines targeted to bodybuilding athletes, Grunewald and Bailey reported over 800 performance claims were made for 624 commercially available supplements.

Although there may be some truth underlying the alleged performance-enhancing mechanisms of these supplements, the effectiveness of most has not been evaluated by scientific research. In a review of nutritional supplements for strength-trained athletes, Williams indicated that there is little or no scientific evidence supporting positive effects on muscle growth, body-fat reduction, or strength enhancement in strength-trained athletes for the following: arginine, lysine, and ornithine (amino acids); inosine; choline; yohimbine; glandular products; vitamin B_{12}; carnitine; chromium; boron; magnesium; medium-chain triglycerides; omega-3 fatty acids; gamma oryzanol; and Smilax. In general, these viewpoints were supported by Clarkson and Rawson, Coleman and others, and Kreider in their recent reviews. Most of these nutrients and dietary supplements, and others such as vanadium and HMB, have been discussed in previous chapters and have been found to be ineffective or inadequately researched.

As noted in chapter 6, creatine monohydrate supplementation does appear to increase body weight, and numerous studies have reported gains in strength, particularly in high-intensity resistance exercises with short-term recovery. Although early increases in body weight may be primarily water, an increased resistance-training capacity may lead to muscle gains over time. Numerous studies support this finding. You may wish to review the discussion of creatine supplementation on pages 217–223.

Several other dietary supplements marketed to athletes are patterned after anabolic/androgenic steroids. In general, as noted in chapter 13, research indicates such supplements do not increase muscle mass and may cause adverse health effects.

In a recent symposium sponsored by the Gatorade Sports Science Institute, five experts on muscle-building supplements provided this advice: Train hard, follow a sound diet with adequate energy, protein, and carbohydrate, and don't rely on dietary supplements. If you do use supplements, be sure to consult with an expert, such as a sports-oriented dietitian or physician, not the clerk at a health food store.

As indicated in chapter 1, many of these products are costly and some can have adverse effects on one's health. *Caveat emptor.*

What is an example of a balanced diet that will help me gain weight?

As with losing weight, the Food Exchange System may serve as the basis for a sound weight-gaining diet. Foods must be selected for high nutrient value as well as additional Calories to support the weight gain. In a recent review regarding healthy muscle gains, Susan Kleiner indicated the new school of thought is shifting away from high-meat, high-milk, high-fat diets, and toward high-Calorie, high-carbohydrate, increased-protein diets. Interestingly, research by Tucker and his associates indicated that women who undertook a resistance-training program seemed to modify their diets favorably, reducing the percentage of energy from dietary fat and increasing the percentage of energy from carbohydrate. As blood glucose and muscle glycogen may help provide energy for high-volume resistance training, Haff and others noted that it may be advisable for athletes to ingest carbohydrate supplements before, during, and immediately after training.

The following suggestions may be helpful for those trying to gain weight.

Milk exchange—Drink 1% or 2% milk instead of skim milk, which will add 15–30 Calories per glass. Prepare milk shakes with dry milk powder and supplement with fruit. Add low-fat cheeses to sandwiches or snacks. Eat yogurt supplemented with fruit. The milk exchange is high in protein.

Meat exchange—Increase your intake of lean meats, poultry, and fish. Legumes such as beans and dried peas are high in protein, carbohydrate, and Calories and low in fat. Use nuts, seeds, and limited amounts of peanut butter for snacks. The meat exchange is also high in protein.

Starch exchange—Increase your consumption of whole-grain products. Pasta and rice are nutritious side dishes that provide adequate Calories. Starchy vegetables like potatoes are also nutritious sources of Calories. Breads and muffins can possibly be supplemented with fruits and nuts. Whole-grain breakfast cereals can provide substantial Calories and even make a tasty dessert or snack with added fruit. The starch exchange is high in complex carbohydrates but also contains about 15 percent of its Calories as protein.

Fruit exchange—Add fruit to other food exchanges. Drink more fruit juices, which are high in both Calories and nutrients. Dried fruits such as apricots, pineapple, dates, and raisins are high in Calories and make excellent snacks.

Vegetable exchange—Use fresh vegetables like broccoli and cauliflower as snacks with melted low-fat cheese or a nutritious dip.

Fat exchange—Try to minimize the intake of saturated fats, using monounsaturated and polyunsaturated fats instead, particularly olive and canola oils. Salad dressings and soft margarine added to vegetables can increase their caloric content.

Beverages—Milk and juices are nutritious and high in Calories. Those who drink alcohol should obtain only limited amounts of Calories in this way. Some liquid supplements are available commercially and may contain 300–400 Calories with substantial amounts of protein. However, check the label for fat and sugar content.

Snacks—Eat three balanced meals per day supplemented with two or three snacks. Dried fruits, nuts, and seeds are excellent snacks. Some of the high-Calorie, high-nutrient liquid meals and sports bars on the market also make good snacks.

Table 12.3 presents an example of a high-Calorie diet plan based upon the Food Exchange System. It consists of three main meals and three snacks and totals about 4,000 Calories with 160 grams of protein, which is 16 percent of the Calories. It is also high in carbohydrate, which may increase insulin release, facilitating amino acid transport into the muscle to help promote protein synthesis. Carbohydrate also spares the use of protein as an energy source. Alternative foods may be substituted from the food exchange list presented in appendix E. This suggested diet provides the necessary nutrients, Calories, and protein essential to increased development of muscle mass and yet fewer than 30 percent of the Calories are derived from fat. The total number of Calories can be adjusted to meet individual needs.

Meal plans may be adjusted to the energy needs of individual athletes. For example, Lambert and others note that competitive bodybuilders should consume a diet that contains about 55–60 percent carbohydrate, 25–30 percent protein, and 15–20 percent fat for both the off-season and pre-contest phases. However, during the off-season the diet should be slightly hyperenergetic (approximately 15 percent increase in energy intake) and during the pre-contest phase the diet should be hypoenergetic (approximately 15 percent decrease in energy intake). For 6–12 weeks prior to competition, bodybuilders attempt to retain muscle mass and reduce body fat to low levels, so they need to be in negative energy balance to facilitate oxidation of body fat. Lambert and others recommend the diet contain 30 percent protein at this time to help prevent loss of muscle mass and possibly also provide a thermic effect to help burn fat.

For more detailed meal plans, the interested reader is referred to *Nutrient Timing* by John Ivy and Robert Portman.

Would such a high-Calorie diet be ill advised for some individuals?

As noted in chapter 5, one of the general recommendations for an improved diet is to reduce the consumption of fats, particularly saturated fats. Unfortunately, many high-Calorie diets are also high in fats. If there is a history of heart disease in the family or if an individual is known to have high blood lipid levels, then high-fat diets are contraindicated. Individuals with kidney problems also may have difficulty processing high-protein diets because of the increased need to excrete urea. Any person initiating such a

weight-gaining program as advised here should be aware of his or her medical history.

Selection of food for a weight-gaining diet, if done wisely, can satisfy the criteria for healthful nutrition. Foods high in complex carbohydrates with moderate amounts of protein and a moderate fat content are able to provide substantial amounts of Calories and nutrients and yet minimize health risks that have been associated with the typical American and Canadian diet. To gain weight wisely, you need to continue to eat healthful foods, but just more of them.

TABLE 12.3 A high-Calorie diet based on the Food Exchange System

Exchange		Calories
Breakfast		
Milk	8 ounces 2% milk	120
Meat	1 poached egg	80
	2 ounces lean ham	110
Starch	2 slices whole wheat toast	160
Fruit	8 ounces orange juice	120
Other	1 tablespoon jelly	50
Mid-morning snack		
Fruit	8 ounces apricot nectar	160
Starch	2 slices whole wheat bread	160
Meat	1 tablespoon peanut butter	100
Lunch		
Milk	8 ounces 2% milk	120
Meat	4 ounces lean sandwich meat	220
Starch	2 slices whole wheat bread	160
	2 granola cookies	100
Fruit	1 banana	120
Vegetable, starchy	1 order French fries	300
Afternoon snack		
Fruit	1/4 cup raisins	120
Dinner		
Milk	8 ounces 2% milk	120
Meat	5 ounces salmon	275
Starch	2 slices whole wheat bread	160
Fruit	1 piece apple pie	350
Vegetable, starchy	1 cup peas	160
	1 sweet potato, candied	300
Evening snack		
Fruit	1/2 cup dried peaches	210
Milk	8 ounces 2% milk with banana	240
Total		4,015

► The Food Exchange System can serve as the basis for increasing caloric intake to gain body weight if the aspirant eats greater quantities of nutritious foods from each of the six lists, in three balanced meals plus several high-Calorie, high-nutrient snacks.

► The individual attempting to gain body weight should obtain necessary protein for muscle synthesis through a well-balanced diet, rather than by consuming expensive protein supplements.

► Although creatine supplementation may help increase muscle mass during resistance training, most dietary supplements marketed to strength-trained individuals are not effective or have not been evaluated by scientific research.

Check for Yourself

Using the information presented in the text, calculate the additional number of Calories you would need in your daily diet to accumulate a weight gain of 0.5 pound per week. What foods could you add to your daily diet to provide these Calories?

APPLICATION EXERCISE

If you have time and are interested, start a resistance-training program, using the principles in the text. Record your 1RM for an exercise (such as the bench press) initially and every two weeks for several months. Use a tape measure to determine body girth changes in the upper arm, chest, waist, and upper thigh. If you have access to skinfold calipers or other measures of body composition, keep similar records. Use a model comparable to those presented, (adjusting the numbers in the vertical column to represent weight lifted for 1 RM, millimeters for skinfold measurement, and centimeters or inches for girth measurement), graph the results, and compare to the text discussion.

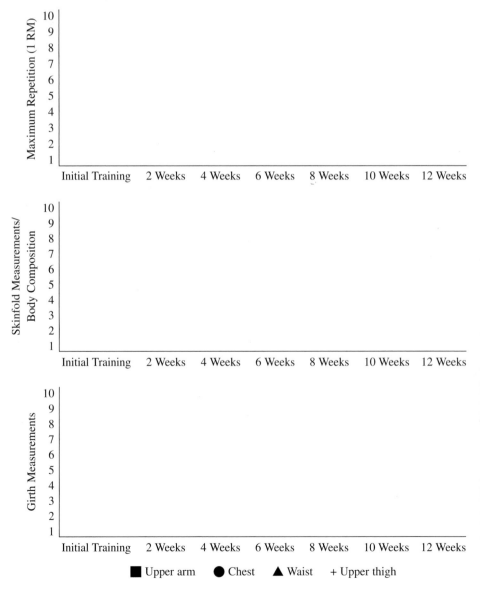

1. Which of the following would be least recommended for someone who wants to gain weight healthfully?
   (a) stop smoking
   (b) set a goal of about 0.5 pound per week
   (c) get enough rest and sleep
   (d) start a resistance training program
   (e) drink more caffeinated beverages

2. Which of the following is not one of the basic principles of resistance training?
   (a) overload
   (b) specificity
   (c) progressive resistance
   (d) aerobic
   (e) sequence

3. The bench press exercise is designed to have the greatest effect on which group of muscles?
   (a) calf
   (b) thigh
   (c) back
   (d) chest
   (e) abdominal

4. The standing lateral raise is designed to have the greatest effect on which group of muscles?
   (a) shoulder
   (b) thigh
   (c) calf
   (d) chest
   (e) abdominal

5. Resistance training will stimulate muscle growth by a variety of mechanisms. Which of the following is considered to be least likely according to your text discussion?
   (a) Individual muscle cells and myofibrils increase in size.

   (b) Myofibrils in each cell may multiply.
   (c) Connective tissue in muscle may increase and thicken.
   (d) Muscle cells will increase water content by binding to increased glycogen.
   (e) Muscle fibers themselves increase rapidly in number.

6. For the purpose of gaining weight, which type of resistance-training equipment is best according to research findings, provided equal amounts of resistance work are done on each?
   (a) isokinetic concentric machines
   (b) isometric devices
   (c) isotonic eccentric free weights
   (d) isotonic concentric free weights
   (e) no equipment is better than any other

7. Which dietary supplement has the most research supporting its potential to help increase muscle mass and weight gain during a resistance-training program?
   (a) HMB
   (b) chromium
   (c) creatine
   (d) ginseng
   (e) carnitine

8. Research suggests that proper resistance training may confer some significant health benefits. Which of the following is least likely?
   (a) increased strength to prevent falls and injury as one ages
   (b) increased bone mineral density to help prevent osteoporosis
   (c) increased testosterone levels to help reduce serum HDL-cholesterol

   (d) improved muscle mass and insulin sensitivity to help prevent type 2 diabetes
   (e) improved body image and psychological health

9. Which of the following would be the least likely dietary recommendation for someone trying to gain weight in lean mass?
   (a) Drink plenty of drinks with caffeine, like soda and coffee.
   (b) Increase the intake of high-Calorie, high nutrient foods.
   (c) Keep the intake of saturated fats to a minimum.
   (d) Eat three balanced meals a day supplemented with snacks.
   (e) Supplement the diet with high-Calorie, high nutrient liquids.

10. To gain one pound of muscle weight per week on a weight-training program, an individual might need an additional 14 grams of protein per day above the RDA, in addition to increased Calories. Which of the following would not supply that amount of protein daily?
    (a) 2 glasses of skim milk
    (b) 1 glass of orange juice and 2 eggs
    (c) 1 slice of toast, 1 egg, and 1 ounce of ham
    (d) 1 glass of orange juice, 2 slices of toast, and 1 banana
    (e) 2 ounces of cheese

Answers to multiple choice questions:
1. e; 2. d; 3. d; 4. a; 5. e; 6. e; 7. c; 8. c; 9. a; 10. d.

1. Explain the strength-endurance continuum as a training concept.
2. List the five basic principles of resistance training and provide an example of each.

3. Discuss the physiological means whereby resistance training leads to increases in muscle growth.
4. Describe at least five of the potential health benefits associated with resistance training.

5. Discuss appropriate safety precautions to use during resistance training, especially with use of free weights.

Books

Bahrke, M., and Yesalis, C. 2002. *Performance-Enhancing Substances in Sport and Exercise.* Champaign, IL: Human Kinetics.

Fleck, S., and Kraemer, W. 2004. *Designing Resistance Training Programs.* Champaign, IL: Human Kinetics.

Ivy, J., and Portman, R. 2004. *Nutrient Timing: The Future of Sports Nutrition.* North Bergen, NJ: Basic Health Publications.

National Academy of Sciences. 2002. *Dietary Reference Intakes for Energy, Carbohydrate, Fiber, Fat, Protein and Amino Acids.* Washington, DC: National Academy Press.

Pope, H., et al. 2000. *The Adonis Complex.* New York: Free Press.

Reuben, D. 1996. *Dr. David Reuben's Quick Weight-Gain Program.* New York: Crown Publishers.

U. S. Department of Health and Human Services. 2000. *Healthy People 2010.* Washington, DC: U. S. Government Printing Office.

Reviews

American College of Sports Medicine. 2002. Position stand: Progression models in resistance training for healthy adults. *Medicine & Science in Sports & Exercise* 34:364–80.

American College of Sports Medicine position stand. Exercise and type 2 diabetes. *Medicine & Science in Sports & Exercise* 32:1345–60.

American College of Sports Medicine. 1998. Position stand: The recommended quantity and quality of exercise for developing and maintaining cardiorespiratory and muscular fitness, and flexibility in healthy adults. *Medicine & Science in Sports & Exercise* 30:975–91.

American Academy of Pediatrics. 1983. Weight training and weight lifting: Information for the pediatrician. *Physician and Sportsmedicine* 11 (March): 157–61.

Bartels, R. 1992. Weight training. How to lift—and eat—for strength and power. *Physician and Sportsmedicine* 20 (March): 223–34.

Carson, J. 1997. The regulation of gene expression in hypertrophying skeletal muscle. *Exercise and Sport Sciences Reviews* 25:301–20.

Clarkson, P. M., and Rawson, E. S. 1999. Nutritional supplements to increase muscle mass. *Critical Reviews in Food Science and Nutrition* 39:317–28.

Coleman, E., et al. 2002. Herbal supplements and sport performance. *Sports Science Exchange Roundtable* 13 (4):1–4.

Consumers Union. 2000. A 12-step program for safe exercise. *Consumer Reports on Health* 12 (4):8–9.

Deschenes, M., and Kraemer, W. 2002. Performance and physiologic adaptations to resistance training. *American Journal of Physical and Medical Rehabilitation* 81:S3–S16.

Evans, W. 1996. Reversing sarcopenia: How weight training can build strength and vitality. *Geriatrics* 51 (5): 46–54.

Faigenbaum, A. 2003. Youth resistance training. *President's Council on Physical Fitness and Sports Research Digest* 4 (3):1–8.

Fitts, R., and Widrick, J. 1996. Muscle mechanics: Adaptations with exercise-training. *Exercise and Sport Sciences Reviews* 24:427–73.

Foran, B. 1985. Advantages and disadvantages of isokinetics, variable resistance, and free weights. *National Strength and Conditioning Association Journal* 7:24–25.

Forbes, G. 1999. Body composition: Influence of nutrition, disease, growth and aging. In *Modern Nutrition in Health and Disease,* eds. M. Shils, et al. Baltimore: Williams & Wilkins.

Gatorade Sports Science Institute. 1999. "Muscle builder" supplements. *Sports Science Exchange* 10 (3):1–4.

Gatorade Sports Science Institute. 1995. Methods of weight gain in athletes. *Sports Science Exchange Roundtable* 6 (3): 1–4.

Guy, J., and Micheli, L. 2001. Strength training for children and adolescents. *Journal of the American Academy of Orthopedic Surgery* 9:29–36.

Haff, G., et al. 2003. Carbohydrate supplementation and resistance training. *Journal of Strength and Conditioning Research* 17:187–96.

Houston, M. E. 1999. Gaining weight: The scientific basis of increasing skeletal muscle mass. *Canadian Journal of Applied Physiology* 24:305–16.

Kell, R., et al. 2001. Musculoskeletal fitness, health outcomes and quality of life. *Sports Medicine* 31:863–73.

Kleiner, S. 1995. Healthy muscle gains. *Physician and Sportsmedicine* 23 (4): 21–22.

Kraemer, W., et al. 2003. Strength training basics. *Physician and Sportsmedicine* 31 (8):39–45.

Kraemer, W., et al. 1998. Resistance training and elite athletes: Adaptations and program considerations. *Journal of Orthopaedic and Sports Physical Therapy* 28:110–19.

Kraemer, W., et al. 1996. Strength and power training: Physiological mechanisms of adaptation. *Exercise and Sport Sciences Reviews* 24:363–97.

Kreider, R. B. 1999. Dietary supplements and the promotion of muscle growth with resistance exercise. *Sports Medicine* 27:97–110.

Lambert, C., et al. 2004. Macronutrient considerations for the sport of bodybuilding. *Sports Medicine* 34:317–27.

Layne, J. E., and Nelson, M. E. 1999. The effects of progressive resistance training on bone density: A review. *Medicine & Science in Sports & Exercise* 31:25–30.

Lemon, P. 1996. Is increased dietary protein necessary or beneficial for individuals with a physically active lifestyle? *Nutrition Reviews* 54:S169–S175.

Lodhia, K., et al. 2005. Peripheral nerve injuries in weight training. *Physician and Sportsmedicine* 33 (7):24–37.

National Strength and Conditioning Association. 1987. Breathing during weight training. *National Strength and Conditioning Association Journal* 9:17–24.

Payne, V., et al. 1997. Resistance training in children and youth: A meta-analysis. *Research Quarterly for Exercise and Sport* 68:80–88.

Phillips, S. 2004. Protein requirements and supplementation in strength sports. *Nutrition* 20:689–95.

Pollock, M. L. 1999. Symposium: Resistance training for health and disease. *Medicine & Science in Sports & Exercise* 31:10–45.

Rasmussen, B., and Phillips, S. 2003. Contractile and nutritional regulation of human muscle growth. *Exercise and Sport Sciences Reviews* 31:127–31.

Tipton, K., and Wolfe, R. 2001. Exercise, protein metabolism, and muscle growth. *International Journal of Sport Nutrition and Exercise Metabolism* 11:109–32.

Volek, J. 2004. Strength nutrition. *Current Sports Medicine Reports* 2:189–93.

Williams, M. 1993. Nutritional supplements for strength trained athletes. *Sports Science Exchange* 6 (47): 1–6.

Winett, R., and Carpinelli, R. 2001. Potential health-related benefits of resistance training. *Preventive Medicine* 33:503–13.

Wolfe, B., et al. 2004. Quantitative analysis of single- versus multiple-set programs in resistance training. *Journal of Strength and Conditioning Research* 18:35–47.

Specific Studies

Andersen, L., et al. 2005. The effect of resistance training combined with timed ingestion of protein on muscle fiber size and muscle strength. *Metabolism* 54:151–56.

Bartels, R., et al. 1989. Effect of chronically increased consumption of energy and carbohydrate on anabolic adaptations to strenuous weight training. In *Report of the Ross Symposium on the Theory and Practice of Athletic Nutrition: Bridging the Gap,* eds. J. Storlie and A. Grandjean. Columbus, OH: Ross Laboratories.

Børsheim, E., et al. 2004. Effect of an amino acid, protein, and carbohydrate mixture on net muscle protein balance after resistance exercise. *International Journal of Sport Nutrition and Exercise Metabolism* 14:255–71.

Depcik, E., and Williams, L. 2004. Weight training and body satisfaction of body-image-disturbed women. *Journal of Applied Sport Psychology* 16:287–99.

Faigenbaum, A. D., et al. 1999. The effects of different resistance training protocols on muscular strength and endurance development in children. *Pediatrics* 104:e5

Feigenbaum, M. S., and Pollock, M. L. 1999. Prescription of resistance exercise training for health and disease. *Medicine & Science in Sports & Exercise* 31:38–45.

Fenicchia, L., et al. 2004. Influence of resistance exercise training on glucose control in women with type 2 diabetes. *Metabolism* 53:284–89.

Galuska, D., et al. 2002. The epidemiology of U.S. adults who regularly engage in resistance training. *Research Quarterly for Exercise and Sport* 73:330–34.

Grunewald, K., and Bailey, R. 1993. Commercially marketed supplements for bodybuilding athletes. *Sports Medicine* 15:90–103.

Harber, M., et al. 2004. Skeletal muscle and hormonal adaptations to circuit weight training in untrained men. *Scandinavian Journal of Medicine and Science in Sports* 14:176–85.

Keith, R., et al. 1996. Nutritional status and lipid profiles of trained steroid-using bodybuilders. *International Journal of Sport Nutrition* 6:247–54.

Kraemer, W., and Ratamess, N. 2005. Progression and resistance training. *President's Council on Physical Fitness and Sports Research Digest* 6 (3):1–8.

Kraemer, W. J., et al. 1998. Hormonal responses to consecutive days of heavy-resistance exercise with or without nutritional supplementation. *Journal of Applied Physiology* 85:1544–55.

MacDougall, J., et al. 1992. Factors affecting blood pressure during heavy weight lifting and static contractions. *Journal of Applied Physiology* 73:1590–97.

McLafferty, C., et al. 2004. Resistance training is associated with improved mood in healthy older adults. *Perceptual and Motor Skills* 98:947–57.

Melanson, E., et al. 2002. Resistance and aerobic exercise have similar effects on 24-h nutrient oxidation. *Medicine & Science in Sports & Exercise* 34:1783–1800.

O'Hagan, F., et al. 1995. Response to resistance training in young women and men. *International Journal of Sports Medicine* 16:314–21.

Pickett, T., et al. 2005. Men, muscles, and body image: Comparisons of competitive bodybuilders, weight trainers, and athletically active controls. *British Journal of Sports Medicine* 39:217–22.

Pope, H. G., et al. 1997. Muscle dysmorphia: An underrecognized form of body dysmorphic disorder. *Psychosomatics* 38:548–57.

Roy, B.D., et al. 2000. Macronutrient intake and whole body protein metabolism following resistance exercise. *Medicine & Science in Sports & Exercise* 32:1412–18.

Schuenke, M., et al. 2002. Effect of an acute period of resistance exercise on excess post-exercise oxygen consumption: Implications for body mass management. *European Journal of Applied Physiology* 86:411–17.

Starkey, D., et al. 1996. Effect of resistance training volume on strength and muscle thickness. *Medicine & Science in Sports & Exercise* 28:1311–20.

Staron, R., et al. 1989. Effects of heavy resistance weight training on muscle fiber size and composition in females. *Medicine & Science in Sports & Exercise* 21:S71.

Sturmi, J., and Rutecki, G. 1995. When competitive bodybuilders collapse. *Physician and Sportsmedicine* 23 (11): 49–53.

Tucker, L., et al. 1996. Participation in a strength training program leads to improved dietary intake in adult women. *Journal of the American Dietetic Association* 96:388–90.

Whipple, T., et al. 2004. Acute effects of moderate intensity resistance exercise on bone cell activity. *International Journal of Sports Medicine* 25:496–501.

Food Drugs and Related Supplements

CHAPTER THIRTEEN

LEARNING OBJECTIVES

After studying this chapter, you should be able to:

1. Explain the metabolic, physiological, and psychological effects of alcohol in the body, and evaluate its efficacy as an ergogenic acid.

2. Explain the possible beneficial and detrimental effects of alcohol consumption on health.

3. List and explain the several theories whereby caffeine supplementation is proposed to be an effective ergogenic aid, and summarize its effect on exercise performance.

4. Explain the possible beneficial and detrimental effects of caffeine in the body, and cite current recommendations for coffee consumption.

5. Understand the potential health problems associated with dietary supplements containing stimulants such as ephedra.

6. Describe the theory underlying the use of sodium bicarbonate as an ergogenic aid, and understand the current research findings regarding its efficacy to enhance exercise performance.

7. Identify drugs and related dietary supplements used by physically active individuals to stimulate muscle building and summarize the effects on exercise performance and potential health risks associated with their use.

8. Explain the theory as to how ginseng may enhance sport performance, and highlight the research findings regarding its ergogenic efficacy.

9. List those drugs or dietary supplements discussed in this chapter whose use is prohibited in sports.

Introduction

As noted in chapter 1, winning in sports is dependent not only on genetic endowment with physiological, psychological, and biomechanical attributes inherent to success in any given sport, but also on optimal training of those attributes. However, over the years athletes have attempted to go beyond training to gain a competitive edge on their opponents, and have used a wide variety of ergogenic aids in the process.

The most historic and popular international sporting event is the Olympic Games. The first Olympics were held in Greece, starting in 776 BC and continuing for over 1,000 years, being cancelled in 393 AD because they were regarded as a pagan ritual. Similar to today, athletes who were successful in these ancient Olympics achieved fame and fortune. Most elite athletes had personal trainers, called *paidotribes,* to plan their exercise program and their diet to prepare them for competition. Several famous Greek scientists, including Galen and Pythagoras, were paidotribes who advocated specific, but different, diets for their athletes; Galen promoted beans as a staple of the athlete's diet, whereas Pythagoras prohibited them. During these early Olympic Games various plants served as sources of drugs. For example, certain mushrooms contained hallucinogens while *Strychnos nux vamica* was the source of strychnine; in small doses both could serve as a stimulant. Athletes in the ancient Olympics were reported to consume such plants for their potential ergogenic effect.

The modern Olympic Games were resurrected in 1896 and continue today with competition among thousands of athletes in dozens of sports. As in the ancient Olympics, athletes in the modern Olympics have been reported to use drugs in attempts to obtain that competitive edge. As several of these drugs are found in some common foods or beverages that we may consume, they have been referred to as *food drugs.* Additionally, some plant extracts may be marketed as dietary supplements designed to imitate ergogenic drugs. Others, particularly herbals, may be used for their pharmaceutical effects by practitioners of alternative medicine.

In this chapter, we will evaluate the effects of several food drugs and related dietary supplements on exercise performance and health. Two very common food drugs, alcohol and caffeine, have been studied for their ergogenic effects for over 100 years, and have been used by athletes as a means to enhance performance since the early 1900s. Each has also been studied extensively for possible health effects, both positive and negative. The dietary supplement Ma Huang contains ephedra, or ephedrine, a stimulant theorized to enhance exercise performance, particularly when combined with caffeine. Ephedrine has also been studied for its potential health effects. Sodium bicarbonate, or baking soda, is used in many food products, and has been studied for eighty years as a means to enhance performance; it also has been marketed as part of a dietary supplement for athletes. Several anabolic hormones, and related steroid drugs, are used to increase muscle mass and have been popular with strength/power athletes for over 50 years. Because the use of such drugs has been controlled and illegal for sport competition for many years, companies have marketed prohormones, or precursors to these hormones, as dietary supplements to avoid drug regulations. However, these prohormones have also recently been classified as controlled drugs and their use is illegal in sports. Use of these anabolic agents may also pose serious health risks. Finally, several herbals, most notably ginseng, are used in alternative medicine for various purposes, one being enhancement of physical performance.

For the interested reader, a complete list of the drugs mentioned in this chapter, plus others, may be found at the World Anti-Doping (WADA) Website, www.wadaama.org.

Alcohol: Ergogenic Effects and Health Implications

The alcohol produced for human consumption is ethyl alcohol, or **ethanol**. Ethanol may be classified as a psychoactive drug, a toxin, or a nutrient.

What is the alcohol and nutrient content of typical alcoholic beverages?

Alcohol is a transparent, colorless liquid derived from the fermentation of sugars in fruits, vegetables, and grains. Although classified legally as a drug, alcohol is a component of many common beverages served throughout the world. In the United States, alcohol is consumed mainly as a natural ingredient of beer, wine, and liquors. Although the alcohol content may vary in different types, in general, beer is about 4–5 percent alcohol, wine is about 12–14 percent alcohol, and typical bar liquor (whiskey, rum, gin, vodka) is about 40–45 percent alcohol (figure 13.1). The term **proof** is a measure of the alcohol content in a beverage and is double the percentage; an 86-proof bottle of whiskey is 43 percent alcohol, while a 150-proof bottle of Caribbean rum is 75 percent alcohol.

One drink of alcohol is the equivalent of one-half ounce of pure ethyl alcohol or the equivalent of about 13–14 grams of alcohol. The following amounts of beer, wine, and liquor contain approximately equal amounts of alcohol and are classified as one drink:

12 ounces (one bottle) of beer
4 ounces (one wine glass) of wine
1.25 ounces (one jigger or shot glass) of liquor

However, some beers may contain 10 percent alcohol, some wines are fortified to 18–24 percent, and some liquors are 50–75 percent. Such beverages would provide significantly more alcohol per standard drink. Technically, alcohol may be classified as a nutrient because it provides energy, one of the major functions of food. Alcohol contains about 7 Calories per gram, almost twice the value of an equal amount of carbohydrate or protein. Beer and wine also contain some carbohydrate, a source of additional Calories. In general, a bottle of regular beer has about 150 Calories, while a 4-ounce glass of wine or a shot glass of liquor contains about 100 Calories. Table 13.1 provides an approximate analysis of the caloric content of common alcoholic beverages and nonalcoholic beer.

In general, the alcohol Calories found in beer, wine, and liquor are empty Calories. Although wine and beer contain trace amounts of protein, vitamins, minerals, and phytochemicals, liquor is void of any nutrient value.

What is the metabolic fate of alcohol in the body?

About 20 percent of the alcohol ingested may be absorbed by the stomach; the remainder passes on to the intestine for absorption. The absorption is rapid, particularly if the digestive tract is empty. The alcohol enters the blood and is distributed to the various tissues, being diluted by the water content of the body. A small portion of the alcohol, about 3–10 percent, is excreted from the body through the breath, urine, or sweat, but the majority is metabolized by the liver, the organ that metabolizes other drugs. As the blood circulates, the liver of an average adult male will metabolize about one-third ounce (8–10 grams) of alcohol per hour, or somewhat less than the amount of alcohol in one drink.

Although alcohol is derived from the fermentation of carbohydrates, it is metabolized in the body like fat. The liver helps convert the metabolic by-products of alcohol into fatty acids, which may be stored in the liver or transported into the blood. Several other compounds, such as lactate, acetate, and acetaldehyde, may also be released into the blood. These products may eventually be utilized for energy and converted into carbon dioxide and water. A schematic of alcohol metabolism is presented in figure 13.2.

As noted, the liver of a 150-pound male can metabolize only about one-third ounce of alcohol, or less than one drink, per hour. The rate is lower in smaller individuals and higher in larger individuals. Thus, consumption of alcohol at a rate greater than one drink per hour will result in an accumulation of alcohol in the blood; this is measured as the **blood alcohol concentration (BAC)** in grams per 100 milliliters of blood. For the average male, one drink will result in a BAC of about 0.025; four drinks in an hour would lead to a BAC of approximately 0.10.

Is alcohol an effective ergogenic aid?

For over a century, athletes have consumed alcohol just prior to or during competition in attempts to improve performance. Alcohol has been alleged to alter energy metabolism, improve physiological processes, or modify psychological factors so as to benefit the athlete. Let us look at the available research to evaluate the truth of these allegations.

Use as an energy source Although alcohol contains a relatively large number of Calories and its metabolic pathways in the body are short, the available evidence suggests that it is not utilized to any significant extent during exercise. First, the major sources of energy for exercise are carbohydrates and fats, which are in ample supply in most individuals. Alcohol may help form fats, but there is no evidence that it can substitute for other fat sources in the body. Even if it could, this would be of no benefit because the body has more than enough fat to supply energy

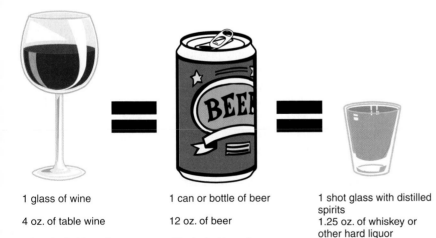

1 glass of wine

4 oz. of table wine

12% alcohol by volume

4 × 0.12 = 0.48 oz.
of ethyl alcohol per serving

1 can or bottle of beer

12 oz. of beer

4% alcohol by volume

12 × 0.04 = 0.48 oz.
of ethyl alcohol per serving

1 shot glass with distilled spirits
1.25 oz. of whiskey or other hard liquor
40% alcohol by volume or 80 proof

1.25 × 0.40 = 0.50 oz.
of ethyl alcohol per serving

FIGURE 13.1 Alcohol equivalencies in typical beverages.

TABLE 13.1 Caloric content of typical alcoholic beverages

		Carbohydrate		Alcohol		Total
Beverage	Amount	Grams	Calories	Grams	Calories	Calories
Beer, regular	12 ounces	13	52	13	91	150
Beer, light	12 ounces	7	28	11	77	109
Beer, nonalcoholic	12 ounces	12	48	1	7	55
Beer, alcohol-free	12 ounces	12	48	0	0	48
Wine, table	4 ounces	4	16	12	84	100
Liquor, 80 proof	1.25 ounces	0	0	14	98	100

The small discrepancies in the calculation of total Calories for beer and liquor may be attributed to a small protein content in beer and trace amounts of carbohydrate in liquor.

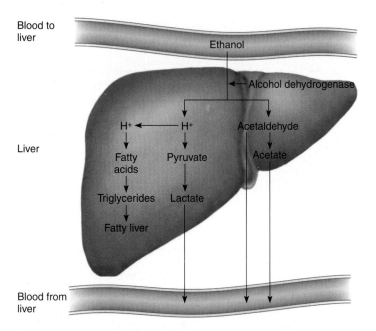

FIGURE 13.2 Simplified metabolic pathways of ethanol (alcohol) in the liver. Hydrogen ions are removed from ethanol as it is converted to acetaldehyde, which may be released into the blood for transport to other tissues. The excess hydrogen ions may combine with fatty acids to form triglycerides or with pyruvate to form lactate. Excessive accumulation of triglycerides may lead to the development of a fatty liver and eventually to cirrhosis.

during prolonged exercise. Second, the by-products of alcohol metabolism that are released by the liver into the blood may enter the skeletal muscles but appear to be of little importance to exercising muscle. Third, even if the energy from alcohol could be used, it would represent an uneconomical source. The amount of oxygen needed to release the Calories from alcohol is greater than for an equivalent amount of carbohydrate and fat. And lastly, the rate at which the liver metabolizes alcohol limits its use as an energy source during exercise, particularly in an individual working at a high level of intensity. In summary, these four factors suggest alcohol is not a key energy source during exercise, and even if it were, it would not offer any advantages over natural supplies of carbohydrate and fat. Recent research with carbon labeling revealed alcohol did not significantly modify endogenous carbohydrate and fat utilization during exercise.

Effect on exercise metabolism Numerous studies have evaluated the potential ergogenic effect of alcohol intake, both in small and large amounts, just prior to various exercise protocols. In general, the resultant effects depend on the alcohol dose and the type of exercise performance.

Research supports the finding that alcohol in small amounts (one to two drinks) neither improves nor deteriorates physiological processes associated with maximal aerobic exercise, including VO_2 max and maximal heart rate; neither does it affect other indicators of maximal aerobic performance such as exercise tests to exhaustion. For example, one study reported an apparent trend toward a deterioration in performance with increased alcohol intake, but there was no adverse effect on 5-mile (8 km) treadmill run time. Moreover, tests of anaerobic performance, such as strength and local muscular endurance, also are not affected.

However, a few studies have reported some potential adverse effects of consuming alcohol before or during submaximal exercise. Most of the studies alluded to above were conducted on males. A recent study reported some adverse acute effects of moderate alcohol consumption on cardiovascular and metabolic responses in females. In a submaximal cycling exercise task for 30 minutes, ingestion of alcohol increased the heart rate, oxygen consumption, blood pressure, and blood lactate, which the investigators indicated were negative effects. Earlier studies have also shown similar effects in males, including decreased pumping capacity of the heart with high BACs. Moreover, some recent research reported a significant decrease in aerobic endurance when alcohol was ingested before and during a treadmill run at about 80–85 percent VO_2 max, which may have been associated with an impaired glucose metabolism. Impaired performance has also been reported in both an 800-meter and 1500-meter run following alcohol consumption, and the detrimental effect was greater with increasing BACs from 0.01 to 0.10.

Several metabolic effects of alcohol intake could impair endurance performance. Alcohol reduces gluconeogenesis by the liver and glucose uptake by the legs during the latter stages of exercise. In prolonged exercise, such as marathons, these effects could lead to an earlier onset of hypoglycemia or muscle glycogen depletion and a subsequent decrease in performance. Moreover, some studies have reported reduced absorption of vitamin B_1 associated with moderate intakes of alcohol. Theoretically, this could impair physical performance of an endurance nature because vitamin B_1 is involved in the aerobic metabolism of carbohydrate.

Alcohol ingestion may also increase urine production by decreasing release of the anti-diuretic hormone. This effect could possibly impair temperature regulation during exercise under warm/hot environmental conditions. Starting a prolonged endurance event under warm/hot conditions in a dehydrated state could certainly impair performance. As a rehydration fluid after dehydration, drinks containing 4 percent alcohol or more, such as beer, tend to delay the recovery process as measured by restoration of blood and plasma volume.

Additional research is merited to document any adverse effects of alcohol on cardiovascular or metabolic processes during exercise, but at this time it appears that alcohol intake before or during aerobic and anaerobic endurance exercise is not ergogenic and may be **ergolytic**, or impairing exercise performance.

Effect on psychological processes   Alcohol also has been used as an ergogenic aid for its psychological effects. It is a narcotic, a depressant, that affects the brain. As a depressant, alcohol would not be advocated as a means to improve performance; however, some have contended that increased feelings of self-confidence, reduced anxiety levels, and a perceived decrease in sensitivity to pain may offset any depressant effects and possibly benefit performance. Moreover, alcohol in small doses may exert a paradoxical stimulation effect. Parts of the brain that normally inhibit behavior may be depressed by alcohol, leading to a transitory sensation of excitement.

Although these effects may occur, research does not support the use of alcohol in sports involving psychological processes such as perceptual-motor abilities. Perceptual-motor activities involve the perception of a stimulus, integration of this stimulus by the brain, and an appropriate motor response (movement). The evidence overwhelmingly supports the conclusion that alcohol adversely affects psychomotor performance skills, such as reaction time, balance, hand/eye coordination, and visual perception. These are important in events with rapidly changing stimuli, such as tennis.

In one form of athletic competition, such as marksmanship in riflery, pistol shooting, dart throwing, and archery, alcohol may be used to decrease hand muscle tremor and thereby improve accuracy for competition. Although research generally is not support-

ive of an improved performance, one study with archers revealed a tendency toward reduced tremor with low blood alcohol levels, resulting in a smoother release. However, no actual performance data were revealed. Throwing accuracy improved in darts at a BAC of 0.02, but was impaired at a BAC of 0.05. This area of study merits additional research.

Social drinking and sports   Only a limited number of studies have been conducted relative to the effect of social drinking upon physical performance, but there is rather general agreement that light social drinking will not impair performance on the following day. Tests of reaction time, strength, power, and cardiovascular performance were not adversely affected following the consumption of one drink the night before. On the other hand, heavy drinking may impair performance on the following day owing to hangover effects, involuntary eye movement, or dehydration.

The use of alcohol by Olympic athletes had been banned previously by the IOC, but because wine and beer are commonly consumed as a part of many traditional European meals it was removed from the banned list prior to the 1972 Olympics. However, individual sports federations within the IOC still may consider alcohol use during competition as grounds for disqualification. At the present time, only several sports, such as those that involve shooting competition, ban the use of alcohol.

In his review, Williams noted that although alcohol consumption is not prohibited for use by most athletes, there are no data supporting an ergogenic effect, and some data to suggest an ergolytic effect. This viewpoint was supported by Burke and Maughan in a recent review. Athletes who drink socially should do so in moderation, and possibly abstain 24 hours prior to a prolonged endurance contest.

What effect can drinking alcohol have upon my health?

Consumption of alcoholic beverages is a popular pastime worldwide. People drink mainly for social reasons, but when and how much they drink may have a significant impact on their health and the health of others. As Klatsky recently noted, the basic disparity underlying all alcohol-health relations is between the effects of lighter and heavier drinking. Although many of the effects of alcohol may negatively affect health status, some effects may be positive. "Both the negative and the positive effects are detailed in a recent National Institute on Alcohol Abuse and Alcoholism (NIAAA) state-of-the-science report on the effects of moderate drinking."

Negative Effects   Alcohol affects all cells in the body, and many of these effects may have significant health implications. Room and others noted that alcohol is causally related to more than 60 different medical conditions, and is a major challenge to public health. Drinking alcoholic beverages, particularly in large amounts, is associated with over 100,000 deaths per year.

Direct toxic effects   Alcohol has a direct toxic effect on the intestinal walls; it tends to impair the absorption of vitamins such as thiamin (B_1). Individuals who drink alcohol also have a higher incidence rate of pharyngeal and esophageal cancer, which may possibly be associated with the direct effect of alcohol as it contacts these tissues during ingestion. Combining alcohol with certain medication such as aspirin or nonsteroidal anti-inflammatory agents (ibuprofen) may promote gastrointestinal bleeding. Drinking alcohol may also aggravate certain health conditions, such as peptic ulcers.

Liver function The liver is the only organ in the body that metabolizes alcohol, and alcohol may affect liver function in several ways. It may interfere with the metabolism of other drugs, increasing the effect of some and lessening the effects of others. Even with a balanced diet high in protein, consuming six drinks a day for less than a month has been shown to cause significant accumulation of fat in the liver. If continued for five years or more, the liver cells degenerate. Eventually the damaged liver cells are replaced by non-functioning scar tissue, a condition known as **cirrhosis.** As liver function deteriorates, fat, carbohydrate, and protein metabolism are not regulated properly; this has possible pathological consequences for other body organs such as the kidney, pancreas, and heart.

Nutrients, such as specific lipids from soybeans, are being studied as a means to help prevent this liver degeneration. Some scientists theorize that wine, because it contains antioxidants, may help prevent oxidative stress and subsequent liver damage, and may thus be the alcoholic beverage with less damaging effects. However, liver damage is one of the most consistent adverse effects of excess alcohol intake.

Mental processes Following absorption, the most immediate effects of alcohol are on the brain; often these effects are paradoxical. Although alcohol is a depressant, a small amount often exerts a stimulating effect because it may release some of the normal inhibitory control mechanisms in the brain. For the most part, however, alcohol acts as a depressant, and its effects on the brain are dose-dependent. The effects occur in a hierarchical fashion related to the development of the brain. In general, alcohol first affects the higher brain centers. With increasing dosages, lower levels of brain function become depressed with subsequent disturbance of normal functions. This hierarchy of brain functions, from higher levels to lower levels, and some of the functions affected by alcohol may be generalized as follows:

Thinking and reasoning—Judgment
Perceptual-motor responses—Reaction time
Fine motor coordination—Muscles of speech
Gross motor coordination—Walking
Visual processes—Double vision
Alertness—Sleep, coma
Respiratory control—Respiratory failure, death

An overview of the effects of increasing blood alcohol content on mental and physical functions is presented in table 13.2.

Youth and gender may influence the mental effects of alcohol. Monti and others reported that heavy drinking during the teenage years may cause permanent brain damage, including impaired memory. Mann and others noted that women become dependent

TABLE 13.2 Typical effects of increasing blood alcohol content		
Number of drinks* consumed in 2 hours	Blood** alcohol content	Typical effects
2–3	.02–.04	Reduced tension, relaxed feeling, relief from daily stress
4–5	.06–.09	Legally drunk in some states, impaired judgment, a high feeling, impaired fine motor ability and coordination
6–8	.11–.16	Legally drunk in all states, slurred speech, impaired gross motor coordination, staggering gait
9–12	.18–.25	Loss of control of voluntary activity, erratic behavior, impaired vision
13–18	.27–.39	Stuporous, total loss of coordination
19 and above	>.40	Coma, depression of respiratory centers, death

*One drink = 12 ounces regular beer
4 ounces wine
1.25 ounces liquor
**BAC based on body weight of 160 pounds (72.6 KG). The BAC will increase proportionally for individuals weighing less (such as a 120-pound female) and will decrease proportionally for individuals weighing more (such as a 200-pound football player). For example, four to five drinks in 2 hours could lead to a BAC of 0.08–0.12 in a 120-pound individual.

on alcohol quicker and suffer adverse effects, such as brain atrophy, faster as compared to men.

If you want to avoid mental impairment associated with alcohol, abstinence is the simplest approach. For those who do drink, abstinence is advised under certain conditions. The acute effects of excessive alcohol consumption include impairment of both motor coordination and judgment—two factors that are extremely important in the safe operation of an automobile. At the least, being arrested for drunk driving may have serious social and personal consequences. At the worst, alcohol is involved as a cause of nearly one-half of all automobile fatalities—20,000 deaths per year in the United States alone. As the saying goes, "Don't drink and drive!"

Alcohol usage also is correlated highly with aggressive tendencies. Laboratory studies have indicated aggressive behavior is directly related to the quantity of alcohol consumed. In a recent meta-analysis investigating the role of alcohol in fatal nontraffic injuries, Smith and others concluded that alcohol was an important factor in homicides, suicides, and unintentional injury deaths. Alcohol abuse is also associated with sexual abuse.

Most of these adverse effects are associated with excessive alcohol intake, particularly as practiced in binge drinking. Recent surveys indicate that almost half of college students binge, and one of the most significant factors underlying alcohol-related behavior problems is the amount of alcohol consumed; the greater the amount of alcohol consumed, the more serious the problem. According to the NIAAA, nationally there are more than 1,400 alcohol-related deaths each year among college students, most due to automobile accidents, but several attributed to heavy binge drinking with resultant respiratory failure.

Many physically active individuals, including competitive athletes, consume alcohol on a regular basis. In their periodic study of NCAA athletes, Green and others recently noted that alcohol was the most widely used drug, with over 80 percent of athletes using alcohol within the past year. O'Brien and Lyons indicated that alcohol-related problems may be more prevalent in the athletic population due to their risk-taking mentality.

DNA damage   Laboratory research has shown that *in vitro* (that is, in a test tube) alcohol and acetaldehyde cause changes in DNA (the genetic material in body cells) comparable to changes elicited by carcinogens. This DNA damage may occur at an alcohol concentration equivalent to one to two drinks. In those who drink, this finding could be related to the increased risk of certain forms of cancer, including pharyngeal and esophageal cancer as mentioned earlier, and also breast and colon cancer.

One of the most debated issues is the risk of breast cancer. Possible mechanisms have been identified; in addition to potential DNA damage, alcohol ingestion may also increase estrogen levels, a factor that increases breast cancer risk. Research associating increased incidence of breast cancer with alcohol consumption is epidemiological in nature. The NIAAA indicated that the effect of alcohol intake on the risk for breast cancer remains controversial. In summary, the NIAAA noted that the overall evidence from epidemiologic data seems to indicate that alcohol may be associated with an increase in the risk of breast cancer in the population overall, but the relative effect of moderate consumption is small at the individual level; the increase in risk is most clearly evident for women with a family history of breast cancer and those using estrogen replacement therapy. The NIAAA recommends that women, in conjunction with their health care provider, should weigh their potential increased risk for breast cancer against their potential reduced risk for cardiovascular disease in determining whether alcohol consumption should be reduced.

Women who drink should abstain during pregnancy because even moderate consumption of alcohol, or even a single drinking binge, may affect DNA in the embryo and fetus. The term **fetal alcohol syndrome (FAS)** refers to the effects upon the development of a fetus if a mother consumes alcohol while pregnant. The incidence rate of FAS is very high in the United States, and FAS is currently the major cause of mental retardation in the Western world. The child may experience retardation in growth and mental development as well as facial birth defects (figure 13.3). **Fetal alcohol effects (FAE)** may be observed in children when full-blown FAS is not present. Children with FAE are easily distracted and have poor attention spans. Both FAS and FAE are associated with learning dis-

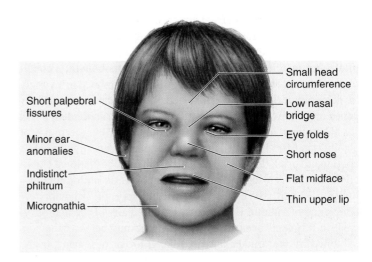

FIGURE 13.3   Common facial characteristics of children with fetal alcohol syndrome (FAS).

orders in children. No "safe" amount of alcohol during pregnancy has been determined. Thus, the U.S. Surgeon General indicated that the safest approach is abstinence.

Obesity   Alcohol is a significant source of Calories, about 7 per gram, somewhat comparable to the caloric content of fat. Recent research has indicated that if small amounts of alcohol (5 percent of daily caloric intake) are interchanged for an equivalent caloric intake from carbohydrates, there is no effect on daily energy expenditure. In other words, alcohol Calories themselves will not increase body fat as long as total daily caloric intake matches daily caloric expenditure. In general, the NIAAA indicates that the relationship between moderate alcohol consumption and obesity remains inconclusive.

However, Yeomans noted that alcohol may increase energy intake in several ways. Alcohol stimulates the appetite, increasing food intake, and alcohol contains energy. Angelo Tremblay, an esteemed scientist in weight control, and his colleagues recently found that alcohol has no inhibitory effect on food intake and its energy content, and when consumed in conjunction with a high-fat diet promotes overfeeding, a primary determinant of obesity. Additionally, Jequier notes that alcohol ingestion reduces fat oxidation and favors a positive fat balance. These points may underlie the conclusion of the recent study by Wannamethee and others, mainly that higher alcohol consumption is positively associated with both overall and abdominal adiposity, irrespective of the type of drink or whether the alcohol is drunk with meals or not. As noted in chapter 11, reducing alcoholic intake may be an important component of an effective weight control program.

Excessive drinking and alcoholism   Heavy alcohol consumption aggravates most of the health problems mentioned above and may lead to addiction. Some research has shown that three or more drinks per day increase the risk of developing high blood pressure and may increase blood lipid levels. These conditions are associated with cardiovascular disease, and heavy alcohol consumption is linked to sudden death from heart failure and stroke.

Alcohol abuse is the major drug problem in the United States, posing a problem for one in seven males and one in sixteen females, or about one out of every ten drinkers. Excessive intake of alcohol may lead to a disorder known as **alcoholism,** a condition whose etiology is unknown but probably is related to a variety of physiological, psychological, and sociological factors. Many genes are likely to be involved in increasing an individual's risk for alcoholism, and Gordis indicates that heavy, long-term use of alcohol modifies brain cells in such a way that certain individuals continue to drink despite growing difficulties. The National Council on Alcoholism suggests that there is no pat definition for alcoholism; it may be evidenced by a variety of behaviors. A deficiency of vitamin B may contribute to many of the neuropsychiatric problems seen in alcoholism. The number of behaviors exhibited by the drinker may be related to various stages in the progression toward alcoholism. Appendix C, a questionnaire developed by the National Council on Alcoholism, provides for an assessment of these behaviors.

Positive Effects   On the positive side, most recent epidemiological research and reviews have shown that light to moderate consumption of alcohol is associated with lessened mortality. For example, in a recent meta-analysis of the relationship of alcohol consumption to all-cause mortality, Holman and others noted that light drinking (less than 2 drinks per day in males; less than 1 drink per day in females) was associated with a lower relative risk for all-cause mortality compared to abstainers, but that the relative risk returned to normal with moderate alcohol intake and increased to 1.37 for heavy drinkers, those taking six or more drinks daily. Research suggests that light to moderate alcohol intake reduces risk of coronary heart disease and stroke, a major factor in reducing risk for all-cause mortality. The mechanism is not known, but several have been proposed based on epidemiological and experimental studies.

One theory suggests small amounts of alcohol induce a relaxation effect, which may reduce emotional stress, a risk factor associated with CHD. Another theory suggests alcohol decreases platelet aggregability (clotting ability) by increasing the activity of a clot-dissolving enzyme in the blood. Still another theory, proposed by Antinoro and others, indicates that moderate amounts of alcohol may improve blood flow to the brain, which they theorize may help prevent or delay certain brain diseases, such as Alzheimer's and Parkinson's, and might help prevent certain forms of stroke. Other mechanisms may be working as well, such as an enhanced insulin sensitivity, which may help in the prevention of the metabolic syndrome and diabetes, both risk factors for CHD.

The most prevalent theory involves the effect of alcohol to raise levels of HDL-cholesterol, the form of cholesterol that protects against the development of CHD (see discussion on pages 174–177). A significant number of studies have supported this effect, although the mechanisms have not been determined. Some studies have shown an increase in one form of cholesterol, HDL_2, which is believed to be protective. Other studies note an increase in HDL_3, which may also elicit a protective effect. Gaziano and others noted alcohol may reduce the risk of heart disease by raising the levels of both HDL_2 and HDL_3. However, Hines and others noted individuals with a specific genetic predisposition may benefit more from alcohol intake, as they may produce a form of alcohol dehydrogenase that metabolizes alcohol more slowly, leading to greater increases in HDL-cholesterol.

Some investigators have theorized that the consumption of certain types of alcoholic beverages, most notably red wine, is responsible for the reported health benefits. Pigments in red wine contain polyphenols and other phytochemicals that may help prevent coronary heart disease by favorable actions on various processes. For example, de Lorimier indicates that phenolic compounds in wine can also increase HDL, have antioxidant activity, decrease platelet aggregation, and promote vasodilation—all potentially beneficial. Chopra and others noted also that alcohol-free red wine may provide some similar health benefits. However, Denke indicates that there is no evidence to support endorsement of one type of alcoholic beverage over another, noting that beer has its own nutritional value. Compared to wine, beer contains more protein and B vitamins, is rich in flavonoids, and has an equivalent antioxidant content, but of different specific antioxidants derived from barley and hops. In a recent study, Mukamal and others found that men who consumed alcohol 3–4 days per week experienced a reduced risk of myocardial infarction, but the type of beverage consumed did not substantially alter this effect.

Although these factors may be important, Naimi and others contend that individuals who drink moderately may practice other lifestyle behaviors that reduce the risk for CHD. For example, Smothers and Bertolucci recently reported that people who moderate their alcohol intake also engage in more leisure-time activity, which may play an explanatory role in the alcohol-heart disease relationship. As noted in chapter 1, exercise itself may reduce the risk of CHD. Nevertheless, data from the National Runners' Health Study, as reported by Williams, reveals that men's blood pressure increases in association with the amount of alcohol intake, regardless of running level. Thus, it should be reemphasized that although there appear to be some positive health effects associated with light to moderate alcohol intake, or at least no detrimental effects, heavier drinking is another matter.

Because of the potential for abuse, addiction, and all types of injuries, abstinence from alcohol or prudent consumption is generally recommended by health authorities. "Low risk" drinking is an emerging term to represent light to moderate alcohol intake. As noted above, abstinence is the best policy for pregnant women or if you plan to operate a motor vehicle. Health professionals, however, generally support the view that low risk drinking, along with a balanced diet, should not pose any health problem to the average healthy individual. The definition of moderation has varied, but the NIAAA recently indicated that except for individuals at particular risk, consumption of 2 drinks a day for men and 1 for women is unlikely to increase health risks. As risks for some conditions and diseases do increase at higher levels of consumption, men should be cautioned to not exceed 4 drinks on any day and women to not exceed 3 on any day.

Nevertheless, although there are actually some possible health benefits associated with alcohol consumption in moderation, health authorities caution that these potential benefits are not sufficient cause to start drinking if you currently abstain. The NIAAA stipulates that *moderate alcohol use* should not be construed as *healthy alcohol use,* because numerous individual differences, such as age, genetics, and metabolic rate, may affect the response to alcohol. You should consult with your physician if you are considering drinking for its possible health benefits.

Key Concept Recap

▶ One drink of alcohol contains approximately 13–14 grams of alcohol, or about one-half ounce. One drink is typically the equivalent of 12 ounces of beer, 4 ounces of wine, and 1.25 ounces of 40 proof whiskey. However, the alcohol content in some beverages may be substantially greater.

▶ Alcohol is not an effective ergogenic aid, and in fact may actually impair athletic performance, that is, it is ergolytic.

▶ Consumption of alcohol in moderation appears to cause no major health problems for the normal, healthy adult, and may actually confer some health benefits. However, alcohol may be contraindicated for some, such as women during pregnancy. Heavy drinking is associated with numerous health problems.

Check for Yourself

Visit a local beer/wine store that carries a wide variety of products, including microbrews and fortified wines. Check the labels for percentage alcohol content, listing those from lowest to highest. Calculate how much alcohol would be in a standard drink from each.

Caffeine: Ergogenic Effects and Health Implications

Various stimulants have been used in attempts to enhance health and sports performance including caffeine.

What is caffeine and in what food products is it found?

Caffeine is an odorless, bitter, white alkaloid that appears naturally in many plants, and is found in many of the foods and beverages that we consume every day, such as coffee, tea, colas, caffeinated waters, juices, sports drinks and sports bars, and chocolate; it is the most popular social drug in the United States (figure 13.4). It is also found in various dietary supplements, such as kola nuts and guarana, and even some over-the-counter stimulant supplements targeted to athletes; most recently, caffeine has been marketed as *performance candy,* such as Jolt Caffeine-Energy Gum and Buzz Bites, a chocolate chew candy. Yet caffeine is legally classified as a drug and has some powerful physiological effects on the human body. A normal therapeutic dose of caf-

FIGURE 13.4 Caffeine is the most popular social drug in the United States. About 90 percent of all adults consume caffeine in one form or another, mainly as coffee.

feine may range from 100–300 milligrams. Some approximate amounts in the beverages we consume are 80–135 mg in a cup of perked coffee, 40–60 mg in a cup of tea, and 35–45 mg in a can of cola. The caffeine content of various products is presented in table 13.3.

What effects does caffeine have on the body that may benefit exercise performance?

Caffeine functions as a stimulant of the nervous system. Its primary mode of action is to block the neurotransmitter adenosine, and thus influence a wide variety of metabolic processes throughout the body. Caffeine stimulates heart function, blood circulation, and release of epinephrine (adrenaline) from the adrenal gland. Epinephrine, also a stimulant, augments these effects and also, in conjunction with caffeine, stimulates a wide variety of tissues. Together they potentiate muscle contraction, raise the rate of muscle and liver glycogen breakdown, increase release of FFA from adipose tissue, and increase use of muscle triglycerides. One of the most observed effects at rest is an increase in blood levels of FFA. These varied physiological responses are mediated by the action of caffeine, or epinephrine, to enhance appropriate intracellular functions in specific cells; functions such as increased calcium release to excite muscle contraction or elevated enzymic activity to release FFA from adipose tissue cells. Caffeine also enhances

TABLE 13.3 Caffeine content in selected products

Product	Serving size	Caffeine (milligrams)
Coffee, brewed	8 ounce cup	80–135
Coffee, instant	8 ounce cup	65–100
Coffee, decaffeinated	8 ounce cup	3–4
Tea, brewed	8 ounce cup	40–60
Tea, green	8 ounce cup	15
Hot cocoa	8 ounce cup	15
Sodas, cola	12 ounce can	35–45
Sodas, high caffeine	12 ounce can	55–70
Energy drinks	8 ounce can	80
Performance candy	1 Buzz Bite	100
Stimulants	1 Vivarin tablet	200
Dietary supplements	5 grams guarana	250

Note: Check labels of over-the-counter stimulants and dietary supplements for caffeine content.

psychological processes, increasing alertness and a feeling of well-being. Caffeine is degraded rapidly in the liver to dimethylxanthines, metabolites which may also affect metabolism favorably.

Overall, caffeine may influence central and peripheral metabolic processes, as well as psychological processes, to help delay the onset of fatigue and has been theorized to enhance performance in many types of exercise, including endurance, strength, speed, and power.

Does caffeine enhance exercise performance?

Caffeine has been studied for its possible ergogenic effects for nearly 100 years. Early research focused on improvements in strength, power, and psychomotor parameters such as reaction time. However, since research by Costill's laboratory in the late 1970s suggested caffeine could increase endurance, many researchers have investigated the effects of caffeine on fat metabolism as a means to enhance performance of endurance athletes, such as marathoners, primarily because of caffeine's alleged potential to spare the use of muscle glycogen. In recent years, increased research attention has also refocused on the ergogenic potential of caffeine in tasks of higher exercise intensity and shorter duration.

Literally hundreds of studies have been conducted to test the ergogenic effectiveness of caffeine. Considerable differences exist in the experimental designs of caffeine studies in such aspects as caffeine delivery system (caffeine in coffee or capsule form), caf-

feine dosage (3–15 mg per kg body weight), the type of exercise task (power, strength, reaction time, short-term endurance, prolonged endurance), the intensity of the exercise (submaximal exercise, maximal exercise), the training status of the subject (trained, untrained), the preexercise diet (high-carbohydrate, mixed), the subjects' caffeine status (user, abstainer), and individual variability (reactor, nonreactor). These differences complicate interpretation of the results. Additionally, some investigators have combined caffeine with other related stimulants, such as ephedrine and theophylline.

Overall, research indicates that caffeine supplementation may be an effective ergogenic for a variety of exercise tests and may improve performance by different mechanisms. Several reviews and a meta-analysis regarding the effect of caffeine on physical performance have been published recently, and the interested reader is referred to the articles by Graham, Doherty and Smith, and Kalmar and Cafarelli. Based on these reviews and an independent analysis of key studies, the following points represent a general summary of the available research.

Effect on Mental Alertness Caffeine can increase alertness, which may improve simple reaction time. Doses of 200 milligrams have been effective, particularly when subjects are mentally fatigued. Hogervorst and others recently noted that caffeine, as part of a carbohydrate-electrolyte solution, improved cognitive function in endurance-trained athletes following a maximal 1-hour time trial on a bicycle ergometer. Larger doses, above 400 milligrams, may increase nervousness and anxiousness in some individuals, and thus may adversely affect performance in events characterized by fine motor skills and control of hand steadiness, such as pistol shooting.

Effect on Muscle Contraction Caffeine may increase the release of calcium from the sarcoplasmic reticulum in the muscle, possibly increasing the force of muscle contraction. Tarnopolsky and Cupido recently evaluated this direct effect of caffeine on muscle contraction in both habitual and nonhabitual caffeine users, stimulating the muscle electrically at different intensities to induce a 2-minute tetanic contraction. They found that caffeine potentiated the force of muscle contraction during the last minute of stimulation and suggested that the data support the hypothesis that some of the ergogenic effect of caffeine in endurance exercise performance occurs directly at the skeletal muscle level. Some studies support such a direct effect. Kalmar and Cafarelli reported significant improvement in a maximal isometric endurance task just over 1 minute in duration. In his recent review, Graham noted that although there are fewer studies with resistance exercise, the available literature would suggest that caffeine could increase endurance in repeated contractions.

Effect on High-intensity Exercise The vast majority of earlier studies revealed that caffeine did not improve performance in events characterized by strength, speed, power, or local muscular endurance, nor in endurance events lasting less than 30 minutes, and this is the general conclusion of the review by Williams, which focuses on high-intensity exercise performance. More recent studies are inconsistent. Several support this general conclusion. For example, in a recent well-controlled crossover study, Paton and others investigated the effect of caffeine (6 mg/kg) on repeated 20-meter sprints in well-trained male team-sport athletes and observed no significant effect on mean sprint performance and fatigue over ten sprints.

However, other recent well-designed, double-blind, placebo, crossover studies have shown caffeine-induced improvement in several high-intensity exercise tasks. For example, Bruce and others reported increased mean power and improved 2000-meter rowing time in eight competitive rowers; Collomp and others reported faster 100-meter swim times in highly trained swimmers; Wiles and others noted significantly faster run times for 1,500 meters, particularly increased speed in the latter part of the race, in trained middle-distance runners; MacIntosh and Wright found significantly faster times in a 1,500-meter swim; Jackman and others reported increased time to exhaustion when exercising at 100 percent VO_2 max, a time approaching 5 minutes. Stuart and others reported significant improvements in repetitive bouts of speed and power typical of high-intensity team sports such as rugby.

The enhanced performance noted in these exercise tasks may be attributed to psychological factors. In support of this point, Cole and others recently had subjects perform cycling tasks at several set ratings of perceived exertion (RPE), which is a scale representing how psychologically stressful the exercise appeared to be. In the three levels of RPE used, the subjects produced more work in 10 minutes following caffeine ingestion as compared to the placebo. Although the subjects perceived the work tasks to be identical by the RPE scale, they actually generated more work with caffeine.

Effect on FFA Mobilization and Use   It is well established that caffeine may raise serum FFA levels at rest just before exercise, but there appears to be some controversy regarding serum FFA levels during exercise when trials with and without caffeine are compared. A number of studies that involved subjects who consumed caffeine beverages regularly and who also used a small dose of caffeine (5 mg/kg) have reported no significant differences between caffeine and placebo trials. The most likely reason is that exercise itself, as a stressor, stimulates epinephrine release and raises FFA levels comparable to the small dose. However, other studies that have involved subjects who were not regular caffeine users or who abstained from caffeine use for 4–7 days and which also employed large doses of caffeine (15 mg/kg) have noted significantly higher levels of FFA during exercise compared to placebo trials. Bucci reported fifteen studies in which caffeine increased FFA over the effect of exercise alone. Whether or not there are changes in plasma FFA may be irrelevant, for as Tarnopolsky notes, plasma concentrations do not provide us with appropriate information regarding the flux of the FFA, that is, the rate at which it appears in the blood from the adipose tissue and the rate of entry into the muscle cell.

Even though caffeine may elevate FFA during exercise, whether the use of fat as an energy source is increased during exercise is debatable. Several reviewers have noted an inconsistency in the results when the respiratory quotient (RQ) was used to assess fuel utilization; the RQ may serve as a general guide to the percentage use of carbohydrate and fat during submaximal, mild-to moderate-intensity exercise.

Several recent studies provide strong evidence that caffeine may not increase fat utilization during exercise. Graham and others monitored fatty acid metabolism directly at the leg level during exercise and found that caffeine (6 mg/kg), although stimulating the sympathetic nervous system, did not alter the fat metabolism in the monitored leg. In a related study, Mora-Rodriguez and Coyle infused epinephrine intravenously in low, moderate, and high amounts to evaluate the effect on fat utilization during low-intensity exercise. Although elevations in plasma epinephrine progressively increased whole body lipolysis, fatty acid oxidation decreased. Based on the most recent research, Graham noted that it appears unlikely that increased fat oxidation is the prime ergogenic mechanism underlying caffeine use as an ergogenic aid.

Effect on Muscle Glycogen Sparing   Previously, several well-designed studies had supported the concept that caffeine would increase fat utilization and spare muscle glycogen, which could contribute to enhanced endurance performance. About 25 years ago, Essig noted that caffeine elicited an increased utilization of muscle triglycerides during exercise and spared the use of muscle glycogen. In studies that have taken muscle biopsies, caffeine has been shown to exert a glycogen-sparing effect. Well-designed studies headed by Lawrence Spriet and Terry Graham from Guelph University in Canada show clearly that caffeine will spare the use of muscle glycogen during the first 15 minutes of exercise, supporting the research findings of Essig years ago. In the study by Spriet and others, no crossover design was used, for all subjects received the placebo first and then 1 week later, the caffeine. Muscle biopsies were taken at the point of exhaustion in the placebo trial. During the caffeine trial, the subjects were stopped for a muscle biopsy at the exact same time they reached exhaustion in the placebo trial; they were still performing but were stopped for the biopsy and then continued cycling. The muscle glycogen was higher in the caffeine trial compared to the placebo trial, strong evidence of a glycogen-sparing effect that allowed the athletes to continue to cycle.

However, more recent studies suggest caffeine does not spare muscle glycogen during exercise. As noted above, Graham and others found no effect of caffeine on fat metabolism during exercise while monitoring fuel use at the leg level, and they also reported no effect on carbohydrate metabolism. In another study from Graham's research group, Greer and others reported that neither caffeine (6 mg/kg) nor the related stimulant theophylline (4.5 mg/kg) affected muscle glycogen utilization during cycling exercise at 80 percent VO_2 max until exhaustion. Laurent and others used nuclear magnetic resonance spectroscopy to evaluate muscle glycogen levels before and after exercise (cycling 2 hours at 65 percent VO_2 max), and found that caffeine (6 mg/kg) did not spare use of muscle glycogen in glycogen-loaded subjects. Thus, based on current research findings from his own and other research groups, Graham indicated that caffeine does not appear to induce a glycogen-sparing effect during exercise.

Effect on Aerobic Endurance Performance   As the duration of the endurance event increases to an hour or more, the research indicates, although not uniformly so, that caffeine may enhance performance. In many studies with improved performance, the psychological effect of caffeine was hypothesized as the cause. A number of studies have shown that caffeine may exert a stimulating effect on psychological processes, such as alertness and mood, which may diminish the perception of effort during exercise and thereby improve performance.

Several recent well-designed studies have shown significant increases in epinephrine levels during exercise following caffeine ingestion, both in elite and recreational athletes. Epinephrine responses to caffeine ingestion may be greater in nonusers versus habitual caffeine users. Epinephrine may exert a stimulating psychological effect, although the mechanism underlying improved performance has not been determined.

Numerous studies have reported significant improvements in endurance performance following caffeine ingestion. For example, in a recent study Greer and others reported that both caffeine (6 mg/kg) and theophylline (4.5 mg/kg), enhanced performance during cycling exercise at 80 percent VO_2 max until exhaustion. In their classic study, Graham and Spriet used elite distance runners as subjects and found that caffeine improved mean run time to exhaustion at 85 percent of VO_2 max from 49.2 minutes following the placebo to 71.0 minutes after caffeine (9 mg/kg body weight), a 44 percent improvement. Performance on a comparable cycling test to exhaustion revealed similar results. In most studies, the caffeine was taken 1 hour prior to performance, but French and others found that caffeine was effective even if taken immediately before the performance task.

In their recent meta-analysis, Doherty and Smith confirmed the ergogenic effects of caffeine in a variety of exercise tasks, particularly so in tests of aerobic endurance (see figure 13.5). Jeukendrup and Martin, in their review on how to improve cycling performance, quantified the ergogenic effects of caffeine, suggesting that low doses could improve 40-kilometer cycling performance by 55–84 seconds. No wonder caffeine is popular with professional cyclists.

Effect of Dietary Carbohydrates   Previous research has shown that carbohydrate loading and having a high-carbohydrate breakfast prior to competition may negate the metabolic effects of caffeine. High-carbohydrate levels stimulate insulin release, which appears to block the effect of caffeine in raising FFA levels. However, given the conflicting data as to whether or not plasma FFA accurately reflect the FFA flux, this observation may not be too meaningful. Moreover, the subjects in the study by Graham and Spriet did load with carbohydrates for several days prior to the exercise task, both in the placebo and caffeine trials, and it did not appear to affect the ergogenic effect of caffeine adversely. Research has also shown that caffeine ingestion does not impede the resynthesis of muscle glycogen during the carbohydrate-loading protocol.

FIGURE 13.5   Caffeine may enhance performance in a wide variety of exercise endeavors, particularly events involving aerobic endurance.

Effect of Caffeine Status   One possible factor determining whether caffeine is an effective ergogenic aid is the caffeine status of the subjects. In many of the studies that report an ergogenic effect, subjects abstained from caffeine use for 2–4 days prior to the experiment; they became caffeine-free for several days to possibly heighten the caffeine effect when taken. This abstention period was based on some research reporting no effects of caffeine on epinephrine or FFA levels if subjects abstained for less than 1 day. Other research documented a decreased sensitivity to caffeine following 6 weeks of increased caffeine ingestion; that is, the epinephrine level was decreased during exercise following this period of increased caffeine intake. However, in a recent review, Graham and Spriet suggest that caffeine withdrawal may have little effect on actual performance, and that subjects may consume caffeine products up to the day of the event.

Effect of Delivery System   Another factor influencing caffeine's effectiveness may be how it is consumed. Graham and others compared the effects of consuming the same dose of caffeine in coffee or as a capsule in water. In a well-designed, double-blind, repeated-measures study with 5 trials (3 caffeine and 2 placebo), they found that although the plasma epinephrine increased with the coffee, the increase was significantly greater with the caffeine capsule. Additionally, the caffeine capsule was the only treatment to improve exercise performance, a treadmill run to exhaustion at 85 percent VO_2 max. They suggested some component or components in coffee may moderate the effect of caffeine. However, other studies have reported significant ergogenic effects when coffee was used to deliver caffeine. Moreover, McLellan and Bell recently reported that consuming coffee 30 minutes prior to taking capsulated caffeine did not negate its beneficial ergogenic effect on cycling endurance performance. Drinking coffee would not seem to impair the potential ergogenic effect of caffeine tablets.

Effect as a Diuretic   Caffeine is a diuretic and also stimulates metabolism. Theoretically, increased water losses and an elevated metabolism before competition could impair exercise performance under warm, humid environmental conditions, possibly because of retarded sweat losses and excessive increases in body temperature. However, research has shown no changes in sweat loss, plasma volume, or body temperature following caffeine ingestion. Moreover, Cohen and others reported that caffeine ingestion did not impair performance in a 13.1-mile (21.1 km) half-marathon run outdoors under hot, humid conditions. Although running performance was not impaired by caffeine, neither was it improved. In a recent review of over ten studies comparing caffeinated beverages with water consumption, Armstrong noted there were few differences between the two regarding body fluid retention and urine production. Armstrong concluded that athletes will not incur detrimental fluid-electrolyte imbalances if they consume caffeinated beverages in moderation and eat a typical diet. Additionally, Armstrong and others recently reported that consuming caffeine, either 3 or 6 milligrams per kilogram body weight for five days, did not cause hypohydration, and questioned the widely accepted notion that caffeine consumption acts chronically as a diuretic.

Effect of Dosage: Legality and Safety   Caffeine use has been widespread in sports for over a century, and its legality has varied. The International Olympic Committee (IOC) banned the use of caffeine as a drug prior to the 1972 Olympics. However, because caffeine is a natural ingredient in some beverages that athletes consume, the IOC removed it from the doping list from 1972 to 1982. The use of large amounts of caffeine was again banned for the 1984 Olympic games, probably because research had suggested that caffeine could artificially improve performance. Olympic athletes were permitted to consume small amounts of caffeine, but the use of large doses was grounds for disqualification. Until 2004, the maximal dose that could be used without exceeding the legal limit for doping approximated 8–10 mg/kg body weight. For a 70-kg athlete this would be 560–700 milligrams of caffeine, or about 4–6 cups of coffee or 3 Vivarin tablets. In their study Bruce and others found that many subjects consuming 9 mg caffeine/kg body weight exceeded the legal limit for doping in effect at that time. However, effective January 1,

2004, the World Anti-Doping Agency (WADA), in conjunction with the medical commission of the International Olympic Committee, removed caffeine from the list of stimulants prohibited for use by athletes. Although research suggests that caffeine is an effective ergogenic aid for various types of athletic endeavors, WADA felt that the doping list should be adjusted to reflect changing times. The removal of caffeine from the prohibited list may be a reflection of the increased prevalence of caffeinated beverages, such as specialty coffees, fortified colas, energy drinks, and even sport drinks. These drinks, which may be larger and contain more caffeine, may be consumed in quantity by athletes.

Currently, athletes need not worry about drinking caffeinated beverages and then being tested positive for use of caffeine as a performance-enhancing substance. However, a recent report suggested WADA is once again considering returning caffeine to the list of restricted performance-enhancing substances.

Individuality   In general, studies have not reported a decrease in performance following caffeine ingestion. However, it should be noted that individuals vary in their responses to any drug. For example, in several of the studies the investigators reported that some subjects had adverse reactions to the caffeine and thus had an impaired performance.

Caffeine appears to be an effective ergogenic aid in doses that are both safe and legal. However, some athletes believe taking caffeine may be considered unethical because it is an artificial means of enhancing performance. Given its safety and legality, the decision to use caffeine as a performance-enhancer rests with the ethical standards of the individual athlete. Although combining ephedrine with caffeine may increase the ergogenic effect of caffeine alone, ephedrine use may be illegal—so its use to increase sports performance is unethical.

Self-experimentation   If you are considering using caffeine as a potential ergogenic aid, it is wise to experiment with its use in training prior to use in competition. You might start by taking 200–400 milligrams of caffeine about an hour prior to some of your workouts. For example, if you are a distance runner, do your long runs periodically with and without the coffee or other caffeine source, and judge for yourself if it works for you. To make it a more valid case study, have someone randomly give you, blinded, a placebo (vitamin capsule) or caffeine capsule before the runs, but without informing you which until you have done each several times. Try this procedure also after abstaining from caffeine for 4–5 days. Keep a record of your feelings and times after the runs so you can compare differences.

Does drinking coffee, tea, or other caffeinated beverages pose any significant health risk?

This is one of the most hotly debated questions over the past quarter century, as about 90 percent of American adults use caffeine in one form or another, mainly coffee. In the early 1970s and 1980s a number of epidemiological studies linked coffee or caffeine consumption with the development of a variety of health problems, including heart disease and associated risk factors such as high serum cholesterol and high blood pressure; pancreatic cancer; fibrocystic breast disease; osteoporosis; and pregnancy-related problems such as infertility, miscarriages, low birth weight, and birth defects. Conversely, other epidemiological studies have shown no relationship between coffee or caffeine consumption and these health problems. Investigators have looked at a variety of factors, including different sources of caffeine such as coffee versus tea, regular versus decaffeinated coffee, and even the method of preparing coffee, such as filtered versus boiled.

Many of the earlier reported adverse findings associated with caffeine consumption were derived from rather small epidemiological studies or from animal research using rather high doses of caffeine. However, more contemporary, larger epidemiological studies have been conducted, and several recent reviews have evaluated these reports and summarized the effect of caffeine on a variety of health problems. The following represent the key points presented in the reviews by James, Signorello and McLaughlin, Daly and Fredholm, Tufts University, and the Consumers Union, as well as other independent sources.

Cardiovascular Disease and Associated Risk Factors

Caffeine is a stimulant that may affect heart function. In some individuals it may cause a slight arrhythmia, or irregular heart beat. However, recent research by Frost and Vestergaard reported that low to moderate consumption of caffeine, as coffee, does not cause the most common type of serious arrhythmia known as atrial fibrillation.

Caffeine may also acutely increase blood pressure in individuals who are caffeine sensitive and also in individuals who are under stress. Not all studies have shown that increased caffeine use is associated with high blood pressure. However, in a recent critical review of dietary caffeine and blood pressure, James concluded that findings from experimental and epidemiologic studies converge to show that blood pressure remains reactive to the pressor effects of caffeine in the diet; overall, the impact of dietary caffeine on population blood pressure levels is likely to be modest, probably increasing blood pressure by about 4 and 2 mmHg for systolic and diastolic blood pressure, respectively.

Several recent reviews have investigated the relationship between coffee consumption and serum lipid levels, noting an inconsistency in the results of most studies. Some studies have shown that both caffeinated and decaffeinated coffee may raise serum cholesterol, but others have reported no effects. In some cases where the cholesterol levels rose, the authors noted the increases were of little clinical significance. Increased serum cholesterol levels have been associated with the method of preparation, particularly boiling coffee as practiced in Scandinavia and other parts of the world. Several cholesterol-raising substances (cafestol and kahweol) have been found in the oil droplets formed in the boiling process. These substances are removed when coffee is filtered, the major means of coffee preparation used in the United States and Canada.

Homocysteine may be a risk factor for CHD, and Verhoef and others recently found that coffee may increase homocysteine levels in the blood. The increase is partly attributed to its caffeine content, but other factors may contribute as well. Caffeine raised homocysteine levels 5 percent, while coffee containing caffeine raised it 11 percent. The effect of such an increase on the risk of CHD has not been determined.

On a positive note, Salazar-Martinez and others, in a large epidemiological study, reported that total caffeine intake from coffee and other sources was associated with a statistically significantly lower risk for type 2 diabetes in both men and women; the relative risk (RR) was lower for those who drank 4 to 5 or more cups of coffee a day. The investigators suggest caffeine may increase the body's sensitivity to insulin, while others suggest coffee contains various nutrients, such as magnesium and various phytochemicals that may help the body regulate glucose metabolism.

Based on contemporary research, most health professional groups, such as the American Heart Association, recommend that moderate coffee consumption, about 1–2 cups daily, is safe and not associated with heart disease. However, the effects of consuming greater amounts of coffee are not as well known. James indicated that the effect of caffeine to increase blood pressure could account for premature deaths in the region of 14 percent for coronary heart disease and 20 percent for stroke, and indicates that strategies for encouraging reduced dietary levels of caffeine deserve serious consideration. Individuals who are hypertensive, or who are under stress, or who may have other risk factors for heart disease, should consult their physician regarding the use of caffeine.

Cancer

The American Cancer Society, after reviewing the available scientific evidence, indicated there is no known association between the consumption of coffee, tea, or other caffeinated beverages and the development of any type of cancer. In support of this viewpoint, Michels and others presented data from two large epidemiological studies involving men and women, and reported that the consumption of caffeinated coffee, tea with caffeine, or caffeine was not associated with incidence of colon or rectal cancer.

Fibrocystic Breast Disease

Fibrocystic breast disease involves the development of benign fibrous lumps in the breast tissue that might develop tenderness or become painful. Although an earlier anecdotal report suggested an association with caffeine intake, a major study by the National Cancer Institute (NCI) revealed no evidence supporting such an association. Both the NCI and a health committee of the American Medical Association stated there is no association between caffeine intake and fibrocystic breast disease.

Osteoporosis

Factors underlying the development of osteoporosis are discussed in detail in chapter 8. Essentially, calcium loss may lead to osteoporosis. For now, we may note that caffeine tends to accelerate the loss of calcium from bones and lead to its excretion in the urine. However, the amount is very small, approximating only 5 milligrams of calcium loss for every cup of coffee. Using 2 tablespoons of milk in the coffee would replace the amount of lost calcium. In a recent report, the National Institutes of Health indicated caffeine use does not cause significant losses of calcium. However, drinking milk or eating calcium-rich foods is highly recommended if you drink caffeinated beverages.

Pregnancy-Related Health Problems Animal research has suggested that very high doses of caffeine, administered directly into the stomach via tubes, could impair fertility or interfere with fetal development, causing detrimental pregnancy consequences such as miscarriage, low birth weight, or birth defects. However, other animal research, administering caffeine in fluids as normally consumed by humans, did not produce such effects. In a recent meta-analysis of 32 human studies, Fernandes and others concluded that there is a small, but statistically significant, increase in the risks for spontaneous abortion and low birthweight babies in pregnant women consuming more than 150 milligrams of caffeine per day. However, the authors noted that they could not control for other possible confounders, such as smoking and alcohol use. In a subsequent review, Signorello and McLaughlin indicated that most of the studies were biased, and concluded that evidence for a causal link between caffeine intake and spontaneous abortion remains inconclusive. The Food and Drug Administration and the American Dietetic Association recommend that pregnant women consider abstaining from caffeine use, or if they do drink caffeine beverages to do so in moderation. In its recent report, the Consumers Union recommended they drink no more than two cups of coffee a day to avoid the possible risk of miscarriage.

Drinking caffeine beverages when breast feeding may make the child jittery as caffeine gets into breast milk.

Weight Control Caffeine use may stimulate metabolism, increasing the resting metabolic rate about 10 percent for several hours, an effect which theoretically could facilitate weight loss. Greenway notes that caffeine has a long history of safe, non-prescription use as a weight-loss supplement, and that the benefits of treating obesity appear to outweigh the small associated risk. Nevertheless, excessive amounts may cause adverse effects in some individuals, especially when combined with ephedrine as discussed below. Proper weight-control procedures are discussed in chapters 10 and 11.

Sleeplessness Caffeine use, particularly before retiring for the night, may delay the onset of sleep because of its stimulant effects.

Gastric Distress Some individuals experience stomach irritation due to increased secretion of gastric acids following ingestion of caffeinated beverages. In such cases, individuals should consult their physician or avoid caffeine.

Caffeine Naivete Abstainers or those who consume little caffeine may experience nervousness, irritability, headaches, or insomnia with moderate doses, although long-term consumption of coffee leads to development of tolerance and reduction of these "coffee nerves" symptoms. Youngstedt and others recently reported that moderate aerobic exercise may reduce the anxiety sometimes associated with caffeine intake.

Caffeine Dependence In a recent cover story for *National Geographic*, coffee was labeled a the world's most popular psychoactive drug—buzzing our brains, fraying our nerves, and robbing our sleep. Yet we simply refuse to survive without it. Although not classified as an addictive drug, some individuals may develop caffeine dependence, often referred to as caffeinism; caffeine dependence is listed in the *Diagnostic and Statistical Manual of Mental Disorders* published by the American Psychiatric Association. Juliano and Griffiths noted that caffeine-dependent individuals may experience various symptoms upon caffeine withdrawal, including headaches and nervousness, fatigue or drowsiness, depression, irritability, and difficulty concentrating. However, caffeine dependence is not considered a serious form of drug abuse.

Death Although rare, death may result from overdoses of caffeine-containing diet or stimulant pills. Individuals who take several different over-the-counter dietary supplements may be taking substantial amounts of caffeine along with other drugs. Such combinations, in excess, may be fatal.

Summary In general though, most professional health organizations note that caffeine is regarded to be a safe drug. If you are healthy and are not on medications, several cups of coffee or caffeinated beverages should pose no health problems. Where moderation is recommended, the dosage is the equivalent of less than 300 milligrams of caffeine per day, or about 2 cups of coffee. And we are talking 6-ounce cups of coffee or so, not the supersize 20-ounce cups or higher from local convenience stores.

Caffeine may actually confer some possible health benefits. Caffeine increases alertness, promotes clearer thinking, and diminishes drowsiness. These factors may contribute to safer automobile operation under certain conditions. Coffee intake is one of the few techniques Horne and Reyner reported as useful to prevent vehicle accidents related to sleepiness. Some of these mental effects may underlie the findings of the study by Ascherio and others indicating that coffee may fend off Parkinson's disease.

Key Concept Recap

▶ Caffeine is a stimulant drug, and can affect a variety of metabolic and psychological processes in the body that may impact exercise performance and health.

▶ Research suggests that caffeine may improve performance in a variety of athletic endeavors, particularly prolonged aerobic endurance exercise. An effective dose is approximately 5 milligrams per kilogram body weight.

▶ In general, caffeine is regarded to be a safe drug, but physicians may recommend abstinence or use in moderation for some individuals. Various health professionals define moderation as 1–2 cups per day.

Check for Yourself

Procure an automatic blood pressure monitor, or have a colleague record your blood pressure. While resting, record your blood pressure several times over a course of 15–20 minutes. Drink a cup of coffee or two, and then record your blood pressure again, about every 15 minutes over the course of an hour, again while resting. Plot the results. Does caffeine affect your blood pressure?

Ephedra (ephedrine): Ergogenic Effects and Health Implications

What is ephedra (ephedrine)?

Ephedra sinica, a plant most commonly referred to as **ephedra,** contains a variety of naturally occurring alkaloids, including **ephedrine** and pseudoephedrine. The Chinese version of ephedra is known as **ma huang** (see figure 13.6). Ephedrine is considered the most active alkaloid, and its synthetic version is ephedrine hydrochloride. Pure ephedrine is regulated as a drug, and the FDA allows only very small amounts in over-the-counter drugs such as cold medications.

Like caffeine, ephedrine is a stimulant and because it is derived from the plant ma huang, it may be classified as a dietary supplement. Ephedra or ephedrine-containing dietary supplements have been marketed to promote weight loss, increase energy, and enhance sports performance, with such names as Xtream Lean, MetabolLoss, Ripped Force, and Performance Orange. Dosages in such products may vary, but 20–25 milligrams per tablet is about average; recommended doses from supplement manufacturers may total 70–90 milligrams per day. However, Haller and others note that product inconsistency is common and the actual content of ephedrine may vary from that specified on the label.

As noted below, ephedrine use may pose some serious health risks. In 2004, the FDA prohibited the sale of ephedra or ephedrine-containing dietary supplements. However, the FDA ruling has been challenged in the courts, and as of this writing ephedrine-containing products are back in the marketplace.

FIGURE 13.6 Seeds of Ephedra sinica, or Ma Huang. The seeds may be processed into tablets for sale as a dietary supplement.

Does ephedrine enhance exercise performance?

In general, although a powerful stimulant, ephedrine by itself has not been shown to consistently enhance exercise performance. In their recent review, Rawson and Clarkson concluded that although there are few studies of the efficacy of ephedrine in improving exercise performance, these studies are consistent in their findings of no ergogenic effects. Shekelle and others, in a meta-analysis, supported this viewpoint, as did Magkos and Kavouras in their recent review, indicating that ephedrine and related alkaloids have not been shown, *as yet,* to result in any significant performance improvements. However, subsequent research has supported an ergogenic effect of ephedrine. Jacobs and others reported that the acute ingestion of caffeine and ephedrine, as well as ephedrine alone, increases local muscular endurance during the first set of traditional resistance-training exercise; however, the performance enhancement was attributed primarily to the effects of ephedrine as there was no additive effect of caffeine. If ephedrine remains in the marketplace, additional research appears to be merited.

Ephedrine with caffeine   Graham indicated that the combination of ephedrine with caffeine has been suggested to be more potent than caffeine alone. Several recent studies by Bell and associates, working with Ira Jacobs at the Defence and Civil Institute of Environmental Medicine in Canada, have shown that caffeine/ephedrine combinations may enhance exercise performance in various exercise performance tasks, many of a military nature. Using pharmaceutical-grade caffeine and ephedrine doses approximating 4–5 mg/kg and 0.8–1.0 kg, respectively, they reported significant improvements in exercise tasks such as a 30-second Wingate test of anaerobic capacity, a maximal cycle ergometer performance about 12.5 minutes in duration, the Canadian Forces Warrior Test (3.2-kilometer run wearing combat gear weighing about 11 kilograms), and a 10-kilometer run wearing similar gear. In their recent review, Magkos and Kavouras indicated that caffeine-ephedrine combinations have been reported in several instances to confer a greater ergogenic benefit than either drug by itself. Research appears to support an ergogenic effect of caffeine/ephedrine supplementation in a number of studies, several involving exercise tasks of a military nature that may be applicable to enhancement of sports performance.

Legality in sports   Use of ephedrine, ephedra, and ma huang in competition is prohibited by WADA and the IOC. However, caffeine, as well as pseudoephedrine, has been removed from the WADA doping list. Nevertheless, ephedrine appears to be popular with athletes. In one survey, Bents and others reported that more than half of college ice hockey players admitted using ephedrine, even when knowing such use was prohibited by the NCAA. As ephedra is banned in competition only, athletes may use it in training. Magkos and Kavouras suggested that caffeine-ephedra mixtures may become one of the most popular ergogenic aids. Indeed, sports bars containing caffeine and ephedrine from ma huang are commercially available.

Do dietary supplements containing ephedra pose any health risks?

Of all dietary supplements, the Consumers Union noted that the herbal supplement ephedra may be the most hazardous. Bent and others noted that ephedra use is associated with a greatly increased risk for adverse reactions compared with other herbs; they indicated that ephedra products accounted for 64 percent of all adverse reactions to herbs in the United States even though these products represented less than 1 percent of herbal product sales.

Use of ephedra has been associated with numerous health problems. Maglione and others reported adverse psychiatric effects of ephedra use, including psychosis, severe depression, mania or agitation, hallucinations, sleep disturbance, and suicidal ideation. Haller and others implicated ephedra with seizures. Naik and Freudenberger indicated ephedra was associated with heart arrhythmias, myocardial infarction, cardiac arrest, and even sudden death. Haller and others reported that although ephedra alone may be dangerous, ephedra combined with caffeine exaggerates the potential adverse risks.

The Ephedra Education Council notes that 100 milligrams of ephedrine per day is safe, and may be useful for individuals on a weight-loss program mainly by increasing the resting metabolic rate. However, this dose may cause problems in individuals with existing disease, such as high blood pressure or heart disease, who are attempting to lose weight. Moreover, some individuals may exceed the recommended dosage. Indeed, Haller and Benowitz noted that ephedrine misuse may be associated with significant health risks.

In recent years, the deaths of several prominent collegiate and professional athletes made headlines when it was discovered they were using ephedra-containing supplements during training under warm environmental conditions. The risk-taking behavior associated with sports participants is well known, so athletes taking more than the recommended dose is one of the major problems. Additionally, the purity and amount of ephedra in a product are not well controlled. Given these possibilities, and given its physiological effects, ephedrine could be involved in such tragedies.

Synephrine Ephedra-free dietary supplements have recently been marketed for weight loss (see figure 13.7). These products may contain synephrine, an extract from the Seville orange, or bitter, or sour orange. Synephrine is a dietary supplement in the United States, but classified as a drug in Europe. Synephrine is structurally similar to ephedrine, and has been marketed as a safe alternative to ephedra.

However, the Consumers Union indicates there is little evidence that synephrine is effective or safe, and experts suspect it could cause the same kinds of problems that ephedra does, particularly when it is combined with caffeine. Bent and others reported that synephrine was of no statistically significant benefit for weight loss. Bouchard and others reported a case study indicating that synephrine may be associated with ischemic stroke.

For individuals interested in weight loss, safer approaches are available, as detailed in chapter 11.

FIGURE 13.7 Ephedra-free dietary supplements are marketed for weight loss; many contain synephrine, a compound similar to ephedrine (see text for discussion).

Key Concept Recap

▶ Ephedra, or ma huang, although classified as a dietary supplement, contains a potent stimulant drug, ephedrine.

▶ In general, research suggests that ephedra or ephedrine supplementation does not enhance exercise or sport performance. However, supplementation with caffeine/ephedrine compounds has been shown to enhance performance in various exercise tasks.

▶ Use of ephedra or ephedrine-containing supplements has been associated with serious health problems, including psychiatric disorders and increased cardiovascular risk factors.

Check for Yourself

Visit a local health food store that primarily sells dietary supplements, including sports supplements. Ask the clerk to show you products containing ephedra or ephedrine for weight loss and enhanced sport performance, and also ask if there are any health risks related to their use. Record the response for class discussion.

Sodium Bicarbonate: Ergogenic Effects, Safety, and Legality

What is sodium bicarbonate?

Sodium bicarbonate is an alkaline salt found naturally in the human body. It is the major component of the alkaline reserve in the blood, whose major function is to help control excess acidity by buffering acids. Thus, sodium bicarbonate is also known as a buffer salt. Its action is comparable to that of medications you may take to control an upset stomach caused by gastric acidity. Sodium bicarbonate may be purchased in a supermarket as baking soda (see figure 13.8), and it also has been marketed to athletes as part of a sports supplement.

Does sodium bicarbonate, or soda loading, enhance physical performance?

During high-intensity anaerobic exercise, sodium bicarbonate helps buffer the lactic acid that is produced when the lactic acid energy system is utilized. You may recall from chapter 3 that the accumulation of excess lactic acid in the muscle cell may interfere with the optimal functioning of various enzymes and thus lead to fatigue. The natural supply of sodium bicarbonate that you have in your blood can help delay the onset of fatigue during anaerobic exercise. It may facilitate the removal of the hydrogen ions associated with lactic acid from the muscle cell, thereby mitigating the adverse effects of the increased acidity (see figure 13.9). However, fatigue is inevitable if the rate of lactic acid production exceeds the capacity of your sodium bicarbonate supply to buffer it. Theoretically, an increase in the alkaline reserve could delay the onset of fatigue.

Alkaline salt supplementation has been studied for its ergogenic potential on all three human energy systems, but mainly the lactic acid energy system. Most studies have used a double-blind placebo design in which all subjects took all treatments. In the popular literature, sodium bicarbonate supplementation has been referred to as *soda loading,* from baking soda, or *buffer boosting,* for increasing the natural blood buffer content.

Lactic Acid Energy System Over a half-century ago, German scientists reported that the ingestion of sodium bicarbonate and other alkaline salts could help improve anaerobic work capacity. Since then, many studies have failed to support this finding, but now a substantial number of well-controlled experiments by highly respected investigators in sport nutrition research have provided supportive data.

FIGURE 13.8 Baking soda is a commercial version of sodium bicarbonate.

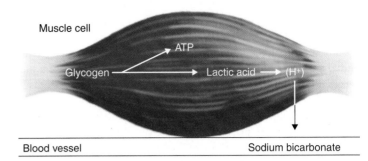

FIGURE 13.9 Alkaline salts, such as sodium bicarbonate, are theorized to reduce the acidity in the muscle cell by facilitating the efflux of hydrogen ions from the cell interior, promoting a more homeostatic environment for continued muscle contraction.

The usual experimental protocol has been to have subjects, about 1–3 hours before the exercise task, ingest a dosage of 0.15–0.30 grams of sodium bicarbonate per kilogram body weight. Recent research by McNaughton has indicated 0.30 grams per kilogram body weight appears to be the optimum dose, with higher dosages providing no additional benefits. This amount totals less than 1 ounce for the average adult. Some studies have used sodium citrate in similar dosages, because it has been shown to increase the alkaline reserve. The exercise task selected was normally one that stressed the lactic acid energy system, or about 1–3 minutes of maximal exercise. Often these exercise tasks were classified as supramaximal, because they used workloads greater than 100 percent VO_2 max. Repeated bouts of intense exercise interspersed with short rest periods have also been used, such as five 100-yard swims with a 2-minute rest between each.

A recent study by Raymer and others, using magnetic resonance spectroscopy, provided support for the main theory underlying the ergogenic efficacy of sodium bicarbonate supplementation. They reported that sodium bicarbonate ingestion delayed the onset of intracellular acidification during incremental exercise, which would help maintain a more homeostatic cellular environment to delay the onset of fatigue.

Based on the available scientific evidence, sodium bicarbonate supplementation does appear to enhance performance in exercise tasks dependent upon the lactic acid energy system (see figure 13.10). A consistent finding is an increased serum pH following sodium bicarbonate supplementation, the desired effect to induce buffering of lactic acid. Regarding other factors that have been investigated, approximately half of the well-controlled laboratory studies suggest that ingestion of sodium bicarbonate will reduce acidosis in the muscle cell, decrease the psychological sensation of fatigue at a standardized level of exercise, and increase performance in high-intensity anaerobic exercise tasks to exhaustion. Most studies provided the alkaline salt supplement an hour or more prior to exercise testing, but McNaughton and others have recently shown that chronic bicarbonate ingestion for a period of 5 days also provided ergogenic benefits on 60-second high-intensity exercise performance. Various field studies have reported significant improvements in events that primarily use the lactic acid energy system, such as 400 or 800 meters in highly trained track athletes, 100-meter swims in experienced

FIGURE 13.10 Sodium bicarbonate may enhance sports performance in a variety of events dependent primarily upon the lactic acid energy system (anaerobic glycolysis), such as the 400-meter sprint in track.

swimmers, and 5-kilometer bicycle races in trained cyclists. In support of these field studies showing improved performance following sodium bicarbonate supplementation, a recent laboratory study by Van Montfoort and others, comparing different sodium mixtures, reported that sodium bicarbonate improved run time to exhaustion in a test designed to evaluate the lactic acid energy system; the run to exhaustion approximated 77–82 seconds.

However, as with most research with nutritional ergogenic aids, not all studies find positive effects. For example, Kozak-Collins and her associates recently reported that sodium bicarbonate supplementation taken at moderate altitude did not improve the performance of competitive female cyclists on repeated 1-minute interval cycle tasks at 95 percent VO_2 max, nor did van Someren and others find any benefits on repeated 45-second high-intensity cycling bouts. Using well-trained wrestlers as subjects, Aschenbach and others reported no ergogenic effect of sodium bicarbonate during high-intensity arm ergometry involving eight 15-second maximal effort intervals with 20 seconds recovery. Portington and others also reported no effects of sodium bicarbonate supplementation on 5 maximal sets of leg press repetitions, but indicated the exercise intensity may have been lower compared to studies that have shown ergogenic effects. It should also be noted that although performance was not improved in these studies, neither was it impaired.

Several recent reviews by Matson and Tran, McNaughton, and Requena, have all concluded that sodium bicarbonate is an effective ergogenic aid in events that may depend primarily on the lactic acid energy system. Matson and Tran provided the most convincing analysis, using the meta-analytic technique to statistically compare the effects reported in twenty-nine of the best studies. In general, they noted that the ingestion of sodium bicarbonate enhanced performance, and in studies that measured exercise time to exhaustion, there was a mean improvement of 27 percent. The majority of the studies conducted subsequent to these reviews have indicated sodium bicarbonate or sodium citrate supplementation was an effective ergogenic aid.

ATP-PCr Energy System Based on the available scientific data, alkaline salt supplementation does not appear to be an effective ergogenic aid for exercise tasks dependent primarily upon the ATP-PCr energy system, since most studies have reported no beneficial effects on performance in exercise bouts lasting less than 30 seconds or in resistive exercise tasks stressing strength, power, or short-term local muscle endurance. For example, McNaughton and Cedaro reported no ergogenic effect on maximal cycle ergometer performance in either 10-second or 30-second trials. This lack of an ergogenic effect is most likely because such exercise tasks do not maximally stress the normal alkaline reserve. However, Price and others reported that ingestion of sodium bicarbonate improved performance in multiple, intermittent 14-second maximal sprints (one sprint every 3 minutes) during a 30-minute cycle ergometer trial. Moreover, Bishop and Claudius reported that sodium bicarbonate ingestion can improve intermittent-sprint performance. The test protocol involved two 36-minute halves with prints interspersed with lesser intensity exercise tasks, and the investigators suggested sodium bicarbonate may be a useful supplement for team-sport athletes. Performance in these multiple sprints may have been somewhat dependent on the lactic acid energy system.

Oxygen Energy System Although sodium bicarbonate has been studied mainly for its buffering effects, the sodium content could theoretically expand blood volume and benefit aerobic endurance performance. The effect of alkaline salt supplementation on performance in events that depend increasingly on the oxygen energy system, such as events approximating 4 minutes or more in duration, are equivocal. Several studies have shown ergogenic effects. McNaughton and Cedaro reported an increased cycle ergometer work output in a 4-minute trial, as did Linossier and others in an exhausting exercise task at 120 percent of VO_2 peak lasting 4–5 minutes. Bird and others found that sodium bicarbonate supplementation improved 1,500-meter run performance while Shave and others found that sodium citrate, as compared to a sodium chloride placebo, improved performance in a 3,000-meter run by almost 11 seconds. Using well-trained male college runners as subjects, Oopik and others found that sodium citrate supplementation improved performance in a simulated 5-kilometer treadmill run by 30 seconds. Although primarily aerobic in nature, such exercise tasks may still depend somewhat on the lactic acid energy system. However, several studies have shown ergogenic effects of alkaline salt supplementation on exercise tasks that depend primarily on oxidative metabolism. Potteiger and others reported that sodium citrate supplementation significantly improved performance by 1.7 minutes in 30-kilometer cycling performance, and McNaughton and others reported that sodium bicarbonate supplementation, compared to the placebo trial, produced a 13 percent improvement in maximal cycle ergometer work over 60 minutes.

Conversely, other studies report no ergogenic effect of alkaline salt supplementation. Potteiger and others reported no beneficial effect of sodium bicarbonate supplementation to male runners on performance in a run to exhaustion at 110 percent of the lactate threshold following 30 minutes of running at the lactate threshold. Ball and Maughan also reported no significant effect of sodium citrate supplementation on cycle ergometer endurance at 100 percent VO_2 max. Stephens and others reported that although sodium bicarbonate supplementation induced a small muscle alkalosis, there was no effect on exercise performance. The exercise task consisted of cycling at 77 percent VO_2 max for 30 minutes, and then completing a set workload as fast as possible, which took about another 30 minutes. In a well-designed crossover study involving endurance-trained cyclists using their own bikes, Schabort and others also found no effect of varying doses of sodium citrate (0.2, 0.4, and 0.6 g/kg) on cycling endurance. The laboratory cycling protocol was designed to compare with an actual 40-kilometer road race, with 10 sets of sprints within the 40-kilometer distance. Although the sodium citrate produced dose-dependent changes in blood alkalinity, there was no significant effect on total 40-kilometer time nor on the various sprint performance times. Other studies have shown no ergogenic effects on 1,500-meter run performance. Additional research is needed to clarify this equivocality.

Stephens and others indicated that sodium bicarbonate ingestion has been shown to increase both muscle glycogenolysis and glycolysis during brief submaximal exercise, which could be detrimental to performance during more prolonged, exhaustive exercise. However, no studies have evaluated this potential ergolytic effect.

Is sodium bicarbonate supplementation safe and legal?

The dosage of sodium bicarbonate used in most of these studies, about 300 milligrams per kilogram body weight, appears to be effective yet medically safe. Relative to possible disadvantages, several investigators have noted that some subjects developed gastrointestinal distress, including nausea and diarrhea. Shave and others noted a high potential for gastrointestinal distress in their study that used 0.5 grams of sodium citrate per kilogram body weight, and suggested that this may limit the use of this strategy by athletes in competition. Excessive doses could lead to alkalosis, with symptoms of apathy, irritability, and possible muscle spasms. Given the potential gastrointestinal distress often associated with an acute high dose of sodium

bicarbonate, research by McNaughton and Thompson suggests that a chronic loading protocol, or taking the same total amount of sodium bicarbonate spread over a 6-day period, may be just as effective.

Use of sodium bicarbonate currently is not prohibited by WADA. As noted, sodium bicarbonate (baking soda) use by athletes has been dubbed *soda loading,* possibly to liken it to *carbohydrate loading.* As you may recall, the purpose of carbohydrate loading is to increase the storage of muscle and liver glycogen as a means to prevent fatigue in prolonged endurance events. Soda loading is viewed by some in a similar context, an attempt to increase the supply of a natural body ingredient helpful as a means to delay fatigue. However, because sodium bicarbonate may be regarded as a drug, it remains to be seen whether this technique will be deemed illegal. Tim Noakes, in the recent edition of his classic text *Lore of Running,* indicated that the use of sodium bicarbonate may be prohibited by the International Olympic Committee in the near future. Currently there is no test to detect its use, except for urinary pH, which can also be affected by some antacids, and at present sodium bicarbonate is considered to be legal for use in sports.

Key Concept Recap

▶ Sodium bicarbonate supplementation appears to be an effective ergogenic aid in exercise tasks that depend primarily upon the lactic acid energy system (anaerobic glycolysis), such as a 400-meter dash in track.

▶ Sodium bicarbonate supplementation may also enhance performance in other types of exercise tasks involved in various sports, such as multiple sprints and high-intensity endurance runs, if such activities depend somewhat on the lactic acid energy system.

▶ Ingestion of sodium bicarbonate is generally regarded as safe, but may cause acute gastrointestinal distress and diarrhea. Supplementation over a longer time frame may be effective and less likely to cause intestinal problems.

Anabolic Hormones and Dietary Supplements: Ergogenic Effects and Health Implications

Several hormones in the body may exert significant anabolic effects on body composition by stimulating protein synthesis, particularly insulin, human growth hormone (HGH), and testosterone. As noted in previous chapters, several nutrient supplements, such as specific amino acids, have been utilized in attempts to increase the secretion of these hormones for anabolic purposes. Two of these hormones, HGH and testosterone, as well as drugs patterned after testosterone, have been used directly to increase muscle mass. Additionally, several prohormones that may be converted into testosterone have been marked as dietary supplements.

Is human growth hormone (HGH) an effective, safe, and legal ergogenic aid?

HGH is a natural hormone secreted by the anterior pituitary gland in the brain; HGH is an anabolic hormone that stimulates bone growth and the development of muscle tissue through its effects on protein, carbohydrate, and fat metabolism. A detailed discussion of the role of HGH is beyond the scope of this text. It is important to note, however, that extensive research into its effects began only recently when genetically engineered versions (recombinant HGH, or rHGH) of the natural body hormone became available in the early 1990s. rHGH injections are therapeutic for individuals with impaired HGH pituitary production or secretion. Available data suggest that in elderly men, who normally have reduced levels of HGH, injections of the hormone modify body composition, decreasing body fat and increasing lean body mass. However, in a recent review, Frisch indicated that the increase in lean body mass in rHGH-treated individuals was not due to increased muscle contractile protein but rather to water and connective tissue. Several studies have supported this viewpoint, particularly when rHGH is used during resistance training. For example, Yarasheski and others studied the effect of rHGH versus a placebo on adult males who weight-trained for 12 weeks. They reported significant increases in lean body mass in the group receiving rHGH, but there were no significant increases in skeletal muscle protein synthesis and size, as measured by magnetic resonance imaging, or in muscular strength, over the effects produced by weight training alone in the placebo group. They suggested that rHGH may influence the development of other tissues. More recently, Taaffe and others reported no significant increase in muscle fiber size, as determined by muscle biopsy, following 10 weeks of resistance training and rHGH injections. Several other well-controlled studies reported similar findings with rHGH supplementation to experienced resistance-trained athletes. However, Healy and others recently reported that HGH injections exerted an anabolic effect during rest and exercise and increased whole body protein in endurance-trained athletes, but whether the increase was muscle mass was not determined. Nevertheless, these investigators indicated that short-term administration of HGH may have short-term benefits for physical performance. The interested reader is referred to the recent review by Dean, who noted that there is no evidence of increased muscle strength with HGH use in trained athletes. The reader is referred also to recent reviews by Kraemer and others, Frisch, and Zachwieja and Yarasheski.

Some athletes use rHGH to train harder and build muscle, and anecdotal reports suggest that it may work for these intended purposes. However, at present, there are no good scientific data to support an ergogenic effect of rHGH on muscle size, strength, or power beyond the effect generated by a proper weight-training program. Additionally, HGH use by athletes is prohibited by the International Olympic Committee.

The potential adverse health effects of rHGH are substantial, including insulin resistance, high blood pressure, and increased risk of congestive heart failure. Most researchers also caution that the long-term health risks of HGH administration, either as rHGH

or produced by amino acid supplementation, are unknown. This is particularly distressing as one report indicated approximately 5 percent of high school students have used HGH. In some pathological conditions, the pituitary gland secretes excess HGH, which is associated with acromegaly, or thickening of soft tissues in the face, hands, and feet. Excess HGH may also cause enlargement of body organs, such as the liver, and may lead to diabetes.

Are testosterone and anabolic/androgenic steroids (AAS) effective, safe, and legal ergogenic aids?

Testosterone, the male steroid sex hormone produced by the testes, was one of the first anabolic agents used in attempts to enhance physical performance, possibly as early as the 1936 Berlin Olympic Games. As documented in the study by Bhasin and the review by Evans, testosterone is a very effective ergogenic aid, increasing lean muscle mass, decreasing body fat, and increasing strength even without resistance training; these anabolic effects were augmented in subjects who also trained. Testosterone must be injected because ingested testosterone will be catabolized by digestive enzymes. Although injected testosterone use is still prevalent among various athletic groups, oral drug forms of testosterone have been developed, as noted here.

Anabolic/androgenic steroids (AAS) represent a class of synthetic drugs designed to mimic the effects of testosterone. The chemical structure of testosterone may be modified in attempts to maximize the anabolic muscle-building effects and minimize the androgenic male secondary sex characteristics; both oral and injectable AAS have been developed.

In the United States, AAS are classified as Schedule III drugs under the Controlled Substances Act, and may be used medically for several conditions, such as treatment of anemia, osteoporosis, and gonadal dysfunction. Earlier research suggested that AAS may be useful in older males by helping to prevent sarcopenia (loss of muscle) with the aging process, but Liu and others indicate AAS supplementation is not recommended because of potential health problems, as noted below.

AAS are the drugs of choice for many strength athletes and bodybuilders to improve performance and appearance. AAS have been used by professional athletes for years, as documented in the revealing book, *Wild Times, Rampant 'Roids, Smash Hits, and How Baseball Got Big* written by a former professional baseball player.

Bahrke and others noted that recent surveys indicate the use of AAS is also prevalent among adolescent athletes, particularly boys in strength-related sports. Their use is even common among young male nonathletes, and increasing numbers of teen-age girls, according to Yesalis and others, who desire to increase muscle mass for an enhanced self-image. Faigenbaum and others recently reported AAS use in middle-school students, ages 9–13, with the belief that they improved sports performance and physical appearance. In general, surveys have indicated that approximately 4–6 percent of boys and 1–2 percent of girls have used AAS.

Although resistance training does not cause drug use, DuRant and others recently noted that adolescent AAS users in the United

States, both athletes and nonathletes, are more likely to engage in strength training. AAS use is also associated with use of other recreational drugs. Thus, young adolescent athletes and nonathletes engaged in strength training should be educated about the health risks associated with AAS use.

The effects of AAS on body composition and strength have been studied rather extensively, and although there may be some flaws in the experimental designs used, most reviewers agree that AAS use may increase muscle mass and strength and decrease total body fat, a judgment supported by recent reviews of laboratory studies that included meta-analysis as part of the evaluative criteria. The increased muscle mass may be attributed to hypertrophy and the formation of new muscle fibers, in which key roles are played by the androgen receptors, as depicted in figure 13.11.

However, AAS use has been associated with a number of medical problems, as documented in recent reviews by Hartgens and Kuipers, and Yesalis and Bahrke. Some are relatively minor such as acne and loss of hair. AAS may also adversely affect psychological processes, leading to increased aggression, hostility, depression, and possible suicide attempts, and an increased tendency to commit violent crimes, including homicide. Continued use may predispose adults to coronary heart disease by inducing structural changes in the heart-muscle, decreasing HDL-cholesterol, and increasing blood pressure as documented in both epidemiological and experimental studies, and recently reviewed by Nnakwe. Prolonged steroid use may possibly lead to impaired development of tendons, decreasing their strength and contributing to a potential for rupture. Prolonged use has resulted in severe liver diseases, including cancer. Anabolic steroids may cause premature cessation of bone growth in children and adolescents and may result in the appearance of several male secondary sex characteristics in females, some of which may be irreversible, such as deepening of the voice. Table 13.4 highlights many of the health problems associated with abuse of AAS.

However, many of the adverse health effects of AAS use appear to be reversible. For example, Hartgens and others found that bodybuilders who cycled off AAS steroids for 3 months had similar lipoprotein profiles and liver enzymes as their non-drug-using counterparts. Moreover, earlier reviews noted that although the

short-term health effects of AAS have been increasingly studied and reviewed, and while AAS use has been associated with adverse and even fatal effects, the incidence of serious effects thus far reported has been extremely low. However, subsequent to these reviews, Urhausen and others reported that several years after discontinuation of anabolic steroid abuse, strength athletes (bodybuilders and powerlifters) who used AAS showed a slight concentric left ventricular hypertrophy in comparison with AAS-free strength athletes; left ventricular hypertrophy increases the risk of heart attack.

TABLE 13.4 Possible Health Risks Associated with Use of Anabolic/Androgenic Steroids (AAS)

Cosmetic-related effects

Facial and body acne
Female-like breast enlargement in males (gynecomastia)
Premature baldness
Masculinization in females
Facial and body hair growth in females
Premature closure of growth centers in adolescents, leading to stunted growth
Deepening of the voice in females

Psychological effects

Increased aggressiveness and possible violent behavior

Reproductive effects

Reduction of testicular size
Reduction of sperm production
Decreased libido
Impotence in males
Enlargement of the prostate gland
Enlargement of the clitoris

Cardiovascular risk factors and diseases

Atherosclerotic serum lipid profile
   Decreased HDL-cholesterol
   Increased LDL-cholesterol
High blood pressure
Impaired glucose tolerance
Increase size of left ventricle
Stroke
Heart disease

Liver function

Jaundice
Peliosis hepatis (blood-filled cysts)
Liver tumors

Athletic injuries

Tendon rupture

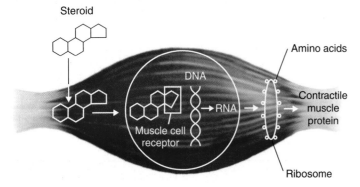

FIGURE 13.11 Anabolic steroids picked up by androgen in the cell nucleus initiate the process of protein formation in cells such as muscle fibers, leading to muscle hypertrophy.

Because of the potential health risks, one of the risk-reduction objectives in *Healthy People 2010* is the reduction of AAS use among high school students. Moreover, the U.S. Congress has passed legislation to classify AAS as controlled substances, thus limiting their production and distribution by pharmaceutical companies. Penalties may be severe. Additionally, most individuals obtain these drugs illegally on the black market where quality is not controlled, and chemical analysis has revealed some potentially hazardous constituents in these "homemade" drugs. AAS users are known to use other illicit drugs as well, each carrying independent health risks.

As is obvious, the use of testosterone or AAS for the purpose of gaining body weight and strength is not recommended. Moreover, their use by athletes is grounds for disqualification for future competition. The American College of Sports Medicine has developed a position statement on the use of anabolic steroids in sports. Although an extensive discussion of AAS is beyond the scope of this text, the ACSM report provides a detailed review for the interested reader, as does the most recent review by Yesalis and Bahrke.

Are anabolic prohormone dietary supplements effective, safe, and legal ergogenic aids?

Several dietary supplements marketed to athletes as potent anabolic agents are of special interest, particularly dehydroepiandrosterone (DHEA), androstenedione, and related compounds. These supplements are classified as prohormones because they are precursors for testosterone and are thus theorized to increase muscle mass and decrease body fat. They may be derived from certain plants, such as wild yams. Although these prohormones have been marketed as dietary supplements, in 2005 the FDA classified them as controlled drugs, similar to anabolic steroids.

Dehydroepiandrosterone (DHEA) and its sulfated metabolite (DHEAS) are produced in the body by the adrenal and gonadal glands, and may be converted into androstenedione with subsequent conversion to testosterone in peripheral tissues, including fat and muscle tissue. Body levels of DHEA are high in young adulthood and gradually decrease to low levels with aging. Although Abbasi and others reported a low, but significant, inverse relationship between natural DHEA levels and body fat in men aged 60–80 years, there are no data supporting beneficial effects of DHEA supplementation. Using well-controlled experimental designs, recent studies by Wallace and Brown and their associates revealed no significant effects of DHEA supplementation (50–100 milligrams/day for 8–12 weeks) on serum testosterone levels, lean body mass, or muscular strength in either healthy middle-aged or young men involved in resistance training.

DHEA has also been marketed as an anti-aging agent to help prevent the development of chronic diseases, but in a recent review, Sirrs and Bebb indicated no good scientific data support this speculation. They caution against use of DHEA supplements as high serum DHEA levels have been associated with several health risks, including several forms of cancer. Nevertheless, a recent study by Villareal and others provided some preliminary data supporting positive effects of DHEA supplementation on bone mineral density, body fat, and lean body mass in elderly subjects with very low levels of natural DHEA. The authors recommended additional research. These data with elderly subjects with very low DHEA levels do not support DHEA supplementation to young or middle-aged individuals. For example, Conrad Earnest, an expert in anabolic dietary supplements, reported that DHEA supplementation at relatively low doses (50–150 milligrams) does not enhance serum testosterone in young men. Moreover, Acacio and others found that six months supplementation with DHEA to young men aged 18–42 elevated levels of a metabolite that raised concerns about the potential negative impact of DHEA supplementation on the prostate gland.

Androstenedione and related compounds, such as androstenediol and norandrostenediol are potent anabolic agents, one step removed from the formation of testosterone. Androstenedione received considerable notoriety during the 1998 baseball season when Mark McGwire, who established a home run record at that time, acknowledged using the dietary supplement. Subsequently, androstenedione-related products flooded the marketplace for resistance-trained individuals, even though no reputable research was available supporting beneficial effects.

Based on previous research with testosterone, Leder and others suggest large doses of androstenedione may be ergogenic, particularly with individuals who take multiple doses daily. However, several subsequent studies have evaluated the ergogenic effects of androstenedione supplementation, and most have shown no beneficial effects. In a short-term study, Rasmussen and others found no effect of oral androstenedione supplementation (100 milligrams/day for 5 days) on serum testosterone or muscle protein anabolism in young men. In a more prolonged study, Wallace and others reported no significant effects of androstenedione supplementation (100 milligrams/day for 12 weeks) on serum testosterone levels, lean body mass, or muscular strength in resistance-trained middle-aged men. Using three individual 100-milligram androstenedione doses daily (total 300 milligrams/day), King and others reported no significant effects on serum testosterone, body fat, lean body mass, muscle fiber diameter, or muscular strength in young men during 8 weeks of resistance training. Other studies, using somewhat higher doses, reported positive findings. Leder and others, although finding no significant effects of a 100-milligram dose, reported significant increases in serum testosterone in adult men following a 300-milligram dose, but no exercise performance was measured. Earnest and others also reported significant, but small, increases in total testosterone with a 200-milligram dose of androstenedione, but not androstenediol, supplementation. In a study with young women, Brown and others reported that androstenedione intake (100 or 300 milligrams) significantly increased serum testosterone concentrations.

Recent reviews do not support an ergogenic effect of androstenedione and its congeners. Earnest noted that even though increases in testosterone following androstenedione ingestion have been found to be statistically significant, they have not been accompanied by favorable changes in protein synthesis or metabolism, muscle mass or lean body mass, or strength. These findings have also been supported in reviews by Tim Ziegenfuss and Ron Maughan.

Use of androstenedione and its congeners may be associated with increased health risks. Earnest indicated that androstenedione supplementation has been associated with impaired lipid metabolism, such as decreased HDL-cholesterol and increased LDL-cholesterol, which might increase risk for cardiovascular disease. Several studies have reported significant increases in estrogen hormones (estradiol or estrone), which could exert feminizing effects in males, such as gynecomastia (breast enlargement). Other adverse effects on gonadal hormones may be associated with testicular shrinkage and infertility. Leder also notes women and children who use such supplements may be at risk. Unfortunately, given the recency of such supplements, no long-term safety data are available.

For athletes who may be tested for doping, the use of DHEA or androstenedione and related prohormones has been banned by WADA and the International Olympic Committee; their use has also been banned by other sports organizations, including the National Collegiate Athletic Association and the National Football League. Although anabolic metabolic prohormones are currently banned for sale in the United States, a number of substitutes for these products are being marketed on the Internet. However, athletes should be aware that such products may be contaminated. In a recent study, Geyer and others secured 634 nutritional supplements from 13 countries, and 14.8 percent contained anabolic androgenic steroids not declared on the label, and the administration of some of the supplements resulted in positive doping tests.

Key Concept Recap

▶ The use of anabolic drugs or hormones to increase body weight may be effective but may also lead to a variety of health problems.

▶ Research has shown that prohormone dietary supplements marketed as anabolic agents, such as androstenedione, do not effectively increase muscle mass or strength. Moreover, such prohormones have been classified as controlled anabolic steroids and their use is illegal.

Check for Yourself

Go to the Internet search engine www.google.com, type in anabolic steroids, and check the advertisements and information related to laws and use of such products. Share the information with your classmates. Now that androstenediol products are illegal, check advertisements for various replacements, such as androstenetrione.

Ginseng, Herbals, and Exercise and Sports Performance

Numerous herbals, which may be regulated as drugs in some countries, have been marketed as ergogenic aids for athletes.

Unfortunately, with the exception of ginseng and related products, limited research has evaluated their ability to enhance exercise or sport performance.

Do ginseng or ciwujia enhance exercise or sport performance?

Ginseng and ciwujia are comparable herbs, and both have been studied for their potential effects on exercise or sport performance.

Ginseng   Extracts derived from the plant family Araliaceae contain numerous chemicals that may influence human physiology, the most important being the glycosides, or ginsenosides. Collectively, these extracts are referred to as **ginseng,** and their physiologic effects vary depending on the plant species, the part of the plant used, and the place of origin. The most common forms of ginseng include Chinese or Korean (Panax ginseng), American (Panax quinquefolium), Japanese (Panax japonicum), and Russian/Siberian (Eleutherococcus senticosus). Eleutherococcus senticosus is a totally different plant from Araliaceae, but it is recognized by some as a legitimate form of ginseng and its ginsenosides are also referred to as eleutherosides. The type and amount of ginsenosides present vary greatly among the different forms of ginseng.

Using such labels as Ginseng Energy, ginseng has been marketed in various forms as a means of enhancing health and physical performance (see figure 13.12). Although the underlying mechanisms are unknown, ginseng is believed to influence neural and hormonal activity in the body and has also been theorized to enhance the immune system. The most prevalent theory suggests ginseng may stimulate the hypothalamus, the part of the brain that controls the pituitary gland, an endocrine gland often referred to as the master gland. The pituitary gland releases hormones that influence other endocrine glands in the body, such as the adrenal gland. The adrenal gland releases cortisol, a hormone involved in the response to stress. The Russians conducted much of the early research with ginseng, and used the term "adaptogens" to characterize its ability to increase resistance to the catabolic effects of stress. Because excessive stress is believed to influence the development of a number of chronic diseases, particularly coronary heart disease, ginseng has been used for its alleged therapeutic properties.

The Russians believed that ginseng helped develop resistance not only to mental stress but also to the physical stress of intense exercise training. Other theories suggest ginseng supplementation may influence physical performance in other ways as well, such as increased cardiac function, blood flow, and oxygen transport during exercise; increased oxygen utilization and decreased lactic acid levels during exercise; enhanced muscle glycogen synthesis after exercise; and a positive effect on nitrogen or protein balance. In essence, given these theorized antistress effects, restorative effects, and metabolic effects, ginseng supplementation is theorized to enhance sport performance by allowing athletes to train more intensely and by influencing physiological processes associated with an antifatiguing effect that increase stamina during competition. It should be noted that although numerous theories have

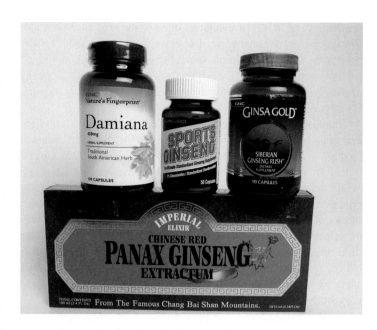

FIGURE 13.12 Various gingseng products are available as dietary supplements, some being marketed directly to athletes.

been advanced in attempts to explain the alleged ergogenic effects of ginseng supplementation, an underlying mechanism has yet to be determined.

Although numerous studies investigated the ergogenic possibilities of ginseng supplementation, few were well-controlled. Research design flaws included no control or placebo group, no double-blind protocol, no randomization of order of treatment, and no statistical analysis. Highlighting these methodological problems in an extensive 1994 review of the ergogenic effect of ginseng supplementation, Michael Bahrke and William Morgan concluded that there is a lack of controlled research demonstrating the ability of ginseng to improve or prolong performance.

Subsequent to the review by Bahrke and Morgan, several well-controlled studies evaluated the ergogenic effects of both standardized ginseng extracts and commercial products and reported no significant effects. For example, Dowling and others reported no effect of Eleutherococcus senticosus on metabolic (oxygen uptake and lactic acid accumulation), physiologic (heart rate and ventilation), or psychologic (ratings of perceived exertion) responses to submaximal and maximal running. Using a similar research protocol but with cycling, Engels and Wirth reported no ergogenic effect of Panax ginseng. Other well-controlled studies by Engels and his associates have found no ergogenic effect of Panax ginseng on high-intensity, interval anaerobic exercise protocols. However, Ziemba and others reported that although Panax ginseng did not influence exercise capacity in soccer players, it did improve multiple-choice reaction time before and during a cycling exercise task. Such an effect may be of benefit to athletes who must react quickly in sports. This finding merits additional research.

Overall, in a recent update of their 1994 review, which includes an additional 35 reports, Bahrke and Morgan note that although more well-controlled research is needed, they again concluded that there is an absence of compelling research evidence regarding the efficacy of ginseng use to improve physical performance in humans. In an analysis of herbal supplements and exercise performance, Williams and Branch cited several other recent major reviews supporting the conclusions of Bahrke and Morgan. Most recently, Goulet and Dionne reviewed studies evaluating the effect of Eleutherococcus senticosus on exercise performance, and concluded that it offers no advantage during exercise endurance tests ranging in duration from 6 to 120 minutes.

Most commercial ginseng preparations appear to have relatively low acute or chronic toxicity when taken in dosages recommended by the manufacturer. Coon and Ernst noted that the most commonly experienced adverse events of Panax ginseng are headache and sleep and gastrointestinal disorders. In general, they found that Panax ginseng, when taken alone and not combined with other substances, is rarely associated with adverse effects. These effects may be attributed to the postulated stimulant effect of ginseng, or possibly to additional substances in the commercial preparation, such as the stimulant ephedrine. For athletes involved in sports that may use drug testing, the use of ginseng products containing ephedrine could lead to disqualification.

Some research suggests long-term ginseng supplementation may prevent some adverse effects of stress on the immune system. Although not studied extensively in athletes, a healthier immune system could help prevent illness or some of the symptoms of the overtraining syndrome during high-intensity training. However, Engels and others recently reported Panax ginseng had no significant effect on immune functions during recovery from intense anaerobic exercise.

Given the available scientific evidence, ginseng supplements cannot be recommended. The consumer should also be aware that commercial ginseng products may suffer from quality control. A recent assay of fifty commercial ginseng preparations indicated that over 10 percent of the products contained no detectable ginsenosides, and the amount in the remaining products varied from 1.9–9.0 percent. Many commercial products contain alcohol.

Individuals who desire to experiment with long-term ginseng supplementation should consult with their physicians, because ginseng use may exacerbate various health problems, such as high blood pressure.

Ciwujia **Ciwujia,** a Chinese herb, is similar to ginseng. Cheuvront and others indicate that ciwujia is extracted from Araliaceae, the same plant family as Panax ginseng. Along with Plowman and others, they also note that it may be derived from the leaves of Eleutherococcus senticosus. Ciwujia is the main active ingredient in the commercial product, Endurox™. Endurox™ is marketed to endurance athletes, and literature published by its manufacturers suggest that it can increase fat oxidation (possibly sparing muscle glycogen), increase oxygen consumption, reduce lactate accumulation, and improve heart rate recovery after exercise. However, most of these claims are based on clinical trials with poor experimental designs. Plowman and others noted that none of the studies followed a randomized crossover or double-blind protocol, nor was the use of a placebo mentioned. None have been published in peer-reviewed journals.

Two recent studies by Plowman, Cheuvront, and their associates, using double-blind, placebo-controlled, crossover experimental designs and published in peer-reviewed journals, reported that supplementation with Endurox™ (800 mg for 7–10 days) had no significant effect on heart rate, oxygen consumption, respiratory exchange ratio (a measure of fat oxidation), lactic acid accumulation, or ratings of perceived exertion during either cycle ergometer or stair-climbing exercise. The investigators indicated their studies did not verify the claims made for Endurox™.

Based on the available evidence, products containing ciwujia do not appear to enhance exercise performance, and thus are not recommended for use by endurance athletes.

What herbals are effective ergogenic aids?

As noted earlier, caffeine may be derived from various herbals, such as guarana and the kola nut, whereas ephedra is a constituent of ma huang. Other than these and ginseng, athletes have experimented with a variety of other herbals, including cayenne for energy and gamma-oryzanol to increase muscle mass.

Kundrat, in a report on herbs and athletes, indicated that double-blind, placebo-controlled human research on herb use by athletes is limited or nonexistent. One reason may be that, at least in the United States, herbs are regulated as dietary supplements and are not required to be standardized, so there is little consistency among different brands. Moreover, herbal sport supplements may often contain several herbals and other substances in a commercial product, so it is difficult to isolate the potential ergogenic effect of a single ingredient.

Studies conducted with such commercial herbal-based sports supplements, such as the recent study by Earnest and others, generally report no significant ergogenic effects.

Nevertheless, several reviews of herbal supplementation and exercise performance are available. In their review, Williams and Branch noted that much of what we know about the efficacy of herbal supplements as ergogenics is based on anecdotal data and poorly controlled studies. However, based on their analysis, they concluded that none of the following herbals have sufficient research support as a means of enhancing exercise or sport performance: bee pollen, capsicum, gamma-oryzanol, ginkgo biloba, kava kava, St. John's wort, Tribulus terrestris, and yohimbine.

Subsequent to these reviews, several other herbals have been studied for their purported ergogenic potential. The herb Cordyceps sinensis is a health tonic from China; although it is rare, a synthetic version is now available; one version is CordyMax Cs-4. Cordyceps sinesis is theorized to have favorable effects on the heart and circulation to improve oxidative capacity and endurance performance. However, Parcell and others reported that 5 weeks of CordyMax Cs-4 supplementation had no effect on aerobic capacity of endurance-trained male cyclists.

Rhodiola rosea, like ginseng, is categorized as an adaptogen, and has been theorized to enhance endurance performance through a stimulating effect. In a preliminary study, De Bock and others found that an acute dose (200 milligrams) of Rhodiola rosea improved time to exhaustion by 3 percent on a cycle ergometer, but there was no significant effect following four weeks of supplementation with 200 milligrams daily. There was no effect on maximal strength or various measures of reaction time or movement time. The improved time to exhaustion following an acute dose may have been a chance finding, and this study merits replication; as the authors noted, it was a preliminary study.

Cytoseira canariensis has been marketed as a new sports supplement designed to increase muscle mass and decrease body fat by inhibiting myostatin. Myostatin is a protein known as a growth and differentiation factor, and its role is to inhibit (not promote) the growth of muscles. Theoretically, by inhibiting the effects of myostatin, muscle growth may be increased. However, Darryn Willoughby, an exercise scientist at Baylor University, reported that 1,200 milligrams/day of Cystoseira canariensis supplementation during 12 weeks of resistance training had no effect on serum myostatin levels, not did it have any effect on muscle mass, muscle strength, or body fat.

Kundrat indicated that athletes should be concerned about the safety of herbals, as there may be some side effects or herb-drug interactions. For athletes using herbals for weight loss, Pittler concluded that the potential health risks recommended against such use due to an increased risk relative to benefit. Athletes contemplating using herbals should consult with their health care professional.

Key Concept Recap

► Results from well-controlled research indicate that ginseng and related adaptogens, such as ciwujia, are not effective ergogenic aids.

► There is limited well-controlled research regarding the effect of herbals on exercise or sport performance, and that which is available suggests herbal sports supplements are not effective ergogenic aids.

If you or one of your colleagues is physically trained or an athlete, you might want to conduct a small case study with caffeine. Either of you should be physically trained to run a mile, swim 500 meters, or some comparable exercise task of 5–10 minutes of high-intensity exercise. Other exercise tasks of shorter duration may be selected. The activity is best done indoors to control environmental conditions. One of you can serve as the investigator and the other as the subject. A third colleague will administer the treatment on a double-blind basis. Randomly, over a 5-week period, the subject will participate in five trials, each involving maximal performance for the selected activity. Thirty minutes before the test, the subject should consume either two caffeine tablets, each containing 200 milligrams of caffeine (Vivarin or comparable over-the-counter tablet) or a comparable placebo (two multivitamin tablets) with some water. The subject's eyes should be closed while taking the tablets. Here is the weekly protocol.

Week 1—Learning protocol; no placebo or caffeine
Week 2—Placebo or caffeine
Week 3—Caffeine or placebo (opposite of week 2)
Week 4—Placebo or caffeine
Week 5—Caffeine or placebo (opposite of week 4)

Record the performance times for each, average the two placebo and two caffeine trials, and compare the results for improvement, if any.

Caffeine Trial

	Week 1 (no placebo or caffeine)	Week 2 (placebo or caffeine)	Week 3 (opposite of week 2)	Week 4 (placebo or caffeine)	Week 5 (opposite of week 4)
Performance Time					

1. Of the drugs and supplements discussed in this chapter, which have the most research supporting their ability to enhance exercise or sports performance?
   (a) caffeine and androstenedione
   (b) gingseng and ephedrine
   (c) alcohol and DHEA
   (d) androstenedione and ephedrine
   (e) sodium bicarbonate and caffeine

2. About how many milligrams of caffeine are in a 6-ounce cup of perked coffee?
   (a) 25–30
   (b) 100–125
   (c) 300–400
   (d) 500–600
   (e) 1,000

3. Which of the following is not a physiological effect of caffeine?
   (a) decreases the metabolic rate
   (b) stimulates the central nervous system
   (c) increases the secretion of epinephrine
   (d) increases heart rate and force of contraction
   (e) increases force of skeletal muscle contractility

4. For an average-size male adult (150 pounds), the consumption of four (4) drinks within a very short period of time would elevate the blood alcohol concentration (BAC) to about what level?
   (a) 0.01
   (b) 0.02
   (c) 0.05
   (d) 0.10
   (e) 0.15

5. As a potential ergogenic aid, sodium bicarbonate would be most likely suited to which type of athlete?
   (a) marathon runner (26.2 miles)
   (b) 100-meter sprinter (track)
   (c) 400-meter sprinter (track)
   (d) pole vaulter (field)
   (e) discus thrower (field)

6. Increasing reearch suggests that moderate alcohol consumption, or "low risk" drinking, may reduce the risk of CHD and all-cause mortality. All of the following, except which, are hypothesized to contribute to this reduced risk?
   (a) a relaxation effect and reduced anxiety

   (b) decreased platelet aggregability (decreased possibility of blood clots)
   (c) increased blood flow to the brain
   (d) reduces caloric intake, induces weight loss, and prevents metabolic syndrome
   (e) an increase in HDL-cholesterol

7. Research generally supports the theory that caffeine may enhance performance in long-distance endurance events. Which of the following is the *least* likely hypothesis?
   (a) It may exert a psychological stimulating effect.
   (b) It stimulates the release of epineprhine from the adrenal gland.
   (c) It decreases the use of both free fatty acids and muscle glycogen.
   (d) It may decrease the perception of effort during exercise.
   (e) It may exert a direct effect on the muscles to increase muscle contractile force.

8. Anabolic/androgenic steroids (AAS) are drugs popular with individuals with

muscle dysmorphia, or those who desire to increase muscle mass even though already very muscular. AAS are designed to mimic mainly the anabolic effects of which natural hormone in the body?
- (a) insulin
- (b) human growth hormone (HGH)
- (c) testosterone
- (d) androsterone
- (e) estrogen

9. Which of the following dietary supplements marketed to strength-trained individuals are precursors, or prohormones, for testosterone?
- (a) creatine and conjugated linoleic acid
- (b) gamma oryzanol and ginseng
- (c) Cordycepts sinensis and Cytoseira canariensis
- (d) HMB and tribulous terrestris
- (e) androstenedione and DHEA

10. Which of the following ergogenic aids are currently permitted for use by athletes in all sports competitions according to the doping list created by the World Anti-Doping Agency (WADA)?
- (a) caffeine and ephedrine
- (b) sodium bicarbonate and caffeine
- (c) caffeine and alcohol
- (d) androstenedione and DHEA
- (e) ginseng and ephedrine

Answers to multiple choice questions: 1. e; 2. b; 3. a; 4. d; 5. c; 6. d; 7. c; 8. c; 9. e; 10. b.

Review Questions—Essay

1. Discuss both the potential beneficial and adverse health effects of consuming various amounts of alcohol.

2. Discuss the efficacy, safety, and legality of caffeine supplementation as an ergogenic aid for aerobic endurance athletes.

3. Discuss the efficacy, safety, and legality of sodium bicarbonate supplementation as an ergogenic aid. In which types of sports would it appear to be most effective?

4. Compare and contrast the effects of testosterone, versus its congeners DHEA and androstenedione, as ergogenic aids for the development of muscle mass and strength. Discuss possible health risks associated with use of each.

5. What is ginseng, why is it purpoted to be an ergogenic aid, and does research support its efficacy as an ergogenic?

References

Books

Bahrke, M., and Yesalis, C. 2002. *Performance-Enhancing Substances in Sport and Exercise.* Champaign, IL: Human Kinetics.

Bucci, L. 1993. *Nutrients as Ergogenic Aids for Sports and Exercise.* Boca Raton, FL: CRC Press.

Noakes, T. 2003. *Love of Running.* Champaign, IL: Human Kinetics.

Reviews

American College of Sports Medicine. 1987. American College of Sports Medicine position stand on use of anabolic-androgenic steroids in sports. *Medicine & Science in Sports & Exercise* 19:534–39.

Antinoro, L. 2001. Battling brain diseases: Diet links to Alzheimer's and Parkinson's. *Environmental Nutrition* 24 (4):1, 4.

Armstrong, L. 2002. Caffeine, body fluid-electrolyte balance, and exercise performance. *International Journal of Sport Nutrition and Exercise Metabolism* 12:189–206.

Association of Women's Health, Obstetric and Neonatal Nurses. 1994. Caffeine and women's health. Washington, DC: International Food Information Council Foundation.

Avisar, R., et al. 2002. Effect of coffee consumption on intraocular pressure. *Annals of Pharmacotherapy* 36:992–95.

Bahrke, M. S., and Morgan. W. P. 2000. Evaluation of the ergogenic properties of ginseng: An update. *Sports Medicine* 29:113–33.

Bahrke, M. S., and Morgan. W. P. 1994. Evaluation of the ergogenic properties of ginseng. *Sports Medicine* 18:229–48.

Bent, S., et al. 2004. Safety and efficacy of citrus aurantium for weight loss. *American Journal of Cardiology* 94:1359–61.

Burke, L., and Maughan, R. 2000. Alcohol in Sport. In *Nutrition in Sport,* ed. R. J. Maughan. Oxford: Blackwell Scientific.

Consumers Union. 2004. Coffee or tea? Battle of the brews. *Consumer Reports on Health* 17 (2):6.

Consumers Union. 2004. Ephedra: Heart dangers in disguise. *Consumer Reports* 69 (1):22–23.

Consumers Union. 2001. Coffee: How much is too much? *Consumer Reports* 66 (5):64–65.

Consumers Union. 1997. What caffeine can do for you—and to you. *Consumers Reports on Health* 9:97–101.

Coon, J., and Ernst, E. 2002. Panax ginseng: A systematic review of adverse effects and drug interactions. *Drug Safety* 25:323–44.

Daly, J. W., and Fredholm, B. B. 1998. Caffeine: An atypical drug of dependence. *Drug and Alcohol Dependence* 51:199–206.

Dean, H. 2002. Does exogenous growth hormone improve athletic performance? *Clinical Journal of Sport Medicine* 12:250–53.

de Lorimier, A. 2000. Alcohol, wine, and health. *American Journal of Surgery* 180:357–61.

Denke, M. 2000. Nutritional and health benefits of beer. *American Journal of the Medical Sciences* 320:320–26.

Doherty, M., and Smith, P. 2004. Effect of caffeine ingestion on exercise testing: A meta-analysis. *International Journal of Sport Nutrition and Exercise Metabolism* 14:626–46.

Earnest, C. 2001. Dietary androgen supplements: Separating substance from hype. *Physician and Sportsmedicine* 29 (5):63–79.

Evans, N. 2004. Current concepts in anabolic-androgenic steroids. *American Journal of Sports Medicine* 32:534–42.

Fernandes, O., et al. 1998. Moderate to heavy caffeine consumption during pregnancy and relationship to spontaneous abortion and abnormal fetal growth: A meta-analysis. *Reproductive Toxicology* 12:435–44.

Food and Drug Administration. 2004. Crackdown on "Andro" products. *FDA Consumer* 38 (3):26.

Frisch, H. 1999. Growth hormone and body composition in athletes. *Journal of Endocrinological Investigations* 22 (5 Supplement):106–9.

Gordis, E. 1999. Research on alcohol problems. *Kappa Phi Journal* 79 (4):24–27, 37.

Goulet, E., and Dionne, I. 2005. Assessment of the effects of eleutherococcus senticosus on endurance performance. *International Journal of Sport Nutrition and Exercise Metabolism* 15:75–83.

Graham, T. 2001. Caffeine, coffee, and ephedrine: Impact on exercise performance and metabolism. *Canadian Journal of Applied Physiology* 26:S103–19.

Graham, T., and Spriet, L. 1996. Caffeine and exercise performance. *Sports Science Exchange* 9(1):1–5.

Greenway, F. 2001. The safety and efficacy of pharmaceutical and herbal caffeine and ephedrine use as a weight loss agent. *Obesity Reviews* 2:199–211.

Haller, C., et al. 2005. Seizures reported in association with use of dietary supplements. *Clinical Toxicology* 43:23–30.

Haller, C., and Benowitz, N. 2000. Adverse cardiovascular and central nervous system events associated with dietary supplements containing ephedra alkaloids. *New England Journal of Medicine* 343:1833–38.

Hartgens, F., and Kuipers, H. 2004. Effects of androgenic-anabolic steroids in athletes. *Sports Medicine* 34:513–54.

Holman, C.D., et al. 1996. Meta-analysis of alcohol and all-cause mortality. *Medical Journal of Australia* 164:141–45.

Horne, J., and Reyner, L. 1999. Vehicle accidents related to sleep: A review. *Occupational and Environmental Medicine* 56:289–94.

James, J. 2004. Critical review of dietary caffeine and blood pressure: A relationship that should be taken more seriously. *Psychosomatic Medicine* 66:63–71.

Jequier, E. 1999. Alcohol intake and body weight: A paradox. *American Journal of Clinical Nutrition* 69:173–74.

Jeukendrup, A., and Martin, J. 2001. Improving cycling performance: How should we spend our time and money? *Sports Medicine* 31:559–69.

Juliano, L., and Griffiths, R. 2004. A critical review of caffeine withdrawal: Empirical validation of symptoms and signs, incidence, severity, and associated features. *Psychopharmacology* 176:1–29.

Kalmar, J., and Cafarelli, E. 2004. Caffeine: A valuable tool to study central fatigue in humans. *Exercise and Sport Sciences Reviews* 32:143–47.

Klatsky, A. 2002. Alcohol and cardiovascular disease: A historical review. *New York Academy of Sciences* 957:7–15.

Koppes, L., et al. 2005. Moderate alcohol consumption lowers the risk of type 2 diabetes: A meta-analysis of prospective observational studies. *Diabetes Care* 28:719–25.

Kraemer, W., et al. 2002. Growth hormone: Physiological effects of exogenous administration. In *Performance-Enhancing Substances in Sport and Exercise,* eds. M. Bahrke and C. Yesalis. Champaign, IL: Human Kinetics.

Kundrat, S. 2005. Herbs and athletes. *Sports Science Exchange* 18 (1):1–6.

Liu, P., et al. 2004. Clinical review 171: The rationale, efficacy and safety of androgen therapy in older men: Future research and current practice recommendations. *Journal of Clinical Endocrinology and Metabolism* 89:4789–96.

Luetkemeier, M. J., et al. 1997. Dietary sodium and plasma volume levels with exercise. *Sports Medicine* 23:279–86.

Magkos, F., and Kavouras, S. 2004. Caffeine and ephedrine: Physiological, metabolic and performance-enhancing effects. *Sports Medicine* 34:971–89.

Maglione, M., et al. 2005. Psychiatric effects of ephedra use: An analysis of Food and Drug Administration reports of adverse events. *American Journal of Psychiatry* 162:189–91.

Matson, L., and Tran, Z. V. 1993. Effects of sodium bicarbonate ingestion on anaerobic performance: A meta-analytic review. *International Journal of Sport Nutrition* 3:2–28.

Maughan, R., et al. 2004. Dietary supplements. *Journal of Sports Sciences* 22:95–113.

McNaughton, L. R. 2000. Bicarbonate and citrate. In *Nutrition in Sport,* ed. R. J. Maughan. Oxford: Blackwell Science.

Monti, P., et al. 2005. Adolescence: Booze, brains, and behavior. *Alcoholism: Clinical & Experimental Research* 29:207–20.

National Institute on Alcohol Abuse and Alcoholism. 2003. *State of the science report on the effects of moderate drinking.* National Institutes of Health. December 19, 2003.

Nnakwe, N. 1996. Anabolic steroids and cardiovascular risk in athletes. *Nutrition Today* 31 (5): 206–8.

O'Brien, C., and Lyons, F. 2000. Alcohol and the athlete. *Sports Medicine* 29:295–300.

Pittler, M., et al. 2005. Adverse events of herbal food supplements for body weight reduction: Systematic review. *Obesity Reviews* 6:93–111.

Rawson, E., and Clarkson, P. 2002. Ephedrine as an ergogenic aid. In *Performance-Enhancing Substances in Sport and Exercise,* eds. M. Bahrke and C. Yesalis. Champaign, IL: Human Kinetics.

Reid, T. 2005. Caffeine. *National Geographic* 207 (1):2–33.

Requena, B., et al. 2005. Sodium bicarbonate and sodium citrate: Ergogenic aids. *Journal of Strength and Conditioning Research* 19:213–24.

Room, R., et al. 2005. Alcohol and public health. *Lancet* 365:519–30.

Shekelle, P., et al. 2003. Efficacy and safety of ephedra and ephedrine for weight loss and athletic performance: A meta-analysis. *JAMA* 289:1537–45.

Signorello, L., and McLaughlin, J. 2004. Maternal caffeine consumption and spontaneous abortion: A review of the epidemiologic evidence. *Epidemiology* 15:229–39.

Sirrs, S. M., and Bebb, R. A. 1999. DHEA: Panacea or snake oil? *Canadian Family Physician* 45:1723–28.

Smith, G., et al. 1999. Fatal nontraffic injuries involving alcohol: A meta-analysis. *Annals of Emergency Medicine* 33:699, 701.

Tarnopolsky, M. 1993. Protein, caffeine, and sports. *Physician and Sportsmedicine* 21 (March): 137–49.

Tufts University. 2001. New findings on caffeine and your health. *Health & Nutrition Letter.* 19(1):1–3.

Wechsler, H., et al. 1994. Health and behavioral consequences of binge drinking in college. *Journal of the American Medical Association* 272:1672–77.

Williams, J. 1991. Caffeine, neuromuscular function and high-intensity exercise performance. *Journal of Sports Medicine and Physical Fitness* 31:481–89.

Williams, M., and Branch, J. 2002. Herbals as ergogenic aids. In *Performance Enhancing Substances in Sports and Exercise,* eds. M. Bahrke and C. Yesalis. Champaign, IL: Human Kinetics.

Williams, M. H. 2000. Smoking, alcohol, ergogenic aids, doping and the endurance performer. In *Endurance in Sport,* eds. R. J. Shephard and P.O Astrand. Oxford: Blackwell Science.

Yeomans, M. 2004. Effects of alcohol on food and energy intake in human subjects: Evidence for passive and active over-consumption of energy. *British Journal of Nutrition* 92:S31–S34.

Yesalis, C., and Bahrke, M. 2005. Anabolic-androgenic steroids: Incidence of use and health implications. *President's Council on Physical Fitness and Sports Research Digest* 5 (5):1–8.

Zachwieja, J. J., and Yarasheski, K. E. 1999. Does growth hormone therapy in conjunction with resistance exercise increase muscle force production and muscle mass in men and women aged 60 years or older? *Physical Therapy* 79:76–82.

Ziegenfuss, T., et al. 2002. Effects of prohomones supplementation in humans: A review. *Canadian Journal of Applied Physiology* 27:628–46.

Specific Studies

Abbasi, A., et al. 1998. Association of dehydroepiandrosterone sulfate, body composition, and physical fitness in independent community-dwelling older men and women. *Journal of the American Geriatric Society* 46:263–73.

Acacio, B., et al. 2004. Pharmacokinetics of dehydroepiandrosterone and its metabolites after long-term daily oral administration to healthy young men. *Fertility and Sterility* 81:595–604.

Armstrong, L., et al. 2005. Fluid, electrolyte, and renal indices of hydration during 11 days of controlled caffeine consumption. *International Journal of Sport Nutrition and Exercise Metabolism* 15:252–65.

Aschenbach, W., et al. 2000. Effect of oral sodium loading on high-intensity arm ergometry in college wrestlers. *Medicine & Science in Sports & Exercise* 32:669–75.

Ascherio, A., et al. 2001. Prospective study of caffeine consumption and risk of Parkinson's disease in men and women. *Annals of Neurology* 50:56–63.

Bahrke, M. S., et al. 1998. Anabolic-androgenic steroid abuse and performance-enhancing drugs among adolescents. *Child and Adolescent Psychiatric Clinics of North America* 7:821–38.

Ball, D., and Maughan, R. J. 1997. The effect of sodium citrate ingestion on the metabolic response to intense exercise following diet manipulation in man. *Experimental Physiology* 82:1041–56.

Battram, D., et al. 2004. Caffeine ingestion does not impede the resynthesis of proglycogen and macroglycogen after prolonged exercise and carbohydrate supplementation in humans. *Journal of Applied Physiology* 96:943–50.

Bell, D., et al. 2002. Effect of ingesting caffeine and ephedrine on 10-km run performance. *Medicine & Science in Sports & Exercise* 34:344–49.

Bell, D., et al. 2001. Effect of caffeine and ephedrine ingestion on anaerobic exercise performance. *Medicine & Science in Sports & Exercise* 33:1399–1403.

Bell, D., et al. 2000. Reducing the dose of combined caffeine and ephedrine preserves the ergogenic effect. *Aviation, Space, and Environmental Medicine* 71:415–19.

Bell, D. G., and Jacobs, I. 1999. Combined caffeine and ephedrine ingestion improves run times of Canadian Forces Warrior Test. *Aviation and Space Environmental Medicine* 70:325–29.

Bell, D. G., et al. 1998. Effects of caffeine, ephedrine and their combination on time to exhaustion during high-intensity exercise. *European Journal of Applied Physiology* 77:427–33.

Bents, R., et al. 2004. Ephedrine, pseudoephedrine, and amphetamine prevalence in college hockey players. *Physician and Sportsmedicine* 32 (9):30–34.

Bhasin, S., et al. 1996. The effects of supraphysiologic doses of testosterone on muscle size and strength in normal men. *New England Journal of Medicine* 335:1–7.

Bird, S., et al. 1995. The effect of sodium bicarbonate ingestion on 1500-m racing time. *Journal of Sports Sciences* 13:399–403.

Bishop, D., and Claudius, B. 2005. Effects of induced metabolic alkalosis on prolonged intermittent-sprint performance. *Medicine & Science in Sports & Exercise* 37:759–67.

Borg, G., et al. 1990. Effect of alcohol on perceived exertion in relation to heart rate and blood lactate. *European Journal of Applied Physiology* 60:382–84.

Bouchard, N., et al. 2005. Ischemic stroke associated with use of an ephedra-free dietary supplement containing synephrine. *Mayo Clinic Proceedings* 80:541–45.

Brown, G., et al. 1999. Effect of oral DHEA on serum testosterone and adaptations to resistance training in young men. *Journal of Applied Physiology* 87:2274–83.

Brown, G., et al. 2004. Changes in serum testosterone and estradiol concentrations following acute androstenedione ingestion in young women. *Hormone and Metabolic Research* 36:62–66.

Bruce, C., et al. 2000. Enhancement of 2000-m rowing performance after caffeine ingestion. *Medicine & Science in Sports & Exercise* 32:1958–63.

Cheuvront, S. N., et al. 1999. Effect of ENDUROX™ on metabolic responses to submaximal exercise. *International Journal of Sport Nutrition* 9:434–42.

Chopra, M., et al. 2000. Nonalcoholic red wine extract and quercetin inhibit LDL oxidation without affecting plasma antioxidant vitamin and carotenoid concentrations. *Clinical Chemistry* 46:1162–70.

Cohen, B., et al. 1996. Effects of caffeine ingestion on endurance racing in heat and humidity. *European Journal of Applied Physiology* 73:358–63.

Cole, K., et al. 1996. Effect of caffeine ingestion on perception of effort and subsequent work production. *International Journal of Sport Nutrition* 6:14–23.

Collomp, K., et al. 1992. Effects of caffeine ingestion on sprint performance in trained and untrained swimmers. *European Journal of Applied Physiology* 64:377–80.

Costill, D., et al. 1978. Effects of caffeine ingestion on metabolism and exercise performance. *Medicine & Science in Sports* 10:155–58.

De Bock, K., et al. 2004. Acute Rhodiola rosea intake can improve endurance exercise performance. *International Journal of Sport Nutrition and Exercise Metabolism* 14:298–307.

Dowling, E. A., et al. 1996. Effect of Eleutherococcus senticosus on submaximal and maximal exercise performance. *Medicine & Science in Sport & Exercise,* 28:482–89.

DuRant, R., et al. 1995. Anabolic-steroid use, strength training, and multiple drug use among adolescents in the United States. *Pediatrics* 96:23–28.

Earnest, C., et al. 2004. Effects of a commercial herbal-based formula on exercise performance in cyclists. *Medicine & Science in Sports & Exercise* 36:504–09.

Earnest, C. P., et al. 2000. In vivo 4-androstene-3, 17-dione and 4-androstene-3 beta, 17 beta-diol supplementation in young men. *European Journal of Applied Physiology* 81:229–32.

Engels, H., et al. 2003. Effects of ginseng on secretory IgA, performance, and recovery from interval exercise. *Medicine & Science in Sports & Exercise* 35:690–96.

Engels, H., et al. 2001. Effects of ginseng supplementation on supramaximal exercise performance and short-term recovery. *Journal of Strength and Conditioning Research* 15:290–95.

Engels, H., and Wirth, J. 1997. No ergogenic effect of ginseng (Panax ginseng C.A. Meyer) during graded maximal aerobic exercise. *Journal of the American Dietetic Association* 97:1110–15.

Essig, D., et al. 1980. Muscle glycogen and triglyceride use during leg cycling following caffeine ingestion. *Medicine & Science in Sports & Exercise* 12:109.

Faigenbaum, A. D., et al. 1998. Anabolic steroid use by male and female middle school students. *Pediatrics* 101:e6.

Fraenkel-Conrat, H., and Singer, B. 1988. Nucleoside adducts are formed by cooperative reactions of acetaldehyde and alcohols: Possible mechanism for the role of alcohol in carcinogenesis. *Proceedings of the National Academy of Sciences* 85:3758–61.

French, C., et al. 1991. Caffeine ingestion during exercise to exhaustion in elite distance runners. *The Journal of Sports Medicine and Physical Fitness* 31:425–32.

Frost, L., and Vestergaard, P. 2005. Caffeine and risk of atrial fibrillation or flutter: The Danish Diet, Cancer, and Health Study. *American Journal of Clinical Nutrition* 81:578–82.

Gaziano, J., et al. 1993. Moderate alcohol intake, increased levels of high-density lipoprotein and its subfractions, and decreased risk of myocardial infarction. *New England Journal of Medicine* 329:1829–34.

Geyer, H., et al. 2004. Analysis of non-hormonal nutritional supplements for anabolic-androgenic steroids: Results of an international study. *International Journal of Sports Medicine* 25:124–29.

Graham, T., et al. 2000. Caffeine ingestion does not alter carbohydrate or fat metabolism in human skeletal muscle during exercise. *Journal of Physiology* 529:837–47.

Graham, T., and Spriet, L. 1991. Performance and metabolic responses to a high caffeine dose during prolonged exercise. *Journal of Applied Physiology* 71:2292–98.

Graham, T. E., et al. 1998. Metabolic and exercise endurance effects of coffee and caffeine ingestion. *Journal of Applied Physiology* 85:883–89.

Green, G., et al. 2001. NCAA study of substance use and abuse habits of college student-athletes. *Clinical Journal of Sport Medicine* 11:51–56.

Greer, F., et al. 2000. Comparison of caffeine and theophylline ingestion: Exercise metabolism and endurance. *Journal of Applied Physiology* 89:1837–44.

Haller, C., et al. 2004. Enhanced stimulant and metabolic effects of combined ephedrine and caffeine. *Clinical Pharmacology and Therapeutics* 75:259–73.

Hartgens, F., et al. 1996. Body composition, cardiovascular risk factors and liver function in long term androgenic-anabolic steroids-using bodybuilders three months after drug withdrawal. *International Journal of Sports Medicine* 17:429–33.

Healy, M., et al. 2003. High dose growth hormone exerts an anabolic effect at rest and during exercise in endurance-trained athletes. *Journal of Clinical Endocrinology and Metabolism* 88:5221–26.

Hines, L., et al. 2001. Genetic variation in alcohol dehydrogenase and the beneficial effect of moderate alcohol consumption on myocardial infarction. *New England Journal of Medicine* 344:549–55.

Hogervorst, E., et al. 1999. Caffeine improves cognitive performance after strenuous physical exercise. *International Journal of Sports Medicine* 20:354–61.

Jackman, M., et al. 1996. Metabolic catecholamine, and endurance responses to caffeine during intense exercise. *Journal of Applied Physiology* 81:1658–63.

Jacobs, L., et al. 2004. Effects of ephedrine, caffeine, and their combination on muscular endurance. *Medicine & Science in Sports & Exercise* 35:987–94.

Kalmar, J. M., and Cafarelli, E. 1999. Effects of caffeine on neuromuscular function. *Journal of Applied Physiology* 87:801–8.

Kendrick, Z., et al. 1993. Effect of ethanol on metabolic responses to treadmill running in well-trained men. *Journal of Clinical Pharmacology* 33:136–39.

King, D. S., et al. 1999. Effect of oral androstenedione on serum testosterone and adaptations to resistance training in young men. *JAMA* 281:2020–28.

Kozak-Collins, K., et al. 1994. Sodium bicarbonate ingestion does not improve performance in women cyclists. *Medicine & Science in Sports & Exercise* 26:1510–15.

Kraemer, W. J., et al. 1998. Hormonal responses to consecutive days of heavy-resistance exercise with or without nutritional supplementation. *Journal of Applied Physiology* 85:1544–55.

Lane, J. D., et al. 1998. Caffeine raises blood pressure at work. *Psychosomatic Medicine* 60:327–30.

Laurent, D., et al. 2000. Effects of caffeine on muscle glycogen utilization and the neuroendocrine axis during exercise. *Journal of Clinical Endocrinology and Metabolism* 85:2170–75.

Leder, B. Z., et al. 2000. Oral androstenedione administration and serum testosterone concentrations in young men. *JAMA* 283:779–82

Linossier, M. T., et al. 1997. Effect of sodium citrate on performance and metabolism of human skeletal muscle during supramaximal cycling exercise. *European Journal of Applied Physiology* 76:48–54.

MacIntosh, B., and Wright, B. 1995. Caffeine ingestion and performance of a 1,500-metre swim. *Canadian Journal of Applied Physiology* 20:168–77.

Mann, K., et al. 2005. Neuroimaging of gender differences in alcohol dependence: Are women more vulnerable? *Alcoholism: Clinical & Experimental Research* 29:896–901.

McLellan, T., and Bell, D. 2004. The impact of prior coffee consumption on the subsequent ergogenic effect of anhydrous caffeine. *International Journal of Sport Nutrition and Exercise Metabolism* 14:698–708.

McNaughton, L., and Thompson, D. 2001. Acute versus chronic sodium bicarbonate ingestion and anaerobic work and power output. *Journal of Sports Medicine and Physical Fitness* 41:456–62.

McNaughton, L., and Cedaro, R. 1992. Sodium citrate ingestion and its effects on maximal anaerobic exercise of different durations. *European Journal of Applied Physiology* 64:36–41.

McNaughton, L., et al. 1999. Sodium bicarbonate can be used as an ergogenic aid in high-intensity, competitive cycle ergometry of 1 h duration. *European Journal of Applied Physiology* 80:64–69.

McNaughton, L., et al. 1999. Effects of chronic bicarbonate ingestion on the performance of high-intensity work. *European Journal of Applied Physiology* 80:333–36.

Mero, A., et al. 2004. Combined creatine and sodium bicarbonate supplementation enhances interval swimming. *Journal of Strength and Conditioning Research* 18:306–10.

Michels, K., et al. 2005. Coffee, tea, and caffeine consumption and incident of colon and rectal cancer. *Journal of the National Cancer Institute* 97:282–92.

Mora-Rodriguez, R., and Coyle, E. 2000. Effects of plasma epinephrine on fat metabolism during exercise: Interactions with exercise intensity. *American Journal of Physiology. Endocrinology and Metabolism* 278:E669–76.

Mukamal, K., et al. 2003. Roles of drinking pattern and type of alcohol consumed in coronary heart disease in men. *New England Journal of Medicine* 348:109–18.

Naik, S., and Freudenberger, R. 2004. Ephedra-associated cardiomyopathy. *Annals of Pharmacotherapy* 38:400–03.

Naimi, T., et al. 2005. Cardiovascular risk factors and confounders among nondrinking and moderate-drinking U.S. adults. *American Journal of Preventive Medicine* 28:369–73.

Oopik, V., et al. 2003. Effects of sodium citrate ingestion before exercise on endurance performance in well-trained college runners. *British Journal of Sports Medicine* 37:485–89.

Parcell, A., et al. 2004. Cordyceps Sinensis (CordyMax Cs-4) supplementation does not improve endurance exercise performance. *International Journal of Sport Nutrition and Exercise Metabolism* 14:236–42.

Paton, C., et al. 2001. Little effect of caffeine ingestion on repeated sprints in team-sport athletes. *Medicine & Science in Sports & Exercise* 33:822–25.

Plowman, S., et al. 1999. The effects of ENDUROX™ on the physiological responses to stair-stepping exercise. *Research Quarterly for Exercise and Sport* 70:385–88.

Portington, K. J., et al. 1998. Effect of induced alkalosis on exhaustive leg press performance. *Medicine & Science in Sports & Exercise* 30:523–28.

Potteiger, J., et al. 1996. The effects of buffer ingestion on metabolic factors related to distance running performance. *European Journal of Applied Physiology* 72:365–71.

Potteiger, J. A., et al. 1996. Sodium citrate ingestion enhances 30 km cycling performance. *International Journal of Sports Medicine* 17:7–11.

Price, M., et al. 2003. Effects of sodium bicarbonate ingestion on prolonged intermittent exercise. *Medicine & Science in Sports & Exercise* 35:1303–08.

Rasmussen, B. B., et al. 2000. Androstenedione does not stimulate muscle protein anabolism in young healthy men. *Journal of Clinical Endocrinology and Metabolism* 85:55–59.

Raymer, G., et al. 2004. Metabolic effects of induced alkalosis during progressive forearm exercise to fatigue. *Journal of Applied Physiology* 96:2050–56.

Salazar-Martinez, E., et al. 2004. Coffee consumption and risk for type 2 diabetes mellitus. *Annals of Internal Medicine* 140:1–8.

Schabort, E., et al. 2000. Dose-related elevations in venous pH with citrate ingestion do not alter 40-km cycling time-trial performance. *European Journal of Applied Physiology* 83:320–27.

Shave, R., et al. 2001. The effects of sodium citrate ingestion on 3,000-meter time-trial performance. *Journal of Strength and Conditioning Research* 15:230–34.

Smothers, B., and Bertolucci, D. 2001. Alcohol consumption and health-promoting behavior in a U.S. hosuehold sample: Leisure-time physical activity. *Journal of Studies on Alcohol* 62:467–76.

Spriet, D., et al. 1992. Caffeine ingestion and muscle metabolism during prolonged exercise in humans. *American Journal of Physiology* 262:E891–E898.

Stephens, T., et al. 2002. Effect of sodium bicarbonate on muscle metabolism during intense endurance cycling. *Medicine & Science in Sports & Exercise* 34:614–21.

Stuart, G., et al. 2005. Multiple effects of caffeine on simulated high-intensity team-sport performance. *Medicine & Science in Sports & Exercise* 37:1998–2005.

Taaffe, D. R., et al. 1996. Lack of effect of recombinant human growth hormone (GH) on muscle morphology and GH-insulin-like growth factor expression in resistance-trained elderly men. *Journal of Clinical Endocrinology and Metabolism* 81:421–25.

Tarnopolsky, M., and Cupido, C. 2000. Caffeine potentiates low frequency skeletal muscle force in habitual and nonhabitual caffeine consumers. *Journal of Applied Physiology* 89:1719–24.

Tremblay, A., et al. 1995. Alcohol and a high-fat diet: A combination favoring overfeeding. *American Journal of Clinical Nutrition* 62:639–44.

Urhausen, A., et al. 2004. Are the cardiac effects of anabolic steroid abuse in strength athletes reversible? *Heart* 90:496–501.

Van Montfoort, M., et al. 2004. Effects of ingestion of bicarbonate, citrate, lactate, and chloride on sprint running. *Medicine & Science in Sports & Exercise* 36:1239–43.

van Someren, K., et al. 1998. An investigation into the effects of sodium citrate ingestion on high-intensity exercise performance. *International Journal of Sport Nutrition* 8:356–63.

Verhoef, P., et al. 2002. Contribution of caffeine to the homocysteine-raising effect of coffee: A randomized controlled trial in humans. *American Journal of Clinical Nutrition* 76:1244–48.

Villareal, D.T., et al. 2000. Effects of DHEA replacement on bone mineral density and body composition in elderly women or men. *Clinical Endocrinology* 53:561–68.

Wallace, M. B., et al. 1999. Effects of dehydroepiandrosterone vs androstenedione supplementation in men. *Medicine & Science in Sports & Exercise* 31:1788–92.

Wannamethee, S., et al. 2005. Alcohol and adioposity: Effects of quantity and type of drink and time relation with meals. *International Journal of Obesity* 29:1436–44.

Wiles, J., et al. 1992. Effect of caffeinated coffee on running speed, respiratory factors, blood lactate and perceived exertion during 1,500-meter treadmill running. *British Journal of Sports Medicine* 26:116–20.

Williams, P. T. 1997. Interactive effects of exercise, alcohol, and vegetarian diet on coronary artery disease risk factors in 9242 runners: The National Runners' Health Study. *American Journal of Clinical Nutrition* 66:1197–206.

Willoughby, D. 2004. Effects of an alleged myostatin-binding supplement and heavy resistance training on serum myostatin, muscle strength and mass, and body composition. *International Journal of Sport Nutrition and Exercise Metabolism* 14:461–72.

Winklemayer, W., et al. 2005. Habitual caffeine intake and the risk of hypertension in women. *JAMA* 294:2330–35.

Yarasheski, K., et al. 1993. Short-term growth hormone treatment does not increase muscle protein synthesis in experienced weight lifters. *Journal of Applied Physiology* 74:3073–76.

Yesalis, C., et al. 1997. Trends in anabolic-androgenic steroid use among adolescents. *Archives of Pediatric and Adolescent Medicine* 151:1197–1206.

Youngstedt, S. D., et al. 1998. Acute exercise reduces caffeine-induced anxiogenesis. *Medicine & Science in Sports & Exercise* 30:740–45.

Ziemba, A. W., et al. 1999. Ginseng treatment improves psychomotor performance at rest and during graded exercise in young athletes. *International Journal of Sport Nutrition* 9:371–77.

Units of Measurement: English System— Metric System Equivalents

The Metric System and Equivalents

To measure ingredients, a standardized system known as the System Internationale (SI) has been established that is interpreted on an international basis. The SI is based on the metric system. However, in the United States we also employ another set of measure and weight, the English system. In the field of dietetics, both systems are employed. The following tables give the quantities of the measures besides stating equivalents. With this information it is possible to calculate in either system of measure and weight.

Household Measures (Approximations)

For easy computing purposes, the cubic centimeter (cc) is considered equivalent to 1 gram:

$$1 \text{ cc} = 1 \text{ gram} = 1 \text{ milliliter (ml)}$$

For easy computing purposes, 1 ounce equals 30 grams or 30 cubic centimeters.

1 quart	=	960 grams
1 pint	=	480 grams
1 cup	=	240 grams
1/2 cup	=	120 grams
1 glass (8 ounces)	=	240 grams
1/2 glass (4 ounces)	=	120 grams
1 orange juice glass	=	100–120 grams
1 tablespoon	=	15 grams
1 teaspoon	=	5 grams

Level Measures and Weights

1 teaspoon	=	5 cc or 5 ml
		5 grams
3 teaspoons	=	1 tablespoon
		15 cc
		15 grams
2 tablespoons	=	30 cc
		30 grams
		1 ounce (fluid)
4 tablespoons	=	1/4 cup
		60 cc
		60 grams
8 tablespoons	=	1/2 cup
		120 cc
		120 grams
16 tablespoons	=	1 cup
		240 grams
		240 ml (fluid)
		8 ounces (fluid)
		1/2 pound
2 cups	=	1 pint
		480 grams
		480 ml (fluid)
		16 ounces (fluid)
		1 pound
4 cups	=	2 pints
		1 quart
		960 cc
		960 ml (fluid)
		2 pounds
4 quarts	=	1 gallon

Units of Weight

		Ounce	Pound	Gram	Kilogram
1 ounce	=	1.0	0.06	28.4	0.028
1 pound	=	16.0	1.0	454	0.454
1 gram	=	0.035	.002	1.0	0.001
1 kilogram	=	35.3	2.2	1,000	1.0

Units of Volume

		Ounce	Pint	Quart	Milliliter	Liter
1 ounce	=	1.0	0.062	0.031	29.57	0.029
1 pint	=	16.0	1.0	0.5	473	.473
1 quart	=	32.0	2.0	1.0	946	.946
1 milliliter	=	0.034	0.002	0.001	1.0	0.001
1 liter	=	33.8	2.112	1.056	1,000	1.0

Units of Length

		Millimeter	Centimeter	Inch	Foot	Yard	Meter
1 millimeter	=	1.0	0.1	0.0394	0.0033	0.0011	0.001
1 centimeter	=	10.0	1.0	0.394	0.033	0.011	0.01
1 inch	=	25.4	2.54	1.0	0.083	0.028	0.025
1 foot	=	304.8	30.48	12.0	1.0	0.333	0.305
1 yard	=	914.4	91.44	36.0	3.0	1.0	0.914
1 meter	=	1,000	100	39.37	3.28	1.094	1.0

1 kilometer	=	1,000 meters	= 0.62 mile
1 mile	=	1,760 yards	=1.61 kilometers

Units of mechanical, thermal, and chemical energy (approximate equivalents)

	Foot-pounds	Kilogram-meters	Kilojoules	Watts*	Kilocalories	Oxygen**
I foot-pound	I	0.138	0.00136	0.0226	0.00032	0.000064
I kilogram-meter	7.23	I	0.0098	0.163	0.0023	0.00046
I kilojoule	737	102	I	16.66	0.239	0.047
I watt*	44.27	6.12	0.06	I	0.0143	0.0028
I kilocalorie	3,088	427	4.18	0.00024	I	0.198
I liter oxygen**	15,585	2,154	21.1	351.9	5.047	I

Note: Read all tables across, such as I watt equals 44.27 foot-pounds; I foot-pound equals 0.0226 watt.

*Watts are units of power expressed per minute.

**Equivalents are based upon one liter of oxygen metabolizing carbohydrate. Energy equivalents would be slightly less on a mixed diet of carbohydrate, fat, and protein. For example, I liter of oxygen would equal only 4.82 kilocalories on such a mixed diet.

Approximate Caloric Expenditure per Minute for Various Physical Activities

Body weight												
Kilograms	**45**	**48**	**50**	**52**	**55**	**57**	**59**	**61**	**64**	**66**	**68**	**70**
Pounds	**100**	**105**	**110**	**115**	**120**	**125**	**130**	**135**	**140**	**145**	**150**	**155**
Sedentary activities												
Lying quietly	1.0	1.0	1.1	1.1	1.2	1.3	1.3	1.4	1.4	1.5	1.5	1.5
Sitting and writing, card playing, etc.	1.2	1.3	1.4	1.5	1.5	1.6	1.7	1.7	1.8	1.8	1.9	2.0
Standing with light work, cleaning, etc.	2.7	2.9	3.0	3.1	3.3	3.4	3.5	3.7	3.8	3.9	4.1	4.2
Physical activities												
Archery	3.1	3.3	3.5	3.6	3.8	4.0	4.1	4.3	4.5	4.6	4.8	4.9
Badminton												
Recreational singles	3.6	3.8	4.0	4.2	4.4	4.6	4.7	4.9	5.1	5.3	5.4	5.6
Social doubles	2.7	2.9	3.0	3.1	3.3	3.4	3.5	3.7	3.8	3.9	4.1	4.2
Competitive	5.9	6.1	6.4	6.7	7.0	7.3	7.6	7.9	8.2	8.5	8.8	9.1
Baseball												
Player	3.1	3.3	3.4	3.6	3.8	4.0	4.1	4.3	4.4	4.5	4.7	4.8
Pitcher	3.9	4.1	4.3	4.5	4.7	4.9	5.1	5.3	5.5	5.7	5.9	6.0
Basketball												
Half court	3.0	3.1	3.3	3.5	3.6	3.8	3.9	4.1	4.2	4.4	4.5	4.7
Recreational	4.9	5.2	5.5	5.7	6.0	6.2	6.5	6.7	7.0	7.2	7.5	7.7
Vigorous competition	6.5	6.8	7.2	7.5	7.8	8.2	8.5	8.8	9.2	9.5	9.9	10.2
Bicycling, level												
(mph) (min/mile)												
5 12:00	1.9	2.0	2.1	2.2	2.3	2.4	2.5	2.6	2.7	2.8	2.9	3.0
10 6:00	4.2	4.4	4.6	4.8	5.1	5.3	5.5	5.7	5.9	6.1	6.4	6.6
15 4:00	7.3	7.6	8.0	8.4	8.7	9.1	9.5	9.8	10.0	10.5	10.9	11.3
20 3:00	10.7	11.2	11.7	12.3	12.8	13.3	13.9	14.4	14.9	15.5	16.0	16.5
Bowling	2.7	2.8	3.0	3.1	3.3	3.4	3.5	3.7	3.8	3.9	4.1	4.2
Calisthenics												
Light type	3.4	3.6	3.8	4.0	4.1	4.3	4.5	4.7	4.8	5.0	5.2	5.4
Timed vigorous	9.7	10.1	10.6	11.1	11.6	12.1	12.6	13.1	13.6	14.1	14.6	15.1
Canoeing												
(mph) (min/mile)												
2.5 24	1.9	2.0	2.1	2.2	2.3	2.4	2.5	2.6	2.7	2.8	2.9	3.0
4.0 15	4.4	4.6	4.9	5.1	5.3	5.5	5.8	6.0	6.2	6.4	6.7	6.9
5.0 12	5.7	6.0	6.3	6.6	6.9	7.2	7.5	7.8	8.1	8.4	8.7	9.0

When using this appendix, keep these points in mind.

A. The figures are approximate and include the resting energy expenditure (REE). Thus, the total cost of the exercise includes not only the energy expended by the exercise itself, but also the amount you would have used anyway during the same period. Suppose you ran for 1 hour and the calculated energy cost was 800 Calories. During that same time at rest, your REE may have been 75 Calories, so the net cost of the exercise is 725 Calories.

B. The figures in the table are only for the time you are performing the activity. For example, in an hour of basketball, you may exercise strenuously for only 35 to 40 minutes, as you may take time-outs and may rest during foul shots. In general, record only the amount of time that you are actually exercising during the activity.

C. The energy cost, expressed in Calories per minute, will vary for different physical activities in a given individual depending on several factors. For example, the caloric cost of bicycling will vary depending on the type of bicycle, going uphill and downhill, and wind resistance. Walking with hand weights or ankle weights will increase energy output. Energy cost for swimming at a certain pace will depend on swimming efficiency, so the less efficient swimmer will expend more Calories. Thus, the values expressed here are approximations and may be increased or decreased depending upon various factors that influence energy cost for a specific physical activity.

D. Not all body weights could be listed, but you may approximate by using the closest weight listed.

E. There may be small differences between males and females, but not enough to make a significant difference in the total caloric value for most exercises.

Body weight

73	75	77	80	82	84	86	89	91	93	95	98	100
160	165	170	175	180	185	190	195	200	205	210	215	220
1.6	1.6	1.7	1.7	1.8	1.8	1.9	1.9	2.0	2.0	2.1	2.1	2.2
2.0	2.1	2.2	2.2	2.3	2.4	2.4	2.5	2.5	2.6	2.7	2.7	2.8
4.4	4.5	4.6	4.8	4.9	5.0	5.2	5.3	5.4	5.6	5.7	5.9	6.0
5.1	5.3	5.4	5.6	5.7	5.9	6.0	6.2	6.4	6.5	6.7	6.9	7.0
5.8	6.0	6.2	6.4	6.6	6.7	6.9	7.1	7.3	7.4	7.6	7.8	8.0
4.4	4.5	4.6	4.8	4.9	5.0	5.2	5.3	5.4	5.6	5.7	5.9	6.0
9.4	9.7	10.0	10.3	10.6	10.9	11.2	11.5	11.8	12.1	12.4	12.7	13.0
5.0	5.2	5.3	5.5	5.6	5.8	5.9	6.1	6.3	6.4	6.6	6.8	6.9
6.3	6.5	6.7	6.9	7.1	7.3	7.4	7.7	7.9	8.0	8.2	8.5	8.6
4.8	5.0	5.1	5.3	5.4	5.6	5.7	5.9	6.0	6.2	6.4	6.5	6.7
8.0	8.2	8.5	8.7	9.0	9.2	9.5	9.7	10.0	10.2	10.5	10.7	11.0
10.5	10.9	11.2	11.5	11.9	12.2	12.5	12.9	13.2	13.5	13.8	14.2	14.5
3.1	3.2	3.3	3.4	3.5	3.6	3.7	3.8	3.9	4.0	4.1	4.2	4.3
6.8	7.0	7.2	7.4	7.6	7.9	8.1	8.3	8.5	8.7	8.9	9.1	9.4
11.6	12.0	12.4	12.7	13.1	13.4	13.8	14.2	14.5	14.9	15.3	15.6	16.0
17.1	17.6	18.1	18.7	19.2	19.7	20.3	20.8	21.3	21.9	22.4	22.9	23.5
4.4	4.5	4.6	4.8	4.9	5.0	5.2	5.3	5.5	5.6	5.7	5.9	6.0
5.5	5.7	5.9	6.1	6.3	6.4	6.6	6.8	7.0	7.1	7.3	7.5	7.7
15.6	16.1	16.6	17.1	17.6	18.1	18.6	19.1	19.6	20.0	20.5	21.0	21.5
3.1	3.2	3.3	3.4	3.5	3.6	3.7	3.8	3.9	4.0	4.1	4.2	4.3
7.1	7.4	7.6	7.8	8.0	8.2	8.5	8.7	8.9	9.1	9.4	9.6	9.8
9.3	9.5	9.8	10.1	10.4	10.7	11.0	11.3	11.6	11.9	12.2	12.5	12.8

Body weight

	Kilograms 45	48	50	52	55	57	59	61	64	66	68	70
	Pounds 100	105	110	115	120	125	130	135	140	145	150	155
Dancing												
Moderately (waltz)	3.1	3.3	3.5	3.6	3.8	4.0	4.1	4.3	4.5	4.6	4.8	4.9
Active (square, disco)	4.5	4.7	5.0	5.2	5.4	5.6	5.9	6.1	6.3	6.6	6.8	7.0
Aerobic (vigorously)	6.0	6.3	6.7	7.0	7.3	7.6	7.9	8.2	8.5	8.8	9.1	9.4
Fencing												
Moderately	3.3	3.5	3.6	3.8	4.0	4.1	4.3	4.5	4.6	4.8	5.0	5.2
Vigorously	6.6	7.0	7.3	7.7	8.0	8.3	8.7	9.0	9.4	9.7	10.0	10.4
Football												
Moderate	3.3	3.5	3.6	3.8	4.0	4.1	4.3	4.5	4.6	4.8	5.0	5.2
Touch, vigorous	5.5	5.8	6.1	6.4	6.6	6.9	7.2	7.5	7.8	8.0	8.3	8.6
Golf												
Twosome (carry clubs)	3.6	3.8	4.0	4.2	4.4	4.6	4.7	4.9	5.1	5.3	5.4	5.6
Foursome (carry clubs)	2.7	2.9	3.0	3.1	3.3	3.4	3.5	3.7	3.8	3.9	4.1	4.2
Power-cart	1.9	2.0	2.1	2.2	2.3	2.4	2.5	2.6	2.7	2.8	2.9	3.0
Handball												
Moderate	6.5	6.8	7.2	7.5	7.8	8.2	8.5	8.8	9.2	9.5	9.9	10.2
Competitive	7.7	8.0	8.4	8.8	9.2	9.6	10.0	10.4	10.8	11.1	11.5	11.9
Hiking, pack (3 mph)	4.5	4.7	5.0	5.2	5.4	5.6	5.9	6.1	6.3	6.6	6.8	7.0
Hockey, field	5.0	6.3	6.7	7.0	7.3	7.6	7.9	8.2	8.5	8.8	9.1	9.4
Hockey, ice	6.6	7.0	7.3	7.7	8.0	8.3	8.7	9.0	9.4	9.7	10.0	10.4
Horseback riding												
Walk	1.9	2.0	2.1	2.2	2.3	2.4	2.5	2.6	2.7	2.8	2.9	3.0
Sitting to trot	2.7	2.9	3.0	3.1	3.3	3.4	3.5	3.7	3.8	3.9	4.1	4.2
Posting to trot	4.2	4.4	4.6	4.8	5.1	5.3	5.5	5.7	5.9	6.1	6.4	6.6
Gallop	5.7	6.0	6.3	6.6	6.9	7.2	7.5	7.8	8.1	8.4	8.7	9.0
Horseshoes	2.5	2.6	2.8	2.9	3.0	3.1	3.3	3.4	3.5	3.7	3.8	3.9
Jogging (see Running)												
Judo	8.5	8.9	9.3	9.8	10.2	10.6	11.0	11.5	11.9	12.3	12.8	13.2
Karate	8.5	8.9	9.3	9.8	10.2	10.6	11.0	11.5	11.9	12.3	12.8	13.2
Mountain climbing	6.5	6.8	7.2	7.5	7.8	8.2	8.5	8.8	9.2	9.5	9.8	10.2
Paddle ball	5.7	6.0	6.3	6.6	6.9	7.2	7.5	7.8	8.1	8.4	8.7	9.0
Pool (billiards)	1.5	1.6	1.6	1.7	1.8	1.9	1.9	2.0	2.1	2.2	2.2	2.3
Racquetball	6.5	6.8	7.1	7.5	7.8	8.1	8.4	8.8	9.1	9.4	9.8	10.1
Roller skating (9 mph)	4.2	4.4	4.6	4.8	5.1	5.3	5.5	5.7	5.9	6.1	6.4	6.6

Running (steady state)

(mph)	(min/mile)												
5.0	12:00	6.0	6.3	6.6	7.0	7.3	7.6	7.9	8.2	8.5	8.8	9.1	9.4
5.5	10:55	6.7	7.0	7.3	7.7	8.0	8.4	8.7	9.0	9.4	9.7	10.0	10.4
6.0	10:00	7.2	7.6	8.0	8.4	8.7	9.1	9.5	9.8	10.2	10.6	10.9	11.3
7.0	8:35	8.5	8.9	9.3	9.8	10.2	10.6	11.0	11.5	11.9	12.3	12.8	13.2
8.0	7:30	9.7	10.2	10.7	11.2	11.6	12.1	12.6	13.1	13.6	14.1	14.6	15.1
9.0	6:40	10.8	11.3	11.9	12.4	12.9	13.5	14.0	14.6	15.1	15.7	16.2	16.8
10.0	6:00	12.1	12.7	13.3	13.9	14.5	15.1	15.7	16.4	17.0	17.6	18.2	18.8
11.0	5:28	13.3	14.0	14.6	15.3	16.0	16.7	17.3	18.0	18.7	19.4	20.0	20.7
12.0	5:00	14.5	15.2	16.0	16.7	17.4	18.2	18.9	19.7	20.4	21.1	21.9	22.6

		45	48	50	52	55	57	59	61	64	66	68	70
Sailing, small boat		2.7	2.9	3.0	3.1	3.3	3.4	3.5	3.7	3.8	3.9	4.1	4.2
Skating, ice (9 mph)		4.2	4.4	4.6	4.8	5.1	5.2	5.5	5.7	5.9	6.1	6.4	6.6
Skating, in-line (13 mph)		9.5	10.0	10.5	10.9	11.5	12.0	12.4	12.8	13.4	13.9	14.3	14.7

Skiing, cross-country

(mph)	(min/mile)												
2.5	24:00	5.0	5.2	5.5	5.7	6.0	6.2	6.5	6.7	7.0	7.2	7.5	7.8
4.0	15:00	6.5	6.8	7.2	7.5	7.8	8.2	8.5	8.8	9.2	9.5	9.9	10.2
5.0	12:00	7.7	8.0	8.4	8.8	9.2	9.6	10.0	10.4	10.8	11.1	11.5	11.9

APPENDIX B Approximate Caloric Expenditure per Minute for Various Physical Activities

73 160	75 165	77 170	80 175	82 180	84 185	86 190	89 195	91 200	93 205	95 210	98 215	100 220
5.1	5.3	5.4	5.6	5.7	5.9	6.0	6.2	6.4	6.5	6.7	6.9	7.0
7.3	7.5	7.7	7.9	8.2	8.4	8.6	8.9	9.1	9.3	9.5	9.8	10.0
9.7	10.0	10.3	10.6	10.9	11.2	11.5	11.8	12.1	12.4	12.7	13.0	13.3
5.3	5.5	5.7	5.8	6.0	6.2	6.3	6.5	6.7	6.8	7.0	7.1	7.3
10.7	11.0	11.4	11.7	12.1	12.4	12.7	13.1	13.4	13.8	14.1	14.4	14.8
5.3	5.5	5.7	5.8	6.0	6.2	6.3	6.5	6.7	6.8	7.0	7.1	7.3
8.9	9.2	9.4	9.7	10.0	10.3	10.6	10.8	11.1	11.4	11.7	12.0	12.2
5.8	6.0	6.2	6.4	6.6	6.7	6.9	7.1	7.3	7.4	7.6	7.8	8.0
4.4	4.5	4.6	4.8	4.9	5.0	5.2	5.3	5.4	5.6	5.7	5.9	6.0
3.1	3.2	3.3	3.4	3.5	3.6	3.7	3.8	3.9	4.0	4.1	4.2	4.3
10.5	10.9	11.2	11.5	11.9	12.2	12.5	12.9	13.2	13.5	13.8	14.2	14.5
12.3	12.7	13.1	13.5	13.9	14.3	14.7	15.0	15.4	15.8	16.2	16.6	17.0
7.3	7.5	7.7	7.9	8.2	8.4	8.6	8.9	9.1	9.3	9.5	9.8	10.0
9.7	10.0	10.3	10.6	10.9	11.2	11.5	11.8	12.1	12.4	12.7	13.0	13.3
10.7	11.0	11.4	11.7	12.1	12.4	12.7	13.1	13.4	13.8	14.1	14.4	14.8
3.1	3.2	3.3	3.4	3.5	3.6	3.7	3.8	3.9	4.0	4.1	4.2	4.3
4.4	4.5	4.6	4.8	4.9	5.0	5.2	5.3	5.4	5.6	5.7	5.9	6.0
6.8	7.0	7.2	7.4	7.6	7.9	8.1	8.3	8.5	8.7	8.9	9.1	9.4
9.3	9.5	9.8	10.1	10.4	10.7	11.0	11.3	11.6	11.9	12.2	12.5	12.8
4.0	4.2	4.3	4.4	4.5	4.7	4.8	4.9	5.2	5.2	5.3	5.4	5.6
13.6	14.1	14.5	14.9	15.4	15.8	16.2	16.6	17.1	17.5	17.9	18.4	18.8
13.6	14.1	14.5	14.9	15.4	15.8	16.2	16.6	17.1	17.5	17.9	18.4	18.8
10.5	10.8	11.2	11.5	11.8	12.1	12.5	12.8	13.1	13.5	13.8	14.1	14.5
9.3	9.5	9.8	10.1	10.4	10.7	11.0	11.2	11.6	11.9	12.2	12.5	12.8
2.4	2.5	2.6	2.6	2.7	2.8	2.9	2.9	3.0	3.1	3.2	3.2	3.3
10.4	10.7	11.1	11.4	11.7	12.0	12.4	12.7	13.0	13.4	13.7	14.0	14.4
6.8	7.0	7.2	7.4	7.6	7.9	8.1	8.3	8.5	8.7	8.9	9.1	9.4
9.7	10.0	10.3	10.6	10.9	11.2	11.6	11.9	12.2	12.5	12.8	13.1	13.4
10.7	11.1	11.4	11.7	12.1	12.4	12.8	13.1	13.4	13.8	14.1	14.5	14.8
11.7	12.0	12.4	12.8	13.1	13.5	13.8	14.3	14.6	15.0	15.4	15.7	16.1
13.6	14.1	14.5	14.9	15.4	15.8	16.2	16.6	17.1	17.5	17.9	18.4	18.8
15.6	16.1	16.6	17.1	17.6	18.1	18.5	19.0	19.5	20.0	20.5	21.0	21.5
17.3	17.9	18.4	19.0	19.5	20.1	20.6	21.2	21.7	22.2	22.8	23.3	23.9
19.4	20.0	20.7	21.3	21.9	22.5	23.1	23.7	24.2	24.8	25.4	26.0	26.7
21.4	22.1	22.7	23.4	24.1	24.8	25.4	26.1	26.8	27.5	28.1	28.8	29.5
23.3	24.1	24.8	25.6	26.3	27.0	27.8	28.5	29.2	30.0	30.7	31.5	32.2
4.4	4.5	4.6	4.8	4.9	5.0	5.2	5.3	5.4	5.6	5.7	5.9	6.0
6.8	7.0	7.2	7.4	7.6	7.9	8.1	8.3	8.5	8.7	8.9	9.1	9.4
15.3	15.7	16.2	16.8	17.2	17.6	18.1	18.7	19.1	19.5	20.0	20.6	21.0
8.0	8.3	8.5	8.8	9.0	9.3	9.5	9.8	10.0	10.3	10.6	10.8	11.1
10.5	10.9	11.2	11.5	11.9	12.2	12.5	12.9	13.2	13.5	13.8	14.2	14.5
12.3	12.7	13.1	13.5	13.9	14.3	14.7	15.0	15.4	15.8	16.2	16.6	17.0

| Kilograms | 45 | 48 | 50 | 52 | 55 | 57 | 59 | 61 | 64 | 66 | 68 | 70 |
Pounds	100	105	110	115	120	125	130	135	140	145	150	155
Skiing, downhill	6.5	6.8	7.2	7.5	7.8	8.2	8.5	8.8	9.2	9.5	9.9	10.2
Soccer	5.9	6.2	6.6	6.9	7.2	7.5	7.8	8.1	8.4	8.7	9.0	9.3
Squash												
Normal	6.7	7.0	7.3	7.7	8.0	8.4	8.7	9.1	9.5	9.8	10.1	10.5
Competition	7.7	8.0	8.4	8.8	9.2	9.6	10.0	10.4	10.8	11.1	11.5	11.9
Swimming (yards/min)												
Backstroke												
25	2.5	2.6	2.8	2.9	3.0	3.1	3.3	3.4	3.5	3.7	3.8	3.9
30	3.5	3.7	3.9	4.1	4.2	4.4	4.6	4.8	4.9	5.1	5.3	5.5
35	4.5	4.7	5.0	5.2	5.4	5.6	5.9	6.1	6.3	6.6	6.8	7.0
40	5.5	5.8	6.1	6.4	6.6	6.9	7.2	7.5	7.8	8.0	8.3	8.6
Breaststroke												
20	3.1	3.3	3.5	3.6	3.8	4.0	4.1	4.3	4.5	4.6	4.8	4.9
30	4.7	5.0	5.2	5.4	5.7	5.9	6.2	6.4	6.7	6.9	7.1	7.4
40	6.3	6.7	7.0	7.3	7.6	8.0	8.3	8.6	8.9	9.3	9.6	9.9
Front crawl												
20	3.1	3.3	3.5	3.6	3.8	4.0	4.1	4.3	4.5	4.6	4.8	4.9
25	4.0	4.2	4.4	4.6	4.8	5.0	5.2	5.4	5.6	5.8	6.0	6.2
35	4.8	5.1	5.4	5.6	5.9	6.1	6.4	6.6	6.8	7.0	7.3	7.5
45	5.7	6.0	6.3	6.6	6.9	7.2	7.5	7.8	8.1	8.4	8.7	9.0
50	7.0	7.4	7.7	8.1	8.5	8.8	9.2	9.5	9.9	10.3	10.6	11.0
Table tennis	3.4	3.6	3.8	4.0	4.1	4.3	4.5	4.7	4.8	5.0	5.2	5.4
Tennis												
Singles, recreational	5.0	5.2	5.5	5.7	6.0	6.2	6.5	6.7	7.0	7.2	7.5	7.8
Doubles, recreational	3.4	3.6	3.8	4.0	4.1	4.3	4.5	4.7	4.8	5.0	5.2	5.4
Competition	6.4	6.7	7.1	7.4	7.7	8.1	8.4	8.7	9.1	9.4	9.8	10.1
Volleyball												
Moderate, recreational	2.9	3.0	3.2	3.3	3.5	3.6	3.8	3.9	4.1	4.2	4.4	4.5
Vigorous, competition	6.5	6.8	7.1	7.5	7.8	8.1	8.4	8.8	9.1	9.4	9.8	10.1
Walking												
(mph) (min/mile)												
1.0 60:00	1.5	1.6	1.7	1.8	1.8	1.9	2.0	2.1	2.2	2.2	2.3	2.4
2.0 30:00	2.1	2.2	2.3	2.4	2.5	2.6	2.8	2.9	3.0	3.1	3.2	3.3
2.3 26:00	2.3	2.4	2.5	2.7	2.8	2.9	3.0	3.1	3.2	3.4	3.5	3.6
3.0 20:00	2.7	2.9	3.0	3.1	3.3	3.4	3.5	3.7	3.8	3.9	4.1	4.2
3.2 18:45	3.1	3.3	3.4	3.6	3.8	4.0	4.1	4.3	4.4	4.5	4.7	4.8
3.5 17:10	3.3	3.5	3.7	3.9	4.0	4.2	4.4	4.6	4.7	4.9	5.1	5.3
4.0 15:00	4.2	4.4	4.6	4.8	5.1	5.3	5.5	5.7	5.9	6.1	6.4	6.6
4.5 13:20	4.7	5.0	5.2	5.4	5.7	5.9	6.2	6.4	6.7	6.9	7.1	7.4
5.0 12:00	5.4	5.7	6.0	6.3	6.5	6.8	7.1	7.4	7.7	7.9	8.2	8.4
5.4 11:10	6.2	6.6	6.9	7.2	7.5	7.9	8.2	8.5	8.8	9.2	9.5	9.8
5.8 10:20	7.7	8.0	8.4	8.8	9.2	9.6	10.0	10.4	10.8	11.1	11.5	11.9
Water skiing	5.0	5.2	5.5	5.7	6.0	6.2	6.5	6.7	7.0	7.2	7.5	7.8
Weight training	5.2	5.4	5.7	6.0	6.2	6.5	6.8	7.0	7.3	7.6	7.8	8.1
Wrestling	8.5	8.9	9.3	9.8	10.2	10.6	11.0	11.5	11.9	12.3	12.8	13.2

Body weight

73 160	75 165	77 170	80 175	82 180	84 185	86 190	89 195	91 200	93 205	95 210	98 215	100 220
10.5	10.9	11.2	11.5	11.9	12.2	12.5	12.9	13.2	13.5	13.8	14.2	14.5
9.6	9.9	10.2	10.5	10.8	11.1	11.4	11.7	12.0	12.3	12.6	12.9	13.2
10.8	11.2	11.5	11.8	12.2	12.5	12.9	13.2	13.5	13.9	14.2	14.6	14.9
12.3	12.7	13.1	13.5	13.9	14.3	14.7	15.0	15.4	15.8	16.2	16.6	17.0
4.0	4.2	4.3	4.4	4.5	4.7	4.8	4.9	5.1	5.2	5.3	5.4	5.6
5.6	5.8	6.0	6.2	6.4	6.5	6.7	6.9	7.1	7.2	7.4	7.6	7.8
7.3	7.5	7.7	7.9	8.2	8.4	8.6	8.9	9.1	9.3	9.5	9.8	10.0
8.9	9.2	9.4	9.7	10.0	10.3	10.6	10.8	11.1	11.4	11.7	12.0	12.2
5.1	5.3	5.4	5.6	5.7	5.9	6.0	6.2	6.4	6.5	6.7	6.9	7.0
7.6	7.9	8.1	8.3	8.6	8.8	9.1	9.3	9.5	9.8	10.0	10.3	10.5
10.2	10.5	10.9	11.2	11.5	11.9	12.2	12.5	12.8	13.1	13.5	13.8	14.1
5.1	5.3	5.4	5.6	5.7	5.9	6.0	6.2	6.4	6.5	6.7	6.9	7.0
6.4	6.6	6.8	7.0	7.2	7.4	7.6	7.8	8.0	8.2	8.4	8.6	8.8
7.8	8.0	8.3	8.5	8.8	9.0	9.2	9.4	9.7	9.9	10.2	10.4	10.7
9.3	9.5	9.8	10.1	10.4	10.7	11.0	11.3	11.6	11.9	12.2	12.5	12.8
11.3	11.7	12.0	12.4	12.8	13.1	13.5	13.8	14.2	14.5	14.9	15.2	15.6
5.5	5.7	5.9	6.1	6.3	6.4	6.6	6.8	7.0	7.1	7.3	7.5	7.7
8.0	8.3	8.5	8.8	9.0	9.3	9.5	9.8	10.0	10.3	10.6	10.8	11.1
5.5	5.7	5.9	6.1	6.3	6.4	6.6	6.8	7.0	7.1	7.3	7.5	7.7
10.4	10.8	11.1	11.4	11.8	12.1	12.4	12.8	13.1	13.4	13.7	14.1	14.4
4.7	4.8	5.0	5.1	5.3	5.4	5.6	5.7	5.9	6.0	6.1	6.3	6.4
10.4	10.7	11.1	11.4	11.7	12.0	12.4	12.7	13.0	13.4	13.7	14.0	14.4
2.4	2.5	2.6	2.7	2.8	2.9	2.9	3.0	3.1	3.2	3.2	3.3	3.4
3.4	3.5	3.6	3.7	3.9	4.0	4.1	4.2	4.3	4.4	4.5	4.6	4.7
3.7	3.8	4.0	4.1	4.2	4.3	4.4	4.5	4.7	4.8	4.9	5.0	5.1
4.4	4.5	4.6	4.8	4.9	5.0	5.2	5.3	5.4	5.6	5.7	5.9	6.0
5.0	5.2	5.3	5.5	5.6	5.8	5.9	6.1	6.3	6.4	6.6	6.8	6.9
5.4	5.6	5.8	6.0	6.2	6.3	6.5	6.7	6.9	7.0	7.2	7.4	7.6
6.8	7.0	7.2	7.4	7.6	7.9	8.1	8.3	8.5	8.7	8.9	9.1	9.4
7.6	7.9	8.1	8.3	8.6	8.8	9.1	9.3	9.5	9.8	10.0	10.3	10.5
8.7	9.0	9.2	9.5	9.8	10.1	10.4	10.6	10.9	11.2	11.5	11.8	12.0
10.1	10.4	10.8	11.1	11.4	11.8	12.1	12.4	12.7	13.0	13.4	13.7	14.0
12.3	12.7	13.1	13.5	13.9	14.3	14.7	15.0	15.4	15.8	16.2	16.6	17.0
8.0	8.3	8.5	8.8	9.0	9.3	9.5	9.8	10.0	10.3	10.6	10.8	11.1
8.3	8.6	8.9	9.1	9.4	9.7	9.9	10.2	10.5	10.7	11.0	11.2	11.5
13.6	14.1	14.5	14.9	15.4	15.8	16.2	16.6	17.1	17.5	17.9	18.4	18.8

Self-Test on Drinking Habits and Alcoholism

Here is a self-test to help you review the role alcohol plays in your life. These questions incorporate some of the common symptoms of alcoholism. This test is intended to help you determine if you or someone you know needs to find out more about alcoholism; it is not intended to be used to establish the diagnosis of alcoholism.

	Yes	No
1. Do you drink heavily when you are disappointed, under pressure, or have had a quarrel with someone?	____	____
2. Have you ever been unable to remember part of the previous evening, even though your friends say you didn't pass out?	____	____
3. When drinking with other people, do you try to have a few extra drinks when others won't know about it?	____	____
4. Are you in more of a hurry to get your first drink of the day than you used to be?	____	____
5. Do you sometimes feel a little guilty about your drinking?	____	____
6. When you're sober, do you sometimes regret things you did or said while drinking?	____	____
7. Have you tried switching brands or drinks, or following different plans to control your drinking?	____	____
8. Have you sometimes failed to keep promises you made to yourself about controlling or cutting down on your drinking?	____	____
9. Have you ever had a DWI (driving while intoxicated) or DUI (driving under the influence of alcohol) violation, or any other legal problem related to your drinking?	____	____
10. Do you try to avoid family or close friends while you are drinking?	____	____

Any "yes" answer indicates you may be at greater risk for alcoholism. More than one "yes" answer may indicate the presence of an alcohol-related problem or alcoholism, and the need for consultation with an alcoholism professional. To find out more, contact the National Council on Alcoholism and Drug Dependence in your area.

Reprinted courtesy of the National Council on Alcoholism and Drug Dependence.

Determination of Healthy Body Weight

There are a number of different techniques utilized to determine a healthy body weight. The following three methods offer you an estimate of an appropriate body weight. Method A is based on the Body Mass Index (BMI). Method B is based upon body-fat percentage. Method C, the waist circumference, does not determine a desirable body weight but provides an assessment of desirable body-fat distribution.

Method A

The BMI uses the metric system, so you need to determine your weight in kilograms and your height in meters. The formula is

$$\frac{\text{Body weight in kilograms}}{(\text{Height in meters})^2}$$

Dividing your body weight in pounds by 2.2 will give you your weight in kilograms. Multiplying your height in inches by 0.0254 will give you your height in meters.

Your weight in kilograms =

$$\frac{(\text{Your weight in pounds})}{2.2} = \underline{\hspace{1cm}}$$

Your height in meters =

$(\text{Your height in inches}) \times 0.0254 = \underline{\hspace{1cm}}$

$$\text{BMI} = \frac{\text{Body weight in kilograms}}{(\text{Height in meters})^2} = \underline{\hspace{1cm}}$$

Or you may use your weight in pounds and height in inches with the following formula:

$$\text{BMI} = \frac{\text{Body weight in pounds} \times 705}{\text{Height in inches}^2}$$

A BMI range of 18.5 to 25 is considered to be normal, but a suggested desirable range for females is 21.3 to 22.1 and for males is 21.9 to 22.4. Individuals with BMI values between 25.0–29.9 are classified as overweight, those from 30.0–39.9 are classified as obese, while those 40 and above are classified as extremely obese. The higher the BMI, the greater the health risks faced by the individual, particularly diabetes, high blood pressure, and heart disease.

If you want to lower your body weight to a more desirable BMI, such as 22, use the following formula to determine what that weight should be; the weight is expressed in kilograms, so multiplying it by 2.2 will give you the desired weight in pounds.

$$\text{Kilograms body weight} =$$
$$\text{Desired BMI} \times (\text{Height in meters})^2$$

Here's a brief example for a woman who weighs 187 pounds and is 5′9″ tall; her BMI calculates to be 27.7, so her weight poses a health risk. If she wants to achieve a BMI of 23, she will need to reduce her weight to 155 pounds.

$$\text{Kilograms body weight} = 23 \times (1.753)^2 = 70.6$$

$$70.6 \text{ kg} \times 2.2 = 155 \text{ pounds}$$

To calculate your desirable body weight:

$$\text{Kilograms body weight} =$$

$$(\text{Your desired BMI}) \times (\text{Your height in meters})^2$$

$\text{Kilograms body weight} = \underline{\hspace{1cm}} \times \underline{\hspace{1cm}}$

$\underline{\hspace{1cm}} \text{ kg} \times 2.2 = \underline{\hspace{1cm}} \text{ pounds}$

Method B

For this method, you will need to know your body-fat percentage as determined by the procedure described in table D.1 or

TABLE D.1   Generalized equations for predicting body fat

Measure the appropriate skinfolds for women (triceps, thigh, and suprailium sites) or men (chest, abdomen, and thigh sites) as illustrated in figures D.1–D.4. You may use either the appropriate formula or the appropriate table in appendix D to obtain the predicted body-fat percentage.

Women*	Men**
$BD = 1.0994921 - 0.0009929 (X_1) + 0.0000023 (X_1)^2 - 0.0001392 (X_2)$	$BD = 1.10938 - 0.0008267 (X_1) + 0.0000016 (X_1)^2 - 0.0002574 (X_2)$
BD = Body density	BD = Body density
X_1 = Sum of triceps, thigh, and suprailium skinfolds	X_1 = Sum of chest, abdomen, and thigh skinfolds
X_2 = Age	X_2 = Age
	To calculate percent body fat, plug into Siri's equation. $$\left(\frac{4.95}{BD} - 4.5 \right) \times 100$$

*From Jackson, A., Pollock, M., and Ward, A. 1980. Generalized equations for predicting body density of women. *Medicine & Science in Sports & Exercise* 12:175–182.
**Jackson, A., and Pollock, M. 1978. Generalized equations for predicting body density of men. *British Journal of Nutrition* 40:497–504.

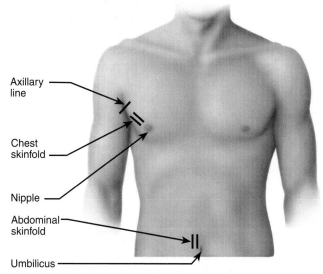

FIGURE D.1 The chest and abdomen skinfold. Chest—A diagonal fold is taken between the axilla and the nipple. Use a midway point. Abdomen—A vertical fold is taken about 2.5 centimeters (1 inch) to the side of the umbilicus.

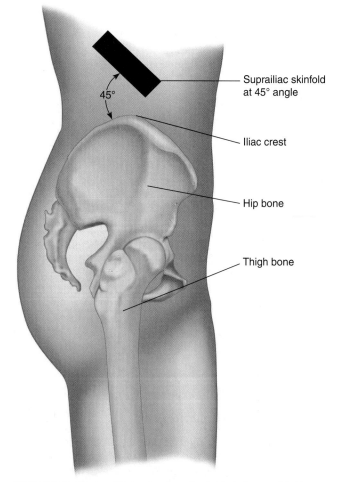

FIGURE D.2 The suprailiac skinfold. A diagonal fold is taken at about a 45-degree angle just above the crest of the ilium.

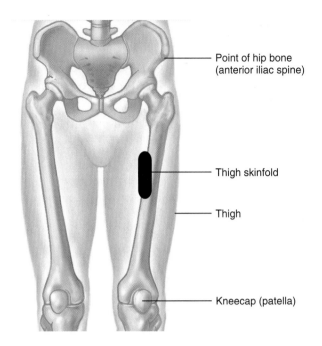

FIGURE D.3 The thigh skinfold. A vertical fold is taken on the front of the thigh midway between the anterior iliac spine and the patella.

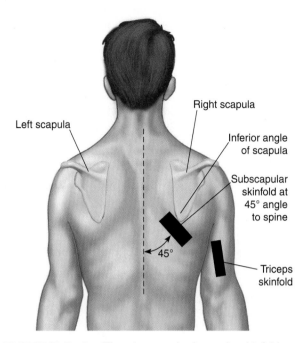

FIGURE D.4 The triceps and subscapular skinfolds. In the triceps skinfold, a vertical fold is taken over the triceps muscle one-half the distance from the acromion process to the olecranon process at the elbow. The subscapular skinfold is taken just below the lower angle of the scapula, at about a 45-degree angle to the spinal column.

another appropriate technique. You will also need to determine the body-fat percentage you desire to have. You may use table 10.2 on page 373 as a guideline.

You will need to do the following calculations for the formula:

1. Determine your current lean body weight (LBW). Multiply your current body weight in pounds by your current percent body fat expressed as a decimal (20 percent would be .20) to obtain your pounds of body fat. Subtract your pounds of body fat from your current weight to give you your lean body weight (LBW).
2. Determine your desired body-fat percentage and express it as a decimal.

$$\text{Desired body weight} = \frac{\text{LBM}}{1.00 - \text{Desired \% body fat}}$$

As an example, suppose we have a 200-pound male who is currently at 25 percent body fat but desires to get down to 20 percent as his first goal. Multiplying his current weight by his current percent body fat yields 50 pounds of body fat ($200 \times .25 = 50$); subtracting this from his current weight yields a LBM of 150 ($200 - 50$). If we plug his desired percent of 20 into the formula, he will need to reach a body weight of 187.5 to achieve this first goal.

$$\text{Desired body weight} = \frac{150}{1.00 - .20} = \frac{150}{.8} = 187.5$$

Your current body weight _____

Your current percent body fat _____

Your pounds of body fat _____

Your LBW _____

Your desired percent body fat _____

$$\text{Desired body weight} \frac{\text{LBW}}{1.00 - ?} = \underline{\quad} = \underline{\quad}$$

Method C

The waist circumference is a measure of regional fat distribution. Using a flexible (preferably metal) tape, measure the narrowest section of the bare waist as seen from the front while standing. Wear tight clothing. Do not compress skin and fat with pressure from the tape. The waist measurement may be used as a simple screening technique for abdominal obesity. Females with a waist of 35 inches or over, and men with a waist of 40 inches or over may be at increased risk.

Waist girth _____

In the following table, use both your BMI and waist measurement to evaluate your risk of associated disease.

Risk of Associated Disease According to BMI and Waist Size

BMI		Waist less than or equal to 40 in. (men) or 35 in. (women)	Waist greater than 40 in. (men) or 35 in. (women)
18.5 or less	Underweight	—	N/A
18.5 – 24.9	Normal	—	N/A
25.0 – 29.9	Overweight	Increased	High
30.0 – 34.9	Obese	High	Very High
35.0 – 39.9	Obese	Very High	Very High
40 or greater	Extremely Obese	Extremely High	Extremely High

Note: Recent research suggests waist sizes greater than 37 inches in men and 31.5 inches in women may increase health risks when accompanied by other conditions, such as high blood pressure.

Source: www.consumer.gov/weightloss.bmi.htm

Percent fat estimate for men: sum of chest, abdomen, and thigh skinfolds

Sum of skinfolds (mm)	Under 22	23–27	28–32	33–37	38–42	43–47	48–52	53–57	Over 57
8–10	1.3	1.8	2.3	2.9	3.4	3.9	4.5	5.0	5.5
11–13	2.2	2.8	3.3	3.9	4.4	4.9	5.5	6.0	6.5
14–16	3.2	3.8	4.3	4.8	5.4	5.9	6.4	7.0	7.5
17–19	4.2	4.7	5.3	5.8	6.3	6.9	7.4	8.0	8.5
20–22	5.1	5.7	6.2	6.8	7.3	7.9	8.4	8.9	9.5
23–25	6.1	6.6	7.2	7.7	8.3	8.8	9.4	9.9	10.5
26–28	7.0	7.6	8.1	8.7	9.2	9.8	10.3	10.9	11.4
29–31	8.0	8.5	9.1	9.6	10.2	10.7	11.3	11.8	12.4
32–34	8.9	9.4	10.0	10.5	11.1	11.6	12.2	12.8	13.3
35–37	9.8	10.4	10.9	11.5	12.0	12.6	13.1	13.7	14.3
38–40	10.7	11.3	11.8	12.4	12.9	13.5	14.1	14.6	15.2
41–43	11.6	12.2	12.7	13.3	13.8	14.4	15.0	15.5	16.1
44–46	12.5	13.1	13.6	14.2	14.7	15.3	15.9	16.4	17.0
47–49	13.4	13.9	14.5	15.1	15.6	16.2	16.8	17.3	17.9
50–52	14.3	14.8	15.4	15.9	16.5	17.1	17.6	18.2	18.8
53–55	15.1	15.7	16.2	16.8	17.4	17.9	18.5	19.1	19.7
56–58	16.0	16.5	17.1	17.7	18.2	18.8	19.4	20.0	20.5
59–61	16.9	17.4	17.9	18.5	19.1	19.7	20.2	20.8	21.4
62–64	17.6	18.2	18.8	19.4	19.9	20.5	21.1	21.7	22.2
65–67	18.5	19.0	19.6	20.2	20.8	21.3	21.9	22.5	23.1
68–70	19.3	19.9	20.4	21.0	21.6	22.2	22.7	23.3	23.9
71–73	20.1	20.7	21.2	21.8	22.4	23.0	23.6	24.1	24.7
74–76	20.9	21.5	22.0	22.6	23.2	23.8	24.4	25.0	25.5
77–79	21.7	22.2	22.8	23.4	24.0	24.6	25.2	25.8	26.3
80–82	22.4	23.0	23.6	24.2	24.8	25.4	25.9	26.5	27.1
83–85	23.2	23.8	24.4	25.0	25.5	26.1	26.7	27.3	27.9
86–88	24.0	24.5	25.1	25.7	26.3	26.9	27.5	28.1	28.7
89–91	24.7	25.3	25.9	26.5	27.1	27.6	28.2	28.8	29.4
92–94	25.4	26.0	26.6	27.2	27.8	28.4	29.0	29.6	30.2
95–97	26.1	26.7	27.3	27.9	28.5	29.1	29.7	30.3	30.9
98–100	26.9	27.4	28.0	28.6	29.2	29.8	30.4	31.0	31.6
101–103	27.5	28.1	28.7	29.3	29.9	30.5	31.1	31.7	32.3
104–106	28.2	28.8	29.4	30.0	30.6	31.2	31.8	32.4	33.0
107–109	28.9	29.5	30.1	30.7	31.3	31.9	32.5	33.1	33.7
110–112	29.6	30.2	30.8	31.4	32.0	32.6	33.2	33.8	34.4
113–115	30.2	30.8	31.4	32.0	32.6	33.2	33.8	34.5	35.1
116–118	30.9	31.5	32.1	32.7	33.3	33.9	34.5	35.1	35.7
119–121	31.5	32.1	32.7	33.3	33.9	34.5	35.1	35.7	36.4
122–124	32.1	32.7	33.3	33.9	34.5	35.1	35.8	36.4	37.0
125–127	32.7	33.3	33.9	34.5	35.1	35.8	36.4	37.0	37.6

From A. S. Jackson and M. L. Pollock, "Practical Assessment of Body Composition," May 1985, in *Physician and Sportsmedicine*. Reprinted with permission of McGraw-Hill, Inc.

Percent fat estimate for women: sum of triceps, suprailium, and thigh skinfolds

Sum of skinfolds (mm)	Age to last year								
	Under 22	23–27	28–32	33–37	38–42	43–47	48–52	53–57	Over 57
23–25	9.7	9.9	10.2	10.4	10.7	10.9	11.2	11.4	11.7
26–28	11.0	11.2	11.5	11.7	12.0	12.3	12.5	12.7	13.0
29–31	12.3	12.5	12.8	13.0	13.3	13.5	13.8	14.0	14.3
32–34	13.6	13.8	14.0	14.3	14.5	14.8	15.0	15.3	15.5
35–37	14.8	15.0	15.3	15.5	15.8	16.0	16.3	16.5	16.8
38–40	16.0	16.3	16.5	16.7	17.0	17.2	17.5	17.7	18.0
41–43	17.2	17.4	17.7	17.9	18.2	18.4	18.7	18.9	19.2
44–46	18.3	18.6	18.8	19.1	19.3	19.6	19.8	20.1	20.3
47–49	19.5	19.7	20.0	20.2	20.5	20.7	21.0	21.2	21.5
50–52	20.6	20.8	21.1	21.3	21.6	21.8	22.1	22.3	22.6
53–55	21.7	21.9	22.1	22.4	22.6	22.9	23.1	23.4	23.6
56–58	22.7	23.0	23.2	23.4	23.7	23.9	24.2	24.4	24.7
59–61	23.7	24.0	24.2	24.5	24.7	25.0	25.2	25.5	25.7
62–64	24.7	25.0	25.2	25.5	25.7	26.0	26.2	26.4	26.7
65–67	25.7	25.9	26.2	26.4	26.7	26.9	27.2	27.4	27.7
68–70	26.6	26.9	27.1	27.4	27.6	27.9	28.1	28.4	28.6
71–73	27.5	27.8	28.0	28.3	28.5	28.8	29.0	29.3	29.5
74–76	28.4	28.7	28.9	29.2	29.4	29.7	29.9	30.2	30.4
77–79	29.3	29.5	29.8	30.0	30.3	30.5	30.8	31.0	31.3
80–82	30.1	30.4	30.6	30.9	31.1	31.4	31.6	31.9	32.1
83–85	30.9	31.2	31.4	31.7	31.9	32.2	32.4	32.7	32.9
86–88	31.7	32.0	32.2	32.5	32.7	32.9	33.2	33.4	33.7
89–91	32.5	32.7	33.0	33.2	33.5	33.7	33.9	34.2	34.4
92–94	33.2	33.4	33.7	33.9	34.2	34.4	34.7	34.9	35.2
95–97	33.9	34.1	34.4	34.6	34.9	35.1	35.4	35.6	35.9
98–100	34.6	34.8	35.1	35.3	35.5	35.8	36.0	36.3	36.5
101–103	35.3	35.4	35.7	35.9	36.2	36.4	36.7	36.9	37.2
104–106	35.8	36.1	36.3	36.6	36.8	37.1	37.3	37.5	37.8
107–109	36.4	36.7	36.9	37.1	37.4	37.6	37.9	38.1	38.4
110–112	37.0	37.2	37.5	37.7	38.0	38.2	38.5	38.7	38.9
113–115	37.5	37.8	38.0	38.2	38.5	38.7	39.0	39.2	39.5
116–118	38.0	38.3	38.5	38.8	39.0	39.3	39.5	39.7	40.0
119–121	38.5	38.7	39.0	39.2	39.5	39.7	40.0	40.2	40.5
122–124	39.0	39.2	39.4	39.7	39.9	40.2	40.4	40.7	40.9
125–127	39.4	39.6	39.9	40.1	40.4	40.6	40.9	41.1	41.4
128–130	39.8	40.0	40.3	40.5	40.8	41.0	41.3	41.5	41.8

From A. S. Jackson and M. L. Pollock, "Practical Assessment of Body Composition," May 1985, in *Physician and Sportsmedicine*. Reprinted with permission of McGraw-Hill, Inc.

Exchange Lists for Meal Planning*

What Are Exchange Lists?

Exchange lists are foods listed together because they are alike. Each serving of a food has about the same amount of carbohydrate, protein, fat, and Calories as the other foods on that list. That is why any food on a list can be "exchanged" or traded for any other food on the same list. For example, you can trade the slice of bread you might eat for breakfast for one-half cup of cooked cereal. Each of these foods equals one starch choice.

Exchange Lists

Foods are listed with their serving sizes, which are usually measured after cooking. When you begin, you should measure the size of each serving. This may help you learn to "eyeball" correct serving sizes.

The following chart shows the amount of nutrients in one serving from each list.

The exchange lists provide you with a lot of food choices (foods from the basic food groups, foods with added sugars,

Groups/Lists	Carbohydrate (grams)	Protein (grams)	Fat (grams)	Calories
Carbohydrate group				
Starch	15	3	1 or less	80
Fruit	15	—	—	60
Milk				
Skim	12	8	0–3	90
Low-fat	12	8	5	120
Whole	12	8	8	150
Other carbohydrates	15	varies	varies	varies
Vegetables	5	2	—	25
Meat and meat substitutes group				
Very lean	—	7	0–1	35
Lean	—	7	3	55
Medium-fat	—	7	5	75
High-fat	—	7	8	100
Fat group	—	—	5	45

*The Exchange Lists are the basis of a meal planning system designed by a committee of the American Diabetes Association and the American Dietetic Association. While designed primarily for people with diabetes and others who must follow special diets, the Exchange Lists are based on principles of good nutrition that apply to everyone.

© 1995 American Diabetes Association, Inc., American Dietetic Association.

free foods, combination foods, and fast foods). This gives you variety in your meals. Several foods, such as dried beans and peas, bacon, and peanut butter, are on two lists. This gives you flexibility in putting your meals together. Whenever you choose new foods or vary your meal plan, monitor your blood glucose to see how these different foods affect your blood glucose level.

Most foods in the Carbohydrate group have about the same amount of carbohydrate per serving. You can exchange starch, fruit, or milk choices in your meal plan. Vegetables are in this group but contain only about 5 grams of carbohydrate.

A Word about Food Labels

Exchange information is based on foods found in grocery stores. However, food companies often change the ingredients in their products. That is why you need to check the Nutrition Facts panel of the food label.

The Nutrition Facts tell you the number of Calories and grams of carbohydrate, protein, and fat in one serving. Compare these numbers with the exchange information in this appendix to see how many exchanges you will be eating. In this way, food labels can help you add foods to your meal plans.

Ask your dietitian to help you use food label information to plan your meals, or read pages 60–65 for more tips on how to use food labels.

Getting Started!

See your dietitian regularly when you are first learning how to use your meal plan and the exchange lists. Your meal plan can be adjusted to fit changes in your lifestyle, such as work, school, vacation, or travel. Regular nutrition counseling can help you make positive changes in your eating habits.

Careful eating habits will help you feel better and be healthier, too. Best wishes and good eating with *Exchange Lists for Meal Planning.*

Starch List

Cereals, grains, pasta, breads, crackers, snacks, starchy vegetables, and cooked dried beans, peas, and lentils are starches. In general, one starch is:

- 1/2 cup of cereal, grain, pasta, or starchy vegetable
- 1 ounce of a bread product, such as 1 slice of bread
- 3/4 to 1 ounce of most snack foods. (Some snack foods may also have added fat.)

Nutrition tips

1. Most starch choices are good sources of B vitamins.
2. Foods made from whole grains are good sources of fiber.
3. Dried beans and peas are a good source of protein and fiber.

Selection tips

1. Choose starches made with little fat as often as you can.
2. Starchy vegetables prepared with fat count as one starch and one fat.
3. Bagels or muffins can be 2, 3, or 4 ounces in size, and can, therefore, count as 2, 3, or 4 starch choices. Check the size you eat.
4. Dried beans, peas, and lentils are also found on the Meat and Meat Substitutes list.
5. Regular potato chips and tortilla chips are found on the Other Carbohydrates list.
6. Most of the serving sizes are measured after cooking.
7. Always check Nutrition Facts on the food label.

One starch exchange equals
15 grams carbohydrate,
3 grams protein,
0–1 grams fat, and
80 Calories.

Bread

Bagel	1/2 (1 oz)
Bread, reduced-calorie	2 slices (1 1/2 oz)
Bread, white, whole wheat, pumpernickel, rye	1 slice (1 oz)
Bread sticks, crisp, 4 in. long ×1/2 in.	2 (2/3 oz)
English muffin	1/2
Hot dog or hamburger bun	1/2 (1 oz)
Pita, 6 in. across	1/2
Roll, plain, small	1 (1 oz)
Raisin bread, unfrosted	1 slice (1 oz)
Tortilla, corn, 6 in. across	1
Tortilla, flour, 7–8 in. across	1
Waffle, 4 1/2 in. square, reduced-fat	1

Cereals and grains

Bran cereals	1/2 cup
Bulgur	1/2 cup
Cereals	1/2 cup
Cereals, unsweetened, ready-to-eat	3/4 cup
Cornmeal (dry)	3 Tbsp
Couscous	1/3 cup
Flour (dry)	3 Tbsp
Granola, low-fat	1/4 cup
Grape-Nuts	1/4 cup
Grits	1/2 cup
Kasha	1/2 cup
Millet	1/4 cup
Muesli	1/4 cup
Oats	1/2 cup
Pasta	1/2 cup
Puffed cereal	1 1/2 cups
Rice milk	1/2 cup
Rice, white or brown	1/3 cup

Shredded Wheat . . . . 1/2 cup
Sugar-frosted cereal . . . . 1/2 cup
Wheat germ. . . . . 3 Tbsp

Starchy vegetables

Baked beans. . . . . 1/3 cup
Corn . . . . 1/2 cup
Corn on cob, medium . . . . 1 (5 oz)
Mixed vegetables with corn, peas, or pasta . . . . 1 cup
Peas, green. . . . . 1/2 cup
Plantain . . . . 1/2 cup
Potato, baked or boiled. . . . . 1 small (3 oz)
Potato, mashed . . . . 1/2 cup
Squash, winter (acorn, butternut) . . . . 1 cup
Yam, sweet potato, plain. . . . . 1/2 cup

Crackers and snacks

Animal crackers. 8
Graham crackers, 2 1/2 in. square 3
Matzoh . . . . 3/4 oz
Melba toast . . . . 4 slices
Oyster crackers 24
Popcorn (popped, no fat added
    or low-fat microwave) . . . . 3 cups
Pretzels. . . . . 3/4 oz
Rice cakes, 4 in. across 2
Saltine-type crackers. 6
Snack chips, fat-free (tortilla, potato) . . . . 15–20 (3/4 oz)
Whole wheat crackers, no fat added . . . . 2–5 (3/4 oz)

Dried beans, peas, and lentils (Count as 1 starch exchange, plus 1 very lean meat exchange.)

Beans and peas (garbanzo, pinto,
    kidney, white, split, black-eyed) . . . . 1/2 cup
Lima beans. . . . . 2/3 cup
Lentils . . . . 1/2 cup
Miso ⬛ . . . . 3 Tbsp

⬛ = 400 mg or more of sodium per serving.

Starchy foods prepared with fat (Count as 1 starch exchange, plus 1 fat exchange.)

Biscuit, 2 1/2 in. across 1
Chow mein noodles. . . . . 1/2 cup
Corn bread, 2 in. cube. 1 (2 oz)
Crackers, round butter type. 6
Croutons . . . . 1 cup
French-fried potatoes . . . . 16–25 (3 oz)
Granola. . . . . 1/4 cup
Muffin, small . . . . 1 (1 1/2 oz)
Pancake, 4 in. across 2
Popcorn, microwave. . . . . 3 cups

Sandwich crackers, cheese or peanut butter filling 3
Stuffing, bread (prepared). . . . . 1/3 cup
Taco shell, 6 in. across. 2
Waffle, 4 1/2 in. square 1
Whole wheat crackers, fat added. . . . . 4–6 (1 oz)

Some food you buy uncooked will weigh less after you cook it. Starches often swell in cooking so a small amount of uncooked starch will become a much larger amount of cooked food. The following table shows some of the changes.

Food (Starch group)	Uncooked	Cooked
Oatmeal	3 Tbsp	1/2 cup
Cream of Wheat	2 Tbsp	1/2 cup
Grits	3 Tbsp	1/2 cup
Rice	2 Tbsp	1/3 cup
Spaghetti	1/4 cup	1/2 cup
Noodles	1/3 cup	1/2 cup
Macaroni	1/4 cup	1/2 cup
Dried beans	1/4 cup	1/2 cup
Dried peas	1/4 cup	1/2 cup
Lentils	3 Tbsp	1/2 cup

Common measurements

3 tsp = 1 Tbsp	4 ounces = 1/2 cup
4 Tbsp = 1/4 cup	8 ounces = 1 cup
5 1/3 Tbsp = 1/3 cup	1 cup = 1/2 pint

Fruit List

Fresh, frozen, canned, and dried fruits and fruit juices are on this list. In general, one fruit exchange is:

- 1 small to medium fresh fruit
- 1/2 cup of canned or fresh fruit or fruit juice
- 1/4 cup of dried fruit

Nutrition tips

1. Fresh, frozen, and dried fruits have about 2 grams of fiber per choice. Fruit juices contain very little fiber.
2. Citrus fruits, berries, and melons are good sources of vitamin C.

Selection tips

1. Count 1/2 cup cranberries or rhubarb sweetened with sugar substitutes as free foods.
2. Read the Nutrition Facts on the food label. If one serving has more than 15 grams of carbohydrate, you will need to adjust the size of the serving you eat or drink.
3. Portion sizes for canned fruits are for the fruit and a small amount of juice.
4. Whole fruit is more filling than fruit juice and may be a better choice.

5. Food labels for fruits may contain the words "no sugar added" or "unsweetened." This means that no sucrose (table sugar) has been added.
6. Generally, fruit canned in extra light syrup has the same amount of carbohydrate per serving as the "no sugar added" or the juice pack. All canned fruits on the fruit list are based on one of these three types of pack.

One fruit exchange equals
15 grams carbohydrate and
60 Calories.

The weight includes skin, core, seeds, and rind.

Fruit

Apple, unpeeled, small	1 (4 oz)
Applesauce, unsweetened	1/2 cup
Apples, dried	4 rings
Apricots, fresh	4 whole (5 1/2 oz)
Apricots, dried	8 halves
Apricots, canned	1/2 cup
Banana, small	1 (4 oz)
Blackberries	3/4 cup
Blueberries	3/4 cup
Cantaloupe, small	1/3 melon (11 oz) or 1 cup cubes
Cherries, sweet, fresh	12 (3 oz)
Cherries, sweet, canned	1/2 cup
Dates	3
Figs, fresh	1 1/2 large or 2 medium (3 1/2 oz)
Figs, dried	1 1/2
Fruit cocktail	1/2 cup
Grapefruit, large	1/2 (11 oz)
Grapefruit sections, canned	3/4 cup
Grapes, small	17 (3 oz)
Honeydew melon	1 slice (10 oz) or 1 cup cubes
Kiwi	1 (3 1/2 oz)
Mandarin oranges, canned	3/4 cup
Mango, small	1/2 fruit (5 1/2 oz) or 1/2 cup
Nectarine, small	1 (5 oz)
Orange, small	1 (6 1/2 oz)
Papaya	1/2 fruit (8 oz) or 1 cup cubes
Peach, medium, fresh	1 (6 oz)
Peaches, canned	1/2 cup
Pear, large, fresh	1/2 (4 oz)
Pears, canned	1/2 cup
Pineapple, fresh	3/4 cup
Pineapple, canned	1/2 cup
Plums, small	2 (5 oz)
Plums, canned	1/2 cup
Prunes, dried	3
Raisins	2 Tbsp
Raspberries	1 cup
Strawberries	1 1/4 cup whole berries
Tangerines, small	2 (8 oz)
Watermelon	1 slice (13 1/2 oz) or 1 1/4 cup cubes

Fruit juice

Apple juice/cider	1/2 cup
Cranberry juice cocktail	1/3 cup
Cranberry juice cocktail, reduced-calorie	1 cup
Fruit juice blends, 100% juice	1/3 cup
Grape juice	1/3 cup
Grapefruit juice	1/2 cup
Orange juice	1/2 cup
Pineapple juice	1/2 cup
Prune juice	1/3 cup

Milk List

Different types of milk and milk products are on this list. Cheeses are on the Meat list and cream and other dairy fats are on the Fat list. Based on the amount of fat they contain, milks are divided into skim/very low-fat milk, low-fat milk, and whole milk. One choice of these includes:

	Carbohydrate (grams)	Protein (grams)	Fat (grams)	Calories
Skim/very low-fat	12	8	0–3	90
Low-fat	12	8	5	120
Whole	12	8	8	150

Nutrition tips

1. Milk and yogurt are good sources of calcium and protein. Check the food label.
2. The higher the fat content of milk and yogurt, the greater the amount of saturated fat and cholesterol. Choose lower-fat varieties.
3. For those who are lactose intolerant, look for lactose-reduced or lactose-free varieties of milk.

Selection tips

1. One cup equals 8 fluid ounces or 1/2 pint.
2. Look for chocolate milk, frozen yogurt, and ice cream on the Other Carbohydrates list.
3. Nondairy creamers are on the Free Foods list.
4. Look for rice milk on the Starch list.
5. Look for soy milk on the Medium-fat Meat list.

One milk exchange equals
12 grams carbohydrate and
8 grams protein.

Skim and very low-fat milk (0–3 grams fat per serving)

Skim milk	1 cup
1/2% milk	1 cup
1% milk	1 cup

Nonfat or low-fat buttermilk	1 cup
Evaporated skim milk	1/2 cup
Nonfat dry milk	1/3 cup dry
Plain nonfat yogurt	3/4 cup
Nonfat or low-fat fruit-flavored yogurt sweetened with aspartame or with a nonnutritive sweetener	1 cup

Low-fat (5 grams fat per serving)

2% milk	1 cup
Plain low-fat yogurt	3/4 cup
Sweet acidophilus milk	1 cup

Whole milk (8 grams fat per serving)

Whole milk	1 cup
Evaporated whole milk	1/2 cup
Goat's milk	1 cup
Kefir	1 cup

Other Carbohydrates List

You can substitute food choices from this list for a starch, fruit, or milk choice on your meal plan. Some choices will also count as one or more fat choices.

Nutrition tips

1. These foods can be substituted in your meal plan, even though they contain added sugars or fat. However, they do not contain as many important vitamins and minerals as the choices on the Starch, Fruit, or Milk list.
2. When planning to include these foods in your meal, be sure to include foods from all the lists to eat a balanced meal.

Selection tips

1. Because many of these foods are concentrated sources of carbohydrate and fat, the portion sizes are often very small.
2. Always check Nutrition Facts on the food label. It will be your most accurate source of information.
3. Many fat-free or reduced-fat products made with fat replacers contain carbohydrate. When eaten in large amounts, they may need to be counted. Talk with your dietitian to determine how to count these in your meal plan.
4. Look for fat-free salad dressings in smaller amounts on the Free Foods list.

One exchange equals
15 grams carbohydrate, or
1 starch, or 1 fruit, or 1 milk.

Food	Serving size	Exchanges per serving
Angel food cake, unfrosted	1/12th cake	2 carbohydrates
Brownie, small, unfrosted	2 in. square	1 carbohydrate, 1 fat
Cake, unfrosted	2 in. square	1 carbohydrate, 1 fat
Cake, frosted	2 in. square	2 carbohydrates, 1 fat
Cookie, fat-free	2 small	1 carbohydrate
Cookie or sandwich cookie with creme filling	2 small	1 carbohydrate, 1 fat
Cupcake, frosted	1 small	2 carbohydrates, 1 fat
Cranberry sauce, jellied	1/4 cup	2 carbohydrates
Doughnut, plain cake	1 medium (1 1/2 oz)	1 1/2 carbohydrates, 2 fats
Doughnut, glazed	3 3/4 in. across (2 oz)	2 carbohydrates, 2 fats
Fruit juice bars, frozen, 100% juice	1 bar (3 oz)	1 carbohydrate
Fruit snacks, chewy (pureed fruit concentrate)	1 roll (3/4 oz)	1 carbohydrate
Fruit spreads, 100% fruit	1 Tbsp	1 carbohydrate
Gelatin, regular	1/2 cup	1 carbohydrate
Gingersnaps	3	1 carbohydrate
Granola bar	1 bar	1 carbohydrate, 1 fat
Granola bar, fat-free	1 bar	2 carbohydrates
Hummus	1/3 cup	1 carbohydrate, 1 fat
Ice cream	1/2 cup	1 carbohydrate, 2 fats
Ice cream, light	1/2 cup	1 carbohydrate, 1 fat
Ice cream, fat-free, no sugar added	1/2 cup	1 carbohydrate
Jam or jelly, regular	1 Tbsp	1 carbohydrate
Milk, chocolate, whole	1 cup	2 carbohydrates, 1 fat
Pie, fruit, 2 crusts	1/6 pie	3 carbohydrates, 2 fats
Pie, pumpkin or custard	1/8 pie	1 carbohydrate, 2 fats
Potato chips	12–18 (1 oz)	1 carbohydrate, 2 fats

Food	Serving size	Exchanges per serving
Pudding, regular (made with low-fat milk)	1/2 cup	2 carbohydrates
Pudding, sugar-free (made with low-fat milk)	1/2 cup	1 carbohydrate
Salad dressing, fat free ⓘ	1/4 cup	1 carbohydrate
Sherbet, sorbet	1/2 cup	2 carbohydrates
Spaghetti or pasta sauce, canned ⓘ	1/2 cup	1 carbohydrate, 1 fat
Sweet roll or Danish	1 (2 1/2 oz)	2 1/2 carbohydrates, 2 fats
Syrup, light	2 Tbsp	1 carbohydrate
Syrup, regular	1 Tbsp	1 carbohydrate
Syrup, regular	1/4 cup	4 carbohydrates
Tortilla chips	6–12 (1 oz)	1 carbohydrate, 2 fats
Yogurt, frozen, low-fat, fat-free	1/3 cup	1 carbohydrate, 0–1 fat
Yogurt, frozen, fat-free, no sugar added	1/2 cup	1 carbohydrate
Yogurt, low-fat with fruit	1 cup	3 carbohydrates, 0–1 fat
Vanilla wafers	5	1 carbohydrate, 1 fat

ⓘ = 400 mg or more sodium per exchange.

Vegetable List

Vegetables that contain small amounts of carbohydrates and Calories are on this list. Vegetables contain important nutrients. Try to eat at least 2 or 3 vegetable choices each day. In general, one vegetable exchange is:

- 1/2 cup of cooked vegetables or vegetable juice
- 1 cup of raw vegetables

If you eat 1 to 2 vegetable choices at a meal or snack, you do not have to count the Calories or carbohydrates because they contain small amounts of these nutrients.

Nutrition tips

1. Fresh and frozen vegetables have less added salt than canned vegetables. Drain and rinse canned vegetables if you want to remove some salt.
2. Choose more dark green and dark yellow vegetables, such as spinach, broccoli, romaine, carrots, chilies, and peppers.
3. Broccoli, brussels sprouts, cauliflower, greens, peppers, spinach, and tomatoes are good sources of vitamin C.
4. Vegetables contain 1 to 4 grams of fiber per serving.

Selection tips

1. A 1-cup portion of broccoli is a portion about the size of a light bulb.
2. Tomato sauce is different from spaghetti sauce, which is on the Other Carbohydrates list.
3. Canned vegetables and juices are available without added salt.
4. If you eat more than 4 cups of raw vegetables or 2 cups of cooked vegetables at one meal, count them as 1 carbohydrate choice.

5. Starchy vegetables such as corn, peas, winter squash, and potatoes that contain larger amounts of Calories and carbohydrates are on the Starch list.

One vegetable exchange equals
5 grams carbohydrate,
2 grams protein,
0 grams fat, and
25 Calories.

Artichoke
Artichoke hearts
Asparagus
Beans (green, wax, Italian)
Bean sprouts
Beets
Broccoli
Brussels sprouts
Cabbage
Carrots
Cauliflower
Celery
Cucumber
Eggplant
Green onions or scallions
Greens (collard, kale, mustard, turnip)
Kohlrabi
Leeks
Mixed vegetables (without corn, peas, or pasta)
Mushrooms
Okra
Onions
Pea pods
Peppers (all varieties)
Radishes
Salad greens (endive, escarole, lettuce, romaine, spinach)
Sauerkraut ⓘ

Spinach
Summer squash
Tomato
Tomatoes, canned
Tomato sauce ⚑
Tomato/vegetable juice ⚑
Turnips
Water chestnuts
Watercress
Zucchini

⚑ = 400 mg or more sodium per exchange.

Meat and Meat Substitutes List

Meat and meat substitutes that contain both protein and fat are on this list. In general, one meat exchange is:

- 1 oz meat, fish, poultry, or cheese
- 1/2 cup dried beans

Based on the amount of fat they contain, meats are divided into very lean, lean, medium-fat, and high-fat lists. This is done so you can see which ones contain the least amount of fat. One ounce (one exchange) of each of these includes:

	Carbohydrate (grams)	Protein (grams)	Fat (grams)	Calories
Very lean	0	7	0-1	35
Lean	0	7	3	55
Medium-fat	0	7	5	75
High-fat	0	7	8	100

Nutrition tips

1. Choose very lean and lean meat choices whenever possible. Items from the high-fat group are high in saturated fat, cholesterol, and Calories and can raise blood cholesterol levels.
2. Meats do not have any fiber.
3. Dried beans, peas, and lentils are good sources of fiber.
4. Some processed meats, seafood, and soy products may contain carbohydrate when consumed in large amounts. Check the Nutrition Facts on the label to see if the amount is close to 15 grams. If so, count it as a carbohydrate choice as well as a meat choice.

Selection tips

1. Weigh meat after cooking and removing bones and fat. Four ounces of raw meat is equal to 3 ounces of cooked meat. Some examples of meat portions are:

   - 1 ounce cheese = 1 meat choice and is about the size of a 1-inch cube

   - 2 ounces meat = 2 meat choices, such as
     1 small chicken leg or thigh
     1/2 cup cottage cheese or tuna
   - 3 ounces meat = 3 meat choices and is about the size of a deck of cards, such as
     1 medium pork chop
     1 small hamburger
     1/2 of a whole chicken breast
     1 unbreaded fish fillet

2. Limit your choices from the high-fat group to three times per week or less.
3. Most grocery stores stock Select and Choice grades of meat. Select grades of meat are the leanest meats.
4. Choice grades contain a moderate amount of fat, and Prime cuts of meat have the highest amount of fat. Restaurants usually serve Prime cuts of meat.
5. "Hamburger" may contain added seasoning and fat, but ground beef does not.
6. Read labels to find products that are low in fat and cholesterol (5 grams or less of fat per serving).
7. Dried beans, peas, and lentils are also found on the Starch list.
8. Peanut butter, in smaller amounts, is also found on the Fats list.
9. Bacon, in smaller amounts, is also found on the Fats list.

Meal planning tips

1. Bake, roast, broil, grill, poach, steam, or boil these foods rather than frying.
2. Place meat on a rack so the fat will drain off during cooking.
3. Use a nonstick spray and a nonstick pan to brown or fry foods.
4. Trim off visible fat before or after cooking.
5. If you add flour, bread crumbs, coating mixes, fat, or marinades when cooking, ask your dietitian how to count it in your meal plan.

Very lean meat and substitutes list (One exchange equals 0 grams carbohydrate, 7 grams protein, 0–1 grams fat, and 35 Calories.)

One very lean meat exchange is equal to any one of the following items.

Poultry: Chicken or turkey (white meat, no skin), Cornish hen (no skin) . . . . 1 oz
Fish: Fresh or frozen cod, flounder, haddock, halibut, trout; tuna fresh or canned in water . . . . 1 oz
Shellfish: Clams, crab, lobster, scallops, shrimp, imitation shellfish . . . . 1 oz
Game: Duck or pheasant (no skin), venison, buffalo, ostrich . . . . 1 oz

Cheese with 1 gram or less fat per ounce:
   Nonfat or low-fat cottage cheese . . . . 1/4 cup
   Fat-free cheese . . . . 1 oz
Other: Processed sandwich meat with 1 gram
or less fat per ounce, such as deli thin, shave meats,
chipped beef 🍶,
turkey ham . . . . 1 oz
   Egg whites 2
   Egg substitutes, plain . . . . 1/4 cup
   Hot dogs with 1 gram or less fat per ounce 🍶 . . . . . 1 oz
   Kidney (high in cholesterol) . . . . 1 oz
   Sausage with 1 gram or less fat per ounce . . . . 1 oz

Count as one very lean meat and one starch exchange.

   Dried beans, peas, lentils (cooked) . . . . 1/2 cup

🍶 = 400 mg or more sodium per exchange.

Lean meat and substitutes list (One exchange equals 0 grams carbohydrate, 7 grams protein, 3 grams fat, and 55 Calories.)

One lean meat exchange is equal to any one of the following
items.

   Beef: USDA Select or Choice grades of lean beef
      trimmed of fat, such as round, sirloin, and flank
      steak; tenderloin; roast (rib, chuck, rump);
      steak (T-bone, Porterhouse, cubed),
      ground round. . . . . 1 oz
   Pork: Lean pork, such as fresh ham; canned,
      cured, or boiled ham; Canadian bacon 🍶;
      tenderloin, center loin chop . . . . 1 oz
   Lamb: Roast, chop, leg . . . . 1 oz
   Veal: Lean chop, roast . . . . 1 oz
   Poultry: Chicken, turkey (dark meat, no skin),
      chicken white meat (with skin), domestic
      duck or goose (well-drained of fat, no skin). . . . . 1 oz
   Fish:
      Herring (uncreamed or smoked) . . . . 1 oz
      Oysters. . . . . 6 medium
      Salmon (fresh or canned), catfish . . . . 1 oz
      Sardines (canned) . . . . 2 medium
      Tuna (canned in oil, drained). . . . . 1 oz
   Game: Goose (no skin), rabbit . . . . 1 oz
   Cheese:
      4.5%-fat cottage cheese . . . . 1/4 cup
      Grated Parmesan . . . . 2 Tbsp
      Cheeses with 3 grams or less fat per ounce . . . . . . 1 oz
   Other:
      Hot dogs with 3 grams or less fat per ounce. . . 1 1/2 oz
      Processed sandwich meat with 3 grams or
         less fat per ounce, such as turkey pastrami
         or kielbasa. . . . . 1 oz
      Liver, heart (high in cholesterol). . . . . 1 oz

Medium-fat meat and substitutes list (One exchange equals 0 grams carbohydrate, 7 grams protein, 5 grams fat, and 75 Calories.)

One medium-fat meat exchange is equal to any one of the following items.

   Beef: Most beef products fall into this category
      (ground beef, meatloaf, corned beef, short ribs,
      prime grades of meat trimmed of fat, such
      as prime rib) . . . . 1 oz
   Pork: Top loin, chop, Boston butt, cutlet . . . . 1 oz
   Lamb: Rib roast, ground . . . . 1 oz
   Veal: Cutlet (ground or cubed, unbreaded) . . . . 1 oz
   Poultry: Chicken dark meat (with skin), ground
      turkey or ground chicken, fried chicken
      (with skin). . . . . 1 oz
   Fish: Any fried fish product . . . . 1 oz
   Cheese: With 5 grams or less fat per ounce
      Feta . . . . 1 oz
      Mozzarella . . . . 1 oz
      Ricotta. . . . . 1/4 cup (2 oz)
   Other:
      Egg (high in cholesterol, limit to 3 per week) 1
      Sausage with 5 grams or less fat per ounce . . . . 1 oz
      Soy milk . . . . 1 cup
      Tempeh . . . . 1/4 cup
      Tofu . . . . 4 oz or 1/2 cup

High-fat meat and substitutes list (One exchange equals 0 grams carbohydrate, 7 grams protein, 8 grams fat, and 100 Calories.)

Remember these items are high in saturated fat, cholesterol,
and Calories and may raise blood cholesterol levels if eaten
on a regular basis. One high-fat meat exchange is equal to any
one of the following items.

   Pork: Spareribs, ground pork, pork sausage . . . . 1 oz
   Cheese: All regular cheeses, such as American 🍶,
      cheddar, Monterey Jack, Swiss . . . . 1 oz
   Other: Processed sandwich meats with 8 grams
      or less fat per ounce, such as bologna, pimento
      loaf, salami . . . . 1 oz
      Sausage, such as bratwurst, Italian,
      knockwurst, Polish, smoked 🍶 . . . . 1 oz
      Hot dog (turkey or chicken) 🍶 1 (10/lb)
      Bacon . . . . 3 slices (20 slices/lb)

Count as one high-fat meat plus one fat exchange.

   Hot dog (beef, pork, or combination) 🍶 1 (10/lb)

   Peanut butter (contains unsaturated fat). . . . . 2 Tbsp

🍶 = 400 mg or more sodium per exchange.

Fat List

Fats are divided into three groups, based on the main type of fat they contain: monounsaturated, polyunsaturated, and saturated. Small amounts of monounsaturated and polyunsaturated fats in the foods we eat are linked with good health benefits. Saturated fats are linked with heart disease and cancer. In general, one fat exchange is:

- 1 teaspoon of regular margarine or vegetable oil
- 1 tablespoon of regular salad dressing

Nutrition tips

1. All fats are high in Calories. Limit serving sizes for good nutrition and health.
2. Nuts and seeds contain small amounts of fiber, protein, and magnesium.
3. If blood pressure is a concern, choose fats in the unsalted form to help lower sodium intake, such as unsalted peanuts.

Selection tips

1. Check the Nutrition Facts on food labels for serving sizes. One fat exchange is based on a serving size containing 5 grams of fat.
2. When selecting regular margarine, choose those with liquid vegetable oil as the first ingredient. Soft margarines are not as saturated as stick margarines. Soft margarines are healthier choices. Avoid those listing hydrogenated or partially hydrogenated fat as the first ingredient.
3. When selecting low-fat margarines, look for liquid vegetable oil as the second ingredient. Water is usually the first ingredient.
4. When used in smaller amounts, bacon and peanut butter are counted as fat choices. When used in larger amounts, they are counted as high-fat meat choices.
5. Fat-free salad dressings are on the Other Carbohydrates list and the Free Foods list.
6. See the Free Foods list for nondairy coffee creamers, whipped topping, and fat-free products, such as margarines, salad dressings, mayonnaise, sour cream, cream cheese, and nonstick cooking spray.

Monounsaturated fats list
(One fat exchange equals 5 grams fat and 45 Calories.)

Avocado, medium . . . . 1/8 (1 oz)
Oil (canola, olive, peanut). 1 tsp
Olives: ripe (black). . . . . 8 large
  green, stuffed 🧂 . . . . 10 large
Nuts
  almonds, cashews . . . . 6 nuts
  mixed (50% peanuts). 6 nuts

  peanuts . . . . 10 nuts
  pecans . . . . 4 halves
Peanut butter, smooth or crunchy . . . . 2 tsp
Sesame seeds . . . . 1 Tbsp
Tahini paste . . . . 2 tsp

Polyunsaturated fats list
(One fat exchange equals 5 grams fat and 45 Calories.)

Margarine: stick, tub, or squeeze . . . . 1 tsp
  lower-fat (30% to 50% vegetable oil). . . . . 1 Tbsp
Mayonnaise: regular . . . . 1 tsp
  reduced-fat . . . . 1 Tbsp
Nuts, walnuts, English. . . . . 4 halves
Oil (corn, safflower, soybean) . . . . 1 tsp
Salad dressing: regular 🧂 . . . . 1 Tbsp
  reduced-fat . . . . 2 Tbsp
Miracle Whip Salad Dressing®: regular. . . . . 2 tsp
  reduced-fat . . . . 1 Tbsp
Seeds: pumpkin, sunflower . . . . 1 Tbsp

🧂 = 400 mg or more sodium per exchange.

Saturated fats list* (One fat exchange equals 5 grams of fat and 45 Calories.)

Bacon, cooked . . . . 1 slice (20 slices/lb)
Bacon, grease. . . . . 1 tsp
Butter: stick . . . . 1 tsp
  whipped . . . . 2 tsp
  reduced-fat . . . . 1 Tbsp
Chitterlings, boiled. . . . . 2 Tbsp (1/2 oz)
Coconut, sweetened, shredded . . . . 2 Tbsp
Cream, half and half. . . . . 2 Tbsp
Cream cheese: regular . . . . 1 Tbsp (1/2 oz)
  reduced-fat. . . . . 2 Tbsp (1 oz)
Fatback or salt pork, see below†
Shortening or lard . . . . 1 tsp
Sour cream: regular . . . . 2 Tbsp
  reduced-fat . . . . 3 Tbsp

*Saturated fats can raise blood cholesterol levels.

†Use a piece 1 in. × 1 in. × 1/4 in. if you plan to eat the fatback cooked with vegetables. Use a piece 2 in. × 1 in. × 1/2 in. when eating only the vegetables with the fatback removed.

Free Foods List

A *free food* is any food or drink that contains less than 20 Calories or less than 5 grams of carbohydrate per serving. Foods with a serving size listed should be limited to three servings per day. Be sure to spread them out throughout the day. If you eat all three servings at one time, it could affect your blood glucose level. Foods listed without a serving size can be eaten as often as you like.

Fat-free or reduced-fat foods

Cream cheese, fat-free . . . . 1 Tbsp
Creamers, nondairy, liquid . . . . 1 Tbsp
Creamers, nondairy, powdered . . . . 2 tsp
Mayonnaise, fat-free . . . . 1 Tbsp
Mayonnaise, reduced-fat . . . . 1 tsp
Margarine, fat-free . . . . 4 Tbsp
Margarine, reduced-fat . . . . 1 tsp
Miracle Whip®, nonfat . . . . 1 Tbsp
Miracle Whip®, reduced-fat . . . . 1 tsp
Nonstick cooking spray
Salad dressing, fat-free . . . . 1 Tbsp
Salad dressing, fat-free, Italian . . . . 2 Tbsp
Salsa . . . . 1/4 cup
Sour cream, fat-free, reduced-fat . . . . 1 Tbsp
Whipped topping, regular or light . . . . 2 Tbsp

Sugar-free or low-sugar foods

Candy, hard, sugar-free . . . . 1 candy
Gelatin dessert, sugar-free
Gelatin, unflavored
Gum, sugar-free
Jam or jelly, low-sugar or light . . . . 2 tsp
Sugar substitutes†
Syrup, sugar-free . . . . 2 Tbsp

†Sugar substitutes, alternatives, or replacements that are approved by the Food and Drug Administration (FDA) are safe to use. Common brand names include:

Equal® (aspartame)

Sprinkle Sweet® (saccharin)

Sweet One® (acesulfame K)

Sweet-10® (saccharin)

Sugar Twin® (saccharin)

Sweet 'n Low® (saccharin)

Drinks

Bouillon, broth, consommé ▮
Bouillon or broth, low-sodium
Carbonated or mineral water
Cocoa powder, unsweetened . . . . 1 Tbsp
Coffee
Club soda
Diet soft drinks, sugar-free
Drink mixes, sugar-free
Tea
Tonic water, sugar-free

Condiments

Catsup . . . . 1 Tbsp
Horseradish
Lemon juice
Lime juice
Mustard
Pickles, dill ▮ . . . . 1 1/2 large
Soy sauce, regular or light ▮
Taco sauce . . . . 1 Tbsp
Vinegar

Seasonings

Be careful with seasonings that contain sodium or are salts, such as garlic or celery salt, and lemon pepper.

Flavoring extracts
Garlic
Herbs, fresh or dried
Pimento
Spices
Tabasco® or hot pepper sauce
Wine, used in cooking
Worcestershire sauce

▮ = 400 mg or more of sodium per choice.

Combination Foods List

Many of the foods we eat are mixed together in various combinations. These combination foods do not fit into any one exchange list. Often it is hard to tell what is in a casserole dish or prepared food item. This is a list of exchanges for some typical combination foods. This list will help you fit these foods into your meal plan. Ask your dietitian for information about any other combination foods you would like to eat.

Food entrees	Serving size	Exchanges per serving
Tuna noodle casserole, lasagna, spaghetti with meatballs, chili with beans, macaroni and cheese 🅸	1 cup (8 oz)	2 carbohydrates, 2 medium-fat meats
Chow mein (without noodles or rice)	2 cups (16 oz)	1 carbohydrate, 2 lean meats
Pizza, cheese, thin crust 🅸	1/4 of 10 in. (5 oz)	2 carbohydrates, 2 medium-fat meats, 1 fat
Pizza, meat topping, thin crust 🅸	1/4 of 10 in. (5 oz)	2 carbohydrates, 2 medium-fat meats, 2 fats
Pot pie 🅸	1 (7 oz)	2 carbohydrates, 1 medium-fat meat, 4 fats

Frozen entrees	Serving size	Exchanges per serving
Salisbury steak with gravy, mashed potato 🅸	1 (11 oz)	2 carbohydrates, 3 medium-fat meats, 3–4 fats
Turkey with gravy, mashed potato, dressing 🅸	1 (11 oz)	2 carbohydrates, 2 medium-fat meats, 2 fats
Entree with less than 300 calories 🅸	1 (8 oz)	2 carbohydrates, 3 lean meats

Soups	Serving size	Exchanges per serving
Bean 🅸	1 cup	1 carbohydrate, 1 very lean meat
Cream (made with water) 🅸	1 cup (8 oz)	1 carbohydrate, 1 fat
Split pea (made with water) 🅸	1/2 cup (4 oz)	1 carbohydrate
Tomato (made with water) 🅸	1 cup (8 oz)	1 carbohydrate
Vegetable beef, chicken noodle, or other broth-type 🅸	1 cup (8 oz)	1 carbohydrate

🅸 = 400 mg or more sodium per exchange.

Fast Foods*

Food entrees	Serving size	Exchanges per serving
Burritos with beef 🅸	2	4 carbohydrates, 2 medium-fat meats, 2 fats
Chicken nuggets 🅸	6	1 carbohydrate, 2 medium-fat meats, 1 fat
Chicken breast and wing, breaded and fried 🅸	1 each	1 carbohydrate, 4 medium-fat meats, 2 fats
Fish sandwich/tartar sauce 🅸	1	3 carbohydrates, 1 medium-fat meat, 3 fats
French fries, thin	20–25	2 carbohydrates, 2 fats
Hamburger, regular	1	2 carbohydrates, 2 medium-fat meats
Hamburger, large 🅸	1	2 carbohydrates, 3 medium-fat meats, 1 fat
Hot dog with a bun 🅸	1	1 carbohydrate, 1 high-fat meat, 1 fat
Individual pan pizza 🅸	1	5 carbohydrates, 3 medium-fat meats, 3 fats
Soft-serve cone 🅸	1 medium	2 carbohydrates, 1 fat
Submarine sandwich 🅸	1 sub (6 in.)	3 carbohydrates, 1 vegetable, 2 medium-fat meats, 1 fat
Taco, hard shell 🅸	1 (6 oz)	2 carbohydrates, 2 medium-fat meats, 2 fats
Taco, soft shell	1 (3 oz)	1 carbohydrate, 1 medium-fat meat, 1 fat

🅸 = 400 mg or more of sodium per serving.

*Ask at your fast-food restaurant for nutrition information about your favorite fast foods.

Calories, Percent Fat, Cholesterol Sodium, and Dietary Fiber in Selected Fast-Food Restaurant Products

Product	Calories	% Fat Calories	Cholesterol (mg)	Sodium (mg)	Dietary Fiber (g)
Arby's (www.arbys.com)					
Regular roast beef	320	34	45	950	2
Beef'n Cheddar	440	41	50	1270	2
Chicken breast fillet	500	44	55	1220	3
Roast chicken club	470	49	65	1320	2
Market Fresh roast turkey/swiss	720	35	90	1790	5
Martha's Vineyard salad	250	28	60	490	4
Burger King (www.burgerking.com)					
Dutch apple pie	300	40	0	240	1
Double cheeseburger	530	53	100	600	1
Side garden salad with fat-free honey mustard dressing	20	0	0	240	1
Onion rings (king size) with zesty dippy sauce	700	54	15	1020	6
Vanilla milk shake	540	33	80	320	0
Croissan'wich with sausage/egg/cheese	470	62	180	1060	1
BK veggie burger	420	35	10	1090	7
Hardee's (www.hardees.com)					
Country Ham biscuit	440	55	35	1710	0
Hot dog	420	64	55	1200	1
Monster thickburger	1410	68	229	2740	2
Cole slaw, small	170	53	10	140	2
Charbroiled chicken sandwich	590	39	80	1180	4
Apple turnover	290	48	5	350	1
KFC (www.KFC.com)					
Green beans	50	28	5	570	2
BBQ baked beans	230	4	0	720	7
Mashed potatoes with gravy	130	30	0	380	1
Breast (original recipe) without skin or dressing	140	19	95	410	0
Side breast (extra crispy)	460	54	135	1230	0
Honey BBQ sandwich	300	27	55	920	1

Product	Calories	% Fat Calories	Cholesterol (mg)	Sodium (mg)	Dietary Fiber (g)
Long John Silver's (www.longjohnsilvers.com)					
Ultimate fish sandwich	470	42	45	1200	3
Battered shrimp (8 pieces)	360	63	130	1310	1
Baked cod (1 piece)	120	33	90	240	0
Hush puppies, side order	60	45	0	200	1
McDonald's (www.mcdonalds.com)					
Hamburger	260	80	30	530	1
Big Mac	560	48	80	1010	48
Premium grilled chicken sandwich	410	20	80	1210	20
Chicken McNuggets (6 pieces)	250	52	35	670	0
French fries (large)	520	43	0	330	7
Hotcakes with margarine and syrup	600	25	20	620	2
Egg McMuffin	290	35	235	850	2
Fruit and walnut salad	120	11	5	85	6
Salad dressing, creamy Caesar (2 oz)	190	90	20	500	0
Pizza Hut (www.pizzahut.com)					
Thin 'N Crispy cheese, 1 medium slice	200	40	25	490	1
Pan, cheese, Veggie Lover's medium slice	260	38	15	470	2
Fit N' Delicious diced chicken	170	24	15	460	2
Personal pan pizza, pepperoni (whole pizza)	660	40	60	1370	4
Cherry dessert pizza, 1 slice	240	30	0	250	1
Subway (www.subway.com)					
Subway Club (6 inches)	320	50	35	1310	4
Turkey breast (6 inches)	280	40	20	1020	4
Tuna deli (6 inches)	350	48	30	750	3
Veggie Delite (6 inches)	230	30	0	520	4
Sweet onion Chicken Teriyaki (6 inches)	380	45	50	1230	4
Taco Bell (www.tacobell.com)					
Bean burrito, Fresco style	350	20	0	1220	9
Taco, beef, regular	170	53	25	350	1
Soft taco, beef, regular	210	43	25	620	1
Chicken Ranchero, taco, Fresco style	170	21	25	560	2
Nachos Supreme, regular	450	51	35	810	5
Chicken Quesadilla, regular	540	50	80	1380	5
Wendy's (www.wendys.com)					
Classic Single w/ Everything	430	42	65	890	2
Ultimate Chicken grilled sandwich	360	16	70	1090	2
Plain potato, baked	270	0	0	25	7
Potato with broccoli and cheese	440	29	10	540	9
Spring mix salad	180	50	30	230	4
Low-fat honey mustard dressing	110	25	0	340	0
Chili (large)	330	24	55	1140	8
Baja Fresh (www.bajafresh.com)					
Burrito Ultimo, steak	1150	41	165	2200	9
Burrito Mexicano, chicken	960	20	75	2290	21
Grilled veggie burrito	970	38	65	1900	17
Bare burrito, steak	730	18	100	2350	19
Veggie & cheese bare burrito	580	15	15	1990	20

Energy Pathways of Carbohydrate, Fat, and Protein

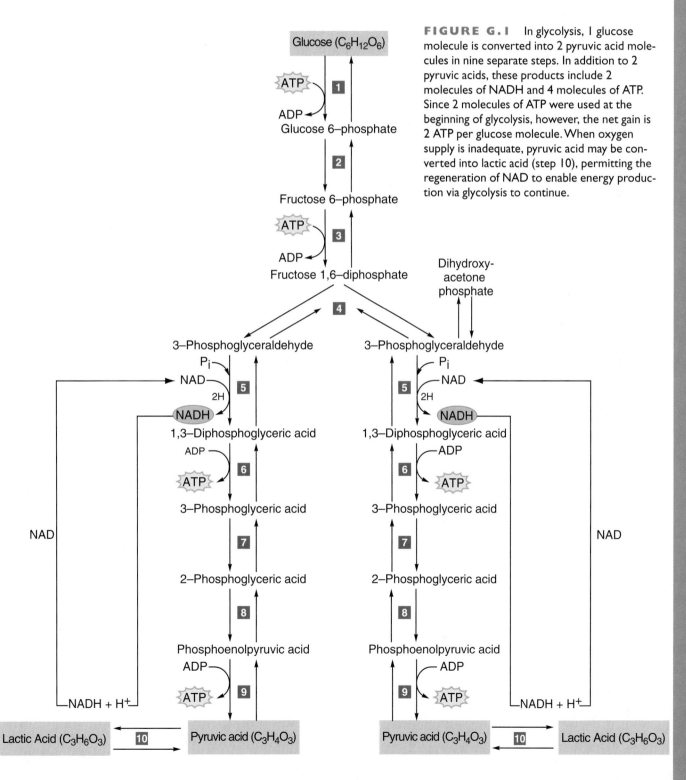

FIGURE G.1 In glycolysis, 1 glucose molecule is converted into 2 pyruvic acid molecules in nine separate steps. In addition to 2 pyruvic acids, these products include 2 molecules of NADH and 4 molecules of ATP. Since 2 molecules of ATP were used at the beginning of glycolysis, however, the net gain is 2 ATP per glucose molecule. When oxygen supply is inadequate, pyruvic acid may be converted into lactic acid (step 10), permitting the regeneration of NAD to enable energy production via glycolysis to continue.

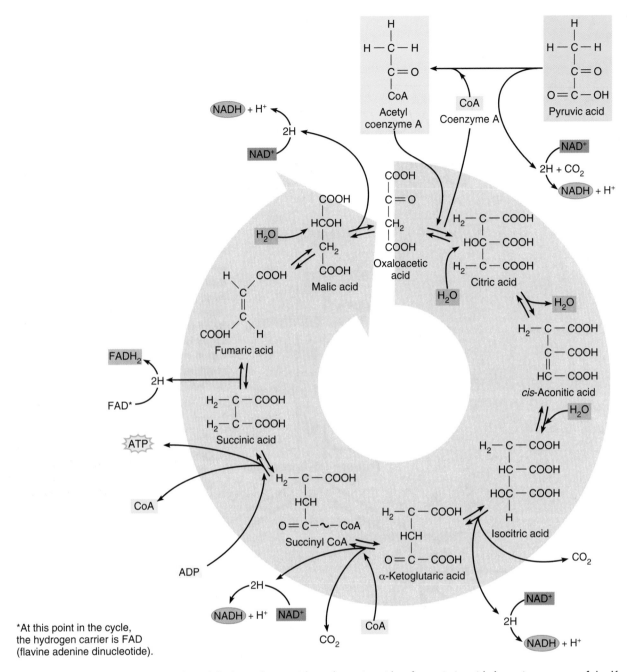

FIGURE G.2 The Krebs cycle. Acetyl CoA combines with oxaloacetic acid to form citric acid. At various stages of the Krebs cycle, hydrogen ions and electrons are removed by NAD (nicotinamide adenine dinucleotide) and FAD (flavin adenine dinucleotide) for passage through the electron transport system and the generation of ATP. Only small amounts of high energy phosphates are generated directly in the Krebs cycle as most are generated via electron transport and the associated oxidative phosphorylation (see figure G.3).

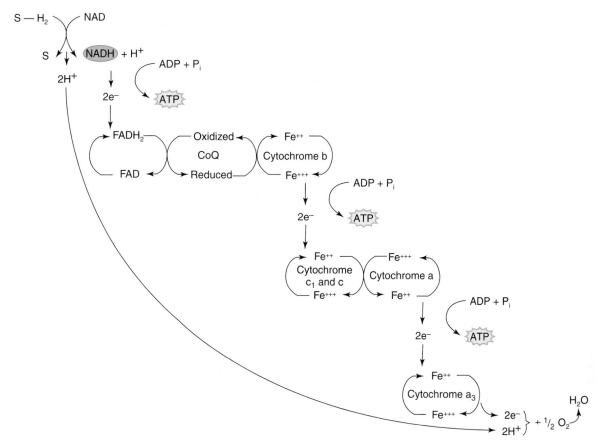

FIGURE G.3 Electron transport and oxidative phosphorylation. Each element in the electron transport chain alternately becomes reduced and then oxidized as it transports electrons to the next member of the chain. This process provides energy for the formation of ATP. At the end of the electron transport chain, the electrons are donated to oxygen, which becomes reduced (by the addition of 2 hydrogen atoms) to water.

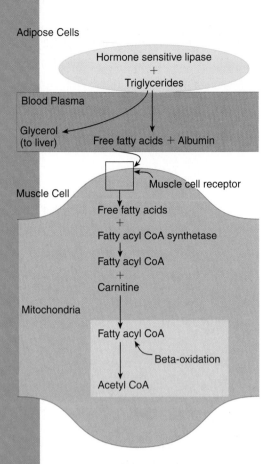

Adipose Cells

FIGURE G.4 Energy pathways for fatty acids. Triglycerides in the adipose tissue may be catabolized by hormone-sensitive lipase, with the fatty acids being released to the plasma and binding with albumin; the glycerol component is transported to the liver for metabolism. A receptor at the muscle cell transports the fatty acid into the muscle cell where it is converted into fatty acyl CoA by an enzyme (fatty acyl CoA synthetase). The fatty acyl CoA is then transported into the mitochondria with carnitine (in an enzyme complex) as a carrier. The fatty acyl CoA, which is a combination of acetyl CoA units, then undergoes beta-oxidation, a process that splits off the acetyl CoA units for entrance into the Krebs cycle.

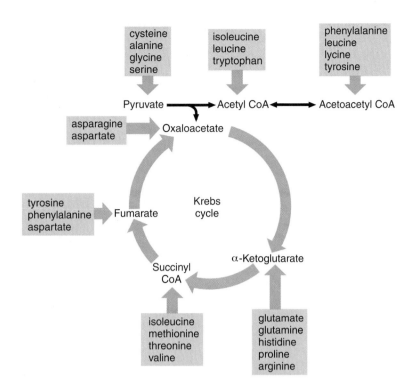

FIGURE G.5 Metabolic fates of various amino acids. Various amino acids, after deamination, may enter into energy pathways at different sites.

Small Steps: 120 Small Steps to a Healthier Diet and Increased Physical Activity

1. Walk to work.
2. Use fat-free milk over whole milk.
3. Do sit-ups in front of the TV.
4. Walk during lunch hour.
5. Drink water before a meal.
6. Eat leaner red meat & poultry.
7. Eat half your dessert.
8. Walk instead of driving whenever you can.
9. Take family walk after dinner.
10. Skate to work instead of driving.
11. Avoid food portions larger than your fist.
12. Mow lawn with push mower.
13. Increase the fiber in your diet.
14. Walk to your place of worship instead of driving.
15. Walk kids to school.
16. Get a dog and walk it.
17. Join an exercise group.
18. Drink diet soda.
19. Replace Sunday drive with Sunday walk.
20. Do yard work.
21. Eat off smaller plates.
22. Get off a stop early & walk.
23. Don't eat late at night.
24. Skip seconds.
25. Work around the house.
26. Skip buffets.
27. Grill, steam, or bake instead of frying.
28. Bicycle to the store instead of driving.
29. Take dog to the park.
30. Ask your doctor about taking a multivitamin.
31. Go for a half-hour walk instead of watching TV.
32. Use vegetable oils over solid fats.
33. More carrots, less cake.
34. Fetch the newspaper yourself.
35. Sit up straight at work.
36. Wash the car by hand.
37. Don't skip meals.
38. Eat more celery sticks.
39. Run when running errands.
40. Pace the sidelines at kids' athletic games.
41. Take wheels off luggage.
42. Choose an activity that fits into your daily life.
43. Try your burger with just lettuce, tomato, and onion.
44. Ask a friend to exercise with you.
45. Make time in your day for physical activity.
46. Exercise with a video if the weather is bad.
47. Bike to the barbershop or beauty salon instead of driving.
48. Keep to a regular eating schedule.
49. If you find it difficult to be active after work, try it before work.
50. Take a walk or do desk exercises instead of a cigarette or coffee break.
51. Perform gardening or home repair activities.
52. Avoid laborsaving devices.
53. Take small trips on foot to get your body moving.
54. Play with your kids 30 minutes a day.
55. Dance to music.
56. Keep a pair of comfortable walking or running shoes in your car and office.
57. Make a Saturday morning walk a group habit.
58. Walk briskly in the mall.
59. Choose activities you enjoy & you'll be more likely to stick with them.
60. Stretch before bed to give you more energy when you wake.
61. Take the long way to the water cooler.
62. Explore new physical activities.
63. Vary your activities, for interest and to broaden the range of benefits.

64. Reward and acknowledge your efforts.
65. Choose fruit for dessert.
66. Consume alcoholic beverages in moderation, if at all.
67. Take stairs instead of the escalator.
68. Conduct an inventory of your meal/snack and physical activity patterns.
69. Share an entrée with a friend.
70. Grill fruit or vegetables.
71. Eat before grocery shopping.
72. Choose a checkout line without a candy display.
73. Make a grocery list before you shop.
74. Buy 100% fruit juices over soda and sugary drinks.
75. Stay active in winter. Play with your kids.
76. Flavor foods with herbs, spices, and other low-fat seasonings.
77. Remove skin from poultry before cooking to lower fat content.
78. Eat before you get too hungry.
79. Don't skip breakfast.
80. Stop eating when you are full.
81. Snack on fruits and vegetables.
82. Top your favorite cereal with apples or bananas.
83. Try brown rice or whole wheat pasta.
84. Include several servings of whole-grain food daily.
85. When eating out, choose a small or medium portion.
86. If main dishes are too big, choose an appetizer or a side dish instead.
87. Ask for salad dressing "on the side."
88. Don't take seconds.
89. Park farther from destination and walk.
90. Try a green salad instead of fries.
91. Bake or broil fish.
92. Walk instead of sitting around.
93. Eat sweet foods in small amounts.
94. Take your dog on longer walks.
95. Drink lots of water.
96. Cut back on added fats or oils in cooking or spreads.
97. Walk the beach instead of sunbathing.
98. Walk to a co-worker's desk instead of e-mailing or calling them.
99. Carry your groceries instead of pushing a cart.
100. Use a snow shovel instead of a snow blower.
101. Cut high-Calorie foods like cheese and chocolate into smaller pieces and eat only a few pieces.
102. Use nonfat or low-fat sour cream, mayo, sauces, dressings, and other condiments.
103. Replace sugar-sweetened beverages with water and add a twist of lemon or lime.
104. Replace high-saturated fat/high Calorie seasonings with herbs grown in a small herb garden in your kitchen window.
105. Refrigerate prepared soups before you eat them. As the soup cools, the fat will rise to the top. Skim it off the surface for reduced-fat content.
106. When eating out, ask your server to put half your entrée in a to-go bag.
107. Substitute vegetables for other ingredients in your sandwich.
108. Every time you eat a meal, sit down, chew slowly, and pay attention to flavors and textures.
109. Try a new fruit or vegetable. (Ever had jicama, plantain, bok choy, starfruit, or papaya?)
110. Make up a batch of brownies with applesauce instead of oil or shortening.
111. Instead of eating out, bring a healthy, low-Calorie lunch to work.
112. Ask your sweetie to bring you fruit or flowers instead of chocolate.
113. Speak up for the salad bar when your co-workers are picking a restaurant for lunch, and remember Calories count, so pay attention to how much and what you eat.
114. When walking, go up the hills instead of around them.
115. Walk briskly through the mall and shop 'til you drop . . . pounds.
116. Clean your closet and donate clothes that are too big.
117. Take your body measurements to gauge progress.
118. Buy a set of hand weights and play a round of Simon Says with your kids. You do it with the weights; they do it without.
119. Swim with your kids.
120. Wear a SmallSteps bracelet to remind you to live a healthier lifestyle every day.

Source: www.SmallStep.Gov

Sample Menu for a 2000-Calorie Food Pattern

Sample Menus for a 2000 calorie food pattern

Averaged over a week, this seven day menu provides all of the recommended amounts of nutrients and food from each food group. (Italicized foods are part of the dish or food that precedes it.)

Food Group	Daily Average
GRAINS	Total Grains (oz eq) 6.0
	Whole Grains 3.4
	Refined Grains 2.6
VEGETABLES*	Total Veg* (cups) 2.6
FRUITS	Fruits (cups) 2.1
MILK	Milk (cups) 3.1
MEAT & BEANS	Meat/ Beans (oz eq) 5.6
OILS	Oils (tsp/grams) 7.2 tsp/32.4 g

Nutrient	Daily Average
Calories	1994
Protein, g	98
Protein, % kcal	20
Carbohydrate, g	264
Carbohydrate, % kcal	53
Total fat, g	67
Total fat, % kcal	30
Saturated fat, g	16
Saturated fat, % kcal	7.0
Monounsaturated fat, g	23
Polyunsaturated fat, g	23
Linoleic Acid, g	21
Alpha-linolenic Acid, g	1.1
Cholesterol, mg	207
Total dietary fiber, g	31
Potassium, mg	4715
Sodium, mg*	1948
Calcium, mg	1389
Magnesium, mg	432
Copper, mg	1.9
Iron, mg	21
Phosphorus, mg	1830
Zinc, mg	14
Thiamin, mg	1.9
Riboflavin, mg	2.5
Niacin Equivalents, mg	24
Vitamin B6, mg	2.9
Vitamin B12, mcg	18.4
Vitamin C, mg	190
Vitamin E, mg (AT)	18.9
Vitamin A, mcg (RAE)	1430
Dietary Folate Equivalents, mcg	558

*Vegetable subgroups	(weekly totals)
Dark-Green Veg (cups)	3.3
Orange Veg (cups)	2.3
Beans/ Peas (cups)	3.0
Starchy Veg (cups)	3.4
Other Veg (cups)	6.6

* Starred items are foods that are labelled as no-salt-added, low-sodium, or low-salt versions of the foods. They can also be prepared from scratch with little or no added salt. All other foods are regular commercial products which contain variable levels of sodium. Average sodium level of the 7-day menu assumes no-salt-added in cooking or at the table.

Day 1

BREAKFAST

Breakfast burrito
1 flour tortilla (7" diameter)
1 scrambled egg (in 1 tsp soft margarine)
1/3 cup black beans*
2 tbsp salsa
1 cup orange juice
1 cup fat-free milk

LUNCH

Roast beef sandwich
1 whole grain sandwich bun
3 ounces lean roast beef
2 slices tomato
1/4 cup shredded romaine lettuce
1/8 cup sauteed mushrooms (in 1 tsp oil)
1 1/2 ounce part-skim mozzarella cheese
1 tsp yellow mustard
3/4 cup baked potato wedges*
1 tbsp ketchup
1 unsweetened beverage

DINNER

Stuffed broiled salmon
5 ounce salmon filet
1 ounce bread stuffing mix
1 tbsp chopped onions
1 tbsp diced celery
2 tsp canola oil
1/2 cup saffron (white) rice
1 ounce slivered almonds
1/2 cup steamed broccoli
1 tsp soft margarine
1 cup fat-free milk

SNACKS

1 cup cantaloupe

Day 2

BREAKFAST

Hot cereal
1/2 cup cooked oatmeal
2 tbsp raisins
1 tsp soft margarine
1/2 cup fat-free milk
1 cup orange juice

LUNCH

Taco salad
2 ounces tortilla chips
2 ounces ground turkey, sauteed in
2 tsp sunflower oil
1/2 cup black beans*
1/2 cup iceberg lettuce
2 slices tomato
1 ounce low-fat cheddar cheese
2 tbsp salsa
1/2 cup avocado
1 tsp lime juice
1 unsweetened beverage

DINNER

Spinach lasagna
1 cup lasagna noodles, cooked (2 oz dry)
2/3 cup cooked spinach
1/2 cup ricotta cheese
1/2 cup tomato sauce tomato bits*
1 ounce part-skim mozzarella cheese
1 ounce whole wheat dinner roll
1 cup fat-free milk

SNACKS

1/2 ounce dry-roasted almonds*
1/4 cup pineapple
2 tbsp raisins

Day 3

BREAKFAST

Cold cereal
1 cup bran flakes
1 cup fat-free milk
1 small banana
1 slice whole wheat toast
1 tsp soft margarine
1 cup prune juice

LUNCH

Tuna fish sandwich
2 slices rye bread
3 ounces tuna (packed in water, drained)
2 tsp mayonnaise
1 tbsp diced celery
1/4 cup shredded romaine lettuce
2 slices tomato
1 medium pear
1 cup fat-free milk

DINNER

Roasted chicken breast
3 ounces boneless skinless chicken breast*
1 large baked sweet potato
1/2 cup peas and onions
1 ounce whole wheat dinner roll
1 tsp soft margarine
1 cup leafy greens salad
3 tsp sunflower oil and vinegar dressing

SNACKS

1/4 cup dried apricots
1 cup low-fat fruited yogurt

Day 4

BREAKFAST

1 whole wheat English muffin
2 tsp soft margarine
1 tbsp jam or preserves
1 medium grapefruit
1 hard-cooked egg
1 unsweetened beverage

LUNCH

White bean-vegetable soup
1 1/4 cup chunky vegetable soup
1/2 cup white beans*
2 ounce breadstick
8 baby carrots
1 cup fat-free milk

DINNER

Rigatoni with meat sauce
1 cup rigatoni pasta (2 ounces dry)
1/2 cup tomato sauce tomato bits*
2 ounces extra lean cooked ground beef (sauteed in 2 tsp vegetable oil)
3 tbsp grated Parmesan cheese
Spinach salad
1 cup baby spinach leaves
1/2 cup tangerine slices
1/2 ounce chopped walnuts
3 tsp sunflower oil and vinegar dressing
1 cup fat-free milk

SNACKS

1 cup low-fat fruited yogurt

* Starred items are foods that are labeled as no-salt-added, low-sodium, or low-salt versions of the foods. They can also be prepared from scratch with little or no added salt. All other foods are regular commercial products which contain variable levels of sodium. Average sodium level of the 7-day menu assumes no-salt-added in cooking or at the table

Source: www.MyPyramid.gov

Day 5

BREAKFAST

Cold cereal
1 cup puffed wheat cereal
1 tbsp raisins
1 cup fat-free milk
1 small banana
1 slice whole wheat toast
1 tsp soft margarine
1 tsp jelly

LUNCH

Smoked turkey sandwich
2 ounces whole wheat pita bread
1/4 cup romaine lettuce
2 slices tomato
3 ounces sliced smoked turkey breast*
1 tbsp mayo-type salad dressing
1 tsp yellow mustard
1/2 cup apple slices
1 cup tomato juice*

DINNER

Grilled top loin steak
5 ounces grilled top loin steak
3/4 cup mashed potatoes
2 tsp soft margarine
1/2 cup steamed carrots
1 tbsp honey
2 ounces whole wheat dinner roll
1 tsp soft margarine
1 cup fat-free milk

SNACKS

1 cup low-fat fruited yogurt

Day 6

BREAKFAST

French toast
2 slices whole wheat French toast
2 tsp soft margarine
2 tbsp maple syrup
1/2 medium grapefruit
1 cup fat-free milk

LUNCH

Vegetarian chili on baked potato
1 cup kidney beans*
1/2 cup tomato sauce w/ tomato tidbits*
3 tbsp chopped onions
1 ounce low-fat cheddar cheese
1 tsp vegetable oil
1 medium baked potato
1/2 cup cantaloupe
3/4 cup lemonade

DINNER

Hawaiian pizza
2 slices cheese pizza
1 ounce canadian bacon
1/4 cup pineapple
2 tbsp mushrooms
2 tbsp chopped onions
Green salad
1 cup leafy greens
3 tsp sunflower oil and vinegar dressing
1 cup fat-free milk

SNACKS

5 whole wheat crackers*
1/8 cup hummus
1/2 cup fruit cocktail (in water or juice)

Day 7

BREAKFAST

Pancakes
3 buckwheat pancakes
2 tsp soft margarine
3 tbsp maple syrup
1/2 cup strawberries
3/4 cup honeydew melon
1/2 cup fat-free milk

LUNCH

Manhattan clam chowder
3 ounces canned clams (drained)
3/4 cup mixed vegetables*
1 cup canned tomatoes*
10 whole wheat crackers*
1 medium orange
1 cup fat-free milk

DINNER

Vegetable stir-fry
4 ounces tofu (firm)
1/4 cup green and red bell peppers
1/2 cup bok choy
2 tbsp vegetable oil
1 cup brown rice
1 cup lemon-flavored iced tea

SNACKS

1 ounce sunflower seeds*
1 large banana
1 cup low-fat fruited yogurt

Glossary

Acceptable Macronutrient Distribution Range (AMDR)   A range of dietary intakes for carbohydrate, fat, and protein that is associated with reduced risk of chronic disease while providing adequate nutrients.

acclimatization   The ability of the body to undergo physiological adaptations so that the stress of a given environment, such as high environmental temperature, is less severe.

acetaldehyde   An intermediate breakdown product of alcohol.

acetic acid   A naturally occurring saturated fatty acid; a precursor for the Krebs cycle when converted into acetyl CoA.

acetyl CoA   The major fuel for the oxidative processes in the body, being derived from the breakdown of glucose and fatty acids.

acid-base balance   A relative balance of acid and base products in the body so that an optimal pH is maintained in the tissues, particularly the blood.

acidosis   A disturbance of the normal acid-base balance in which excess acids accumulate in the body. Lactic acid production during exercise may lead to acidosis.

acrylamide   A cancer-causing agent that may be produced by prolonged, high-temperature cooking.

activity-stat   Center in the brain theorized to regulate daily physical activity.

acute exercise bout   A single bout of exercise that will produce various physiological reactions dependent upon the nature of the exercise; a single workout.

added sugars   Refined sugars added to foods during commercial food processing.

additives   Substances added to food to improve flavor, color, texture, stability, or for similar purposes.

adenosine triphosphate   *See* ATP.

Adequate Intake (AI)   Recommended dietary intake comparable to the RDA, but based on less scientific evidence.

adipokines   Substances released from adipose (fat) cells that function as hormones in other parts of the body.

Adonis complex   A disturbed body image in which muscular individuals consider themselves too thin or not sufficiently muscular; also known as muscle dysmorphia.

adrenaline   A hormone secreted by the adrenal medulla; it is a stimulant and prepares the body for "fight or flight."

aerobic   Relating to energy processes that occur in the presence of oxygen.

aerobic glycolysis   Oxidative processes in the cell that liberate energy in the metabolism of the carbohydrate glycogen.

aerobic lipolysis   Oxidative processes in the cell that liberate energy in the metabolism of fats.

aerobic walking   Rapid walking designed to elevate the heart rate so that a training effect will occur; more strenuous than ordinary leisure walking.

Air Displacement Plethysmography
A procedure to measure body composition via displacement of air in a special chamber; comparable to water displacement in underwater weighing techniques to evaluate body composition.

alanine   A nonessential amino acid.

alcohol   A colorless liquid with depressant effects; ethyl alcohol or ethanol is the alcohol designed for human consumption.

alcohol dehydrogenase   An enzyme in the liver that initiates the breakdown of alcohol to acetaldehyde.

alcoholism   A rather undefined term used to describe individuals who abuse the effect of alcohol; an addiction or habituation that may result in physical and/or psychological withdrawal effects.

aldosterone   The main electrolyte-regulating hormone secreted by the adrenal cortex; primarily controls sodium and potassium balance.

allithiamine   A derivative of thiamine.

alpha-ketoacid   Specific acids associated with different amino acids and released upon deamination or transamination; for example, the breakdown of glutamate yields alpha-ketoglutarate.

alpha-linolenic acid   An omega-3 fatty acid considered to be an essential nutrient.

alpha-tocopherol   The most biologically active alcohol in vitamin E.

alpha-tocopherol equivalent   The amount of other forms of tocopherol to equal the vitamin E activity of one milligram of alpha-tocopherol.

AMDR   *See* Acceptable Macronutrient Distribution Range.

amenorrhea   Absence or cessation of menstruation.

amino acids   The chief structural material of protein, consisting of an amino group (NH_2) and an acid group (COOH) plus other components.

amino group   The nitrogen-containing component of amino acids (NH_2).

aminostatic theory   A theory suggesting that hunger is controlled by the presence or absence of amino acids in the blood acting upon a receptor in the hypothalamus.

ammonia   A metabolic by-product of the oxidation of glutamine; it may be transformed into urea for excretion from the body.

amylopectin   A branched-chain starch.

amylose   A straight-chain starch that is more resistant to digestion compared to amylopectin.

anabolic/androgenic steroids (AAS)
Drugs designed to mimic the actions of testosterone to build muscle tissue (anabolism) while minimizing the androgenic effects (masculinization).

anabolism   Constructive metabolism, the process whereby simple body compounds are formed into more complex ones.

anaerobic   Relating to energy processes that occur in the absence of oxygen.

anaerobic glycolysis   Metabolic processes in the cell that liberate energy in the metabolism of the carbohydrate glycogen without the involvement of oxidation.

anaerobic threshold   The intensity of exercise at which the individual begins to increase the proportion of energy derived from anaerobic means, principally the lactic acid system. *Also see* steady-state threshold and OBLA.

android-type obesity Male-type obesity in which the body fat accumulates in the abdominal area and is a more significant risk factor for chronic disease than is gynoid-type obesity.

androstenedione An androgen produced in the body that is converted to testosterone; marketed as a dietary supplement.

anemia In general, subnormal levels of circulating RBCs and hemoglobin; there are many different types of anemia.

angina The pain experienced under the breastbone or in other areas of the upper body when the heart is deprived of oxygen.

anhidrotic heat exhaustion Heat exhaustion associated with diminished secretion or absence of sweat.

anion A negatively charged ion, or electrolyte.

anorexia athletica A form of anorexia nervosa observed in athletes involved in sports in which low percentages of body fat may enhance performance, such as gymnastics and ballet.

anorexia nervosa A serious nervous condition, particularly among teenage girls and young women, marked by a loss of appetite and leading to various degrees of emaciation.

anthropometry Use of body girths and diameters to evaluate body composition.

antibodies Protein substances developed in the body in reaction to the presence of a foreign substance, called an antigen; natural antibodies are also present in the blood. They are protective in nature.

antidiuretic hormone (ADH) Hormone secreted by the pituitary gland; its major action is to conserve body water by decreasing urine formation.

antinutrients Substances in foods that can adversely affect nutrient status.

antioxidant A compound that may protect other compounds from the effects of oxygen. The antioxidant itself interferes with oxidative processes.

antipromoters Compounds that block the actions of promoters, agents associated with the development of certain diseases, such as cancer.

apolipoprotein A class of special proteins associated with the formation of lipoproteins. A variety of apolipoproteins have been identified and are involved in the specific functions of the different lipoproteins.

appetite A pleasant desire for food for the purpose of enjoyment that is developed through previous experience; believed to be controlled in humans by an appetite center, or appestat, in the hypothalamus.

arginine An essential amino acid.

arteriosclerosis Hardening of the arteries; *also see* atherosclerosis.

ascorbic acid Vitamin C.

aspartame An artificial sweetener made from amino acids.

aspartates Salts of aspartic acid, an amino acid.

atherosclerosis A specific form of arteriosclerosis characterized by the formation of plaque on the inner layers of the arterial wall.

athletic amenorrhea The cessation of menstruation in athletes, believed to be caused by factors associated with participation in strenuous physical activity.

ATP Adenosine triphosphate, a high-energy phosphate compound found in the body; one of the major forms of energy available for immediate use in the body.

ATPase The enzyme involved in the splitting of ATP and the release of energy.

ATP-PCr system The energy system for fast, powerful muscle contractions; uses ATP as the immediate energy source, the spent ATP being quickly regenerated by breakdown of the PCr. ATP and PCr are high-energy phosphates in the muscle cell.

baking soda A commercial form of sodium bicarbonate.

basal energy expenditure (BEE) The basal metabolic rate (BMR) total energy expenditure over 24 hours.

basal metabolic rate (BMR) The measurement of energy expenditure in the body under resting, postabsorptive conditions, indicative of the energy needed to maintain life under these basal conditions.

Basic Four Food Groups Grouping of foods into four categories that can be used as a means to educate individuals on how to obtain essential nutrients. The four groups are meat, milk, bread-cereal, and fruit-vegetable.

bee pollen A nutritional product containing minute amounts of protein and some vitamins that has been advertised to be possibly ergogenic for some athletes.

behavior modification Relative to weight-control methods, behavioral patterns, or the way one acts, may be modified to help achieve weight loss.

beriberi A deficiency disease attributed to lack of thiamin (vitamin B_1) in the diet.

beta-carotene A precursor for vitamin A found in plants.

beta glucan Gummy form of water-soluble fiber useful in reducing serum cholesterol; oats are a good source.

beta-oxidation Process in the cells whereby 2-carbon units of acetic acid are removed from long-chain fatty acids for conversion to acetyl CoA and oxidation via the Krebs cycle.

bile A fluid secreted by the liver into the intestine that aids in the breakdown process of fats.

bile salts Active salts found in bile; cholesterol is part of their structure.

binge-purge syndrome An eating behavior characterized by excessive hunger leading to gorging, followed by guilt and purging by vomiting. *Also see* bulimia nervosa.

bioavailability In relation to nutrients in food, the amount that may be absorbed into the body.

bioelectrical impedance analysis (BIA) A method to calculate percentage of body fat by measuring electrical resistance due to the water content of the body.

bioengineered foods Foods modified by genetic engineering to produce desirable traits.

biotin A component of the B complex.

bisphosphonates Drugs used to inhibit bone resorption, but not mineralization, to help prevent bone loss and increase bone mineral density; Fosamax is one brand.

blood alcohol content (BAC) The concentration of alcohol in the blood, usually expressed as milligram percent.

blood alcohol level *See* blood alcohol content.

blood glucose Blood sugar; the means by which carbohydrate is carried in the blood; normal range is 70-120 mg/ml.

blood pressure The pressure of the blood in the blood vessels; usually used to refer to arterial blood pressure. *Also see* systolic blood pressure and diastolic blood pressure.

BMI *See* Body Mass Index.

body image The image or impression the individual has of his or her body. A poor body image may lead to personality problems.

Body Mass Index (BMI) An index calculated by a ratio of height to weight, used as a measure of obesity.

body plethysmography A body composition technique using a special chamber to measure air displacement; similar to water displacement theory associated with underwater weighing.

branched-chain amino acids (BCAA) Three essential amino acids (leucine, isoleucine, and valine) that help form muscle tissue.

bread exchange   One bread exchange in the Food Exchange System contains 15 grams of carbohydrate, 3 grams of protein, and 80 Calories.

brown fat   A special form of adipose tissue that is designed to produce heat; small amounts are found in humans in the area of vital organs such as the heart and lungs.

buffer boosting   Term associated with use of sodium bicarbonate as an ergogenic aid to increase the acid-buffering capacity of the blood.

bulimia nervosa   An eating disorder involving a loss of control over the impulse to binge; the binge-purge syndrome.

bulk-up method   A method of weight training designed to increase muscle mass; uses high resistance and moderate volume with many different muscle groups.

caffeine   A stimulant drug found in many food products such as coffee, tea, and cola drinks; stimulates the central nervous system.

calciferol   A synthetic vitamin D.

calcitriol   The hormone form of vitamin D.

calcium   A silver-white metallic element essential to human nutrition.

caloric concept of weight control   The concept that Calories are the basis of weight control. Excess Calories will add body weight while caloric deficiencies will contribute to weight loss.

caloric deficit   A negative caloric balance whereby more Calories are expended than consumed; a weight loss will occur.

Calorie   A Calorie is a measure of heat energy. A small calorie represents the amount of heat needed to raise one gram of water one degree Celsius. A large Calorie (kilocalorie, KC, or C) is 1,000 small calories.

calorimeter   A device used to measure the caloric value of a given food, or heat production of animals or humans.

carbohydrates   A group of compounds containing carbon, hydrogen, and oxygen. Glucose, glycogen, sugar, starches, fiber, cellulose, and the various saccharides are all carbohydrates.

carbohydrate loading   A dietary method used by endurance-type athletes to help increase the carbohydrate (glycogen) levels in their muscles and liver.

carcinogenicity   The potential of a substance to cause cancer.

carnitine   A chemical that facilitates the transfer of fatty acids into the mitochondria for subsequent oxidation.

catabolism   Destructive metabolism whereby complex chemical compounds in the body are degraded to simpler ones.

catalase   An enzyme that helps neutralize free radicals.

cation   A positively charged ion or electrolyte.

cellulite   A name given to the lumpy fat that often appears in the thigh and hip region of women. Cellulite is simply normal fat in small compartments formed by connective tissue, but may contain other compounds that bind water.

cellulose   The fibrous carbohydrate that provides the structural backbone for plants; plant fiber.

Celsius   A thermometer scale that has a freezing point of 0° and a boiling point of 100°; also known as the centigrade scale.

central fatigue   Fatigue caused by suboptimal functioning of neurotransmitters, most likely in the brain.

cerebrospinal fluid (CSF)   The fluid found in the brain and spinal cord.

chloride   A compound of chlorine present in a salt form carrying a negative charge; Cl^-, an anion.

cholecalciferol   The product of irradiation of 7-dehydrocholesterol found in the skin. *Also see* vitamin D_3.

cholesterol   A fat-like pearly substance, an alcohol, found in all animal fat and oils; a main constituent of some body tissues and body compounds.

choline   A substance associated with the B complex that is widely distributed in both plant and animal tissues; involved in carbohydrate, fat, and protein metabolism.

chondroitin   Formed in the body from amino acids and involved in cartilage formation; marked as a dietary supplement.

chromium   A whitish metal essential to human nutrition; it is involved in carbohydrate metabolism via its role with insulin.

chronic fatigue syndrome   Prolonged fatigue (over 6 months) of unknown cause characterized by mental depression and physical fatigue; may be observed in endurance athletes.

chronic-training effect   Physiological changes in the body, brought on by repeated bouts of exercise, that will help make the body more efficient during exercise.

chylomicron   A particle of emulsified fat found in the blood following the digestion and assimilation of fat.

circuit aerobics   A combination of aerobic and weight-training exercises designed to

elicit the specific benefits of each type of exercise.

circuit training   A method of training in which exercises are arranged in a circuit or sequence. May be designed with weight training to help convey an aerobic training effect.

cirrhosis   A degenerative disease of the liver, one cause being excessive consumption of alcohol.

***cis* fatty acids**   The chemical structure of unsaturated fatty acids in which the hydrogen ions are on the same side of the double bond.

Ciwujia   A chinese herb theorized to be ergogenic.

clinical obesity   Obesity determined by a clinical procedure.

Clostridium   A bacteria commonly involved in food poisoning.

cobalamin   The cobalt-containing complex common to all members of the vitamin B_{12} group; often used to designate cyanocobalamin.

cobalt   A gray, hard metal that is a component of vitamin B_{12}.

coenzyme   An activator of an enzyme; many vitamins are coenzymes.

coenzyme Q10   *See* CoQ10.

colon   The large intestine.

complementary proteins   Combining plant foods such as rice and beans so that essential amino acids deficient in one of the foods are provided by the other in order to obtain a balanced intake of essential amino acids.

complete protein   A protein that contains all nine essential amino acids in the proper proportions. Animal protein is complete protein.

complex carbohydrates   A term used to describe foods high in starch, such as bread, cereals, fruits, and vegetables as contrasted to simple carbohydrates such as table sugar.

concentric method   A method of weight training in which the muscle shortens.

conduction   In relation to body temperature, the transfer of heat from one substance to another by direct contact.

convection   In relation to body temperature, the transfer of heat by way of currents in either air or water.

copper   A reddish metallic element essential to human nutrition; it functions with iron in the formation of hemoglobin and the cytochromes.

CoQ10   A coenzyme involved in the electron transport system in the mitochondria.

core temperature The temperature of the deep tissues of the body, usually measured orally or rectally; *also see* shell temperature.

Cori cycle Cycle involving muscle breakdown of glucose to lactate, lactate transport via blood to the liver for reconversion to glucose, and glucose returning to the muscle.

coronary artery disease (CAD) Atherosclerosis in the coronary arteries.

coronary heart disease (CHD) A degenerative disease of the heart caused primarily by arteriosclerosis or atherosclerosis of the coronary vessels of the heart.

coronary occlusion Closure of coronary arteries that may precipitate a heart attack; occlusion may be partial or complete closure.

coronary risk factors Behaviors (smoking) or body properties (cholesterol levels) that may predispose an individual to coronary heart disease.

coronary thrombosis Occlusion (closure) of coronary arteries, usually by a blood clot.

cortisol A hormone secreted by the adrenal cortex with gluconeogenic potential, helping to convert amino acids to glucose.

creatine A nitrogen-containing compound found in the muscles, usually complexed with phosphate to form phosphocreatine.

crossover concept The concept that as exercise intensity increases, at some point carbohydrate rather than fat becomes the predominant fuel for muscle contraction.

cruciferous vegetables Vegetables in the cabbage family, such as broccoli, cauliflower, kale, and all cabbages.

cyanocobalamin Vitamin B_{12}.

cysteine A breakdown product of cystine. It is also a sulfur-containing amino acid.

cystine A sulfur-containing amino acid.

cytochromes Any one of a class of pigment compounds that play an important role in cellular oxidative processes.

Daily Reference Values (DRVs) The DRVs are recommended daily intakes for the macronutrients (carbohydrate, fat, and protein) as well as cholesterol, sodium, and potassium. On a food label, the DRV is based on a 2,000 Calorie diet.

Daily Value (DV) A term used in food labeling; the DV is based on a daily energy intake of 2,000 Calories and for the food labeled, presents the percentage of the RDI and the DRV recommended for healthy Americans. *See* RDI and DRV.

deamination Removal of an amine group, or nitrogen, from an amino acid.

dehydration A reduction of the body water to below the normal level of hydration; water output exceeds water intake.

dehydroepiandrosterone (DHEA) A natural steroid hormone produced endogenously by the adrenal gland. May be marketed as a nutritional sports ergogenic as derived from herbal precursors.

depressant Drugs or agents that will depress or lower the level of bodily functions, particularly central nervous system functioning.

DHAP Dihydroxyacetone and pyruvate, the combination of two by-products of glycolysis.

DHEA *See* dehydroepiandrosterone.

Diabesity Term coined to highlight the relationship between the development of diabetes following the onset of obesity.

diabetes mellitus A disorder of carbohydrate metabolism due to disturbances in production or utilization of insulin; results in high blood glucose levels and loss of sugar in the urine.

diarrhea Frequent passage of a watery fecal discharge due to a gastrointestinal disturbance.

diastolic blood pressure The blood pressure in the arteries when the heart is at rest between beats.

dietary fiber Nondigestible carbohydrates and lignin that are intrinsic and intact in plants.

Dietary Folate Equivalents (DFE) Used in estimating folate requirements, adjusting for the greater degree of absorption of folic acid (free form) compared with folate naturally found in foods. One microgram food folate equals 0.5 to 0.6 folic acid added to foods or as a supplement.

dietary-induced thermogenesis (DIT) The increase in the basal metabolic rate following the ingestion of a meal. Heat production is increased.

Dietary Reference Intakes (DRI) Standards for recommended dietary intakes, consisting of various values. *See also* AI, EAR, RDA, AMDR, and UL.

dietary supplement A food product, added to the total diet, that contains either vitamins, minerals, herbs, botanicals, amino acids, metabolites, constituents, extracts, or combinations of these ingredients.

Dietary Supplement Health and Education Act (DSHEA) Act passed by the United States Congress defining a dietary supplement (*see* dietary supplement); legislation to control advertising and marketing.

2,3-diphosphoglyceride A by-product of carbohydrate metabolism in the red blood cell; helps the hemoglobin unload oxygen to the tissues.

disaccharides Any one of a class of sugars that yield two monosaccharides on hydrolysis; sucrose is the most common.

dispensable amino acids *See* nonessential animo acids.

diuretics A class of agents that stimulate the formation of urine; used as a means to reduce body fluids.

diverticulosis Weak spots in the wall of the large intestine that may bulge out like a weak spot in a tire inner tube. May become infected leading to diverticulitis.

DNA Deoxyribonucleic acid; a complex protein found in chromosomes that is the carrier of genetic information and the basis of heredity.

docasahexanoic acid (DHA) Docasahexanoic acid, an omega-3 fatty acid found in fatty fish.

doping Official term used by WADA and the International Olympic Committee to depict the use of drugs in sports in attempts to enhance performance.

doubly-labeled water technique A technique using labeled water to study energy metabolism.

dual energy X-ray absorptiometry (DEXA, DXA) A computerized X-ray technique at two energy levels to image body fat, lean tissues, and bone mineral content.

dumping syndrome Movement of fluid from the blood to the intestines by osmosis. May occur when a concentrated sugar solution is consumed in large quantities, causing symptoms such as weakness and gastrointestinal distress.

duration concept One of the major concepts of aerobic exercise; duration refers to the amount of time spent exercising during each session.

EAH *See* exercise-associated hyponatremia.

eating disorder A psychological disorder centering on the avoidance, excessive consumption, or purging of food, such as anorexia nervosa and bulimia nervosa.

eccentric method A weight-training method in which the muscle undergoes a lengthening contraction.

eicosanoids Derivatives of fatty acid oxidation in the body, including prostaglandins, thromboxanes, and leukotrienes.

eicosapentaenoic acid (EPA) An omega-3 fatty acid found in fatty fish.

electrolyte A substance that, when in a solution, conducts an electric current.

electrolyte solution A solution that contains ions and can conduct electricity; often the ions of salts such as sodium and chloride are called electrolytes; *also see* ions.

electron transfer system A highly structured array of chemical compounds in the cell that transport electrons and harness energy for later use.

element Relative to chemistry, a substance that cannot be subdivided into substances different from itself; many elements are essential to human life.

endocrine system The body system consisting of glands that secrete hormones, which have a wide variety of effects throughout the body.

energy The ability to do work; energy exists in various forms, notably mechanical, heat, and chemical in the human body.

English system A measurement system based upon the foot, pound, quart, and other nonmetric units; *also see* metric system.

enzyme A complex protein in the body that serves as a catalyst, facilitating reactions between various substances without being changed itself.

Ephedra Term used for the plant Ephedra sinica, a source of ephedrine.

ephedrine A stimulant with somewhat weaker effects than amphetamine; found in some commercial dietary supplements; also known as ephedra.

epidemiological research A study of certain populations to determine the relationship of various risk factors to epidemic diseases or health problems.

epinephrine A hormone secreted by the adrenal medulla that stimulates numerous body processes to enhance energy production, particularly during intense exercise.

epithelial cells The layer of cells that covers the outside and inside surfaces of the body, including the skin and the lining of the gastrointestinal system.

ergogenic aids Work-enhancing agents that are used in attempts to increase athletic or physical performance capacity.

ergogenic effect The physiological or psychological effect that an ergogenic substance is designed to produce.

ergolytic effect An agent or substance that may lead to decreases in work productivity or physical performance. *See also* ergogenic effect.

Escherichia A bacteria commonly involved in food poisoning.

essential amino acids Those amino acids that must be obtained in the diet and cannot

be synthesized in the body. Also known as indispensable amino acids.

essential fat Fat in the body that is an essential part of the tissues, such as cell membrane structure, nerve coverings, and the brain; *also see* storage fat.

essential fatty acid Those unsaturated fatty acids that may not be synthesized in the body and must be obtained in the diet, e.g., linoleic fatty acid.

essential nutrients Those nutrients found to be essential to human life and optimal functioning.

ester Compound formed from the combination of an organic acid and an alcohol.

Estimated Average Requirement (EAR) Nutrient intake value estimated to meet the requirements of half the healthy individuals in a group.

Estimated Energy Requirement (EER) The daily dietary intake predicted to maintain energy balance for an individual of a defined age, gender, height, weight, and level of physical activity consistent with good health.

Estimated Minimal Requirement (EMR) Part of the RDA pertaining to the minimal daily requirement for sodium, chloride, and potassium.

Estimated Safe and Adequate Daily Dietary Intakes (ESADDI) Part of the previous RDA. Daily allowances for selected nutrients that are based upon available scientific evidence to be safe and adequate to meet human needs.

ethanol Alcohol; ethyl alcohol.

ethyl alcohol Alcohol; ethanol.

evaporation The conversion of a liquid to a vapor, which consumes energy; evaporation of sweat cools the body by using body heat as the energy source.

exercise A form of structured physical activity generally designed to enhance physical fitness; exercise usually refers to strenuous physical activity.

exercise-associated hyponatrimia (EAH) Term associated with the decline in serum sodium levels during prolonged exercise with excessive fluid intake and/or sodium losses; see also water intoxication.

exercise frequency In an aerobic exercise program, the number of times per week that an individual exercises.

exercise intensity The tempo, speed, or resistance of an exercise. Intensity can be increased by working faster, doing more work in a given amount of time.

exercise metabolic rate (EMR) An increased metabolic rate due to the need for increased energy production; during exercise, the resting energy expenditure (REE) may be increased more than twenty-fold.

exercise sequence *See* principle of exercise sequence.

exercise stimulus The means whereby one elicits a physiological response; running, for example, can be the stimulus to increase the heart rate and other physiological functions.

exercisenomics General term regarding the effects of exercise on genetic expression and resultant metabolic adaptations.

exertional heat stroke Heat stroke that is precipitated by exercise in a warm or hot environment.

experimental research Study that manipulates an independent variable (cause) to observe the outcome on a dependent variable (effect).

extracellular water Body water that is located outside the cells; often subdivided into the intravascular water and the intercellular, or interstitial, water.

facilitated diffusion Process whereby glucose combines with a special protein carrier molecule at the membrane surface, facilitating glucose transport into the cell; insulin promotes facilitated diffusion in some cells.

faddism Relative to nutrition, the use of dietary fads based upon theoretical principles that may or may not be valid; usually used in a negative sense, as in quackery.

fasting Starvation; abstinence from eating that may be partial or complete.

fast-twitch fibers Muscle fibers characterized by high contractile speed.

fat exchange A fat exchange in the Food Exchange System contains 5 grams of fat and 45 Calories.

fat-free mass The remaining mass of the human body following the extraction of all fat.

fatigue A generalized or specific feeling of tiredness that may have a multitude of causes; may be mental or physical.

fat loading A term to describe practices used to maximize the use of fats as an energy source during exercise, particularly a low-carbohydrate, high-fat diet.

fat patterning The deposition of fat in specific areas of the human body, such as the stomach, thighs, or hips. Genetics plays an important role in fat patterning.

fats Triglycerides; a combination, or ester, of three fatty acids and glycerol.

fat substitutes   Various substances used as substitutes for fats in food products; two popular brands are Simplesse and Olestra.

fatty acids   Any one of a number of aliphatic acids containing only carbon, oxygen, and hydrogen; they may be saturated or unsaturated.

female athlete triad   The triad of disordered eating, amenorrhea, and osteoporosis sometimes seen in female athletes involved in sports where excess body weight may be detrimental to performance.

female-type obesity   *See* gynoid-type obesity.

ferritin   The form in which iron is stored in the tissues.

fetal alcohol effects (FAE)   Symptoms noted in children born to women who consumed alcohol during pregnancy; not as severe as fetal alcohol syndrome.

fetal alcohol syndrome (FAS)   The cluster of physical and mental symptoms seen in the child of a mother who consumes excessive alcohol during pregnancy.

fiber   In general, the indigestible carbohydrate in plants that forms the structural network; *also see* cellulose.

First Law of Thermodynamics   The law that energy cannot be created or destroyed; energy can be converted from one form to another.

flatulence   Gas or air in the gastrointestinal tract, particularly the intestines.

fluoride   A salt of hydrofluoric acid; a compound of fluorine that may be helpful in the prevention of tooth decay.

folacin   Collective term for various forms of folic acid.

folate   Salt of folic acid; form found in foods.

folic acid   A water-soluble vitamin that appears to be essential in preventing certain types of anemia.

food additives   *See* additives.

food allergy   An adverse immune response to an otherwise harmless food. *Also see* food hypersensitivity.

food cultism   Treating a particular food as if it possesses special properties, such as prevention or treatment of disease or improvement of athletic performance, usually without scientific justification.

Food and Drug Administration (FDA)   Federal agency tasked with the responsibilities to monitor safety of foods and drugs sold in the United States.

Food Exchange System   The system developed by the American Dietetic Association and other health groups that categorizes foods by content of carbohydrate, fat, protein, and Calories. Used as a basis for diet planning.

food hypersensitivity   Some individuals may develop clinical symptoms, such as migraine headaches, gastrointestinal distress, or hives and itching when certain foods are eaten.

food intolerance   A general term for any adverse reaction to a food or food component not involving the immune system; an example is lactose intolerance.

food poisoning   Foodborne illness caused by bacteria such as Salmonella, Escherichia, Staphylococcus, and Clostridium.

foot-pound   A unit of work whereby the weight of 1 pound is moved through a distance of 1 foot.

Fosamax   A commercial bisphosphonate product.

free fatty acids (FFA)   Acids formed by the hydrolysis of triglycerides.

free radicals   An atom or compound in which there is an unpaired electron. Thought to cause cellular damage.

fructose   A monosaccharide known as levulose or fruit sugar; found in all sweet fruits.

fruit exchange   One fruit exchange in the Food Exchange System contains 15 grams of carbohydrate and 60 Calories.

fruitarian   A type of vegetarian who subsides solely on fruits, fruit products, and nuts.

fTRP:BCAA ratio   The ratio of free tryptophan to branched-chain amino acids; a high ratio is theorized to elicit fatigue in prolonged endurance events.

functional fiber   Isolated, nondigestible carbohydrates that have beneficial effects in humans.

functional foods   Food products containing nutrients designed to provide health benefits beyond basic nutrition.

galactose   A monosaccharide formed when lactose is hydrolyzed into glucose and galactose.

gastric emptying   The rate at which substances, particularly fluids, empty from the stomach; high gastric emptying rates are advisable for sports drinks.

generally recognized as safe (GRAS)   A classification for food additives indicating that they most likely are not harmful for human consumption.

ghrelin   Hormone released by an empty stomach to stimulate the appetite.

ginseng   A general term for a variety of natural chemical plant extracts derived from the family Araliaceae; extract contains ginsenosides and other chemicals that may influence human physiology.

glucagon   A hormone secreted by the pancreas; basically it exerts actions just the opposite of insulin, i.e., it responds to hypoglycemia and helps to increase blood sugar levels.

glucarate   A compound found in cruciferous vegetables that is thought to block the actions of cancer-causing agents.

glucogenic amino acids   Amino acids that may undergo deamination and be converted into glucose through the process of gluconeogenesis.

gluconeogenesis   The formation of carbohydrates from molecules that are not themselves carbohydrate, such as amino acids and the glycerol from fat.

glucosamine   Formed in the body from amino acids and involved in cartilage formation; marketed as a dietary supplement.

glucose   A monosaccharide; a thick, sweet, syrupy liquid.

glucose-alanine cycle   The cycle in which alanine is released from the muscle and is converted to glucose in the liver.

glucose-electrolyte solutions   Solutions designed to replace sweat losses; contain varying proportions of water, glucose, sodium, potassium, chloride, and other electrolytes.

glucose polymer   A combination of several glucose molecules into a more complex carbohydrate.

glucose polymer solutions   Fluid replacement beverages containing primarily water and glucose polymers.

glucostatic theory   The theory that hunger and satiety are controlled by the glucose level in the blood; the receptors that respond to the blood glucose level are in the hypothalamus.

GLUT-4   Receptors in cell membranes that transport glucose from the blood to the cell interior.

glutathione peroxidase   An enzyme that helps neutralize free radicals.

glycemic index   An index expressing the effects of various foods on the rate and amount of increase in blood glucose levels.

Glycerate   A commercial product containing glycerol; marketed to athletes.

glycerin   *See* glycerol.

glycerol   Glycerin, a clear syrupy liquid; an alcohol that combines with fatty acids to form triglycerides.

glycogen   A polysaccharide that is the chief storage form of carbohydrate in animals; it is stored primarily in the liver and muscles.

glycogen-sparing effect   The theory that certain dietary techniques, such as the use of caffeine, may facilitate the oxidation of fatty acids for energy and thus spare the utilization of glycogen.

glycolysis   The degradation of sugars into smaller compounds; the main quantitative anaerobic energy process in the muscle tissue.

gout   The deposit of uric acid by-products in and about the joints contributing to inflammation and pain; usually occurs in the knee or foot.

gram calorie   A small calorie; *see* Calorie.

gums   A form of water-soluble dietary fiber found in plants.

gynoid-type obesity   Female-type obesity; body fat is deposited primarily about the hips and thighs. *Also see* android-type obesity.

HDL   High-density lipoprotein; a protein-lipid complex in the blood that facilitates the transport of triglycerides, cholesterol, and phospholipids. *Also see* HDL cholesterol.

HDL-cholesterol   High-density lipoprotein cholesterol; one mechanism whereby cholesterol is transported in the blood. High HDL levels are somewhat protective against CHD.

health-related fitness   Those components of physical fitness whose improvement have health benefits, such as cardiovascular fitness, body composition, flexibility, and muscular strength and endurance.

Healthy Eating Index (HEI)   USDA computerized dietary analysis to assess personal diets to provide an overall rating as related to health.

heat-balance equation   Heat balance is dependent upon the interrelationships of metabolic heat production and loss or gain of heat by radiation, convection, conduction, and evaporation.

heat cramps   Painful muscular cramps or tetany following prolonged exercise in the heat without water or salt replacement.

heat exhaustion   Weakness or dizziness from overexertion in a hot environment.

heat index   The apparent temperature determined by combining air temperature and relative humidity.

heat stroke   Elevated body temperature of 105.8° F or greater caused by exposure to excessive heat gains or production and diminished heat loss.

heat syncope   Fainting caused by excessive heat exposure.

hematuria   Blood or red blood cells in the urine.

heme iron   The iron in the diet associated with hemoglobin in animal meats.

hemicellulose   A form of dietary fiber found in plants. Differs from cellulose in that it may be hydrolyzed by dilute acids outside of the body. Not hydrolyzed in the body.

hemochromatosis   Presence of excessive iron in the body resulting in an enlarged liver and bronze pigmentation of the skin.

hemoglobin   The protein-iron pigment in the red blood cells that transports oxygen.

hemolysis   A rupturing of red blood cells with a release of hemoglobin into the plasma.

hepatitis   An inflammatory condition of the liver.

heterocyclic amines (HCA)   Carcinogens formed in foods that have been charred by excess grilling or broiling.

hidden fat   In foods, the fat that is not readily apparent, such as the high fat content of cheese.

high blood pressure   *See* hypertension.

high-density lipoprotein   *See* HDL.

high-fructose corn syrup   A common high-Calorie sweetener used as a food additive; derived from the partial hydrolysis of corn starch.

histidine   An essential amino acid.

HMB   Beta-hydroxy-beta-methylbutyrate, a metabolic by-product of the amino acid leucine, alleged to retard the breakdown of muscle protein during strenuous exercise.

homeostasis   A term used to describe a condition of normalcy in the internal body environment.

homocysteine   A metabolic by-product of amino acid metabolism; elevated blood levels are associated with increased risk of vascular diseases.

hormone   A chemical substance produced by specific body cells, secreted into the blood and then acting on specific target tissues.

hormone sensitive lipase (HSL)   An enzyme that catalyzes triglycerides into free fatty acids and glycerol.

HR max   The normal maximal heart rate of an individual during exercise.

HR reserve   The mathematical difference, or reserve, between the resting HR and maximal HR. A percentage of this reserve may be added to the resting HR to determine exercise intensity.

human growth hormone (HGH)   A hormone released by the pituitary gland that regulates growth; also involved in fatty acid metabolism; rHGH is a genetically engineered form.

hunger   A basic physiological desire to eat that is normally caused by a lack of food; may be accompanied by stomach contractions.

hunger center   A collection of nerve cells in the hypothalamus that is involved in the control of feeding reflexes.

hydrodensitometry   Another term for the underwater weighing technique.

hydrogenated fats   Fats to which hydrogen has been added, usually causing them to be saturated.

hydrolysis   A mechanism for splitting substances into smaller compounds by the addition of water; enzyme action.

hypercholesteremia   Elevated blood cholesterol levels.

hyperglycemia   Elevated blood glucose levels.

hyperhydration   The practice of increasing the body-water stores by fluid consumption prior to an athletic event; a state of increased water content in the body.

hyperkalemia   An increased concentration of potassium in the blood.

hyperlipidemia   Elevated blood lipid levels.

hyperplasia   The formation of new body cells.

hypertension   A condition with various causes whereby the blood pressure is higher than normal.

hyperthermia   Unusually high body temperature; fever.

hypertonic   Relative to osmotic pressure, a solution that has a greater concentration of solute or salts, hence higher osmotic pressure, in comparison to another solution.

hypertriglyceridemia   Elevated blood levels of triglycerides.

hypertrophy   Excessive growth of a cell or organ; in pathology, an abnormal growth.

hypervitaminosis   A pathological condition due to an excessive vitamin intake, particularly the fat-soluble vitamins A and D.

hypoglycemia   A low blood sugar level.

hypohydration   A state of decreased water content in the body caused by dehydration.

hypokalemia   A decreased concentration of potassium in the blood.

hyponatremia   A decreased concentration of sodium in the blood.

hypothalamus   A part of the brain involved in the control of involuntary activity in the body; contains many centers for neural control such as temperature, hunger, appetite, and thirst.

hypothermia Unusually low body temperature.

hypotonic Having an osmotic pressure lower than that of the solution to which it is compared.

IGF *See* insulin-like growth factor.

incomplete protein Protein food that does not possess the proper amount of essential amino acids; characteristic of plant foods in general.

Index of Nutritional Quality (INQ) A mathematical means of determining the quality of any given food relative to its content of a specific nutrient.

indicator nutrients These eight nutrients, if provided in adequate supply through a varied diet, should provide adequate amounts of the other essential nutrients. The eight are protein, vitamin A, thiamin, riboflavin, niacin, vitamin C, calcium, and iron.

indispensable amino acids *See* essential amino acids.

indoles Phytochemicals believed to help prevent various diseases.

infrared interactance Use of infrared technology to estimate body composition.

initial fitness level The physical fitness level of an individual prior to the onset of a physical conditioning program.

in-line skating An exercise-skating technique with specially-designed shoes for use on sidewalks and similar surfaces.

inosine A nucleoside of the purine family that serves as a base for the formation of a variety of compounds in the body; theorized to be ergogenic.

inositol A member of the B complex, although its role in human nutrition has not been established; not classified as a vitamin.

INQ *See* Index of Nutritional Quality.

insensible perspiration Perspiration on the skin not detectable by ordinary senses.

insoluble dietary fiber Dietary fiber that is not soluble in water, such as cellulose. *Also see* soluble dietary fiber.

insulin A hormone secreted by the pancreas involved in carbohydrate metabolism.

Insulin-like growth factor (IGF) A growth factor found in the blood which resembles insulin; produced in response to growth hormone release.

insulin response Blood insulin levels rise following the ingestion of sugar and the resultant hyperglycemia; the insulin causes the sugar to be taken up by the muscles and fat cells, possibly creating a reactive hypoglycemia.

intercellular water Body water found between the cells; also known as interstitial water.

intermittent high-intensity exercise Short-term bouts of high-intensity exercise interspersed with short periods of recovery.

International Unit (IU) International Unit; a method of expressing the quantity of some substance, such as vitamins, which is an internationally developed and accepted standard.

International Unit System (SI) *Le Systeme International d'Unite,* or the International System of Units; a system of measurement based upon the metric system.

interstitial water *See* intercellular water.

interval training A method of physical training in which periods of activity are interspersed with periods of rest.

intestinal absorption The rate at which substances, particularly fluids and nutrients, are absorbed into the body; a fast rate of intestinal absorption is a desirable characteristic of sports drinks.

intracellular water Body water that is found within the cells.

intravascular water Body water found in the vascular system, or blood vessels.

involuntary dehydration Unintentional loss of body fluids during exercise under warm or hot environmental conditions.

IOC International Olympic Committee.

iodine A nonmetallic element that is necessary for the proper development and functioning of the thyroid gland.

ions Particles with an electrical charge; anions are negative and cations are positive.

iron A metallic element essential for the development of several chemical compounds in the body, notably hemoglobin.

iron-deficiency anemia Anemia caused by an inadequate intake or absorption of iron, resulting in impaired hemoglobin formation.

iron deficiency without anemia A condition in which the hemoglobin levels are normal but several indices of iron status in the body are below normal levels.

irradiation Process whereby foods are subjected to ionizing radiation to kill bacteria.

ischemia Lack of blood supply.

isoflavones Phytochemicals believed to help prevent various diseases.

isokinetic Literally meaning "same speed"; in weight training an isokinetic machine is used to control the speed of muscle contraction.

isoleucine An essential amino acid.

isometric Literally meaning "same length"; in weight training the resistance is set so that the muscle will not shorten.

isotonic Literally meaning "equal tension or pressure"; in weight training the resistance is set so there is supposed to be equal tension in the muscle through a range of motion, but this is rarely achieved owing to movement of body parts. Isotonic also means equal osmotic pressures between two solutions.

jogging A term used to designate slow running; although the distinction between running and jogging is relative to the individual involved, a common value used for jogging is a 9-minute mile or slower.

joule A measure of work in the metric system; a newton of force applied through a distance of one meter.

ketogenesis The formation of ketones in the body from other substances, such as fats and proteins.

ketogenic amino acids Amino acids that may be deaminated, converted into ketones and eventually into fat.

ketones An organic compound containing a carbonyl group; ketone acids in the body, such as acetone, are the end products of fat metabolism.

ketosis The accumulation of excess ketones in the blood; since ketones are acids, acidosis occurs.

key-nutrient concept The concept that if certain key nutrients are adequately supplied by the diet, the other essential nutrients will also be present in adequate amounts. *Also see* indicator nutrients.

kidney stones Compounds in the pelvis of the kidney formed from various salts such as carbonates, oxalates, and phosphates.

kilocalorie (KC) A large Calorie; *see* Calorie.

kilogram A unit of mass in the metric system; in ordinary terms, 1 kilogram is the equivalent of 2.2 pounds.

kilogram-meter (KGM) A measure of work in the metric system whereby 1 kilogram of weight is moved through a distance of 1 meter; however, the joule is the recommended unit to express work.

kilojoule One thousand joules; one kilojoule (kJ) is approximately 0.25 kilocalorie.

Krebs cycle The main oxidative reaction sequence in the body that generates ATP; also known as the citric acid or tricarboxylic acid cycle.

lactic acid The anaerobic end product of glycolysis; it has been implicated as a causative factor in the etiology of fatigue.

lactic acid system The energy system that produces ATP anaerobically by the breakdown of glycogen to lactic acid; used primarily in events of maximal effort for one to two minutes.

lactose A white crystalline disaccharide that yields glucose and galactose upon hydrolysis; also known as milk sugar.

lactose intolerance Gastrointestinal disturbances due to an intolerance to lactose in milk; caused by deficiency of lactase, an enzyme that digests lactose.

lactovegetarian A vegetarian who includes milk products in the diet as a form of high-quality protein.

LDL Low-density lipoprotein; a protein-lipid complex in the blood that facilitates the transport of triglycerides, cholesterol, and phospholipids. *Also see* LDL-cholesterol.

LDL-cholesterol Low-density lipoprotein cholesterol; a mechanism whereby cholesterol is transported in the blood. High blood levels are associated with increased incidence of CHD.

lean body mass The body weight minus the body fat, composed primarily of muscle, bone, and other nonfat tissue.

lecithin A fatty substance of a class known as phospholipids; said to have the therapeutic properties of phosphorous.

legume The fruit or pod of vegetables including soybeans, kidney beans, lima beans, garden peas, black-eyed peas, and lentils; high in protein.

leptin Regulatory hormone produced by fat cells; when released into the circulation, it influences the hypothalamus to control appetite.

leucine An essential amino acid.

leukotrienes Eicosanoids that possess hormone-like activity in numerous cells in the body.

levulose Fructose.

lignin A noncarbohydrate form of dietary fiber.

limiting amino acid An amino acid deficient in a specific plant food, making it an incomplete protein; methionine is a limiting amino acid in legumes while lysine is deficient in grain products.

linoleic acid An essential fatty acid.

lipase An enzyme that catabolizes fats into fatty acids and glycerol.

lipids A class of fats or fat-like substances characterized by their insolubility in water and solubility in fat solvents; triglycerides, fatty acids, phospholipids, and cholesterol are important lipids in the body.

lipoic acid A coenzyme that functions in oxidative decarboxylation, or removal of carbon dioxide from a compound.

lipoprotein A combination of lipid and protein possessing the general properties of proteins. Practically all the lipids of the plasma are present in this form.

lipoprotein (a) Serum lipid factor very similar to the LDL, being in the upper LDL density range and containing apolipoprotein (a); high levels are associated with increased risk for CHD.

lipoprotein lipase An enzyme involved in the metabolism of lipoproteins.

lipostatic theory The theory that hunger and satiety are controlled by the lipid level in the blood.

liquid meals Food in a liquid form designed to provide a balanced intake of essential nutrients.

liquid-protein diets Protein in a liquid form; a common form consists of protein predigested into simple amino acids.

liver glycogen The major storage form of carbohydrate in the liver.

long-chain fatty acids (LCFA) Fatty acids containing chains with 12 or more carbons.

long-haul concept Relative to weight control, the idea that weight loss via exercise should be gradual, and one should not expect to lose large amounts of weight in a short time.

L-tryptophan One form of tryptophan. L is for levo (left), or the direction in which polarized light is rotated when various organic compounds are analyzed.

lycopene A carotenoid that serves as an antioxidant.

lysine An essential amino acid.

macrominerals Those minerals essential to human nutrition with an RDA in excess of 100 mg/day: calcium, magnesium, phosphorous, sodium, potassium, chloride.

macronutrients Dietary nutrients needed by the body in daily amounts greater than a few grams, such as carbohydrate, fat, protein, and water.

magnesium A white metallic mineral element essential in human nutrition.

magnetic resonance imaging (MRI) Magnetic-field and radio-frequency waves used to image body tissues; useful for imaging visceral fat.

ma huang A Chinese plant extract theorized to be ergogenic; contains ephedrine, a stimulant.

major minerals *See* macrominerals.

male-type obesity *See* android-type obesity.

malnutrition Poor nutrition that may be due to inadequate amounts of essential nutrients. Too many Calories leading to obesity is also a form of malnutrition. *Also see* subclinical malnutrition.

maltodextrin A glucose polymer that exerts lesser osmotic effects compared with glucose; used in a variety of sports drinks as the source of carbohydrate.

maltose A white crystalline disaccharide that yields two molecules of glucose upon hydrolysis.

manganese A metallic element essential in human nutrition.

maximal heart rate *See* HR max.

maximal heart rate reserve The difference between the maximal HR and resting HR. A percentage of this reserve, usually 60-90 percent, is added to the resting HR to get the target HR for aerobics training programs.

maximal oxygen uptake *See* VO$_2$ max.

meat exchange One very lean meat exchange in the Food Exchange System contains 0-1 gram of fat, 7 grams of protein, and 35 Calories; a lean meat exchange contains 3 grams of fat, 7 grams of protein and 55 Calories; a medium-fat meat exchange has an additional 2 grams of fat and totals 75 Calories; a high-fat exchange has 5 additional grams of fat and totals 100 Calories.

Mediterranean Food Guide Pyramid A food group approach to healthful nutrition that includes basic food groups, but also lists olive oil and wine as components of the diet.

medium-chain fatty acids (MCFA) Fatty acids containing chains with 6-12 carbons.

medium-chain triglycerides (MCTs) Triglycerides containing fatty acids with carbon chain lengths of 6-12 carbons.

megadose An excessive amount of a substance in comparison to a normal dose of RDA; usually used to refer to vitamins.

menoquinone The animal form of vitamin K.

meta-analysis A statistical technique to summarize the findings of numerous studies in an attempt to provide a quantitatively based conclusion.

metabolic aftereffects of exercise The theory that the aftereffects of exercise will cause the metabolic rate to be elevated for a time, thus expending Calories and contributing to weight loss.

metabolic rate The energy expended to maintain all physical and chemical changes occurring in the body.

metabolic syndrome The syndrome of symptoms often seen with android-type obesity, particularly hyperinsulinemia, hypertriglyceridemia, and hypertension.

metabolic water The water that is a by-product of the oxidation of carbohydrate, fat, and protein in the body.

metabolism The sum total of all physical and chemical processes occurring in the body.

metalloenzyme An enzyme that needs a mineral component, such as zinc, in order to function effectively.

methionine An essential amino acid.

methylmercury An industrial waste product dumped in the seas that may accumulate in large fish; may lead to subsequent nerve damage in children or pregnant females who eat contaminated fish.

metric system A method of measurement based upon units of ten.

MET A measurement unit of energy expenditure; one MET equals approximately 3.5 ml O_2/kg body weight/minute.

microgram One millionth of a gram (µg).

micronutrients Dietary nutrients needed by the body in daily amounts less than a few grams, such as vitamins and minerals.

milk exchange One skim milk exchange in the Food Exchange System contains 12 grams of carbohydrate, 8 grams of protein, a trace of fat, and 90 Calories. A low-fat exchange contains 120 Calories whereas whole milk has 150 Calories.

milligram One thousandth of a gram.

millimole One thousandth of a mole.

mineral An inorganic element occurring in nature.

mitochondria Structures within the cells that serve as the location for the aerobic production of ATP.

mole One mole is the gram molecular weight of a compound, which is the quantity of a substance that equals its molecular weight.

molybdenum A hard, heavy, silvery-white metallic element.

monosaccharides Simple sugars (glucose, fructose, and galactose) that cannot be broken down by hydrolysis.

monounsaturated fatty acids (MUFA) Fatty acids that have a single double bond.

morbid obesity Severe obesity in which the incidence of life-threatening diseases is increased significantly.

MPF factor Muscle protein factor; an unknown property of meat, fish, and poultry that facilitates the absorption of nonheme iron found in plant foods.

muscle dysmorphia *See* Adonis complex.

muscle glycogen The form in which carbohydrate is stored in the muscle.

muscle hypertrophy An increase in the size of the muscle.

myocardial infarction Death of heart tissue following cessation of blood flow; may be caused by coronary occlusion.

myoglobin An iron-containing compound, similar to hemoglobin, found in the muscle tissues; it binds oxygen in the muscle cells.

MyPyramid The graphic and program representing the healthful food guidelines presented by the United States Department of Agriculture.

narcotic Any agent that produces insensibility to pain.

National Weight Control Registry A registry of individuals who have lost at least 30 pounds and have kept if off for a year.

Nautilus A brand of exercise equipment designed for strength-training programs; uses a principle to help provide optimal resistance throughout the full range of motion.

NCAA National Collegiate Athletic Association.

negative caloric balance A condition whereby the caloric output exceeds the caloric intake, thus contributing to a weight loss.

negative nitrogen balance A condition in which dietary protein is insufficient to meet the nitrogen needs of the body. More nitrogen is excreted than is retained in the body.

net protein utilization (NPU) A technique used to assess protein quality.

neural tube defects (NTD) Birth defects involving incomplete formation of the neural tube in the spinal column of newborn children; may lead to paralysis; may be prevented by adequate folate intake.

neuropeptide Y (NPY) Neuropeptide produced in the hypothalamus; a potent appetite stimulant.

neutron activation analysis A sophisticated, noninvasive method of analyzing body structure and function.

newton A unit of force that will accelerate 1 kilogram of mass 1 meter per second per second.

niacin Nicotinamide; nicotinic acid; part of the B complex and an important part of several coenzymes involved in aerobic energy processes in the cells.

niacin equivalent A unit of measure of niacin activity in a food related to both the amount of niacin present and that obtainable from tryptophan; about 60 mg tryptophan can be converted to 1 mg niacin.

nickel A silvery-white metallic element.

nicotinamide An amide of nicotinic acid; niacin.

nicotinic acid Niacin.

nitrogen A colorless, tasteless, odorless gas comprising about 80 percent of the atmospheric gas; an essential component of protein that is formed in plants during their developmental process.

nitrogen balance A dietary state in which the input and output of nitrogen is balanced so that the body neither gains nor loses protein tissue.

nonessential amino acids Amino acids that may be formed in the body and thus need not be obtained in the diet; also known as dispensable amino acids. *See* essential amino acids.

nonessential nutrient A nutrient that may be formed in the body from excess amounts of other nutrients.

nonexercise activity thermogenesis (NEAT) Thermogenesis, or heat production by the body, that accompanies physical activity other than volitional exercise.

nonheme iron Iron that is found in plant foods; *see* heme iron.

nonprotein nitrogen Nitrogen in the body and foods that is associated with nonprotein compounds.

normohydration The state of normal hydration, or normal body-water levels, as compared with hypohydration and hyperhydration.

nutraceutical A nutrient that may function as a pharmaceutical when taken in certain quantities.

nutrient Substances found in food that provide energy, promote growth and repair of tissues, and regulate metabolism.

nutrient density A concept related to the degree of concentration of nutrients in a given food; *also see* the related concept INQ.

nutrigenomics General term regarding the effects of nutrition on genetic expression and resultant metabolic adaptions.

nutrition The study of foods and nutrients and their effect on health, growth, and development of the individual.

nutritional labeling A listing of selected key nutrients and Calories on the label of commercially prepared food products.

obesity An excessive accumulation of body fat; usually reserved for those individuals who are 20-30 percent or more above the average weight for their size.

octacosanol A solid white alcohol found in wheat germ oil.

odds ratio (OR) A probability estimate; OR of 1.0 is normal.

Olestra A commercially produced substitute for dietary fat.

oligomenorrhea Intermittent periods of amenorrhea.

omega-3 fatty acids Polyunsaturated fatty acids that have a double bond between the third and fourth carbon from the terminal, or omega, carbon. EPA and DHA found in fish oils are theorized to prevent coronary heart disease.

onset of blood lactic acid (OBLA) The intensity level of exercise at which the blood lactate begins to accumulate rapidly.

oral contraceptives Birth control pills used to prevent conception.

oral rehydration therapy (ORT) Fluids balanced in nutrients that help restore normal hydration levels in the body and prevent excessive dehydration.

organic foods Foods that are stated to be grown without the use of man-made chemicals such as pesticides and artificial fertilizers.

orlistat A prescription drug for weight loss that blocks the digestion of dietary fat.

osmolality Osmotic concentration determined by the ionic concentration of the dissolved substance per unit of solvent.

osmoreceptors Receptors in the body that react to changes in the osmotic pressure of the blood.

osmotic pressure A pressure that produces a diffusion between solutions that have different concentrations.

osteomalacia A disease characterized by softening of the bones, leading to brittleness and increased deformity; caused by a deficiency of vitamin D.

osteoporosis Increased porosity or softening of the bone.

overload principle *See* principle of overload.

overtraining syndrome Symptoms associated with excessive training, such as tiredness, sleeplessness, and elevated heart rate.

overweight Body weight greater than that which is considered normal; *also see* obesity.

ovolactovegetarian A vegetarian who also consumes eggs and milk products as a source of high-quality animal protein.

ovovegetarian A vegetarian who includes eggs in the diet to help obtain adequate amounts of protein.

oxalates Salts of oxalic acid, which are found in green leafy vegetables such as spinach and beet greens.

oxidized LDL An oxidized form of low-density lipoprotein that has increased atherogenic potential.

oxygen consumption The total amount of oxygen utilized in the body for the production of energy; it is directly related to the metabolic rate.

oxygen system The energy system that produces ATP via the oxidation of various foodstuffs, primarily fats and carbohydrates.

paidotribe Individuals who served as personal trainers in ancient Greece to advise athletes on proper diet and exercise training programs.

pangamic acid A term often associated with "vitamin B_{15}," the essentiality of which has not been established; often contains calcium gluconate and dimethylglycine.

pantothenic acid A vitamin of the B complex.

para-aminobenzoic acid (PABA) Although not a vitamin, often grouped with the B complex.

partially hydrogenated fats Polyunsaturated fats that are not fully saturated with hydrogen through a hydrogenation process; *also see* trans fatty acids.

peak bone mass The concept of maximizing the amount of bone mineral content during the formative years of childhood and young adulthood.

pectin A form of soluble dietary fiber found in some fruits.

pellagra A deficiency disease caused by inadequate amounts of niacin in the diet.

pentose A simple sugar containing five carbons instead of six as in glucose.

peptides Small compounds formed by the union of two or more amino acids; known also as dipeptides, tripeptides, etc., depending upon the number of amino acids combined.

perceptual-motor activities Physical activities characterized by the perception of a given stimulus and culminating in an appropriate motor, or movement, response.

peripheral vascular disease Atherosclerosis or blockage of the peripheral arteries.

pernicious anemia A severe progressive form of anemia that may be fatal if not treated with vitamin B_{12}. Usually caused by inability to absorb B_{12}, not a dietary deficiency of B_{12}.

pescovegetarian A vegetarian who eats fish, but not poultry.

pesticides Poisons used to destroy pests of various types, including plants and animals.

pH The abbreviation used to express the level of acidity of a solution; a low pH represents high acidity.

phenylalanine An essential amino acid.

phenylketonuria (PKU) Congenital lack of an enzyme to metabolize phenylalanine, an essential amino acid. May lead to mental retardation if not detected early in life.

phosphagens Compounds such as ATP and phosphocreatine that serve as a source of high energy in the body cells.

phosphates Salts of phosphoric acid, purported to possess ergogenic qualities.

phosphocreatine (PCr) A high-energy phosphate compound found in the body cells; part of the ATP-PCr energy system.

phospholipids Lipids containing phosphorus that in hydrolysis yield fatty acids, glycerol, and a nitrogenous compound. Lecithin is an example.

phosphorus A nonmetallic element essential to human nutrition.

phosphorus:calcium ratio The ratio of calcium to phosphorus intake in the diet; the normal ratio is 1:1.

photon absorptiometry An analytical, noninvasive technique designed to assess bone density.

phylloquinone Vitamin K; essential in the blood clotting process.

physical activity Any activity that involves human movement; in relation to health and physical fitness, physical activity is often classified as structured and unstructured.

Physical Activity Level (PAL) Increase in energy expenditure through physical activity based on energy expended through daily walking mileage or equivalent activities; National Academy of Sciences lists four PAL categories: sedentary, low active, active, and very active.

Physical Activity Pyramid A guide to weekly physical activity, including aerobic endurance, muscular strength and endurance, and flexibility.

Physical Activity Quotient (PA)
Coefficient used to calculate estimated energy requirement (EER) based on categories of physical activity levels (PAL).

physical conditioning Methods used to increase the efficiency or capacity of a given body system so as to improve physical or athletic performance.

physical fitness A set of abilities individuals possess to perform specific types of physical activity. *Also see* health-related fitness and sports-related fitness.

phytates Salts of phytic acids; produced in the body during the digestion of certain grain products; can combine with some minerals such as iron and possibly decrease their absorption.

phytochemicals Chemical substances, other than nutrients, found in plants that are theorized to possess medicinal properties to help prevent various diseases.

phytoestrogens Phytochemicals that may compete with natural endogenous estrogens; believed to help prevent certain forms of cancer associated with excess estrogen activity in the body.

picolinate A natural derivative of tryptophan; commercially it is bound to chromium as a means of enhancing chromium absorption.

plaque The material that forms in the inner layer of the artery and contributes to atherosclerosis. It contains cholesterol, lipids, and other debris.

platelet aggregability Function of platelets to promote clumping together of red blood cells.

polypeptides A combination of a number of simple amino acids; *also see* peptide.

polysaccharide A carbohydrate that upon hydrolysis will yield more than ten monosaccharides.

polyunsaturated fatty acids Fats that contain two or more double bonds and thus are open to hydrogenation.

positive caloric balance A condition whereby caloric intake exceeds caloric output; the resultant effect is a weight gain.

Positive Health Lifestyle A lifestyle characterized by health behaviors designed to promote health and longevity by helping to prevent many of the chronic diseases afflicting modern society.

postabsorptive state The period after a meal has been absorbed from the gastrointestinal tract; in BMR tests it is usually a period of approximately 12 hours.

potassium A metallic element essential in human nutrition; it is the principal cation present in the intracellular fluids.

power Work divided by time; the ability to produce work in a given period of time.

power-endurance continuum In relation to strength training, the concept that power or strength is developed by high resistance and few repetitions, whereas endurance is developed by low resistance and many repetitions.

PRE Progressive resistive exercise.

pre-event nutrition Dietary intake prior to athletic competition; may refer to a 2- to 3-day period prior to an event or the immediate pre-event meal.

premenstrual syndrome (PMS) A condition associated with a wide variety of symptoms during the time prior to menses.

principle of exercise sequence Relative to a weight-training workout, the lifting sequence is designed so that different muscle groups are utilized sequentially so as to be fresh for each exercise.

principle of overload The major concept of physical training whereby one imposes a stress greater than that normally imposed upon a particular body system.

principle of progressive resistance exercise (PRE) A training technique, primarily with weights, whereby resistance is increased as the individual develops increased strength levels.

principle of recuperation A principle of physical conditioning whereby adequate rest periods are taken for recuperation to occur so that exercise may be continued.

principle of specificity of training The principle that physical training should be designed to mimic the specific athletic event in which one competes. Specific human energy systems and neuromuscular skills should be stressed.

Pritikin program A dietary program developed by Nathan Pritikin, which severely restricts the intake of certain foods like fats and cholesterol and greatly increases the consumption of complex carbohydrates.

profile of mood states (POMS) An inventory to evaluate mood states such as anger, vigor, etc.

proline A nonessential amino acid.

promoters Substances or agents necessary to support or promote the development of a disease once it is initiated.

proof Relative to alcohol content, proof is twice the percentage of alcohol in a solution; 80-proof whiskey is 40 percent alcohol.

prostaglandins Eicosanoids that possess hormone-like activity in numerous cells in the body.

proteases Enzymes that catalyze proteins.

protein Any one of a group of complex organic compounds containing nitrogen; formed from various combinations of amino acids.

protein-Calorie insufficiency A major health problem in certain parts of the world where the population suffers from inadequate intake of protein and total Calories.

protein complementarity The practice among vegetarians of eating foods together from two or more different food groups, usually legumes, nuts, or beans with grain products, in order to ensure a balanced intake of essential amino acids.

Protein Digestibility Corrected Amino Acid Score (PDCAAS) A scientific measure used to assess the quality of protein in foods with values from 1.0 to 0.0, with 1.0 being the highest quality.

protein-sparing effect An adequate intake of energy Calories, as from carbohydrate, will decrease somewhat the rate of protein catabolism in the body and hence spare protein. This is the basis of the protein-sparing modified fast, or diet.

proteinuria The presence of proteins in the urine.

provitamin A Carotene, a substance in the diet from which the body may form vitamin A.

Prudent Healthy Diet A diet plan based upon healthful eating principles that is designed to help prevent or treat common chronic diseases in the United States, Canada, and Mexico, particularly cardiovascular disease and cancer.

psyllium A plant product that contains both water-soluble and insoluble dietary fiber.

purines The end products of nucleoprotein metabolism, which may be formed in the body; they are nonprotein nitrogen compounds that are eventually degraded to uric acid.

pyridoxal A component of the vitamin B group.

pyridoxamine A part of the vitamin B group; an analog of pyridoxine.

pyridoxine A component of the vitamin B complex, vitamin B_6.

pyruvate The end product of glycolysis. Under aerobic conditions it may be converted into acetyl CoA, whereas under anaerobic conditions it is converted into lactic acid.

PYY Peptide YY (PYY), a gut hormone fragment produced by the intestines; affects neurons in the hypothalamus to reduce appetite and food intake.

quackery Misrepresentation of the facts to deceive the consumer.

quality Calories Calories in foods that are accompanied by substantial amounts of nutrients. Skim milk contains quality Calories as it provides considerable amounts of protein, calcium, and other nutrients, while cola drinks provide similar Calories but no nutrients.

radiation Electromagnetic waves given off by an object; the body radiates heat to a cool environment.

radura International symbol of radiation; used on labels for irradiated foods.

rating of perceived exertion (RPE) A subjective rating, on a numerical scale, used to express the perceived difficulty of a given work task.

reactive hypoglycemia A decrease in blood glucose caused by an excessive insulin response to hyperglycemia associated with a substantial intake of high-glycemic-index foods.

Recommended Dietary Allowances (RDA) The levels of intake of essential nutrients considered to be adequate to meet the known nutritional needs of practically all healthy persons.

recommended dietary goals Dietary goals for U.S. citizens that have been established by a U.S. Senate subcommittee on nutrition; goals stress dietary reduction of fat, cholesterol, salt, and sugar, and increase of complex carbohydrates.

recuperation principle *See* principle of recuperation.

Reference Daily Intakes (RDIs) The RDI is used in food labeling as the recommended daily intake for protein and selected vitamins and minerals. It replaces the old U.S. RDA (United States Recommended Daily Allowance).

regional fat distribution Deposition of fat in different regions of the body. *See also* android- and gynoid-type obesity.

relative humidity The percentage of moisture in the air compared to the amount of moisture needed to cause saturation, which is taken as 100.

relative risk (RR) A probability estimate; RR of 1.0 is normal.

relative-weight method A method of determining obesity by comparing the weight of an individual to standardized height and weight tables.

repetition maximum (RM) In weight training, the amount of weight that can be lifted for a specific number of repetitions.

repetitions In relation to weight training or interval training, the number of times that an exercise is done.

resistin An adipokine secreted by adipose tissue that is thought to increase insulin resistance and development of type 2 diabetes.

resistin Substance secreted by adipose tissue that is reported to induce insulin resistance, linking obesity to diabetes.

resting energy expenditure (REE) The energy required to drive all physiological processes while in a state of rest.

resting metabolic rate (RMR) *Also see* BMR and REE.

retinol Vitamin A.

retinol equivalent (RE) A measure of vitamin A activity in food as measured by preformed vitamin A or carotene, provitamin A; 1 RE equals 5 IU.

rHGH *See* human growth hormone.

riboflavin Vitamin B_2, a member of the B complex.

ribose A five-carbon sugar found in several body compounds, such as riboflavin.

risk factor Associated factors that increase the risk for a given disease; for example, cigarette smoking and lung cancer.

RNA Ribonucleic acid; nuclear material involved in the formation of proteins in cells.

running Although the distinction between running and jogging is relative to the individual involved, a common value used for running is 7 mph or faster.

saccharide A series of carbohydrates ranging from simple sugars (monosaccharides) to complex carbohydrates (polysaccharides).

saccharine An artificial sweetener made from coal tar.

Salmonella A bacteria commonly involved in food poisoning.

salt-depletion heat exhaustion Weakness caused by excessive loss of electrolytes due to excessive sweating.

sarcopenia Loss of muscle mass associated with the aging process.

satiety center A group of nerve cells in the hypothalamus that responds to certain stimuli in the blood and provides a sensation of satiety.

saturated fatty acids Fats that have all chemical bonds filled.

SCAN Sports and Cardiovascular Nutritionists, a practice group of the American Dietetic Association focusing on applications of nutrition to sport and wellness.

scurvy A deficiency caused by a lack of vitamin C in the diet; symptoms include weakness, bleeding gums, and anemia.

SDA Specific dynamic action; often used to represent the increased energy cost observed during the metabolism of protein in the body. *Also see* dietary-induced thermogenesis and TEF.

Seasonal affective disorder (SAD) Symptoms associated with various seasons of the year, e.g., depression in winter months.

secondary amenorrhea Cessation of menstruation after the onset of puberty; primary amenorrhea is the lack of menstruation prior to menarche.

Sedentary Death Syndrome (SeDS) Term associated with a sedentary lifestyle and related health problems that predispose to premature death.

selenium A nonmetallic element resembling sulfur; an essential nutrient.

semivegetarian An individual who refrains from eating red meat but includes white meat such as fish and chicken in a diet stressing vegetarian concepts.

serotonin A neurotransmitter in the brain; may induce a sense of relaxation and drowsiness, possibly associated with fatigue; may also depress the appetite.

serum lipid level The concentration of lipids in the blood serum.

set-point theory The weight-control theory that postulates that each individual has an established normal body weight. Any deviation from this set point will lead to changes in body metabolism to return the individual to the normal weight.

sets In weight training, a certain number of repetitions constitutes a set; for example, a lifter may do three sets of six repetitions per set.

settling-point theory Theory that the body weight set point may be increased or decreased through interactions of genetics and the environment; an environment rich in high-fat foods may lead to a higher set point so that the body settles in at a higher weight and fat content.

shell temperature The temperature of the skin; *also see* core temperature.

short-chain fatty acids (SCFA) Fatty acids with chains containing less than six carbons.

sibutramine A prescription drug for weight loss that suppresses the appetite by affecting brain neurotransmitters.

silicon A nonmetallic element.

simple carbohydrates Usually used to refer to table sugar, or sucrose, a disaccharide; may refer also to other disaccharides and the monosaccharides.

Simplesse A commercially produced fat substitute derived from protein.

skinfold technique A technique used to compute an individual's percentage of body fat; various skinfolds are measured and a regression formula is used to compute the body fat.

sling psychrometer A device that incorporates both a dry-bulb and wet-bulb thermometer, thus providing a heat-stress index incorporating both temperature and relative humidity.

slow-twitch fibers Red muscle fibers that have a slow contraction speed; designed for aerobic-type activity.

Smilax A commercial plant extract theorized to produce anabolic effects.

soda loading Term associated with use of baking soda (sodium bicarbonate) as an ergogenic aid.

sodium A soft metallic element; combines with chloride to form salt; the major extracellular cation in the human body.

sodium bicarbonate $NaHCO_3$; a sodium salt of carbonic acid that serves as a buffer of acids in the blood, often referred to as the alkaline reserve.

sodium citrate A white powder used as a blood buffer; *see also* sodium bicarbonate.

soluble dietary fiber Dietary fibers in plants such as gums and pectins that are soluble in water.

specific dynamic action *See* SDA.

specific heat The amount of energy or heat needed to raise the temperature of a unit of mass, such as 1 kilogram of body tissue, 1 degree Celsius.

specificity of training *See* principle of specificity of training.

sport nutrition The application of nutritional principles to sport with the intent of maximizing performance.

sports anemia A temporary condition of low hemoglobin levels often observed in athletes during the early stages of training.

sports bars Commercial food products targeted to athletes and physically active individuals containing various concentrations of carbohydrate, fat, and protein; some products contain other nutrients, such as antioxidants.

sports drinks Popular term for various glucose-electrolyte fluid replacement drinks.

sports gels Commercial food products targeted to athletes; consist primarily of carbohydrate in a gel form.

sports-related fitness Components of physical fitness that, when improved, have implications for enhanced sport performance, such as agility and power.

sports supplements Dietary supplements marketed to athletes and physically active individuals.

spot reducing The theory that exercising a specific body part, such as the thighs, will facilitate the loss of body fat from that spot.

standard error of measurement or estimate A measure of variability about the mean. Sixty-eight percent of the population is within one standard error above and below the mean, while about 95 percent is within two standard errors.

standardized exercise An exercise task that conforms to a specific standardized protocol.

Staphylococcus A bacteria commonly involved in food poisoning.

steady state A level of metabolism, usually during exercise, when the oxygen consumption satisfies the energy expenditure and the individual is performing in an aerobic state.

steady-state threshold The intensity level of exercise above which the production of energy appears to shift rapidly to anaerobic mechanisms, such as when a rapid rise in blood lactic acid exists. The oxygen system will still supply a major portion of the energy, but the lactic acid system begins to contribute an increasing share.

sterols Substances similar to fats because of their solubility characteristics; the most commonly known sterol is cholesterol.

stimulus period In exercise programs, the time period over which the stimulus is applied, such as a HR of 150 for 15 minutes.

storage fat Fat that accumulates and is stored in the adipose tissue; *also see* essential fat.

strength-endurance continuum In relation to strength training, the concept that power or strength is developed by high resistance and few repetitions and that endurance is developed by low resistance and many repetitions.

structured physical activity A planned program of physical activities usually designed to enhance physical fitness; structured physical activity is often referred to as exercise.

subclinical malnutrition A nutrient-deficiency state in which no clinical signs of the nutrient deficiency are observable, but other nonspecific symptoms such as fatigue may be present.

subcutaneous fat The body fat found immediately under the skin; evaluated by skinfold calipers.

sucrose Table sugar, a disaccharide; yields glucose and fructose upon hydrolysis.

sulfur A pale yellow nonmetallic element essential in human nutrition; component of the sulfur-containing amino acids.

sumo wrestling A form of wrestling in Japan.

superoxide dismutase An enzyme in body cells that helps neutralize free radicals.

Syndrome X *See* metabolic syndrome.

synephrine A dietary supplement marketed for fat loss; synephrine is derived from a fruit plant known as bitter orange. Used as an alterative to Ephedra, or ephedrine.

systolic blood pressure The blood pressure in the arteries when the heart is contracting and pumping blood.

target heart-rate range In an aerobic exercise program, the heart-rate level that will provide the stimulus for a beneficial training effect.

taurine A vitamin-like compound synthesized from amino acids, mainly methionine and cysteine.

testosterone The male sex hormone responsible for male secondary sex characteristics at puberty; it has anabolic and androgenic effects.

thermic effect of exercise (TEE) Increased muscular contraction produces additional heat.

thermic effect of food (TEF) The increased body heat production associated with the digestion, assimilation, and metabolism of energy nutrients in a meal just consumed.

thermogenesis The production of heat; metabolic processes in the body generate heat constantly.

thiamin Vitamin B_1.

threonine An essential amino acid.

threshold stimulus The minimal level of exercise intensity needed to stimulate gains in physical fitness.

thromboxanes Eicosanoids that possess hormone-like activity in numerous cells in the body.

thyroxine A hormone secreted by the thyroid gland that is involved in the control of the metabolic rate.

tin A white metallic element.

tocopherol Generic name for an alcohol that has the activity of vitamin E.

Tolerable Upper Intake Levels (UL) The highest level of daily nutrient intake likely to pose no adverse health risks.

tonicity Tension or pressure as related to fluids; fluids with high osmolality exhibit hypertonicity while fluids with low osmolality exhibit hypotonicity.

total body electrical impedance A sophisticated method of measuring the resistance provided by water in the body as a means to predict body composition.

total body fat The sum total of the body's storage fat and essential fat stores.

total daily energy expenditure (TDEE) The total amount of energy expended during the day, including REE, TEF, and TEE.

total fiber Sum of dietary fiber and functional fiber.

trabecular bone The spongy bone structure found inside the bone, as contrasted with the more compact bone on the outside.

trace minerals Those minerals essential to human nutrition that have an RDA less than 100 mg.

trans fatty acids Unsaturated fatty acids in which the hydrogen ions are on opposite sides of the double bond.

triglycerides One of the many fats formed by the union of glycerol and fatty acids.

triose A simple sugar having three carbon atoms.

tryptophan An essential amino acid.

Type I muscle fiber The slow-twitch red fiber that provides energy primarily by the oxygen system.

Type IIa muscle fiber The fast-twitch red fiber that provides energy by both the oxygen system and the lactic acid system.

Type IIb muscle fiber The fast-twitch white fiber that provides energy primarily by the lactic acid system.

tyrosine A nonessential amino acid.

ubiquinone *See* CoQ$_{10}$.

uncoupling protein (UPC) A protein believed to stimulate thermogenesis in fat tissues; uncouples thermogenesis with the production of ATP, so no ATP is generated in this process.

underwater weighing A technique for measuring the percentage of body fat in humans.

United States Recommended Daily Allowances *See* U.S. RDA.

Universal Gym A brand name for exercise equipment, particularly weights for strength development.

unsaturated fatty acids Fatty acids that contain double or triple bonds and hence can add hydrogen atoms.

unstructured physical activity Many of the normal, daily physical activities that are generally not planned as exercise, such as walking to work, climbing stairs, gardening, domestic activities, and games and other childhood pursuits.

urea The chief nitrogenous constituent of urine and the final product of the decomposition of proteins in the body.

uric acid A crystalline end product of purine metabolism; commonly involved in gout and the formation of kidney stones.

USDA United States Department of Agriculture.

USOC United States Olympic Committee.

U.S. RDA The United States Recommended Daily Allowances; the RDA figures used on labels, representing the percentage of the RDA for a given nutrient contained in a serving of the food. The U.S. RDA are now known as the Reference Daily Intake (RDI).

valine An essential amino acid.

Valsalva phenomenon A condition in which a forceful exhalation is attempted against a closed epiglottis and no air escapes; such a straining may cause the person to faint.

vanadium A light gray metallic element.

vanadyl sulfate A salt form of vanadium; marketed for its anabolic potential.

vascular water The body water contained in the blood vessels; a part of the extracellular water.

vasodilation An increase in the size of the blood vessels, usually referring to the arterial system.

vegan Vegetarian who eats no animal products.

vegetable exchange One vegetable exchange in the Food Exchange System contains 5 grams of carbohydrate, 2 grams of protein, and 25 Calories.

vegetarian One whose food is of vegetable or plant origin; *also see* lactovegetarian, ovovegetarian, ovolactovegetarian, pescovegetarian, semivegetarian, and vegan.

very-low-Calorie diet (VLCD) A diet containing less than 800 Calories per day.

very low-density lipoprotein *See* VLDL.

visceral fat The deep fat found in the abdominal area; needs special measuring techniques, such as MRI.

vitamin, natural Often referred to as a vitamin derived from natural sources; i.e., food in nature; contrast with vitamin, synthetic.

vitamin, synthetic An artificial vitamin commercially produced from the separate components of the vitamin.

vitamin A Retinol, an unsaturated aliphatic alcohol; fat soluble.

vitamin B$_1$ Thiamin; the antineuritic vitamin.

vitamin B$_2$ Riboflavin.

vitamin B$_6$ Pyridoxine and related compounds.

vitamin B$_{12}$ Cyanocobalamin.

vitamin B$_{15}$ Not a vitamin but marketed as one; usual composition is calcium gluconate and dimethylglycine (DMG).

vitamin C Ascorbic acid; the antiscorbutic vitamin.

vitamin D Any one of related sterols that have antirachitic properties; fat soluble.

vitamin D$_3$ The prohormone form of vitamin D, also known as cholecalciferol, formed in the skin by irradiation from the sun. Released into the blood and eventually converted by the kidney to the hormone form of vitamin D.

vitamin deficiency Subnormal body-vitamin levels due to inadequate intake or absorption; specific disorders are linked with deficiencies of specific vitamins.

vitamin E Various forms of tocotrienols and tocopherols; fat soluble.

vitamin K The antihemorrhagic, or clotting vitamin; fat soluble.

vitamins A general term for a number of substances deemed essential for the normal metabolic functioning of the body.

VLDL Very low-density lipoproteins; a protein-lipid complex in the blood that transports triglycerides, cholesterol, and phospholipids; has a very low density. *Also see* HDL-cholesterol and LDL-cholesterol.

voluntary dehydration Intentional loss of body fluids in attempts to reduce body mass for sports competition; techniques include exercise, sauna, and diuretics.

VO$_2$ max Maximal oxygen uptake; measured during exercise, the maximal amount of oxygen consumed reflects the body's ability to utilize oxygen as an energy source; equals the cardiac output times the arteriovenous oxygen difference.

WADA World Anti-Doping Agency.

waist circumference The circumference of the waist at its most narrow point as seen from the front; used as a measure of regional adeposity.

warm-down A phase after an exercise session during which the individual gradually tapers the level of activity—for example, by jogging slowly after a fast run.

warm-up   Low-level exercises used to increase the muscle temperature and/or stretch the muscles prior to a strenuous exercise bout.

water   A tasteless, colorless, odorless fluid essential to life; composed of two parts hydrogen and one part oxygen (H_2O).

water-depletion heat exhaustion Weakness caused by excessive loss of body fluids such as through exercise-induced dehydration in a hot or warm environment.

water intoxication   Consumption of excessive amounts of water leading to dilution of body electrolytes. *See also* hyponatremia.

watt   A unit of power in the SI; one watt equals about 6 kilogram-meters per minute.

WBGT Index   Wet-bulb globe thermometer index; a heat-stress index based upon four factors measured by the wet-bulb globe thermometer.

weight cycling   Repetitive loss and regain of body weight; often called yo-yo dieting.

wet-bulb globe thermometer   A device that takes into account the various factors determining heat stress: air temperature, air movement, radiation heat, and humidity.

wheat germ oil   Oil extracted from the embryo of wheat, high in linoleic fatty acid, vitamin E, and octacosanol.

work   Effort expended to accomplish something; in terms of physics, force times distance.

xerophthalmia   Dryness of the conjunctiva and cornea of the eye, which may lead to blindness if untreated; caused by a deficiency of vitamin A.

xylitol   A sugar alcohol that may be obtained from fruits.

yohimbine   A plant extract theorized to stimulate testosterone production and elicit anabolic effects.

zinc   A blue-white crystalline metallic element essential to human nutrition.

zone diet   A high-protein diet plan; the 40-30-30 plan consisting of 40 percent Calories from carbohydrate, and 30 percent each from protein and fat.

Photo Credits

Chapter 1

Page 2: © Fruits & Vegetables, OS1/PhotoDisc/Getty; p. 3: © Fruits & Vegetables, OS1/PhotoDisc; figure 1.2: R-F Website/Getty Images; p. 8: © Supporting Cast: Teens, OS39/PhotoDisc/Getty; figure 1.6: © Sygma/CORBIS; p. 15 (top): © Fruits & Vegetables, OS1/PhotoDisc/Getty; p. 15 (bottom): © Sporting Goods, OS25/PhotoDisc/Getty; p. 17: © Fruits & Vegetables, OS1/PhotoDisc/Getty; figure 1.7: © Vol. 67/PhotoDisc/Getty; figure 1.9: © Mauro Femariello/Photo Researchers, Inc.

Chapter 2

Page 40: © Fruits & Vegetables, OS1/PhotoDisc/Getty; p. 42 (top): © Supporting Cast: Teens, OS39/PhotoDisc/Getty; figure 2.2a-f: © Greg Kidd and Joanne Scott; p. 44 (top): © Fruits & Vegetables, OS1/PhotoDisc/Getty; p. 44 (bottom): © Fruits & Vegetables, OS1/PhotoDisc/Getty; figure 2.5: © DV023/Digital Vision/Getty; p. 48 (left): © Supporting Cast: Teens, OS39/PhotoDisc/Getty; p. 48 (right): © Fruits & Vegetables, OS1/PhotoDisc/Getty; figure 2.7a: © The McGraw-Hill Companies, Inc./Sabina Dowell, photographer; figure 2.7b: © Greg Kidd and Joanne Scott; figure 2.8: © Brian Leatart/FoodPix/Jupiterimages; figure 2.9: © The McGraw-Hill Companies, Inc./Sabina Dowell, photographer; p. 23: © Supporting Cast: Teens, OS39/PhotoDisc/Getty; p. 24: © Supporting Cast: Teens, OS39/PhotoDisc/Getty; figure 2.11: © The McGraw-Hill Companies, Inc./Sabina Dowell, photographer; p. 35: © Supporting Cast: Teens, OS39/PhotoDisc/Getty; p. 37: © Market Fresh, OS49/PhotoDisc/Getty; p. 40 (all): © Fruits & Vegetables, OS1/PhotoDisc/Getty.

Chapter 3

Figure 3.3: © Samual Ashfield/SPL/Photo Researchers, Inc.; figure 3.4: © Delicious Delights/Corbis RF; figure 3.6: © People in Sports/Corbis RF; p. 92: © Supporting Cast: Teens, OS39/PhotoDisc/Getty; p. 93 (both): © Supporting Cast: Teens, OS39/PhotoDisc/Getty; figure 3.14: © Yoav Levy/Phototake; p. 96 (bottom): © Supporting Cast: Teens, OS39/PhotoDisc/Getty; figure 3.16: © Vol. 10/PhotoDisc/Getty; p. 98: © Sporting Goods, OS25/PhotoDisc/Getty; p. 100: © Supporting Cast: Teens, OS39/PhotoDisc/Getty.

Chapter 4

Figure 4.3: © Randy Mayor/FoodPix/Jupiterimages; p. 119: © Fruits & Vegetables, OS1/PhotoDisc/Getty; p. 123: © Market Fresh, OS49/PhotoDisc/Getty; p. 126: © Recreational Sports, Vol. 82/PhotoDisc/Getty; p. 133: © Sporting Goods, OS25/PhotoDisc/Getty; p. 137: © Market Fresh, OS49/PhotoDisc/Getty; p. 138: © Sporting Goods, OS25/PhotoDisc/Getty; p. 140: © Familiar Objects, OS57/PhotoDisc/Getty; p. 143: © Contemporary Cuisine, Vol. 30/PhotoDisc/Getty; p. 145: © Food and Dining, Vol. 12/PhotoDisc/Getty.

Chapter 5

Figure 5.4: © The McGraw-Hill Companies, Inc./John Thoeming, photographer; p. 166, p. 171, p. 173 (left): © Sporting Goods, OS25/PhotoDisc/Getty; p. 173 (right): © Supporting Cast: Teens, OS39/PhotoDisc/Getty; figure 5.17: © Journal-Courier/The Image Works.

Chapter 6

Figure 6.3: © The McGraw-Hill Companies, Inc./John Thoeming, photographer; p. 205: © Contemporary Health, Vol. 83/ PhotoDisc/Getty.

Chapter 7

Page 244: © Health and Well Being, Vol. 67/PhotoDisc/Getty; p. 250, p. 253: © Fruits & Vegetables, OS1/PhotoDisc/Getty; p. 255: © Market Fresh, OS49/PhotoDisc/Getty; p. 257: © Childís Play, OS47/PhotoDisc/Getty; p. 261, p. 269: © Sporting Goods, OS25/PhotoDisc/Getty.

Chapter 8

Page 287: © Sports & Fitness, Vol. 103/Corbis RF; p. 292: © American Food Basics, Vol. 4/Corbis RF; p. 302: © Food Essentials, Vol. 20/ PhotoDisc/Getty; p. 309: © Sports & Fitness, Vol. 103/Corbis.

Chapter 9

Page 321: © Food Essentials, Vol. 20/PhotoDisc/Getty; figure 9.1: © People in Sports/Corbis RF; figure 9.4: © The McGraw-Hill Companies, Inc./John Thoeming, photographer; p. 327: © Fruits & Vegetables, OS1/PhotoDisc/Getty; figure 9.9: © Clive Brunskill/ Getty; p. 336: © Fruits & Vegetables, OS1/PhotoDisc/ Getty; p. 348: © Health and Well Being, Vol. 67/PhotoDisc/Getty; figure 9.12: © Tony Duffy/Getty; p. 354: © Contemporary Health, Vol. 83/ PhotoDisc/Getty.

Chapter 10

Figure 10 2: Rick O'Quinn/University of Georgia; figure 10.3: Photo courtesy of Life Measurement Instruments; p. 370: © Sports & Fitness, Vol. 103/Corbis; p. 381 (top): © Sporting Goods, OS25/PhotoDisc/Getty; p. 381 (bottom): © Sports & Fitness, Vol. 103/Corbis; p. 385: © Sports & Fitness, Vol. 103/Corbis.

Chapter 11

Page 410: © Sports & Fitness, Vol. 103/Corbis; figure 11.3: © The McGraw-Hill Companies, Inc./John Thoeming, photographer; figure 11.5a (golf ball): © Vol. 127/Corbis RF; figure 11.5b (tennis ball): © Sporting Goods, OS25/PhotoDisc/Getty; figure 11.5c (yo-yo): R-F website/Corbis; figure 11.5d (mouse): © Vol. 127/Corbis RF; figure 11.5e (baseball): © Sporting Goods, OS25/PhotoDisc/ Getty; figure 11.5f (fist): © OS02/PhotoDisc/ Getty; figure 11.6: © Ariel Skelley/CORBIS; p. 426: © Sports & Fitness, Vol. 103/Corbis; figure 11.11: © RNT Productions/ CORBIS; p. 435: © Sports & Fitness, Vol. 103/Corbis.

Chapter 12

Page 454: © Sports & Fitness, Vol. 103/Corbis; figure 12.2: © Vol. 51/PhotoDisc/Getty; figure 12.12: © Rachel Epstein/PhotoEdit.

Chapter 13

Page 481: © Contemporary Cuisine, Vol. 30/PhotoDisc/Getty; figure 13.4: © Vol. 66/PhotoDisc/Getty; figure 13.5: © The McGraw-Hill Companies, Inc./Lars A. Niki, photographer; p. 489: © Contemporary Cuisine, Vol. 30/PhotoDisc/Getty; figure 13.6: © Vol. 59/PhotoDisc/Getty; figure 13.7: © The McGraw-Hill Companies, Inc./Jill Braaten, photographer; figure 13.8: © The McGraw-Hill Companies, Inc./Jill Braaten, photographer; figure 13.10: © Sports & Fitness CD/Corbis RF; figure 13.12: © The McGraw-Hill Companies, Inc./Jill Braaten, photographer.

Index

USA Track & Field (USATF), 341
Utter, A. C., 129

V

Vainio, H., 267
Valsalva phenomenon (Valsalva maneuver), 465
Valtin, H., 321
Vanadium, 306–307
Vandenberghe, K., 138, 221
van der Beek, E., 250, 256
van der Vusse, G. J., 165, 166
van Dijk, R., 257
van Erp-Bart, A., 257
Van Hall, G., 141, 215
Van Loan, M. D., 302, 369
van Loon, L., 122, 133, 165, 173
Van Montfoort, M., 495
Van Nieuwenhoven, M., 343
van Someren, K., 495
van Staveren, W., 376
Vanstone, C., 183
Van Zyl, C., 170
Vegans, 54
Vegetarian diets, 54–60
    becoming vegetarian and, 59
    healthfulness of nonvegetarian diet compared with, 57–59
    nutritional concerns about, 55–57
    physical performance potential and, 60
    protein sources in, 199
    types of, 54, 55
Vegetarian Times Complete Cookbook, 59
Veicsteinas, A., 168
Vema, S., 307
Venables, M., 166
Venkatraman, J. T., 168, 169
Ventura, J., 212
Verhaar, H., 245
Verhoef, P., 490
Very-low-calorie diets (VLCDs), 384, 422
Very low density lipoproteins (VLDL), 162–163
Vestergaard, P., 490
Vieth, R., 245
Viitala, P., 260
Villani, R., 172
Villareal, D. T., 499
Vincent, J., 304
Vinceti, M., 305
Virk, R. S., 252
Visceral fat, 366
Vitamin A, 241, 242–243, 244
Vitamin B$_1$, 242–243, 248–250
Vitamin B$_2$, 242–243, 250
Vitamin B$_6$, 242–243, 251–252
Vitamin B$_{12}$, 242–243, 252–253
Vitamin B complex, 256–257
Vitamin C, 242–243, 257–259
Vitamin D, 242–243, 244–246
Vitamin E, 242–243, 246–247
Vitamin Intervention for Stroke Prevention (VISP) study, 257
Vitamin K, 242–243, 247–248

Vitamins, 237–271. *See also specific vitamins*
    deficiencies of, 240–241
    ergogenic aspects of, 259–263
    essential, 240, 242–243
    fat-soluble, 241, 242–243, 244–248, 270
    functions of, 238–240
    health and, 263–271
    megadoses of, 265
    in vegetarian diet, 56, 57–59
    water-soluble, 242–243, 248–259, 270
Vitamin supplements, 21
    ergogenic aspects of, 259–263
    health aspects of, 263–271
Volek, J. S., 218, 222, 223, 411, 412, 469
Volpe, S., 304
Volumetrics Eating Plan, The, 412
VO$_2$ max, 95, 96, 123
von Fraunhofer, J., 142
Vorona, R., 376
Voy, R., 24
Vukovich, M., 173, 223
Vuori, I., 12

W

Wacher, S., 172
Wadden, T., 375, 383, 406, 442
Wagenmakers, A., 172, 173, 202, 212
Wagner, D. R., 347, 368, 369, 370
Waist circumference, 369, 371, 372, 521–523
Walberg-Rankin, J. W., 127, 203, 206, 390, 405
Walker, J., 139
Walker, L. S., 304
Walking, energy metabolism during, 98–99
Wallace, M. B., 499
Waller, M., 297
Walzem, R., 208
Wang, L., 381
Wang, W., 65
Wannamethee, S., 483
Warber, J., 256
Ward, A., 520
Ward-Smith, A. J., 95, 104
Warm-down, 430
Warm-up, 430
Warren, M. P., 289, 387, 388
Water, 320–324
    body. *See* Body water; Dehydration; Hydration; Hyperhydration
    ergogenic aspects of, 346
    functions of, 324
    health and, 324, 348
    metabolic, 321
    nutritional supplementation of, 21
    requirements for, 320–321
    substances in, 321–322
Water-depletion heat exhaustion, 349, 351
Water intoxication, 341
Water-soluble vitamins, 242–243, 270

Watson, P., 214, 261
WBGT Index, 329
Weaver, C. M., 246, 287, 288, 292, 298
Webb, D., 262, 267
Weber, P., 248, 259
Websites, as information source, 25
Webster, B., 284
Webster, M., 250, 255
Weggemans, R., 182
Weibel, E., 104
Weideman, C., 209
Weight, L., 261, 297
Weight control, 399–444
    behavior modification for, 406–408
    caffeine and, 491
    caloric concept of, 401–402
    Calorie/kilogram requirement to maintain weight and, 402–404
    comprehensive weight-control programs for, 441–444
    determining amount of weight to lose for, 405
    dietary modifications for. *See* Dieting
    exercise programs for, 423–441
    prevention in, 443–444
    safe amount of weight loss and, 405
Weight-Control Information Network (WIN), 444
Weight cycling, 384–385
Weight gaining. *See* Gaining weight
Weight loss
    excessive, 382–390
    spot reducing and, 439
Weight-loss drugs and supplements, 383–384
Weight Watchers, 400, 441, 442
Weigle, D., 412
Weilbrauch, M., 143
Weiss, B., 67
Weiss, M., 224
Weller, E., 293
Wellman, N., 27–28
Welsh, R., 128
Weltan, S. M., 125
Weltzin, T., 385
Wesson, M., 216
Westman, E., 412
Weston, S., 262
Wheeler, K. B., 72
Whey proteins, 208, 209–210
White, J. A., 335
White fat, 373
Wild Times, Rampant 'Roids, Smash Hits, and How Baseball Got Big, 497
Wiles, J., 210, 487
Willett, W. C., 285, 375
Williams, C., 14, 67, 127, 130, 132, 138, 139, 261
Williams, J., 486
Williams, M. H., 99, 212, 214, 215, 218, 219, 223, 470, 481, 501, 502
Williams, P. J., 186, 383, 484
Willoughby, D., 220, 502

Wilson, A. K., 297
Wilson, G., 386
Winett, R., 467
Wing, R., 441
Wingo, J., 347
Winnick, J., 128
Wirth, J., 501
Wolfe, B., 455
Wolfe, R., 127, 165, 166, 201, 203, 206, 207, 469
Wood, O., 69
Wood, P., 186, 429
Wood, R., 296
Work, 82
World Anti-Doping Agency (WADA)
    on anabolic prohormones, 500
    on caffeine, 489
    on ephedrine, 492
World Health Organization (WHO), 40
Worthington, V., 67
Wright, B., 487
Wroble, R. R., 390
Wurzelmann, J., 300
Wyatt, K. M., 252

X

Xerophthalmia, 244

Y

Yaguchi, H., 203
Yarasheski, K. E., 497
Yaspelkis, B. B., 130, 333
Yates, A., 40
Yeomans, M., 483
Yesalis, C., 497, 498, 499
Ylikoski, T., 262
YMCA, 443
Yoshizumi, W., 221
Young, A., 333
Young athletes
    weight-reduction programs for, 443
    weight restriction in, 385
Yo-yo syndrome, 384–385
Yquel, R., 218

Z

Zachman, R. D., 244
Zachwieja, J. J., 343, 390, 439, 497
Zanker, C., 289
Zeaxanthin, 58
Zeisel, S., 256
Zemel, M., 287
Zeni, A., 429
Zhang, K., 85
Zhang, M., 224
Zhang, S., 253
Ziegenfuss, T., 141, 500
Ziegler, P., 15, 259
Ziemba, A. E., 501
Zierler, K., 121, 125, 163
Zinc, 281, 295, 301–302, 309
Zitterman, A., 247, 248
Zone, The (Sears), 171
Zone diet, 210, 412

Median heights and weights and recommended energy intake

Category	Age (years) or condition	Weight (kg)	Weight (lb)	Height (cm)	Height (in)	REE[a] (kcal/day)	Average energy allowance (kcal)[b] Multiples of REE	Per kg	Per day[c]
Infants	0.0–0.5	6	13	60	24	320		108	650
	0.5–1.0	9	20	71	28	500		98	850
Children	1–3	13	29	90	35	740		102	1,300
	4–6	20	44	112	44	950		90	1,800
	7–10	28	62	132	52	1,130		70	2,000
Males	11–14	45	99	157	62	1,440	1.70	55	2,500
	15–18	66	145	176	69	1,760	1.67	45	3,000
	19–24	72	160	177	70	1,780	1.67	40	2,900
	25–50	79	174	176	70	1,800	1.60	37	2,900
	51+	77	170	173	68	1,530	1.50	30	2,300
Females	11–14	46	101	157	62	1,310	1.67	47	2,200
	15–18	55	120	163	64	1,370	1.60	40	2,200
	19–24	58	128	164	65	1,350	1.60	38	2,200
	25–50	63	138	163	64	1,380	1.55	36	2,200
	51+	65	143	160	63	1,280	1.50	30	1,900
Pregnant	1st trimester								+ 0
	2nd trimester								+ 300
	3rd trimester								+ 300
Lactating	1st 6 months								+ 500
	2nd 6 months								+ 500

[a]REE is resting energy expenditure; see chapter 3 for explanation. Calculation is based on Food and Agriculture Organization equations, then rounded.

[b]In the range of light to moderate activity, the coefficient of variation is ± 20%. Thus, for an individual with an average energy allowance of 2,500 Calories per day, the typical range might be 2,000–3,000, which is plus or minus 500 Calories (.20 × 2,500). See chapter 3 for expanded discussion of energy requirement based upon physical activity levels.

[c]Figure is rounded.

Dietary Reference Intakes (DRIs): Tolerable Upper Intake Levels (UL[a]), Vitamins

Food and Nutrition Board, Institute of Medicine, National Academies

Life Stage Group	Vitamin A (µg/d)[b]	Vitamin C (mg/d)	Vitamin D (µg/d)	Vitamin E (mg/d)[c,d]	Vitamin K	Thiamin	Riboflavin	Niacin (mg/d)[d]	Vitamin B-6 (mg/d)	Folate (µg/d)[d]	Vitamin B-12	Pantothenic Acid	Biotin	Choline (g/d)	Carotenoids[e]
Infants															
0–6 mo	600	ND[f]	25	ND	ND	ND	ND	ND	ND	ND	ND	ND	ND	ND	ND
7–12 mo	600	ND	25	ND	ND	ND	ND	ND	ND	ND	ND	ND	ND	ND	ND
Children															
1–3 y	600	400	50	200	ND	ND	ND	10	30	300	ND	ND	ND	1.0	ND
4–8 y	900	650	50	300	ND	ND	ND	15	40	400	ND	ND	ND	1.0	ND
Males, Females															
9–13 y	1,700	1,200	50	600	ND	ND	ND	20	60	600	ND	ND	ND	2.0	ND
14–18 y	2,800	1,800	50	800	ND	ND	ND	30	80	800	ND	ND	ND	3.0	ND
19–70 y	3,000	2,000	50	1,000	ND	ND	ND	35	100	1,000	ND	ND	ND	3.5	ND
>70 y	3,000	2,000	50	1,000	ND	ND	ND	35	100	1,000	ND	ND	ND	3.5	ND
Pregnancy															
≤18 y	2,800	1,800	50	800	ND	ND	ND	30	80	800	ND	ND	ND	3.0	ND
19–50 y	3,000	2,000	50	1,000	ND	ND	ND	35	100	1,000	ND	ND	ND	3.5	ND
Lactation															
≤18 y	2,800	1,800	50	800	ND	ND	ND	30	80	800	ND	ND	ND	3.0	ND
19–50 y	3,000	2,000	50	1,000	ND	ND	ND	35	100	1,000	ND	ND	ND	3.5	ND

[a]UL = The maximum level of daily nutrient intake that is likely to pose no risk of adverse effects. Unless otherwise specified, the UL represents total intake from food, water, and supplements. Due to lack of suitable data, ULs could not be established for vitamin K, thiamin, riboflavin, vitamin B-12, pantothenic acid, biotin, or carotenoids. In the absence of ULs, extra caution may be warranted in consuming levels above recommended intakes.

[b]As preformed vitamin A only.

[c]As α-tocopherol; applies to any form of supplemental α-tocopherol.

[d]The ULs for vitamin E, niacin, and folate apply to synthetic forms obtained from supplements, fortified foods, or a combination of the two.

[e]β-Carotene supplements are advised only to serve as a provitamin A source for individuals at risk of vitamin A deficiency.

[f]ND = Not determinable due to lack of data of adverse effects in this age group and concern with regard to lack of ability to handle excess amounts. Source of intake should be from food only to prevent high levels of intake.

SOURCES: Dietary Reference Intakes for Calcium, Phosphorus, Magnesium, Vitamin D, and Fluoride (1997); Dietary Reference Intakes for Thiamin, Riboflavin, Niacin, Vitamin B-6, Folate, Vitamin B-12, Pantothenic Acid, Biotin, and Choline (1998); Dietary Reference Intakes for Vitamin C, Vitamin E, Selenium, and Carotenoids (2000); and Dietary Reference Intakes for Vitamin A, Vitamin K, Arsenic, Boron, Chromium, Copper, Iodine, Iron, Manganese, Molybdenum, Nickel, Silicon, Vanadium, and Zinc (2001). These reports may be accessed via www.nap.edu.